THE AUTHORISED DAILY PRAYER BOOK OF THE UNITED HEBREW CONGREGATIONS OF THE COMMONWEALTH

סדר תפילות כל השנה

כמנהג פולין – מנהג אנגליה

התרגום המקורי ע״י

ה״ר שמעון ב״ר רבי יהודה סינגער זצ״ל

עם תרגום ופירוש

ע״י הרב הכולל

ממוה״ר **יעקב צבי זקס** זצ״ל

עם הוספות תחת השגחת

הרב הכולל

ממוה״ר **אפרים יצחק מירוויס** שליט״א

Celebrating 150 Years

The US

לונדון

שנת ענ״י באמת ישע״ך

THE AUTHORISED

DAILY PRAYER BOOK

OF THE

UNITED HEBREW CONGREGATIONS
OF THE COMMONWEALTH

ORIGINAL TRANSLATION
by the Rev. Simeon Singer

WITH A TRANSLATION AND COMMENTARY BY
Chief Rabbi Lord Jonathan Sacks זצ"ל

ENLARGED UNDER THE DIRECTION OF
Chief Rabbi Ephraim Mirvis

Published to celebrate the
150th anniversary of the United Synagogue (1870–2020)

KOREN

5782 – 2022

The Authorised Daily Prayer Book
of the United Hebrew Congregations of the Commonwealth
First Koren Edition, 2022

FIRST EDITION 1890
SECOND EDITION 1962
THIRD (CENTENARY) EDITION 1990
Enlarged 1992
Revised 1998
FOURTH EDITION 2006
US 150TH ANNIVERSARY EDITION 2022

Koren Publishers Jerusalem
POB 4044, Jerusalem 91040, ISRAEL
POB 8531, New Milford, CT 06776, USA
www.korenpub.co.il

Printed in the PRC

Standard Size, Hardcover, ISBN 978-965-7767-74-0
Pocket Size, Hardcover, ISBN 978-965-7767-73-3
Large Size, Hardcover, ISBN 978-965-7767-75-7
Standard Size, Leather, ISBN 978-965-7767-95-5
Pocket Size, Leather, ISBN 978-965-7767-94-8
Large Size, Leather, ISBN 978-965-7767-96-2

NSS01

Dedicated to the memory of

Bobby Fisch

זאב בן משה דוד הכהן ז"ל

by wife Rosemary and children

CONTENTS

SERVICES FOR FESTIVALS & NEW MOON

BLESSINGS

PREFACE TO THE FIRST EDITION

A COMPLETE DAILY PRAYER BOOK, IN Hebrew and English, equally suitable for use in Synagogues, families and schools, has never yet been within the reach of the community at large. The present volume is intended to supply this primal necessity. It owes its origin to the generosity and public spirit of Mrs. Nathaniel Montefiore, by whom the entire cost of production has been defrayed. It is, therefore, now possible for all who can afford the outlay of one shilling to obtain a book which could not otherwise have been offered to the public except at a far higher price.

No pains have been spared to render the work of permanent value, and worthy of its place as the Authorised Prayer Book of the United Hebrew Congregations of the British Empire. As it was practically complete before the death of the late Chief Rabbi, Dr. N.M. Adler, it was enabled to receive and to be issued with the stamp of his sanction and authorisation.

The main objects kept in view in the production of the book have been to furnish a correct text (for the greater part of which S. Baer's *Abodath Israel* has served as the basis), and a satisfactory translation, and to combine with these fundamental requirements the not insignificant advantages of good paper, clear type and strong binding.

To render the volume still more suitable for general use, a number of Prayers for special occasions have been introduced. Of these, the Prayers to be said at the Consecration of a House, and upon the Sick and Death Bed, have been written or arranged by the Rev Dr. Hermann Adler, the Prayer in the House of Mourning and the Thanksgiving to be offered up by Women after their Confinement are the same that have been in use for some years past, having been drawn up by the late Chief Rabbi. The Marriage Service and Morning and Evening Prayers for Children have also been introduced.

The English translation is entirely new. Its aim has been to unite accuracy and even literalness with due regard to English idiom, and to that simplicity of style and diction which befits the language of prayer. It should be noted that the Biblical passages were translated by an accomplished scholar upon the basis of the Revised Version, the text or margin of which rendering has, upon the whole, been closely followed.

Thanks are due to the Rev. Dr. H. Adler, Dr. Friedlander and Mr. I. Abrahams, for many valuable suggestions as well as for much assistance while the book was passing through the press.

The copyright of the book is vested in the Jewish Association for the Diffusion of Religious Knowledge.

S. Singer

London, *Tammuz*, 5650 – July 1890

PREFACE

SINCE 1890, ONE OF THE MOST distinctive historical features of United Synagogue and similar communities has been the Authorised Daily Prayer Book, known for many decades as the 'Singers Siddur' after its first editor, Rev Simeon Singer. This edition is published in celebration of the United Synagogue's 150th anniversary which took place in 2020.

It is a central feature of our communal legacy, representing the familiar styles of our services as well as informing us of our traditions, prayers and beliefs. Helping us to express ourselves spiritually and remind ourselves daily of the values and responsibilities of a Jew, it brings out 'the language of the soul', to use the phrase employed by the late Rabbi Lord Sacks of blessed memory in his majestic essay written for his 2006 edition.

The antecedent for this is ancient and is particularly found in the Amida, the central part of each service. Fascinatingly, the Talmudic scholar Rabbi Chiya Bar Abba (Berachot 34b) who lived in the Land of Israel in the second century CE, tells us that, when possible, we must pray in a room which has windows. His source is the conduct of the Biblical figure Daniel, who lived in Babylonia and publicly prayed by a window facing towards Jerusalem, to set an example for his fellow Jews.

At that time, as the Amida began to develop into the form which we have, Jews needed a structure for prayer as well as maintaining their practices and beliefs now they were in exile. The development of fixed texts for daily prayer was a crucial element in achieving this and to help us apply the values articulated by our prayers to the societies in which we lived.

Although the prayers and values in the siddur are timeless, its setting and structure must speak to each generation. Augmenting the work of Rabbi Lord Sacks, Chief Rabbi Ephraim Mirvis has in this edition continued the chain started by Rev Singer to ensure we have a siddur with translation, commentary, layout and rubric which are appropriate for our times. It is our hope and prayer that it will enhance our appreciation of our prayers and our community even further.

I extend my sincere thanks to all of those involved in bringing this edition to fruition. In particular, I thank the Chief Rabbi and the Fisch family who have been generous partners and are committed to the values and practices of the United Synagogue.

The bulk of this edition is the work of Rabbi Sacks. Even though, very sadly, we are now bereft of him, we are committed to perpetuating the legacy of his translation, commentary and explanatory essay about prayer.

Our ultimate gratitude is to the Almighty for giving us the opportunity to be part of the Jewish people, as the words of the siddur express most eloquently.

I hope you will use this siddur for many years to come.

Michael Goldstein
President of the United Synagogue
Sivan, 5782 – May 2022

JUST AS THIS EDITION WAS GOING to print, we heard the sad news of the passing of Her Majesty Queen Elizabeth II. The United Synagogue held a memorial service at St John's Wood United Synagogue on 14 September, 2022, addressed by Chief Rabbi Ephraim Mirvis and former Prime Minister, the Rt Hon Theresa May MP. For 70 years, the Queen has been a constant for generations of United Synagogue members, the wider Jewish community and the nation at large. Across the country, every week, without exception, we say the Prayer for the Royal Family in our shuls. Since 1952 when Her Majesty the Queen ascended to the throne, there have been more than a dozen versions of the Prayer for the Royal Family to reflect changes to the royal family: marriages and, sadly, deaths. The one constant in the prayer throughout the last seventy years has been "Our Sovereign Lady, Queen Elizabeth". With a heavy heart, we have now updated the prayer in this siddur as we join together to pray that God blesses our new King Charles III and puts a spirit and wisdom into his heart and into the heart of all of his counsellors.

Michael Goldstein
Ellul, 5782 – September 2022

INTRODUCTION

Chief Rabbi Ephraim Mirvis

תפילות אבות תקנום "PRAYER WAS established by our Patriarchs". With these words, the Talmud (Berachot 26b) traces the laws, traditions and customs of our prayer back to the very origins of our faith, when their seeds were sown by Abraham, Isaac and Jacob.

Since that time, historical developments have influenced and shaped both the essence of *tefillah* and the various associated traditions which continue to this day. The dispersion of our people and the vicissitudes of Jewish life over the course of millennia are reflected in prayers that were introduced at pivotal points in our history, while geographical distances simultaneously contributed to the development of distinct customs that became sacred to the communities that adopted them.

In this context, we treasure our Minhag Anglia, which reflects our historic customs and practices. These were first incorporated in a prayer book in 1890 by Rev Simeon Singer, under the authority of Chief Rabbi Nathan Marcus Adler. Since then, the Authorised Daily Prayer Book of the United Hebrew Congregations of the Commonwealth has been reset and enlarged on many occasions. New editions have included improvements of the typeface, additional prayers, rubrics and commentaries. The history of Singer's, as it has always affectionately been known, is an affirmation of the close connection between Jewish prayer and tradition. This publication, which celebrates the 150th anniversary of the United Synagogue, is the latest addition to this ongoing chain of the Anglo-Jewish tradition of which we are so immensely proud.

Since the publication of the first Authorised Daily Prayer Book, the Jewish people have endured the most horrific suffering through two World Wars, persecution in many countries and most tragically, the Shoah. We have also been blessed to witness the establishment of the State of Israel and a post-war rejuvenation of Torah study and commitment to Jewish life. Confronted with growing levels of assimilation within an increasingly secular environment, the British Jewish community continues to flourish. The closing of our Synagogues over periods of lockdown during the Coronavirus pandemic and the limitations placed upon communal activity highlighted for us just how central our places of worship are and how life-enhancing our prayer services continue to be.

I was privileged to serve on the Singer's Prayer Book Committee, which produced the previous (fourth) edition under the inspirational leadership of Elkan Levy and with the generous support of Everard and Mina Goodman. The ambitious project was made possible thanks to the dedication and talent of Simon Goulden, together with valuable contributions given by the other committee members, Rabbi Mordechai Ginsbury, Geoffrey Hartnell and Josephine Wayne. Many dozens of others contributed valuable time and expertise to enable the siddur to see the light of day.

In his preface, Elkan Levy wrote: "We believe that this new edition of the Authorised Daily Prayer Book will not only restore Anglo-Jewry's pride in its own liturgy, but will enable future generations with devotion and clarity to approach the Almighty "*Shomea tefillah* – He who listens to prayer". So it proved to be.

The fourth edition saw the most significant enhancement of the Authorised Daily Prayer Book, which was carried out by my predecessor, Rabbi Lord Jonathan Sacks, whose masterful translation and explanatory notes were widely welcomed and praised. In this new edition, in recognition of his profound scholarship and incalculable contribution to our community, Rabbi Lord Sacks' work is preserved in full. His contribution to our understanding of daily prayer, which is so evident in this publication, continues to make a deep global impact.

In this expanded edition, to celebrate our unique Anglo-Jewish tradition, we have included significant writings relating to prayer by my immediate past predecessors, Rabbi Lord Jakobovits and Rabbi Lord Sacks. We have also added the Torah readings and Haftarot for festivals to the siddur. As a result, apart from Rosh Hashanah and Yom Kippur, this is the only prayer book one will need to have for all our daily, Shabbat and festival services.

We are indebted to Dayan Ivan Binstock for authoring the Guide to the Jewish Year, incorporating the customs of the United Synagogue, which appears at the back of this siddur. This authoritative codification of our practice is the first of its kind and is therefore a most significant addition to the Authorised Daily Prayer Book.

I am indebted as ever to the professional staff of my office, led so ably by Ari Jesner and I am particularly grateful to Dan Bacall, Michelle Bauernfreund and Mark Frazer for their work on this project.

I am grateful to the professional teams, both at Koren and the United Synagogue, whose input to this project has been invaluable.

This siddur is lovingly dedicated to the memory of Bobby Fisch. A charismatic, generous and popular congregational leader, Bobby had a transformative impact on the Finchley community. It was my privilege to be Bobby's partner in steering the Finchley community forward. Like many others, I shall forever be indebted to him for his inspiration, sage advice and encouragement.

Committed to our passionate continuation of the halachic process built on an unbroken chain that connects the Jews of today with the Torah given by God to Moses and the Jewish people at Mount Sinai, the United Synagogue infuses the lives of individuals, families and entire communities with the relevance of our timeless tradition and reveals how timely it remains in the 21st century. Nothing reflects this better than the Authorised Daily Prayer Book, which links our heritage of the past with the needs of the present and our aspirations for the future.

RESPONSIBILITY THROUGH PRAYER

Our prayers often take us back to the pivotal historic event which launched us as a people. *Zecher litziat Mitzrayim* – recalling the exodus of the Israelites from Egypt, inspires perpetual national joy. The Torah is careful not to describe our long, yearned for freedom as *chofesh,* which has the connotation of free time, but rather *cherut,* which implies liberty for the sake of responsibility. Upon emerging from Egypt, the newly crowned 'Kingdom of Priests and Holy Nation' was given the Torah with a Divinely inspired mandate for responsible living.

In this spirit, the central theme of Jewish prayer is our daily expression of *achrayut* – Jewish responsibility. The Siddur inspires us to excel in all three levels of *achrayu*t – responsibility to God, responsibility to ourselves and responsibility to others.

Responsibility to God

The Talmud, in recounting the last moments of the great sage, Rabbi Eliezer (Berachot 28b) says, "When Rabbi Eliezer fell ill, his students came to visit him. They said, "Rabbi, teach us a way to conduct ourselves, so that we may thereby merit eternal life." His answer concluded, "When you pray, know before whom you are standing. In this way, you will merit eternal life."

Rabbi Eliezer here calls upon us to recognise the awesome nature of prayer and the extraordinary opportunity it presents to us, to communicate directly in a one-to-one encounter with God. If we relate to prayer as we would, at the very least, to an audience with a human monarch, we would appreciate the remarkable opportunity that is presented to us every single day. It is with this in mind that many Holy Arks in our Synagogues display the words, דע לפני מי אתה עומד – Know before Whom you stand (Berachot 28a).

In the Book of Genesis, the prayer of Abraham is described as *amidah* – standing, while the prayer of Isaac is described as *sichah* – conversation. These terms reflect the dual nature of our prayerful relationship with God. *Amidah* requires that we be acutely aware of the fact that we are standing before none other than the Creator of the World. Together with that, we are privileged to be given the gift of *sichah,* an invitation to communicate privately and intimately with God, who is a loving parent figure and a trusted, loyal friend. One of our great challenges in prayer is to strike the right balance between these distinctly different facets of our relationship with the Almighty.

This is why we acknowledge that God is *Avinu Malkenu* – both our loving father and also our awesome and omnipresent King. In a similar vein, our blessings commence *Baruch atah Hashem* – Blessed are You, Lord, addressing God in the informal second person, and then continue *Elokeinu Melech ha'olam* – our God, King of the universe, in the third person, inspiring us to have the required respect and humility as we stand before Him.

The Book of Genesis describes one of the earliest prayers on record. When fleeing from his twin brother Esau, Jacob "encountered the place" (Genesis 28:11). Our Sages explain this 'encounter' to be a reference to prayer. Rabbi Moshe Feinstein (1895–1986) explains that Jacob was concerned about his capacity and that of his future family, to maintain their faith against the odds, whilst living in the Diaspora. Through this highly impactful encounter, the Almighty taught Jacob that prayer would be the central pillar upon which his faith would be sustained, regardless of his surroundings. Ever since that time, our Houses of Prayer have been at the centre of Jewish life. It is a truism to this day: the stronger one's connection to Synagogue, the stronger one's connection to

Judaism and the stronger one's relationship with God.

Over recent years, it has been wonderful to witness the transformation of many of our Synagogues from Houses of Prayer into powerhouses of Jewish religious, educational, social and cultural excellence. Yet, at the heart of it all, remains our tradition of *tefillah betzibur* – communal prayer. The unprecedented, challenging loss of this particular aspect of Jewish life had a dramatic impact during the Coronavirus pandemic, when we deeply missed the transformative power of *tefillah betzibur* to lift us during times of adversity.

Throughout our history, particularly in the Diaspora, the Beit HaKnesset or Synagogue has lived up to its name, meaning 'house of gathering', through being the focal point of Jewish life. In addition, as the German name 'Shul' indicates, our Synagogues have served as life-sustaining centres of Jewish education, in recognition of the teaching of the Mishna: "And the study of Torah supersedes all precepts" (Peah 1:1).

Our service of the Almighty is enhanced by the quality of our Synagogue services and the *ruach* (atmosphere) that they invoke. These are essential elements of the appeal that our services must maintain in order to inspire our congregants. The reality of attitudes within our ever-changing world is that traditional loyalty to the community is insufficient to guarantee Synagogue attendance and a meaningful connection to Judaism in the long term. The *ruach* achieved in prayer is the unique ingredient which lifts the soul and brings us closer to the Divine.

Responsibility to ourselves

In our Shabbat afternoon service, before taking the Torah scroll from the Ark, we chant the words *va'ani tefilati* – "as for me, my prayer" (Psalm 69:14). These words inspire us to deepen our understanding of ourselves through prayer. Spiritually speaking, we are what we pray, as highlighted by King David when he wrote the words, "I am prayer" (Psalms 109:4).

The Book of Genesis describes the eventful meeting of Rebecca and Isaac. Having travelled from Mesopotamia to marry Isaac, Rebecca saw him for the first time when he was praying, having entered a field to meditate with God. "And Rebecca lifted her eyes and, when she saw Isaac, she fell from the camel" (Genesis 24:64). The Midrash explains: Rebecca observed Isaac immersed in prayer. Overcome by this sacred, awe-inspiring vision, she lost her balance and fell off the camel. Such was the manner in which Isaac's prayers defined him as a true man of God.

Indeed, our prayers inspire us to be responsible to ourselves by sanctifying every precious moment of life and to appreciate depths of our spirituality which we otherwise would not discover. Prayer leads us to transformative introspection in which we recognise our personal strengths and weaknesses and are inspired to engage in *teshuva*, the journey back to being the people God had intended us to be.

Every aspect of Jewish life is infused with the aspiration to have a positive outlook on the world. Nothing helps us to realise this goal as effectively as our *tefillah*.

While the *minhag* (custom) and *nusach* (text) of siddurim can differ from community to community, there is one feature of the siddur which is standard – its order. The term *siddur* is derived from the word *seder*, meaning 'order' and this is reflected in a universally accepted framework for prayer. This makes it easy for anyone entering any Synagogue to readily find their place.

However, there is one feature of the order of the siddur which is surprising. Every siddur commences with the *Shacharit* (morning) service, followed by the *Mincha* (afternoon) service, which is followed, in turn, by *Ma'ariv* (the evening service). Yet, from the Biblical account of the days of creation in Genesis, we learn that *erev* (evening) precedes *boker* (morning). Consequently, the days on our calendar start in the evening, as is reflected in the commencement times for Shabbat, Festivals, Yahrzeits and so on. This is why Machzorim (prayer books for festivals) always begin with the Mincha and Ma'ariv prayers. So why, therefore, do our daily siddurim not also commence this way?

Night-time is a symbol of fear and dread, while the morning is charged with a renewed spirit of hope and promise. Our approach to daily prayer reflects our eternal spirit of optimism and positivity. Of course, many of our prayers are a cry for God's help in times of personal or national uncertainty and crisis. However, in addition, we turn to the Almighty to offer our gratitude for His ongoing blessings and support. In this spirit, we give prominence to our prayers of thanksgiving by standing when we recite them. Grateful for the gift of every breath of life, our hope in the Lord powers us through every day. The structure of the siddur inspires us to recognise that, just as day precedes night, so light can overcome darkness and hope may prevail under even the most challenging circumstances. This is beautifully reflected in the order of the prayerful sentiments expressed by the Psalmist, "to declare Your lovingkindness in the morning, and Your faithfulness in the night." (Psalm 92:3)

Responsibility to Others

Achrayut, meaning responsibility, is derived from the word *acher,* meaning 'other'. At the heart of Jewish prayer is a deep concern for the welfare of others and a desire to enable them to benefit from the blessings of the Almighty.

A treasured feature of our prayer services on festivals is *duchaning,* the Priestly Blessing. Amongst the many interesting laws related to this precept, the following question arises: What happens if there are only ten people in Synagogue and all of them are *kohanim*? Is there still a requirement for *duchaning?* The Shulchan Aruch addresses this issue: "If a Synagogue is comprised entirely of *Kohanim;* if there are only ten, they all get up to *duchan*" (Orach Chaim 12:25). This presents an extraordinary scenario. During the repetition of the Amidah, every single person in Synagogue steps forward. They chant the blessing "Blessed are you, Lord our God, King of the Universe, who has sanctified us with the holiness of Aaron and commanded us to bless His people Israel with love" and then turn to bless an entirely empty room!

Mindful of this perplexing situation, the Shulchan Aruch asks, "Who are they blessing?" and provides a powerful answer: "They are blessing their brethren in the fields".

Emerging from this *halacha* is a profound message with relevance well beyond *Kohanim* and *duchaning.* If there are only *Kohanim* in Shul, that must be because everyone else has gone out to work in the fields. How do we relate to those who are not present in Synagogue? Not only are the *Kohanim* commanded to bless them, but to bless them "with love". Our responsibility to them is not diminished by their absence. This is why the prayers of the siddur are primarily in the plural, for our engagement with the Almighty through *tefillah* is not only for ourselves. Everyone counts and we have a responsibility for all.

In a similar vein, Jewish tradition records the astonishing paradox of a prayer in which God is asked not to answer a prayer.

In Temple times, Yom Kippur was the only day of the year on which the High Priest entered the Holy of Holies in Jerusalem. The holiest person, in the holiest place, on the holiest day of the year, had a unique opportunity to offer a special, brief prayer to God. He concluded with the words: "And do not hearken to the prayers of travellers." Why?

People who are on the go, such as travellers and tourists, invariably hope and pray for sunny weather. If God was agreeable to such transient prayers, which are offered on every day of the year, there would be no rain. Our food supply and economy would be ruined.

When standing before the Almighty, we understandably focus on our own needs and requirements, yet we must also constantly be mindful of the needs of others. Empathy for all of God's creatures must be a central element of our prayers. We have a responsibility to society as a whole and the environment of which we are a part.

Empathy alone, however, is not enough. In *Anim Zemirot*, we chant the words, *Vayeshavucha lefi ma'asecha* – we recount God's value according to His deeds. Similarly, as we strive to emulate the Almighty, it is our actions which count. Prayerful empathy for the plight of others must precipitate meaningful action for their sakes. As we turn heavenwards filled with *bitachon* – trust in the Almighty, He calls upon us to engage in *hishtadlut* – our efforts, in partnership with Him. Our supplications from the heart in prayer must therefore be accompanied by selfless acts of kindness and social responsibility.

The very act of communal prayer itself cultivates an awareness of others. The Book of Proverbs (14:28) teaches: "The glory of the King (God) is to be found in the midst of a multitude of people". So, whilst it is permissible for us to pray privately, it is preferable for us to pray where there is a *minyan*. We pray *with* and therefore *for* others.

This notion that we are stronger as a collective is amplified in the Torah through a fascinating mathematical conundrum. When describing an age of blessing for the Jewish nation, the Book of Leviticus (26:8) states: "Five of you will pursue a hundred, and a hundred of you will pursue ten thousand...". If five can successfully pursue one hundred, each individual has the power to take on twenty enemy soldiers. Therefore, one hundred should have the power to overcome two thousand. Yet, the Torah tells us "a hundred of you will pursue ten thousand!"

Highlighting the seemingly disproportionate ratios in the verse, Rashi explains that one cannot compare the impact of the commitment of a small group to that of a large group. Through being part of a larger group, latent potential is released and the individual power of each participant is significantly enhanced.

In this spirit, when the Talmud (Berachot 8a) asks: When is it an acceptable time for prayer? our Sages answer: At the time when the community prays together.

Empowered by a deep sense of responsibility for one another, when we congregate as a community, united in prayer, strengthened in the knowledge that we belong to something greater than ourselves, an *et ratzon* is achieved – a propitious moment and a time of goodwill before God.

The quest to live up to these responsibilities was what led to the inception, 150 years ago, of the United Synagogue, when it adopted the name *Kehillah Kedoshah Knesset Yisrael* – the holy community, the congregation of Israel. Ever since that time, its communities have created countless 'propitious moments' of goodwill before God. In Synagogues where everyone counts, our 'communities of faith,' filled with optimism and hope, continue to bring entire congregations together in a spirit of unity.

Imbued with a deep sense of responsibility to God, to ourselves and to others, may we continue to be inspired by authentic, inclusive and modern Torah Judaism within a welcoming, warm and spiritually uplifting space for many years to come.

ACKNOWLEDGEMENTS

The fourth edition of the Authorised Daily Prayer Book and the enlarged 150th anniversary edition were made possible by the talent and expertise of the following people:

Professor David Aberbach
Anthony Angel
Rabbi Raymond Apple
Jon Barron
Joanna Benarroch
Dayan Ivan Binstock
Rev Michael Binstock
Rabbi Shmuel Bloom
Barry Bloombaum
Immanuel Burton
Richard Carr
David Collins
Joy Conway *zt'l*
Mark Creeger
Nadav Ezra
Paul Faiman
Rebbetzen Jacqueline Feldman
Raphäel Freedman
Harvey Freeman
Rabbi Philip Ginsbury
Rabbi Mordechai Ginsbury
Rabbi Doniel Golomb
Simon Goulden
Chief Rabbi Cyril Harris zt'l
Geoffrey Hartnell
Rev Moshe Haschel
Richard Herman
Dr Simon Hochhauser
Simon Jackson
Rabbi Shlomo Katanka
Ivor Katz
Rabbi Michael Laitner
Ashley Leboff
Irene Leeman
Elkan Levy
Rabbi Dovid Lewis
Rabbi Nicky Liss
Ian Metcalfe
Alan Mitchell
Gerald Normie
Professor Stefan Reif
Jonathan Renshaw
Laurie Reznik
Annabel Ries
Joanna Rose
Jessica Sacks
Rebbetzen Judy Salasnik
Doreen Samuels
Peter Sheldon
Rabbi Geoffrey Shisler
Rabbi Daniel Sturgess
Stuart Taylor
Richard Verber
Josephine Wayne
Syma Weinberg
Sorelle Weinstein
Dr Steven Wilson
Rabbi Saul Zneimer

THE AUTHORISED
Daily Prayer Book

תפילת שחרית לחול

Morning Service for Weekdays

השכמת הבוקר

On waking up in the morning, say:

מוֹדֶה (Women say מוֹדָה) אֲנִי לְפָנֶיךָ, מֶלֶךְ חַי וְקַיָּם, שֶׁהֶחֱזַרְתָּ בִּי נִשְׁמָתִי בְּחֶמְלָה, רַבָּה אֱמוּנָתֶךָ.

After washing one's hands, say:

רֵאשִׁית חָכְמָה יִרְאַת יהוה, שֵׂכֶל טוֹב לְכָל עֹשֵׂיהֶם, תְּהִלָּתוֹ עוֹמֶדֶת לָעַד. תּוֹרָה צִוָּה לָנוּ מֹשֶׁה מוֹרָשָׁה קְהִלַּת יַעֲקֹב. שְׁמַע בְּנִי מוּסַר אָבִיךָ וְאַל תִּטֹּשׁ תּוֹרַת אִמֶּךָ. תּוֹרָה תְּהִי אֱמוּנָתִי וְאֵל שַׁדַּי בְּעֶזְרָתִי. בָּרוּךְ שֵׁם כְּבוֹד מַלְכוּתוֹ לְעוֹלָם וָעֶד.

Those who do not wear a tallit gadol, holding the tallit katan in readiness to wear it, say:

בָּרוּךְ אַתָּה יהוה אֱלֹהֵינוּ מֶלֶךְ הָעוֹלָם אֲשֶׁר קִדְּשָׁנוּ בְּמִצְוֹתָיו וְצִוָּנוּ עַל מִצְוַת צִיצִית.

תפילת שחרית

On arrival at the synagogue, say:

וַאֲנִי בְּרֹב חַסְדְּךָ אָבוֹא בֵיתֶךָ, אֶשְׁתַּחֲוֶה אֶל־הֵיכַל קָדְשְׁךָ בְּיִרְאָתֶךָ. בְּבֵית אֱלֹהִים נְהַלֵּךְ בְּרָגֶשׁ.

On entering the synagogue, say:

מַה טֹּבוּ אֹהָלֶיךָ יַעֲקֹב מִשְׁכְּנֹתֶיךָ יִשְׂרָאֵל. וַאֲנִי בְּרֹב חַסְדְּךָ אָבוֹא בֵיתֶךָ, אֶשְׁתַּחֲוֶה אֶל־הֵיכַל קָדְשְׁךָ בְּיִרְאָתֶךָ. יהוה אָהַבְתִּי מְעוֹן בֵּיתֶךָ, וּמְקוֹם מִשְׁכַּן כְּבוֹדֶךָ. וַאֲנִי אֶשְׁתַּחֲוֶה וְאֶכְרָעָה, אֶבְרְכָה לִפְנֵי־יהוה עֹשִׂי. וַאֲנִי תְפִלָּתִי לְךָ יהוה, עֵת רָצוֹן, אֱלֹהִים בְּרָב־חַסְדֶּךָ, עֲנֵנִי בֶּאֱמֶת יִשְׁעֶךָ.

PRAYERS ON WAKING

מוֹדֶה אֲנִי *I thank you*: These words are to be said immediately on waking from sleep. In them we thank God for life itself, renewed each day. Sleep, said the Sages, is "one-sixtieth of death". Waking, therefore, is a miniature rebirth. Despite its brevity, this sentence articulates a transformative act of faith: the recognition that life is a gift from God. Expressing gratitude at the fact of being alive, we prepare ourselves to celebrate and sanctify the new day.

ON WAKING

On waking up in the morning, say:

מוֹדֶה I thank You, living and eternal King, for giving me back my soul in mercy. Great is Your faithfulness.

After washing one's hands, say:

רֵאשִׁית Wisdom begins in awe of the LORD; all who fulfil [His commandments] gain good understanding; His praise is everlasting. The Torah Moses commanded us is the heritage of the congregation of Jacob. Listen, my son, to your father's instruction, and do not forsake your mother's teaching. May the Torah be my faith and Almighty GOD my help. Blessed be the name of His glorious kingdom for ever and all time.

Those who do not wear a tallit gadol, holding the tallit katan in readiness to wear it, say:

בָּרוּךְ Blessed are You LORD our GOD, King of the universe, who has made us holy through His commandments and has commanded us concerning the precept of tzitzit.

MORNING SERVICE

On arrival at the synagogue, say:

וַאֲנִי As for me, in Your great lovingkindness, I will come into Your house. I will bow down to Your holy Temple in awe of You. We will walk with the throng to GOD's house.

On entering the synagogue, say:

מַה טֹּבוּ How goodly are your tents, Jacob, Your dwelling places, Israel. As for me, in Your great lovingkindness, I will come into Your house. I will bow down to Your holy Temple in awe of You. LORD, I love the habitation of Your house, the place where Your glory dwells. As for me, I will bow in worship; I will bend the knee before the LORD my Maker. As for me, may my prayer come to You, LORD, at a time of favour. GOD, in Your great lovingkindness, answer me with Your faithful salvation.

מַה טֹּבוּ *How goodly*: Tradition interpreted "tents" and "dwelling places" as synagogues and houses of study (*Sanhedrin* 105a), which are the vehicles of Jewish continuity through the generations. Rav Kook explained the difference between the two: We use a tent when we are on a journey; we have a dwelling place where we feel at home. Together they represent the twin needs of the soul: to grow on the one hand, and to be rooted in eternal values on the other.

עטיפת טלית

Meditation before putting on the טַלִּית:

הִנְנִי מִתְעַטֵּף בְּטַלִּית שֶׁל־צִיצִת כְּדֵי לְקַיֵּם מִצְוַת בּוֹרְאִי, כַּכָּתוּב בַּתּוֹרָה, וְעָשׂוּ לָהֶם צִיצִת עַל־כַּנְפֵי בִגְדֵיהֶם לְדֹרֹתָם, וּכְשֵׁם שֶׁאֲנִי מִתְכַּסֶּה בְטַלִּית בָּעוֹלָם הַזֶּה כֵּן תִּזְכֶּה נִשְׁמָתִי לְהִתְלַבֵּשׁ בְּטַלִּית נָאָה לָעוֹלָם הַבָּא בְּגַן עֵדֶן, אָמֵן.

Unfold the טַלִּית and, before wrapping oneself in it, say:

בָּרוּךְ אַתָּה יהוה אֱלֹהֵינוּ מֶלֶךְ הָעוֹלָם, אֲשֶׁר קִדְּשָׁנוּ בְּמִצְוֹתָיו וְצִוָּנוּ לְהִתְעַטֵּף בַּצִּיצִת.

After wrapping oneself in it, say:

מַה־יָּקָר חַסְדְּךָ אֱלֹהִים, וּבְנֵי אָדָם בְּצֵל כְּנָפֶיךָ יֶחֱסָיוּן. יִרְוְיֻן מִדֶּשֶׁן בֵּיתֶךָ, וְנַחַל עֲדָנֶיךָ תַשְׁקֵם. כִּי־עִמְּךָ מְקוֹר חַיִּים, בְּאוֹרְךָ נִרְאֶה־אוֹר. מְשֹׁךְ חַסְדְּךָ לְיֹדְעֶיךָ וְצִדְקָתְךָ לְיִשְׁרֵי־לֵב.

הנחת תפילין

Meditation before putting on the תְּפִלִּין:

הִנְנִי מְכַוֵּן בְּהַנָּחַת תְּפִלִּין לְקַיֵּם מִצְוַת בּוֹרְאִי, שֶׁצִּוָּנוּ לְהָנִיחַ תְּפִלִּין, כַּכָּתוּב בַּתּוֹרָה, וּקְשַׁרְתָּם לְאוֹת עַל־יָדֶךָ, וְהָיוּ לְטֹטָפֹת בֵּין עֵינֶיךָ. וְהֵם אַרְבַּע פָּרָשִׁיּוֹת אֵלּוּ, שְׁמַע, וְהָיָה אִם־שָׁמֹעַ, קַדֶּשׁ, וְהָיָה כִּי יְבִיאֲךָ, שֶׁיֵּשׁ בָּהֶם יִחוּדוֹ וְאַחְדוּתוֹ יִתְבָּרַךְ שְׁמוֹ, וְשֶׁנִּזְכֹּר נִסִּים וְנִפְלָאוֹת שֶׁעָשָׂה עִמָּנוּ בְּהוֹצִיאוֹ אֹתָנוּ מִמִּצְרַיִם, וַאֲשֶׁר לוֹ הַכֹּחַ וְהַמֶּמְשָׁלָה בָּעֶלְיוֹנִים וּבַתַּחְתּוֹנִים לַעֲשׂוֹת בָּהֶם כִּרְצוֹנוֹ. וְצִוָּנוּ לְהָנִיחַ עַל־הַיָּד, לְזִכְרוֹן זְרוֹעוֹ הַנְּטוּיָה, וְשֶׁהִיא נֶגֶד הַלֵּב, לְשַׁעְבֵּד בָּזֶה תַּאֲוַת וּמַחְשְׁבוֹת לִבֵּנוּ לַעֲבוֹדָתוֹ, יִתְבָּרַךְ שְׁמוֹ. וְעַל־הָרֹאשׁ נֶגֶד הַמֹּחַ, שֶׁהַנְּשָׁמָה

TALLIT AND TEFILLIN

The *mitzvah* of *tzitzit*, placing tassels on the corner of our garments, is to recall us constantly to our vocation: "Thus you will be reminded to keep all My commandments, and be holy to your God." Over the course of time, the fulfilment of this commandment took two different forms: the *tallit*, worn as a robe during prayer, *over* our clothes, and the *tallit katan*, worn as an undergarment *beneath* our outer clothes. Though they fulfil a single commandment, they were deemed so different as to warrant two different blessings.

TALLIT

Meditation before putting on the *tallit*:

I am about to wrap myself in this tasselled robe (*tallit*) to fulfil the commandment of my Creator, as is written in the Torah: "They shall make tassels on the corners of their garments for all generations." And just as I cover myself with the *tallit* in this world, so may my soul be worthy of being clothed in a beautiful *tallit* in the World to Come in the Garden of Eden. Amen.

Unfold the *tallit* and, before wrapping oneself in it, say:

בָּרוּךְ Blessed are You, LORD our GOD, King of the Universe, who has made us holy through His commandments, and has commanded us to wrap ourselves in the tasselled garment.

After wrapping oneself in it, say:

מַה־יָּקָר How precious is Your lovingkindness, O LORD, and the children of men find refuge under the shadow of Your wings. They are filled with the rich plenty of Your house. You give them drink from Your river of delights. For with You is the fountain of life; in Your light, we see light. Continue Your lovingkindness to those who know You, and Your righteousness to the upright in heart.

TEFILLIN

Meditation before putting on the *tefillin*:

By putting on the *tefillin* I hereby intend to fulfil the commandment of my Creator who commanded us to wear *tefillin*, as it is written in the Torah: "Bind them as a sign on your hand, and they shall be an emblem on the centre of your head." They contain these four sections of the Torah: one beginning with *Shema* (Deuteronomy 6:4–9); another with *Vehayah im shamo-a* (ibid. 11:13–21); the third with *Kaddesh* (Exodus 13:1–10); and the fourth with *Vehayah ki yevi-acha* (ibid. 11–16). These proclaim the uniqueness and unity of GOD, blessed be His name. They also remind us of the miracles and wonders which He did for us when He brought us out of Egypt, and that He has the power and the dominion over the highest and the lowest to deal with them as He pleases. He commanded us to place one of the *tefillin* on the arm in memory of His "outstretched arm" (of redemption), setting it opposite the heart, to subject the desires and designs of our heart to His service, blessed be His name. The other is to be on the

---

Tefillin: The word *tefillin* (called *totafot* in the Torah) means "emblem, sign, insignia", the visible symbol of an abstract idea. *Tefillin* are our reminder of the commandment of the *Shema*: "Love GOD your LORD with all your heart, all your soul and all your might". *All your heart* – this is the *tefillin* on the upper arm opposite the heart. *All your soul* – this is the head-*tefillin* opposite the seat of consciousness,

שֶׁבְּמוֹחִי, עִם־חוּשַׁי וְכֹחוֹתַי, כֻּלָּם יִהְיוּ מְשֻׁעְבָּדִים לַעֲבוֹדָתוֹ, יִתְבָּרַךְ שְׁמוֹ. וּמִשֶּׁפַע מִצְוַת תְּפִלִּין יִתְמַשֵּׁךְ עָלַי לִהְיוֹת לִי חַיִּים אֲרֻכִּים, וְשֶׁפַע קֹדֶשׁ, וּמַחֲשָׁבוֹת קְדוֹשׁוֹת בְּלִי הִרְהוּר חֵטְא וְעָוֹן כְּלָל, וְשֶׁלֹּא יְפַתֵּנוּ וְלֹא יִתְגָּרֶה בָּנוּ יֵצֶר הָרָע, וְיַנִּיחֵנוּ לַעֲבֹד אֶת־יהוה כַּאֲשֶׁר עִם־לְבָבֵנוּ, אָמֵן.

Stand while putting on the תְּפִלִּין. Place the hand-תְּפִלִּין on the biceps of the left arm (or right arm if you are left-handed) and, before tightening the strap, say:

בָּרוּךְ אַתָּה יהוה אֱלֹהֵינוּ מֶלֶךְ הָעוֹלָם, אֲשֶׁר קִדְּשָׁנוּ בְּמִצְוֹתָיו וְצִוָּנוּ לְהָנִיחַ תְּפִלִּין.

Wrap the strap of the hand-תְּפִלִּין seven times around the arm. Place the head-תְּפִלִּין above the hairline, centrally (i.e. above the space midway between the eyes), and say:

בָּרוּךְ אַתָּה יהוה אֱלֹהֵינוּ מֶלֶךְ הָעוֹלָם, אֲשֶׁר קִדְּשָׁנוּ בְּמִצְוֹתָיו וְצִוָּנוּ עַל־מִצְוַת תְּפִלִּין.

Adjust the strap of the head-תְּפִלִּין and say:

בָּרוּךְ שֵׁם כְּבוֹד מַלְכוּתוֹ לְעוֹלָם וָעֶד.

After putting on the head-תְּפִלִּין, wind the strap of the hand-תְּפִלִּין three times around the middle finger, saying:

וְאֵרַשְׂתִּיךְ לִי לְעוֹלָם. וְאֵרַשְׂתִּיךְ לִי בְּצֶדֶק וּבְמִשְׁפָּט וּבְחֶסֶד וּבְרַחֲמִים. וְאֵרַשְׂתִּיךְ לִי בֶּאֱמוּנָה, וְיָדַעַתְּ אֶת־יהוה.

After putting on the תְּפִלִּין, say:

שמות יג:א–י

וַיְדַבֵּר יהוה אֶל־מֹשֶׁה לֵּאמֹר. קַדֶּשׁ־לִי כָל־בְּכוֹר, פֶּטֶר כָּל־רֶחֶם בִּבְנֵי יִשְׂרָאֵל בָּאָדָם וּבַבְּהֵמָה, לִי הוּא. וַיֹּאמֶר מֹשֶׁה אֶל־הָעָם. זָכוֹר אֶת־הַיּוֹם הַזֶּה אֲשֶׁר יְצָאתֶם מִמִּצְרַיִם, מִבֵּית עֲבָדִים, כִּי בְּחֹזֶק יָד הוֹצִיא יהוה אֶתְכֶם מִזֶּה, וְלֹא יֵאָכֵל חָמֵץ. הַיּוֹם אַתֶּם יֹצְאִים, בְּחֹדֶשׁ הָאָבִיב. וְהָיָה כִי־יְבִיאֲךָ יהוה אֶל־אֶרֶץ הַכְּנַעֲנִי וְהַחִתִּי וְהָאֱמֹרִי וְהַחִוִּי וְהַיְבוּסִי אֲשֶׁר נִשְׁבַּע לַאֲבֹתֶיךָ לָתֶת לָךְ, אֶרֶץ זָבַת חָלָב וּדְבָשׁ, וְעָבַדְתָּ אֶת־הָעֲבֹדָה הַזֹּאת בַּחֹדֶשׁ הַזֶּה. שִׁבְעַת יָמִים תֹּאכַל

---

the soul. *All your might* – this is the strap of the hand-*tefillin,* symbolising action, power, might. *Tefillin* thus symbolise the love for GOD in emotion (heart), thought (head) and deed (hand). *The LORD spoke* – this commandment is alluded to or mentioned in the four passages in the Torah which are contained in the *tefillin.* These are two; the others are the first and second paragraphs of the *Shema.*

head, opposite the brain, so that the mind, whose seat is in the brain, together with my other senses and faculties, may be subjected to His service, blessed be His name. May the spiritual influence of the commandment of the *tefillin* be with me so that I may have a long life, a flow of holiness, and sacred thoughts, free from any suggestion of sin or iniquity. May the evil inclination neither incite nor entice us, but leave us to serve the LORD, as it is in our hearts to do. Amen.

Stand while putting on the *tefillin*. Place the hand-*tefillin* on the biceps of the left arm (or right arm if you are left-handed) and, before tightening the strap, say:

בָּרוּךְ Blessed are You, LORD our GOD, King of the Universe, who has made us holy through His commandments, and has commanded us to put on *tefillin*.

Wrap the strap of the hand-*tefillin* seven times around the arm. Place the head-*tefillin* above the hairline, centrally (i.e. above the space midway between the eyes), and say:

בָּרוּךְ Blessed are You, LORD our GOD, King of the Universe, who has made us holy through His commandments, and has commanded us about the commandment of *tefillin*.

Adjust the strap of the head-*tefillin* and say:

בָּרוּךְ Blessed be the name of His glorious kingdom for ever and all time.

After putting on the head-*tefillin*, wind the strap of the hand-*tefillin* three times around the middle finger, saying:

וְאֵרַשְׂתִּיךְ I will betroth You to Me for ever; I will betroth you to Me in righteousness and justice, lovingkindness and compassion; I will betroth you to Me in faithfulness; and you shall know the LORD.

After putting on the *tefillin*, say:

EXODUS 13:1–10.

The LORD spoke to Moses, saying, "Consecrate to Me every firstborn male. The first offspring of every womb among the Israelites, whether man or beast, belongs to Me." Then Moses said to the people, "Remember this day on which you left Egypt, the slave-house, when the LORD brought you out of it with a mighty hand. No leaven shall be eaten. You are leaving on this day, in the month of Aviv. When the LORD brings you into the land of the Canaanites, Hittites, Amorites, Hivites and Jebusites, the land He swore to your ancestors to give you, a land flowing with milk and honey, you are to observe this service in this same month. For seven days you shall eat unleavened bread, and make the seventh day a festival to the LORD. Unleavened bread shall be eaten throughout the seven days. No leavened bread may be seen in your posses-

---

וְאֵרַשְׂתִּיךְ *I will betroth you to Me*: These exquisite lines from the Book of Hosea speak of GOD's covenant with Israel as a marriage – a mutual pledge of faith, born of love. Wrapping the strap of the hand-*tefillin* around the middle finger like a wedding ring, we remind ourselves of GOD's love for Israel, and Israel's love for GOD.

מַצֹּת, וּבַיּוֹם הַשְּׁבִיעִי חַג לַיהוה. מַצּוֹת יֵאָכֵל אֵת שִׁבְעַת הַיָּמִים, וְלֹא־יֵרָאֶה לְךָ חָמֵץ, וְלֹא־יֵרָאֶה לְךָ שְׂאֹר בְּכָל־גְּבֻלֶךָ. וְהִגַּדְתָּ לְבִנְךָ בַּיּוֹם הַהוּא לֵאמֹר: בַּעֲבוּר זֶה עָשָׂה יהוה לִי בְּצֵאתִי מִמִּצְרָיִם. וְהָיָה לְךָ לְאוֹת עַל־יָדְךָ וּלְזִכָּרוֹן בֵּין עֵינֶיךָ, לְמַעַן תִּהְיֶה תּוֹרַת יהוה בְּפִיךָ, כִּי בְּיָד חֲזָקָה הוֹצִאֲךָ יהוה מִמִּצְרָיִם. וְשָׁמַרְתָּ אֶת־הַחֻקָּה הַזֹּאת לְמוֹעֲדָהּ, מִיָּמִים יָמִימָה.

שמות יג:יא–טז

וְהָיָה כִּי־יְבִאֲךָ יהוה אֶל־אֶרֶץ הַכְּנַעֲנִי כַּאֲשֶׁר נִשְׁבַּע לְךָ וְלַאֲבֹתֶיךָ, וּנְתָנָהּ לָךְ. וְהַעֲבַרְתָּ כָל־פֶּטֶר־רֶחֶם לַיהוה, וְכָל־פֶּטֶר שֶׁגֶר בְּהֵמָה אֲשֶׁר יִהְיֶה לְךָ, הַזְּכָרִים לַיהוה. וְכָל־פֶּטֶר חֲמֹר תִּפְדֶּה בְשֶׂה, וְאִם־לֹא תִפְדֶּה וַעֲרַפְתּוֹ, וְכֹל בְּכוֹר אָדָם בְּבָנֶיךָ תִּפְדֶּה. וְהָיָה כִּי־יִשְׁאָלְךָ בִנְךָ מָחָר לֵאמֹר, מַה־זֹּאת, וְאָמַרְתָּ אֵלָיו, בְּחֹזֶק יָד הוֹצִיאָנוּ יהוה מִמִּצְרַיִם מִבֵּית עֲבָדִים. וַיְהִי כִּי־הִקְשָׁה פַרְעֹה לְשַׁלְּחֵנוּ, וַיַּהֲרֹג יהוה כָּל־בְּכוֹר בְּאֶרֶץ מִצְרַיִם, מִבְּכֹר אָדָם וְעַד־בְּכוֹר בְּהֵמָה, עַל־כֵּן אֲנִי זֹבֵחַ לַיהוה כָּל־פֶּטֶר רֶחֶם הַזְּכָרִים, וְכָל־בְּכוֹר בָּנַי אֶפְדֶּה. וְהָיָה לְאוֹת עַל־יָדְכָה וּלְטוֹטָפֹת בֵּין עֵינֶיךָ, כִּי בְּחֹזֶק יָד הוֹצִיאָנוּ יהוה מִמִּצְרָיִם.

אדון עולם

אֲדוֹן **עוֹלָם** אֲשֶׁר מָלַךְ, בְּטֶרֶם כָּל־יְצִיר נִבְרָא.
לְעֵת נַעֲשָׂה בְחֶפְצוֹ כֹּל, אֲזַי מֶלֶךְ שְׁמוֹ נִקְרָא.
וְאַחֲרֵי כִּכְלוֹת הַכֹּל, לְבַדּוֹ יִמְלוֹךְ נוֹרָא.
וְהוּא הָיָה וְהוּא הֹוֶה, וְהוּא יִהְיֶה בְּתִפְאָרָה.
וְהוּא אֶחָד וְאֵין שֵׁנִי, לְהַמְשִׁיל לוֹ לְהַחְבִּירָה.
בְּלִי רֵאשִׁית בְּלִי תַכְלִית, וְלוֹ הָעֹז וְהַמִּשְׂרָה.
וְהוּא אֵלִי וְחַי גֹּאֲלִי, וְצוּר חֶבְלִי בְּעֵת צָרָה.
וְהוּא נִסִּי וּמָנוֹס לִי, מְנָת כּוֹסִי בְּיוֹם אֶקְרָא.
בְּיָדוֹ אַפְקִיד רוּחִי, בְּעֵת אִישַׁן וְאָעִירָה.
וְעִם־רוּחִי גְּוִיָּתִי, יהוה לִי וְלֹא אִירָא.

אֲדוֹן עוֹלָם *Lord of the universe*: A magnificent poem, attributed by some to the Spanish Jewish poet Solomon ibn Gabirol (1021–1070). Its power lies in its effortless transition from abstract theology to personal experience. The first six lines speak of God in cosmic terms; the last four lines turn to God as a personal presence. Though He is unfathomably vast, He is also intensely close. I face the world without fear because I rest in His everlasting arms.

sion, and no leaven shall be seen anywhere within your borders. On that day you shall tell your son, 'This is because of what the LORD did for me when I left Egypt.' [These words] shall also be a sign on your hand, and a reminder above your forehead, so that the LORD's Torah may always be in your mouth, because with a mighty hand the LORD brought you out of Egypt. You shall therefore keep this statute at its appointed time from year to year."

EXODUS 13:11–16

After the LORD has brought you into the land of the Canaanites, as He swore to you and your ancestors, and He has given it to you, you shall set apart for the LORD the first offspring of every womb. All the firstborn males of your cattle belong to the LORD. Every firstling donkey you shall redeem with a lamb. If you do not redeem it, you must break its neck. Every firstborn among your sons you must redeem. If, in time to come, your son asks you, "What does this mean?" you shall say to him, "With a mighty hand the LORD brought us out of Egypt, out of the slave-house. When Pharaoh stubbornly refused to let us leave, the LORD killed all the firstborn in the land of Egypt, both man and beast. That is why I sacrifice to the LORD the first male offspring of every womb, and redeem all the firstborn of my sons." [These words] shall be a sign on your hand and as an emblem above your forehead, that with a mighty hand the LORD brought us out of Egypt.

ADON OLAM

אֲדוֹן עוֹלָם LORD of the universe, who reigned
before the birth of any thing –
When by His will all things were made
then was His name proclaimed King.
And when all things shall cease to be
He alone will reign in awe.
He was, He is, and He shall be
glorious for evermore.
He is One, there is none else,
alone, unique, beyond compare;
Without beginning, without end,
His might, His rule are everywhere.
He is my GOD; my Redeemer lives.
He is the Rock on whom I rely –
My banner and my safe retreat,
my cup, my portion when I cry.
Into His hand my soul I place,
when I awake and when I sleep.
GOD is with me, I shall not fear;
body and soul from harm will He keep.

יגדל

יִגְדַּל אֱלֹהִים חַי וְיִשְׁתַּבַּח, נִמְצָא וְאֵין עֵת אֶל מְצִיאוּתוֹ.
אֶחָד וְאֵין יָחִיד כְּיִחוּדוֹ, נֶעְלָם וְגַם אֵין סוֹף לְאַחְדּוּתוֹ.
אֵין לוֹ דְּמוּת הַגּוּף וְאֵינוֹ גוּף, לֹא נַעֲרוֹךְ אֵלָיו קְדֻשָּׁתוֹ.
קַדְמוֹן לְכָל דָּבָר אֲשֶׁר נִבְרָא, רִאשׁוֹן וְאֵין רֵאשִׁית לְרֵאשִׁיתוֹ.
הִנּוֹ אֲדוֹן עוֹלָם לְכָל נוֹצָר, יוֹרֶה גְדֻלָּתוֹ וּמַלְכוּתוֹ.
שֶׁפַע נְבוּאָתוֹ נְתָנוֹ, אֶל אַנְשֵׁי סְגֻלָּתוֹ וְתִפְאַרְתּוֹ.
לֹא קָם בְּיִשְׂרָאֵל כְּמֹשֶׁה עוֹד, נָבִיא וּמַבִּיט אֶת תְּמוּנָתוֹ.
תּוֹרַת אֱמֶת נָתַן לְעַמּוֹ אֵל, עַל יַד נְבִיאוֹ נֶאֱמַן בֵּיתוֹ.
לֹא יַחֲלִיף הָאֵל וְלֹא יָמִיר דָּתוֹ, לְעוֹלָמִים לְזוּלָתוֹ.
צוֹפֶה וְיוֹדֵעַ סְתָרֵינוּ, מַבִּיט לְסוֹף דָּבָר בְּקַדְמָתוֹ.
גּוֹמֵל לְאִישׁ חֶסֶד כְּמִפְעָלוֹ, נוֹתֵן לְרָשָׁע רָע כְּרִשְׁעָתוֹ.
יִשְׁלַח לְקֵץ יָמִין מְשִׁיחֵנוּ, לִפְדּוֹת מְחַכֵּי קֵץ יְשׁוּעָתוֹ.
מֵתִים יְחַיֶּה אֵל בְּרֹב חַסְדּוֹ, בָּרוּךְ עֲדֵי־עַד שֵׁם תְּהִלָּתוֹ.

בָּרוּךְ אַתָּה יהוה אֱלֹהֵינוּ מֶלֶךְ הָעוֹלָם, אֲשֶׁר קִדְּשָׁנוּ בְּמִצְוֹתָיו, וְצִוָּנוּ עַל נְטִילַת יָדָיִם.

בָּרוּךְ אַתָּה יהוה אֱלֹהֵינוּ מֶלֶךְ הָעוֹלָם, אֲשֶׁר יָצַר אֶת־הָאָדָם בְּחָכְמָה, וּבָרָא בוֹ נְקָבִים נְקָבִים, חֲלוּלִים חֲלוּלִים. גָּלוּי וְיָדוּעַ לִפְנֵי כִסֵּא כְבוֹדֶךָ, שֶׁאִם יִפָּתֵחַ אֶחָד מֵהֶם, אוֹ

יִגְדַּל *Great is the living God*: A poetic setting of Maimonides' Thirteen Principles of Jewish faith, written by Rabbi Daniel bar Judah (Rome, fourteenth century), each line representing one of the principles. Like *Adon Olam*, the presence of *Yigdal* in the Siddur reminds us that it is not only a book of prayer but also the supreme book of Jewish faith. Judaism contains little systematic theology. We speak *to* God more than we speak *about* God. Yet Judaism *is* a faith whose distinctive beliefs find their home in the prayer book. We do not analyse faith in academic detachment. We sing it, affirming faith with joy.

YIGDAL

יִגְדַּל Great is the living God and praised.
He exists, and His existence is beyond time.
He is One, and there is no unity like His.
Unfathomable, His oneness is infinite.
He has neither bodily form nor substance;
His holiness is beyond compare.
He preceded all that was created.
He was first: there was no beginning to His beginning.
Behold He is Master of the Universe; to every creature
He shows His greatness and majesty.
The rich flow of His prophecy He gave
to His treasured people in whom He gloried.
Never in Israel has there arisen another like Moses,
a prophet who beheld God's image.
God gave His people a Torah of truth
by the hand of His prophet, most faithful of His house.
God will not alter or change His law
for any other, for eternity.
He sees and knows our secret thoughts;
as soon as something is begun, He foresees its end.
He rewards people with lovingkindness according to their deeds;
He punishes the wicked according to his wickedness.
At the end of days He will send our Messiah,
to redeem those who await His final salvation.
God will revive the dead in His great lovingkindness.
Blessed for evermore is His glorious name!

בָּרוּךְ Blessed are You, Lord our God, King of the Universe, who has made us holy through His commandments, and has commanded us about washing hands.

בָּרוּךְ Blessed are You, Lord our God, King of the Universe, who formed man in wisdom and created in him many orifices and cavities. It is revealed and known before the throne of Your glory that were one

---

אֲשֶׁר יָצַר *Who formed man in wisdom*: A blessing of thanks for the intricate wonders of the human body. *Were one of them to be ruptured or blocked* – even the smallest variation in the human genome can cause potentially fatal illness. The more we understand of the complexity of life, the more we appreciate "How myriad are

יִסָּתֵם אֶחָד מֵהֶם, אִי אֶפְשַׁר לְהִתְקַיֵּם וְלַעֲמוֹד לְפָנֶיךָ. בָּרוּךְ אַתָּה יהוה, רוֹפֵא כָל־בָּשָׂר וּמַפְלִיא לַעֲשׂוֹת.

ברכות התורה

בָּרוּךְ אַתָּה יהוה אֱלֹהֵינוּ מֶלֶךְ הָעוֹלָם, אֲשֶׁר קִדְּשָׁנוּ בְּמִצְוֹתָיו, וְצִוָּנוּ לַעֲסוֹק בְּדִבְרֵי תוֹרָה.

וְהַעֲרֶב־נָא יהוה אֱלֹהֵינוּ אֶת דִּבְרֵי תוֹרָתְךָ בְּפִינוּ וּבְפִי עַמְּךָ בֵּית יִשְׂרָאֵל, וְנִהְיֶה אֲנַחְנוּ וְצֶאֱצָאֵינוּ וְצֶאֱצָאֵי עַמְּךָ בֵּית יִשְׂרָאֵל, כֻּלָּנוּ יוֹדְעֵי שְׁמֶךָ וְלוֹמְדֵי תוֹרָתֶךָ. בָּרוּךְ אַתָּה יהוה, הַמְלַמֵּד תּוֹרָה לְעַמּוֹ יִשְׂרָאֵל.

בָּרוּךְ אַתָּה יהוה אֱלֹהֵינוּ מֶלֶךְ הָעוֹלָם, אֲשֶׁר בָּחַר־בָּנוּ מִכָּל־הָעַמִּים וְנָתַן־לָנוּ אֶת־תּוֹרָתוֹ. בָּרוּךְ אַתָּה יהוה, נוֹתֵן הַתּוֹרָה.

במדבר ו:כד–כו

יְבָרֶכְךָ יהוה וְיִשְׁמְרֶךָ. יָאֵר יהוה פָּנָיו אֵלֶיךָ וִיחֻנֶּךָּ. יִשָּׂא יהוה פָּנָיו אֵלֶיךָ, וְיָשֵׂם לְךָ שָׁלוֹם.

משנה פאה א:א

אֵלּוּ דְבָרִים שֶׁאֵין לָהֶם שִׁעוּר, הַפֵּאָה וְהַבִּכּוּרִים וְהָרַאְיוֹן וּגְמִילוּת חֲסָדִים וְתַלְמוּד תּוֹרָה.

---

your works, O God; You have made them all with wisdom; the earth is full of Your creations" (Psalm 104:24). This blessing is a rejection of the idea that the spirit alone is holy, and physical life bereft of God.

BLESSINGS OVER THE TORAH

The history of Judaism is a story of the love of a people for the Book of Books, the Torah. As a preliminary to study, we pronounce two blessings and a prayer. The first, "who has made us holy with His commandments", is a blessing over the commandment to engage in study of the Torah, a declaration that we do not simply study as an intellectual or cultural exercise but as the fulfilment of a Divine commandment. This is followed

of them to be ruptured or blocked, it would be impossible to survive and stand before You. Blessed are You, LORD, Healer of all flesh who does wondrous deeds.

BLESSINGS OVER THE TORAH

בָּרוּךְ Blessed are You, LORD our GOD, King of the Universe, who has made us holy through His commandments, and has commanded us to engage in study of the words of Torah.

וְהַעֲרֶב־נָא Please, LORD our GOD, make the words of Your Torah sweet in our mouth and in the mouth of Your people, the house of Israel, so that we, our descendants and the descendants of Your people, the house of Israel, may all know Your name and study Your Torah. Blessed are You, LORD, who teaches Torah to His people Israel.

בָּרוּךְ Blessed are You, LORD our GOD, King of the Universe, who has chosen us from all the peoples and given us His Torah. Blessed are You, LORD, Giver of the Torah.

NUMBERS 6:24–26

יְבָרֶכְךָ May the LORD bless you and protect you. May the LORD make His face shine on you and be gracious to you. May the LORD turn His face toward you and grant you peace.

MISHNAH PEAH 1:1

אֵלּוּ These are the things for which there is no fixed measure: the corner of the field, first-fruits, appearances before the LORD [on festivals, with offerings], acts of kindness and the study of Torah.

---

by a prayer that GOD make Torah study sweet, and help us to hand it on to our children. The final blessing, "Who has chosen us", is a blessing of acknowledgement that chosenness means responsibility, and is inseparably linked to the study and practice of Torah.

So as to follow the blessings immediately with an act that fulfils the commandment, we read three texts whose recitation forms an act of study. The Talmud (*Kiddushin* 30a) rules that Torah study must be divided into three: study of 1. Torah; 2. Mishnah; and 3. Talmud. Hence we read: 1. a biblical text, the priestly blessings; 2. a passage from the Mishnah about commandments that have no fixed measure; and 3. a passage from

תלמוד בבלי, שבת קכז:א

אֵלּוּ דְבָרִים שֶׁאָדָם אוֹכֵל פֵּרוֹתֵיהֶם בָּעוֹלָם הַזֶּה וְהַקֶּרֶן קַיֶּמֶת לוֹ לָעוֹלָם הַבָּא, וְאֵלּוּ הֵן, כִּבּוּד אָב וָאֵם, וּגְמִילוּת חֲסָדִים, וְהַשְׁכָּמַת בֵּית הַמִּדְרָשׁ שַׁחֲרִית וְעַרְבִית, וְהַכְנָסַת אוֹרְחִים, וּבִקּוּר חוֹלִים, וְהַכְנָסַת כַּלָּה, וּלְוָיַת הַמֵּת, וְעִיּוּן תְּפִלָּה, וַהֲבָאַת שָׁלוֹם בֵּין אָדָם לַחֲבֵרוֹ, וְתַלְמוּד תּוֹרָה כְּנֶגֶד כֻּלָּם.

אֱלֹהַי, נְשָׁמָה שֶׁנָּתַתָּ בִּי טְהוֹרָה הִיא. אַתָּה בְרָאתָהּ אַתָּה יְצַרְתָּהּ, אַתָּה נְפַחְתָּהּ בִּי, וְאַתָּה מְשַׁמְּרָהּ בְּקִרְבִּי, וְאַתָּה עָתִיד לִטְּלָהּ מִמֶּנִּי, וּלְהַחֲזִירָהּ בִּי לֶעָתִיד לָבוֹא. כָּל־זְמַן שֶׁהַנְּשָׁמָה בְקִרְבִּי, מוֹדֶה אֲנִי לְפָנֶיךָ, יהוה אֱלֹהַי וֵאלֹהֵי אֲבוֹתַי, רִבּוֹן כָּל־הַמַּעֲשִׂים, אֲדוֹן כָּל־הַנְּשָׁמוֹת. בָּרוּךְ אַתָּה יהוה, הַמַּחֲזִיר נְשָׁמוֹת לִפְגָרִים מֵתִים.

ברכות השחר

The Leader starts from here.

בָּרוּךְ אַתָּה יהוה אֱלֹהֵינוּ מֶלֶךְ הָעוֹלָם, אֲשֶׁר נָתַן לַשֶּׂכְוִי בִינָה לְהַבְחִין בֵּין יוֹם וּבֵין לָיְלָה.

בָּרוּךְ אַתָּה יהוה אֱלֹהֵינוּ מֶלֶךְ הָעוֹלָם, שֶׁלֹּא עָשַׂנִי נָכְרִי.

בָּרוּךְ אַתָּה יהוה אֱלֹהֵינוּ מֶלֶךְ הָעוֹלָם, שֶׁלֹּא עָשַׂנִי עָבֶד.

---

the Talmud about the reward of good deeds in this world and the next.

אֱלֹהַי *My God, the soul You placed within me is pure*: An affirmation of Jewish belief in the freedom and responsibility of each human being. The soul as such is pure. We have good instincts and bad, and we must choose between them. The blessing ends with a reference to the resurrection of the dead, returning to the theme of the first words said in the morning.

בָּרוּךְ אַתָּה *Blessed are You*: These bless-

BABYLONIAN TALMUD, SHABBAT 127A

אֵלּוּ These are the things whose fruits we eat in this world but whose full reward awaits us in the World to Come: honouring parents, acts of kindness, arriving early at the house of study morning and evening, hospitality to strangers, visiting the sick, helping the needy bride, attending to the dead, devotion in prayer, and bringing peace between people – but the study of Torah is equal to them all.

אֱלֹהַי My God, the soul You placed within me is pure. You created it, You formed it, You breathed it into me, and You guard it while it is within me. One day You will take it from me, and restore it to me in the time to come. As long as the soul is within me, I will thank You, Lord my God and God of my ancestors, Master of all works, Lord of all souls. Blessed are You, Lord, who restores souls to lifeless bodies.

MORNING BLESSINGS

The Leader starts from here.

בָּרוּךְ Blessed are You, Lord our God, King of the Universe, who gives the heart understanding to distinguish day from night.

Blessed are You, Lord our God, King of the Universe, who has not made me a heathen.

Blessed are You, Lord our God, King of the Universe, who has not made me a slave.

---

ings, itemised in the Talmud (*Berachot* 60b), were originally said at home to accompany the various stages of waking and rising. "Who gives sight to the blind" was said on opening one's eyes, "Who clothes the naked" on putting on clothes, and so on. Several medieval authorities, however, held that they should be said in the synagogue.

Their purpose is to make us conscious of what we might otherwise take for granted. Praise is an act of focused attention, foregrounding what is usually in the background of awareness. "The world is full of the light of God, but to see it we must learn to open our eyes" (Rabbi Nachman of Bratslav).

Who gives the heart: This is the translation according to Rabbi Asher; Rashi and Abudraham read it, "the cockerel". According to Rabbi Asher's reading, the first blessing mirrors the first request of the *Amidah*, for human understanding, as well as the first act of creation in which God created light, separating it from darkness.

Men say:

בָּרוּךְ אַתָּה יהוה אֱלֹהֵינוּ מֶלֶךְ הָעוֹלָם, שֶׁלֹּא עָשַׂנִי אִשָּׁה.

Women say:

בָּרוּךְ אַתָּה יהוה אֱלֹהֵינוּ מֶלֶךְ הָעוֹלָם, שֶׁעָשַׂנִי כִּרְצוֹנוֹ.

בָּרוּךְ אַתָּה יהוה אֱלֹהֵינוּ מֶלֶךְ הָעוֹלָם, פּוֹקֵחַ עִוְרִים.

בָּרוּךְ אַתָּה יהוה אֱלֹהֵינוּ מֶלֶךְ הָעוֹלָם, מַלְבִּישׁ עֲרֻמִּים.

בָּרוּךְ אַתָּה יהוה אֱלֹהֵינוּ מֶלֶךְ הָעוֹלָם, מַתִּיר אֲסוּרִים.

בָּרוּךְ אַתָּה יהוה אֱלֹהֵינוּ מֶלֶךְ הָעוֹלָם, זוֹקֵף כְּפוּפִים.

בָּרוּךְ אַתָּה יהוה אֱלֹהֵינוּ מֶלֶךְ הָעוֹלָם, רוֹקַע הָאָרֶץ עַל־הַמָּיִם.

בָּרוּךְ אַתָּה יהוה אֱלֹהֵינוּ מֶלֶךְ הָעוֹלָם, שֶׁעָשָׂה־לִּי כָּל־צָרְכִּי.

בָּרוּךְ אַתָּה יהוה אֱלֹהֵינוּ מֶלֶךְ הָעוֹלָם, אֲשֶׁר הֵכִין מִצְעֲדֵי־גָבֶר.

בָּרוּךְ אַתָּה יהוה אֱלֹהֵינוּ מֶלֶךְ הָעוֹלָם, אוֹזֵר יִשְׂרָאֵל בִּגְבוּרָה.

בָּרוּךְ אַתָּה יהוה אֱלֹהֵינוּ מֶלֶךְ הָעוֹלָם, עוֹטֵר יִשְׂרָאֵל בְּתִפְאָרָה.

בָּרוּךְ אַתָּה יהוה אֱלֹהֵינוּ מֶלֶךְ הָעוֹלָם, הַנּוֹתֵן לַיָּעֵף כֹּחַ.

שֶׁלֹּא עָשַׂנִי *Who has not made me a heathen, a slave, a woman*: These three blessings are mentioned in the Talmud (*Menachot* 43b). They have nothing to do with hierarchies of dignity, for we believe that every human being is equally formed in the image of God. Rather, they are acknowledgments of the special responsibilities of Jewish life. Heathens, slaves and women are exempt from certain commandments which apply to Jewish men. In these blessings, we express our faith that the commandments are not a burden but a cherished vocation.

שֶׁעָשַׂנִי כִּרְצוֹנוֹ *Who has made me accord-*

Men say:

Blessed are You, LORD our GOD, King of the Universe, who has not made me a woman.

Women say:

Blessed are You, LORD our GOD, King of the Universe, who has made me according to His will.

Blessed are You, LORD our GOD, King of the Universe, who has given sight to the blind.

Blessed are You, LORD our GOD, King of the Universe, who clothes the naked.

Blessed are You, LORD our GOD, King of the Universe, who sets captives free.

Blessed are You, LORD our GOD, King of the Universe, who raises those bowed down.

Blessed are You, LORD our GOD, King of the Universe, who spreads the earth above the waters.

Blessed are You, LORD our GOD, King of the Universe, who provides me with all I need.

Blessed are You, LORD our GOD, King of the Universe, who makes firm the steps of man.

Blessed are You, LORD our GOD, King of the Universe, who girds Israel with strength.

Blessed are You, LORD our GOD, King of the Universe, who crowns Israel with glory.

Blessed are You, LORD our GOD, King of the Universe, who gives strength to the weary.

---

ing to His will: Women embrace their vocation positively, unlike the negative formula ("who has *not* made me") used by men. Women ("the mother of all life", Genesis 3:20) are able to experience the Divine more closely than men by bringing new life into the world, the most profound of all creative acts. Whereas men thank GOD for the ability to *act* in accordance with GOD's will, women thank GOD existentially: "who has *made* me according to His will".

בָּרוּךְ אַתָּה יהוה אֱלֹהֵינוּ מֶלֶךְ הָעוֹלָם, הַמַּעֲבִיר שֵׁנָה מֵעֵינָי וּתְנוּמָה מֵעַפְעַפָּי. וִיהִי רָצוֹן מִלְּפָנֶיךָ, יהוה אֱלֹהֵינוּ וֵאלֹהֵי אֲבוֹתֵינוּ, שֶׁתַּרְגִּילֵנוּ בְּתוֹרָתֶךָ וְדַבְּקֵנוּ בְּמִצְוֹתֶיךָ, וְאַל תְּבִיאֵנוּ לֹא לִידֵי חֵטְא, וְלֹא לִידֵי עֲבֵירָה וְעָוֹן, וְלֹא לִידֵי נִסָּיוֹן, וְלֹא לִידֵי בִזָּיוֹן, וְאַל תַּשְׁלֶט־בָּנוּ יֵצֶר הָרָע. וְהַרְחִיקֵנוּ מֵאָדָם רָע וּמֵחָבֵר רָע. וְדַבְּקֵנוּ בְּיֵצֶר הַטּוֹב וּבְמַעֲשִׂים טוֹבִים, וְכוֹף אֶת־יִצְרֵנוּ לְהִשְׁתַּעְבֶּד־לָךְ. ← וּתְנֵנוּ הַיּוֹם וּבְכָל־יוֹם לְחֵן וּלְחֶסֶד וּלְרַחֲמִים בְּעֵינֶיךָ, וּבְעֵינֵי כָל רוֹאֵינוּ, וְתִגְמְלֵנוּ חֲסָדִים טוֹבִים. בָּרוּךְ אַתָּה יהוה, גּוֹמֵל חֲסָדִים טוֹבִים לְעַמּוֹ יִשְׂרָאֵל.

יְהִי רָצוֹן מִלְּפָנֶיךָ, יהוה אֱלֹהַי וֵאלֹהֵי אֲבוֹתַי, שֶׁתַּצִּילֵנִי הַיּוֹם וּבְכָל־יוֹם מֵעַזֵּי פָנִים וּמֵעַזּוּת פָּנִים, מֵאָדָם רָע, וּמֵחָבֵר רָע, וּמִשָּׁכֵן רָע, וּמִפֶּגַע רָע, וּמִשָּׂטָן הַמַּשְׁחִית, מִדִּין קָשֶׁה וּמִבַּעַל־דִּין קָשֶׁה, בֵּין שֶׁהוּא בֶן־בְּרִית, וּבֵין שֶׁאֵינוֹ בֶן־בְּרִית.

לְעוֹלָם יְהֵא אָדָם יְרֵא־שָׁמַיִם בַּסֵּתֶר וּבַגָּלוּי, וּמוֹדֶה עַל־הָאֱמֶת, וְדוֹבֵר אֱמֶת בִּלְבָבוֹ, וְיַשְׁכֵּם וְיֹאמַר,

---

הַמַּעֲבִיר *Who removes sleep from my eyes*: Having thanked God for the blessings with which we are surrounded, we conclude by asking for His help in dedicating our lives to His service, undeterred by obstacles that may stand in our way. The prayer ends with thanksgiving for God's kindness, reminding us of the verse from Psalms (92:3): "To proclaim Your loving-kindness in the morning and Your faithfulness at night."

יְהִי רָצוֹן *May it be Your will*: A meditation composed by Rabbi Judah the Prince (late second–early third century), redactor of the Mishnah and leader of the Jewish community in Israel. We are social beings, influenced by our environment (Maimonides), therefore we pray to be protected from harmful people, events and temptations. The prayer reflects the "social fabric of faith" (Lord Jakobovits).

בָּרוּךְ Blessed are You, LORD our GOD, King of the Universe, who removes sleep from my eyes and slumber from my eyelids. And may it be Your will, LORD our GOD and GOD of our ancestors, to accustom us to Your Torah, and make us attached to Your commandments. Lead us not into error, transgression, iniquity, temptation or disgrace. Do not let the evil instinct dominate us. Keep us far from a bad man and a bad companion. Help us attach ourselves to the good instinct and to good deeds and bend our instincts to be subservient to You. ➔ Grant us, this day and every day, grace, lovingkindness and compassion in Your eyes and in the eyes of all who see us, and bestow lovingkindness upon us. Blessed are You, LORD, who bestows lovingkindness on His people Israel.

יְהִי May it be Your will, LORD my GOD and GOD of my ancestors, to save me today and every day, from the arrogant and from arrogance itself, from a bad man, a bad friend, a bad neighbour, a bad mishap, a destructive adversary, a harsh trial and a harsh opponent, whether or not he is a son of the covenant.

לְעוֹלָם A person should always be GOD-fearing, privately and publicly, acknowledging the truth and speaking it in his heart. He should rise early and say:

לְעוֹלָם *A person should always*: This whole section until "Who sanctifies Your name among the multitudes" appears in the tenth-century Midrash, *Tanna DeVei Eliyyahu* (ch. 21). Some believe that it dates from a period of persecution under the Persian ruler Yazdegerd II who, in 456 CE, forbade the observance of Shabbat and the reading of the Torah. Jews continued to practise their faith in secret, saying prayers at times and in ways that would not be detected by their persecutors. This explains the reference to fearing GOD "privately" and "speaking truth in the heart" (that is, the secret practice of Judaism) and the recitation here of the first lines of the *Shema*, which could not be said at the normal time. The final blessing, "Who sanctifies Your name among the multitudes", refers to the martyrdom of those who went to their deaths rather than renounce their faith. Martyrdom is called *Kiddush HaShem*, "sanctifying [GOD's] name".

רִבּוֹן כָּל־הָעוֹלָמִים, לֹא עַל צִדְקוֹתֵינוּ אֲנַחְנוּ מַפִּילִים תַּחֲנוּנֵינוּ לְפָנֶיךָ, כִּי עַל־רַחֲמֶיךָ הָרַבִּים. מָה אֲנַחְנוּ, מֶה חַיֵּינוּ, מֶה חַסְדֵּנוּ, מַה צִּדְקֵנוּ, מַה־יְּשׁוּעָתֵנוּ, מַה־כֹּחֵנוּ, מַה־גְּבוּרָתֵנוּ. מַה נֹּאמַר לְפָנֶיךָ, יהוה אֱלֹהֵינוּ וֵאלֹהֵי אֲבוֹתֵינוּ, הֲלֹא כָּל־הַגִּבּוֹרִים כְּאַיִן לְפָנֶיךָ, וְאַנְשֵׁי הַשֵּׁם כְּלֹא הָיוּ, וַחֲכָמִים כִּבְלִי מַדָּע, וּנְבוֹנִים כִּבְלִי הַשְׂכֵּל. כִּי רוֹב מַעֲשֵׂיהֶם תֹּהוּ, וִימֵי חַיֵּיהֶם הֶבֶל לְפָנֶיךָ, וּמוֹתַר הָאָדָם מִן־הַבְּהֵמָה אָיִן, כִּי הַכֹּל הָבֶל.

אֲבָל אֲנַחְנוּ עַמְּךָ, בְּנֵי בְרִיתֶךָ, בְּנֵי אַבְרָהָם אֹהַבְךָ שֶׁנִּשְׁבַּעְתָּ לּוֹ בְּהַר הַמּוֹרִיָּה, זֶרַע יִצְחָק יְחִידוֹ שֶׁנֶּעֱקַד עַל־גַּב הַמִּזְבֵּחַ, עֲדַת יַעֲקֹב בִּנְךָ בְּכוֹרֶךָ, שֶׁמֵּאַהֲבָתְךָ שֶׁאָהַבְתָּ אֹתוֹ וּמִשִּׂמְחָתְךָ שֶׁשָּׂמַחְתָּ־בּוֹ, קָרָאתָ אֶת־שְׁמוֹ יִשְׂרָאֵל וִישֻׁרוּן.

לְפִיכָךְ אֲנַחְנוּ חַיָּבִים לְהוֹדוֹת לְךָ, וּלְשַׁבֵּחֲךָ, וּלְפָאֶרְךָ, וּלְבָרֵךְ וּלְקַדֵּשׁ וְלָתֵת־שֶׁבַח וְהוֹדָיָה לִשְׁמֶךָ. אַשְׁרֵינוּ, מַה־טּוֹב חֶלְקֵנוּ, וּמַה־נָּעִים גּוֹרָלֵנוּ, וּמַה־יָּפָה יְרֻשָּׁתֵנוּ. ← אַשְׁרֵינוּ, שֶׁאֲנַחְנוּ מַשְׁכִּימִים וּמַעֲרִיבִים, עֶרֶב וָבֹקֶר וְאוֹמְרִים פַּעֲמַיִם בְּכָל־יוֹם,

All, aloud:

שְׁמַע יִשְׂרָאֵל, יהוה אֱלֹהֵינוּ, יהוה אֶחָד.

Quietly:

בָּרוּךְ שֵׁם כְּבוֹד מַלְכוּתוֹ לְעוֹלָם וָעֶד.

רִבּוֹן *Master of all worlds*: This passage also appears in the *Ne'ilah* prayer on Yom Kippur. It expresses the paradox of the human condition in the presence of God. We know how small we are and how brief our lives. *Fleeting breath* – the Hebrew word *hevel* – the key word of the opening chapters of Ecclesiastes, from which

רִבּוֹן Master of all worlds, not because of our righteousness do we lay our pleas before You, but because of Your great compassion. What are we? What are our lives? What is our lovingkindness? What is our righteousness? What is our salvation? What is our strength? What is our might? What shall we say before You, LORD our GOD and GOD of our ancestors? Are not all the mighty like nothing before You, the men of renown as if they had never been, the wise as if they know nothing, and the understanding as if they lack intelligence? For their many works are in vain, and the days of their lives like a fleeting breath before You. The pre-eminence of man over the animals is nothing, for all is but a fleeting breath.

אֲבָל Yet we are Your people, the children of Your covenant, the children of Abraham, Your beloved, to whom You made a promise on Mount Moriah; the offspring of Isaac his only one who was bound on the altar; the congregation of Jacob Your firstborn son whom – because of the love with which You loved him and the joy with which You rejoiced in him – You called Israel and Yeshurun.

לְפִיכָךְ Therefore it is our duty to thank You, and to praise, glorify, bless, sanctify and give praise and thanks to Your name. Happy are we, how good is our portion, how lovely our fate, how beautiful our heritage. ➔ Happy are we who, early and late, evening and morning, say twice each day –

All, aloud:

Listen, Israel: the LORD is our GOD, the LORD is One.

Quietly:

Blessed be the name of His glorious kingdom for ever and all time.

---

this line is taken – has been translated as "vain, meaningless, empty, futile". However, it literally means "a short breath". It conveys a sense of the brevity and insubstantiality of life as a physical phenomenon. All that lives soon dies, and is as if it had never been. *Yet* – You created us, made us, chose us. We are infinitesi-

אַתָּה הוּא עַד שֶׁלֹּא נִבְרָא הָעוֹלָם, אַתָּה הוּא מִשֶּׁנִּבְרָא הָעוֹלָם, אַתָּה הוּא בָּעוֹלָם הַזֶּה, וְאַתָּה הוּא לָעוֹלָם הַבָּא. קַדֵּשׁ אֶת־שִׁמְךָ עַל־מַקְדִּישֵׁי שְׁמֶךָ, וְקַדֵּשׁ אֶת־שִׁמְךָ בְּעוֹלָמֶךָ. ◂ וּבִישׁוּעָתְךָ תָּרוּם וְתַגְבִּהַּ קַרְנֵנוּ. בָּרוּךְ אַתָּה יהוה, מְקַדֵּשׁ אֶת־שִׁמְךָ בָּרַבִּים.

אַתָּה הוּא יהוה אֱלֹהֵינוּ, בַּשָּׁמַיִם וּבָאָרֶץ וּבִשְׁמֵי הַשָּׁמַיִם הָעֶלְיוֹנִים. אֱמֶת, אַתָּה הוּא רִאשׁוֹן, וְאַתָּה הוּא אַחֲרוֹן, וּמִבַּלְעָדֶיךָ אֵין אֱלֹהִים. קַבֵּץ קֹוֶיךָ מֵאַרְבַּע כַּנְפוֹת הָאָרֶץ. יַכִּירוּ וְיֵדְעוּ כָּל־בָּאֵי עוֹלָם כִּי אַתָּה־הוּא הָאֱלֹהִים לְבַדְּךָ לְכֹל מַמְלְכוֹת הָאָרֶץ. אַתָּה עָשִׂיתָ אֶת־הַשָּׁמַיִם וְאֶת־הָאָרֶץ, אֶת־הַיָּם, וְאֵת כָּל־אֲשֶׁר בָּם. וּמִי בְּכָל־מַעֲשֵׂה יָדֶיךָ בָּעֶלְיוֹנִים אוֹ בַתַּחְתּוֹנִים שֶׁיֹּאמַר לְךָ, מַה־תַּעֲשֶׂה. אָבִינוּ שֶׁבַּשָּׁמַיִם, עֲשֵׂה עִמָּנוּ חֶסֶד בַּעֲבוּר שִׁמְךָ הַגָּדוֹל שֶׁנִּקְרָא עָלֵינוּ, וְקַיֶּם־לָנוּ יהוה אֱלֹהֵינוּ מַה שֶּׁכָּתוּב, בָּעֵת הַהִיא אָבִיא אֶתְכֶם, וּבָעֵת קַבְּצִי אֶתְכֶם, כִּי־אֶתֵּן אֶתְכֶם לְשֵׁם וְלִתְהִלָּה בְּכֹל עַמֵּי הָאָרֶץ, בְּשׁוּבִי אֶת־שְׁבוּתֵיכֶם לְעֵינֵיכֶם, אָמַר יהוה.

קרבנות

במדבר כח:א–ח

וַיְדַבֵּר יהוה אֶל־מֹשֶׁה לֵּאמֹר. צַו אֶת־בְּנֵי יִשְׂרָאֵל וְאָמַרְתָּ אֲלֵהֶם, אֶת־קָרְבָּנִי לַחְמִי לְאִשַּׁי, רֵיחַ נִיחֹחִי, תִּשְׁמְרוּ

אַתָּה הוּא *It was You who existed*: This prayer, with its emphasis on the changelessness of God, may have been incorporated at a time of persecution, expressing the refusal of Jews to abandon their faith. God does not alter or revoke His cov-

mally small, yet brushed by the wings of Infinity. We are dust; yet *we are Your people, children of Your covenant*, descendants of those You singled out to be witnesses to the world of Your existence and majesty.

אַתָּה הוּא It was You who existed before the world was created, it is You now that the world has been created, it is You in this world and You in the World to Come. Sanctify Your name through those who sanctify Your name, and sanctify it throughout Your world. ➔ By Your salvation may our pride be exalted and raised high. Blessed are You, LORD, who sanctifies Your name among the multitudes.

אַתָּה הוּא You are the LORD our GOD in heaven and on earth, and in the highest heaven of heavens. Truly, You are the first and You are the last, and besides You there is no GOD. Gather those who hope in You from the four quarters of the earth. May all mankind recognise and know that You alone are GOD over all the kingdoms on earth. You made the heavens and the earth, the sea and all they contain. Who among all the works of Your hands, above and below, can say to You, "What are You doing?" Heavenly Father, deal kindly with us for the sake of Your great name by which we are called, and fulfil for us, LORD our GOD, that which is written: "At that time I will bring you home, and at that time I will gather you, for I will give you renown and praise among all the peoples of the earth when I bring back your exiles before your eyes, says the LORD."

OFFERINGS

NUMBERS 28:1–8

וַיְדַבֵּר The LORD said to Moses, "Command the Israelites and tell them: 'Be careful to offer to Me at the appointed time My food-offering con-

---

enant, therefore we may not renounce our religion or identity: "I, GOD, do not change; so you, children of Jacob, are not destroyed" (Malachi 3:6).

אַתָּה הוּא *You are the LORD our GOD*: This second prayer, for the end of exile, culminates with the verse from Zephaniah (3:20) which speaks of the ingathering of Jews and of a time when "I will give you renown and praise among all the peoples on earth." This entire sequence of prayers is eloquent testimony to how Jews sustained faith and hope, dignity and pride, during some of the most prolonged periods of persecution in history.

OFFERINGS

There now follows a second cycle of study, with the same structure as the first, with passages from: 1. the Torah; 2. the

commentary continues on page 28

לְהַקְרִיב לִי בְּמוֹעֲדוֹ. וְאָמַרְתָּ לָהֶם, זֶה הָאִשֶּׁה אֲשֶׁר תַּקְרִיבוּ לַיהוה, כְּבָשִׂים בְּנֵי־שָׁנָה תְמִימִם, שְׁנַיִם לַיּוֹם, עֹלָה תָמִיד. אֶת־הַכֶּבֶשׂ אֶחָד תַּעֲשֶׂה בַבֹּקֶר, וְאֵת הַכֶּבֶשׂ הַשֵּׁנִי תַּעֲשֶׂה בֵּין הָעַרְבָּיִם. וַעֲשִׂירִית הָאֵיפָה סֹלֶת לְמִנְחָה, בְּלוּלָה בְּשֶׁמֶן כָּתִית רְבִיעִת הַהִין. עֹלַת תָּמִיד, הָעֲשֻׂיָה בְּהַר סִינַי, לְרֵיחַ נִיחֹחַ, אִשֶּׁה לַיהוה. וְנִסְכּוֹ רְבִיעִת הַהִין לַכֶּבֶשׂ הָאֶחָד, בַּקֹּדֶשׁ הַסֵּךְ נֶסֶךְ שֵׁכָר לַיהוה. וְאֵת הַכֶּבֶשׂ הַשֵּׁנִי תַּעֲשֶׂה בֵּין הָעַרְבָּיִם, כְּמִנְחַת הַבֹּקֶר וּכְנִסְכּוֹ תַּעֲשֶׂה, אִשֵּׁה רֵיחַ נִיחֹחַ לַיהוה.

ויקרא א:יא

וְשָׁחַט אֹתוֹ עַל יֶרֶךְ הַמִּזְבֵּחַ צָפֹנָה לִפְנֵי יהוה, וְזָרְקוּ בְּנֵי אַהֲרֹן הַכֹּהֲנִים אֶת־דָּמוֹ עַל־הַמִּזְבֵּחַ סָבִיב.

On שַׁבָּת, say (במדבר כח:ט–י):

וּבְיוֹם הַשַּׁבָּת שְׁנֵי־כְבָשִׂים בְּנֵי־שָׁנָה תְּמִימִם, וּשְׁנֵי עֶשְׂרֹנִים סֹלֶת מִנְחָה בְּלוּלָה בַשֶּׁמֶן, וְנִסְכּוֹ. עֹלַת שַׁבַּת בְּשַׁבַּתּוֹ, עַל־עֹלַת הַתָּמִיד וְנִסְכָּהּ.

On רֹאשׁ חֹדֶשׁ, say (במדבר כח:יא–טו):

וּבְרָאשֵׁי חָדְשֵׁיכֶם תַּקְרִיבוּ עֹלָה לַיהוה, פָּרִים בְּנֵי־בָקָר שְׁנַיִם, וְאַיִל אֶחָד, כְּבָשִׂים בְּנֵי־שָׁנָה שִׁבְעָה, תְּמִימִם. וּשְׁלֹשָׁה עֶשְׂרֹנִים סֹלֶת מִנְחָה בְּלוּלָה בַשֶּׁמֶן לַפָּר הָאֶחָד, וּשְׁנֵי עֶשְׂרֹנִים סֹלֶת מִנְחָה בְּלוּלָה בַשֶּׁמֶן לָאַיִל הָאֶחָד. וְעִשָּׂרֹן עִשָּׂרוֹן, סֹלֶת מִנְחָה בְּלוּלָה בַשֶּׁמֶן, לַכֶּבֶשׂ הָאֶחָד, עֹלָה רֵיחַ נִיחֹחַ, אִשֶּׁה לַיהוה. וְנִסְכֵּיהֶם חֲצִי הַהִין יִהְיֶה לַפָּר, וּשְׁלִישִׁת הַהִין לָאַיִל, וּרְבִיעִת הַהִין לַכֶּבֶשׂ יָיִן, זֹאת עֹלַת חֹדֶשׁ בְּחָדְשׁוֹ לְחָדְשֵׁי הַשָּׁנָה. וּשְׂעִיר עִזִּים אֶחָד לְחַטָּאת לַיהוה, עַל־עֹלַת הַתָּמִיד יֵעָשֶׂה, וְנִסְכּוֹ.

---

sumed by fire, as an aroma pleasing to Me.' Tell them: 'This is the fire-offering you shall offer to the LORD – two lambs a year old without blemish, as a regular burnt-offering each day. Prepare one lamb in the morning and the other towards evening, together with a grain-offering of a tenth of an ephah of fine flour mixed with a quarter of a hin of oil from pressed olives. This is the regular burnt-offering instituted at Mount Sinai as a pleasing aroma, a fire-offering made to the LORD. Its libation is to be a quarter of a hin (of wine) with each lamb, poured in the sanctuary as a libation of strong drink to the LORD. Prepare the second lamb in the afternoon, along with the same grain-offering and libation as in the morning. This is a fire-offering, an aroma pleasing to the LORD.'"

LEVITICUS 1:11

וְשָׁחַט He shall slaughter it at the north side of the altar before the LORD, and Aaron's sons the priests shall sprinkle its blood against the altar on all sides.

On Shabbat, say (NUMBERS 28:9–10):

On the Sabbath day, make an offering of two lambs a year old, without blemish, together with two-tenths of an ephah of fine flour mixed with oil as a meal-offering, and its appropriate libation. This is the burnt-offering for every Sabbath, in addition to the regular daily burnt-offering and its libation.

On Rosh Chodesh, say (NUMBERS 28:11–15):

On your new moons, present as a burnt-offering to the LORD, two young bulls, one ram, and seven yearling lambs without blemish. There shall be a meal-offering of three-tenths of an ephah of fine flour mixed with oil for each bull, two-tenths of an ephah of fine flour mixed with oil for the ram, and one-tenth of an ephah of fine flour mixed with oil for each lamb. This is the burnt-offering – a fire-offering of pleasing aroma to the LORD. Their libations shall be: half a hin of wine for each bull, a third of a hin for the ram, and a quarter of a hin for each lamb. This is the monthly burnt-offering to be made at each new moon throughout the year. One male goat should be offered as a sin-offering to GOD, in addition to the regular daily burnt-offering and its libation.

הלכות קרבנות

משנה זבחים פרק ה

[א] **אֵיזֶהוּ** מְקוֹמָן שֶׁל־זְבָחִים. קָדְשֵׁי קָדָשִׁים שְׁחִיטָתָן בַּצָּפוֹן. פַּר וְשָׂעִיר שֶׁל יוֹם הַכִּפּוּרִים שְׁחִיטָתָן בַּצָּפוֹן, וְקִבּוּל דָּמָן בִּכְלִי שָׁרֵת בַּצָּפוֹן. וְדָמָן טָעוּן הַזָּיָה עַל־בֵּין הַבַּדִּים, וְעַל הַפָּרֹכֶת, וְעַל־מִזְבַּח הַזָּהָב. מַתָּנָה אַחַת מֵהֶן מְעַכֶּבֶת. שְׁיָרֵי הַדָּם הָיָה שׁוֹפֵךְ עַל יְסוֹד מַעֲרָבִי שֶׁלַּמִּזְבֵּחַ הַחִיצוֹן, אִם־לֹא נָתַן, לֹא עִכֵּב.

[ב] **פָּרִים** הַנִּשְׂרָפִים וּשְׂעִירִים הַנִּשְׂרָפִים שְׁחִיטָתָן בַּצָּפוֹן, וְקִבּוּל דָּמָן בִּכְלִי שָׁרֵת בַּצָּפוֹן. וְדָמָן טָעוּן הַזָּיָה עַל־הַפָּרֹכֶת וְעַל־מִזְבַּח הַזָּהָב. מַתָּנָה אַחַת מֵהֶן מְעַכֶּבֶת. שְׁיָרֵי הַדָּם הָיָה שׁוֹפֵךְ עַל יְסוֹד מַעֲרָבִי שֶׁלַּמִּזְבֵּחַ הַחִיצוֹן, אִם־לֹא נָתַן, לֹא עִכֵּב. אֵלּוּ וָאֵלּוּ נִשְׂרָפִין בְּבֵית הַדָּשֶׁן.

[ג] **חַטֹּאת** הַצִּבּוּר וְהַיָּחִיד אֵלּוּ הֵן חַטֹּאת הַצִּבּוּר, שְׂעִירֵי רָאשֵׁי חֳדָשִׁים וְשֶׁל־מוֹעֲדוֹת שְׁחִיטָתָן בַּצָּפוֹן, וְקִבּוּל דָּמָן בִּכְלִי שָׁרֵת בַּצָּפוֹן. וְדָמָן טָעוּן אַרְבַּע מַתָּנוֹת עַל אַרְבַּע קְרָנוֹת. כֵּיצַד, עָלָה בַכֶּבֶשׁ, וּפָנָה לַסּוֹבֵב וּבָא־לוֹ לְקֶרֶן דְּרוֹמִית מִזְרָחִית, מִזְרָחִית צְפוֹנִית, צְפוֹנִית מַעֲרָבִית, מַעֲרָבִית דְּרוֹמִית. שְׁיָרֵי הַדָּם הָיָה שׁוֹפֵךְ עַל יְסוֹד דְּרוֹמִי. וְנֶאֱכָלִין לִפְנִים מִן־הַקְּלָעִים, לְזִכְרֵי כְהֻנָּה, בְּכָל־מַאֲכָל, לְיוֹם וָלַיְלָה, עַד חֲצוֹת.

Mishnah; and 3. the Talmud (see below). The passages from the Torah relate to the daily, weekly and monthly sacrifices because, in the absence of the Temple, the Sages held that study of the laws about sacrifice was a substitute for sacrifice itself (*Ta'anit* 27b). The passage from the Mishnah (*Zevachim* 5) is also about sacri-

LAWS OF OFFERINGS

MISHNAH ZEVACHIM, CHAPTER 5

1. **אֵיזֶהוּ** What is the location for sacrifices? The holiest offerings were slaughtered on the north side. The bull and he-goat of the Day of Atonement were slaughtered on the north side. Their blood was received in a sacred vessel on the north side, and had to be sprinkled between the poles (of the ark), toward the veil (screening the Holy of Holies), and on the golden altar. (The omission of) one of these sprinklings invalidated (the atonement ceremony). The leftover blood was to be poured onto the western base of the outer altar. If this was not done, however, the omission did not invalidate (the ceremony).

2. **פָּרִים** The bulls and he-goats that were completely burnt were slaughtered on the north side, their blood was received in a sacred vessel on the north side, and had to be sprinkled towards the veil and on the golden altar. (The omission of) one of these sprinklings invalidated (the ceremony). The leftover blood was to be poured onto the western base of the outer altar. If this was not done, however, the omission did not invalidate (the ceremony). All these offerings were burnt where the altar ashes were deposited.

3. **חַטֹּאת** The communal and individual sin-offerings – these are the communal sin-offerings: the he-goats offered on the New Moon and Festivals were slaughtered on the north side, their blood was received in a sacred vessel on the north side, and required four sprinklings, one on each of the four corners of the altar. How was this done? The priest ascended the ramp and turned (right) onto the surrounding ledge. He came to the south-east corner, then went to the north-east, then to the north-west, then to the south-west. The leftover blood he poured onto the southern base. (The meat of these offerings), prepared in any manner, was eaten within the (courtyard) curtains, by males of the priesthood, on that day and the following night, until midnight.

4. **הָעוֹלָה** The burnt-offering was among the holiest of sacrifices. It was

---

fices, and was chosen because it does not contain any disagreement between the Sages, and thus accords with the rule that one should pray "after a decided *halachah*", that is, an item of Jewish law about which there is no debate. Some congregations include additional passages; our custom is to follow the text as it exists in the earliest Siddurim, those of Rabbi Amram Gaon and Rabbi Saadiah Gaon.

[ד] **הָעוֹלָה** קֹדֶשׁ קָדָשִׁים. שְׁחִיטָתָהּ בַּצָּפוֹן, וְקִבּוּל דָּמָהּ בִּכְלִי שָׁרֵת בַּצָּפוֹן. וְדָמָהּ טָעוּן שְׁתֵּי מַתָּנוֹת שֶׁהֵן אַרְבַּע, וּטְעוּנָה הַפְשֵׁט וְנִתּוּחַ, וְכָלִיל לָאִשִּׁים.

[ה] **זִבְחֵי** שַׁלְמֵי צִבּוּר וַאֲשָׁמוֹת, אֵלּוּ הֵן אֲשָׁמוֹת, אֲשַׁם גְּזֵלוֹת, אֲשַׁם מְעִילוֹת, אֲשַׁם שִׁפְחָה חֲרוּפָה, אֲשַׁם נָזִיר, אֲשַׁם מְצוֹרָע, אָשָׁם תָּלוּי. שְׁחִיטָתָן בַּצָּפוֹן, וְקִבּוּל דָּמָן בִּכְלִי שָׁרֵת בַּצָּפוֹן, וְדָמָן טָעוּן שְׁתֵּי מַתָּנוֹת שֶׁהֵן אַרְבַּע. וְנֶאֱכָלִין לִפְנִים מִן הַקְּלָעִים לְזִכְרֵי כְהֻנָּה, בְּכָל־מַאֲכָל, לְיוֹם וָלַיְלָה, עַד חֲצוֹת.

[ו] **הַתּוֹדָה** וְאֵיל נָזִיר קָדָשִׁים קַלִּים. שְׁחִיטָתָן בְּכָל־מָקוֹם בָּעֲזָרָה, וְדָמָן טָעוּן שְׁתֵּי מַתָּנוֹת שֶׁהֵן אַרְבַּע. וְנֶאֱכָלִין בְּכָל־הָעִיר, לְכָל־אָדָם, בְּכָל־מַאֲכָל, לְיוֹם וָלַיְלָה, עַד חֲצוֹת. הַמּוּרָם מֵהֶם כַּיּוֹצֵא בָהֶם, אֶלָּא שֶׁהַמּוּרָם נֶאֱכָל לַכֹּהֲנִים, לִנְשֵׁיהֶם וְלִבְנֵיהֶם וּלְעַבְדֵיהֶם.

[ז] **שְׁלָמִים** קָדָשִׁים קַלִּים. שְׁחִיטָתָן בְּכָל־מָקוֹם בָּעֲזָרָה, וְדָמָן טָעוּן שְׁתֵּי מַתָּנוֹת שֶׁהֵן אַרְבַּע. וְנֶאֱכָלִין בְּכָל־הָעִיר, לְכָל־אָדָם, בְּכָל־מַאֲכָל, לִשְׁנֵי יָמִים וְלַיְלָה אֶחָד. הַמּוּרָם מֵהֶם כַּיּוֹצֵא בָהֶם, אֶלָּא שֶׁהַמּוּרָם נֶאֱכָל לַכֹּהֲנִים, לִנְשֵׁיהֶם וְלִבְנֵיהֶם וּלְעַבְדֵיהֶם.

[ח] **הַבְּכוֹר** וְהַמַּעֲשֵׂר וְהַפֶּסַח קָדָשִׁים קַלִּים. שְׁחִיטָתָן בְּכָל־מָקוֹם בָּעֲזָרָה, וְדָמָן טָעוּן מַתָּנָה אֶחָת, וּבִלְבָד שֶׁיִּתֵּן כְּנֶגֶד הַיְסוֹד. שִׁנָּה בַאֲכִילָתָן, הַבְּכוֹר נֶאֱכָל לַכֹּהֲנִים, וְהַמַּעֲשֵׂר לְכָל־אָדָם. וְנֶאֱכָלִין בְּכָל־הָעִיר, בְּכָל־מַאֲכָל, לִשְׁנֵי יָמִים וְלַיְלָה אֶחָד. הַפֶּסַח אֵינוֹ נֶאֱכָל אֶלָּא בַלַּיְלָה, וְאֵינוֹ נֶאֱכָל

slaughtered on the north side, its blood was received in a sacred vessel on the north side, and required two sprinklings (at opposite corners of the altar), making four in all. The offering had to be flayed, dismembered and wholly consumed by fire.

5. **זִבְחֵי** The communal peace-offerings and the guilt-offerings – these are the guilt-offerings: the guilt-offering for robbery; the guilt-offering for profane use of sacred object; the guilt-offering (for violating) a betrothed maidservant; the guilt-offering of a Nazirite (who had become defiled by a corpse); the guilt-offering of a leper (at his cleansing); and the guilt-offering in case of doubt. All these were slaughtered on the north side, their blood was received in a sacred vessel on the north side, and required two sprinklings (at opposite corners of the altar), making four in all. (The meat of these offerings), prepared in any manner, was eaten within the (courtyard) curtains, by males of the priesthood, on that day and the following night, until midnight.

6. **הַתּוֹדָה** The thanksgiving-offering and the ram of a Nazirite were offerings of lesser holiness. They could be slaughtered anywhere in the Temple court, and their blood required two sprinklings (at opposite corners of the altar), making four in all. The meat of these offerings, prepared in any manner, was eaten anywhere within the city (Jerusalem), by anyone during that day and the following night until midnight. This also applied to the portion of these sacrifices (given to the priests), except that the priests' portion was only to be eaten by the priests, their wives, children and servants.

7. **שְׁלָמִים** Peace-offerings were (also) of lesser holiness. They could be slaughtered anywhere in the Temple court, and their blood required two sprinklings (at opposite corners of the altar), making four in all. The meat of these offerings, prepared in any manner, was eaten anywhere within the city (Jerusalem), by anyone, for two days and one night. This also applied to the portion of these sacrifices (given to the priests), except that the priests' portion was only to be eaten by the priests, their wives, children and servants.

8. **הַבְּכוֹר** The firstborn and tithe of cattle and the Passover lamb were sacrifices of lesser holiness. They could be slaughtered anywhere in the Temple court, and their blood required only one sprinkling, which had to be done at the base of the altar. They differed in their consumption: the firstborn was eaten only by priests, while the tithe could be eaten by anyone. Both could be eaten anywhere within the city, prepared in any manner, during two days and one night. The Passover lamb had to be eaten that night un-

אֶלָּא עַד חֲצוֹת, וְאֵינוֹ נֶאֱכָל אֶלָּא לִמְנוּיָו, וְאֵינוֹ נֶאֱכָל אֶלָּא צָלִי.

ברייתא דרבי ישמעאל

רַבִּי יִשְׁמָעֵאל אוֹמֵר, בִּשְׁלֹשׁ־עֶשְׂרֵה מִדּוֹת הַתּוֹרָה נִדְרֶשֶׁת. [א] מִקַּל וָחֹמֶר. [ב] וּמִגְּזֵרָה שָׁוָה. [ג] מִבִּנְיַן אָב מִכָּתוּב אֶחָד, וּמִבִּנְיַן אָב מִשְּׁנֵי כְתוּבִים. [ד] מִכְּלָל וּפְרָט. [ה] וּמִפְּרָט וּכְלָל. [ו] כְּלָל וּפְרָט וּכְלָל, אִי אַתָּה דָן אֶלָּא כְּעֵין הַפְּרָט. [ז] מִכְּלָל שֶׁהוּא צָרִיךְ לִפְרָט, וּמִפְּרָט שֶׁהוּא צָרִיךְ לִכְלָל. [ח] כָּל־דָּבָר שֶׁהָיָה בִּכְלָל, וְיָצָא מִן־הַכְּלָל לְלַמֵּד, לֹא לְלַמֵּד עַל־עַצְמוֹ יָצָא, אֶלָּא לְלַמֵּד עַל־הַכְּלָל כֻּלּוֹ יָצָא. [ט] כָּל־דָּבָר שֶׁהָיָה בִּכְלָל, וְיָצָא לִטְעוֹן טוֹעַן אֶחָד שֶׁהוּא כְעִנְיָנוֹ, יָצָא לְהָקֵל וְלֹא לְהַחֲמִיר. [י] כָּל־דָּבָר שֶׁהָיָה בִּכְלָל, וְיָצָא לִטְעוֹן טוֹעַן אַחֵר שֶׁלֹּא כְעִנְיָנוֹ, יָצָא לְהָקֵל וּלְהַחֲמִיר. [יא] כָּל־דָּבָר שֶׁהָיָה בִּכְלָל, וְיָצָא לִדּוֹן בַּדָּבָר הֶחָדָשׁ, אִי אַתָּה יָכוֹל לְהַחֲזִירוֹ לִכְלָלוֹ, עַד שֶׁיַּחֲזִירֶנּוּ הַכָּתוּב לִכְלָלוֹ בְּפֵרוּשׁ. [יב] דָּבָר הַלָּמֵד מֵעִנְיָנוֹ, וְדָבָר הַלָּמֵד מִסּוֹפוֹ. [יג] וְכֵן שְׁנֵי כְתוּבִים הַמַּכְחִישִׁים זֶה אֶת־זֶה, עַד שֶׁיָּבֹא הַכָּתוּב הַשְּׁלִישִׁי וְיַכְרִיעַ בֵּינֵיהֶם.

← יְהִי רָצוֹן מִלְּפָנֶיךָ, יהוה אֱלֹהֵינוּ וֵאלֹהֵי אֲבוֹתֵינוּ, שֶׁיִּבָּנֶה בֵּית הַמִּקְדָּשׁ בִּמְהֵרָה בְיָמֵינוּ, וְתֵן חֶלְקֵנוּ בְּתוֹרָתֶךָ. וְשָׁם נַעֲבָדְךָ בְּיִרְאָה, כִּימֵי עוֹלָם וּכְשָׁנִים קַדְמוֹנִיּוֹת.

THE INTERPRETIVE PRINCIPLES OF RABBI ISHMAEL

This passage is included as an item of Talmud, defined in its broadest sense as "deducing conclusions from premises, developing implications of statements, comparing dicta, and studying the hermeneutical principles by which the Torah is interpreted" (Maimonides, *Laws of Torah Study* 1:11). It was chosen because it appears at the beginning of the *Sifra*, the halachic commentary to Leviticus, which is the source of most of the laws of offerings. It also reminds us

til midnight. It could only be eaten by those who had been numbered for it, and eaten only roasted.

THE INTERPRETIVE PRINCIPLES OF RABBI ISHMAEL

רַבִּי יִשְׁמָעֵאל Rabbi Ishmael says: The Torah is expounded by thirteen principles: 1. An inference from a lenient law to a strict one, and vice versa. 2. An inference drawn from identical words in two passages. 3. A general principle derived from one text or two related texts. 4. A general law followed by specific examples (where the law applies exclusively to those examples). 5. A specific example followed by a general law (where the law applies to everything implied in the general statement). 6. A general law followed by specific examples and concluding with a general law: here you may infer only cases similar to the examples. 7. When a general statement requires clarification by a specific example, or a specific example requires clarification by a general statement (then rules 4 and 5 do not apply). 8. When a particular case, already included in the general statement, is expressly mentioned to teach something new, that special provision applies to all other cases included in the general statement. 9. When a particular case, though included in the general statement, is expressly mentioned with a provision similar to the general law, such a case is singled out to lessen the severity of the law, not to increase it. 10. When a particular case, though included in the general statement, is explicitly mentioned with a provision differing from the general law, it is singled out to lessen in some respects, and in others to increase, the severity of the law. 11. When a particular case, though included in the general statement, is explicitly mentioned with a new provision, the terms of the general statement no longer apply to it, unless Scripture indicates explicitly that they do apply. 12. A matter elucidated from its context, or from the following passage. 13. Also, when two passages (seem to) contradict each other, (they are to be elucidated by) a third passage that reconciles them.

→ May it be Your will, LORD our GOD and GOD of our ancestors, that the Temple be speedily rebuilt in our days, and grant us our share in Your Torah. And may we serve You there in reverence, as in the days of old and as in former years.

---

of the indissoluble connection between the Written Law (the Mosaic books) and the Oral Law (Mishnah, Midrash and Talmud). Rabbi Ishmael's principles show how the latter can be derived from the former.

קדיש דרבנן

The transliteration can be found at the end of the Siddur.

Mourner:

יִתְגַּדַּל וְיִתְקַדַּשׁ שְׁמֵהּ רַבָּא. (Cong. אָמֵן) בְּעָלְמָא דִּי־בְרָא כִּרְעוּתֵהּ. וְיַמְלִיךְ מַלְכוּתֵהּ, בְּחַיֵּיכוֹן וּבְיוֹמֵיכוֹן וּבְחַיֵּי דִי־כָל־ בֵּית יִשְׂרָאֵל, בַּעֲגָלָא וּבִזְמַן קָרִיב. וְאִמְרוּ אָמֵן. (Cong. אָמֵן)

All:

יְהֵא שְׁמֵהּ רַבָּא מְבָרַךְ לְעָלַם וּלְעָלְמֵי עָלְמַיָּא.

Mourner:

יִתְבָּרַךְ וְיִשְׁתַּבַּח וְיִתְפָּאַר וְיִתְרוֹמַם וְיִתְנַשֵּׂא וְיִתְהַדַּר וְיִתְעַלֶּה וְיִתְהַלָּל שְׁמֵהּ דְּקֻדְשָׁא בְּרִיךְ הוּא (Cong. בְּרִיךְ הוּא) לְעֵלָּא (Between רֹאשׁ הַשָּׁנָה and יוֹם כִּפּוּר add לְעֵלָּא) מִן־כָּל־בִּרְכָתָא וְשִׁירָתָא תֻּשְׁבְּחָתָא וְנֶחֱמָתָא, דַּאֲמִירָן בְּעָלְמָא. וְאִמְרוּ אָמֵן. (Cong. אָמֵן)

עַל יִשְׂרָאֵל וְעַל רַבָּנָן, וְעַל תַּלְמִידֵיהוֹן וְעַל כָּל תַּלְמִידֵי תַלְמִידֵיהוֹן, וְעַל כָּל־מָן דְּעָסְקִין בְּאוֹרַיְתָא, דִּי בְּאַתְרָא הָדֵן וְדִי בְּכָל־אֲתַר וַאֲתַר. יְהֵא לְהוֹן וּלְכוֹן שְׁלָמָא רַבָּא, חִנָּא וְחִסְדָּא וְרַחֲמִין, וְחַיִּין אֲרִיכִין, וּמְזוֹנָא רְוִיחָא, וּפֻרְקָנָא מִן־קֳדָם אֲבוּהוֹן דִּי בִשְׁמַיָּא. וְאִמְרוּ אָמֵן. (Cong. אָמֵן)

יְהֵא שְׁלָמָא רַבָּא מִן־שְׁמַיָּא, וְחַיִּים טוֹבִים עָלֵינוּ וְעַל־כָּל־ יִשְׂרָאֵל. וְאִמְרוּ אָמֵן. (Cong. אָמֵן)

Bow, take three steps back, then bow, first left, then right, then centre, while saying:

עֹשֶׂה שָׁלוֹם בִּמְרוֹמָיו, הוּא בְּרַחֲמָיו יַעֲשֶׂה שָׁלוֹם עָלֵינוּ, וְעַל־כָּל־יִשְׂרָאֵל. וְאִמְרוּ אָמֵן. (Cong. אָמֵן)

On שַׁבָּת, יוֹם טוֹב and הוֹשַׁעְנָא רַבָּה continue on page 322.

LAWS OF KADDISH

1. *Kaddish* requires the presence of a *minyan*, that is, ten adult males.

2. It is our custom to say *Kaddish* standing.

3. It is also our custom that all mourners recite *Kaddish* in unison.

THE RABBIS' KADDISH

The transliteration can be found at the end of the Siddur.

Mourner:

יִתְגַּדַּל Magnified and sanctified may His great name be, in the world He created by His will. May He establish His kingdom in your lifetime and in your days, and in the lifetime of all the House of Israel, swiftly and soon – and say: Amen.

All:

May His great name be blessed for ever and all time.

Mourner:

Blessed and praised, glorified and exalted, raised and honoured, uplifted and lauded be the name of the Holy One, blessed be He, (between Rosh Hashanah and Yom Kippur add 'well') beyond any blessing, song, praise and consolation uttered in the world – and say: Amen.

To Israel, to the teachers, their disciples and their disciples' disciples, and to all who engage in the study of Torah, here or elsewhere, may there come to them and you great peace, grace, kindness and compassion, long life, ample sustenance and deliverance from their Father in Heaven – and say: Amen.

May there be great peace from heaven, and good life for us and all Israel – and say: Amen.

Bow, take three steps back, then bow, first left, then right, then centre, while saying:

May He who makes peace in His high places, in His compassion make peace for us and all Israel – and say: Amen.

On Shabbat, Festivals and Hoshana Rabba, continue on page 323.

---

4. The Sages attached particular significance to the response, "May His great name be blessed for ever and all time." This should be said with full concentration by all present.

THE RABBIS' KADDISH

The *Kaddish*, one of the most important of all prayers, had its origins not in the synagogue but in the house of study. It grew out of a custom, still widely practised, of ending every discourse or sermon with the hope that we may speedily see the coming of the messianic age, when the sovereignty of God will be recognised by all the dwellers on earth. It is written mainly in Aramaic, the language most widely spoken by Jews in the first centuries of the Common Era.

מזמור לפני פסוקי דזמרה

תהלים ל

מִזְמוֹר שִׁיר חֲנֻכַּת הַבַּיִת לְדָוִד. אֲרוֹמִמְךָ יהוה כִּי דִלִּיתָנִי, וְלֹא־שִׂמַּחְתָּ אֹיְבַי לִי. יהוה אֱלֹהָי, שִׁוַּעְתִּי אֵלֶיךָ וַתִּרְפָּאֵנִי. יהוה, הֶעֱלִיתָ מִן־שְׁאוֹל נַפְשִׁי, חִיִּיתַנִי מִיָּרְדִי־בוֹר. זַמְּרוּ לַיהוה חֲסִידָיו, וְהוֹדוּ לְזֵכֶר קָדְשׁוֹ. כִּי רֶגַע בְּאַפּוֹ, חַיִּים בִּרְצוֹנוֹ, בָּעֶרֶב יָלִין בֶּכִי וְלַבֹּקֶר רִנָּה. וַאֲנִי אָמַרְתִּי בְשַׁלְוִי, בַּל אֶמּוֹט לְעוֹלָם. יהוה בִּרְצוֹנְךָ הֶעֱמַדְתָּה לְהַרְרִי עֹז, הִסְתַּרְתָּ פָנֶיךָ הָיִיתִי נִבְהָל. אֵלֶיךָ יהוה אֶקְרָא, וְאֶל־אֲדֹנָי אֶתְחַנָּן. מַה־בֶּצַע בְּדָמִי, בְּרִדְתִּי אֶל שָׁחַת, הֲיוֹדְךָ עָפָר, הֲיַגִּיד אֲמִתֶּךָ. שְׁמַע־יהוה וְחָנֵּנִי, יהוה הֱיֵה עֹזֵר לִי. ⇐ הָפַכְתָּ מִסְפְּדִי לְמָחוֹל לִי, פִּתַּחְתָּ שַׂקִּי, וַתְּאַזְּרֵנִי שִׂמְחָה. לְמַעַן יְזַמֶּרְךָ כָבוֹד וְלֹא יִדֹּם, יהוה אֱלֹהַי לְעוֹלָם אוֹדֶךָּ.

קדיש יתום

The transliteration can be found at the end of the Siddur.

Mourner:

יִתְגַּדַּל וְיִתְקַדַּשׁ שְׁמֵהּ רַבָּא. (Cong. אָמֵן) בְּעָלְמָא דִּי־בְרָא כִרְעוּתֵהּ. וְיַמְלִיךְ מַלְכוּתֵהּ, בְּחַיֵּיכוֹן וּבְיוֹמֵיכוֹן וּבְחַיֵּי דְכָל־בֵּית יִשְׂרָאֵל, בַּעֲגָלָא וּבִזְמַן קָרִיב. וְאִמְרוּ אָמֵן. (Cong. אָמֵן)

All:

יְהֵא שְׁמֵהּ רַבָּא מְבָרַךְ לְעָלַם וּלְעָלְמֵי עָלְמַיָּא.

It has come to have five forms: 1. half-*Kaddish,* recited to mark the beginning or end of a section of the prayers; 2. full *Kaddish* (*titkabal*), to mark the end of the *Amidah* and its associated meditations; 3. the Mourner's *Kaddish*; 4. *Kaddish de-Rabbanan,* said after a passage from the Oral Law; 5. the *Kaddish* of Renewal, said only at the conclusion of a tractate of the Talmud, or by a child at the funeral of a parent.

The *Kaddish deRabbanan* is a prayer

A PSALM BEFORE VERSES OF PRAISE

PSALM 30

מִזְמוֹר A psalm of David. A song for the dedication of the House. I will exalt You, LORD, for You have lifted me up, and not let my enemies rejoice over me. LORD, my GOD, I cried to You for help and You healed me. LORD, You lifted my soul from the grave; You spared me from going down to the pit. Sing to the LORD, you His devoted ones, and give thanks to His holy name. For His anger is for a moment, but His favour for a lifetime. At night there may be weeping, but in the morning there is joy. When I felt secure, I said, "I shall never be shaken." LORD, when You favoured me, You made me stand firm as a mountain, but when You hid Your face, I was terrified. To You, LORD, I called; I pleaded with my LORD: "What gain would there be if I died and went down to the grave? Can dust thank You? Can it declare Your truth? Hear, LORD, and be gracious to me; LORD, be my help." ➔ You have turned my sorrow into dancing. You have removed my sackcloth and clothed me with joy, so that my soul may sing to You and not be silent. LORD my GOD, for ever will I thank You.

MOURNER'S KADDISH

The transliteration can be found at the end of the Siddur.

Mourner:

יִתְגַּדַּל Magnified and sanctified may His great name be, in the world He created by His will. May He establish His kingdom in your lifetime and in your days, and in the lifetime of all the House of Israel, swiftly and soon – and say: Amen.

All:

May His great name be blessed for ever and all time.

not only for the establishment of GOD's kingdom but also for the teachers of Torah and their disciples. It is characteristic of Judaism's value system that this is the first *Kaddish* we say each morning. Judaism is a faith whose passion is education, whose heroes are teachers, and whose citadels are schools and houses of study. To learn, to teach, to internalise GOD's will, to join our minds with the great Sages and scholars of the past – this is a supreme expression of Judaism, and the one from which all else flows.

Mourner:

יִתְבָּרַךְ וְיִשְׁתַּבַּח וְיִתְפָּאַר וְיִתְרוֹמַם וְיִתְנַשֵּׂא וְיִתְהַדָּר
וְיִתְעַלֶּה וְיִתְהַלָּל שְׁמֵהּ דְּקֻדְשָׁא בְּרִיךְ הוּא (Cong. בְּרִיךְ הוּא)
לְעֵלָּא (Between רֹאשׁ הַשָּׁנָה and יוֹם כִּפּוּר add לְעֵלָּא) מִן־כָּל־בִּרְכָתָא
וְשִׁירָתָא תֻּשְׁבְּחָתָא וְנֶחֱמָתָא, דַּאֲמִירָן בְּעָלְמָא. וְאִמְרוּ
אָמֵן. (Cong. אָמֵן)

יְהֵא שְׁלָמָא רַבָּא מִן־שְׁמַיָּא, וְחַיִּים עָלֵינוּ וְעַל־כָּל־יִשְׂרָאֵל.
וְאִמְרוּ אָמֵן. (Cong. אָמֵן)

Bow, take three steps back, then bow, first left, then right, then centre, while saying:

עֹשֶׂה שָׁלוֹם בִּמְרוֹמָיו, הוּא יַעֲשֶׂה שָׁלוֹם עָלֵינוּ, וְעַל־כָּל־
יִשְׂרָאֵל, וְאִמְרוּ אָמֵן. (Cong. אָמֵן)

PESUKEI DE-ZIMRA / VERSES OF PRAISE
"A person should first recount the praise of the Holy One, blessed be He, and then pray" (*Berachot* 32b), hence the passages that follow, known as the "Verses of Praise". The morning service from this point until the end is constructed in three movements, whose themes are: 1. *Creation*: God as He is in nature; 2. *Revelation*: God as He is in Torah and prayer; and 3. *Redemption*: God as He is in history and our lives. The theme of the Verses of Praise is Creation – God as Architect and Maker of a universe of splendour and diversity, whose orderliness testifies to the single creative will which underlies all that exists. The Psalms tell this story not in scientific prose but majestic poetry, not *proving* but *proclaiming* the One at the heart of all.

LAWS OF VERSES OF PRAISE:

1. From the beginning of the Verses of Praise to the end of the *Amidah*, there should be no talking. It is permitted, however, to answer Amen and to respond to *Bar'chu*, *Kaddish* and *Kedushah*.

2. One who arrives late and finds the congregation already saying the Verses of Praise should do the following so as to be able to say *Bar'chu* and subsequent prayers together with the congregation: 1. put on *tallit* and *tefillin*, saying the appropriate blessings; 2. make the blessings over washing hands, אֲשֶׁר יָצַר "who formed man in wisdom", and אֱלֹהַי, נְשָׁמָה "My God, the soul You placed in me is pure"; 3. say the blessings over the Torah (page 14); 4. say בָּרוּךְ שֶׁאָמַר "Blessed is He who spoke" and אַשְׁרֵי "Happy are those"; 5. on weekdays, say יִשְׁתַּבַּח "May Your name be praised for ever", and on Shabbat and Festivals, נִשְׁמַת "The soul of all that lives". If there is more time, one should say other passages in the following order of priority: 1. Psalm 148; 2. Psalm 150; 3. Psalms 146, 147, 149; 4. וַיְבָרֶךְ דָּוִיד "David blessed"; 5. הודו "Thank

Mourner:

Blessed and praised, glorified and exalted, raised and honoured, uplifted and lauded be the name of the Holy One, blessed be He, (between Rosh Hashanah and Yom Kippur add 'well') beyond any blessing, song, praise and consolation uttered in the world – and say: Amen.

May there be great peace from heaven, and life for us and all Israel – and say: Amen.

Bow, take three steps back, then bow, first left, then right, then centre, while saying:

May He who makes peace in His high places, make peace for us and all Israel – and say: Amen.

---

the LORD"; 6. Psalm 100. On Shabbat, the daily psalms take priority over those added on Shabbat.

3. If there is no time to say any of the Verses of Praise before *Bar'chu*, one should say prayers with the congregation, and at the end of the service go back and say the full Verses of Praise except for בָּרוּךְ שֶׁאָמַר "Blessed is He who spoke" and יִשְׁתַּבַּח "May Your name be praised for ever".

The core elements of *Pesukei de-Zimra* are: 1. Psalm 145 (*Ashrei*), a prayer to which the Sages attached particular significance, specifying that it should be said three times daily; and 2. Psalms 146–150 which form the culmination and crescendo of the Book of Psalms as a whole. These six psalms correspond to the six days of creation; others are added on Shabbat and Festivals. Around this inner core other passages have been woven: some from other biblical books and others from selected verses in the Book of Psalms. The section begins and ends with a paragraph of blessings: "Blessed is He who spoke" (*Baruch She'amar*) at the beginning, and "May Your Name be praised for ever" (*Yishtabach*) at the end.

בָּרוּךְ שֶׁאָמַר *Blessed is He*: An introductory blessing to the Verses of Praise, in two parts. The first is a ten-part litany of praise to GOD as Creator, each phrase introduced with the word Blessed (the second phrase, "Blessed is He", is not a separate verse but was originally a congregational response). The number ten corresponds to the ten times the word *Vayomer*, "And He said", appears in the story of creation in Genesis 1, hence the rabbinic saying that "With ten utterances the world was created."

Blessed are You: The second half of the blessing is a prelude to the biblical verses that follow, mainly from the Book of Psalms ("With the songs of Your servant David we will exalt You") but also from the books of Chronicles and Nehemiah ("extolled by the mouth of His people"). To emphasise the significance of this declaration, we recite it standing and, at the end, kiss the two front fringes of the *tallit*.

פסוקי דזמרה

The following is recited standing, while holding the front two צִיצִיּוֹת of the טַלִּית.
They are kissed and released at the end of the blessing.

בָּרוּךְ שֶׁאָמַר וְהָיָה הָעוֹלָם, בָּרוּךְ הוּא.
בָּרוּךְ עֹשֶׂה בְרֵאשִׁית,
בָּרוּךְ אוֹמֵר וְעוֹשֶׂה,
בָּרוּךְ גּוֹזֵר וּמְקַיֵּם,
בָּרוּךְ מְרַחֵם עַל הָאָרֶץ,
בָּרוּךְ מְרַחֵם עַל הַבְּרִיּוֹת,
בָּרוּךְ מְשַׁלֵּם שָׂכָר־טוֹב לִירֵאָיו,
בָּרוּךְ חַי לָעַד וְקַיָּם לָנֶצַח,
בָּרוּךְ פּוֹדֶה וּמַצִּיל,
בָּרוּךְ שְׁמוֹ.

בָּרוּךְ אַתָּה יהוה אֱלֹהֵינוּ מֶלֶךְ הָעוֹלָם, הָאֵל הָאָב הָרַחֲמָן הַמְהֻלָּל בְּפִי עַמּוֹ, מְשֻׁבָּח וּמְפֹאָר בִּלְשׁוֹן חֲסִידָיו וַעֲבָדָיו, וּבְשִׁירֵי דָוִד עַבְדֶּךָ. נְהַלֶּלְךָ יהוה אֱלֹהֵינוּ, בִּשְׁבָחוֹת וּבִזְמִירוֹת. נְגַדֶּלְךָ וּנְשַׁבֵּחֲךָ וּנְפָאֶרְךָ וְנַזְכִּיר שִׁמְךָ וְנַמְלִיכְךָ, מַלְכֵּנוּ אֱלֹהֵינוּ. ◄ יָחִיד, חֵי הָעוֹלָמִים, מֶלֶךְ מְשֻׁבָּח וּמְפֹאָר עֲדֵי־עַד שְׁמוֹ הַגָּדוֹל. בָּרוּךְ אַתָּה יהוה, מֶלֶךְ מְהֻלָּל בַּתִּשְׁבָּחוֹת.

דברי הימים א׳ טז:ח–לו

הוֹדוּ לַיהוה קִרְאוּ בִשְׁמוֹ, הוֹדִיעוּ בָעַמִּים עֲלִילֹתָיו. שִׁירוּ לוֹ, זַמְּרוּ־לוֹ, שִׂיחוּ בְּכָל־נִפְלְאֹתָיו. הִתְהַלְלוּ בְּשֵׁם קָדְשׁוֹ, יִשְׂמַח לֵב מְבַקְשֵׁי יהוה. דִּרְשׁוּ יהוה וְעֻזּוֹ, בַּקְּשׁוּ פָנָיו תָּמִיד. זִכְרוּ נִפְלְאֹתָיו אֲשֶׁר עָשָׂה, מֹפְתָיו וּמִשְׁפְּטֵי־פִיהוּ. זֶרַע יִשְׂרָאֵל עַבְדּוֹ, בְּנֵי יַעֲקֹב בְּחִירָיו. הוּא יהוה אֱלֹהֵינוּ, בְּכָל־הָאָרֶץ מִשְׁפָּטָיו. זִכְרוּ לְעוֹלָם בְּרִיתוֹ, דָּבָר צִוָּה לְאֶלֶף

VERSES OF PRAISE

The following is recited standing, while holding the two front *tzitziot* of the *tallit*. They are kissed and released at the end of the blessing.

בָּרוּךְ Blessed is He who spoke and the world came into being, blessed is He.
Blessed is He who creates the universe.
Blessed is He who speaks and acts.
Blessed is He who decrees and fulfils.
Blessed is He who shows compassion to the earth.
Blessed is He who shows compassion to all creatures.
Blessed is He who gives a good reward to those who fear Him.
Blessed is He who lives for ever and exists to eternity.
Blessed is He who redeems and saves.
Blessed is His name.
Blessed are You, LORD our GOD, King of the Universe, GOD, compassionate Father, extolled by the mouth of His people, praised and glorified by the tongue of His devoted ones and those who serve Him. With the songs of Your servant David we will praise You, O LORD our GOD. With praises and psalms we will magnify and praise You, glorify You and make mention of Your name. We will proclaim Your kingship, our King, our GOD, ➔ the only One, life of the universe, the King whose great name is praised and glorified to all eternity. Blessed are You, LORD, the King extolled with songs of praise.

I CHRONICLES 16:8–36

הוֹדוּ Thank the LORD, call on His name, make His acts known among the peoples. Sing to Him, make music to Him, tell of all His wonders. Glory in His holy name; let the hearts of those who seek the LORD rejoice. Search out the LORD and His strength; seek His presence at all times. Remember the wonders He has done, His miracles, and the judgements He pronounced. O descendants of Israel His servant, sons of Jacob His chosen ones: He is the LORD our GOD. His judgements are throughout the earth. Remember His covenant for ever, the word He commanded for a thousand generations. He made it with Abraham,

דּוֹר. אֲשֶׁר כָּרַת אֶת־אַבְרָהָם, וּשְׁבוּעָתוֹ לְיִצְחָק. וַיַּעֲמִידֶהָ לְיַעֲקֹב לְחֹק, לְיִשְׂרָאֵל בְּרִית עוֹלָם. לֵאמֹר, לְךָ אֶתֵּן אֶרֶץ־כְּנָעַן, חֶבֶל נַחֲלַתְכֶם. בִּהְיוֹתְכֶם מְתֵי מִסְפָּר, כִּמְעַט וְגָרִים בָּהּ. וַיִּתְהַלְּכוּ מִגּוֹי אֶל־גּוֹי, וּמִמַּמְלָכָה אֶל־עַם אַחֵר. לֹא־הִנִּיחַ לְאִישׁ לְעָשְׁקָם, וַיּוֹכַח עֲלֵיהֶם מְלָכִים. אַל־תִּגְּעוּ בִּמְשִׁיחָי, וּבִנְבִיאַי אַל־תָּרֵעוּ. שִׁירוּ לַיהוה כָּל־הָאָרֶץ, בַּשְּׂרוּ מִיּוֹם־אֶל־יוֹם יְשׁוּעָתוֹ. סַפְּרוּ בַגּוֹיִם אֶת־כְּבוֹדוֹ, בְּכָל־הָעַמִּים נִפְלְאֹתָיו. ← כִּי גָדוֹל יהוה וּמְהֻלָּל מְאֹד, וְנוֹרָא הוּא עַל־כָּל־אֱלֹהִים. כִּי כָּל־אֱלֹהֵי הָעַמִּים אֱלִילִים | וַיהוה שָׁמַיִם עָשָׂה. הוֹד וְהָדָר לְפָנָיו, עֹז וְחֶדְוָה בִּמְקֹמוֹ. הָבוּ לַיהוה מִשְׁפְּחוֹת עַמִּים, הָבוּ לַיהוה כָּבוֹד וָעֹז. הָבוּ לַיהוה כְּבוֹד שְׁמוֹ, שְׂאוּ מִנְחָה וּבֹאוּ לְפָנָיו, הִשְׁתַּחֲווּ לַיהוה בְּהַדְרַת־קֹדֶשׁ. חִילוּ מִלְּפָנָיו כָּל־הָאָרֶץ, אַף־תִּכּוֹן תֵּבֵל בַּל־תִּמּוֹט. יִשְׂמְחוּ הַשָּׁמַיִם וְתָגֵל הָאָרֶץ, וְיֹאמְרוּ בַגּוֹיִם, יהוה מָלָךְ. יִרְעַם הַיָּם וּמְלוֹאוֹ, יַעֲלֹץ הַשָּׂדֶה וְכָל־אֲשֶׁר־בּוֹ. אָז יְרַנְּנוּ עֲצֵי הַיָּעַר, מִלִּפְנֵי יהוה, כִּי־בָא לִשְׁפּוֹט אֶת־הָאָרֶץ. הוֹדוּ לַיהוה כִּי טוֹב, כִּי לְעוֹלָם חַסְדּוֹ. וְאִמְרוּ הוֹשִׁיעֵנוּ אֱלֹהֵי יִשְׁעֵנוּ, וְקַבְּצֵנוּ וְהַצִּילֵנוּ מִן־הַגּוֹיִם, לְהֹדוֹת לְשֵׁם קָדְשֶׁךָ, לְהִשְׁתַּבֵּחַ בִּתְהִלָּתֶךָ. בָּרוּךְ יהוה אֱלֹהֵי יִשְׂרָאֵל מִן־הָעוֹלָם וְעַד־הָעֹלָם, וַיֹּאמְרוּ כָל־הָעָם, אָמֵן, וְהַלֵּל לַיהוה.

← רוֹמְמוּ יהוה אֱלֹהֵינוּ וְהִשְׁתַּחֲווּ לַהֲדֹם רַגְלָיו, קָדוֹשׁ הוּא. רוֹמְמוּ יהוה אֱלֹהֵינוּ וְהִשְׁתַּחֲווּ לְהַר קָדְשׁוֹ, כִּי קָדוֹשׁ יהוה אֱלֹהֵינוּ. וְהוּא רַחוּם יְכַפֵּר עָוֹן וְלֹא יַשְׁחִית, וְהִרְבָּה לְהָשִׁיב אַפּוֹ, וְלֹא יָעִיר כָּל־חֲמָתוֹ. אַתָּה יהוה לֹא־תִכְלָא רַחֲמֶיךָ מִמֶּנִּי, חַסְדְּךָ וַאֲמִתְּךָ תָּמִיד יִצְּרוּנִי. זְכֹר רַחֲמֶיךָ

vowed it to Isaac, and confirmed it to Jacob as a statute and to Israel as an everlasting covenant, saying, "To you I will give the land of Canaan as your allotted heritage." You were then small in number, few, strangers there, wandering from nation to nation, from one kingdom to another, but He let no man oppress them, and for their sake He rebuked kings: "Do not touch My anointed ones, and do My prophets no harm." Sing to the LORD, all the earth, proclaim His salvation daily. Declare His glory among the nations, His marvels among all the peoples. For great is the LORD and greatly to be praised; He is awesome beyond all heavenly powers. ➔ For all the gods of the peoples are mere idols; it was the LORD who made the heavens. Before Him are majesty and splendour; there is strength and beauty in His holy place. Render to the LORD, O families of the peoples, render to the LORD honour and might. Render to the LORD the glory due to His name; bring an offering and come before Him; bow down to the LORD in the splendour of holiness. Tremble before Him, all the earth; the world stands firm, it will not be shaken. Let the heavens rejoice and the earth be glad; let them declare among the nations, "The LORD is King." Let the sea roar, and all that is in it; let the fields be jubilant, and all they contain. Then the trees of the forest will sing for joy before the LORD, for He is coming to judge the earth. Give thanks to the LORD, for He is good; His lovingkindness endures for ever. Say: "Save us, GOD of our salvation; gather us and rescue us from the nations, to acknowledge Your holy name and glory in Your praise. Blessed is the LORD, GOD of Israel, from eternity to eternity." And all the people said "Amen" and "Praise the LORD".

➔ Exalt the Lord our God and bow before His footstool: He is holy. Exalt the Lord our God and bow at His holy mountain; for holy is the Lord our God. He is compassionate. He forgives iniquity and does not destroy. Repeatedly He suppresses His anger, not rousing His full wrath.

הודו *Thank the LORD*: A psalm of thanksgiving composed by King David to celebrate the moment when the Ark of the Covenant was brought to Jerusalem.

רוֹמְמוּ *Exalt*: This paragraph is a selection of verses from the Book of Psalms on the theme of hope and trust in GOD.

יהוה וַחֲסָדֶיךָ, כִּי מֵעוֹלָם הֵמָּה. תְּנוּ עֹז לֵאלֹהִים עַל־יִשְׂרָאֵל גַּאֲוָתוֹ, וְעֻזּוֹ בַּשְּׁחָקִים. נוֹרָא אֱלֹהִים מִמִּקְדָּשֶׁיךָ, אֵל יִשְׂרָאֵל הוּא נֹתֵן עֹז וְתַעֲצֻמוֹת לָעָם, בָּרוּךְ אֱלֹהִים. אֵל־נְקָמוֹת יהוה, אֵל נְקָמוֹת הוֹפִיעַ. הִנָּשֵׂא שֹׁפֵט הָאָרֶץ, הָשֵׁב גְּמוּל עַל־גֵּאִים. לַיהוה הַיְשׁוּעָה, עַל־עַמְּךָ בִרְכָתֶךָ סֶּלָה. ◄ יהוה צְבָאוֹת עִמָּנוּ, מִשְׂגָּב־לָנוּ אֱלֹהֵי יַעֲקֹב סֶלָה. יהוה צְבָאוֹת, אַשְׁרֵי אָדָם בֹּטֵחַ בָּךְ. יהוה הוֹשִׁיעָה, הַמֶּלֶךְ יַעֲנֵנוּ בְיוֹם־קָרְאֵנוּ. הוֹשִׁיעָה אֶת־עַמֶּךָ, וּבָרֵךְ אֶת־נַחֲלָתֶךָ, וּרְעֵם וְנַשְּׂאֵם עַד־הָעוֹלָם. נַפְשֵׁנוּ חִכְּתָה לַיהוה, עֶזְרֵנוּ וּמָגִנֵּנוּ הוּא. כִּי־בוֹ יִשְׂמַח לִבֵּנוּ, כִּי בְשֵׁם קָדְשׁוֹ בָטָחְנוּ. יְהִי־חַסְדְּךָ יהוה עָלֵינוּ, כַּאֲשֶׁר יִחַלְנוּ לָךְ. הַרְאֵנוּ יהוה חַסְדֶּךָ, וְיֶשְׁעֲךָ תִּתֶּן־לָנוּ. קוּמָה עֶזְרָתָה לָּנוּ, וּפְדֵנוּ לְמַעַן חַסְדֶּךָ. אָנֹכִי יהוה אֱלֹהֶיךָ הַמַּעַלְךָ מֵאֶרֶץ מִצְרָיִם, הַרְחֶב־פִּיךָ וַאֲמַלְאֵהוּ. אַשְׁרֵי הָעָם שֶׁכָּכָה לּוֹ, אַשְׁרֵי הָעָם שֶׁיהוה אֱלֹהָיו. ◄ וַאֲנִי בְּחַסְדְּךָ בָטַחְתִּי, יָגֵל לִבִּי בִּישׁוּעָתֶךָ, אָשִׁירָה לַיהוה, כִּי גָמַל עָלָי.

The following psalm is said while standing. It is omitted on the day before פֶּסַח, the day before יוֹם כִּפּוּר and חוֹל הַמּוֹעֵד פֶּסַח.

תהלים ק

מִזְמוֹר לְתוֹדָה, הָרִיעוּ לַיהוה כָּל־הָאָרֶץ. עִבְדוּ אֶת־יהוה בְּשִׂמְחָה, בֹּאוּ לְפָנָיו בִּרְנָנָה. דְּעוּ כִּי יהוה הוּא אֱלֹהִים, הוּא עָשָׂנוּ, וְלוֹ אֲנַחְנוּ, עַמּוֹ וְצֹאן מַרְעִיתוֹ. בֹּאוּ שְׁעָרָיו בְּתוֹדָה, חֲצֵרֹתָיו בִּתְהִלָּה, הוֹדוּ לוֹ, בָּרְכוּ שְׁמוֹ. ◄ כִּי־טוֹב יהוה, לְעוֹלָם חַסְדּוֹ, וְעַד־דֹּר וָדֹר אֱמוּנָתוֹ.

מִזְמוֹר לְתוֹדָה *A psalm of thanksgiving*: This psalm accompanied the *korban todah*, a thanksgiving offering (Leviticus 7:11), brought to express gratitude for coming safely through a hazardous situation (recovering from illness, completing a potentially dangerous journey or being released from captivity). Nowadays, we make the *HaGomel* blessing (which is said after surviving illness, childbirth or

You, O LORD: do not withhold Your compassion from me. May Your lovingkindness and truth always guard me. Remember, LORD, Your acts of compassion and love, for they have existed for ever. Ascribe power to GOD, whose majesty is over Israel and whose might is in the skies. You are awesome, GOD, in Your holy places. It is the GOD of Israel who gives might and strength to the people, may GOD be blessed. GOD of retribution, LORD, GOD of retribution, appear. Arise, Judge of the earth, to repay the arrogant their just deserts. Salvation belongs to the LORD; may Your blessing rest upon Your people, Selah! ➔ The LORD of hosts is with us, the GOD of Jacob is our stronghold, Selah! Lord of hosts, happy is the one who trusts in You. O Lord, save. May the King answer us on the day we call. Save Your people and bless Your heritage; tend them and carry them for ever. Our soul longs for the LORD; He is our Help and Shield. For in Him our hearts rejoice, for in His holy name we have trusted. May your lovingkindness, LORD, be upon us, as we have put our hope in You. Show us, LORD, Your lovingkindness and grant us Your salvation. Arise, help us and redeem us for the sake of Your love. I am the LORD your GOD who brought you up from the land of Egypt: open your mouth wide and I will fill it. Happy is the people for whom this is so; happy is the people whose LORD is GOD. ➔ As for me, I trust in Your lovingkindness; my heart rejoices in Your salvation. I will sing to the LORD for He has been good to me.

The following psalm is said while standing. It is omitted on the day before Pesach, the day before Yom Kippur and the Intermediate Days of Pesach.

PSALM 100

מִזְמוֹר A psalm of thanksgiving. Shout joyously to the LORD, all the earth. Serve the LORD with joy. Come before Him with jubilation. Know that the LORD is GOD. He made us and we are His. We are His people and the flock He tends. Enter His gates with thanksgiving, His courts with praise. Thank Him and bless His name. ➔ For the LORD is good, His lovingkindness is everlasting, and His faithfulness is for every generation.

---

danger) in place of the sacrifice. The psalm first appeared as part of the daily service in Yemenite and French prayer books of the Middle Ages. Its presence here is to emphasise the mood of thankfulness that dominates this section of the prayers.

יְהִי כְבוֹד יהוה לְעוֹלָם, יִשְׂמַח יהוה בְּמַעֲשָׂיו. יְהִי שֵׁם יהוה מְבֹרָךְ, מֵעַתָּה וְעַד־עוֹלָם. מִמִּזְרַח־שֶׁמֶשׁ עַד־מְבוֹאוֹ, מְהֻלָּל שֵׁם יהוה. רָם עַל־כָּל־גּוֹיִם | יהוה, עַל הַשָּׁמַיִם כְּבוֹדוֹ. יהוה שִׁמְךָ לְעוֹלָם, יהוה זִכְרְךָ לְדֹר־וָדֹר. יהוה בַּשָּׁמַיִם הֵכִין כִּסְאוֹ, וּמַלְכוּתוֹ בַּכֹּל מָשָׁלָה. יִשְׂמְחוּ הַשָּׁמַיִם וְתָגֵל הָאָרֶץ, וְיֹאמְרוּ בַגּוֹיִם יהוה מָלָךְ. יהוה מֶלֶךְ, יהוה מָלָךְ, יהוה יִמְלֹךְ לְעֹלָם וָעֶד. יהוה מֶלֶךְ עוֹלָם וָעֶד, אָבְדוּ גוֹיִם מֵאַרְצוֹ. יהוה הֵפִיר עֲצַת גּוֹיִם, הֵנִיא מַחְשְׁבוֹת עַמִּים. רַבּוֹת מַחֲשָׁבוֹת בְּלֶב־אִישׁ, וַעֲצַת יהוה הִיא תָקוּם. עֲצַת יהוה לְעוֹלָם תַּעֲמֹד, מַחְשְׁבוֹת לִבּוֹ לְדֹר וָדֹר. כִּי הוּא אָמַר וַיֶּהִי, הוּא צִוָּה וַיַּעֲמֹד. כִּי־בָחַר יהוה בְּצִיּוֹן, אִוָּהּ לְמוֹשָׁב לוֹ. כִּי יַעֲקֹב בָּחַר לוֹ יָהּ, יִשְׂרָאֵל לִסְגֻלָּתוֹ. כִּי לֹא־יִטֹּשׁ יהוה עַמּוֹ, וְנַחֲלָתוֹ לֹא יַעֲזֹב. ← וְהוּא רַחוּם יְכַפֵּר עָוֹן וְלֹא יַשְׁחִית, וְהִרְבָּה לְהָשִׁיב אַפּוֹ, וְלֹא יָעִיר כָּל־חֲמָתוֹ. יהוה הוֹשִׁיעָה, הַמֶּלֶךְ יַעֲנֵנוּ בְיוֹם־קָרְאֵנוּ.

אשרי

אַשְׁרֵי יוֹשְׁבֵי בֵיתֶךָ, עוֹד יְהַלְלוּךָ סֶּלָה.
אַשְׁרֵי הָעָם שֶׁכָּכָה לּוֹ, אַשְׁרֵי הָעָם שֶׁיהוה אֱלֹהָיו.

תהלים קמה

תְּהִלָּה לְדָוִד,

אֲרוֹמִמְךָ אֱלוֹהַי הַמֶּלֶךְ, וַאֲבָרְכָה שִׁמְךָ לְעוֹלָם וָעֶד.
בְּכָל יוֹם אֲבָרְכֶךָּ, וַאֲהַלְלָה שִׁמְךָ לְעוֹלָם וָעֶד.
גָּדוֹל יהוה וּמְהֻלָּל מְאֹד, וְלִגְדֻלָּתוֹ אֵין חֵקֶר.
דּוֹר לְדוֹר יְשַׁבַּח מַעֲשֶׂיךָ, וּגְבוּרֹתֶיךָ יַגִּידוּ.

יְהִי May the LORD's glory be for ever; may the LORD rejoice in His works. May the LORD's name be blessed, now and for ever. From the rising of the sun to its setting, may the LORD's name be praised. The LORD is high above all nations; His glory is above the heavens. LORD, Your name is for ever. Your renown, LORD, is for all generations. The LORD has established His throne in heaven; His kingdom rules all. Let the heavens rejoice and the earth be glad. Let them say among the nations, "The LORD is King." The LORD is King, the LORD was King, the LORD will be King for ever and all time. The LORD is King for ever and all time; nations will perish from His land. The LORD foils the plans of nations; He frustrates the intentions of peoples. Many are the intentions in a person's mind, but the LORD's plan prevails. The LORD's plan shall stand for ever, His mind's intent for all generations. For He spoke and it was; He commanded and it stood firm. For the LORD has chosen Zion; He desired it for His dwelling. For the LORD has chosen Jacob to Himself, Israel as His special treasure. For the LORD will not abandon His people nor will He forsake His heritage. ◆ He is compassionate. He forgives iniquity and does not destroy. Repeatedly He suppresses His anger, not rousing His full wrath. LORD, save! May the King answer us on the day we call.

ASHREI

אַשְׁרֵי Happy are those who dwell in Your House;
they shall continue to praise You, Selah!
Happy are the people for whom this is so;
happy are the people whose GOD is the LORD.

PSALM 145

A song of praise by David.

I will exalt You, my GOD, the King,
and bless Your name for ever and all time.
Every day I will bless You,
and praise Your name for ever and all time.
GOD is great and greatly to be praised;
His greatness is unfathomable.
One generation will praise Your works to the next,
and tell of Your mighty deeds.

הֲדַר כְּבוֹד הוֹדֶךָ, וְדִבְרֵי נִפְלְאֹתֶיךָ אָשִׂיחָה.
וֶעֱזוּז נוֹרְאוֹתֶיךָ יֹאמֵרוּ, וּגְדֻלָּתְךָ אֲסַפְּרֶנָּה.
זֵכֶר רַב־טוּבְךָ יַבִּיעוּ, וְצִדְקָתְךָ יְרַנֵּנוּ.
חַנּוּן וְרַחוּם יהוה, אֶרֶךְ אַפַּיִם וּגְדָל־חָסֶד.
טוֹב יהוה לַכֹּל, וְרַחֲמָיו עַל כָּל מַעֲשָׂיו.
יוֹדוּךָ יהוה כָּל מַעֲשֶׂיךָ, וַחֲסִידֶיךָ יְבָרְכוּכָה.
כְּבוֹד מַלְכוּתְךָ יֹאמֵרוּ, וּגְבוּרָתְךָ יְדַבֵּרוּ.
לְהוֹדִיעַ לִבְנֵי הָאָדָם גְּבוּרֹתָיו, וּכְבוֹד הֲדַר מַלְכוּתוֹ.
מַלְכוּתְךָ מַלְכוּת כָּל עֹלָמִים, וּמֶמְשַׁלְתְּךָ בְּכָל דּוֹר וָדֹר.
סוֹמֵךְ יהוה לְכָל הַנֹּפְלִים, וְזוֹקֵף לְכָל הַכְּפוּפִים.
עֵינֵי כֹל אֵלֶיךָ יְשַׂבֵּרוּ, וְאַתָּה נוֹתֵן לָהֶם אֶת אָכְלָם בְּעִתּוֹ.
פּוֹתֵחַ אֶת יָדֶךָ, וּמַשְׂבִּיעַ לְכָל־חַי רָצוֹן.
צַדִּיק יהוה בְּכָל דְּרָכָיו, וְחָסִיד בְּכָל מַעֲשָׂיו.
קָרוֹב יהוה לְכָל קֹרְאָיו, לְכֹל אֲשֶׁר יִקְרָאֻהוּ בֶאֱמֶת.
רְצוֹן יְרֵאָיו יַעֲשֶׂה, וְאֶת שַׁוְעָתָם יִשְׁמַע, וְיוֹשִׁיעֵם.
שׁוֹמֵר יהוה אֶת כָּל אֹהֲבָיו, וְאֵת כָּל־הָרְשָׁעִים יַשְׁמִיד.
◄ תְּהִלַּת יהוה יְדַבֶּר פִּי, וִיבָרֵךְ כָּל־בָּשָׂר שֵׁם קָדְשׁוֹ לְעוֹלָם וָעֶד.
וַאֲנַחְנוּ נְבָרֵךְ יָהּ, מֵעַתָּה וְעַד־עוֹלָם, הַלְלוּיָהּ.

תהלים קמו

הַלְלוּיָהּ, הַלְלִי נַפְשִׁי אֶת־יהוה. אֲהַלְלָה יהוה בְּחַיָּי, אֲזַמְּרָה לֵאלֹהַי בְּעוֹדִי. אַל־תִּבְטְחוּ בִנְדִיבִים, בְּבֶן־אָדָם שֶׁאֵין לוֹ תְשׁוּעָה. תֵּצֵא רוּחוֹ, יָשֻׁב לְאַדְמָתוֹ, בַּיּוֹם הַהוּא אָבְדוּ עֶשְׁתֹּנֹתָיו. אַשְׁרֵי שֶׁאֵל יַעֲקֹב בְּעֶזְרוֹ, שִׂבְרוֹ עַל־יהוה אֱלֹהָיו. עֹשֶׂה שָׁמַיִם וָאָרֶץ, אֶת־הַיָּם וְאֶת־כָּל־אֲשֶׁר־בָּם, הַשֹּׁמֵר אֱמֶת לְעוֹלָם. עֹשֶׂה מִשְׁפָּט לַעֲשׁוּקִים, נֹתֵן

On the glorious splendour of Your majesty I will meditate,
and on the acts of Your wonders.
They shall talk of the power of Your awesome deeds,
and I will tell of Your greatness.
They shall recite the record of Your great goodness,
and sing with joy of Your righteousness.
The LORD is gracious and compassionate,
slow to anger and great in lovingkindness.
The LORD is good to all,
and His compassion extends to all His works.
All Your works shall thank You, LORD,
and Your devoted ones shall bless You.
They shall talk of the glory of Your kingship,
and speak of Your might.
To make known to mankind His mighty deeds
and the glorious majesty of His kingship.
Your kingdom is an everlasting kingdom,
and Your reign is for all generations.
The LORD supports all who fall,
and raises all who are bowed down.
All raise their eyes to You in hope,
and You give them their food in due season.
You open Your hand,
and satisfy every living thing with Your favour.
The LORD is righteous in all His ways,
and kind in all He does.
The LORD is close to all who call on Him,
to all who call on Him in truth.
He fulfils the will of those who revere Him;
He hears their cry and saves them.
The LORD guards all who love Him,
but all the wicked He will destroy.
→ My mouth shall speak the praise of the LORD,
and all creatures shall bless His holy name for ever and all time.
We will bless the LORD now and for ever. Halleluyah!

PSALM 146

הַלְלוּיָהּ Halleluyah! Praise the LORD, O my soul. I will praise the LORD all my life; I will sing to my GOD as long as I live. Put not your trust in princes, or in mortal man who cannot save. His breath expires, he

לֶחֶם לָרְעֵבִים, יהוה מַתִּיר אֲסוּרִים. יהוה פֹּקֵחַ עִוְרִים,
יהוה זֹקֵף כְּפוּפִים, יהוה אֹהֵב צַדִּיקִים. יהוה שֹׁמֵר אֶת
גֵּרִים, יָתוֹם וְאַלְמָנָה יְעוֹדֵד, וְדֶרֶךְ רְשָׁעִים יְעַוֵּת. ‹ יִמְלֹךְ
יהוה לְעוֹלָם, אֱלֹהַיִךְ צִיּוֹן לְדֹר וָדֹר, הַלְלוּיָהּ.

תהלים קמז

הַלְלוּיָהּ, כִּי־טוֹב זַמְּרָה אֱלֹהֵינוּ, כִּי־נָעִים נָאוָה תְהִלָּה.
בּוֹנֵה יְרוּשָׁלַיִם יהוה, נִדְחֵי יִשְׂרָאֵל יְכַנֵּס. הָרוֹפֵא לִשְׁבוּרֵי־
לֵב, וּמְחַבֵּשׁ לְעַצְּבוֹתָם. מוֹנֶה מִסְפָּר לַכּוֹכָבִים, לְכֻלָּם
שֵׁמוֹת יִקְרָא. גָּדוֹל אֲדוֹנֵינוּ וְרַב־כֹּחַ, לִתְבוּנָתוֹ אֵין מִסְפָּר.
מְעוֹדֵד עֲנָוִים יהוה, מַשְׁפִּיל רְשָׁעִים עֲדֵי־אָרֶץ. עֱנוּ לַיהוה
בְּתוֹדָה, זַמְּרוּ לֵאלֹהֵינוּ בְכִנּוֹר. הַמְכַסֶּה שָׁמַיִם בְּעָבִים,
הַמֵּכִין לָאָרֶץ מָטָר, הַמַּצְמִיחַ הָרִים חָצִיר. נוֹתֵן לִבְהֵמָה
לַחְמָהּ, לִבְנֵי עֹרֵב אֲשֶׁר יִקְרָאוּ. לֹא בִגְבוּרַת־הַסּוּס יֶחְפָּץ,
לֹא־בְשׁוֹקֵי הָאִישׁ יִרְצֶה. רוֹצֶה יהוה אֶת־יְרֵאָיו, אֶת־
הַמְיַחֲלִים לְחַסְדּוֹ. שַׁבְּחִי יְרוּשָׁלַיִם אֶת יהוה, הַלְלִי אֱלֹהַיִךְ
צִיּוֹן. כִּי־חִזַּק בְּרִיחֵי שְׁעָרָיִךְ, בֵּרַךְ בָּנַיִךְ בְּקִרְבֵּךְ. הַשָּׂם
גְּבוּלֵךְ שָׁלוֹם, חֵלֶב חִטִּים יַשְׂבִּיעֵךְ. הַשֹּׁלֵחַ אִמְרָתוֹ אָרֶץ,
עַד־מְהֵרָה יָרוּץ דְּבָרוֹ. הַנֹּתֵן שֶׁלֶג כַּצָּמֶר, כְּפוֹר כָּאֵפֶר
יְפַזֵּר. מַשְׁלִיךְ קַרְחוֹ כְפִתִּים, לִפְנֵי קָרָתוֹ מִי יַעֲמֹד. יִשְׁלַח
דְּבָרוֹ וְיַמְסֵם, יַשֵּׁב רוּחוֹ יִזְּלוּ מָיִם. ‹ מַגִּיד דְּבָרָיו לְיַעֲקֹב,
חֻקָּיו וּמִשְׁפָּטָיו לְיִשְׂרָאֵל. לֹא עָשָׂה כֵן לְכָל־גּוֹי, וּמִשְׁפָּטִים
בַּל־יְדָעוּם, הַלְלוּיָהּ.

תהלים קמח

הַלְלוּיָהּ, הַלְלוּ אֶת־יהוה מִן־הַשָּׁמַיִם, הַלְלוּהוּ בַּמְּרוֹמִים.
הַלְלוּהוּ כָל־מַלְאָכָיו, הַלְלוּהוּ כָּל־צְבָאָו. הַלְלוּהוּ שֶׁמֶשׁ

returns to the earth; on that day his plans come to an end. Happy is he whose help is the God of Jacob, whose hope is in the Lord his God who made heaven and earth, the sea and all they contain; He who keeps faith for ever. He secures justice for the oppressed. He gives food to the hungry. The Lord sets captives free. The Lord gives sight to the blind. The Lord raises those bowed down. The Lord loves the righteous. The Lord protects the stranger. He gives courage to the orphan and widow. He thwarts the way of the wicked. → The Lord shall reign for ever. He is your God, O Zion, for all generations. Halleluyah!

PSALM 147

הַלְלוּיָהּ Halleluyah! How good it is to sing songs to our God; how pleasant and fitting to praise Him. The Lord rebuilds Jerusalem. He gathers the scattered exiles of Israel. He heals the brokenhearted and binds up their wounds. He counts the number of the stars, calling each by name. Great is our Lord and mighty in power; His understanding has no limit. The Lord gives courage to the humble, but casts the wicked to the ground. Sing to the Lord in thanks; make music to our God on the harp. He covers the sky with clouds. He provides the earth with rain and makes grass grow on the hills. He gives food to the cattle and to the ravens when they cry. He does not take delight in the strength of horses nor pleasure in the fleetness of man. The Lord takes pleasure in those who fear Him, who put their hope in His loving care. Praise the Lord, Jerusalem; sing to your God, Zion, for He has strengthened the bars of your gates and blessed your children in your midst. He has brought peace to your borders, and satisfied you with the finest wheat. He sends His commandment to earth; swiftly runs His word. He spreads snow like fleece, sprinkles frost like ashes, scatters hail like crumbs. Who can stand His cold? He sends His word and melts them; He makes the wind blow and the waters flow. → He has declared his words to Jacob, His statutes and laws to Israel. He has done this for no other nation; such laws they do not know. Halleluyah!

PSALM 148

הַלְלוּיָהּ Halleluyah! Praise the Lord from the heavens, praise Him in the heights. Praise Him, all His angels, praise Him, all His hosts.

וְיָרֵחַ, הַלְלְוּהוּ כָּל־כּוֹכְבֵי אוֹר. הַלְלְוּהוּ שְׁמֵי הַשָּׁמָיִם, וְהַמַּיִם אֲשֶׁר מֵעַל הַשָּׁמָיִם. יְהַלְלוּ אֶת־שֵׁם יהוה, כִּי הוּא צִוָּה וְנִבְרָאוּ. וַיַּעֲמִידֵם לָעַד לְעוֹלָם, חָק־נָתַן וְלֹא יַעֲבוֹר. הַלְלוּ אֶת־יהוה מִן־הָאָרֶץ, תַּנִּינִים וְכָל־תְּהֹמוֹת. אֵשׁ וּבָרָד שֶׁלֶג וְקִיטוֹר, רוּחַ סְעָרָה עֹשָׂה דְבָרוֹ. הֶהָרִים וְכָל־גְּבָעוֹת, עֵץ פְּרִי וְכָל־אֲרָזִים. הַחַיָּה וְכָל־בְּהֵמָה, רֶמֶשׂ וְצִפּוֹר כָּנָף. מַלְכֵי־אֶרֶץ וְכָל־לְאֻמִּים, שָׂרִים וְכָל־שֹׁפְטֵי אָרֶץ. בַּחוּרִים וְגַם־בְּתוּלוֹת, זְקֵנִים עִם־נְעָרִים. ◄ יְהַלְלוּ אֶת־שֵׁם יהוה, כִּי־נִשְׂגָּב שְׁמוֹ לְבַדּוֹ, הוֹדוֹ עַל־אֶרֶץ וְשָׁמָיִם. וַיָּרֶם קֶרֶן לְעַמּוֹ, תְּהִלָּה לְכָל־חֲסִידָיו, לִבְנֵי יִשְׂרָאֵל עַם קְרֹבוֹ, הַלְלוּיָהּ.

תהלים קמט

הַלְלוּיָהּ, שִׁירוּ לַיהוה שִׁיר חָדָשׁ, תְּהִלָּתוֹ בִּקְהַל חֲסִידִים. יִשְׂמַח יִשְׂרָאֵל בְּעֹשָׂיו, בְּנֵי־צִיּוֹן יָגִילוּ בְמַלְכָּם. יְהַלְלוּ שְׁמוֹ בְמָחוֹל, בְּתֹף וְכִנּוֹר יְזַמְּרוּ־לוֹ. כִּי־רוֹצֶה יהוה בְּעַמּוֹ, יְפָאֵר עֲנָוִים בִּישׁוּעָה. יַעְלְזוּ חֲסִידִים בְּכָבוֹד, יְרַנְּנוּ עַל־מִשְׁכְּבוֹתָם. רוֹמְמוֹת אֵל בִּגְרוֹנָם, וְחֶרֶב פִּיפִיּוֹת בְּיָדָם. לַעֲשׂוֹת נְקָמָה בַּגּוֹיִם, תּוֹכֵחוֹת בַּלְאֻמִּים. ◄ לֶאְסֹר מַלְכֵיהֶם בְּזִקִּים, וְנִכְבְּדֵיהֶם בְּכַבְלֵי בַרְזֶל. לַעֲשׂוֹת בָּהֶם מִשְׁפָּט כָּתוּב, הָדָר הוּא לְכָל־חֲסִידָיו, הַלְלוּיָהּ.

תהלים קנ

הַלְלוּיָהּ,
הַלְלוּ־אֵל בְּקָדְשׁוֹ, הַלְלְוּהוּ בִּרְקִיעַ עֻזּוֹ.
הַלְלְוּהוּ בִגְבוּרֹתָיו, הַלְלְוּהוּ כְּרֹב גֻּדְלוֹ.
הַלְלְוּהוּ בְּתֵקַע שׁוֹפָר, הַלְלְוּהוּ בְּנֵבֶל וְכִנּוֹר.
הַלְלְוּהוּ בְתֹף וּמָחוֹל, הַלְלְוּהוּ בְּמִנִּים וְעוּגָב.

Praise Him, sun and moon, praise Him, all shining stars. Praise Him, highest heavens and the waters above the heavens. Let them praise the name of the LORD, for He commanded and they were created. He established them for ever and all time, issuing a decree that will never change. Praise the LORD from the earth: sea monsters and all the deep seas, fire and hail, snow and mist, storm winds that obey His word; mountains and all hills, fruit trees and all cedars, wild animals and all cattle, creeping things and winged birds; kings of the earth and all nations, princes and all judges on earth; youths and maidens, old and young. ➾ Let them praise the name of the LORD, for His name alone is sublime; His majesty is above earth and heaven. He has raised the pride of His people, for the glory of all His devoted ones, the children of Israel, the people close to Him. Halleluyah!

PSALM 149

הַלְלוּיָהּ Halleluyah! Sing to the LORD a new song, His praise in the assembly of the devoted. Let Israel rejoice in its Maker; let the children of Zion exult in their King. Let them praise His name with dancing; sing praises to Him with timbrel and harp. For the LORD delights in His people; He adorns the humble with salvation. Let the devoted revel in glory; let them sing for joy on their beds. Let high praises of GOD be in their throats, and a two-edged sword in their hand: to impose retribution on the nations, punishment on the peoples, ➾ binding their kings with chains, their nobles with iron fetters, carrying out the judgement written against them. This is the glory of all His devoted ones. Halleluyah!

PSALM 150

הַלְלוּיָהּ Halleluyah!
Praise GOD in His holy place;
    praise Him in the heavens of His power.
Praise Him for His mighty deeds;
    praise Him for His surpassing greatness.
Praise Him with blasts of the ram's horn;
    praise Him with the harp and lyre.
Praise Him with timbrel and dance;
    praise Him with strings and flute.

← הַלְלְוּהוּ בְצִלְצְלֵי־שָׁמַע, הַלְלְוּהוּ בְּצִלְצְלֵי־תְרוּעָה.
כֹּל הַנְּשָׁמָה תְּהַלֵּל יָהּ, הַלְלוּיָהּ.
כֹּל הַנְּשָׁמָה תְּהַלֵּל יָהּ, הַלְלוּיָהּ.

בָּרוּךְ יהוה לְעוֹלָם, אָמֵן וְאָמֵן. בָּרוּךְ יהוה מִצִּיּוֹן, שֹׁכֵן יְרוּשָׁלָיִם, הַלְלוּיָהּ. בָּרוּךְ יהוה אֱלֹהִים אֱלֹהֵי יִשְׂרָאֵל, עֹשֵׂה נִפְלָאוֹת לְבַדּוֹ. ← וּבָרוּךְ שֵׁם כְּבוֹדוֹ לְעוֹלָם, וְיִמָּלֵא כְבוֹדוֹ אֶת־כָּל־הָאָרֶץ, אָמֵן וְאָמֵן.

Stand from this point until after בָּרְכוּ on page 62.

דברי הימים א׳ כט:י–יג

וַיְבָרֶךְ דָּוִיד אֶת־יהוה לְעֵינֵי כָּל־הַקָּהָל, וַיֹּאמֶר דָּוִיד, בָּרוּךְ אַתָּה יהוה, אֱלֹהֵי יִשְׂרָאֵל אָבִינוּ, מֵעוֹלָם וְעַד־עוֹלָם. לְךָ יהוה הַגְּדֻלָּה וְהַגְּבוּרָה וְהַתִּפְאֶרֶת וְהַנֵּצַח וְהַהוֹד, כִּי־כֹל בַּשָּׁמַיִם וּבָאָרֶץ, לְךָ יהוה הַמַּמְלָכָה וְהַמִּתְנַשֵּׂא לְכֹל לְרֹאשׁ. וְהָעֹשֶׁר וְהַכָּבוֹד מִלְּפָנֶיךָ, וְאַתָּה מוֹשֵׁל בַּכֹּל, וּבְיָדְךָ כֹּחַ וּגְבוּרָה, וּבְיָדְךָ לְגַדֵּל וּלְחַזֵּק לַכֹּל. וְעַתָּה אֱלֹהֵינוּ מוֹדִים אֲנַחְנוּ לָךְ, וּמְהַלְלִים לְשֵׁם תִּפְאַרְתֶּךָ.

נחמיה ט:ו–יא

אַתָּה־הוּא יהוה לְבַדֶּךָ, אַתָּה עָשִׂיתָ אֶת־הַשָּׁמַיִם, שְׁמֵי הַשָּׁמַיִם וְכָל־צְבָאָם, הָאָרֶץ וְכָל־אֲשֶׁר עָלֶיהָ, הַיַּמִּים וְכָל־אֲשֶׁר בָּהֶם, וְאַתָּה מְחַיֶּה אֶת־כֻּלָּם, וּצְבָא הַשָּׁמַיִם לְךָ מִשְׁתַּחֲוִים. ← אַתָּה הוּא יהוה הָאֱלֹהִים אֲשֶׁר בָּחַרְתָּ בְּאַבְרָם, וְהוֹצֵאתוֹ מֵאוּר כַּשְׂדִּים, וְשַׂמְתָּ שְּׁמוֹ אַבְרָהָם.
וּמָצָאתָ אֶת־לְבָבוֹ נֶאֱמָן לְפָנֶיךָ,
וְכָרוֹת עִמּוֹ הַבְּרִית לָתֵת אֶת־אֶרֶץ הַכְּנַעֲנִי הַחִתִּי הָאֱמֹרִי וְהַפְּרִזִּי וְהַיְבוּסִי וְהַגִּרְגָּשִׁי, לָתֵת לְזַרְעוֹ, וַתָּקֶם אֶת־דְּבָרֶיךָ,

→ Praise Him with clashing cymbals;
praise Him with resounding cymbals.
Let all that breathes praise the LORD. Halleluyah!
Let all that breathes praise the LORD. Halleluyah!

בָּרוּךְ Blessed be the LORD for ever. Amen and Amen. Blessed from Zion be the LORD who dwells in Jerusalem. Halleluyah! Blessed be the LORD, GOD of Israel, who alone does wonders. → Blessed be His glorious name for ever, and may all the earth be filled with His glory. Amen and Amen.

Stand from this point until after "Bless the LORD" on page 63.

I CHRONICLES 29:10–13

וַיְבָרֶךְ David blessed the LORD in front of the entire assembly. David said, "Blessed are You, LORD, GOD of our father Israel, for ever and ever. Yours, LORD, are the greatness and the power, the glory, majesty and splendour, for everything in heaven and earth is Yours. Yours, LORD, is the kingdom; You are exalted as head over all. Both riches and honour are in Your gift and You reign over all things. In Your hand are strength and might. It is in Your power to make great and give strength to all. Therefore, our GOD, we thank You and praise Your glorious name."

NEHEMIAH 9:6–11

אַתָּה־הוּא You alone are the LORD. You made the heavens, even the highest heavens, and all their hosts, the earth and all that is on it, the seas and all they contain. You give life to them all, and the hosts of heaven worship You. → You are the LORD GOD who chose Abram and brought him out of Ur of the Chaldees, changing his name to Abraham. You found his heart faithful towards You –
And You made a covenant with him to give to his descendants the land of the Canaanites, Hittites, Amorites, Perizzites, Jebusites and Girgashites. You fulfilled Your promise for You are righteous. You saw the suffering of our ancestors in Egypt. You heard their cry at the Sea of Reeds. You sent signs and wonders against Pharaoh, all his servants and all the people of his land, because You knew how arrogantly

כִּי צַדִּיק אָתָּה. וַתֵּרֶא אֶת־עֳנִי אֲבֹתֵינוּ בְּמִצְרָיִם, וְאֶת־
זַעֲקָתָם שָׁמַעְתָּ עַל־יַם־סוּף. וַתִּתֵּן אֹתֹת וּמֹפְתִים בְּפַרְעֹה
וּבְכָל־עֲבָדָיו וּבְכָל־עַם אַרְצוֹ, כִּי יָדַעְתָּ כִּי הֵזִידוּ עֲלֵיהֶם,
וַתַּעַשׂ־לְךָ שֵׁם כְּהַיּוֹם הַזֶּה. ◄ וְהַיָּם בָּקַעְתָּ לִפְנֵיהֶם, וַיַּעַבְרוּ
בְתוֹךְ־הַיָּם בַּיַּבָּשָׁה, וְאֶת־רֹדְפֵיהֶם הִשְׁלַכְתָּ בִמְצוֹלֹת, כְּמוֹ־
אֶבֶן בְּמַיִם עַזִּים.

שירת הים

שמות יד:ל–טו:יט

וַיּוֹשַׁע יְהוָה בַּיּוֹם הַהוּא אֶת־יִשְׂרָאֵל מִיַּד מִצְרָיִם וַיַּרְא
יִשְׂרָאֵל אֶת־מִצְרַיִם מֵת עַל־שְׂפַת הַיָּם: ◄ וַיַּרְא יִשְׂרָאֵל
אֶת־הַיָּד הַגְּדֹלָה אֲשֶׁר עָשָׂה יְהוָה בְּמִצְרַיִם, וַיִּירְאוּ הָעָם
אֶת־יְהוָה, וַיַּאֲמִינוּ בַּיהוָה וּבְמֹשֶׁה עַבְדּוֹ:

אָז יָשִׁיר־מֹשֶׁה וּבְנֵי יִשְׂרָאֵל אֶת־הַשִּׁירָה הַזֹּאת לַיהוָה וַיֹּאמְרוּ
לֵאמֹר אָשִׁירָה לַיהוָה כִּי־גָאֹה גָּאָה סוּס
וְרֹכְבוֹ רָמָה בַיָּם: עָזִּי וְזִמְרָת יָהּ וַיְהִי־לִי
לִישׁוּעָה זֶה אֵלִי וְאַנְוֵהוּ אֱלֹהֵי
אָבִי וַאֲרֹמְמֶנְהוּ: יְהוָה אִישׁ מִלְחָמָה יְהוָה
שְׁמוֹ: מַרְכְּבֹת פַּרְעֹה וְחֵילוֹ יָרָה בַיָּם וּמִבְחַר
שָׁלִשָׁיו טֻבְּעוּ בְיַם־סוּף: תְּהֹמֹת יְכַסְיֻמוּ יָרְדוּ בִמְצוֹלֹת כְּמוֹ־
אָבֶן: יְמִינְךָ יְהוָה נֶאְדָּרִי בַּכֹּחַ יְמִינְךָ
יְהוָה תִּרְעַץ אוֹיֵב: וּבְרֹב גְּאוֹנְךָ תַּהֲרֹס
קָמֶיךָ תְּשַׁלַּח חֲרֹנְךָ יֹאכְלֵמוֹ כַּקַּשׁ: וּבְרוּחַ
אַפֶּיךָ נֶעֶרְמוּ מַיִם נִצְּבוּ כְמוֹ־נֵד
נֹזְלִים קָפְאוּ תְהֹמֹת בְּלֶב־יָם: אָמַר
אוֹיֵב אֶרְדֹּף אַשִּׂיג אֲחַלֵּק שָׁלָל תִּמְלָאֵמוֹ

the Egyptians treated them. You created for Yourself renown that remains to this day. → You divided the sea before them, so that they passed through the sea on dry land, but You cast their pursuers into the depths, like a stone into mighty waters.

THE SONG AT THE SEA

EXODUS 14:30–15:19

וַיּוֹשַׁע That day the LORD saved Israel from the hands of the Egyptians, and Israel saw the Egyptians lying dead on the seashore. → When Israel saw the great power the LORD had displayed against the Egyptians, the people feared the LORD, and believed in the LORD and in His servant, Moses.

אָז Then Moses and the Israelites sang this song to the LORD, saying:
I will sing to the LORD, for He has triumphed gloriously;
horse and rider He has hurled into the sea.
The LORD is my strength and song; He has become my salvation.
This is my GOD, and I will beautify Him,
my father's GOD, and I will exalt Him.
The LORD is a Master of war; LORD is His name.
Pharaoh's chariots and army He cast into the sea;
the best of his officers drowned in the Sea of Reeds.
The deep waters covered them;
they went down to the depths like a stone.
Your right hand, LORD, is majestic in power.
Your right hand, LORD, shatters the enemy.
In the greatness of Your majesty, You overthrew those who rose against You.
You sent out Your fury; it consumed them like stubble.
By the blast of Your nostrils the waters piled up.
The surging waters stood straight like a wall;
the deeps congealed in the heart of the sea.
The enemy said, "I will pursue. I will overtake. I will divide the spoil.
My desire shall have its fill of them.
I will draw my sword. My hand will destroy them."

נַפְשִׁי   אָרִיק חַרְבִּי תּוֹרִישֵׁמוֹ יָדִי: נָשַׁפְתָּ
בְרוּחֲךָ כִּסָּמוֹ יָם   צָלֲלוּ כַּעוֹפֶרֶת בְּמַיִם
אַדִּירִים: מִי־כָמֹכָה בָּאֵלִם יְהֹוָה   מִי
כָּמֹכָה נֶאְדָּר בַּקֹּדֶשׁ   נוֹרָא תְהִלֹּת עֹשֵׂה
פֶלֶא: נָטִיתָ יְמִינְךָ תִּבְלָעֵמוֹ אָרֶץ: נָחִיתָ
בְחַסְדְּךָ עַם־זוּ גָּאָלְתָּ   נֵהַלְתָּ בְעָזְּךָ אֶל־נְוֵה
קָדְשֶׁךָ:   שָׁמְעוּ עַמִּים יִרְגָּזוּן   חִיל
אָחַז יֹשְׁבֵי פְּלָשֶׁת: אָז נִבְהֲלוּ אַלּוּפֵי
אֱדוֹם   אֵילֵי מוֹאָב יֹאחֲזֵמוֹ רָעַד   נָמֹגוּ
כֹּל יֹשְׁבֵי כְנָעַן: תִּפֹּל עֲלֵיהֶם אֵימָתָה
וָפַחַד   בִּגְדֹל זְרוֹעֲךָ יִדְּמוּ כָּאָבֶן   עַד־
יַעֲבֹר עַמְּךָ יְהֹוָה   עַד־יַעֲבֹר עַם־זוּ
קָנִיתָ:   תְּבִאֵמוֹ וְתִטָּעֵמוֹ בְּהַר נַחֲלָתְךָ   מָכוֹן
לְשִׁבְתְּךָ פָּעַלְתָּ יְהֹוָה   מִקְּדָשׁ אֲדֹנָי כּוֹנְנוּ
יָדֶיךָ:   יְהֹוָה | יִמְלֹךְ לְעֹלָם וָעֶד: יהוה | יִמְלֹךְ לְעָלַם וָעֶד.

כִּי בָא סוּס פַּרְעֹה בְּרִכְבּוֹ וּבְפָרָשָׁיו בַּיָּם, וַיָּשֶׁב יהוה עֲלֵהֶם אֶת־מֵי הַיָּם, וּבְנֵי יִשְׂרָאֵל הָלְכוּ בַיַּבָּשָׁה בְּתוֹךְ הַיָּם. ← כִּי לַיהוה הַמְּלוּכָה, וּמֹשֵׁל בַּגּוֹיִם. וְעָלוּ מוֹשִׁעִים בְּהַר צִיּוֹן, לִשְׁפֹּט אֶת־הַר עֵשָׂו, וְהָיְתָה לַיהוה הַמְּלוּכָה. וְהָיָה יהוה לְמֶלֶךְ עַל־כָּל־הָאָרֶץ, בַּיּוֹם הַהוּא יִהְיֶה יהוה אֶחָד וּשְׁמוֹ אֶחָד. וּבְתוֹרָתְךָ כָּתוּב לֵאמֹר, שְׁמַע יִשְׂרָאֵל יהוה אֱלֹהֵינוּ יהוה אֶחָד.

ברכה שלאחר פסוקי דזמרה

יִשְׁתַּבַּח שִׁמְךָ לָעַד מַלְכֵּנוּ, הָאֵל הַמֶּלֶךְ הַגָּדוֹל וְהַקָּדוֹשׁ, בַּשָּׁמַיִם וּבָאָרֶץ. כִּי לְךָ נָאֶה יהוה אֱלֹהֵינוּ וֵאלֹהֵי אֲבוֹתֵינוּ,

You blew with Your wind; the sea covered them.
They sank like lead in the mighty waters.
Who is like You, LORD, among the mighty?
Who is like You – majestic in holiness, awesome in glory, working wonders?
You stretched out Your right hand,
the earth swallowed them.
In Your lovingkindness, You led the people You redeemed.
In Your strength, You guided them to Your holy abode.
Nations heard and trembled;
terror gripped Philistia's inhabitants.
The chiefs of Edom were dismayed,
Moab's leaders were seized with trembling,
the people of Canaan melted away.
Fear and dread fell upon them.
By the power of Your arm, they were still as stone –
until Your people crossed, O LORD,
until the people You acquired crossed over.
You will bring them and plant them on the mountain of Your heritage –
the place, LORD, You made for Your dwelling,
the sanctuary, LORD, Your hands established.
The LORD will reign for ever and all time.
The LORD will reign for ever and all time.

When Pharaoh's horses, chariots and riders went into the sea, the LORD brought the waters of the sea back over them, but the Israelites walked on dry land through the sea. ➔ For kingship is the LORD's and He rules over the nations. Saviours shall go up to Mount Zion to judge Mount Esau, and the LORD's shall be the kingdom. Then shall the LORD be King over all the earth. On that day shall the LORD be One and His name One, as it is written in Your Torah, saying: Listen, Israel: the LORD is our GOD, the LORD is ONE.

BLESSING AFTER VERSES OF PRAISE

יִשְׁתַּבַּח May Your name be praised for ever, our King, the great and

שִׁיר וּשְׁבָחָה, הַלֵּל וְזִמְרָה, עֹז וּמֶמְשָׁלָה, נֶצַח גְּדֻלָּה וּגְבוּרָה, תְּהִלָּה וְתִפְאֶרֶת, קְדֻשָּׁה וּמַלְכוּת, ← בְּרָכוֹת וְהוֹדָאוֹת מֵעַתָּה וְעַד־עוֹלָם. בָּרוּךְ אַתָּה יהוה, אֵל מֶלֶךְ גָּדוֹל בַּתִּשְׁבָּחוֹת, אֵל הַהוֹדָאוֹת, אֲדוֹן הַנִּפְלָאוֹת, הַבּוֹחֵר בְּשִׁירֵי זִמְרָה, מֶלֶךְ, אֵל, חֵי הָעוֹלָמִים.

Between רֹאשׁ הַשָּׁנָה and יוֹם כִּפּוּר, and on הוֹשַׁעְנָא רַבָּה, some congregations say this psalm responsively, verse by verse. The Ark is opened for this psalm.

תהלים קל

שִׁיר הַמַּעֲלוֹת, מִמַּעֲמַקִּים קְרָאתִיךָ יהוה. אֲדֹנָי שִׁמְעָה בְקוֹלִי, תִּהְיֶינָה אָזְנֶיךָ קַשֻּׁבוֹת, לְקוֹל תַּחֲנוּנָי. אִם עֲוֹנוֹת תִּשְׁמָר־יָהּ, אֲדֹנָי מִי יַעֲמֹד. כִּי עִמְּךָ הַסְּלִיחָה, לְמַעַן תִּוָּרֵא. קִוִּיתִי יהוה קִוְּתָה נַפְשִׁי, וְלִדְבָרוֹ הוֹחָלְתִּי. נַפְשִׁי לַאדֹנָי, מִשֹּׁמְרִים לַבֹּקֶר, שֹׁמְרִים לַבֹּקֶר. יַחֵל יִשְׂרָאֵל אֶל יהוה, כִּי־עִם־יהוה הַחֶסֶד, וְהַרְבֵּה עִמּוֹ פְדוּת. וְהוּא יִפְדֶּה אֶת יִשְׂרָאֵל, מִכֹּל עֲוֹנוֹתָיו.

The Leader says חֲצִי קַדִּישׁ.

Leader:

יִתְגַּדַּל וְיִתְקַדַּשׁ שְׁמֵהּ רַבָּא. (Cong. אָמֵן) בְּעָלְמָא דִּי־בְרָא כִרְעוּתֵהּ. וְיַמְלִיךְ מַלְכוּתֵהּ, בְּחַיֵּיכוֹן וּבְיוֹמֵיכוֹן וּבְחַיֵּי דִי־כָל־בֵּית יִשְׂרָאֵל, בַּעֲגָלָא וּבִזְמַן קָרִיב. וְאִמְרוּ אָמֵן. (Cong. אָמֵן)

All:

יְהֵא שְׁמֵהּ רַבָּא מְבָרַךְ לְעָלַם וּלְעָלְמֵי עָלְמַיָּא.

Leader:

יִתְבָּרַךְ וְיִשְׁתַּבַּח וְיִתְפָּאַר וְיִתְרוֹמַם וְיִתְנַשֵּׂא וְיִתְהַדַּר וְיִתְעַלֶּה וְיִתְהַלָּל שְׁמֵהּ דְּקֻדְשָׁא בְּרִיךְ הוּא (Cong. בְּרִיךְ הוּא) לְעֵלָּא (Between רֹאשׁ הַשָּׁנָה and יוֹם כִּפּוּר add לְעֵלָּא) מִן־כָּל־בִּרְכָתָא וְשִׁירָתָא תֻּשְׁבְּחָתָא וְנֶחֱמָתָא, דַּאֲמִירָן בְּעָלְמָא. וְאִמְרוּ אָמֵן. (Cong. אָמֵן)

holy GOD, King in heaven and on earth. For to You, LORD our GOD and GOD of our ancestors, it is right to offer song and praise, hymn and psalm, strength and dominion, eternity, greatness and power, song of praise and glory, holiness and kingship, → blessings and thanks, from now and for ever. Blessed are You, LORD, GOD and King, exalted in praises, GOD of thanksgivings, Master of wonders, who delights in hymns of song, King, GOD, Giver of life to the world.

Between Rosh Hashanah and Yom Kippur, and on Hoshana Rabba, some congregations say this psalm responsively, verse by verse. The Ark is opened for this psalm.

PSALM 130

שִׁיר A song of ascents. From the depths I have called to You, O LORD. LORD, hear my voice; let Your ears be attentive to my plea. If You, LORD, should keep account of sins, who could stand? But with You there is forgiveness, that You may be held in awe. I wait for the LORD, my soul waits, and in His word I put my hope. My soul waits for the LORD more than watchmen wait for the morning, more than watchmen wait for the morning. Israel, put your hope in the LORD, for with the LORD there is lovingkindness, and great is His power to redeem. It is He who will redeem Israel from all their sins.

The Leader says half-*Kaddish*.

Leader:

יִתְגַּדַּל Magnified and sanctified may His great name be, in the world He created by His will. May He establish His kingdom in your lifetime and in your days, and in the lifetime of all the House of Israel, swiftly and soon – and say: Amen.

All:

May His great name be blessed for ever and all time.

Leader:

Blessed and praised, glorified and exalted, raised and honoured, uplifted and lauded be the name of the Holy One, blessed be He, (between Rosh Hashanah and Yom Kippur add 'well') beyond any blessing, song, praise and consolation uttered in the world – and say: Amen.

The Leader says the following, both the Leader and Congregation bowing at בָּרְכוּ, standing straight at God's name:

בָּרְכוּ אֶת יהוה הַמְבֹרָךְ.

The Congregation, followed by the Leader, responds, bowing at בָּרוּךְ, standing straight at God's name:

בָּרוּךְ יהוה הַמְבֹרָךְ לְעוֹלָם וָעֶד.

ברכות קריאת שמע

בָּרוּךְ אַתָּה יהוה אֱלֹהֵינוּ מֶלֶךְ הָעוֹלָם, יוֹצֵר אוֹר וּבוֹרֵא חֹשֶׁךְ, עֹשֶׂה שָׁלוֹם וּבוֹרֵא אֶת הַכֹּל.

הַמֵּאִיר לָאָרֶץ וְלַדָּרִים עָלֶיהָ בְּרַחֲמִים, וּבְטוּבוֹ מְחַדֵּשׁ בְּכָל־יוֹם תָּמִיד מַעֲשֵׂה בְרֵאשִׁית. מָה רַבּוּ מַעֲשֶׂיךָ יהוה, כֻּלָּם בְּחָכְמָה עָשִׂיתָ, מָלְאָה הָאָרֶץ קִנְיָנֶךָ. הַמֶּלֶךְ הַמְרוֹמָם לְבַדּוֹ מֵאָז, הַמְשֻׁבָּח וְהַמְפֹאָר וְהַמִּתְנַשֵּׂא מִימוֹת עוֹלָם. אֱלֹהֵי עוֹלָם, בְּרַחֲמֶיךָ הָרַבִּים רַחֵם עָלֵינוּ, אֲדוֹן עֻזֵּנוּ, צוּר מִשְׂגַּבֵּנוּ, מָגֵן יִשְׁעֵנוּ, מִשְׂגָּב בַּעֲדֵנוּ.

אֵל בָּרוּךְ גְּדוֹל דֵּעָה, הֵכִין וּפָעַל זָהֳרֵי חַמָּה, טוֹב יָצַר כָּבוֹד לִשְׁמוֹ, מְאוֹרוֹת נָתַן סְבִיבוֹת עֻזּוֹ, פִּנּוֹת צְבָאָיו קְדוֹשִׁים רוֹמְמֵי שַׁדַּי, תָּמִיד מְסַפְּרִים כְּבוֹד־אֵל וּקְדֻשָּׁתוֹ. תִּתְבָּרַךְ יהוה אֱלֹהֵינוּ עַל־שֶׁבַח מַעֲשֵׂה יָדֶיךָ, וְעַל־מְאוֹרֵי־אוֹר שֶׁעָשִׂיתָ, יְפָאֲרוּךָ, סֶּלָה.

THE SHEMA AND ITS BLESSINGS

The Verses of Praise are a prelude to prayer. We now move to congregational prayer, at whose heart are the *Shema* and the *Amidah* (the "standing" prayer). Saying the *Shema* twice daily (morning and evening, "when you lie down and when you rise up") is a biblical institution, and was part of the order of service in Temple times. The transition to congregational prayer is marked by a call – "Bless God" – to those present to join together in prayer as a community.

The Leader says the following, both the Leader and Congregation bowing at "Bless", standing straight at "The LORD":

Bless the LORD, the blessed One.

The Congregation, followed by the Leader, responds, bowing at "Bless", standing straight at "The LORD":

Bless the LORD, the blessed One, for ever and all time.

BLESSINGS OF THE SHEMA

בָּרוּךְ Blessed are You, LORD our GOD, King of the Universe, who forms light and creates darkness, makes peace and creates all.

הַמֵּאִיר In compassion He gives light to the earth and its inhabitants, and in His goodness continually renews the work of creation, day after day. How many are Your works, O LORD. You made them all in wisdom. The earth is full of Your creations. He is the King exalted alone since the beginning of time – praised, glorified and elevated since the world began. Eternal GOD, in Your great compassion, have compassion on us, LORD of our strength, Rock of our refuge, Shield of our salvation, You are our stronghold.

The blessed GOD, great in knowledge, prepared and made the rays of the sun. He who is good formed glory for His name, surrounding His power with radiant stars. The leaders of His hosts, the holy ones, exalt the Almighty, constantly proclaiming GOD's glory and holiness. Be blessed, LORD our GOD, for the magnificence of Your handiwork and for the radiant lights You have made. May they glorify You, Selah!

אֵל בָּרוּךְ *The blessed GOD*: An alphabetical acrostic of 22 words. Although the first blessing is about creation as a whole, the morning prayer emphasises the element of which we are most conscious at the start of the day: the creation of light. Of this, there are two forms: the physical light of the sun, moon and stars, made on the fourth day of creation, and the spiritual light created on the first day ("Let there be light"). The prayer modulates from the first to the second: from the universe as we see it to the mystical vision of GOD enthroned in glory surrounded by angels.

תִּתְבָּרַךְ צוּרֵנוּ מַלְכֵּנוּ וְגוֹאֲלֵנוּ, בּוֹרֵא קְדוֹשִׁים. יִשְׁתַּבַּח שִׁמְךָ לָעַד מַלְכֵּנוּ, יוֹצֵר מְשָׁרְתִים, וַאֲשֶׁר מְשָׁרְתָיו כֻּלָּם עוֹמְדִים בְּרוּם עוֹלָם, וּמַשְׁמִיעִים בְּיִרְאָה יַחַד בְּקוֹל דִּבְרֵי אֱלֹהִים־חַיִּים וּמֶלֶךְ עוֹלָם. כֻּלָּם אֲהוּבִים, כֻּלָּם בְּרוּרִים, כֻּלָּם גִּבּוֹרִים, וְכֻלָּם עֹשִׂים בְּאֵימָה וּבְיִרְאָה רְצוֹן קוֹנָם.
← וְכֻלָּם פּוֹתְחִים אֶת־פִּיהֶם בִּקְדֻשָּׁה וּבְטָהֳרָה, בְּשִׁירָה וּבְזִמְרָה, וּמְבָרְכִים וּמְשַׁבְּחִים וּמְפָאֲרִים וּמַעֲרִיצִים וּמַקְדִּישִׁים וּמַמְלִיכִים

אֶת־שֵׁם הָאֵל הַמֶּלֶךְ הַגָּדוֹל הַגִּבּוֹר וְהַנּוֹרָא קָדוֹשׁ הוּא.
← וְכֻלָּם מְקַבְּלִים עֲלֵיהֶם עֹל מַלְכוּת שָׁמַיִם זֶה מִזֶּה, וְנוֹתְנִים רְשׁוּת זֶה לָזֶה, לְהַקְדִּישׁ לְיוֹצְרָם, בְּנַחַת רוּחַ בְּשָׂפָה בְרוּרָה וּבִנְעִימָה קְדוֹשָׁה, כֻּלָּם כְּאֶחָד עוֹנִים וְאוֹמְרִים בְּיִרְאָה,

All, aloud:

קָדוֹשׁ קָדוֹשׁ קָדוֹשׁ יהוה צְבָאוֹת, מְלֹא כָל־הָאָרֶץ כְּבוֹדוֹ.

← וְהָאוֹפַנִּים וְחַיּוֹת הַקֹּדֶשׁ בְּרַעַשׁ גָּדוֹל מִתְנַשְּׂאִים לְעֻמַּת שְׂרָפִים. לְעֻמָּתָם מְשַׁבְּחִים וְאוֹמְרִים,

All, aloud:

בָּרוּךְ כְּבוֹד־יהוה מִמְּקוֹמוֹ.

לָאֵל בָּרוּךְ נְעִימוֹת יִתֵּנוּ. לַמֶּלֶךְ אֵל חַי וְקַיָּם, זְמִירוֹת יֹאמֵרוּ, וְתִשְׁבָּחוֹת יַשְׁמִיעוּ. כִּי הוּא לְבַדּוֹ פּוֹעֵל גְּבוּרוֹת, עֹשֶׂה חֲדָשׁוֹת, בַּעַל מִלְחָמוֹת, זוֹרֵעַ צְדָקוֹת, מַצְמִיחַ יְשׁוּעוֹת, בּוֹרֵא רְפוּאוֹת, נוֹרָא תְהִלּוֹת, אֲדוֹן הַנִּפְלָאוֹת.

The three blessings and the three paragraphs of the *Shema* form six passages, leading up to the seventh, the *Amidah*. In Judaism, seven is the number of the holy. For the main commentary on this section of the prayers, see page 370.

תִּתְבָּרַךְ May You be blessed, our Rock, King and Redeemer, Creator of holy beings. May Your name be praised for ever, our King, Creator of the ministering angels, all of whom stand in the universe's heights, proclaiming together, in awe, aloud, the words of the living God, the eternal King. They are all beloved, all pure, all mighty, and all perform in awe and reverence the will of their Maker. ➝ All open their mouths in holiness and purity, with song and psalm, and bless, praise, glorify, revere, sanctify and declare the sovereignty of –

The name of the great, mighty and awesome God and King, holy is He. ➝ All accept on themselves, one from another, the yoke of the kingdom of heaven, granting permission to one another to sanctify the One who formed them, in serene spirit, pure speech and sacred melody, and all, as one, respond, saying in awe:

All, aloud:

Holy, holy, holy is the Lord of hosts:
the whole world is filled with His glory.

➝ Then the Ophanim and the Holy Chayot, with a roar of noise, raise themselves toward the Seraphim and, facing them, give praise, saying:

All, aloud:

Blessed be the Lord's glory from His place.

לָאֵל To the blessed God they offer melodies. To the King, living and eternal God, they say psalms and proclaim praises. For it is He alone who does mighty deeds and creates new things. He is Master of battles. He sows righteousness and makes salvation grow. He creates cures. He is revered in praises, the Lord of wonders who, in His goodness, continually renews the work of creation, day after day, as it

---

The theme of this section of the service is *revelation*: God as He has disclosed Himself in the words of the Torah. So at its heart are three passages from the Torah, known collectively by their first word, *Shema*. Around it are three blessings, two before and one after the *Shema*. Like the morning service as a whole, their themes are creation, revelation and redemption. The first (continuing the theme of the Verses of Praise) is about creation, renewed daily. The second ("You have loved us") is about revelation: the Torah, given in love. The third ("True and firm") is about redemption.

הַמְחַדֵּשׁ בְּטוּבוֹ בְּכָל־יוֹם תָּמִיד מַעֲשֵׂה בְרֵאשִׁית. כָּאָמוּר, לְעֹשֵׂה אוֹרִים גְּדֹלִים, כִּי לְעוֹלָם חַסְדּוֹ. ◄ אוֹר חָדָשׁ עַל־צִיּוֹן תָּאִיר, וְנִזְכֶּה כֻלָּנוּ מְהֵרָה לְאוֹרוֹ. בָּרוּךְ אַתָּה יהוה, יוֹצֵר הַמְּאוֹרוֹת.

אַהֲבָה רַבָּה אֲהַבְתָּנוּ יהוה אֱלֹהֵינוּ, חֶמְלָה גְדוֹלָה וִיתֵרָה חָמַלְתָּ עָלֵינוּ. אָבִינוּ מַלְכֵּנוּ, בַּעֲבוּר אֲבוֹתֵינוּ שֶׁבָּטְחוּ בְךָ, וַתְּלַמְּדֵם חֻקֵּי חַיִּים, כֵּן תְּחָנֵּנוּ וּתְלַמְּדֵנוּ. אָבִינוּ הָאָב הָרַחֲמָן הַמְרַחֵם, רַחֵם עָלֵינוּ, וְתֵן בְּלִבֵּנוּ לְהָבִין וּלְהַשְׂכִּיל, לִשְׁמֹעַ לִלְמֹד וּלְלַמֵּד, לִשְׁמֹר וְלַעֲשׂוֹת וּלְקַיֵּם אֶת־כָּל־דִּבְרֵי תַלְמוּד תּוֹרָתֶךָ בְּאַהֲבָה. וְהָאֵר עֵינֵינוּ בְּתוֹרָתֶךָ, וְדַבֵּק לִבֵּנוּ בְּמִצְוֹתֶיךָ, וְיַחֵד לְבָבֵנוּ לְאַהֲבָה וּלְיִרְאָה אֶת שְׁמֶךָ, וְלֹא נֵבוֹשׁ לְעוֹלָם וָעֶד. כִּי בְשֵׁם קָדְשְׁךָ הַגָּדוֹל וְהַנּוֹרָא בָּטָחְנוּ, נָגִילָה וְנִשְׂמְחָה בִּישׁוּעָתֶךָ.

At this point, gather the four צִיצִיּוֹת, holding them in the left hand.

וַהֲבִיאֵנוּ לְשָׁלוֹם מֵאַרְבַּע כַּנְפוֹת הָאָרֶץ, וְתוֹלִיכֵנוּ קוֹמְמִיּוּת לְאַרְצֵנוּ. כִּי אֵל פּוֹעֵל יְשׁוּעוֹת אָתָּה, וּבָנוּ בָחַרְתָּ מִכָּל־עַם וְלָשׁוֹן. ◄ וְקֵרַבְתָּנוּ לְשִׁמְךָ הַגָּדוֹל סֶלָה בֶּאֱמֶת, לְהוֹדוֹת לְךָ וּלְיַחֶדְךָ בְּאַהֲבָה. בָּרוּךְ אַתָּה יהוה, הַבּוֹחֵר בְּעַמּוֹ יִשְׂרָאֵל בְּאַהֲבָה.

The Shema. The *Shema* is the oldest and greatest of our prayers, part of the liturgy since Temple times, recited evening and morning, "when you lie down and when you rise". Its opening line is among the first words taught to a Jewish child, and among the last words spoken by those who went to their deaths because they were Jews. It is the supreme declaration of faith.

The *Shema* contains no human requests, no praise, no plea. It is a set of biblical readings. It is less a prayer than a prelude to prayer. In prayer, we speak to God. In the *Shema*, God, through the Torah, speaks to us. The word *Shema* itself means "listen", and the recital of the *Shema* is a supreme act of faith-as-listening: to the voice that brought the universe into being, created us in love and guides us through our lives.

is said, "[Praise] Him who made the great lights, for His love endures for ever". → May You make a new light shine over Zion, and may we all soon be worthy of its light. Blessed are You, LORD, who forms the radiant lights.

אַהֲבָה You have loved us with great love, LORD our GOD, and with surpassing compassion have You had compassion on us. Our Father, our King, for the sake of our ancestors who trusted in You, and to whom You taught the laws of life, be gracious also to us and teach us. Our Father, compassionate Father, ever compassionate, have compassion on us. Instil in our hearts the desire to understand and discern, to listen, learn and teach, to observe, perform and fulfil all the teachings of Your Torah in love. Enlighten our eyes in Your Torah and let our hearts cling to Your commandments. Unite our hearts to love and revere Your name, so that we may never be ashamed. And because we have trusted in Your holy, great and revered name, may we be glad and rejoice in Your salvation.

At this point, gather the four *tzitziot* of the *tallit*, holding them in the left hand.

Bring us back in peace from the four quarters of the earth and lead us upright to our land, for You are a GOD who performs acts of salvation. You chose us from all peoples and tongues, → bringing us close to Your great name for ever in truth, that we may thank You and proclaim Your Oneness in love. Blessed are You, LORD, who chooses His people Israel in love.

The first paragraph represents *kabbalat ol malchut shamayim*, "acceptance of the yoke of the kingship of heaven". We pledge allegiance to the One GOD, sovereign of the universe, to whose authority all earthly powers are answerable. We do so not in fear but in love and with the totality of our being: all our heart, our soul, our might. That love suffuses all we do, from our relationship with our children to the homes we make.

The second paragraph represents *kabbalat ol mitzvot*, "acceptance of the commandments". Whereas the first paragraph speaks to us as individuals, the second speaks to us as a people, defined by our covenant with GOD and its 613 commandments. "Our nation is only a nation in virtue of its Torah", said Rabbi Saadia Gaon, and our collective fate depends on our collective faith. The third paragraph speaks of *tzitzit*, a perennial reminder of GOD's commandments. It then leads into the theme of the exodus from Egypt, which we are commanded to remember "all the days of our lives".

שמע

When prayers are not said with a מִנְיָן, say:

אֵל מֶלֶךְ נֶאֱמָן.

Cover the eyes with the right hand while saying the following verse:

דברים ו:ד–ט

שְׁמַ֖ע יִשְׂרָאֵ֑ל יְהוָ֥ה אֱלֹהֵ֖ינוּ יְהוָ֥ה ׀ אֶחָֽד׃

Quietly:

בָּרוּךְ שֵׁם כְּבוֹד מַלְכוּתוֹ לְעוֹלָם וָעֶד.

Touch the hand-תְּפִלִּין at ° and the head-תְּפִלִּין at °°.

וְאָהַבְתָּ֗ אֵ֚ת יְהוָ֣ה אֱלֹהֶ֔יךָ בְּכׇל־לְבָבְךָ֥ וּבְכׇל־נַפְשְׁךָ֖ וּבְכׇל־
מְאֹדֶֽךָ׃ וְהָי֞וּ הַדְּבָרִ֣ים הָאֵ֗לֶּה אֲשֶׁ֨ר אָנֹכִ֧י מְצַוְּךָ֛ הַיּ֖וֹם עַל־
לְבָבֶֽךָ׃ וְשִׁנַּנְתָּ֤ם לְבָנֶ֙יךָ֙ וְדִבַּרְתָּ֖ בָּ֑ם בְּשִׁבְתְּךָ֤ בְּבֵיתֶ֙ךָ֙ וּבְלֶכְתְּךָ֣
בַדֶּ֔רֶךְ וּֽבְשׇׁכְבְּךָ֖ וּבְקוּמֶֽךָ׃ °וּקְשַׁרְתָּ֥ם לְא֖וֹת עַל־יָדֶ֑ךָ °°וְהָי֥וּ
לְטֹטָפֹ֖ת בֵּ֥ין עֵינֶֽיךָ׃ וּכְתַבְתָּ֛ם עַל־מְזֻז֥וֹת בֵּיתֶ֖ךָ וּבִשְׁעָרֶֽיךָ׃

Touch the hand-תְּפִלִּין at ° and the head-תְּפִלִּין at °°.

דברים יא:יג–כא

וְהָיָ֗ה אִם־שָׁמֹ֤עַ תִּשְׁמְעוּ֙ אֶל־מִצְוֺתַ֔י אֲשֶׁ֧ר אָנֹכִ֛י מְצַוֶּ֥ה
אֶתְכֶ֖ם הַיּ֑וֹם לְאַהֲבָ֞ה אֶת־יְהוָ֤ה אֱלֹהֵיכֶם֙ וּלְעׇבְד֔וֹ בְּכׇל־
לְבַבְכֶ֖ם וּבְכׇל־נַפְשְׁכֶֽם׃ וְנָתַתִּ֧י מְטַֽר־אַרְצְכֶ֛ם בְּעִתּ֖וֹ יוֹרֶ֣ה
וּמַלְק֑וֹשׁ וְאָסַפְתָּ֣ דְגָנֶ֔ךָ וְתִירֹשְׁךָ֖ וְיִצְהָרֶֽךָ׃ וְנָתַתִּ֛י עֵ֥שֶׂב
בְּשָׂדְךָ֖ לִבְהֶמְתֶּ֑ךָ וְאָכַלְתָּ֖ וְשָׂבָֽעְתָּ׃ הִשָּׁמְר֣וּ לָכֶ֔ם פֶּ֥ן־יִפְתֶּ֖ה
לְבַבְכֶ֑ם וְסַרְתֶּ֗ם וַעֲבַדְתֶּם֙ אֱלֹהִ֣ים אֲחֵרִ֔ים וְהִשְׁתַּחֲוִיתֶ֖ם
לָהֶֽם׃ וְחָרָ֨ה אַף־יְהוָ֜ה בָּכֶ֗ם וְעָצַ֤ר אֶת־הַשָּׁמַ֙יִם֙ וְלֹא־יִהְיֶ֣ה
מָטָ֔ר וְהָ֣אֲדָמָ֔ה לֹ֥א תִתֵּ֖ן אֶת־יְבוּלָ֑הּ וַאֲבַדְתֶּ֣ם מְהֵרָ֗ה מֵעַל֙
הָאָ֣רֶץ הַטֹּבָ֔ה אֲשֶׁ֥ר יְהוָ֖ה נֹתֵ֥ן לָכֶֽם׃ וְשַׂמְתֶּם֙ אֶת־דְּבָרַ֣י
אֵ֔לֶּה עַל־לְבַבְכֶ֖ם וְעַל־נַפְשְׁכֶ֑ם °וּקְשַׁרְתֶּ֨ם אֹתָ֤ם לְאוֹת֙ עַל־
יֶדְכֶ֔ם °°וְהָי֥וּ לְטוֹטָפֹ֖ת בֵּ֥ין עֵינֵיכֶֽם׃ וְלִמַּדְתֶּ֥ם אֹתָ֛ם אֶת־

THE SHEMA

When prayers are not said with a *minyan*, say:

God, faithful King!

Cover the eyes with the right hand while saying the following verse:

DEUTERONOMY 6:4–9

Listen, Israel: the Lord is our God, the Lord is One.

Quietly:

Blessed be the name of His glorious kingdom for ever and ever.

Touch the hand-*tefillin* at ° and the head-*tefillin* at °°.

וְאָהַבְתָּ Love the Lord your God with all your heart, with all your soul, and with all your might. These words which I command you today shall be on your heart. Teach them repeatedly to your children, speaking of them when you sit at home and when you travel on the way, when you lie down and when you rise. °Bind them as a sign on your hand, and °°they shall be an emblem between your eyes. Write them on the doorposts of your house and gates.

Touch the hand-*tefillin* at ° and the head-*tefillin* at °°.

DEUTERONOMY 11:13–21

וְהָיָה If you indeed heed My commandments with which I charge you today, to love the Lord your God and worship Him with all your heart and with all your soul, I will give rain in your land in its season, the early and late rain; and you shall gather in your grain, wine and oil. I will give grass in your field for your cattle, and you shall eat and be satisfied. Be careful lest your heart be tempted and you go astray and worship other gods, bowing down to them. Then the Lord's anger will flare against you and He will close the heavens so that there will be no rain. The land will not yield its crops, and you will perish swiftly from the good land that the Lord is giving you. Therefore set these, My words, on your heart and soul. °Bind them as a sign on your hand, °°and they shall be an emblem between your eyes. Teach them to your children, speaking of them when you sit at home and when you travel on the way, when you lie down and when you rise. Write them

בְּנֵיכֶם לְדַבֵּר בָּם בְּשִׁבְתְּךָ בְּבֵיתֶךָ וּבְלֶכְתְּךָ בַדֶּרֶךְ וּבְשָׁכְבְּךָ וּבְקוּמֶךָ: וּכְתַבְתָּם עַל־מְזוּזוֹת בֵּיתֶךָ וּבִשְׁעָרֶיךָ: לְמַעַן יִרְבּוּ יְמֵיכֶם וִימֵי בְנֵיכֶם עַל הָאֲדָמָה אֲשֶׁר נִשְׁבַּע יהוה לַאֲבֹתֵיכֶם לָתֵת לָהֶם כִּימֵי הַשָּׁמַיִם עַל־הָאָרֶץ:

Transfer the צִיצִיּוֹת to the right hand, kissing them at °.

במדבר טו:לז–מא

וַיֹּאמֶר יהוה אֶל־מֹשֶׁה לֵּאמֹר: דַּבֵּר אֶל־בְּנֵי יִשְׂרָאֵל וְאָמַרְתָּ אֲלֵהֶם וְעָשׂוּ לָהֶם °צִיצִת עַל־כַּנְפֵי בִגְדֵיהֶם לְדֹרֹתָם וְנָתְנוּ עַל־°צִיצִת הַכָּנָף פְּתִיל תְּכֵלֶת: וְהָיָה לָכֶם °לְצִיצִת וּרְאִיתֶם אֹתוֹ וּזְכַרְתֶּם אֶת־כָּל־מִצְוֹת יהוה וַעֲשִׂיתֶם אֹתָם וְלֹא תָתוּרוּ אַחֲרֵי לְבַבְכֶם וְאַחֲרֵי עֵינֵיכֶם אֲשֶׁר־אַתֶּם זֹנִים אַחֲרֵיהֶם: לְמַעַן תִּזְכְּרוּ וַעֲשִׂיתֶם אֶת־כָּל־מִצְוֹתָי וִהְיִיתֶם קְדֹשִׁים לֵאלֹהֵיכֶם: אֲנִי יהוה אֱלֹהֵיכֶם אֲשֶׁר הוֹצֵאתִי אֶתְכֶם מֵאֶרֶץ מִצְרַיִם לִהְיוֹת לָכֶם לֵאלֹהִים אֲנִי יהוה אֱלֹהֵיכֶם: °**אֱמֶת** –

The Leader repeats:

← יהוה אֱלֹהֵיכֶם, אֱמֶת –

At °, kiss the צִיצִיּוֹת and release them.

וְיַצִּיב וְנָכוֹן וְקַיָּם וְיָשָׁר וְנֶאֱמָן וְאָהוּב וְחָבִיב וְנֶחְמָד וְנָעִים וְנוֹרָא וְאַדִּיר וּמְתֻקָּן וּמְקֻבָּל וְטוֹב וְיָפֶה הַדָּבָר הַזֶּה עָלֵינוּ לְעוֹלָם וָעֶד. אֱמֶת אֱלֹהֵי עוֹלָם מַלְכֵּנוּ צוּר יַעֲקֹב, מָגֵן יִשְׁעֵנוּ, לְדֹר וָדֹר הוּא קַיָּם, וּשְׁמוֹ קַיָּם, וְכִסְאוֹ נָכוֹן, וּמַלְכוּתוֹ וֶאֱמוּנָתוֹ לָעַד קַיֶּמֶת. וּדְבָרָיו חָיִים וְקַיָּמִים, נֶאֱמָנִים וְנֶחֱמָדִים °לָעַד וּלְעוֹלְמֵי עוֹלָמִים. ← עַל־אֲבוֹתֵינוּ וְעָלֵינוּ, עַל־בָּנֵינוּ וְעַל־דּוֹרוֹתֵינוּ, וְעַל־כָּל־דּוֹרוֹת זֶרַע יִשְׂרָאֵל עֲבָדֶיךָ.

on the doorposts of your house and gates, so that you and your children may live long in the land that the LORD swore to your ancestors to give them, for as long as the heavens are above the earth.

Transfer the *tzitziot* to the right hand, kissing them at °.

NUMBERS 15:37–41

וַיֹּאמֶר The LORD spoke to Moses, saying: Speak to the Israelites and tell them to make °tassels on the corners of their garments for all generations. They shall attach to the °tassel at each corner a thread of blue. This shall be your °tassel, and you shall see it and remember all of the LORD's commandments and keep them, not straying after your heart and after your eyes, following your own sinful desires. Thus you will be reminded to keep all My commandments, and be holy to your GOD. I am the LORD your GOD, who brought you out of the land of Egypt to be your GOD. I am the LORD your GOD. °True –

The Leader repeats:

→ The LORD your GOD is true –

At °, kiss the *tzitziot* and release them.

וְיַצִּיב And firm, established and enduring, right, faithful, beloved, cherished, delightful, pleasant, awesome, mighty, perfect, accepted, good and beautiful is this faith for us for ever. True is the eternal GOD, our King, Rock of Jacob, Shield of our salvation. He exists and His name exists through all generations. His throne is established, His kingship and faithfulness endure for ever. His words live and persist, faithful and desirable °for ever and all time. → So they were for our ancestors, so they are for us, and so they will be for our children and all our generations and for all future generations of the seed of Israel, Your servants.

וְיַצִּיב *And firm*: This blessing, joining the *Shema* to the *Amidah*, goes back to Temple times. The Sages emphasised that there must be no separation between the last words of the *Shema*, "I am the LORD your GOD", and the first word of the prayer, "*True* and firm", or between its last words, "who redeemed Israel", and the beginning of the *Amidah* (*Berachot* 14b, 9b). The connection between the two is *redemption*, the theme of this blessing. The *Shema* ends by speaking about redemption in the past. In the *Amidah* we pray for redemption in the future. Connecting past and future is "truth" – our faith in GOD and in His covenant with us.

עַל־הָרִאשׁוֹנִים וְעַל־הָאַחֲרוֹנִים, דָּבָר טוֹב וְקַיָּם לְעוֹלָם וָעֶד, אֱמֶת וֶאֱמוּנָה חֹק וְלֹא יַעֲבֹר. אֱמֶת שָׁאַתָּה הוּא יהוה אֱלֹהֵינוּ וֵאלֹהֵי אֲבוֹתֵינוּ, ◄ מַלְכֵּנוּ מֶלֶךְ אֲבוֹתֵינוּ, גּוֹאֲלֵנוּ גּוֹאֵל אֲבוֹתֵינוּ, יוֹצְרֵנוּ צוּר יְשׁוּעָתֵנוּ, פּוֹדֵנוּ וּמַצִּילֵנוּ מֵעוֹלָם הוּא שְׁמֶךָ, אֵין אֱלֹהִים זוּלָתֶךָ.

עֶזְרַת אֲבוֹתֵינוּ אַתָּה הוּא מֵעוֹלָם, מָגֵן וּמוֹשִׁיעַ לִבְנֵיהֶם אַחֲרֵיהֶם בְּכָל־דּוֹר וָדוֹר. בְּרוּם עוֹלָם מוֹשָׁבֶךָ, וּמִשְׁפָּטֶיךָ וְצִדְקָתְךָ עַד־אַפְסֵי אָרֶץ. אַשְׁרֵי אִישׁ שֶׁיִּשְׁמַע לְמִצְוֹתֶיךָ, וְתוֹרָתְךָ וּדְבָרְךָ יָשִׂים עַל־לִבּוֹ. אֱמֶת אַתָּה הוּא אָדוֹן לְעַמֶּךָ וּמֶלֶךְ גִּבּוֹר לָרִיב רִיבָם. אֱמֶת אַתָּה הוּא רִאשׁוֹן וְאַתָּה הוּא אַחֲרוֹן, וּמִבַּלְעָדֶיךָ אֵין לָנוּ מֶלֶךְ גּוֹאֵל וּמוֹשִׁיעַ. מִמִּצְרַיִם גְּאַלְתָּנוּ יהוה אֱלֹהֵינוּ, וּמִבֵּית עֲבָדִים פְּדִיתָנוּ. כָּל־בְּכוֹרֵיהֶם הָרָגְתָּ, וּבְכוֹרְךָ גָּאָלְתָּ, וְיַם־סוּף בָּקַעְתָּ, וְזֵדִים טִבַּעְתָּ, וִידִידִים הֶעֱבַרְתָּ, וַיְכַסּוּ מַיִם צָרֵיהֶם, אֶחָד מֵהֶם לֹא נוֹתָר. עַל־זֹאת שִׁבְּחוּ אֲהוּבִים וְרוֹמְמוּ אֵל, וְנָתְנוּ יְדִידִים זְמִירוֹת שִׁירוֹת וְתִשְׁבָּחוֹת, בְּרָכוֹת וְהוֹדָאוֹת, לְמֶלֶךְ אֵל חַי וְקַיָּם, רָם וְנִשָּׂא, גָּדוֹל וְנוֹרָא, מַשְׁפִּיל גֵּאִים, וּמַגְבִּיהַּ שְׁפָלִים, מוֹצִיא אֲסִירִים, וּפוֹדֶה עֲנָוִים, וְעוֹזֵר דַּלִּים, וְעוֹנֶה לְעַמּוֹ בְּעֵת שַׁוְּעָם אֵלָיו.

Stand and take three steps back.

◄ תְּהִלּוֹת לְאֵל עֶלְיוֹן, בָּרוּךְ הוּא וּמְבֹרָךְ. מֹשֶׁה וּבְנֵי יִשְׂרָאֵל לְךָ עָנוּ שִׁירָה בְּשִׂמְחָה רַבָּה, וְאָמְרוּ כֻלָּם,

מִי־כָמֹכָה בָּאֵלִים יהוה, מִי כָּמֹכָה נֶאְדָּר בַּקֹּדֶשׁ, נוֹרָא תְהִלֹּת עֹשֵׂה פֶלֶא. ◄ שִׁירָה חֲדָשָׁה שִׁבְּחוּ גְאוּלִים לְשִׁמְךָ עַל־שְׂפַת הַיָּם, יַחַד כֻּלָּם הוֹדוּ וְהִמְלִיכוּ וְאָמְרוּ,

עַל־הָרִאשׁוֹנִים For the early and the later generations this faith has proved good and enduring for ever – true and faithful, an irrevocable law. True – You are the LORD: our GOD and GOD of our ancestors, ➾ our King and King of our ancestors, our Redeemer and Redeemer of our ancestors, our Maker, Rock of our salvation, our Deliverer and Rescuer: this has ever been Your name. There is no GOD but You.

עֶזְרַת You have always been the help of our ancestors, Shield and Saviour of their children after them in every generation. Your dwelling is in the heights of the universe, and Your judgements and righteousness reach to the ends of the earth. Happy is the one who obeys Your commandments and takes to heart Your teaching and Your word. True – You are the Master of Your people and a mighty King who pleads their cause. True – You are the first and You are the last. Beside You, we have no king, redeemer or saviour. From Egypt You redeemed us, LORD our GOD, and from the slave-house You delivered us. All their firstborn You killed, but Your firstborn You redeemed. You split the Sea of Reeds and drowned the arrogant. You brought Your beloved ones across. The water covered their foes; not one of them was left. For this, the beloved ones praised and exalted GOD, the cherished ones sang psalms, songs and praises, blessings and thanksgivings to the King, the living and enduring GOD. High and exalted, great and awesome, He humbles the haughty and raises the lowly, freeing captives and redeeming those in need, helping the poor and answering His people when they cry out to Him.

Stand and take three steps back.

➾ Praises to GOD Most High, the Blessed One who is blessed. Moses and the children of Israel recited to You a song with great joy, and they all exclaimed:

מִי־כָמֹכָה "Who is like You, Lord, among the mighty? Who is like You, majestic in holiness, awesome in praises, doing wonders?"

➾ With a new song, the redeemed people praised Your name at the seashore. Together they all gave thanks, proclaimed Your kingship, and declared:

יהוה | יִמְלֹךְ לְעוֹלָם וָעֶד.

Congregants should end the following blessing together with the Leader so as to be able to move directly from the words גָּאַל יִשְׂרָאֵל to the עֲמִידָה, without the interruption of saying אמן.

← **צוּר** יִשְׂרָאֵל, קוּמָה בְּעֶזְרַת יִשְׂרָאֵל, וּפְדֵה כִנְאֻמֶךָ יְהוּדָה וְיִשְׂרָאֵל. גֹּאֲלֵנוּ יהוה צְבָאוֹת שְׁמוֹ, קְדוֹשׁ יִשְׂרָאֵל. בָּרוּךְ אַתָּה יהוה, גָּאַל יִשְׂרָאֵל.

עמידה

The following prayer, until קַדְמוֹנִיּוֹת, on page 96, is said standing with feet together. The עֲמִידָה is first said silently; then, if there is a מִנְיָן, it is repeated aloud by the Leader. Take three steps forward. At the points indicated by ▼, bend the knees at the first word, bow at the second, and stand straight before God's name.

אֲדֹנָי, שְׂפָתַי תִּפְתָּח, וּפִי יַגִּיד תְּהִלָּתֶךָ.

אבות

▼**בָּרוּךְ** אַתָּה יהוה אֱלֹהֵינוּ וֵאלֹהֵי אֲבוֹתֵינוּ, אֱלֹהֵי אַבְרָהָם, אֱלֹהֵי יִצְחָק, וֵאלֹהֵי יַעֲקֹב, הָאֵל הַגָּדוֹל הַגִּבּוֹר וְהַנּוֹרָא, אֵל עֶלְיוֹן, גּוֹמֵל חֲסָדִים טוֹבִים וְקוֹנֵה הַכֹּל, וְזוֹכֵר חַסְדֵי אָבוֹת, וּמֵבִיא גוֹאֵל לִבְנֵי בְנֵיהֶם, לְמַעַן שְׁמוֹ בְּאַהֲבָה.

LAWS OF THE AMIDAH:

1. The *Amidah* is said standing, facing Jerusalem (in practice, this usually means facing the synagogue wall containing the Ark), with feet together.
2. During the *Amidah*, we must be especially conscious of standing in the presence of God. To symbolise entry to the Divine presence, we take three steps forward before beginning the prayer (having first taken three steps back), and at the end bow and take three steps back, bowing first left, then right, then forward.
3. At four points during the *Amidah* (indicated by the symbol ▼ in the text), we bow, bending the knees at the first word, bowing at the second, and standing straight before saying God's name.
4. The *Amidah* is said quietly. We alone should be able to hear what we are saying (based on the biblical precedent of Hannah whose "lips moved but her voice was not heard", 1 Samuel 1:13). It should be said with complete concentration.
5. If, before one has finished the silent *Amidah*, the Leader begins the repetition and reaches *Kedushah*, one should pause, listen with full attention to the *Kedushah*, and then return to one's prayer. One should not interrupt one's own prayer by saying the congregational responses aloud.

"The LORD shall reign for ever and ever."

Congregants should end the following blessing together with the Leader so as to be able to move directly from the words "redeemed Israel" to the *Amidah*, without the interruption of saying Amen.

→ צוּר Rock of Israel! Arise to the help of Israel. Deliver, as You promised, Judah and Israel. Our Redeemer is the LORD of hosts; His name, the Holy One of Israel. Blessed are You, LORD, who redeemed Israel.

AMIDAH: THE STANDING PRAYER

The following prayer, until "in former years", on page 97, is said standing with feet together.

The *Amidah* is first said silently; then, if there is a *minyan*, it is repeated aloud by the Leader.

Take three steps forward. At the points indicated by ▾, bend the knees at the first word, bow at the second, and stand straight before GOD's name.

O LORD, open my lips, so that my mouth may declare Your praise.

PATRIARCHS

▾בָּרוּךְ Blessed are You, LORD our GOD and GOD of our Fathers, GOD of Abraham, GOD of Isaac and GOD of Jacob; the great, mighty and awesome GOD, GOD Most High, who bestows acts of lovingkindness and creates all, who remembers the lovingkindness of the Fathers and will bring a Redeemer to their children's children for the sake of His name, in love.

AMIDAH: THE STANDING PRAYER

The *Amidah* is the summit of prayer: in it, we enter the holy of holies of religious experience. We say it standing because we are conscious of being in the unmediated presence of GOD. The name *Amidah* is also related to its earliest setting: prayers said by the people of the *Ma'amad*, groups of laymen who, in Second Temple times, accompanied their local "watch" (*mishmar*) of priests who officiated in the Temple on a one-in-24-week rota. The *Ma'amad* was one of the prototypes of congregational prayer.

According to tradition, the *Amidah* in embryonic form dates back to the Great Assembly in the time of Ezra following the Jews' return from Babylon. Several centuries later, it was canonised in a fuller form by Shimon HaPakuli in the days of Rabban Gamliel II.

It is often called the *Shemoneh Esreh*, "Eighteen", because it originally consisted of eighteen blessings (now, nineteen). It has a three-part structure: 1. *praise* (blessings 1–3); 2. *requests* (blessings 4–16); and 3. *thanks* (17–19). Each of these has a tripartite form. The first and last sections each contain three blessings. The middle section is composed of twelve blessings, six personal requests and six collective ones. The first three personal requests are for spiritual goods (wisdom, repentance and forgiveness). The second are

Between רֹאשׁ הַשָּׁנָה and יוֹם כִּפּוּר, add:

זָכְרֵנוּ לְחַיִּים, מֶלֶךְ חָפֵץ בַּחַיִּים, וְכָתְבֵנוּ בְּסֵפֶר הַחַיִּים, לְמַעַנְךָ אֱלֹהִים חַיִּים.

מֶלֶךְ עוֹזֵר וּמוֹשִׁיעַ וּמָגֵן. ▾בָּרוּךְ אַתָּה יהוה, מָגֵן אַבְרָהָם.

גבורות

אַתָּה גִּבּוֹר לְעוֹלָם אֲדֹנָי, מְחַיֵּה מֵתִים אַתָּה, רַב לְהוֹשִׁיעַ.

From after שְׂמְחַת תּוֹרָה until פֶּסַח, add:

מַשִּׁיב הָרְוּחַ וּמוֹרִיד הַגֶּשֶׁם.

מְכַלְכֵּל חַיִּים בְּחֶסֶד, מְחַיֵּה מֵתִים בְּרַחֲמִים רַבִּים, סוֹמֵךְ נוֹפְלִים, וְרוֹפֵא חוֹלִים, וּמַתִּיר אֲסוּרִים, וּמְקַיֵּם אֱמוּנָתוֹ לִישֵׁנֵי עָפָר. מִי כָמְוֹךָ בַּעַל גְּבוּרוֹת, וּמִי דּוֹמֶה לָּךְ, מֶלֶךְ מֵמִית וּמְחַיֶּה וּמַצְמִיחַ יְשׁוּעָה.

for physical goods (deliverance, healing and livelihood). The first three national requests are for physical events (ingathering of exiles, justice, and an end to internal conflicts). The second three are for the nation's spiritual needs (the righteous and pious, the rebuilding of Jerusalem, and the restoration of the Davidic monarchy). One blessing, "Listen to our voice" (the sixteenth, last of the "request" blessings), stands outside this structure because it is a prayer about prayer itself. It is also the point at which individuals can add their personal requests.

Blessing 1: Patriarchs. In these opening chords we refer back to the dawn of our people's history – the days of the patriarchs, Abraham, Isaac and Jacob. In so doing, we echo Moses, who constantly referred to the patriarchs when praying for forgiveness for the people. God's love for, and covenant with, those who first heard His call is the supreme ground on which we stand when we turn to Him in prayer. The paragraph ends with a reference to Abraham, who was the first person to heed God's call. *For Your sake, O God of life* – the phrase literally means "Living God". The translation, however, conveys the poetic structure of this short but powerful prayer: four phrases, each ending with the word *chayyim*, "life".

Blessing 2: Divine might. The fivefold reference to the resurrection of the dead reflects the controversy between the Sadducees and Pharisees in the late Second Temple era. The Sadducees rejected belief in resurrection; the Pharisees, whose heirs we are, affirmed it. Belief that those who died will one day live again is one of Judaism's great principles of hope, set out in the vision of Ezekiel of the valley

Between Rosh Hashanah and Yom Kippur, add:

Remember us for life, O King who desires life, and write us in the book of life – for Your sake, O God of life.

King, Helper, Saviour, Shield: ▾Blessed are You, Lord, Shield of Abraham.

DIVINE MIGHT

אַתָּה You are eternally mighty, Lord. You give life to the dead and have great power to save.

From after Simchat Torah until Pesach, add:

He makes the wind blow and the rain fall.

He sustains the living with lovingkindness, and with great compassion revives the dead. He supports the fallen, heals the sick, sets captives free, and keeps His faith with those who sleep in the dust. Who is like You, Master of might, and to whom can You be compared, O King who brings death and gives life, and makes salvation grow?

---

of dry bones that came to life once more. Jews kept hope alive; hope kept the Jewish people alive.

Kedushah. The *Kedushah* is the supreme moment of holiness in prayer. It takes several different forms. Common to them all is that they are built around the two supreme mystical visions in the Hebrew Bible, of Isaiah (6) and Ezekiel (1–3). The prophet sees God enthroned in glory, surrounded by angels singing His praises. Isaiah hears them singing, "Holy, holy, holy is the Lord of Hosts: the whole world is filled with His glory." Ezekiel (3:12) hears them singing, "Blessed is the Lord's glory from His place." Together they constitute the most sublime expression of prayer as praise in the presence of God.

In the morning, *Kedushah* is said three times at different points in the service. There is *Kedushat Yotzer*, which appears in the first of the three *Shema* blessings (page 62), *Kedushah de-Amidah*, said here during the Leader's repetition; and *Kedushah de-Sidra*, towards the end of the service. The first and third do not require a *minyan* and are said sitting. The second requires a *minyan* and is said standing. The reason is that the first and third are descriptions of the song of the angels; the second is a re-enactment. We stand, feet together, rising on our toes, as if we too were angels.

In the *Kedushah* we move beyond the priestly prayer-as-sacrifice and the prophetic prayer-as-dialogue to prayer as a mystic experience. So holy is it that in Israel in ancient times it was said only on Shabbat and festivals. The Zohar interprets Jacob's vision of a ladder stretching

Between רֹאשׁ הַשָּׁנָה and יוֹם כִּפּוּר, add:

מִי כָמְוֹךָ אַב הָרַחֲמִים, זוֹכֵר יְצוּרָיו לַחַיִּים בְּרַחֲמִים.

וְנֶאֱמָן אַתָּה לְהַחֲיוֹת מֵתִים. בָּרוּךְ אַתָּה יהוה, מְחַיֵּה הַמֵּתִים.

When saying the עֲמִידָה silently, go to אַתָּה קָדוֹשׁ on page 80.

קדושה

During the Leader's repetition, the following is said standing, with feet together, rising on the toes at the words indicated by ▲.

Congregation then Leader: נְקַדֵּשׁ אֶת־שִׁמְךָ בָּעוֹלָם, כְּשֵׁם שֶׁמַּקְדִּישִׁים אוֹתוֹ בִּשְׁמֵי מָרוֹם, כַּכָּתוּב עַל יַד נְבִיאֶךָ, וְקָרָא זֶה אֶל־זֶה וְאָמַר.

Congregation and Leader: ▲קָדוֹשׁ ▲קָדוֹשׁ ▲קָדוֹשׁ יהוה צְבָאוֹת, מְלֹא כָל־הָאָרֶץ כְּבוֹדוֹ.

Leader: לְעֻמָּתָם בָּרוּךְ יֹאמֵרוּ.

Congregation and Leader: ▲בָּרוּךְ כְּבוֹד־יהוה, מִמְּקוֹמוֹ.

Leader: וּבְדִבְרֵי קָדְשְׁךָ כָּתוּב לֵאמֹר.

Congregation and Leader: ▲יִמְלֹךְ יהוה לְעוֹלָם, אֱלֹהַיִךְ צִיּוֹן לְדֹר וָדֹר, הַלְלוּיָהּ.

Leader: לְדוֹר וָדוֹר נַגִּיד גָּדְלֶךָ וּלְנֵצַח נְצָחִים קְדֻשָּׁתְךָ נַקְדִּישׁ, וְשִׁבְחֲךָ אֱלֹהֵינוּ מִפִּינוּ לֹא יָמוּשׁ לְעוֹלָם וָעֶד, כִּי אֵל מֶלֶךְ גָּדוֹל וְקָדוֹשׁ אָתָּה. בָּרוּךְ אַתָּה יהוה, *הָאֵל הַקָּדוֹשׁ.

*Between רֹאשׁ הַשָּׁנָה and יוֹם כִּפּוּר, end the blessing:

הַמֶּלֶךְ הַקָּדוֹשׁ.

The Leader continues with אתה חונן overleaf.

Between Rosh Hashanah and Yom Kippur, add:

Who is like You, compassionate Father, who remembers His creatures in compassion, for life?

Faithful are You to revive the dead. Blessed are You, LORD, who revives the dead.

When saying the *Amidah* silently, go to "You are holy" on page 81.

KEDUSHAH

During the Leader's repetition, the following is said standing, with feet together, rising on the toes at the words indicated by ▲:

Congregation then Leader: נְקַדֵּשׁ We will sanctify Your name on earth, as they sanctify it in the highest heavens, as is written by Your prophet, "And they [the angels] call to one another saying:

Congregation and Leader: ▲Holy, ▲holy, ▲holy is the LORD of Hosts the whole world is filled with His glory."

Leader: Those facing them say "Blessed – "

Congregation and Leader: "▲Blessed is the LORD's glory from His place."

Leader: And in Your Holy Writings it is written thus:

Congregation and Leader: "▲The LORD shall reign forever. He is your GOD, Zion, from generation to generation, Halleluyah!"

Leader: From generation to generation we will declare Your greatness, and we will proclaim Your holiness for evermore. Your praise, our GOD, shall never leave our mouth, for You, GOD, are a great and holy King. Blessed are You, LORD, *the holy GOD.

*Between Rosh Hashanah and Yom Kippur, end the blessing:

the holy King.

The Leader continues with "You grace humanity" overleaf.

from earth to heaven, with angels ascending and descending (Genesis 28:12), as a metaphor for prayer, and this, too, is part of the meaning of *Kedushah*. We have climbed the ladder from earth to heaven. As the leader repeats the prayer on behalf of the entire community, we reach the summit of religious experience.

קדושת השם

אַתָּה קָדוֹשׁ וְשִׁמְךָ קָדוֹשׁ, וּקְדוֹשִׁים בְּכָל־יוֹם יְהַלְלְוּךָ סֶּלָה. בָּרוּךְ אַתָּה יהוה, *הָאֵל הַקָּדוֹשׁ.

*Between רֹאשׁ הַשָּׁנָה and יוֹם כִּפּוּר, end the blessing:
הַמֶּלֶךְ הַקָּדוֹשׁ.

דעת

אַתָּה חוֹנֵן לְאָדָם דַּעַת, וּמְלַמֵּד לֶאֱנוֹשׁ בִּינָה. חָנֵּנוּ מֵאִתְּךָ דֵּעָה בִּינָה וְהַשְׂכֵּל. בָּרוּךְ אַתָּה יהוה, חוֹנֵן הַדָּעַת.

תשובה

הֲשִׁיבֵנוּ אָבִינוּ לְתוֹרָתֶךָ, וְקָרְבֵנוּ מַלְכֵּנוּ לַעֲבוֹדָתֶךָ, וְהַחֲזִירֵנוּ בִּתְשׁוּבָה שְׁלֵמָה לְפָנֶיךָ. בָּרוּךְ אַתָּה יהוה, הָרוֹצֶה בִּתְשׁוּבָה.

סליחה

סְלַח־לָנוּ אָבִינוּ כִּי חָטָאנוּ, מְחַל־לָנוּ מַלְכֵּנוּ כִּי פָשָׁעְנוּ,* כִּי מוֹחֵל וְסוֹלֵחַ אָתָּה. בָּרוּךְ אַתָּה יהוה, חַנּוּן, הַמַּרְבֶּה לִסְלוֹחַ.

*On Fast Days, some congregations say סְלִיחוֹת during the Leader's repetition at this point; others do so after the end of the repetition.

Blessing 3: Holiness. The threefold reference to holiness ("You are holy and Your name is holy, and holy ones praise You daily") mirrors the threefold declaration of the angels in Isaiah's vision: "Holy, holy, holy is the Lord of Hosts". *Kadosh*, "holy", means "set apart, distinct". When used of God, it refers to His transcendence, the fact that He stands outside nature, creating and sustaining it. When used of Israel, it means that we too are summoned to stand apart from the idols of the age, living instead in close and continuous proximity to God.

The first three paragraphs of the *Amidah* form a composite unit. The first speaks of the beginning of covenantal time in the days of the patriarchs. The second is about the end of time: resurrection. The third is about holiness, beyond space and time.

Blessing 4: Knowledge. This is the first of the "request" blessings. King Solomon,

HOLINESS

אַתָּה You are holy and Your name is holy, and holy ones praise You daily, Selah! Blessed are You, LORD, *the holy GOD.

*Between Rosh Hashanah and Yom Kippur, end the blessing:
the holy King.

KNOWLEDGE

אַתָּה You grace humanity with knowledge and teach mortals understanding. Grace us with the knowledge, understanding and discernment that come from You. Blessed are You, LORD, who graciously grants knowledge.

REPENTANCE

הֲשִׁיבֵנוּ Bring us back, our Father, to Your Torah. Draw us near, our King, to Your service. Lead us back to You in perfect repentance. Blessed are You, LORD, who desires repentance.

FORGIVENESS

סְלַח־לָנוּ Forgive us, our Father, for we have sinned. Pardon us, our King, for we have transgressed; *for You pardon and forgive. Blessed are You, LORD, the gracious One who repeatedly forgives.

*On Fast Days, some congregations say *Selichot* during the Leader's repetition at this point; others do so after the end of the repetition.

---

when asked by GOD to name the thing he most desired (1 Kings 3:5–15), asked for wisdom; so do we. Knowledge is prior to emotion, because "the heart is deceitful above all things" (Jeremiah 17:9). Untutored emotion can be misdirected, even destructive.

This paragraph replicates the structure of the *Amidah* as a whole. It begins with praise ("You grace humanity with knowledge"), proceeds to request ("Grace us with the knowledge"), and ends in acknowledgement ("Who graciously grants knowledge").

Blessing 5: Repentance. Knowledge and understanding allow us to see where we have drifted from the right path of life. So we ask GOD to help us find the way back to repentance.

Blessing 6: Forgiveness. Repentance involves asking GOD to forgive us. This applies to sins between us and GOD. Sins between us and our fellow human beings are only forgiven when we have apologised to, and tried to obtain the forgiveness of, those we have wronged. Knowledge, repentance and forgiveness

גאולה

רְאֵה בְעָנְיֵנוּ, וְרִיבָה רִיבֵנוּ, וּגְאָלֵנוּ מְהֵרָה לְמַעַן שְׁמֶךָ, כִּי גוֹאֵל חָזָק אָתָּה. בָּרוּךְ אַתָּה יהוה, גּוֹאֵל יִשְׂרָאֵל.

On Fast Days, the Leader adds:

עֲנֵנוּ יהוה עֲנֵנוּ, בְּיוֹם צוֹם־תַּעֲנִיתֵנוּ, כִּי בְצָרָה־גְדוֹלָה אֲנָחְנוּ. אַל־תֵּפֶן אֶל־רִשְׁעֵנוּ, וְאַל תַּסְתֵּר פָּנֶיךָ מִמֶּנּוּ, וְאַל־תִּתְעַלַּם מִתְּחִנָּתֵנוּ. הֱיֵה נָא קָרוֹב לְשַׁוְעָתֵנוּ, יְהִי נָא חַסְדְּךָ לְנַחֲמֵנוּ, טֶרֶם נִקְרָא אֵלֶיךָ עֲנֵנוּ, כַּדָּבָר שֶׁנֶּאֱמַר, וְהָיָה טֶרֶם יִקְרָאוּ וַאֲנִי אֶעֱנֶה, עוֹד הֵם מְדַבְּרִים וַאֲנִי אֶשְׁמָע. כִּי אַתָּה יהוה הָעוֹנֶה בְּעֵת צָרָה, פּוֹדֶה וּמַצִּיל בְּכָל עֵת צָרָה וְצוּקָה. בָּרוּךְ אַתָּה יהוה, הָעוֹנֶה בְּעֵת צָרָה.

רפואה

רְפָאֵנוּ יהוה וְנֵרָפֵא, הוֹשִׁיעֵנוּ וְנִוָּשֵׁעָה, כִּי תְהִלָּתֵנוּ אָתָּה, וְהַעֲלֵה רְפוּאָה שְׁלֵמָה לְכָל מַכּוֹתֵינוּ,* כִּי אֵל מֶלֶךְ רוֹפֵא נֶאֱמָן וְרַחֲמָן אָתָּה. בָּרוּךְ אַתָּה יהוה, רוֹפֵא, חוֹלֵי עַמּוֹ יִשְׂרָאֵל.

*The following prayer for a sick person may be said here:

וִיהִי רָצוֹן מִלְּפָנֶיךָ, יהוה אֱלֹהֵינוּ וֵאלֹהֵי אֲבוֹתֵינוּ, שֶׁתִּשְׁלַח מְהֵרָה רְפוּאָה שְׁלֵמָה מִן הַשָּׁמַיִם, רְפוּאַת הַנֶּפֶשׁ וּרְפוּאַת הַגּוּף לַחוֹלֶה/לַחוֹלָה (name בֶּן/בַּת mother's name) בְּתוֹךְ שְׁאָר חוֹלֵי יִשְׂרָאֵל.

are the three primary needs of the mind and soul.

Blessing 7: Redemption. The commentators explain that this request is not for national redemption, the subject of later blessings. Here the reference is to release from personal crises: captivity, persecution, misfortune or affliction. Rabbi Samson Raphael Hirsch distinguishes between the first two phrases thus: "Look on our affliction" refers to suffering not caused by others, while "Plead our cause" refers to those who seek our harm. Rational argument is often insufficient to cure hatred; therefore we place our fate

REDEMPTION

רְאֵה Look on our affliction, plead our cause, and redeem us soon for Your name's sake, for You are a powerful Redeemer. Blessed are You, Lord, the Redeemer of Israel.

On Fast Days, the Leader adds:

עֲנֵנוּ Answer us, Lord, answer us on our Fast Day, for we are in great distress. Look not at our wickedness. Do not hide Your face from us and do not ignore our plea. Be near to our cry; please let Your lovingkindness comfort us. Even before we call to You, answer us, as is said, "Before they call, I will answer. While they are still speaking, I will hear". For You, Lord, are the One who answers in time of distress, redeems and rescues in all times of trouble and anguish. Blessed are You, Lord, who answers in time of distress.

HEALING

רְפָאֵנוּ Heal us, Lord, and we shall be healed. Save us and we shall be saved, for You are our praise. Bring complete recovery for all our ailments,* for You, God, King, are a faithful and compassionate Healer. Blessed are You, Lord, Healer of the sick of His people Israel.

---

*The following prayer for a sick person may be said here:

May it be Your will, O Lord our God and God of our ancestors, that You speedily send a complete recovery from heaven, a healing of both soul and body, to the patient (name), son/daughter of (mother's name) among the other afflicted of Israel.

---

in the hands of God, asking Him to heal hostility (Rabbi J.H. Hertz). *For Your name's sake* – may we be spared suffering not for our own sake but so that we may be free to worship You without distraction (Rabbi Jacob Zvi Mecklenburg). *Redeemer of Israel* – in the present, as opposed to the blessing immediately prior to the *Amidah*, which refers to acts of Divine redemption in the past.

Answer us: A special prayer to be said on public fasts (*Ta'anit* 11a). The Leader recites it at this point in the repetition of the morning and afternoon *Amidah*. Individuals say it in the afternoon only, as part of the 16th blessing, without the concluding benediction.

Blessing 8: Healing. We pray that medical treatment be successful, and that God Himself be part of the healing process. We are both body and soul: the health of one affects that of the other.

ברכת השנים

בָּרֵךְ עָלֵינוּ יהוה אֱלֹהֵינוּ אֶת הַשָּׁנָה הַזֹּאת וְאֶת כָּל מִינֵי תְבוּאָתָהּ לְטוֹבָה,

From the second day of פֶּסַח until December 4th (in a year before a civil leap year, 5th), say:

וְתֵן בְּרָכָה

From December 5th (in the year before a civil leap year, 6th) until פֶּסַח, say:

וְתֵן טַל וּמָטָר לִבְרָכָה

עַל־פְּנֵי הָאֲדָמָה, וְשַׂבְּעֵנוּ מִטּוּבֶךָ, וּבָרֵךְ שְׁנָתֵנוּ כַּשָּׁנִים הַטּוֹבוֹת. בָּרוּךְ אַתָּה יהוה, מְבָרֵךְ הַשָּׁנִים.

קיבוץ גלויות

תְּקַע בְּשׁוֹפָר גָּדוֹל לְחֵרוּתֵנוּ, וְשָׂא נֵס לְקַבֵּץ גָּלֻיּוֹתֵינוּ, וְקַבְּצֵנוּ יַחַד מֵאַרְבַּע כַּנְפוֹת הָאָרֶץ. בָּרוּךְ אַתָּה יהוה, מְקַבֵּץ, נִדְחֵי עַמּוֹ יִשְׂרָאֵל.

השבת המשפט

הָשִׁיבָה שׁוֹפְטֵינוּ כְּבָרִאשׁוֹנָה, וְיוֹעֲצֵינוּ כְּבַתְּחִלָּה, וְהָסֵר מִמֶּנּוּ יָגוֹן וַאֲנָחָה, וּמְלוֹךְ עָלֵינוּ אַתָּה יהוה לְבַדְּךָ בְּחֶסֶד וּבְרַחֲמִים, וְצַדְּקֵנוּ בַּמִּשְׁפָּט. בָּרוּךְ אַתָּה יהוה, *מֶלֶךְ, אוֹהֵב צְדָקָה וּמִשְׁפָּט.

---

*Between רֹאשׁ הַשָּׁנָה and יוֹם כִּפּוּר, end the blessing:

הַמֶּלֶךְ הַמִּשְׁפָּט.

Blessing 9: Prosperity. We pray for God's blessing on our efforts to earn a livelihood. Israel's agriculture depends on rain, so this blessing includes – during the winter months – a prayer for rain. Israel is a land that teaches its inhabitants the need for prayer. *Grant dew and rain* – unlike the praise "He makes the wind blow and the rain fall" (page 76), which we begin saying on Shemini Atzeret, the actual prayer for rain is said later to coincide with the rainy season itself. In Israel, it is said from 7 Cheshvan. Outside Israel, it is said from the 60th day after "Takufat Tishrei", the Jewish equivalent of the autumnal equinox.

Blessing 10: Ingathering of exiles. With this paragraph, the requests change from individual to collective hopes. They begin with three prayers for political-historical renewal: the return of exiles, the res-

PROSPERITY

בָּרֵךְ Bless this year for us, LORD our GOD, and all its types of produce for good.

From the second day of Pesach until December 4th (in a year before a civil leap year, 5th), say:	From December 5th (in the year before a civil leap year, 6th) until Pesach, say:
Grant blessing	Grant dew and rain as a blessing

on the face of the earth, and from Your goodness satisfy us, blessing our year as the best of years. Blessed are You, LORD, who blesses the years.

INGATHERING OF EXILES

תְּקַע Sound the great shofar for our freedom, raise high the banner to gather our exiles, and gather us together from the four quarters of the earth. Blessed are You, LORD, who gathers the dispersed of His people Israel.

JUSTICE

הָשִׁיבָה Restore our judges as at first and our counsellors as at the beginning, and remove from us sorrow and sighing. May You alone, LORD, reign over us with lovingkindness and compassion, and vindicate us in justice. Blessed are You, LORD, *the King who loves righteousness and justice.

---

*Between Rosh Hashanah and Yom Kippur, end the blessing:
the King of justice.

---

toration of independence, and an end to the factionalism that caused great damage to the Israelites from the biblical era to the end of the Second Temple period. *Sound the great shofar*: A reference to Isaiah 27:13, "On that day a great shofar will sound". *Raise high the banner*: Isaiah 11:12, "He will raise a banner for the nations and gather the exiles of Israel; He will assemble the scattered people of Judah from the four quarters of the earth."

Blessing 11: Justice. A prayer for self-government. The "Judges" in the biblical book of that name were not merely judges in a legal sense; they were leaders of the people (Rabbi Abraham ben HaRambam). The prayer for the restoration of judges, following the ingathering of exiles, is thus a plea for the return of national sovereignty. *Remove from us sorrow and sighing* – the plaint of a people who have known the full precariousness of being dependent on the goodwill of others.

ברכת המינים

וְלַמַּלְשִׁינִים אַל־תְּהִי תִקְוָה, וְכָל הָרִשְׁעָה כְּרֶגַע תֹּאבֵד, וְכָל אוֹיְבֶיךָ מְהֵרָה יִכָּרֵתוּ, וּמַלְכוּת זָדוֹן מְהֵרָה תְעַקֵּר וּתְשַׁבֵּר וּתְמַגֵּר וְתַכְנִיעַ בִּמְהֵרָה בְיָמֵינוּ. בָּרוּךְ אַתָּה יהוה, שֹׁבֵר אוֹיְבִים וּמַכְנִיעַ זֵדִים.

על הצדיקים

עַל־הַצַּדִּיקִים וְעַל־הַחֲסִידִים, וְעַל־זִקְנֵי עַמְּךָ בֵּית יִשְׂרָאֵל, וְעַל־פְּלֵיטַת סוֹפְרֵיהֶם, וְעַל־גֵּרֵי הַצֶּדֶק וְעָלֵינוּ, יֶהֱמוּ רַחֲמֶיךָ יהוה אֱלֹהֵינוּ, וְתֵן שָׂכָר טוֹב לְכָל הַבּוֹטְחִים בְּשִׁמְךָ בֶּאֱמֶת, וְשִׂים חֶלְקֵנוּ עִמָּהֶם לְעוֹלָם, וְלֹא נֵבוֹשׁ כִּי־בְךָ בָּטָחְנוּ. בָּרוּךְ אַתָּה יהוה, מִשְׁעָן וּמִבְטָח לַצַּדִּיקִים.

בנין ירושלים

וְלִירוּשָׁלַיִם עִירְךָ בְּרַחֲמִים תָּשׁוּב, וְתִשְׁכּוֹן בְּתוֹכָהּ כַּאֲשֶׁר דִּבַּרְתָּ, וּבְנֵה אוֹתָהּ בְּקָרוֹב בְּיָמֵינוּ בִּנְיַן עוֹלָם, וְכִסֵּא דָוִד מְהֵרָה לְתוֹכָהּ תָּכִין. בָּרוּךְ אַתָּה יהוה, בּוֹנֵה יְרוּשָׁלָיִם.

משיח בן דוד

אֶת־צֶמַח דָּוִד עַבְדְּךָ מְהֵרָה תַצְמִיחַ, וְקַרְנוֹ תָּרוּם בִּישׁוּעָתֶךָ, כִּי לִישׁוּעָתְךָ קִוִּינוּ כָּל־הַיּוֹם. בָּרוּךְ אַתָּה יהוה, מַצְמִיחַ קֶרֶן יְשׁוּעָה.

Blessing 12: Against Informers. The text of this paragraph underwent several changes during the centuries. Its original object was the sectarianism that split the Jewish world during the late Second Temple period. There were Jews in the Hellenistic age who turned against their own people. Faith (*emunah*) in Judaism involves the idea of loyalty – to a people and its heritage. This prayer is a protest against disloyalty.

The Talmud says that, to formulate this prayer, Rabban Gamliel turned to Shmuel HaKatan. Rav Kook pointed out that the only other reference to Shmuel HaKatan in rabbinic literature says that he used to say: "Do not rejoice when your enemy falls." Only a person who deeply loved his fellow human beings could be entrusted with the task of constructing this prayer, which must be free of animosity and *schadenfreude*.

Blessing 13: The righteous. After mention-

AGAINST INFORMERS

וְלַמַּלְשִׁינִים For the slanderers let there be no hope, and may all wickedness perish in an instant. May all Your enemies swiftly be cut down. May You swiftly uproot, crush, cast down and humble the kingdom of arrogance swiftly in our days. Blessed are You, LORD, who destroys enemies and humbles the arrogant.

THE RIGHTEOUS

עַל־הַצַּדִּיקִים To the righteous, the pious, the elders of Your people the house of Israel, the remnant of their scholars, the righteous converts, and to us, may Your compassion be aroused, LORD our GOD. Grant a good reward to all who sincerely trust in Your name. Set our lot with them for ever, so that we may never be ashamed, for in You we trust. Blessed are You, LORD, who is the support and trust of the righteous.

REBUILDING JERUSALEM

וְלִירוּשָׁלַיִם To Jerusalem, Your city, may You return in compassion, and may You dwell in it as You promised. May You rebuild it rapidly in our days as an everlasting structure, and instal within it soon the throne of David. Blessed are You, LORD, who builds Jerusalem.

KINGDOM OF DAVID

אֶת־צֶמַח May the offshoot of Your servant David soon flower, and may his pride be raised high by Your salvation, for we wait for Your salvation all day. Blessed are You, LORD, who makes the glory of salvation flourish.

---

ing those who harm the Jewish people, we go on to describe those who endow it with greatness: the righteous, the pious, the elders, scholars and converts. *The remnant of their scholars* is a reference to those Jews who endured religious persecution under the Greeks and Romans, and later in Europe survived the Crusades to the Holocaust. Judaism lost many of its greatest scholars as martyrs.

Blessing 14: Rebuilding Jerusalem. Jerusalem is the home of the Jewish soul, the place to which we turn in prayer and for whose restoration Jews prayed in every generation. The Book of Psalms has left us an indelible description of how Jews felt when the city fell to the Babylonians in the sixth century BCE: "By the rivers of Babylon we sat and wept when we remembered Zion…May my tongue cling to the roof of my mouth if I do not remember you, if I do not consider Jerusalem my highest joy" (Psalm 137). Jerusalem is mentioned more than 600 times in the Hebrew Bible.

Blessing 15: Kingdom of David. David was promised by GOD that the monar-

שומע תפילה

שְׁמַע קוֹלֵנוּ יהוה אֱלֹהֵינוּ, חוּס וְרַחֵם עָלֵינוּ, וְקַבֵּל בְּרַחֲמִים וּבְרָצוֹן אֶת־תְּפִלָּתֵנוּ, כִּי אֵל שׁוֹמֵעַ תְּפִלּוֹת וְתַחֲנוּנִים, אָתָּה. וּמִלְּפָנֶיךָ מַלְכֵּנוּ, רֵיקָם אַל תְּשִׁיבֵנוּ, כִּי אַתָּה שׁוֹמֵעַ תְּפִלַּת עַמְּךָ יִשְׂרָאֵל בְּרַחֲמִים. בָּרוּךְ אַתָּה יהוה, שׁוֹמֵעַ תְּפִלָּה.

עבודה

רְצֵה יהוה אֱלֹהֵינוּ בְּעַמְּךָ יִשְׂרָאֵל וּבִתְפִלָּתָם, וְהָשֵׁב אֶת־הָעֲבוֹדָה לִדְבִיר בֵּיתֶךָ. וְאִשֵּׁי יִשְׂרָאֵל וּתְפִלָּתָם בְּאַהֲבָה תְקַבֵּל בְּרָצוֹן, וּתְהִי לְרָצוֹן תָּמִיד עֲבוֹדַת יִשְׂרָאֵל עַמֶּךָ.

On רֹאשׁ חֹדֶשׁ and חוֹל הַמּוֹעֵד, say:

אֱלֹהֵינוּ וֵאלֹהֵי אֲבוֹתֵינוּ, יַעֲלֶה, וְיָבֹא, וְיַגִּיעַ, וְיֵרָאֶה, וְיֵרָצֶה, וְיִשָּׁמַע, וְיִפָּקֵד, וְיִזָּכֵר זִכְרוֹנֵנוּ וּפִקְדּוֹנֵנוּ, וְזִכְרוֹן אֲבוֹתֵינוּ, וְזִכְרוֹן מָשִׁיחַ בֶּן דָּוִד עַבְדֶּךָ, וְזִכְרוֹן יְרוּשָׁלַיִם עִיר קָדְשֶׁךָ, וְזִכְרוֹן כָּל־עַמְּךָ בֵּית יִשְׂרָאֵל לְפָנֶיךָ, לִפְלֵיטָה וּלְטוֹבָה, וּלְחֵן וּלְחֶסֶד וּלְרַחֲמִים, וּלְחַיִּים וּלְשָׁלוֹם בְּיוֹם

On רֹאשׁ חֹדֶשׁ:	On פֶּסַח:	On סֻכּוֹת:
רֹאשׁ הַחֹדֶשׁ	חַג הַמַּצּוֹת	חַג הַסֻּכּוֹת

הַזֶּה. זָכְרֵנוּ יהוה אֱלֹהֵינוּ בּוֹ לְטוֹבָה, וּפָקְדֵנוּ בוֹ לִבְרָכָה, וְהוֹשִׁיעֵנוּ בוֹ לְחַיִּים. וּבִדְבַר יְשׁוּעָה וְרַחֲמִים, חוּס וְחָנֵּנוּ וְרַחֵם עָלֵינוּ וְהוֹשִׁיעֵנוּ, כִּי אֵלֶיךָ עֵינֵינוּ, כִּי אֵל מֶלֶךְ חַנּוּן וְרַחוּם אָתָּה.

---

chy would always be the heritage of his children. The Davidic monarchy came to an end with the Babylonian conquest. It will be restored in the messianic age. The word "Messiah" in Hebrew means "anointed"; that is, a duly appointed king of Davidic descent.

Blessing 16: Response to Prayer. An all-inclusive prayer, that our prayers be heard.

RESPONSE TO PRAYER

שְׁמַע Listen to our voice, LORD our GOD. Spare us and have compassion on us, and in compassion and favour accept our prayer, for You, GOD, listen to prayers and pleas. Do not turn us away, O our King, empty-handed from Your presence, for You listen with compassion to the prayer of Your people Israel. Blessed are You, LORD, who listens to prayer.

TEMPLE SERVICE

רְצֵה Find favour, LORD our GOD, in Your people Israel and their prayer. Restore the service to Your most holy house, and accept in love and favour the fire-offerings of Israel and their prayer. May the service of Your people Israel always find favour with You.

On Rosh Chodesh and the Intermediate Days of Festivals, say:

אֱלֹהֵינוּ Our GOD and GOD of our ancestors, may there rise, come, reach, appear, be favoured, heard, regarded and remembered before You, our recollection and remembrance, as well as the remembrance of our ancestors, and of the Messiah son of David Your servant, and of Jerusalem Your holy city, and of all Your people the House of Israel – for deliverance and well-being, grace, lovingkindness and compassion, life and peace, on this day of:

On Rosh Chodesh:	On Pesach:	On Sukkot:
Rosh Chodesh.	the Festival of Matzot.	the Festival of Sukkot.

On it remember us, LORD our GOD, for good, recollect us for blessing, and deliver us for life. In accord with Your promise of salvation and compassion, spare us and be gracious to us; have compassion on us and deliver us, for our eyes are turned to You because You, GOD, are a gracious and compassionate King.

At this point in the silent *Amidah*, the individual can include any of his or her personal requests.

Blessing 17: Temple Service. The last three blessings, called by the Sages "Thanksgiving", are linked because they were said by the priests in the Temple (*Tamid* 5:1). This paragraph was originally a prayer that the day's sacrifices be accepted. The priests then said *Modim*, "We give thanks to You" and blessed the people. According to *Tosafot*, this means that they said the threefold Priestly Blessing, but ac-

וְתֶחֱזֶינָה עֵינֵינוּ בְּשׁוּבְךָ לְצִיּוֹן בְּרַחֲמִים. בָּרוּךְ אַתָּה יהוה, הַמַּחֲזִיר שְׁכִינָתוֹ לְצִיּוֹן.

הודאה

▽ Bow at the first five words.

▽**מוֹדִים** אֲנַחְנוּ לָךְ, שָׁאַתָּה הוּא יהוה אֱלֹהֵינוּ וֵאלֹהֵי אֲבוֹתֵינוּ לְעוֹלָם וָעֶד. צוּר חַיֵּינוּ, מָגֵן יִשְׁעֵנוּ אַתָּה הוּא לְדוֹר וָדוֹר. נוֹדֶה לְּךָ וּנְסַפֵּר תְּהִלָּתֶךָ עַל חַיֵּינוּ הַמְּסוּרִים בְּיָדֶךָ, וְעַל נִשְׁמוֹתֵינוּ הַפְּקוּדוֹת לָךְ, וְעַל נִסֶּיךָ שֶׁבְּכָל־יוֹם עִמָּנוּ, וְעַל נִפְלְאוֹתֶיךָ וְטוֹבוֹתֶיךָ שֶׁבְּכָל־עֵת, עֶרֶב וָבֹקֶר וְצָהֳרָיִם. הַטּוֹב כִּי לֹא־כָלוּ רַחֲמֶיךָ, וְהַמְרַחֵם כִּי לֹא־תַמּוּ חֲסָדֶיךָ, מֵעוֹלָם קִוִּינוּ לָךְ.

During the Leader's repetition, the Congregation says quietly:

▽**מוֹדִים** אֲנַחְנוּ לָךְ, שָׁאַתָּה הוּא יהוה אֱלֹהֵינוּ וֵאלֹהֵי אֲבוֹתֵינוּ, אֱלֹהֵי כָל־בָּשָׂר, יוֹצְרֵנוּ, יוֹצֵר בְּרֵאשִׁית. בְּרָכוֹת וְהוֹדָאוֹת לְשִׁמְךָ הַגָּדוֹל וְהַקָּדוֹשׁ, עַל שֶׁהֶחֱיִיתָנוּ וְקִיַּמְתָּנוּ. כֵּן תְּחַיֵּנוּ וּתְקַיְּמֵנוּ, וְתֶאֱסוֹף גָּלֻיּוֹתֵינוּ לְחַצְרוֹת קָדְשֶׁךָ, לִשְׁמוֹר חֻקֶּיךָ וְלַעֲשׂוֹת רְצוֹנֶךָ, וּלְעָבְדְּךָ בְּלֵבָב שָׁלֵם, עַל שֶׁאֲנַחְנוּ מוֹדִים לָךְ. בָּרוּךְ אֵל הַהוֹדָאוֹת.

On חֲנֻכָּה and פּוּרִים, say:

עַל הַנִּסִּים, וְעַל הַפֻּרְקָן, וְעַל הַגְּבוּרוֹת, וְעַל הַתְּשׁוּעוֹת, וְעַל הַמִּלְחָמוֹת, שֶׁעָשִׂיתָ לַאֲבוֹתֵינוּ בַּיָּמִים הָהֵם בַּזְּמַן הַזֶּה.

---

cording to Maimonides it means that they said the prayer beginning "Grant peace".

Blessing 18: *Thanksgiving.* The root *y-d-h* has three meanings: 1. to bow (see Targum to II Samuel 16:4), hence we bow at the beginning and end of this blessing; 2. to confess or profess; and 3. to thank. The blessing begins as a confession of faith, and moves to thanks for God's blessings which surround us continually. *For Your miracles which are with us every day* – Nachmanides explained the difference between a "revealed" and a "hidden" miracle. Revealed miracles stand outside the laws of nature; hidden miracles

וְתֶחֱזֶינָה And may our eyes witness Your return to Zion in compassion. Blessed are You, LORD, who restores His Presence to Zion.

THANKSGIVING

▽ Bow at the first nine words.

מוֹדִים▽ We give thanks to You, for You are the LORD our GOD and GOD of our ancestors for ever and all time. You are the Rock of our lives, Shield of our salvation from generation to generation. We will thank You and declare Your praise for our lives, which are entrusted into Your hand; our souls, which are placed in Your charge; for Your miracles which are with us every day; and for Your wonders and favours at all times, evening, morning and midday. You are good – for Your compassion never fails. You are compassionate – for Your lovingkindnesses never cease. We have always placed our hope in You.

During the Leader's repetition, the Congregation says quietly:

מוֹדִים▽ We give thanks to You, for You are the LORD our GOD and GOD of our ancestors, GOD of all flesh, who formed us and formed the universe. Blessings and thanks are due to Your great and holy name for giving us life and sustaining us. May You continue to give us life and sustain us; and may You gather our exiles to Your holy courts, to keep Your decrees, do Your will and serve You with a perfect heart, for it is for us to give You thanks. Blessed be GOD to whom thanksgiving is due.

On Chanukah and Purim, say:

עַל הַנִּסִּים [We thank You also] for the miracles, the redemption, the mighty deeds, and the victories in battle which You performed for our ancestors in those days at this time.

---

take place within them. GOD is present not only in signs and wonders, but also in the very laws that govern the universe. To see the miraculous in the everyday is part of the Judaic vision, beautifully expressed in these lines.

Blessing 19: Peace. Shalom means more than the English word "peace": it also means "completeness, perfection, harmonious interaction". The prophets of Israel were the first in history to conceive of peace as an ideal, most famously in the

On חֲנֻכָּה, say:

בִּימֵי מַתִּתְיָהוּ בֶּן־יוֹחָנָן כֹּהֵן גָּדוֹל חַשְׁמוֹנַאי וּבָנָיו, כְּשֶׁעָמְדָה מַלְכוּת יָוָן הָרְשָׁעָה עַל־עַמְּךָ יִשְׂרָאֵל, לְהַשְׁכִּיחָם תּוֹרָתֶךָ, וּלְהַעֲבִירָם מֵחֻקֵּי רְצוֹנֶךָ. וְאַתָּה בְּרַחֲמֶיךָ הָרַבִּים, עָמַדְתָּ לָהֶם בְּעֵת צָרָתָם, רַבְתָּ אֶת־רִיבָם, דַּנְתָּ אֶת־דִּינָם, נָקַמְתָּ אֶת־נִקְמָתָם. מָסַרְתָּ גִבּוֹרִים בְּיַד חַלָּשִׁים, וְרַבִּים בְּיַד מְעַטִּים, וּטְמֵאִים בְּיַד טְהוֹרִים, וּרְשָׁעִים בְּיַד צַדִּיקִים, וְזֵדִים בְּיַד עוֹסְקֵי תוֹרָתֶךָ. וּלְךָ עָשִׂיתָ שֵׁם גָּדוֹל וְקָדוֹשׁ בְּעוֹלָמֶךָ, וּלְעַמְּךָ יִשְׂרָאֵל עָשִׂיתָ תְּשׁוּעָה גְדוֹלָה וּפֻרְקָן כְּהַיּוֹם הַזֶּה. וְאַחַר כֵּן בָּאוּ בָנֶיךָ לִדְבִיר בֵּיתֶךָ, וּפִנּוּ אֶת־הֵיכָלֶךָ, וְטִהֲרוּ אֶת־מִקְדָּשֶׁךָ, וְהִדְלִיקוּ נֵרוֹת בְּחַצְרוֹת קָדְשֶׁךָ, וְקָבְעוּ שְׁמוֹנַת יְמֵי חֲנֻכָּה אֵלּוּ, לְהוֹדוֹת וּלְהַלֵּל לְשִׁמְךָ הַגָּדוֹל.

On פּוּרִים, say:

בִּימֵי מָרְדְּכַי וְאֶסְתֵּר בְּשׁוּשַׁן הַבִּירָה, כְּשֶׁעָמַד עֲלֵיהֶם הָמָן הָרָשָׁע, בִּקֵּשׁ לְהַשְׁמִיד לַהֲרוֹג וּלְאַבֵּד אֶת־כָּל־הַיְּהוּדִים, מִנַּעַר וְעַד זָקֵן, טַף וְנָשִׁים בְּיוֹם אֶחָד, בִּשְׁלוֹשָׁה־עָשָׂר לְחֹדֶשׁ שְׁנֵים־עָשָׂר, הוּא־חֹדֶשׁ אֲדָר, וּשְׁלָלָם לָבוֹז. וְאַתָּה בְּרַחֲמֶיךָ הָרַבִּים הֵפַרְתָּ אֶת־עֲצָתוֹ, וְקִלְקַלְתָּ אֶת־מַחֲשַׁבְתּוֹ, וַהֲשֵׁבוֹתָ גְּמוּלוֹ בְּרֹאשׁוֹ, וְתָלוּ אוֹתוֹ וְאֶת־בָּנָיו עַל־הָעֵץ.

וְעַל כֻּלָּם יִתְבָּרַךְ וְיִתְרוֹמַם שִׁמְךָ מַלְכֵּנוּ תָּמִיד לְעוֹלָם וָעֶד.

Between רֹאשׁ הַשָּׁנָה and יוֹם כִּפּוּר, say:

וּכְתוֹב לְחַיִּים טוֹבִים כָּל־בְּנֵי בְרִיתֶךָ.

וְכֹל הַחַיִּים יוֹדוּךָ סֶּלָה, וִיהַלְלוּ אֶת־שִׁמְךָ בֶּאֱמֶת, הָאֵל יְשׁוּעָתֵנוּ וְעֶזְרָתֵנוּ סֶלָה. ▾בָּרוּךְ אַתָּה יהוה, הַטּוֹב שִׁמְךָ וּלְךָ נָאֶה לְהוֹדוֹת.

On Chanukah, say:

בִּימֵי In the days of Mattityahu, son of Yochanan the High Priest, the Hasmonean, and his sons, the wicked Greek kingdom rose up against Your people Israel to make them forget Your Torah and to force them to transgress the statutes of Your will. It was then that You in Your great compassion stood by them in the time of their distress. You championed their cause, judged their claim, and avenged their wrong. You delivered the strong into the hands of the weak, the many into the hands of the few, the impure into the hands of the pure, the wicked into the hands of the righteous, and the arrogant into the hands of those who were engaged in the study of Your Torah. You made for Yourself great and holy renown in Your world, and for Your people Israel You performed a great salvation and redemption on this day. Your children then entered the holiest part of Your house, cleansed Your Temple, purified Your sanctuary, kindled lights in Your holy courts, and designated these eight days of Chanukah for giving thanks and praise to Your great name.

On Purim, say:

בִּימֵי In the days of Mordechai and Esther, in Shushan the capital, the wicked Haman rose up against them and sought to destroy, slay and exterminate all the Jews, young and old, children and women, on one day, the thirteenth day of the twelfth month, which is the month of Adar, and to plunder their possessions. Then You in Your great compassion thwarted his counsel, frustrated his plans, and caused his scheme to recoil on his own head, so that they hanged him and his sons on the gallows.

וְעַל For all these things may Your name be blessed and exalted, our King, continually, for ever and all time.

Between Rosh Hashanah and Yom Kippur, say:

And write, for a good life, all the children of Your covenant.

Let all that lives thank You, Selah! and praise Your name in truth, God, our Saviour and Help, Selah! ▾Blessed are You, Lord, whose name is "the Good" and to whom thanks are due.

During the repetition of the עֲמִידָה, the Leader says the following, except at a שִׁבְעָה and on תִּשְׁעָה בְּאָב:

אֱלֹהֵינוּ וֵאלֹהֵי אֲבוֹתֵינוּ, בָּרְכֵנוּ בַּבְּרָכָה הַמְשֻׁלֶּשֶׁת, בַּתּוֹרָה הַכְּתוּבָה עַל יְדֵי מֹשֶׁה עַבְדֶּךָ, הָאֲמוּרָה מִפִּי אַהֲרֹן וּבָנָיו כֹּהֲנִים, עַם קְדוֹשֶׁךָ, כָּאָמוּר.

יְבָרֶכְךָ יהוה, וְיִשְׁמְרֶךָ. (Cong.: כֵּן יְהִי רָצוֹן)

יָאֵר יהוה פָּנָיו אֵלֶיךָ וִיחֻנֶּךָּ. (Cong.: כֵּן יְהִי רָצוֹן)

יִשָּׂא יהוה פָּנָיו אֵלֶיךָ וְיָשֵׂם לְךָ שָׁלוֹם. (Cong.: כֵּן יְהִי רָצוֹן)

ברכת שלום

שִׂים שָׁלוֹם, טוֹבָה, וּבְרָכָה, חֵן, וָחֶסֶד וְרַחֲמִים עָלֵינוּ וְעַל כָּל־יִשְׂרָאֵל עַמֶּךָ. בָּרְכֵנוּ אָבִינוּ, כֻּלָּנוּ כְּאֶחָד בְּאוֹר פָּנֶיךָ, כִּי בְאוֹר פָּנֶיךָ נָתַתָּ לָּנוּ, יהוה אֱלֹהֵינוּ, תּוֹרַת חַיִּים וְאַהֲבַת חֶסֶד, וּצְדָקָה, וּבְרָכָה, וְרַחֲמִים, וְחַיִּים, וְשָׁלוֹם. וְטוֹב בְּעֵינֶיךָ לְבָרֵךְ אֶת־עַמְּךָ יִשְׂרָאֵל, בְּכָל־עֵת וּבְכָל־שָׁעָה בִּשְׁלוֹמֶךָ. *בָּרוּךְ אַתָּה יהוה, הַמְבָרֵךְ אֶת עַמּוֹ יִשְׂרָאֵל בַּשָּׁלוֹם.

*Between רֹאשׁ הַשָּׁנָה and יוֹם כִּפּוּר, substitute the following:

בְּסֵפֶר חַיִּים בְּרָכָה וְשָׁלוֹם, וּפַרְנָסָה טוֹבָה, נִזָּכֵר וְנִכָּתֵב לְפָנֶיךָ, אֲנַחְנוּ וְכָל־עַמְּךָ בֵּית יִשְׂרָאֵל, לְחַיִּים טוֹבִים וּלְשָׁלוֹם. בָּרוּךְ אַתָּה יהוה, עֹשֵׂה הַשָּׁלוֹם.

The Leader's repetition ends at this point.

אֱלֹהַי, נְצוֹר לְשׁוֹנִי מֵרָע, וּשְׂפָתַי מִדַּבֵּר מִרְמָה, וְלִמְקַלְלַי נַפְשִׁי תִדֹּם, וְנַפְשִׁי כֶּעָפָר לַכֹּל תִּהְיֶה. פְּתַח לִבִּי בְּתוֹרָתֶךָ,

words of Isaiah: "Nation shall not lift up sword against nation; neither shall they learn war anymore." Peace is the ultimate hope of monotheism, with its belief that the world is the product of a single will, not the blind clash of conflicting elements.

אֱלֹהַי *Guard my tongue*: A private medi-

During the repetition of the *Amidah*, the Leader says the following, except in a house of mourning during *shivah* week and on the Ninth of Av:

אֱלֹהֵינוּ Our God and God of our fathers, bless us with the threefold blessing in the Torah, written by the hand of Moses Your servant and pronounced by Aaron and his sons the priests, Your holy people, as it is said:

May the Lord bless you and protect you. (Cong.: May it be Your will.)

May the Lord make His face shine on you and be gracious to you. (Cong.: May it be Your will.)

May the Lord turn His face towards you, and give you peace. (Cong.: May it be Your will.)

PEACE

שִׂים Grant peace, goodness and blessing, grace, lovingkindness and compassion to us and all Israel Your people. Bless us, our Father, all as one, with the light of Your face, for by the light of Your face You have given us, Lord our God, the Torah of life and love of kindness, righteousness, blessing, compassion, life and peace. May it be good in Your eyes to bless Your people Israel at every time, in every hour, with Your peace. *Blessed are You, Lord, who blesses His people Israel with peace.

*Between Rosh Hashanah and Yom Kippur, substitute the following:

In the book of life, blessing, peace and prosperity, may we and all Your people the house of Israel be remembered and written before You for a good life, and for peace. Blessed are You, Lord, who makes peace.

The Leader's repetition ends at this point.

אֱלֹהַי My God, guard my tongue from evil and my lips from deceitful speech. To those who curse me, let my soul be silent; may

tation composed by the fourth-century scholar Mar son of Ravina. It beautifully mirrors the opening meditation, "O Lord, open my lips." Having asked God to teach us what to say in His presence, we now ask Him to teach us what *not* to say in the presence of other human beings. We ask for help not to respond in kind to those who seek our harm. "The way of the righteous is to suffer humiliation but not to inflict it; to hear themselves insulted but not to reply" (*Yoma* 23a).

וּבְמִצְוֹתֶיךָ תִּרְדּוֹף נַפְשִׁי. וְכׇל הַחוֹשְׁבִים עָלַי רָעָה, מְהֵרָה הָפֵר עֲצָתָם וְקַלְקֵל מַחֲשַׁבְתָּם. עֲשֵׂה לְמַעַן שְׁמֶךָ, עֲשֵׂה לְמַעַן יְמִינֶךָ, עֲשֵׂה לְמַעַן קְדֻשָּׁתֶךָ, עֲשֵׂה לְמַעַן תּוֹרָתֶךָ. לְמַעַן יֵחָלְצוּן יְדִידֶיךָ, הוֹשִׁיעָה יְמִינְךָ וַעֲנֵנִי. יִהְיוּ לְרָצוֹן אִמְרֵי־פִי וְהֶגְיוֹן לִבִּי לְפָנֶיךָ, יהוה צוּרִי וְגוֹאֲלִי.

Bow, take three steps back, then bow, first left, then right, then centre, while saying:

עֹשֶׂה שָׁלוֹם בִּמְרוֹמָיו, הוּא יַעֲשֶׂה שָׁלוֹם עָלֵינוּ, וְעַל־כׇּל־יִשְׂרָאֵל, וְאִמְרוּ אָמֵן.

יְהִי רָצוֹן מִלְּפָנֶיךָ יהוה אֱלֹהֵינוּ וֵאלֹהֵי אֲבוֹתֵינוּ, שֶׁיִּבָּנֶה בֵּית הַמִּקְדָּשׁ בִּמְהֵרָה בְיָמֵינוּ, וְתֵן חֶלְקֵנוּ בְּתוֹרָתֶךָ. וְשָׁם נַעֲבׇדְךָ בְּיִרְאָה, כִּימֵי עוֹלָם וּכְשָׁנִים קַדְמוֹנִיּוֹת. וְעָרְבָה לַיהוה מִנְחַת יְהוּדָה וִירוּשָׁלָיִם, כִּימֵי עוֹלָם וּכְשָׁנִים קַדְמוֹנִיּוֹת.

When praying with a מִנְיָן, the עֲמִידָה is repeated aloud by the Leader.

In emergencies and special cases of urgency only, the following short form of the עֲמִידָה may be said (though not when וְתֵן טַל וּמָטָר לִבְרָכָה is said).

First say from אֲדֹנָי on page 74 until הַקָּדוֹשׁ on page 80, then say:

הֲבִינֵנוּ יהוה אֱלֹהֵינוּ לָדַעַת דְּרָכֶיךָ, וּמוֹל אֶת לְבָבֵנוּ לְיִרְאָתֶךָ, וְתִסְלַח לָנוּ לִהְיוֹת גְּאוּלִים, וְרַחֲקֵנוּ מִמַּכְאוֹב, וְדַשְּׁנֵנוּ בִּנְאוֹת אַרְצֶךָ, וּנְפוּצוֹתֵינוּ מֵאַרְבַּע כַּנְפוֹת הָאָרֶץ תְּקַבֵּץ, וְהַתּוֹעִים עַל דַּעְתְּךָ יִשָּׁפֵטוּ, וְעַל הָרְשָׁעִים תָּנִיף יָדֶךָ, וְיִשְׂמְחוּ צַדִּיקִים בְּבִנְיַן עִירֶךָ וּבְתִקּוּן הֵיכָלֶךָ וּבִצְמִיחַת קֶרֶן לְדָוִד עַבְדֶּךָ וּבַעֲרִיכַת נֵר לְבֶן־יִשַׁי מְשִׁיחֶךָ, טֶרֶם נִקְרָא אַתָּה תַעֲנֶה. בָּרוּךְ אַתָּה יהוה, שׁוֹמֵעַ תְּפִלָּה.

Continue with רְצֵה on page 88 until קַדְמוֹנִיּוֹת on above.

On רֹאשׁ חֹדֶשׁ, חוֹל הַמּוֹעֵד, חֲנֻכָּה, יוֹם הָעַצְמָאוּת and יוֹם יְרוּשָׁלַיִם, say הַלֵּל on page 618.

LAWS OF SHORT FORM OF THE AMIDAH:
1. The shortened form is used only in cases of genuine emergency, for example, if there is no time to say the full *Amidah* with concentration, or in the case of one who is seriously ill.
2. It is not said on the evening after Shabbat or festivals, or when "Grant dew and rain" is said.

my soul be to all like the dust. Open my heart to Your Torah and let my soul pursue Your commandments. As for all who plan evil against me, swiftly thwart their counsel and frustrate their plans. Act for the sake of Your name; act for the sake of Your right hand; act for the sake of Your holiness; act for the sake of Your Torah. That Your beloved ones may be delivered, save with Your right hand and answer me. May the words of my mouth and the meditation of my heart find favour before You, LORD, my Rock and Redeemer.

Bow, take three steps back, then bow, first left, then right, then centre, while saying:

May He who makes peace in His high places, make peace for us and all Israel – and say: Amen.

יְהִי May it be Your will, LORD our GOD and GOD of our ancestors, that the Temple be rebuilt speedily in our days, and grant us a share in Your Torah. And there we will serve You with reverence, as in the days of old and as in former years. Then the offering of Judah and Jerusalem will be pleasing to the LORD as in the days of old and as in former years.

When praying with a *minyan*, the *Amidah* is repeated aloud by the Leader.

In emergencies and special cases of urgency only, the following short form of the *Amidah* may be said (though not when "Grant dew and rain" is said). First say from "O LORD" on page 75 until "the holy GOD" on page 81, then say:

הֲבִינֵנוּ Grant us understanding, LORD our GOD, to know Your ways. Sensitise our hearts so that we may revere You, and forgive us so that we may be redeemed. Keep us far from suffering and satisfy us with the pastures of Your land. Gather our scattered people from the four quarters of the earth. May those who go astray be judged according to Your will: raise Your hand against the wicked. May the righteous rejoice in the rebuilding of Your city, the restoration of Your Temple, the flowering of Your servant David's glory, and the radiant light of the son of Jesse, Your anointed. May You answer us even before we call. Blessed are You, LORD, who hears prayer.

Continue with "Find favour" on page 89 until "former years" on above.

On Rosh Chodesh, the Intermediate Days of Pesach and Sukkot, Chanukah, Yom Ha'Atzma'ut and Yom Yerushalayim, say *Hallel* on page 619.

אבינו מלכנו

Between רֹאשׁ הַשָּׁנָה and יוֹם כִּפּוּר (and in most congregations on Fast Days except תִּשְׁעָה בְּאָב), the following until וְהוֹשִׁיעֵנוּ on page 102 is said morning and afternoon. It is not said on Friday afternoon, שַׁבָּת, or the day before יוֹם כִּפּוּר, unless it is a Friday, in which case it is said in שַׁחֲרִית only.

The Ark is opened.

אָבִינוּ מַלְכֵּנוּ, חָטָאנוּ לְפָנֶיךָ.

אָבִינוּ מַלְכֵּנוּ, אֵין לָנוּ מֶלֶךְ אֶלָּא אָתָּה.

אָבִינוּ מַלְכֵּנוּ, עֲשֵׂה עִמָּנוּ לְמַעַן שְׁמֶךָ.

Between רֹאשׁ הַשָּׁנָה and יוֹם כִּפּוּר, say:

אָבִינוּ מַלְכֵּנוּ, חַדֵּשׁ עָלֵינוּ שָׁנָה טוֹבָה.

On Fast Days, say:

אָבִינוּ מַלְכֵּנוּ, בָּרֵךְ עָלֵינוּ שָׁנָה טוֹבָה.

אָבִינוּ מַלְכֵּנוּ, בַּטֵּל מֵעָלֵינוּ כָּל־גְּזֵרוֹת קָשׁוֹת.

אָבִינוּ מַלְכֵּנוּ, בַּטֵּל מַחְשְׁבוֹת שׂוֹנְאֵינוּ.

אָבִינוּ מַלְכֵּנוּ, הָפֵר עֲצַת אוֹיְבֵינוּ.

אָבִינוּ מַלְכֵּנוּ, כַּלֵּה כָּל צַר וּמַשְׂטִין מֵעָלֵינוּ.

אָבִינוּ מַלְכֵּנוּ, סְתוֹם פִּיּוֹת מַשְׂטִינֵנוּ וּמְקַטְרִיגֵנוּ.

אָבִינוּ מַלְכֵּנוּ, כַּלֵּה דֶּבֶר וְחֶרֶב וְרָעָב וּשְׁבִי וּמַשְׁחִית מִבְּנֵי בְרִיתֶךָ.

אָבִינוּ מַלְכֵּנוּ, מְנַע מַגֵּפָה מִנַּחֲלָתֶךָ.

אָבִינוּ מַלְכֵּנוּ, סְלַח וּמְחַל לְכָל־עֲוֹנוֹתֵינוּ.

אָבִינוּ מַלְכֵּנוּ, מְחֵה וְהַעֲבֵר פְּשָׁעֵינוּ וְחַטֹּאתֵינוּ מִנֶּגֶד עֵינֶיךָ.

אָבִינוּ מַלְכֵּנוּ, מְחוֹק בְּרַחֲמֶיךָ הָרַבִּים כָּל שִׁטְרֵי חוֹבוֹתֵינוּ.

AVINU MALKENU

Between Rosh Hashanah and Yom Kippur (and in most congregations on Fast Days except the Ninth of Av), the following until "and save us" on page 103 is said morning and afternoon. It is not said on Friday afternoon, Shabbat, or the day before Yom Kippur, unless it is a Friday, in which case it is said in the Morning Service only.

The Ark is opened.

אָבִינוּ מַלְכֵּנוּ Our Father, our King, we have sinned before You.
Our Father, our King, we have no king but You.
Our Father, our King, deal kindly with us for the sake of Your name.

Between Rosh Hashanah and Yom Kippur, say:
Our Father, our King, renew for us a good year.

On Fast Days, say:
Our Father our King, bless us with a good year.

Our Father, our King, nullify all harsh decrees against us.
Our Father, our King, nullify the plans of those who hate us.
Our Father, our King, thwart the counsel of our enemies.
Our Father, our King, rid us of every oppressor and adversary.
Our Father, our King, close the mouths of our adversaries and accusers.
Our Father, our King, eradicate pestilence, sword, famine, captivity and destruction from the people of Your covenant.
Our Father, our King, withhold the plague from Your heritage.
Our Father, our King, forgive and pardon all our iniquities.
Our Father, our King, wipe away and remove our transgressions and sins from Your sight.
Our Father, our King, erase in Your abundant mercy all records of our sins.

אָבִינוּ מַלְכֵּנוּ *Our Father, our King*: A prayer attributed, in its earliest form, to Rabbi Akiva. The opening two words juxtapose the two aspects of our relationship with God. He is our King and we are His subjects; He is our parent and we are His children. The first relationship is governed by justice, the second by love, compassion and forgiveness. By placing the words in the reverse order, we mirror both history and faith: history because God called us His children ("My child, My firstborn, Israel") at Mount Sinai before He became Israel's king; faith because we ask God to let His parental love temper the severity of justice.

The following verses are said responsively, first by the Leader, then by the Congregation:

אָבִינוּ מַלְכֵּנוּ, הַחֲזִירֵנוּ בִּתְשׁוּבָה שְׁלֵמָה לְפָנֶיךָ.
אָבִינוּ מַלְכֵּנוּ, שְׁלַח רְפוּאָה שְׁלֵמָה לְחוֹלֵי עַמֶּךָ.
אָבִינוּ מַלְכֵּנוּ, קְרַע רְוֹעַ גְּזַר דִּינֵנוּ.
אָבִינוּ מַלְכֵּנוּ, זָכְרֵנוּ בְּזִכְרוֹן טוֹב לְפָנֶיךָ.

Between רֹאשׁ הַשָּׁנָה and יוֹם כִּפּוּר, say:

אָבִינוּ מַלְכֵּנוּ, כָּתְבֵנוּ בְּסֵפֶר חַיִּים טוֹבִים.
אָבִינוּ מַלְכֵּנוּ, כָּתְבֵנוּ בְּסֵפֶר גְּאֻלָּה וִישׁוּעָה.
אָבִינוּ מַלְכֵּנוּ, כָּתְבֵנוּ בְּסֵפֶר פַּרְנָסָה וְכַלְכָּלָה.
אָבִינוּ מַלְכֵּנוּ, כָּתְבֵנוּ בְּסֵפֶר זְכֻיּוֹת.
אָבִינוּ מַלְכֵּנוּ, כָּתְבֵנוּ בְּסֵפֶר סְלִיחָה וּמְחִילָה.

On Fast Days, say:

אָבִינוּ מַלְכֵּנוּ, זָכְרֵנוּ לְחַיִּים טוֹבִים.
אָבִינוּ מַלְכֵּנוּ, זָכְרֵנוּ לִגְאֻלָּה וִישׁוּעָה.
אָבִינוּ מַלְכֵּנוּ, זָכְרֵנוּ לְפַרְנָסָה וְכַלְכָּלָה.
אָבִינוּ מַלְכֵּנוּ, זָכְרֵנוּ לִזְכֻיּוֹת.
אָבִינוּ מַלְכֵּנוּ, זָכְרֵנוּ לִסְלִיחָה וּמְחִילָה.

End of responsive reading.

אָבִינוּ מַלְכֵּנוּ, הַצְמַח לָנוּ יְשׁוּעָה בְּקָרוֹב.
אָבִינוּ מַלְכֵּנוּ, הָרֵם קֶרֶן יִשְׂרָאֵל עַמֶּךָ.
אָבִינוּ מַלְכֵּנוּ, הָרֵם קֶרֶן מְשִׁיחֶךָ.
אָבִינוּ מַלְכֵּנוּ, מַלֵּא יָדֵינוּ מִבִּרְכוֹתֶיךָ.
אָבִינוּ מַלְכֵּנוּ, מַלֵּא אֲסָמֵינוּ שָׂבָע.
אָבִינוּ מַלְכֵּנוּ, שְׁמַע קוֹלֵנוּ, חוּס וְרַחֵם עָלֵינוּ.
אָבִינוּ מַלְכֵּנוּ, קַבֵּל בְּרַחֲמִים וּבְרָצוֹן אֶת־תְּפִלָּתֵנוּ.
אָבִינוּ מַלְכֵּנוּ, פְּתַח שַׁעֲרֵי שָׁמַיִם לִתְפִלָּתֵנוּ.
אָבִינוּ מַלְכֵּנוּ, זְכוֹר כִּי עָפָר אֲנָחְנוּ.

The following verses are said responsively, first by the Leader, then by the Congregation:

Our Father, our King, bring us back to You in perfect repentance.
Our Father, our King, send a complete healing to the sick of Your people.
Our Father, our King, tear up the evil decree against us.
Our Father, our King, remember us with favour.

Between Rosh Hashanah and Yom Kippur, say:

Our Father, our King, write us in the book of good life.
Our Father, our King, write us in the book of redemption and salvation.
Our Father, our King, write us in the book of livelihood and sustenance.
Our Father, our King, write us in the book of merit.
Our Father, our King, write us in the book of pardon and forgiveness.

On Fast Days, say:

Our Father, our King, remember us for a good life.
Our Father, our King, remember us for redemption and salvation.
Our Father, our King, remember us for livelihood and sustenance.
Our Father, our King, remember us for merit.
Our Father, our King, remember us for pardon and forgiveness.

End of responsive reading.

Our Father, our King, let salvation soon flourish for us.
Our Father, our King, raise the honour of Your people Israel.
Our Father, our King, raise the honour of Your anointed.
Our Father, our King, fill our hands with Your blessings.
Our Father, our King, fill our storehouses with abundance.
Our Father, our King, hear our voice, pity and be compassionate to us.
Our Father, our King, accept, with compassion and favour, our prayer.
Our Father, our King, open the gates of heaven to our prayer.
Our Father, our King, please do not turn us away from You empty-handed.
Our Father, our King, remember that we are dust.

אָבִינוּ מַלְכֵּנוּ, נָא אַל תְּשִׁיבֵנוּ רֵיקָם מִלְּפָנֶיךָ.
אָבִינוּ מַלְכֵּנוּ, תְּהֵא הַשָּׁעָה הַזֹּאת שְׁעַת רַחֲמִים וְעֵת
רָצוֹן מִלְּפָנֶיךָ.
אָבִינוּ מַלְכֵּנוּ, חֲמוֹל עָלֵינוּ וְעַל עוֹלָלֵנוּ וְטַפֵּנוּ.
אָבִינוּ מַלְכֵּנוּ, עֲשֵׂה לְמַעַן הֲרוּגִים עַל שֵׁם קָדְשֶׁךָ.
אָבִינוּ מַלְכֵּנוּ, עֲשֵׂה לְמַעַן טְבוּחִים עַל יִחוּדֶךָ.
אָבִינוּ מַלְכֵּנוּ, עֲשֵׂה לְמַעַן בָּאֵי בָאֵשׁ וּבַמַּיִם עַל קִדּוּשׁ
שְׁמֶךָ.
אָבִינוּ מַלְכֵּנוּ, נְקוֹם לְעֵינֵינוּ נִקְמַת דַּם עֲבָדֶיךָ הַשָּׁפוּךְ.
אָבִינוּ מַלְכֵּנוּ, עֲשֵׂה לְמַעַנְךָ אִם לֹא לְמַעֲנֵנוּ.
אָבִינוּ מַלְכֵּנוּ, עֲשֵׂה לְמַעַנְךָ וְהוֹשִׁיעֵנוּ.
אָבִינוּ מַלְכֵּנוּ, עֲשֵׂה לְמַעַן רַחֲמֶיךָ הָרַבִּים.
אָבִינוּ מַלְכֵּנוּ, עֲשֵׂה לְמַעַן שִׁמְךָ הַגָּדוֹל הַגִּבּוֹר וְהַנּוֹרָא,
שֶׁנִּקְרָא עָלֵינוּ.
← אָבִינוּ מַלְכֵּנוּ, חָנֵּנוּ וַעֲנֵנוּ, כִּי אֵין בָּנוּ מַעֲשִׂים, עֲשֵׂה
עִמָּנוּ צְדָקָה וָחֶסֶד וְהוֹשִׁיעֵנוּ.

The Ark is closed.

TACHANUN: PLEADING WITH GOD

This section of the prayers, known as *Tachanun*, "plea", is a return to private prayer, which began with the silent *Amidah*. The Siddur preserves a careful balance between the two ways in which we address GOD: as individuals with our personal hopes and fears, and as members of a community whose fate and aspirations we share. First we pray individually (the silent *Amidah*), then communally (the Leader's repetition), then individually in *Tachanun* again.

Knowing that our time in the direct presence of the supreme King of kings is drawing to an end, we approach Him directly, seeking, as it were, a private audience. Our voices drop; we whisper our deepest thoughts; we express our feelings of inadequacy and vulnerability. We know we are unworthy: we say nothing in our defence except that we have absolute faith in GOD.

The word *Tachanun* derives from the root *ch-n-n* meaning "to show favour, to be gracious, to forgive". What differentiates *Tachanun* from other modes of prayer is the extent to which we emphasise our failings and our lack of good deeds. We express our dependence on GOD's unconditional grace and mercy.

Our Father, our King, may this moment be a moment of compassion and a time of favour before You.
Our Father, our King, have pity on us, our children and our infants.
Our Father, our King, act for the sake of those who were killed for Your holy name.
Our Father, our King, act for the sake of those who were slaughtered for proclaiming Your Unity.
Our Father, our King, act for the sake of those who went through fire and water to sanctify Your name.
Our Father, our King, avenge before our eyes the spilt blood of Your servants.
Our Father, our King, act for Your sake, if not for ours.
Our Father, our King, act for Your sake, and save us.
Our Father, our King, act for the sake of Your abundant compassion.
Our Father, our King, act for the sake of Your great, mighty and awesome name by which we are called.
→ Our Father, our King, be gracious to us and answer us, though we have no worthy deeds; act with us in charity and lovingkindness and save us.

The Ark is closed.

Tachanun is the chamber music rather than the symphony of the soul, and it has a unique intensity of tone.

The practice of following public prayer with private intercession goes back to Temple times. After the daily sacrifice, "The Levites sang the Psalm [of the day]. When they reached the end of each section [the Psalm was divided into three parts] they blew the shofar and the people prostrated themselves" (*Tamid* 7:3). Some communities continued the custom of prostration, with face to the ground, even after the destruction of the Temple. We preserve a trace of that gesture by resting our head on our arm and covering our faces as we say Psalm 6. The Reader's repetition of the *Amidah* stands in place of the daily sacrifice, which is why we subsequently "fall on our faces".

The custom of attaching special significance to Mondays and Thursdays is also ancient. Already in the Second Temple period, Mondays and Thursdays were days on which the pious would fast. According to tradition, Moses began his ascent of Mount Sinai to receive the second tablets on a Thursday and descended forty days later on a Monday (the tenth of Tishrei, Yom Kippur). The second tablets were a sign of God's forgiveness. Hence these days were seen as "days of favour". They were also market days when people would come from villages to towns. Congregations were larger; the Torah was read; law courts were in session. The

תחנון

תַּחֲנוּן is not said on the following mornings: 1. On שַׁבָּת or יוֹם טוֹב (including חוֹל הַמּוֹעֵד), רֹאשׁ חֹדֶשׁ, during the whole month of נִיסָן, on יוֹם הָעַצְמָאוּת, ל״ג בָּעֹמֶר, יוֹם יְרוּשָׁלַיִם and the first eight days of סִיוָן, on תִּשְׁעָה בְּאָב and ט״ו בְּאָב, from עֶרֶב רֹאשׁ הַשָּׁנָה, עֶרֶב יוֹם כִּפּוּר until and including the day after שִׂמְחַת תּוֹרָה, חֲנֻכָּה, ט״ו בִּשְׁבָט, פּוּרִים, שׁוּשָׁן פּוּרִים, and the 14th and 15th of אֲדָר רִאשׁוֹן in a Jewish leap year. 2. In the presence of a bridegroom on the day of his Wedding and for the subsequent six days. 3. In a house of mourning during the week of שִׁבְעָה. 4. On the occasion of a בְּרִית מִילָה, if prayers are said where the ceremony will take place later that day or if the father, סַנְדָּק or מוֹהֵל is present.

On Sundays, Tuesdays, Wednesdays and Fridays begin with, וַיֹּאמֶר דָּוִד on page 112.

On Mondays and Thursdays, say the following quietly while standing until וַיֹּאמֶר דָּוִד on page 112.

וְהוּא רַחוּם יְכַפֵּר עָוֹן וְלֹא יַשְׁחִית, וְהִרְבָּה לְהָשִׁיב אַפּוֹ וְלֹא יָעִיר כָּל חֲמָתוֹ. אַתָּה יהוה, לֹא תִכְלָא רַחֲמֶיךָ מִמֶּנּוּ, חַסְדְּךָ וַאֲמִתְּךָ תָּמִיד יִצְּרוּנוּ. הוֹשִׁיעֵנוּ יהוה אֱלֹהֵינוּ וְקַבְּצֵנוּ מִן הַגּוֹיִם, לְהוֹדוֹת לְשֵׁם קָדְשֶׁךָ, לְהִשְׁתַּבֵּחַ בִּתְהִלָּתֶךָ. אִם עֲוֹנוֹת תִּשְׁמָר־יָהּ אֲדֹנָי מִי יַעֲמֹד. כִּי עִמְּךָ הַסְּלִיחָה, לְמַעַן תִּוָּרֵא. לֹא כַחֲטָאֵינוּ תַּעֲשֶׂה־לָּנוּ, וְלֹא כַעֲוֹנוֹתֵינוּ תִּגְמֹל עָלֵינוּ. אִם עֲוֹנֵינוּ עָנוּ בָנוּ, יהוה עֲשֵׂה לְמַעַן שְׁמֶךָ. זְכֹר רַחֲמֶיךָ יהוה וַחֲסָדֶיךָ, כִּי מֵעוֹלָם הֵמָּה. יַעֲנֵנוּ יהוה בְּיוֹם צָרָה, יְשַׂגְּבֵנוּ שֵׁם אֱלֹהֵי יַעֲקֹב. יהוה הוֹשִׁיעָה, הַמֶּלֶךְ יַעֲנֵנוּ בְיוֹם קָרְאֵנוּ. אָבִינוּ מַלְכֵּנוּ חָנֵּנוּ

A tradition, found in the Gaonic literature, dates these prayers to the period of persecution under the Romans, when three exiles crossed the Mediterranean, found temporary refuge and then suffered renewed oppression. Some passages may have been added in the wake of the Gothic and Frankish persecutions in the seventh century. Their mood bespeaks the tears of Jews throughout the centuries of exile who experienced persecution, expulsion, humiliation, and often heightened atmosphere was the setting for more extended penitential prayer.

One of the classic biblical instances of supplication was Daniel's prayer on behalf of the exiles in Babylon (Daniel 9). Sections of that prayer, together with other verses from the prophetic books and Psalms, form the core of these paragraphs. There are three sections, each containing eighteen mentions of God's name: thus we say them quietly, standing, as if they were forms of the *Amidah*.

TACHANUN

Tachanun is not said on the following mornings: 1. On Shabbat or Festivals (including Intermediate Days), Rosh Chodesh, during the whole month of Nisan, on Yom Ha'Atzma'ut, Lag BaOmer and Yom Yerushalayim, the first eight days of Sivan, the Ninth of Av and the 15th of Av, the day before Rosh Hashanah, from the day before Yom Kippur until and including the day after Simchat Torah, Chanukah, the 15th of Shevat, Purim, Shushan Purim and the 14th and 15th of Adar Rishon in a Jewish leap year. 2. In the presence of a bridegroom on the day of his wedding and for the subsequent six days. 3. In a house of mourning during the week of *Shivah*. 4. On the occasion of a *Brit Milah*, if prayers are said where the ceremony will take place later that day or if the father, *sandek* or *mohel* is present.

On Sundays, Tuesdays, Wednesdays and Fridays, begin with "David said" on page 113.

On Mondays and Thursdays, say the following quietly while standing until "David said", on page 113.

וְהוּא רַחוּם He is compassionate. He forgives iniquity and does not destroy. Repeatedly He suppresses His anger, not rousing His full wrath. LORD, do not withhold Your compassion from us. May Your lovingkindness and truth always protect us. Save us, LORD our GOD, and gather us from among the nations, that we may give thanks to Your holy name and glory in Your praise. If You, LORD, were to keep account of sins, LORD, who could stand? But with You is forgiveness, that You may be revered. Do not deal with us according to our sins; do not repay us according to our iniquities. Though our iniquities testify against us, LORD, act for Your name's sake. Remember,

---

bloodshed at the hands of those amongst whom they lived. Even in times of freedom, we continue to say these prayers, keeping faith with our ancestors and remembering their tears.

What is remarkable about the prayers is the absence of anger or despair. If we ever doubt the power of prayer to transform the human situation, here we find an answer. Despite being treated as a pariah people, Jews never allowed themselves to be defined by their enemies. They wept and gave voice to pain: "GOD, see how low our glory has sunk among the nations. They abhor us as if we were impure." Yet they remained the people of the covenant, children of the Divine promise, unbroken and unbreakable. Prayer sustains hope, and hope defeats tragedy. In these profound and moving words, Jews found the strength to survive.

With its intense penitential mood, *Tachanun* is not said on days of festive joy; nor is it said on the Ninth of Av or in the house of a mourner.

וְהוּא רַחוּם *He is compassionate*: Penitential prayers woven from a variety of biblical texts, from Genesis and Exodus, Isaiah, Jeremiah and Joel, Lamentations,

וַעֲנֵנוּ, כִּי אֵין בָּנוּ מַעֲשִׂים, צְדָקָה עֲשֵׂה עִמָּנוּ לְמַעַן שְׁמֶךָ. אֲדוֹנֵינוּ אֱלֹהֵינוּ, שְׁמַע קוֹל תַּחֲנוּנֵינוּ, וּזְכָר־לָנוּ אֶת־בְּרִית אֲבוֹתֵינוּ וְהוֹשִׁיעֵנוּ לְמַעַן שְׁמֶךָ. וְעַתָּה אֲדֹנָי אֱלֹהֵינוּ, אֲשֶׁר הוֹצֵאתָ אֶת עַמְּךָ מֵאֶרֶץ מִצְרַיִם בְּיָד חֲזָקָה וַתַּעַשׂ־לְךָ שֵׁם כַּיּוֹם הַזֶּה, חָטָאנוּ רָשָׁעְנוּ. אֲדֹנָי, כְּכָל־צִדְקֹתֶיךָ יָשָׁב־נָא אַפְּךָ וַחֲמָתְךָ מֵעִירְךָ יְרוּשָׁלַיִם הַר קָדְשֶׁךָ, כִּי בַחֲטָאֵינוּ וּבַעֲוֹנוֹת אֲבוֹתֵינוּ, יְרוּשָׁלַיִם וְעַמְּךָ לְחֶרְפָּה לְכָל־סְבִיבוֹתֵינוּ. וְעַתָּה שְׁמַע אֱלֹהֵינוּ אֶל תְּפִלַּת עַבְדְּךָ וְאֶל תַּחֲנוּנָיו, וְהָאֵר פָּנֶיךָ עַל מִקְדָּשְׁךָ הַשָּׁמֵם, לְמַעַן אֲדֹנָי.

הַטֵּה אֱלֹהַי אָזְנְךָ וּשְׁמָע, פְּקַח עֵינֶיךָ וּרְאֵה שֹׁמְמֹתֵינוּ, וְהָעִיר אֲשֶׁר נִקְרָא שִׁמְךָ עָלֶיהָ, כִּי לֹא עַל צִדְקוֹתֵינוּ אֲנַחְנוּ מַפִּילִים תַּחֲנוּנֵינוּ לְפָנֶיךָ, כִּי עַל רַחֲמֶיךָ הָרַבִּים. אֲדֹנָי שְׁמָעָה, אֲדֹנָי סְלָחָה, אֲדֹנָי הַקְשִׁיבָה וַעֲשֵׂה, אַל תְּאַחַר, לְמַעַנְךָ אֱלֹהַי, כִּי שִׁמְךָ נִקְרָא עַל עִירְךָ וְעַל עַמֶּךָ. אָבִינוּ הָאָב הָרַחֲמָן, הַרְאֵנוּ אוֹת לְטוֹבָה וְקַבֵּץ נְפוּצוֹתֵינוּ מֵאַרְבַּע כַּנְפוֹת הָאָרֶץ, יַכִּירוּ וְיֵדְעוּ כָּל־הַגּוֹיִם, כִּי אַתָּה יהוה אֱלֹהֵינוּ. וְעַתָּה יהוה אָבִינוּ אָתָּה, אֲנַחְנוּ הַחֹמֶר וְאַתָּה יֹצְרֵנוּ, וּמַעֲשֵׂה יָדְךָ כֻּלָּנוּ. הוֹשִׁיעֵנוּ לְמַעַן שְׁמֶךָ, צוּרֵנוּ מַלְכֵּנוּ וְגוֹאֲלֵנוּ. חוּסָה יהוה עַל־עַמֶּךָ וְאַל־תִּתֵּן נַחֲלָתְךָ לְחֶרְפָּה לִמְשָׁל־בָּם גּוֹיִם. לָמָּה יֹאמְרוּ בָעַמִּים, אַיֵּה

Daniel and Psalms. Lacking a Temple and sacrifices, we offer God our tears in their place: "The sacrifices of God are a broken spirit; a broken and humbled heart, God, You will not despise" (Psalm 51:19).

וְעַתָּה *And now*: A prayer uttered by Daniel (9:15–19) in the first year of the reign of Xerxes, when he foresaw that the desolation of Jerusalem would last for seventy years. Fasting, dressed in sackcloth and ashes, he pleaded to God to forgive the people and bring an end to their suffering. These words play a key part in the *Selichot* (penitential prayers) on Fast Days.

אֲנַחְנוּ הַחֹמֶר *We are the clay and You are our potter*: A verse from Isaiah (64:7)

LORD, Your compassion and lovingkindness, for they are everlasting. May the LORD answer us when we are in distress; may the name of Jacob's GOD protect us. LORD, save. May the King answer us when we call. Our Father, our King, be gracious to us and answer us, though we have no worthy deeds; act charitably with us for Your name's sake. LORD our GOD, hear the sound of our pleas. Remember for us the covenant of our ancestors, and save us for Your name's sake. And now, My LORD, our GOD, who took Your people out of the land of Egypt with a mighty hand, creating for Yourself renown to this day: we have sinned and acted wrongly. LORD, in keeping with all Your righteousness, please turn Your wrath and anger away from Jerusalem, Your holy mountain. Because of our sins and the iniquities of our ancestors, Jerusalem and Your people have become the scorn of all those around us. And now, our GOD, heed Your servant's prayer and pleas, and let Your face shine on Your desolate Sanctuary, for Your sake, O LORD.

Incline Your ear, my GOD, and hear. Open Your eyes and see our desolation and that of the city called by Your name. Not because of our righteousness do we lay our pleas before You, but because of Your great compassion. LORD, hear! LORD, forgive! LORD, listen and act! Do not delay – for Your sake, my GOD, because Your city and Your people are called by Your name. Our Father, compassionate Father, show us a sign for good, and gather our scattered ones from the four quarters of the earth. Let all the nations recognise and know that You are the LORD our GOD. And now, LORD, You are our Father. We are the clay and You are our potter; we are all the work of Your hand. Save us for the sake of Your name, our Rock, our King and our Redeemer. Pity Your people, LORD. Let not Your heritage become an object of scorn, a byword among nations. Why should they say among the

---

which became the basis of one of the liturgical poems on *Kol Nidrei* night. The passage weaves together three appeals to GOD's compassion: 1. we are Your children and You our parent: have mercy on us as a parent forgives a child; 2. we are Your creation and You are our Creator: save us as an artist saves his most precious works of art; 3. we are Your witnesses, bearers of Your name: therefore save us for the sake of Your name. Let not the nations say, seeing our suffering, "Where is GOD?"

אֱלֹהֵיהֶם. יָדַעְנוּ כִּי חָטָאנוּ וְאֵין מִי יַעֲמֹד בַּעֲדֵנוּ, שִׁמְךָ הַגָּדוֹל יַעֲמָד־לָנוּ בְּעֵת צָרָה. יָדַעְנוּ כִּי אֵין בָּנוּ מַעֲשִׂים, צְדָקָה עֲשֵׂה עִמָּנוּ לְמַעַן שְׁמֶךָ. כְּרַחֵם אָב עַל בָּנִים, כֵּן תְּרַחֵם יהוה עָלֵינוּ, וְהוֹשִׁיעֵנוּ לְמַעַן שְׁמֶךָ. חֲמֹל עַל־עַמֶּךָ, רַחֵם עַל נַחֲלָתֶךָ, חוּסָה נָּא כְּרֹב רַחֲמֶיךָ. חָנֵּנוּ וַעֲנֵנוּ, כִּי לְךָ יהוה הַצְּדָקָה, עֹשֵׂה נִפְלָאוֹת בְּכָל־עֵת.

הַבֶּט־נָא רַחֶם־נָא עַל עַמְּךָ מְהֵרָה לְמַעַן שְׁמֶךָ. בְּרַחֲמֶיךָ הָרַבִּים, יהוה אֱלֹהֵינוּ, חוּס וְרַחֵם וְהוֹשִׁיעָה צֹאן מַרְעִיתֶךָ, וְאַל יִמְשָׁל בָּנוּ קֶצֶף, כִּי לְךָ עֵינֵינוּ תְלוּיוֹת. הוֹשִׁיעֵנוּ לְמַעַן שְׁמֶךָ, רַחֵם עָלֵינוּ לְמַעַן בְּרִיתֶךָ. הַבִּיטָה וַעֲנֵנוּ בְּעֵת צָרָה, כִּי לְךָ יהוה הַיְשׁוּעָה. בְּךָ תוֹחַלְתֵּנוּ, אֱלוֹהַּ סְלִיחוֹת, אָנָּא סְלַח נָא אֵל טוֹב וְסַלָּח, כִּי אֵל מֶלֶךְ חַנּוּן וְרַחוּם אָתָּה.

אָנָּא מֶלֶךְ חַנּוּן וְרַחוּם, זְכוֹר וְהַבֵּט לִבְרִית בֵּין הַבְּתָרִים, וְתֵרָאֶה לְפָנֶיךָ עֲקֵדַת יָחִיד לְמַעַן יִשְׂרָאֵל. אָבִינוּ מַלְכֵּנוּ חָנֵּנוּ וַעֲנֵנוּ, כִּי שִׁמְךָ הַגָּדוֹל נִקְרָא עָלֵינוּ, עֹשֵׂה נִפְלָאוֹת בְּכָל־עֵת, עֲשֵׂה עִמָּנוּ כְּחַסְדֶּךָ. חַנּוּן וְרַחוּם, הַבִּיטָה וַעֲנֵנוּ בְּעֵת צָרָה, כִּי לְךָ יהוה הַיְשׁוּעָה. אָבִינוּ מַלְכֵּנוּ, מַחֲסֵנוּ, אַל תַּעַשׂ עִמָּנוּ כְּרֹעַ מַעֲלָלֵינוּ. זְכֹר רַחֲמֶיךָ יהוה וַחֲסָדֶיךָ, וּכְרֹב טוּבְךָ הוֹשִׁיעֵנוּ וַחֲמָל־נָא עָלֵינוּ, כִּי אֵין לָנוּ אֱלוֹהַּ אַחֵר מִבַּלְעָדֶיךָ צוּרֵנוּ. אַל תַּעַזְבֵנוּ יהוה אֱלֹהֵינוּ, אַל תִּרְחַק מִמֶּנּוּ, כִּי נַפְשֵׁנוּ קָצְרָה מֵחֶרֶב וּמִשְּׁבִי וּמִדֶּבֶר וּמִמַּגֵּפָה וּמִכָּל־צָרָה וְיָגוֹן. הַצִּילֵנוּ, כִּי לְךָ קִוִּינוּ, וְאַל־תַּכְלִימֵנוּ יהוה אֱלֹהֵינוּ. וְהָאֵר פָּנֶיךָ בָּנוּ, וּזְכָר לָנוּ אֶת בְּרִית אֲבוֹתֵינוּ, וְהוֹשִׁיעֵנוּ לְמַעַן שְׁמֶךָ. רְאֵה בְצָרוֹתֵינוּ וּשְׁמַע קוֹל תְּפִלָּתֵנוּ, כִּי אַתָּה שׁוֹמֵעַ תְּפִלַּת כָּל־פֶּה.

peoples, "Where is their God?" We know we have sinned and that there is no-one to stand up for us. Let Your great name stand up for us in time of trouble. We know we have no merits of our own: therefore deal with us charitably for Your name's sake. As a father has compassion on his children, so, Lord, have compassion on us, and save us for the sake of Your name. Have mercy on Your people; have compassion for Your heritage; take pity in Your great compassion. Be gracious to us and answer us, for righteousness is Yours, Lord. Always You do wondrous things.

Please look, please swiftly have compassion for Your people for Your name's sake. In Your great compassion, Lord our God, have pity and compassion, and rescue the flock You tend. Let us not be ruled by wrath, for our eyes are turned towards You. Save us for Your name's sake. Have compassion on us for the sake of Your covenant. Look and answer us in time of trouble, for Yours, Lord, is the power to save. Our hope is in You, God of forgiveness. Please forgive, good and forgiving God, for You are a gracious, compassionate God and King.

Please, gracious and compassionate King, remember and call to mind the Covenant between the Pieces [with Abraham] and let the binding of his only son [Isaac] appear before You for Israel's sake. Our Father, our King, be gracious to us and answer us, for we are called by Your great name. You who work miracles at all times, deal with us according to Your lovingkindness. Gracious and compassionate One, look and answer us in time of trouble, for salvation is Yours, Lord. Our Father, our King, our Refuge, do not act with us according to our evil deeds. Remember, Lord, Your tender mercies and Your love. Save us in Your great goodness, and have mercy on us, for we have no other God but You, our Rock. Do not abandon us, Lord our God, do not be distant from us, for we are worn out by the sword and captivity, pestilence and plague, and by every trouble and sorrow. Rescue us, for in You lies our hope. Put us not to shame, Lord our God. Let Your face shine upon us. Remember for us the covenant of our ancestors and save us for Your name's sake. See our troubles and heed the voice of our prayer, for You heed the prayer of every mouth.

אֵל רַחוּם וְחַנּוּן, רַחֵם עָלֵינוּ וְעַל־כָּל־מַעֲשֶׂיךָ, כִּי אֵין כָּמְוֹךָ. יהוה אֱלֹהֵינוּ, אָנָּא שָׂא נָא פְשָׁעֵינוּ. אָבִינוּ מַלְכֵּנוּ צוּרֵנוּ וְגוֹאֲלֵנוּ, אֵל חַי וְקַיָּם הַחֲסִין בַּכֹּחַ, חָסִיד וָטוֹב עַל כָּל מַעֲשֶׂיךָ, כִּי אַתָּה הוּא יהוה אֱלֹהֵינוּ. אֵל אֶרֶךְ אַפַּיִם וּמָלֵא רַחֲמִים, עֲשֵׂה עִמָּנוּ כְּרֹב רַחֲמֶיךָ, וְהוֹשִׁיעֵנוּ לְמַעַן שְׁמֶךָ. שְׁמַע מַלְכֵּנוּ תְּפִלָּתֵנוּ, וּמִיַּד אוֹיְבֵינוּ הַצִּילֵנוּ. שְׁמַע מַלְכֵּנוּ תְּפִלָּתֵנוּ וּמִכָּל־צָרָה וְיָגוֹן הַצִּילֵנוּ. אָבִינוּ מַלְכֵּנוּ אַתָּה, וְשִׁמְךָ עָלֵינוּ נִקְרָא, אַל תַּנִּיחֵנוּ. אַל תַּעַזְבֵנוּ אָבִינוּ, וְאַל תִּטְּשֵׁנוּ בּוֹרְאֵנוּ, וְאַל תִּשְׁכָּחֵנוּ יוֹצְרֵנוּ, כִּי אֵל מֶלֶךְ חַנּוּן וְרַחוּם אָתָּה.

אֵין כָּמְוֹךָ חַנּוּן וְרַחוּם יהוה אֱלֹהֵינוּ, אֵין כָּמְוֹךָ אֵל אֶרֶךְ אַפַּיִם וְרַב חֶסֶד וֶאֱמֶת. הוֹשִׁיעֵנוּ בְּרַחֲמֶיךָ הָרַבִּים, מֵרַעַשׁ וּמֵרֹגֶז הַצִּילֵנוּ. זְכֹר לַעֲבָדֶיךָ לְאַבְרָהָם לְיִצְחָק וּלְיַעֲקֹב, אַל־תֵּפֶן אֶל־קָשְׁיֵנוּ וְאֶל־רִשְׁעֵנוּ וְאֶל־חַטָּאתֵנוּ. שׁוּב מֵחֲרוֹן אַפֶּךָ וְהִנָּחֵם עַל־הָרָעָה לְעַמֶּךָ. וְהָסֵר מִמֶּנּוּ מַכַּת הַמָּוֶת כִּי רַחוּם אָתָּה, כִּי כֵן דַּרְכֶּךָ, עֹשֶׂה חֶסֶד חִנָּם בְּכָל־דּוֹר וָדוֹר. חוּסָה יהוה עַל־עַמֶּךָ וְהַצִּילֵנוּ מִזַּעְמֶךָ, וְהָסֵר מִמֶּנּוּ מַכַּת הַמַּגֵּפָה וּגְזֵרָה קָשָׁה, כִּי אַתָּה שׁוֹמֵר יִשְׂרָאֵל. לְךָ אֲדֹנָי הַצְּדָקָה וְלָנוּ בֹּשֶׁת הַפָּנִים. מַה־נִּתְאוֹנֵן, וּמַה־נֹּאמַר, מַה־נְּדַבֵּר, וּמַה־נִּצְטַדָּק. נַחְפְּשָׂה דְרָכֵינוּ וְנַחְקֹרָה, וְנָשְׁוּבָה אֵלֶיךָ, כִּי יְמִינְךָ פְשׁוּטָה לְקַבֵּל שָׁבִים. אָנָּא יהוה הוֹשִׁיעָה נָּא, אָנָּא יהוה הַצְלִיחָה נָא. אָנָּא יהוה עֲנֵנוּ בְיוֹם קָרְאֵנוּ. לְךָ יהוה חִכִּינוּ, לְךָ יהוה קִוִּינוּ, לְךָ יהוה נְיַחֵל. אַל־תֶּחֱשֶׁה וּתְעַנֵּנוּ, כִּי נָאֲמוּ גוֹיִם, אָבְדָה תִקְוָתָם. כָּל־בֶּרֶךְ וְכָל־קוֹמָה לְךָ לְבַד תִּשְׁתַּחֲוֶה.

O Compassionate and gracious God, have compassion on us and on all Your works, for there is none like You, Lord our God. Please, we beg You, forgive our sins, our Father, our King, our Rock, our Redeemer, living and eternal God, mighty in strength, loving and good to all Your works, for You are the Lord our God. O God, slow to anger and full of compassion, act with us according to Your great compassion and save us for Your name's sake. Hear our prayer, our King, and save us from our enemies' hands. Heed our prayer, our King, and save us from all distress and sorrow. You are our Father, our King. We are called by Your name. Do not desert us. Do not abandon us, our Father. Do not cast us away, our Creator. Do not forget us, our Maker – for You are a gracious and compassionate God and King.

There is none like You in grace and compassion, Lord our God. There is none like You, God, slow to anger and abounding in lovingkindness and truth. Save us in Your great compassion; rescue us from storm and turmoil. Remember Your servants Abraham, Isaac and Jacob; do not attend to our stubbornness, wickedness and sinfulness. Turn from Your fierce anger, and relent from the evil meant for Your people. Remove from us the scourge of death, for You are compassionate. This is Your way, to show unearned lovingkindness to every generation. Have pity on Your people, Lord, and save us from Your wrath. Remove from us the scourge of plague and the harsh decree, for You are the Guardian of Israel. You are right, my Lord, and we are shamefaced. How can we complain? What can we say? What can we plead? How can we justify ourselves? Let us search our ways and examine them and return to You, for Your right hand is outstretched to receive those who return. Please, Lord, please save. Please, Lord, please send success. Please, Lord, answer us when we call. For You, Lord, we wait. For You, Lord, we hope. For You, Lord, we long. Do not be silent while we suffer, for the nations are saying, "Their hope is lost." To You alone every knee must bend, and those who hold themselves high bow down.

הַפּוֹתֵחַ יָד בִּתְשׁוּבָה לְקַבֵּל פּוֹשְׁעִים וְחַטָּאִים, נִבְהֲלָה
נַפְשֵׁנוּ מֵרֹב עִצְבוֹנֵנוּ, אַל תִּשְׁכָּחֵנוּ נֶצַח. קוּמָה וְהוֹשִׁיעֵנוּ,
כִּי חָסִינוּ בָךְ. אָבִינוּ מַלְכֵּנוּ, אִם אֵין בָּנוּ צְדָקָה וּמַעֲשִׂים
טוֹבִים, זְכָר־לָנוּ אֶת־בְּרִית אֲבוֹתֵינוּ וְעֵדוּתֵינוּ בְּכָל יוֹם,
יהוה אֶחָד. הַבִּיטָה בְעָנְיֵנוּ כִּי רַבּוּ מַכְאוֹבֵינוּ וְצָרוֹת לְבָבֵנוּ.
חוּסָה יהוה עָלֵינוּ בְּאֶרֶץ שִׁבְיֵנוּ וְאַל־תִּשְׁפּוֹךְ חֲרוֹנְךָ עָלֵינוּ,
כִּי אֲנַחְנוּ עַמְּךָ בְּנֵי בְרִיתֶךָ. אֵל, הַבִּיטָה דַּל כְּבוֹדֵנוּ בַּגּוֹיִם,
וְשִׁקְּצוּנוּ כְּטֻמְאַת הַנִּדָּה. עַד־מָתַי עֻזְּךָ בַּשֶּׁבִי, וְתִפְאַרְתְּךָ
בְּיַד־צָר. עוֹרְרָה גְבוּרָתְךָ וְקִנְאָתְךָ עַל אוֹיְבֶיךָ. הֵם יֵבֹשׁוּ
וְיֵחַתּוּ מִגְּבוּרָתָם, וְאַל יִמְעֲטוּ לְפָנֶיךָ תְּלָאוֹתֵינוּ. מַהֵר
יְקַדְּמוּנוּ רַחֲמֶיךָ בְּיוֹם צָרָתֵנוּ, וְאִם־לֹא לְמַעֲנֵנוּ, לְמַעַנְךָ
פְעַל, וְאַל־תַּשְׁחִית זֵכֶר שְׁאֵרִיתֵנוּ. וְחֹן אֹם הַמְיַחֲדִים שִׁמְךָ
פַּעֲמַיִם בְּכָל־יוֹם תָּמִיד בְּאַהֲבָה וְאוֹמְרִים, שְׁמַע יִשְׂרָאֵל
יהוה אֱלֹהֵינוּ יהוה אֶחָד.

נפילת אפים

On Sundays, Tuesdays, Wednesdays and Fridays, begin here. The following, until לֹא נֵדַע on page 118, is said sitting. When praying in a place where there is a סֵפֶר תּוֹרָה, one should rest one's head on the arm on which the תְּפִלִּין are not worn.

וַיֹּאמֶר דָּוִד אֶל־גָּד, צַר־לִי מְאֹד, נִפְּלָה־נָּא בְיַד־יהוה, כִּי־
רַבִּים רַחֲמָיו, וּבְיַד אָדָם אַל־אֶפֹּלָה. רַחוּם וְחַנּוּן חָטָאתִי
לְפָנֶיךָ. יהוה מָלֵא רַחֲמִים, רַחֵם עָלַי וְקַבֵּל תַּחֲנוּנָי.

תהילים ו:ב–יא

יהוה, אַל־בְּאַפְּךָ תוֹכִיחֵנִי, וְאַל־בַּחֲמָתְךָ תְיַסְּרֵנִי. חָנֵּנִי
יהוה, כִּי־אֻמְלַל אָנִי, רְפָאֵנִי יהוה, כִּי נִבְהֲלוּ עֲצָמָי. וְנַפְשִׁי

הַפּוֹתֵחַ יָד *You who hold out an open hand*: God's forgiveness stretches beyond strict retribution: "I do not desire the death of the wicked, but rather that they turn from their ways and live" (Ezekiel 33:11).

וַיֹּאמֶר דָּוִד *David said to Gad*: Words spoken by David during a moment of crisis (II Samuel 24). The king had sinned by taking a census of the people. God, through the prophet Gad, offered him a

You who hold out an open hand of repentance to receive transgressors and sinners – our soul is overwhelmed by our great sorrow. Do not forget us for ever. Arise and save us, for we seek refuge in You. Our Father, our King, though we lack righteousness and good deeds, remember for us the covenant of our fathers, and our testimonies daily that "The LORD is One." Look on our affliction, for many are our sufferings and heartaches. Have pity on us, LORD, in the land of our captivity. Do not pour out Your wrath on us, for we are Your people, the children of Your covenant. GOD, see how low our glory has sunk among the nations. They abhor us as if we were impure. How long will Your strength be captive, and Your glory in the hand of the foe? Arouse Your strength and zeal against Your enemies. Let them be shamed and deprived of power. Let not our hardships seem small to You. Swiftly may Your compassion reach us in the day of our distress. If not for our sake, act for Yours, so that the memory of our survivors be not destroyed. Be gracious to the nation who, in constant love, proclaim twice daily the unity of Your name, saying, "Listen, Israel, the LORD is our GOD, the LORD is One."

LOWERING THE HEAD

On Sundays, Tuesdays, Wednesdays and Fridays, begin here. The following, until "what to do" on page 119, is said sitting. When praying in a place where there is a Torah scroll, one should rest one's head on the arm on which the *tefillin* are not worn.

וַיֹּאמֶר דָּוִד David said to Gad, "I am in great distress. Let us fall into GOD's hand, for His mercy is great; but do not let me fall into the hand of man." Compassionate and gracious One, I have sinned before You. LORD, full of compassion, have compassion on me and accept my pleas.

PSALM 6:2–11

LORD, do not rebuke me in Your anger or chastise me in Your wrath. Be gracious to me, LORD, for I am weak. Heal me, LORD, for my bones

---

choice: famine, war, or punishment directly from heaven. David replied: it is better to be punished by GOD than suffer the cruelty of man.

LORD, do not rebuke me: A psalm of intense emotional power, spoken out of fear's heart of darkness. *The LORD has heard my pleas* – from the deepest pain, strength is born, when prayer becomes the ladder on which we climb from the pit of despair to the free air of hope.

נִבְהֲלָה מְאֹד, וְאַתָּה יהוה, עַד־מָתָי. שׁוּבָה יהוה, חַלְּצָה נַפְשִׁי, הוֹשִׁיעֵנִי לְמַעַן חַסְדֶּךָ. כִּי אֵין בַּמָּוֶת זִכְרֶךָ, בִּשְׁאוֹל מִי יוֹדֶה־לָּךְ. יָגַעְתִּי בְּאַנְחָתִי, אַשְׂחֶה בְכָל־לַיְלָה מִטָּתִי, בְּדִמְעָתִי עַרְשִׂי אַמְסֶה. עָשְׁשָׁה מִכַּעַס עֵינִי, עָתְקָה בְּכָל־צוֹרְרָי. סוּרוּ מִמֶּנִּי כָּל־פֹּעֲלֵי אָוֶן, כִּי שָׁמַע יהוה קוֹל בִּכְיִי. שָׁמַע יהוה תְּחִנָּתִי, יהוה תְּפִלָּתִי יִקָּח. יֵבֹשׁוּ וְיִבָּהֲלוּ מְאֹד כָּל־אֹיְבָי, יָשֻׁבוּ יֵבֹשׁוּ רָגַע.

Sit upright. On Mondays and Thursdays, say the following.

On Sundays, Tuesdays, Wednesdays and Fridays, continue with שׁוֹמֵר יִשְׂרָאֵל on page 116.

יהוה אֱלֹהֵי יִשְׂרָאֵל, שׁוּב מֵחֲרוֹן אַפֶּךָ וְהִנָּחֵם עַל הָרָעָה לְעַמֶּךָ.

הַבֵּט מִשָּׁמַיִם וּרְאֵה כִּי הָיִינוּ לַעַג וָקֶלֶס בַּגּוֹיִם, נֶחְשַׁבְנוּ כַּצֹּאן לַטֶּבַח יוּבָל, לַהֲרוֹג וּלְאַבֵּד וּלְמַכָּה וּלְחֶרְפָּה. וּבְכָל־זֹאת שִׁמְךָ לֹא שָׁכָחְנוּ, נָא אַל תִּשְׁכָּחֵנוּ.

יהוה אֱלֹהֵי יִשְׂרָאֵל, שׁוּב מֵחֲרוֹן אַפֶּךָ וְהִנָּחֵם עַל הָרָעָה לְעַמֶּךָ.

זָרִים אוֹמְרִים אֵין תּוֹחֶלֶת וְתִקְוָה, חֹן אֹם לְשִׁמְךָ מְקַוֶּה, טָהוֹר יְשׁוּעָתֵנוּ קָרְבָה, יָגַעְנוּ וְלֹא הוּנַח לָנוּ, רַחֲמֶיךָ יִכְבְּשׁוּ אֶת־כַּעַסְךָ מֵעָלֵינוּ. אָנָּא שׁוּב מֵחֲרוֹנְךָ, וְרַחֵם סְגֻלָּה אֲשֶׁר בָּחָרְתָּ.

יהוה אֱלֹהֵי יִשְׂרָאֵל, שׁוּב מֵחֲרוֹן אַפֶּךָ וְהִנָּחֵם עַל הָרָעָה לְעַמֶּךָ.

חוּסָה יהוה עָלֵינוּ בְּרַחֲמֶיךָ, וְאַל־תִּתְּנֵנוּ בִּידֵי אַכְזָרִים. לָמָּה יֹאמְרוּ הַגּוֹיִם אַיֵּה נָא אֱלֹהֵיהֶם, לְמַעַנְךָ עֲשֵׂה עִמָּנוּ

הַבֵּט מִשָּׁמַיִם *Look down from heaven*: These heart-rending words were already known in Europe in the eleventh century, and recall the terrible persecutions Jews suffered during the early Middle Ages.

וּבְכָל־זֹאת *Yet, despite all this*: After the

are in agony. My soul is in anguish, and You, O LORD – how long? Turn, LORD, set my soul free; save me for the sake of Your love. For no-one remembers You when he is dead. Who can praise You from the grave? I am weary with my sighing. Every night I drench my bed, I soak my couch with my tears. My eye grows dim from grief, worn out because of all my foes. Leave me, all you evildoers, for the LORD has heard the sound of my weeping. The LORD has heard my pleas. The LORD will accept my prayer. All my enemies will be shamed and utterly dismayed. They will turn back in sudden shame.

Sit upright. On Mondays and Thursdays, say the following.

On Sundays, Tuesdays, Wednesdays and Fridays, continue with "Guardian of Israel" on page 117.

LORD, GOD of Israel, turn away from Your fierce anger,
and relent from the evil against Your people.

Look down from heaven and see how we have become an object of scorn and derision among the nations. We are regarded as sheep led to the slaughter, to be killed, destroyed, beaten and humiliated. Yet, despite all this, we have not forgotten Your name. Please do not forget us.

LORD, GOD of Israel, turn away From Your fierce anger,
and relent from the evil against Your people.

Strangers say, "You have no hope or expectation." Be gracious to the nation whose hope is in Your name. O Pure One, bring our deliverance close. We are exhausted. We are given no rest. May Your compassion suppress Your anger against us. Please turn away from Your fierce anger, and have compassion on the people You chose as Your own.

LORD, GOD of Israel, turn away from Your fierce anger,
and relent from the evil against Your people.

Have pity on us, LORD, in Your compassion, and do not hand us over to cruel oppressors. Why should the nations say, "Where is their GOD now?" For Your own sake, deal kindly with us, and do not delay. Please

---

Holocaust, the concentration camp at Theresienstadt was excavated. A hidden room was discovered, which had served as a secret place in which the prisoners would pray. On one of its walls were written the words: "Yet, despite all this, we have not forgotten Your name. Please do not forget us."

חֶסֶד וְאַל תְּאַחַר. אָנָּא שׁוּב מֵחֲרוֹנְךָ, וְרַחֵם סְגֻלָּה אֲשֶׁר בָּחָרְתָּ.

יהוה אֱלֹהֵי יִשְׂרָאֵל, שׁוּב מֵחֲרוֹן אַפֶּךָ וְהִנָּחֵם עַל הָרָעָה לְעַמֶּךָ.

קוֹלֵנוּ תִשְׁמַע וְתָחֹן, וְאַל־תִּטְּשֵׁנוּ בְּיַד אוֹיְבֵינוּ לִמְחוֹת אֶת־שְׁמֵנוּ. זְכֹר אֲשֶׁר נִשְׁבַּעְתָּ לַאֲבוֹתֵינוּ כְּכוֹכְבֵי הַשָּׁמַיִם אַרְבֶּה אֶת־זַרְעֲכֶם, וְעַתָּה נִשְׁאַרְנוּ מְעַט מֵהַרְבֵּה. וּבְכָל־זֹאת שִׁמְךָ לֹא שָׁכָחְנוּ, נָא אַל־תִּשְׁכָּחֵנוּ.

יהוה אֱלֹהֵי יִשְׂרָאֵל, שׁוּב מֵחֲרוֹן אַפֶּךָ וְהִנָּחֵם עַל הָרָעָה לְעַמֶּךָ.

עָזְרֵנוּ אֱלֹהֵי יִשְׁעֵנוּ עַל־דְּבַר כְּבוֹד־שְׁמֶךָ, וְהַצִּילֵנוּ וְכַפֵּר עַל־חַטֹּאתֵינוּ לְמַעַן שְׁמֶךָ.

יהוה אֱלֹהֵי יִשְׂרָאֵל, שׁוּב מֵחֲרוֹן אַפֶּךָ וְהִנָּחֵם עַל הָרָעָה לְעַמֶּךָ.

On all days, continue here:

שׁוֹמֵר יִשְׂרָאֵל, שְׁמוֹר שְׁאֵרִית יִשְׂרָאֵל, וְאַל־יֹאבַד יִשְׂרָאֵל, הָאוֹמְרִים, שְׁמַע יִשְׂרָאֵל.

שׁוֹמֵר גּוֹי אֶחָד, שְׁמוֹר שְׁאֵרִית עַם אֶחָד, וְאַל יֹאבַד גּוֹי אֶחָד, הַמְיַחֲדִים שִׁמְךָ, יהוה אֱלֹהֵינוּ יהוה אֶחָד.

שׁוֹמֵר גּוֹי קָדוֹשׁ, שְׁמוֹר שְׁאֵרִית עַם קָדוֹשׁ, וְאַל־יֹאבַד גּוֹי קָדוֹשׁ, הַמְשַׁלְּשִׁים בְּשִׁלּוּשׁ קְדֻשָּׁה לְקָדוֹשׁ.

מִתְרַצֶּה בְּרַחֲמִים וּמִתְפַּיֵּס בְּתַחֲנוּנִים, הִתְרַצֶּה וְהִתְפַּיֵּס לְדוֹר עָנִי, כִּי אֵין עוֹזֵר.

אָבִינוּ מַלְכֵּנוּ, חָנֵּנוּ וַעֲנֵנוּ, כִּי אֵין בָּנוּ מַעֲשִׂים, עֲשֵׂה עִמָּנוּ צְדָקָה וָחֶסֶד וְהוֹשִׁיעֵנוּ.

שׁוֹמֵר יִשְׂרָאֵל *Guardian of Israel*: A three-line prayer set in motion by a phrase from Psalm 121: "See: the *Guardian of Israel* neither slumbers nor sleeps". An example of early liturgical poetry, it has the same structure as the poem preced-

turn away from Your fierce anger, and have compassion on the people You chose as Your own.

LORD, GOD of Israel, turn away from Your fierce anger,
and relent from the evil against Your people.

Heed our voice and be gracious. Do not abandon us into the hand of our enemies to blot out our name. Remember what You promised our fathers: "I will make your descendants as many as the stars of heaven" – yet now we are only a few left from many. Yet, despite all this, we have not forgotten Your name. Please do not forget us.

LORD, GOD of Israel, turn away from Your fierce anger,
and relent from the evil against Your people.

Help us, GOD of our salvation, for the sake of the glory of Your name. Save us and pardon our sins for Your name's sake.

LORD, GOD of Israel, turn away from Your fierce anger,
and relent from the evil against Your people.

On all days, continue here:

שׁוֹמֵר Guardian of Israel, guard the remnant of Israel, and let not Israel perish, who declare, "Listen, Israel."

Guardian of a unique nation, guard the remnant of a unique people, and let not that unique nation perish, who proclaim the unity of Your name [saying], "The LORD is our GOD, the LORD is One."

Guardian of a holy nation, guard the remnant of that holy nation, and let not the holy nation perish, who three times repeat the threefold declaration of holiness to the Holy One.

You who are conciliated by calls for compassion and placated by pleas, be conciliated and placated toward an afflicted generation, for there is no other help.

Our Father, our King, be gracious to us and answer us, though we have no worthy deeds; act with us in charity and lovingkindness and save us.

---

ing the morning *Amidah*, "Rock of Israel! Arise to the help of Israel…" and the prayer said on the Ten Days of Penitence, "Remember us for life, King who desires life…" In each case the stanza contains four lines, all ending with the same word (Rabbi Jeffrey Cohen). The prayer was transferred from the penitential prayers known as *Selichot* to the Daily Service.

Stand at ▲.

וַאֲנַחְנוּ לֹא נֵדַע ▲מַה־נַּעֲשֶׂה, כִּי עָלֶיךָ עֵינֵינוּ. זְכֹר רַחֲמֶיךָ יהוה וַחֲסָדֶיךָ, כִּי מֵעוֹלָם הֵמָּה. יְהִי־חַסְדְּךָ יהוה עָלֵינוּ, כַּאֲשֶׁר יִחַלְנוּ לָךְ. אַל תִּזְכָּר־לָנוּ עֲוֹנוֹת רִאשׁוֹנִים, מַהֵר יְקַדְּמוּנוּ רַחֲמֶיךָ, כִּי דַלּוֹנוּ מְאֹד. חָנֵּנוּ יהוה חָנֵּנוּ, כִּי־רַב שָׂבַעְנוּ בוּז. בְּרֹגֶז רַחֵם תִּזְכּוֹר. כִּי הוּא יָדַע יִצְרֵנוּ, זָכוּר כִּי עָפָר אֲנָחְנוּ. ◆ עָזְרֵנוּ אֱלֹהֵי יִשְׁעֵנוּ עַל־דְּבַר כְּבוֹד־שְׁמֶךָ, וְהַצִּילֵנוּ וְכַפֵּר עַל־חַטֹּאתֵינוּ לְמַעַן שְׁמֶךָ.

The Leader says חֲצִי קַדִּישׁ.

Leader:

יִתְגַּדַּל וְיִתְקַדַּשׁ שְׁמֵהּ רַבָּא. (Cong. אָמֵן) בְּעָלְמָא דִּי־בְרָא כִרְעוּתֵהּ. וְיַמְלִיךְ מַלְכוּתֵהּ, בְּחַיֵּיכוֹן וּבְיוֹמֵיכוֹן וּבְחַיֵּי דִי־כָל־בֵּית יִשְׂרָאֵל, בַּעֲגָלָא וּבִזְמַן קָרִיב. וְאִמְרוּ אָמֵן. (Cong. אָמֵן)

All:

יְהֵא שְׁמֵהּ רַבָּא מְבָרַךְ לְעָלַם וּלְעָלְמֵי עָלְמַיָּא.

Leader:

יִתְבָּרַךְ וְיִשְׁתַּבַּח וְיִתְפָּאַר וְיִתְרוֹמַם וְיִתְנַשֵּׂא וְיִתְהַדַּר וְיִתְעַלֶּה וְיִתְהַלָּל שְׁמֵהּ דְּקֻדְשָׁא בְּרִיךְ הוּא (Cong. בְּרִיךְ הוּא) לְעֵלָּא (לְעֵלָּא Between רֹאשׁ הַשָּׁנָה and יוֹם כִּפּוּר add) מִן־כָּל־בִּרְכָתָא וְשִׁירָתָא תֻּשְׁבְּחָתָא וְנֶחֱמָתָא, דַּאֲמִירָן בְּעָלְמָא. וְאִמְרוּ אָמֵן. (Cong. אָמֵן)

וַאֲנַחְנוּ לֹא נֵדַע *We do not know*: A line taken from the prayer of King Jehoshaphat when the nation was confronted by a coalition of hostile powers intent on war (II Chronicles 20:12). Our custom is to stand after these words. Abudraham explains that this is because – like Moses pleading on behalf of the people – we have prayed in every posture, sitting (before the *Amidah*), standing (during the *Amidah*), and "falling on our faces" (during *Tachanun*). We have exhausted the repertoire of prayer and do not know what else to do. We stand at this point to signal that our private supplications have come to an end.

Stand at ▲.

וַאֲנַחְנוּ We do not know what to do, ▲but our eyes are turned to You. Remember, LORD, Your compassion and lovingkindness, for they are everlasting. May Your lovingkindness, LORD, be with us, for we have put our hope in You. Do not hold against us the sins of those who came before us. May Your mercies meet us swiftly, for we have been brought very low. Be gracious to us, LORD, be gracious to us, for we are sated with contempt. In wrath, remember mercy. He knows our nature; He remembers that we are dust. ➔ Help us, GOD of our salvation, for the sake of the glory of Your name. Save us and grant atonement for our sins for Your name's sake.

The Leader says half-*Kaddish*.

Leader:

יִתְגַּדַּל Magnified and sanctified may His great name be, in the world He created by His will. May He establish His kingdom in your lifetime and in your days, and in the lifetime of all the House of Israel, swiftly and soon – and say: Amen.

All:

May His great name be blessed for ever and all time.

Leader:

Blessed and praised, glorified and exalted, raised and honoured, uplifted and lauded be the name of the Holy One, blessed be He, (between Rosh Hashanah and Yom Kippur add 'well') beyond any blessing, song, praise and consolation uttered in the world – and say: Amen.

READING OF THE TORAH

From earliest times, the public reading of the Torah has been a constitutive element of the spiritual life of Israel. At Mount Sinai, to confirm the covenant between the people and GOD, Moses "took the Book of the Covenant and read it aloud to the people" (Exodus 24:7). The penultimate commandment of the Torah specifies that every seven years (on Sukkot following the sabbatical year) there should be a national assembly at which "the people, men, women, children and the strangers in your communities" were to hear the Torah proclaimed "so that they may listen and learn to fear the LORD your GOD and observe faithfully all the words of this Torah" (Deuteronomy 31:12).

At critical moments during the biblical era, when the people had drifted from their faith, national renewal was marked by a public Torah reading. King Jehoshaphat sent out officers who "taught throughout Judah, having with them a

On Mondays and Thursdays, חֲנֻכָּה ,חוֹל הַמּוֹעֵד ,רֹאשׁ חֹדֶשׁ,
פּוּרִים and Fast Days, the תּוֹרָה is read when prayers are said with a מִנְיָן.

On days when the תּוֹרָה is not read, continue with אַשְׁרֵי on page 132.

The following two paragraphs are not said on חוֹל הַמּוֹעֵד,
שׁוּשַׁן פּוּרִים ,פּוּרִים ,חֲנֻכָּה ,תִּשְׁעָה בְּאָב ,עֶרֶב פֶּסַח ,רֹאשׁ חֹדֶשׁ
and the 14th and 15th of אֲדָר רִאשׁוֹן in a Jewish leap year, יוֹם הָעַצְמָאוּת,
יוֹם יְרוּשָׁלַיִם, or in a house of mourning during the week of שִׁבְעָה.

אֵל אֶרֶךְ אַפַּיִם וְרַב־חֶסֶד וֶאֱמֶת, אַל־בְּאַפְּךָ תוֹכִיחֵנוּ. חוּסָה יהוה עַל עַמֶּךָ, וְהוֹשִׁיעֵנוּ מִכָּל רָע. חָטָאנוּ לְךָ אָדוֹן, סְלַח נָא כְּרוֹב רַחֲמֶיךָ אֵל.

אֵל אֶרֶךְ אַפַּיִם וְרַב חֶסֶד וֶאֱמֶת, אַל־תַּסְתֵּר פָּנֶיךָ מִמֶּנּוּ. חוּסָה יהוה עַל יִשְׂרָאֵל עַמֶּךָ, וְהַצִּילֵנוּ מִכָּל־רָע. חָטָאנוּ לְךָ אָדוֹן, סְלַח־נָא כְּרוֹב רַחֲמֶיךָ אֵל.

קריאת התורה

The Ark is opened and the Congregation stands. All say:

וַיְהִי בִּנְסֹעַ הָאָרֹן, וַיֹּאמֶר מֹשֶׁה, קוּמָה יהוה וְיָפֻצוּ אֹיְבֶיךָ, וְיָנֻסוּ מְשַׂנְאֶיךָ מִפָּנֶיךָ. כִּי מִצִּיּוֹן תֵּצֵא תוֹרָה, וּדְבַר יהוה מִירוּשָׁלָיִם. בָּרוּךְ שֶׁנָּתַן תּוֹרָה לְעַמּוֹ יִשְׂרָאֵל בִּקְדֻשָּׁתוֹ.

The סֵפֶר תּוֹרָה is handed to the Leader, who holds it on
his right, bows toward the Ark and says:

גַּדְּלוּ לַיהוה אִתִּי, וּנְרוֹמְמָה שְׁמוֹ יַחְדָּו.

The Ark is closed.

All:

לְךָ יהוה הַגְּדֻלָּה וְהַגְּבוּרָה וְהַתִּפְאֶרֶת וְהַנֵּצַח וְהַהוֹד, כִּי כֹל בַּשָּׁמַיִם וּבָאָרֶץ, לְךָ יהוה הַמַּמְלָכָה וְהַמִּתְנַשֵּׂא לְכֹל

---

scroll of the Lord's Torah. They circulated throughout the towns of Judah and taught the people" (II Chronicles 17:9).

King Josiah assembled "all the men of Judah, the inhabitants of Jerusalem, the priests, the Levites, and all the people, young and old alike and read to them the entire Book of the Covenant which had been found in the Lord's Temple" (II Chronicles 34:30).

On Mondays and Thursdays, Rosh Chodesh, the Intermediate Days of Festivals, Chanukah, Purim and Fast Days, the Torah is read when prayers are said with a *minyan*.

On days when the Torah is not read, continue with "Happy are those" on page 133.

The following two paragraphs are not said on the Intermediate Days of festivals, Rosh Chodesh, the day before Pesach, the Ninth of Av, Chanukah, Purim, Shushan Purim and the 14th and 15th of Adar Rishon in a Jewish leap year, Yom Ha'Atzma'ut, Yom Yerushalayim, or in a house of mourning during the week of *shivah*.

אֵל God, slow to anger, abounding in lovingkindness and truth, do not rebuke us in Your anger. Have pity on Your people, Lord, and save us from all evil. We have sinned against You, Lord. Please forgive in accordance with Your great compassion, God.

אֵל God, slow to anger, abounding in lovingkindness and truth, do not hide Your face from us. Have pity on Israel Your people, Lord, and deliver us from all evil. We have sinned against You, Lord. Please forgive in accordance with Your great compassion, God.

READING OF THE TORAH

The Ark is opened and the Congregation stands. All say:

וַיְהִי בִּנְסֹעַ Whenever the Ark set out, Moses would say, "Arise, Lord, and may Your enemies be scattered. May those who hate You flee before You." For the Torah shall come forth from Zion, and the word of the Lord from Jerusalem. Blessed is He who in His Holiness gave the Torah to His people Israel.

The Torah scroll is handed to the Leader, who holds it on his right, bows toward the Ark and says:

Magnify the Lord with me, and let us exalt His name together.

The Ark is closed.

All:

לְךָ Yours, Lord, are the greatness and the power, the glory and the majesty and splendour, for everything in heaven and earth is Yours. Yours, Lord, is the kingdom; You are exalted as head over all. Exalt

The Book of Nehemiah (8:1–12) contains a graphic description of the return of the Babylonian exiles to Israel. Ezra gathered the people at the Temple and read the Torah to them "from dawn until midday", assisted by Levites who "interpreted it and explained its meaning, so that they understood the verses".

These were national occasions. At a more local level, tradition holds that Mo-

לְראשׁ. רוֹמְמוּ יהוה אֱלֹהֵינוּ וְהִשְׁתַּחֲווּ לַהֲדֹם רַגְלָיו, קָדוֹשׁ הוּא. רוֹמְמוּ יהוה אֱלֹהֵינוּ וְהִשְׁתַּחֲווּ לְהַר קָדְשׁוֹ, כִּי קָדוֹשׁ יהוה אֱלֹהֵינוּ.

אַב הָרַחֲמִים הוּא יְרַחֵם עַם עֲמוּסִים, וְיִזְכֹּר בְּרִית אֵיתָנִים, וְיַצִּיל נַפְשׁוֹתֵינוּ מִן־הַשָּׁעוֹת הָרָעוֹת, וְיִגְעַר בְּיֵצֶר הָרַע מִן הַנְּשׂוּאִים, וְיָחֹן אוֹתָנוּ לִפְלֵיטַת עוֹלָמִים, וִימַלֵּא מִשְׁאֲלוֹתֵינוּ בְּמִדָּה טוֹבָה יְשׁוּעָה וְרַחֲמִים.

The סֵפֶר תּוֹרָה is placed on the reading desk and is prepared for reading.

A mourner, during the week of שִׁבְעָה, may not read the תּוֹרָה (unless he is the only person capable of so doing), nor may he be called to the reading of the תּוֹרָה.

The Leader says:

וְתִגָּלֶה וְתֵרָאֶה מַלְכוּתוֹ עָלֵינוּ בִּזְמַן קָרוֹב, וְיָחֹן פְּלֵטָתֵנוּ וּפְלֵטַת עַמּוֹ בֵּית יִשְׂרָאֵל לְחֵן וּלְחֶסֶד וּלְרַחֲמִים וּלְרָצוֹן. וְנֹאמַר אָמֵן. הַכֹּל הָבוּ גֹדֶל לֵאלֹהֵינוּ וּתְנוּ כָבוֹד לַתּוֹרָה.

A כֹּהֵן, if present, is called up to the reading thus:

כֹּהֵן קְרָב, יַעֲמֹד (פלוני בֶּן פלוני) הַכֹּהֵן.

If no כֹּהֵן is present, a לֵוִי or יִשְׂרָאֵל is called up thus:

אֵין כַּאן כֹּהֵן, יַעֲמֹד (פלוני בֶּן פלוני הַלֵּוִי/הַיִּשְׂרָאֵל) בִּמְקוֹם כֹּהֵן.

בָּרוּךְ שֶׁנָּתַן תּוֹרָה לְעַמּוֹ יִשְׂרָאֵל בִּקְדֻשָּׁתוֹ.

All:

וְאַתֶּם הַדְּבֵקִים בַּיהוה אֱלֹהֵיכֶם, חַיִּים כֻּלְּכֶם הַיּוֹם.

---

ses instituted the practice that the Torah be read on Shabbat, Festivals and their Intermediate Days, and Rosh Chodesh. Ezra ordained that it also be read on Mondays and Thursdays (market days in ancient times) and on Shabbat afternoons (*Yerushalmi Megillah* 4:1). The public reading of the Torah is as ancient an institution as prayer itself.

The synagogue thus became not only a house of prayer but also a house of study. The result is a dynamic tension between speaking and listening. In prayer, we speak to God. In study we listen to God speaking to us, His word unchanged and undiminished across the centuries.

The assembly convened by Ezra, when the Torah was not only read but also explained, became the model for educational activities within the synagogue, of

the LORD our GOD and bow to His footstool; He is holy. Exalt the LORD our GOD, and bow at His holy mountain, for holy is the LORD our GOD.

אַב הָרַחֲמִים May the Father of compassion have compassion on the people borne by Him. May He remember the covenant with the mighty [patriarchs], and deliver us from evil times. May He reproach the evil instinct in the people carried by Him, and graciously grant that we be an everlasting remnant. May He fulfil in good measure our requests for salvation and compassion.

The Torah scroll is placed on the reading desk and is prepared for reading.

A mourner, during the week of *shivah*, may not read the Torah (unless he is the only person capable of so doing), nor may he be called to the reading of the Torah.

The Leader says:

וְתִגָּלֶה May His kingship over us be soon revealed and made manifest. May He be gracious to our surviving remnant, the remnant of His people the house of Israel in grace, lovingkindness, compassion and favour, and let us say Amen. Let us all render greatness to our GOD and give honour to the Torah.

A Cohen, if present, is called up to the reading thus:

Let the Cohen come forward. Arise (Hebrew name), the Cohen.

If no Cohen is present, a Levi or Yisrael is called up thus:

As there is no Cohen, arise (Hebrew name) in place of a Cohen.

Blessed is He who, in His holiness, gave the Torah to His people Israel.

All:

You who cling to the LORD your GOD are all alive today.

---

which the *derashah* ("sermon", or more precisely, "exposition") is only one of many forms. To an unparalleled degree, Judaism is predicated on universal literacy and lifelong learning. The Torah is not just written on parchment; it is meant to be engraved on the Jewish soul.

Keri'at ha-Torah, translated as "the reading of the Torah", also means "the proclamation of the Torah". The public reading symbolically affirms the Torah as the written constitution of the Jewish people as a nation under the sovereignty of GOD. It is a re-enactment of the revelation at Mount Sinai when the Israelites first became a nation, bound by the Torah's laws, summoned to translate its ideals into life.

For the laws on being called to the Torah, see page 409.

The appropriate תּוֹרָה portions are to be found on pages 846–921.

The reader shows the עוֹלֶה (the person called to the תּוֹרָה) the section to be read. The עוֹלֶה touches the scroll at that place with the צִיצִית of his טַלִּית, which he then kisses. Holding the handles of the scroll, he says:

בָּרְכוּ אֶת יהוה הַמְבֹרָךְ.

The Congregation responds:

בָּרוּךְ יהוה הַמְבֹרָךְ לְעוֹלָם וָעֶד.

The עוֹלֶה continues:

בָּרוּךְ יהוה הַמְבֹרָךְ לְעוֹלָם וָעֶד.

בָּרוּךְ אַתָּה יהוה אֱלֹהֵינוּ מֶלֶךְ הָעוֹלָם, אֲשֶׁר־בָּחַר בָּנוּ מִכָּל־הָעַמִּים, וְנָתַן לָנוּ אֶת־תּוֹרָתוֹ. בָּרוּךְ אַתָּה יהוה, נוֹתֵן הַתּוֹרָה.

After the reading, the עוֹלֶה says:

בָּרוּךְ אַתָּה יהוה אֱלֹהֵינוּ מֶלֶךְ הָעוֹלָם, אֲשֶׁר נָתַן־לָנוּ תּוֹרַת־אֱמֶת, וְחַיֵּי עוֹלָם נָטַע בְּתוֹכֵנוּ. בָּרוּךְ אַתָּה יהוה, נוֹתֵן הַתּוֹרָה.

One who has survived a situation of danger (safe arrival after a hazardous journey, release from captivity or recovery from serious illness) says:

בָּרוּךְ אַתָּה יהוה אֱלֹהֵינוּ מֶלֶךְ הָעוֹלָם, הַגּוֹמֵל לְחַיָּבִים טוֹבוֹת, שֶׁגְּמָלַנִי כָּל־טוֹב.

The Congregation responds:

אָמֵן. מִי שֶׁגְּמָלְךָ כָּל־טוֹב, הוּא יִגְמָלְךָ כָּל־טוֹב, סֶלָה.

The appropriate Torah portions are to be found on pages 846–921.

The reader shows the *oleh* (the person called to the Torah) the section to be read. The *oleh* touches the scroll at that place with the *tzitzit* of his *tallit,* which he then kisses. Holding the handles of the scroll, he says:

Bar'chu et Adonai haM'vorach.

Bless the LORD, the blessed One.

The Congregation responds:

Baruch Adonai haM'vorach le-olam va-ed.

Bless the LORD, the blessed One, for ever and all time.

The *oleh* continues:

Baruch Adonai haM'vorach le-olam va-ed.

Baruch atah Adonai, Eloheinu Melech ha-olam, asher bachar banu mikol ha-amim, venatan lanu et Torato, baruch atah Adonai, noten haTorah.

Bless the LORD, the blessed One, for ever and all time.

Blessed are You, LORD our GOD, King of the Universe, who has chosen us from all peoples and has given us His Torah. Blessed are You, LORD, Giver of the Torah.

After the reading, the *oleh* says:

Baruch atah Adonai, Eloheinu Melech ha-olam, asher natan lanu Torat emet, v'chayei olam nata b'tochenu, baruch atah Adonai, noten haTorah.

Blessed are You, LORD our GOD, King of the Universe, who has given us the Torah of truth, planting everlasting life in our midst. Blessed are You, LORD, Giver of the Torah.

One who has survived a situation of danger (safe arrival after a hazardous journey, release from captivity or recovery from serious illness) says:

Baruch atah Adonai, Eloheinu Melech ha-olam, hagomel l'chayavim tovot, sheg'malani kol tov.

Blessed are You, LORD our GOD, King of the Universe, who bestows good on the unworthy, who has bestowed on me much good.

The Congregation responds:

Amen. May He who bestowed much good on you continue to bestow on you much good, Selah.

Special מִי שֶׁבֵּרַךְ and memorial prayers may be said at this point. See page 922.

After a בַּר מִצְוָה has finished the תּוֹרָה blessing, his father says aloud:

בָּרוּךְ שֶׁפְּטָרַנִי מֵעָנְשׁוֹ שֶׁל זֶה.

The Leader says חֲצִי קַדִּישׁ.

Leader:

יִתְגַּדַּל וְיִתְקַדַּשׁ שְׁמֵהּ רַבָּא. (Cong. אָמֵן) בְּעָלְמָא דִּי־בְרָא כִרְעוּתֵהּ. וְיַמְלִיךְ מַלְכוּתֵהּ, בְּחַיֵּיכוֹן וּבְיוֹמֵיכוֹן וּבְחַיֵּי דִי־כָל־בֵּית יִשְׂרָאֵל, בַּעֲגָלָא וּבִזְמַן קָרִיב. וְאִמְרוּ אָמֵן. (Cong. אָמֵן)

All:

יְהֵא שְׁמֵהּ רַבָּא מְבָרַךְ לְעָלַם וּלְעָלְמֵי עָלְמַיָּא.

Leader:

יִתְבָּרַךְ וְיִשְׁתַּבַּח וְיִתְפָּאַר וְיִתְרוֹמַם וְיִתְנַשֵּׂא וְיִתְהַדַּר וְיִתְעַלֶּה וְיִתְהַלָּל שְׁמֵהּ דְּקֻדְשָׁא בְּרִיךְ הוּא (Cong. בְּרִיךְ הוּא) לְעֵלָּא (Between רֹאשׁ הַשָּׁנָה and יוֹם כִּפּוּר add לְעֵלָּא) מִן־כָּל־בִּרְכָתָא וְשִׁירָתָא תֻּשְׁבְּחָתָא וְנֶחֱמָתָא, דַּאֲמִירָן בְּעָלְמָא. וְאִמְרוּ אָמֵן. (Cong. אָמֵן)

After the reading, the סֵפֶר תּוֹרָה is lifted, and the Congregation says:

וְזֹאת הַתּוֹרָה אֲשֶׁר־שָׂם מֹשֶׁה לִפְנֵי בְּנֵי יִשְׂרָאֵל, עַל־פִּי יהוה בְּיַד־מֹשֶׁה.

LAWS OF RAISING AND BINDING THE TORAH SCROLL

1. The Ashkenazi custom is to raise the Torah scroll after the reading; Sephardim do so before the reading.

2. Care should be taken that the person called to raise the scroll is strong enough to do so, holding it steadily. One who feels that he lacks the physical strength should decline the *mitzvah*.

3. Before the raising, the scroll should be rolled to a point where a seam is exposed, where two pieces of parchment have been sown together, so that if an accident should occur, the tear will occur at the seam, not in the parchment itself.

4. Before the raising, the scroll should be opened so that when it is lifted and shown to the congregation, three columns of the script are exposed.

5. On raising the Torah, the person holding it should turn so that all present can see the ex-

Special blessings and memorial prayers may be said at this point. See page 922.

After a *Bar Mitzvah* boy has finished the Torah blessing, his father says aloud:

Blessed is He who has released me from
the responsibility for this child.

The Leader says half-*Kaddish*.

Leader:

יִתְגַּדַּל may His great name be, in the world He created by His will. May He establish His kingdom in your lifetime and in your days, and in the lifetime of all the House of Israel, swiftly and soon – and say: Amen.

All:

May His great name be blessed for ever and all time.

Leader:

Blessed and praised, glorified and exalted, raised and honoured, uplifted and lauded be the name of the Holy One, blessed be He, (between Rosh Hashanah and Yom Kippur add 'well') beyond any blessing, song, praise and consolation uttered in the world – and say: Amen.

After the reading, the Torah scroll is lifted, and the Congregation says:

וְזֹאת This is the Torah that Moses placed before the children of Israel, at the Lord's commandment, by the hand of Moses.

---

posed script. Facing the Ark, he should turn in a clockwise direction, i. e. to the right.

6. While the Torah is being raised, all present should stand.

7. The person binding the scroll should not touch the parchment with his hands.

8. The knot or buckle of the strap by which the scroll is bound should be facing inward, i.e. toward the person holding the scroll.

9. On days when a *haftarah* is said, the reader should not normally begin until the Torah scroll has been rolled and bound.

10. When the scroll is being returned to the Ark, all should stand until the Ark is closed.

בָּרוּךְ שֶׁפְּטָרַנִי *Blessed is He who has released me*: A blessing mentioned in the early rabbinic literature (*Bereishit Rabbah* 63:10). Until a child reaches maturity, the parents bear the responsibility for his or her acts. The blessing testifies that the child is now an independent moral agent. Parenthood is a supreme responsibility in Judaism. In the only passage to explain why Abraham was chosen, the Torah says, "I have chosen him so that he will instruct his children and his household after him to keep the way of the Lord, doing righteousness and justice" (Genesis 18:19).

On those Mondays and Thursdays when תַּחֲנוּן is said, the Leader says the following while the סֵפֶר תּוֹרָה is being bound:

יְהִי רָצוֹן מִלִּפְנֵי אָבִינוּ שֶׁבַּשָּׁמַיִם, לְכוֹנֵן אֶת־בֵּית חַיֵּינוּ, וּלְהָשִׁיב אֶת־שְׁכִינָתוֹ בְּתוֹכֵנוּ, בִּמְהֵרָה בְיָמֵינוּ. וְנֹאמַר אָמֵן.

יְהִי רָצוֹן מִלִּפְנֵי אָבִינוּ שֶׁבַּשָּׁמַיִם, לְרַחֵם עָלֵינוּ וְעַל פְּלֵיטָתֵנוּ, וְלִמְנֹעַ מַשְׁחִית וּמַגֵּפָה מֵעָלֵינוּ וּמֵעַל כָּל־עַמּוֹ בֵּית יִשְׂרָאֵל. וְנֹאמַר אָמֵן.

יְהִי רָצוֹן מִלִּפְנֵי אָבִינוּ שֶׁבַּשָּׁמַיִם, לְקַיֶּם־בָּנוּ חַכְמֵי יִשְׂרָאֵל, הֵם וּנְשֵׁיהֶם וּבְנֵיהֶם וּבְנוֹתֵיהֶם וְתַלְמִידֵיהֶם וְתַלְמִידֵי תַלְמִידֵיהֶם, בְּכָל־מְקוֹמוֹת מוֹשְׁבוֹתֵיהֶם. וְנֹאמַר אָמֵן.

יְהִי רָצוֹן מִלִּפְנֵי אָבִינוּ שֶׁבַּשָּׁמַיִם, שֶׁנִּשְׁמַע וְנִתְבַּשֵּׂר בְּשׂוֹרוֹת טוֹבוֹת, יְשׁוּעוֹת וְנֶחָמוֹת, וִיקַבֵּץ נִדָּחֵינוּ מֵאַרְבַּע כַּנְפוֹת הָאָרֶץ. וְנֹאמַר אָמֵן.

All:

אַחֵינוּ כָּל־בֵּית־יִשְׂרָאֵל, הַנְּתוּנִים בְּצָרָה וּבְשִׁבְיָה, הָעוֹמְדִים בֵּין בַּיָּם וּבֵין בַּיַּבָּשָׁה, הַמָּקוֹם יְרַחֵם עֲלֵיהֶם וְיוֹצִיאֵם מִצָּרָה לִרְוָחָה, וּמֵאֲפֵלָה לְאוֹרָה, וּמִשִּׁעְבּוּד לִגְאֻלָּה, הַשְׁתָּא בַּעֲגָלָא וּבִזְמַן קָרִיב. וְנֹאמַר אָמֵן.

The leader takes the סֵפֶר תּוֹרָה and says:

יְהַלְלוּ אֶת־שֵׁם יהוה, כִּי נִשְׂגָּב שְׁמוֹ לְבַדּוֹ.

Congregation:

הוֹדוֹ עַל אֶרֶץ וְשָׁמָיִם. וַיָּרֶם קֶרֶן לְעַמּוֹ,
תְּהִלָּה לְכָל־חֲסִידָיו, לִבְנֵי יִשְׂרָאֵל עַם קְרֹבוֹ, הַלְלוּיָהּ.

On those Mondays and Thursdays when *Tachanun* is said, the Leader says the following while the Torah scroll is being bound:

יְהִי רָצוֹן May it be the will of our Father in heaven to establish (the Temple), home of our life, and to restore His Presence to our midst, swiftly in our days – and let us say, Amen.

יְהִי רָצוֹן May it be the will of our Father in heaven to have compassion on us and our remnant, and to keep destruction and plague away from us and from all His people the house of Israel – and let us say, Amen.

יְהִי רָצוֹן May it be the will of our Father in heaven to preserve among us the Sages of Israel: them, their wives, their sons and daughters, their disciples and their disciples' disciples, in all their dwelling places – and let us say, Amen.

יְהִי רָצוֹן May it be the will of our Father in heaven that we may hear and be given good tidings of salvation and consolation, and that our dispersed be gathered from the four corners of the earth – and let us say, Amen.

All:

אַחֵינוּ As for our brothers of the whole house of Israel who are in distress or captivity, on sea or land, may the All-present have compassion on them and lead them from distress to relief, from darkness to light, and from oppression to freedom, now, swiftly and soon – and let us say, Amen.

The Leader takes the Torah scroll and says:

יְהַלְלוּ Let them praise the name of the Lord, for His name alone is sublime.

Congregation:

הוֹדוֹ His majesty is above earth and heaven. He has raised the horn of His people, for the glory of all His devoted ones, the children of Israel, the people close to Him. Halleluyah!

While the סֵפֶר תּוֹרָה is returned to the Ark, say:

תהלים כד

לְדָוִד מִזְמוֹר, לַיהוה הָאָרֶץ וּמְלוֹאָהּ, תֵּבֵל וְיֹשְׁבֵי בָהּ. כִּי־הוּא עַל יַמִּים יְסָדָהּ, וְעַל נְהָרוֹת יְכוֹנְנֶהָ. מִי־יַעֲלֶה בְהַר יהוה, וּמִי־יָקוּם בִּמְקוֹם קָדְשׁוֹ. נְקִי כַפַּיִם וּבַר לֵבָב, אֲשֶׁר לֹא־נָשָׂא לַשָּׁוְא נַפְשִׁי וְלֹא נִשְׁבַּע לְמִרְמָה. יִשָּׂא בְרָכָה מֵאֵת יהוה, וּצְדָקָה מֵאֱלֹהֵי יִשְׁעוֹ. זֶה דּוֹר דֹּרְשָׁיו, מְבַקְשֵׁי פָנֶיךָ, יַעֲקֹב, סֶלָה. שְׂאוּ שְׁעָרִים רָאשֵׁיכֶם, וְהִנָּשְׂאוּ פִּתְחֵי עוֹלָם, וְיָבוֹא מֶלֶךְ הַכָּבוֹד. מִי זֶה מֶלֶךְ הַכָּבוֹד, יהוה עִזּוּז וְגִבּוֹר, יהוה גִּבּוֹר מִלְחָמָה. שְׂאוּ שְׁעָרִים רָאשֵׁיכֶם, וּשְׂאוּ פִּתְחֵי עוֹלָם, וְיָבֹא מֶלֶךְ הַכָּבוֹד. ◄ מִי הוּא זֶה מֶלֶךְ הַכָּבוֹד, יהוה צְבָאוֹת הוּא מֶלֶךְ הַכָּבוֹד, סֶלָה.

While the סֵפֶר תּוֹרָה is placed into the Ark, say:

וּבְנֻחֹה יֹאמַר, שׁוּבָה יהוה רִבְבוֹת אַלְפֵי יִשְׂרָאֵל. קוּמָה יהוה לִמְנוּחָתֶךָ, אַתָּה וַאֲרוֹן עֻזֶּךָ. כֹּהֲנֶיךָ יִלְבְּשׁוּ צֶדֶק, וַחֲסִידֶיךָ יְרַנֵּנוּ. בַּעֲבוּר דָּוִד עַבְדֶּךָ אַל־תָּשֵׁב פְּנֵי מְשִׁיחֶךָ. כִּי לֶקַח טוֹב נָתַתִּי לָכֶם, תּוֹרָתִי אַל־תַּעֲזֹבוּ. עֵץ־חַיִּים הִיא לַמַּחֲזִיקִים בָּהּ, וְתֹמְכֶיהָ מְאֻשָּׁר. דְּרָכֶיהָ דַרְכֵי־נֹעַם, וְכָל־נְתִיבוֹתֶיהָ שָׁלוֹם. ◄ הֲשִׁיבֵנוּ יהוה אֵלֶיךָ וְנָשׁוּבָה, חַדֵּשׁ יָמֵינוּ כְּקֶדֶם.

The Ark is closed.

לְדָוִד מִזְמוֹר *A psalm of David*: A psalm of joyous procession to the Temple. It begins with creation, "The earth is the Lord's", and moves directly to the moral requirements of the religious life: "Who may climb the mountain of the Lord?" Just as God created an orderly universe, so we are commanded to create an orderly society. Worshipping God at the Temple may not be divorced from honesty and integrity in everyday life. The latter part of the psalm, "Lift up your heads, O gates", was said by King Solomon when the Ark, containing the tablets of the covenant, was first brought into the Temple (*Shabbat* 30a). As the Torah scroll is returned to the Ark, we recall that historic scene.

While the Torah scroll is returned to the Ark, say:

PSALM 24

לְדָוִד A psalm of David. The earth is the LORD's and all it contains, the world and all who live in it. For He founded it on the seas and established it on the streams. Who may climb the mountain of the LORD? Who may stand in His holy place? He who has clean hands and a pure heart, who has not taken My name in vain, or sworn deceitfully. He shall receive blessing from the LORD, and just reward from GOD, his salvation. This is a generation of those who seek Him, the descendants of Jacob who seek Your presence, Selah! Lift up your heads, O gates; be uplifted, eternal doors, so that the King of glory may enter. Who is the King of glory? It is the LORD, strong and mighty, the LORD mighty in battle. Lift up your heads, O gates; be uplifted, eternal doors, so that the King of glory may enter. ➔ Who is he, the King of glory? The LORD of hosts, He is the King of glory, Selah!

While the Torah scroll is placed into the Ark, say:

וּבְנֻחֹה When the Ark came to rest, Moses would say: "Return, O LORD, to the myriad thousands of Israel." Advance, LORD, to Your resting place, You and Your mighty Ark. Your priests are clothed in righteousness, and Your devoted ones sing in joy. For the sake of Your servant David, do not reject Your anointed one. For I give you good instruction; do not forsake My Torah. It is a tree of life to those who grasp it, and those who uphold it are happy. Its ways are ways of pleasantness, and all its paths are peace. ➔ Turn us back, O LORD, to You, and we will return. Renew our days as of old.

The Ark is closed.

וּבְנֻחֹה יֹאמַר *When the Ark came to rest*: These words, taken from Numbers 10:36, recall the journeys of the Israelites through the wilderness in the days of Moses. They parallel the words we say when the scroll is taken out, "Whenever the Ark set out" (page 120), said by the Israelites when they began a new journey. Throughout the centuries, wherever Jews went, they took the Torah with them: it became their "portable homeland". *It is a tree of life to those who grasp it* – though Adam and Eve were forbidden to eat the fruit of the tree of life (Genesis 3:22), the Torah is our intimation of eternity in the midst of time. Immortality is a matter, not of *how long* we live, but of *how* we live.

סיום תפילה

אשרי

אַשְׁרֵי יוֹשְׁבֵי בֵיתֶךָ, עוֹד יְהַלְלְוּךָ סֶּלָה.
אַשְׁרֵי הָעָם שֶׁכָּכָה לּוֹ, אַשְׁרֵי הָעָם שֶׁיהוה אֱלֹהָיו.

תהלים קמה

תְּהִלָּה לְדָוִד,
אֲרוֹמִמְךָ אֱלוֹהַי הַמֶּלֶךְ, וַאֲבָרְכָה שִׁמְךָ לְעוֹלָם וָעֶד.
בְּכָל יוֹם אֲבָרְכֶךָּ, וַאֲהַלְלָה שִׁמְךָ לְעוֹלָם וָעֶד.
גָּדוֹל יהוה וּמְהֻלָּל מְאֹד, וְלִגְדֻלָּתוֹ אֵין חֵקֶר.
דּוֹר לְדוֹר יְשַׁבַּח מַעֲשֶׂיךָ, וּגְבוּרֹתֶיךָ יַגִּידוּ.
הֲדַר כְּבוֹד הוֹדֶךָ, וְדִבְרֵי נִפְלְאֹתֶיךָ אָשִׂיחָה.
וֶעֱזוּז נוֹרְאוֹתֶיךָ יֹאמֵרוּ, וּגְדֻלָּתְךָ אֲסַפְּרֶנָּה.
זֵכֶר רַב־טוּבְךָ יַבִּיעוּ, וְצִדְקָתְךָ יְרַנֵּנוּ.
חַנּוּן וְרַחוּם יהוה, אֶרֶךְ אַפַּיִם וּגְדָל־חָסֶד.
טוֹב יהוה לַכֹּל, וְרַחֲמָיו עַל כָּל מַעֲשָׂיו.
יוֹדוּךָ יהוה כָּל מַעֲשֶׂיךָ, וַחֲסִידֶיךָ יְבָרְכוּכָה.
כְּבוֹד מַלְכוּתְךָ יֹאמֵרוּ, וּגְבוּרָתְךָ יְדַבֵּרוּ.

CONCLUSION OF THE MORNING SERVICE
The final section of the prayers now begins. It interweaves two distinct elements: one is a formal conclusion to the morning service, including *Aleinu* and the psalm for the day, with an emphasis on the theme of Redemption, and the other is study. It was the custom in ancient times, and in many places today, to devote time after prayer to Torah learning. This originally included texts from the prophetic books. The close of a study session was marked by a series of prayers beginning "You are the Holy One". The *Kaddish* had its origin in such sessions.

The link between these two ideas – redemption and Torah study – is created in an inspired fashion, by reading two consecutive verses from Isaiah, the first of which speaks of redemption ("A redeemer will come to Zion"), and the second of which talks of Torah study ("My words I have placed in your mouth will not depart from your mouth, or from

CONCLUSION OF SERVICE

ASHREI

אַשְׁרֵי Happy are those who dwell in Your House;
they shall continue to praise you, Selah!
Happy are the people for whom this is so;
happy are the people whose God is the Lord.

PSALM 145

A song of praise by David.

I will exalt You, my God, the King,
and bless Your name for ever and all time.
Every day I will bless You,
and praise Your name for ever and all time.
God is great and greatly to be praised;
His greatness is unfathomable.
One generation will praise Your works to the next,
and tell of Your mighty deeds.
On the glorious splendour of Your majesty I will meditate,
and on the acts of Your wonders.
They shall talk of the power of Your awesome deeds,
and I will tell of Your greatness.
They shall recite the record of Your great goodness,
and sing with joy of Your righteousness.
The Lord is gracious and compassionate,
slow to anger and great in lovingkindness.
The Lord is good to all,
and His compassion extends to all His works.
All Your works shall thank You, Lord,
and Your devoted ones shall bless You.
They shall talk of the glory of Your kingship,
and speak of Your might.

---

the mouths of your children"). Thus are joined study, the *internalisation* of God's word, and redemption, the *externalisation* of God's word as we prepare to enter the world of work, striving to live by the Torah's commandments.

אַשְׁרֵי *Happy are those*: Just as we say *Ashrei before* the *Shema* and the *Amidah*, so do we say it *after*, following the custom of "the pious of old" who devoted time before prayer in preparation, and afterward in meditation. According to the Talmud, the practice was based on the first line of *Ashrei* itself: "Happy are those who dwell in Your House."

לְהוֹדִיעַ לִבְנֵי הָאָדָם גְּבוּרֹתָיו, וּכְבוֹד הֲדַר מַלְכוּתוֹ.
מַלְכוּתְךָ מַלְכוּת כָּל עֹלָמִים, וּמֶמְשַׁלְתְּךָ בְּכָל דּוֹר וָדֹר.
סוֹמֵךְ יהוה לְכָל הַנֹּפְלִים, וְזוֹקֵף לְכָל הַכְּפוּפִים.
עֵינֵי כֹל אֵלֶיךָ יְשַׂבֵּרוּ, וְאַתָּה נוֹתֵן לָהֶם אֶת אָכְלָם בְּעִתּוֹ.
פּוֹתֵחַ אֶת יָדֶךָ, וּמַשְׂבִּיעַ לְכָל־חַי רָצוֹן.
צַדִּיק יהוה בְּכָל דְּרָכָיו, וְחָסִיד בְּכָל מַעֲשָׂיו.
קָרוֹב יהוה לְכָל קֹרְאָיו, לְכֹל אֲשֶׁר יִקְרָאֻהוּ בֶאֱמֶת.
רְצוֹן יְרֵאָיו יַעֲשֶׂה, וְאֶת שַׁוְעָתָם יִשְׁמַע, וְיוֹשִׁיעֵם.
שׁוֹמֵר יהוה אֶת כָּל אֹהֲבָיו, וְאֵת כָּל־הָרְשָׁעִים יַשְׁמִיד.
← תְּהִלַּת יהוה יְדַבֶּר פִּי, וִיבָרֵךְ כָּל־בָּשָׂר שֵׁם קָדְשׁוֹ לְעוֹלָם וָעֶד.
וַאֲנַחְנוּ נְבָרֵךְ יָהּ, מֵעַתָּה וְעַד־עוֹלָם, הַלְלוּיָהּ.

The following paragraph is not said on חוֹל הַמּוֹעֵד ,רֹאשׁ חֹדֶשׁ ,עֶרֶב פֶּסַח ,תִּשְׁעָה בְּאָב ,חֲנֻכָּה, the day before יוֹם כִּפּוּר ,פּוּרִים ,שׁוּשַׁן פּוּרִים, and the 14th and 15th of אֲדָר רִאשׁוֹן in a Jewish leap year, יוֹם הָעַצְמָאוּת ,יוֹם יְרוּשָׁלַיִם, or in a house of mourning during the week of שִׁבְעָה.

תהלים כ

לַמְנַצֵּחַ מִזְמוֹר לְדָוִד. יַעַנְךָ יהוה בְּיוֹם צָרָה, יְשַׂגֶּבְךָ שֵׁם אֱלֹהֵי יַעֲקֹב. יִשְׁלַח עֶזְרְךָ מִקֹּדֶשׁ, וּמִצִּיּוֹן יִסְעָדֶךָּ. יִזְכֹּר כָּל מִנְחֹתֶיךָ, וְעוֹלָתְךָ יְדַשְּׁנֶה סֶלָה. יִתֶּן לְךָ כִלְבָבֶךָ וְכָל־עֲצָתְךָ יְמַלֵּא. נְרַנְּנָה בִּישׁוּעָתֶךָ, וּבְשֵׁם אֱלֹהֵינוּ נִדְגֹּל, יְמַלֵּא יהוה כָּל־מִשְׁאֲלוֹתֶיךָ. עַתָּה יָדַעְתִּי כִּי הוֹשִׁיעַ יהוה מְשִׁיחוֹ, יַעֲנֵהוּ מִשְּׁמֵי קָדְשׁוֹ, בִּגְבֻרוֹת יֵשַׁע יְמִינוֹ. אֵלֶּה בָרֶכֶב, וְאֵלֶּה בַסּוּסִים, וַאֲנַחְנוּ בְּשֵׁם יהוה אֱלֹהֵינוּ נַזְכִּיר. הֵמָּה כָּרְעוּ וְנָפָלוּ וַאֲנַחְנוּ קַמְנוּ וַנִּתְעוֹדָד. ← יהוה הוֹשִׁיעָה, הַמֶּלֶךְ יַעֲנֵנוּ בְיוֹם קָרְאֵנוּ.

Psalm 20: A prayer for protection from harm. As prayer reaches its close, and we prepare to re-enter the outside world with its hazards and dangers, we ask God to keep us from harm. Because of the solemnity of its mood, it is omitted on festivals or in a house of mourning, so as not to subtract from the joy of the former, or add to the grief of the latter.

To make known to mankind His mighty deeds
and the glorious majesty of His kingship.
Your kingdom is an everlasting kingdom,
and Your reign is for all generations.
The LORD supports all who fall,
and raises all who are bowed down.
All raise their eyes to You in hope,
and You give them their food in due season.
You open Your hand,
and satisfy every living thing with Your favour.
The LORD is righteous in all His ways,
and kind in all He does.
The LORD is close to all who call on Him,
to all who call on Him in truth.
He fulfils the will of those who revere Him;
He hears their cry and saves them.
The LORD guards all who love Him,
but all the wicked He will destroy.
→ My mouth shall speak the praise of the LORD,
and all creatures shall bless His holy name for ever and all time.
We will bless the LORD now and for ever. Halleluyah!

The following paragraph is not said on the Intermediate Days of Festivals, Rosh Chodesh, the day before Pesach, the Ninth of Av, the day before Yom Kippur, Chanukah, Purim, Shushan Purim and the 14th and 15th of Adar Rishon in a Jewish leap year, Yom Ha'Atzma'ut, Yom Yerushalayim, or in a house of mourning during the week of *shivah*.

PSALM 20

לַמְנַצֵּחַ For the director of music. A psalm of David. May the LORD answer you when you are in distress; may the name of Jacob's GOD protect you. May He send you help from the Sanctuary and support from Zion. May He remember all your meal-offerings and accept your burnt-offerings, Selah! May He give you your heart's desire and make all your plans succeed. We will shout for joy at Your salvation and lift a banner in the name of our GOD. May the LORD grant all your requests. Now I know that the LORD saves His anointed; He answers him from His holy heaven with the saving power of His right hand. Some trust in chariots, others in horses, but we call on the name of the LORD our GOD. They are brought to their knees and fall, but we rise up and stand firm. → LORD, save. May the King answer us on the day we call.

The words in bold type are said aloud together by the Leader and Congregation.

וּבָא לְצִיּוֹן גּוֹאֵל, וּלְשָׁבֵי פֶשַׁע בְּיַעֲקֹב נְאֻם יהוה. וַאֲנִי, זֹאת בְּרִיתִי אוֹתָם, אָמַר יהוה, רוּחִי אֲשֶׁר עָלֶיךָ, וּדְבָרַי אֲשֶׁר שַׂמְתִּי בְּפִיךָ, לֹא יָמוּשׁוּ מִפִּיךָ וּמִפִּי זַרְעֲךָ וּמִפִּי זֶרַע זַרְעֲךָ, אָמַר יהוה, מֵעַתָּה וְעַד עוֹלָם, ‹ וְאַתָּה קָדוֹשׁ יוֹשֵׁב תְּהִלּוֹת יִשְׂרָאֵל. וְקָרָא זֶה אֶל־זֶה וְאָמַר, **קָדוֹשׁ, קָדוֹשׁ, קָדוֹשׁ יהוה צְבָאוֹת, מְלֹא כָל הָאָרֶץ כְּבוֹדוֹ.** וּמְקַבְּלִין דֵּין מִן דֵּין וְאָמְרִין, קַדִּישׁ בִּשְׁמֵי מְרוֹמָא עִלָּאָה בֵּית שְׁכִינְתֵּהּ, קַדִּישׁ עַל אַרְעָא עוֹבַד גְּבוּרְתֵּהּ, קַדִּישׁ לְעָלַם וּלְעָלְמֵי עָלְמַיָּא, יהוה צְבָאוֹת, מַלְיָא כָל־אַרְעָא זִיו יְקָרֵהּ. ‹ וַתִּשָּׂאֵנִי רוּחַ, וָאֶשְׁמַע אַחֲרַי קוֹל רַעַשׁ גָּדוֹל, **בָּרוּךְ כְּבוֹד יהוה מִמְּקוֹמוֹ.** וּנְטָלַתְנִי רוּחָא, וְשִׁמְעֵת בַּתְרַי קָל זִיעַ סַגִּיא דִּמְשַׁבְּחִין וְאָמְרִין, בְּרִיךְ יְקָרָא דַיהוה מֵאֲתַר בֵּית שְׁכִינְתֵּהּ. **יהוה יִמְלֹךְ לְעֹלָם וָעֶד.** יהוה מַלְכוּתֵהּ קָאֵם לְעָלַם וּלְעָלְמֵי עָלְמַיָּא.

יהוה אֱלֹהֵי אַבְרָהָם יִצְחָק וְיִשְׂרָאֵל אֲבוֹתֵינוּ, שָׁמְרָה זֹּאת לְעוֹלָם, לְיֵצֶר מַחְשְׁבוֹת לְבַב עַמֶּךָ, וְהָכֵן לְבָבָם אֵלֶיךָ. וְהוּא רַחוּם, יְכַפֵּר עָוֹן וְלֹא יַשְׁחִית, וְהִרְבָּה לְהָשִׁיב אַפּוֹ, וְלֹא יָעִיר כָּל־חֲמָתוֹ. כִּי אַתָּה אֲדֹנָי טוֹב וְסַלָּח, וְרַב חֶסֶד לְכָל־קוֹרְאֶיךָ. צִדְקָתְךָ צֶדֶק לְעוֹלָם, וְתוֹרָתְךָ אֱמֶת. תִּתֵּן אֱמֶת לְיַעֲקֹב, חֶסֶד לְאַבְרָהָם, אֲשֶׁר נִשְׁבַּעְתָּ לַאֲבוֹתֵינוּ מִימֵי קֶדֶם. בָּרוּךְ אֲדֹנָי יוֹם יוֹם יַעֲמָס־לָנוּ, הָאֵל יְשׁוּעָתֵנוּ סֶלָה. יהוה צְבָאוֹת עִמָּנוּ, מִשְׂגָּב לָנוּ אֱלֹהֵי יַעֲקֹב סֶלָה. יהוה צְבָאוֹת, אַשְׁרֵי אָדָם בֹּטֵחַ בָּךְ. יהוה הוֹשִׁיעָה, הַמֶּלֶךְ יַעֲנֵנוּ בְיוֹם קָרְאֵנוּ.

The words in bold type are said aloud together by the Leader and Congregation.

וּבָא לְצִיּוֹן גּוֹאֵל "A redeemer will come to Zion, to those in Jacob who repent of their sins," declares the LORD. "As for Me, this is My covenant with them," says the LORD. "My spirit, that is on you, and My words I have placed in your mouth will not depart from your mouth, or from the mouth of your children, or from the mouth of their descendants from this time on and forever," says the LORD. ➜ You are the Holy One, enthroned on the praises of Israel. And (the angels) call to one another, saying, "**Holy, holy, holy is the LORD of hosts. The whole earth is full of His glory.**" And they receive permission from one another, saying: "Holy in the highest heavens, home of His presence; holy on earth, the work of His strength; holy for ever and all time is the LORD of hosts; the whole earth is full of His radiant glory." Then a wind lifted me up and I heard behind me the sound of a great noise, saying, "**Blessed is the LORD's glory from His place.**" ➜ Then a wind lifted me up and I heard behind me the sound of a great tempest of those who uttered praise, saying, "Blessed is the LORD's glory from the place of the home of His Presence." **The LORD shall reign for ever and all time**. The LORD's kingdom is established for ever and all time.

LORD, GOD of Abraham, Isaac and Israel, our ancestors, may You keep this for ever so that it forms the thoughts in Your people's heart, and directs their heart towards You. He is compassionate. He forgives iniquity and does not destroy. Repeatedly He suppresses His anger, not rousing His full wrath. For You, my LORD, are good and forgiving, abundantly kind to all who call on You. Your righteousness is eternally righteous, and Your Torah is truth. Grant truth to Jacob, lovingkindness to Abraham, as You promised our ancestors in ancient times. Blessed is the LORD who day after day bears our burden, for GOD is our salvation, Selah! The LORD of hosts is with us; the GOD of Jacob is our refuge, Selah! LORD of hosts, happy is the one who trusts in You. LORD, save. May the King answer us on the day we call.

וּבָא לְצִיּוֹן גּוֹאֵל *A redeemer will come to Zion*: These two verses are all that remain of the ancient custom of studying prophetic texts after prayer. *You are the Holy One* – the third and final *Kedushah* of the morning service, known as *Kedushah*

בָּרוּךְ אֱלֹהֵינוּ שֶׁבְּרָאֲנוּ לִכְבוֹדוֹ, וְהִבְדִּילָנוּ מִן הַתּוֹעִים, וְנָתַן לָנוּ תּוֹרַת אֱמֶת, וְחַיֵּי עוֹלָם נָטַע בְּתוֹכֵנוּ. הוּא יִפְתַּח לִבֵּנוּ בְּתוֹרָתוֹ, וְיָשֵׂם בְּלִבֵּנוּ אַהֲבָתוֹ וְיִרְאָתוֹ וְלַעֲשׂוֹת רְצוֹנוֹ וּלְעָבְדוֹ בְּלֵבָב שָׁלֵם, לְמַעַן לֹא נִיגַע לָרִיק, וְלֹא נֵלֵד לַבֶּהָלָה.

יְהִי רָצוֹן מִלְּפָנֶיךָ יהוה אֱלֹהֵינוּ וֵאלֹהֵי אֲבוֹתֵינוּ, שֶׁנִּשְׁמֹר חֻקֶּיךָ בָּעוֹלָם הַזֶּה, וְנִזְכֶּה וְנִחְיֶה וְנִרְאֶה וְנִירַשׁ טוֹבָה וּבְרָכָה לִשְׁנֵי יְמוֹת הַמָּשִׁיחַ וּלְחַיֵּי הָעוֹלָם הַבָּא. לְמַעַן יְזַמֶּרְךָ כָבוֹד וְלֹא יִדֹּם, יהוה אֱלֹהַי לְעוֹלָם אוֹדֶךָּ. בָּרוּךְ הַגֶּבֶר אֲשֶׁר יִבְטַח בַּיהוה, וְהָיָה יהוה מִבְטַחוֹ. בִּטְחוּ בַיהוה עֲדֵי־עַד, כִּי בְּיָהּ יהוה צוּר עוֹלָמִים. וְיִבְטְחוּ בְךָ יוֹדְעֵי שְׁמֶךָ, כִּי לֹא עָזַבְתָּ דֹרְשֶׁיךָ, יהוה. ‹ יהוה חָפֵץ לְמַעַן צִדְקוֹ, יַגְדִּיל תּוֹרָה וְיַאְדִּיר.

On רֹאשׁ חֹדֶשׁ and יוֹם טוֹב, the Leader says חֲצִי קַדִּישׁ, page 126. This is then followed by מוּסָף. The מוּסָף for רֹאשׁ חֹדֶשׁ is on page 630, for יוֹם טוֹב on page 670.

On other days, the Leader says קַדִּישׁ תִּתְקַבַּל:

קדיש תתקבל

Leader:

יִתְגַּדַּל וְיִתְקַדַּשׁ שְׁמֵהּ רַבָּא. (Cong. אָמֵן) בְּעָלְמָא דִּי־בְרָא כִרְעוּתֵהּ. וְיַמְלִיךְ מַלְכוּתֵהּ, בְּחַיֵּיכוֹן וּבְיוֹמֵיכוֹן וּבְחַיֵּי דְכָל־בֵּית יִשְׂרָאֵל, בַּעֲגָלָא וּבִזְמַן קָרִיב. וְאִמְרוּ אָמֵן. (Cong. אָמֵן)

All:

יְהֵא שְׁמֵהּ רַבָּא מְבָרַךְ לְעָלַם וּלְעָלְמֵי עָלְמַיָּא.

---

de-Sidra. Here, it is incorporated into an act of study. Hence the verses of the *Kedushah* are followed by their Aramaic translations and expansions (Aramaic was for a long time the language of study).

Blessed is our God who created us for His glory, separating us from those who go astray; who gave us the Torah of truth, planting within us eternal life. May He open our heart to His Torah, imbuing our heart with the love and awe of Him, that we may do His will and serve Him with a perfect heart, so that we neither toil in vain nor give birth to confusion.

May it be Your will, O Lord our God and God of our ancestors, that we keep Your laws in this world, and thus be worthy to live, see and inherit goodness and blessing in the Messianic Age and in the life of the World to Come, so that my soul may sing to You and not be silent. Lord, my God, for ever I will thank You. Blessed is the man who trusts in the Lord, whose trust is in the Lord alone. Trust in the Lord for evermore, for God the Lord is an everlasting Rock. Those who know Your name trust in You, for You, Lord, do not forsake those who seek You. ✧ The Lord desired, for the sake of Israel's merit, to make the Torah great and glorious.

On Rosh Chodesh and festivals, the Leader says half-*Kaddish*, page 127. This is then followed by *Musaf*. The *Musaf* for Rosh Chodesh is on page 631, for festivals on page 671.

On other days, the Leader says full *Kaddish*:

FULL KADDISH

Leader:

יִתְגַּדַּל Magnified and sanctified may His great name be, in the world He created by His will. May He establish His kingdom in your lifetime and in your days, and in the lifetime of all the House of Israel, swiftly and soon – and say: Amen.

All:

May His great name be blessed for ever and all time.

בָּרוּךְ אֱלֹהֵינוּ *Blessed is our God*: There now follow a concluding blessing and a prayer. The blessing marks the end of a Torah study session (the counterpart of the two opening benedictions in the Blessings of Dawn). The prayer, by contrast, looks forward to the future, personal and collective: personal – may God help us to keep His commandments, and collective – may we see the coming of the Messianic Age.

Leader:

יִתְבָּרַךְ וְיִשְׁתַּבַּח וְיִתְפָּאַר וְיִתְרוֹמַם וְיִתְנַשֵּׂא וְיִתְהַדָּר וְיִתְעַלֶּה וְיִתְהַלָּל שְׁמֵהּ דְּקֻדְשָׁא בְּרִיךְ הוּא (Cong. בְּרִיךְ הוּא) לְעֵלָּא (Between רֹאשׁ הַשָּׁנָה and יוֹם כִּפּוּר add לְעֵלָּא) מִן־כָּל־בִּרְכָתָא וְשִׁירָתָא תֻּשְׁבְּחָתָא וְנֶחֱמָתָא, דַּאֲמִירָן בְּעָלְמָא. וְאִמְרוּ אָמֵן. (Cong. אָמֵן)

תִּתְקַבַּל צְלוֹתְהוֹן וּבָעוּתְהוֹן דְּכָל־יִשְׂרָאֵל קֳדָם אֲבוּהוֹן דִּי בִשְׁמַיָּא. וְאִמְרוּ אָמֵן. (Cong. אָמֵן)

יְהֵא שְׁלָמָא רַבָּא מִן־שְׁמַיָּא, וְחַיִּים עָלֵינוּ וְעַל־כָּל־יִשְׂרָאֵל. וְאִמְרוּ אָמֵן. (Cong. אָמֵן)

Bow, take three steps back, then bow, first left, then right, then centre, while saying:

עֹשֶׂה שָׁלוֹם בִּמְרוֹמָיו, הוּא יַעֲשֶׂה שָׁלוֹם עָלֵינוּ, וְעַל־כָּל־יִשְׂרָאֵל. וְאִמְרוּ אָמֵן. (Cong. אָמֵן)

עלינו

Stand while saying עָלֵינוּ. Bow at ▾.

עָלֵינוּ לְשַׁבֵּחַ לַאֲדוֹן הַכֹּל, לָתֵת גְּדֻלָּה לְיוֹצֵר בְּרֵאשִׁית, שֶׁלֹּא עָשָׂנוּ כְּגוֹיֵי הָאֲרָצוֹת, וְלֹא שָׂמָנוּ כְּמִשְׁפְּחוֹת הָאֲדָמָה. שֶׁלֹּא שָׂם חֶלְקֵנוּ כָּהֶם, וְגֹרָלֵנוּ כְּכָל־הֲמוֹנָם. ▾וַאֲנַחְנוּ כּוֹרְעִים וּמִשְׁתַּחֲוִים וּמוֹדִים, לִפְנֵי מֶלֶךְ מַלְכֵי הַמְּלָכִים הַקָּדוֹשׁ בָּרוּךְ הוּא. שֶׁהוּא נוֹטֶה שָׁמַיִם וְיוֹסֵד אָרֶץ, וּמוֹשַׁב יְקָרוֹ בַּשָּׁמַיִם מִמַּעַל, וּשְׁכִינַת עֻזּוֹ בְּגָבְהֵי מְרוֹמִים. הוּא אֱלֹהֵינוּ, אֵין עוֹד. אֱמֶת מַלְכֵּנוּ, אֶפֶס זוּלָתוֹ, כַּכָּתוּב בְּתוֹרָתוֹ, וְיָדַעְתָּ הַיּוֹם וַהֲשֵׁבֹתָ אֶל־לְבָבֶךָ,

---

עָלֵינוּ *It is our duty*: Since the twelfth or thirteenth centuries it has become the custom to bring all services to a close with the magnificent prayer known as *Aleinu*, a construct of two paragraphs, composed at different times and in different styles,

Leader:

Blessed and praised, glorified and exalted, raised and honoured, uplifted and lauded be the name of the Holy One, blessed be He, (between Rosh Hashanah and Yom Kippur add 'well') beyond any blessing, song, praise and consolation uttered in the world – and say: Amen.

May the prayers and pleas of all Israel be accepted by their Father in heaven – and say: Amen.

May there be great peace from heaven, and life for us and all Israel – and say: Amen.

Bow, take three steps back, then bow, first left, then right, then centre, while saying:

May He who makes peace in His high places, make peace for us and all Israel – and say: Amen.

ALEINU

Stand while saying *Aleinu*. Bow at ▾.

עָלֵינוּ It is our duty to praise the Master of all, and ascribe greatness to the Author of creation, who has not made us like the nations of the lands nor placed us like the families of the earth; who has not made our portion like theirs, nor our destiny like all their multitudes. Therefore ▾we bow in worship and thank the Supreme King of kings, the Holy One, blessed be He, who extends the heavens and establishes the earth, whose throne of glory is in the heavens above, and whose power's presence is in the highest of heights. He is our God; there is no other. Truly He is our King, there is none else, as it is written in His Torah "You shall know and take to heart this day

---

which together make a striking statement of the particularity of Jewish faith and its universal aspiration for humanity.

The first paragraph, a text of great antiquity, was originally used (and still is) as an introduction to the Blessing of Kingship in the *Musaf* of Rosh Hashanah. Less a prayer than a declaration of faith, it speaks of the singular vocation of the Jewish people as bearers of the message of monotheism. Twice, the prayer uses the expression, "There is no other", forcefully expressed in Hebrew by two monosyllabic words, *ein od.*

כִּי יהוה הוּא הָאֱלֹהִים בַּשָּׁמַיִם מִמַּעַל וְעַל־הָאָרֶץ מִתָּחַת, אֵין עוֹד.

עַל־כֵּן נְקַוֶּה לְּךָ יהוה אֱלֹהֵינוּ לִרְאוֹת מְהֵרָה בְּתִפְאֶרֶת עֻזֶּךָ, לְהַעֲבִיר גִּלּוּלִים מִן הָאָרֶץ, וְהָאֱלִילִים כָּרוֹת יִכָּרֵתוּן, לְתַקֵּן עוֹלָם בְּמַלְכוּת שַׁדַּי. וְכָל־בְּנֵי בָשָׂר יִקְרְאוּ בִשְׁמֶךָ, לְהַפְנוֹת אֵלֶיךָ כָּל־רִשְׁעֵי אָרֶץ. יַכִּירוּ וְיֵדְעוּ כָּל־יוֹשְׁבֵי תֵבֵל, כִּי לְךָ תִּכְרַע כָּל־בֶּרֶךְ, תִּשָּׁבַע כָּל־לָשׁוֹן. לְפָנֶיךָ יהוה אֱלֹהֵינוּ יִכְרְעוּ וְיִפֹּלוּ, וְלִכְבוֹד שִׁמְךָ יְקָר יִתֵּנוּ. וִיקַבְּלוּ כֻלָּם אֶת־עוֹל מַלְכוּתֶךָ, וְתִמְלֹךְ עֲלֵיהֶם מְהֵרָה לְעוֹלָם וָעֶד. כִּי הַמַּלְכוּת שֶׁלְּךָ הִיא וּלְעוֹלְמֵי עַד תִּמְלוֹךְ בְּכָבוֹד, כַּכָּתוּב בְּתוֹרָתֶךָ, יהוה יִמְלֹךְ לְעֹלָם וָעֶד. ← וְנֶאֱמַר, וְהָיָה יהוה לְמֶלֶךְ עַל־כָּל־הָאָרֶץ, בַּיּוֹם הַהוּא יִהְיֶה יהוה אֶחָד וּשְׁמוֹ אֶחָד.

Some congregations add:

אַל תִּירָא מִפַּחַד פִּתְאֹם, וּמִשֹּׁאַת רְשָׁעִים כִּי תָבֹא. עֻצוּ עֵצָה וְתֻפָר, דַּבְּרוּ דָבָר וְלֹא יָקוּם, כִּי עִמָּנוּ אֵל. וְעַד זִקְנָה אֲנִי הוּא, וְעַד שֵׂיבָה אֲנִי אֶסְבֹּל, אֲנִי עָשִׂיתִי וַאֲנִי אֶשָּׂא, וַאֲנִי אֶסְבֹּל וַאֲמַלֵּט.

קדיש יתום

The transliteration can be found at the end of the Siddur.

Mourner:

יִתְגַּדַּל וְיִתְקַדַּשׁ שְׁמֵהּ רַבָּא. (Cong. אָמֵן) בְּעָלְמָא דִּי־בְרָא כִרְעוּתֵהּ. וְיַמְלִיךְ מַלְכוּתֵהּ, בְּחַיֵּיכוֹן וּבְיוֹמֵיכוֹן וּבְחַיֵּי דִי־כָל־בֵּית יִשְׂרָאֵל, בַּעֲגָלָא וּבִזְמַן קָרִיב. וְאִמְרוּ אָמֵן. (Cong. אָמֵן)

The second paragraph turns to God and to the future, to a time when all humanity will acknowledge the One God, a vision eloquently spoken of by the prophet Zechariah, from whose book the final verse is taken. It contains a phrase – "to perfect the world under the sovereignty of God" – which became a lead-

that the LORD is GOD, in heaven above and on earth below. There is no other."

עַל־כֵּן Therefore we place our hope in You, LORD our GOD, that we may soon see the glory of Your power, when You will remove abominations from the earth, and idols will be utterly destroyed, when the world will be perfected under the sovereignty of the Almighty, when all humanity will call on Your name, and the earth's wicked will all turn to You. All the world's inhabitants will realise and know that to You every knee must bow and every tongue swear loyalty. Before You, LORD our GOD, they will kneel and bow down and give honour to Your glorious name. They will all accept the yoke of Your kingdom, and You will reign over them soon and for ever. For the kingdom is Yours, and to all eternity You will reign in glory, as it is written in Your Torah: "The LORD will reign for ever and ever." ➛ And it is said: "Then the LORD shall be King over all the earth: on that day the LORD shall be One and His name One."

Some congregations add:

Have no fear of sudden terror or of the ruin that overtakes the wicked. Devise your strategy, but it will be thwarted; propose your plan, but it will not stand, for GOD is with us. When you grow old, I will still be the same. When your hair turns grey, I will still carry you. I made you, I will bear you, I will carry you, and I will rescue you.

MOURNER'S KADDISH

The transliteration can be found at the end of the Siddur.

Mourner:

יִתְגַּדַּל may His great name be, in the world He created by His will. May He establish His kingdom in your lifetime and in your days, and in the lifetime of all the House of Israel, swiftly and soon – and say: Amen.

---

ing theme of Lurianic mysticism in the sixteenth century (*tikkun olam*).

No prayer more eloquently expresses the dual nature of the Jewish people: its singular history as the nation chosen to be GOD's witnesses on earth, and its universal aspiration for the time when all the inhabitants of earth will recognise the GOD in whose image we are formed.

All:

יְהֵא שְׁמֵהּ רַבָּא מְבָרַךְ לְעָלַם וּלְעָלְמֵי עָלְמַיָּא.

Mourner:

יִתְבָּרַךְ וְיִשְׁתַּבַּח וְיִתְפָּאַר וְיִתְרוֹמַם וְיִתְנַשֵּׂא וְיִתְהַדָּר
וְיִתְעַלֶּה וְיִתְהַלָּל שְׁמֵהּ דְּקֻדְשָׁא בְּרִיךְ הוּא (Cong. בְּרִיךְ הוּא)
לְעֵלָּא (Between רֹאשׁ הַשָּׁנָה and יוֹם כִּפּוּר add לְעֵלָּא) מִן־כָּל־בִּרְכָתָא
וְשִׁירָתָא תֻּשְׁבְּחָתָא וְנֶחֱמָתָא, דַּאֲמִירָן בְּעָלְמָא. וְאִמְרוּ
אָמֵן. (Cong. אָמֵן)

יְהֵא שְׁלָמָא רַבָּא מִן־שְׁמַיָּא, וְחַיִּים עָלֵינוּ וְעַל־כָּל־יִשְׂרָאֵל.
וְאִמְרוּ אָמֵן. (Cong. אָמֵן)

Bow, take three steps back, then bow, first left, then right, then centre, while saying:

עֹשֶׂה שָׁלוֹם בִּמְרוֹמָיו, הוּא יַעֲשֶׂה שָׁלוֹם עָלֵינוּ, וְעַל־כָּל־
יִשְׂרָאֵל. וְאִמְרוּ אָמֵן. (Cong. אָמֵן)

שיר של יום

One of the following psalms is said on the appropriate day of the week as indicated. After the psalm, קַדִּישׁ יָתוֹם on page 142 is said.

On חֲנֻכָּה, מִזְמוֹר שִׁיר חֲנֻכַּת הַבַּיִת is also added, page 36, after the daily psalm. On רֹאשׁ חֹדֶשׁ, add Psalm 104, page 154. From the second day of רֹאשׁ חֹדֶשׁ אֱלוּל until (and including) שְׁמִינִי עֲצֶרֶת, add Psalm 27, page 156.

Sunday

הַיּוֹם יוֹם רִאשׁוֹן בְּשַׁבָּת, שֶׁבּוֹ הָיוּ הַלְוִיִּם אוֹמְרִים בְּבֵית הַמִּקְדָּשׁ.

תהלים כד

לְדָוִד מִזְמוֹר, לַיהוה הָאָרֶץ וּמְלוֹאָהּ, תֵּבֵל וְיֹשְׁבֵי בָהּ.
כִּי־הוּא עַל יַמִּים יְסָדָהּ, וְעַל נְהָרוֹת יְכוֹנְנֶהָ. מִי־יַעֲלֶה
בְהַר יהוה, וּמִי־יָקוּם בִּמְקוֹם קָדְשׁוֹ. נְקִי כַפַּיִם וּבַר לֵבָב,
אֲשֶׁר לֹא־נָשָׂא לַשָּׁוְא נַפְשִׁי, וְלֹא נִשְׁבַּע לְמִרְמָה. יִשָּׂא

THE DAILY PSALM
A special psalm was said in the Temple on each of the seven days of the week. We say them still, in memory of those days and in hope of future restoration.

All:

May His great name be blessed for ever and all time.

Mourner:

Blessed and praised, glorified and exalted, raised and honoured, uplifted and lauded be the name of the Holy One, blessed be He, (between Rosh Hashanah and Yom Kippur add 'well') beyond any blessing, song, praise and consolation uttered in the world – and say: Amen.

May there be great peace from heaven, and life for us and all Israel – and say: Amen.

Bow, take three steps back, then bow, first left, then right, then centre, while saying:

May He who makes peace in His high places, make peace for us and all Israel – and say: Amen.

THE DAILY PSALM

One of the following psalms is said on the appropriate day of the week as indicated. After the psalm, the Mourner's *Kaddish* on page 143 is said.

On Chanukah, Psalm 30 is also added, page 37, after the daily psalm. On Rosh Chodesh, add Psalm 104, page 155. From the second day of Rosh Chodesh Ellul until (and including) Shemini Atzeret, add Psalm 27, page 157.

Sunday

Today is the first day of the week,
on which the Levites used to say this psalm in the Temple:

PSALM 24

לְדָוִד A psalm of David. The earth is the LORD's and all it contains, the world and all who live in it. For He founded it on the seas and established it on the streams. Who may climb the mountain of the LORD? Who may stand in His holy place? He who has clean hands and a pure heart, who has not taken My name in vain or sworn deceitfully. He shall receive a blessing from the LORD, and just reward from

Sunday: Psalm 24. לְדָוִד מִזְמוֹר The opening verses mirror the act of creation, reminding us that each week mirrors the seven days of creation itself. The psalm also alludes to the Temple, built on "the mountain of the LORD". The connection between the two is based on the idea that the Temple was a microcosm of the universe, and its construction a human counterpart to the Divine creation of the cosmos.

בְּרָכָה מֵאֵת יהוה, וּצְדָקָה מֵאֱלֹהֵי יִשְׁעוֹ. זֶה דּוֹר דֹּרְשָׁיו, מְבַקְשֵׁי פָנֶיךָ יַעֲקֹב סֶלָה. שְׂאוּ שְׁעָרִים רָאשֵׁיכֶם, וְהִנָּשְׂאוּ פִּתְחֵי עוֹלָם, וְיָבוֹא מֶלֶךְ הַכָּבוֹד. מִי זֶה מֶלֶךְ הַכָּבוֹד, יהוה עִזּוּז וְגִבּוֹר, יהוה גִּבּוֹר מִלְחָמָה. שְׂאוּ שְׁעָרִים רָאשֵׁיכֶם, וּשְׂאוּ פִּתְחֵי עוֹלָם, וְיָבֹא מֶלֶךְ הַכָּבוֹד. ← מִי הוּא זֶה מֶלֶךְ הַכָּבוֹד, יהוה צְבָאוֹת, הוּא מֶלֶךְ הַכָּבוֹד סֶלָה.

Monday

הַיּוֹם יוֹם שֵׁנִי בְּשַׁבָּת, שֶׁבּוֹ הָיוּ הַלְוִיִּם אוֹמְרִים בְּבֵית הַמִּקְדָּשׁ.

תהלים מח

שִׁיר מִזְמוֹר לִבְנֵי קֹרַח. גָּדוֹל יהוה וּמְהֻלָּל מְאֹד, בְּעִיר אֱלֹהֵינוּ, הַר קָדְשׁוֹ. יְפֵה נוֹף, מְשׂוֹשׂ כָּל־הָאָרֶץ, הַר צִיּוֹן יַרְכְּתֵי צָפוֹן, קִרְיַת מֶלֶךְ רָב. אֱלֹהִים בְּאַרְמְנוֹתֶיהָ נוֹדַע לְמִשְׂגָּב. כִּי הִנֵּה הַמְּלָכִים נוֹעֲדוּ, עָבְרוּ יַחְדָּו. הֵמָּה רָאוּ כֵּן תָּמָהוּ, נִבְהֲלוּ נֶחְפָּזוּ. רְעָדָה אֲחָזָתַם שָׁם, חִיל כַּיּוֹלֵדָה. בְּרוּחַ קָדִים תְּשַׁבֵּר אֳנִיּוֹת תַּרְשִׁישׁ. כַּאֲשֶׁר שָׁמַעְנוּ כֵּן רָאִינוּ בְּעִיר יהוה צְבָאוֹת, בְּעִיר אֱלֹהֵינוּ, אֱלֹהִים יְכוֹנְנֶהָ עַד־עוֹלָם סֶלָה. דִּמִּינוּ אֱלֹהִים חַסְדֶּךָ, בְּקֶרֶב הֵיכָלֶךָ. כְּשִׁמְךָ אֱלֹהִים כֵּן תְּהִלָּתְךָ, עַל קַצְוֵי אֶרֶץ, צֶדֶק מָלְאָה יְמִינֶךָ. יִשְׂמַח הַר צִיּוֹן, תָּגֵלְנָה בְּנוֹת יְהוּדָה, לְמַעַן מִשְׁפָּטֶיךָ. סֹבּוּ צִיּוֹן וְהַקִּיפוּהָ, סִפְרוּ מִגְדָּלֶיהָ. שִׁיתוּ לִבְּכֶם לְחֵילָה, פַּסְּגוּ אַרְמְנוֹתֶיהָ, לְמַעַן תְּסַפְּרוּ לְדוֹר אַחֲרוֹן. ← כִּי זֶה אֱלֹהִים אֱלֹהֵינוּ עוֹלָם וָעֶד, הוּא יְנַהֲגֵנוּ עַל־מוּת.

Monday: Psalm 48. שִׁיר מִזְמוֹר לִבְנֵי קֹרַח A hymn of praise to the beauty and endurance of Jerusalem, the city that outlived all those who sought to conquer it. "A score of conquerors have held it as their choicest prize; and more than a dozen times has it been utterly destroyed. The Babylonians burnt it, and deported its population; the Romans slew a million of its inhabitants, razed it to the ground, passed

the God of his salvation. This is a generation of those who seek Him, the descendants of Jacob who seek Your presence, Selah! Lift up your heads, O gates; be uplifted, eternal doors, so that the King of glory may enter. Who is the King of glory? It is the Lord, strong and mighty, the Lord mighty in battle. Lift up your heads, O gates; be uplifted, eternal doors, that the King of glory may enter. ➔ Who is He, the King of glory? The Lord of hosts, He is the King of glory, Selah!

Monday

Today is the second day of the week,
on which the Levites used to say this psalm in the Temple:

PSALM 48

שִׁיר מִזְמוֹר A song. A psalm of the sons of Korach. Great is the Lord and greatly to be praised in the city of God, on His holy mountain – beautiful in its heights, joy of all the earth, Mount Zion on its northern side, city of the great King. In its citadels God is known as a stronghold. See how the kings joined forces, advancing together. They saw, they were astounded, they panicked, they fled. There fear seized them, like the pains of a woman giving birth, like ships of Tarshish wrecked by an eastern wind. What we had heard, now we have seen, in the city of the God of hosts, in the city of our God. May God preserve it for ever, Selah! In the midst of Your Temple, God, we meditate on Your love. As is Your name, God, so is Your praise: it reaches to the ends of the earth. Your right hand is filled with righteousness. Let Mount Zion rejoice, let the towns of Judah be glad, because of Your judgements. Walk around Zion and encircle it. Count its towers, note its strong walls, view its citadels, so that you may tell a future generation ➔ that this is God, our God, for ever and ever. He will guide us for evermore.

---

the ploughshare over it, and strewed its furrows with salt; Hadrian banished its very name from the lips of men, changed it to *Aelia Capitolina*, and prohibited any Jew from entering its precincts on pain of death. Persians and Arabs, Barbarians and Crusaders and Turks took it and retook it, ravaged it and burnt it; and yet, marvellous to relate, it ever rises from its ashes to renewed life and glory. It is the Eternal City of the Eternal People" (Rabbi J.H. Hertz).

Tuesday

הַיּוֹם יוֹם שְׁלִישִׁי בְּשַׁבָּת, שֶׁבּוֹ הָיוּ הַלְוִיִּם אוֹמְרִים בַּמִּקְדָּשׁ.

תהלים פב

מִזְמוֹר לְאָסָף, אֱלֹהִים נִצָּב בַּעֲדַת־אֵל, בְּקֶרֶב אֱלֹהִים יִשְׁפֹּט. עַד מָתַי תִּשְׁפְּטוּ־עָוֶל, וּפְנֵי רְשָׁעִים תִּשְׂאוּ סֶלָה. שִׁפְטוּ־דָל וְיָתוֹם, עָנִי וָרָשׁ הַצְדִּיקוּ. פַּלְּטוּ־דַל וְאֶבְיוֹן, מִיַּד רְשָׁעִים הַצִּילוּ. לֹא יָדְעוּ וְלֹא יָבִינוּ, בַּחֲשֵׁכָה יִתְהַלָּכוּ, יִמּוֹטוּ כָּל־מוֹסְדֵי אָרֶץ. אֲנִי אָמַרְתִּי אֱלֹהִים אַתֶּם, וּבְנֵי עֶלְיוֹן כֻּלְּכֶם. אָכֵן כְּאָדָם תְּמוּתוּן, וּכְאַחַד הַשָּׂרִים תִּפֹּלוּ. ← קוּמָה אֱלֹהִים שָׁפְטָה הָאָרֶץ, כִּי אַתָּה תִנְחַל בְּכָל־הַגּוֹיִם.

Wednesday

הַיּוֹם יוֹם רְבִיעִי בְּשַׁבָּת, שֶׁבּוֹ הָיוּ הַלְוִיִּם אוֹמְרִים בַּמִּקְדָּשׁ.

תהלים צד

אֵל נְקָמוֹת יהוה, אֵל נְקָמוֹת הוֹפִיעַ. הִנָּשֵׂא שֹׁפֵט הָאָרֶץ, הָשֵׁב גְּמוּל עַל־גֵּאִים. עַד־מָתַי רְשָׁעִים, יהוה, עַד מָתַי רְשָׁעִים יַעֲלֹזוּ. יַבִּיעוּ יְדַבְּרוּ עָתָק, יִתְאַמְּרוּ כָּל־פֹּעֲלֵי אָוֶן. עַמְּךָ יהוה יְדַכְּאוּ, וְנַחֲלָתְךָ יְעַנּוּ. אַלְמָנָה וְגֵר יַהֲרֹגוּ, וִיתוֹמִים יְרַצֵּחוּ. וַיֹּאמְרוּ לֹא יִרְאֶה־יָּהּ, וְלֹא יָבִין אֱלֹהֵי יַעֲקֹב. בִּינוּ בֹּעֲרִים בָּעָם, וּכְסִילִים מָתַי תַּשְׂכִּילוּ. הֲנֹטַע אֹזֶן הֲלֹא יִשְׁמָע, אִם־יֹצֵר עַיִן הֲלֹא יַבִּיט. הֲיֹסֵר גּוֹיִם הֲלֹא יוֹכִיחַ, הַמְלַמֵּד אָדָם דָּעַת. יהוה יֹדֵעַ מַחְשְׁבוֹת אָדָם,

---

Tuesday: Psalm 82. מִזְמוֹר לְאָסָף The psalm for Tuesday is about judges and justice. Justice, the application of law, brings order to society as scientific law brings order to the cosmos. Justice ultimately belongs to God. A judge must therefore act with humility and integrity, bringing Divine order to human chaos. "A judge who delivers a true judgement becomes a partner of the Holy One blessed be He in the work of creation" (*Shabbat* 10a).

Tuesday

Today is the third day of the week,
on which the Levites used to say this psalm in the Temple:

PSALM 82

מִזְמוֹר לְאָסָף A psalm of Asaph. God stands in the Divine assembly. Among the judges He delivers judgement. How long will you judge unjustly, showing favour to the wicked? Selah. Do justice to the weak and the fatherless. Vindicate the poor and destitute. Rescue the weak and needy. Save them from the hand of the wicked. They do not know nor do they understand. They walk about in darkness while all the earth's foundations shake. I once said, "You are like gods, all of you are sons of the Most High." But you shall die like mere men, you will fall like any prince. ➔ Arise, O Lord, judge the earth, for all the nations are Your possession.

Wednesday

Today is the fourth day of the week,
on which the Levites used to say this psalm in the Temple:

PSALM 94

אֵל נְקָמוֹת God of retribution, Lord, God of retribution, appear! Rise up, Judge of the earth. Repay to the arrogant what they deserve. How long shall the wicked, Lord, how long shall the wicked triumph? They pour out insolent words. All the evildoers are full of boasting. They crush Your people, Lord, and oppress Your inheritance. They kill the widow and the stranger. They murder the fatherless. They say, "The Lord does not see. The God of Jacob pays no heed." Take heed, you most brutish people. You fools, when will you grow wise? Will He who implants the ear not hear? Will He who formed the eye not see? Will He who disciplines nations – He who teaches man knowledge – not

---

Wednesday: Psalm 94. אֵל נְקָמוֹת יהוה The psalm, marking the midweek, of intense power about the connection between religious faith and ethical conduct and their opposite: lack of faith and a failure of humanity. When man begins to worship himself, he dreams of becoming a god but ends by becoming lower than the beasts. Appropriately, some communities recite this psalm on Yom HaShoah, Holocaust Memorial Day (27 Nisan).

כִּי הֵמָּה הָבֶל. אַשְׁרֵי הַגֶּבֶר אֲשֶׁר תְּיַסְּרֶנּוּ יָּהּ, וּמִתּוֹרָתְךָ תְלַמְּדֶנּוּ. לְהַשְׁקִיט לוֹ מִימֵי רָע, עַד יִכָּרֶה לָרָשָׁע שָׁחַת. כִּי לֹא־יִטֹּשׁ יהוה עַמּוֹ, וְנַחֲלָתוֹ לֹא יַעֲזֹב. כִּי עַד־צֶדֶק יָשׁוּב מִשְׁפָּט, וְאַחֲרָיו כָּל־יִשְׁרֵי־לֵב. מִי־יָקוּם לִי עִם־מְרֵעִים, מִי־יִתְיַצֵּב לִי עִם־פֹּעֲלֵי אָוֶן. לוּלֵי יהוה עֶזְרָתָה לִּי, כִּמְעַט שָׁכְנָה דוּמָה נַפְשִׁי. אִם אָמַרְתִּי מָטָה רַגְלִי, חַסְדְּךָ יהוה יִסְעָדֵנִי. בְּרֹב שַׂרְעַפַּי בְּקִרְבִּי, תַּנְחוּמֶיךָ יְשַׁעַשְׁעוּ נַפְשִׁי. הַיְחָבְרְךָ כִּסֵּא הַוּוֹת, יֹצֵר עָמָל עֲלֵי־חֹק. יָגוֹדּוּ עַל נֶפֶשׁ צַדִּיק, וְדָם נָקִי יַרְשִׁיעוּ. וַיְהִי יהוה לִי לְמִשְׂגָּב, וֵאלֹהַי לְצוּר מַחְסִי. וַיָּשֶׁב עֲלֵיהֶם אֶת־אוֹנָם, וּבְרָעָתָם יַצְמִיתֵם, יַצְמִיתֵם יהוה אֱלֹהֵינוּ. ◄ לְכוּ נְרַנְּנָה לַיהוה, נָרִיעָה לְצוּר יִשְׁעֵנוּ.

Thursday

הַיּוֹם יוֹם חֲמִישִׁי בְּשַׁבָּת, שֶׁבּוֹ הָיוּ הַלְוִיִּם אוֹמְרִים בְּבֵית הַמִּקְדָּשׁ.

תהלים פא

לַמְנַצֵּחַ עַל־הַגִּתִּית לְאָסָף. הַרְנִינוּ לֵאלֹהִים עוּזֵּנוּ, הָרִיעוּ לֵאלֹהֵי יַעֲקֹב. שְׂאוּ זִמְרָה וּתְנוּ־תֹף, כִּנּוֹר נָעִים עִם־נָבֶל. תִּקְעוּ בַחֹדֶשׁ שׁוֹפָר, בַּכֶּסֶה לְיוֹם חַגֵּנוּ. כִּי חֹק לְיִשְׂרָאֵל הוּא, מִשְׁפָּט לֵאלֹהֵי יַעֲקֹב. עֵדוּת בִּיהוֹסֵף שָׂמוֹ, בְּצֵאתוֹ עַל־אֶרֶץ מִצְרָיִם, שְׂפַת לֹא־יָדַעְתִּי אֶשְׁמָע. הֲסִירוֹתִי מִסֵּבֶל שִׁכְמוֹ, כַּפָּיו מִדּוּד תַּעֲבֹרְנָה. בַּצָּרָה קָרָאתָ, וָאֲחַלְּצֶךָּ, אֶעֶנְךָ בְּסֵתֶר רַעַם, אֶבְחָנְךָ עַל־מֵי מְרִיבָה, סֶלָה. שְׁמַע עַמִּי וְאָעִידָה בָּךְ, יִשְׂרָאֵל אִם־תִּשְׁמַע־לִי. לֹא יִהְיֶה

Thursday: Psalm 81. לַמְנַצֵּחַ GOD pleads with His people: a classic expression of one of the great themes of the prophetic literature, the Divine pathos – GOD's love for, but exasperation with, His children. "If only My people would listen to Me".

punish? The LORD knows that the thoughts of man are a mere fleeting breath. Happy is the man whom You discipline, LORD, the one You instruct in Your Torah, giving him tranquility in days of trouble, until a pit is dug for the wicked. For the LORD will not forsake His people, nor abandon His heritage. Judgement shall again accord with justice, and all the upright in heart will follow it. Who will rise up for me against the wicked? Who will stand up for me against wrongdoers? Had the LORD not been my help, I would soon have dwelt in death's silence. When I thought my foot was slipping, Your lovingkindness, LORD, gave me support. When I was filled with anxiety, Your consolations soothed my soul. Can a corrupt throne be allied with You? Can injustice be framed into law? They join forces against the life of the righteous, and condemn the innocent to death. But the LORD is my stronghold, my GOD is the Rock of my refuge. He will bring back on them their wickedness, and destroy them for their evil deeds. The LORD our GOD will destroy them. ➔ Come, let us sing to the LORD; let us shout for joy to the Rock of our salvation.

Thursday

Today is the fifth day of the week,
on which the Levites used to say this psalm in the Temple:

PSALM 81

לַמְנַצֵּחַ For the Director of Music; on the Gittit. By Asaph. Sing for joy to GOD, our strength. Shout aloud to the GOD of Jacob. Raise a song, beat the drum, play the sweet harp and lyre. Sound the ram's horn on the new moon, on our feast day when the moon is hidden. For it is a statute for Israel, an ordinance of the GOD of Jacob. He established it as a testimony for Joseph when He went forth against the land of Egypt, where I heard a language that I did not know. I relieved his shoulder of the burden. His hands were freed from the builder's basket. In distress you called and I rescued you. I answered you from the secret place of thunder; I tested you at the waters of Meribah, Selah! Hear, My people, and I will warn you. Israel, if you would only listen to Me! Let there be no strange god among you. Do not bow down to

בְּךָ אֵל זָר, וְלֹא תִשְׁתַּחֲוֶה לְאֵל נֵכָר. אָנֹכִי יהוה אֱלֹהֶיךָ, הַמַּעַלְךָ מֵאֶרֶץ מִצְרָיִם, הַרְחֶב פִּיךָ וַאֲמַלְאֵהוּ. וְלֹא־שָׁמַע עַמִּי לְקוֹלִי, וְיִשְׂרָאֵל לֹא אָבָה לִי. וָאֲשַׁלְּחֵהוּ בִּשְׁרִירוּת לִבָּם, יֵלְכוּ בְּמוֹעֲצוֹתֵיהֶם. לוּ עַמִּי שֹׁמֵעַ לִי, יִשְׂרָאֵל בִּדְרָכַי יְהַלֵּכוּ. כִּמְעַט אוֹיְבֵיהֶם אַכְנִיעַ, וְעַל צָרֵיהֶם אָשִׁיב יָדִי. מְשַׂנְאֵי יהוה יְכַחֲשׁוּ־לוֹ, וִיהִי עִתָּם לְעוֹלָם. ← וַיַּאֲכִילֵהוּ מֵחֵלֶב חִטָּה, וּמִצּוּר דְּבַשׁ אַשְׂבִּיעֶךָ.

Friday

הַיּוֹם יוֹם שִׁשִּׁי בְּשַׁבָּת, שֶׁבּוֹ הָיוּ הַלְוִיִּם אוֹמְרִים בְּמִקְדָּשׁ.

תהלים צג

יהוה מָלָךְ, גֵּאוּת לָבֵשׁ, לָבֵשׁ יהוה עֹז הִתְאַזָּר, אַף־תִּכּוֹן תֵּבֵל בַּל־תִּמּוֹט. נָכוֹן כִּסְאֲךָ מֵאָז, מֵעוֹלָם אָתָּה. נָשְׂאוּ נְהָרוֹת יהוה, נָשְׂאוּ נְהָרוֹת קוֹלָם, יִשְׂאוּ נְהָרוֹת דָּכְיָם. מִקֹּלוֹת מַיִם רַבִּים, אַדִּירִים מִשְׁבְּרֵי־יָם, אַדִּיר בַּמָּרוֹם יהוה. ← עֵדֹתֶיךָ נֶאֶמְנוּ מְאֹד לְבֵיתְךָ נַאֲוָה־קֹדֶשׁ, יהוה לְאֹרֶךְ יָמִים.

שַׁבָּת

הַיּוֹם יוֹם שַׁבַּת קֹדֶשׁ, שֶׁבּוֹ הָיוּ הַלְוִיִּם אוֹמְרִים בְּמִקְדָּשׁ.

תהלים צב

מִזְמוֹר שִׁיר לְיוֹם הַשַּׁבָּת. טוֹב לְהֹדוֹת לַיהוה, וּלְזַמֵּר לְשִׁמְךָ עֶלְיוֹן. לְהַגִּיד בַּבֹּקֶר חַסְדֶּךָ, וֶאֱמוּנָתְךָ בַּלֵּילוֹת. עֲלֵי־עָשׂוֹר וַעֲלֵי־נָבֶל, עֲלֵי הִגָּיוֹן בְּכִנּוֹר. כִּי שִׂמַּחְתַּנִי יהוה בְּפָעֳלֶךָ, בְּמַעֲשֵׂי יָדֶיךָ אֲרַנֵּן. מַה־גָּדְלוּ מַעֲשֶׂיךָ יהוה,

---

Friday: Psalm 93. יהוה מָלָךְ Speaking as it does of the completion of creation ("the world is firmly established"), this psalm is appropriate for the sixth day, when "the heavens and the earth were finished and all their hosts."

an alien god. I am the LORD your GOD who brought you out of the land of Egypt. Open your mouth wide and I will fill it. But My people would not listen to Me. Israel would have none of Me. So I left them to their stubborn hearts, letting them follow their own devices. If only My people would listen to Me, if Israel would walk in My ways, I would soon subdue their enemies, and turn My hand against their foes. Those who hate the LORD would cower before Him and their doom would last for ever. ➜ He would feed Israel with the finest wheat – with honey from the rock I would satisfy you.

Friday

Today is the sixth day of the week,
on which the Levites used to say this psalm in the Temple:

PSALM 93

יהוה מָלָךְ LORD reigns. He is robed in majesty. The LORD is robed, girded with strength. The world is firmly established; it cannot be moved. Your throne stands firm as of old; You are eternal. Rivers lift up, LORD, rivers lift up their voice, rivers lift up their crashing waves. Mightier than the noise of many waters, than the mighty waves of the sea is the LORD on high. ➜ Your testimonies are very sure; holiness adorns Your house, LORD, for evermore.

Shabbat

Today is the holy Sabbath,
on which the Levites used to say this psalm in the Temple:

PSALM 92

מִזְמוֹר A psalm. A song for the Sabbath day. It is good to thank the LORD and sing psalms to Your name, Most High – to tell of Your lovingkindness in the morning and Your faithfulness at night, to the music of the ten-stringed lyre and the melody of the harp. For You have made me rejoice by Your work, O LORD; I sing for joy at the deeds of Your hands. How great are Your deeds, LORD, and how very deep Your thoughts. A boor cannot know, nor can a fool understand, that though the wicked spring up like grass and all evildoers flourish, it is only that they may be destroyed for ever. But You, LORD, are eter-

מְאֹד עָמְקוּ מַחְשְׁבֹתֶיךָ. אִישׁ בַּעַר לֹא יֵדָע, וּכְסִיל לֹא־
יָבִין אֶת־זֹאת. בִּפְרֹחַ רְשָׁעִים כְּמוֹ־עֵשֶׂב, וַיָּצִיצוּ כָּל־פֹּעֲלֵי
אָוֶן, לְהִשָּׁמְדָם עֲדֵי־עַד. וְאַתָּה מָרוֹם לְעֹלָם יהוה. כִּי־הִנֵּה
אֹיְבֶיךָ יהוה, כִּי־הִנֵּה אֹיְבֶיךָ יֹאבֵדוּ, יִתְפָּרְדוּ כָּל־פֹּעֲלֵי אָוֶן.
וַתָּרֶם כִּרְאֵים קַרְנִי, בַּלֹּתִי בְּשֶׁמֶן רַעֲנָן. וַתַּבֵּט עֵינִי בְּשׁוּרָי,
בַּקָּמִים עָלַי מְרֵעִים, תִּשְׁמַעְנָה אָזְנָי. ‹ צַדִּיק כַּתָּמָר
יִפְרָח, כְּאֶרֶז בַּלְּבָנוֹן יִשְׂגֶּה. שְׁתוּלִים בְּבֵית יהוה, בְּחַצְרוֹת
אֱלֹהֵינוּ יַפְרִיחוּ. עוֹד יְנוּבוּן בְּשֵׂיבָה, דְּשֵׁנִים וְרַעֲנַנִּים יִהְיוּ.
לְהַגִּיד כִּי־יָשָׁר יהוה, צוּרִי, וְלֹא עַוְלָתָה בּוֹ.

On רֹאשׁ חֹדֶשׁ, the following psalm is said:

תהלים קד

בָּרְכִי נַפְשִׁי אֶת־יהוה, יהוה אֱלֹהַי גָּדַלְתָּ מְאֹד, הוֹד וְהָדָר
לָבָשְׁתָּ. עֹטֶה אוֹר כַּשַּׂלְמָה, נוֹטֶה שָׁמַיִם כַּיְרִיעָה. הַמְקָרֶה
בַמַּיִם עֲלִיּוֹתָיו, הַשָּׂם־עָבִים רְכוּבוֹ, הַמְהַלֵּךְ עַל־כַּנְפֵי־
רוּחַ. עֹשֶׂה מַלְאָכָיו רוּחוֹת, מְשָׁרְתָיו אֵשׁ לֹהֵט. יָסַד אֶרֶץ
עַל־מְכוֹנֶיהָ, בַּל־תִּמּוֹט עוֹלָם וָעֶד. תְּהוֹם כַּלְּבוּשׁ כִּסִּיתוֹ,
עַל־הָרִים יַעַמְדוּ מָיִם. מִן־גַּעֲרָתְךָ יְנוּסוּן, מִן־קוֹל רַעַמְךָ
יֵחָפֵזוּן. יַעֲלוּ הָרִים, יֵרְדוּ בְקָעוֹת, אֶל־מְקוֹם זֶה יָסַדְתָּ
לָהֶם. גְּבוּל־שַׂמְתָּ בַּל־יַעֲבֹרוּן, בַּל־יְשׁוּבוּן לְכַסּוֹת הָאָרֶץ.
הַמְשַׁלֵּחַ מַעְיָנִים בַּנְּחָלִים, בֵּין הָרִים יְהַלֵּכוּן. יַשְׁקוּ כָּל־
חַיְתוֹ שָׂדָי, יִשְׁבְּרוּ פְרָאִים צְמָאָם. עֲלֵיהֶם עוֹף־הַשָּׁמַיִם
יִשְׁכּוֹן, מִבֵּין עֳפָאיִם יִתְּנוּ־קוֹל. מַשְׁקֶה הָרִים מֵעֲלִיּוֹתָיו,
מִפְּרִי מַעֲשֶׂיךָ תִּשְׂבַּע הָאָרֶץ. מַצְמִיחַ חָצִיר לַבְּהֵמָה,
וְעֵשֶׂב לַעֲבֹדַת הָאָדָם, לְהוֹצִיא לֶחֶם מִן־הָאָרֶץ. וְיַיִן יְשַׂמַּח
לְבַב־אֱנוֹשׁ, לְהַצְהִיל פָּנִים מִשָּׁמֶן, וְלֶחֶם לְבַב־אֱנוֹשׁ

nally exalted. For behold Your enemies, LORD, behold Your enemies will perish; all evildoers will be scattered. You have raised my pride like that of a wild ox; I am anointed with fresh oil. My eyes shall look in triumph on my adversaries; my ears shall hear the downfall of the wicked who rise against me. ➔ The righteous will flourish like a palm tree and grow tall like a cedar in Lebanon. Planted in the LORD's house, blossoming in our GOD's courtyards, they will still bear fruit in old age, and stay vigorous and fresh, proclaiming that the LORD is upright: He is my Rock, in whom there is no wrong.

On Rosh Chodesh, the following psalm is said:

PSALM 104

בָּרְכִי נַפְשִׁי Bless the LORD, my soul. LORD, my GOD, You are very great, clothed in majesty and splendour, wrapped in a robe of light. You have spread out the heavens like a tent. He has laid the beams of His lofts in the waters. He makes the clouds His chariot, riding on the wings of the wind. He makes the winds His messengers, flames of fire His ministers. He has fixed the earth on its foundations so that it will never be shaken. You covered it with the deep like a cloak; the waters stood above the mountains. At Your rebuke they fled; at the sound of Your thunder they rushed away, flowing over the hills, pouring down into the valleys to the place You appointed for them. You fixed a boundary they were not to pass, so that they would never cover the earth again. He makes springs flow in the valleys; they make their way between the hills, giving drink to all the beasts of the field; the wild donkeys quench their thirst. The birds of the sky dwell beside them, singing among the foliage. He waters the mountains from His lofts: the earth is sated with the fruit of Your work. He makes grass grow for the cattle, and plants for the use of man, that He may produce bread from the earth, wine to cheer the heart of man, oil to make the face shine, and bread to sustain man's heart. The trees of the LORD drink their fill, the cedars of Lebanon which He planted. There, birds build their nests; the stork makes its home in the cypresses. High hills are for the wild goats; crags are shelter for the badgers. He made the moon

יִסְעָד. יִשְׂבְּעוּ עֲצֵי יהוה, אַרְזֵי לְבָנוֹן אֲשֶׁר נָטָע. אֲשֶׁר־שָׁם צִפֳּרִים יְקַנֵּנוּ, חֲסִידָה בְּרוֹשִׁים בֵּיתָהּ. הָרִים הַגְּבֹהִים לַיְּעֵלִים, סְלָעִים מַחְסֶה לַשְׁפַנִּים. עָשָׂה יָרֵחַ לְמוֹעֲדִים, שֶׁמֶשׁ יָדַע מְבוֹאוֹ. תָּשֶׁת חֹשֶׁךְ וִיהִי לָיְלָה, בּוֹ תִרְמֹשׂ כָּל־חַיְתוֹ־יָעַר. הַכְּפִירִים שֹׁאֲגִים לַטָּרֶף, וּלְבַקֵּשׁ מֵאֵל אָכְלָם. תִּזְרַח הַשֶּׁמֶשׁ יֵאָסֵפוּן, וְאֶל־מְעוֹנֹתָם יִרְבָּצוּן. יֵצֵא אָדָם לְפָעֳלוֹ, וְלַעֲבֹדָתוֹ עֲדֵי־עָרֶב. מָה־רַבּוּ מַעֲשֶׂיךָ יהוה, כֻּלָּם בְּחָכְמָה עָשִׂיתָ, מָלְאָה הָאָרֶץ קִנְיָנֶךָ. זֶה הַיָּם, גָּדוֹל וּרְחַב יָדָיִם, שָׁם רֶמֶשׂ וְאֵין מִסְפָּר, חַיּוֹת קְטַנּוֹת עִם־גְּדֹלוֹת. שָׁם אֳנִיּוֹת יְהַלֵּכוּן, לִוְיָתָן זֶה יָצַרְתָּ לְשַׂחֶק־בּוֹ. כֻּלָּם אֵלֶיךָ יְשַׂבֵּרוּן, לָתֵת אָכְלָם בְּעִתּוֹ. תִּתֵּן לָהֶם, יִלְקֹטוּן, תִּפְתַּח יָדְךָ, יִשְׂבְּעוּן טוֹב. תַּסְתִּיר פָּנֶיךָ יִבָּהֵלוּן, תֹּסֵף רוּחָם יִגְוָעוּן, וְאֶל־עֲפָרָם יְשׁוּבוּן. תְּשַׁלַּח רוּחֲךָ יִבָּרֵאוּן, וּתְחַדֵּשׁ פְּנֵי אֲדָמָה. יְהִי כְבוֹד יהוה לְעוֹלָם, יִשְׂמַח יהוה בְּמַעֲשָׂיו. הַמַּבִּיט לָאָרֶץ וַתִּרְעָד, יִגַּע בֶּהָרִים וְיֶעֱשָׁנוּ. אָשִׁירָה לַיהוה בְּחַיָּי, אֲזַמְּרָה לֵאלֹהַי בְּעוֹדִי. ◂ יֶעֱרַב עָלָיו שִׂיחִי, אָנֹכִי אֶשְׂמַח בַּיהוה. יִתַּמּוּ חַטָּאִים מִן־הָאָרֶץ, וּרְשָׁעִים עוֹד אֵינָם, בָּרְכִי נַפְשִׁי אֶת־יהוה, הַלְלוּיָהּ.

קַדִּישׁ יָתוֹם can be found on page 142.

From the second day of רֹאשׁ חֹדֶשׁ אֱלוּל until (and including) שְׁמִינִי עֲצֶרֶת, the following psalm is said every evening and morning. Until the day before עֶרֶב רֹאשׁ הַשָּׁנָה, the שׁוֹפָר is sounded before the reading of the psalm.

תהלים כז

לְדָוִד, יהוה אוֹרִי וְיִשְׁעִי, מִמִּי אִירָא, יהוה מָעוֹז חַיַּי, מִמִּי אֶפְחָד. בִּקְרֹב עָלַי מְרֵעִים לֶאֱכֹל אֶת בְּשָׂרִי, צָרַי וְאֹיְבַי לִי, הֵמָּה כָשְׁלוּ וְנָפָלוּ. אִם תַּחֲנֶה עָלַי מַחֲנֶה, לֹא יִירָא לִבִּי, אִם תָּקוּם עָלַי מִלְחָמָה, בְּזֹאת אֲנִי בוֹטֵחַ. אַחַת שָׁאַלְתִּי

to mark the seasons, and makes the sun know when to set. You bring darkness and it is night; then all the beasts of the forests stir. The young lions roar for prey, seeking their food from God. When the sun rises they slink away and seek rest in their lairs. Man goes out to his work and his labour until evening. How many are Your works, Lord; You made them all with wisdom; the earth Is full of Your creations. There is the vast, immeasurable sea with its countless swarming creatures, living things great and small. There ships sail. There is Leviathan You formed to sport there. All of them look to You in hope, to give them their food when it is due. What You give them, they gather up. When You open Your hand, they are sated with good. When You hide Your face, they are dismayed. When You take away their breath, they die and return to dust. When You send back Your breath, they are created, giving new life to the earth. May the glory of the Lord be for ever; may the Lord rejoice in His works. When He looks at the earth, it trembles. When He touches the mountains, they pour forth smoke. I will sing to the Lord as long as I live; I will sing psalms to my God all my life. ➔ May my meditation be pleasing to Him; I shall rejoice in the Lord. May sinners vanish from the earth, and the wicked be no more. Bless the Lord, my soul. Halleluyah!

Mourner's *Kaddish* can be found on page 143.

From the second day of Rosh Chodesh Ellul until (and including) Shemini Atzeret, the following psalm is said every evening and morning. Until the day before the Eve of Rosh Hashanah, the shofar is sounded before the reading of the psalm.

PSALM 27

לְדָוִד A psalm of David. The Lord is my light and my salvation – whom then shall I fear? The Lord is the stronghold of my life – of whom shall I be afraid? When evil men close in on me to devour my flesh, it is they, my enemies and foes, who stumble and fall. Should

---

Psalm 27: לְדָוִד A magnificent expression of trust in God's protection and unfailing love. An early Midrash (*Leviticus Rabbah* 21:4) relates it to the festivals of Tishrei: "*The* Lord *is my light* – on Rosh Hashanah, *and my salvation* – on Yom Kippur". The phrase, "He will keep me safe in His pavilion [*beSukkoh*]" suggested Sukkot. It was accordingly adopted as a prayer for the penitential period up to and including these holy days, beginning on Rosh Chodesh Ellul.

מֵאֵת יהוה, אוֹתָהּ אֲבַקֵּשׁ, שִׁבְתִּי בְּבֵית יהוה כָּל יְמֵי חַיַּי, לַחֲזוֹת בְּנֹעַם יהוה, וּלְבַקֵּר בְּהֵיכָלוֹ. כִּי יִצְפְּנֵנִי בְּסֻכֹּה בְּיוֹם רָעָה, יַסְתִּרֵנִי בְּסֵתֶר אָהֳלוֹ, בְּצוּר יְרוֹמְמֵנִי. וְעַתָּה יָרוּם רֹאשִׁי עַל אֹיְבַי סְבִיבוֹתַי, וְאֶזְבְּחָה בְאָהֳלוֹ זִבְחֵי תְרוּעָה, אָשִׁירָה וַאֲזַמְּרָה לַיהוה. שְׁמַע יהוה קוֹלִי אֶקְרָא, וְחָנֵּנִי וַעֲנֵנִי. לְךָ אָמַר לִבִּי בַּקְּשׁוּ פָנָי, אֶת פָּנֶיךָ יהוה אֲבַקֵּשׁ. אַל תַּסְתֵּר פָּנֶיךָ מִמֶּנִּי, אַל תַּט בְּאַף עַבְדֶּךָ, עֶזְרָתִי הָיִיתָ, אַל תִּטְּשֵׁנִי וְאַל תַּעַזְבֵנִי, אֱלֹהֵי יִשְׁעִי. כִּי אָבִי וְאִמִּי עֲזָבוּנִי, וַיהוה יַאַסְפֵנִי. הוֹרֵנִי יהוה דַּרְכֶּךָ, וּנְחֵנִי בְּאֹרַח מִישׁוֹר, לְמַעַן שׁוֹרְרָי. אַל תִּתְּנֵנִי בְּנֶפֶשׁ צָרָי, כִּי קָמוּ בִי עֵדֵי שֶׁקֶר, וִיפֵחַ חָמָס. ◆ לוּלֵא הֶאֱמַנְתִּי לִרְאוֹת בְּטוּב יהוה בְּאֶרֶץ חַיִּים. קַוֵּה אֶל יהוה, חֲזַק וְיַאֲמֵץ לִבֶּךָ, וְקַוֵּה אֶל יהוה.

קַדִּישׁ יָתוֹם can be found on page 142.

The following psalm is said in the house of mourning during the week of שִׁבְעָה, on the days when תַּחֲנוּן is said:

תהלים מט

לַמְנַצֵּחַ לִבְנֵי קֹרַח מִזְמוֹר. שִׁמְעוּ־זֹאת כָּל־הָעַמִּים, הַאֲזִינוּ כָּל־יֹשְׁבֵי חָלֶד. גַּם־בְּנֵי אָדָם, גַּם־בְּנֵי־אִישׁ, יַחַד עָשִׁיר וְאֶבְיוֹן. פִּי יְדַבֵּר חָכְמוֹת, וְהָגוּת לִבִּי תְבוּנוֹת. אַטֶּה לְמָשָׁל אָזְנִי, אֶפְתַּח בְּכִנּוֹר חִידָתִי. לָמָּה אִירָא בִּימֵי רָע, עֲוֹן עֲקֵבַי יְסֻבֵּנִי. הַבֹּטְחִים עַל־חֵילָם, וּבְרֹב עָשְׁרָם יִתְהַלָּלוּ. אָח לֹא־פָדֹה יִפְדֶּה אִישׁ, לֹא יִתֵּן לֵאלֹהִים כָּפְרוֹ. וְיֵקַר פִּדְיוֹן נַפְשָׁם, וְחָדַל לְעוֹלָם. וִיחִי־עוֹד לָנֶצַח, לֹא יִרְאֶה הַשָּׁחַת. כִּי יִרְאֶה חֲכָמִים יָמוּתוּ, יַחַד כְּסִיל וָבַעַר יֹאבֵדוּ, וְעָזְבוּ לַאֲחֵרִים חֵילָם. קִרְבָּם בָּתֵּימוֹ לְעוֹלָם, מִשְׁכְּנֹתָם לְדֹר וָדֹר, קָרְאוּ בִשְׁמוֹתָם עֲלֵי אֲדָמוֹת. וְאָדָם בִּיקָר בַּל־יָלִין, נִמְשַׁל כַּבְּהֵמוֹת נִדְמוּ. זֶה דַרְכָּם, כֵּסֶל לָמוֹ, וְאַחֲרֵיהֶם

an army besiege me, my heart would not fear. Should war break out against me, still I would be confident. One thing I ask of the LORD, only this do I seek: to live in the house of the LORD all the days of my life, to gaze on the beauty of the LORD and worship in His Temple. For He will keep me safe in His pavilion on the day of trouble. He will hide me under the cover of His tent. He will set me high upon a rock. Now my head is high above my enemies who surround me. I will sacrifice in His tent with shouts of joy. I will sing and chant praises to the LORD. LORD, hear my voice when I call. Be gracious to me and answer me. On Your behalf my heart says, "Seek My face." Your face, LORD, will I seek. Do not hide Your face from me. Do not turn Your servant away in anger. You have been my help. Do not reject or forsake me, GOD, my Saviour. Were my father and my mother to forsake me, the LORD would take me in. Teach me Your way, LORD, and lead me on a level path, because of my oppressors. Do not abandon me to the will of my foes, for false witnesses have risen against me, breathing violence. ➻ Were it not for my faith that I shall see the LORD's goodness in the land of the living…Hope in the LORD. Be strong and of good courage, and hope in the LORD!

Mourner's *Kaddish* can be found on page 143.

The following psalm is said in a house of mourning during the week of *shivah*, on the days when *Tachanun* is said:

PSALM 49

לַמְנַצֵּחַ For the director of music. Of the sons of Korach. A sacred song. Hear this, all you peoples. Listen, all inhabitants of the World, low and high, rich and poor alike. My mouth will speak words of wisdom; the utterance of my heart will give understanding. I listen with care to a parable; I expound my mystery to the music of the harp. Why should I fear when evil days come, when the wickedness of my foes surrounds me, trusting in their wealth, boasting of their great riches? No man can redeem his brother or pay GOD the price of his release, for the ransom of a life is costly; no payment is ever enough that would let him live for ever, never seeing the grave. For all can see that wise men die, that the foolish and senseless all perish and leave their wealth to

בְּפִיהֶם יִרְצוּ, סֶלָה. כַּצֹּאן לִשְׁאוֹל שַׁתּוּ, מָוֶת יִרְעֵם, וַיִּרְדּוּ בָם יְשָׁרִים לַבֹּקֶר, וְצוּרָם לְבַלּוֹת שְׁאוֹל מִזְּבֻל לוֹ. אַךְ־אֱלֹהִים יִפְדֶּה־נַפְשִׁי מִיַּד שְׁאוֹל, כִּי יִקָּחֵנִי סֶלָה. אַל־תִּירָא כִּי יַעֲשִׁר אִישׁ, כִּי־יִרְבֶּה כְּבוֹד בֵּיתוֹ. כִּי לֹא בְמוֹתוֹ יִקַּח הַכֹּל, לֹא־יֵרֵד אַחֲרָיו כְּבוֹדוֹ. כִּי נַפְשׁוֹ בְּחַיָּיו יְבָרֵךְ, וְיוֹדֻךָ כִּי־תֵיטִיב לָךְ. תָּבוֹא עַד־דּוֹר אֲבוֹתָיו, עַד־נֵצַח לֹא יִרְאוּ־אוֹר. ◂ אָדָם בִּיקָר וְלֹא יָבִין, נִמְשַׁל כַּבְּהֵמוֹת נִדְמוּ.

קַדִּישׁ יָתוֹם can be found on page 142.

The following psalm is said in the house of mourning during the week of שִׁבְעָה, on the days when תַּחֲנוּן is not said:

תהלים טז

מִכְתָּם לְדָוִד, שָׁמְרֵנִי אֵל כִּי־חָסִיתִי בָךְ. אָמַרְתְּ לַיהוה, אֲדֹנָי אָתָּה, טוֹבָתִי בַּל־עָלֶיךָ. לִקְדוֹשִׁים אֲשֶׁר־בָּאָרֶץ הֵמָּה, וְאַדִּירֵי כָּל־חֶפְצִי־בָם. יִרְבּוּ עַצְּבוֹתָם אַחֵר מָהָרוּ, בַּל־אַסִּיךְ נִסְכֵּיהֶם מִדָּם, וּבַל־אֶשָּׂא אֶת־שְׁמוֹתָם עַל־שְׂפָתָי. יהוה, מְנָת־חֶלְקִי וְכוֹסִי, אַתָּה תּוֹמִיךְ גּוֹרָלִי. חֲבָלִים נָפְלוּ־לִי בַּנְּעִמִים, אַף־נַחֲלָת שָׁפְרָה עָלָי. אֲבָרֵךְ אֶת־יהוה אֲשֶׁר יְעָצָנִי, אַף־לֵילוֹת יִסְּרוּנִי כִלְיוֹתָי. שִׁוִּיתִי יהוה לְנֶגְדִּי תָמִיד, כִּי מִימִינִי בַּל־אֶמּוֹט. לָכֵן שָׂמַח לִבִּי וַיָּגֶל כְּבוֹדִי, אַף־בְּשָׂרִי יִשְׁכֹּן לָבֶטַח. כִּי לֹא־תַעֲזֹב נַפְשִׁי לִשְׁאוֹל, לֹא־תִתֵּן חֲסִידְךָ לִרְאוֹת שָׁחַת. ◂ תּוֹדִיעֵנִי אֹרַח חַיִּים, שֹׂבַע שְׂמָחוֹת אֶת־פָּנֶיךָ, נְעִמוֹת בִּימִינְךָ נֶצַח.

קַדִּישׁ יָתוֹם can be found on page 142.

Psalms in a house of mourning. Bereavement is not only a time of loss but also of reflection and repentance, as we think about mortality and the values for which we live (Maimonides, *Laws of Mourning*, 13:12). Psalm 49 is a powerful reminder that wealth is ephemeral, wisdom eternal. Psalm 16 is a poem of trust in God's protection in this life, and in eternal life in the World to Come.

others. They think their houses will remain for ever, their dwellings for all generations; they give their names to their estates. But man, despite his splendour, does not endure; he is like the beasts that perish. Such is the fate of the foolish and their followers who approve their words, Selah. Like sheep they are destined for the grave: death will be their shepherd. The upright will rule over them in the morning. Their forms will decay in the grave, far from their mansions. But God will redeem my life from the grave; He will surely take me to Himself, Selah. Do not be overawed when a man grows rich, when the glory of his house increases, for he will take nothing with him when he dies; his wealth will not descend with him. Though while he lived he counted himself blessed – men always praise you when you prosper – he will join the generation of his ancestors who will never again see the light. → A man who, despite his splendour, lacks understanding is like the beasts that perish.

Mourner's *Kaddish* can be found on page 143.

The following psalm is said in a house of mourning during the week of *shivah*, on the days when *Tachanun* is not said:

PSALM 16

מִכְתָּם לְדָוִד Protect me, God, for in You I have found refuge. I have said to the Lord: You are my Lord: from You alone comes the good I enjoy. All my delight is in the holy ones, the mighty in the land. Those who run after other gods multiply their sorrows. I shall never offer them libations of blood, nor will their names pass my lips. The Lord is my allotted portion and my cup: You direct my fate. The lines have fallen for me in pleasant places; I am well content with my inheritance. I will bless the Lord who has guided me; at night my innermost being admonishes me. I have set the Lord before me at all times. He is at my right hand: I shall not be shaken. Therefore my heart is glad, my spirit rejoices, and my body rests secure. For You will not abandon me to the grave, nor let Your faithful one see the pit. → You will teach me the path of life. In Your presence is fullness of joy; at Your right hand, bliss for evermore.

Mourner's *Kaddish* can be found on page 143.

Some say the following daily, after the end of morning prayers:

עשרת הדברות

שמות כ:א–יז

וַיְדַבֵּר אֱלֹהִים אֵת כָּל־הַדְּבָרִים הָאֵלֶּה לֵאמֹר.

[א] **אָנֹכִי** יְהוָה אֱלֹהֶיךָ אֲשֶׁר הוֹצֵאתִיךָ מֵאֶרֶץ מִצְרַיִם מִבֵּית עֲבָדִים.

[ב] **לֹא־יִהְיֶה** לְךָ אֱלֹהִים אֲחֵרִים עַל־פָּנָי. לֹא־תַעֲשֶׂה לְךָ פֶּסֶל וְכָל־תְּמוּנָה אֲשֶׁר בַּשָּׁמַיִם מִמַּעַל וַאֲשֶׁר בָּאָרֶץ מִתָּחַת וַאֲשֶׁר בַּמַּיִם מִתַּחַת לָאָרֶץ. לֹא־תִשְׁתַּחֲוֶה לָהֶם וְלֹא תָעָבְדֵם כִּי אָנֹכִי יְהוָה אֱלֹהֶיךָ אֵל קַנָּא פֹּקֵד עֲוֹן אָבֹת עַל־בָּנִים עַל־שִׁלֵּשִׁים וְעַל־רִבֵּעִים לְשֹׂנְאָי. וְעֹשֶׂה חֶסֶד לַאֲלָפִים לְאֹהֲבַי וּלְשֹׁמְרֵי מִצְוֹתָי.

[ג] **לֹא** תִשָּׂא אֶת־שֵׁם־יְהוָה אֱלֹהֶיךָ לַשָּׁוְא כִּי לֹא יְנַקֶּה יהוה אֵת אֲשֶׁר־יִשָּׂא אֶת־שְׁמוֹ לַשָּׁוְא.

[ד] **זָכוֹר** אֶת־יוֹם הַשַּׁבָּת לְקַדְּשׁוֹ. שֵׁשֶׁת יָמִים תַּעֲבֹד וְעָשִׂיתָ כָּל־מְלַאכְתֶּךָ. וְיוֹם הַשְּׁבִיעִי שַׁבָּת לַיהוָה אֱלֹהֶיךָ לֹא־תַעֲשֶׂה כָל־מְלָאכָה אַתָּה | וּבִנְךָ וּבִתֶּךָ עַבְדְּךָ וַאֲמָתְךָ וּבְהֶמְתֶּךָ וְגֵרְךָ אֲשֶׁר בִּשְׁעָרֶיךָ. כִּי שֵׁשֶׁת־יָמִים עָשָׂה יהוה אֶת־הַשָּׁמַיִם וְאֶת־הָאָרֶץ אֶת־הַיָּם וְאֶת־כָּל־אֲשֶׁר־בָּם וַיָּנַח בַּיּוֹם הַשְּׁבִיעִי עַל־כֵּן בֵּרַךְ יְהוָה אֶת־יוֹם הַשַּׁבָּת וַיְקַדְּשֵׁהוּ.

[ה] **כַּבֵּד** אֶת־אָבִיךָ וְאֶת־אִמֶּךָ לְמַעַן יַאֲרִכוּן יָמֶיךָ עַל הָאֲדָמָה אֲשֶׁר־יְהוָה אֱלֹהֶיךָ נֹתֵן לָךְ.

[ו] **לֹא** תִרְצָח.

Some say the following daily after the end of morning prayers:

THE TEN COMMANDMENTS

EXODUS 20:1–17

God spoke all these words, saying:

1. אָנֹכִי I am the Lord your God who brought you out of the land of Egypt, from the slave-house.

2. לֹא־יִהְיֶה Have no other gods beside Me. Do not make a sculptured image for yourself, or any likeness of what is in the heavens above, or on the earth below, or in the waters under the earth. Do not bow down to them or worship them, for I am the Lord your God, a zealous God, visiting the guilt of the parents on the children to the third and fourth generation, if they also reject Me; but showing kindness to thousands of generations of those who love Me and keep My commandments.

3. לֹא Do not take the name of the Lord your God in vain. The Lord will not leave unpunished one who utters His name in vain.

4. זָכוֹר Remember the Sabbath and keep it holy. Six days you shall labour and do all your work, but the seventh day is a Sabbath of the Lord your God; on it you shall not do any work – you, your son or daughter, your male or female slaves, your cattle, or the stranger within your gates. For in six days the Lord made heaven and earth and sea, and all that is in them, and rested on the seventh day; therefore the Lord blessed the Sabbath day and made it holy.

5. כַּבֵּד Honour your father and your mother, so that you may live long in the land that the Lord your God is giving you.

6. לֹא Do not murder.

The Ten Commandments: In Temple times, the Ten Commandments were recited as part of the daily prayers, immediately prior to the *Shema*. The practice was discontinued when sectarians maintained that only these, and not the other commandments, were from God (*Berachot* 12a). So deep was the attachment of Jews to this "sublime summary of human duties" (Rabbi J.H. Hertz), however, that the custom developed to say it privately after the end of the morning service.

[ז] **לֹ֖א** תִּנְאָֽף׃

[ח] **לֹ֖א** תִּגְנֹֽב׃

[ט] **לֹֽא־**תַעֲנֶ֥ה בְרֵעֲךָ֖ עֵ֥ד שָֽׁקֶר׃

[י] **לֹ֥א** תַחְמֹ֖ד בֵּ֣ית רֵעֶ֑ךָ לֹֽא־תַחְמֹ֞ד אֵ֣שֶׁת רֵעֶ֗ךָ וְעַבְדּ֤וֹ וַאֲמָתוֹ֙ וְשׁוֹר֣וֹ וַחֲמֹר֔וֹ וְכֹ֖ל אֲשֶׁ֥ר לְרֵעֶֽךָ׃

שלשה עשר עקרים

[א] **אֲנִי** מַאֲמִין בֶּאֱמוּנָה שְׁלֵמָה, שֶׁהַבּוֹרֵא יִתְבָּרַךְ שְׁמוֹ הוּא בּוֹרֵא וּמַנְהִיג לְכָל־הַבְּרוּאִים, וְהוּא לְבַדּוֹ עָשָׂה וְעוֹשֶׂה וְיַעֲשֶׂה לְכָל־הַמַּעֲשִׂים.

[ב] **אֲנִי** מַאֲמִין בֶּאֱמוּנָה שְׁלֵמָה, שֶׁהַבּוֹרֵא יִתְבָּרַךְ שְׁמוֹ הוּא יָחִיד וְאֵין יְחִידוּת כָּמְוֹהוּ בְּשׁוּם פָּנִים, וְהוּא לְבַדּוֹ אֱלֹהֵינוּ, הָיָה הֹוֶה וְיִהְיֶה.

[ג] **אֲנִי** מַאֲמִין בֶּאֱמוּנָה שְׁלֵמָה, שֶׁהַבּוֹרֵא יִתְבָּרַךְ שְׁמוֹ אֵינוֹ גוּף, וְלֹא יַשִּׂיגְוּהוּ מַשִּׂיגֵי הַגּוּף, וְאֵין לוֹ שׁוּם דִּמְיוֹן כְּלָל.

[ד] **אֲנִי** מַאֲמִין בֶּאֱמוּנָה שְׁלֵמָה, שֶׁהַבּוֹרֵא יִתְבָּרַךְ שְׁמוֹ הוּא רִאשׁוֹן וְהוּא אַחֲרוֹן.

[ה] **אֲנִי** מַאֲמִין בֶּאֱמוּנָה שְׁלֵמָה, שֶׁהַבּוֹרֵא יִתְבָּרַךְ שְׁמוֹ לוֹ לְבַדּוֹ רָאוּי לְהִתְפַּלֵּל, וְאֵין רָאוּי לְהִתְפַּלֵּל לְזוּלָתוֹ.

[ו] **אֲנִי** מַאֲמִין בֶּאֱמוּנָה שְׁלֵמָה, שֶׁכָּל־דִּבְרֵי הַנְּבִיאִים אֱמֶת.

[ז] **אֲנִי** מַאֲמִין בֶּאֱמוּנָה שְׁלֵמָה, שֶׁנְּבוּאַת מֹשֶׁה רַבֵּנוּ עָלָיו הַשָּׁלוֹם הָיְתָה אֲמִתִּית, וְשֶׁהוּא הָיָה אָב לַנְּבִיאִים, לַקּוֹדְמִים לְפָנָיו וְלַבָּאִים אַחֲרָיו.

7. לֹא Do not commit adultery.

8. לֹא Do not steal.

9. לֹא Do not testify as a false witness against your neighbour.

10. לֹא Do not be envious of your neighbour's house. Do not be envious of your neighbour's wife, his male or female slave, his ox, his ass, or anything else that is your neighbour's.

THE THIRTEEN PRINCIPLES OF JEWISH FAITH

1. אֲנִי I believe with perfect faith that the Creator, blessed be His name, creates and rules all creatures, and that He alone made, makes, and will make, all things.

2. אֲנִי I believe with perfect faith that the Creator, blessed be His name, is One; that there is no oneness like His in any way; and that He alone is our God who was, is, and ever will be.

3. אֲנִי I believe with perfect faith that the Creator, blessed be His name, is not physical, that no physical attributes can apply to Him, and that there is nothing whatsoever to compare to Him.

4. אֲנִי I believe with perfect faith that the Creator, blessed be His name, is first and last.

5. אֲנִי I believe with perfect faith that the Creator, blessed be His name, is the only one to whom it is proper to pray, and that it is improper to pray to anyone else.

6. אֲנִי I believe with perfect faith that all the words of the prophets are true.

7. אֲנִי I believe with perfect faith that the prophecy of Moses our teacher, peace be to him, was true, and that he was the father of the prophets – those who preceded him and those who followed him.

[ח] **אֲנִי** מַאֲמִין בֶּאֱמוּנָה שְׁלֵמָה, שֶׁכָּל־הַתּוֹרָה הַמְּצוּיָה עַתָּה בְיָדֵינוּ הִיא הַנְּתוּנָה לְמשֶׁה רַבֵּינוּ עָלָיו הַשָּׁלוֹם.

[ט] **אֲנִי** מַאֲמִין בֶּאֱמוּנָה שְׁלֵמָה, שֶׁזֹּאת הַתּוֹרָה לֹא תְהִי מֻחְלֶפֶת וְלֹא תְהִי תּוֹרָה אַחֶרֶת מֵאֵת הַבּוֹרֵא יִתְבָּרַךְ שְׁמוֹ.

[י] **אֲנִי** מַאֲמִין בֶּאֱמוּנָה שְׁלֵמָה, שֶׁהַבּוֹרֵא יִתְבָּרַךְ שְׁמוֹ יוֹדֵעַ כָּל־מַעֲשֵׂה בְנֵי אָדָם וְכָל־מַחְשְׁבוֹתָם, שֶׁנֶּאֱמַר, הַיֹּצֵר יַחַד לִבָּם, הַמֵּבִין אֶל־כָּל־מַעֲשֵׂיהֶם.

[יא] **אֲנִי** מַאֲמִין בֶּאֱמוּנָה שְׁלֵמָה, שֶׁהַבּוֹרֵא יִתְבָּרַךְ שְׁמוֹ גּוֹמֵל טוֹב לְשׁוֹמְרֵי מִצְוֹתָיו וּמַעֲנִישׁ לְעוֹבְרֵי מִצְוֹתָיו.

[יב] **אֲנִי** מַאֲמִין בֶּאֱמוּנָה שְׁלֵמָה, בְּבִיאַת הַמָּשִׁיחַ וְאַף־עַל־פִּי שֶׁיִּתְמַהְמֵהַּ, עִם כָּל־זֶה אֲחַכֶּה־לּוֹ בְּכָל יוֹם שֶׁיָּבוֹא.

[יג] **אֲנִי** מַאֲמִין בֶּאֱמוּנָה שְׁלֵמָה, שֶׁתִּהְיֶה תְּחִיַּת הַמֵּתִים בְּעֵת שֶׁיַּעֲלֶה רָצוֹן מֵאֵת הַבּוֹרֵא יִתְבָּרַךְ שְׁמוֹ וְיִתְעַלֶּה זִכְרוֹ לָעַד וּלְנֵצַח נְצָחִים.

לִישׁוּעָתְךָ קִוִּיתִי יהוה. קִוִּיתִי יהוה לִישׁוּעָתְךָ. יהוה לִישׁוּעָתְךָ קִוִּיתִי. לְפֻרְקָנָךְ סַבְּרֵית יהוה. סַבְּרֵית יהוה לְפֻרְקָנָךְ. יהוה לְפֻרְקָנָךְ סַבְּרֵית.

The Thirteen Principles of Jewish Faith: A prose counterpart to the poetic *Yigdal,* both of which summarise the principles set out by Moses Maimonides

8. אֲנִי I believe with perfect faith that the entire Torah now in our hands is the same one that was given to Moses our teacher, peace be upon him.

9. אֲנִי I believe with perfect faith that this Torah will not be changed, nor will there be any other Torah from the Creator, blessed be His name.

10. אֲנִי I believe with perfect faith that the Creator, blessed be His name, knows all the deeds and thoughts of humanity, as it is said, "He fashions the hearts of them all, comprehending all their deeds".

11. אֲנִי I believe with perfect faith that the Creator, blessed be His name, rewards those who keep His commandments, and punishes those who transgress them.

12. אֲנִי I believe with perfect faith in the coming of the Messiah, and though he may delay, I wait daily for his coming.

13. אֲנִי I believe with perfect faith that the dead will live again at a time of the Creator's choosing: blessed be His name and exalted be His mention for ever and all time.

לִישׁוּעָתְךָ For Your salvation I hope, O Lord. I hope, O Lord, for Your salvation. O Lord, for Your salvation, I hope.

(1135–1204). The first five are about God: 1. His existence; 2. His unity; 3. His incorporeality; 4. His eternity; and 5. the belief that He alone is to be worshipped. The next four are about revelation: belief in 6. prophecy; 7. the unique status of Moses as the greatest of the prophets; 8. the Divine authorship of the Torah; and 9. the immutability of the Torah. The last four are about reward, punishment and justice: 10. God knows our thoughts and deeds; 11. He rewards and punishes; 12. He will send the Messiah; and 13. in time to come, He will bring the dead back to life again. The presence of this passage is a reminder that the Siddur is not just a book of prayer but also of faith.

תפילות מנחה ומעריב לחול

Afternoon and Evening Services for Weekdays

תפלת מנחה לחול

אשרי

אַשְׁרֵי יוֹשְׁבֵי בֵיתֶךָ, עוֹד יְהַלְלְוּךָ סֶּלָה.
אַשְׁרֵי הָעָם שֶׁכָּכָה לּוֹ, אַשְׁרֵי הָעָם שֶׁיהוה אֱלֹהָיו.

תהלים קמה

תְּהִלָּה לְדָוִד,
אֲרוֹמִמְךָ אֱלוֹהַי הַמֶּלֶךְ, וַאֲבָרְכָה שִׁמְךָ לְעוֹלָם וָעֶד.
בְּכָל יוֹם אֲבָרְכֶךָּ, וַאֲהַלְלָה שִׁמְךָ לְעוֹלָם וָעֶד.
גָּדוֹל יהוה וּמְהֻלָּל מְאֹד, וְלִגְדֻלָּתוֹ אֵין חֵקֶר.
דּוֹר לְדוֹר יְשַׁבַּח מַעֲשֶׂיךָ, וּגְבוּרֹתֶיךָ יַגִּידוּ.
הֲדַר כְּבוֹד הוֹדֶךָ, וְדִבְרֵי נִפְלְאֹתֶיךָ אָשִׂיחָה.
וֶעֱזוּז נוֹרְאוֹתֶיךָ יֹאמֵרוּ, וּגְדֻלָּתְךָ אֲסַפְּרֶנָּה.
זֵכֶר רַב־טוּבְךָ יַבִּיעוּ, וְצִדְקָתְךָ יְרַנֵּנוּ.
חַנּוּן וְרַחוּם יהוה, אֶרֶךְ אַפַּיִם וּגְדָל־חָסֶד.
טוֹב יהוה לַכֹּל, וְרַחֲמָיו עַל כָּל מַעֲשָׂיו.
יוֹדוּךָ יהוה כָּל מַעֲשֶׂיךָ, וַחֲסִידֶיךָ יְבָרְכוּכָה.
כְּבוֹד מַלְכוּתְךָ יֹאמֵרוּ, וּגְבוּרָתְךָ יְדַבֵּרוּ.
לְהוֹדִיעַ לִבְנֵי הָאָדָם גְּבוּרֹתָיו, וּכְבוֹד הֲדַר מַלְכוּתוֹ.

AFTERNOON SERVICE
The afternoon service corresponds to the daily afternoon sacrifice (Numbers 28:4). *Minchah*, the "meal offering", was not unique to the afternoon. The prayer may have acquired this name because of the verse in Psalms (141:2): "May my prayer be like incense before You, the lifting up of my hands like the afternoon offering (*minchat arev*)." The Sages attached special significance to this prayer, noting that Elijah's prayer was answered at this time (1 Kings 18:36).

Its form is simple. It begins with *Ashrei* as a prelude to prayer, the third of three times we say it daily. The *Amidah* is the same as in the morning with two changes. In the Reader's repetition, the

AFTERNOON SERVICE FOR WEEKDAYS

ASHREI

אַשְׁרֵי Happy are those who dwell in Your House;
they shall continue to praise you, Selah!
Happy are the people for whom this is so;
happy are the people whose God is the Lord.

PSALM 145

A song of praise by David.

I will exalt You, my God, the King,
and bless Your name for ever and all time.
Every day I will bless You,
and praise Your name for ever and all time.
God is great and greatly to be praised;
His greatness is unfathomable.
One generation will praise Your works to the next,
and tell of Your mighty deeds.
On the glorious splendour of Your majesty I will meditate,
and on the acts of Your wonders.
They shall talk of the power of Your awesome deeds,
and I will tell of Your greatness.
They shall recite the record of Your great goodness,
and sing with joy of Your righteousness.
The Lord is gracious and compassionate,
slow to anger and great in lovingkindness.
The Lord is good to all,
and His compassion extends to all His works.
All Your works shall thank You, Lord,
and Your devoted ones shall bless You.
They shall talk of the glory of Your kingship,
and speak of Your might.
To make known to mankind His mighty deeds
and the glorious majesty of His kingship.

---

passage referring to the priestly blessing is not said, since in the Temple the priests did not bless the congregation in the afternoon. Likewise, a shorter form of the final blessing (associated with the priestly blessing in the Temple) is said. *Tachanun* is said on days when it is said in the morning, except on the afternoon before Shabbat and festivals. The service ends with *Aleinu*.

מַלְכוּתְךָ מַלְכוּת כָּל עֹלָמִים, וּמֶמְשַׁלְתְּךָ בְּכָל דּוֹר וָדֹר.
סוֹמֵךְ יהוה לְכָל הַנֹּפְלִים, וְזוֹקֵף לְכָל הַכְּפוּפִים.
עֵינֵי כֹל אֵלֶיךָ יְשַׂבֵּרוּ, וְאַתָּה נוֹתֵן לָהֶם אֶת אָכְלָם בְּעִתּוֹ.
פּוֹתֵחַ אֶת יָדֶךָ, וּמַשְׂבִּיעַ לְכָל־חַי רָצוֹן.
צַדִּיק יהוה בְּכָל דְּרָכָיו, וְחָסִיד בְּכָל מַעֲשָׂיו.
קָרוֹב יהוה לְכָל קֹרְאָיו, לְכֹל אֲשֶׁר יִקְרָאֻהוּ בֶאֱמֶת.
רְצוֹן יְרֵאָיו יַעֲשֶׂה, וְאֶת שַׁוְעָתָם יִשְׁמַע, וְיוֹשִׁיעֵם.
שׁוֹמֵר יהוה אֶת כָּל אֹהֲבָיו, וְאֵת כָּל־הָרְשָׁעִים יַשְׁמִיד.
← תְּהִלַּת יהוה יְדַבֶּר פִּי, וִיבָרֵךְ כָּל־בָּשָׂר שֵׁם קָדְשׁוֹ לְעוֹלָם וָעֶד.
וַאֲנַחְנוּ נְבָרֵךְ יָהּ, מֵעַתָּה וְעַד־עוֹלָם, הַלְלוּיָהּ.

The Leader says חֲצִי קַדִּישׁ.

Leader:

יִתְגַּדַּל וְיִתְקַדַּשׁ שְׁמֵהּ רַבָּא. (Cong. אָמֵן) בְּעָלְמָא דִּי־בְרָא כִרְעוּתֵהּ. וְיַמְלִיךְ מַלְכוּתֵהּ, בְּחַיֵּיכוֹן וּבְיוֹמֵיכוֹן וּבְחַיֵּי דִּי־כָל־ בֵּית יִשְׂרָאֵל, בַּעֲגָלָא וּבִזְמַן קָרִיב. וְאִמְרוּ אָמֵן. (Cong. אָמֵן)

All:

יְהֵא שְׁמֵהּ רַבָּא מְבָרַךְ לְעָלַם וּלְעָלְמֵי עָלְמַיָּא.

Leader:

יִתְבָּרַךְ וְיִשְׁתַּבַּח וְיִתְפָּאַר וְיִתְרוֹמַם וְיִתְנַשֵּׂא וְיִתְהַדַּר וְיִתְעַלֶּה וְיִתְהַלָּל שְׁמֵהּ דְּקֻדְשָׁא בְּרִיךְ הוּא (Cong. בְּרִיךְ הוּא) לְעֵלָּא (Between רֹאשׁ הַשָּׁנָה and יוֹם כִּפּוּר add לְעֵלָּא) מִן־כָּל־בִּרְכָתָא וְשִׁירָתָא תֻּשְׁבְּחָתָא וְנֶחֱמָתָא, דַּאֲמִירָן בְּעָלְמָא. וְאִמְרוּ אָמֵן. (Cong. אָמֵן)

On Fast days, turn to page 120 for קְרִיאַת הַתּוֹרָה.
שְׁמוֹת לב:א–י, יא–יד and יְשַׁעְיָה מה:ו–מו:ח are read on pages 908–909.
After the סֵפֶר תּוֹרָה is returned to the Ark, the Leader says חֲצִי קַדִּישׁ.

Your kingdom is an everlasting kingdom,
and Your reign is for all generations.
The LORD supports all who fall,
and raises all who are bowed down.
All raise their eyes to You in hope,
and You give them their food in due season.
You open Your hand,
and satisfy every living thing with Your favour.
The LORD is righteous in all His ways,
and kind in all He does.
The LORD is close to all who call on Him,
to all who call on Him in truth.
He fulfils the will of those who revere Him;
He hears their cry and saves them.
The LORD guards all who love Him,
but all the wicked He will destroy.
→ My mouth shall speak the praise of the LORD,
and all creatures shall bless His holy name for ever and all time.
We will bless the LORD now and for ever. Halleluyah!

The Leader says half-*Kaddish*.

Leader:

יִתְגַּדַּל Magnified and sanctified may His great name be, in the world He created by His will. May He establish His kingdom in your lifetime and in your days, and in the lifetime of all the House of Israel, swiftly and soon – and say: Amen.

All:

May His great name be blessed for ever and all time.

Leader:

Blessed and praised, glorified and exalted, raised and honoured, uplifted and lauded be the name of the Holy One, blessed be He, (between Rosh Hashanah and Yom Kippur add 'well') beyond any blessing, song, praise and consolation uttered in the world – and say: Amen.

On Fast days, turn to page 121 for the Torah reading.
Exodus 32:1–10, 11–14 and Isaiah 55:6–56:8 are read on pages 908–909.
After the Torah scroll is returned to the Ark, the Leader says half-*Kaddish*.

עמידה

The following prayer, until קַדְמוֹנִיּוֹת, on page 192, is said standing with feet together.

The עֲמִידָה is first said silently; then, if there is a מִנְיָן, it is repeated aloud by the Leader.

Take three steps back, then forward. At the points indicated by ▾, bend the knees at the first word, bow at the second, and stand straight before God's name..

אֲדֹנָי, שְׂפָתַי תִּפְתָּח, וּפִי יַגִּיד תְּהִלָּתֶךָ.

אבות

▾**בָּרוּךְ** אַתָּה יהוה אֱלֹהֵינוּ וֵאלֹהֵי אֲבוֹתֵינוּ, אֱלֹהֵי אַבְרָהָם, אֱלֹהֵי יִצְחָק, וֵאלֹהֵי יַעֲקֹב, הָאֵל הַגָּדוֹל הַגִּבּוֹר וְהַנּוֹרָא, אֵל עֶלְיוֹן, גּוֹמֵל חֲסָדִים טוֹבִים וְקוֹנֵה הַכֹּל, וְזוֹכֵר חַסְדֵי אָבוֹת, וּמֵבִיא גוֹאֵל לִבְנֵי בְנֵיהֶם, לְמַעַן שְׁמוֹ בְּאַהֲבָה.

Between רֹאשׁ הַשָּׁנָה and יוֹם כִּפּוּר, add:

זָכְרֵנוּ לַחַיִּים, מֶלֶךְ חָפֵץ בַּחַיִּים, וְכָתְבֵנוּ בְּסֵפֶר הַחַיִּים, לְמַעַנְךָ אֱלֹהִים חַיִּים.

מֶלֶךְ עוֹזֵר וּמוֹשִׁיעַ וּמָגֵן. ▾בָּרוּךְ אַתָּה יהוה, מָגֵן אַבְרָהָם.

גבורות

אַתָּה גִּבּוֹר לְעוֹלָם אֲדֹנָי, מְחַיֵּה מֵתִים אַתָּה, רַב לְהוֹשִׁיעַ.

From after שִׂמְחַת תּוֹרָה until פֶּסַח, add:

מַשִּׁיב הָרוּחַ וּמוֹרִיד הַגֶּשֶׁם.

מְכַלְכֵּל חַיִּים בְּחֶסֶד, מְחַיֵּה מֵתִים בְּרַחֲמִים רַבִּים, סוֹמֵךְ נוֹפְלִים, וְרוֹפֵא חוֹלִים, וּמַתִּיר אֲסוּרִים, וּמְקַיֵּם אֱמוּנָתוֹ לִישֵׁנֵי עָפָר. מִי כָמוֹךָ בַּעַל גְּבוּרוֹת, וּמִי דּוֹמֶה לָּךְ, מֶלֶךְ מֵמִית וּמְחַיֶּה וּמַצְמִיחַ יְשׁוּעָה.

אֲדֹנָי שְׂפָתַי תִּפְתָּח *O Lord, open my lips*: Standing in the presence of God, we feel our inadequacy. The greatest of the prophets felt tongue-tied. Moses said, "I am not a man of words…I am heavy of speech and tongue." Isaiah said, "I am

AMIDAH: THE STANDING PRAYER

The following prayer, until "in former years", on page 193, is said standing with feet together.

The *Amidah* is first said silently; then, if there is a *minyan*, it is repeated aloud by the Leader.

Take three steps back, then forward. At the points indicated by ▾, bend the knees at the first word, bow at the second, and stand straight before GOD's name.

O LORD, open my lips, so that my mouth may declare Your praise.

PATRIARCHS

▾בָּרוּךְ Blessed are You, LORD our GOD and GOD of our Fathers, GOD of Abraham, GOD of Isaac and GOD of Jacob; the great, mighty and awesome GOD, GOD Most High, who bestows acts of lovingkindness and creates all, who remembers the lovingkindness of the Fathers and will bring a Redeemer to their children's children for the sake of His name, in love.

Between Rosh Hashanah and Yom Kippur, add:
Remember us for life, O King who desires life, and write us in the book of life – for Your sake, O GOD of life.

King, Helper, Saviour, Shield: ▾Blessed are You, LORD, Shield of Abraham.

DIVINE MIGHT

אַתָּה You are eternally mighty, LORD. You give life to the dead and have great power to save.

From after Simchat Torah until Pesach, add:
He makes the wind blow and the rain fall.

He sustains the living with lovingkindness, and with great compassion revives the dead. He supports the fallen, heals the sick, sets captives free, and keeps His faith with those who sleep in the dust. Who is like You, Master of might, and to whom can You be compared, O King who brings death and gives life, and makes salvation grow?

a man of unclean lips." Jeremiah said, "I cannot speak for I am a child." So our first prayer is for Divine help in the act of prayer itself.

Between רֹאשׁ הַשָּׁנָה and יוֹם כִּפּוּר, add:

מִי כָמְוֹךָ אַב הָרַחֲמִים, זוֹכֵר יְצוּרָיו לְחַיִּים בְּרַחֲמִים.

וְנֶאֱמָן אַתָּה לְהַחֲיוֹת מֵתִים. בָּרוּךְ אַתָּה יהוה, מְחַיֵּה הַמֵּתִים.

When saying the עֲמִידָה silently, go to אַתָּה קָדוֹשׁ overleaf.

קדושה

During the Leader's repetition, the following is said standing, with feet together, rising on the toes at the words indicated by ▲.

Congregation then Leader: נְקַדֵּשׁ אֶת־שִׁמְךָ בָּעוֹלָם, כְּשֵׁם שֶׁמַּקְדִּישִׁים אוֹתוֹ בִּשְׁמֵי מָרוֹם, כַּכָּתוּב עַל יַד נְבִיאֶךָ, וְקָרָא זֶה אֶל־זֶה וְאָמַר.

Congregation and Leader: ▲קָדוֹשׁ ▲קָדוֹשׁ ▲קָדוֹשׁ יהוה צְבָאוֹת, מְלֹא כָל־הָאָרֶץ כְּבוֹדוֹ.

Leader: לְעֻמָּתָם בָּרוּךְ יֹאמֵרוּ.

Congregation and Leader: ▲בָּרוּךְ כְּבוֹד־יהוה, מִמְּקוֹמוֹ.

Leader: וּבְדִבְרֵי קָדְשְׁךָ כָּתוּב לֵאמֹר.

Congregation and Leader: ▲יִמְלֹךְ יהוה לְעוֹלָם, אֱלֹהַיִךְ צִיּוֹן לְדֹר וָדֹר, הַלְלוּיָהּ.

Leader: לְדוֹר וָדוֹר נַגִּיד גָּדְלֶךָ וּלְנֵצַח נְצָחִים קְדֻשָּׁתְךָ נַקְדִּישׁ, וְשִׁבְחֲךָ אֱלֹהֵינוּ מִפִּינוּ לֹא יָמוּשׁ לְעוֹלָם וָעֶד, כִּי אֵל מֶלֶךְ גָּדוֹל וְקָדוֹשׁ אָתָּה. בָּרוּךְ אַתָּה יהוה, *הָאֵל הַקָּדוֹשׁ.

*Between רֹאשׁ הַשָּׁנָה and יוֹם כִּפּוּר, end the blessing:

הַמֶּלֶךְ הַקָּדוֹשׁ.

Between Rosh Hashanah and Yom Kippur, add:

Who is like You, compassionate Father, who remembers His creatures in compassion, for life?

Faithful are You to revive the dead. Blessed are You, LORD, who revives the dead.

When saying the *Amidah* silently, go to "You are holy" overleaf.

KEDUSHAH

During the Leader's repetition, the following is said standing, with feet together, rising on the toes at the words indicated by ▲:

Congregation then Leader — נְקַדֵּשׁ We will sanctify Your name on earth, as they sanctify it in the highest heavens, as is written by Your prophet, "And they [the angels] call to one another saying:

Congregation and Leader — ▲Holy, ▲holy, ▲holy is the LORD of Hosts the whole world is filled with His glory."

Leader — Those facing them say "Blessed – "

Congregation and Leader — "▲Blessed is the LORD's glory from His place."

Leader — And in Your Holy Writings it is written thus:

Congregation and Leader — "▲The LORD shall reign forever. He is your GOD, Zion, from generation to generation, Halleluyah!"

Leader — From generation to generation we will declare Your greatness, and we will proclaim Your holiness for evermore. Your praise, our GOD, shall never leave our mouth, for You, GOD, are a great and holy King. Blessed are You, LORD, *the holy GOD.

*Between Rosh Hashanah and Yom Kippur, end the blessing:

the holy King.

הַמֶּלֶךְ הַקָּדוֹשׁ *The holy King*: During the Ten Days of Repentance we substitute this phrase for "the holy GOD", to emphasise that these are days of judgement in which we are especially conscious of Divine sovereignty over all humanity. For this reason too, in the eleventh paragraph we substitute "the King of justice" for the usual ending.

קדושת השם

אַתָּה קָדוֹשׁ וְשִׁמְךָ קָדוֹשׁ, וּקְדוֹשִׁים בְּכָל־יוֹם יְהַלְלְוּךָ סֶּלָה. בָּרוּךְ אַתָּה יהוה, *הָאֵל הַקָּדוֹשׁ.

---

*Between רֹאשׁ הַשָּׁנָה and יוֹם כִּפּוּר, end the blessing:

הַמֶּלֶךְ הַקָּדוֹשׁ.

דעת

אַתָּה חוֹנֵן לְאָדָם דַּעַת, וּמְלַמֵּד לֶאֱנוֹשׁ בִּינָה. חָנֵּנוּ מֵאִתְּךָ דֵּעָה בִּינָה וְהַשְׂכֵּל. בָּרוּךְ אַתָּה יהוה, חוֹנֵן הַדָּעַת.

תשובה

הֲשִׁיבֵנוּ אָבִינוּ לְתוֹרָתֶךָ, וְקָרְבֵנוּ מַלְכֵּנוּ לַעֲבוֹדָתֶךָ, וְהַחֲזִירֵנוּ בִּתְשׁוּבָה שְׁלֵמָה לְפָנֶיךָ. בָּרוּךְ אַתָּה יהוה, הָרוֹצֶה בִּתְשׁוּבָה.

סליחה

סְלַח־לָנוּ אָבִינוּ כִּי חָטָאנוּ, מְחַל־לָנוּ מַלְכֵּנוּ כִּי פָשָׁעְנוּ, כִּי מוֹחֵל וְסוֹלֵחַ אָתָּה. בָּרוּךְ אַתָּה יהוה, חַנּוּן, הַמַּרְבֶּה לִסְלֽוֹחַ.

גאולה

רְאֵה בְעָנְיֵנוּ, וְרִיבָה רִיבֵנוּ, וּגְאָלֵנוּ מְהֵרָה לְמַעַן שְׁמֶךָ, כִּי גּוֹאֵל חָזָק אָתָּה. בָּרוּךְ אַתָּה יהוה, גּוֹאֵל יִשְׂרָאֵל.

On Fast Days, the Leader adds:

עֲנֵנוּ יהוה עֲנֵנוּ, בְּיוֹם צוֹם־תַּעֲנִיתֵנוּ, כִּי בְצָרָה־גְדוֹלָה אֲנָחְנוּ. אַל־תֵּפֶן אֶל־רִשְׁעֵנוּ, וְאַל תַּסְתֵּר פָּנֶיךָ מִמֶּנּוּ, וְאַל־תִּתְעַלַּם מִתְּחִנָּתֵנוּ. הֱיֵה נָא קָרוֹב לְשַׁוְעָתֵנוּ, יְהִי נָא חַסְדְּךָ לְנַחֲמֵנוּ, טֶרֶם נִקְרָא אֵלֶיךָ עֲנֵנוּ, כַּדָּבָר שֶׁנֶּאֱמַר, וְהָיָה טֶרֶם יִקְרָאוּ וַאֲנִי אֶעֱנֶה, עוֹד הֵם מְדַבְּרִים וַאֲנִי אֶשְׁמָע. כִּי אַתָּה יהוה הָעוֹנֶה

HOLINESS

אַתָּה You are holy and Your name is holy, and holy ones praise You daily, Selah! Blessed are You, LORD, *the holy GOD.

---

* Between Rosh Hashanah and Yom Kippur, end the blessing:
the holy King.

KNOWLEDGE

אַתָּה You grace humanity with knowledge and teach mortals understanding. Grace us with the knowledge, understanding and discernment that come from You. Blessed are You, LORD, who graciously grants knowledge.

REPENTANCE

הֲשִׁיבֵנוּ Bring us back, our Father, to Your Torah. Draw us near, our King, to Your service. Lead us back to You in perfect repentance. Blessed are You, LORD, who desires repentance.

FORGIVENESS

סְלַח־לָנוּ Forgive us, our Father, for we have sinned. Pardon us, our King, for we have transgressed; for You pardon and forgive. Blessed are You, LORD, the gracious One who repeatedly forgives.

REDEMPTION

רְאֵה Look on our affliction, plead our cause, and redeem us soon for Your name's sake, for You are a powerful Redeemer. Blessed are You, LORD, the Redeemer of Israel.

On Fast Days, the Leader adds:

עֲנֵנוּ Answer us, LORD, answer us on our Fast Day, for we are in great distress. Look not at our wickedness. Do not hide Your face from us and do not ignore our plea. Be near to our cry; please let Your lovingkindness comfort us. Even before we call to You, answer us, as is said, "Before they call, I will answer. While they are still speaking, I will hear". For You, LORD, are the One who answers in

בְּעֵת צָרָה, פּוֹדֶה וּמַצִּיל בְּכָל עֵת צָרָה וְצוּקָה. בָּרוּךְ אַתָּה יהוה, הָעוֹנֶה בְּעֵת צָרָה.

רפואה

רְפָאֵנוּ יהוה וְנֵרָפֵא, הוֹשִׁיעֵנוּ וְנִוָּשֵׁעָה, כִּי תְהִלָּתֵנוּ אָתָּה, וְהַעֲלֵה רְפוּאָה שְׁלֵמָה לְכָל מַכּוֹתֵינוּ,* כִּי אֵל מֶלֶךְ רוֹפֵא נֶאֱמָן וְרַחֲמָן אָתָּה. בָּרוּךְ אַתָּה יהוה, רוֹפֵא, חוֹלֵי עַמּוֹ יִשְׂרָאֵל.

---

*The following prayer for a sick person may be said here:

וִיהִי רָצוֹן מִלְּפָנֶיךָ, יהוה אֱלֹהֵינוּ וֵאלֹהֵי אֲבוֹתֵינוּ, שֶׁתִּשְׁלַח מְהֵרָה רְפוּאָה שְׁלֵמָה מִן הַשָּׁמַיִם, רְפוּאַת הַנֶּפֶשׁ וּרְפוּאַת הַגּוּף לַחוֹלֶה/לַחוֹלָה (if known, add Hebrew name בֶּן/בַּת mother's name) בְּתוֹךְ שְׁאָר חוֹלֵי יִשְׂרָאֵל.

ברכת השנים

בָּרֵךְ עָלֵינוּ יהוה אֱלֹהֵינוּ אֶת הַשָּׁנָה הַזֹּאת וְאֶת כָּל מִינֵי תְבוּאָתָהּ לְטוֹבָה,

From the second day of פֶּסַח until December 4th (in a year before a civil leap year, 5th), say:

וְתֵן בְּרָכָה

From December 5th (in the year before a civil leap year, 6th) until פֶּסַח, say:

וְתֵן טַל וּמָטָר לִבְרָכָה

עַל־פְּנֵי הָאֲדָמָה, וְשַׂבְּעֵנוּ מִטּוּבֶךָ, וּבָרֵךְ שְׁנָתֵנוּ כַּשָּׁנִים הַטּוֹבוֹת. בָּרוּךְ אַתָּה יהוה, מְבָרֵךְ הַשָּׁנִים.

קיבוץ גלויות

תְּקַע בְּשׁוֹפָר גָּדוֹל לְחֵרוּתֵנוּ, וְשָׂא נֵס לְקַבֵּץ גָּלֻיּוֹתֵינוּ, וְקַבְּצֵנוּ יַחַד מֵאַרְבַּע כַּנְפוֹת הָאָרֶץ. בָּרוּךְ אַתָּה יהוה, מְקַבֵּץ, נִדְחֵי עַמּוֹ יִשְׂרָאֵל.

time of distress, redeems and rescues in all times of trouble and anguish. Blessed are You, LORD, who answers in time of distress.

HEALING

רְפָאֵנוּ Heal us, LORD, and we shall be healed. Save us and we shall be saved, for You are our praise. Bring complete recovery for all our ailments,* for You, GOD, King, are a faithful and compassionate Healer. Blessed are You, LORD, Healer of the sick of His people Israel.

---

*The following prayer for a sick person may be said here:
May it be Your will, O LORD our GOD and GOD of our ancestors, that You speedily send a complete recovery from heaven, a healing of both soul and body, to the patient (name), son/daughter of (mother's name) among the other afflicted of Israel.

PROSPERITY

בָּרֵךְ Bless this year for us, LORD our GOD, and all its types of produce for good.

From the second day of Pesach until December 4th (in a year before a civil leap year, 5th), say:	From December 5th (in the year before a civil leap year, 6th) until Pesach, say:
Grant blessing	Grant dew and rain as a blessing

on the face of the earth, and from Your goodness satisfy us, blessing our year as the best of years. Blessed are You, LORD, who blesses the years.

INGATHERING OF EXILES

תְּקַע Sound the great shofar for our freedom, raise high the banner to gather our exiles, and gather us together from the four quarters of the earth. Blessed are You, LORD, who gathers the dispersed of His people Israel.

השבת המשפט

הָשִׁיבָה שׁוֹפְטֵינוּ כְּבָרִאשׁוֹנָה, וְיוֹעֲצֵינוּ כְּבַתְּחִלָּה, וְהָסֵר מִמֶּנּוּ יָגוֹן וַאֲנָחָה, וּמְלוֹךְ עָלֵינוּ אַתָּה יהוה לְבַדְּךָ בְּחֶסֶד וּבְרַחֲמִים, וְצַדְּקֵנוּ בַּמִּשְׁפָּט. בָּרוּךְ אַתָּה יהוה, *מֶלֶךְ, אוֹהֵב צְדָקָה וּמִשְׁפָּט.

*Between רֹאשׁ הַשָּׁנָה and יוֹם כִּפּוּר, end the blessing:
הַמֶּלֶךְ הַמִּשְׁפָּט.

ברכת המינים

וְלַמַּלְשִׁינִים אַל־תְּהִי תִקְוָה, וְכָל הָרִשְׁעָה כְּרֶגַע תֹּאבֵד, וְכָל אוֹיְבֶיךָ מְהֵרָה יִכָּרֵתוּ, וּמַלְכוּת זָדוֹן מְהֵרָה תְעַקֵּר וּתְשַׁבֵּר וּתְמַגֵּר וְתַכְנִיעַ בִּמְהֵרָה בְיָמֵינוּ. בָּרוּךְ אַתָּה יהוה, שׁוֹבֵר אוֹיְבִים וּמַכְנִיעַ זֵדִים.

על הצדיקים

עַל־הַצַּדִּיקִים וְעַל־הַחֲסִידִים, וְעַל־זִקְנֵי עַמְּךָ בֵּית יִשְׂרָאֵל, וְעַל־פְּלֵיטַת סוֹפְרֵיהֶם, וְעַל־גֵּרֵי הַצֶּדֶק וְעָלֵינוּ, יֶהֱמוּ רַחֲמֶיךָ יהוה אֱלֹהֵינוּ, וְתֵן שָׂכָר טוֹב לְכֹל הַבּוֹטְחִים בְּשִׁמְךָ בֶּאֱמֶת, וְשִׂים חֶלְקֵנוּ עִמָּהֶם לְעוֹלָם, וְלֹא נֵבוֹשׁ כִּי־בְךָ בָטָחְנוּ. בָּרוּךְ אַתָּה יהוה, מִשְׁעָן וּמִבְטָח לַצַּדִּיקִים.

בנין ירושלים

וְלִירוּשָׁלַיִם עִירְךָ בְּרַחֲמִים תָּשׁוּב, וְתִשְׁכּוֹן בְּתוֹכָהּ כַּאֲשֶׁר דִּבַּרְתָּ, וּבְנֵה אוֹתָהּ בְּקָרוֹב בְּיָמֵינוּ בִּנְיַן עוֹלָם, וְכִסֵּא דָוִד מְהֵרָה לְתוֹכָהּ תָּכִין.* בָּרוּךְ אַתָּה יהוה, בּוֹנֵה יְרוּשָׁלָיִם.

*On תִּשְׁעָה בְּאָב, the Congregation say:

נַחֵם יהוה אֱלֹהֵינוּ אֶת־אֲבֵלֵי צִיּוֹן, וְאֶת־אֲבֵלֵי יְרוּשָׁלָיִם, וְאֶת־הָעִיר הָאֲבֵלָה וְהֶחֳרֵבָה וְהַבְּזוּיָה וְהַשּׁוֹמֵמָה, הָאֲבֵלָה מִבְּלִי בָנֶיהָ, וְהֶחֳרֵבָה מִמְּעוֹנוֹתֶיהָ, וְהַבְּזוּיָה מִכְּבוֹדָהּ, וְהַשּׁוֹמֵמָה

JUSTICE

הָשִׁיבָה Restore our judges as at first and our counsellors as at the beginning, and remove from us sorrow and sighing. May You alone, LORD, reign over us with lovingkindness and compassion, and vindicate us in justice. Blessed are You, LORD,*the King who loves righteousness and justice.

---

*Between Rosh Hashanah and Yom Kippur, end the blessing:
the King of justice.

AGAINST INFORMERS

וְלַמַּלְשִׁינִים For the slanderers let there be no hope, and may all wickedness perish in an instant. May all Your enemies swiftly be cut down. May You swiftly uproot, crush, cast down and humble the kingdom of arrogance swiftly in our days. Blessed are You, LORD, who destroys enemies and humbles the arrogant.

THE RIGHTEOUS

עַל־הַצַּדִּיקִים To the righteous, the pious, the elders of Your people the house of Israel, the remnant of their scholars, the righteous converts, and to us, may Your compassion be aroused, LORD our GOD. Grant a good reward to all who sincerely trust in Your name. Set our lot with them for ever, so that we may never be ashamed, for in You we trust. Blessed are You, LORD, who is the support and trust of the righteous.

REBUILDING JERUSALEM

וְלִירוּשָׁלַיִם To Jerusalem, Your city, may You return in compassion, and may You dwell in it as You promised. May You rebuild it rapidly in our days as an everlasting structure, and instal within it soon the throne of David. *Blessed are You, LORD, who builds Jerusalem.

---

*On the Ninth of Av, the Congregation say:
נַחֵם Console, O LORD our GOD, the mourners of Zion and the mourners of Jerusalem, and the city that is in sorrow, laid waste, scorned and desolate; that grieves for the loss of its children, that

מֵאֵין יוֹשֵׁב. וְהִיא יוֹשֶׁבֶת וְרֹאשָׁהּ חָפוּי כְּאִשָּׁה עֲקָרָה שֶׁלֹּא יָלָדָה. וַיְבַלְּעוּהָ לִגְיוֹנוֹת, וַיִּירָשׁוּהָ עוֹבְדֵי זָרִים, וַיָּטִילוּ אֶת־עַמְּךָ יִשְׂרָאֵל לֶחָרֶב, וַיַּהַרְגוּ בְזָדוֹן חֲסִידֵי עֶלְיוֹן, עַל־כֵּן צִיּוֹן בְּמַר תִּבְכֶּה, וִירוּשָׁלַיִם תִּתֵּן קוֹלָהּ. לִבִּי לִבִּי עַל חַלְלֵיהֶם, מֵעַי מֵעַי עַל חַלְלֵיהֶם, כִּי אַתָּה יהוה בָּאֵשׁ הִצַּתָּהּ, וּבָאֵשׁ אַתָּה עָתִיד לִבְנוֹתָהּ, כָּאָמוּר, וַאֲנִי אֶהְיֶה־לָּהּ, נְאֻם־יהוה, חוֹמַת אֵשׁ סָבִיב, וּלְכָבוֹד אֶהְיֶה בְתוֹכָהּ. בָּרוּךְ אַתָּה יהוה, מְנַחֵם צִיּוֹן וּבוֹנֵה יְרוּשָׁלָיִם.

משיח בן דוד

אֶת־צֶמַח דָּוִד עַבְדְּךָ מְהֵרָה תַצְמִיחַ, וְקַרְנוֹ תָּרוּם בִּישׁוּעָתֶךָ, כִּי לִישׁוּעָתְךָ קִוִּינוּ כָּל־הַיּוֹם. בָּרוּךְ אַתָּה יהוה, מַצְמִיחַ קֶרֶן יְשׁוּעָה.

שומע תפילה

שְׁמַע קוֹלֵנוּ יהוה אֱלֹהֵינוּ, חוּס וְרַחֵם עָלֵינוּ, וְקַבֵּל בְּרַחֲמִים וּבְרָצוֹן אֶת־תְּפִלָּתֵנוּ, כִּי אֵל שׁוֹמֵעַ תְּפִלּוֹת וְתַחֲנוּנִים, אָתָּה. וּמִלְּפָנֶיךָ מַלְכֵּנוּ, רֵיקָם אַל תְּשִׁיבֵנוּ,* כִּי אַתָּה שׁוֹמֵעַ תְּפִלַּת עַמְּךָ יִשְׂרָאֵל בְּרַחֲמִים. בָּרוּךְ אַתָּה יהוה, שׁוֹמֵעַ תְּפִלָּה.

---

*On Fast Days, the Congregation adds:

עֲנֵנוּ יהוה עֲנֵנוּ, בְּיוֹם צוֹם־תַּעֲנִיתֵנוּ, כִּי בְצָרָה־גְדוֹלָה אֲנָחְנוּ. אַל־תֵּפֶן אֶל־רִשְׁעֵנוּ, וְאַל תַּסְתֵּר פָּנֶיךָ מִמֶּנּוּ, וְאַל־תִּתְעַלַּם מִתְּחִנָּתֵנוּ. הֱיֵה נָא קָרוֹב לְשַׁוְעָתֵנוּ, יְהִי נָא חַסְדְּךָ לְנַחֲמֵנוּ, טֶרֶם נִקְרָא אֵלֶיךָ עֲנֵנוּ, כַּדָּבָר שֶׁנֶּאֱמַר, וְהָיָה טֶרֶם יִקְרָאוּ וַאֲנִי אֶעֱנֶה, עוֹד הֵם מְדַבְּרִים וַאֲנִי אֶשְׁמָע. כִּי אַתָּה יהוה הָעוֹנֶה בְּעֵת צָרָה, פּוֹדֶה וּמַצִּיל בְּכָל עֵת צָרָה וְצוּקָה.

is laid waste of its dwellings, robbed of its glory, desolate without inhabitants. She sits with her head covered like a barren childless woman. Legions have devoured her; idolaters have taken possession of her; they have put Your people Israel to the sword and deliberately killed the devoted followers of the Most High. Therefore Zion weeps bitterly, and Jerusalem raises her voice. My heart, my heart grieves for those they killed; I am in anguish, I am in anguish for those they killed. For You, O LORD, consumed it with fire and with fire You will rebuild it in the future, as is said, "And I myself will be a wall of fire around it, says the LORD, and I will be its glory within." Blessed are You, LORD, who consoles Zion and rebuilds Jerusalem.

KINGDOM OF DAVID

אֶת־צֶמַח May the offshoot of Your servant David soon flower, and may his pride be raised high by Your salvation, for we wait for Your salvation all day. Blessed are You, LORD, who makes the glory of salvation flourish.

RESPONSE TO PRAYER

שְׁמַע Listen to our voice, LORD our GOD. Spare us and have compassion on us, and in compassion and favour accept our prayer, for You, GOD, listen to prayers and pleas. Do not turn us away, O our King, empty-handed from Your presence, *for You listen with compassion to the prayer of Your people Israel. Blessed are You, LORD, who listens to prayer.

---

*On Fast Days, the Congregation adds:

עֲנֵנוּ Answer us, LORD, answer us on our Fast Day, for we are in great distress. Look not at our wickedness. Do not hide Your face from us and do not ignore our plea. Be near to our cry; please let Your lovingkindness comfort us. Even before we call to You, answer us, as is said, "Before they call, I will answer. While they are still speaking, I will hear". For You, LORD, are the One who answers in time of distress, redeems and rescues in all times of trouble and anguish. Blessed are You, LORD, who answers in time of distress.

עבודה

רְצֵה יהוה אֱלֹהֵינוּ בְּעַמְּךָ יִשְׂרָאֵל וּבִתְפִלָּתָם, וְהָשֵׁב אֶת־הָעֲבוֹדָה לִדְבִיר בֵּיתֶךָ. וְאִשֵּׁי יִשְׂרָאֵל וּתְפִלָּתָם בְּאַהֲבָה תְקַבֵּל בְּרָצוֹן, וּתְהִי לְרָצוֹן תָּמִיד עֲבוֹדַת יִשְׂרָאֵל עַמֶּךָ.

On רֹאשׁ חֹדֶשׁ and חוֹל הַמּוֹעֵד, say:

אֱלֹהֵינוּ וֵאלֹהֵי אֲבוֹתֵינוּ, יַעֲלֶה, וְיָבֹא, וְיַגִּיעַ, וְיֵרָאֶה, וְיֵרָצֶה, וְיִשָּׁמַע, וְיִפָּקֵד, וְיִזָּכֵר זִכְרוֹנֵנוּ וּפִקְדוֹנֵנוּ, וְזִכְרוֹן אֲבוֹתֵינוּ, וְזִכְרוֹן מָשִׁיחַ בֶּן דָּוִד עַבְדֶּךָ, וְזִכְרוֹן יְרוּשָׁלַיִם עִיר קָדְשֶׁךָ, וְזִכְרוֹן כָּל־עַמְּךָ בֵּית יִשְׂרָאֵל לְפָנֶיךָ, לִפְלֵיטָה וּלְטוֹבָה, וּלְחֵן וּלְחֶסֶד וּלְרַחֲמִים, וּלְחַיִּים וּלְשָׁלוֹם בְּיוֹם

On רֹאשׁ חֹדֶשׁ:	On פֶּסַח:	On סֻכּוֹת:
רֹאשׁ הַחֹדֶשׁ	חַג הַמַּצּוֹת	חַג הַסֻּכּוֹת

הַזֶּה. זָכְרֵנוּ יהוה אֱלֹהֵינוּ בּוֹ לְטוֹבָה, וּפָקְדֵנוּ בוֹ לִבְרָכָה, וְהוֹשִׁיעֵנוּ בוֹ לְחַיִּים. וּבִדְבַר יְשׁוּעָה וְרַחֲמִים, חוּס וְחָנֵּנוּ וְרַחֵם עָלֵינוּ וְהוֹשִׁיעֵנוּ, כִּי אֵלֶיךָ עֵינֵינוּ, כִּי אֵל מֶלֶךְ חַנּוּן וְרַחוּם אָתָּה.

וְתֶחֱזֶינָה עֵינֵינוּ בְּשׁוּבְךָ לְצִיּוֹן בְּרַחֲמִים. בָּרוּךְ אַתָּה יהוה, הַמַּחֲזִיר שְׁכִינָתוֹ לְצִיּוֹן.

הודאה

▽ Bow at the first five words

▽**מוֹדִים** אֲנַחְנוּ לָךְ, שָׁאַתָּה הוּא יהוה אֱלֹהֵינוּ וֵאלֹהֵי אֲבוֹתֵינוּ לְעוֹלָם וָעֶד. צוּר חַיֵּינוּ, מָגֵן יִשְׁעֵנוּ אַתָּה הוּא לְדוֹר וָדוֹר. נוֹדֶה לְּךָ וּנְסַפֵּר תְּהִלָּתֶךָ עַל חַיֵּינוּ הַמְּסוּרִים בְּיָדֶךָ, וְעַל נִשְׁמוֹתֵינוּ הַפְּקוּדוֹת לָךְ, וְעַל

During the Leader's repetition, the Congregation says quietly:

▽**מוֹדִים** אֲנַחְנוּ לָךְ, שָׁאַתָּה הוּא יהוה אֱלֹהֵינוּ וֵאלֹהֵי אֲבוֹתֵינוּ, אֱלֹהֵי כָל־בָּשָׂר, יוֹצְרֵנוּ, יוֹצֵר בְּרֵאשִׁית. בְּרָכוֹת וְהוֹדָאוֹת לְשִׁמְךָ הַגָּדוֹל וְהַקָּדוֹשׁ, עַל

TEMPLE SERVICE

רְצֵה Find favour, LORD our GOD, in Your people Israel and their prayer. Restore the service to Your most holy house, and accept in love and favour the fire-offerings of Israel and their prayer. May the service of Your people Israel always find favour with You.

On Rosh Chodesh and the Intermediate Days of Festivals, say:

אֱלֹהֵינוּ Our GOD and GOD of our ancestors, may there rise, come, reach, appear, be favoured, heard, regarded and remembered before You, our recollection and remembrance, as well as the remembrance of our ancestors, and of the Messiah son of David Your servant, and of Jerusalem Your holy city, and of all Your people the House of Israel – for deliverance and well-being, grace, lovingkindness and compassion, life and peace, on this day of:

On Rosh Chodesh:	On Pesach:	On Sukkot:
Rosh Chodesh.	the Festival of Matzot.	the Festival of Sukkot.

On it remember us, LORD our GOD, for good; recollect us for blessing, and deliver us for life. In accord with Your promise of salvation and compassion, spare us and be gracious to us; have compassion on us and deliver us, for our eyes are turned to You because You, GOD, are a gracious and compassionate King.

וְתֶחֱזֶינָה And may our eyes witness Your return to Zion in compassion. Blessed are You, LORD, who restores His Presence to Zion.

THANKSGIVING

▽ Bow at the first nine words

מוֹדִים▽ We give thanks to You, for You are the LORD our GOD and GOD of our ancestors for ever and all time. You are the Rock of our lives, Shield of our salvation from generation to generation. We will thank You and declare Your praise for our lives, which are entrusted into Your hand; our souls, which are placed in Your charge; for Your miracles which are

During the Leader's repetition, the Congregation says quietly:

מוֹדִים▽ We give thanks to You, for You are the LORD our GOD and GOD of our ancestors, GOD of all flesh, who formed us and formed the universe. Blessings and thanks are due to Your great and holy name for giving us life and sustaining us. May You continue to give

נִסֶּיךָ שֶׁבְּכָל־יוֹם עִמָּנוּ, וְעַל נִפְלְאוֹתֶיךָ וְטוֹבוֹתֶיךָ שֶׁבְּכָל־עֵת, עֶרֶב וָבֹקֶר וְצָהֳרָיִם. הַטּוֹב כִּי לֹא־כָלוּ רַחֲמֶיךָ, וְהַמְרַחֵם כִּי לֹא־תַמּוּ חֲסָדֶיךָ, מֵעוֹלָם קִוִּינוּ לָךְ.

שֶׁהֶחֱיִיתָנוּ וְקִיַּמְתָּנוּ. כֵּן תְּחַיֵּנוּ וּתְקַיְּמֵנוּ, וְתֶאֱסוֹף גָּלֻיּוֹתֵינוּ לְחַצְרוֹת קָדְשֶׁךָ, לִשְׁמוֹר חֻקֶּיךָ וְלַעֲשׂוֹת רְצוֹנֶךָ, וּלְעָבְדְּךָ בְּלֵבָב שָׁלֵם, עַל שֶׁאֲנַחְנוּ מוֹדִים לָךְ. בָּרוּךְ אֵל הַהוֹדָאוֹת.

On חֲנֻכָּה and פּוּרִים, say:

עַל הַנִּסִּים, וְעַל הַפֻּרְקָן, וְעַל הַגְּבוּרוֹת, וְעַל הַתְּשׁוּעוֹת, וְעַל הַמִּלְחָמוֹת, שֶׁעָשִׂיתָ לַאֲבוֹתֵינוּ בַּיָּמִים הָהֵם בַּזְּמַן הַזֶּה.

On חֲנֻכָּה, say:

בִּימֵי מַתִּתְיָהוּ בֶּן־יוֹחָנָן כֹּהֵן גָּדוֹל חַשְׁמוֹנַאי וּבָנָיו, כְּשֶׁעָמְדָה מַלְכוּת יָוָן הָרְשָׁעָה עַל־עַמְּךָ יִשְׂרָאֵל, לְהַשְׁכִּיחָם תּוֹרָתֶךָ, וּלְהַעֲבִירָם מֵחֻקֵּי רְצוֹנֶךָ. וְאַתָּה בְּרַחֲמֶיךָ הָרַבִּים, עָמַדְתָּ לָהֶם בְּעֵת צָרָתָם, רַבְתָּ אֶת־רִיבָם, דַּנְתָּ אֶת־דִּינָם, נָקַמְתָּ אֶת־נִקְמָתָם. מָסַרְתָּ גִבּוֹרִים בְּיַד חַלָּשִׁים, וְרַבִּים בְּיַד מְעַטִּים, וּטְמֵאִים בְּיַד טְהוֹרִים, וּרְשָׁעִים בְּיַד צַדִּיקִים, וְזֵדִים בְּיַד עוֹסְקֵי תוֹרָתֶךָ. וּלְךָ עָשִׂיתָ שֵׁם גָּדוֹל וְקָדוֹשׁ בְּעוֹלָמֶךָ, וּלְעַמְּךָ יִשְׂרָאֵל עָשִׂיתָ תְּשׁוּעָה גְדוֹלָה וּפֻרְקָן כְּהַיּוֹם הַזֶּה. וְאַחַר כֵּן בָּאוּ בָנֶיךָ לִדְבִיר בֵּיתֶךָ, וּפִנּוּ אֶת־הֵיכָלֶךָ, וְטִהֲרוּ אֶת־מִקְדָּשֶׁךָ, וְהִדְלִיקוּ נֵרוֹת בְּחַצְרוֹת קָדְשֶׁךָ, וְקָבְעוּ שְׁמוֹנַת יְמֵי חֲנֻכָּה אֵלּוּ, לְהוֹדוֹת וּלְהַלֵּל לְשִׁמְךָ הַגָּדוֹל.

On פּוּרִים, say:

בִּימֵי מָרְדְּכַי וְאֶסְתֵּר בְּשׁוּשַׁן הַבִּירָה, כְּשֶׁעָמַד עֲלֵיהֶם הָמָן הָרָשָׁע, בִּקֵּשׁ לְהַשְׁמִיד לַהֲרוֹג וּלְאַבֵּד אֶת־כָּל־הַיְּהוּדִים, מִנַּעַר וְעַד זָקֵן, טַף וְנָשִׁים בְּיוֹם אֶחָד, בִּשְׁלוֹשָׁה־עָשָׂר לְחֹדֶשׁ שְׁנֵים־עָשָׂר, הוּא־חֹדֶשׁ אֲדָר, וּשְׁלָלָם לָבוֹז. וְאַתָּה בְּרַחֲמֶיךָ הָרַבִּים הֵפַרְתָּ אֶת־עֲצָתוֹ, וְקִלְקַלְתָּ אֶת־מַחֲשַׁבְתּוֹ, וַהֲשֵׁבוֹתָ גְּמוּלוֹ בְּרֹאשׁוֹ, וְתָלוּ אוֹתוֹ וְאֶת־בָּנָיו עַל־הָעֵץ.

with us every day; and for Your wonders and favours at all times, evening, morning and midday. You are good – for Your compassion never fails. You are compassionate – for Your loving-kindnesses never cease. We have always placed our hope in You.

us life and sustain us; and may You gather our exiles to Your holy courts, to keep Your decrees, do Your will and serve You with a perfect heart, for it is for us to give You thanks. Blessed be GOD to whom thanksgiving is due.

On Chanukah and Purim, say:

עַל הַנִּסִּים [We thank You also] for the miracles, the redemption, the mighty deeds, and the victories in battle which You performed for our ancestors in those days at this time.

On Chanukah, say:

בִּימֵי In the days of Mattityahu, son of Yochanan the High Priest, the Hasmonean, and his sons, the wicked Greek kingdom rose up against Your people Israel to make them forget Your Torah and to force them to transgress the statutes of Your will. It was then that You in Your great compassion stood by them in the time of their distress. You championed their cause, judged their claim, and avenged their wrong. You delivered the strong into the hands of the weak, the many into the hands of the few, the impure into the hands of the pure, the wicked into the hands of the righteous, and the arrogant into the hands of those who were engaged in the study of Your Torah. You made for Yourself great and holy renown in Your world, and for Your people Israel You performed a great salvation and redemption on this day. Your children then entered the holiest part of Your house, cleansed Your Temple, purified Your sanctuary, kindled lights in Your holy courts, and designated these eight days of Chanukah for giving thanks and praise to Your great name.

On Purim, say:

בִּימֵי In the days of Mordechai and Esther, in Shushan the capital, the wicked Haman rose up against them and sought to destroy, slay and exterminate all the Jews, young and old, children and women, on one day, the thirteenth day of the twelfth month, which is the month of Adar, and to plunder their possessions. Then You in Your great compassion thwarted his counsel, frustrated his plans, and caused his scheme to recoil on his own head, so that they hanged him and his sons on the gallows.

וְעַל כֻּלָּם יִתְבָּרַךְ וְיִתְרוֹמַם שִׁמְךָ מַלְכֵּנוּ תָּמִיד לְעוֹלָם וָעֶד.

Between רֹאשׁ הַשָּׁנָה and יוֹם כִּפּוּר, say:

וּכְתוֹב לְחַיִּים טוֹבִים כָּל־בְּנֵי בְרִיתֶךָ.

וְכֹל הַחַיִּים יוֹדוּךָ סֶּלָה, וִיהַלְלוּ אֶת־שִׁמְךָ בֶּאֱמֶת, הָאֵל יְשׁוּעָתֵנוּ וְעֶזְרָתֵנוּ סֶלָה. ▾בָּרוּךְ אַתָּה יהוה, הַטּוֹב שִׁמְךָ וּלְךָ נָאֶה לְהוֹדוֹת.

During the repetition of the עֲמִידָה on Fast Days, the Leader says the following:

אֱלֹהֵינוּ וֵאלֹהֵי אֲבוֹתֵינוּ, בָּרְכֵנוּ בַּבְּרָכָה הַמְשֻׁלֶּשֶׁת, בַּתּוֹרָה, הַכְּתוּבָה עַל יְדֵי מֹשֶׁה עַבְדֶּךָ, הָאֲמוּרָה מִפִּי אַהֲרֹן וּבָנָיו כֹּהֲנִים, עַם קְדוֹשֶׁךָ, כָּאָמוּר.

יְבָרֶכְךָ יהוה, וְיִשְׁמְרֶךָ. (Cong.: כֵּן יְהִי רָצוֹן)

יָאֵר יהוה פָּנָיו אֵלֶיךָ וִיחֻנֶּךָּ. (Cong.: כֵּן יְהִי רָצוֹן)

יִשָּׂא יהוה פָּנָיו אֵלֶיךָ וְיָשֵׂם לְךָ שָׁלוֹם. (Cong.: כֵּן יְהִי רָצוֹן)

ברכת שלום

*__שָׁלוֹם__ רָב עַל יִשְׂרָאֵל עַמְּךָ תָּשִׂים לְעוֹלָם, כִּי אַתָּה הוּא מֶלֶךְ אָדוֹן לְכָל הַשָּׁלוֹם. וְטוֹב בְּעֵינֶיךָ לְבָרֵךְ אֶת עַמְּךָ יִשְׂרָאֵל בְּכָל עֵת וּבְכָל שָׁעָה בִּשְׁלוֹמֶךָ.

---

*On Fast Days, substitute:

שִׂים שָׁלוֹם, טוֹבָה, וּבְרָכָה, חֵן, וָחֶסֶד וְרַחֲמִים עָלֵינוּ וְעַל כָּל־יִשְׂרָאֵל עַמֶּךָ. בָּרְכֵנוּ אָבִינוּ, כֻּלָּנוּ כְּאֶחָד בְּאוֹר פָּנֶיךָ, כִּי בְאוֹר פָּנֶיךָ נָתַתָּ לָּנוּ, יהוה אֱלֹהֵינוּ, תּוֹרַת חַיִּים וְאַהֲבַת חֶסֶד, וּצְדָקָה, וּבְרָכָה, וְרַחֲמִים, וְחַיִּים, וְשָׁלוֹם. וְטוֹב בְּעֵינֶיךָ לְבָרֵךְ אֶת־עַמְּךָ יִשְׂרָאֵל, בְּכָל־עֵת וּבְכָל־שָׁעָה בִּשְׁלוֹמֶךָ.

וְעַל For all these things may Your name be blessed and exalted, our King, continually, for ever and all time.

Between Rosh Hashanah and Yom Kippur, say:
And write, for a good life, all the children of Your covenant.

Let all that lives thank You, Selah! and praise Your name in truth, God, our Saviour and Help, Selah! ▾Blessed are You, Lord, whose name is "the Good" and to whom thanks are due.

During the repetition of the *Amidah* on Fast Days, the Leader says the following:
אֱלֹהֵינוּ Our God and God of our fathers, bless us with the threefold blessing in the Torah, written by the hand of Moses Your servant and pronounced by Aaron and his sons the priests, Your holy people, as it is said:
May the Lord bless you and protect you. (Cong.: May it be Your will.)
May the Lord make His face shine on you and be gracious to you.
(Cong.: May it be Your will.)
May the Lord turn His face towards you, and give you peace.
(Cong.: May it be Your will.)

PEACE

שָׁלוֹם *Grant great peace to Your people Israel for ever, for You are the sovereign Lord of all peace; and may it be good in Your eyes to bless Your people Israel at every time, at every hour, with Your peace.

*On Fast Days, substitute:
שִׂים Grant peace, goodness and blessing, grace, lovingkindness and compassion to us and all Israel Your people. Bless us, our Father, all as one, with the light of Your face, for by the light of Your face You have given us, Lord our God, the Torah of life and love of kindness, righteousness, blessing, compassion, life and peace. May it be good in Your eyes to bless Your people Israel at every time, in every hour, with Your peace.

*בָּרוּךְ אַתָּה יהוה, הַמְבָרֵךְ אֶת עַמּוֹ יִשְׂרָאֵל בַּשָּׁלוֹם.

---

*Between רֹאשׁ הַשָּׁנָה and יוֹם כִּפּוּר, substitute the following:

בְּסֵפֶר חַיִּים בְּרָכָה וְשָׁלוֹם, וּפַרְנָסָה טוֹבָה, נִזָּכֵר וְנִכָּתֵב לְפָנֶיךָ, אֲנַחְנוּ וְכָל־עַמְּךָ בֵּית יִשְׂרָאֵל, לְחַיִּים טוֹבִים וּלְשָׁלוֹם. בָּרוּךְ אַתָּה יהוה, עוֹשֵׂה הַשָּׁלוֹם.

The Leader's repetition ends at this point.

אֱלֹהַי, נְצוֹר לְשׁוֹנִי מֵרָע, וּשְׂפָתַי מִדַּבֵּר מִרְמָה, וְלִמְקַלְלַי נַפְשִׁי תִדּוֹם, וְנַפְשִׁי כֶּעָפָר לַכֹּל תִּהְיֶה. פְּתַח לִבִּי בְּתוֹרָתֶךָ, וּבְמִצְוֹתֶיךָ תִּרְדּוֹף נַפְשִׁי. וְכֹל הַחוֹשְׁבִים עָלַי רָעָה, מְהֵרָה הָפֵר עֲצָתָם וְקַלְקֵל מַחְשְׁבוֹתָם. עֲשֵׂה לְמַעַן שְׁמֶךָ, עֲשֵׂה לְמַעַן יְמִינֶךָ, עֲשֵׂה לְמַעַן קְדֻשָּׁתֶךָ, עֲשֵׂה לְמַעַן תּוֹרָתֶךָ. לְמַעַן יֵחָלְצוּן יְדִידֶיךָ, הוֹשִׁיעָה יְמִינְךָ וַעֲנֵנִי. יִהְיוּ לְרָצוֹן אִמְרֵי־פִי וְהֶגְיוֹן לִבִּי לְפָנֶיךָ, יהוה צוּרִי וְגוֹאֲלִי.

Bow, take three steps back, then bow, first left, then right, then centre, while saying:

עֹשֶׂה שָׁלוֹם בִּמְרוֹמָיו, הוּא יַעֲשֶׂה שָׁלוֹם עָלֵינוּ, וְעַל־כָּל־יִשְׂרָאֵל, וְאִמְרוּ אָמֵן.

יְהִי רָצוֹן מִלְּפָנֶיךָ יהוה אֱלֹהֵינוּ וֵאלֹהֵי אֲבוֹתֵינוּ, שֶׁיִּבָּנֶה בֵּית הַמִּקְדָּשׁ בִּמְהֵרָה בְיָמֵינוּ, וְתֵן חֶלְקֵנוּ בְּתוֹרָתֶךָ. וְשָׁם נַעֲבָדְךָ בְּיִרְאָה, כִּימֵי עוֹלָם וּכְשָׁנִים קַדְמוֹנִיּוֹת. וְעָרְבָה לַיהוה מִנְחַת יְהוּדָה וִירוּשָׁלָיִם, כִּימֵי עוֹלָם וּכְשָׁנִים קַדְמוֹנִיּוֹת.

When praying with a מִנְיָן, the עֲמִידָה is repeated aloud by the Leader.

אבינו מלכנו

Between רֹאשׁ הַשָּׁנָה and יוֹם כִּפּוּר and in most congregations on Fast Days (except תִּשְׁעָה בְּאָב), including תַּעֲנִית אֶסְתֵּר when observed on Thursday אָבִינוּ מַלְכֵּנוּ on page 98 is said at this point. It is not said on Friday afternoon, עֶרֶב יוֹם כִּפּוּר, or on ערב פורים.

*Blessed are You, LORD, who blesses His people Israel with peace.

---

*Between Rosh Hashanah and Yom Kippur, substitute the following::

In the book of life, blessing, peace and prosperity, may we and all Your people the house of Israel be remembered and written before You for a good life, and for peace. Blessed are You, LORD, who makes peace.

The Leader's repetition ends at this point.

אֱלֹהַי My GOD, guard my tongue from evil and my lips from deceitful speech. To those who curse me, let my soul be silent; may my soul be to all like the dust. Open my heart to Your Torah and let my soul pursue Your commandments. As for all who plan evil against me, swiftly thwart their counsel and frustrate their plans. Act for the sake of Your name; act for the sake of Your right hand; act for the sake of Your holiness; act for the sake of Your Torah. That Your beloved ones may be delivered, save with Your right hand and answer me. May the words of my mouth and the meditation of my heart find favour before You, LORD, my Rock and Redeemer.

Bow, take three steps back, then bow, first left, then right, then centre, while saying:

May He who makes peace in His high places, make peace for us and all Israel – and say: Amen.

יְהִי May it be Your will, LORD our GOD and GOD of our ancestors, that the Temple be rebuilt speedily in our days, and grant us a share in Your Torah. And there we will serve You with reverence, as in the days of old and as in former years. Then the offering of Judah and Jerusalem will be pleasing to the LORD as in the days of old and as in former years.

When praying with a *minyan*, the *Amidah* is repeated aloud by the Leader.

AVINU MALKENU

Between Rosh Hashanah and Yom Kippur and in most congregations on Fast Days (except the Ninth of Av), including the Fast of Esther, when observed on Thursday, *Avinu Malkenu* on page 99 is said at this point. It is not said on Friday afternoon, the eve of Yom Kippur, or the eve of Purim.

תחנון

תַּחֲנוּן is not said on Friday afternoons and on the following days: 1. רֹאשׁ חֹדֶשׁ and the preceding afternoon, during the whole month of נִיסָן, on ל״ג בָּעֹמֶר, יוֹם הָעַצְמָאוּת, יוֹם יְרוּשָׁלַיִם and the preceding afternoons, the first eight days of סִיוָן, on תִּשְׁעָה בְּאָב and ט״ו בְּאָב and the preceding afternoons, from עֶרֶב רֹאשׁ הַשָּׁנָה, עֶרֶב יוֹם כִּפּוּר until and including the day after שִׂמְחַת תּוֹרָה, on חֲנֻכָּה, ט״ו בִּשְׁבָט and the preceding afternoons, on פּוּרִים and שׁוּשַׁן פּוּרִים and פורים קטן and שושן פורים קטן which falls on 14th and 15th אֲדָר רִאשׁוֹן in a Jewish leap year and the preceding afternoons. 2. In the presence of a bridegroom on the day of his wedding and for the subsequent six days. 3. In a house of mourning during the week of שִׁבְעָה. 4. On the occasion of a בְּרִית מִילָה, if prayers are said where the ceremony will take place later that day or if the father, סַנְדָּק or מוֹהֵל is present.

נפילת אפים

Say until יֵבֹשׁוּ רָגַע while sitting, with the head resting on the left arm. This applies only when prayers are said in a place containing a סֵפֶר תּוֹרָה; otherwise, sit with head erect.

וַיֹּאמֶר דָּוִד אֶל־גָּד, צַר־לִי מְאֹד, נִפְּלָה־נָּא בְיַד־יהוה, כִּי־רַבִּים רַחֲמָיו, וּבְיַד אָדָם אַל־אֶפֹּלָה. רַחוּם וְחַנּוּן חָטָאתִי לְפָנֶיךָ. יהוה מָלֵא רַחֲמִים, רַחֵם עָלַי וְקַבֵּל תַּחֲנוּנָי.

תהילים ו:ב–יא

יהוה, אַל־בְּאַפְּךָ תוֹכִיחֵנִי, וְאַל־בַּחֲמָתְךָ תְיַסְּרֵנִי. חָנֵּנִי יהוה, כִּי־אֻמְלַל אָנִי, רְפָאֵנִי יהוה, כִּי נִבְהֲלוּ עֲצָמָי. וְנַפְשִׁי נִבְהֲלָה מְאֹד, וְאַתָּה יהוה, עַד־מָתָי. שׁוּבָה יהוה, חַלְּצָה נַפְשִׁי, הוֹשִׁיעֵנִי לְמַעַן חַסְדֶּךָ. כִּי אֵין בַּמָּוֶת זִכְרֶךָ, בִּשְׁאוֹל מִי יוֹדֶה־לָּךְ. יָגַעְתִּי בְאַנְחָתִי, אַשְׂחֶה בְכָל־לַיְלָה מִטָּתִי, בְּדִמְעָתִי עַרְשִׂי אַמְסֶה. עָשְׁשָׁה מִכַּעַס עֵינִי, עָתְקָה בְּכָל־צוֹרְרָי. סוּרוּ מִמֶּנִּי כָּל־פֹּעֲלֵי אָוֶן, כִּי שָׁמַע יהוה קוֹל בִּכְיִי. שָׁמַע יהוה תְּחִנָּתִי, יהוה תְּפִלָּתִי יִקָּח. יֵבֹשׁוּ וְיִבָּהֲלוּ מְאֹד כָּל־אֹיְבָי, יָשֻׁבוּ יֵבֹשׁוּ רָגַע.

Sit upright and say:

שׁוֹמֵר יִשְׂרָאֵל, שְׁמוֹר שְׁאֵרִית יִשְׂרָאֵל, וְאַל־יֹאבַד יִשְׂרָאֵל, הָאוֹמְרִים, שְׁמַע יִשְׂרָאֵל.

שׁוֹמֵר גּוֹי אֶחָד, שְׁמוֹר שְׁאֵרִית עַם אֶחָד, וְאַל יֹאבַד גּוֹי אֶחָד, הַמְיַחֲדִים שִׁמְךָ, יהוה אֱלֹהֵינוּ יהוה אֶחָד.

TACHANUN

Tachanun is not said on Friday afternoons and the following days: 1. Rosh Chodesh and the preceding afternoon, during the whole month of Nisan, on Yom Ha'Atzma'ut, Lag BaOmer, Yom Yerushalayim and the preceding afternoons, the first eight days of Sivan, on the 9th and 15th of Av and the preceding afternoons, the day before Rosh Hashanah, from the day before Yom Kippur until and including the day after Simchat Torah, on Chanukah, the 15th of Shevat and the preceding afternoons, on Purim and Shushan Purim, on Purim Katan and on Shushan Purim Katan which falls on the 14th and 15th of Adar Rishon in a Jewish leap year, and the preceding afternoons. 2. In the presence of a bridegroom on the day of his wedding and for the subsequent six days. 3. In a house of mourning during the week of *shivah*. 4. On the occasion of a *Brit Milah*, if prayers are said where the ceremony will take place later that day or if the father, *sandek* or *mohel* is present.

LOWERING THE HEAD

Say until "sudden shame" while sitting, with the head resting on the left arm. This applies only when prayers are said in a place containing a Torah scroll; otherwise, sit with head erect.

וַיֹּאמֶר דָּוִד David said to Gad, "I am in great distress. Let us fall into God's hand, for His mercy is great; but do not let me fall into the hand of man." Compassionate and gracious One, I have sinned before You. LORD, full of compassion, have compassion on me and accept my pleas.

PSALM 6:2–11

LORD, do not rebuke me in Your anger or chastise me in Your wrath. Be gracious to me, LORD, for I am weak. Heal me, LORD, for my bones are in agony. My soul is in anguish, and You, O LORD – how long? Turn, LORD, set my soul free; save me for the sake of Your love. For no-one remembers You when he is dead. Who can praise You from the grave? I am weary with my sighing. Every night I drench my bed, I soak my couch with my tears. My eye grows dim from grief, worn out because of all my foes. Leave me, all you evildoers, for the LORD has heard the sound of my weeping. The LORD has heard my pleas. The LORD will accept my prayer. All my enemies will be shamed and utterly dismayed. They will turn back in sudden shame.

Sit upright and say:

שׁוֹמֵר Guardian of Israel, guard the remnant of Israel, and let not Israel perish, who declare, "Listen, Israel."

Guardian of a unique nation, guard the remnant of a unique people, and let not that unique nation perish, who proclaim the unity of

שׁוֹמֵר גּוֹי קָדוֹשׁ, שְׁמוֹר שְׁאֵרִית עַם קָדוֹשׁ, וְאַל־יֹאבַד
גּוֹי קָדוֹשׁ, הַמְשַׁלְּשִׁים בְּשָׁלוֹשׁ קְדֻשּׁוֹת לְקָדוֹשׁ.
מִתְרַצֶּה בְּרַחֲמִים וּמִתְפַּיֵּס בְּתַחֲנוּנִים, הִתְרַצֶּה וְהִתְפַּיֵּס
לְדוֹר עָנִי, כִּי אֵין עוֹזֵר.
אָבִינוּ מַלְכֵּנוּ, חָנֵּנוּ וַעֲנֵנוּ, כִּי אֵין בָּנוּ מַעֲשִׂים, עֲשֵׂה
עִמָּנוּ צְדָקָה וָחֶסֶד וְהוֹשִׁיעֵנוּ.

Stand at ▲.

וַאֲנַחְנוּ לֹא נֵדַע ▲מַה־נַּעֲשֶׂה, כִּי עָלֶיךָ עֵינֵינוּ. זְכֹר רַחֲמֶיךָ יהוה וַחֲסָדֶיךָ, כִּי מֵעוֹלָם הֵמָּה. יְהִי־חַסְדְּךָ יהוה עָלֵינוּ, כַּאֲשֶׁר יִחַלְנוּ לָךְ. אַל תִּזְכָּר־לָנוּ עֲוֹנוֹת רִאשׁוֹנִים, מַהֵר יְקַדְּמוּנוּ רַחֲמֶיךָ, כִּי דַלּוֹנוּ מְאֹד. חָנֵּנוּ יהוה חָנֵּנוּ, כִּי־רַב שָׂבַעְנוּ בוּז. בְּרֹגֶז רַחֵם תִּזְכּוֹר. כִּי הוּא יָדַע יִצְרֵנוּ, זָכוּר כִּי עָפָר אֲנָחְנוּ. ❖ עָזְרֵנוּ אֱלֹהֵי יִשְׁעֵנוּ עַל־דְּבַר כְּבוֹד־שְׁמֶךָ, וְהַצִּילֵנוּ וְכַפֵּר עַל־חַטֹּאתֵינוּ לְמַעַן שְׁמֶךָ.

The Leader says קַדִּישׁ תִּתְקַבַּל.

קדיש תתקבל

Leader:

יִתְגַּדַּל וְיִתְקַדַּשׁ שְׁמֵהּ רַבָּא. (Cong. אָמֵן) בְּעָלְמָא דִּי־בְרָא כִרְעוּתֵהּ. וְיַמְלִיךְ מַלְכוּתֵהּ, בְּחַיֵּיכוֹן וּבְיוֹמֵיכוֹן וּבְחַיֵּי דִי־כָל־בֵּית יִשְׂרָאֵל, בַּעֲגָלָא וּבִזְמַן קָרִיב. וְאִמְרוּ אָמֵן. (Cong. אָמֵן)

All:

יְהֵא שְׁמֵהּ רַבָּא מְבָרַךְ לְעָלַם וּלְעָלְמֵי עָלְמַיָּא.

Leader:

יִתְבָּרַךְ וְיִשְׁתַּבַּח וְיִתְפָּאַר וְיִתְרוֹמַם וְיִתְנַשֵּׂא וְיִתְהַדַּר וְיִתְעַלֶּה וְיִתְהַלַּל שְׁמֵהּ דִּי־קֻדְשָׁא בְּרִיךְ הוּא (Cong. בְּרִיךְ הוּא) לְעֵלָּא (Between רֹאשׁ הַשָּׁנָה and יוֹם כִּפּוּר add לְעֵלָּא) מִן־כָּל־בִּרְכָתָא

Your name [saying], "The LORD is our GOD, the LORD is One."

Guardian of a holy nation, guard the remnant of that holy nation, and let not the holy nation perish, who three times repeat the threefold declaration of holiness to the Holy One.

You who are conciliated by calls for compassion and placated by pleas, be conciliated and placated toward an afflicted generation, for there is no other help.

Our Father, our King, be gracious to us and answer us, though we have no worthy deeds; act with us in charity and lovingkindness and save us.

Stand at ▲.

וַאֲנַחְנוּ We do not know what to do, ▲but our eyes are turned to You. Remember, LORD, Your compassion and lovingkindness, for they are everlasting. May Your lovingkindness, LORD, be with us, for we have put our hope in You. Do not hold against us the sins of those who came before us. May Your mercies meet us swiftly, for we have been brought very low. Be gracious to us, LORD, be gracious to us, for we are sated with contempt. In wrath, remember mercy. He knows our nature; He remembers that we are dust. ➔ Help us, GOD of our salvation, for the sake of the glory of Your name. Save us and grant atonement for our sins for Your name's sake.

The Leader says full *Kaddish*.

FULL KADDISH

Leader:

יִתְגַּדַּל Magnified and sanctified may His great name be, in the world He created by His will. May He establish His kingdom in your lifetime and in your days, and in the lifetime of all the House of Israel, swiftly and soon – and say: Amen.

All:

May His great name be blessed for ever and all time.

Leader:

Blessed and praised, glorified and exalted, raised and honoured, up-

וְשִׁירָתָא תֻּשְׁבְּחָתָא וְנֶחֱמָתָא, דַּאֲמִירָן בְּעָלְמָא. וְאִמְרוּ אָמֵן. (Cong. אָמֵן)

תִּתְקַבַּל צְלוֹתְהוֹן וּבָעוּתְהוֹן דְּכָל־יִשְׂרָאֵל קֳדָם אֲבוּהוֹן דִּי בִשְׁמַיָּא. וְאִמְרוּ אָמֵן. (Cong. אָמֵן)

יְהֵא שְׁלָמָא רַבָּא מִן־שְׁמַיָּא, וְחַיִּים עָלֵינוּ וְעַל־כָּל־יִשְׂרָאֵל. וְאִמְרוּ אָמֵן. (Cong. אָמֵן)

Bow, take three steps back, then bow, first left, then right, then centre, while saying:

עֹשֶׂה שָׁלוֹם בִּמְרוֹמָיו, הוּא יַעֲשֶׂה שָׁלוֹם עָלֵינוּ, וְעַל־כָּל־יִשְׂרָאֵל, וְאִמְרוּ אָמֵן. (Cong. אָמֵן)

עלינו

Stand while saying עָלֵינוּ. Bow at ▾.

עָלֵינוּ לְשַׁבֵּחַ לַאֲדוֹן הַכֹּל, לָתֵת גְּדֻלָּה לְיוֹצֵר בְּרֵאשִׁית, שֶׁלֹּא עָשָׂנוּ כְּגוֹיֵי הָאֲרָצוֹת, וְלֹא שָׂמָנוּ כְּמִשְׁפְּחוֹת הָאֲדָמָה. שֶׁלֹּא שָׂם חֶלְקֵנוּ כָּהֶם, וְגוֹרָלֵנוּ כְּכָל־הֲמוֹנָם. ▾וַאֲנַחְנוּ כּוֹרְעִים וּמִשְׁתַּחֲוִים וּמוֹדִים, לִפְנֵי מֶלֶךְ מַלְכֵי הַמְּלָכִים הַקָּדוֹשׁ בָּרוּךְ הוּא. שֶׁהוּא נוֹטֶה שָׁמַיִם וְיוֹסֵד אָרֶץ, וּמוֹשַׁב יְקָרוֹ בַּשָּׁמַיִם מִמַּעַל, וּשְׁכִינַת עֻזּוֹ בְּגָבְהֵי מְרוֹמִים. הוּא אֱלֹהֵינוּ, אֵין עוֹד. אֱמֶת מַלְכֵּנוּ, אֶפֶס זוּלָתוֹ, כַּכָּתוּב בְּתוֹרָתוֹ, וְיָדַעְתָּ הַיּוֹם וַהֲשֵׁבֹתָ אֶל־לְבָבֶךָ, כִּי יהוה הוּא הָאֱלֹהִים בַּשָּׁמַיִם מִמַּעַל וְעַל־הָאָרֶץ מִתָּחַת, אֵין עוֹד.

עַל־כֵּן נְקַוֶּה לְךָ יהוה אֱלֹהֵינוּ לִרְאוֹת מְהֵרָה בְּתִפְאֶרֶת עֻזֶּךָ, לְהַעֲבִיר גִּלּוּלִים מִן הָאָרֶץ, וְהָאֱלִילִים כָּרוֹת יִכָּרֵתוּן, לְתַקֵּן עוֹלָם בְּמַלְכוּת שַׁדַּי. וְכָל־בְּנֵי בָשָׂר יִקְרְאוּ בִשְׁמֶךָ, לְהַפְנוֹת אֵלֶיךָ כָּל־רִשְׁעֵי אָרֶץ. יַכִּירוּ וְיֵדְעוּ כָּל־יוֹשְׁבֵי תֵבֵל, כִּי לְךָ תִּכְרַע כָּל־בֶּרֶךְ, תִּשָּׁבַע כָּל־לָשׁוֹן. לְפָנֶיךָ יהוה

lifted and lauded be the name of the Holy One, blessed be He, (between Rosh Hashanah and Yom Kippur add 'well') beyond any blessing, song, praise and consolation uttered in the world – and say: Amen.

May the prayers and pleas of all Israel be accepted by their Father in heaven – and say: Amen.

May there be great peace from heaven, and life for us and all Israel – and say: Amen.

Bow, take three steps back, then bow, first left, then right, then centre, while saying:

May He who makes peace in His high places, make peace for us and all Israel – and say: Amen.

ALEINU

Stand while saying *Aleinu*. Bow at ▼.

עָלֵינוּ It is our duty to praise the Master of all, and ascribe greatness to the Author of creation, who has not made us like the nations of the lands nor placed us like the families of the earth; who has not made our portion like theirs, nor our destiny like all their multitudes. Therefore ▼we bow in worship and thank the Supreme King of kings, the Holy One, blessed be He, who extends the heavens and establishes the earth, whose throne of glory is in the heavens above, and whose power's presence is in the highest of heights. He is our God; there is no other. Truly He is our King, there is none else, as it is written in His Torah: "You shall know and take to heart this day that the Lord is God, in heaven above and on earth below. There is no other."

עַל־כֵּן Therefore we place our hope in You, Lord our God, that we may soon see the glory of Your power, when You will remove abominations from the earth, and idols will be utterly destroyed, when the world will be perfected under the sovereignty of the Almighty, when all humanity will call on Your name, and the earth's wicked will all turn to You. All the world's inhabitants will realise and know that to You every knee must bow and every tongue swear loyalty. Before You,

אֱלֹהֵינוּ יִכְרְעוּ וְיִפֹּלוּ, וְלִכְבוֹד שִׁמְךָ יְקָר יִתֵּנוּ. וִיקַבְּלוּ כֻלָּם אֶת־עוֹל מַלְכוּתֶךָ, וְתִמְלֹךְ עֲלֵיהֶם מְהֵרָה לְעוֹלָם וָעֶד. כִּי הַמַּלְכוּת שֶׁלְּךָ הִיא וּלְעוֹלְמֵי עַד תִּמְלוֹךְ בְּכָבוֹד, כַּכָּתוּב בְּתוֹרָתֶךָ, יהוה יִמְלֹךְ לְעוֹלָם וָעֶד. ← וְנֶאֱמַר, וְהָיָה יהוה לְמֶלֶךְ עַל־כָּל־הָאָרֶץ, בַּיּוֹם הַהוּא יִהְיֶה יהוה אֶחָד וּשְׁמוֹ אֶחָד.

Some congregations add:

אַל תִּירָא מִפַּחַד פִּתְאֹם, וּמִשֹּׁאַת רְשָׁעִים כִּי תָבֹא. עֻצוּ עֵצָה וְתֻפָר, דַּבְּרוּ דָבָר וְלֹא יָקוּם, כִּי עִמָּנוּ אֵל. וְעַד זִקְנָה אֲנִי הוּא, וְעַד שֵׂיבָה אֲנִי אֶסְבֹּל, אֲנִי עָשִׂיתִי וַאֲנִי אֶשָּׂא, וַאֲנִי אֶסְבֹּל וַאֲמַלֵּט.

קדיש יתום

The transliteration can be found at the end of the Siddur.

Mourner:

יִתְגַּדַּל וְיִתְקַדַּשׁ שְׁמֵהּ רַבָּא. (Cong. אָמֵן) בְּעָלְמָא דִּי־בְרָא כִרְעוּתֵהּ. וְיַמְלִיךְ מַלְכוּתֵהּ, בְּחַיֵּיכוֹן וּבְיוֹמֵיכוֹן וּבְחַיֵּי דְכָל־בֵּית יִשְׂרָאֵל, בַּעֲגָלָא וּבִזְמַן קָרִיב. וְאִמְרוּ אָמֵן. (Cong. אָמֵן)

All:

יְהֵא שְׁמֵהּ רַבָּא מְבָרַךְ לְעָלַם וּלְעָלְמֵי עָלְמַיָּא.

Mourner:

יִתְבָּרַךְ וְיִשְׁתַּבַּח וְיִתְפָּאַר וְיִתְרוֹמַם וְיִתְנַשֵּׂא וְיִתְהַדָּר וְיִתְעַלֶּה וְיִתְהַלָּל שְׁמֵהּ דְּקֻדְשָׁא בְּרִיךְ הוּא (Cong. בְּרִיךְ הוּא) לְעֵלָּא (Between רֹאשׁ הַשָּׁנָה and יוֹם כִּפּוּר add לְעֵלָּא) מִן־כָּל־בִּרְכָתָא וְשִׁירָתָא תֻּשְׁבְּחָתָא וְנֶחֱמָתָא, דַּאֲמִירָן בְּעָלְמָא. וְאִמְרוּ אָמֵן. (Cong. אָמֵן)

יְהֵא שְׁלָמָא רַבָּא מִן־שְׁמַיָּא, וְחַיִּים עָלֵינוּ וְעַל־כָּל־יִשְׂרָאֵל. וְאִמְרוּ אָמֵן. (Cong. אָמֵן)

Bow, take three steps back, then bow, first left, then right, then centre, while saying:

עֹשֶׂה שָׁלוֹם בִּמְרוֹמָיו, הוּא יַעֲשֶׂה שָׁלוֹם עָלֵינוּ, וְעַל־כָּל־יִשְׂרָאֵל, וְאִמְרוּ אָמֵן. (Cong. אָמֵן)

LORD our GOD, they will kneel and bow down and give honour to Your glorious name. They will all accept the yoke of Your kingdom, and You will reign over them soon and for ever. For the kingdom is Yours, and to all eternity You will reign in glory, as it is written in Your Torah: "The LORD will reign for ever and ever." → And it is said: "Then the LORD shall be King over all the earth: on that day the LORD shall be One and His name One."

Some congregations add:

Have no fear of sudden terror or of the ruin that overtakes the wicked. Devise your strategy, but it will be thwarted; propose your plan, but it will not stand, for GOD is with us. When you grow old, I will still be the same. When your hair turns grey, I will still carry you. I made you, I will bear you, I will carry you, and I will rescue you.

MOURNER'S KADDISH

The transliteration can be found at the end of the Siddur.

Mourner:

יִתְגַּדַּל Magnified and sanctified may His great name be, in the world He created by His will. May He establish His kingdom in your lifetime and in your days, and in the lifetime of all the House of Israel, swiftly and soon – and say: Amen.

All:

May His great name be blessed for ever and all time.

Mourner:

Blessed and praised, glorified and exalted, raised and honoured, uplifted and lauded be the name of the Holy One, blessed be He, (between Rosh Hashanah and Yom Kippur add 'well') beyond any blessing, song, praise and consolation uttered in the world – and say: Amen.

May there be great peace from heaven, and life for us and all Israel – and say: Amen.

Bow, take three steps back, then bow, first left, then right, then centre, while saying:

May He who makes peace in His high places, make peace for us and all Israel – and say: Amen.

מעריב לחול

וְהוּא רַחוּם יְכַפֵּר עָוֹן וְלֹא יַשְׁחִית, וְהִרְבָּה לְהָשִׁיב אַפּוֹ, וְלֹא יָעִיר כָּל־חֲמָתוֹ. יהוה הוֹשִׁיעָה, הַמֶּלֶךְ יַעֲנֵנוּ בְיוֹם־קָרְאֵנוּ.

The Leader says the following, the Leader and Congregation bowing at בָּרְכוּ, standing straight at God's name:

בָּרְכוּ אֶת יהוה הַמְבֹרָךְ.

The Congregation, followed by the Leader, responds, bowing at בָּרוּךְ, standing straight at God's name:

בָּרוּךְ יהוה הַמְבֹרָךְ לְעוֹלָם וָעֶד.

ברכות קריאת שמע

בָּרוּךְ אַתָּה יהוה אֱלֹהֵינוּ מֶלֶךְ הָעוֹלָם, אֲשֶׁר בִּדְבָרוֹ מַעֲרִיב עֲרָבִים, בְּחָכְמָה פּוֹתֵחַ שְׁעָרִים, וּבִתְבוּנָה מְשַׁנֶּה עִתִּים וּמַחֲלִיף אֶת הַזְּמַנִּים וּמְסַדֵּר אֶת הַכּוֹכָבִים בְּמִשְׁמְרוֹתֵיהֶם בָּרָקִיעַ כִּרְצוֹנוֹ. בּוֹרֵא יוֹם וָלָיְלָה, גּוֹלֵל אוֹר מִפְּנֵי חֹשֶׁךְ וְחֹשֶׁךְ מִפְּנֵי אוֹר. ← וּמַעֲבִיר יוֹם וּמֵבִיא לָיְלָה, וּמַבְדִּיל בֵּין יוֹם וּבֵין לָיְלָה, יהוה צְבָאוֹת שְׁמוֹ. אֵל חַי וְקַיָּם, תָּמִיד יִמְלוֹךְ עָלֵינוּ, לְעוֹלָם וָעֶד. בָּרוּךְ אַתָּה יהוה, הַמַּעֲרִיב עֲרָבִים.

EVENING SERVICE
The saying of *Shema* at night ("when you lie down") is a biblical imperative. In early post-Temple times there were some who held that the evening *Amidah* was non-obligatory since – unlike the morning and afternoon services – there was no daily sacrifice to which it corresponded (*Berachot* 27b–28a). So widespread was its observance, however, that it was eventually deemed obligatory. Notwithstanding, since the *Amidah* at night does not correspond to a sacrifice, it is not repeated by the Reader.

Tradition identifies the evening prayer with Jacob, who had his most intense religious experiences at night, especially the vision most associated with prayer: the

EVENING SERVICE FOR WEEKDAYS

וְהוּא רַחוּם He is compassionate. He forgives iniquity and does not destroy. Repeatedly He suppresses His anger, not rousing His full wrath. LORD, save! King, answer us on the day we call.

The Leader says the following, the Leader and Congregation bowing at "Bless", standing straight at "The LORD":

Bless the LORD, the blessed One.

The Congregation, followed by the Leader, responds, bowing at "Bless", standing straight at "The LORD":

Bless the LORD, the blessed One, for ever and all time.

BLESSINGS OF THE SHEMA

בָּרוּךְ Blessed are You, LORD our GOD, King of the Universe, who by His word brings on evenings, by His wisdom opens the gates of heaven, with understanding makes time change and the seasons rotate, and by His will orders the stars in their constellations in the sky. He creates day and night, rolling away the light before the darkness, and darkness before the light. ✧ He makes the day pass and brings on night, distinguishing day from night: the LORD of hosts is His name. May the living and enduring GOD rule over us for ever and all time. Blessed are You, LORD, who brings on evenings.

---

ladder stretching from earth to heaven on which angels ascended and descended. During that vision, GOD promised Jacob that "I will protect you wherever you go". The evening service represents our trust in GOD during the dark and dangers of night.

וְהוּא רַחוּם *He is compassionate*: A prelude to prayer, from the Book of Psalms, that serves as a brief equivalent to the Verses of Praise in the morning service. The verse, Psalm 78:38, contains thirteen words which are reminiscent of the thirteen attributes of Divine mercy.

בָּרְכוּ אֶת יהוה *Bless the LORD*: As in the morning service, a call to the congregation to join in communal prayer, derived from the verse: "Magnify the LORD with me; let us exalt His name together" (Psalm 34:4).

הַמַּעֲרִיב עֲרָבִים *Who by His word brings*

אַהֲבַת עוֹלָם בֵּית יִשְׂרָאֵל עַמְּךָ אָהָבְתָּ. תּוֹרָה וּמִצְוֹת, חֻקִּים וּמִשְׁפָּטִים, אוֹתָנוּ לִמַּדְתָּ. עַל כֵּן יהוה אֱלֹהֵינוּ, בְּשָׁכְבֵנוּ וּבְקוּמֵנוּ נָשִׂיחַ בְּחֻקֶּיךָ, וְנִשְׂמַח בְּדִבְרֵי תוֹרָתֶךָ, וּבְמִצְוֹתֶיךָ לְעוֹלָם וָעֶד. ← כִּי הֵם חַיֵּינוּ, וְאֹרֶךְ יָמֵינוּ, וּבָהֶם נֶהְגֶּה יוֹמָם וָלָיְלָה. וְאַהֲבָתְךָ, אַל תָּסִיר מִמֶּנּוּ לְעוֹלָמִים. בָּרוּךְ אַתָּה יהוה, אוֹהֵב עַמּוֹ יִשְׂרָאֵל.

שמע

When prayers are not said with a מִנְיָן, say:

אֵל מֶלֶךְ נֶאֱמָן.

Cover the eyes with the right hand while saying the following verse:

דברים ו:ד–ט

שְׁמַע יִשְׂרָאֵל יהוה אֱלֹהֵינוּ יהוה | אֶחָד׃

Quietly:

בָּרוּךְ שֵׁם כְּבוֹד מַלְכוּתוֹ לְעוֹלָם וָעֶד.

וְאָהַבְתָּ אֵת יהוה אֱלֹהֶיךָ בְּכָל־לְבָבְךָ וּבְכָל־נַפְשְׁךָ וּבְכָל־מְאֹדֶךָ׃ וְהָיוּ הַדְּבָרִים הָאֵלֶּה אֲשֶׁר אָנֹכִי מְצַוְּךָ הַיּוֹם עַל־לְבָבֶךָ׃ וְשִׁנַּנְתָּם לְבָנֶיךָ וְדִבַּרְתָּ בָּם בְּשִׁבְתְּךָ בְּבֵיתֶךָ וּבְלֶכְתְּךָ בַדֶּרֶךְ וּבְשָׁכְבְּךָ וּבְקוּמֶךָ׃ וּקְשַׁרְתָּם לְאוֹת עַל־יָדֶךָ וְהָיוּ לְטֹטָפֹת בֵּין עֵינֶיךָ׃ וּכְתַבְתָּם עַל־מְזֻזוֹת בֵּיתֶךָ וּבִשְׁעָרֶיךָ׃

דברים יא:יג–כא

וְהָיָה אִם־שָׁמֹעַ תִּשְׁמְעוּ אֶל־מִצְוֺתַי אֲשֶׁר אָנֹכִי מְצַוֶּה אֶתְכֶם הַיּוֹם לְאַהֲבָה אֶת־יהוה אֱלֹהֵיכֶם וּלְעָבְדוֹ בְּכָל־

---

on evenings: Praise of God as Creator of the universe, and hence of time itself. As with the morning service, the two blessings before the *Shema*, and the one immediately following, speak in turn of the three key elements of Jewish faith: creation, revelation and redemption.

אַהֲבַת עוֹלָם *With everlasting love*: A counterpart to the morning blessing, "You have

אַהֲבַת עוֹלָם With everlasting love have You loved Your people, the House of Israel. You have taught us Torah and commandments, decrees and laws of justice. Therefore, Lord our God, when we lie down and when we rise up we will speak of Your decrees, rejoicing in the words of Your Torah and Your commandments for ever. ➔ For they are our life and the length of our days; on them will we meditate day and night. May You never take away Your love from us. Blessed are You, Lord, who loves His people Israel.

THE SHEMA

When prayers are not said with a *minyan*, say:

God, faithful King!

Cover the eyes with the right hand while saying the following verse:

DEUTERONOMY 6:4–9

Listen, Israel: the Lord is our God, the Lord is One.

Quietly:

Blessed be the name of His glorious kingdom for ever and ever.

וְאָהַבְתָּ Love the Lord your God with all your heart, with all your soul, and with all your might. These words which I command you today shall be on your heart. Teach them repeatedly to your children, speaking of them when you sit at home and when you travel on the way, when you lie down and when you rise. Bind them as a sign on your hand, and they shall be an emblem between your eyes. Write them on the doorposts of your house and gates.

DEUTERONOMY 11:13–21

וְהָיָה If you indeed heed My commandments with which I charge you

---

loved us with great love". Both speak of Divine love in terms of revelation: God's gift to Israel of the Torah and its commandments. In the same way that God binds Himself to His people through word and deed, so do we bind ourselves to Him by the words of Torah and the deeds of the commandments. No simpler or more profound statement exists of the love of Jews for the life of the commandments than the phrase, "For they are our life and the length of our days".

לְבַבְכֶם וּבְכׇל־נַפְשְׁכֶם: וְנָתַתִּי מְטַר־אַרְצְכֶם בְּעִתּוֹ יוֹרֶה
וּמַלְקוֹשׁ וְאָסַפְתָּ דְגָנֶךָ וְתִירֹשְׁךָ וְיִצְהָרֶךָ: וְנָתַתִּי עֵשֶׂב
בְּשָׂדְךָ לִבְהֶמְתֶּךָ וְאָכַלְתָּ וְשָׂבָעְתָּ: הִשָּׁמְרוּ לָכֶם פֶּן־יִפְתֶּה
לְבַבְכֶם וְסַרְתֶּם וַעֲבַדְתֶּם אֱלֹהִים אֲחֵרִים וְהִשְׁתַּחֲוִיתֶם
לָהֶם: וְחָרָה אַף־יהוה בָּכֶם וְעָצַר אֶת־הַשָּׁמַיִם וְלֹא־יִהְיֶה
מָטָר וְהָאֲדָמָה לֹא תִתֵּן אֶת־יְבוּלָהּ וַאֲבַדְתֶּם מְהֵרָה מֵעַל
הָאָרֶץ הַטֹּבָה אֲשֶׁר יהוה נֹתֵן לָכֶם: וְשַׂמְתֶּם אֶת־דְּבָרַי
אֵלֶּה עַל־לְבַבְכֶם וְעַל־נַפְשְׁכֶם וּקְשַׁרְתֶּם אֹתָם לְאוֹת עַל־
יֶדְכֶם וְהָיוּ לְטוֹטָפֹת בֵּין עֵינֵיכֶם: וְלִמַּדְתֶּם אֹתָם אֶת־
בְּנֵיכֶם לְדַבֵּר בָּם בְּשִׁבְתְּךָ בְּבֵיתֶךָ וּבְלֶכְתְּךָ בַדֶּרֶךְ וּבְשׇׁכְבְּךָ
וּבְקוּמֶךָ: וּכְתַבְתָּם עַל־מְזוּזוֹת בֵּיתֶךָ וּבִשְׁעָרֶיךָ: לְמַעַן
יִרְבּוּ יְמֵיכֶם וִימֵי בְנֵיכֶם עַל הָאֲדָמָה אֲשֶׁר נִשְׁבַּע יהוה
לַאֲבֹתֵיכֶם לָתֵת לָהֶם כִּימֵי הַשָּׁמַיִם עַל־הָאָרֶץ:

במדבר טו:לז–מא

וַיֹּאמֶר יהוה אֶל־מֹשֶׁה לֵּאמֹר: דַּבֵּר אֶל־בְּנֵי יִשְׂרָאֵל
וְאָמַרְתָּ אֲלֵהֶם וְעָשׂוּ לָהֶם צִיצִת עַל־כַּנְפֵי בִגְדֵיהֶם לְדֹרֹתָם
וְנָתְנוּ עַל־צִיצִת הַכָּנָף פְּתִיל תְּכֵלֶת: וְהָיָה לָכֶם לְצִיצִת
וּרְאִיתֶם אֹתוֹ וּזְכַרְתֶּם אֶת־כׇּל־מִצְוֺת יהוה וַעֲשִׂיתֶם אֹתָם
וְלֹא תָתוּרוּ אַחֲרֵי לְבַבְכֶם וְאַחֲרֵי עֵינֵיכֶם אֲשֶׁר־אַתֶּם זֹנִים
אַחֲרֵיהֶם: לְמַעַן תִּזְכְּרוּ וַעֲשִׂיתֶם אֶת־כׇּל־מִצְוֺתָי וִהְיִיתֶם
קְדֹשִׁים לֵאלֹהֵיכֶם: אֲנִי יהוה אֱלֹהֵיכֶם אֲשֶׁר הוֹצֵאתִי
אֶתְכֶם מֵאֶרֶץ מִצְרַיִם לִהְיוֹת לָכֶם לֵאלֹהִים אֲנִי יהוה
אֱלֹהֵיכֶם: **אֱמֶת** –

The Leader repeats:

← יהוה אֱלֹהֵיכֶם, אֱמֶת –

וֶאֱמוּנָה כׇּל־זֹאת, וְקַיָּם עָלֵינוּ, כִּי הוּא יהוה אֱלֹהֵינוּ וְאֵין

today, to love the LORD your GOD and worship Him with all your heart and with all your soul, I will give rain in your land in its season, the early and late rain; and you shall gather in your grain, wine and oil. I will give grass in your field for your cattle, and you shall eat and be satisfied. Be careful lest your heart be tempted and you go astray and worship other gods, bowing down to them. Then the LORD's anger will flare against you and He will close the heavens so that there will be no rain. The land will not yield its crops, and you will perish swiftly from the good land that the LORD is giving you. Therefore set these, My words, on your heart and soul. Bind them as a sign on your hand, and they shall be an emblem between your eyes. Teach them to your children, speaking of them when you sit at home and when you travel on the way, when you lie down and when you rise. Write them on the doorposts of your house and gates, so that you and your children may live long in the land that the LORD swore to your ancestors to give them, for as long as the heavens are above the earth.

NUMBERS 15:37–41

וַיֹּאמֶר The LORD spoke to Moses, saying: Speak to the Israelites and tell them to make tassels on the corners of their garments for all generations. They shall attach to the tassel at each corner a thread of blue. This shall be your tassel, and you shall see it and remember all of the LORD's commandments and keep them, not straying after your heart and after your eyes, following your own sinful desires. Thus you will be reminded to keep all My commandments, and be holy to your GOD. I am the LORD your GOD, who brought you out of the land of Egypt to be your GOD. I am the LORD your GOD. True –

The Leader repeats:

→ The LORD your GOD is true –

וֶאֱמוּנָה – and faithful is all this, and firmly established for us that He

---

אֱמֶת וֶאֱמוּנָה *True and faithful*: A blessing about redemption, parallel to the blessing "True and firm" in the morning. The special emphasis on faithfulness at night echoes the phrase from Psalm 92: "to tell of Your love in the morning, and Your faithfulness at night."

זוּלָתוֹ, וַאֲנַחְנוּ יִשְׂרָאֵל עַמּוֹ. הַפּוֹדֵנוּ מִיַּד מְלָכִים, מַלְכֵּנוּ הַגּוֹאֲלֵנוּ מִכַּף כָּל־הֶעָרִיצִים. הָאֵל הַנִּפְרָע לָנוּ מִצָּרֵינוּ, וְהַמְשַׁלֵּם גְּמוּל לְכָל־אֹיְבֵי נַפְשֵׁנוּ. הָעֹשֶׂה גְדֹלוֹת עַד־אֵין חֵקֶר, וְנִפְלָאוֹת עַד־אֵין מִסְפָּר. הַשָּׂם נַפְשֵׁנוּ בַּחַיִּים, וְלֹא־נָתַן לַמּוֹט רַגְלֵנוּ. הַמַּדְרִיכֵנוּ עַל בָּמוֹת אוֹיְבֵינוּ, וַיָּרֶם קַרְנֵנוּ עַל־כָּל־שׂוֹנְאֵנוּ. הָעֹשֶׂה־לָּנוּ נִסִּים וּנְקָמָה בְּפַרְעֹה, אוֹתוֹת וּמוֹפְתִים בְּאַדְמַת בְּנֵי־חָם. הַמַּכֶּה בְעֶבְרָתוֹ כָּל־בְּכוֹרֵי מִצְרָיִם, וַיּוֹצֵא אֶת־עַמּוֹ יִשְׂרָאֵל מִתּוֹכָם לְחֵרוּת עוֹלָם. הַמַּעֲבִיר בָּנָיו בֵּין גִּזְרֵי יַם־סוּף, אֶת־רוֹדְפֵיהֶם וְאֶת־שׂוֹנְאֵיהֶם בִּתְהוֹמוֹת טִבַּע. וְרָאוּ בָנָיו גְּבוּרָתוֹ, שִׁבְּחוּ וְהוֹדוּ לִשְׁמוֹ. ◂ וּמַלְכוּתוֹ בְּרָצוֹן קִבְּלוּ עֲלֵיהֶם. מֹשֶׁה וּבְנֵי יִשְׂרָאֵל לְךָ עָנוּ שִׁירָה בְּשִׂמְחָה רַבָּה, וְאָמְרוּ כֻלָּם,

מִי־כָמֹכָה בָּאֵלִם יהוה, מִי־כָּמֹכָה נֶאְדָּר בַּקֹּדֶשׁ, נוֹרָא תְהִלֹּת, עֹשֵׂה פֶלֶא. ◂ מַלְכוּתְךָ רָאוּ בָנֶיךָ בּוֹקֵעַ יָם לִפְנֵי מֹשֶׁה, זֶה אֵלִי עָנוּ, וְאָמְרוּ, **יהוה יִמְלֹךְ לְעֹלָם וָעֶד.** ◂ וְנֶאֱמַר, כִּי־פָדָה יהוה אֶת־יַעֲקֹב, וּגְאָלוֹ מִיַּד חָזָק מִמֶּנּוּ. בָּרוּךְ אַתָּה יהוה, גָּאַל יִשְׂרָאֵל.

הַשְׁכִּיבֵנוּ יהוה אֱלֹהֵינוּ לְשָׁלוֹם, וְהַעֲמִידֵנוּ מַלְכֵּנוּ לְחַיִּים, וּפְרוֹשׂ עָלֵינוּ סֻכַּת שְׁלוֹמֶךָ, וְתַקְּנֵנוּ בְּעֵצָה טוֹבָה מִלְּפָנֶיךָ, וְהוֹשִׁיעֵנוּ לְמַעַן שְׁמֶךָ, וְהָגֵן בַּעֲדֵנוּ, וְהָסֵר מֵעָלֵינוּ אוֹיֵב, דֶּבֶר, וְחֶרֶב, וְרָעָב, וְיָגוֹן, וְהָסֵר שָׂטָן מִלְּפָנֵינוּ וּמֵאַחֲרֵנוּ, וּבְצֵל כְּנָפֶיךָ תַּסְתִּירֵנוּ, כִּי אֵל שׁוֹמְרֵנוּ וּמַצִּילֵנוּ אָתָּה, כִּי אֵל מֶלֶךְ חַנּוּן וְרַחוּם אָתָּה. ◂ וּשְׁמוֹר צֵאתֵנוּ וּבוֹאֵנוּ, לְחַיִּים וּלְשָׁלוֹם מֵעַתָּה וְעַד עוֹלָם. בָּרוּךְ אַתָּה יהוה, שׁוֹמֵר עַמּוֹ יִשְׂרָאֵל לָעַד.

is the LORD our GOD, and there is none beside Him, and that we, Israel, are His people. He is our King, who redeems us from the hand of kings and delivers us from the grasp of all tyrants. He is our GOD, who on our behalf repays our foes and brings just retribution on our mortal enemies; who performs great deeds beyond understanding and wonders beyond number; who kept us alive, not letting our foot slip; who led us on the high places of our enemies, raising our pride above all our foes; who did miracles for us and brought vengeance against Pharaoh; who performed signs and wonders in the land of Ham's children; who smote in His wrath all the firstborn of Egypt, and brought out His people Israel from their midst into everlasting freedom; who led His children through the divided Reed Sea, plunging their pursuers and enemies into the depths. When His children saw His might, they gave praise and thanks to His name, ➛ and willingly accepted His Sovereignty. Moses and the children of Israel then sang a song to You with great joy, and they all exclaimed:

מִי־כָמְֹכָה "Who is like You, LORD, among the mighty? Who is like You, majestic in holiness, awesome in praises, doing wonders?"
➛ Your children beheld Your majesty as You parted the sea before Moses. "This is my GOD!" they responded, and then said: **"The Lord shall reign for ever and ever."** ➛ And it is said, "For the LORD has redeemed Jacob and rescued him from a power stronger than his own." Blessed are You, LORD, who redeemed Israel.

הַשְׁכִּיבֵנוּ Help us lie down, O LORD our GOD, in peace, and rise up, O our King, to life. Spread over us Your canopy of peace. Direct us with Your good counsel, and save us for the sake of Your name. Shield us and remove from us every enemy, plague, sword, famine and sorrow. Remove the adversary from before and behind us. Shelter us in the shadow of Your wings, for You, GOD, are our Guardian and Deliverer; You, GOD, are a gracious and compassionate King. ➛ Guard our going out and our coming in, for life and peace, from now and for ever. Blessed are You, LORD, who guards His people Israel for ever.

הַשְׁכִּיבֵנוּ *Help us lie down*: This blessing, which has no parallel in the morning service, is a prayer for protection against the hazards of the night.

בָּרוּךְ יהוה לְעוֹלָם, אָמֵן וְאָמֵן. בָּרוּךְ יהוה מִצִּיּוֹן, שֹׁכֵן יְרוּשָׁלָיִם, הַלְלוּיָהּ. בָּרוּךְ יהוה אֱלֹהִים אֱלֹהֵי יִשְׂרָאֵל, עֹשֵׂה נִפְלָאוֹת לְבַדּוֹ. וּבָרוּךְ שֵׁם כְּבוֹדוֹ לְעוֹלָם, וְיִמָּלֵא כְבוֹדוֹ אֶת־כָּל־הָאָרֶץ, אָמֵן וְאָמֵן. יְהִי כְבוֹד יהוה לְעוֹלָם, יִשְׂמַח יהוה בְּמַעֲשָׂיו. יְהִי שֵׁם יהוה מְבֹרָךְ, מֵעַתָּה וְעַד עוֹלָם. כִּי לֹא־יִטֹּשׁ יהוה אֶת־עַמּוֹ בַּעֲבוּר שְׁמוֹ הַגָּדוֹל, כִּי הוֹאִיל יהוה לַעֲשׂוֹת אֶתְכֶם לוֹ לְעָם. וַיַּרְא כָּל־הָעָם וַיִּפְּלוּ עַל־פְּנֵיהֶם, וַיֹּאמְרוּ, יהוה הוּא הָאֱלֹהִים, יהוה הוּא הָאֱלֹהִים. וְהָיָה יהוה לְמֶלֶךְ עַל־כָּל־הָאָרֶץ, בַּיּוֹם הַהוּא יִהְיֶה יהוה אֶחָד וּשְׁמוֹ אֶחָד. יְהִי חַסְדְּךָ יהוה עָלֵינוּ, כַּאֲשֶׁר יִחַלְנוּ לָךְ. הוֹשִׁיעֵנוּ אֱלֹהֵי יִשְׁעֵנוּ, וְקַבְּצֵנוּ וְהַצִּילֵנוּ מִן־הַגּוֹיִם, לְהוֹדוֹת לְשֵׁם קָדְשֶׁךָ, לְהִשְׁתַּבֵּחַ בִּתְהִלָּתֶךָ. כָּל־גּוֹיִם אֲשֶׁר עָשִׂיתָ יָבוֹאוּ וְיִשְׁתַּחֲווּ לְפָנֶיךָ אֲדֹנָי, וִיכַבְּדוּ לִשְׁמֶךָ. כִּי־גָדוֹל אַתָּה וְעֹשֵׂה נִפְלָאוֹת, אַתָּה אֱלֹהִים לְבַדֶּךָ. וַאֲנַחְנוּ עַמְּךָ וְצֹאן מַרְעִיתֶךָ, נוֹדֶה לְּךָ לְעוֹלָם, לְדוֹר וָדֹר נְסַפֵּר תְּהִלָּתֶךָ. בָּרוּךְ יהוה בַּיּוֹם, בָּרוּךְ יהוה בַּלָּיְלָה. בָּרוּךְ יהוה בְּשָׁכְבֵנוּ. בָּרוּךְ יהוה בְּקוּמֵנוּ. כִּי בְיָדְךָ נַפְשׁוֹת הַחַיִּים וְהַמֵּתִים. אֲשֶׁר בְּיָדוֹ נֶפֶשׁ כָּל־חָי, וְרוּחַ כָּל־בְּשַׂר־אִישׁ. בְּיָדְךָ אַפְקִיד רוּחִי, פָּדִיתָה אוֹתִי, יהוה אֵל אֱמֶת. אֱלֹהֵינוּ שֶׁבַּשָּׁמַיִם יַחֵד שִׁמְךָ, וְקַיֵּם מַלְכוּתְךָ תָּמִיד, וּמְלֹךְ עָלֵינוּ לְעוֹלָם וָעֶד.

יִרְאוּ עֵינֵינוּ וְיִשְׂמַח לִבֵּנוּ וְתָגֵל נַפְשֵׁנוּ בִּישׁוּעָתְךָ בֶּאֱמֶת, בֶּאֱמֹר לְצִיּוֹן מָלַךְ אֱלֹהָיִךְ. יהוה מֶלֶךְ, יהוה מָלָךְ, יהוה

בָּרוּךְ יהוה לְעוֹלָם *Blessed be the* Lord *for ever*: This passage originated among Babylonian Jewry at a time when synagogues were not permitted within the

בָּרוּךְ Blessed be the LORD for ever. Amen and Amen. Blessed from Zion be the LORD who dwells in Jerusalem. Halleluyah. Blessed be the LORD, GOD of Israel, who alone does wondrous things. Blessed be His glorious name for ever, and may the whole earth be filled with His glory. Amen and Amen. May the glory of the LORD endure for ever; may the LORD rejoice in His works. May the name of the LORD be blessed now and for all time. For the sake of His great name the LORD will not abandon His people, for the LORD vowed to make you His own. When all the people saw [GOD's wonders] they fell on their faces and said: "The LORD, He is GOD; the LORD, He is GOD." The LORD shall be King over all the earth; on that day the LORD will be One and His name One. May Your love, LORD, be upon us, as we have put our hope in You. Save us, GOD our Saviour, gather us and deliver us from the nations, to thank Your holy name, and glory in Your praise. All the nations You made shall come and bow before You, LORD, and pay honour to Your name, for You are great and You perform wonders: You alone are GOD. We, Your people, the flock Your pasture, will praise You for ever. For all generations we will relate Your praise. Blessed is the LORD by day, blessed is the LORD by night. Blessed is the LORD when we lie down; blessed is the LORD when we rise. For in Your hand are the souls of the living and the dead, (as it is written:) "In His hand is every living soul, and the breath of all mankind." Into Your hand I entrust my spirit: You redeemed me, LORD, GOD of truth. Our GOD in heaven, bring unity to Your name, establish Your kingdom constantly and reign over us for ever and all time.

יִרְאוּ May our eyes see, our hearts rejoice, and our souls be glad in Your true salvation, when Zion is told, "Your GOD reigns". The LORD is King, the LORD was King, the LORD will be King for ever and all

---

town and were built in the fields outside. This made attendance at synagogue potentially hazardous at night. This prayer, with its eighteen references to GOD, was originally recited as a substitute for the evening *Amidah* – possibly to shorten the evening service in synagogue so that participants could return home before dark. When conditions changed, the prayer was retained. Since it was a substitute for the weekday *Amidah*, it is not said on Shabbat or festivals.

יִמְלוֹךְ לְעוֹלָם וָעֶד. ◂ כִּי הַמַּלְכוּת שֶׁלְּךָ הִיא, וּלְעוֹלְמֵי עַד תִּמְלוֹךְ בְּכָבוֹד, כִּי אֵין לָנוּ מֶלֶךְ אֶלָּא אָתָּה. בָּרוּךְ אַתָּה יהוה, הַמֶּלֶךְ בִּכְבוֹדוֹ תָּמִיד יִמְלוֹךְ עָלֵינוּ לְעוֹלָם וָעֶד, וְעַל כָּל־מַעֲשָׂיו.

The Leader says חֲצִי קַדִּישׁ.

Leader:

יִתְגַּדַּל וְיִתְקַדַּשׁ שְׁמֵהּ רַבָּא. (Cong. אָמֵן) בְּעָלְמָא דִּי־בְרָא כִרְעוּתֵהּ, וְיַמְלִיךְ מַלְכוּתֵהּ, בְּחַיֵּיכוֹן וּבְיוֹמֵיכוֹן וּבְחַיֵּי דְכָל־בֵּית יִשְׂרָאֵל, בַּעֲגָלָא וּבִזְמַן קָרִיב. וְאִמְרוּ אָמֵן. (Cong. אָמֵן)

All:

יְהֵא שְׁמֵהּ רַבָּא מְבָרַךְ לְעָלַם וּלְעָלְמֵי עָלְמַיָּא.

Leader:

יִתְבָּרַךְ וְיִשְׁתַּבַּח וְיִתְפָּאַר וְיִתְרוֹמַם וְיִתְנַשֵּׂא וְיִתְהַדָּר וְיִתְעַלֶּה וְיִתְהַלָּל שְׁמֵהּ דְּקֻדְשָׁא בְּרִיךְ הוּא (Cong. בְּרִיךְ הוּא) לְעֵֽלָּא (Between רֹאשׁ הַשָּׁנָה and יוֹם כִּפּוּר add לְעֵֽלָּא) מִן־כָּל־בִּרְכָתָא וְשִׁירָתָא תֻּשְׁבְּחָתָא וְנֶחֱמָתָא, דַּאֲמִירָן בְּעָלְמָא. וְאִמְרוּ אָמֵן. (Cong. אָמֵן)

עמידה

The following prayer, until קַדְמוֹנִיּוֹת, on page 228, is said silently, standing with feet together.

Take three steps back, then forward. At the points indicated by ▾, bend the knees at the first word, bow at the second, and stand straight before God's name.

אֲדֹנָי, שְׂפָתַי תִּפְתָּח, וּפִי יַגִּיד תְּהִלָּתֶךָ.

אבות

▾בָּרוּךְ אַתָּה יהוה אֱלֹהֵינוּ וֵאלֹהֵי אֲבוֹתֵינוּ, אֱלֹהֵי אַבְרָהָם, אֱלֹהֵי יִצְחָק, וֵאלֹהֵי יַעֲקֹב, הָאֵל הַגָּדוֹל הַגִּבּוֹר וְהַנּוֹרָא,

time. → For sovereignty is Yours, and to all eternity You will reign in glory, for we have no king but You. Blessed are You, Lord, the King who in His glory will constantly reign over us and all His creation for ever and all time.

The Leader says half-*Kaddish*.

Leader:

יִתְגַּדַּל Magnified and sanctified may His great name be, in the world He created by His will. May He establish His kingdom in your lifetime and in your days, and in the lifetime of all the House of Israel, swiftly and soon – and say: Amen.

All:

May His great name be blessed for ever and all time.

Leader:

Blessed and praised, glorified and exalted, raised and honoured, uplifted and lauded be the name of the Holy One, blessed be He, (between Rosh Hashanah and Yom Kippur add 'well') beyond any blessing, song, praise and consolation uttered in the world – and say: Amen.

AMIDAH: THE STANDING PRAYER

The following prayer, until "in former years", on page 229, is said silently, standing with feet together.

Take three steps back, then forward. At the points indicated by ▼, bend the knees at the first word, bow at the second, and stand straight before God's name.

O Lord, open my lips, so that my mouth may declare Your praise.

PATRIARCHS

▼**בָּרוּךְ** Blessed are You, Lord our God and God of our Fathers, God of Abraham, God of Isaac and God of Jacob; the great, mighty and awesome God, God Most High, who bestows acts of lovingkindness and creates all, who remembers the lovingkindness of the Fathers and

אֵל עֶלְיוֹן, גּוֹמֵל חֲסָדִים טוֹבִים וְקוֹנֵה הַכֹּל, וְזוֹכֵר חַסְדֵי אָבוֹת, וּמֵבִיא גוֹאֵל לִבְנֵי בְנֵיהֶם, לְמַעַן שְׁמוֹ בְּאַהֲבָה.

Between רֹאשׁ הַשָּׁנָה and יוֹם כִּפּוּר, add:

זָכְרֵנוּ לַחַיִּים, מֶלֶךְ חָפֵץ בַּחַיִּים, וְכָתְבֵנוּ בְּסֵפֶר הַחַיִּים, לְמַעַנְךָ אֱלֹהִים חַיִּים.

מֶלֶךְ עוֹזֵר וּמוֹשִׁיעַ וּמָגֵן. ▼בָּרוּךְ אַתָּה יהוה, מָגֵן אַבְרָהָם.

גבורות

אַתָּה גִּבּוֹר לְעוֹלָם אֲדֹנָי, מְחַיֵּה מֵתִים אַתָּה, רַב לְהוֹשִׁיעַ.

From after שִׂמְחַת תּוֹרָה until פֶּסַח, add:

מַשִּׁיב הָרוּחַ וּמוֹרִיד הַגָּשֶׁם.

מְכַלְכֵּל חַיִּים בְּחֶסֶד, מְחַיֵּה מֵתִים בְּרַחֲמִים רַבִּים, סוֹמֵךְ נוֹפְלִים, וְרוֹפֵא חוֹלִים, וּמַתִּיר אֲסוּרִים, וּמְקַיֵּם אֱמוּנָתוֹ לִישֵׁנֵי עָפָר. מִי כָמוֹךָ בַּעַל גְּבוּרוֹת, וּמִי דּוֹמֶה לָּךְ, מֶלֶךְ מֵמִית וּמְחַיֶּה וּמַצְמִיחַ יְשׁוּעָה.

Between רֹאשׁ הַשָּׁנָה and יוֹם כִּפּוּר, add:

מִי כָמוֹךָ אַב הָרַחֲמִים, זוֹכֵר יְצוּרָיו לַחַיִּים בְּרַחֲמִים.

וְנֶאֱמָן אַתָּה לְהַחֲיוֹת מֵתִים. בָּרוּךְ אַתָּה יהוה, מְחַיֵּה הַמֵּתִים.

קדושת השם

אַתָּה קָדוֹשׁ וְשִׁמְךָ קָדוֹשׁ, וּקְדוֹשִׁים בְּכָל־יוֹם יְהַלְלוּךָ סֶּלָה. בָּרוּךְ אַתָּה יהוה, *הָאֵל הַקָּדוֹשׁ.

*Between רֹאשׁ הַשָּׁנָה and יוֹם כִּפּוּר, end the blessing:

הַמֶּלֶךְ הַקָּדוֹשׁ.

will bring a Redeemer to their children's children for the sake of His name, in love.

Between Rosh Hashanah and Yom Kippur, add:

Remember us for life, O King who desires life, and write us in the book of life – for Your sake, O God of life.

King, Helper, Saviour, Shield: ▾Blessed are You, Lord, Shield of Abraham.

DIVINE MIGHT

אַתָּה You are eternally mighty, Lord. You give life to the dead and have great power to save.

From after Simchat Torah until Pesach, add:

He makes the wind blow and the rain fall.

He sustains the living with lovingkindness, and with great compassion revives the dead. He supports the fallen, heals the sick, sets captives free, and keeps His faith with those who sleep in the dust. Who is like You, Master of might, and to whom can You be compared, O King who brings death and gives life, and makes salvation grow?

Between Rosh Hashanah and Yom Kippur, add:

Who is like You, compassionate Father, who remembers His creatures in compassion, for life?

Faithful are You to revive the dead. Blessed are You, Lord, who revives the dead.

HOLINESS

אַתָּה You are holy and Your name is holy, and holy ones praise You daily, Selah! Blessed are You, Lord, *the holy God.

*Between Rosh Hashanah and Yom Kippur, end the blessing:

the holy King.

דעת

אַתָּה חוֹנֵן לְאָדָם דַּעַת, וּמְלַמֵּד לֶאֱנוֹשׁ בִּינָה.

After שַׁבָּת or a יוֹם טוֹב, say:

אַתָּה חוֹנַנְתָּנוּ לְמַדַּע תּוֹרָתֶךָ, וַתְּלַמְּדֵנוּ לַעֲשׂוֹת חֻקֵּי רְצוֹנֶךָ וַתַּבְדֵּל יהוה אֱלֹהֵינוּ בֵּין קֹדֶשׁ לְחוֹל בֵּין אוֹר לְחֹשֶׁךְ, בֵּין יִשְׂרָאֵל לָעַמִּים, בֵּין יוֹם הַשְּׁבִיעִי לְשֵׁשֶׁת יְמֵי הַמַּעֲשֶׂה. אָבִינוּ מַלְכֵּנוּ, הָחֵל עָלֵינוּ הַיָּמִים הַבָּאִים לִקְרָאתֵנוּ לְשָׁלוֹם חֲשׂוּכִים מִכָּל־חֵטְא וּמְנֻקִּים מִכָּל־עָוֹן וּמְדֻבָּקִים בְּיִרְאָתֶךָ. וְ...

חָנֵּנוּ מֵאִתְּךָ דֵּעָה בִּינָה וְהַשְׂכֵּל. בָּרוּךְ אַתָּה יהוה, חוֹנֵן הַדָּעַת.

תשובה

הֲשִׁיבֵנוּ אָבִינוּ לְתוֹרָתֶךָ, וְקָרְבֵנוּ מַלְכֵּנוּ לַעֲבוֹדָתֶךָ, וְהַחֲזִירֵנוּ בִּתְשׁוּבָה שְׁלֵמָה לְפָנֶיךָ. בָּרוּךְ אַתָּה יהוה, הָרוֹצֶה בִּתְשׁוּבָה.

סליחה

סְלַח־לָנוּ אָבִינוּ כִּי חָטָאנוּ, מְחַל־לָנוּ מַלְכֵּנוּ כִּי פָשָׁעְנוּ, כִּי מוֹחֵל וְסוֹלֵחַ אָתָּה. בָּרוּךְ אַתָּה יהוה, חַנּוּן, הַמַּרְבֶּה לִסְלֹחַ.

גאולה

רְאֵה בְעָנְיֵנוּ, וְרִיבָה רִיבֵנוּ, וּגְאָלֵנוּ מְהֵרָה לְמַעַן שְׁמֶךָ, כִּי גּוֹאֵל חָזָק אָתָּה. בָּרוּךְ אַתָּה יהוה, גּוֹאֵל יִשְׂרָאֵל.

אַתָּה חוֹנַנְתָּנוּ *You have graced us*: From Talmudic times, this paragraph has been the way of marking *Havdalah* – the transition between holy and secular time – within the *Amidah* prayer. *Havdalah* is repeated as a separate ceremony in the synagogue after prayer, and then again at home. Its positioning here, in the prayer for knowledge, indicates the essential connection between the human mind and the

KNOWLEDGE

אַתָּה You grace humanity with knowledge and teach mortals understanding.

After Shabbat or a Festival, say:

אַתָּה חוֹנַנְתָּנוּ You have graced us with the knowledge of Your Torah, and taught us to perform the statutes of Your will. You have distinguished, Lord our God, between sacred and profane, light and darkness, Israel and the nations, and between the seventh day and the six days of work. Our Father, our King, may the days approaching us bring peace; may we be free from all sin, cleansed from all iniquity, holding fast to our reverence of You. And…

Grace us with the knowledge, understanding and discernment that come from You. Blessed are You, Lord, who graciously grants knowledge.

REPENTANCE

הֲשִׁיבֵנוּ Bring us back, our Father, to Your Torah. Draw us near, our King, to Your service. Lead us back to You in perfect repentance. Blessed are You, Lord, who desires repentance.

FORGIVENESS

סְלַח־לָנוּ Forgive us, our Father, for we have sinned. Pardon us, our King, for we have transgressed; for You pardon and forgive. Blessed are You, Lord, the gracious One who repeatedly forgives.

REDEMPTION

רְאֵה Look on our affliction, plead our cause, and redeem us soon for Your name's sake, for You are a powerful Redeemer. Blessed are You, Lord, the Redeemer of Israel.

---

ability to make distinctions ("If there is no knowledge", says the Talmud, "how can there be distinction?"). In nature there are no sharp boundaries. Day shades gradually into night; winter into spring; life into sentience. According to the Torah, what links man to God is our ability to separate, classify and name, and thus to see order amidst seeming chaos. As we begin the working week, we acknowledge the Divine order of creation as the necessary prelude to human acts of creation.

רפואה

רְפָאֵנוּ יהוה וְנֵרָפֵא, הוֹשִׁיעֵנוּ וְנִוָּשֵׁעָה, כִּי תְהִלָּתֵנוּ אָתָּה, וְהַעֲלֵה רְפוּאָה שְׁלֵמָה לְכָל מַכּוֹתֵינוּ,* כִּי אֵל מֶלֶךְ רוֹפֵא נֶאֱמָן וְרַחֲמָן אָתָּה. בָּרוּךְ אַתָּה יהוה, רוֹפֵא, חוֹלֵי עַמּוֹ יִשְׂרָאֵל.

---

*The following prayer for a sick person may be said here:

וִיהִי רָצוֹן מִלְּפָנֶיךָ, יהוה אֱלֹהֵינוּ וֵאלֹהֵי אֲבוֹתֵינוּ, שֶׁתִּשְׁלַח מְהֵרָה רְפוּאָה שְׁלֵמָה מִן הַשָּׁמַיִם, רְפוּאַת הַנֶּפֶשׁ וּרְפוּאַת הַגּוּף לַחוֹלֶה/לַחוֹלָה (if known, add Hebrew name בֶּן/בַּת mother's name) בְּתוֹךְ שְׁאָר חוֹלֵי יִשְׂרָאֵל.

ברכת השנים

בָּרֵךְ עָלֵינוּ יהוה אֱלֹהֵינוּ אֶת הַשָּׁנָה הַזֹּאת וְאֶת כָּל מִינֵי תְבוּאָתָהּ לְטוֹבָה,

From חוֹל הַמּוֹעֵד פֶּסַח until December 3rd (in a year before a civil leap year, 4th), say:

וְתֵן בְּרָכָה

From December 4th (in the year before a civil leap year, 5th) until פֶּסַח, say:

וְתֵן טַל וּמָטָר לִבְרָכָה

עַל־פְּנֵי הָאֲדָמָה, וְשַׂבְּעֵנוּ מִטּוּבֶךָ, וּבָרֵךְ שְׁנָתֵנוּ כַּשָּׁנִים הַטּוֹבוֹת. בָּרוּךְ אַתָּה יהוה, מְבָרֵךְ הַשָּׁנִים.

קיבוץ גלויות

תְּקַע בְּשׁוֹפָר גָּדוֹל לְחֵרוּתֵנוּ, וְשָׂא נֵס לְקַבֵּץ גָּלֻיּוֹתֵינוּ, וְקַבְּצֵנוּ יַחַד מֵאַרְבַּע כַּנְפוֹת הָאָרֶץ. בָּרוּךְ אַתָּה יהוה, מְקַבֵּץ, נִדְחֵי עַמּוֹ יִשְׂרָאֵל.

תְּקַע בְּשׁוֹפָר גָּדוֹל *Sound the great shofar*: The reference is to Isaiah 27:13, "In that day a great ram's horn shall be sounded, and the strayed in the land of Assyria and the expelled in the land of Egypt shall come and worship the LORD on the holy mount in Jerusalem." The shofar is a symbol with many meanings. Rabbi Saadia Gaon enumerated ten: 1. the creation of the universe, when we sound it on Rosh Hashanah, cre-

HEALING

רְפָאֵנוּ Heal us, LORD, and we shall be healed. Save us and we shall be saved, for You are our praise. Bring complete recovery for all our ailments,* for You, GOD, King, are a faithful and compassionate Healer. Blessed are You, LORD, Healer of the sick of His people Israel.

*The following prayer for a sick person may be said here:

May it be Your will, O LORD our GOD and GOD of our ancestors, that You speedily send a complete recovery from heaven, a healing of both soul and body, to the patient (name), son/daughter of (mother's name) among the other afflicted of Israel.

PROSPERITY

בָּרֵךְ Bless this year for us, LORD our GOD, and all its types of produce for good.

From the Intermediate Days of Pesach until December 3rd (in a year before a civil leap year, 4th), say:	From December 4th (in the year before a civil leap year, 5th) until Pesach, say:
Grant blessing	Grant dew and rain as a blessing

on the face of the earth, and from Your goodness satisfy us, blessing our year as the best of years. Blessed are You, LORD, who blesses the years.

INGATHERING OF EXILES

תְּקַע Sound the great shofar for our freedom, raise high the banner to gather our exiles, and gather us together from the four quarters of the earth. Blessed are You, LORD, who gathers the dispersed of His people Israel.

ation's anniversary; 2. Divine judgement, of which the shofar is a herald; 3. the revelation at Mount Sinai, when the people heard "the sound of a ram's horn, growing louder and louder" (Exodus 19:19); 4. the teachings of the prophets who were commanded to "sound the horn and warn the people" (Ezekial 33:3); 5. Israel's battles against its enemies, when it heard "the blare of horns, the alarms of war" (Jeremiah 4:19); 6. the binding of Isaac, for whom a ram was substituted (Genesis 22:13); 7. the fear of heaven (Amos 3:6); 8. the Day of Judgement (Zephaniah 1:14–16); 9. the ingathering of exiles; and 10. the end of days (Isaiah 18:3).

השבת המשפט

הָשִׁיבָה שׁוֹפְטֵינוּ כְּבָרִאשׁוֹנָה, וְיוֹעֲצֵינוּ כְּבַתְּחִלָּה, וְהָסֵר מִמֶּנּוּ יָגוֹן וַאֲנָחָה, וּמְלוֹךְ עָלֵינוּ אַתָּה יהוה לְבַדְּךָ בְּחֶסֶד וּבְרַחֲמִים, וְצַדְּקֵנוּ בַּמִּשְׁפָּט. בָּרוּךְ אַתָּה יהוה, *מֶלֶךְ, אוֹהֵב צְדָקָה וּמִשְׁפָּט.

---

*Between ראש הַשָּׁנָה and יוֹם כִּפּוּר, end the blessing:

הַמֶּלֶךְ הַמִּשְׁפָּט.

ברכת המינים

וְלַמַּלְשִׁינִים אַל־תְּהִי תִקְוָה, וְכָל הָרִשְׁעָה כְּרֶגַע תֹּאבֵד, וְכָל אוֹיְבֶיךָ מְהֵרָה יִכָּרֵתוּ, וּמַלְכוּת זָדוֹן מְהֵרָה תְעַקֵּר וּתְשַׁבֵּר וּתְמַגֵּר וְתַכְנִיעַ בִּמְהֵרָה בְיָמֵינוּ. בָּרוּךְ אַתָּה יהוה, שׁוֹבֵר אוֹיְבִים וּמַכְנִיעַ זֵדִים.

על הצדיקים

עַל־הַצַּדִּיקִים וְעַל־הַחֲסִידִים, וְעַל־זִקְנֵי עַמְּךָ בֵּית יִשְׂרָאֵל, וְעַל־פְּלֵיטַת סוֹפְרֵיהֶם, וְעַל־גֵּרֵי הַצֶּדֶק וְעָלֵינוּ, יֶהֱמוּ רַחֲמֶיךָ יהוה אֱלֹהֵינוּ, וְתֵן שָׂכָר טוֹב לְכָל הַבּוֹטְחִים בְּשִׁמְךָ בֶּאֱמֶת, וְשִׂים חֶלְקֵנוּ עִמָּהֶם לְעוֹלָם, וְלֹא נֵבוֹשׁ כִּי־בְךָ בָּטָחְנוּ. בָּרוּךְ אַתָּה יהוה, מִשְׁעָן וּמִבְטָח לַצַּדִּיקִים.

בנין ירושלים

וְלִירוּשָׁלַיִם עִירְךָ בְּרַחֲמִים תָּשׁוּב, וְתִשְׁכּוֹן בְּתוֹכָהּ כַּאֲשֶׁר דִּבַּרְתָּ, וּבְנֵה אוֹתָהּ בְּקָרוֹב בְּיָמֵינוּ בִּנְיַן עוֹלָם, וְכִסֵּא דָוִד מְהֵרָה לְתוֹכָהּ תָּכִין. בָּרוּךְ אַתָּה יהוה, בּוֹנֵה יְרוּשָׁלָיִם.

משיח בן דוד

אֶת־צֶמַח דָּוִד עַבְדְּךָ מְהֵרָה תַצְמִיחַ, וְקַרְנוֹ תָּרוּם בִּישׁוּעָתֶךָ, כִּי לִישׁוּעָתְךָ קִוִּינוּ כָּל־הַיּוֹם. בָּרוּךְ אַתָּה יהוה, מַצְמִיחַ קֶרֶן יְשׁוּעָה.

JUSTICE

הָשִׁיבָה Restore our judges as at first and our counsellors as at the beginning, and remove from us sorrow and sighing. May You alone, LORD, reign over us with lovingkindness and compassion, and vindicate us in justice. Blessed are You, LORD,*the King who loves righteousness and justice.

*Between Rosh Hashanah and Yom Kippur, end the blessing:
the King of justice.

AGAINST INFORMERS

וְלַמַּלְשִׁינִים For the slanderers let there be no hope, and may all wickedness perish in an instant. May all Your enemies swiftly be cut down. May You swiftly uproot, crush, cast down and humble the kingdom of arrogance swiftly in our days. Blessed are You, LORD, who destroys enemies and humbles the arrogant.

THE RIGHTEOUS

עַל־הַצַּדִּיקִים To the righteous, the pious, the elders of Your people the house of Israel, the remnant of their scholars, the righteous converts, and to us, may Your compassion be aroused, LORD our GOD. Grant a good reward to all who sincerely trust in Your name. Set our lot with them for ever, so that we may never be ashamed, for in You we trust. Blessed are You, LORD, who is the support and trust of the righteous.

REBUILDING JERUSALEM

וְלִירוּשָׁלַיִם To Jerusalem, Your city, may You return in compassion, and may You dwell in it as You promised. May You rebuild it rapidly in our days as an everlasting structure, and instal within it soon the throne of David. Blessed are You, LORD, who builds Jerusalem.

KINGDOM OF DAVID

אֶת־צֶמַח May the offshoot of Your servant David soon flower, and may his pride be raised high by Your salvation, for we wait for Your salvation all day. Blessed are You, LORD, who makes the glory of salvation flourish.

שומע תפילה

שְׁמַע קוֹלֵנוּ יהוה אֱלֹהֵינוּ, חוּס וְרַחֵם עָלֵינוּ, וְקַבֵּל בְּרַחֲמִים וּבְרָצוֹן אֶת־תְּפִלָּתֵנוּ, כִּי אֵל שׁוֹמֵעַ תְּפִלּוֹת וְתַחֲנוּנִים אָתָּה. וּמִלְּפָנֶיךָ מַלְכֵּנוּ, רֵיקָם אַל תְּשִׁיבֵנוּ, כִּי אַתָּה שׁוֹמֵעַ תְּפִלַּת עַמְּךָ יִשְׂרָאֵל בְּרַחֲמִים. בָּרוּךְ אַתָּה יהוה, שׁוֹמֵעַ תְּפִלָּה.

עבודה

רְצֵה יהוה אֱלֹהֵינוּ בְּעַמְּךָ יִשְׂרָאֵל וּבִתְפִלָּתָם, וְהָשֵׁב אֶת־הָעֲבוֹדָה לִדְבִיר בֵּיתֶךָ. וְאִשֵּׁי יִשְׂרָאֵל וּתְפִלָּתָם בְּאַהֲבָה תְקַבֵּל בְּרָצוֹן, וּתְהִי לְרָצוֹן תָּמִיד עֲבוֹדַת יִשְׂרָאֵל עַמֶּךָ.

On רֹאשׁ חֹדֶשׁ and חוֹל הַמּוֹעֵד, say:

אֱלֹהֵינוּ וֵאלֹהֵי אֲבוֹתֵינוּ, יַעֲלֶה, וְיָבֹא, וְיַגִּיעַ, וְיֵרָאֶה, וְיֵרָצֶה, וְיִשָּׁמַע, וְיִפָּקֵד, וְיִזָּכֵר זִכְרוֹנֵנוּ וּפִקְדוֹנֵנוּ, וְזִכְרוֹן אֲבוֹתֵינוּ, וְזִכְרוֹן מָשִׁיחַ בֶּן דָּוִד עַבְדֶּךָ, וְזִכְרוֹן יְרוּשָׁלַיִם עִיר קָדְשֶׁךָ, וְזִכְרוֹן כָּל־עַמְּךָ בֵּית יִשְׂרָאֵל לְפָנֶיךָ, לִפְלֵיטָה וּלְטוֹבָה, וּלְחֵן וּלְחֶסֶד וּלְרַחֲמִים, וּלְחַיִּים וּלְשָׁלוֹם בְּיוֹם

On רֹאשׁ חֹדֶשׁ:	On פֶּסַח:	On סֻכּוֹת:
רֹאשׁ הַחֹדֶשׁ	חַג הַמַּצּוֹת	חַג הַסֻּכּוֹת

הַזֶּה. זָכְרֵנוּ יהוה אֱלֹהֵינוּ בּוֹ לְטוֹבָה, וּפָקְדֵנוּ בוֹ לִבְרָכָה, וְהוֹשִׁיעֵנוּ בוֹ לְחַיִּים. וּבִדְבַר יְשׁוּעָה וְרַחֲמִים, חוּס וְחָנֵּנוּ וְרַחֵם עָלֵינוּ וְהוֹשִׁיעֵנוּ, כִּי אֵלֶיךָ עֵינֵינוּ, כִּי אֵל מֶלֶךְ חַנּוּן וְרַחוּם אָתָּה.

וְתֶחֱזֶינָה עֵינֵינוּ בְּשׁוּבְךָ לְצִיּוֹן בְּרַחֲמִים. בָּרוּךְ אַתָּה יהוה, הַמַּחֲזִיר שְׁכִינָתוֹ לְצִיּוֹן.

הודאה

▽ Bow at the first five words.

▽**מוֹדִים** אֲנַחְנוּ לָךְ, שָׁאַתָּה הוּא יהוה אֱלֹהֵינוּ וֵאלֹהֵי אֲבוֹתֵינוּ לְעוֹלָם וָעֶד. צוּר חַיֵּינוּ, מָגֵן יִשְׁעֵנוּ אַתָּה הוּא

RESPONSE TO PRAYER

שְׁמַע Listen to our voice, LORD our GOD. Spare us and have compassion on us, and in compassion and favour accept our prayer, for You, GOD, listen to prayers and pleas. Do not turn us away, O our King, empty-handed from Your presence, for You listen with compassion to the prayer of Your people Israel. Blessed are You, LORD, who listens to prayer.

TEMPLE SERVICE

רְצֵה Find favour, LORD our GOD, in Your people Israel and their prayer. Restore the service to Your most holy house, and accept in love and favour the fire-offerings of Israel and their prayer. May the service of Your people Israel always find favour with You.

On Rosh Chodesh and the Intermediate Days of Festivals, say:

אֱלֹהֵינוּ Our GOD and GOD of our ancestors, may there rise, come, reach, appear, be favoured, heard, regarded and remembered before You, our recollection and remembrance, as well as the remembrance of our ancestors, and of the Messiah son of David Your servant, and of Jerusalem Your holy city, and of all Your people the House of Israel – for deliverance and well-being, grace, lovingkindness and compassion, life and peace, on this day of:

On Rosh Chodesh:	On Pesach:	On Sukkot:
Rosh Chodesh.	the Festival of Matzot.	the Festival of Sukkot.

On it remember us, LORD our GOD, for good, recollect us for blessing, and deliver us for life. In accord with Your promise of salvation and compassion, spare us and be gracious to us, have compassion on us and deliver us, for our eyes are turned to You because You, GOD, are a gracious and compassionate King.

וְתֶחֱזֶינָה And may our eyes witness Your return to Zion in compassion. Blessed are You, LORD, who restores His Presence to Zion.

THANKSGIVING

▽ Bow at the first nine words.

מוֹדִים▽ We give thanks to You, for You are the LORD our GOD and GOD of our ancestors for ever and all time. You are the Rock of our lives, Shield of our salvation from generation to generation. We

לְדוֹר וָדוֹר. נוֹדֶה לְּךָ וּנְסַפֵּר תְּהִלָּתֶךָ עַל חַיֵּינוּ הַמְּסוּרִים בְּיָדֶךָ, וְעַל נִשְׁמוֹתֵינוּ הַפְּקוּדוֹת לָךְ, וְעַל נִסֶּיךָ שֶׁבְּכָל־יוֹם עִמָּנוּ, וְעַל נִפְלְאוֹתֶיךָ וְטוֹבוֹתֶיךָ שֶׁבְּכָל־עֵת, עֶרֶב וָבֹקֶר וְצָהֳרָיִם. הַטּוֹב כִּי לֹא־כָלוּ רַחֲמֶיךָ, וְהַמְרַחֵם כִּי לֹא־תַמּוּ חֲסָדֶיךָ, מֵעוֹלָם קִוִּינוּ לָךְ.

On חֲנֻכָּה and פּוּרִים, say:

עַל הַנִּסִּים, וְעַל הַפֻּרְקָן, וְעַל הַגְּבוּרוֹת, וְעַל הַתְּשׁוּעוֹת, וְעַל הַמִּלְחָמוֹת, שֶׁעָשִׂיתָ לַאֲבוֹתֵינוּ בַּיָּמִים הָהֵם בַּזְּמַן הַזֶּה.

On חֲנֻכָּה, say:

בִּימֵי מַתִּתְיָהוּ בֶּן־יוֹחָנָן כֹּהֵן גָּדוֹל חַשְׁמוֹנַאי וּבָנָיו, כְּשֶׁעָמְדָה מַלְכוּת יָוָן הָרְשָׁעָה עַל־עַמְּךָ יִשְׂרָאֵל, לְהַשְׁכִּיחָם תּוֹרָתֶךָ, וּלְהַעֲבִירָם מֵחֻקֵּי רְצוֹנֶךָ. וְאַתָּה בְּרַחֲמֶיךָ הָרַבִּים, עָמַדְתָּ לָהֶם בְּעֵת צָרָתָם, רַבְתָּ אֶת־רִיבָם, דַּנְתָּ אֶת־דִּינָם, נָקַמְתָּ אֶת־נִקְמָתָם. מָסַרְתָּ גִבּוֹרִים בְּיַד חַלָּשִׁים, וְרַבִּים בְּיַד מְעַטִּים, וּטְמֵאִים בְּיַד טְהוֹרִים, וּרְשָׁעִים בְּיַד צַדִּיקִים, וְזֵדִים בְּיַד עוֹסְקֵי תוֹרָתֶךָ. וּלְךָ עָשִׂיתָ שֵׁם גָּדוֹל וְקָדוֹשׁ בְּעוֹלָמֶךָ, וּלְעַמְּךָ יִשְׂרָאֵל עָשִׂיתָ תְּשׁוּעָה גְדוֹלָה וּפֻרְקָן כְּהַיּוֹם הַזֶּה. וְאַחַר כֵּן בָּאוּ בָנֶיךָ לִדְבִיר בֵּיתֶךָ, וּפִנּוּ אֶת־הֵיכָלֶךָ, וְטִהֲרוּ אֶת־מִקְדָּשֶׁךָ, וְהִדְלִיקוּ נֵרוֹת בְּחַצְרוֹת קָדְשֶׁךָ, וְקָבְעוּ שְׁמוֹנַת יְמֵי חֲנֻכָּה אֵלּוּ, לְהוֹדוֹת וּלְהַלֵּל לְשִׁמְךָ הַגָּדוֹל.

On פּוּרִים, say:

בִּימֵי מָרְדְּכַי וְאֶסְתֵּר בְּשׁוּשַׁן הַבִּירָה, כְּשֶׁעָמַד עֲלֵיהֶם הָמָן הָרָשָׁע, בִּקֵּשׁ לְהַשְׁמִיד לַהֲרוֹג וּלְאַבֵּד אֶת־כָּל־הַיְּהוּדִים, מִנַּעַר וְעַד זָקֵן, טַף וְנָשִׁים בְּיוֹם אֶחָד, בִּשְׁלוֹשָׁה־עָשָׂר לְחֹדֶשׁ שְׁנֵים־עָשָׂר, הוּא־חֹדֶשׁ אֲדָר, וּשְׁלָלָם לָבוֹז. וְאַתָּה בְּרַחֲמֶיךָ הָרַבִּים הֵפַרְתָּ אֶת־עֲצָתוֹ, וְקִלְקַלְתָּ אֶת־מַחֲשַׁבְתּוֹ, וַהֲשֵׁבוֹתָ גְּמוּלוֹ בְּרֹאשׁוֹ, וְתָלוּ אוֹתוֹ וְאֶת־בָּנָיו עַל־הָעֵץ.

---

will thank You and declare Your praise for our lives which are entrusted into Your hand; our souls which are placed in Your charge; for Your miracles which are with us every day; and for Your wonders and favours at all times, evening, morning and midday. You are good – for Your compassion never fails. You are compassionate – for Your lovingkindnesses never cease. We have always placed our hope in You.

On Chanukah and Purim, say:

עַל הַנִּסִּים [We thank You also] for the miracles, the redemption, the mighty deeds, and the victories in battle which You performed for our ancestors in those days at this time.

On Chanukah, say:

בִּימֵי In the days of Mattityahu, son of Yochanan the High Priest, the Hasmonean, and his sons, the wicked Greek kingdom rose up against Your people Israel to make them forget Your Torah and to force them to transgress the statutes of Your will. It was then that You in Your great compassion stood by them in the time of their distress. You championed their cause, judged their claim, and avenged their wrong. You delivered the strong into the hands of the weak, the many into the hands of the few, the impure into the hands of the pure, the wicked into the hands of the righteous, and the arrogant into the hands of those who were engaged in the study of Your Torah. You made for Yourself great and holy renown in Your world, and for Your people Israel You performed a great salvation and redemption on this day. Your children then entered the holiest part of Your house, cleansed Your Temple, purified Your sanctuary, kindled lights in Your holy courts, and designated these eight days of Chanukah for giving thanks and praise to Your great name.

On Purim, say:

בִּימֵי In the days of Mordechai and Esther, in Shushan the capital, the wicked Haman rose up against them and sought to destroy, slay and exterminate all the Jews, young and old, children and women, on one day, the thirteenth day of the twelfth month, which is the month of Adar, and to plunder their possessions. Then You in Your great compassion thwarted his counsel, frustrated his plans, and caused his scheme to recoil on his own head, so that they hanged him and his sons on the gallows.

וְעַל כֻּלָּם יִתְבָּרַךְ וְיִתְרוֹמַם שִׁמְךָ מַלְכֵּנוּ תָּמִיד לְעוֹלָם וָעֶד.

Between רֹאשׁ הַשָּׁנָה and יוֹם כִּפּוּר, say:

וּכְתוֹב לְחַיִּים טוֹבִים כָּל־בְּנֵי בְרִיתֶךָ.

וְכֹל הַחַיִּים יוֹדְוּךָ סֶּלָה, וִיהַלְלוּ אֶת־שִׁמְךָ בֶּאֱמֶת, הָאֵל יְשׁוּעָתֵנוּ וְעֶזְרָתֵנוּ סֶלָה. ▾בָּרוּךְ אַתָּה יהוה, הַטּוֹב שִׁמְךָ וּלְךָ נָאֶה לְהוֹדוֹת.

שלום

שָׁלוֹם רָב עַל יִשְׂרָאֵל עַמְּךָ תָּשִׂים לְעוֹלָם, כִּי אַתָּה הוּא מֶלֶךְ אָדוֹן לְכָל הַשָּׁלוֹם. וְטוֹב בְּעֵינֶיךָ לְבָרֵךְ אֶת עַמְּךָ יִשְׂרָאֵל בְּכָל עֵת וּבְכָל שָׁעָה בִּשְׁלוֹמֶךָ. *בָּרוּךְ אַתָּה יהוה, הַמְבָרֵךְ אֶת עַמּוֹ יִשְׂרָאֵל בַּשָּׁלוֹם.

---

*Between רֹאשׁ הַשָּׁנָה and יוֹם כִּפּוּר, substitute the following:

בְּסֵפֶר חַיִּים בְּרָכָה וְשָׁלוֹם, וּפַרְנָסָה טוֹבָה, נִזָּכֵר וְנִכָּתֵב לְפָנֶיךָ, אֲנַחְנוּ וְכָל־עַמְּךָ בֵּית יִשְׂרָאֵל, לְחַיִּים טוֹבִים וּלְשָׁלוֹם. בָּרוּךְ אַתָּה יהוה, עוֹשֵׂה הַשָּׁלוֹם.

אֱלֹהַי, נְצוֹר לְשׁוֹנִי מֵרָע, וּשְׂפָתַי מִדַּבֵּר מִרְמָה, וְלִמְקַלְלַי נַפְשִׁי תִדֹּם, וְנַפְשִׁי כֶּעָפָר לַכֹּל תִּהְיֶה. פְּתַח לִבִּי בְּתוֹרָתֶךָ, וּבְמִצְוֹתֶיךָ תִּרְדֹּף נַפְשִׁי. וְכָל הַחוֹשְׁבִים עָלַי רָעָה, מְהֵרָה הָפֵר עֲצָתָם וְקַלְקֵל מַחֲשַׁבְתָּם. עֲשֵׂה לְמַעַן שְׁמֶךָ, עֲשֵׂה לְמַעַן יְמִינֶךָ, עֲשֵׂה לְמַעַן קְדֻשָּׁתֶךָ, עֲשֵׂה לְמַעַן תּוֹרָתֶךָ. לְמַעַן יֵחָלְצוּן יְדִידֶיךָ, הוֹשִׁיעָה יְמִינְךָ וַעֲנֵנִי. יִהְיוּ לְרָצוֹן אִמְרֵי־פִי וְהֶגְיוֹן לִבִּי לְפָנֶיךָ, יהוה צוּרִי וְגוֹאֲלִי.

Bow, take three steps back, then bow, first left, then right, then centre, while saying:

עֹשֶׂה שָׁלוֹם בִּמְרוֹמָיו, הוּא יַעֲשֶׂה שָׁלוֹם עָלֵינוּ, וְעַל־כָּל־יִשְׂרָאֵל, וְאִמְרוּ אָמֵן.

וְעַל For all these things may Your name be blessed and exalted, our King, continually, for ever and all time.

Between Rosh Hashanah and Yom Kippur, say:
And write, for a good life, all the children of Your covenant.

Let all that lives thank You, Selah! and praise Your name in truth, God, our Saviour and Help, Selah! ▼Blessed are You, Lord, whose name is "the Good" and to whom thanks are due.

PEACE

שָׁלוֹם Grant great peace to Your people Israel for ever, for You are the sovereign Lord of all peace; and may it be good in Your eyes to bless Your people Israel at every time, at every hour, with Your peace.*Blessed are You, Lord, who blesses His people Israel with peace.

---

*Between Rosh Hashanah and Yom Kippur, substitute the following:
In the book of life, blessing, peace and prosperity, may we and all Your people the house of Israel be remembered and written before You for a good life, and for peace. Blessed are You, Lord, who makes peace.

אֱלֹהַי My God, guard my tongue from evil and my lips from deceitful speech. To those who curse me, let my soul be silent; may my soul be to all like the dust. Open my heart to Your Torah and let my soul pursue Your commandments. As for all who plan evil against me, swiftly thwart their counsel and frustrate their plans. Act for the sake of Your name; act for the sake of Your right hand; act for the sake of Your holiness; act for the sake of Your Torah. That Your beloved ones may be delivered, save with Your right hand and answer me. May the words of my mouth and the meditation of my heart find favour before You, Lord, my Rock and Redeemer.

Bow, take three steps back, then bow, first left, then right, then centre, while saying:
May He who makes peace in His high places, make peace for us and all Israel – and say: Amen.

יְהִי רָצוֹן מִלְּפָנֶיךָ יהוה אֱלֹהֵינוּ וֵאלֹהֵי אֲבוֹתֵינוּ, שֶׁיִּבָּנֶה בֵּית הַמִּקְדָּשׁ בִּמְהֵרָה בְיָמֵינוּ, וְתֵן חֶלְקֵנוּ בְּתוֹרָתֶךָ. וְשָׁם נַעֲבָדְךָ בְּיִרְאָה, כִּימֵי עוֹלָם וּכְשָׁנִים קַדְמוֹנִיּוֹת. וְעָרְבָה לַיהוה מִנְחַת יְהוּדָה וִירוּשָׁלָיִם, כִּימֵי עוֹלָם וּכְשָׁנִים קַדְמוֹנִיּוֹת.

At the end of שַׁבָּת, turn to page 580.

On other days, the Leader says קַדִּישׁ תִּתְקַבַּל.

קדיש תתקבל

Leader:

יִתְגַּדַּל וְיִתְקַדַּשׁ שְׁמֵהּ רַבָּא. (Cong. אָמֵן) בְּעָלְמָא דִּי בְרָא כִרְעוּתֵהּ. וְיַמְלִיךְ מַלְכוּתֵהּ, בְּחַיֵּיכוֹן וּבְיוֹמֵיכוֹן וּבְחַיֵּי דְכָל־בֵּית יִשְׂרָאֵל, בַּעֲגָלָא וּבִזְמַן קָרִיב. וְאִמְרוּ אָמֵן. (Cong. אָמֵן)

All:

יְהֵא שְׁמֵהּ רַבָּא מְבָרַךְ לְעָלַם וּלְעָלְמֵי עָלְמַיָּא.

Leader:

יִתְבָּרַךְ וְיִשְׁתַּבַּח וְיִתְפָּאַר וְיִתְרוֹמַם וְיִתְנַשֵּׂא וְיִתְהַדַּר וְיִתְעַלֶּה וְיִתְהַלָּל שְׁמֵהּ דְּקֻדְשָׁא בְּרִיךְ הוּא (Cong. בְּרִיךְ הוּא) לְעֵלָּא (Between רֹאשׁ הַשָּׁנָה and יוֹם כִּפּוּר add לְעֵלָּא) מִן כָּל־בִּרְכָתָא וְשִׁירָתָא תֻּשְׁבְּחָתָא וְנֶחֱמָתָא, דַּאֲמִירָן בְּעָלְמָא. וְאִמְרוּ אָמֵן. (Cong. אָמֵן)

תִּתְקַבַּל צְלוֹתְהוֹן וּבָעוּתְהוֹן דְּכָל־יִשְׂרָאֵל קֳדָם אֲבוּהוֹן דִּי בִשְׁמַיָּא. וְאִמְרוּ אָמֵן. (Cong. אָמֵן)

יְהֵא שְׁלָמָא רַבָּא מִן־שְׁמַיָּא, וְחַיִּים עָלֵינוּ וְעַל־כָּל־יִשְׂרָאֵל. וְאִמְרוּ אָמֵן. (Cong. אָמֵן)

Bow, take three steps back, then bow, first left, then right, then centre, while saying:

עֹשֶׂה שָׁלוֹם בִּמְרוֹמָיו, הוּא יַעֲשֶׂה שָׁלוֹם עָלֵינוּ, וְעַל־כָּל־יִשְׂרָאֵל, וְאִמְרוּ אָמֵן. (Cong. אָמֵן)

יְהִי May it be Your will, LORD our GOD and GOD of our ancestors, that the Temple be rebuilt speedily in our days, and grant us a share in Your Torah. And there we will serve You with reverence, as in the days of old and as in former years. Then the offering of Judah and Jerusalem will be pleasing to the LORD as in the days of old and as in former years.

At the end of Shabbat, turn to page 581.

On other days, the Leader says full *Kaddish*.

FULL KADDISH

Leader:

יִתְגַּדַּל Magnified and sanctified may His great name be, in the world He created by His will. May He establish His kingdom in your lifetime and in your days, and in the lifetime of all the House of Israel, swiftly and soon – and say: Amen.

All:

May His great name be blessed for ever and all time.

Leader:

Blessed and praised, glorified and exalted, raised and honoured, uplifted and lauded be the name of the Holy One, blessed be He, (between Rosh Hashanah and Yom Kippur add 'well') beyond any blessing, song, praise and consolation uttered in the world – and say: Amen.

May the prayers and pleas of all Israel be accepted by their Father in heaven – and say: Amen.

May there be great peace from heaven, and life for us and all Israel – and say: Amen.

Bow, take three steps back, then bow, first left, then right, then centre, while saying:

May He who makes peace in His high places, make peace for us and all Israel – and say: Amen.

יְהִי רָצוֹן *May it be Your will*: A quotation from Ethics of the Fathers (5:23), said here as a reminder of the connection between prayer and sacrifice, and of our longing to see the Temple rebuilt. The next verse, taken from the last of the prophets, Malachi (3:4), epitomises our messianic hope.

From the second night of פֶּסַח until the night before שָׁבוּעוֹת, the עֹמֶר is counted here on page 238. At this point on פּוּרִים, מְגִלַּת אֶסְתֵּר is read and on תִּשְׁעָה בְּאָב, מְגִלַּת אֵיכָה is read.

עלינו

Stand while saying עָלֵינוּ. Bow at ▼.

עָלֵינוּ לְשַׁבֵּחַ לַאֲדוֹן הַכֹּל, לָתֵת גְּדֻלָּה לְיוֹצֵר בְּרֵאשִׁית, שֶׁלֹּא עָשָׂנוּ כְּגוֹיֵי הָאֲרָצוֹת, וְלֹא שָׂמָנוּ כְּמִשְׁפְּחוֹת הָאֲדָמָה. שֶׁלֹּא שָׂם חֶלְקֵנוּ כָּהֶם, וְגֹרָלֵנוּ כְּכָל־הֲמוֹנָם. ▼וַאֲנַחְנוּ כּוֹרְעִים וּמִשְׁתַּחֲוִים וּמוֹדִים, לִפְנֵי מֶלֶךְ מַלְכֵי הַמְּלָכִים הַקָּדוֹשׁ בָּרוּךְ הוּא. שֶׁהוּא נוֹטֶה שָׁמַיִם וְיוֹסֵד אָרֶץ, וּמוֹשַׁב יְקָרוֹ בַּשָּׁמַיִם מִמַּעַל, וּשְׁכִינַת עֻזּוֹ בְּגָבְהֵי מְרוֹמִים. הוּא אֱלֹהֵינוּ, אֵין עוֹד. אֱמֶת מַלְכֵּנוּ, אֶפֶס זוּלָתוֹ, כַּכָּתוּב בְּתוֹרָתוֹ, וְיָדַעְתָּ הַיּוֹם וַהֲשֵׁבֹתָ אֶל־לְבָבֶךָ, כִּי יהוה הוּא הָאֱלֹהִים בַּשָּׁמַיִם מִמַּעַל וְעַל־הָאָרֶץ מִתָּחַת, אֵין עוֹד.

עַל־כֵּן נְקַוֶּה לְּךָ יהוה אֱלֹהֵינוּ לִרְאוֹת מְהֵרָה בְּתִפְאֶרֶת עֻזֶּךָ, לְהַעֲבִיר גִּלּוּלִים מִן הָאָרֶץ, וְהָאֱלִילִים כָּרוֹת יִכָּרֵתוּן, לְתַקֵּן עוֹלָם בְּמַלְכוּת שַׁדַּי. וְכָל־בְּנֵי בָשָׂר יִקְרְאוּ בִשְׁמֶךָ, לְהַפְנוֹת אֵלֶיךָ כָּל־רִשְׁעֵי אָרֶץ. יַכִּירוּ וְיֵדְעוּ כָּל־יוֹשְׁבֵי תֵבֵל, כִּי לְךָ תִּכְרַע כָּל־בֶּרֶךְ, תִּשָּׁבַע כָּל־לָשׁוֹן. לְפָנֶיךָ יהוה אֱלֹהֵינוּ יִכְרְעוּ וְיִפֹּלוּ, וְלִכְבוֹד שִׁמְךָ יְקָר יִתֵּנוּ. וִיקַבְּלוּ כֻלָּם אֶת־עוֹל מַלְכוּתֶךָ, וְתִמְלֹךְ עֲלֵיהֶם מְהֵרָה לְעוֹלָם וָעֶד. כִּי הַמַּלְכוּת שֶׁלְּךָ הִיא וּלְעוֹלְמֵי עַד תִּמְלוֹךְ בְּכָבוֹד, כַּכָּתוּב בְּתוֹרָתֶךָ, יהוה יִמְלֹךְ לְעֹלָם וָעֶד. ← וְנֶאֱמַר, וְהָיָה יהוה לְמֶלֶךְ עַל־כָּל־הָאָרֶץ, בַּיּוֹם הַהוּא יִהְיֶה יהוה אֶחָד וּשְׁמוֹ אֶחָד.

Some congregations add:

אַל תִּירָא מִפַּחַד פִּתְאֹם, וּמִשֹּׁאַת רְשָׁעִים כִּי תָבֹא. עֻצוּ עֵצָה וְתֻפָר, דַּבְּרוּ דָבָר וְלֹא יָקוּם, כִּי עִמָּנוּ אֵל. וְעַד זִקְנָה אֲנִי הוּא, וְעַד שֵׂיבָה אֲנִי אֶסְבֹּל, אֲנִי עָשִׂיתִי וַאֲנִי אֶשָּׂא, וַאֲנִי אֶסְבֹּל וַאֲמַלֵּט.

From the second night of Pesach until the night before Shavuot, the Omer is counted here on page 239. At this point on Purim, the Book of Esther is read and on the Ninth of Av, the Book of Lamentations is read.

ALEINU

Stand while saying *Aleinu*. Bow at ▾.

עָלֵינוּ It is our duty to praise the Master of all, and ascribe greatness to the Author of creation, who has not made us like the nations of the lands nor placed us like the families of the earth; who has not made our portion like theirs, nor our destiny like all their multitudes. Therefore ▾we bow in worship and thank the Supreme King of kings, the Holy One, blessed be He, who extends the heavens and establishes the earth, whose throne of glory is in the heavens above, and whose power's presence is in the highest of heights. He is our God; there is no other. Truly He is our King, there is none else, as it is written in His Torah: "You shall know and take to heart this day that the Lord is God, in heaven above and on earth below. There is no other."

עַל־כֵּן Therefore we place our hope in You, Lord our God, that we may soon see the glory of Your power, when You will remove abominations from the earth, and idols will be utterly destroyed, when the world will be perfected under the sovereignty of the Almighty, when all humanity will call on Your name, and the earth's wicked will all turn to You. All the world's inhabitants will realise and know that to You every knee must bow and every tongue swear loyalty. Before You, Lord our God, they will kneel and bow down and give honour to Your glorious name. They will all accept the yoke of Your kingdom, and You will reign over them soon and for ever. For the kingdom is Yours, and to all eternity You will reign in glory, as it is written in Your Torah: "The Lord will reign for ever and ever." ➔ And it is said: "Then the Lord shall be King over all the earth: on that day the Lord shall be One and His name One."

Some congregations add:

Have no fear of sudden terror or of the ruin that overtakes the wicked. Devise your strategy, but it will be thwarted; propose your plan, but it will not stand, for God is with us. When you grow old, I will still be the same. When your hair turns grey, I will still carry you. I made you, I will bear you, I will carry you, and I will rescue you.

קדיש יתום

The transliteration can be found at the end of the Siddur.

Mourner:

יִתְגַּדַּל וְיִתְקַדַּשׁ שְׁמֵהּ רַבָּא. (Cong. אָמֵן) **בְּעָלְמָא דִּי־בְרָא כִרְעוּתֵהּ. וְיַמְלִיךְ מַלְכוּתֵהּ, בְּחַיֵּיכוֹן וּבְיוֹמֵיכוֹן וּבְחַיֵּי דְכָל־בֵּית יִשְׂרָאֵל, בַּעֲגָלָא וּבִזְמַן קָרִיב. וְאִמְרוּ אָמֵן.** (Cong. אָמֵן)

All:

יְהֵא שְׁמֵהּ רַבָּא מְבָרַךְ לְעָלַם וּלְעָלְמֵי עָלְמַיָּא.

Mourner:

יִתְבָּרַךְ וְיִשְׁתַּבַּח וְיִתְפָּאַר וְיִתְרוֹמַם וְיִתְנַשֵּׂא וְיִתְהַדָּר וְיִתְעַלֶּה וְיִתְהַלָּל שְׁמֵהּ דְּקֻדְשָׁא בְּרִיךְ הוּא (Cong. בְּרִיךְ הוּא) **לְעֵֽלָּא** (Between רֹאשׁ הַשָּׁנָה and יוֹם כִּפּוּר add **לְעֵֽלָּא**) **מִן־כָּל־בִּרְכָתָא וְשִׁירָתָא תֻּשְׁבְּחָתָא וְנֶחֱמָתָא, דִּי־אֲמִירָן בְּעָלְמָא. וְאִמְרוּ אָמֵן.** (Cong. אָמֵן)

יְהֵא שְׁלָמָא רַבָּא מִן־שְׁמַיָּא, וְחַיִּים עָלֵינוּ וְעַל־כָּל־יִשְׂרָאֵל. וְאִמְרוּ אָמֵן. (Cong. אָמֵן)

Bow, take three steps back, then bow, first left, then right, then centre, while saying:

עֹשֶׂה שָׁלוֹם בִּמְרוֹמָיו, הוּא יַעֲשֶׂה שָׁלוֹם עָלֵינוּ, וְעַל־כָּל־יִשְׂרָאֵל, וְאִמְרוּ אָמֵן. (Cong. אָמֵן)

From the second night of רֹאשׁ חֹדֶשׁ אֱלוּל until and including שְׁמִינִי עֲצֶרֶת,
this psalm is said, followed by קַדִּישׁ יָתוֹם.

תהלים כז

לְדָוִד, יהוה אוֹרִי וְיִשְׁעִי, מִמִּי אִירָא, יהוה מָעוֹז חַיַּי, מִמִּי אֶפְחָד. בִּקְרֹב עָלַי מְרֵעִים לֶאֱכֹל אֶת בְּשָׂרִי, צָרַי וְאֹיְבַי לִי, הֵמָּה כָשְׁלוּ וְנָפָלוּ. אִם תַּחֲנֶה עָלַי מַחֲנֶה, לֹא יִירָא לִבִּי,

MOURNER'S KADDISH

The transliteration can be found at the end of the Siddur.

Mourner:

יִתְגַּדַּל may His great name be, in the world He created by His will. May He establish His kingdom in your lifetime and in your days, and in the lifetime of all the House of Israel, swiftly and soon – and say: Amen.

All:

May His great name be blessed for ever and all time.

Mourner:

Blessed and praised, glorified and exalted, raised and honoured, uplifted and lauded be the name of the Holy One, blessed be He, (between Rosh Hashanah and Yom Kippur add 'well') beyond any blessing, song, praise and consolation uttered in the world – and say: Amen.

May there be great peace from heaven, and life for us and all Israel – and say: Amen.

Bow, take three steps back, then bow, first left, then right, then centre, while saying:

May He who makes peace in His high places, make peace for us and all Israel – and say: Amen.

From the second night of Rosh Chodesh Ellul until and including Shemini Atzeret, this psalm is said, followed by Mourner's *Kaddish.*

PSALM 27

לְדָוִד A psalm of David. The LORD is my light and my salvation – whom then shall I fear? The LORD is the stronghold of my life – of whom shall I be afraid? When evil men close in on me to devour my flesh, it is they, my enemies and foes, who stumble and fall. Should an army besiege me, my heart would not fear. Should war break out against me, still I would be confident. One thing I ask of the LORD, only this do I seek: to live in the house of the LORD all the days of my life, to gaze on the beauty of the LORD and worship in His Temple.

אִם תָּקוּם עָלַי מִלְחָמָה, בְּזֹאת אֲנִי בוֹטֵחַ. אַחַת שָׁאַלְתִּי מֵאֵת יהוה, אוֹתָהּ אֲבַקֵּשׁ, שִׁבְתִּי בְּבֵית יהוה כָּל יְמֵי חַיַּי, לַחֲזוֹת בְּנֹעַם יהוה, וּלְבַקֵּר בְּהֵיכָלוֹ. כִּי יִצְפְּנֵנִי בְּסֻכֹּה בְּיוֹם רָעָה, יַסְתִּרֵנִי בְּסֵתֶר אָהֳלוֹ, בְּצוּר יְרוֹמְמֵנִי. וְעַתָּה יָרוּם רֹאשִׁי עַל אֹיְבַי סְבִיבוֹתַי, וְאֶזְבְּחָה בְאָהֳלוֹ זִבְחֵי תְרוּעָה, אָשִׁירָה וַאֲזַמְּרָה לַיהוה. שְׁמַע יהוה קוֹלִי אֶקְרָא, וְחָנֵּנִי וַעֲנֵנִי. לְךָ אָמַר לִבִּי בַּקְּשׁוּ פָנָי, אֶת פָּנֶיךָ יהוה אֲבַקֵּשׁ. אַל תַּסְתֵּר פָּנֶיךָ מִמֶּנִּי, אַל תַּט בְּאַף עַבְדֶּךָ, עֶזְרָתִי הָיִיתָ, אַל תִּטְּשֵׁנִי וְאַל תַּעַזְבֵנִי, אֱלֹהֵי יִשְׁעִי. כִּי אָבִי וְאִמִּי עֲזָבוּנִי, וַיהוה יַאַסְפֵנִי. הוֹרֵנִי יהוה דַּרְכֶּךָ, וּנְחֵנִי בְּאֹרַח מִישׁוֹר, לְמַעַן שׁוֹרְרָי. אַל תִּתְּנֵנִי בְּנֶפֶשׁ צָרָי, כִּי קָמוּ בִי עֵדֵי שֶׁקֶר, וִיפֵחַ חָמָס. ◂ לוּלֵא הֶאֱמַנְתִּי לִרְאוֹת בְּטוּב יהוה בְּאֶרֶץ חַיִּים. קַוֵּה אֶל יהוה, חֲזַק וְיַאֲמֵץ לִבֶּךָ, וְקַוֵּה אֶל יהוה.

קַדִּישׁ יָתוֹם can be found on page 232.

The following psalm is said in a house of mourning during the week of שִׁבְעָה, on the days when תַּחֲנוּן is said:

תהלים מט

לַמְנַצֵּחַ לִבְנֵי קֹרַח מִזְמוֹר. שִׁמְעוּ־זֹאת כָּל־הָעַמִּים, הַאֲזִינוּ כָּל־יֹשְׁבֵי חָלֶד. גַּם־בְּנֵי אָדָם, גַּם־בְּנֵי־אִישׁ, יַחַד עָשִׁיר וְאֶבְיוֹן. פִּי יְדַבֵּר חָכְמוֹת, וְהָגוּת לִבִּי תְבוּנוֹת. אַטֶּה לְמָשָׁל אָזְנִי, אֶפְתַּח בְּכִנּוֹר חִידָתִי. לָמָּה אִירָא בִּימֵי רָע, עֲוֺן עֲקֵבַי יְסֻבֵּנִי. הַבֹּטְחִים עַל־חֵילָם, וּבְרֹב עָשְׁרָם יִתְהַלָּלוּ. אָח לֹא־פָדֹה יִפְדֶּה אִישׁ, לֹא יִתֵּן לֵאלֹהִים כָּפְרוֹ. וְיֵקַר פִּדְיוֹן נַפְשָׁם, וְחָדַל לְעוֹלָם. וִיחִי־עוֹד לָנֶצַח, לֹא יִרְאֶה הַשָּׁחַת. כִּי יִרְאֶה חֲכָמִים יָמוּתוּ, יַחַד כְּסִיל וָבַעַר יֹאבֵדוּ, וְעָזְבוּ לַאֲחֵרִים חֵילָם. קִרְבָּם בָּתֵּימוֹ לְעוֹלָם, מִשְׁכְּנֹתָם לְדֹר

For He will keep me safe in His pavilion on the day of trouble. He will hide me under the cover of His tent. He will set me high upon a rock. Now my head is high above my enemies who surround me. I will sacrifice in His tent with shouts of joy. I will sing and chant praises to the LORD. LORD, hear my voice when I call. Be gracious to me and answer me. On Your behalf my heart says, "Seek My face." Your face, LORD, will I seek. Do not hide Your face from me. Do not turn Your servant away in anger. You have been my help. Do not reject or forsake me, GOD, my Saviour. Were my father and my mother to forsake me, the LORD would take me in. Teach me Your way, LORD, and lead me on a level path, because of my oppressors. Do not abandon me to the will of my foes, for false witnesses have risen against me, breathing violence. ➾ Were it not for my faith that I shall see the LORD's goodness in the land of the living… Hope in the LORD. Be strong and of good courage, and hope in the LORD!

Mourner's *Kaddish* can be found on page 233.

The following psalm is said in a house of mourning during the week of *shivah*, on the days when *Tachanun* is said:

PSALM 49

לַמְנַצֵּחַ For the director of music. Of the sons of Korach. A sacred song. Hear this, all you peoples. Listen, all inhabitants of the World, low and high, rich and poor alike. My mouth will speak words of wisdom; the utterance of my heart will give understanding. I listen with care to a parable; I expound my mystery to the music of the harp. Why should I fear when evil days come, when the wickedness of my foes surrounds me, trusting in their wealth, boasting of their great riches? No man can redeem his brother or pay GOD the price of his release, for the ransom of a life is costly; no payment is ever enough that would let him live for ever, never seeing the grave. For all can see that wise men die, that the foolish and senseless all perish and leave their wealth to others. They think their houses will remain for ever, their dwellings for all generations; they give their names to their estates. But man, despite his splendour, does not endure; he is like the beasts that per-

וָדֹר, קָרְאוּ בִשְׁמוֹתָם עֲלֵי אֲדָמוֹת. וְאָדָם בִּיקָר בַּל־יָלִין, נִמְשַׁל כַּבְּהֵמוֹת נִדְמוּ. זֶה דַרְכָּם, כֵּסֶל לָמוֹ, וְאַחֲרֵיהֶם בְּפִיהֶם יִרְצוּ, סֶלָה. כַּצֹּאן לִשְׁאוֹל שַׁתּוּ, מָוֶת יִרְעֵם, וַיִּרְדּוּ בָם יְשָׁרִים לַבֹּקֶר, וְצוּרָם לְבַלּוֹת שְׁאוֹל מִזְּבֻל לוֹ. אַךְ־אֱלֹהִים יִפְדֶּה־נַפְשִׁי מִיַּד שְׁאוֹל, כִּי יִקָּחֵנִי סֶלָה. אַל־תִּירָא כִּי יַעֲשִׁר אִישׁ, כִּי־יִרְבֶּה כְּבוֹד בֵּיתוֹ. כִּי לֹא בְמוֹתוֹ יִקַּח הַכֹּל, לֹא־יֵרֵד אַחֲרָיו כְּבוֹדוֹ. כִּי נַפְשׁוֹ בְּחַיָּיו יְבָרֵךְ, וְיוֹדֻךָ כִּי־תֵיטִיב לָךְ. תָּבוֹא עַד־דּוֹר אֲבוֹתָיו, עַד־נֵצַח לֹא יִרְאוּ־אוֹר. ◄ אָדָם בִּיקָר וְלֹא יָבִין, נִמְשַׁל כַּבְּהֵמוֹת נִדְמוּ.

קַדִּישׁ יָתוֹם can be found on page 232.

The following psalm is said in the house of mourning during the week of שִׁבְעָה, on the days when תַּחֲנוּן is not said:

תהלים טז

מִכְתָּם לְדָוִד, שָׁמְרֵנִי אֵל כִּי־חָסִיתִי בָךְ. אָמַרְתְּ לַיהוה, אֲדֹנָי אָתָּה, טוֹבָתִי בַּל־עָלֶיךָ. לִקְדוֹשִׁים אֲשֶׁר־בָּאָרֶץ הֵמָּה, וְאַדִּירֵי כָּל־חֶפְצִי־בָם. יִרְבּוּ עַצְּבוֹתָם אַחֵר מָהָרוּ, בַּל־אַסִּיךְ נִסְכֵּיהֶם מִדָּם, וּבַל־אֶשָּׂא אֶת־שְׁמוֹתָם עַל־שְׂפָתָי. יהוה, מְנָת־חֶלְקִי וְכוֹסִי, אַתָּה תּוֹמִיךְ גּוֹרָלִי. חֲבָלִים נָפְלוּ־לִי בַּנְּעִמִים, אַף־נַחֲלָת שָׁפְרָה עָלָי. אֲבָרֵךְ אֶת־יהוה אֲשֶׁר יְעָצָנִי, אַף־לֵילוֹת יִסְּרוּנִי כִלְיוֹתָי. שִׁוִּיתִי יהוה לְנֶגְדִּי תָמִיד, כִּי מִימִינִי בַּל־אֶמּוֹט. לָכֵן שָׂמַח לִבִּי וַיָּגֶל כְּבוֹדִי, אַף־בְּשָׂרִי יִשְׁכֹּן לָבֶטַח. כִּי לֹא־תַעֲזֹב נַפְשִׁי לִשְׁאוֹל, לֹא־תִתֵּן חֲסִידְךָ לִרְאוֹת שָׁחַת. ◄ תּוֹדִיעֵנִי אֹרַח חַיִּים, שֹׂבַע שְׂמָחוֹת אֶת־פָּנֶיךָ, נְעִמוֹת בִּימִינְךָ נֶצַח.

קַדִּישׁ יָתוֹם can be found on page 232.

ish. Such is the fate of the foolish and their followers who approve their words, Selah. Like sheep they are destined for the grave: death will be their shepherd. The upright will rule over them in the morning. Their forms will decay in the grave, far from their mansions. But God will redeem my life from the grave; He will surely take me to Himself, Selah. Do not be overawed when a man grows rich, when the glory of his house increases, for he will take nothing with him when he dies; his wealth will not descend with him. Though while he lived he counted himself blessed – men always praise you when you prosper – he will join the generation of his ancestors who will Never again see the light. ➔ A man who, despite his splendour, lacks understanding is like the beasts that perish.

Mourner's *Kaddish* can be found on page 233.

The following psalm is said in the house of mourning during the week of *shivah*, on the days when *Tachanun* is not said:

PSALM 16

מִכְתָּם לְדָוִד Protect me, God, for in You I have found refuge. I have said to the Lord: You are my Lord: from You alone comes the good I enjoy. All my delight is in the holy ones, the mighty in the land. Those who run after other gods multiply their sorrows. I shall never offer them libations of blood, nor will their names pass my lips. The Lord is my allotted portion and my cup: You direct my fate. The lines have fallen for me in pleasant places; I am well content with my inheritance. I will bless the Lord who has guided me; at night my innermost being admonishes me. I have set the Lord before me at all times. He is at my right hand: I shall not be shaken. Therefore my heart is glad, my spirit rejoices, and my body rests secure. For You will not abandon me to the grave, nor let Your faithful one see the pit. ➔ You will teach me the path of life. In Your presence is fullness of joy; at Your right hand, bliss for evermore.

Mourner's *Kaddish* can be found on page 233.

סדר ספירת העומר

The עֹמֶר is counted each night from the second night of פֶּסַח until the night before שָׁבֻעוֹת.

הִנְנִי מְקַיֵּם מִצְוַת עֲשֵׂה שֶׁל־סְפִירַת הָעֹמֶר כְּמוֹ שֶׁכָּתוּב בַּתּוֹרָה, וּסְפַרְתֶּם לָכֶם מִמָּחֳרַת הַשַּׁבָּת מִיּוֹם הֲבִיאֲכֶם אֶת־עֹמֶר הַתְּנוּפָה שֶׁבַע שַׁבָּתוֹת תְּמִימֹת תִּהְיֶינָה, עַד מִמָּחֳרַת הַשַּׁבָּת הַשְּׁבִיעִית תִּסְפְּרוּ חֲמִשִּׁים יוֹם.

בָּרוּךְ אַתָּה יהוה אֱלֹהֵינוּ מֶלֶךְ הָעוֹלָם, אֲשֶׁר קִדְּשָׁנוּ בְּמִצְוֹתָיו וְצִוָּנוּ עַל סְפִירַת הָעֹמֶר.

1. הַיּוֹם יוֹם אֶחָד לָעֹמֶר.
2. הַיּוֹם שְׁנֵי יָמִים לָעֹמֶר.
3. הַיּוֹם שְׁלֹשָׁה יָמִים לָעֹמֶר.
4. הַיּוֹם אַרְבָּעָה יָמִים לָעֹמֶר.
5. הַיּוֹם חֲמִשָּׁה יָמִים לָעֹמֶר.
6. הַיּוֹם שִׁשָּׁה יָמִים לָעֹמֶר.
7. הַיּוֹם שִׁבְעָה יָמִים שֶׁהֵם שָׁבוּעַ אֶחָד לָעֹמֶר.
8. הַיּוֹם שְׁמוֹנָה יָמִים שֶׁהֵם שָׁבוּעַ אֶחָד וְיוֹם אֶחָד לָעֹמֶר.
9. הַיּוֹם תִּשְׁעָה יָמִים שֶׁהֵם שָׁבוּעַ אֶחָד וּשְׁנֵי יָמִים לָעֹמֶר.
10. הַיּוֹם עֲשָׂרָה יָמִים שֶׁהֵם שָׁבוּעַ אֶחָד וּשְׁלֹשָׁה יָמִים לָעֹמֶר.
11. הַיּוֹם אַחַד עָשָׂר יוֹם שֶׁהֵם שָׁבוּעַ אֶחָד וְאַרְבָּעָה יָמִים לָעֹמֶר.
12. הַיּוֹם שְׁנֵים עָשָׂר יוֹם שֶׁהֵם שָׁבוּעַ אֶחָד וַחֲמִשָּׁה יָמִים לָעֹמֶר.
13. הַיּוֹם שְׁלֹשָׁה עָשָׂר יוֹם שֶׁהֵם שָׁבוּעַ אֶחָד וְשִׁשָּׁה יָמִים לָעֹמֶר.
14. הַיּוֹם אַרְבָּעָה עָשָׂר יוֹם שֶׁהֵם שְׁנֵי שָׁבוּעוֹת לָעֹמֶר.
15. הַיּוֹם חֲמִשָּׁה עָשָׂר יוֹם שֶׁהֵם שְׁנֵי שָׁבוּעוֹת וְיוֹם אֶחָד לָעֹמֶר.
16. הַיּוֹם שִׁשָּׁה עָשָׂר יוֹם שֶׁהֵם שְׁנֵי שָׁבוּעוֹת וּשְׁנֵי יָמִים לָעֹמֶר.
17. הַיּוֹם שִׁבְעָה עָשָׂר יוֹם שֶׁהֵם שְׁנֵי שָׁבוּעוֹת וּשְׁלֹשָׁה יָמִים לָעֹמֶר.

COUNTING THE OMER
When the Temple stood, on the day after the first day of Pesach an offering was made of an Omer (approximately four kilos) of new barley grain. There then began a count of forty-nine days – seven complete weeks – and on the fiftieth day, the festival of Shavuot was celebrated. When the Temple was destroyed, the Sages ordained that we should continue

COUNTING OF THE OMER

The Omer is counted each night from the second night of Pesach until the night before Shavuot.

הִנְנִי I am about to fulfil the positive commandment of Counting the Omer, as is written in the Torah: "You shall count seven complete weeks from the day following the [Passover] rest day, when you brought the Omer as a wave-offering. To the day after the seventh week, you shall count fifty days."

בָּרוּךְ Blessed are You, LORD our GOD, King of the Universe, who has made us holy through His commandments, and has commanded us about counting the Omer.

1. Today is the first day of the Omer.
2. Today is the second day of the Omer.
3. Today is the third day of the Omer.
4. Today is the fourth day of the Omer.
5. Today is the fifth day of the Omer.
6. Today is the sixth day of the Omer.
7. Today is the seventh day, making one week of the Omer.
8. Today is the eighth day, making one week and one day of the Omer.
9. Today is the ninth day, making one week and two days of the Omer.
10. Today is the tenth day, making one week and three days of the Omer.
11. Today is the eleventh day, making one week and four days of the Omer.
12. Today is the twelfth day, making one week and five days of the Omer.
13. Today is the thirteenth day, making one week and six days of the Omer.
14. Today is the fourteenth day, making two weeks of the Omer.
15. Today is the fifteenth day, making two weeks and one day of the Omer.
16. Today is the sixteenth day, making two weeks and two days of the Omer.
17. Today is the seventeenth day, making two weeks and three days of the Omer.

---

to count the days as a memory of this practice. The forty-nine days, connecting the Exodus from Egypt with the giving of the Torah at Mount Sinai, are a time of preparation and growth – of leaving a world of slavery and getting ready to enter a world of personal, social and spiritual responsibility. The Jewish mystics attached special significance to this period of the year as one in which the various facets of the soul were cleansed, one by one.

18. הַיּוֹם שְׁמוֹנָה עָשָׂר יוֹם שֶׁהֵם שְׁנֵי שָׁבוּעוֹת וְאַרְבָּעָה יָמִים לָעֹמֶר.
19. הַיּוֹם תִּשְׁעָה עָשָׂר יוֹם שֶׁהֵם שְׁנֵי שָׁבוּעוֹת וַחֲמִשָּׁה יָמִים לָעֹמֶר.
20. הַיּוֹם עֶשְׂרִים יוֹם שֶׁהֵם שְׁנֵי שָׁבוּעוֹת וְשִׁשָּׁה יָמִים לָעֹמֶר.
21. הַיּוֹם אֶחָד וְעֶשְׂרִים יוֹם שֶׁהֵם שְׁלשָׁה שָׁבוּעוֹת לָעֹמֶר.
22. הַיּוֹם שְׁנַיִם וְעֶשְׂרִים יוֹם שֶׁהֵם שְׁלשָׁה שָׁבוּעוֹת וְיוֹם אֶחָד לָעֹמֶר.
23. הַיּוֹם שְׁלשָׁה וְעֶשְׂרִים יוֹם שֶׁהֵם שְׁלשָׁה שָׁבוּעוֹת וּשְׁנֵי יָמִים לָעֹמֶר.
24. הַיּוֹם אַרְבָּעָה וְעֶשְׂרִים יוֹם שֶׁהֵם שְׁלשָׁה שָׁבוּעוֹת וּשְׁלשָׁה יָמִים לָעֹמֶר.
25. הַיּוֹם חֲמִשָּׁה וְעֶשְׂרִים יוֹם שֶׁהֵם שְׁלשָׁה שָׁבוּעוֹת וְאַרְבָּעָה יָמִים לָעֹמֶר.
26. הַיּוֹם שִׁשָּׁה וְעֶשְׂרִים יוֹם שֶׁהֵם שְׁלשָׁה שָׁבוּעוֹת וַחֲמִשָּׁה יָמִים לָעֹמֶר.
27. הַיּוֹם שִׁבְעָה וְעֶשְׂרִים יוֹם שֶׁהֵם שְׁלשָׁה שָׁבוּעוֹת וְשִׁשָּׁה יָמִים לָעֹמֶר.
28. הַיּוֹם שְׁמוֹנָה וְעֶשְׂרִים יוֹם שֶׁהֵם אַרְבָּעָה שָׁבוּעוֹת לָעֹמֶר.
29. הַיּוֹם תִּשְׁעָה וְעֶשְׂרִים יוֹם שֶׁהֵם אַרְבָּעָה שָׁבוּעוֹת וְיוֹם אֶחָד לָעֹמֶר.
30. הַיּוֹם שְׁלשִׁים יוֹם שֶׁהֵם אַרְבָּעָה שָׁבוּעוֹת וּשְׁנֵי יָמִים לָעֹמֶר.
31. הַיּוֹם אֶחָד וּשְׁלשִׁים יוֹם שֶׁהֵם אַרְבָּעָה שָׁבוּעוֹת וּשְׁלשָׁה יָמִים לָעֹמֶר.
32. הַיּוֹם שְׁנַיִם וּשְׁלשִׁים יוֹם שֶׁהֵם אַרְבָּעָה שָׁבוּעוֹת וְאַרְבָּעָה יָמִים לָעֹמֶר.
33. הַיּוֹם שְׁלשָׁה וּשְׁלשִׁים יוֹם שֶׁהֵם אַרְבָּעָה שָׁבוּעוֹת וַחֲמִשָּׁה יָמִים לָעֹמֶר.
34. הַיּוֹם אַרְבָּעָה וּשְׁלשִׁים יוֹם שֶׁהֵם אַרְבָּעָה שָׁבוּעוֹת וְשִׁשָּׁה יָמִים לָעֹמֶר.
35. הַיּוֹם חֲמִשָּׁה וּשְׁלשִׁים יוֹם שֶׁהֵם חֲמִשָּׁה שָׁבוּעוֹת לָעֹמֶר.
36. הַיּוֹם שִׁשָּׁה וּשְׁלשִׁים יוֹם שֶׁהֵם חֲמִשָּׁה שָׁבוּעוֹת וְיוֹם אֶחָד לָעֹמֶר.
37. הַיּוֹם שִׁבְעָה וּשְׁלשִׁים יוֹם שֶׁהֵם חֲמִשָּׁה שָׁבוּעוֹת וּשְׁנֵי יָמִים לָעֹמֶר.
38. הַיּוֹם שְׁמוֹנָה וּשְׁלשִׁים יוֹם שֶׁהֵם חֲמִשָּׁה שָׁבוּעוֹת וּשְׁלשָׁה יָמִים לָעֹמֶר.
39. הַיּוֹם תִּשְׁעָה וּשְׁלשִׁים יוֹם שֶׁהֵם חֲמִשָּׁה שָׁבוּעוֹת וְאַרְבָּעָה יָמִים לָעֹמֶר.
40. הַיּוֹם אַרְבָּעִים יוֹם שֶׁהֵם חֲמִשָּׁה שָׁבוּעוֹת וַחֲמִשָּׁה יָמִים לָעֹמֶר.
41. הַיּוֹם אֶחָד וְאַרְבָּעִים יוֹם שֶׁהֵם חֲמִשָּׁה שָׁבוּעוֹת וְשִׁשָּׁה יָמִים לָעֹמֶר:
42. הַיּוֹם שְׁנַיִם וְאַרְבָּעִים יוֹם שֶׁהֵם שִׁשָּׁה שָׁבוּעוֹת לָעֹמֶר.
43. הַיּוֹם שְׁלשָׁה וְאַרְבָּעִים יוֹם שֶׁהֵם שִׁשָּׁה שָׁבוּעוֹת וְיוֹם אֶחָד לָעֹמֶר.
44. הַיּוֹם אַרְבָּעָה וְאַרְבָּעִים יוֹם שֶׁהֵם שִׁשָּׁה שָׁבוּעוֹת וּשְׁנֵי יָמִים לָעֹמֶר.
45. הַיּוֹם חֲמִשָּׁה וְאַרְבָּעִים יוֹם שֶׁהֵם שִׁשָּׁה שָׁבוּעוֹת וּשְׁלשָׁה יָמִים לָעֹמֶר.
46. הַיּוֹם שִׁשָּׁה וְאַרְבָּעִים יוֹם שֶׁהֵם שִׁשָּׁה שָׁבוּעוֹת וְאַרְבָּעָה יָמִים לָעֹמֶר.
47. הַיּוֹם שִׁבְעָה וְאַרְבָּעִים יוֹם שֶׁהֵם שִׁשָּׁה שָׁבוּעוֹת וַחֲמִשָּׁה יָמִים לָעֹמֶר.
48. הַיּוֹם שְׁמוֹנָה וְאַרְבָּעִים יוֹם שֶׁהֵם שִׁשָּׁה שָׁבוּעוֹת וְשִׁשָּׁה יָמִים לָעֹמֶר.
49. הַיּוֹם תִּשְׁעָה וְאַרְבָּעִים יוֹם שֶׁהֵם שִׁבְעָה שָׁבוּעוֹת לָעֹמֶר.

18. Today is the eighteenth day, making two weeks and four days of the Omer.
19. Today is the nineteenth day, making two weeks and five days of the Omer.
20. Today is the twentieth day, making two weeks and six days of the Omer.
21. Today is the twenty-first day, making three weeks of the Omer.
22. Today is the twenty-second day, making three weeks and one day of the Omer.
23. Today is the twenty-third day, making three weeks and two days of the Omer.
24. Today is the twenty-fourth day, making three weeks and three days of the Omer.
25. Today is the twenty-fifth day, making three weeks and four days of the Omer.
26. Today is the twenty-sixth day, making three weeks and five days of the Omer.
27. Today is the twenty-seventh day, making three weeks and six days of the Omer.
28. Today is the twenty-eighth day, making four weeks of the Omer.
29. Today is the twenty-ninth day, making four weeks and one day of the Omer.
30. Today is the thirtieth day, making four weeks and two days of the Omer.
31. Today is the thirty-first day, making four weeks and three days of the Omer.
32. Today is the thirty-second day, making four weeks and four days of the Omer.
33. Today is the thirty-third day, making four weeks and five days of the Omer.
34. Today is the thirty-fourth day, making four weeks and six days of the Omer.
35. Today is the thirty-fifth day, making five weeks of the Omer.
36. Today is the thirty-sixth day, making five weeks and one day of the Omer.
37. Today is the thirty-seventh day, making five weeks and two days of the Omer.
38. Today is the thirty-eighth day, making five weeks and three days of the Omer.
39. Today is the thirty-ninth day, making five weeks and four days of the Omer.
40. Today is the fortieth day, making five weeks and five days of the Omer.
41. Today is the forty-first day, making five weeks and six days of the Omer.
42. Today is the forty-second day, making six weeks of the Omer.
43. Today is the forty-third day, making six weeks and one day of the Omer.
44. Today is the forty-fourth day, making six weeks and two days of the Omer.
45. Today is the forty-fifth day, making six weeks and three days of the Omer.
46. Today is the forty-sixth day, making six weeks and four days of the Omer.
47. Today is the forty-seventh day, making six weeks and five days of the Omer.
48. Today is the forty-eighth day, making six weeks and six days of the Omer.
49. Today is the forty-ninth day, making seven weeks of the Omer.

הָרַחֲמָן הוּא יַחֲזִיר לָנוּ עֲבוֹדַת בֵּית הַמִּקְדָּשׁ לִמְקוֹמָהּ. יְהִי רָצוֹן מִלְּפָנֶיךָ, יהוה אֱלֹהֵינוּ וֵאלֹהֵי אֲבוֹתֵינוּ, שֶׁיִּבָּנֶה בֵּית הַמִּקְדָּשׁ בִּמְהֵרָה בְיָמֵינוּ, וְתֵן חֶלְקֵנוּ בְּתוֹרָתֶךָ. וְשָׁם נַעֲבָדְךָ בְּיִרְאָה כִּימֵי עוֹלָם וּכְשָׁנִים קַדְמוֹנִיּוֹת.

תהלים סז
Some add the following:

לַמְנַצֵּחַ בִּנְגִינֹת מִזְמוֹר שִׁיר. אֱלֹהִים יְחָנֵּנוּ וִיבָרְכֵנוּ יָאֵר פָּנָיו אִתָּנוּ סֶלָה. לָדַעַת בָּאָרֶץ דַּרְכֶּךָ בְּכָל־גּוֹיִם יְשׁוּעָתֶךָ. יוֹדוּךָ עַמִּים אֱלֹהִים יוֹדוּךָ עַמִּים כֻּלָּם. יִשְׂמְחוּ וִירַנְּנוּ לְאֻמִּים כִּי־תִשְׁפֹּט עַמִּים מִישֹׁר וּלְאֻמִּים בָּאָרֶץ תַּנְחֵם סֶלָה. יוֹדוּךָ עַמִּים אֱלֹהִים יוֹדוּךָ עַמִּים כֻּלָּם. אֶרֶץ נָתְנָה יְבוּלָהּ יְבָרְכֵנוּ אֱלֹהִים אֱלֹהֵינוּ. יְבָרְכֵנוּ אֱלֹהִים וְיִירְאוּ אוֹתוֹ כָּל־אַפְסֵי־אָרֶץ.

אָנָּא, בְּכֹחַ גְּדֻלַּת יְמִינְךָ, תַּתִּיר צְרוּרָה.
קַבֵּל רִנַּת עַמְּךָ, שַׂגְּבֵנוּ, טַהֲרֵנוּ, נוֹרָא.
נָא גִבּוֹר, דּוֹרְשֵׁי יִחוּדְךָ, כְּבָבַת שָׁמְרֵם.
בָּרְכֵם, טַהֲרֵם, רַחֲמֵם, צִדְקָתְךָ תָּמִיד גָּמְלֵם.
חֲסִין קָדוֹשׁ, בְּרוֹב טוּבְךָ נַהֵל עֲדָתֶךָ.
יָחִיד גֵּאֶה, לְעַמְּךָ פְּנֵה, זוֹכְרֵי קְדֻשָּׁתֶךָ.
שַׁוְעָתֵנוּ קַבֵּל וּשְׁמַע צַעֲקָתֵנוּ, יוֹדֵעַ תַּעֲלֻמוֹת.
בָּרוּךְ שֵׁם כְּבוֹד מַלְכוּתוֹ לְעוֹלָם וָעֶד.

רִבּוֹן הָעוֹלָמִים, אַתָּה צִוִּיתָנוּ עַל יְדֵי מֹשֶׁה עַבְדְּךָ לִסְפּוֹר סְפִירַת הָעֹמֶר, כְּדֵי לְטַהֲרֵנוּ מִטֻּמְאוֹתֵינוּ, כְּמוֹ שֶׁנֶּאֱמַר: וּסְפַרְתֶּם לָכֶם מִמָּחֳרַת הַשַּׁבָּת מִיּוֹם הֲבִיאֲכֶם אֶת עֹמֶר הַתְּנוּפָה, שֶׁבַע שַׁבָּתוֹת תְּמִימֹת תִּהְיֶינָה. עַד מִמָּחֳרַת הַשַּׁבָּת הַשְּׁבִיעִת תִּסְפְּרוּ חֲמִשִּׁים יוֹם. כְּדֵי שֶׁיִּטָּהֲרוּ נַפְשׁוֹת עַמְּךָ יִשְׂרָאֵל מִזֻּהֲמָתָם. בְּכֵן יְהִי רָצוֹן מִלְּפָנֶיךָ יהוה אֱלֹהֵינוּ וֵאלֹהֵי אֲבוֹתֵינוּ, שֶׁבִּזְכוּת הַסְּפִירָה שֶׁסָּפַרְתִּי, יְתֻקַּן כָּל־מַה שֶּׁפָּגַמְתִּי וְאֶטָּהֵר וְאֶתְקַדֵּשׁ בִּקְדֻשָּׁה שֶׁל־מַעְלָה, אָמֵן סֶלָה.

לַמְנַצֵּחַ *Psalm 67*: Selected to be said at this time because the Psalm (excluding the first verse, which is a superscription and not part of the Psalm itself) contains forty-nine words, corresponding to the days of the counting of the Omer.

אָנָּא, בְּכֹחַ *Please, by the power*: A hymn in seven lines, each of six words, whose initial letters spell out a mystical 42-letter name of God. It is attributed to Rabbi Nechunya ben ha-Kanah (second half of the first century CE).

הָרַחֲמָן May the compassionate One restore the Temple service to its place. May it be Your will, LORD our GOD and GOD of our ancestors, that the Temple be rebuilt speedily in our days, and grant us a share in Your Torah. And there we will serve You with reverence, as in the days of old and as in former years.

PSALM 67

Some add the following:

לַמְנַצֵּחַ For the director of music. With stringed instruments. A psalm. A song. May GOD be gracious to us and bless us. May He make His face shine on us, Selah. Then will Your way be known on earth, Your salvation among all the nations. Let the peoples praise You, GOD; let all peoples praise You. Let nations rejoice and sing for joy, for You judge the peoples with equity, and guide the nations of the earth, Selah. Let the peoples praise You, GOD; let all peoples praise You. The earth has yielded its harvest. May GOD, our GOD, bless us. GOD will bless us, and all the ends of the earth will fear Him.

אָנָּא Please, by the power of Your great right hand, set the captive nation free.
Accept Your people's prayer. Strengthen us, purify us, You who are revered.
Please, mighty One, guard like the pupil of the eye those who seek Your unity.
Bless them, cleanse them, have compassion on them, grant them your righteousness always.
Mighty One, holy One, in Your great goodness guide Your congregation.
Only One, Exalted One, turn to Your people, who proclaim Your holiness.
Accept our plea and heed our cry, You who know all secret thoughts.
Blessed be the name of His glorious kingdom for ever and all time.

רִבּוֹן הָעוֹלָמִים Master of the Universe, You command us through Your servant Moses to count the Omer, to cleanse our impurities, as You have written in Your Torah: 'You shall count seven complete weeks from the day following the [Passover] rest day, when you brought the Omer as a wave offering. To the day after the seventh week, you shall count fifty days.' This is so that the souls of Your people Israel may be purified from their uncleanliness. May it also be Your will, LORD our GOD and GOD of our ancestors, that by the merit of this counting the Omer, any defect on my part may be repaired. May I be cleansed and sanctified with Your holiness on high. Amen. Selah.

רִבּוֹן הָעוֹלָמִים *Master of the Universe*: a prayer emphasising the idea that the counting of the Omer is a time of spiritual purification

סדר קריאת שמע על המטה

If מעריב was said before nightfall, then complete
the full three paragraphs of שמע on page 204 and 206:

בָּרוּךְ אַתָּה יהוה אֱלֹהֵינוּ מֶלֶךְ הָעוֹלָם. הַמַּפִּיל חֶבְלֵי שֵׁנָה עַל־עֵינַי וּתְנוּמָה עַל־עַפְעַפָּי. וִיהִי רָצוֹן מִלְּפָנֶיךָ יהוה אֱלֹהַי וֵאלֹהֵי אֲבוֹתַי שֶׁתַּשְׁכִּיבֵנִי לְשָׁלוֹם וְתַעֲמִידֵנִי לְשָׁלוֹם. וְאַל יְבַהֲלוּנִי רַעְיוֹנַי וַחֲלוֹמוֹת רָעִים וְהִרְהוּרִים רָעִים. וּתְהִי מִטָּתִי שְׁלֵמָה לְפָנֶיךָ. וְהָאֵר עֵינַי פֶּן־אִישַׁן הַמָּוֶת. כִּי אַתָּה הַמֵּאִיר לְאִישׁוֹן בַּת־עָיִן. בָּרוּךְ אַתָּה יהוה. הַמֵּאִיר לָעוֹלָם כֻּלּוֹ בִּכְבוֹדוֹ.

אֵל מֶלֶךְ נֶאֱמָן.

Cover the eyes with the right hand while saying the following verse:

דברים ו:ד–ט

שְׁמַע יִשְׂרָאֵל יהוָה אֱלֹהֵינוּ יהוָה | אֶחָד:

Quietly:

בָּרוּךְ שֵׁם כְּבוֹד מַלְכוּתוֹ לְעוֹלָם וָעֶד.

וְאָהַבְתָּ אֵת יהוה אֱלֹהֶיךָ בְּכָל־לְבָבְךָ וּבְכָל־נַפְשְׁךָ וּבְכָל־מְאֹדֶךָ: וְהָיוּ הַדְּבָרִים הָאֵלֶּה אֲשֶׁר אָנֹכִי מְצַוְּךָ הַיּוֹם עַל־לְבָבֶךָ: וְשִׁנַּנְתָּם לְבָנֶיךָ וְדִבַּרְתָּ בָּם בְּשִׁבְתְּךָ בְּבֵיתֶךָ וּבְלֶכְתְּךָ בַדֶּרֶךְ וּבְשָׁכְבְּךָ וּבְקוּמֶךָ: וּקְשַׁרְתָּם לְאוֹת עַל־יָדֶךָ וְהָיוּ לְטֹטָפֹת בֵּין עֵינֶיךָ: וּכְתַבְתָּם עַל־מְזֻזוֹת בֵּיתֶךָ וּבִשְׁעָרֶיךָ:

וִיהִי נֹעַם אֲדֹנָי אֱלֹהֵינוּ עָלֵינוּ וּמַעֲשֵׂה יָדֵינוּ כּוֹנְנָה עָלֵינוּ וּמַעֲשֵׂה יָדֵינוּ כּוֹנְנֵהוּ.

PRAYERS BEFORE SLEEP AT NIGHT
Just as our first words in the morning should be words of prayer, so should our last at night. The night prayers consist of: 1. a prayer for peaceful sleep and a safe awakening, mentioned in the Talmud (*Berachot* 60b); 2. the first paragraph of the *Shema*, ensuring these words are with us "when we lie down"; 3. Psalm 91, a prayer for protection from danger;

PRAYERS BEFORE SLEEP AT NIGHT

If Ma'ariv was said before nightfall, then complete the full three paragraphs of Shema on page 204 and 206.

בָּרוּךְ Blessed are You, LORD our GOD, King of the Universe, who makes the bonds of sleep fall on my eyes, and slumber on my eyelids. May it be Your will, LORD my GOD and GOD of my fathers, that You make me lie down in peace and arise in peace. Let not my imagination, bad dreams or troubling thoughts disturb me. May my bed be flawless before You. Enlighten my eyes lest I sleep the sleep of death, for it is You who illuminate the pupil of the eye. Blessed are You, LORD, who gives light to the whole world in His glory.

GOD, faithful King!

Cover the eyes with the right hand while saying the following verse:

DEUTERONOMY 6:4–9

Listen, Israel, the LORD is our GOD, the LORD is One.

Quietly:

Blessed be the name of His glorious kingdom for ever and ever.

וְאָהַבְתָּ Love the LORD your GOD with all your heart, with all your soul, and with all your might. These words which I command you today shall be on your heart. Teach them repeatedly to your children, speaking of them when you sit at home and when you travel on the way, when you lie down and when you rise. Bind them as a sign on your hand, and they shall be an emblem between your eyes. Write them on the doorposts of your house and gates.

וִיהִי May the pleasantness of the LORD our GOD be upon us. Establish for us the work of our hands, O establish the work of our hands.

---

4. Psalm 3, chosen because of its reference to night: "I lie down to sleep and I wake again, for the LORD supports me"; 5. *Help us lie down* – three paragraphs from the evening service; 6. *May the angel who rescued me from all harm*, a series of biblical verses about safety and security; 7. A verse about angels, based on "The LORD's angel encamps around those who fear Him, and He rescues them" (Psalm 34:8) and "He will command His angels about you, to guard you in all your ways" (Psalm

תהלים צא

יֹשֵׁב בְּסֵתֶר עֶלְיוֹן, בְּצֵל שַׁדַּי יִתְלוֹנָן. אֹמַר לַיהוה מַחְסִי וּמְצוּדָתִי, אֱלֹהַי אֶבְטַח־בּוֹ. כִּי הוּא יַצִּילְךָ מִפַּח יָקוּשׁ, מִדֶּבֶר הַוּוֹת. בְּאֶבְרָתוֹ יָסֶךְ לָךְ, וְתַחַת כְּנָפָיו תֶּחְסֶה, צִנָּה וְסֹחֵרָה אֲמִתּוֹ. לֹא־תִירָא מִפַּחַד לָיְלָה, מֵחֵץ יָעוּף יוֹמָם. מִדֶּבֶר בָּאֹפֶל יַהֲלֹךְ, מִקֶּטֶב יָשׁוּד צָהֳרָיִם. יִפֹּל מִצִּדְּךָ אֶלֶף, וּרְבָבָה מִימִינֶךָ, אֵלֶיךָ לֹא יִגָּשׁ. רַק בְּעֵינֶיךָ תַבִּיט, וְשִׁלֻּמַת רְשָׁעִים תִּרְאֶה. כִּי־אַתָּה יהוה מַחְסִי, עֶלְיוֹן שַׂמְתָּ מְעוֹנֶךָ. לֹא־תְאֻנֶּה אֵלֶיךָ רָעָה, וְנֶגַע לֹא־יִקְרַב בְּאָהֳלֶךָ. כִּי מַלְאָכָיו יְצַוֶּה־לָּךְ, לִשְׁמָרְךָ בְּכָל־דְּרָכֶיךָ. עַל־כַּפַּיִם יִשָּׂאוּנְךָ, פֶּן תִּגֹּף בָּאֶבֶן רַגְלֶךָ. עַל־שַׁחַל וָפֶתֶן תִּדְרֹךְ, תִּרְמֹס כְּפִיר וְתַנִּין. כִּי בִי חָשַׁק וַאֲפַלְּטֵהוּ, אֲשַׂגְּבֵהוּ כִּי־יָדַע שְׁמִי. יִקְרָאֵנִי וְאֶעֱנֵהוּ, עִמּוֹ אָנֹכִי בְצָרָה, אֲחַלְּצֵהוּ וַאֲכַבְּדֵהוּ. אֹרֶךְ יָמִים אַשְׂבִּיעֵהוּ, וְאַרְאֵהוּ בִּישׁוּעָתִי. אֹרֶךְ יָמִים אַשְׂבִּיעֵהוּ, וְאַרְאֵהוּ בִּישׁוּעָתִי.

תהלים ג:ב–ט

יהוה מָה־רַבּוּ צָרָי, רַבִּים קָמִים עָלָי. רַבִּים אֹמְרִים לְנַפְשִׁי, אֵין יְשׁוּעָתָה לּוֹ בֵאלֹהִים סֶלָה. וְאַתָּה יהוה מָגֵן בַּעֲדִי, כְּבוֹדִי וּמֵרִים רֹאשִׁי. קוֹלִי אֶל־יהוה אֶקְרָא, וַיַּעֲנֵנִי מֵהַר קָדְשׁוֹ סֶלָה. אֲנִי שָׁכַבְתִּי וָאִישָׁנָה, הֱקִיצוֹתִי, כִּי יהוה יִסְמְכֵנִי. לֹא־אִירָא מֵרִבְבוֹת עָם, אֲשֶׁר סָבִיב שָׁתוּ עָלָי. קוּמָה יהוה, הוֹשִׁיעֵנִי אֱלֹהַי, כִּי־הִכִּיתָ אֶת־כָּל־אֹיְבַי לֶחִי, שִׁנֵּי רְשָׁעִים שִׁבַּרְתָּ. לַיהוה הַיְשׁוּעָה, עַל־עַמְּךָ בִרְכָתֶךָ סֶּלָה.

הַשְׁכִּיבֵנוּ יהוה אֱלֹהֵינוּ לְשָׁלוֹם, וְהַעֲמִידֵנוּ מַלְכֵּנוּ לְחַיִּים, וּפְרוֹשׂ עָלֵינוּ סֻכַּת שְׁלוֹמֶךָ, וְתַקְּנֵנוּ בְּעֵצָה טוֹבָה מִלְּפָנֶיךָ, וְהוֹשִׁיעֵנוּ לְמַעַן שְׁמֶךָ, וְהָגֵן בַּעֲדֵנוּ, וְהָסֵר מֵעָלֵינוּ אוֹיֵב, דֶּבֶר, וְחֶרֶב, וְרָעָב, וְיָגוֹן, וְהָסֵר שָׂטָן מִלְּפָנֵינוּ וּמֵאַחֲרֵינוּ, וּבְצֵל כְּנָפֶיךָ

91:11); 8. Psalm 128, about work, recalling the phrase from Ecclesiastes (5:11), "Sweet is the sleep of one who labours"; 9. *Tremble, and do not sin*, from Psalm

PSALM 91

יֹשֵׁב He who lives in the shelter of the Most High dwells in the shadow of the Almighty. I say of GOD, my refuge and stronghold, my LORD in whom I trust, that He will save you from the fowler's snare and the deadly pestilence. With His pinions He will cover you, and beneath His wings you will find shelter; His faithfulness is an encircling shield. You need not fear terror by night, nor the arrow that flies by day; not the pestilence that stalks in darkness, nor the plague that ravages at noon. A thousand may fall at your side, ten thousand at your right hand, but it will not come near you. You will only look with your eyes and see the punishment of the wicked. Because you said, "GOD is my refuge", taking the Most High as your shelter, no harm will befall you, no plague come near your tent, for He will command His angels about you, to guard you in all your ways. They will lift you in their hands, lest your foot stumble on a stone. You will tread on lions and vipers; you will trample on young lions and snakes. [GOD says:] "Because he loves Me, I will rescue him; I will protect him, because he acknowledges My name. When he calls on Me, I will answer him; I will be with him in distress, I will deliver him and bring him honour. With long life I will satisfy him and show him My salvation. With long life I will satisfy him and show him My salvation.

PSALM 3: 2–9

יהוה LORD, how numerous are my enemies, how many rise against me. Many say of me: "There is no help for him in GOD", Selah. But You, LORD, are a shield around me. You are my glory; You raise my head high. I cry aloud to the LORD, and He answers me from His holy mountain, Selah. I lie down to sleep and I wake again, for the LORD supports me. I will not fear the myriad forces ranged against me on all sides. Arise, LORD, save me, O my GOD; strike all my enemies across the cheek; break the teeth of the wicked. From the LORD comes deliverance; may Your blessing rest upon Your people, Selah.

הַשְׁכִּיבֵנוּ Help us lie down, O LORD our GOD, in peace, and rise up, O our King, to life. Spread over us Your canopy of peace. Direct us with Your good counsel, and save us for the sake of Your name. Shield us and

---

4:5, mentioned in the Talmud (*Berachot* 4b) as an appropriate verse before sleep; and 10. *Adon Olam*, said here because of its closing lines with their reference to entrusting our souls and bodies to GOD's safekeeping at night.

תַּסְתִּירֵנוּ, כִּי אֵל שׁוֹמְרֵנוּ וּמַצִּילֵנוּ אָתָּה, כִּי אֵל מֶלֶךְ חַנּוּן וְרַחוּם אָתָּה. וּשְׁמוֹר צֵאתֵנוּ וּבוֹאֵנוּ, לְחַיִּים וּלְשָׁלוֹם מֵעַתָּה וְעַד עוֹלָם.

בָּרוּךְ יהוה בַּיּוֹם, בָּרוּךְ יהוה בַּלָּיְלָה. בָּרוּךְ יהוה בְּשָׁכְבֵנוּ. בָּרוּךְ יהוה בְּקוּמֵנוּ. כִּי בְיָדְךָ נַפְשׁוֹת הַחַיִּים וְהַמֵּתִים. אֲשֶׁר בְּיָדוֹ נֶפֶשׁ כָּל־חָי, וְרוּחַ כָּל־בְּשַׂר־אִישׁ. בְּיָדְךָ אַפְקִיד רוּחִי, פָּדִיתָה אוֹתִי, יהוה אֵל אֱמֶת. אֱלֹהֵינוּ שֶׁבַּשָּׁמַיִם יַחֵד שִׁמְךָ, וְקַיֵּם מַלְכוּתְךָ תָּמִיד, וּמְלוֹךְ עָלֵינוּ לְעוֹלָם וָעֶד.

יִרְאוּ עֵינֵינוּ וְיִשְׂמַח לִבֵּנוּ וְתָגֵל נַפְשֵׁנוּ בִּישׁוּעָתְךָ בֶּאֱמֶת בֶּאֱמוֹר לְצִיּוֹן מָלַךְ אֱלֹהָיִךְ. יהוה מֶלֶךְ, יהוה מָלָךְ, יהוה יִמְלוֹךְ לְעוֹלָם וָעֶד. כִּי הַמַּלְכוּת שֶׁלְּךָ הִיא וּלְעוֹלְמֵי עַד תִּמְלוֹךְ בְּכָבוֹד כִּי אֵין לָנוּ מֶלֶךְ אֶלָּא אָתָּה.

הַמַּלְאָךְ הַגֹּאֵל אֹתִי מִכָּל־רָע יְבָרֵךְ אֶת־הַנְּעָרִים, וְיִקָּרֵא בָהֶם שְׁמִי, וְשֵׁם אֲבֹתַי אַבְרָהָם וְיִצְחָק, וְיִדְגּוּ לָרֹב בְּקֶרֶב הָאָרֶץ. וַיֹּאמֶר, אִם־שָׁמוֹעַ תִּשְׁמַע לְקוֹל יהוה אֱלֹהֶיךָ, וְהַיָּשָׁר בְּעֵינָיו תַּעֲשֶׂה, וְהַאֲזַנְתָּ לְמִצְוֹתָיו, וְשָׁמַרְתָּ כָּל־חֻקָּיו, כָּל־הַמַּחֲלָה אֲשֶׁר־שַׂמְתִּי בְמִצְרַיִם לֹא־אָשִׂים עָלֶיךָ, כִּי אֲנִי יהוה רֹפְאֶךָ. וַיֹּאמֶר יהוה אֶל הַשָּׂטָן, יִגְעַר יהוה בְּךָ הַשָּׂטָן, וְיִגְעַר יהוה בְּךָ הַבֹּחֵר בִּירוּשָׁלָםִ, הֲלוֹא זֶה אוּד מֻצָּל מֵאֵשׁ. הִנֵּה מִטָּתוֹ שֶׁלִּשְׁלֹמֹה, שִׁשִּׁים גִּבֹּרִים סָבִיב לָהּ, מִגִּבֹּרֵי יִשְׂרָאֵל. כֻּלָּם אֲחֻזֵי חֶרֶב, מְלֻמְּדֵי מִלְחָמָה, אִישׁ חַרְבּוֹ עַל־יְרֵכוֹ מִפַּחַד בַּלֵּילוֹת.

יְבָרֶכְךָ יהוה וְיִשְׁמְרֶךָ. יָאֵר יהוה פָּנָיו אֵלֶיךָ וִיחֻנֶּךָּ. יִשָּׂא יהוה פָּנָיו אֵלֶיךָ, וְיָשֵׂם לְךָ שָׁלוֹם.

Say three times:

הִנֵּה לֹא יָנוּם וְלֹא יִישָׁן, שׁוֹמֵר יִשְׂרָאֵל.

remove from us every enemy, plague, sword, famine and sorrow. Remove the adversary from before and behind us. Shelter us in the shadow of Your wings, for You, God, are our Guardian and Deliverer; You, God, are a gracious and compassionate King. Guard our going out and our coming in, for life and peace, from now and for ever.

בָּרוּךְ Blessed is the Lord by day, blessed is the Lord by night. Blessed is the Lord when we lie down; blessed is the Lord when we rise. For in Your hand are the souls of the living and the dead, [as it is written:] "In His hand is every living soul, and the breath of all mankind." Into Your hand I entrust my spirit: You redeemed me, Lord, God of truth. Our God in heaven, bring unity to Your name, establish Your kingdom constantly and reign over us for ever and all time.

יִרְאוּ May our eyes see, our hearts rejoice, and our souls be glad in Your true salvation, when Zion is told, "Your God reigns". The Lord is King, the Lord was King, and the Lord will be King for ever and all time. For sovereignty is Yours, and to all eternity You will reign in glory, for we have no king but You.

הַמַּלְאָךְ May the angel who rescued me from all harm, bless these boys. May they be called by my name and the names of my fathers Abraham and Isaac, and may they increase greatly on the earth. He said, "If you listen carefully to the voice of the Lord your God and do what is right in His eyes, if you pay attention to His commandments and keep all His statutes, I will not bring on you any of the diseases I brought on the Egyptians, for I am the Lord who heals you." The Lord said to the accuser, "The Lord shall rebuke you, accuser. The Lord who has chosen Jerusalem shall rebuke you! Is not this man a burning stick snatched from the fire?" Look! It is Solomon's bed, escorted by sixty warriors, the noblest of Israel, all of them wearing the sword, experienced in battle, each with his sword at his side, prepared for the terrors of the night.

יְבָרֶכְךָ May the Lord bless you and protect you. May the Lord make His face shine on you and be gracious to you. May the Lord turn His face toward you and give you peace.

Say three times:

הִנֵּה See – the Guardian of Israel neither slumbers nor sleeps.

Say three times:

לִישׁוּעָתְךָ קִוִּיתִי יהוה. קִוִּיתִי יהוה לִישׁוּעָתְךָ. יהוה לִישׁוּעָתְךָ קִוִּיתִי.

Say three times:

בְּשֵׁם יהוה אֱלֹהֵי יִשְׂרָאֵל, מִימִינִי מִיכָאֵל, וּמִשְּׂמֹאלִי גַּבְרִיאֵל, וּמִלְּפָנַי אוּרִיאֵל, וּמֵאֲחוֹרַי רְפָאֵל, וְעַל רֹאשִׁי שְׁכִינַת אֵל.

תהלים קכח

שִׁיר הַמַּעֲלוֹת, אַשְׁרֵי כָּל־יְרֵא יהוה, הַהֹלֵךְ בִּדְרָכָיו. יְגִיעַ כַּפֶּיךָ כִּי תֹאכֵל, אַשְׁרֶיךָ וְטוֹב לָךְ. אֶשְׁתְּךָ כְּגֶפֶן פֹּרִיָּה בְּיַרְכְּתֵי בֵיתֶךָ, בָּנֶיךָ כִּשְׁתִלֵי זֵיתִים, סָבִיב לְשֻׁלְחָנֶךָ. הִנֵּה כִי־כֵן יְבֹרַךְ גָּבֶר יְרֵא יהוה. יְבָרֶכְךָ יהוה מִצִּיּוֹן, וּרְאֵה בְּטוּב יְרוּשָׁלָםִ, כֹּל יְמֵי חַיֶּיךָ. וּרְאֵה־בָנִים לְבָנֶיךָ, שָׁלוֹם עַל־יִשְׂרָאֵל.

Say three times:

רִגְזוּ וְאַל־תֶּחֱטָאוּ, אִמְרוּ בִלְבַבְכֶם עַל־מִשְׁכַּבְכֶם, וְדֹמּוּ סֶלָה.

אֲדוֹן עוֹלָם אֲשֶׁר מָלַךְ, בְּטֶרֶם כָּל־יְצִיר נִבְרָא.
לְעֵת נַעֲשָׂה בְחֶפְצוֹ כֹּל, אֲזַי מֶלֶךְ שְׁמוֹ נִקְרָא.
וְאַחֲרֵי כִּכְלוֹת הַכֹּל, לְבַדּוֹ יִמְלוֹךְ נוֹרָא.
וְהוּא הָיָה וְהוּא הֹוֶה, וְהוּא יִהְיֶה בְּתִפְאָרָה.
וְהוּא אֶחָד וְאֵין שֵׁנִי, לְהַמְשִׁיל לוֹ לְהַחְבִּירָה.
בְּלִי רֵאשִׁית בְּלִי תַכְלִית, וְלוֹ הָעֹז וְהַמִּשְׂרָה.
וְהוּא אֵלִי וְחַי גֹּאֲלִי, וְצוּר חֶבְלִי בְּעֵת צָרָה.
וְהוּא נִסִּי וּמָנוֹס לִי, מְנָת כּוֹסִי בְּיוֹם אֶקְרָא.
בְּיָדוֹ אַפְקִיד רוּחִי, בְּעֵת אִישַׁן וְאָעִירָה.
וְעִם־רוּחִי גְּוִיָּתִי, יהוה לִי וְלֹא אִירָא.

Say three times:

לִישׁוּעָתְךָ For Your salvation I hope, LORD. I hope, LORD, for Your salvation. LORD, for Your salvation I hope.

Say three times:

בְּשֵׁם In the name of the LORD, GOD of Israel: may Michael be at my right hand, Gabriel, at my left; in front of me, Uriel, behind me, Raphael; and above my head the Presence of GOD.

PSALM 128

שִׁיר הַמַּעֲלוֹת A song of ascents. Happy are all who fear the LORD, who walk in His ways. When you eat the fruit of your labour, happy and fortunate are you. Your wife shall be like a fruitful vine within your house; your sons like olive saplings around your table. So shall the man who fears the LORD be blessed. May the LORD bless you from Zion; may you see the good of Jerusalem all the days of your life; and may you live to see your children's children. Peace be on Israel!

Say three times:

רִגְזוּ Tremble, and do not sin. Search your heart as you lie on your bed, and be silent. Selah.

אֲדוֹן עוֹלָם LORD of the universe, who reigned
before the birth of any thing –
When by His will all things were made
then was His name proclaimed King.
And when all things shall cease to be
He alone will reign in awe.
He was, He is, and He shall be
glorious for evermore.
He is One, there is none else,
alone, unique, beyond compare;
Without beginning, without end,
His might, His rule are everywhere.
He is my GOD; my Redeemer lives.
He is the Rock on whom I rely –
My banner and my safe retreat,
my cup, my portion when I cry.
Into His hand my soul I place,
when I awake and when I sleep.
GOD is with me, I shall not fear;
body and soul from harm will He keep.

❦ תפילות לשבת ❦

Services for Shabbat

קבלת שבת

הדלקת הנרות

For יום טוב lighting, including when שבת coincides with יום טוב,
see page 645. It is a tradition to give צְדָקָה before kindling the שַׁבָּת lights.

Meditation before lighting the שַׁבָּת candles. Add the words in brackets if you have children.

רִבּוֹן הָעוֹלָמִים, הִנֵּה בָּאתִי לְהַדְלִיק אֶת הַנֵּרוֹת לִכְבוֹד הַשַּׁבָּת, כַּכָּתוּב, וְקָרָאתָ לַשַּׁבָּת עֹנֶג לִקְדוֹשׁ יהוה מְכֻבָּד. וּבִזְכוּת מִצְוָה זוֹ, תַּשְׁפִּיעַ עָלַי וְעַל בְּנֵי בֵיתִי, שֶׁפַע הַחַיִּים שֶׁתְּחָנֵּנוּ וּתְבָרְכֵנוּ בְּרֹב בְּרָכוֹת, וְתַשְׁכֵּן שְׁכִינָתְךָ בְּתוֹכֵנוּ.

אַב הָרַחֲמִים, אָנָּא מְשֹׁךְ חַסְדְּךָ עָלַי וְעַל קְרוֹבַי הָאֲהוּבִים (וְזַכֵּנִי לְגַדֵּל בָּנַי וּבְנוֹתַי) לָלֶכֶת בְּדַרְכֵי יְשָׁרִים לְפָנֶיךָ, דְּבֵקִים בַּתּוֹרָה, וּבְמַעֲשִׂים טוֹבִים. הַרְחֵק מֵעָלֵינוּ כָּל חֶרְפָּה, תּוּגָה, וְיָגוֹן, וְשִׂים שָׁלוֹם אוֹרָה וְשִׂמְחָה בִּמְעוֹנֵנוּ, כִּי עִמְּךָ מְקוֹר חַיִּים, בְּאוֹרְךָ נִרְאֶה־אוֹר, אָמֵן.

Cover the eyes with the hands after lighting the candles, and say:

בָּרוּךְ אַתָּה יהוה אֱלֹהֵינוּ מֶלֶךְ הָעוֹלָם, אֲשֶׁר קִדְּשָׁנוּ בְּמִצְוֹתָיו, וְצִוָּנוּ לְהַדְלִיק נֵר שֶׁל שַׁבָּת.

CANDLE LIGHTING

Lighting candles is a positive rabbinic commandment, symbolising *shalom bayit*, domestic peace. By creating peace in the home, we are helping to make peace in the world.

The Shabbat candles also symbolise the light of the Divine presence, which illuminates relationships within the home. Rabbi Akiva noted that the Hebrew words for man (*ish*) and woman (*ishah*) both contain the letters of *esh*, "fire". Each contains one extra letter – *yod* in the case of man, *heh* in the case of woman, and these two letters together spell one of the names of God. He concluded: "When husband and wife are worthy, the Divine presence dwells between them" (*Sotah* 17a).

The ancient custom is for women to perform this commandment since they are the primary guardians of the home. Our custom is to light two candles, representing the two dimensions

WELCOMING SHABBAT

CANDLE LIGHTING

For Yom Tov candle lighting, including when Shabbat coincides with Yom Tov, see page 645. It is a tradition to give money to charity before kindling the Shabbat lights.

Meditation before lighting the Shabbat candles. Add the words in brackets if you have children.

רִבּוֹן Master of the Universe: I am about to fulfil the commandment of lighting lights in honour of the Sabbath, as it is written: "You shall call the Sabbath a delight, the holy day of the Lord, a day to be honoured". In the merit of this commandment, may You bestow on me and my family a full life. Be gracious to us. May You bless us with many blessings, and cause Your Presence to dwell among us.

אַב Compassionate Father, extend Your lovingkindness to me and my loved ones (and grant me the privilege of raising my children) so that they walk before You in the ways of the upright, holding fast to Your Torah and to good deeds. Keep far from us any shame, grief and sorrow. Set peace, light and joy in our home, for with You is the source of life; in Your light, we see light. Amen.

Cover the eyes with the hands after lighting the candles, and say:

בָּרוּךְ Blessed are You, Lord our God, King of the Universe, who has made us holy through His commandments, and has commanded us to light the Sabbath light.

---

of Shabbat: *shamor*, "guarding", observing the prohibitions of Shabbat, and *zachor*, "remembering", keeping its positive commandments.

Normally we make a blessing over a commandment *before* performing it. In the case of Shabbat lights, however, the blessing is made afterward, so that the lighting precedes mental acceptance of the day and its prohibitions. The blessing is made while covering one's eyes, so that the blessing follows the act but precedes its benefit. It is also customary at this point to say a prayer for the welfare of one's family that their lives may be illuminated by the Torah and its teachings.

WELCOMING SHABBAT

Already in Talmudic times Shabbat was seen as a bride, and the day itself as a wedding. "Rabbi Chanina robed himself and stood on the eve of Shabbat at sunset and said, 'Come, let us go and welcome Shabbat the queen.' Rabbi Yannai donned his robes and said, 'Come O bride, come O bride'" (*Shabbat* 119a).

Many congregations sing the following before קַבָּלַת שַׁבָּת:

ידיד נפש

יְדִיד נֶפֶשׁ, אָב הָרַחֲמָן, מְשֹׁךְ עַבְדְּךָ אֶל רְצוֹנָךְ,
יָרוּץ עַבְדְּךָ כְּמוֹ אַיָּל, יִשְׁתַּחֲוֶה מוּל הֲדָרָךְ,
כִּי יֶעֱרַב לוֹ יְדִידוּתָךְ, מִנֹּפֶת צוּף וְכָל טָעַם.

הָדוּר, נָאֶה, זִיו הָעוֹלָם, נַפְשִׁי חוֹלַת אַהֲבָתָךְ,
אָנָּא, אֵל נָא, רְפָא נָא לָהּ, בְּהַרְאוֹת לָהּ נֹעַם זִיוָךְ,
אָז תִּתְחַזֵּק וְתִתְרַפֵּא, וְהָיְתָה לָךְ שִׁפְחַת עוֹלָם.

וָתִיק, יֶהֱמוּ רַחֲמֶיךָ, וְחוּס נָא עַל בֵּן אוֹהֲבָךְ,
כִּי זֶה כַּמֶּה נִכְסֹף נִכְסַף לִרְאוֹת בְּתִפְאֶרֶת עֻזָּךְ,
אָנָּא, אֵלִי, מַחְמַד לִבִּי, חְוּשָׁה נָּא, וְאַל תִּתְעַלָּם.

הִגָּלֵה נָא וּפְרֹשׂ, חָבִיב, עָלַי אֶת סֻכַּת שְׁלוֹמָךְ,
תָּאִיר אֶרֶץ מִכְּבוֹדָךְ, נָגִילָה וְנִשְׂמְחָה בָךְ.
מַהֵר, אָהוּב, כִּי בָא מוֹעֵד, וְחָנֵּנִי כִּימֵי עוֹלָם.

In the late sixteenth century, this idea was developed with fresh intensity by a remarkable group of Jewish mystics in Tzefat. They included Rabbi Moses Cordovero who developed the custom of saying special psalms to greet the incoming Shabbat; his brother-in-law Rabbi Shlomo Alkabets, composer of the song *Lecha Dodi*; Rabbi Eliezer Azikri, author of *Yedid Nefesh*; and Rabbi Isaac Luria, greatest of the Tzefat mystics, whose thought brought new depth to our understanding of prayer and observance of Shabbat as acts that help heal the spiritual fractures of the world.

By the twelfth century, the custom existed to say Psalm 92 as a song of welcome to Shabbat. The Tzefat kabbalists did more. Dressed in white, they would go out into the fields as the sun set, singing psalms and songs to the Shabbat bride. That is the origin of the six extra psalms we say (95–99, 29) prior to *Lecha Dodi*. A further reminder of the original custom is our practice of turning round to face West at the last verse of the song, facing, as they did, the setting sun, to welcome the incoming bride. To emphasise the non-statutory character of *Kabbalat Shabbat*, in some synagogues

Many congregations sing the following before the Welcoming Shabbat Service:

YEDID NEFESH

י Beloved of the soul, Father of compassion,
draw Your servant close to Your will.
Like a deer will Your servant run
and fall prostrate before Your beauty.
To him Your love is sweeter
than honey from the comb, than any taste.

ה Glorious, beautiful, radiance of the world,
my soul is sick with love for You.
Please, God, heal her now
by showing her Your tender radiance.
Then she will recover her strength and be healed,
Be Your servant for eternity.

ו Ancient of Days, let Your mercy be aroused;
please have pity on Your beloved child.
How long have I yearned
to see the glory of Your strength.
Please, my God, my heart's desire –
hasten; do not hide Yourself.

ה Reveal Yourself, beloved, and spread over me
the tabernacle of Your peace.
Let the earth shine with Your glory,
let us be overjoyed and rejoice in You.
Hurry, beloved, for the appointed time has come,
and be gracious to me as in the times of old.

---

the custom is for the Reader to recite it from the reading desk rather than the usual prayer lectern.

יְדִיד נֶפֶשׁ *Beloved of the soul*: A song of passionate intensity, composed by the Tzefat kabbalist Rabbi Eliezer Azikri. In language reminiscent of The Song of Songs, it speaks of Israel's love of God. *Do not hide Yourself* in exile. *The appointed time* of redemption. The initial letters of the four verses spell God's holiest name.

On יוֹם טוֹב or שַׁבָּת חוֹל הַמּוֹעֵד or on the evening immediately after יוֹם טוֹב, the service begins with מִזְמוֹר שִׁיר on page 270. On יוֹם טוֹב falling on a weekday, the service begins with בָּרְכוּ on page 274.

Mourners during the week of שִׁבְעָה leave the synagogue at this point, returning after לְכָה דוֹדִי on page 270.

תהלים צה

לְכוּ נְרַנְּנָה לַיהוה, נָרִיעָה לְצוּר יִשְׁעֵנוּ. נְקַדְּמָה פָנָיו בְּתוֹדָה, בִּזְמִרוֹת נָרִיעַ לוֹ. כִּי אֵל גָּדוֹל יהוה, וּמֶלֶךְ גָּדוֹל עַל־כָּל־אֱלֹהִים. אֲשֶׁר בְּיָדוֹ מֶחְקְרֵי־אָרֶץ, וְתוֹעֲפוֹת הָרִים לוֹ. אֲשֶׁר־לוֹ הַיָּם וְהוּא עָשָׂהוּ, וְיַבֶּשֶׁת יָדָיו יָצָרוּ. בֹּאוּ נִשְׁתַּחֲוֶה וְנִכְרָעָה, נִבְרְכָה לִפְנֵי־יהוה עֹשֵׂנוּ. כִּי הוּא אֱלֹהֵינוּ וַאֲנַחְנוּ עַם מַרְעִיתוֹ וְצֹאן יָדוֹ, הַיּוֹם אִם־בְּקֹלוֹ תִשְׁמָעוּ. אַל־תַּקְשׁוּ לְבַבְכֶם כִּמְרִיבָה, כְּיוֹם מַסָּה בַּמִּדְבָּר. אֲשֶׁר נִסּוּנִי אֲבוֹתֵיכֶם, בְּחָנוּנִי גַּם רָאוּ פָעֳלִי. ← אַרְבָּעִים שָׁנָה אָקוּט בְּדוֹר, וָאֹמַר עַם תֹּעֵי לֵבָב הֵם, וְהֵם לֹא־יָדְעוּ דְרָכָי. אֲשֶׁר־נִשְׁבַּעְתִּי בְאַפִּי, אִם־יְבֹאוּן אֶל מְנוּחָתִי.

תהלים צו

שִׁירוּ לַיהוה שִׁיר חָדָשׁ, שִׁירוּ לַיהוה כָּל־הָאָרֶץ. שִׁירוּ לַיהוה בָּרְכוּ שְׁמוֹ, בַּשְּׂרוּ מִיּוֹם־לְיוֹם יְשׁוּעָתוֹ. סַפְּרוּ בַגּוֹיִם כְּבוֹדוֹ, בְּכָל־הָעַמִּים נִפְלְאוֹתָיו. כִּי גָדוֹל יהוה וּמְהֻלָּל מְאֹד, נוֹרָא הוּא עַל־כָּל־אֱלֹהִים. כִּי כָּל־אֱלֹהֵי הָעַמִּים אֱלִילִים, וַיהוה שָׁמַיִם עָשָׂה. הוֹד־וְהָדָר לְפָנָיו, עֹז וְתִפְאֶרֶת בְּמִקְדָּשׁוֹ. הָבוּ לַיהוה מִשְׁפְּחוֹת עַמִּים, הָבוּ לַיהוה כָּבוֹד

לְכוּ נְרַנְּנָה *Psalm 95.* The six psalms said before *Lecha Dodi* represent the six days of the week. The first five appear sequentially in the Book of Psalms (95–99). They speak of the song creation sings to its Creator. These are followed by Psalm 29, understood by some as a description of the Giving of the Torah at Mount Sinai. *Lecha Dodi* looks forward to future redemption, and Psalms 92 and 93 envision the end of days. Thus the entire sequence is structured around the movement from creation to revelation to redemption. *Come, let us sing for joy*: The Psalmist calls on the

On a Festival or its intermediate Shabbat, or on the evening immediately after a Festival, the service begins with Psalm 92 on page 271. On Festivals falling on a weekday, the service begins with "Bless the Lord" on page 275.

Mourners during the week of *shivah* leave the synagogue at this point, returning after "Come, my beloved" on page 271.

PSALM 95

לְכוּ נְרַנְּנָה Come, let us sing for joy to the Lord, let us shout aloud to the Rock of our salvation. Let us greet Him with thanksgiving, shout aloud to Him with songs of praise. For the Lord is the great God, the King great above all powers. In His hand are the depths of the earth, and the mountain peaks are His. The sea is His, for He made it; the dry land too, for His hands formed it. Come, let us bow in worship and bend the knee before the Lord our Maker. For He is our God, and we are the people of His pasture, the flock He tends – today, if you would heed His voice. Do not harden your hearts as you did at Merivah, as you did that day at Massah in the desert, when your ancestors tested and tried Me though they had seen My deeds. ➢ For forty years I strove with that generation. I said, "They are a people whose hearts go astray, who have not understood My ways." So I swore in My anger, "They shall not enter My place of rest."

PSALM 96

שִׁירוּ Sing to the Lord a new song; sing to the Lord all the earth. Sing to the Lord, bless His name; proclaim his deliverance day after day. Declare His glory among the nations, His marvels among all peoples. For great is the Lord and greatly to be praised; He is awesome beyond all heavenly powers. For all the gods of the peoples are mere idols: it was the Lord who made the heavens. Before Him are majesty and

---

people to serve God with joy, redeeming the sin of their ancestors who, though they had been rescued by God from slavery, were ungrateful and argumentative. *Massah and Merivah* (literally, "testing and quarrelling"), were the names given to the place where, after crossing the Reed Sea, the Israelites complained of their lack of water (Exodus 17:1–7). *For forty years*: A reference to the episode of the spies (Numbers 13–14), when the people, demoralised by their report, rebelled. Their fate was to spend forty years in the desert. The Psalmist urges the people to do the opposite: to sing to God with joy.

שִׁירוּ לַיהוה *Psalm 96. Sing to the Lord a new song*: One of the most difficult ideas

וָעֹז. הָבוּ לַיהוה כְּבוֹד שְׁמוֹ, שְׂאוּ־מִנְחָה וּבֹאוּ לְחַצְרוֹתָיו.
הִשְׁתַּחֲווּ לַיהוה בְּהַדְרַת־קֹדֶשׁ, חִילוּ מִפָּנָיו כָּל־הָאָרֶץ.
אִמְרוּ בַגּוֹיִם יהוה מָלָךְ, אַף־תִּכּוֹן תֵּבֵל בַּל־תִּמּוֹט, יָדִין
עַמִּים בְּמֵישָׁרִים. ◁ יִשְׂמְחוּ הַשָּׁמַיִם וְתָגֵל הָאָרֶץ, יִרְעַם
הַיָּם וּמְלֹאוֹ. יַעֲלֹז שָׂדַי וְכָל־אֲשֶׁר־בּוֹ, אָז יְרַנְּנוּ כָּל־עֲצֵי־
יָעַר. לִפְנֵי יהוה כִּי בָא, כִּי בָא לִשְׁפֹּט הָאָרֶץ, יִשְׁפֹּט־תֵּבֵל
בְּצֶדֶק, וְעַמִּים בֶּאֱמוּנָתוֹ.

תהלים צז

יהוה מָלָךְ תָּגֵל הָאָרֶץ, יִשְׂמְחוּ אִיִּים רַבִּים. עָנָן וַעֲרָפֶל
סְבִיבָיו, צֶדֶק וּמִשְׁפָּט מְכוֹן כִּסְאוֹ. אֵשׁ לְפָנָיו תֵּלֵךְ, וּתְלַהֵט
סָבִיב צָרָיו. הֵאִירוּ בְרָקָיו תֵּבֵל, רָאֲתָה וַתָּחֵל הָאָרֶץ. הָרִים
כַּדּוֹנַג נָמַסּוּ מִלִּפְנֵי יהוה, מִלִּפְנֵי אֲדוֹן כָּל־הָאָרֶץ. הִגִּידוּ
הַשָּׁמַיִם צִדְקוֹ, וְרָאוּ כָל־הָעַמִּים כְּבוֹדוֹ. יֵבֹשׁוּ כָּל־עֹבְדֵי
פֶסֶל הַמִּתְהַלְלִים בָּאֱלִילִים, הִשְׁתַּחֲווּ־לוֹ כָּל־אֱלֹהִים.
שָׁמְעָה וַתִּשְׂמַח צִיּוֹן וַתָּגֵלְנָה בְּנוֹת יְהוּדָה, לְמַעַן מִשְׁפָּטֶיךָ
יהוה. כִּי־אַתָּה יהוה עֶלְיוֹן עַל־כָּל־הָאָרֶץ, מְאֹד נַעֲלֵיתָ עַל־
כָּל־אֱלֹהִים. ◁ אֹהֲבֵי יהוה שִׂנְאוּ רָע, שֹׁמֵר נַפְשׁוֹת חֲסִידָיו,
מִיַּד רְשָׁעִים יַצִּילֵם. אוֹר־זָרֻעַ לַצַּדִּיק, וּלְיִשְׁרֵי־לֵב שִׂמְחָה.
שִׂמְחוּ צַדִּיקִים בַּיהוה, וְהוֹדוּ לְזֵכֶר קָדְשׁוֹ.

---

for modern minds to grasp is that the universe might sing for joy at the coming of judgement and justice. Yet we believe not only in one God, Creator of heaven and earth, but also in the inseparable connection between *cosmos* and *ethos,* the world-that-is and the world-that-ought-to-be. God not only created the universe but also *saw that it was good.* From the outset, the universe had an objective moral structure. As the natural world is governed by scientific law, so is the human world is governed by moral law. Hence creation rejoices that *He is coming to judge the earth,* that the world is governed by the rule of right rather than the rule of force.

splendour; there are strength and beauty in His holy place. Render to the LORD, O families of the peoples; render to the LORD glory and might. Render to the LORD the glory due to His name; bring an offering and come into His courts. Bow down to the LORD in the splendour of holiness. Tremble before Him, all the earth. Say among the nations, "The LORD is King." The world stands firm, it will not be shaken. He will judge the peoples with equity. ➔ Let the heavens rejoice and the earth be glad. Let the sea roar, and all that is in it; let the fields be jubilant, and all they contain. Then the trees of the forest will sing for joy before the LORD, for He is coming to judge the earth. He will judge the world with justice, and the peoples with His faithfulness.

PSALM 97

יהוה The LORD reigns, let the earth be glad. Let the many islands rejoice. Clouds and thick darkness surround him; righteousness and justice are the foundation of his throne. Fire goes ahead of Him, consuming his enemies on every side. His lightning lights up the world; the earth sees and trembles. Mountains melt like wax before the LORD, before the LORD of all the earth. The heavens proclaim His righteousness, and all the peoples see His glory. All who worship images and boast in idols are put to shame. Bow down to Him, all you heavenly powers. Zion hears and rejoices, and the towns of Judah are glad because of your judgements, LORD. For You, LORD, are supreme over all the earth; You are exalted far above all heavenly powers. ➔ Let those who love the LORD hate evil, for He protects the lives of his devoted ones, delivering them from the hand of the wicked. Light is sown for the righteous, and joy for the upright in heart. Rejoice in the LORD, you who are righteous, and praise His holy name.

יהוה מָלָךְ *Psalm 97. The LORD reigns, let the earth be glad*: GOD, Maker of the Universe, is the ultimate Sovereign. Therefore all earthly rule and exercise of power is subject to His overarching authority: "GOD reigns". History is not destined to be an endless story of the victory of might over right, the powerful over the powerless. At the heart of reality is a force that makes for justice, giving strength to the weak, and courage to the oppressed. "Light is sown for the righteous, and joy for the upright in heart."

תהלים צח

מִזְמוֹר, שִׁירוּ לַיהוה שִׁיר חָדָשׁ, כִּי־נִפְלָאוֹת עָשָׂה, הוֹשִׁיעָה־לּוֹ יְמִינוֹ וּזְרוֹעַ קָדְשׁוֹ. הוֹדִיעַ יהוה יְשׁוּעָתוֹ, לְעֵינֵי הַגּוֹיִם גִּלָּה צִדְקָתוֹ. זָכַר חַסְדּוֹ וֶאֱמוּנָתוֹ לְבֵית יִשְׂרָאֵל, רָאוּ כָל־אַפְסֵי־אָרֶץ אֵת יְשׁוּעַת אֱלֹהֵינוּ. הָרִיעוּ לַיהוה כָּל־הָאָרֶץ, פִּצְחוּ וְרַנְּנוּ וְזַמֵּרוּ. זַמְּרוּ לַיהוה בְּכִנּוֹר, בְּכִנּוֹר וְקוֹל זִמְרָה. בַּחֲצֹצְרוֹת וְקוֹל שׁוֹפָר, הָרִיעוּ לִפְנֵי הַמֶּלֶךְ יהוה. ‹ יִרְעַם הַיָּם וּמְלֹאוֹ, תֵּבֵל וְיֹשְׁבֵי בָהּ. נְהָרוֹת יִמְחֲאוּ־כָף, יַחַד הָרִים יְרַנֵּנוּ. לִפְנֵי יהוה כִּי בָא לִשְׁפֹּט הָאָרֶץ, יִשְׁפֹּט־תֵּבֵל בְּצֶדֶק, וְעַמִּים בְּמֵישָׁרִים.

תהלים צט

יהוה מָלָךְ יִרְגְּזוּ עַמִּים, יֹשֵׁב כְּרוּבִים תָּנוּט הָאָרֶץ. יהוה בְּצִיּוֹן גָּדוֹל, וְרָם הוּא עַל־כָּל־הָעַמִּים. יוֹדוּ שִׁמְךָ גָּדוֹל וְנוֹרָא קָדוֹשׁ הוּא. וְעֹז מֶלֶךְ מִשְׁפָּט אָהֵב, אַתָּה כּוֹנַנְתָּ מֵישָׁרִים, מִשְׁפָּט וּצְדָקָה בְּיַעֲקֹב אַתָּה עָשִׂיתָ. רוֹמְמוּ יהוה אֱלֹהֵינוּ, וְהִשְׁתַּחֲווּ לַהֲדֹם רַגְלָיו, קָדוֹשׁ הוּא. מֹשֶׁה וְאַהֲרֹן בְּכֹהֲנָיו, וּשְׁמוּאֵל בְּקֹרְאֵי שְׁמוֹ, קֹרְאִים אֶל יהוה וְהוּא יַעֲנֵם. ‹ בְּעַמּוּד עָנָן יְדַבֵּר אֲלֵיהֶם, שָׁמְרוּ עֵדֹתָיו וְחֹק נָתַן־לָמוֹ. יהוה אֱלֹהֵינוּ אַתָּה עֲנִיתָם, אֵל נֹשֵׂא הָיִיתָ לָהֶם, וְנֹקֵם עַל־עֲלִילוֹתָם. רוֹמְמוּ יהוה אֱלֹהֵינוּ וְהִשְׁתַּחֲווּ לְהַר קָדְשׁוֹ, כִּי קָדוֹשׁ יהוה אֱלֹהֵינוּ.

מִזְמוֹר *Psalm 98.* In this celebratory song, the Psalmist describes redemption in the vivid image of a royal arrival. The King who is also Judge and Deliverer is about to come. The trumpets sound a clarion to announce His entrance. A roar is heard, not just from the assembled people but from the universe itself: the sea, the earth, rivers and mountains. All herald His coming with joy, for they know that when He sits in judgement He will resolve all disputes with equity.

PSALM 98

מִזְמוֹר A Psalm. Sing a new song to the LORD, for He has done wondrous things; He has saved by His right hand and His holy arm. The LORD has made His salvation known; He has displayed His righteousness in the sight of the nations. He remembered His lovingkindness and faithfulness to the house of Israel; all the ends of the earth have seen the victory of our LORD. Shout for joy to the LORD, all the earth; burst into song, sing with joy, play music. Play music to the LORD on the harp – on the harp with the sound of singing. With trumpets and the sound of the ram's horn, shout for joy before the LORD, the King. ➔ Let the sea and all that is in it thunder, the world and all who live in it. Let the rivers clap their hands, the mountains sing together for joy – before the LORD, for He is coming to judge the earth. He will judge the world with justice, and the peoples with equity.

PSALM 99

יהוה מָלָךְ The LORD reigns, let the peoples tremble. He sits enthroned on the cherubim, let the earth quake. Great is the LORD in Zion, He is exalted over all the peoples. Let them praise Your name, O great and awesome One: He is holy! The King in His might loves justice. You have established equity. The justice and righteousness in Jacob is Your doing. Exalt the LORD our GOD, and bow at His footstool: He is holy! Moses and Aaron were among his priests; Samuel was among those who called on His name. They called on the LORD and He answered them. ➔ He spoke to them in a pillar of cloud; they observed His testimonies and the statute He gave them. LORD our GOD, You answered them. You were for them a forgiving GOD, though You punished their misdeeds. Exalt the LORD our GOD and bow at His holy mountain, for the LORD our GOD is holy.

יהוה מָלָךְ *Psalm 99.* Having declared GOD's sovereignty, the Psalmist now speaks of His holiness. The three sections of the Psalm each end on this theme. The first two – about GOD's enthronement and His justice, end with the declaration, "He is holy". The third ends with a double use of the word: "Bow at His *holy* mountain, for LORD our GOD is *holy*." *Moses, Aaron, Samuel.* Respectively they represent the three "crowns" of leadership: prophecy, priesthood and kingship.

The following psalm is said standing:

תהלים כט

מִזְמוֹר לְדָוִד, הָבוּ לַיהוה בְּנֵי אֵלִים, הָבוּ לַיהוה כָּבוֹד וָעֹז. הָבוּ לַיהוה כְּבוֹד שְׁמוֹ, הִשְׁתַּחֲווּ לַיהוה בְּהַדְרַת־קֹדֶשׁ. קוֹל יהוה עַל הַמָּיִם, אֵל־הַכָּבוֹד הִרְעִים, יהוה עַל־מַיִם רַבִּים. קוֹל־יהוה בַּכֹּחַ, קוֹל יהוה בֶּהָדָר. קוֹל יהוה שֹׁבֵר אֲרָזִים, וַיְשַׁבֵּר יהוה אֶת־אַרְזֵי הַלְּבָנוֹן. וַיַּרְקִידֵם כְּמוֹ־עֵגֶל, לְבָנוֹן וְשִׂרְיוֹן כְּמוֹ בֶן־רְאֵמִים. קוֹל־יהוה חֹצֵב לַהֲבוֹת אֵשׁ. קוֹל יהוה יָחִיל מִדְבָּר, יָחִיל יהוה מִדְבַּר קָדֵשׁ. ◁ קוֹל יהוה יְחוֹלֵל אַיָּלוֹת, וַיֶּחֱשֹׂף יְעָרוֹת, וּבְהֵיכָלוֹ, כֻּלּוֹ אֹמֵר כָּבוֹד. יהוה לַמַּבּוּל יָשָׁב, וַיֵּשֶׁב יהוה מֶלֶךְ לְעוֹלָם. יהוה, עֹז לְעַמּוֹ יִתֵּן, יהוה יְבָרֵךְ אֶת עַמּוֹ בַשָּׁלוֹם.

The following is recited in some congregations:

אָנָּא, בְּכֹחַ, גְּדֻלַּת יְמִינְךָ, תַּתִּיר צְרוּרָה.
קַבֵּל רִנַּת עַמְּךָ, שַׂגְּבֵנוּ, טַהֲרֵנוּ, נוֹרָא.
נָא גִבּוֹר, דּוֹרְשֵׁי יִחוּדְךָ, כְּבָבַת שָׁמְרֵם.
בָּרְכֵם, טַהֲרֵם, רַחֲמֵם, צִדְקָתְךָ תָּמִיד גָּמְלֵם.
חֲסִין קָדוֹשׁ, בְּרוֹב טוּבְךָ נַהֵל עֲדָתֶךָ.
יָחִיד גֵּאֶה, לְעַמְּךָ פְּנֵה, זוֹכְרֵי קְדֻשָּׁתֶךָ.
שַׁוְעָתֵנוּ קַבֵּל וּשְׁמַע צַעֲקָתֵנוּ, יוֹדֵעַ תַּעֲלוּמוֹת
בָּרוּךְ שֵׁם כְּבוֹד מַלְכוּתוֹ לְעוֹלָם וָעֶד.

Moses was the greatest of the prophets, Aaron the first High Priest, and Samuel the man who anointed Israel's first kings, Saul and David.

מִזְמוֹר לְדָוִד *Psalm 29.* This psalm, powerful in both imagery and language, breaks the sequence of the previous psalms (95–99). Many interpret it as a poetic description of the giving of the Torah. The Talmud Yerushalmi (*Berachot* 4:3) relates its seven mentions of the word *kol*, "voice", to the seven blessings of the *Shabbat Amidah.* Its mood is significant. It describes an earth-shattering storm which subsides, so that the last word of the psalm is "peace." So will the storm of human history one day be transfigured into peace. Redemption stands to history as does Shabbat to the six days of creation.

The following psalm is said standing:

PSALM 29

מִזְמוֹר לְדָוִד A psalm of David. Render to the LORD, you angelic powers, render to the LORD glory and might. Render to the LORD the glory due to His name. Bow to the LORD in the beauty of holiness. The LORD's voice echoes over the waters; the GOD of glory thunders; the LORD is over the mighty waters. The LORD's voice in power, the LORD's voice in beauty, the LORD's voice breaks cedars, the LORD shatters the cedars of Lebanon. He makes Lebanon skip like a calf, Sirion like a young wild ox. The LORD's voice cleaves flames of fire. The LORD's voice makes the desert quake, the LORD shakes the desert of Kadesh. ➾ The LORD's voice makes hinds calve and strips the forests bare, and in His temple all say: "Glory!" The LORD sat enthroned at the Flood, the LORD sits enthroned as King for ever. The LORD will give strength to His people; the LORD will bless His people with peace.

The following is recited in some congregations:

אָנָּא Please, by the power of Your great right hand,
set the captive nation free.

Accept Your people's prayer. Strengthen us, purify us,
You who are revered.

Please, mighty One, guard like the pupil of the eye
those who seek Your unity.

Bless them, cleanse them, have compassion on them,
grant them your righteousness always.

Mighty One, holy One, in Your great goodness
guide Your congregation.

Only One, Exalted One, turn to Your people,
who proclaim Your holiness.

Accept our plea and heed our cry,
You who know all secret thoughts.

Blessed be the name of His glorious kingdom for
ever and all time.

אָנָּא בְּכֹחַ *Please, by the power*: A hymn in seven lines, each of six words, whose initial letters spell out a mystical 42-letter name of GOD. It is attributed to Rabbi Nechunya ben ha-Kanah (second half of the first century CE).

לְכָה דוֹדִי לִקְרַאת כַּלָּה,
פְּנֵי שַׁבָּת נְקַבְּלָה.
לְכָה דוֹדִי לִקְרַאת כַּלָּה, פְּנֵי שַׁבָּת נְקַבְּלָה.

שָׁמוֹר וְזָכוֹר בְּדִבּוּר אֶחָד,
הִשְׁמִיעָנוּ אֵל הַמְיֻחָד,
יהוה אֶחָד וּשְׁמוֹ אֶחָד,
לְשֵׁם וּלְתִפְאֶרֶת וְלִתְהִלָּה.
לְכָה דוֹדִי לִקְרַאת כַּלָּה, פְּנֵי שַׁבָּת נְקַבְּלָה.

לִקְרַאת שַׁבָּת לְכוּ וְנֵלְכָה,
כִּי הִיא מְקוֹר הַבְּרָכָה,
מֵרֹאשׁ מִקֶּדֶם נְסוּכָה,
סוֹף מַעֲשֶׂה בְּמַחֲשָׁבָה תְּחִלָּה.
לְכָה דוֹדִי לִקְרַאת כַּלָּה, פְּנֵי שַׁבָּת נְקַבְּלָה.

מִקְדַּשׁ מֶלֶךְ עִיר מְלוּכָה,
קוּמִי צְאִי מִתּוֹךְ הַהֲפֵכָה,
רַב לָךְ שֶׁבֶת בְּעֵמֶק הַבָּכָא,
וְהוּא יַחֲמוֹל עָלַיִךְ חֶמְלָה.
לְכָה דוֹדִי לִקְרַאת כַּלָּה, פְּנֵי שַׁבָּת נְקַבְּלָה.

לְכָה דוֹדִי *Come, my Beloved*: This song – the one original composition introduced into this service by the Tzefat kabbalists – was written by Rabbi Shlomo Alkabets. It is a work of surpassing beauty, speaking in turn of Shabbat, Jerusalem, the Jewish people, and the Messiah, before returning in its last verse to the Shabbat again. Artfully woven from biblical quotations, many of them drawn from Isaiah's prophecies of consolation, together with Talmudic and midrashic ideas, its first eight verses form an acrostic, spelling out the name of its author, Shlomo ha-Levi.

לְכָה דוֹדִי Come, my Beloved, to greet the bride;
let us welcome the Sabbath.

Come, my Beloved, to greet the bride;
let us welcome the Sabbath.

שָׁמוֹר "Observe" and "Remember" in one act of speech,
The One and Only God made us hear.
The Lord is One and His name is One,
For renown, for splendour, and for praise.

Come, my Beloved, to greet the bride;
let us welcome the Sabbath.

לִקְרַאת To greet the Sabbath, come let us go,
For of blessing, she is the source.
From the outset, as of old, ordained:
Last in deed, first in thought.

Come, my Beloved, to greet the bride;
let us welcome the Sabbath.

מִקְדַּשׁ Sanctuary of the King, royal city,
Arise, go forth from your ruined state.
Too long have you dwelt in the valley of tears.
He will shower compassion on you.

Come, my Beloved, to greet the bride;
let us welcome the Sabbath.

שָׁמוֹר *"Observe" and "Remember" in one act of speech*: This refers to two versions of the Ten Commandments. In the first (Exodus 20:8), Israel was commanded to "Remember" the Sabbath; in the second (Deuteronomy 5:12) to "observe" it. According to the Sages, both were uttered at the same time. "Observe" refers to the negative commandment of Shabbat, the prohibition against work, while "Remember" refers to the positive commandment, to sanctify it in word and deed. The idea that both were spoken simultaneously teaches that the negative and positive aspects of holy time are inseparable. The prohibition against work creates space for rest and joy.

מִקְדַּשׁ *Sanctuary of the King, royal city*: In this and the next four verses, the

הִתְנַעֲרִי מֵעָפָר קוּמִי,
לִבְשִׁי בִּגְדֵי תִפְאַרְתֵּךְ עַמִּי,
עַל יַד בֶּן יִשַׁי בֵּית הַלַּחְמִי,
קָרְבָה אֶל נַפְשִׁי גְאָלָהּ.
לְכָה דוֹדִי לִקְרַאת כַּלָּה, פְּנֵי שַׁבָּת נְקַבְּלָה.

הִתְעוֹרְרִי הִתְעוֹרְרִי,
כִּי בָא אוֹרֵךְ קוּמִי אוֹרִי,
עוּרִי עוּרִי שִׁיר דַּבֵּרִי,
כְּבוֹד יהוה עָלַיִךְ נִגְלָה.
לְכָה דוֹדִי לִקְרַאת כַּלָּה, פְּנֵי שַׁבָּת נְקַבְּלָה.

לֹא תֵבֹשִׁי וְלֹא תִכָּלְמִי,
מַה תִּשְׁתּוֹחֲחִי וּמַה תֶּהֱמִי,
בָּךְ יֶחֱסוּ עֲנִיֵּי עַמִּי,
וְנִבְנְתָה עִיר עַל תִּלָּהּ.
לְכָה דוֹדִי לִקְרַאת כַּלָּה, פְּנֵי שַׁבָּת נְקַבְּלָה.

וְהָיוּ לִמְשִׁסָּה שֹׁאסָיִךְ,
וְרָחֲקוּ כָּל מְבַלְּעָיִךְ,
יָשִׂישׂ עָלַיִךְ אֱלֹהָיִךְ,
כִּמְשׂוֹשׂ חָתָן עַל כַּלָּה.
לְכָה דוֹדִי לִקְרַאת כַּלָּה, פְּנֵי שַׁבָּת נְקַבְּלָה.

---

poet speaks of the desolate condition of Jerusalem and the Jewish people in his day. Using language drawn from Isaiah, he turns first to Jerusalem, then

הִתְנַעֲרִי Shake off the dust, arise!
Put on your clothes of glory, My people.
Through the son of Jesse the Bethlehemite,
Draw near to my soul and redeem it.

Come, my Beloved, to greet the bride;
let us welcome the Sabbath.

הִתְעוֹרְרִי Wake up, wake up,
For your light has come: rise, shine!
Awake, awake, break out in song,
For the LORD's glory is revealed on you.

Come, my Beloved, to greet the bride;
let us welcome the Sabbath.

לֹא תֵבוֹשִׁי Do not be ashamed, do not be confounded.
Why be downcast? Why do you mourn?
In you the needy of My people find shelter,
And the city shall be rebuilt on its hill.

Come, my Beloved, to greet the bride;
let us welcome the Sabbath.

וְהָיוּ Those who despoiled you shall be despoiled,
And all who devoured you shall be far away.
Your GOD will rejoice over you
As a bridegroom rejoices over his bride.

Come, my Beloved, to greet the bride;
let us welcome the Sabbath.

---

to the Jewish people, then to the land of Israel itself, summoning them to shake off their grief and rouse themselves to new glory. These verses radiate the hope born of faith, the victory of joy over despair.

יָמִין וּשְׂמֹאל תִּפְרֹוֹצִי,
וְאֶת־יהוה תַּעֲרִיצִי,
עַל יַד אִישׁ בֶּן פַּרְצִי,
וְנִשְׂמְחָה וְנָגִילָה.
לְכָה דוֹדִי לִקְרַאת כַּלָּה, פְּנֵי שַׁבָּת נְקַבְּלָה.

Stand and turn to face the rear of the synagogue, as if to greet the incoming bride, bowing at the words בּוֹאִי כַלָּה, then turn forward.

בּוֹאִי בְשָׁלוֹם עֲטֶרֶת בַּעְלָהּ,
גַּם בְּשִׂמְחָה וּבְצָהֳלָה,
תּוֹךְ אֱמוּנֵי עַם סְגֻלָּה,
בּוֹאִי כַלָּה, בּוֹאִי כַלָּה.
לְכָה דוֹדִי לִקְרַאת כַּלָּה, פְּנֵי שַׁבָּת נְקַבְּלָה.

Mourners during the week of שִׁבְעָה return to the synagogue at this point. They are greeted with the following words of consolation:

הַמָּקוֹם יְנַחֵם אֶתְכֶם בְּתוֹךְ שְׁאָר אֲבֵלֵי צִיּוֹן וִירוּשָׁלָיִם.

On שַׁבָּת חוֹל הַמּוֹעֵד or יוֹם טוֹב or on the evening immediately after יוֹם טוֹב, the service begins here.

תהלים צב

מִזְמוֹר שִׁיר לְיוֹם הַשַּׁבָּת. טוֹב לְהֹדוֹת לַיהוה, וּלְזַמֵּר לְשִׁמְךָ עֶלְיוֹן. לְהַגִּיד בַּבֹּקֶר חַסְדֶּךָ, וֶאֱמוּנָתְךָ בַּלֵּילוֹת. עֲלֵי־עָשׂוֹר וַעֲלֵי־נָבֶל, עֲלֵי הִגָּיוֹן בְּכִנּוֹר. כִּי שִׂמַּחְתַּנִי יהוה בְּפָעֳלֶךָ, בְּמַעֲשֵׂי יָדֶיךָ אֲרַנֵּן. מַה־גָּדְלוּ מַעֲשֶׂיךָ יהוה, מְאֹד עָמְקוּ מַחְשְׁבֹתֶיךָ. אִישׁ בַּעַר לֹא יֵדָע, וּכְסִיל לֹא־

בּוֹאִי בְשָׁלוֹם *Come in peace* – at this point our custom is to turn round to greet the Shabbat bride, as did the mystics in the fields of Tzefat.

מִזְמוֹר *A Psalm. A song for the Sabbath day*: This Psalm, sung by the Levites on Shabbat, was already understood by the Sages as "a song for the time to come, for the day which will be all Shabbat and rest in life everlasting". Shabbat is not merely a day of rest, it is a rehearsal, within time,

יָמִין Right and left you shall spread out,
And GOD you will revere.
Through the descendant of Peretz,
We shall rejoice and we shall be glad.

Come, my Beloved, to greet the bride;
let us welcome the Sabbath.

Stand and turn to face to the rear of the synagogue, as if to greet the incoming bride, bowing at the words "Enter, O bride!", then turn forward.

בּוֹאִי Come in peace, O crown of her husband;
Come with joy and jubilation,
Among the faithful of the treasured people.
Enter, O bride! Enter, O bride!

Come, my Beloved, to greet the bride;
let us welcome the Sabbath.

Mourners during the week of *Shivah* return to the synagogue at this point. They are greeted with the following words of consolation:

הַמָּקוֹם May the Almighty comfort you among the other mourners of Zion and Jerusalem.

On a Festival or its intermediate Shabbat, or on the evening immediately after a Festival, the service begins here.

PSALM 92

מִזְמוֹר A Psalm. A Song for the Sabbath Day. It is good to thank the LORD and sing psalms to Your name, Most High – to tell of Your lovingkindness in the morning and Your faithfulness at night, to the music of the ten-stringed lyre and the melody of the harp. For You have made me rejoice by Your work, O LORD; I sing for joy at the deeds

---

for the age beyond time when humanity, guided by the call of GOD, moves beyond strife, evil and oppression, to create a world of harmony, respecting the integrity of creation as GOD's work, and the human person as GOD's image.

At that time people looking back at history will see that though evil flourished "like grass", it was shortlived, while the righteous grow slowly but stand tall "like the cedar of Lebanon." Because our time perspective is short, we seem to inhabit a world in which evil prevails. Were we able to see history as a whole, we would know that good wins the final victory; in the long run justice prevails.

יָבִין אֶת־זֹאת. בִּפְרֹחַ רְשָׁעִים כְּמוֹ־עֵשֶׂב, וַיָּצִיצוּ כׇּל־פֹּעֲלֵי
אָוֶן, לְהִשָּׁמְדָם עֲדֵי־עַד. וְאַתָּה מָרוֹם לְעֹלָם יהוה. כִּי־הִנֵּה
אֹיְבֶיךָ יהוה, כִּי־הִנֵּה אֹיְבֶיךָ יֹאבֵדוּ, יִתְפָּרְדוּ כׇּל־פֹּעֲלֵי אָוֶן.
וַתָּרֶם כִּרְאֵים קַרְנִי, בַּלֹּתִי בְּשֶׁמֶן רַעֲנָן. וַתַּבֵּט עֵינִי בְּשׁוּרָי,
בַּקָּמִים עָלַי מְרֵעִים, תִּשְׁמַעְנָה אָזְנָי. ◄ צַדִּיק כַּתָּמָר
יִפְרָח, כְּאֶרֶז בַּלְּבָנוֹן יִשְׂגֶּה. שְׁתוּלִים בְּבֵית יהוה, בְּחַצְרוֹת
אֱלֹהֵינוּ יַפְרִיחוּ. עוֹד יְנוּבוּן בְּשֵׂיבָה, דְּשֵׁנִים וְרַעֲנַנִּים יִהְיוּ.
לְהַגִּיד כִּי־יָשָׁר יהוה, צוּרִי, וְלֹא עַוְלָתָה בּוֹ.

תהלים צג

יהוה מָלָךְ, גֵּאוּת לָבֵשׁ, לָבֵשׁ יהוה עֹז הִתְאַזָּר, אַף־תִּכּוֹן
תֵּבֵל בַּל־תִּמּוֹט. נָכוֹן כִּסְאֲךָ מֵאָז, מֵעוֹלָם אָתָּה. נָשְׂאוּ
נְהָרוֹת יהוה, נָשְׂאוּ נְהָרוֹת קוֹלָם, יִשְׂאוּ נְהָרוֹת דׇּכְיָם.
◄ מִקֹּלוֹת מַיִם רַבִּים, אַדִּירִים מִשְׁבְּרֵי־יָם, אַדִּיר בַּמָּרוֹם
יהוה. עֵדֹתֶיךָ נֶאֶמְנוּ מְאֹד לְבֵיתְךָ נַאֲוָה־קֹּדֶשׁ, יהוה לְאֹרֶךְ
יָמִים.

קדיש יתום

The transliteration can be found at the end of the Siddur.

Mourner:

יִתְגַּדַּל וְיִתְקַדַּשׁ שְׁמֵהּ רַבָּא. (Cong. אָמֵן) בְּעָלְמָא דִּי־בְרָא
כִרְעוּתֵהּ. וְיַמְלִיךְ מַלְכוּתֵהּ, בְּחַיֵּיכוֹן וּבְיוֹמֵיכוֹן וּבְחַיֵּי דְכׇל־
בֵּית יִשְׂרָאֵל, בַּעֲגָלָא וּבִזְמַן קָרִיב. וְאִמְרוּ אָמֵן. (Cong. אָמֵן)

All:

יְהֵא שְׁמֵהּ רַבָּא מְבָרַךְ לְעָלַם וּלְעָלְמֵי עָלְמַיָּא.

Mourner:

יִתְבָּרַךְ וְיִשְׁתַּבַּח וְיִתְפָּאַר וְיִתְרוֹמַם וְיִתְנַשֵּׂא וְיִתְהַדַּר
וְיִתְעַלֶּה וְיִתְהַלָּל שְׁמֵהּ דְּקֻדְשָׁא בְּרִיךְ הוּא (Cong. בְּרִיךְ הוּא)
לְעֵלָּא (On שַׁבַּת שׁוּבָה add לְעֵלָּא) מִן־כׇּל־בִּרְכָתָא וְשִׁירָתָא

of Your hands. How great are Your deeds, LORD, and how very deep Your thoughts. A boor cannot know, nor can a fool understand, that though the wicked spring up like grass and all evildoers flourish, it is only that they may be destroyed for ever. But You, LORD, are eternally exalted. For behold Your enemies, LORD, behold Your enemies will perish; all evildoers will be scattered. You have raised my pride like that of a wild ox; I am anointed with fresh oil. My eyes shall look in triumph on my adversaries, my ears shall hear the downfall of the wicked who rise against me. → The righteous will flourish like a palm tree and grow tall like a cedar in Lebanon. Planted in the LORD's house, blossoming in our GOD's courtyards, they will still bear fruit in old age, and stay vigorous and fresh, proclaiming that the LORD is upright: He is my Rock, in whom there is no wrong.

PSALM 93

יהוה מָלָךְ The LORD reigns. He is robed in majesty. The LORD is robed, girded with strength. The world is firmly established; it cannot be moved. Your throne stands firm as of old; You are eternal. Rivers lift up, LORD, rivers lift up their voice, rivers lift up their crashing waves. → Mightier than the noise of many waters, than the mighty waves of the sea is the LORD on high. Your testimonies are very sure; holiness adorns Your house, LORD, for evermore.

MOURNER'S KADDISH

The transliteration can be found at the end of the Siddur.

Mourner:

יִתְגַּדַּל Magnified and sanctified may His great name be, in the world He created by His will. May He establish His kingdom in your lifetime and in your days, and in the lifetime of all the House of Israel, swiftly and soon – and say: Amen.

All:

May His great name be blessed for ever and all time.

Mourner:

Blessed and praised, glorified and exalted, raised and honoured, uplifted and lauded be the name of the Holy One, blessed be He, (between

תֻּשְׁבְּחָתָא וְנֶחֱמָתָא, דַּאֲמִירָן בְּעָלְמָא. וְאִמְרוּ אָמֵן. (Cong. אָמֵן)

יְהֵא שְׁלָמָא רַבָּא מִן־שְׁמַיָּא, וְחַיִּים עָלֵינוּ וְעַל־כָּל־יִשְׂרָאֵל. וְאִמְרוּ אָמֵן. (Cong. אָמֵן)

Bow, take three steps back, then bow, first left, then right, then centre, while saying:

עֹשֶׂה שָׁלוֹם בִּמְרוֹמָיו, הוּא יַעֲשֶׂה שָׁלוֹם עָלֵינוּ, וְעַל־כָּל־יִשְׂרָאֵל. וְאִמְרוּ אָמֵן. (Cong. אָמֵן)

מעריב לשבת ויום טוב

On יום טוב falling on a weekday, the service begins here.

The Leader says the following, both Leader and Congregation bowing at בָּרְכוּ, standing straight at God's name:

בָּרְכוּ אֶת יהוה הַמְבֹרָךְ.

The Congregation, followed by the Leader, responds, bowing at בָּרוּךְ, standing straight at God's name:

בָּרוּךְ יהוה הַמְבֹרָךְ לְעוֹלָם וָעֶד.

ברכות קריאת שמע

בָּרוּךְ אַתָּה יהוה אֱלֹהֵינוּ מֶלֶךְ הָעוֹלָם, אֲשֶׁר בִּדְבָרוֹ מַעֲרִיב עֲרָבִים, בְּחָכְמָה פּוֹתֵחַ שְׁעָרִים, וּבִתְבוּנָה מְשַׁנֶּה עִתִּים וּמַחֲלִיף אֶת הַזְּמַנִּים וּמְסַדֵּר אֶת הַכּוֹכָבִים בְּמִשְׁמְרוֹתֵיהֶם בָּרָקִיעַ כִּרְצוֹנוֹ. בּוֹרֵא יוֹם וָלָיְלָה, גּוֹלֵל אוֹר מִפְּנֵי חֹשֶׁךְ וְחֹשֶׁךְ מִפְּנֵי אוֹר. ◂ וּמַעֲבִיר יוֹם וּמֵבִיא לָיְלָה, וּמַבְדִּיל בֵּין יוֹם וּבֵין לָיְלָה, יהוה צְבָאוֹת שְׁמוֹ. אֵל חַי וְקַיָּם, תָּמִיד

אֲשֶׁר בִּדְבָרוֹ מַעֲרִיב עֲרָבִים *Who by His word brings on evenings*: The three key Jewish beliefs are creation (that God made the universe), revelation (that God speaks to mankind), and redemption (that God rescues humanity, teaching us how to act with justice and compassion). The blessings surrounding the *Shema* are con-

Rosh Hashanah and Yom Kippur add 'well') beyond any blessing, song, praise and consolation uttered in the world – and say: Amen.

May there be great peace from heaven, and life for us and all Israel – and say: Amen.

Bow, take three steps back, then bow, first left, then right, then centre, while saying:

May He who makes peace in His high places, make peace for us and all Israel – and say: Amen.

EVENING SERVICE FOR SHABBAT AND FESTIVALS

On a Festival falling on a weekday, the service begins here.

The Leader says the following, both Leader and Congregation bowing at "Bless" standing straight at "The Lord":

Bless the Lord, the blessed One.

The Congregation, followed by the Leader, responds, bowing at "Bless", standing straight at "The Lord":

Bless the Lord, the blessed One, for ever and all time.

BLESSINGS OF THE SHEMA

בָּרוּךְ Blessed are You, Lord our God, King of the Universe, who by His word brings on evenings, by His wisdom opens the gates of heaven, with understanding makes time change and the seasons rotate, and by His will orders the stars in their constellations in the sky. He creates day and night, rolling away the light before the darkness, and darkness before the light. ➔ He makes the day pass and brings on night, distinguishing day from night: the Lord of hosts is His name.

---

structed on this pattern. This, the first, speaks of creation – heaven and earth, light and darkness, day and night. The next speaks of revelation, God's gift of the Torah to the children of Israel. The third, immediately after the *Shema*, speaks of redemption ("who redeemed Israel"). The Siddur is our tutorial in belief, teaching us to see the world through the eyes of faith.

יִמְלוֹךְ עָלֵינוּ, לְעוֹלָם וָעֶד. בָּרוּךְ אַתָּה יהוה, הַמַּעֲרִיב עֲרָבִים.

אַהֲבַת עוֹלָם בֵּית יִשְׂרָאֵל עַמְּךָ אָהָבְתָּ. תּוֹרָה וּמִצְוֹת, חֻקִּים וּמִשְׁפָּטִים, אוֹתָנוּ לִמַּדְתָּ. עַל כֵּן יהוה אֱלֹהֵינוּ, בְּשָׁכְבֵנוּ וּבְקוּמֵנוּ נָשִׂיחַ בְּחֻקֶּיךָ, וְנִשְׂמַח בְּדִבְרֵי תוֹרָתֶךָ, וּבְמִצְוֹתֶיךָ לְעוֹלָם וָעֶד. ◄ כִּי הֵם חַיֵּינוּ, וְאֹרֶךְ יָמֵינוּ, וּבָהֶם נֶהְגֶּה יוֹמָם וָלָיְלָה. וְאַהֲבָתְךָ, אַל תָּסִיר מִמֶּנּוּ לְעוֹלָמִים. בָּרוּךְ אַתָּה יהוה, אוֹהֵב עַמּוֹ יִשְׂרָאֵל.

שמע

When prayers are not said with a מִנְיָן, say:

אֵל מֶלֶךְ נֶאֱמָן.

Cover the eyes with the right hand while saying the following verse:

דברים ו:ד–ט

שְׁמַע יִשְׂרָאֵל יהוה אֱלֹהֵינוּ יהוה | אֶחָד׃

Quietly:

בָּרוּךְ שֵׁם כְּבוֹד מַלְכוּתוֹ לְעוֹלָם וָעֶד.

וְאָהַבְתָּ אֵת יהוה אֱלֹהֶיךָ בְּכָל־לְבָבְךָ וּבְכָל־נַפְשְׁךָ וּבְכָל־מְאֹדֶךָ׃ וְהָיוּ הַדְּבָרִים הָאֵלֶּה אֲשֶׁר אָנֹכִי מְצַוְּךָ הַיּוֹם עַל־לְבָבֶךָ׃ וְשִׁנַּנְתָּם לְבָנֶיךָ וְדִבַּרְתָּ בָּם בְּשִׁבְתְּךָ בְּבֵיתֶךָ וּבְלֶכְתְּךָ בַדֶּרֶךְ וּבְשָׁכְבְּךָ וּבְקוּמֶךָ׃ וּקְשַׁרְתָּם לְאוֹת עַל־יָדֶךָ וְהָיוּ לְטֹטָפֹת בֵּין עֵינֶיךָ׃ וּכְתַבְתָּם עַל־מְזֻזוֹת בֵּיתֶךָ וּבִשְׁעָרֶיךָ׃

אַהֲבַת עוֹלָם *With everlasting love*: Nothing more eloquently refutes the idea that Judaism is a dry, legalistic religion than this magnificent poem in which the people of Israel pour out their thanks for the gift of Torah and its “commandments, laws and decrees of justice”. Here, law becomes love and love becomes law. God unites us to Him by teaching us how to act in accordance with His will – which

May the living and enduring God rule over us for ever and all time. Blessed are You, Lord, who brings on evenings.

אַהֲבַת עוֹלָם With everlasting love have You loved Your people, the House of Israel. You have taught us Torah and commandments, decrees and laws of justice. Therefore, Lord our God, when we lie down and when we rise up we will speak of Your decrees, rejoicing in the words of Your Torah and Your commandments for ever. → For they are our life and the length of our days; on them will we meditate day and night. May You never take away Your love from us. Blessed are You, Lord, who loves His people Israel.

THE SHEMA

When prayers are not said with a *minyan*, say:

God, faithful King!

Cover the eyes with the right hand while saying the following verse:

DEUTERONOMY 6:4–9

Listen, Israel: the Lord is our God, the Lord is One.

Quietly:

Blessed be the name of His glorious kingdom for ever and ever.

וְאָהַבְתָּ Love the Lord your God with all your heart, with all your soul, and with all your might. These words which I command you today shall be on your heart. Teach them repeatedly to your children, speaking of them when you sit at home and when you travel on the way, when you lie down and when you rise. Bind them as a sign on your hand, and they shall be an emblem between your eyes. Write them on the doorposts of your house and gates.

---

becomes in turn "our life and the length of our days".

שְׁמַע יִשְׂרָאֵל *Listen, Israel*: *Shema* means not only "to hear" but also "to listen, understand, internalise, respond and obey." It is translated here as "Listen" because listening is active, while hearing is passive. This, the most famous line of Jewish prayer, is a call to action on the part of the mind, emotion and will. It asks us to reflect on, strive to understand, and to

דברים יא:יג–כא

וְהָיָ֗ה אִם־שָׁמֹ֤עַ תִּשְׁמְעוּ֙ אֶל־מִצְוֺתַ֔י אֲשֶׁ֧ר אָנֹכִ֛י מְצַוֶּ֥ה
אֶתְכֶ֖ם הַיּ֑וֹם לְאַהֲבָ֞ה אֶת־יְהוָ֤ה אֱלֹהֵיכֶם֙ וּלְעׇבְד֔וֹ בְּכׇל־
לְבַבְכֶ֖ם וּבְכׇל־נַפְשְׁכֶֽם׃ וְנָתַתִּ֧י מְטַֽר־אַרְצְכֶ֛ם בְּעִתּ֖וֹ יוֹרֶ֣ה
וּמַלְק֑וֹשׁ וְאָסַפְתָּ֣ דְגָנֶ֔ךָ וְתִֽירֹשְׁךָ֖ וְיִצְהָרֶֽךָ׃ וְנָתַתִּ֛י עֵ֥שֶׂב
בְּשָׂדְךָ֖ לִבְהֶמְתֶּ֑ךָ וְאָכַלְתָּ֖ וְשָׂבָֽעְתָּ׃ הִשָּׁמְר֣וּ לָכֶ֔ם פֶּ֥ן יִפְתֶּ֖ה
לְבַבְכֶ֑ם וְסַרְתֶּ֗ם וַעֲבַדְתֶּם֙ אֱלֹהִ֣ים אֲחֵרִ֔ים וְהִשְׁתַּחֲוִיתֶ֖ם
לָהֶֽם׃ וְחָרָ֨ה אַף־יְהוָ֜ה בָּכֶ֗ם וְעָצַ֤ר אֶת־הַשָּׁמַ֙יִם֙ וְלֹא־יִהְיֶ֣ה
מָטָ֔ר וְהָ֣אֲדָמָ֔ה לֹ֥א תִתֵּ֖ן אֶת־יְבוּלָ֑הּ וַאֲבַדְתֶּ֣ם מְהֵרָ֗ה מֵעַל֙
הָאָ֣רֶץ הַטֹּבָ֔ה אֲשֶׁ֥ר יְהוָ֖ה נֹתֵ֥ן לָכֶֽם׃ וְשַׂמְתֶּם֙ אֶת־דְּבָרַ֣י
אֵ֔לֶּה עַל־לְבַבְכֶ֖ם וְעַל־נַפְשְׁכֶ֑ם וּקְשַׁרְתֶּ֨ם אֹתָ֤ם לְאוֹת֙ עַל־
יֶדְכֶ֔ם וְהָי֥וּ לְטוֹטָפֹ֖ת בֵּ֥ין עֵינֵיכֶֽם׃ וְלִמַּדְתֶּ֥ם אֹתָ֛ם אֶת־
בְּנֵיכֶ֖ם לְדַבֵּ֣ר בָּ֑ם בְּשִׁבְתְּךָ֤ בְּבֵיתֶ֙ךָ֙ וּבְלֶכְתְּךָ֣ בַדֶּ֔רֶךְ וּֽבְשׇׁכְבְּךָ֖
וּבְקוּמֶֽךָ׃ וּכְתַבְתָּ֛ם עַל־מְזוּז֥וֹת בֵּיתֶ֖ךָ וּבִשְׁעָרֶֽיךָ׃ לְמַ֨עַן
יִרְבּ֤וּ יְמֵיכֶם֙ וִימֵ֣י בְנֵיכֶ֔ם עַ֚ל הָאֲדָמָ֔ה אֲשֶׁ֨ר נִשְׁבַּ֧ע יְהוָ֛ה
לַאֲבֹתֵיכֶ֖ם לָתֵ֣ת לָהֶ֑ם כִּימֵ֥י הַשָּׁמַ֖יִם עַל־הָאָֽרֶץ׃

במדבר טו:לז–מא

וַיֹּ֥אמֶר יְהוָ֖ה אֶל־מֹשֶׁ֥ה לֵּאמֹֽר׃ דַּבֵּ֞ר אֶל־בְּנֵ֤י יִשְׂרָאֵל֙
וְאָמַרְתָּ֣ אֲלֵהֶ֔ם וְעָשׂ֨וּ לָהֶ֥ם צִיצִ֛ת עַל־כַּנְפֵ֥י בִגְדֵיהֶ֖ם לְדֹרֹתָ֑ם
וְנָ֥תְנ֛וּ עַל־צִיצִ֥ת הַכָּנָ֖ף פְּתִ֥יל תְּכֵֽלֶת׃ וְהָיָ֣ה לָכֶם֮ לְצִיצִת֒
וּרְאִיתֶ֣ם אֹת֗וֹ וּזְכַרְתֶּם֙ אֶת־כׇּל־מִצְוֺ֣ת יְהוָ֔ה וַעֲשִׂיתֶ֖ם אֹתָ֑ם
וְלֹֽא־תָת֜וּרוּ אַחֲרֵ֤י לְבַבְכֶם֙ וְאַחֲרֵ֣י עֵֽינֵיכֶ֔ם אֲשֶׁר־אַתֶּ֥ם זֹנִ֖ים
אַחֲרֵיהֶֽם׃ לְמַ֣עַן תִּזְכְּר֔וּ וַעֲשִׂיתֶ֖ם אֶת־כׇּל־מִצְוֺתָ֑י וִהְיִיתֶ֥ם
קְדֹשִׁ֖ים לֵאלֹהֵיכֶֽם׃ אֲנִ֞י יְהוָ֣ה אֱלֹהֵיכֶ֗ם אֲשֶׁ֨ר הוֹצֵ֤אתִי
אֶתְכֶם֙ מֵאֶ֣רֶץ מִצְרַ֔יִם לִהְי֥וֹת לָכֶ֖ם לֵאלֹהִ֑ים אֲנִ֖י יְהוָ֥ה
אֱלֹהֵיכֶֽם׃ **אֱמֶת** –

DEUTERONOMY 11:13–21

וְהָיָה If you indeed heed My commandments with which I charge you today, to love the LORD your GOD and worship Him with all your heart and with all your soul, I will give rain in your land in its season, the early and late rain; and you shall gather in your grain, wine and oil. I will give grass in your field for your cattle, and you shall eat and be satisfied. Be careful lest your heart be tempted and you go astray and worship other gods, bowing down to them. Then the LORD's anger will flare against you and He will close the heavens so that there will be no rain. The land will not yield its crops, and you will perish swiftly from the good land that the LORD is giving you. Therefore set these, My words, on your heart and soul. Bind them as a sign on your hand, and they shall be an emblem between your eyes. Teach them to your children, speaking of them when you sit at home and when you travel on the way, when you lie down and when you rise. Write them on the doorposts of your house and gates, so that you and your children may live long in the land that the LORD swore to your ancestors to give them, for as long as the heavens are above the earth.

NUMBERS 15:37–41

וַיֹּאמֶר The LORD spoke to Moses, saying: Speak to the Israelites and tell them to make tassels on the corners of their garments for all generations. They shall attach to the tassel at each corner a thread of blue. This shall be your tassel, and you shall see it and remember all of the LORD's commandments and keep them, not straying after your heart and after your eyes, following your own sinful desires. Thus you will be reminded to keep all My commandments, and be holy to your GOD. I am the LORD your GOD, who brought you out of the land of Egypt to be your GOD. I am the LORD your GOD. **True** –

---

affirm the unity of GOD. GOD speaks in a "still, small voice", and to serve Him is to listen with the totality of our being.

Secular terms for understanding are permeated with visual images. We speak of insight, foresight, vision, observation, perspective; when we understand, we say "I see". Judaism, with its belief in an invisible, transcendent GOD, is a culture of the ear, not the eye. The patriarchs and prophets did not see GOD; they heard Him. To emphasise the non-visual nature of Jewish belief, it is our custom to cover our eyes as we say these words.

The Leader repeats:

← יהוה אֱלֹהֵיכֶם, אֱמֶת –

וֶאֱמוּנָה כָּל־זֹאת, וְקַיָּם עָלֵינוּ, כִּי הוּא יהוה אֱלֹהֵינוּ וְאֵין זוּלָתוֹ, וַאֲנַחְנוּ יִשְׂרָאֵל עַמּוֹ. הַפּוֹדֵנוּ מִיַּד מְלָכִים, מַלְכֵּנוּ הַגּוֹאֲלֵנוּ מִכַּף כָּל־הֶעָרִיצִים. הָאֵל הַנִּפְרָע לָנוּ מִצָּרֵינוּ, וְהַמְשַׁלֵּם גְּמוּל לְכָל־אֹיְבֵי נַפְשֵׁנוּ. הָעֹשֶׂה גְדֹלוֹת עַד־אֵין חֵקֶר, וְנִפְלָאוֹת עַד־אֵין מִסְפָּר. הַשָּׂם נַפְשֵׁנוּ בַּחַיִּים, וְלֹא־נָתַן לַמּוֹט רַגְלֵנוּ. הַמַּדְרִיכֵנוּ עַל בָּמוֹת אוֹיְבֵינוּ, וַיָּרֶם קַרְנֵנוּ עַל־כָּל־שׂוֹנְאֵנוּ. הָעֹשֶׂה־לָּנוּ נִסִּים וּנְקָמָה בְּפַרְעֹה, אוֹתוֹת וּמוֹפְתִים בְּאַדְמַת בְּנֵי־חָם. הַמַּכֶּה בְעֶבְרָתוֹ כָּל־בְּכוֹרֵי מִצְרָיִם, וַיּוֹצֵא אֶת־עַמּוֹ יִשְׂרָאֵל מִתּוֹכָם לְחֵרוּת עוֹלָם. הַמַּעֲבִיר בָּנָיו בֵּין גִּזְרֵי יַם־סוּף, אֶת־רוֹדְפֵיהֶם וְאֶת־שׂוֹנְאֵיהֶם בִּתְהוֹמוֹת טִבַּע. וְרָאוּ בָנָיו גְּבוּרָתוֹ, שִׁבְּחוּ וְהוֹדוּ לִשְׁמוֹ. וּמַלְכוּתוֹ בְּרָצוֹן קִבְּלוּ עֲלֵיהֶם. מֹשֶׁה וּבְנֵי יִשְׂרָאֵל לְךָ עָנוּ שִׁירָה בְּשִׂמְחָה רַבָּה, וְאָמְרוּ כֻלָּם,

מִי־כָמֹכָה בָּאֵלִם יהוה, מִי כָּמֹכָה נֶאְדָּר בַּקֹּדֶשׁ, נוֹרָא תְהִלֹּת, עֹשֵׂה פֶלֶא. ← מַלְכוּתְךָ רָאוּ בָנֶיךָ בּוֹקֵעַ יָם לִפְנֵי מֹשֶׁה, זֶה אֵלִי עָנוּ, וְאָמְרוּ, **יהוה יִמְלֹךְ לְעוֹלָם וָעֶד.**
← וְנֶאֱמַר, כִּי־פָדָה יהוה אֶת־יַעֲקֹב, וּגְאָלוֹ מִיַּד חָזָק מִמֶּנּוּ.
בָּרוּךְ אַתָּה יהוה, גָּאַל יִשְׂרָאֵל.

הַשְׁכִּיבֵנוּ יהוה אֱלֹהֵינוּ לְשָׁלוֹם, וְהַעֲמִידֵנוּ מַלְכֵּנוּ לְחַיִּים, וּפְרוֹשׂ עָלֵינוּ סֻכַּת שְׁלוֹמֶךָ, וְתַקְּנֵנוּ בְּעֵצָה טוֹבָה מִלְּפָנֶיךָ, וְהוֹשִׁיעֵנוּ לְמַעַן שְׁמֶךָ, וְהָגֵן בַּעֲדֵנוּ, וְהָסֵר מֵעָלֵינוּ אוֹיֵב, דֶּבֶר, וְחֶרֶב, וְרָעָב, וְיָגוֹן, וְהָסֵר שָׂטָן מִלְּפָנֵינוּ וּמֵאַחֲרֵינוּ, וּבְצֵל כְּנָפֶיךָ תַּסְתִּירֵנוּ, כִּי אֵל שׁוֹמְרֵנוּ וּמַצִּילֵנוּ אָתָּה,

The Leader repeats:

→ The LORD your GOD is true –

וֶאֱמוּנָה – and faithful is all this, and firmly established for us that He is the LORD our GOD, and there is none beside Him, and that we, Israel, are His people. He is our King, who redeems us from the hand of kings and delivers us from the grasp of all tyrants. He is our GOD, who on our behalf repays our foes and brings just retribution on our mortal enemies; who performs great deeds beyond understanding and wonders beyond number; who kept us alive, not letting our foot slip; who led us on the high places of our enemies, raising our pride above all our foes; who did miracles for us and brought vengeance against Pharaoh, who performed signs and wonders in the land of Ham's children; who smote in His wrath all the firstborn of Egypt, and brought out His people Israel from their midst into everlasting freedom; → who led His children through the divided Reed Sea, plunging their pursuers and enemies into the depths. When His children saw His might, they gave praise and thanks to His name, and willingly accepted His Sovereignty. Moses and the children of Israel then sang a song to You with great joy, and they all exclaimed:

מִי־כָמְכָה **"Who is like You, LORD, among the mighty? Who is like You, majestic in holiness, awesome in praises, doing wonders?"** → Your children beheld Your majesty as You parted the sea before Moses. "This is my GOD!" they responded, and then said: **"The Lord shall reign for ever and ever."** → And it is said, "For the LORD has redeemed Jacob and rescued him from a power stronger than his own. Blessed are You, LORD, who redeemed Israel.

הַשְׁכִּיבֵנוּ Help us lie down, LORD our GOD, in peace, and rise, O our King, to life. Spread over us Your canopy of peace. Direct us with Your good counsel, and save us for the sake of Your name. Shield us and remove from us every enemy, plague, sword, famine and sorrow. Remove the adversary from before and behind us. Shelter us in the shadow of Your wings, for You, GOD, are our Guardian and Deliverer;

כִּי אֵל מֶלֶךְ חַנּוּן וְרַחוּם אָתָּה. וּשְׁמוֹר צֵאתֵנוּ וּבוֹאֵנוּ, לְחַיִּים וּלְשָׁלוֹם מֵעַתָּה וְעַד עוֹלָם. ◄ וּפְרֹשׂ עָלֵינוּ סֻכַּת שְׁלוֹמֶךָ. בָּרוּךְ אַתָּה יהוה, הַפּוֹרֵשׂ סֻכַּת שָׁלוֹם עָלֵינוּ וְעַל כָּל עַמּוֹ יִשְׂרָאֵל וְעַל יְרוּשָׁלָיִם.

On שַׁבָּת, the Congregation stands and, together with the Leader, says:

שמות לא:טז–יז

וְשָׁמְרוּ בְנֵי־יִשְׂרָאֵל אֶת־הַשַּׁבָּת, לַעֲשׂוֹת אֶת־הַשַּׁבָּת לְדֹרֹתָם בְּרִית עוֹלָם. בֵּינִי וּבֵין בְּנֵי יִשְׂרָאֵל אוֹת הִיא לְעוֹלָם, כִּי־שֵׁשֶׁת יָמִים עָשָׂה יהוה אֶת־הַשָּׁמַיִם וְאֶת־הָאָרֶץ, וּבַיּוֹם הַשְּׁבִיעִי שָׁבַת וַיִּנָּפַשׁ.

On פֶּסַח, שָׁבֻעוֹת and סֻכּוֹת (but not חוֹל הַמּוֹעֵד) say:

ויקרא כג:מד

וַיְדַבֵּר מֹשֶׁה אֶת־מֹעֲדֵי יהוה אֶל־בְּנֵי יִשְׂרָאֵל.

The Leader says חֲצִי קַדִּישׁ.

Leader:

יִתְגַּדַּל וְיִתְקַדַּשׁ שְׁמֵהּ רַבָּא. (Cong. אָמֵן) בְּעָלְמָא דִּי־בְרָא כִרְעוּתֵהּ. וְיַמְלִיךְ מַלְכוּתֵהּ, בְּחַיֵּיכוֹן וּבְיוֹמֵיכוֹן וּבְחַיֵּי דִי־כָל־בֵּית יִשְׂרָאֵל, בַּעֲגָלָא וּבִזְמַן קָרִיב. וְאִמְרוּ אָמֵן. (Cong. אָמֵן)

All:

יְהֵא שְׁמֵהּ רַבָּא מְבָרַךְ לְעָלַם וּלְעָלְמֵי עָלְמַיָּא.

Leader:

יִתְבָּרַךְ וְיִשְׁתַּבַּח וְיִתְפָּאַר וְיִתְרוֹמַם וְיִתְנַשֵּׂא וְיִתְהַדָּר וְיִתְעַלֶּה וְיִתְהַלָּל שְׁמֵהּ דְּקֻדְשָׁא בְּרִיךְ הוּא (Cong. בְּרִיךְ הוּא) לְעֵלָּא (On שַׁבָּת שׁוּבָה add לְעֵלָּא) מִן־כָּל־בִּרְכָתָא וְשִׁירָתָא תֻּשְׁבְּחָתָא וְנֶחֱמָתָא, דִּי־אֲמִירָן בְּעָלְמָא. וְאִמְרוּ אָמֵן. (Cong. אָמֵן)

You, God, are a gracious and compassionate King. Guard our going out and our coming in, for life and peace, from now and for ever, → and spread over us Your canopy of peace. Blessed are You, Lord, who spreads a canopy of peace over all His people Israel, and over Jerusalem.

On Shabbat, the Congregation stands and, together with the Leader, says:

EXODUS 31:16–17

וְשָׁמְרוּ The children of Israel must keep the Sabbath, observing the Sabbath in every generation as an everlasting covenant. It is a sign between Me and the children of Israel for ever, for in six days God made the heavens and the earth, but on the seventh day He ceased work and refreshed Himself.

On Festivals (but not on their intermediate days) say:

LEVITICUS 23:44

וַיְדַבֵּר Thus Moses announced the Lord's appointed seasons to the children of Israel.

The Leader says half-*Kaddish*.

Leader:

יִתְגַּדַּל Magnified and sanctified may His great name be, in the world He created by His will. May He establish His kingdom in your lifetime and in your days, and in the lifetime of all the House of Israel, swiftly and soon – and say: Amen.

All:

May His great name be blessed for ever and all time.

Leader:

Blessed and praised, glorified and exalted, raised and honoured, uplifted and lauded be the name of the Holy One, blessed be He, (between Rosh Hashanah and Yom Kippur add 'well') beyond any blessing, song, praise and consolation uttered in the world – and say: Amen.

On יוֹם טוֹב, say the appropriate עֲמִידָה on page 646.

עמידה

The following prayer, until קַדְמוֹנִיּוֹת, on page 294, is said silently, standing with feet together.

Take three steps back, then forward. At the points indicated by ▾, bend the knees at the first word, bow at the second, and stand straight before God's name.

אֲדֹנָי, שְׂפָתַי תִּפְתָּח, וּפִי יַגִּיד תְּהִלָּתֶךָ.

אבות

▾**בָּרוּךְ** אַתָּה יהוה אֱלֹהֵינוּ וֵאלֹהֵי אֲבוֹתֵינוּ, אֱלֹהֵי אַבְרָהָם, אֱלֹהֵי יִצְחָק, וֵאלֹהֵי יַעֲקֹב, הָאֵל הַגָּדוֹל הַגִּבּוֹר וְהַנּוֹרָא, אֵל עֶלְיוֹן, גּוֹמֵל חֲסָדִים טוֹבִים וְקוֹנֵה הַכֹּל, וְזוֹכֵר חַסְדֵי אָבוֹת, וּמֵבִיא גוֹאֵל לִבְנֵי בְנֵיהֶם, לְמַעַן שְׁמוֹ בְּאַהֲבָה.

On שַׁבַּת שׁוּבָה, add:

זָכְרֵנוּ לְחַיִּים, מֶלֶךְ חָפֵץ בַּחַיִּים, וְכָתְבֵנוּ בְּסֵפֶר הַחַיִּים, לְמַעַנְךָ אֱלֹהִים חַיִּים.

מֶלֶךְ עוֹזֵר וּמוֹשִׁיעַ וּמָגֵן. ▾בָּרוּךְ אַתָּה יהוה, מָגֵן אַבְרָהָם.

גבורות

אַתָּה גִּבּוֹר לְעוֹלָם אֲדֹנָי, מְחַיֵּה מֵתִים אַתָּה, רַב לְהוֹשִׁיעַ.

From שְׁמִינִי עֲצֶרֶת until the first day of פֶּסַח, add:

מַשִּׁיב הָרְוּחַ וּמוֹרִיד הַגֶּשֶׁם.

THE FRIDAY NIGHT AMIDAH

On Shabbat and festivals, the *Amidah*, the "standing prayer", consists not of nineteen but seven blessings (on Musaf of Rosh Hashanah, nine). The first and last three are, with minor variations, the same throughout the year. The seventh (middle) blessing is dedicated to the special "sanctity of the day". Uniquely on Shabbat, this blessing is different for each of the three services; evening, morning and afternoon (the Musaf prayer is in a category of its own). The quality of time on Shabbat is different from other days: like a symphony, it has several movements.

On Friday evening, we speak of the Shabbat of creation; in the morning, of the Shabbat of revelation, as it was com-

On Festivals, say the appropriate *Amidah* on page 647.

AMIDAH: THE STANDING PRAYER

The following prayer, until "in former years", on page 295, is said silently, standing with feet together.

Take three steps back, then forward. At the points indicated by ▾, bend the knees at the first word, bow at the second, and stand straight before God's name.

O Lord, open my lips, so that my mouth may declare Your praise.

PATRIARCHS

▾בָּרוּךְ Blessed are You, Lord our God and God of our Fathers, God of Abraham, God of Isaac and God of Jacob; the great, mighty and awesome God, God Most High, who bestows acts of lovingkindness and creates all, who remembers the lovingkindness of the Fathers and will bring a Redeemer to their children's children for the sake of His name, in love.

On the Shabbat of Penitence, add:

Remember us for life, O King who desires life, and write us in the book of life – for Your sake, O God of life.

King, Helper, Saviour, Shield: ▾Blessed are You, Lord, Shield of Abraham.

DIVINE MIGHT

אַתָּה You are eternally mighty, Lord. You give life to the dead and have great power to save.

From Shmini Atzeret until the first day of Pesach, add:

He makes the wind blow and the rain fall.

manded on Mount Sinai; and in the afternoon, we look forward to the Shabbat of redemption. Thus in the evening, we think of the birth of time; in the morning, of historical time, the remembered past and the living present; and in the afternoon, of the culmination of time, and the World to Come of which Shabbat is the foretaste. Shabbat becomes a journey through the three phases of faith: God's creation of the Universe, His self-revelation to humanity, and His redemptive acts – collectively summoning us to build a world at peace with itself because it is at peace with God.

Another interpretation sees in the three stages of Shabbat the three parts

מְכַלְכֵּל חַיִּים בְּחֶסֶד, מְחַיֵּה מֵתִים בְּרַחֲמִים רַבִּים, סוֹמֵךְ נוֹפְלִים, וְרוֹפֵא חוֹלִים, וּמַתִּיר אֲסוּרִים, וּמְקַיֵּם אֱמוּנָתוֹ לִישֵׁנֵי עָפָר. מִי כָמוֹךָ בַּעַל גְּבוּרוֹת, וּמִי דּוֹמֶה לָּךְ, מֶלֶךְ מֵמִית וּמְחַיֶּה וּמַצְמִיחַ יְשׁוּעָה.

On שַׁבַּת שׁוּבָה, add:

מִי כָמְוֹךָ אַב הָרַחֲמִים, זוֹכֵר יְצוּרָיו לַחַיִּים בְּרַחֲמִים.

וְנֶאֱמָן אַתָּה לְהַחֲיוֹת מֵתִים. בָּרוּךְ אַתָּה יהוה, מְחַיֵּה הַמֵּתִים.

קדושת השם

אַתָּה קָדוֹשׁ וְשִׁמְךָ קָדוֹשׁ, וּקְדוֹשִׁים בְּכָל־יוֹם יְהַלְלְוּךָ סֶּלָה. בָּרוּךְ אַתָּה יהוה, *הָאֵל הַקָּדוֹשׁ.

*On שַׁבַּת שׁוּבָה, end the blessing:

הַמֶּלֶךְ הַקָּדוֹשׁ.

קדושת היום

אַתָּה קִדַּשְׁתָּ אֶת־יוֹם הַשְּׁבִיעִי לִשְׁמֶךָ, תַּכְלִית מַעֲשֵׂה שָׁמַיִם וָאָרֶץ, וּבֵרַכְתּוֹ מִכָּל־הַיָּמִים, וְקִדַּשְׁתּוֹ מִכָּל־הַזְּמַנִּים, וְכֵן כָּתוּב בְּתוֹרָתֶךָ.

וַיְכֻלּוּ הַשָּׁמַיִם וְהָאָרֶץ וְכָל־צְבָאָם. וַיְכַל אֱלֹהִים בַּיּוֹם הַשְּׁבִיעִי מְלַאכְתּוֹ אֲשֶׁר עָשָׂה, וַיִּשְׁבֹּת בַּיּוֹם הַשְּׁבִיעִי מִכָּל־

of a wedding: the first part, betrothal, *Kiddushin*; then the marriage itself, *Nisu'in*, symbolised by joy; then *yichud*, the coming together of the bride and groom (Abudraham). This idea, reflected in the language of the *Amidah*, accords with the mystical understanding of the Shabbat as a bride, and the day itself as a marriage of heaven and earth.

אַתָּה קִדַּשְׁתָּ *You sanctified*: As signalled above, the Friday evening blessing speaks of creation: "You sanctified the seventh day for Your Name's sake, as the culmination of the creation of heaven and earth." It

He sustains the living with lovingkindness, and with great compassion revives the dead. He supports the fallen, heals the sick, sets captives free, and keeps His faith with those who sleep in the dust. Who is like You, Master of might, and to whom can You be compared, O King who brings death and gives life, and makes salvation grow?

On the Shabbat of Penitence, add:

Who is like You, compassionate Father, who remembers His creatures in compassion, for life?

Faithful are You to revive the dead. Blessed are You, LORD, who revives the dead.

HOLINESS

אַתָּה You are holy and Your name is holy, and holy ones praise You daily, Selah! Blessed are You, LORD, *the holy GOD.

*On the Shabbat of Penitence, end the blessing:

the holy King.

HOLINESS OF THE DAY

אַתָּה קִדַּשְׁתָּ You sanctified the seventh day for Your name's sake, as the culmination of the creation of heaven and earth. Of all days, You blessed it; of all seasons You sanctified it – and so it is written in Your Torah:

וַיְכֻלּוּ Then the heavens and the earth were completed, and all their array. With the seventh day, GOD completed the work He had done.

---

refers to the beginning of time: the seventh day of creation when GOD rested and the universe was young. And it uses the word "sanctified", the key word of the betrothal declaration under the bridal canopy.

וַיְכֻלּוּ הַשָּׁמַיִם וְהָאָרֶץ *Then the heavens and the earth were completed*: These three verses conclude the biblical account of creation. They contain 35 (5×7) words. The entire creation narrative (Genesis 1:1–2:3) is constructed in multiples of seven. The word "good" appears seven times, the word "GOD" thirty-five times, and the word "earth" twenty-one times. The opening verse contains seven words, the second fourteen, and the complete text 469 (7×67) words. From the very outset, seven dominates, as if to signal from the beginning that the seventh day was the culmination and purpose of creation: "last in deed, first in thought".

מְלַאכְתּוֹ אֲשֶׁר עָשָׂה. וַיְבָרֶךְ אֱלֹהִים אֶת־יוֹם הַשְּׁבִיעִי, וַיְקַדֵּשׁ אֹתוֹ, כִּי בוֹ שָׁבַת מִכָּל־מְלַאכְתּוֹ, אֲשֶׁר־בָּרָא אֱלֹהִים, לַעֲשׂוֹת.

אֱלֹהֵינוּ וֵאלֹהֵי אֲבוֹתֵינוּ, רְצֵה בִמְנוּחָתֵנוּ, קַדְּשֵׁנוּ בְּמִצְוֹתֶיךָ, וְתֵן חֶלְקֵנוּ בְּתוֹרָתֶךָ. שַׂבְּעֵנוּ מִטּוּבֶךָ, וְשַׂמְּחֵנוּ בִּישׁוּעָתֶךָ. וְטַהֵר לִבֵּנוּ לְעָבְדְּךָ בֶּאֱמֶת. וְהַנְחִילֵנוּ יהוה אֱלֹהֵינוּ בְּאַהֲבָה וּבְרָצוֹן שַׁבַּת קָדְשֶׁךָ, וְיָנוּחוּ בָהּ יִשְׂרָאֵל מְקַדְּשֵׁי שְׁמֶךָ. בָּרוּךְ אַתָּה יהוה, מְקַדֵּשׁ הַשַּׁבָּת.

עבודה

רְצֵה יהוה אֱלֹהֵינוּ בְּעַמְּךָ יִשְׂרָאֵל וּבִתְפִלָּתָם, וְהָשֵׁב אֶת־הָעֲבוֹדָה לִדְבִיר בֵּיתֶךָ. וְאִשֵּׁי יִשְׂרָאֵל וּתְפִלָּתָם בְּאַהֲבָה תְקַבֵּל בְּרָצוֹן, וּתְהִי לְרָצוֹן תָּמִיד עֲבוֹדַת יִשְׂרָאֵל עַמֶּךָ.

On רֹאשׁ חֹדֶשׁ and חוֹל הַמּוֹעֵד, say:

אֱלֹהֵינוּ וֵאלֹהֵי אֲבוֹתֵינוּ, יַעֲלֶה, וְיָבֹא, וְיַגִּיעַ, וְיֵרָאֶה, וְיֵרָצֶה, וְיִשָּׁמַע, וְיִפָּקֵד, וְיִזָּכֵר זִכְרוֹנֵנוּ וּפִקְדוֹנֵנוּ, וְזִכְרוֹן אֲבוֹתֵינוּ, וְזִכְרוֹן מָשִׁיחַ בֶּן דָּוִד עַבְדֶּךָ, וְזִכְרוֹן יְרוּשָׁלַיִם עִיר קָדְשֶׁךָ, וְזִכְרוֹן כָּל־עַמְּךָ בֵּית יִשְׂרָאֵל לְפָנֶיךָ, לִפְלֵיטָה וּלְטוֹבָה, וּלְחֵן וּלְחֶסֶד וּלְרַחֲמִים, וּלְחַיִּים וּלְשָׁלוֹם בְּיוֹם

On רֹאשׁ חֹדֶשׁ:	On פֶּסַח:	On סֻכּוֹת:
רֹאשׁ הַחֹדֶשׁ	חַג הַמַּצּוֹת	חַג הַסֻּכּוֹת

הַזֶּה. זָכְרֵנוּ יהוה אֱלֹהֵינוּ בּוֹ לְטוֹבָה, וּפָקְדֵנוּ בוֹ לִבְרָכָה, וְהוֹשִׁיעֵנוּ בוֹ לְחַיִּים. וּבִדְבַר יְשׁוּעָה וְרַחֲמִים, חוּס וְחָנֵּנוּ וְרַחֵם עָלֵינוּ וְהוֹשִׁיעֵנוּ, כִּי אֵלֶיךָ עֵינֵינוּ, כִּי אֵל מֶלֶךְ חַנּוּן וְרַחוּם אָתָּה.

וַיְקַדֵּשׁ אֹתוֹ *And declared it holy*: This is the first time the word "holy" appears in the Torah, indicating that time, not just space, is holy. The Sages noted the similarities between Shabbat and the sanctuary constructed by the Israelites in the

He ceased on the seventh day from all the work He had done. God blessed the seventh day and declared it holy, because on it He ceased from all His work He had created to do.

אֱלֹהֵינוּ Our God and God of our ancestors, may You find favour in our rest. Make us holy through Your commandments and grant us our share in Your Torah. Satisfy us with Your goodness, grant us joy in Your salvation, and purify our hearts to serve You in truth. In love and favour, O Lord our God, grant us as our heritage Your holy Shabbat, so that Israel, who sanctify Your name, may find rest on it. Blessed are You, Lord, who sanctifies the Sabbath.

TEMPLE SERVICE

רְצֵה Find favour, Lord our God, in Your people Israel and their prayer. Restore the service to Your most holy house, and accept in love and favour the fire-offerings of Israel and their prayer. May the service of Your people Israel always find favour with You.

On Rosh Chodesh and the Intermediate Days of Festivals, say:

אֱלֹהֵינוּ Our God and God of our ancestors, may there rise, come, reach, appear, be favoured, heard, regarded and remembered before You, our recollection and remembrance, as well as the remembrance of our ancestors, and of the Messiah son of David Your servant, and of Jerusalem Your holy city, and of all Your people the House of Israel – for deliverance and well-being, grace, lovingkindness and compassion, life and peace, on this day of:

On Rosh Chodesh, say:	On Pesach, say:	On Sukkot, say:
Rosh Chodesh.	the Festival of Matzot.	the Festival of Sukkot.

On it remember us, Lord our God, for good, recollect us for blessing, and deliver us for life. In accord with Your promise of salvation and compassion, spare us and be gracious to us, have compassion on us and deliver us, for our eyes are turned to You because You, God, are a gracious and compassionate King.

---

wilderness. The 39 categories of work performed in the building of the sanctuary are the same as those forbidden on Shabbat. Shabbat is thus a "sanctuary in time", and Israel, the "eternal people", is the nation called on to sanctify time.

וְתֶחֱזֶינָה עֵינֵינוּ בְּשׁוּבְךָ לְצִיּוֹן בְּרַחֲמִים. בָּרוּךְ אַתָּה יהוה, הַמַּחֲזִיר שְׁכִינָתוֹ לְצִיּוֹן.

הודאה

▽ Bow at the first five words.

▽**מוֹדִים** אֲנַחְנוּ לָךְ, שָׁאַתָּה הוּא יהוה אֱלֹהֵינוּ וֵאלֹהֵי אֲבוֹתֵינוּ לְעוֹלָם וָעֶד. צוּר חַיֵּינוּ, מָגֵן יִשְׁעֵנוּ אַתָּה הוּא לְדוֹר וָדוֹר. נוֹדֶה לְּךָ וּנְסַפֵּר תְּהִלָּתֶךָ עַל חַיֵּינוּ הַמְּסוּרִים בְּיָדֶךָ, וְעַל נִשְׁמוֹתֵינוּ הַפְּקוּדוֹת לָךְ, וְעַל נִסֶּיךָ שֶׁבְּכָל־יוֹם עִמָּנוּ, וְעַל נִפְלְאוֹתֶיךָ וְטוֹבוֹתֶיךָ שֶׁבְּכָל־עֵת, עֶרֶב וָבֹקֶר וְצָהֳרָיִם. הַטּוֹב כִּי לֹא־כָלוּ רַחֲמֶיךָ, וְהַמְרַחֵם כִּי לֹא־תַמּוּ חֲסָדֶיךָ, מֵעוֹלָם קִוִּינוּ לָךְ.

On שַׁבַּת חֲנֻכָּה, say:

עַל הַנִּסִּים, וְעַל הַפֻּרְקָן, וְעַל הַגְּבוּרוֹת, וְעַל הַתְּשׁוּעוֹת, וְעַל הַמִּלְחָמוֹת, שֶׁעָשִׂיתָ לַאֲבוֹתֵינוּ בַּיָּמִים הָהֵם בַּזְּמַן הַזֶּה.

בִּימֵי מַתִּתְיָהוּ בֶּן־יוֹחָנָן כֹּהֵן גָּדוֹל חַשְׁמוֹנָאִי וּבָנָיו, כְּשֶׁעָמְדָה מַלְכוּת יָוָן הָרְשָׁעָה עַל־עַמְּךָ יִשְׂרָאֵל, לְהַשְׁכִּיחָם תּוֹרָתֶךָ, וּלְהַעֲבִירָם מֵחֻקֵּי רְצוֹנֶךָ. וְאַתָּה בְּרַחֲמֶיךָ הָרַבִּים, עָמַדְתָּ לָהֶם בְּעֵת צָרָתָם, רַבְתָּ אֶת־רִיבָם, דַּנְתָּ אֶת־דִּינָם, נָקַמְתָּ אֶת־נִקְמָתָם. מָסַרְתָּ גִבּוֹרִים בְּיַד חַלָּשִׁים, וְרַבִּים בְּיַד מְעַטִּים, וּטְמֵאִים בְּיַד טְהוֹרִים, וּרְשָׁעִים בְּיַד צַדִּיקִים, וְזֵדִים בְּיַד עוֹסְקֵי תוֹרָתֶךָ. וּלְךָ עָשִׂיתָ שֵׁם גָּדוֹל וְקָדוֹשׁ בְּעוֹלָמֶךָ, וּלְעַמְּךָ יִשְׂרָאֵל עָשִׂיתָ תְּשׁוּעָה גְדוֹלָה וּפֻרְקָן כְּהַיּוֹם הַזֶּה. וְאַחַר כֵּן בָּאוּ בָנֶיךָ לִדְבִיר בֵּיתֶךָ, וּפִנּוּ אֶת־הֵיכָלֶךָ, וְטִהֲרוּ אֶת־מִקְדָּשֶׁךָ, וְהִדְלִיקוּ נֵרוֹת בְּחַצְרוֹת קָדְשֶׁךָ, וְקָבְעוּ שְׁמוֹנַת יְמֵי חֲנֻכָּה אֵלּוּ, לְהוֹדוֹת וּלְהַלֵּל לְשִׁמְךָ הַגָּדוֹל.

וְתֶחֱזֶינָה And may our eyes witness Your return to Zion in compassion. Blessed are You, LORD, who restores His Presence to Zion.

THANKSGIVING

▽ Bow at the first nine words.

מוֹדִים▽ We give thanks to You, for You are the LORD our GOD and GOD of our ancestors for ever and all time. You are the Rock of our lives, Shield of our salvation from generation to generation. We will thank You and declare Your praise for our lives which are entrusted into Your hand; our souls which are placed in Your charge; for Your miracles which are with us every day; and for Your wonders and favours at all times, evening, morning and midday. You are good – for Your compassion never fails. You are compassionate – for Your lovingkindnesses never cease. We have always placed our hope in You.

On Shabbat Chanukah, say:

עַל הַנִּסִּים [We thank You also] for the miracles, the redemption, the mighty deeds, and the victories in battle which You performed for our ancestors in those days at this time.

בִּימֵי In the days of Mattityahu, son of Yochanan the High Priest, the Hasmonean, and his sons, the wicked Greek kingdom rose up against Your people Israel to make them forget Your Torah and to force them to transgress the statutes of Your will. It was then that You in Your great compassion stood by them in the time of their distress. You championed their cause, judged their claim, and avenged their wrong. You delivered the strong into the hands of the weak, the many into the hands of the few, the impure into the hands of the pure, the wicked into the hands of the righteous, and the arrogant into the hands of those who were engaged in the study of Your Torah. You made for Yourself great and holy renown in Your world, and for Your people Israel You performed a great salvation and redemption on this day. Your children then entered the holiest part of Your house, cleansed Your Temple, purified Your sanctuary, kindled lights in Your holy courts, and designated these eight days of Chanukah for giving thanks and praise to Your great name.

וְעַל כֻּלָּם יִתְבָּרַךְ וְיִתְרוֹמַם שִׁמְךָ מַלְכֵּנוּ תָּמִיד לְעוֹלָם וָעֶד.

On שַׁבָּת שׁוּבָה, add:

וּכְתוֹב לְחַיִּים טוֹבִים כָּל־בְּנֵי בְרִיתֶךָ.

וְכֹל הַחַיִּים יוֹדוּךָ סֶּלָה, וִיהַלְלוּ אֶת־שִׁמְךָ בֶּאֱמֶת, הָאֵל יְשׁוּעָתֵנוּ וְעֶזְרָתֵנוּ סֶלָה. ▾בָּרוּךְ אַתָּה יהוה, הַטּוֹב שִׁמְךָ וּלְךָ נָאֶה לְהוֹדוֹת.

שלום

שָׁלוֹם רָב עַל יִשְׂרָאֵל עַמְּךָ תָּשִׂים לְעוֹלָם, כִּי אַתָּה הוּא מֶלֶךְ אָדוֹן לְכָל הַשָּׁלוֹם. וְטוֹב בְּעֵינֶיךָ לְבָרֵךְ אֶת עַמְּךָ יִשְׂרָאֵל בְּכָל עֵת וּבְכָל שָׁעָה בִּשְׁלוֹמֶךָ. *בָּרוּךְ אַתָּה יהוה, הַמְבָרֵךְ אֶת עַמּוֹ יִשְׂרָאֵל בַּשָּׁלוֹם.

*On שַׁבָּת שׁוּבָה, substitute the following:

בְּסֵפֶר חַיִּים בְּרָכָה וְשָׁלוֹם, וּפַרְנָסָה טוֹבָה, נִזָּכֵר וְנִכָּתֵב לְפָנֶיךָ, אֲנַחְנוּ וְכָל־עַמְּךָ בֵּית יִשְׂרָאֵל, לְחַיִּים טוֹבִים וּלְשָׁלוֹם. בָּרוּךְ אַתָּה יהוה, עֹשֵׂה הַשָּׁלוֹם.

אֱלֹהַי, נְצוֹר לְשׁוֹנִי מֵרָע, וּשְׂפָתַי מִדַּבֵּר מִרְמָה, וְלִמְקַלְלַי נַפְשִׁי תִדֹּם, וְנַפְשִׁי כֶּעָפָר לַכֹּל תִּהְיֶה. פְּתַח לִבִּי בְּתוֹרָתֶךָ, וּבְמִצְוֹתֶיךָ תִּרְדֹּף נַפְשִׁי. וְכֹל הַחוֹשְׁבִים עָלַי רָעָה, מְהֵרָה הָפֵר עֲצָתָם וְקַלְקֵל מַחֲשַׁבְתָּם. עֲשֵׂה לְמַעַן שְׁמֶךָ, עֲשֵׂה לְמַעַן יְמִינֶךָ, עֲשֵׂה לְמַעַן קְדֻשָּׁתֶךָ, עֲשֵׂה לְמַעַן תּוֹרָתֶךָ. לְמַעַן יֵחָלְצוּן יְדִידֶיךָ, הוֹשִׁיעָה יְמִינְךָ וַעֲנֵנִי. יִהְיוּ לְרָצוֹן אִמְרֵי־פִי וְהֶגְיוֹן לִבִּי לְפָנֶיךָ, יהוה צוּרִי וְגוֹאֲלִי.

Bow, take three steps back, then bow, first left, then right, then centre, while saying:

עֹשֶׂה שָׁלוֹם בִּמְרוֹמָיו, הוּא יַעֲשֶׂה שָׁלוֹם עָלֵינוּ, וְעַל־כָּל־יִשְׂרָאֵל, וְאִמְרוּ אָמֵן.

וְעַל For all these things may Your name be blessed and exalted, our King, continually, for ever and all time.

On the Shabbat of Penitence, add:

And write, for a good life, all the children of Your covenant.

Let all that lives thank You, Selah! and praise Your name in truth, God, our Saviour and Help, Selah! ▾Blessed are You, Lord, whose name is "the Good" and to whom thanks is due.

PEACE

שָׁלוֹם Grant great peace to Your people Israel for ever, for You are the sovereign Lord of all peace; and may it be good in Your eyes to bless Your people Israel at every time, at every hour, with Your peace. *Blessed are You, Lord, who blesses His people Israel with peace.

---

*On the Shabbat of Penitence, substitute the following:

In the book of life, blessing, peace and prosperity, may we and all Your people the house of Israel be remembered and written before You for a good life, and for peace. Blessed are You, Lord, who makes peace.

אֱלֹהַי My God, guard my tongue from evil and my lips from deceitful speech. To those who curse me, let my soul be silent; may my soul be to all like the dust. Open my heart to Your Torah and let my soul pursue Your commandments. As for all who plan evil against me, swiftly thwart their counsel and frustrate their plans. Act for the sake of Your name; act for the sake of Your right hand; act for the sake of Your holiness; act for the sake of Your Torah. That Your beloved ones may be delivered, save with Your right hand and answer me. May the words of my mouth and the meditation of my heart find favour before You, Lord, my Rock and Redeemer.

Bow, take three steps back, then bow, first left, then right, then centre, while saying:

May He who makes peace in His high places, make peace for us and all Israel – and say: Amen.

יְהִי רָצוֹן מִלְּפָנֶיךָ יהוה אֱלֹהֵינוּ וֵאלֹהֵי אֲבוֹתֵינוּ, שֶׁיִּבָּנֶה בֵּית הַמִּקְדָּשׁ בִּמְהֵרָה בְיָמֵינוּ, וְתֵן חֶלְקֵנוּ בְּתוֹרָתֶךָ. וְשָׁם נַעֲבָדְךָ בְּיִרְאָה, כִּימֵי עוֹלָם וּכְשָׁנִים קַדְמוֹנִיּוֹת. וְעָרְבָה לַיהוה מִנְחַת יְהוּדָה וִירוּשָׁלָיִם, כִּימֵי עוֹלָם וּכְשָׁנִים קַדְמוֹנִיּוֹת.

The Leader and Congregation stand and say:

וַיְכֻלּוּ הַשָּׁמַיִם וְהָאָרֶץ וְכָל צְבָאָם. וַיְכַל אֱלֹהִים בַּיּוֹם הַשְּׁבִיעִי מְלַאכְתּוֹ אֲשֶׁר עָשָׂה, וַיִּשְׁבֹּת בַּיּוֹם הַשְּׁבִיעִי מִכָּל מְלַאכְתּוֹ אֲשֶׁר עָשָׂה. וַיְבָרֶךְ אֱלֹהִים אֶת יוֹם הַשְּׁבִיעִי, וַיְקַדֵּשׁ אֹתוֹ, כִּי בוֹ שָׁבַת מִכָּל מְלַאכְתּוֹ, אֲשֶׁר־בָּרָא אֱלֹהִים, לַעֲשׂוֹת.

The following until מְקַדֵּשׁ הַשַּׁבָּת on page 296 is said only when praying with a מִנְיָן. It is omitted when the first day of פֶּסַח falls on שַׁבָּת.

Leader:

בָּרוּךְ אַתָּה יהוה אֱלֹהֵינוּ וֵאלֹהֵי אֲבוֹתֵינוּ, אֱלֹהֵי אַבְרָהָם, אֱלֹהֵי יִצְחָק, וֵאלֹהֵי יַעֲקֹב, הָאֵל הַגָּדוֹל הַגִּבּוֹר וְהַנּוֹרָא, אֵל עֶלְיוֹן, קוֹנֵה שָׁמַיִם וָאָרֶץ.

Leader and Congregation:

מָגֵן אָבוֹת בִּדְבָרוֹ, מְחַיֵּה מֵתִים בְּמַאֲמָרוֹ, הָאֵל הַקָּדוֹשׁ (On שַׁבָּת שׁוּבָה change to הַמֶּלֶךְ הַקָּדוֹשׁ) שֶׁאֵין כָּמוֹהוּ, הַמֵּנִיחַ לְעַמּוֹ בְּיוֹם שַׁבַּת קָדְשׁוֹ, כִּי בָם רָצָה לְהָנִיחַ לָהֶם. לְפָנָיו נַעֲבוֹד בְּיִרְאָה וָפַחַד, וְנוֹדֶה לִשְׁמוֹ בְּכָל יוֹם תָּמִיד מֵעֵין הַבְּרָכוֹת. אֵל הַהוֹדָאוֹת, אֲדוֹן הַשָּׁלוֹם, מְקַדֵּשׁ הַשַּׁבָּת וּמְבָרֵךְ שְׁבִיעִי, וּמֵנִיחַ בִּקְדֻשָּׁה לְעַם מְדֻשְּׁנֵי עֹנֶג, זֵכֶר לְמַעֲשֵׂה בְרֵאשִׁית.

Leader:

אֱלֹהֵינוּ וֵאלֹהֵי אֲבוֹתֵינוּ רְצֵה בִמְנוּחָתֵנוּ. קַדְּשֵׁנוּ בְּמִצְוֹתֶיךָ, וְתֵן חֶלְקֵנוּ בְּתוֹרָתֶךָ. שַׂבְּעֵנוּ מִטּוּבֶךָ, וְשַׂמְּחֵנוּ בִּישׁוּעָתֶךָ,

יְהִי May it be Your will, LORD our GOD and GOD of our ancestors, that the Temple be rebuilt speedily in our days, and grant us a share in Your Torah. And there we will serve You with reverence, as in the days of old and as in former years. Then the offering of Judah and Jerusalem will be pleasing to the LORD as in the days of old and as in former years.

The Leader and Congregation stand and say:

וַיְכֻלּוּ Then the heavens and the earth were completed, and all their array. With the seventh day, GOD completed the work He had done. He ceased on the seventh day from all the work He had done. GOD blessed the seventh day and declared it holy, because on it He ceased from all His work He had created to do.

The following until "who sanctifies the Sabbath" on page 297 is said only when praying with a *minyan*. It is omitted when the first day of Pesach falls on Shabbat.

Leader:

בָּרוּךְ Blessed are You, LORD our GOD and GOD of our Fathers, GOD of Abraham, GOD of Isaac and GOD of Jacob, the great, mighty and awesome GOD, GOD Most High, Creator of heaven and earth.

Leader and Congregation:

מָגֵן By His word, He was the Shield of our ancestors. By His promise, He will revive the dead. There is none like the holy GOD (On the Shabbat of Penitence, change to "holy King"), who gives rest to His people on His holy Sabbath day, for He found them worthy of His favour to give them rest. Before Him we will come in worship with reverence and awe, giving thanks to His name daily, continually, with due blessings. He is GOD to whom thanks are due, the LORD of peace who sanctifies the Sabbath and blesses the seventh day, and in holiness gives rest to a people filled with delight, in remembrance of the work of creation.

Leader:

אֱלֹהֵינוּ Our GOD and GOD of our ancestors, may You find favour in our rest. Make us holy through Your commandments and grant us our share in Your Torah. Satisfy us with Your goodness, grant us joy

---

מָגֵן *By His word, He was the Shield of our ancestors*: A summary of the seven blessings of the *Amidah*, which is unique to Friday evening. Tradition ascribes it to the fact that in Babylon, where synagogues were for the most part outside

וְטַהֵר לִבֵּנוּ לְעָבְדְּךָ בֶּאֱמֶת. וְהַנְחִילֵנוּ יהוה אֱלֹהֵינוּ בְּאַהֲבָה וּבְרָצוֹן שַׁבַּת קָדְשֶׁךָ. וְיָנוּחוּ בָהּ יִשְׂרָאֵל מְקַדְּשֵׁי שְׁמֶךָ. בָּרוּךְ אַתָּה יהוה, מְקַדֵּשׁ הַשַּׁבָּת.

The Leader says קַדִּישׁ תִּתְקַבַּל.

קדיש תתקבל

Leader:

יִתְגַּדַּל וְיִתְקַדַּשׁ שְׁמֵהּ רַבָּא. (Cong. אָמֵן) בְּעָלְמָא דִּי־בְרָא כִרְעוּתֵהּ. וְיַמְלִיךְ מַלְכוּתֵהּ, בְּחַיֵּיכוֹן וּבְיוֹמֵיכוֹן וּבְחַיֵּי דְכָל־בֵּית יִשְׂרָאֵל, בַּעֲגָלָא וּבִזְמַן קָרִיב. וְאִמְרוּ אָמֵן. (Cong. אָמֵן)

All:

יְהֵא שְׁמֵהּ רַבָּא מְבָרַךְ לְעָלַם וּלְעָלְמֵי עָלְמַיָּא.

Leader:

יִתְבָּרַךְ וְיִשְׁתַּבַּח וְיִתְפָּאַר וְיִתְרוֹמַם וְיִתְנַשֵּׂא וְיִתְהַדָּר וְיִתְעַלֶּה וְיִתְהַלָּל שְׁמֵהּ דְּקֻדְשָׁא בְּרִיךְ הוּא (Cong. בְּרִיךְ הוּא) לְעֵלָּא (On שַׁבַּת שׁוּבָה add לְעֵלָּא) מִן־כָּל־בִּרְכָתָא וְשִׁירָתָא תֻּשְׁבְּחָתָא וְנֶחֱמָתָא, דַּאֲמִירָן בְּעָלְמָא. וְאִמְרוּ אָמֵן. (Cong. אָמֵן)

תִּתְקַבַּל צְלוֹתְהוֹן וּבָעוּתְהוֹן דְּכָל־יִשְׂרָאֵל קֳדָם אֲבוּהוֹן דִּי בִשְׁמַיָּא. וְאִמְרוּ אָמֵן. (Cong. אָמֵן)

יְהֵא שְׁלָמָא רַבָּא מִן־שְׁמַיָּא, וְחַיִּים עָלֵינוּ וְעַל־כָּל־יִשְׂרָאֵל. וְאִמְרוּ אָמֵן. (Cong. אָמֵן)

Bow, take three steps back, then bow, first left, then right, then centre, while saying:

עֹשֶׂה שָׁלוֹם בִּמְרוֹמָיו, הוּא יַעֲשֶׂה שָׁלוֹם עָלֵינוּ, וְעַל־כָּל־יִשְׂרָאֵל. וְאִמְרוּ אָמֵן. (Cong. אָמֵן)

in Your salvation, and purify our hearts to serve You in truth. In love and favour, LORD our GOD, grant us as our heritage Your holy Sabbath, so that Israel who sanctify Your name may find rest on it. Blessed are You, LORD, who sanctifies the Sabbath.

The Leader says full *Kaddish*.

FULL KADDISH

Leader:

יִתְגַּדַּל Magnified and sanctified may His great name be, in the world He created by His will. May He establish His kingdom in your lifetime and in your days, and in the lifetime of all the House of Israel, swiftly and soon – and say: Amen.

All:

May His great name be blessed for ever and all time.

Leader:

Blessed and praised, glorified and exalted, raised and honoured, uplifted and lauded be the name of the Holy One, blessed be He, (between Rosh Hashanah and Yom Kippur add 'well') beyond any blessing, song, praise and consolation uttered in the world – and say: Amen.

May the prayers and pleas of all Israel be accepted by their Father in heaven – and say: Amen.

May there be great peace from heaven, and life for us and all Israel – and say: Amen.

Bow, take three steps back, then bow, first left, then right, then centre, while saying:

May He who makes peace in His high places, make peace for us and all Israel – and say: Amen.

---

town, going home at night was fraught with danger. This prayer was added for the benefit of latecomers, so that the congregation could leave together.

The following is not said on שַׁבַּת חוֹל הַמּוֹעֵד, on יוֹם טוֹב, or on the evening immediately after יוֹם טוֹב.

משנה שבת פרק ב׳

[א] **בַּמֶּה מַדְלִיקִין** וּבַמָּה אֵין מַדְלִיקִין. אֵין מַדְלִיקִין לֹא בְלֶכֶשׁ, וְלֹא בְחֹסֶן, וְלֹא בְכַלָּךְ, וְלֹא בִפְתִילַת הָאִידָן, וְלֹא בִפְתִילַת הַמִּדְבָּר, וְלֹא בִירוֹקָה שֶׁעַל פְּנֵי הַמָּיִם. לֹא בְזֶפֶת, וְלֹא בְשַׁעֲוָה, וְלֹא בְשֶׁמֶן קִיק, וְלֹא בְשֶׁמֶן שְׂרֵפָה, וְלֹא בְאַלְיָה, וְלֹא בְחֵלֶב. נַחוּם הַמָּדִי אוֹמֵר, מַדְלִיקִין בְּחֵלֶב מְבֻשָּׁל. וַחֲכָמִים אוֹמְרִים, אֶחָד מְבֻשָּׁל וְאֶחָד שֶׁאֵינוֹ מְבֻשָּׁל אֵין מַדְלִיקִין בּוֹ.

[ב] אֵין מַדְלִיקִין בְּשֶׁמֶן שְׂרֵפָה בְּיוֹם טוֹב. רַבִּי יִשְׁמָעֵאל אוֹמֵר, אֵין מַדְלִיקִין בְּעִטְרָן מִפְּנֵי כְבוֹד הַשַּׁבָּת. וַחֲכָמִים מַתִּירִין בְּכָל הַשְּׁמָנִים, בְּשֶׁמֶן שֻׁמְשְׁמִין, בְּשֶׁמֶן אֱגוֹזִים, בְּשֶׁמֶן צְנוֹנוֹת, בְּשֶׁמֶן דָּגִים, בְּשֶׁמֶן פַּקּוּעוֹת, בְּעִטְרָן, וּבְנֵפְט. רַבִּי טַרְפוֹן אוֹמֵר, אֵין מַדְלִיקִין אֶלָּא בְשֶׁמֶן זַיִת בִּלְבָד.

[ג] כָּל הַיּוֹצֵא מִן הָעֵץ אֵין מַדְלִיקִין בּוֹ אֶלָּא פִשְׁתָּן. וְכָל הַיּוֹצֵא מִן הָעֵץ אֵינוֹ מִטַּמֵּא טֻמְאַת אֹהָלִים אֶלָּא פִשְׁתָּן. פְּתִילַת הַבֶּגֶד שֶׁקִּפְּלָהּ וְלֹא הִבְהֲבָהּ. רַבִּי אֱלִיעֶזֶר אוֹמֵר, טְמֵאָה הִיא וְאֵין מַדְלִיקִין בָּהּ. רַבִּי עֲקִיבָא אוֹמֵר, טְהוֹרָה הִיא וּמַדְלִיקִין בָּהּ.

[ד] לֹא יִקֹּב אָדָם שְׁפוֹפֶרֶת שֶׁל בֵּיצָה וִימַלְּאֶנָּה שֶׁמֶן וְיִתְּנֶנָּה עַל פִּי הַנֵּר בִּשְׁבִיל שֶׁתְּהֵא מְנַטֶּפֶת, וַאֲפִילוּ הִיא

בַּמֶּה מַדְלִיקִין *With what wicks may we light?* This, the second chapter of the Mishnah tractate *Shabbat*, was also added to prolong the service for the benefit of latecomers. Its recitation, however, is also related to an ancient controversy

The following is not said on a Festival, on the intermediate Shabbat of a Festival, or on the evening immediately after a Festival.

MISHNAH SHABBAT, CHAPTER 2

1. בַּמֶּה מַדְלִיקִין With what wicks may we light the Sabbath lamp and with what may we not light? We may not use a wick of cedar bast, or uncombed flax, or raw silk, or a wick made of willow bast or desert weed, or seaweed. [For oil] we may not use pitch, or wax, or cotton-seed oil or [contaminated consecrated] oil that must be destroyed by burning, or fat from sheeps' tails, or tallow. Nahum the Mede says: We may use boiled tallow. But the Sages say: Whether boiled or not boiled, we may not use it.

2. [Contaminated consecrated] oil that must be destroyed by burning may not be used for a festival lamp. Rabbi Ishmael says: We may not use tar out of respect for the honour due to the Sabbath. But the Sages permit all these oils: sesame oil, nut oil, radish oil, fish oil, gourd oil, tar or naphtha. Rabbi Tarfon, however, says: We may use only olive oil.

3. No product from a tree may be used as a wick for the Sabbath lamp, except flax. Also no product of a tree can contract "tent" uncleanness, except flax. If a wick was made from a cloth that has been twisted but not singed, Rabbi Eliezer declares, it is susceptible to contamination and may not be used for a Sabbath lamp; but Rabbi Akiva says, it is not susceptible to contamination, and may be used for the Sabbath lamp.

4. One may not pierce an eggshell, fill it with oil, and put it over the mouth of a lamp so that the oil may drip from it into the lamp, even if the vessel is of earthenware, but Rabbi Judah permits it. If, how-

---

between those who accepted the Oral Law and those (Sadducees, and later, Karaites) who denied it. The latter held that the commandment, "Do not light a fire in any of your dwellings on the Sabbath day" (Exodus 35:3), precluded the use of any light; the former held that it excluded only the act of kindling itself, and not the use of a light that had been lit before Shabbat. Hence the study of the section of the Mishnah, part of the Oral Law, that deals with Shabbat lights.

שֶׁל חֶרֶס. וְרַבִּי יְהוּדָה מַתִּיר. אֲבָל אִם חִבְּרָהּ הַיּוֹצֵר מִתְּחִלָּה מֻתָּר, מִפְּנֵי שֶׁהוּא כְּלִי אֶחָד. לֹא יְמַלֵּא אָדָם קְעָרָה שֶׁמֶן וְיִתְּנֶנָּה בְּצַד הַנֵּר וְיִתֵּן רֹאשׁ הַפְּתִילָה בְּתוֹכָהּ בִּשְׁבִיל שֶׁתְּהֵא שׁוֹאֶבֶת. וְרַבִּי יְהוּדָה מַתִּיר.

[ה] הַמְכַבֶּה אֶת הַנֵּר מִפְּנֵי שֶׁהוּא מִתְיָרֵא מִפְּנֵי גוֹיִם, מִפְּנֵי לִסְטִים, מִפְּנֵי רוּחַ רָעָה, אוֹ בִשְׁבִיל הַחוֹלֶה שֶׁיִּישַׁן, פָּטוּר. כְּחָס עַל הַנֵּר, כְּחָס עַל הַשֶּׁמֶן, כְּחָס עַל הַפְּתִילָה, חַיָּב. רַבִּי יוֹסֵי פּוֹטֵר בְּכֻלָּן, חוּץ מִן הַפְּתִילָה, מִפְּנֵי שֶׁהוּא עוֹשָׂהּ פֶּחָם.

[ו] עַל שָׁלֹשׁ עֲבֵרוֹת נָשִׁים מֵתוֹת בִּשְׁעַת לֵדָתָן, עַל שֶׁאֵינָן זְהִירוֹת בְּנִדָּה, בְּחַלָּה, וּבְהַדְלָקַת הַנֵּר.

[ז] שְׁלֹשָׁה דְבָרִים צָרִיךְ אָדָם לוֹמַר בְּתוֹךְ בֵּיתוֹ עֶרֶב שַׁבָּת עִם חֲשֵׁכָה, עִשַּׂרְתֶּם, עֵרַבְתֶּם, הַדְלִיקוּ אֶת הַנֵּר. סָפֵק חֲשֵׁכָה סָפֵק אֵינָהּ חֲשֵׁכָה אֵין מְעַשְּׂרִין אֶת הַוַּדַּאי, וְאֵין מַטְבִּילִין אֶת הַכֵּלִים, וְאֵין מַדְלִיקִין אֶת הַנֵּרוֹת, אֲבָל מְעַשְּׂרִין אֶת הַדְּמַאי, וּמְעָרְבִין, וְטוֹמְנִין אֶת הַחַמִּין.

תלמוד בבלי מסכת ברכות סד:א'

אָמַר רַבִּי אֶלְעָזָר אָמַר רַבִּי חֲנִינָא, תַּלְמִידֵי חֲכָמִים מַרְבִּים שָׁלוֹם בָּעוֹלָם. שֶׁנֶּאֱמַר, וְכָל בָּנַיִךְ לִמּוּדֵי יהוה, וְרַב שְׁלוֹם בָּנָיִךְ. אַל תִּקְרֵי בָּנָיִךְ אֶלָּא בּוֹנָיִךְ. שָׁלוֹם רָב לְאֹהֲבֵי תוֹרָתֶךָ, וְאֵין לָמוֹ מִכְשׁוֹל. יְהִי שָׁלוֹם בְּחֵילֵךְ, שַׁלְוָה בְּאַרְמְנוֹתָיִךְ. לְמַעַן אַחַי וְרֵעָי, אֲדַבְּרָה נָּא שָׁלוֹם בָּךְ. לְמַעַן בֵּית יהוה אֱלֹהֵינוּ, אֲבַקְשָׁה טוֹב לָךְ. ◆ יהוה עֹז לְעַמּוֹ יִתֵּן, יהוה יְבָרֵךְ אֶת עַמּוֹ בַשָּׁלוֹם.

In many congregations, קַדִּישׁ דְּרַבָּנָן on page 34, is said here.

On יום טוב say the appropriate קִדּוּשׁ on page 660.

ever, the potter had originally attached it to the lamp, it is permitted because it constitutes a single vessel. One may not fill a bowl with oil, put it beside a lamp, and put the end of the wick in it so that it draws oil from the bowl; but Rabbi Judah permits this.

5. One who extinguishes a lamp because he is afraid of heathens, robbers, or depression, or to enable a sick person to sleep, is not liable [for violating the Sabbath]. If he did it to spare the lamp, or the oil, or the wick, he is liable. Rabbi Yose absolves him in all these cases except that of sparing the wick, because he thereby turns it into charcoal.

6. For three transgressions women may die in childbirth: for being careless in observing the laws of menstruation, separating challah [dough-offering], and lighting the Sabbath light.

7. One should say three things at home on the eve of the Sabbath just before dark: Have you tithed? Have you prepared the Eruv? Light the Sabbath lamp. If there is doubt whether or not darkness has fallen, we may not tithe definitely untithed produce, nor immerse [unclean] vessels, nor light the Sabbath lamp. We may tithe produce about which there is a doubt whether it has been tithed or not, we may prepare an Eruv, and insulate hot food.

BABYLONIAN TALMUD, BERACHOT 64A

אָמַר Rabbi Eleazar said in the name of Rabbi Chanina: The disciples of the Sages increase peace in the world, as it is said, "And all your children shall be taught of the Lord, and great shall be the peace of your children [*banayich*]". Read not *banayich*, "your children", but *bonayich*, "your builders". Those who love Your Torah have great peace; there is no stumbling block for them. May there be peace within your ramparts, prosperity in your palaces. For the sake of my brothers and friends, I shall say, "Peace be within you." For the sake of the house of the Lord our God, I will seek your good. ➔ May the Lord grant strength to His people; may the Lord bless His people with peace.

In many congregations, the Rabbis' *Kaddish* on page 35 is said here.

On Festivals, say the appropriate *Kiddush* on page 661.

קידוש בבית הכנסת

The Leader takes a cup of wine in his hand, and says:

בָּרוּךְ אַתָּה יהוה אֱלֹהֵינוּ מֶלֶךְ הָעוֹלָם, בּוֹרֵא פְּרִי הַגָּפֶן.

בָּרוּךְ אַתָּה יהוה אֱלֹהֵינוּ מֶלֶךְ הָעוֹלָם, אֲשֶׁר קִדְּשָׁנוּ בְּמִצְוֹתָיו, וְרָצָה בָנוּ, וְשַׁבַּת קָדְשׁוֹ בְּאַהֲבָה וּבְרָצוֹן הִנְחִילָנוּ, זִכָּרוֹן לְמַעֲשֵׂה בְרֵאשִׁית. כִּי הוּא יוֹם תְּחִלָּה לְמִקְרָאֵי קֹדֶשׁ, זֵכֶר לִיצִיאַת מִצְרָיִם. כִּי בָנוּ בָחַרְתָּ, וְאוֹתָנוּ קִדַּשְׁתָּ, מִכָּל־הָעַמִּים. וְשַׁבַּת קָדְשְׁךָ בְּאַהֲבָה וּבְרָצוֹן הִנְחַלְתָּנוּ. בָּרוּךְ אַתָּה יהוה, מְקַדֵּשׁ הַשַּׁבָּת.

The wine is given to children under the age of בַּת־מִצְוָה or בַּר־מִצְוָה to drink.

If there are no children present, the Leader drinks the cup of wine himself.

From the second night of פֶּסַח until the night before שָׁבֻעוֹת, the עֹמֶר is counted here on page 238.

Stand while saying עָלֵינוּ. Bow at ▾.

עָלֵינוּ לְשַׁבֵּחַ לַאֲדוֹן הַכֹּל, לָתֵת גְּדֻלָּה לְיוֹצֵר בְּרֵאשִׁית, שֶׁלֹּא עָשָׂנוּ כְּגוֹיֵי הָאֲרָצוֹת, וְלֹא שָׂמָנוּ כְּמִשְׁפְּחוֹת הָאֲדָמָה. שֶׁלֹּא שָׂם חֶלְקֵנוּ כָּהֶם, וְגֹרָלֵנוּ כְּכָל־הֲמוֹנָם. ▾וַאֲנַחְנוּ כּוֹרְעִים וּמִשְׁתַּחֲוִים וּמוֹדִים, לִפְנֵי מֶלֶךְ מַלְכֵי הַמְּלָכִים הַקָּדוֹשׁ בָּרוּךְ הוּא. שֶׁהוּא נוֹטֶה שָׁמַיִם וְיוֹסֵד אָרֶץ, וּמוֹשַׁב יְקָרוֹ בַּשָּׁמַיִם מִמַּעַל, וּשְׁכִינַת עֻזּוֹ בְּגָבְהֵי מְרוֹמִים. הוּא אֱלֹהֵינוּ, אֵין עוֹד. אֱמֶת מַלְכֵּנוּ, אֶפֶס זוּלָתוֹ, כַּכָּתוּב בְּתוֹרָתוֹ, וְיָדַעְתָּ הַיּוֹם וַהֲשֵׁבֹתָ אֶל־לְבָבֶךָ, כִּי יהוה הוּא הָאֱלֹהִים בַּשָּׁמַיִם מִמַּעַל וְעַל־הָאָרֶץ מִתָּחַת, אֵין עוֹד.

עַל־כֵּן נְקַוֶּה לְּךָ יהוה אֱלֹהֵינוּ לִרְאוֹת מְהֵרָה בְּתִפְאֶרֶת עֻזֶּךָ, לְהַעֲבִיר גִּלּוּלִים מִן הָאָרֶץ, וְהָאֱלִילִים כָּרוֹת יִכָּרֵתוּן,

KIDDUSH IN THE SYNAGOGUE

The Leader takes a cup of wine in his hand, and says:

בָּרוּךְ Blessed are You, LORD our GOD, King of the Universe, who creates the fruit of the vine.

בָּרוּךְ Blessed are You, LORD our GOD, King of the Universe, who has made us holy with His commandments, has favoured us, and in love and favour given us His holy Sabbath as a heritage, a remembrance of the work of creation. It is the first among the holy days of assembly, a remembrance of the exodus from Egypt. For You chose us and sanctified us from all the peoples, and in love and favour gave us Your holy Sabbath as a heritage. Blessed are You, LORD, who sanctifies the Sabbath.

The wine is given to children under the age of *Bar* or *Bat Mitzvah* to drink.

If there are no children present, the Leader drinks the cup of wine himself.

From the second night of Pesach until the night before Shavuot, the *Omer* is counted here on page 239.

ALEINU

Stand while saying *Aleinu*. Bow at ▾.

עָלֵינוּ It is our duty to praise the Master of all, and ascribe greatness to the Author of creation, who has not made us like the nations of the lands nor placed us like the families of the earth; who has not made our portion like theirs, nor our destiny like all their multitudes. Therefore ▾we bow in worship and thank the Supreme King of kings, the Holy One, blessed be He, who extends the heavens and establishes the earth, whose throne of glory is in the heavens above, and whose power's presence is in the highest of heights. He is our GOD; there is no other. Truly He is our King, there is none else, as it is written in His Torah: "You shall know and take to heart this day that the LORD is GOD, in heaven above and on earth below. There is no other."

עַל־כֵּן Therefore we place our hope in You, LORD our GOD, that

---

קִדּוּשׁ *Kiddush. Kiddush* is our way of fulfilling the commandment to "remember" the seventh day. It is said "where we eat the meal". Hence, in the synagogue the wine is not drunk by an adult but by a child, to avoid the possibility of a blessing said in vain. The custom of reciting kiddush in the synagogue goes back to an age when the house of prayer was also a hostel for visitors, who ate their meals nearby.

לְתַקֵּן עוֹלָם בְּמַלְכוּת שַׁדַּי. וְכָל־בְּנֵי בָשָׂר יִקְרְאוּ בִשְׁמֶךָ, לְהַפְנוֹת אֵלֶיךָ כָּל־רִשְׁעֵי אָרֶץ. יַכִּירוּ וְיֵדְעוּ כָּל־יוֹשְׁבֵי תֵבֵל, כִּי לְךָ תִּכְרַע כָּל־בֶּרֶךְ, תִּשָּׁבַע כָּל־לָשׁוֹן. לְפָנֶיךָ יהוה אֱלֹהֵינוּ יִכְרְעוּ וְיִפֹּלוּ, וְלִכְבוֹד שִׁמְךָ יְקָר יִתֵּנוּ. וִיקַבְּלוּ כֻלָּם אֶת־עוֹל מַלְכוּתֶךָ, וְתִמְלֹךְ עֲלֵיהֶם מְהֵרָה לְעוֹלָם וָעֶד. כִּי הַמַּלְכוּת שֶׁלְּךָ הִיא וּלְעוֹלְמֵי עַד תִּמְלוֹךְ בְּכָבוֹד, כַּכָּתוּב בְּתוֹרָתֶךָ, יהוה יִמְלֹךְ לְעוֹלָם וָעֶד. ◆ וְנֶאֱמַר, וְהָיָה יהוה לְמֶלֶךְ עַל־כָּל־הָאָרֶץ, בַּיּוֹם הַהוּא יִהְיֶה יהוה אֶחָד וּשְׁמוֹ אֶחָד.

Some congregations add:

אַל תִּירָא מִפַּחַד פִּתְאֹם, וּמִשֹּׁאַת רְשָׁעִים כִּי תָבֹא. עֻצוּ עֵצָה וְתֻפָר, דַּבְּרוּ דָבָר וְלֹא יָקוּם, כִּי עִמָּנוּ אֵל. וְעַד זִקְנָה אֲנִי הוּא, וְעַד שֵׂיבָה אֲנִי אֶסְבֹּל, אֲנִי עָשִׂיתִי וַאֲנִי אֶשָּׂא, וַאֲנִי אֶסְבֹּל וַאֲמַלֵּט.

קדיש יתום

The transliteration can be found at the end of the Siddur.

Mourner:

יִתְגַּדַּל וְיִתְקַדַּשׁ שְׁמֵהּ רַבָּא. (Cong. אָמֵן) בְּעָלְמָא דִּי־בְרָא כִרְעוּתֵהּ. וְיַמְלִיךְ מַלְכוּתֵהּ, בְּחַיֵּיכוֹן וּבְיוֹמֵיכוֹן וּבְחַיֵּי דִּי־כָל־בֵּית יִשְׂרָאֵל, בַּעֲגָלָא וּבִזְמַן קָרִיב. וְאִמְרוּ אָמֵן. (Cong. אָמֵן)

All:

יְהֵא שְׁמֵהּ רַבָּא מְבָרַךְ לְעָלַם וּלְעָלְמֵי עָלְמַיָּא.

Mourner:

יִתְבָּרַךְ וְיִשְׁתַּבַּח וְיִתְפָּאַר וְיִתְרוֹמַם וְיִתְנַשֵּׂא וְיִתְהַדָּר וְיִתְעַלֶּה וְיִתְהַלָּל שְׁמֵהּ דְּקֻדְשָׁא בְּרִיךְ הוּא (Cong. בְּרִיךְ הוּא) לְעֵלָּא (On שַׁבַּת שׁוּבָה add לְעֵלָּא) מִן־כָּל־בִּרְכָתָא וְשִׁירָתָא תֻּשְׁבְּחָתָא וְנֶחֱמָתָא, דַּאֲמִירָן בְּעָלְמָא. וְאִמְרוּ אָמֵן. (Cong. אָמֵן)

we may soon see the glory of Your power, when You will remove abominations from the earth, and idols will be utterly destroyed, when the world will be perfected under the sovereignty of the Almighty, when all humanity will call on Your name, and the earth's wicked will all turn to You. All the world's inhabitants will realise and know that to You every knee must bow and every tongue swear loyalty. Before You, LORD our GOD, they will kneel and bow down and give honour to Your glorious name. They will all accept the yoke of Your kingdom, and You will reign over them soon and for ever. For the kingdom is Yours, and to all eternity You will reign in glory, as it is written in Your Torah: "The LORD will reign for ever and ever." → And it is said: "Then the LORD shall be King over all the earth: on that day the LORD shall be One and His name One."

Some congregations add:

Have no fear of sudden terror or of the ruin that overtakes the wicked. Devise your strategy, but it will be thwarted; propose your plan, but it will not stand, for GOD is with us. When you grow old, I will still be the same. When your hair turns grey, I will still carry you. I made you, I will bear you, I will carry you, and I will rescue you.

MOURNER'S KADDISH

The transliteration can be found at the end of the Siddur.

Mourner:

יִתְגַּדַּל Magnified and sanctified may His great name be, in the world He created by His will. May He establish His kingdom in your lifetime and in your days, and in the lifetime of all the House of Israel, swiftly and soon – and say: Amen.

All:

May His great name be blessed for ever and all time.

Mourner:

Blessed and praised, glorified and exalted, raised and honoured, uplifted and lauded be the name of the Holy One, blessed be He, (between Rosh Hashanah and Yom Kippur add 'well') beyond any blessing, song, praise and consolation uttered in the world – and say: Amen.

יְהֵא שְׁלָמָא רַבָּא מִן־שְׁמַיָּא, וְחַיִּים עָלֵינוּ וְעַל־כָּל־יִשְׂרָאֵל. וְאִמְרוּ אָמֵן. (Cong. אָמֵן)

Bow, take three steps back, then bow, first left, then right, then centre, while saying:

עֹשֶׂה שָׁלוֹם בִּמְרוֹמָיו, הוּא יַעֲשֶׂה שָׁלוֹם עָלֵינוּ, וְעַל־כָּל־יִשְׂרָאֵל. וְאִמְרוּ אָמֵן. (Cong. אָמֵן)

From the second night of רֹאשׁ חֹדֶשׁ אֱלוּל until (and including) שְׁמִינִי עֲצֶרֶת, the following psalm is said.

תהלים כז

לְדָוִד, יהוה אוֹרִי וְיִשְׁעִי, מִמִּי אִירָא, יהוה מָעוֹז חַיַּי, מִמִּי אֶפְחָד. בִּקְרֹב עָלַי מְרֵעִים לֶאֱכֹל אֶת בְּשָׂרִי, צָרַי וְאֹיְבַי לִי, הֵמָּה כָשְׁלוּ וְנָפָלוּ. אִם תַּחֲנֶה עָלַי מַחֲנֶה, לֹא יִירָא לִבִּי, אִם תָּקוּם עָלַי מִלְחָמָה, בְּזֹאת אֲנִי בוֹטֵחַ. אַחַת שָׁאַלְתִּי מֵאֵת יהוה, אוֹתָהּ אֲבַקֵּשׁ, שִׁבְתִּי בְּבֵית יהוה כָּל יְמֵי חַיַּי, לַחֲזוֹת בְּנֹעַם יהוה, וּלְבַקֵּר בְּהֵיכָלוֹ. כִּי יִצְפְּנֵנִי בְּסֻכֹּה בְּיוֹם רָעָה, יַסְתִּרֵנִי בְּסֵתֶר אָהֳלוֹ, בְּצוּר יְרוֹמְמֵנִי. וְעַתָּה יָרוּם רֹאשִׁי עַל אֹיְבַי סְבִיבוֹתַי, וְאֶזְבְּחָה בְאָהֳלוֹ זִבְחֵי תְרוּעָה, אָשִׁירָה וַאֲזַמְּרָה לַיהוה. שְׁמַע יהוה קוֹלִי אֶקְרָא, וְחָנֵּנִי וַעֲנֵנִי. לְךָ אָמַר לִבִּי בַּקְּשׁוּ פָנָי, אֶת פָּנֶיךָ יהוה אֲבַקֵּשׁ. אַל תַּסְתֵּר פָּנֶיךָ מִמֶּנִּי, אַל תַּט בְּאַף עַבְדֶּךָ, עֶזְרָתִי הָיִיתָ, אַל תִּטְּשֵׁנִי וְאַל תַּעַזְבֵנִי, אֱלֹהֵי יִשְׁעִי. כִּי אָבִי וְאִמִּי עֲזָבוּנִי, וַיהוה יַאַסְפֵנִי. הוֹרֵנִי יהוה דַּרְכֶּךָ, וּנְחֵנִי בְּאֹרַח מִישׁוֹר, לְמַעַן שׁוֹרְרָי. אַל תִּתְּנֵנִי בְּנֶפֶשׁ צָרָי, כִּי קָמוּ בִי עֵדֵי שֶׁקֶר, וִיפֵחַ חָמָס. ← לוּלֵא הֶאֱמַנְתִּי לִרְאוֹת בְּטוּב יהוה בְּאֶרֶץ חַיִּים. קַוֵּה אֶל יהוה, חֲזַק וְיַאֲמֵץ לִבֶּךָ, וְקַוֵּה אֶל יהוה.

קַדִּישׁ יָתוֹם on previous page.

May there be great peace from heaven, and life for us and all Israel – and say: Amen.

Bow, take three steps back, then bow, first left, then right, then centre, while saying:

May He who makes peace in His high places, make peace for us and all Israel – and say: Amen.

From the second night of Rosh Chodesh Ellul until (and including) Shemini Atzeret, the following psalm is said.

PSALM 27

לְדָוִד A psalm of David. The LORD is my light and my salvation – whom then shall I fear? The LORD is the stronghold of my life – of whom shall I be afraid? When evil men close in on me to devour my flesh it is they, my enemies and foes, who stumble and fall. Should an army besiege me, my heart would not fear. Should war break out against me, still I would be confident. One thing I ask of the LORD, only this do I seek: to live in the house of the LORD all the days of my life, to gaze on the beauty of the LORD and worship in His Temple. For He will keep me safe in His pavilion on the day of trouble. He will hide me under the cover of His tent. He will set me high upon a rock. Now my head is high above my enemies who surround me. I will sacrifice in His tent with shouts of joy. I will sing and chant praises to the LORD. LORD, hear my voice when I call. Be gracious to me and answer me. On Your behalf my heart says, "Seek My face." Your face, LORD, will I seek. Do not hide Your face from me. Do not turn Your servant away in anger. You have been my help. Do not reject or forsake me, GOD, my Saviour. Were my father and my mother to forsake me, the LORD would take me in. Teach me Your way, LORD, and lead me on a level path, because of my oppressors. Do not abandon me to the will of my foes, for false witnesses have risen against me, breathing violence. ➔ Were it not for my faith that I shall see the LORD's goodness in the land of the living… Hope in the LORD. Be strong and of good courage, and hope in the LORD!

Mourner's *Kaddish* on previous page.

יגדל

The following is often sung in alternate verses by the Leader and Congregation:

יִגְדַּל אֱלֹהִים חַי וְיִשְׁתַּבַּח, נִמְצָא וְאֵין עֵת אֶל מְצִיאוּתוֹ.
אֶחָד וְאֵין יָחִיד כְּיִחוּדוֹ, נֶעְלָם וְגַם אֵין סוֹף לְאַחְדּוּתוֹ.
אֵין לוֹ דְּמוּת הַגּוּף וְאֵינוֹ גּוּף, לֹא נַעֲרוֹךְ אֵלָיו קְדֻשָּׁתוֹ.
קַדְמוֹן לְכָל דָּבָר אֲשֶׁר נִבְרָא, רִאשׁוֹן וְאֵין רֵאשִׁית לְרֵאשִׁיתוֹ.
הִנּוֹ אֲדוֹן עוֹלָם לְכָל נוֹצָר, יוֹרֶה גְדֻלָּתוֹ וּמַלְכוּתוֹ.
שֶׁפַע נְבוּאָתוֹ נְתָנוֹ, אֶל אַנְשֵׁי סְגֻלָּתוֹ וְתִפְאַרְתּוֹ.
לֹא קָם בְּיִשְׂרָאֵל כְּמֹשֶׁה עוֹד, נָבִיא וּמַבִּיט אֶת תְּמוּנָתוֹ.
תּוֹרַת אֱמֶת נָתַן לְעַמּוֹ אֵל, עַל יַד נְבִיאוֹ נֶאֱמַן בֵּיתוֹ.
לֹא יַחֲלִיף הָאֵל וְלֹא יָמִיר דָּתוֹ, לְעוֹלָמִים לְזוּלָתוֹ.
צוֹפֶה וְיוֹדֵעַ סְתָרֵינוּ, מַבִּיט לְסוֹף דָּבָר בְּקַדְמָתוֹ.
גּוֹמֵל לְאִישׁ חֶסֶד כְּמִפְעָלוֹ, נוֹתֵן לְרָשָׁע רָע כְּרִשְׁעָתוֹ.
יִשְׁלַח לְקֵץ יָמִין מְשִׁיחֵנוּ, לִפְדּוֹת מְחַכֵּי קֵץ יְשׁוּעָתוֹ.
מֵתִים יְחַיֶּה אֵל בְּרֹב חַסְדּוֹ, בָּרוּךְ עֲדֵי־עַד שֵׁם תְּהִלָּתוֹ.

יִגְדַּל *Great*: A poetic setting of Maimonides' thirteen principles of Jewish faith. The first five relate to creation, the next four to revelation, the last four to redemption. Without creation, there would be no universe. Without revelation, there would be no living contact with God. Without redemption, there would be no hope. The service thus ends with a re-affirmation of faith.

SHABBAT AT HOME

Shabbat is a celebration of the Jewish home, and the home is the matrix of Judaism. The prophets compared the relationship between God and Israel with that between husband and wife, and between parent and child. The Hebrew word *emunah,* usually translated as "faith", in fact means "faithfulness, fidelity", the virtue born and sustained within the home. The love between husband and wife is the human redemption of solitude. The love between parent and child is the closest we come to immortality in this world, for it is through our children that we, and what we live for, live on.

Friday night is when, freed from the pressures of work, we can give time and loving attention to one another. It is also the time when we feel most profoundly the *Shechinah*, the Divine presence, in

YIGDAL

The following is often sung in alternate verses by the Leader and Congregation:

יִגְדַּל Great is the living God and praised.
He exists, and His existence is beyond time.

He is One, and there is no unity like His.
Unfathomable, His oneness is infinite.

He has neither bodily form nor substance;
His holiness is beyond compare.

He preceded all that was created.
He was first: there was no beginning to His beginning.

Behold He is Master of the Universe; to every creature
He shows His greatness and majesty.

The rich flow of His prophecy He gave
to His treasured people in whom He gloried.

Never in Israel has there arisen another like Moses,
a prophet who beheld God's image.

God gave His people a Torah of truth
by the hand of His prophet, most faithful of His house.

God will not alter or change His law
for any other, for eternity.

He sees and knows our secret thoughts;
as soon as something is begun, He foresees its end.

He rewards people with lovingkindness according to their deeds;
He punishes the wicked according to his wickedness.

At the end of days He will send our Messiah,
to redeem those who await His final salvation.

God will revive the dead in His great lovingkindness.
Blessed for evermore is His glorious name!

---

the home. Our relationship to God and to those closest to us are both covenantal; that is to say, a mutual pledge of loyalty and love. Through the family and the quality of its relationships, Divine blessings flow into the world.

Before the Friday evening meal, we enact sequentially the values on which the home is built: 1. lighting candles, symbolising domestic Peace; 2. blessing children, our responsibility and continuity; 3. welcoming angels, invisible signs of God's protection; 4. praising "the woman of strength", guardian of the home; 5. *Kiddush*, the dimension of holiness; 6. the blessing over bread, a symbol of sustenance as God's gift; and 7. song and words of Torah, expressing our faith in joy.

קידוש וזמירות לליל שבת

ברכת הבנים

On the evenings of שַׁבָּת and יוֹם טוֹב, it is customary for parents to bless their children.

To sons, say:

יְשִׂמְךָ אֱלֹהִים כְּאֶפְרַיִם וְכִמְנַשֶּׁה.

To daughters, say:

יְשִׂמֵךְ אֱלֹהִים כְּשָׂרָה רִבְקָה רָחֵל וְלֵאָה.

To both sons and daughters:

יְבָרֶכְךָ יהוה וְיִשְׁמְרֶךָ. יָאֵר יהוה פָּנָיו אֵלֶיךָ וִיחֻנֶּךָּ.
יִשָּׂא יהוה פָּנָיו אֵלֶיךָ, וְיָשֵׂם לְךָ שָׁלוֹם.

סעודת ליל שבת

Many people sing each of the four verses of the following song three times:

שָׁלוֹם עֲלֵיכֶם, מַלְאֲכֵי הַשָּׁרֵת, מַלְאֲכֵי עֶלְיוֹן, מִמֶּלֶךְ מַלְכֵי הַמְּלָכִים הַקָּדוֹשׁ בָּרוּךְ הוּא.

בּוֹאֲכֶם לְשָׁלוֹם, מַלְאֲכֵי הַשָּׁלוֹם, מַלְאֲכֵי עֶלְיוֹן, מִמֶּלֶךְ מַלְכֵי הַמְּלָכִים הַקָּדוֹשׁ בָּרוּךְ הוּא.

בָּרְכוּנִי לְשָׁלוֹם, מַלְאֲכֵי הַשָּׁלוֹם, מַלְאֲכֵי עֶלְיוֹן, מִמֶּלֶךְ מַלְכֵי הַמְּלָכִים הַקָּדוֹשׁ בָּרוּךְ הוּא.

צֵאתְכֶם לְשָׁלוֹם, מַלְאֲכֵי הַשָּׁלוֹם, מַלְאֲכֵי עֶלְיוֹן, מִמֶּלֶךְ מַלְכֵי הַמְּלָכִים הַקָּדוֹשׁ בָּרוּךְ הוּא.

BLESSING THE CHILDREN
The custom of parents blessing their children has its origin in the blessing Jacob gave to his grandsons: "By you shall Israel invoke blessings, saying, May God make you like Ephraim and Manasseh" (Genesis 48:20). The blessing for boys repeats this phrase. That for girls invokes the four biblical matriarchs: Sarah, Rebecca, Rachel and Leah. This is followed, in both cases,

KIDDUSH AND SONGS FOR SHABBAT EVENING

BLESSING THE CHILDREN

On the evenings of Shabbat and Festivals, it is customary for parents to bless their children.

To sons, say:

יְשִׂמְךָ May God make you like Ephraim and Manasseh.

To daughters, say:

יְשִׂמֵךְ May God make you like Sarah, Rebecca, Rachel and Leah.

To both sons and daughters:

יְבָרֶכְךָ May the Lord bless you and protect you.
May the Lord make His face shine on you and be gracious to you.
May the Lord turn His face toward you and give you peace.

SHABBAT EVE MEAL

Many people sing each of the four verses of the following song three times:

שָׁלוֹם עֲלֵיכֶם Welcome, ministering angels, angels of the Most High, the supreme King of kings, the Holy One, blessed be He.

בּוֹאֲכֶם Enter in peace, angels of peace, angels of the Most High, the supreme King of kings, the Holy One, blessed be He.

בָּרְכוּנִי Bless me with peace, angels of peace, angels of the Most High, the supreme King of kings, the Holy One, blessed be He.

צֵאתְכֶם Go in peace, angels of peace, angels of the Most High, the supreme King of kings, the Holy One, blessed be He.

---

by the priestly blessing. It is a beautiful custom, symbolising the continuity of the generations in a way that is both tender and deeply spiritual. In the only verse to describe why Abraham was chosen, God says: "I have chosen him so that he will teach his children and his household after him to keep the way of the Lord, doing righteousness and justice" (Genesis 18:21). The bond between parents and children represents the continuity of the covenant across the generations.

שָׁלוֹם עֲלֵיכֶם *Welcome*: A poem based on the Talmudic passage (*Shabbat* 119b) that states that two ministering angels accompany a person on Friday night on his way from synagogue to home. When they see the home prepared for Shabbat, they bless the family. The author of the poem is un-

כִּי מַלְאָכָיו יְצַוֶּה־לָּךְ, לִשְׁמָרְךָ בְּכָל־דְּרָכֶיךָ.
יהוה יִשְׁמָר־צֵאתְךָ וּבוֹאֶךָ, מֵעַתָּה וְעַד־עוֹלָם.

משלי לא:י–לא

אֵשֶׁת חַיִל מִי יִמְצָא, וְרָחֹק מִפְּנִינִים מִכְרָהּ.
בָּטַח בָּהּ לֵב בַּעְלָהּ, וְשָׁלָל לֹא יֶחְסָר.
גְּמָלַתְהוּ טוֹב וְלֹא רָע, כֹּל יְמֵי חַיֶּיהָ.
דָּרְשָׁה צֶמֶר וּפִשְׁתִּים, וַתַּעַשׂ בְּחֵפֶץ כַּפֶּיהָ.
הָיְתָה כָּאֳנִיּוֹת סוֹחֵר, מִמֶּרְחָק תָּבִיא לַחְמָהּ.
וַתָּקָם בְּעוֹד לַיְלָה, וַתִּתֵּן טֶרֶף לְבֵיתָהּ, וְחֹק לְנַעֲרֹתֶיהָ.
זָמְמָה שָׂדֶה וַתִּקָּחֵהוּ, מִפְּרִי כַפֶּיהָ נָטְעָה כָּרֶם.
חָגְרָה בְעוֹז מָתְנֶיהָ, וַתְּאַמֵּץ זְרוֹעֹתֶיהָ.
טָעֲמָה כִּי־טוֹב סַחְרָהּ, לֹא־יִכְבֶּה בַלַּיְלָה נֵרָהּ.
יָדֶיהָ שִׁלְּחָה בַכִּישׁוֹר, וְכַפֶּיהָ תָּמְכוּ פָלֶךְ.
כַּפָּהּ פָּרְשָׂה לֶעָנִי, וְיָדֶיהָ שִׁלְּחָה לָאֶבְיוֹן.
לֹא־תִירָא לְבֵיתָהּ מִשָּׁלֶג, כִּי כָל־בֵּיתָהּ לָבֻשׁ שָׁנִים.
מַרְבַדִּים עָשְׂתָה־לָּהּ, שֵׁשׁ וְאַרְגָּמָן לְבוּשָׁהּ.
נוֹדָע בַּשְּׁעָרִים בַּעְלָהּ, בְּשִׁבְתּוֹ עִם־זִקְנֵי־אָרֶץ.
סָדִין עָשְׂתָה וַתִּמְכֹּר, וַחֲגוֹר נָתְנָה לַכְּנַעֲנִי.
עֹז וְהָדָר לְבוּשָׁהּ, וַתִּשְׂחַק לְיוֹם אַחֲרוֹן.
פִּיהָ פָּתְחָה בְחָכְמָה, וְתוֹרַת־חֶסֶד עַל־לְשׁוֹנָהּ.
צוֹפִיָּה הֲלִיכוֹת בֵּיתָהּ, וְלֶחֶם עַצְלוּת לֹא תֹאכֵל.
קָמוּ בָנֶיהָ וַיְאַשְּׁרוּהָ, בַּעְלָהּ וַיְהַלְלָהּ.
רַבּוֹת בָּנוֹת עָשׂוּ חָיִל, וְאַתְּ עָלִית עַל־כֻּלָּנָה.
שֶׁקֶר הַחֵן וְהֶבֶל הַיֹּפִי, אִשָּׁה יִרְאַת־יהוה הִיא תִתְהַלָּל.
תְּנוּ־לָהּ מִפְּרִי יָדֶיהָ, וִיהַלְלוּהָ בַשְּׁעָרִים מַעֲשֶׂיהָ.

He will command His angels about you, to guard you in all your ways.
May the Lord guard your going out and your return, from now and for all time.

PROVERBS 31:10–31.

אֵשֶׁת חַיִל A woman of strength, who can find? Her worth is far beyond pearls.
Her husband's heart trusts in her, and he has no lack of gain.
She brings him good, not harm, all the days of her life.
She seeks wool and linen, and works with willing hands.
She is like a ship laden with merchandise, bringing her food from afar.
She rises while it is still night, providing food for her household, portions for her maids.
She considers a field and buys it; from her earnings she plants a vineyard.
She girds herself with strength, and braces her arms for her tasks.
She sees that her business goes well; her lamp does not go out at night.
She holds the distaff in her hand, and grasps the spindle with her palms.
She reaches out her palm to the poor, and extends her hand to the needy.
She has no fear for her family when it snows, for all her household is clothed in crimson wool.
She makes elegant coverings; her clothing is fine linen and purple wool.
Her husband is well known in the gates, where he sits with the elders of the land.
She makes linen garments and sells them, and supplies merchants with sashes.
She is clothed with strength and dignity; she can laugh at the days to come.
She opens her mouth with wisdom, and the law of kindness is on her tongue.
She watches over the ways of her household, and never eats the bread of idleness.
Her children rise and call her happy; her husband also praises her:
"Many women have excelled, but you surpass them all."
Charm is deceptive and beauty vain: it is the God-fearing woman who deserves praise.
Give her the reward she has earned; let her deeds bring her praise in the gates.

---

known, but it is first mentioned in mystical circles in the seventeenth century.

אֵשֶׁת חַיִל *A woman of strength*: This text, an alphabetical acrostic, is taken from the closing chapter of the Book of Proverbs. In a series of scenes it describes an ideal woman: active, practical, a businesswoman as well as director of the household, involved in the welfare of strangers as well as her family, a woman of wisdom and kindness, "clothed with strength and dignity". The word *chayil* in the opening phrase signifies strength, both moral and physical. Many of the commentators see the woman in this passage as a symbol of the Divine presence (or Shabbat itself, personified as a bride). Without negating this allegorical meaning, the poem is also a hymn of thanks to the female head of

קידוש לליל שבת

For קִדּוּשׁ on יוֹם טוֹב, see page 660 and on רֹאשׁ הַשָּׁנָה, see page 746. The Leader takes a full cup of wine (or grape juice) in his hand and says:

Quietly:

וַיְהִי־עֶרֶב וַיְהִי בֹקֶר

יוֹם הַשִּׁשִּׁי. וַיְכֻלּוּ הַשָּׁמַיִם וְהָאָרֶץ וְכָל־צְבָאָם. וַיְכַל אֱלֹהִים בַּיּוֹם הַשְּׁבִיעִי מְלַאכְתּוֹ אֲשֶׁר עָשָׂה, וַיִּשְׁבֹּת בַּיּוֹם הַשְּׁבִיעִי מִכָּל־מְלַאכְתּוֹ אֲשֶׁר עָשָׂה. וַיְבָרֶךְ אֱלֹהִים אֶת־יוֹם הַשְּׁבִיעִי וַיְקַדֵּשׁ אֹתוֹ, כִּי בוֹ שָׁבַת מִכָּל־מְלַאכְתּוֹ אֲשֶׁר־בָּרָא אֱלֹהִים, לַעֲשׂוֹת.

When saying קִדּוּשׁ for others, add:

סַבְרִי מָרָנָן וְרַבָּנָן וְרַבּוֹתַי.

בָּרוּךְ אַתָּה יהוה אֱלֹהֵינוּ מֶלֶךְ הָעוֹלָם, בּוֹרֵא פְּרִי הַגָּפֶן.

בָּרוּךְ אַתָּה יהוה אֱלֹהֵינוּ מֶלֶךְ הָעוֹלָם, אֲשֶׁר קִדְּשָׁנוּ בְּמִצְוֹתָיו וְרָצָה בָנוּ, וְשַׁבַּת קָדְשׁוֹ בְּאַהֲבָה וּבְרָצוֹן הִנְחִילָנוּ, זִכָּרוֹן לְמַעֲשֵׂה בְרֵאשִׁית. כִּי הוּא יוֹם תְּחִלָּה לְמִקְרָאֵי קֹדֶשׁ, זֵכֶר לִיצִיאַת מִצְרָיִם. כִּי־בָנוּ בָחַרְתָּ, וְאוֹתָנוּ קִדַּשְׁתָּ, מִכָּל־הָעַמִּים. וְשַׁבַּת קָדְשְׁךָ בְּאַהֲבָה וּבְרָצוֹן הִנְחַלְתָּנוּ. בָּרוּךְ אַתָּה יהוה, מְקַדֵּשׁ הַשַּׁבָּת.

It is customary for all present to drink of the wine.
All then wash their hands, saying, immediately after the washing:

בָּרוּךְ אַתָּה יהוה אֱלֹהֵינוּ מֶלֶךְ הָעוֹלָם, אֲשֶׁר קִדְּשָׁנוּ בְּמִצְוֹתָיו וְצִוָּנוּ עַל נְטִילַת יָדָיִם.

---

the household for the blessings she brings to the family and the home.

קִדּוּשׁ *Kiddush*: In the Ten Commandments, we are commanded to "remember" the Shabbat day. This was understood to mean a verbal declaration, said over a cup of wine: hence *Kiddush*. The Friday night *Kiddush* contains three elements: 1. a biblical reading, referring to

KIDDUSH FOR SHABBAT EVENING

For *Kiddush* on Festivals, see page 661 and on Rosh Hashanah, see page 747.

The Leader takes a full cup of wine (or grape juice) in his hand and says:

Quietly:

And it was evening, and it was morning –

יוֹם הַשִּׁשִּׁי The sixth day. Then the heavens and the earth were completed, and all their array. With the seventh day, God completed the work He had done. He ceased on the seventh day from all the work He had done. God blessed the seventh day and declared it holy, because on it He ceased from all His work He had created to do.

When saying *Kiddush* for others, add:

Please pay attention, my teachers, rabbis and friends.

Blessed are You, Lord our God, King of the Universe, who creates the fruit of the vine.

Blessed are You, Lord our God, King of the Universe, who has made us holy through His commandments, who has favoured us, and in love and favour gave us His holy Sabbath as a heritage, a remembrance of the work of creation. It is the first among the holy days of assembly, a remembrance of the exodus from Egypt. For You chose us and sanctified us from all the peoples, and in love and favour gave us Your holy Sabbath as a heritage. Blessed are You, Lord, who sanctifies the Sabbath.

It is customary for all present to drink of the wine.
All then wash their hands, saying, immediately after the washing:

Blessed are You, Lord our God, King of the Universe, who has made us holy through His commandments, and has commanded us about washing hands.

---

the first Shabbat when God completed creation and rested on the seventh day; 2. a blessing over wine; and 3. a blessing over the day itself.

It is our custom to begin the first paragraph with the last two words of the previous verse so that the first four Hebrew words of *Kiddush* – *Yom Hashishi Vayechulu Hashamayim* – spell out the four-letter name of God. The previous words are said quietly. The blessing over the day recalls the two fundamental beliefs of which Shabbat is a memory: creation and the exodus from Egypt.

Washing hands. The ancient practice of

After washing hands, one should not speak until one has eaten some of the חַלָּה, the שַׁבָּת bread.

Holding both loaves, the person making the blessing says:

בָּרוּךְ אַתָּה יהוה אֱלֹהֵינוּ מֶלֶךְ הָעוֹלָם, הַמּוֹצִיא לֶחֶם מִן הָאָרֶץ.

Some of the bread should be given to each person present.

זמירות לליל שבת

יה רבון

יָהּ רִבּוֹן עָלַם וְעָלְמַיָּא, אַנְתְּ הוּא מַלְכָּא מֶלֶךְ מַלְכַיָּא,
עוֹבַד גְּבוּרְתֵּךְ וְתִמְהַיָּא, שְׁפַר קֳדָמָךְ לְהַחֲוָיָא.
יָהּ רִבּוֹן עָלַם וְעָלְמַיָּא, אַנְתְּ הוּא מַלְכָּא מֶלֶךְ מַלְכַיָּא.

שְׁבָחִין אֲסַדֵּר צַפְרָא וְרַמְשָׁא, לָךְ אֱלָהָא קַדִּישָׁא דִּי בְרָא כָּל
נַפְשָׁא, עִירִין קַדִּישִׁין וּבְנֵי אֱנָשָׁא, חֵיוַת בָּרָא וְעוֹפֵי שְׁמַיָּא.
יָהּ רִבּוֹן עָלַם וְעָלְמַיָּא, אַנְתְּ הוּא מַלְכָּא מֶלֶךְ מַלְכַיָּא.

רַבְרְבִין עוֹבְדֵיךְ וְתַקִּיפִין, מָכִיךְ רָמַיָּא וְזָקִיף כְּפִיפִין,
לוּ יִחְיֶה גְבַר שְׁנִין אַלְפִין, לָא יֵעוֹל גְּבוּרְתֵּךְ בְּחֻשְׁבְּנַיָּא.
יָהּ רִבּוֹן עָלַם וְעָלְמַיָּא, אַנְתְּ הוּא מַלְכָּא מֶלֶךְ מַלְכַיָּא.

אֱלָהָא דִּי לֵהּ יְקַר וּרְבוּתָא, פְּרוֹק יָת עָנָךְ מִפּוּם אַרְיְוָתָא,
וְאַפֵּיק יָת עַמֵּךְ מִגּוֹ גָלוּתָא, עַמֵּךְ דִּי בְחַרְתְּ מִכָּל אֻמַּיָּא.
יָהּ רִבּוֹן עָלַם וְעָלְמַיָּא, אַנְתְּ הוּא מַלְכָּא מֶלֶךְ מַלְכַיָּא.

לְמִקְדָּשֵׁךְ תּוּב וּלְקֹדֶשׁ קֻדְשִׁין, אֲתַר דִּי בֵהּ יֶחֱדוּן רוּחִין וְנַפְשִׁין,
וִיזַמְּרוּן לָךְ שִׁירִין וְרַחֲשִׁין, בִּירוּשְׁלֵם קַרְתָּא דְשׁוּפְרַיָּא.
יָהּ רִבּוֹן עָלַם וְעָלְמַיָּא, אַנְתְּ הוּא מַלְכָּא מֶלֶךְ מַלְכַיָּא.

---

washing hands before eating bread signals the sacred nature of a meal. The table is like the Temple altar; the bread is like consecrated food – hence our custom to dip the bread in salt, as was done with the meal-offering in the Temple (Leviticus 2:13). In this way, the home becomes a miniature sanctuary, and one of the most physical of the body's needs – food – is invested with the charisma of holiness.

After washing hands, one should not speak until one has eaten some of the *challah*, the Shabbat bread.

Holding both loaves, the person making the blessing says:

Blessed are You, LORD our GOD, King of the Universe, who brings forth bread from the earth.

Some of the bread should be given to each person present.

SHABBAT EVE ZEMIROT

YAH RIBON

יָהּ רִבּוֹן Master of all worlds, our GOD, adored, King of kings, over all the LORD: Your wondrous deeds to applaud, we sing to You with one accord.

GOD of all worlds, our GOD, adored; King of kings, over all the LORD.

Early and late my praise shall ring, to You, Holy Author of every thing: Beasts of the field, birds that take wing. Angels and mortals to You shall sing.

GOD of all worlds, our GOD, adored; King of kings, over all the LORD.

Your great good deeds are vast in scale, You humble the proud, You lift the frail. A thousand years would not avail, of Your works to tell the tale.

GOD of all worlds, our GOD, adored; King of kings, over all the LORD.

Yours is the glory, the greatness too, from the lion's jaw, Your flock rescue. Bring Your exiles home to You: The people You chose, deliver anew.

GOD of all worlds, our GOD, adored; King of kings, over all the LORD.

Come back to Your Temple, Your sacred shrine, that there in joy our souls may entwine. In song our voices to combine, when Jerusalem's beauty again will shine.

GOD of all worlds, our GOD, adored; King of kings, over all the LORD.

Blessing over bread. The two loaves are reminders of the double portion of manna that fell on Friday for the Israelites in the wilderness, so that they would not have to collect food on the Shabbat itself (Exodus 16:22). The Hebrew word for bread, *lechem*, comes from the same root as *milchamah*, "war", because livelihood involves competition for scarce resources, and can thus lead to war. The *challot* symbolise bread without war, a foretaste of the future in which "there will be neither famine nor war, neither jealousy nor strife" (Maimonides). *Challah* is the name for the portion of the dough set aside for the priests.

יָהּ רִבּוֹן *Yah ribbon.* A poem in Aramaic composed by Rabbi Israel Najara, who lived in Tzefat in the sixteenth–seventeenth centuries. The initial letters of the verses are an acrostic, spelling out the poet's name. Its theme is GOD's great-

צור משלו

צוּר מִשֶּׁלּוֹ אָכַלְנוּ בָּרְכוּ אֱמוּנַי, שָׂבַעְנוּ וְהוֹתַרְנוּ כִּדְבַר יהוה.

צוּר מִשֶּׁלּוֹ אָכַלְנוּ בָּרְכוּ אֱמוּנַי, שָׂבַעְנוּ וְהוֹתַרְנוּ כִּדְבַר יהוה.

הַזָּן אֶת עוֹלָמוֹ רוֹעֵנוּ אָבִינוּ, אָכַלְנוּ אֶת לַחְמוֹ וְיֵינוֹ שָׁתִינוּ, עַל כֵּן נוֹדֶה לִשְׁמוֹ וּנְהַלְּלוֹ בְּפִינוּ, אָמַרְנוּ וְעָנִינוּ אֵין קָדוֹשׁ כַּיהוה.

צוּר מִשֶּׁלּוֹ אָכַלְנוּ בָּרְכוּ אֱמוּנַי, שָׂבַעְנוּ וְהוֹתַרְנוּ כִּדְבַר יהוה.

בְּשִׁיר וְקוֹל תּוֹדָה נְבָרֵךְ לֵאלֹהֵינוּ, עַל אֶרֶץ חֶמְדָּה טוֹבָה שֶׁהִנְחִיל לַאֲבוֹתֵינוּ, מָזוֹן וְצֵדָה הִשְׂבִּיעַ לְנַפְשֵׁנוּ, חַסְדּוֹ גָּבַר עָלֵינוּ וֶאֱמֶת יהוה.

צוּר מִשֶּׁלּוֹ אָכַלְנוּ בָּרְכוּ אֱמוּנַי, שָׂבַעְנוּ וְהוֹתַרְנוּ כִּדְבַר יהוה.

רַחֵם בְּחַסְדֶּךָ עַל עַמְּךָ צוּרֵנוּ, עַל צִיּוֹן מִשְׁכַּן כְּבוֹדֶךָ זְבוּל בֵּית תִּפְאַרְתֵּנוּ, בֶּן דָּוִד עַבְדֶּךָ יָבוֹא וְיִגְאָלֵנוּ, רוּחַ אַפֵּינוּ מְשִׁיחַ יהוה.

צוּר מִשֶּׁלּוֹ אָכַלְנוּ בָּרְכוּ אֱמוּנַי, שָׂבַעְנוּ וְהוֹתַרְנוּ כִּדְבַר יהוה.

יִבָּנֶה הַמִּקְדָּשׁ עִיר צִיּוֹן תְּמַלֵּא, וְשָׁם נָשִׁיר שִׁיר חָדָשׁ וּבִרְנָנָה נַעֲלֶה, הָרַחֲמָן הַנִּקְדָּשׁ יִתְבָּרַךְ וְיִתְעַלֶּה, עַל כּוֹס יַיִן מָלֵא כְּבִרְכַּת יהוה.

צוּר מִשֶּׁלּוֹ אָכַלְנוּ בָּרְכוּ אֱמוּנַי, שָׂבַעְנוּ וְהוֹתַרְנוּ כִּדְבַר יהוה.

---

ness as Creator of all. In the poignant fourth verse, the poet compares the Jewish people's exile to the plight of sheep confronted by a lion.

צוּר מִשֶּׁלּוֹ *Tzur mishelo*: Composed probably in France in the fourteenth century, author unknown. The song, which has no specific connection with Shabbat, is a poetic prelude to the Grace after Meals. Its first three verses parallel, in theme and language, the first three blessings of

TZUR MISHELO

צוּר מִשֶּׁלּוֹ The Rock from whom we have eaten: Bless Him, my faithful friends; we have sufficed, we have left over, just as the LORD said.

The Rock from whom we have eaten: Bless Him, my faithful friends;
we have sufficed, we have left over, just as the LORD said.

He feeds His world – our Shepherd, our Father, we have eaten of His bread, His wine we have drunk. So let us thank His name, let us praise Him with our mouths, saying, singing: None is holy like the LORD.

The Rock from whom we have eaten: Bless Him, my faithful friends;
we have sufficed, we have left over, just as the LORD said.

With song and sound of thanks, we shall bless our GOD, for the gift He gave our fathers: A good and lovely land. With food and sustenance He has satisfied our souls. His kindness overwhelms us: True is the LORD.

The Rock from whom we have eaten: Bless Him, my faithful friends;
we have sufficed, we have left over, just as the LORD said.

Have compassion in Your love for Your people, our Rock, for Zion, Your home of glory, Temple of our splendour. The son of David Your servant: may he come and redeem us, breath of our life, anointed of the LORD.

The Rock from whom we have eaten: Bless Him, my faithful friends;
we have sufficed, we have left over, just as the LORD said.

May the Temple be rebuilt, Zion's city full again; there we will sing a new song as we go up in joy, to the Compassionate, the Holy One – may He be blessed and raised on high – with a full cup of wine, sign of the blessing of the LORD.

The Rock from whom we have eaten: Bless Him, my faithful friends;
we have sufficed, we have left over, just as the LORD said.

Grace: 1. GOD as Feeder and Sustainer of the world; 2. thanks for the gift of the land of Israel; 3. Zion and the Davidic monarchy together with a prayer for its restoration ("the anointed" means the Messiah). The fourth verse prays for the rebuilding of the Temple. The reference to a "full cup of wine" alludes to the custom, especially at celebratory gatherings, of reciting the Grace over a cup of wine.

יום זה לישראל

יוֹם זֶה לְיִשְׂרָאֵל אוֹרָה וְשִׂמְחָה, שַׁבַּת מְנוּחָה.

צִוִּיתָ פִּקּוּדִים בְּמַעֲמַד הַר סִינַי, שַׁבָּת וּמוֹעֲדִים לִשְׁמוֹר
בְּכָל שָׁנַי, לַעֲרֹךְ לְפָנַי מַשְׂאֵת וַאֲרוּחָה, שַׁבַּת מְנוּחָה.

יוֹם זֶה לְיִשְׂרָאֵל אוֹרָה וְשִׂמְחָה, שַׁבַּת מְנוּחָה.

חֶמְדַּת הַלְּבָבוֹת לְאֻמָּה שְׁבוּרָה, לִנְפָשׁוֹת נִכְאָבוֹת נְשָׁמָה
יְתֵרָה, לְנֶפֶשׁ מְצֵרָה יָסִיר אֲנָחָה, שַׁבַּת מְנוּחָה.

יוֹם זֶה לְיִשְׂרָאֵל אוֹרָה וְשִׂמְחָה, שַׁבַּת מְנוּחָה.

קִדַּשְׁתָּ בֵּרַכְתָּ אוֹתוֹ מִכָּל יָמִים, בְּשֵׁשֶׁת כִּלִּיתָ מְלֶאכֶת
עוֹלָמִים, בּוֹ מָצְאוּ עֲגוּמִים הַשְׁקֵט וּבִטְחָה, שַׁבַּת מְנוּחָה.

יוֹם זֶה לְיִשְׂרָאֵל אוֹרָה וְשִׂמְחָה, שַׁבַּת מְנוּחָה.

לְאִסּוּר מְלָאכָה צִוִּיתָנוּ נוֹרָא, אֶזְכֶּה הוֹד מְלוּכָה אִם שַׁבָּת
אֶשְׁמְרָה, אַקְרִיב שַׁי לַמּוֹרָא, מִנְחָה מֶרְקָחָה, שַׁבַּת מְנוּחָה.

יוֹם זֶה לְיִשְׂרָאֵל אוֹרָה וְשִׂמְחָה, שַׁבַּת מְנוּחָה.

חַדֵּשׁ מִקְדָּשֵׁנוּ, זָכְרָה נֶחֱרֶבֶת, טוּבְךָ, מוֹשִׁיעֵנוּ, תְּנָה
לַנֶּעֱצֶבֶת, בְּשַׁבָּת יוֹשֶׁבֶת בְּזֶמֶר וּשְׁבָחָה, שַׁבַּת מְנוּחָה.

יוֹם זֶה לְיִשְׂרָאֵל אוֹרָה וְשִׂמְחָה, שַׁבַּת מְנוּחָה.

בִּרְכַּת הַמָּזוֹן is on page 756.

יוֹם זֶה לְיִשְׂרָאֵל *Yom Zeh le-Yisrael*: A fragment of a larger song, attributed by some to Rabbi Isaac Luria, by others to an earlier, fifteenth-century author. *Light and joy* – a phrase from the Book of Esther (8:16). *Serenity* – the word *menuchah* signifies more than just "rest"; it also means "ease, quiet, calm, tranquillity, inner peace". Shattered people – the poem dates from a period in which persecution was a fresh and painful memory. The second verse is remarkable for its candid expression, even on the Shabbat, of Jewish grief. *An extra soul* – according to the Sages, on

YOM ZEH LE-YISRAEL

יוֹם זֶה לְיִשְׂרָאֵל This day for Israel is light and joy, a Sabbath of serenity.

At the assembly at Sinai You decreed the laws,
Sabbath and the festivals – to keep them all My years;
Setting a table before Me with courses of fine food –
A Sabbath of serenity.

This day, for Israel, is light and joy, a Sabbath of serenity.

Heart's delight to a shattered people,
To suffering spirits, an extra soul.
From troubled hearts may it banish sighs –
A Sabbath of serenity.

This day, for Israel, is light and joy, a Sabbath of serenity.

You sanctified and blessed it above all other days.
In six days You finished the making of all worlds.
On it sad souls find quiet and safety –
A Sabbath of serenity.

This day, for Israel, is light and joy, a Sabbath of serenity.

All work is forbidden by the revered One's commandment,
I will merit royal glory if I keep the Sabbath day,
Bringing the awesome One a sweetly scented gift –
A Sabbath of serenity.

This day, for Israel, is light and joy, a Sabbath of serenity.

Renew our Sanctuary, remember the ruined city.
Bestow Your goodness, Saviour, on one who is sad,
Yet still she spends the Sabbath in song and praise –
A Sabbath of serenity.

This day, for Israel, is light and joy, a Sabbath of serenity.

Grace after Meals is on page 757.

Shabbat we acquire Shabbat an "extra soul" (*Betzah* 16a). The idea arises from the verb the Torah uses to describe God's rest on Shabbat (Exodus 31:17): *vayinafash*, from *nefesh*, "a soul". The last verse, that speaks of "a grieving people who still spend the Sabbath in song and praise" is testimony to the power of Shabbat to break through the carapace of suffering and reach, even there, hope and joy.

תפילת שחרית לשבת ויום טוב

Begin as on weekdays, from pages 2–34. Then continue:

Some congregations say the Psalm for the Day (weekdays page 144 ff, שַׁבָּת page 152) and additional psalms at this point. קַדִּישׁ יָתוֹם is then said. Others say them later.

מזמור לפני פסוקי דזמרה

תהלים ל

מִזְמוֹר שִׁיר חֲנֻכַּת הַבַּיִת לְדָוִד. אֲרוֹמִמְךָ יהוה כִּי דִלִּיתָֽנִי,
וְלֹא־שִׂמַּחְתָּ אֹיְבַי לִי. יהוה אֱלֹהָי, שִׁוַּֽעְתִּי אֵלֶיךָ וַתִּרְפָּאֵֽנִי.
יהוה הֶעֱלִֽיתָ מִן־שְׁאוֹל נַפְשִׁי, חִיִּיתַֽנִי מִיָּֽרְדִי־בוֹר. זַמְּרוּ
לַיהוה חֲסִידָיו, וְהוֹדוּ לְזֵֽכֶר קָדְשׁוֹ. כִּי רֶֽגַע בְּאַפּוֹ, חַיִּים
בִּרְצוֹנוֹ, בָּעֶֽרֶב יָלִין בֶּֽכִי וְלַבֹּֽקֶר רִנָּה. וַאֲנִי אָמַֽרְתִּי בְשַׁלְוִי,
בַּל אֶמּוֹט לְעוֹלָם. יהוה בִּרְצוֹנְךָ הֶעֱמַֽדְתָּה לְהַרְרִי עֹז,
הִסְתַּֽרְתָּ פָנֶֽיךָ הָיִֽיתִי נִבְהָל. אֵלֶֽיךָ יהוה אֶקְרָא, וְאֶל־
אֲדֹנָי אֶתְחַנָּן. מַה־בֶּֽצַע בְּדָמִי, בְּרִדְתִּי אֶל שָֽׁחַת, הֲיוֹדְךָ
עָפָר, הֲיַגִּיד אֲמִתֶּֽךָ. שְׁמַע־יהוה וְחָנֵּֽנִי, יהוה הֱיֵה עֹזֵר לִי.
← הָפַֽכְתָּ מִסְפְּדִי לְמָחוֹל לִי, פִּתַּֽחְתָּ שַׂקִּי, וַתְּאַזְּרֵֽנִי שִׂמְחָה.
לְמַֽעַן יְזַמֶּרְךָ כָבוֹד וְלֹא יִדֹּם, יהוה אֱלֹהַי לְעוֹלָם אוֹדֶֽךָּ.

מִזְמוֹר שִׁיר *A song for the dedication of the House:* According to Rashi, David wrote this psalm to be sung at the inauguration of the Temple, though he knew it would only take place in the lifetime of his son, Solomon. The psalm first entered the Siddur as a prayer to be said on Chanukah, and was later adopted as part of the daily prayers.

Its content is beautifully suited to be a bridge between the "Blessings of Dawn" and the "Verses of Praise". The connecting

MORNING SERVICE FOR SHABBAT AND FESTIVALS

Begin as on weekdays, from pages 3–35. Then continue:

Some congregations say the Psalm for the Day (weekdays page 145 ff, Shabbat page 153) and additional psalms at this point. The Mourner's *Kaddish* is then said. Others say them later.

A PSALM BEFORE VERSES OF PRAISE

PSALM 30

מִזְמוֹר A psalm of David. A song for the dedication of the House. I will exalt You, LORD, for You have lifted me up, and not let my enemies rejoice over me. LORD, my GOD, I cried to You for help and You healed me. LORD, You lifted my soul from the grave, You spared me from going down to the pit. Sing to the LORD, you His devoted ones, and give thanks to His holy name. For His anger is for a moment, but His favour for a lifetime. At night there may be weeping, but in the morning there is joy. When I felt secure, I said, "I shall never be shaken." LORD, when You favoured me, You made me stand firm as a mountain, but when You hid Your face, I was terrified. To You, LORD, I called; I pleaded with my LORD: "What gain would there be if I died and went down to the grave? Can dust thank You? Can it declare Your truth? Hear, LORD, and be gracious to me; LORD, be my help." → You have turned my sorrow into dancing. You have removed my sackcloth and clothed me with joy, so that my soul may sing to You and not be silent. LORD my GOD, for ever I will thank You.

---

theme is *the restoration of life as a reason for giving praise*. The Psalmist recounts a crisis when his life, hitherto secure, was suddenly in danger. It was then that he prayed to GOD, "What gain would there be if I died and went down to the grave?… Can dust thank You?" So we, waking to the life of a new day, express our sense of joy, "so that my spirit may sing to you and not be silent."

קדיש יתום

The transliteration can be found at the end of the Siddur.

Mourner:

יִתְגַּדַּל וְיִתְקַדַּשׁ שְׁמֵהּ רַבָּא. (Cong. אָמֵן) בְּעָלְמָא דִּי־בְרָא כִרְעוּתֵהּ. וְיַמְלִיךְ מַלְכוּתֵהּ, בְּחַיֵּיכוֹן וּבְיוֹמֵיכוֹן וּבְחַיֵּי דְכָל־בֵּית יִשְׂרָאֵל, בַּעֲגָלָא וּבִזְמַן קָרִיב. וְאִמְרוּ אָמֵן. (Cong. אָמֵן)

All:

יְהֵא שְׁמֵהּ רַבָּא מְבָרַךְ לְעָלַם וּלְעָלְמֵי עָלְמַיָּא.

Mourner:

יִתְבָּרַךְ וְיִשְׁתַּבַּח וְיִתְפָּאַר וְיִתְרוֹמַם וְיִתְנַשֵּׂא וְיִתְהַדָּר וְיִתְעַלֶּה וְיִתְהַלָּל שְׁמֵהּ דְּקֻדְשָׁא בְּרִיךְ הוּא (Cong. בְּרִיךְ הוּא) לְעֵלָּא (On שַׁבָּת שׁוּבָה add לְעֵלָּא) מִן־כָּל־בִּרְכָתָא וְשִׁירָתָא תֻּשְׁבְּחָתָא וְנֶחֱמָתָא, דַּאֲמִירָן בְּעָלְמָא. וְאִמְרוּ אָמֵן. (Cong. אָמֵן)

יְהֵא שְׁלָמָא רַבָּא מִן־שְׁמַיָּא, וְחַיִּים עָלֵינוּ וְעַל־כָּל־יִשְׂרָאֵל. וְאִמְרוּ אָמֵן. (Cong. אָמֵן)

Bow, take three steps back, then bow, first left, then right, then centre, while saying:

עֹשֶׂה שָׁלוֹם בִּמְרוֹמָיו, הוּא יַעֲשֶׂה שָׁלוֹם עָלֵינוּ, וְעַל־כָּל־יִשְׂרָאֵל. וְאִמְרוּ אָמֵן. (Cong. אָמֵן)

MOURNER'S *KADDISH*
The paradox has long been noted that the mourner's *Kaddish* contains no mention of death, bereavement or grief. In Judaism, we emerge from the pain of loss by re-immersing ourselves in life – and thus in God, the source of all life.

The most profound gift we can bring to the memory of one we have lost is to be a source of blessing to the deceased by the good deeds we do in his or her name. When we say *Kaddish*, we are the cause of the congregation saying, in response, "May His great name be blessed for ever

MOURNER'S KADDISH

The transliteration can be found at the end of the Siddur.

Mourner:

יִתְגַּדַּל Magnified and sanctified may His great name be, in the world He created by His will. May He establish His kingdom in your lifetime and in your days, and in the lifetime of all the House of Israel, swiftly and soon – and say: Amen.

All:

May His great name be blessed for ever and all time.

Mourner:

Blessed and praised, glorified and exalted, raised and honoured, uplifted and lauded be the name of the Holy One, blessed be He, (between Rosh Hashanah and Yom Kippur add 'well') beyond any blessing, song, praise and consolation uttered in the world – and say: Amen.

May there be great peace from heaven, and life for us and all Israel – and say: Amen.

Bow, take three steps back, then bow, first left, then right, then centre, while saying:

May He who makes peace in His high places, make peace for us and all Israel – and say: Amen.

---

and ever". This, according to the Talmud, brings great pleasure to God. By causing the congregation to praise God, we show that the recollection of the person we have lost moves us to good deeds – and thus that their memory continues to be a blessing.

PESUKEI DE-ZIMRA / VERSES OF PRAISE
This section of the prayers is based on the Talmudic teaching (*Berachot* 32b) that "The pious men of old used to wait for an hour [before praying], they prayed for an hour, and then waited again for an hour." Prayer requires mental preparation beforehand, as well as a gradual leave-taking afterward. It is impossible to move directly from worldly concerns to the intense concentration required for genuine prayer, and vice versa. The verse cited in support of this practice is "Happy are they that dwell in Your house" (Psalm 144:5), and this verse occupies a prominent place at the heart of the "Verses of Praise". In addition to the six psalms said on weekdays, nine extra psalms are added on Shabbat and Festivals.

פסוקי דזמרה

The following is recited standing, while holding the front two צִיצִיּוֹת of the טַלִּית. They are kissed and released at the end of this blessing:

בָּרוּךְ שֶׁאָמַר וְהָיָה הָעוֹלָם, בָּרוּךְ הוּא.
בָּרוּךְ עֹשֶׂה בְרֵאשִׁית,
בָּרוּךְ אוֹמֵר וְעוֹשֶׂה,
בָּרוּךְ גּוֹזֵר וּמְקַיֵּם,
בָּרוּךְ מְרַחֵם עַל הָאָרֶץ,
בָּרוּךְ מְרַחֵם עַל הַבְּרִיּוֹת,
בָּרוּךְ מְשַׁלֵּם שָׂכָר טוֹב לִירֵאָיו,
בָּרוּךְ חַי לָעַד וְקַיָּם לָנֶצַח,
בָּרוּךְ פּוֹדֶה וּמַצִּיל,
בָּרוּךְ שְׁמוֹ.

בָּרוּךְ אַתָּה יהוה אֱלֹהֵינוּ מֶלֶךְ הָעוֹלָם, הָאֵל הָאָב הָרַחֲמָן הַמְהֻלָּל בְּפִי עַמּוֹ, מְשֻׁבָּח וּמְפֹאָר בִּלְשׁוֹן חֲסִידָיו וַעֲבָדָיו, וּבְשִׁירֵי דָוִד עַבְדֶּךָ. נְהַלֶּלְךָ יהוה אֱלֹהֵינוּ, בִּשְׁבָחוֹת וּבִזְמִירוֹת. נְגַדֶּלְךָ וּנְשַׁבֵּחֲךָ וּנְפָאֶרְךָ וְנַזְכִּיר שִׁמְךָ וְנַמְלִיכְךָ, מַלְכֵּנוּ אֱלֹהֵינוּ. ← יָחִיד, חֵי הָעוֹלָמִים, מֶלֶךְ מְשֻׁבָּח וּמְפֹאָר עֲדֵי־עַד שְׁמוֹ הַגָּדוֹל. בָּרוּךְ אַתָּה יהוה, מֶלֶךְ מְהֻלָּל בַּתִּשְׁבָּחוֹת.

דברי הימים א׳ טז:ח–לו

הוֹדוּ לַיהוה קִרְאוּ בִשְׁמוֹ, הוֹדִיעוּ בָעַמִּים עֲלִילֹתָיו. שִׁירוּ לוֹ, זַמְּרוּ־לוֹ, שִׂיחוּ בְּכָל־נִפְלְאֹתָיו. הִתְהַלְלוּ בְּשֵׁם קָדְשׁוֹ,

---

בָּרוּךְ שֶׁאָמַר *Blessed is He*: An introductory blessing to the Verses of Praise, in two parts. The first is a ten-part litany of praise to God as creator, each phrase introduced with the word Blessed (the second phrase, "Blessed be He", is not a separate verse but originally a congregational response). The number ten corresponds to the ten times the word *Vayomer*, "And He said", appears in the story

VERSES OF PRAISE

The following is recited standing, while holding the two front *tzitziot* of the *tallit*.
They are kissed and released at the end of this blessing:

בָּרוּךְ Blessed is He who spoke and the world came into being, blessed is He.
Blessed is He who creates the universe.
Blessed is He who speaks and acts.
Blessed is He who decrees and fulfils.
Blessed is He who shows compassion to the earth.
Blessed is He who shows compassion to all creatures.
Blessed is He who gives a good reward to those who fear Him.
Blessed is He who lives for ever and exists to eternity.
Blessed is He who redeems and saves.
Blessed is His name.

Blessed are You, LORD our GOD, King of the Universe, GOD, compassionate Father, extolled by the mouth of His people, praised and glorified by the tongue of His devoted ones and those who serve Him. With the songs of Your servant David we will praise You, O LORD our GOD. With praises and psalms we will magnify and praise You, glorify You and make mention of Your name. We will proclaim Your kingship, our King, our GOD, ➻ the only One, life of the Universe, the King whose great name is praised and glorified to all eternity. Blessed are You, LORD, the King extolled with songs of praise.

I CHRONICLES 16:8–36

הודו Thank the LORD, call on His name, make His acts known among the peoples. Sing to Him, make music to Him, tell of all His wonders.

---

of creation in Genesis 1. Hence the rabbinic saying that "With ten utterances the world was created."

Blessed are You: The second half of the blessing is a prelude to the biblical verses that follow, mainly from the Psalms ("With the Psalms of your servant David we will exalt you") but also from the books of Chronicles and Nehemiah ("extolled by the mouth of His people"). To emphasize the significance of this declaration, we recite it standing and, at the end, kiss the two front fringes of the tallit.

הודו *Thank the LORD*: The Bible gives us a vivid account (1 Chronicles 15–16) of the moment when this passage was first re-

יִשְׂמַח לֵב מְבַקְשֵׁי יהוה. דִּרְשׁוּ יהוה וְעֻזּוֹ, בַּקְּשׁוּ פָנָיו תָּמִיד. זִכְרוּ נִפְלְאֹתָיו אֲשֶׁר עָשָׂה, מֹפְתָיו וּמִשְׁפְּטֵי־פִיהוּ. זֶרַע יִשְׂרָאֵל עַבְדּוֹ, בְּנֵי יַעֲקֹב בְּחִירָיו. הוּא יהוה אֱלֹהֵינוּ, בְּכָל־הָאָרֶץ מִשְׁפָּטָיו. זִכְרוּ לְעוֹלָם בְּרִיתוֹ, דָּבָר צִוָּה לְאֶלֶף דּוֹר. אֲשֶׁר כָּרַת אֶת־אַבְרָהָם, וּשְׁבוּעָתוֹ לְיִצְחָק. וַיַּעֲמִידֶהָ לְיַעֲקֹב לְחֹק, לְיִשְׂרָאֵל בְּרִית עוֹלָם. לֵאמֹר, לְךָ אֶתֵּן אֶרֶץ־כְּנָעַן, חֶבֶל נַחֲלַתְכֶם. בִּהְיוֹתְכֶם מְתֵי מִסְפָּר, כִּמְעַט וְגָרִים בָּהּ. וַיִּתְהַלְּכוּ מִגּוֹי אֶל־גּוֹי, וּמִמַּמְלָכָה אֶל־עַם אַחֵר. לֹא־הִנִּיחַ לְאִישׁ לְעָשְׁקָם, וַיּוֹכַח עֲלֵיהֶם מְלָכִים. אַל־תִּגְּעוּ בִּמְשִׁיחָי, וּבִנְבִיאַי אַל־תָּרֵעוּ. שִׁירוּ לַיהוה כָּל־הָאָרֶץ, בַּשְּׂרוּ מִיּוֹם־אֶל־יוֹם יְשׁוּעָתוֹ. סַפְּרוּ בַגּוֹיִם אֶת־כְּבוֹדוֹ, בְּכָל־הָעַמִּים נִפְלְאֹתָיו. כִּי גָדוֹל יהוה וּמְהֻלָּל מְאֹד, וְנוֹרָא הוּא עַל־כָּל־אֱלֹהִים. כִּי כָּל־אֱלֹהֵי הָעַמִּים אֱלִילִים | וַיהוה שָׁמַיִם עָשָׂה. הוֹד וְהָדָר לְפָנָיו, עֹז וְחֶדְוָה בִּמְקֹמוֹ. הָבוּ לַיהוה מִשְׁפְּחוֹת עַמִּים, הָבוּ לַיהוה כָּבוֹד וָעֹז. הָבוּ לַיהוה כְּבוֹד שְׁמוֹ, שְׂאוּ מִנְחָה וּבֹאוּ לְפָנָיו, הִשְׁתַּחֲווּ לַיהוה בְּהַדְרַת־קֹדֶשׁ. חִילוּ מִלְּפָנָיו כָּל־הָאָרֶץ, אַף־תִּכּוֹן תֵּבֵל בַּל־תִּמּוֹט. יִשְׂמְחוּ הַשָּׁמַיִם וְתָגֵל הָאָרֶץ, וְיֹאמְרוּ בַגּוֹיִם, יהוה מָלָךְ. יִרְעַם הַיָּם וּמְלוֹאוֹ, יַעֲלֹץ הַשָּׂדֶה וְכָל־אֲשֶׁר־בּוֹ. אָז יְרַנְּנוּ עֲצֵי הַיָּעַר, מִלִּפְנֵי יהוה, כִּי־בָא לִשְׁפּוֹט אֶת־הָאָרֶץ. הוֹדוּ לַיהוה כִּי טוֹב, כִּי לְעוֹלָם חַסְדּוֹ. וְאִמְרוּ הוֹשִׁיעֵנוּ אֱלֹהֵי יִשְׁעֵנוּ, וְקַבְּצֵנוּ וְהַצִּילֵנוּ מִן־הַגּוֹיִם, לְהֹדוֹת לְשֵׁם

---

cited: when King David brought the Ark of the Covenant to Jerusalem, newly established as the capital of the Jewish state. The ark, which had been captured by the Philistines, was brought back by David to a temporary resting place. Later it was carried into Jerusalem to scenes of great jubilation. As on other momentous occasions in the life of biblical Israel, the leader (here David) reminds the people of the

Glory in His holy name; let the hearts of those who seek the LORD rejoice. Search out the LORD and His strength; seek His presence at all times. Remember the wonders He has done, His miracles and the judgements He pronounced. O descendants of Israel His servant, sons of Jacob His chosen ones: He is the LORD our GOD. His judgements are throughout the earth. Remember His covenant for ever, the word He commanded for a thousand generations. He made it with Abraham, vowed it to Isaac, and confirmed it to Jacob as a statute and to Israel as an everlasting covenant, saying, "To you I will give the land of Canaan as your allotted heritage." You were then small in number, few, strangers there, wandering from nation to nation, from one kingdom to another, but He let no man oppress them, and for their sake He rebuked kings: "Do not touch My anointed ones, and do My prophets no harm." Sing to the LORD, all the earth, proclaim His salvation daily. Declare His glory among the nations, His marvels among all the peoples. For great is the LORD and greatly to be praised; He is awesome beyond all heavenly powers. ➔ For all the gods of the peoples are mere idols; it was the Lord who made the heavens. Before Him are majesty and splendour; there is strength and beauty in His holy place. Render to the LORD, O families of the peoples, render to the LORD honour and might. Render to the LORD the glory due to His name; bring an offering and come before Him; bow down to the LORD in the splendour of holiness. Tremble before Him, all the earth; the world stands firm, it will not be shaken. Let the heavens rejoice and the earth be glad; let them declare among the nations, "The LORD is King." Let the sea roar, and all that is in it; let the fields be jubilant, and all they contain. Then the trees of the forest will sing for joy before the LORD, for He is coming to judge the earth. Give thanks to the LORD, for He is good; His lovingkindness endures for ever. Say: "Save us, GOD of our salvation; gather us and rescue us from the nations, to acknowledge

history of the nation, and its dependence on Divine providence. The passage ends with the response of the people: "And all the people said 'Amen' and 'Praise the LORD'". According to *Seder Olam*, this passage was recited daily (in two halves, one in the morning, the other in the afternoon) as an accompaniment to the sacrifices, from that day until the inauguration of the Temple in the time of Solomon.

קָדְשֶׁךָ, לְהִשְׁתַּבֵּחַ בִּתְהִלָּתֶךָ. בָּרוּךְ יהוה אֱלֹהֵי יִשְׂרָאֵל מִן־הָעוֹלָם, וְעַד־הָעוֹלָם וַיֹּאמְרוּ כָל־הָעָם, אָמֵן, וְהַלֵּל לַיהוה.

← רוֹמְמוּ יהוה אֱלֹהֵינוּ וְהִשְׁתַּחֲווּ לַהֲדֹם רַגְלָיו, קָדוֹשׁ הוּא. רוֹמְמוּ יהוה אֱלֹהֵינוּ וְהִשְׁתַּחֲווּ לְהַר קָדְשׁוֹ, כִּי קָדוֹשׁ יהוה אֱלֹהֵינוּ. וְהוּא רַחוּם יְכַפֵּר עָוֹן וְלֹא יַשְׁחִית, וְהִרְבָּה לְהָשִׁיב אַפּוֹ, וְלֹא יָעִיר כָּל־חֲמָתוֹ. אַתָּה יהוה לֹא־תִכְלָא רַחֲמֶיךָ מִמֶּנִּי, חַסְדְּךָ וַאֲמִתְּךָ תָּמִיד יִצְּרוּנִי. זְכֹר רַחֲמֶיךָ יהוה וַחֲסָדֶיךָ, כִּי מֵעוֹלָם הֵמָּה. תְּנוּ עֹז לֵאלֹהִים עַל־יִשְׂרָאֵל גַּאֲוָתוֹ, וְעֻזּוֹ בַּשְּׁחָקִים. נוֹרָא אֱלֹהִים מִמִּקְדָּשֶׁיךָ, אֵל יִשְׂרָאֵל הוּא נֹתֵן עֹז וְתַעֲצֻמוֹת לָעָם, בָּרוּךְ אֱלֹהִים. אֵל־נְקָמוֹת יהוה, אֵל־נְקָמוֹת הוֹפִיעַ. הִנָּשֵׂא שֹׁפֵט הָאָרֶץ, הָשֵׁב גְּמוּל עַל־גֵּאִים. לַיהוה הַיְשׁוּעָה, עַל־עַמְּךָ בִרְכָתֶךָ סֶּלָה. יהוה צְבָאוֹת עִמָּנוּ, מִשְׂגָּב־לָנוּ אֱלֹהֵי יַעֲקֹב סֶלָה. ← יהוה צְבָאוֹת, אַשְׁרֵי אָדָם בֹּטֵחַ בָּךְ. יהוה הוֹשִׁיעָה, הַמֶּלֶךְ יַעֲנֵנוּ בְיוֹם־קָרְאֵנוּ. הוֹשִׁיעָה אֶת־עַמֶּךָ, וּבָרֵךְ אֶת־נַחֲלָתֶךָ, וּרְעֵם וְנַשְּׂאֵם עַד־הָעוֹלָם. נַפְשֵׁנוּ חִכְּתָה לַיהוה, עֶזְרֵנוּ וּמָגִנֵּנוּ הוּא. כִּי־בוֹ יִשְׂמַח לִבֵּנוּ, כִּי בְשֵׁם קָדְשׁוֹ בָטָחְנוּ. יְהִי־חַסְדְּךָ יהוה עָלֵינוּ, כַּאֲשֶׁר יִחַלְנוּ לָךְ. הַרְאֵנוּ יהוה חַסְדֶּךָ, וְיֶשְׁעֲךָ תִּתֶּן־לָנוּ. קוּמָה עֶזְרָתָה לָּנוּ, וּפְדֵנוּ לְמַעַן חַסְדֶּךָ. אָנֹכִי יהוה אֱלֹהֶיךָ הַמַּעַלְךָ מֵאֶרֶץ מִצְרָיִם, הַרְחֶב־פִּיךָ וַאֲמַלְאֵהוּ. ← אַשְׁרֵי הָעָם שֶׁכָּכָה לּוֹ, אַשְׁרֵי הָעָם שֶׁיהוה אֱלֹהָיו. וַאֲנִי בְּחַסְדְּךָ בָטַחְתִּי, יָגֵל לִבִּי בִּישׁוּעָתֶךָ, אָשִׁירָה לַיהוה, כִּי גָמַל עָלָי.

רוֹמְמוּ *Exalt the* Lord *our* God: A selection of verses from the Book of Psalms, expressing hope and trust in God. The voice in these verses modulates from singular to plural, individual to nation. This frequent shift from public to private and back again is a distinctive feature of Jewish sensibility. We speak to God as individuals, from the depths of our being, yet we are also members of an extended family, a people, a nation, whose fate and destiny we share and on whose behalf we pray.

Your holy name and glory in Your praise. Blessed is the LORD, GOD of Israel, from eternity to eternity." And all the people said "Amen" and "Praise the LORD".

→ Exalt the Lord our God and bow before His footstool: He is holy. Exalt the Lord our God and bow at His holy mountain; for holy is the Lord our God. He is compassionate. He forgives iniquity and does not destroy. Repeatedly He suppresses His anger, not rousing His full wrath. You, O Lord: do not withhold Your compassion from me. May Your lovingkindness and truth always guard me. Remember, Lord, Your acts of compassion and love, for they have existed for ever. Ascribe power to God, whose majesty is over Israel and whose might is in the skies. You are awesome, God, in Your holy places. It is the God of Israel who gives might and strength to the people, may God be blessed. God of retribution, Lord, God of retribution, appear. Arise, Judge of the earth, to repay the arrogant their just deserts. Salvation belongs to the Lord; may Your blessing rest upon Your people, Selah! ← The Lord of hosts is with us, the God of Jacob is our stronghold, Selah! Lord of hosts, happy is the one who trusts in You. O Lord, save. May the King answer us on the day we call. Save Your people and bless Your heritage; tend them and carry them for ever. Our soul longs for the LORD; He is our Help and Shield. For in Him our hearts rejoice, for in His holy name we have trusted. May your lovingkindness, LORD, be upon us, as we have put our hope in You. Show us, LORD, Your lovingkindness and grant us Your salvation. Arise, help us and redeem us for the sake of Your love. I am the LORD your GOD who brought you up from the land of Egypt: open your mouth wide and I will fill it. → Happy is the people for whom this is so; happy is the people whose LORD is GOD. As for me, I trust in Your lovingkindness; my heart rejoices in Your salvation. I will sing to the LORD for He has been good to me.

EXTRA PSALMS FOR SHABBAT AND FESTIVALS

In the earliest Siddurim, we already find the well-established custom of saying extra psalms on Shabbat and Festivals. This is because, work being forbidden, we have more time to pray, and also because on Shabbat we reflect on GOD's creation, a theme of many of the psalms. The Ashkenazi custom is to say nine. Together with the six weekday psalms, they make fifteen, the number associ-

On הוֹשַׁעְנָא רַבָּה, the following psalm is said while standing (תהלים ק):

מִזְמוֹר לְתוֹדָה, הָרִֽיעוּ לַיהוה כָּל־הָאָֽרֶץ. עִבְדוּ אֶת־יהוה בְּשִׂמְחָה, בֹּֽאוּ לְפָנָיו בִּרְנָנָה. דְּעוּ כִּי יהוה הוּא אֱלֹהִים, הוּא עָשָֽׂנוּ, וְלוֹ אֲנַֽחְנוּ, עַמּוֹ וְצֹאן מַרְעִיתוֹ. בֹּֽאוּ שְׁעָרָיו בְּתוֹדָה, חֲצֵרֹתָיו בִּתְהִלָּה, הֽוֹדוּ לוֹ, בָּרְכוּ שְׁמוֹ. ◄ כִּי־טוֹב יהוה, לְעוֹלָם חַסְדּוֹ, וְעַד־דֹּר וָדֹר אֱמוּנָתוֹ.

תהלים יט

לַמְנַצֵּֽחַ מִזְמוֹר לְדָוִד.
הַשָּׁמַיִם מְסַפְּרִים כְּבוֹד־אֵל,
וּמַעֲשֵׂה יָדָיו מַגִּיד הָרָקִֽיעַ.
יוֹם לְיוֹם יַבִּֽיעַ אֹֽמֶר,
וְלַֽיְלָה לְּלַֽיְלָה יְחַוֶּה־דָּֽעַת.
אֵין אֹֽמֶר וְאֵין דְּבָרִים,
בְּלִי נִשְׁמָע קוֹלָם.
בְּכָל הָאָֽרֶץ יָצָא קַוָּם,
וּבִקְצֵה תֵבֵל מִלֵּיהֶם,
לַשֶּֽׁמֶשׁ שָׂם אֹֽהֶל בָּהֶם.
וְהוּא כְּחָתָן יֹצֵא מֵחֻפָּתוֹ,
יָשִׂישׂ כְּגִבּוֹר לָרוּץ אֹֽרַח.
מִקְצֵה הַשָּׁמַיִם מוֹצָאוֹ,
וּתְקוּפָתוֹ עַל קְצוֹתָם,
וְאֵין נִסְתָּר מֵחַמָּתוֹ.

ated with the fifteen Songs of Ascents (Psalms 120–134), and the fifteen steps in the Temple on which the Levites stood and sang their songs.

There is a striking feature to this sequence of additional Psalms. According to one interpretation (Meiri) the phrase "a song of ascents" means one begun softly and continued with ever-increasing volume. The extra psalms begin in Psalm 19

On Hoshana Rabba, the following psalm is said while standing (PSALM 100):

מִזְמוֹר A psalm of thanksgiving. Shout joyously to the LORD, all the earth. Serve the LORD with joy. Come before Him with jubilation. Know that the LORD is GOD. He made us and we are His. We are His people and the flock He tends. Enter His gates with thanksgiving, His courts with praise. Thank Him and bless His name. → For the LORD is good, His lovingkindness is everlasting and His faithfulness is for every generation.

PSALM 19

לַמְנַצֵּחַ For the Conductor. A psalm of David.
The heavens declare the glory of GOD;
the skies proclaim the work of His hands.
Day to day they pour forth speech;
night to night they communicate knowledge.
There is no speech, there are no words,
their voice is not heard,
Yet their music carries throughout the earth,
their words to the end of the world.
In them He has set a tent for the sun.
It emerges like a groom from his marriage chamber,
rejoicing like a champion about to run a race.
It rises at one end of the heaven
and makes its circuit to the other:
nothing is hidden from its heat.

---

with the universe singing a silent song ("their voice cannot be heard") and end in Psalm 93 with a magnificent crescendo ("above the noise of the great and many waters").

לַמְנַצֵּחַ *Psalm 19: The heavens declare the glory of GOD:* A hymn of glory to the universe as GOD's work and the Torah as GOD's word. In the first half of the poem, the Psalmist speaks metaphorically of creation singing a song of praise to its Creator, a silent song yet one that can be heard by those whose ears are attuned to wonder. But GOD's word not only gives life to the natural universe: it instructs the human universe, the world we make by our actions and reactions. The Psalmist pours out his praise of GOD's creation of the world-that-is, and His revelation of the world-that-ought-to-be. *Yet their music* – literally "their line", perhaps the reverberating string of a musical instrument. Alternatively, it may mean the

תּוֹרַת יהוה תְּמִימָה, מְשִׁיבַת נָפֶשׁ,
עֵדוּת יהוה נֶאֱמָנָה, מַחְכִּימַת פֶּתִי.
פִּקּוּדֵי יהוה יְשָׁרִים, מְשַׂמְּחֵי־לֵב,
מִצְוַת יהוה בָּרָה, מְאִירַת עֵינָיִם.
יִרְאַת יהוה טְהוֹרָה, עוֹמֶדֶת לָעַד,
מִשְׁפְּטֵי יהוה אֱמֶת, צָדְקוּ יַחְדָּו.
הַנֶּחֱמָדִים מִזָּהָב וּמִפַּז רָב,
וּמְתוּקִים מִדְּבַשׁ וְנֹפֶת צוּפִים.
גַּם־עַבְדְּךָ נִזְהָר בָּהֶם,
בְּשָׁמְרָם עֵקֶב רָב.
שְׁגִיאוֹת מִי־יָבִין,
מִנִּסְתָּרוֹת נַקֵּנִי.
גַּם מִזֵּדִים חֲשֹׂךְ עַבְדֶּךָ,
אַל יִמְשְׁלוּ־בִי,
אָז אֵיתָם,
וְנִקֵּיתִי מִפֶּשַׁע רָב.
← יִהְיוּ לְרָצוֹן אִמְרֵי־פִי,
וְהֶגְיוֹן לִבִּי לְפָנֶיךָ, יהוה, צוּרִי וְגוֹאֲלִי.

תהלים לד

לְדָוִד, בְּשַׁנּוֹתוֹ אֶת־טַעְמוֹ לִפְנֵי־אֲבִימֶלֶךְ, וַיְגָרְשֵׁהוּ וַיֵּלַךְ.
אֲבָרְכָה אֶת־יהוה בְּכָל־עֵת, תָּמִיד תְּהִלָּתוֹ בְּפִי.
בַּיהוה תִּתְהַלֵּל נַפְשִׁי, יִשְׁמְעוּ עֲנָוִים וְיִשְׂמָחוּ.
גַּדְּלוּ לַיהוה אִתִּי, וּנְרוֹמְמָה שְׁמוֹ יַחְדָּו.
דָּרַשְׁתִּי אֶת יהוה וְעָנָנִי, וּמִכָּל־מְגוּרוֹתַי הִצִּילָנִי.
הִבִּיטוּ אֵלָיו וְנָהָרוּ,
וּפְנֵיהֶם אַל יֶחְפָּרוּ.

The LORD's Torah is perfect, refreshing the soul.
The LORD's testimony is faithful, making the simple wise.
The LORD's precepts are just, gladdening the heart.
The LORD's commandment is radiant, giving light to the eyes.
The fear of the LORD is pure, enduring forever.
The LORD's judgements are true, altogether righteous.
More precious than gold, than much fine gold.
They are sweeter than honey, than honey from the comb.
Your servant, too, is careful of them,
for in observing them there is great reward.
Yet who can discern his errors?
Cleanse me of hidden faults.
Keep Your servant also from wilful sins;
let them not have dominion over me.
Then shall I be blameless,
and innocent of grave sin.
→ May the words of my mouth and the meditation of my heart
find favour before You, LORD, my Rock and my Redeemer.

PSALM 34

לְדָוִד Of David. When he pretended to be insane before Abimelech, who drove him away, and he left.
I will bless the LORD at all times;
His praise will be always on my lips.
My soul will glory in the LORD;
let the lowly hear this and rejoice.
Magnify the LORD with me;
let us exalt His name together.
I sought the LORD, and He answered me;
He saved me from all my fears.
Those who look to Him are radiant;
Their faces are never downcast.

---

line marking a boundary – a reference to the order and "fearful symmetry" of the Universe.

לְדָוִד *Psalm 34*: During the period that David was fleeing from King Saul, he took refuge in the Philistine city of Gath. There,

זֶה עָנִי קָרָא וַיהוה שָׁמֵעַ, וּמִכָּל־צָרוֹתָיו הוֹשִׁיעוֹ.
חֹנֶה מַלְאַךְ־יהוה סָבִיב לִירֵאָיו, וַיְחַלְּצֵם.
טַעֲמוּ וּרְאוּ כִּי־טוֹב יהוה, אַשְׁרֵי הַגֶּבֶר יֶחֱסֶה בּוֹ.
יְראוּ אֶת־יהוה קְדֹשָׁיו, כִּי אֵין מַחְסוֹר לִירֵאָיו.
כְּפִירִים רָשׁוּ וְרָעֵבוּ, וְדֹרְשֵׁי יהוה לֹא־יַחְסְרוּ כָל־טוֹב.
לְכוּ בָנִים שִׁמְעוּ־לִי, יִרְאַת יהוה אֲלַמֶּדְכֶם.
מִי־הָאִישׁ הֶחָפֵץ חַיִּים, אֹהֵב יָמִים לִרְאוֹת טוֹב.
נְצֹר לְשׁוֹנְךָ מֵרָע, וּשְׂפָתֶיךָ מִדַּבֵּר מִרְמָה.
סוּר מֵרָע וַעֲשֵׂה־טוֹב, בַּקֵּשׁ שָׁלוֹם וְרָדְפֵהוּ.
עֵינֵי יהוה אֶל־צַדִּיקִים, וְאָזְנָיו אֶל־שַׁוְעָתָם.
פְּנֵי יהוה בְּעֹשֵׂי רָע, לְהַכְרִית מֵאֶרֶץ זִכְרָם.
צָעֲקוּ וַיהוה שָׁמֵעַ, וּמִכָּל־צָרוֹתָם הִצִּילָם.
קָרוֹב יהוה לְנִשְׁבְּרֵי־לֵב, וְאֶת דַּכְּאֵי־רוּחַ יוֹשִׁיעַ.
רַבּוֹת רָעוֹת צַדִּיק, וּמִכֻּלָּם יַצִּילֶנּוּ יהוה.
שֹׁמֵר כָּל־עַצְמוֹתָיו, אַחַת מֵהֵנָּה לֹא נִשְׁבָּרָה.
תְּמוֹתֵת רָשָׁע רָעָה, וְשֹׂנְאֵי צַדִּיק יֶאְשָׁמוּ.
◀ פּוֹדֶה יהוה נֶפֶשׁ עֲבָדָיו, וְלֹא יֶאְשְׁמוּ כָּל־הַחֹסִים בּוֹ.

---

however, he was recognised and his life was again in danger. Feigning insanity in order to appear harmless, he was dismissed by the king and was able to escape (1 Samuel 21:10–15). The Psalm of thanksgiving that follows is constructed as an alphabetical acrostic. An extra verse has been added at the end to avoid closing on a negative note. *Magnify the* L*ORD* *with me* – this verse is taken by the Sages as the source of the institution of summoning to prayer, as in the Grace after Meals. It is also said on taking the Torah scroll out of the Ark. *Taste and see* – religious experience precedes religious understanding. GOD's goodness has to be felt before it can be thought. *Guard your tongue from evil* – the Sages said about *lashon hara*, evil speech, that it harms the one who says it, the one it is said about, and the one who gives credence to it. *Seek peace and pursue it* – "Seek peace where you are, and pursue it elsewhere" (Avot de-Rabbi Nathan).

This poor man called, and the LORD heard;
He saved him from all his troubles.
The LORD's angel encamps around those who fear Him,
and He rescues them.
Taste and see that the LORD is good;
happy is the man who takes refuge in Him.
Fear the LORD, you His holy ones,
for those who fear Him lack nothing.
Young lions may grow weak and hungry,
but those who seek the LORD lack no good thing.
Come, my children, listen to me;
I will teach you the fear of the LORD.
Who desires life,
loving each day to see good?
Then keep your tongue from evil
and your lips from speaking deceit.
Turn from evil and do good;
seek peace and pursue it.
The eyes of the LORD are on the righteous
and His ears attentive to their cry;
The LORD's face is set against those who do evil,
to erase their memory from the earth.
The righteous cry out, and the LORD hears them;
delivering them from all their troubles.
The LORD is close to the broken-hearted,
and saves those who are crushed in spirit.
Many troubles may befall the righteous,
but the LORD delivers him from them all;
He protects all his bones,
so that none of them will be broken.
Evil will slay the wicked;
the enemies of the righteous will be condemned.
→ The LORD redeems his servants;
none who take refuge in Him shall be condemned.

תהלים צ

תְּפִלָּה לְמֹשֶׁה אִישׁ הָאֱלֹהִים, אֲדֹנָי, מָעוֹן אַתָּה הָיִיתָ לָּנוּ בְּדֹר וָדֹר. בְּטֶרֶם הָרִים יֻלָּדוּ וַתְּחוֹלֵל אֶרֶץ וְתֵבֵל, וּמֵעוֹלָם עַד עוֹלָם אַתָּה אֵל. תָּשֵׁב אֱנוֹשׁ עַד דַּכָּא, וַתֹּאמֶר שׁוּבוּ בְנֵי־אָדָם. כִּי אֶלֶף שָׁנִים בְּעֵינֶיךָ כְּיוֹם אֶתְמוֹל כִּי יַעֲבֹר, וְאַשְׁמוּרָה בַלָּיְלָה. זְרַמְתָּם, שֵׁנָה יִהְיוּ, בַּבֹּקֶר כֶּחָצִיר יַחֲלֹף. בַּבֹּקֶר יָצִיץ וְחָלָף, לָעֶרֶב יְמוֹלֵל וְיָבֵשׁ. כִּי־כָלִינוּ בְאַפֶּךָ, וּבַחֲמָתְךָ נִבְהָלְנוּ. שַׁתָּה עֲוֹנֹתֵינוּ לְנֶגְדֶּךָ, עֲלֻמֵנוּ לִמְאוֹר פָּנֶיךָ. כִּי כָל־יָמֵינוּ פָּנוּ בְעֶבְרָתֶךָ. כִּלִּינוּ שָׁנֵינוּ כְמוֹ הֶגֶה. יְמֵי שְׁנוֹתֵינוּ בָהֶם שִׁבְעִים שָׁנָה, וְאִם בִּגְבוּרֹת שְׁמוֹנִים שָׁנָה, וְרָהְבָּם עָמָל וָאָוֶן, כִּי גָז חִישׁ וַנָּעֻפָה. מִי־יוֹדֵעַ עֹז אַפֶּךָ, וּכְיִרְאָתְךָ עֶבְרָתֶךָ. לִמְנוֹת יָמֵינוּ כֵּן הוֹדַע, וְנָבִא לְבַב חָכְמָה. שׁוּבָה יהוה עַד־מָתָי, וְהִנָּחֵם עַל עֲבָדֶיךָ. שַׂבְּעֵנוּ בַבֹּקֶר חַסְדֶּךָ, וּנְרַנְּנָה וְנִשְׂמְחָה בְּכָל־יָמֵינוּ. שַׂמְּחֵנוּ כִּימוֹת עִנִּיתָנוּ, שְׁנוֹת רָאִינוּ רָעָה. יֵרָאֶה אֶל־עֲבָדֶיךָ פָעֳלֶךָ, וַהֲדָרְךָ עַל בְּנֵיהֶם. ◄ וִיהִי נֹעַם אֲדֹנָי אֱלֹהֵינוּ עָלֵינוּ, וּמַעֲשֵׂה יָדֵינוּ כּוֹנְנָה עָלֵינוּ, וּמַעֲשֵׂה יָדֵינוּ כּוֹנְנֵהוּ.

תהלים צא

יֹשֵׁב בְּסֵתֶר עֶלְיוֹן, בְּצֵל שַׁדַּי יִתְלוֹנָן. אֹמַר לַיהוה מַחְסִי וּמְצוּדָתִי, אֱלֹהַי אֶבְטַח־בּוֹ. כִּי הוּא יַצִּילְךָ מִפַּח יָקוּשׁ, מִדֶּבֶר הַוּוֹת. בְּאֶבְרָתוֹ יָסֶךְ לָךְ, וְתַחַת כְּנָפָיו תֶּחְסֶה, צִנָּה

תְּפִלָּה לְמֹשֶׁה *Psalm 90*: A moving meditation on the eternity of God and the shortness of our lives. *You sweep men away* – a succession of poetic images conveying the brevity of human life: it flows as fast as a swollen river; as quickly as a sleep or a dream; it is like grass in a parched land that withers by the end of the day; it is like a sigh, a mere breath, like a bird that briefly lands then flies away. The speed with which these metaphors succeed one another mirrors the rapidity with which the days and years pass. *Teach us rightly to number our days* – the moral at the heart of the Psalm: Teach us to remember how short life is, that we may spend our time on the things that endure. *May the pleasantness of the Lord our God be*

PSALM 90

תְּפִלָּה לְמֹשֶׁה A prayer of Moses, the man of GOD. LORD, You have been our shelter in every generation. Before the mountains were born, before You brought forth the earth and the world, from everlasting to everlasting You are GOD. You turn men back to dust, saying, "Return, you children of men." For a thousand years in Your sight are like yesterday when it has passed, like a watch in the night. You sweep men away; they sleep. In the morning they are like grass newly grown: in the morning it flourishes and is new, but by evening it withers and dries up. For we are consumed by Your anger, terrified by Your fury. You have set our iniquities before You, our secret sins in the light of Your presence. All our days pass away in Your wrath, we spend our years like a sigh. The span of our life is seventy years, or if we are strong, eighty years; but the best of them is trouble and sorrow, for they quickly pass, and we fly away. Who can know the force of Your anger? Your wrath matches the fear due to You. Teach us rightly to number our days, that we may gain a heart of wisdom. Relent, O LORD! How much longer? Be sorry for Your servants. Satisfy us in the morning with Your lovingkindness, that we may sing and rejoice all our days. Grant us joy for as many days as You have afflicted us, for as many years as we saw trouble. Let Your deeds be seen by Your servants, and Your glory by their children. ➔ May the pleasantness of the LORD our GOD be upon us. Establish for us the work of our hands, O establish the work of our hands.

PSALM 91

יֹשֵׁב בְּסֵתֶר He who lives in the shelter of the Most High dwells in the shadow of the Almighty. I say of the LORD, my refuge and strong-

---

upon us: according to the Sages, this is the blessing Moses gave the Israelites when they finished constructing the Tabernacle, adding, "May the Divine presence rest in the work of your hands."

יֹשֵׁב בְּסֵתֶר *Psalm 91:* A prayer for protection from danger and harm. The psalm uses many images for GOD's protection. To those who trust in Him, He is shelter, shadow, refuge, stronghold. He protects us beneath His wings, and encircles us like a shield. When we are in distress, He is with us. When we are in danger, we are not alone. Trust defeats terror, and faith conquers fear. The first speaker in the Psalm is human; the second, GOD Himself (*Sanhedrin* 103a).

וְסֹחֵרָה אֲמִתּוֹ. לֹא־תִירָא מִפַּחַד לָיְלָה, מֵחֵץ יָעוּף יוֹמָם.
מִדֶּבֶר בָּאֹפֶל יַהֲלֹךְ, מִקֶּטֶב יָשׁוּד צָהֳרָיִם. יִפֹּל מִצִּדְּךָ אֶלֶף,
וּרְבָבָה מִימִינֶךָ, אֵלֶיךָ לֹא יִגָּשׁ. רַק בְּעֵינֶיךָ תַבִּיט, וְשִׁלֻּמַת
רְשָׁעִים תִּרְאֶה. כִּי־אַתָּה יהוה מַחְסִי, עֶלְיוֹן שַׂמְתָּ מְעוֹנֶךָ.
לֹא־תְאֻנֶּה אֵלֶיךָ רָעָה, וְנֶגַע לֹא־יִקְרַב בְּאָהֳלֶךָ. כִּי מַלְאָכָיו
יְצַוֶּה־לָּךְ, לִשְׁמָרְךָ בְּכָל־דְּרָכֶיךָ. עַל־כַּפַּיִם יִשָּׂאוּנְךָ, פֶּן תִּגֹּף
בָּאֶבֶן רַגְלֶךָ. עַל־שַׁחַל וָפֶתֶן תִּדְרֹךְ, תִּרְמֹס כְּפִיר וְתַנִּין.
כִּי בִי חָשַׁק וַאֲפַלְּטֵהוּ, אֲשַׂגְּבֵהוּ כִּי־יָדַע שְׁמִי. יִקְרָאֵנִי
וְאֶעֱנֵהוּ, עִמּוֹ אָנֹכִי בְצָרָה, אֲחַלְּצֵהוּ וַאֲכַבְּדֵהוּ. ← אֹרֶךְ
יָמִים אַשְׂבִּיעֵהוּ, וְאַרְאֵהוּ בִּישׁוּעָתִי. אֹרֶךְ יָמִים אַשְׂבִּיעֵהוּ,
וְאַרְאֵהוּ בִּישׁוּעָתִי.

תהלים קלה

הַלְלוּיָהּ הַלְלוּ אֶת־שֵׁם יהוה, הַלְלוּ עַבְדֵי יהוה. שֶׁעֹמְדִים
בְּבֵית יהוה, בְּחַצְרוֹת בֵּית אֱלֹהֵינוּ. הַלְלוּיָהּ כִּי־טוֹב
יהוה, זַמְּרוּ לִשְׁמוֹ כִּי נָעִים. כִּי־יַעֲקֹב בָּחַר לוֹ יָהּ, יִשְׂרָאֵל
לִסְגֻלָּתוֹ. כִּי אֲנִי יָדַעְתִּי כִּי־גָדוֹל יהוה, וַאֲדֹנֵינוּ מִכָּל־
אֱלֹהִים. כֹּל אֲשֶׁר־חָפֵץ יהוה עָשָׂה, בַּשָּׁמַיִם וּבָאָרֶץ,
בַּיַּמִּים וְכָל־תְּהֹמוֹת. מַעֲלֶה נְשִׂאִים מִקְצֵה הָאָרֶץ, בְּרָקִים
לַמָּטָר עָשָׂה, מוֹצֵא רוּחַ מֵאֹצְרוֹתָיו. שֶׁהִכָּה בְּכוֹרֵי מִצְרָיִם,
מֵאָדָם עַד־בְּהֵמָה. שָׁלַח אוֹתֹת וּמֹפְתִים בְּתוֹכֵכִי מִצְרָיִם,
בְּפַרְעֹה וּבְכָל־עֲבָדָיו. שֶׁהִכָּה גּוֹיִם רַבִּים, וְהָרַג מְלָכִים

הַלְלוּיָהּ *Psalms 135–136*: Two psalms forming a single composite unit, similar in tone, vocabulary and literary structure to the group of Psalms 113–118 known as *Hallel*. Some Sages called these two psalms "The Great *Hallel*" to distinguish them from Psalms 113–118 which they called "The Egyptian *Hallel*" since it contains a reference to the exodus from Egypt (others confined the description to Psalm 136 alone). It is likely that both were written for public worship in the Temple, and both are litanies: a series of invocations said by a leader of prayer, together with congregational responses. Psalm 136, with its refrain "For His lov-

hold, my God in whom I trust, that He will save you from the fowler's snare and the deadly pestilence. With His pinions He will cover you, and beneath His wings you will find shelter; His faithfulness is an encircling shield. You need not fear terror by night, nor the arrow that flies by day; not the pestilence that stalks in darkness, nor the plague that ravages at noon. A thousand may fall at your side, ten thousand at your right hand, but it will not come near you. You will only look with your eyes and see the punishment of the wicked. Because you said "The Lord is my Refuge", taking the Most High as your shelter, no harm will befall you, no plague will come near your tent, for He will command His angels about you, to guard you in all your ways. They will lift you in their hands, lest your foot stumble on a stone. You will tread on lions and vipers, you will trample on young lions and snakes. [God says] "Because he loves Me, I will rescue him; I will protect him, because he acknowledges My name. When he calls on Me, I will answer him, I will be with him in distress, I will deliver him and bring him honour. ➔ With long life I will satisfy him, and show him My salvation. With long life I will satisfy him, and show him My salvation."

PSALM 135

הַלְלוּיָהּ Halleluyah! Praise the name of the Lord. Praise Him, you servants of the Lord who stand in the Lord's house, in the courtyards of the house of our God. Praise the Lord, for the Lord is good; sing praises to His name, for it is lovely. For the Lord has chosen Jacob as His own, Israel as his treasure. For I know that the Lord is great, that our Lord is above all heavenly powers. Whatever pleases the Lord, He does, in heaven and on earth, in the seas and all the depths. He raises clouds from the ends of the earth; He sends lightning with the

---

ingkindness endures forever", is the only psalm in which the congregational responses are set out in full, line by line. In Psalm 135 the responses are likely to have been, for the first section, "Halleluyah" (Praise God), and for the last, "Blessed be the Lord." Psalm 135 is structured in three parts: the first and last speak about the truth of God and the falsity of idols, and the second about God's power over nature and history. The first part is five verses long; the second, seven; the third, nine. *He struck down the firstborn of Egypt* – these lines are paralleled in the next Psalm. *The idols of the nations are silver and gold...You who fear the Lord, bless the Lord* – almost exactly paralleled in *Hallel* (Psalm 115:4–13).

עֲצוּמִים. לְסִיחוֹן מֶלֶךְ הָאֱמֹרִי, וּלְעוֹג מֶלֶךְ הַבָּשָׁן, וּלְכֹל מַמְלְכוֹת כְּנָעַן. וְנָתַן אַרְצָם נַחֲלָה, נַחֲלָה לְיִשְׂרָאֵל עַמּוֹ. יהוה שִׁמְךָ לְעוֹלָם, יהוה זִכְרְךָ לְדֹר־וָדֹר. כִּי־יָדִין יהוה עַמּוֹ, וְעַל־עֲבָדָיו יִתְנֶחָם. עֲצַבֵּי הַגּוֹיִם כֶּסֶף וְזָהָב, מַעֲשֵׂה יְדֵי אָדָם. פֶּה לָהֶם וְלֹא יְדַבֵּרוּ, עֵינַיִם לָהֶם וְלֹא יִרְאוּ. אָזְנַיִם לָהֶם וְלֹא יַאֲזִינוּ, אַף אֵין־יֶשׁ־רוּחַ בְּפִיהֶם. כְּמוֹהֶם יִהְיוּ עֹשֵׂיהֶם, כֹּל אֲשֶׁר בֹּטֵחַ בָּהֶם. ◂ בֵּית יִשְׂרָאֵל בָּרְכוּ אֶת־יהוה, בֵּית אַהֲרֹן בָּרְכוּ אֶת־יהוה. בֵּית הַלֵּוִי בָּרְכוּ אֶת־יהוה, יִרְאֵי יהוה בָּרְכוּ אֶת־יהוה. בָּרוּךְ יהוה מִצִּיּוֹן שֹׁכֵן יְרוּשָׁלָיִם, הַלְלוּיָהּ.

In many congregations, this psalm is said standing.

תהלים קלו

הוֹדוּ לַיהוה כִּי־טוֹב, כִּי לְעוֹלָם חַסְדּוֹ.
הוֹדוּ לֵאלֹהֵי הָאֱלֹהִים, כִּי לְעוֹלָם חַסְדּוֹ.
הוֹדוּ לַאֲדֹנֵי הָאֲדֹנִים, כִּי לְעוֹלָם חַסְדּוֹ.
לְעֹשֵׂה נִפְלָאוֹת גְּדֹלוֹת לְבַדּוֹ, כִּי לְעוֹלָם חַסְדּוֹ.
לְעֹשֵׂה הַשָּׁמַיִם בִּתְבוּנָה, כִּי לְעוֹלָם חַסְדּוֹ.
לְרוֹקַע הָאָרֶץ עַל הַמָּיִם, כִּי לְעוֹלָם חַסְדּוֹ.
לְעֹשֵׂה אוֹרִים גְּדֹלִים, כִּי לְעוֹלָם חַסְדּוֹ.
אֶת־הַשֶּׁמֶשׁ לְמֶמְשֶׁלֶת בַּיּוֹם, כִּי לְעוֹלָם חַסְדּוֹ.
אֶת־הַיָּרֵחַ וְכוֹכָבִים לְמֶמְשְׁלוֹת בַּלָּיְלָה, כִּי לְעוֹלָם חַסְדּוֹ.
לְמַכֵּה מִצְרַיִם בִּבְכוֹרֵיהֶם, כִּי לְעוֹלָם חַסְדּוֹ.
וַיּוֹצֵא יִשְׂרָאֵל מִתּוֹכָם, כִּי לְעוֹלָם חַסְדּוֹ.
בְּיָד חֲזָקָה וּבִזְרוֹעַ נְטוּיָה, כִּי לְעוֹלָם חַסְדּוֹ.
לְגֹזֵר יַם סוּף לִגְזָרִים, כִּי לְעוֹלָם חַסְדּוֹ.
וְהֶעֱבִיר יִשְׂרָאֵל בְּתוֹכוֹ, כִּי לְעוֹלָם חַסְדּוֹ.

rain; He brings out the wind from His storehouses. He struck down the firstborn of Egypt, of both man and animals. He sent signs and wonders into your midst, Egypt – against Pharaoh and all his servants. He struck down many nations and slew mighty kings: Sichon, king of the Amorites, Og, king of Bashan, and all the kingdoms of Canaan, giving their land as a heritage, a heritage for His people Israel. Your name, LORD, endures for ever; Your renown, LORD, for all generations. For the LORD will bring justice to His people, and have compassion on His servants. The idols of the nations are silver and gold, the work of human hands. They have mouths, but cannot speak; eyes, but cannot see; ears, but cannot hear; there is no breath in their mouths. Those who make them will become like them: so will all who trust in them. ➔ House of Israel, bless the LORD. House of Aaron, bless the LORD. House of Levi, bless the LORD. You who fear the LORD, bless the LORD. Blessed is the LORD from Zion, He who dwells in Jerusalem. Halleluyah!

In many congregations, this psalm is said standing.

PSALM 136

הודו Thank the LORD, for He is good, His lovingkindness is for ever.
Thank the GOD of gods, His lovingkindness is for ever.
Thank the LORD of lords, His lovingkindness is for ever.
To the One who alone works great wonders, His lovingkindness is for ever.
Who made the heavens with wisdom, His lovingkindness is for ever.
Who spread the earth upon the waters, His lovingkindness is for ever.
Who made the great lights, His lovingkindness is for ever.
The sun to rule by day, His lovingkindness is for ever.
The moon and the stars to rule by night; His lovingkindness is for ever.
Who struck Egypt through their firstborn, His lovingkindness is for ever.
And brought out Israel from their midst, His lovingkindness is for ever.
With a strong hand and outstretched arm, His lovingkindness is for ever.
Who split the Reed Sea into parts, His lovingkindness is for ever.
And made Israel pass through it, His lovingkindness is for ever.

הודו *Psalm 136*: Originally in the Temple, the leader of prayer said the first half of each verse, to which the congregation responded with the second half. As in sev-

וְנִעֵר פַּרְעֹה וְחֵילוֹ בְיַם סוּף, כִּי לְעוֹלָם חַסְדּוֹ.
לְמוֹלִיךְ עַמּוֹ בַּמִּדְבָּר, כִּי לְעוֹלָם חַסְדּוֹ.
לְמַכֵּה מְלָכִים גְּדֹלִים, כִּי לְעוֹלָם חַסְדּוֹ.
וַיַּהֲרֹג מְלָכִים אַדִּירִים, כִּי לְעוֹלָם חַסְדּוֹ.
לְסִיחוֹן מֶלֶךְ הָאֱמֹרִי, כִּי לְעוֹלָם חַסְדּוֹ.
וּלְעוֹג מֶלֶךְ הַבָּשָׁן, כִּי לְעוֹלָם חַסְדּוֹ.
וְנָתַן אַרְצָם לְנַחֲלָה, כִּי לְעוֹלָם חַסְדּוֹ.
נַחֲלָה לְיִשְׂרָאֵל עַבְדּוֹ, כִּי לְעוֹלָם חַסְדּוֹ.
שֶׁבְּשִׁפְלֵנוּ זָכַר־לָנוּ, כִּי לְעוֹלָם חַסְדּוֹ.
וַיִּפְרְקֵנוּ מִצָּרֵינוּ, כִּי לְעוֹלָם חַסְדּוֹ.
← נֹתֵן לֶחֶם לְכָל־בָּשָׂר, כִּי לְעוֹלָם חַסְדּוֹ.
הוֹדוּ לְאֵל הַשָּׁמָיִם, כִּי לְעוֹלָם חַסְדּוֹ.

תהלים לג

רַנְּנוּ צַדִּיקִים בַּיהוה, לַיְשָׁרִים נָאוָה תְהִלָּה. הוֹדוּ לַיהוה בְּכִנּוֹר, בְּנֵבֶל עָשׂוֹר זַמְּרוּ־לוֹ. שִׁירוּ לוֹ שִׁיר חָדָשׁ, הֵיטִיבוּ נַגֵּן בִּתְרוּעָה. כִּי־יָשָׁר דְּבַר־יהוה, וְכָל־מַעֲשֵׂהוּ בֶּאֱמוּנָה. אֹהֵב צְדָקָה וּמִשְׁפָּט, חֶסֶד יהוה מָלְאָה הָאָרֶץ. בִּדְבַר יהוה, שָׁמַיִם נַעֲשׂוּ, וּבְרוּחַ פִּיו כָּל־צְבָאָם. כֹּנֵס כַּנֵּד מֵי הַיָּם, נֹתֵן בְּאוֹצָרוֹת תְּהוֹמוֹת. יִירְאוּ מֵיהוה כָּל הָאָרֶץ, מִמֶּנּוּ יָגוּרוּ כָּל־יֹשְׁבֵי תֵבֵל. כִּי־הוּא אָמַר וַיֶּהִי, הוּא צִוָּה וַיַּעֲמֹד. יהוה הֵפִיר עֲצַת גּוֹיִם, הֵנִיא מַחְשְׁבוֹת עַמִּים. עֲצַת יהוה לְעוֹלָם תַּעֲמֹד, מַחְשְׁבוֹת לִבּוֹ לְדֹר וָדֹר. אַשְׁרֵי הַגּוֹי אֲשֶׁר־יהוה אֱלֹהָיו, הָעָם בָּחַר לְנַחֲלָה לוֹ. מִשָּׁמַיִם הִבִּיט יהוה, רָאָה אֶת־כָּל־בְּנֵי הָאָדָם. מִמְּכוֹן שִׁבְתּוֹ הִשְׁגִּיחַ, אֶל־כָּל־יֹשְׁבֵי הָאָרֶץ. הַיֹּצֵר יַחַד לִבָּם, הַמֵּבִין אֶל־כָּל־מַעֲשֵׂיהֶם. אֵין הַמֶּלֶךְ נוֹשָׁע בְּרָב־חָיִל, גִּבּוֹר לֹא־יִנָּצֵל בְּרָב־

Casting Pharaoh and his army into the Reed Sea; His lovingkindness is for ever.
Who led His people through the wilderness; His lovingkindness is for ever.
Who struck down great kings, His lovingkindness is for ever.
And slew mighty kings, His lovingkindness is for ever.
Sihon, king of the Amorites, His lovingkindness is for ever.
And Og, king of Bashan, His lovingkindness is for ever.
And gave their land as a heritage, His lovingkindness is for ever.
A heritage for His servant Israel; His lovingkindness is for ever.
Who remembered us in our lowly state, His lovingkindness is for ever.
And rescued us from our tormentors, His lovingkindness is for ever.
→ Who gives food to all flesh, His lovingkindness is for ever.
Give thanks to the God of heaven. His lovingkindness is for ever.

PSALM 33

רַנְּנוּ Sing joyfully to the Lord, you righteous, for praise from the upright is seemly. Give thanks to the Lord with the harp; make music to Him on the ten-stringed lute. Sing Him a new song, play skillfully with shouts of joy. For the Lord's word is right, and all His deeds are done in faith. He loves righteousness and justice; the earth is full of Lord's lovingkindness. By the Lord's word the heavens were made, and all their starry host by the breath of His mouth. He gathers the sea waters as a heap, and places the deep in storehouses. Let all the earth fear the Lord, and all the world's inhabitants stand in awe of Him. For He spoke, and it was; He commanded, and it stood firm. The Lord foils the plans of nations; He thwarts the intentions of peoples. The Lord's plans stand for ever, His heart's intents for all generations. Happy is the nation whose god is the Lord, the people He has chosen as His own. From heaven the Lord looks down and sees all mankind; from His dwelling place He oversees all who live on earth. He forms the hearts of all, and discerns all their deeds. No king is saved by the size of his army; no warrior is delivered by great strength. A

---

eral other psalms, the poem opens with cosmology and ends with history; it begins with God as Creator, and continues with God as Redeemer. The Sages related the twenty-six verses of the Psalm to the twenty-six generations between Adam and the Giving of the Torah – from creation to revelation. Because of its summary of the events of the exodus, it forms part of the *Haggadah* on Pesach.

כֹּחַ. שֶׁקֶר הַסּוּס לִתְשׁוּעָה, וּבְרֹב חֵילוֹ לֹא יְמַלֵּט. הִנֵּה עֵין יהוה אֶל־יְרֵאָיו, לַמְיַחֲלִים לְחַסְדּוֹ. לְהַצִּיל מִמָּוֶת נַפְשָׁם, וּלְחַיּוֹתָם בָּרָעָב. נַפְשֵׁנוּ חִכְּתָה לַיהוה, עֶזְרֵנוּ וּמָגִנֵּנוּ הוּא. ← כִּי־בוֹ יִשְׂמַח לִבֵּנוּ, כִּי בְשֵׁם קָדְשׁוֹ בָטָחְנוּ. יְהִי־חַסְדְּךָ יהוה עָלֵינוּ, כַּאֲשֶׁר יִחַלְנוּ לָךְ.

תהלים צב

מִזְמוֹר שִׁיר לְיוֹם הַשַּׁבָּת. טוֹב לְהֹדוֹת לַיהוה, וּלְזַמֵּר לְשִׁמְךָ עֶלְיוֹן. לְהַגִּיד בַּבֹּקֶר חַסְדֶּךָ, וֶאֱמוּנָתְךָ בַּלֵּילוֹת. עֲלֵי־עָשׂוֹר וַעֲלֵי־נָבֶל, עֲלֵי הִגָּיוֹן בְּכִנּוֹר. כִּי שִׂמַּחְתַּנִי יהוה בְּפָעֳלֶךָ, בְּמַעֲשֵׂי יָדֶיךָ אֲרַנֵּן. מַה־גָּדְלוּ מַעֲשֶׂיךָ יהוה, מְאֹד עָמְקוּ מַחְשְׁבֹתֶיךָ. אִישׁ בַּעַר לֹא יֵדָע, וּכְסִיל לֹא־יָבִין אֶת־זֹאת. בִּפְרֹחַ רְשָׁעִים כְּמוֹ־עֵשֶׂב, וַיָּצִיצוּ כָּל־פֹּעֲלֵי אָוֶן, לְהִשָּׁמְדָם עֲדֵי־עַד. וְאַתָּה מָרוֹם לְעֹלָם יהוה. כִּי־הִנֵּה אֹיְבֶיךָ יהוה, כִּי־הִנֵּה אֹיְבֶיךָ יֹאבֵדוּ, יִתְפָּרְדוּ כָּל־פֹּעֲלֵי אָוֶן. וַתָּרֶם כִּרְאֵים קַרְנִי, בַּלֹּתִי בְּשֶׁמֶן רַעֲנָן. וַתַּבֵּט עֵינִי בְּשׁוּרָי, בַּקָּמִים עָלַי מְרֵעִים, תִּשְׁמַעְנָה אָזְנָי. ← צַדִּיק כַּתָּמָר יִפְרָח, כְּאֶרֶז בַּלְּבָנוֹן יִשְׂגֶּה. שְׁתוּלִים בְּבֵית יהוה, בְּחַצְרוֹת אֱלֹהֵינוּ יַפְרִיחוּ. עוֹד יְנוּבוּן בְּשֵׂיבָה, דְּשֵׁנִים וְרַעֲנַנִּים יִהְיוּ. לְהַגִּיד כִּי־יָשָׁר יהוה, צוּרִי, וְלֹא־עַוְלָתָה בּוֹ.

תהלים צג

יהוה מָלָךְ, גֵּאוּת לָבֵשׁ, לָבֵשׁ יהוה עֹז הִתְאַזָּר, אַף־תִּכּוֹן תֵּבֵל בַּל־תִּמּוֹט. נָכוֹן כִּסְאֲךָ מֵאָז, מֵעוֹלָם אָתָּה. נָשְׂאוּ נְהָרוֹת יהוה, נָשְׂאוּ נְהָרוֹת קוֹלָם, יִשְׂאוּ נְהָרוֹת דָּכְיָם. ← מִקֹּלוֹת מַיִם רַבִּים, אַדִּירִים מִשְׁבְּרֵי־יָם, אַדִּיר בַּמָּרוֹם יהוה. עֵדֹתֶיךָ נֶאֶמְנוּ מְאֹד לְבֵיתְךָ נַאֲוָה־קֹדֶשׁ, יהוה לְאֹרֶךְ יָמִים.

horse is a vain hope for deliverance; despite its great strength, it cannot save. The eye of the LORD is on those who fear Him, on those who place their hope in His unfailing love, to rescue their soul from death, and keep them alive in famine. Our soul waits for the LORD; He is our Help and Shield. ➔ In Him our hearts rejoice, for we trust in His holy name. Let Your unfailing love be upon us, LORD, as we have put our hope in You.

PSALM 92

מִזְמוֹר שִׁיר A Psalm. A Song for the Sabbath Day. It is good to thank the LORD and sing psalms to Your name, Most High – to tell of Your lovingkindness in the morning and Your faithfulness at night, to the music of the ten-stringed lyre and the melody of the harp. For You have made me rejoice by Your work, O LORD; I sing for joy at the deeds of Your hands. How great are Your deeds, LORD, and how very deep Your thoughts. A boor cannot know, nor can a fool understand, that though the wicked spring up like grass and all evildoers flourish, it is only that they may be destroyed for ever. But You, LORD, are eternally exalted. For behold Your enemies, LORD, behold Your enemies will perish; all evildoers will be scattered. You have raised my pride like that of a wild ox; I am anointed with fresh oil. My eyes shall look in triumph on my adversaries, my ears shall hear the downfall of the wicked who rise against me. ➔ The righteous will flourish like a palm tree and grow tall like a cedar in Lebanon. Planted in the LORD's house, blossoming in our GOD's courtyards, they will still bear fruit in old age, and stay vigorous and fresh, proclaiming that the LORD is upright: He is my Rock, in whom there is no wrong.

PSALM 93

יהוה מָלָךְ The LORD reigns. He is robed in majesty. The LORD is robed, girded with strength. The world is firmly established; it cannot be moved. Your throne stands firm as of old; You are eternal. Rivers lift up, LORD, rivers lift up their voice, rivers lift up their crashing waves. ➔ Mightier than the noise of many waters, than the mighty waves of the sea is the LORD on high. Your testimonies are very sure; holiness adorns Your house, LORD, for evermore.

יְהִי כְבוֹד יהוה לְעוֹלָם, יִשְׂמַח יהוה בְּמַעֲשָׂיו. יְהִי שֵׁם יהוה מְבֹרָךְ, מֵעַתָּה וְעַד־עוֹלָם. מִמִּזְרַח־שֶׁמֶשׁ עַד־מְבוֹאוֹ, מְהֻלָּל שֵׁם יהוה. רָם עַל־כָּל־גּוֹיִם | יהוה, עַל הַשָּׁמַיִם כְּבוֹדוֹ. יהוה שִׁמְךָ לְעוֹלָם, יהוה זִכְרְךָ לְדֹר־וָדֹר. יהוה בַּשָּׁמַיִם הֵכִין כִּסְאוֹ, וּמַלְכוּתוֹ בַּכֹּל מָשָׁלָה. יִשְׂמְחוּ הַשָּׁמַיִם וְתָגֵל הָאָרֶץ, וְיֹאמְרוּ בַגּוֹיִם יהוה מָלָךְ. יהוה מֶלֶךְ, יהוה מָלָךְ, יהוה יִמְלֹךְ לְעֹלָם וָעֶד. יהוה מֶלֶךְ עוֹלָם וָעֶד, אָבְדוּ גוֹיִם מֵאַרְצוֹ. יהוה הֵפִיר עֲצַת גּוֹיִם, הֵנִיא מַחְשְׁבוֹת עַמִּים. רַבּוֹת מַחֲשָׁבוֹת בְּלֶב־אִישׁ, וַעֲצַת יהוה הִיא תָקוּם. עֲצַת יהוה לְעוֹלָם תַּעֲמֹד, מַחְשְׁבוֹת לִבּוֹ לְדֹר וָדֹר. כִּי הוּא אָמַר וַיֶּהִי, הוּא צִוָּה וַיַּעֲמֹד. כִּי־בָחַר יהוה בְּצִיּוֹן, אִוָּהּ לְמוֹשָׁב לוֹ. כִּי יַעֲקֹב בָּחַר לוֹ יָהּ, יִשְׂרָאֵל לִסְגֻלָּתוֹ. כִּי לֹא־יִטֹּשׁ יהוה עַמּוֹ, וְנַחֲלָתוֹ לֹא יַעֲזֹב. ◂ וְהוּא רַחוּם יְכַפֵּר עָוֹן וְלֹא יַשְׁחִית, וְהִרְבָּה לְהָשִׁיב אַפּוֹ, וְלֹא יָעִיר כָּל־חֲמָתוֹ. יהוה הוֹשִׁיעָה, הַמֶּלֶךְ יַעֲנֵנוּ בְיוֹם־קָרְאֵנוּ.

אשרי

אַשְׁרֵי יוֹשְׁבֵי בֵיתֶךָ, עוֹד יְהַלְלוּךָ סֶּלָה.
אַשְׁרֵי הָעָם שֶׁכָּכָה לּוֹ, אַשְׁרֵי הָעָם שֶׁיהוה אֱלֹהָיו.

תהלים קמה

תְּהִלָּה לְדָוִד,

אֲרוֹמִמְךָ אֱלוֹהַי הַמֶּלֶךְ, וַאֲבָרְכָה שִׁמְךָ לְעוֹלָם וָעֶד.

יְהִי כְבוֹד *May the Lord's glory*: – An anthology of verses, mainly from Psalms, but also from Chronicles and Proverbs. One verse, "The Lord is King, the Lord was King, the Lord will be King for ever and all time", does not appear in this form in the Bible: it is a combination of three biblical phrases, two from Psalms, one from Exodus (at the end of the Song at the Sea). The verses take us through the following sequence of thought: God created the universe, therefore God is Sovereign over the universe. In the short term it may seem that human beings de-

יְהִי May the LORD's glory be for ever; may the LORD rejoice in His works. May the LORD's name be blessed, now and for ever. From the rising of the sun to its setting, may the LORD's name be praised. The LORD is high above all nations; His glory is above the heavens. LORD, Your name is for ever. Your renown, LORD, is for all generations. The LORD has established His throne in heaven; His kingdom rules all. Let the heavens rejoice and the earth be glad. Let them say among the nations, "The LORD is King." The LORD is King, the LORD was King, the LORD will be King for ever and all time. The LORD is King for ever and all time; nations will perish from His land. The LORD foils the plans of nations; He frustrates the intentions of peoples. Many are the intentions in a person's mind, but the LORD's plan prevails. The LORD's plan shall stand for ever, His mind's intent for all generations. For He spoke and it was; He commanded and it stood firm. For the LORD has chosen Zion; He desired it for His dwelling. For the LORD has chosen Jacob to Himself, Israel as His special treasure. For the LORD will not abandon His people nor will He forsake His heritage. He is compassionate. → He forgives iniquity and does not destroy. Repeatedly He suppresses His anger, not rousing His full wrath. LORD, save! May the King answer us on the day we call.

ASHREI

אַשְׁרֵי Happy are those who dwell in Your House;
they shall continue to praise you, Selah!
Happy are the people for whom this is so;
happy are the people whose GOD is the LORD.

PSALM 145

A song of praise by David.

I will exalt You, my GOD, the King,
and bless Your name for ever and all time.

---

termine their own fate even against the will of heaven. However, it is not so: "The LORD's plan prevails." GOD has chosen a particular people (Zion, Jacob) to exemplify this truth, for Israel is the only nation whose very existence is dependent on its covenant with GOD. Because Israel recognises no ultimate king other than GOD, it turns to Him in prayer.

אַשְׁרֵי *Happy are those*: Psalm 145 is the single most important passage in the Verses of Praise. The Sages saw it as the paradigm of praise, firstly because it is

בְּכָל יוֹם אֲבָרְכֶךָּ, וַאֲהַלְלָה שִׁמְךָ לְעוֹלָם וָעֶד.
גָּדוֹל יהוה וּמְהֻלָּל מְאֹד, וְלִגְדֻלָּתוֹ אֵין חֵקֶר.
דּוֹר לְדוֹר יְשַׁבַּח מַעֲשֶׂיךָ, וּגְבוּרֹתֶיךָ יַגִּידוּ.
הֲדַר כְּבוֹד הוֹדֶךָ, וְדִבְרֵי נִפְלְאֹתֶיךָ אָשִׂיחָה.
וֶעֱזוּז נוֹרְאוֹתֶיךָ יֹאמֵרוּ, וּגְדֻלָּתְךָ אֲסַפְּרֶנָּה.
זֵכֶר רַב־טוּבְךָ יַבִּיעוּ, וְצִדְקָתְךָ יְרַנֵּנוּ.
חַנּוּן וְרַחוּם יהוה, אֶרֶךְ אַפַּיִם וּגְדָל־חָסֶד.
טוֹב יהוה לַכֹּל, וְרַחֲמָיו עַל כָּל מַעֲשָׂיו.
יוֹדוּךָ יהוה כָּל מַעֲשֶׂיךָ, וַחֲסִידֶיךָ יְבָרְכוּכָה.
כְּבוֹד מַלְכוּתְךָ יֹאמֵרוּ, וּגְבוּרָתְךָ יְדַבֵּרוּ.
לְהוֹדִיעַ לִבְנֵי הָאָדָם גְּבוּרֹתָיו, וּכְבוֹד הֲדַר מַלְכוּתוֹ.
מַלְכוּתְךָ מַלְכוּת כָּל עֹלָמִים, וּמֶמְשַׁלְתְּךָ בְּכָל דּוֹר וָדֹר.
סוֹמֵךְ יהוה לְכָל הַנֹּפְלִים, וְזוֹקֵף לְכָל הַכְּפוּפִים.
עֵינֵי כֹל אֵלֶיךָ יְשַׂבֵּרוּ, וְאַתָּה נוֹתֵן לָהֶם אֶת אָכְלָם בְּעִתּוֹ.
פּוֹתֵחַ אֶת יָדֶךָ, וּמַשְׂבִּיעַ לְכָל־חַי רָצוֹן.
צַדִּיק יהוה בְּכָל דְּרָכָיו, וְחָסִיד בְּכָל מַעֲשָׂיו.
קָרוֹב יהוה לְכָל קֹרְאָיו, לְכֹל אֲשֶׁר יִקְרָאֻהוּ בֶאֱמֶת.
רְצוֹן יְרֵאָיו יַעֲשֶׂה, וְאֶת שַׁוְעָתָם יִשְׁמַע, וְיוֹשִׁיעֵם.
שׁוֹמֵר יהוה אֶת כָּל אֹהֲבָיו, וְאֵת כָּל־הָרְשָׁעִים יַשְׁמִיד.
← תְּהִלַּת יהוה יְדַבֶּר פִּי, וִיבָרֵךְ כָּל־בָּשָׂר שֵׁם קָדְשׁוֹ לְעוֹלָם וָעֶד.
וַאֲנַחְנוּ נְבָרֵךְ יָהּ, מֵעַתָּה וְעַד־עוֹלָם, הַלְלוּיָהּ.

---

constructed as an alphabetic acrostic (with the exception of the letter *nun*), thus praising God with all the letters of the alphabet; second, because it contains the verse "You open Your hand and satisfy every living thing with your favour.", encapsulating the idea that God not merely created the universe in the beginning, but also daily sustains it and the life it contains. The Sages ruled that it be said three times daily (twice in the morning service, once in the afternoon).

There are other reasons for its prominence. It is the only one of the 150 Psalms

Every day I will bless You,
and praise Your name for ever and all time.
God is great and greatly to be praised;
His greatness is unfathomable.
One generation will praise Your works to the next,
and tell of Your mighty deeds.
On the glorious splendour of Your majesty I will meditate,
and on the acts of Your wonders.
They shall talk of the power of Your awesome deeds,
and I will tell of Your greatness.
They shall recite the record of Your great goodness,
and sing with joy of Your righteousness.
The Lord is gracious and compassionate,
slow to anger and great in lovingkindness.
The Lord is good to all,
and His compassion extends to all His works.
All Your works shall thank You, Lord,
and Your devoted ones shall bless You.
They shall talk of the glory of Your kingship,
and speak of Your might,
To make known to mankind His mighty deeds
and the glorious majesty of His kingship.
Your kingdom is an everlasting kingdom,
and Your reign is for all generations.
The Lord supports all who fall,
and raises all who are bowed down.
All raise their eyes to You in hope,
and You give them their food in due season.
You open Your hand,
and satisfy every living thing with Your favour.
The Lord is righteous in all His ways,
and kind in all He does.
The Lord is close to all who call on Him,
to all who call on Him in truth.
He fulfils the will of those who revere Him;
He hears their cry and saves them.
The Lord guards all who love Him,
but all the wicked He will destroy.
→ My mouth shall speak the praise of the Lord,
and all creatures shall bless His holy name for ever and all time.
We will bless the Lord now and for ever. Halleluyah!

תהלים קמו

הַלְלוּיָהּ, הַלְלִי נַפְשִׁי אֶת־יהוה. אֲהַלְלָה יהוה בְּחַיָּי, אֲזַמְּרָה לֵאלֹהַי בְּעוֹדִי. אַל־תִּבְטְחוּ בִנְדִיבִים, בְּבֶן־אָדָם שֶׁאֵין לוֹ תְשׁוּעָה. תֵּצֵא רוּחוֹ, יָשֻׁב לְאַדְמָתוֹ, בַּיּוֹם הַהוּא אָבְדוּ עֶשְׁתֹּנֹתָיו. אַשְׁרֵי שֶׁאֵל יַעֲקֹב בְּעֶזְרוֹ, שִׂבְרוֹ עַל־יהוה אֱלֹהָיו. עֹשֶׂה שָׁמַיִם וָאָרֶץ, אֶת־הַיָּם וְאֶת־כָּל־אֲשֶׁר־בָּם, הַשֹּׁמֵר אֱמֶת לְעוֹלָם. עֹשֶׂה מִשְׁפָּט לַעֲשׁוּקִים, נֹתֵן לֶחֶם לָרְעֵבִים, יהוה מַתִּיר אֲסוּרִים. יהוה פֹּקֵחַ עִוְרִים, יהוה זֹקֵף כְּפוּפִים, יהוה אֹהֵב צַדִּיקִים. יהוה שֹׁמֵר אֶת גֵּרִים, יָתוֹם וְאַלְמָנָה יְעוֹדֵד, וְדֶרֶךְ רְשָׁעִים יְעַוֵּת. ◄ יִמְלֹךְ יהוה לְעוֹלָם, אֱלֹהַיִךְ צִיּוֹן לְדֹר וָדֹר, הַלְלוּיָהּ.

תהלים קמז

הַלְלוּיָהּ, כִּי־טוֹב זַמְּרָה אֱלֹהֵינוּ, כִּי־נָעִים נָאוָה תְהִלָּה. בּוֹנֵה יְרוּשָׁלַיִם יהוה, נִדְחֵי יִשְׂרָאֵל יְכַנֵּס. הָרוֹפֵא לִשְׁבוּרֵי־לֵב, וּמְחַבֵּשׁ לְעַצְּבוֹתָם. מוֹנֶה מִסְפָּר לַכּוֹכָבִים, לְכֻלָּם שֵׁמוֹת יִקְרָא. גָּדוֹל אֲדוֹנֵינוּ וְרַב־כֹּחַ, לִתְבוּנָתוֹ אֵין מִסְפָּר. מְעוֹדֵד עֲנָוִים יהוה, מַשְׁפִּיל רְשָׁעִים עֲדֵי־אָרֶץ. עֱנוּ לַיהוה בְּתוֹדָה, זַמְּרוּ לֵאלֹהֵינוּ בְכִנּוֹר. הַמְכַסֶּה שָׁמַיִם בְּעָבִים, הַמֵּכִין לָאָרֶץ מָטָר, הַמַּצְמִיחַ הָרִים חָצִיר. נוֹתֵן לִבְהֵמָה לַחְמָהּ, לִבְנֵי עֹרֵב אֲשֶׁר יִקְרָאוּ. לֹא בִגְבוּרַת הַסּוּס יֶחְפָּץ, לֹא־בְשׁוֹקֵי הָאִישׁ יִרְצֶה. רוֹצֶה יהוה אֶת־יְרֵאָיו, אֶת־הַמְיַחֲלִים לְחַסְדּוֹ. שַׁבְּחִי יְרוּשָׁלַיִם אֶת יהוה, הַלְלִי אֱלֹהַיִךְ צִיּוֹן. כִּי־חִזַּק בְּרִיחֵי שְׁעָרָיִךְ, בֵּרַךְ בָּנַיִךְ בְּקִרְבֵּךְ. הַשָּׂם גְּבוּלֵךְ שָׁלוֹם, חֵלֶב חִטִּים יַשְׂבִּיעֵךְ. הַשֹּׁלֵחַ אִמְרָתוֹ אָרֶץ,

---

to be called *Tehillah le-David*, "A Song of Praise of David". It contains the phrase, "Every day I will bless You", suggesting that it be said daily. Its 21 lines are constructed in three groups of seven verses: 1–7 are about God's praise throughout

PSALM 146

הַלְלוּיָהּ Halleluyah! Praise the LORD, O my soul. I will praise the LORD all my life; I will sing to my GOD as long as I live. Put not your trust in princes or in mortal man who cannot save. His breath expires, he returns to the earth; on that day his plans come to an end. Happy is he whose help is the GOD of Jacob, whose hope is in the LORD his GOD who made heaven and earth, the sea and all they contain; He who keeps faith for ever. He secures justice for the oppressed. He gives food to the hungry. The LORD sets captives free. The LORD gives sight to the blind. The LORD raises those bowed down. The LORD loves the righteous. The LORD protects the stranger. He gives courage to the orphan and widow. He thwarts the way of the wicked. ▸ The LORD shall reign for ever. He is your GOD, O Zion, for all generations. Halleluyah!

PSALM 147

הַלְלוּיָהּ Halleluyah! How good it is to sing songs to our GOD; how pleasant and fitting to praise Him. The LORD rebuilds Jerusalem. He gathers the scattered exiles of Israel. He heals the broken-hearted and binds up their wounds. He counts the number of the stars, calling each by name. Great is our LORD and mighty in power; His understanding has no limit. The LORD gives courage to the humble, but casts the wicked to the ground. Sing to the LORD in thanks; make music to our GOD on the harp. He covers the sky with clouds. He provides the earth with rain and makes grass grow on the hills. He gives food to the cattle and to the ravens when they cry. He does not take delight in the strength of horses nor pleasure in the fleetness of man. The LORD takes pleasure in those who fear Him, who put their hope in His loving care. Praise

---

the generations; 8–14 depict GOD's kingship and compassion; and 15–21 are about prayer how GOD heeds it. The psalm is built on numerical structures (3, 7, 10) that closely resemble the creation narrative in Genesis 1:1–2:3.

To it have been added two verses from other psalms at the beginning, which use the word *Ashrei* (happy) three times, and one at the end. It thus epitomises the Book of Psalms as a whole, which begins with the word *Ashrei* and ends with the word *Halleluyah*.

הַלְלוּיָהּ *Psalm 146*: The contrast between human and Divine rule. Human beings are mortal. They come from dust and return to dust. GOD is eternal, as are

עַד־מְהֵרָה יָרוּץ דְּבָרוֹ. הַנֹּתֵן שֶׁלֶג כַּצָּמֶר, כְּפוֹר כָּאֵפֶר יְפַזֵּר. מַשְׁלִיךְ קַרְחוֹ כְפִתִּים, לִפְנֵי קָרָתוֹ מִי יַעֲמֹד. יִשְׁלַח דְּבָרוֹ וְיַמְסֵם, יַשֵּׁב רוּחוֹ יִזְּלוּ מָיִם. ← מַגִּיד דְּבָרָיו לְיַעֲקֹב, חֻקָּיו וּמִשְׁפָּטָיו לְיִשְׂרָאֵל. לֹא עָשָׂה כֵן לְכָל־גּוֹי, וּמִשְׁפָּטִים בַּל־יְדָעוּם, הַלְלוּיָהּ.

תהלים קמח

הַלְלוּיָהּ, הַלְלוּ אֶת־יהוה מִן־הַשָּׁמַיִם, הַלְלוּהוּ בַּמְּרוֹמִים. הַלְלוּהוּ כָל־מַלְאָכָיו, הַלְלוּהוּ כָּל־צְבָאָיו. הַלְלוּהוּ שֶׁמֶשׁ וְיָרֵחַ, הַלְלוּהוּ כָּל־כּוֹכְבֵי אוֹר. הַלְלוּהוּ שְׁמֵי הַשָּׁמָיִם, וְהַמַּיִם אֲשֶׁר מֵעַל הַשָּׁמָיִם. יְהַלְלוּ אֶת־שֵׁם יהוה, כִּי הוּא צִוָּה וְנִבְרָאוּ. וַיַּעֲמִידֵם לָעַד לְעוֹלָם, חָק־נָתַן וְלֹא יַעֲבוֹר. הַלְלוּ אֶת־יהוה מִן־הָאָרֶץ, תַּנִּינִים וְכָל־תְּהֹמוֹת. אֵשׁ וּבָרָד שֶׁלֶג וְקִיטוֹר, רוּחַ סְעָרָה עֹשָׂה דְבָרוֹ. הֶהָרִים וְכָל־גְּבָעוֹת, עֵץ פְּרִי וְכָל־אֲרָזִים. הַחַיָּה וְכָל־בְּהֵמָה, רֶמֶשׂ וְצִפּוֹר כָּנָף. מַלְכֵי־אֶרֶץ וְכָל־לְאֻמִּים, שָׂרִים וְכָל־שֹׁפְטֵי אָרֶץ. בַּחוּרִים וְגַם־בְּתוּלוֹת, זְקֵנִים עִם־נְעָרִים. ← יְהַלְלוּ אֶת־שֵׁם יהוה, כִּי־נִשְׂגָּב שְׁמוֹ לְבַדּוֹ, הוֹדוֹ עַל־אֶרֶץ וְשָׁמָיִם. וַיָּרֶם קֶרֶן לְעַמּוֹ, תְּהִלָּה לְכָל־חֲסִידָיו, לִבְנֵי יִשְׂרָאֵל עַם קְרֹבוֹ, הַלְלוּיָהּ.

תהלים קמט

הַלְלוּיָהּ, שִׁירוּ לַיהוה שִׁיר חָדָשׁ, תְּהִלָּתוֹ בִּקְהַל חֲסִידִים. יִשְׂמַח יִשְׂרָאֵל בְּעֹשָׂיו, בְּנֵי־צִיּוֹן יָגִילוּ בְמַלְכָּם. יְהַלְלוּ

---

the values by which He governs the affairs of humankind. He brings justice to the oppressed, food to the hungry, freedom to captives, and hope to those at the margins of society. These principles of justice and compassion run through Jewish history as the governing ideals of a society under the sovereignty of God.

הַלְלוּיָהּ *Psalm 147*: A magnificent weaving together of the themes of nature, God's role in Israel's history, and the paradox of Divine distance and closeness. God counts the stars: He rules the cosmos. At the same time, He also "heals the broken-hearted and binds up their wounds": He cares for each of us. What matters ultimately is not power but humility in

the LORD, Jerusalem; sing to your GOD, Zion, for He has strengthened the bars of your gates and blessed your children in your midst. He has brought peace to your borders, and satisfied you with the finest wheat. He sends His commandment to earth; swiftly runs His word. He spreads snow like fleece, sprinkles frost like ashes, scatters hail like crumbs. Who can stand His cold? He sends His word and melts them; He makes the wind blow and the waters flow. ➔ He has declared his words to Jacob, His statutes and laws to Israel. He has done this for no other nation; such laws they do not know. Halleluyah!

PSALM 148

הַלְלוּיָהּ Halleluyah! Praise the LORD from the heavens, praise Him in the heights. Praise Him, all His angels, praise Him, all His hosts. Praise Him, sun and moon, praise Him, all shining stars. Praise Him, highest heavens and the waters above the heavens. Let them praise the name of the LORD, for He commanded and they were created. He established them for ever and all time, issuing a decree that will never change. Praise the LORD from the earth: sea monsters and all the deep seas, fire and hail, snow and mist, storm winds that obey His word; mountains and all hills, fruit trees and all cedars, wild animals and all cattle, creeping things and winged birds; kings of the earth and all nations, princes and all judges on earth; youths and maidens, old and young. ➔ Let them praise the name of the LORD, for His name alone is sublime; His majesty is above earth and heaven. He has raised the pride of His people, for the glory of all His devoted ones, the children of Israel, the people close to Him. Halleluyah!

PSALM 149

הַלְלוּיָהּ Halleluyah! Sing to the LORD a new song, His praise in the assembly of the devoted. Let Israel rejoice in its Maker; let the children

---

the face of GOD. He has chosen Israel uniquely to embody this truth in their constitution as a nation. Therefore He, not a human legislature, is the source of their laws.

הַלְלוּיָהּ *Psalm 148*: A creation Psalm. The entire universe sings a song of praise to GOD. The first half of the Psalm is about the heavens, the second about the earth. Each is a voice in the choral symphony of creation, in which all that exists testifies to its Maker.

הַלְלוּיָהּ *Psalm 149*: A Psalm of thanksgiving for GOD's role in Israel's history,

שְׁמוֹ בְמָחוֹל, בְּתֹף וְכִנּוֹר יְזַמְּרוּ־לוֹ. כִּי־רוֹצֶה יהוה בְּעַמּוֹ, יְפָאֵר עֲנָוִים בִּישׁוּעָה. יַעְלְזוּ חֲסִידִים בְּכָבוֹד, יְרַנְּנוּ עַל־מִשְׁכְּבוֹתָם. רוֹמְמוֹת אֵל בִּגְרוֹנָם, וְחֶרֶב פִּיפִיּוֹת בְּיָדָם. לַעֲשׂוֹת נְקָמָה בַּגּוֹיִם, תּוֹכֵחוֹת בַּלְאֻמִּים. ◂ לֶאְסֹר מַלְכֵיהֶם בְּזִקִּים, וְנִכְבְּדֵיהֶם בְּכַבְלֵי בַרְזֶל. לַעֲשׂוֹת בָּהֶם מִשְׁפָּט כָּתוּב, הָדָר הוּא לְכָל־חֲסִידָיו, הַלְלוּיָהּ.

תהלים קנ

הַלְלוּיָהּ,
הַלְלוּ־אֵל בְּקָדְשׁוֹ, הַלְלוּהוּ בִּרְקִיעַ עֻזּוֹ.
הַלְלוּהוּ בִגְבוּרֹתָיו, הַלְלוּהוּ כְּרֹב גֻּדְלוֹ.
הַלְלוּהוּ בְּתֵקַע שׁוֹפָר, הַלְלוּהוּ בְּנֵבֶל וְכִנּוֹר.
הַלְלוּהוּ בְתֹף וּמָחוֹל, הַלְלוּהוּ בְּמִנִּים וְעוּגָב.
הַלְלוּהוּ בְצִלְצְלֵי־שָׁמַע, הַלְלוּהוּ בְּצִלְצְלֵי־תְרוּעָה.
◂ כֹּל הַנְּשָׁמָה תְּהַלֵּל יָהּ, הַלְלוּיָהּ.
כֹּל הַנְּשָׁמָה תְּהַלֵּל יָהּ, הַלְלוּיָהּ.

בָּרוּךְ יהוה לְעוֹלָם, אָמֵן וְאָמֵן. בָּרוּךְ יהוה מִצִּיּוֹן, שֹׁכֵן יְרוּשָׁלָיִם, הַלְלוּיָהּ. בָּרוּךְ יהוה אֱלֹהִים אֱלֹהֵי יִשְׂרָאֵל, עֹשֵׂה נִפְלָאוֹת לְבַדּוֹ. ◂ וּבָרוּךְ שֵׁם כְּבוֹדוֹ לְעוֹלָם, וְיִמָּלֵא כְבוֹדוֹ אֶת־כָּל־הָאָרֶץ, אָמֵן וְאָמֵן.

הַלְלוּיָהּ *Psalm 150*: The Book of Psalms here reaches its crescendo in a magnificent song whose key word is praise (*Hallel*) which appears in one or other form thirteen times in a single short paragraph. In ancient times it was recited by pilgrims bringing first fruits to Jerusalem, when they reached the Temple Mount (Maimonides, *Bikkurim* 4:17). The repeti-

granting them victory in war and ensuring the ultimate victory of justice over cruelty and aggression. The "two-edged sword" may be a reference to the dual nature of history: on the one hand the house of Israel must fight its own battles, on the other it must always be conscious of the providential pattern of history, the role of God in its survival and success.

of Zion exult in their King. Let them praise His name with dancing, sing praises to Him with timbrel and harp. For the LORD delights in His people; He adorns the humble with salvation. Let the devoted revel in glory; let them sing for joy on their beds. Let high praises of GOD be in their throats, and a two-edged sword in their hand: to impose retribution on the nations, punishment on the peoples, → binding their kings with chains, their nobles with iron fetters, carrying out the judgement written against them. This is the glory of all His devoted ones. Halleluyah!

PSALM 150

הַלְלוּיָהּ Halleluyah!
Praise GOD in His holy place,
  praise Him in the heavens of His power.
Praise Him for His mighty deeds,
  praise Him for His surpassing greatness.
Praise Him with blasts of the ram's horn,
  praise Him with the harp and lyre.
Praise Him with timbrel and dance,
  praise Him with strings and flute.
Praise Him with clashing cymbals,
  praise Him with resounding cymbals.
→ Let all that breathes praise the LORD. Halleluyah!
Let all that breathes praise the LORD. Halleluyah!

בָּרוּךְ Blessed be the LORD for ever. Amen and Amen. Blessed from Zion be the LORD who dwells in Jerusalem. Halleluyah! Blessed be the LORD, GOD of Israel, who alone does wonders. → Blessed be His glorious name for ever, and may all the earth be filled with His glory. Amen and Amen.

---

tion of the last verse is a convention signaling the end of a book or passage.

בָּרוּךְ ה' *Blessed be the LORD*: A passage marking the closure of the Verses of Praise. It is constructed out of three verses from the Book of Psalms, chosen because they open with the word "Blessed".

Stand from this point until נִשְׁמַת on page 362.

דברי הימים א׳ כט:י–יג

וַיְבָרֶךְ דָּוִיד אֶת־יהוה לְעֵינֵי כָּל־הַקָּהָל, וַיֹּאמֶר דָּוִיד, בָּרוּךְ אַתָּה יהוה, אֱלֹהֵי יִשְׂרָאֵל אָבִינוּ, מֵעוֹלָם וְעַד־עוֹלָם. לְךָ יהוה הַגְּדֻלָּה וְהַגְּבוּרָה וְהַתִּפְאֶרֶת וְהַנֵּצַח וְהַהוֹד, כִּי־כֹל בַּשָּׁמַיִם וּבָאָרֶץ, לְךָ יהוה הַמַּמְלָכָה וְהַמִּתְנַשֵּׂא לְכֹל לְרֹאשׁ. וְהָעֹשֶׁר וְהַכָּבוֹד מִלְּפָנֶיךָ, וְאַתָּה מוֹשֵׁל בַּכֹּל, וּבְיָדְךָ כֹּחַ וּגְבוּרָה, וּבְיָדְךָ לְגַדֵּל וּלְחַזֵּק לַכֹּל. וְעַתָּה אֱלֹהֵינוּ מוֹדִים אֲנַחְנוּ לָךְ, וּמְהַלְלִים לְשֵׁם תִּפְאַרְתֶּךָ.

נחמיה ט:ו–יא

אַתָּה־הוּא יהוה לְבַדֶּךָ, אַתָּה עָשִׂיתָ אֶת־הַשָּׁמַיִם, שְׁמֵי הַשָּׁמַיִם וְכָל־צְבָאָם, הָאָרֶץ וְכָל־אֲשֶׁר עָלֶיהָ, הַיַּמִּים וְכָל־אֲשֶׁר בָּהֶם, וְאַתָּה מְחַיֶּה אֶת־כֻּלָּם, וּצְבָא הַשָּׁמַיִם לְךָ מִשְׁתַּחֲוִים. ← אַתָּה הוּא יהוה הָאֱלֹהִים אֲשֶׁר בָּחַרְתָּ בְּאַבְרָם, וְהוֹצֵאתוֹ מֵאוּר כַּשְׂדִּים, וְשַׂמְתָּ שְּׁמוֹ אַבְרָהָם. וּמָצָאתָ אֶת־לְבָבוֹ נֶאֱמָן לְפָנֶיךָ,

וְכָרוֹת עִמּוֹ הַבְּרִית לָתֵת אֶת־אֶרֶץ הַכְּנַעֲנִי הַחִתִּי הָאֱמֹרִי וְהַפְּרִזִּי וְהַיְבוּסִי וְהַגִּרְגָּשִׁי, לָתֵת לְזַרְעוֹ, וַתָּקֶם אֶת־דְּבָרֶיךָ, כִּי צַדִּיק אָתָּה. וַתֵּרֶא אֶת־עֳנִי אֲבֹתֵינוּ בְּמִצְרָיִם, וְאֶת־זַעֲקָתָם שָׁמַעְתָּ עַל־יַם־סוּף. וַתִּתֵּן אֹתֹת וּמֹפְתִים בְּפַרְעֹה וּבְכָל־עֲבָדָיו וּבְכָל־עַם אַרְצוֹ, כִּי יָדַעְתָּ כִּי הֵזִידוּ עֲלֵיהֶם, וַתַּעַשׂ־לְךָ שֵׁם כְּהַיּוֹם הַזֶּה. ← וְהַיָּם בָּקַעְתָּ לִפְנֵיהֶם, וַיַּעַבְרוּ בְתוֹךְ־הַיָּם בַּיַּבָּשָׁה, וְאֶת־רֹדְפֵיהֶם הִשְׁלַכְתָּ בִמְצוֹלֹת, כְּמוֹ־אֶבֶן בְּמַיִם עַזִּים.

וַיְבָרֶךְ דָּוִיד *David blessed*: The first of three passages marking historic transitions in the history of Israel: 1. King David's prayer for the building of the Temple;

Stand from this point until "The soul" on page 363.

I CHRONICLES 29:10–13

וַיְבָרֶךְ David blessed the LORD in front of the entire assembly. David said, "Blessed are You, LORD, GOD of our father Israel, for ever and ever. Yours, LORD, are the greatness and the power, the glory, majesty and splendour, for everything in heaven and earth is Yours. Yours, LORD, is the kingdom; You are exalted as head over all. In Your hand are strength and might. It is in Your power to make great and give strength to all. Therefore, our GOD, we thank You and praise Your glorious name."

NEHEMIAH 9:6–11

אַתָּה־הוּא You alone are the LORD. You made the heavens, even the highest heavens, and all their hosts, the earth and all that is on it, the seas and all they contain. You give life to them all, and the hosts of heaven worship You. ➔ You are the LORD GOD who chose Abram and brought him out of Ur of the Chaldees, changing his name to Abraham. You found his heart faithful towards You –

And You made a covenant with him to give to his descendants the land of the Canaanites, Hittites, Amorites, Perizzites, Jebusites and Girgashites. You fulfilled Your promise for You are righteous. You saw the suffering of our ancestors in Egypt. You heard their cry at the Sea of Reeds. You sent signs and wonders against Pharaoh, all his servants and all the people of his land, because You knew how arrogantly the Egyptians treated them. You created for Yourself renown that remains to this day. ➔ You divided the sea before them, so that they passed through the sea on dry land, but You cast their pursuers into the depths, like a stone into mighty waters.

---

2. the prayer said at the gathering convened by Ezra after the return from the Babylonian exile; and 3. the song Moses and the Israelites sang at the Sea of Reeds, after the waters had miraculously divided, allowing them to cross to safety.

One reason for their presence here is that thus far we have prayed as individuals. Communal prayer is about to begin. The three historic passages are about the constitution of a *community* of prayer.

In the first, David had made Jerusalem the capital of the nation and brought the Ark to it. Now at the end of his life

שירת הים

שמות יד:ל–טו:יט

וַיּוֹשַׁע יְהוָה בַּיּוֹם הַהוּא אֶת־יִשְׂרָאֵל מִיַּד מִצְרָיִם וַיַּרְא
יִשְׂרָאֵל אֶת־מִצְרַיִם מֵת עַל־שְׂפַת הַיָּם: ‹ וַיַּרְא יִשְׂרָאֵל
אֶת־הַיָּד הַגְּדֹלָה אֲשֶׁר עָשָׂה יְהוָה בְּמִצְרַיִם, וַיִּירְאוּ הָעָם
אֶת־יְהוָה, וַיַּאֲמִינוּ בַּיהוָה וּבְמֹשֶׁה עַבְדּוֹ:

אָז יָשִׁיר־מֹשֶׁה וּבְנֵי יִשְׂרָאֵל אֶת־הַשִּׁירָה הַזֹּאת לַיהוָה וַיֹּאמְרוּ
לֵאמֹר אָשִׁירָה לַיהוָה כִּי־גָאֹה גָּאָה סוּס
וְרֹכְבוֹ רָמָה בַיָּם: עָזִּי וְזִמְרָת יָהּ וַיְהִי־לִי
לִישׁוּעָה זֶה אֵלִי וְאַנְוֵהוּ אֱלֹהֵי
אָבִי וַאֲרֹמְמֶנְהוּ: יְהוָה אִישׁ מִלְחָמָה יְהוָה
שְׁמוֹ: מַרְכְּבֹת פַּרְעֹה וְחֵילוֹ יָרָה בַיָּם וּמִבְחַר
שָׁלִשָׁיו טֻבְּעוּ בְיַם־סוּף: תְּהֹמֹת יְכַסְיֻמוּ יָרְדוּ בִמְצוֹלֹת כְּמוֹ־
אָבֶן: יְמִינְךָ יְהוָה נֶאְדָּרִי בַּכֹּחַ יְמִינְךָ
יְהוָה תִּרְעַץ אוֹיֵב: וּבְרֹב גְּאוֹנְךָ תַּהֲרֹס
קָמֶיךָ תְּשַׁלַּח חֲרֹנְךָ יֹאכְלֵמוֹ כַּקַּשׁ: וּבְרוּחַ
אַפֶּיךָ נֶעֶרְמוּ מַיִם נִצְּבוּ כְמוֹ־נֵד
נֹזְלִים קָפְאוּ תְהֹמֹת בְּלֶב־יָם: אָמַר
אוֹיֵב אֶרְדֹּף אַשִּׂיג אֲחַלֵּק שָׁלָל תִּמְלָאֵמוֹ
נַפְשִׁי אָרִיק חַרְבִּי תּוֹרִישֵׁמוֹ יָדִי: נָשַׁפְתָּ
בְרוּחֲךָ כִּסָּמוֹ יָם צָלֲלוּ כַּעוֹפֶרֶת בְּמַיִם

---

he assembled the people and charged them with the sacred task of building the Temple. In the second, after the Babylonian exile, Ezra and Nehemiah summoned the people to reaffirm their historic covenant with God. The third, after the Israelites had crossed the Sea of Reeds, was the moment when they left the land over which Pharaoh ruled. They were now God's people, under His sole domain. Common to all three passages is that they were said at historic moments when the people pledged themselves to be defined as a nation bound together by a sacred task.

Instead of simply moving from indi-

THE SONG AT THE SEA

EXODUS 14:30–15:19

וַיּוֹשַׁע That day the LORD saved Israel from the hands of the Egyptians, and Israel saw the Egyptians lying dead on the seashore. ➔ When Israel saw the great power the LORD had displayed against the Egyptians, the people feared the LORD, and believed in the LORD and in His servant, Moses.

אָז Then Moses and the Israelites sang this song to the LORD, saying:
I will sing to the LORD, for He has triumphed gloriously;
horse and rider He has hurled into the sea.
The LORD is my strength and song; He has become my salvation.
This is my GOD, and I will beautify Him,
my father's GOD, and I will exalt Him.
The LORD is a Master of war; LORD is His name.
Pharaoh's chariots and army He cast into the sea;
the best of his officers drowned in the Sea of Reeds.
The deep waters covered them;
they went down to the depths like a stone.
Your right hand, LORD, is majestic in power.
Your right hand, LORD, shatters the enemy.
In the greatness of Your majesty, You overthrew those who rose against You.
You sent out Your fury; it consumed them like stubble.
By the blast of Your nostrils the waters piled up.
The surging waters stood straight like a wall;
the deeps congealed in the heart of the sea.
The enemy said, "I will pursue. I will overtake. I will divide the spoil.
My desire shall have its fill of them.
I will draw my sword. My hand will destroy them."
You blew with Your wind; the sea covered them.
They sank like lead in the mighty waters.

---

vidual to communal worship, the Siddur takes us through three transformative moments in Jewish history when the people constituted themselves as a nation dedicated to the service of GOD. They were no longer mere individuals (returning exiles, escaping slaves) but a group, a nation, a community of faith.

אַדִּירִים: מִי־כָמֹכָה בָּאֵלִם יְהוָה מִי
כָּמֹכָה נֶאְדָּר בַּקֹּדֶשׁ נוֹרָא תְהִלֹּת עֹשֵׂה
פֶלֶא: נָטִיתָ יְמִינְךָ תִּבְלָעֵמוֹ אָרֶץ: נָחִיתָ
בְחַסְדְּךָ עַם־זוּ גָּאָלְתָּ נֵהַלְתָּ בְעָזְּךָ אֶל־נְוֵה
קָדְשֶׁךָ: שָׁמְעוּ עַמִּים יִרְגָּזוּן חִיל
אָחַז יֹשְׁבֵי פְּלָשֶׁת: אָז נִבְהֲלוּ אַלּוּפֵי
אֱדוֹם אֵילֵי מוֹאָב יֹאחֲזֵמוֹ רָעַד נָמֹגוּ
כֹּל יֹשְׁבֵי כְנָעַן: תִּפֹּל עֲלֵיהֶם אֵימָתָה
וָפַחַד בִּגְדֹל זְרוֹעֲךָ יִדְּמוּ כָּאָבֶן עַד־
יַעֲבֹר עַמְּךָ יְהוָה עַד־יַעֲבֹר עַם־זוּ
קָנִיתָ: תְּבִאֵמוֹ וְתִטָּעֵמוֹ בְּהַר נַחֲלָתְךָ מָכוֹן
לְשִׁבְתְּךָ פָּעַלְתָּ יְהוָה מִקְּדָשׁ אֲדֹנָי כּוֹנְנוּ
יָדֶיךָ: יְהוָה | יִמְלֹךְ לְעֹלָם וָעֶד: יהוה יִמְלֹךְ לְעֹלָם וָעֶד.

כִּי בָא סוּס פַּרְעֹה בְּרִכְבּוֹ וּבְפָרָשָׁיו בַּיָּם, וַיָּשֶׁב יהוה עֲלֵהֶם אֶת־מֵי הַיָּם, וּבְנֵי יִשְׂרָאֵל הָלְכוּ בַיַּבָּשָׁה בְּתוֹךְ הַיָּם. ◄ כִּי לַיהוה הַמְּלוּכָה, וּמֹשֵׁל בַּגּוֹיִם. וְעָלוּ מוֹשִׁעִים בְּהַר צִיּוֹן, לִשְׁפֹּט אֶת־הַר עֵשָׂו, וְהָיְתָה לַיהוה הַמְּלוּכָה. וְהָיָה יהוה לְמֶלֶךְ עַל־כָּל־הָאָרֶץ, בַּיּוֹם הַהוּא יִהְיֶה יהוה אֶחָד וּשְׁמוֹ אֶחָד. וּבְתוֹרָתְךָ כָּתוּב לֵאמֹר, שְׁמַע יִשְׂרָאֵל יהוה אֱלֹהֵינוּ יהוה אֶחָד.

On הוֹשַׁעְנָא רַבָּה continue with the weekday service, from יִשְׁתַּבַּח, on page 58.

נִשְׁמַת כָּל־חַי תְּבָרֵךְ אֶת־שִׁמְךָ יהוה אֱלֹהֵינוּ, וְרוּחַ כָּל־בָּשָׂר תְּפָאֵר וּתְרוֹמֵם זִכְרְךָ מַלְכֵּנוּ תָּמִיד. מִן־הָעוֹלָם וְעַד־

נִשְׁמַת כָּל־חַי *The soul of all that lives:* This magnificent poem is composed of two parts. The first, according to Rabbi Yochanan is the "blessing of the song" mentioned in the Mishnah as a conclusion to saying *Hallel* in the *seder* service on Pesach (*Pesachim* 118a). Just as there, so here, it stands as a conclusion to the reci-

Who is like You, LORD, among the mighty?
Who is like You – majestic in holiness, awesome in glory, working wonders?
You stretched out Your right hand,
the earth swallowed them.
In Your lovingkindness, You led the people You redeemed.
In Your strength, You guided them to Your holy abode.
Nations heard and trembled;
terror gripped Philistia's inhabitants.
The chiefs of Edom were dismayed,
Moab's leaders were seized with trembling,
the people of Canaan melted away.
Fear and dread fell upon them.
By the power of Your arm, they were still as stone –
until Your people crossed, O LORD,
until the people You acquired crossed over.
You will bring them and plant them on the mountain of Your heritage –
the place, LORD, You made for Your dwelling,
the sanctuary, LORD, Your hands established.
The LORD will reign for ever and all time.
The LORD will reign for ever and all time.

When Pharaoh's horses, chariots and riders went into the sea, the LORD brought the waters of the sea back over them, but the Israelites walked on dry land through the sea. → For kingship is the LORD's and He rules over the nations. Saviours shall go up to Mount Zion to judge Mount Esau, and the LORD's shall be the kingdom. Then shall the LORD be King over all the earth. On that day shall the LORD be One and His name One, as it is written in Your Torah, saying: Listen, Israel: the LORD is our GOD, the LORD is One.

On Hoshana Rabba continue with the weekday service, from "May Your name be praised," on page 59.

נִשְׁמַת The soul of all that lives shall bless Your name, LORD our GOD, and the spirit of all flesh shall always glorify and exalt Your remem-

---

tation of Psalms. The second part, beginning "To You alone we give thanks", is mentioned in the Talmud (Berachot 59b) as a thanksgiving prayer for rain.

הָעוֹלָם אַתָּה אֵל, וּמִבַּלְעָדֶיךָ אֵין לָנוּ מֶלֶךְ גּוֹאֵל וּמוֹשִׁיעַ. פּוֹדֶה וּמַצִּיל וּמְפַרְנֵס וּמְרַחֵם בְּכָל־עֵת צָרָה וְצוּקָה, אֵין לָנוּ מֶלֶךְ אֶלָּא אָתָּה. אֱלֹהֵי הָרִאשׁוֹנִים וְהָאַחֲרוֹנִים, אֱלוֹהַּ כָּל־בְּרִיּוֹת, אֲדוֹן כָּל־תּוֹלָדוֹת, הַמְהֻלָּל בְּרֹב הַתִּשְׁבָּחוֹת, הַמְנַהֵג עוֹלָמוֹ בְּחֶסֶד וּבְרִיּוֹתָיו בְּרַחֲמִים. ויהוה לֹא־יָנוּם וְלֹא־יִישָׁן. הַמְעוֹרֵר יְשֵׁנִים, וְהַמֵּקִיץ נִרְדָּמִים, וְהַמֵּשִׂיחַ אִלְּמִים, וְהַמַּתִּיר אֲסוּרִים, וְהַסּוֹמֵךְ נוֹפְלִים, וְהַזּוֹקֵף כְּפוּפִים.

לְךָ לְבַדְּךָ אֲנַחְנוּ מוֹדִים.
אִלּוּ פִינוּ מָלֵא שִׁירָה כַּיָּם,
וּלְשׁוֹנֵנוּ רִנָּה כַּהֲמוֹן גַּלָּיו,
וְשִׂפְתוֹתֵינוּ שֶׁבַח כְּמֶרְחֲבֵי רָקִיעַ,
וְעֵינֵינוּ מְאִירוֹת כַּשֶּׁמֶשׁ וְכַיָּרֵחַ,
וְיָדֵינוּ פְרוּשׂוֹת כְּנִשְׁרֵי שָׁמָיִם,
וְרַגְלֵינוּ קַלּוֹת כָּאַיָּלוֹת,
אֵין אֲנַחְנוּ מַסְפִּיקִים לְהוֹדוֹת לְךָ,
יהוה אֱלֹהֵינוּ וֵאלֹהֵי אֲבוֹתֵינוּ,
וּלְבָרֵךְ אֶת־שְׁמֶךָ עַל־אַחַת מֵאֶלֶף אֶלֶף אַלְפֵי אֲלָפִים
וְרִבֵּי רְבָבוֹת פְּעָמִים הַטּוֹבוֹת שֶׁעָשִׂיתָ עִם אֲבוֹתֵינוּ וְעִמָּנוּ.

מִמִּצְרַיִם גְּאַלְתָּנוּ יהוה אֱלֹהֵינוּ, וּמִבֵּית עֲבָדִים פְּדִיתָנוּ. בְּרָעָב זַנְתָּנוּ, וּבְשָׂבָע כִּלְכַּלְתָּנוּ, מֵחֶרֶב הִצַּלְתָּנוּ, וּמִדֶּבֶר מִלַּטְתָּנוּ, וּמֵחֳלָיִם רָעִים וְנֶאֱמָנִים דִּלִּיתָנוּ. עַד־הֵנָּה עֲזָרוּנוּ רַחֲמֶיךָ, וְלֹא־עֲזָבוּנוּ חֲסָדֶיךָ. וְאַל־תִּטְּשֵׁנוּ יהוה אֱלֹהֵינוּ לָנֶצַח. עַל־כֵּן אֵבָרִים שֶׁפִּלַּגְתָּ בָּנוּ, וְרוּחַ וּנְשָׁמָה שֶׁנָּפַחְתָּ בְּאַפֵּינוּ, וְלָשׁוֹן אֲשֶׁר שַׂמְתָּ בְּפִינוּ, הֵן הֵם יוֹדוּ וִיבָרְכוּ

brance, our King. From eternity to eternity You are GOD. Without You, we have no King, Redeemer or Saviour, who liberates, rescues, sustains and shows compassion in every time of trouble and distress. We have no King but You, GOD of the first and last, GOD of all creatures, Master of all ages, extolled by a multitude of praises, who guides His world with lovingkindness and His creatures with compassion. The LORD neither slumbers nor sleeps. He rouses the sleepers and wakens the slumberers. He makes the dumb speak, sets the bound free, supports the fallen, and raises those bowed down.

לְךָ To You alone we give thanks:
If our mouths were as full of song as the sea,
and our tongue with jubilation as its myriad waves,
if our lips were full of praise like the spacious heavens,
and our eyes shone like the sun and moon,
if our hands were outstretched like eagles of the sky,
and our feet as swift as hinds –
still we could not thank You enough,
LORD our GOD and GOD of our ancestors,
or bless Your name for even one of the thousand thousands
and myriad myriads of favours You did for our ancestors and for us.

מִמִּצְרַיִם You redeemed us from Egypt, LORD our GOD, and freed us from the house of bondage. In famine You nourished us; in times of plenty You sustained us. You delivered us from the sword, saved us from the plague, and spared us from serious and lasting illness. Until now Your mercies have helped us. Your love has not forsaken us. May You, LORD our GOD, never abandon us. Therefore the limbs You formed within us, the spirit and soul You breathed into our nostrils,

---

The first section is an extended meditation on the final words of the Book of Psalms: "Let all that breathes praise the LORD." Hebrew has many words for soul, all deriving from verbs related to breathing. *Neshamah* – the word linking this passage to the end of Psalms – means to breathe deeply, as we are able to do in a state of rest. Hence the Sages said that on Shabbat we have "an extra soul". In the still silence of the turning world it is as if we hear all that lives sing a song of praise to GOD who brought the universe into being, sustains it, and guides the destinies of all things.

The second section is composed

וְיִשַׁבְּחוּ וִיפָאֲרוּ וִירוֹמְמוּ וְיַעֲרִיצוּ וְיַקְדִּישׁוּ וְיַמְלִיכוּ אֶת־שִׁמְךָ מַלְכֵּנוּ. כִּי כָל־פֶּה לְךָ יוֹדֶה, וְכָל־לָשׁוֹן לְךָ תִשָּׁבַע, וְכָל־בֶּרֶךְ לְךָ תִכְרַע, וְכָל־קוֹמָה לְפָנֶיךָ תִשְׁתַּחֲוֶה, וְכָל־לְבָבוֹת יִירָאוּךָ, וְכָל־קֶרֶב וּכְלָיוֹת יְזַמְּרוּ לִשְׁמֶךָ, כַּדָּבָר שֶׁכָּתוּב, כָּל עַצְמוֹתַי תֹּאמַרְנָה, יהוה מִי כָמוֹךָ, מַצִּיל עָנִי מֵחָזָק מִמֶּנּוּ, וְעָנִי וְאֶבְיוֹן מִגֹּזְלוֹ. מִי יִדְמֶה־לָּךְ, וּמִי יִשְׁוֶה־לָּךְ, וּמִי יַעֲרָךְ־לָךְ. הָאֵל הַגָּדוֹל הַגִּבּוֹר וְהַנּוֹרָא, אֵל עֶלְיוֹן, קֹנֵה שָׁמַיִם וָאָרֶץ. ← נְהַלֶּלְךָ וּנְשַׁבֵּחֲךָ וּנְפָאֶרְךָ וּנְבָרֵךְ אֶת־שֵׁם קָדְשֶׁךָ, כָּאָמוּר, לְדָוִד, בָּרְכִי נַפְשִׁי אֶת־יהוה, וְכָל־קְרָבַי אֶת־שֵׁם קָדְשׁוֹ.

On יוֹם טוֹב, the Leader for שַׁחֲרִית begins here.

הָאֵל בְּתַעֲצֻמוֹת עֻזֶּךָ,
הַגָּדוֹל בִּכְבוֹד שְׁמֶךָ,
הַגִּבּוֹר לָנֶצַח וְהַנּוֹרָא בְּנוֹרְאוֹתֶיךָ,
הַמֶּלֶךְ הַיּוֹשֵׁב עַל כִּסֵּא רָם וְנִשָּׂא.

On שַׁבָּת, the Leader for שַׁחֲרִית begins here.

שׁוֹכֵן עַד, מָרוֹם וְקָדוֹשׁ שְׁמוֹ. וְכָתוּב, רַנְּנוּ צַדִּיקִים בַּיהוה, לַיְשָׁרִים נָאוָה תְהִלָּה.

← בְּפִי יְשָׁרִים תִּתְהַלָּל.
וּבְדִבְרֵי צַדִּיקִים תִּתְבָּרַךְ.
וּבִלְשׁוֹן חֲסִידִים תִּתְרוֹמָם.
וּבְקֶרֶב קְדוֹשִׁים תִּתְקַדָּשׁ.

---

around a phrase from Psalms: "All my bones shall say, God, who is like You?" – thus ingeniously linking the Psalms of praise with the Song at the Sea, which contains the same phrase "Who is like You?" Through a fine series of images, the poet expresses the human inability to adequately thank God, itemising how

and the tongue You placed in our mouth – they will thank and bless, praise and glorify, exalt and esteem, hallow and do homage to Your name, O our King. For every mouth shall give thanks to You, every tongue vow allegiance to You, every knee shall bend to You, every upright body shall bow to You, all hearts shall fear You, and our innermost being sing praises to Your name, as is written: "All my bones shall say: LORD, who is like You? You save the poor from one stronger than him, the poor and needy from one who would rob him". Who is like You? Who is equal to You? Who can be compared to You? O great, mighty and awesome GOD, GOD Most High, Maker of heaven and earth. ➔ We will laud, praise and glorify You and bless Your holy name, as it is said: "Of David. Bless the LORD, O my soul, and all that is within me bless His holy name."

On Festivals, the Leader for the Morning Service begins here.

הָאֵל GOD – in Your absolute power,
Great – in the glory of Your name,
Mighty – for ever,
Awesome – in Your awe-inspiring deeds,
The King – enthroned on a high and lofty throne.

On Shabbat, the Leader for the Morning Service begins here.

שׁוֹכֵן עַד He inhabits eternity; exalted and holy is His name. And it is written: "Sing, you righteous, to the LORD; for the upright, praise is seemly."

➔ By the mouth of the upright You shall be praised.
By the words of the righteous You shall be blessed.
By the tongue of the devout You shall be extolled,
And in the midst of the holy You shall be sanctified.

---

the various limbs ("All my bones") may praise Him.

שׁוֹכֵן עַד *He inhabits eternity*: The Reader begins at different points on different holy days of the year. On Shabbat he begins with "He inhabits eternity", emphasising creation; on Festivals, with "You are GOD", laying stress on GOD as He acts in history; on Rosh Hashanah and Yom Kippur, with "You are the King", evoking ideas of justice and judgement.

וּבְמַקְהֲלוֹת רִבְבוֹת עַמְּךָ בֵּית יִשְׂרָאֵל, בְּרִנָּה יִתְפָּאַר שִׁמְךָ מַלְכֵּנוּ בְּכָל דּוֹר וָדוֹר. ◂ שֶׁכֵּן חוֹבַת כָּל־הַיְצוּרִים, לְפָנֶיךָ יהוה אֱלֹהֵינוּ וֵאלֹהֵי אֲבוֹתֵינוּ, לְהוֹדוֹת לְהַלֵּל לְשַׁבֵּחַ לְפָאֵר לְרוֹמֵם לְהַדֵּר לְבָרֵךְ לְעַלֵּה וּלְקַלֵּס, עַל־כָּל־דִּבְרֵי שִׁירוֹת וְתִשְׁבְּחוֹת דָּוִד בֶּן־יִשַׁי עַבְדְּךָ מְשִׁיחֶךָ.

The following prayer is said standing:

יִשְׁתַּבַּח שִׁמְךָ לָעַד מַלְכֵּנוּ, הָאֵל הַמֶּלֶךְ הַגָּדוֹל וְהַקָּדוֹשׁ, בַּשָּׁמַיִם וּבָאָרֶץ. כִּי לְךָ נָאֶה יהוה אֱלֹהֵינוּ וֵאלֹהֵי אֲבוֹתֵינוּ, שִׁיר וּשְׁבָחָה, הַלֵּל וְזִמְרָה, עֹז וּמֶמְשָׁלָה, נֶצַח גְּדֻלָּה וּגְבוּרָה, תְּהִלָּה וְתִפְאֶרֶת, קְדֻשָּׁה וּמַלְכוּת, ◂ בְּרָכוֹת וְהוֹדָאוֹת מֵעַתָּה וְעַד־עוֹלָם. בָּרוּךְ אַתָּה יהוה, אֵל מֶלֶךְ גָּדוֹל בַּתִּשְׁבָּחוֹת, אֵל הַהוֹדָאוֹת, אֲדוֹן הַנִּפְלָאוֹת, הַבּוֹחֵר בְּשִׁירֵי זִמְרָה, מֶלֶךְ, אֵל, חֵי הָעוֹלָמִים.

On שַׁבַּת שׁוּבָה, some congragations say this psalm responsively, verse by verse. The Ark is opened for this psalm.

תהלים קל

שִׁיר הַמַּעֲלוֹת, מִמַּעֲמַקִּים קְרָאתִיךָ יהוה. אֲדֹנָי שִׁמְעָה בְקוֹלִי, תִּהְיֶינָה אָזְנֶיךָ קַשֻּׁבוֹת, לְקוֹל תַּחֲנוּנָי. אִם עֲוֹנוֹת תִּשְׁמָר־יָהּ, אֲדֹנָי מִי יַעֲמֹד. כִּי עִמְּךָ הַסְּלִיחָה, לְמַעַן תִּוָּרֵא. קִוִּיתִי יהוה קִוְּתָה נַפְשִׁי, וְלִדְבָרוֹ הוֹחָלְתִּי. נַפְשִׁי לַאדֹנָי, מִשֹּׁמְרִים לַבֹּקֶר, שֹׁמְרִים לַבֹּקֶר. יַחֵל יִשְׂרָאֵל אֶל יהוה, כִּי־עִם־יהוה הַחֶסֶד, וְהַרְבֵּה עִמּוֹ פְדוּת. וְהוּא יִפְדֶּה אֶת יִשְׂרָאֵל, מִכֹּל עֲוֹנוֹתָיו.

וּבְמַקְהֲלוֹת *And in the assemblies*: The list of nine words for praise corresponds to the nine additional psalms we say on Shabbat and Festivals. The word "assemblies" refers to the large congregations present in synagogues on holy days, reminding us of the Temple, full at such times.

וּבְמַקְהֲלוֹת And in the assemblies of tens of thousands of Your people, the house of Israel, with joyous song shall Your name, our King, be glorified in every generation. ➝ For this is the duty of all creatures before You, LORD our GOD and GOD of our ancestors: to thank, praise, laud, glorify, exalt, honour, bless, raise high and acclaim – even beyond all the words of song and praise of David, son of Jesse, Your servant, Your anointed.

The following prayer is said standing:

יִשְׁתַּבַּח May Your name be praised for ever, our King, the great and holy GOD, King in heaven and on earth. For to You, LORD our GOD and GOD of our ancestors, it is right to offer song and praise, hymn and psalm, strength and dominion, eternity, greatness and power, song of praise and glory, holiness and kingship, ➝ blessings and thanks, from now and for ever. Blessed are You, LORD, GOD and King, exalted in praises, GOD of thanksgivings, Master of wonders, who delights in hymns of song, King, GOD, Giver of life to the world.

On the Shabbat of Penitence, some congragations say this psalm responsively, verse by verse. The Ark is opened for this psalm.

PSALM 130

שִׁיר A song of ascents. From the depths I have called to You, O LORD. LORD, hear my voice; let Your ears be attentive to my plea. If You, LORD, should keep account of sins, who could stand? But with You there is forgiveness, that You may be held in awe. I wait for the LORD, my soul waits, and in His word I put my hope. My soul waits for the LORD more than watchmen wait for the morning, more than watchmen wait for the morning. Israel, put your hope in the LORD, for with the LORD there is lovingkindness, and great is His power to redeem. It is He who will redeem Israel from all their sins.

יִשְׁתַּבַּח שִׁמְךָ *May Your name be praised forever*: The concluding blessing over the Verses of Praise which, like the introductory blessing, is said standing. The fifteen terms of glorification equal the number of Psalms in the Verses of Praise on Shabbat and Festivals, as well as the number of "Songs of Ascents".

The Leader says חֲצִי קַדִּישׁ.

Leader:

יִתְגַּדַּל וְיִתְקַדַּשׁ שְׁמֵהּ רַבָּא. (Cong. אָמֵן) בְּעָלְמָא דִּי־בְרָא כִרְעוּתֵהּ. וְיַמְלִיךְ מַלְכוּתֵהּ, בְּחַיֵּיכוֹן וּבְיוֹמֵיכוֹן וּבְחַיֵּי דְּכָל־בֵּית יִשְׂרָאֵל, בַּעֲגָלָא וּבִזְמַן קָרִיב. וְאִמְרוּ אָמֵן. (Cong. אָמֵן)

All:

יְהֵא שְׁמֵהּ רַבָּא מְבָרַךְ לְעָלַם וּלְעָלְמֵי עָלְמַיָּא.

Leader:

יִתְבָּרַךְ וְיִשְׁתַּבַּח וְיִתְפָּאַר וְיִתְרוֹמַם וְיִתְנַשֵּׂא וְיִתְהַדָּר וְיִתְעַלֶּה וְיִתְהַלָּל שְׁמֵהּ דְּקֻדְשָׁא בְּרִיךְ הוּא (Cong. בְּרִיךְ הוּא) לְעֵלָּא (On שַׁבַּת שׁוּבָה add לְעֵלָּא) מִן־כָּל־בִּרְכָתָא וְשִׁירָתָא תֻּשְׁבְּחָתָא וְנֶחֱמָתָא, דַּאֲמִירָן בְּעָלְמָא. וְאִמְרוּ אָמֵן. (Cong. אָמֵן)

The Leader says the following, both Leader and Congregation bowing at בָּרְכוּ, standing straight at God's name:

בָּרְכוּ אֶת יהוה הַמְבֹרָךְ.

The Congregation, followed by the Leader, responds, bowing at בָּרוּךְ, standing straight at God's name:

בָּרוּךְ יהוה הַמְבֹרָךְ לְעוֹלָם וָעֶד.

ברכות קריאת שמע

בָּרוּךְ אַתָּה יהוה אֱלֹהֵינוּ מֶלֶךְ הָעוֹלָם, יוֹצֵר אוֹר וּבוֹרֵא חֹשֶׁךְ, עֹשֶׂה שָׁלוֹם וּבוֹרֵא אֶת הַכֹּל.

SUMMONS TO PRAYER

בָּרְכוּ *Bless the Lord* – An ancient formula (see Nehemiah 9:5) for summoning the congregation to prayer. From this point onward, communal prayer begins. Prayers of special sanctity require a *minyan*, a quorum of ten adult males. The ten spies who brought back a negative report about the land were called a "congregation". In response to Abraham's prayer

The Leader says half-*Kaddish*.

Leader:

יִתְגַּדַּל Magnified and sanctified may His great name be, in the world He created by His will. May He establish His kingdom in your lifetime and in your days, and in the lifetime of all the House of Israel, swiftly and soon – and say: Amen.

All:

May His great name be blessed for ever and all time.

Leader:

Blessed and praised, glorified and exalted, raised and honoured, uplifted and lauded be the name of the Holy One, blessed be He, (between Rosh Hashanah and Yom Kippur add 'well') beyond any blessing, song, praise and consolation uttered in the world – and say: Amen.

The Leader says the following, both Leader and Congregation bowing at "Bless", standing straight at "The LORD":

Bless the LORD, the blessed One.

The Congregation, followed by the Leader, responds, bowing at "Bless", standing straight at "The LORD":

Bless the LORD, the blessed One, for ever and all time.

BLESSINGS OF THE SHEMA

בָּרוּךְ Blessed are You, LORD our GOD, King of the Universe, who forms light and creates darkness, makes peace and creates all.

---

about Sodom (Genesis 18), GOD assured him that if it contained ten righteous individuals, their merits would save the city. Ten is thus the minimum number to constitute a community. When the Temple stood, sacrifices were offered daily on behalf of the entire Jewish people. Since then, though Jews have been scattered and dispersed, wherever ten gather in prayer it is as if the whole Jewish people were present. The community is a microcosm of the nation.

BLESSINGS OF THE SHEMA

יוֹצֵר אוֹר *Who forms light: A statement of faith that all things* – good and apparently bad – come from the One GOD. The prayer is based on a verse in Isaiah

On a יום טוב which occurs on a weekday, say:

הַמֵּאִיר לָאָרֶץ וְלַדָּרִים עָלֶיהָ בְּרַחֲמִים, וּבְטוּבוֹ מְחַדֵּשׁ בְּכָל־יוֹם תָּמִיד מַעֲשֵׂה בְרֵאשִׁית. מָה רַבּוּ מַעֲשֶׂיךָ יהוה, כֻּלָּם בְּחָכְמָה עָשִׂיתָ, מָלְאָה הָאָרֶץ קִנְיָנֶךָ. הַמֶּלֶךְ הַמְרוֹמָם לְבַדּוֹ מֵאָז, הַמְשֻׁבָּח וְהַמְפֹאָר וְהַמִּתְנַשֵּׂא מִימוֹת עוֹלָם. אֱלֹהֵי עוֹלָם, בְּרַחֲמֶיךָ הָרַבִּים רַחֵם עָלֵינוּ, אֲדוֹן עֻזֵּנוּ, צוּר מִשְׂגַּבֵּנוּ, מָגֵן יִשְׁעֵנוּ, מִשְׂגָּב בַּעֲדֵנוּ. אֵל בָּרוּךְ גְּדוֹל דֵּעָה, הֵכִין וּפָעַל זָהֳרֵי חַמָּה, טוֹב יָצַר כָּבוֹד לִשְׁמוֹ, מְאוֹרוֹת נָתַן סְבִיבוֹת עֻזּוֹ, פִּנּוֹת צְבָאָיו קְדוֹשִׁים רוֹמְמֵי שַׁדַּי, תָּמִיד מְסַפְּרִים כְּבוֹד־אֵל וּקְדֻשָּׁתוֹ. ← תִּתְבָּרַךְ יהוה אֱלֹהֵינוּ עַל־שֶׁבַח מַעֲשֵׂה יָדֶיךָ, וְעַל־מְאוֹרֵי־אוֹר שֶׁעָשִׂיתָ, יְפָאֲרוּךָ, סֶּלָה.

Now turn to תִּתְבָּרַךְ on page 378.

On שַׁבָּת, and יום טוב falling on שַׁבָּת, continue as follows:

הַכֹּל יוֹדְוּךָ, וְהַכֹּל יְשַׁבְּחוּךָ, וְהַכֹּל יֹאמְרוּ אֵין קָדוֹשׁ כַּיהוה. הַכֹּל יְרוֹמְמְוּךָ סֶּלָה, יוֹצֵר הַכֹּל. הָאֵל הַפּוֹתֵחַ בְּכָל־יוֹם דַּלְתוֹת שַׁעֲרֵי מִזְרָח, וּבוֹקֵעַ חַלּוֹנֵי רָקִיעַ, מוֹצִיא חַמָּה מִמְּקוֹמָהּ וּלְבָנָה מִמְּכוֹן שִׁבְתָּהּ, וּמֵאִיר לָעוֹלָם כֻּלּוֹ וּלְיוֹשְׁבָיו, שֶׁבָּרָא בְּמִדַּת רַחֲמִים. הַמֵּאִיר לָאָרֶץ וְלַדָּרִים עָלֶיהָ בְּרַחֲמִים, וּבְטוּבוֹ מְחַדֵּשׁ בְּכָל־יוֹם תָּמִיד מַעֲשֵׂה

(45:7). The original has the phrase "makes peace and creates evil"; this last word has been changed to "all" to avoid speaking of evil in the context of prayer. The verse is directed against *dualism*: the perennial temptation to see in the suffering of the world, a force (evil, darkness, the devil) independent of, and opposed to, God. Dualism sees strife and war, contest and conquest, as part of the structure of reality itself. So profoundly did Judaism reject this idea, that it placed this counter-affirmation at the beginning of our collective prayers.

הַכֹּל יוֹדְוּךָ *All will thank You*: A short poem built around the last word of the previous line, "All", which is repeated here five times, four times at the beginning of a phrase, and once at the end. In monotheism, to worship anything less than the All is idolatry – be it worship of the self, the race, the nation, the ruler or the political system.

On a Festival which occurs on a weekday, say:

הַמֵּאִיר In compassion He gives light to the earth and its inhabitants, and in His goodness continually renews the work of creation, day after day. How many are Your works, O LORD. You made them all in wisdom. The earth is full of Your creations. He is the King exalted alone since the beginning of time – praised, glorified and elevated since the world began. Eternal GOD, in Your great compassion, have compassion on us, LORD of our strength, Rock of our refuge, Shield of our salvation, You are our stronghold. The blessed GOD, great in knowledge, prepared and made the rays of the sun. He who is good formed glory for His name, surrounding His power with radiant stars. The leaders of His hosts, the holy ones, exalt the Almighty, constantly proclaiming GOD's glory and holiness. ➔ Be blessed, LORD our GOD, for the magnificence of Your handiwork and for the radiant lights You have made. May they glorify You, Selah!

Now turn to "May You be blessed" on page 379.

On Shabbat, and a Festival falling on Shabbat, continue as follows:

הַכֹּל All will thank You. All will praise You. All will declare: Nothing is holy as is the LORD. All will exalt You, Selah, You who form all – the GOD who daily opens the doors of the gates of the East and cleaves the windows of the sky, who brings out the sun from its place and the moon from its abode, giving light to the whole world and its inhabitants whom He created by the attribute of compassion. In compassion He gives light to the earth and its inhabitants, and in His goodness daily, continually, renews the work of creation. He is the King

---

The paragraphs that follow are an expansion of the usual first blessing before the *Shema*. The first, but not the other blessings, is enlarged in honour of the Shabbat, because its theme is creation, and Shabbat is "a remembrance of the work of creation".

בְּכָל־יוֹם תָּמִיד *Daily, continually, renews the work of creation*: Rabbi Judah Halevi explained the difference between creation-from-something (*Yetzirah*) and creation-from-nothing (*Beriah*). When a carpenter makes a table from wood, the table continues to exist after the creative act is finished. When one makes something from nothing, however, the creative act must be continually renewed, otherwise the creation would cease to be. Divine creation is creation-from-nothing, and is thus perpetually re-enacted. This prayer invites us to a sense of wonder at the fact of existence: "Not *how* the world is, but *that* it is, is the mystical."

בְרֵאשִׁית. הַמֶּלֶךְ הַמְרוֹמָם לְבַדּוֹ מֵאָז, הַמְשֻׁבָּח וְהַמְפֹאָר וְהַמִּתְנַשֵּׂא מִימוֹת עוֹלָם. אֱלֹהֵי עוֹלָם, בְּרַחֲמֶיךָ הָרַבִּים רַחֵם עָלֵינוּ, אֲדוֹן עֻזֵּנוּ, צוּר מִשְׂגַּבֵּנוּ, מָגֵן יִשְׁעֵנוּ, מִשְׂגָּב בַּעֲדֵנוּ.

אֵין כְּעֶרְכֶּךָ, וְאֵין זוּלָתֶךָ,
אֶפֶס בִּלְתֶּךָ, וּמִי דּוֹמֶה לָּךְ.
← אֵין כְּעֶרְכְּךָ יהוה אֱלֹהֵינוּ בָּעוֹלָם הַזֶּה,
וְאֵין זוּלָתְךָ מַלְכֵּנוּ לְחַיֵּי הָעוֹלָם הַבָּא.
אֶפֶס בִּלְתְּךָ גּוֹאֲלֵנוּ לִימוֹת הַמָּשִׁיחַ,
וְאֵין דּוֹמֶה לְּךָ מוֹשִׁיעֵנוּ לִתְחִיַּת הַמֵּתִים.

אל אדון

אֵל אָדוֹן עַל־כָּל־הַמַּעֲשִׂים,
בָּרוּךְ וּמְבֹרָךְ בְּפִי כָּל־נְשָׁמָה,
גָּדְלוֹ וְטוּבוֹ מָלֵא עוֹלָם,
דַּעַת וּתְבוּנָה סוֹבְבִים אוֹתוֹ.
הַמִּתְגָּאֶה עַל חַיּוֹת הַקֹּדֶשׁ,
וְנֶהְדָּר בְּכָבוֹד עַל הַמֶּרְכָּבָה,
זְכוּת וּמִישׁוֹר לִפְנֵי כִסְאוֹ,
חֶסֶד וְרַחֲמִים לִפְנֵי כְבוֹדוֹ.
טוֹבִים מְאוֹרוֹת שֶׁבָּרָא אֱלֹהֵינוּ,
יְצָרָם בְּדַעַת בְּבִינָה וּבְהַשְׂכֵּל,
כֹּחַ וּגְבוּרָה נָתַן בָּהֶם,
לִהְיוֹת מוֹשְׁלִים בְּקֶרֶב תֵּבֵל.

אֵין כְּעֶרְכְּךָ *None can be compared to You*: a fourfold statement of the uniqueness of God, each phrase of which is then expanded in the following lines. The

who alone was exalted since time began, praised, glorified and raised high from days of old. Eternal God, in Your great compassion, have compassion on us, Lord of our strength, Rock of our refuge, Shield of our salvation, Stronghold of our safety.

אֵין כְּעֶרְכֶּךָ None can be compared to You, there is none besides You; None without You. Who is like You?

› None can be compared to You, Lord our God – in this world.
There is none besides You, our King – in the life of the World to Come.
There is none but You, our Redeemer – in the days of the Messiah.
There is none like You, our Saviour – at the resurrection of the dead.

EL ADON

אֵל אָדוֹן God, Lord of all creation,
the Blessed, is blessed by every soul.
His greatness and goodness fill the world;
knowledge and wisdom surround Him.
Exalted above the holy Chayot,
adorned in glory on the Chariot;
Merit and right are before His throne,
kindness and compassion before His glory.
Good are the radiant stars our God created,
He formed them with knowledge, understanding and deliberation.
He gave them strength and might
to rule throughout the world;

---

fourfold structure of many early rabbinic prayers reflects the influence of Jewish mysticism, which saw reality in terms of four dimensions of increasing spirituality: the world of action, *Asiyah*; the world of formation, *Yetzirah*; the world of creation, *Beriah*; and the world of Emanation, *Atzilut*.

This world...the World to Come – the prayer itemises four time-zones: 1. this world that we inhabit now; 2. the World to Come, according to Maimonides, the realm of the soul after death; 3. the days of the Messiah, when the Temple will be rebuilt, the rule of David will be restored and peace and justice will prevail in the affairs of mankind; and 4. the resurrection of the dead, the final denouement of history, when those who have died will live again.

אֵל אָדוֹן *God, Lord of all creation*: A hymn of praise to God as Creator of the heavens, stars and celestial forces. The poem, structured in verses of four phrases, each with four words (except

מְלֵאִים זִיו וּמְפִיקִים נֹגַהּ,
נָאֶה זִיוָם בְּכָל־הָעוֹלָם,
שְׂמֵחִים בְּצֵאתָם, וְשָׂשִׂים בְּבוֹאָם
עוֹשִׂים בְּאֵימָה רְצוֹן קוֹנָם.
פְּאֵר וְכָבוֹד נוֹתְנִים לִשְׁמוֹ,
צָהֳלָה וְרִנָּה לְזֵכֶר מַלְכוּתוֹ,
קָרָא לַשֶּׁמֶשׁ וַיִּזְרַח אוֹר,
רָאָה וְהִתְקִין צוּרַת הַלְּבָנָה.
שֶׁבַח נוֹתְנִים־לוֹ כָּל צְבָא מָרוֹם.
תִּפְאֶרֶת וּגְדֻלָּה, שְׂרָפִים וְאוֹפַנִּים וְחַיּוֹת הַקֹּדֶשׁ.

לָאֵל אֲשֶׁר שָׁבַת מִכָּל־הַמַּעֲשִׂים, בַּיּוֹם הַשְּׁבִיעִי הִתְעַלָּה וְיָשַׁב עַל־כִּסֵּא כְבוֹדוֹ, תִּפְאֶרֶת עָטָה לְיוֹם הַמְּנוּחָה, עֹנֶג קָרָא לְיוֹם הַשַּׁבָּת. זֶה שֶׁבַח שֶׁל יוֹם הַשְּׁבִיעִי, שֶׁבּוֹ שָׁבַת אֵל מִכָּל־מְלַאכְתּוֹ. וְיוֹם הַשְּׁבִיעִי מְשַׁבֵּחַ וְאוֹמֵר, מִזְמוֹר שִׁיר לְיוֹם הַשַּׁבָּת, טוֹב לְהוֹדוֹת לַיהוה. לְפִיכָךְ יְפָאֲרוּ וִיבָרְכוּ לָאֵל כָּל־יְצוּרָיו. שֶׁבַח יְקָר וּגְדֻלָּה יִתְּנוּ לָאֵל מֶלֶךְ יוֹצֵר כֹּל, הַמַּנְחִיל מְנוּחָה לְעַמּוֹ יִשְׂרָאֵל בִּקְדֻשָּׁתוֹ בְּיוֹם שַׁבַּת קֹדֶשׁ. שִׁמְךָ יהוה אֱלֹהֵינוּ יִתְקַדַּשׁ, וְזִכְרְךָ מַלְכֵּנוּ יִתְפָּאַר, בַּשָּׁמַיִם מִמַּעַל וְעַל־הָאָרֶץ מִתָּחַת. תִּתְבָּרַךְ מוֹשִׁיעֵנוּ עַל־שֶׁבַח מַעֲשֵׂה יָדֶיךָ, וְעַל מְאוֹרֵי־אוֹר שֶׁעָשִׂיתָ, יְפָאֲרוּךָ, סֶּלָה.

---

the last two, which have six words), is an alphabetical acrostic. It is longer than its weekday counterpart in honour of Shabbat. On weekdays each letter corresponds to a word; on Shabbat to a complete phrase. The poem contains traces of *Merkavah* ("Chariot") mysticism, based on Ezekiel's vision of the Divine chariot (Ezekiel 1).

לָאֵל *To God who rested*: A prayer on the theme of "the Sabbath of creation" at the

Full of splendour, radiating light,
beautiful is their splendour throughout the world;
Glad as they go forth, joyous as they return,
they fulfill with awe their Creator's will.

Glory and honour they give to His name,
jubilation and song at the mention of His majesty.
He called the sun into being and it shone with light.
He looked and fashioned the form of the moon.

All the hosts on high give Him praise;
the Seraphim, Ophanim and holy Chayot
ascribe glory and greatness –

לָאֵל To God who rested from all works, and on the seventh day ascended and sat on His throne of glory. He robed the day of rest in glory and called the Sabbath day a delight. This is the praise of the seventh day, that on it God rested from all His work. The seventh day itself gives praise, saying, "A psalm, a song for the Sabbath day. It is good to give thanks to the Lord". Therefore let all He has formed glorify and bless God. Let them give praise, honour and grandeur to God, the King, who formed all things and in His holiness gave a heritage of rest to His people Israel on the holy Sabbath day. May Your name, O Lord our God, be sanctified, and Your renown, O our King, be glorified in the heavens above and on earth below. May You be blessed, our Deliverer, by the praises of Your handiwork, and by the radiant lights You have made: may they glorify You. Selah!

---

dawn of time. Here, time itself is personified. Shabbat becomes a living presence, "robed in glory". The passage reflects a midrashic tradition that, at creation, each day sang its own song to God. The Sabbath sang Psalm 92 – the Midrash taking its opening phrase to mean not "a song for the Sabbath day" but "a song sung by the Sabbath day".

Shabbat is a unique institution. The year is determined by the sun; the month by the phases of the moon, but there is no Shabbat in nature: nothing that corresponds to the seven-day cycle of work and rest, creation and cessation, doing and being.

The Sages say that the creation of the first man and woman, their sin and their sentence to exile from the Garden of Eden all took place on the sixth day. Out of compassion, God allowed them to stay one full day in the Garden: the seventh day. Thus, the Shabbat is as close as we come to Paradise regained.

תִּתְבָּרַךְ צוּרֵנוּ מַלְכֵּנוּ וְגֹאֲלֵנוּ, בּוֹרֵא קְדוֹשִׁים. יִשְׁתַּבַּח שִׁמְךָ לָעַד מַלְכֵּנוּ, יוֹצֵר מְשָׁרְתִים, וַאֲשֶׁר מְשָׁרְתָיו כֻּלָּם עוֹמְדִים בְּרוּם עוֹלָם, וּמַשְׁמִיעִים בְּיִרְאָה יַחַד בְּקוֹל דִּבְרֵי אֱלֹהִים־חַיִּים וּמֶלֶךְ עוֹלָם. ← כֻּלָּם אֲהוּבִים, כֻּלָּם בְּרוּרִים, כֻּלָּם גִּבּוֹרִים, וְכֻלָּם עֹשִׂים בְּאֵימָה וּבְיִרְאָה רְצוֹן קוֹנָם. וְכֻלָּם פּוֹתְחִים אֶת־פִּיהֶם בִּקְדֻשָּׁה וּבְטָהֳרָה, בְּשִׁירָה וּבְזִמְרָה, וּמְבָרְכִים וּמְשַׁבְּחִים וּמְפָאֲרִים וּמַעֲרִיצִים וּמַקְדִּישִׁים וּמַמְלִיכִים

אֶת־שֵׁם הָאֵל הַמֶּלֶךְ הַגָּדוֹל הַגִּבּוֹר וְהַנּוֹרָא קָדוֹשׁ הוּא.

← וְכֻלָּם מְקַבְּלִים עֲלֵיהֶם עֹל מַלְכוּת שָׁמַיִם זֶה מִזֶּה, וְנוֹתְנִים רְשׁוּת זֶה לָזֶה, לְהַקְדִּישׁ לְיוֹצְרָם, בְּנַחַת רוּחַ בְּשָׂפָה בְרוּרָה וּבִנְעִימָה קְדוֹשָׁה, כֻּלָּם כְּאֶחָד עוֹנִים וְאוֹמְרִים בְּיִרְאָה,

All, aloud:

קָדוֹשׁ קָדוֹשׁ קָדוֹשׁ יהוה צְבָאוֹת, מְלֹא כָל־הָאָרֶץ כְּבוֹדוֹ.

← וְהָאוֹפַנִּים וְחַיּוֹת הַקֹּדֶשׁ בְּרַעַשׁ גָּדוֹל מִתְנַשְּׂאִים לְעֻמַּת שְׂרָפִים. לְעֻמָּתָם מְשַׁבְּחִים וְאוֹמְרִים,

All, aloud:

בָּרוּךְ כְּבוֹד־יהוה מִמְּקוֹמוֹ.

קדושת יוצר THE HOLINESS PRAYER
Two prophets, Isaiah and Ezekiel, saw mystical visions of God among His heavenly host, the choir of angels. These visions, together with the words the prophets heard the angels sing ("Holy, holy, holy" in Isaiah's vision, "Blessed be the glory of God from his place" in Ezekiel's), form the heart of *Kedushah*, the "Holiness" prayer. This is recited three times in the morning prayers – before the *Shema*, during the Reader's repetition of the *Amidah*, and towards the end of prayer, except on Shabbat when the third is transferred to the afternoon.

This section of the prayers – the vision of the heavenly throne and the angels – is part of the mystical tradition in

תִּתְבָּרַךְ May You be blessed, our Rock, King and Redeemer, Creator of holy beings. May Your name be praised for ever, our King, Creator of the ministering angels, all of whom stand in the universe's heights, proclaiming together, in awe, aloud, the words of the living God, the eternal King. ➝ They are all beloved, all pure, all mighty, and all perform in awe and reverence the will of their Maker. All open their mouths in holiness and purity, with song and psalm, and bless, praise, glorify, revere, sanctify and declare the sovereignty of –
The name of the great, mighty and awesome God and King, holy is He. ➝ All accept on themselves, one from another, the yoke of the kingdom of heaven, granting permission to one another to sanctify the One who formed them, in serene spirit, pure speech and sacred melody, and all, as one, respond, saying in awe:

All, aloud:

Holy, holy, holy is the Lord of hosts:
the whole world is filled with His glory.

➝ Then the Ophanim and the Holy Chayot, with a roar of noise, raise themselves toward the Seraphim and, facing them, give praise, saying:

All, aloud:

Blessed be the Lord's glory from His place.

Judaism. Prayer is Jacob's ladder, stretching from earth to heaven, with "angels of the Lord" ascending and descending. The three *Kedushot* represent, respectively, the ascent, the summit, and the descent: the journey of the soul from earth to heaven and back again, transformed by our experience of the Divine.

וְהָאוֹפַנִּים וְחַיּוֹת שְׂרָפִים *Ophanim, Chayot, Seraphim*: Three kinds of angels seen by Isaiah and Ezekiel in their visions. Serafim are angels of fire. Chayot are "living beings" surrounded by fire. Ophanim are "wheels within wheels". They form a heavenly retinue surrounding the Divine throne, an angelic choir singing God's praises. *Sacred melody* – the text, according to our custom, consists of three two-word phrases: tranquil spirit (*nachat ru'ach*), pure speech (*safah berurah*), and sacred melody (*neimah kedoshah).* They summarise the ideal elements of prayer: spiritual *tranquillity*, cognitive *clarity*, and aesthetic *beauty*.

לְאֵל בָּרוּךְ נְעִימוֹת יִתֵּנוּ. לְמֶלֶךְ אֵל חַי וְקַיָּם, זְמִירוֹת יֹאמֵרוּ, וְתִשְׁבָּחוֹת יַשְׁמִיעוּ. כִּי הוּא לְבַדּוֹ פּוֹעֵל גְּבוּרוֹת, עֹשֶׂה חֲדָשׁוֹת, בַּעַל מִלְחָמוֹת, זוֹרֵעַ צְדָקוֹת, מַצְמִיחַ יְשׁוּעוֹת, בּוֹרֵא רְפוּאוֹת, נוֹרָא תְהִלּוֹת, אֲדוֹן הַנִּפְלָאוֹת. הַמְחַדֵּשׁ בְּטוּבוֹ בְּכָל־יוֹם תָּמִיד מַעֲשֵׂה בְרֵאשִׁית. כָּאָמוּר, לְעֹשֵׂה אוֹרִים גְּדֹלִים, כִּי לְעוֹלָם חַסְדּוֹ. ← אוֹר חָדָשׁ עַל־צִיּוֹן תָּאִיר, וְנִזְכֶּה כֻלָּנוּ מְהֵרָה לְאוֹרוֹ. בָּרוּךְ אַתָּה יהוה, יוֹצֵר הַמְּאוֹרוֹת.

אַהֲבָה רַבָּה אֲהַבְתָּנוּ יהוה אֱלֹהֵינוּ, חֶמְלָה גְדוֹלָה וִיתֵרָה חָמַלְתָּ עָלֵינוּ. אָבִינוּ מַלְכֵּנוּ, בַּעֲבוּר אֲבוֹתֵינוּ שֶׁבָּטְחוּ בְךָ, וַתְּלַמְּדֵם חֻקֵּי חַיִּים, כֵּן תְּחָנֵּנוּ וּתְלַמְּדֵנוּ. אָבִינוּ הָאָב הָרַחֲמָן הַמְרַחֵם, רַחֵם עָלֵינוּ, וְתֵן בְּלִבֵּנוּ לְהָבִין וּלְהַשְׂכִּיל, לִשְׁמֹעַ לִלְמֹד וּלְלַמֵּד, לִשְׁמֹר וְלַעֲשׂוֹת וּלְקַיֵּם אֶת־כָּל־דִּבְרֵי תַלְמוּד תּוֹרָתֶךָ בְּאַהֲבָה. וְהָאֵר עֵינֵינוּ בְּתוֹרָתֶךָ, וְדַבֵּק לִבֵּנוּ בְּמִצְוֹתֶיךָ, וְיַחֵד לְבָבֵנוּ לְאַהֲבָה וּלְיִרְאָה אֶת שְׁמֶךָ, וְלֹא נֵבוֹשׁ לְעוֹלָם וָעֶד. כִּי בְשֵׁם קָדְשְׁךָ הַגָּדוֹל וְהַנּוֹרָא בָּטָחְנוּ, נָגִילָה וְנִשְׂמְחָה בִּישׁוּעָתֶךָ.

At this point, gather the four צִיצִיּוֹת, holding them in the left hand.

וַהֲבִיאֵנוּ לְשָׁלוֹם מֵאַרְבַּע כַּנְפוֹת הָאָרֶץ, וְתוֹלִיכֵנוּ קוֹמְמִיּוּת לְאַרְצֵנוּ. כִּי אֵל פּוֹעֵל יְשׁוּעוֹת אָתָּה, וּבָנוּ בָחַרְתָּ מִכָּל־עַם וְלָשׁוֹן. ← וְקֵרַבְתָּנוּ לְשִׁמְךָ הַגָּדוֹל סֶלָה בֶּאֱמֶת, לְהוֹדוֹת לְךָ וּלְיַחֶדְךָ בְּאַהֲבָה. בָּרוּךְ אַתָּה יהוה, הַבּוֹחֵר בְּעַמּוֹ יִשְׂרָאֵל בְּאַהֲבָה.

אַהֲבָה רַבָּה *You have loved us*: One of the supreme expressions of love in the liturgy. Having spoken of GOD's relationship to the universe, we now speak of His relationship to us, moving from cosmic grandeur to spiritual intimacy. The phrase *Our Father, compassionate Father, ever compassionate, have compas-*

לְאֵל To the blessed God they offer melodies. To the King, living and eternal God, they say psalms and proclaim praises. For it is He alone who does mighty deeds and creates new things. He is Master of battles. He sows righteousness and makes salvation grow. He creates cures. He is revered in praises, the Lord of wonders who, in His goodness, continually renews the work of creation, day after day, as it is said, "[Praise] Him who made the great lights, for His love endures for ever". ➔ May You make a new light shine over Zion, and may we all soon be worthy of its light. Blessed are You, Lord, who forms the radiant lights.

אַהֲבָה You have loved us with great love, Lord our God, and with surpassing compassion have You had compassion on us. Our Father, our King, for the sake of our ancestors who trusted in You, and to whom You taught the laws of life, be gracious also to us and teach us. Our Father, compassionate Father, ever compassionate, have compassion on us. Instil in our hearts the desire to understand and discern, to listen, learn and teach, to observe, perform and fulfil all the teachings of Your Torah in love. Enlighten our eyes in Your Torah, and let our hearts cling to Your commandments. Unite our hearts to love and revere Your name, so that we may never be ashamed. And because we have trusted in Your holy, great and revered name, may we be glad and rejoice in Your salvation.

At this point, gather the four *tzitziot*, holding them in the left hand.

Bring us back in peace from the four quarters of the earth and lead us upright to our land, for You are a God who performs acts of salvation. You chose us from all peoples and tongues, ➔ bringing us close to Your great name for ever in truth, that we may thank You and proclaim Your Oneness in love. Blessed are You, Lord, who chooses His people Israel in love.

---

sion on us, with its twofold repetition of "father" and threefold mention of compassion in the space of six Hebrew words, is one of the most concentrated expressions of the love and trust we feel in and for God – the God who said, "My child, My firstborn, Israel". The channel through which this love flows is the Torah, God's covenant with His people. This contains "the laws of life" in a double sense: laws that *guide* us in life, and laws that *give* us life.

שמע

When prayers are not said with a מִנְיָן, say:

אֵל מֶלֶךְ נֶאֱמָן.

Cover the eyes with the right hand while saying the following verse:

דברים ו:ד–ט

שְׁמַע יִשְׂרָאֵל יהוה אֱלֹהֵינוּ יהוה | אֶחָד:

Quietly:

בָּרוּךְ שֵׁם כְּבוֹד מַלְכוּתוֹ לְעוֹלָם וָעֶד.

וְאָהַבְתָּ אֵת יהוה אֱלֹהֶיךָ בְּכָל־לְבָבְךָ וּבְכָל־נַפְשְׁךָ וּבְכָל־מְאֹדֶךָ: וְהָיוּ הַדְּבָרִים הָאֵלֶּה אֲשֶׁר אָנֹכִי מְצַוְּךָ הַיּוֹם עַל־לְבָבֶךָ: וְשִׁנַּנְתָּם לְבָנֶיךָ וְדִבַּרְתָּ בָּם בְּשִׁבְתְּךָ בְּבֵיתֶךָ וּבְלֶכְתְּךָ בַדֶּרֶךְ וּבְשָׁכְבְּךָ וּבְקוּמֶךָ: וּקְשַׁרְתָּם לְאוֹת עַל־יָדֶךָ וְהָיוּ לְטֹטָפֹת בֵּין עֵינֶיךָ: וּכְתַבְתָּם עַל־מְזֻזוֹת בֵּיתֶךָ וּבִשְׁעָרֶיךָ:

דברים יא:יג–כא

וְהָיָה אִם־שָׁמֹעַ תִּשְׁמְעוּ אֶל־מִצְוֹתַי אֲשֶׁר אָנֹכִי מְצַוֶּה אֶתְכֶם הַיּוֹם לְאַהֲבָה אֶת־יהוה אֱלֹהֵיכֶם וּלְעָבְדוֹ בְּכָל־

THE SHEMA

שְׁמַע *Listen, Israel:* The word *Shema* is untranslatable in English. It means 1. listen, 2. hear, 3. reflect on, 4. understand, 5. internalise, 6. respond in action, and hence 7. obey. In rabbinic Hebrew it developed yet other senses, such as "transmit, know about, infer, learn". I have translated it here as "Listen" rather than the traditional "Hear" because listening is active, hearing passive. The *Shema* is a call to an act of mind and soul, to meditate on, internalise and affirm the oneness of God.

Most civilisations have been cultures of the eye. Judaism, with its belief in the invisible God who transcends the universe, and its prohibition against visual representations of God, is supremely a civilisation of the ear. The patriarchs and prophets did not see God; they heard Him. Hence the key verb in Judaism is *Shema*, "listen". To give dramatic force to the idea that God is heard, not seen, we cover our eyes with our hand as we say these words.

ה' אֱלֹהֵינוּ *The Lord is our God*: The Sages called this declaration "acceptance of the yoke of the kingship of Heaven", meaning that we take God as our Sovereign, and our covenant with Him as the essence of our existence as a people.

THE SHEMA

When prayers are not said with a *minyan*, say:

God, faithful King!

Cover the eyes with the right hand while saying the following verse:

DEUTERONOMY 6:4–9

Listen, Israel: the Lord is our God, the Lord is One.

Quietly:

Blessed be the name of His glorious kingdom for ever and ever.

וְאָהַבְתָּ Love the Lord your God with all your heart, with all your soul, and with all your might. These words which I command you today shall be on your heart. Teach them repeatedly to your children, speaking of them when you sit at home and when you travel on the way, when you lie down and when you rise. Bind them as a sign on your hand, and they shall be an emblem between your eyes. Write them on the doorposts of your house and gates.

DEUTERONOMY 11:13–21

וְהָיָה If you indeed heed My commandments with which I charge you today, to love the Lord your God and worship Him with all your

---

The Lord is One – among the many meanings of this phrase are: 1. there is only one God; 2. God is a unity, indivisible; 3. God is the only ultimate reality; 4. God is One despite the many appearances He has had throughout history; and 5. God alone is our King. This great sentence is the supreme declaration of Jewish faith: among the first Hebrew words learned by a child, often the last words of martyrs.

בָּרוּךְ שֵׁם *Blessed be the name*: This was the congregational response to the utterance in the Temple of the Tetragrammaton, God's holiest name. It is said here as a memory of the Temple service, but silently (except on Yom Kippur) because it is not part of the biblical text.

וְשִׁנַּנְתָּם *Teach them repeatedly*: Education is the responsibility, not only of schools, but also of parents. In Judaism, parents are educators, the home a matrix of learning, and education a conversation across the generations. Alshich connects this verse with the earlier one ("Love God"): How do we teach our children? By showing them what we love.

וְהָיָה, אִם־שָׁמֹעַ תִּשְׁמְעוּ *If you indeed heed My commandments*: The Sages called this

לְבַבְכֶם וּבְכָל־נַפְשְׁכֶם: וְנָתַתִּי מְטַר־אַרְצְכֶם בְּעִתּוֹ יוֹרֶה
וּמַלְקוֹשׁ וְאָסַפְתָּ דְגָנֶךָ וְתִירֹשְׁךָ וְיִצְהָרֶךָ: וְנָתַתִּי עֵשֶׂב
בְּשָׂדְךָ לִבְהֶמְתֶּךָ וְאָכַלְתָּ וְשָׂבָעְתָּ: הִשָּׁמְרוּ לָכֶם פֶּן־יִפְתֶּה
לְבַבְכֶם וְסַרְתֶּם וַעֲבַדְתֶּם אֱלֹהִים אֲחֵרִים וְהִשְׁתַּחֲוִיתֶם
לָהֶם: וְחָרָה אַף־יהוה בָּכֶם וְעָצַר אֶת־הַשָּׁמַיִם וְלֹא־יִהְיֶה
מָטָר וְהָאֲדָמָה לֹא תִתֵּן אֶת־יְבוּלָהּ וַאֲבַדְתֶּם מְהֵרָה מֵעַל
הָאָרֶץ הַטֹּבָה אֲשֶׁר יהוה נֹתֵן לָכֶם: וְשַׂמְתֶּם אֶת־דְּבָרַי
אֵלֶּה עַל־לְבַבְכֶם וְעַל־נַפְשְׁכֶם וּקְשַׁרְתֶּם אֹתָם לְאוֹת עַל־
יֶדְכֶם וְהָיוּ לְטוֹטָפֹת בֵּין עֵינֵיכֶם: וְלִמַּדְתֶּם אֹתָם אֶת־
בְּנֵיכֶם לְדַבֵּר בָּם בְּשִׁבְתְּךָ בְּבֵיתֶךָ וּבְלֶכְתְּךָ בַדֶּרֶךְ וּבְשָׁכְבְּךָ
וּבְקוּמֶךָ: וּכְתַבְתָּם עַל־מְזוּזוֹת בֵּיתֶךָ וּבִשְׁעָרֶיךָ: לְמַעַן
יִרְבּוּ יְמֵיכֶם וִימֵי בְנֵיכֶם עַל הָאֲדָמָה אֲשֶׁר נִשְׁבַּע יהוה
לַאֲבֹתֵיכֶם לָתֵת לָהֶם כִּימֵי הַשָּׁמַיִם עַל־הָאָרֶץ:

Transfer the צִיצִית to the right hand, kissing them at °.

במדבר טו:לז–מא

וַיֹּאמֶר יהוה אֶל־מֹשֶׁה לֵּאמֹר: דַּבֵּר אֶל־בְּנֵי יִשְׂרָאֵל
וְאָמַרְתָּ אֲלֵהֶם וְעָשׂוּ לָהֶם °צִיצִת עַל־כַּנְפֵי בִגְדֵיהֶם
לְדֹרֹתָם וְנָתְנוּ עַל־°צִיצִת הַכָּנָף פְּתִיל תְּכֵלֶת: וְהָיָה לָכֶם
°לְצִיצִת וּרְאִיתֶם אֹתוֹ וּזְכַרְתֶּם אֶת־כָּל־מִצְוֹת יהוה
וַעֲשִׂיתֶם אֹתָם וְלֹא תָתֻרוּ אַחֲרֵי לְבַבְכֶם וְאַחֲרֵי עֵינֵיכֶם
אֲשֶׁר־אַתֶּם זֹנִים אַחֲרֵיהֶם: לְמַעַן תִּזְכְּרוּ וַעֲשִׂיתֶם אֶת־
כָּל־מִצְוֹתָי וִהְיִיתֶם קְדֹשִׁים לֵאלֹהֵיכֶם: אֲנִי יהוה אֱלֹהֵיכֶם
אֲשֶׁר הוֹצֵאתִי אֶתְכֶם מֵאֶרֶץ מִצְרַיִם לִהְיוֹת לָכֶם לֵאלֹהִים
אֲנִי יהוה אֱלֹהֵיכֶם: °**אֱמֶת** –

The Leader repeats:

← יהוה אֱלֹהֵיכֶם, אֱמֶת –

heart and with all your soul, I will give rain in your land in its season, the early and late rain; and you shall gather in your grain, wine and oil. I will give grass in your field for your cattle, and you shall eat and be satisfied. Be careful lest your heart be tempted and you go astray and worship other gods, bowing down to them. Then the LORD's anger will flare against you and He will close the heavens so that there will be no rain. The land will not yield its crops, and you will perish swiftly from the good land that the LORD is giving you. Therefore set these, My words, on your heart and soul. Bind them as a sign on your hand, and they shall be an emblem between your eyes. Teach them to your children, speaking of them when you sit at home and when you travel on the way, when you lie down and when you rise. Write them on the doorposts of your house and gates, so that you and your children may live long in the land that the LORD swore to your ancestors to give them, for as long as the heavens are above the earth.

Transfer the *tzitziot* to the right hand, kissing them at °.

NUMBERS 15:37–41

וַיֹּאמֶר The LORD spoke to Moses, saying: Speak to the Israelites and tell them to make °tassels on the corners of their garments for all generations. They shall attach to the °tassel at each corner a thread of blue. This shall be your °tassel, and you shall see it and remember all of the LORD's commandments and keep them, not straying after your heart and after your eyes, following your own sinful desires. Thus you will be reminded to keep all My commandments, and be holy to your GOD. I am the LORD your GOD, who brought you out of the land of Egypt to be your GOD. I am the LORD your GOD. °**True** –

The Leader repeats:

→ The LORD your GOD is true –

"acceptance of the yoke of the commands". Having declared GOD our Sovereign, we go on to accept the laws He has given us, understanding that Israel's fate as a nation depends on its fidelity to them.

וַיֹּאמֶר ה' *The LORD spoke*: This paragraph was included in the *Shema* because: 1. it deals with the third outward sign, *tzitzit*, which belongs together with the two mentioned in the previous paragraphs, *tefillin* and *mezuzah*; and 2. it mentions the exodus, which we are commanded to remember "all the days of your life". *After your heart and your eyes* – a principle of Judaism, as of cognitive psychology, is

At °, kiss the ציציות and release them.

וְיַצִּיב וְנָכוֹן וְקַיָּם וְיָשָׁר וְנֶאֱמָן וְאָהוּב וְחָבִיב וְנֶחְמָד וְנָעִים וְנוֹרָא וְאַדִּיר וּמְתֻקָּן וּמְקֻבָּל וְטוֹב וְיָפֶה הַדָּבָר הַזֶּה עָלֵינוּ לְעוֹלָם וָעֶד. אֱמֶת אֱלֹהֵי עוֹלָם מַלְכֵּנוּ צוּר יַעֲקֹב, מָגֵן יִשְׁעֵנוּ, לְדֹר וָדֹר הוּא קַיָּם, וּשְׁמוֹ קַיָּם, וְכִסְאוֹ נָכוֹן, וּמַלְכוּתוֹ וֶאֱמוּנָתוֹ לָעַד קַיָּמֶת. וּדְבָרָיו חָיִים וְקַיָּמִים, נֶאֱמָנִים וְנֶחֱמָדִים °לָעַד וּלְעוֹלְמֵי עוֹלָמִים. ‹ עַל־אֲבוֹתֵינוּ וְעָלֵינוּ, עַל־בָּנֵינוּ וְעַל־דּוֹרוֹתֵינוּ, וְעַל כָּל־דּוֹרוֹת זֶרַע יִשְׂרָאֵל עֲבָדֶיךָ.

עַל־הָרִאשׁוֹנִים וְעַל־הָאַחֲרוֹנִים, דָּבָר טוֹב וְקַיָּם לְעוֹלָם וָעֶד, אֱמֶת וֶאֱמוּנָה חֹק וְלֹא יַעֲבֹר. אֱמֶת שָׁאַתָּה הוּא יהוה אֱלֹהֵינוּ וֵאלֹהֵי אֲבוֹתֵינוּ, ‹ מַלְכֵּנוּ מֶלֶךְ אֲבוֹתֵינוּ, גּוֹאֲלֵנוּ גּוֹאֵל אֲבוֹתֵינוּ, יוֹצְרֵנוּ צוּר יְשׁוּעָתֵנוּ, פּוֹדֵנוּ וּמַצִּילֵנוּ מֵעוֹלָם הוּא שְׁמֶךָ, אֵין אֱלֹהִים זוּלָתֶךָ.

עֶזְרַת אֲבוֹתֵינוּ אַתָּה הוּא מֵעוֹלָם, מָגֵן וּמוֹשִׁיעַ לִבְנֵיהֶם אַחֲרֵיהֶם בְּכָל־דּוֹר וָדוֹר. בְּרוּם עוֹלָם מוֹשָׁבֶךָ, וּמִשְׁפָּטֶיךָ וְצִדְקָתְךָ עַד־אַפְסֵי אָרֶץ. אַשְׁרֵי אִישׁ שֶׁיִּשְׁמַע לְמִצְוֹתֶיךָ, וְתוֹרָתְךָ וּדְבָרְךָ יָשִׂים עַל־לִבּוֹ. אֱמֶת אַתָּה הוּא אָדוֹן לְעַמֶּךָ וּמֶלֶךְ גִּבּוֹר לָרִיב רִיבָם. אֱמֶת אַתָּה הוּא רִאשׁוֹן

---

that our perceptions are filtered through our beliefs and emotions. What we feel affects what we see. The heart controls the eye.

אֱמֶת וְיַצִּיב *True and firm*: Fifteen adjectives mirroring the fifteen "Songs of Ascents" and the fifteen steps to the Temple courtyard. The prayer is structured around a six-part repetition of the word *Emet*: "true", mirroring the six-part sequence – the three paragraphs of the *Shema* and its three surrounding blessings – which leads up to the *Amidah*, the holiest of prayers, as the six days of the week lead to Shabbat, holiest of days.

The meaning of the word "true" here

At °, kiss the *tzitziot* and release them.

וְיַצִּיב And firm, established and enduring, right, faithful, beloved, cherished, delightful, pleasant, awesome, mighty, perfect, accepted, good and beautiful is this faith for us for ever. True is the eternal God, our King, Rock of Jacob, Shield of our salvation. He exists and His name exists through all generations. His throne is established, His kingship and faithfulness endure for ever. His words live and persist, faithful and desirable °for ever and all time. ➔ So they were for our ancestors, so they are for us, and so they will be for our children and all our generations and for all future generations of the seed of Israel, Your servants.

עַל־הָרִאשׁוֹנִים For the early and the later generations this faith has proved good and enduring for ever – true and faithful, an irrevocable law. True – You are the Lord: our God and God of our ancestors, ➔ our King and King of our ancestors, our Redeemer and Redeemer of our ancestors, our Maker, Rock of our salvation, our Deliverer and Rescuer: this has ever been Your name. There is no God but You.

עֶזְרַת You have always been the help of our ancestors, Shield and Saviour of their children after them in every generation. Your dwelling is in the heights of the Universe, and Your judgements and righteousness reach to the ends of the earth. Happy is the one who obeys Your commandments and takes to heart Your teaching and Your word. True – You are the Master of Your people and a mighty King who pleads their cause. True – You are the first and You are the last. Beside You we have no King, Redeemer or Saviour. From Egypt You redeemed

---

is similar to the word Amen said after a blessing. It is an act of affirmation and ratification, reminding us that the *Shema* is less a prayer than a declaration of faith. The passage recapitulates the main ideas of the *Shema*. Its primary emphasis, though, is on redemption. It contains the word "redeem" eight times, and is filled with redemption-related terms – deliverance, rescue, help, shield, saviour, as well as redemptive activity – pleading a cause, raising the lowly, redeeming the meek, and helping the needy. Redemption refers to God's activity in history, liberating slaves, rewarding the faithful, and ensuring justice.

וְאַתָּה הוּא אַחֲרוֹן, וּמִבַּלְעָדֶיךָ אֵין לָנוּ מֶלֶךְ גּוֹאֵל וּמוֹשִׁיעַ. מִמִּצְרַיִם גְּאַלְתָּנוּ יהוה אֱלֹהֵינוּ, וּמִבֵּית עֲבָדִים פְּדִיתָנוּ. כָּל־בְּכוֹרֵיהֶם הָרָגְתָּ, וּבְכוֹרְךָ גָּאָלְתָּ, וְיַם־סוּף בָּקַעְתָּ, וְזֵדִים טִבַּעְתָּ, וִידִידִים הֶעֱבַרְתָּ, וַיְכַסּוּ מַיִם צָרֵיהֶם, אֶחָד מֵהֶם לֹא נוֹתָר. עַל־זֹאת שִׁבְּחוּ אֲהוּבִים וְרוֹמְמוּ אֵל, וְנָתְנוּ יְדִידִים זְמִירוֹת שִׁירוֹת וְתִשְׁבָּחוֹת, בְּרָכוֹת וְהוֹדָאוֹת, לְמֶלֶךְ אֵל חַי וְקַיָּם, רָם וְנִשָּׂא, גָּדוֹל וְנוֹרָא, מַשְׁפִּיל גֵּאִים, וּמַגְבִּיהַּ שְׁפָלִים, מוֹצִיא אֲסִירִים, וּפוֹדֶה עֲנָוִים, וְעוֹזֵר דַּלִּים, וְעוֹנֶה לְעַמּוֹ בְּעֵת שַׁוְּעָם אֵלָיו.

Stand and take three steps back.

← תְּהִלּוֹת לְאֵל עֶלְיוֹן, בָּרוּךְ הוּא וּמְבוֹרָךְ. מֹשֶׁה וּבְנֵי יִשְׂרָאֵל לְךָ עָנוּ שִׁירָה בְּשִׂמְחָה רַבָּה, וְאָמְרוּ כֻלָּם,

מִי־כָמֹכָה בָּאֵלִים יהוה, מִי כָּמֹכָה נֶאְדָּר בַּקֹּדֶשׁ, נוֹרָא תְהִלֹּת עֹשֵׂה פֶלֶא. ← שִׁירָה חֲדָשָׁה שִׁבְּחוּ גְאוּלִים לְשִׁמְךָ עַל־שְׂפַת הַיָּם, יַחַד כֻּלָּם הוֹדוּ וְהִמְלִיכוּ וְאָמְרוּ,

יהוה יִמְלֹךְ לְעוֹלָם וָעֶד.

Congregants should end the following blessing together with the Leader so as to be able to move directly from the words גָּאַל יִשְׂרָאֵל to the עֲמִידָה, without the interruption of saying אמן.

← **צוּר יִשְׂרָאֵל**, קוּמָה בְּעֶזְרַת יִשְׂרָאֵל, וּפְדֵה כִנְאֻמֶךָ יְהוּדָה וְיִשְׂרָאֵל. גֹּאֲלֵנוּ יהוה צְבָאוֹת שְׁמוֹ, קְדוֹשׁ יִשְׂרָאֵל. בָּרוּךְ אַתָּה יהוה, גָּאַל יִשְׂרָאֵל.

גָּאַל יִשְׂרָאֵל *Who redeemed Israel*: The Sages attached great significance to the principle of "juxtaposing redemption and prayer", insisting that nothing should interrupt the transition from the words "who redeemed Israel" to the *Amidah* itself. The act of prayer *is* ultimately a request for redemption, a plea for God to intervene

us, Lord our God, and from the slave-house You delivered us. All their firstborn You killed, but Your firstborn You redeemed. You split the Sea of Reeds and drowned the arrogant. You brought Your beloved ones across. The water covered their foes; not one of them was left. For this, the beloved ones praised and exalted God, the cherished ones sang psalms, songs and praises, blessings and thanksgivings to the King, the living and enduring God. High and exalted, great and awesome, He humbles the haughty and raises the lowly, freeing captives and redeeming those in need, helping the poor and answering His people when they cry out to Him.

Stand and take three steps back.

➔ Praises to God Most High, the Blessed One who is blessed. Moses and the children of Israel recited to You a song with great joy, and they all exclaimed:

מִי־כָמֹכָה "Who is like You, Lord, among the mighty? Who is like You, majestic in holiness, awesome in praises, doing wonders?"

➔ With a new song, the redeemed people praised Your name at the seashore. Together they all gave thanks, proclaimed Your kingship, and declared:

"The Lord shall reign for ever and ever."

Congregants should end the following blessing together with the Leader so as to be able to move directly from the words "redeemed Israel" to the *Amidah*, without the interruption of saying Amen.

➔ **צוּר יִשְׂרָאֵל** Rock of Israel! Arise to the help of Israel. Deliver, as You promised, Judah and Israel. Our Redeemer is the Lord of hosts; His name, the Holy One of Israel. Blessed are You, Lord, who redeemed Israel.

---

in our lives and the life of our people. The God of the philosophers is a dimension of reality but not a personal presence, a shaper of history. One may meditate on such a being, but we cannot speak to Him, lay our innermost thoughts before Him, and place our fate in His hands. The God of the prophets – the God of redemption – is encountered in events, in history, in life (Judah Halevi, *Kuzari*).

עמידה

On a יוֹם טוֹב, say the appropriate עֲמִידָה on page 646.

The following prayer, until קַדְמוֹנִיּוֹת, on page 402, is said standing with feet together.

The עֲמִידָה is first said silently; then, if there is a מִנְיָן, it is repeated aloud by the Leader.

Take three steps forward. At the points indicated by ▾, bend the knees at the first word, bow at the second, and stand straight before GOD's name.

אֲדֹנָי, שְׂפָתַי תִּפְתָּח, וּפִי יַגִּיד תְּהִלָּתֶךָ.

אבות

▾**בָּרוּךְ** אַתָּה יהוה אֱלֹהֵינוּ וֵאלֹהֵי אֲבוֹתֵינוּ, אֱלֹהֵי אַבְרָהָם, אֱלֹהֵי יִצְחָק, וֵאלֹהֵי יַעֲקֹב, הָאֵל הַגָּדוֹל הַגִּבּוֹר וְהַנּוֹרָא, אֵל עֶלְיוֹן, גּוֹמֵל חֲסָדִים טוֹבִים וְקוֹנֵה הַכֹּל, וְזוֹכֵר חַסְדֵי אָבוֹת, וּמֵבִיא גוֹאֵל לִבְנֵי בְנֵיהֶם, לְמַעַן שְׁמוֹ בְּאַהֲבָה.

On שַׁבַּת שׁוּבָה, add:

זָכְרֵנוּ לַחַיִּים, מֶלֶךְ חָפֵץ בַּחַיִּים, וְכָתְבֵנוּ בְּסֵפֶר הַחַיִּים, לְמַעַנְךָ אֱלֹהִים חַיִּים.

מֶלֶךְ עוֹזֵר וּמוֹשִׁיעַ וּמָגֵן. ▾בָּרוּךְ אַתָּה יהוה, מָגֵן אַבְרָהָם.

גבורות

אַתָּה גִּבּוֹר לְעוֹלָם אֲדֹנָי, מְחַיֵּה מֵתִים אַתָּה, רַב לְהוֹשִׁיעַ.

From after שְׂמְחַת תּוֹרָה until פֶּסַח add:

מַשִּׁיב הָרוּחַ וּמוֹרִיד הַגֶּשֶׁם.

מְכַלְכֵּל חַיִּים בְּחֶסֶד, מְחַיֵּה מֵתִים בְּרַחֲמִים רַבִּים, סוֹמֵךְ נוֹפְלִים, וְרוֹפֵא חוֹלִים, וּמַתִּיר אֲסוּרִים, וּמְקַיֵּם אֱמוּנָתוֹ לִישֵׁנֵי עָפָר. מִי כָמוֹךָ בַּעַל גְּבוּרוֹת, וּמִי דּוֹמֶה לָּךְ, מֶלֶךְ מֵמִית וּמְחַיֶּה וּמַצְמִיחַ יְשׁוּעָה.

On שַׁבַּת שׁוּבָה, add:

מִי כָמוֹךָ אַב הָרַחֲמִים, זוֹכֵר יְצוּרָיו לַחַיִּים בְּרַחֲמִים.

AMIDAH: THE STANDING PRAYER

On a Festival, say the appropriate *Amidah* on page 647.

The following prayer, until *Kadmoniot*, on page 403, is said standing with feet together.

The *Amidah* is first said silently; then, if there is a *minyan*, it is repeated aloud by the Leader.

Take three steps forward. At the points indicated by ▾, bend the knees at the first word, bow at the second, and stand straight before GOD's name.

O LORD, open my lips, so that my mouth may declare Your praise.

PATRIARCHS

▾בָּרוּךְ Blessed are You, LORD our GOD and GOD of our Fathers, GOD of Abraham, GOD of Isaac and GOD of Jacob; the great, mighty and awesome GOD, GOD most high, who bestows acts of lovingkindness and creates all, who remembers the lovingkindness of the Fathers and will bring a Redeemer to their children's children for the sake of His name, in love.

On the Shabbat of Penitence, add:

Remember us for life, O King who desires life, and write us in the book of life – for Your sake, O GOD of life.

King, Helper, Saviour, Shield: ▾Blessed are You, LORD, Shield of Abraham.

DIVINE MIGHT

אַתָּה You are eternally mighty, LORD. You give life to the dead and have great power to save.

From after Simchat Torah until Pesach, add:

He makes the wind blow and the rain fall.

He sustains the living with lovingkindness, and with great compassion revives the dead. He supports the fallen, heals the sick, sets captives free, and keeps His faith with those who sleep in the dust. Who is like You, Master of might, and to whom can You be compared, O King who brings death and gives life, and makes salvation grow?

On the Shabbat of Penitence say:

Who is like You, compassionate Father, who remembers His creatures in compassion, for life?

וְנֶאֱמָן אַתָּה לְהַחֲיוֹת מֵתִים. בָּרוּךְ אַתָּה יהוה, מְחַיֵּה הַמֵּתִים.

When saying the עֲמִידָה silently, go to אַתָּה קָדוֹשׁ overleaf.

קדושה

During the Leader's repetition, the following is said standing, with feet together, rising on the toes at the words indicated by ▲.

Congregation then Leader: נְקַדֵּשׁ אֶת־שִׁמְךָ בָּעוֹלָם, כְּשֵׁם שֶׁמַּקְדִּישִׁים אוֹתוֹ בִּשְׁמֵי מָרוֹם, כַּכָּתוּב עַל יַד נְבִיאֶךָ, וְקָרָא זֶה אֶל־זֶה וְאָמַר.

Congregation and Leader: ▲קָדוֹשׁ ▲קָדוֹשׁ ▲קָדוֹשׁ יהוה צְבָאוֹת, מְלֹא כָל־הָאָרֶץ כְּבוֹדוֹ.

Congregation then Leader: אָז בְּקוֹל רַעַשׁ גָּדוֹל אַדִּיר וְחָזָק מַשְׁמִיעִים קוֹל, מִתְנַשְּׂאִים לְעֻמַּת שְׂרָפִים, לְעֻמָּתָם בָּרוּךְ יֹאמֵרוּ.

Congregation and Leader: ▲בָּרוּךְ כְּבוֹד־יהוה, מִמְּקוֹמוֹ.

Congregation then Leader: מִמְּקוֹמְךָ מַלְכֵּנוּ תוֹפִיעַ, וְתִמְלֹךְ עָלֵינוּ, כִּי מְחַכִּים אֲנַחְנוּ לָךְ. מָתַי תִּמְלֹךְ בְּצִיּוֹן, בְּקָרוֹב בְּיָמֵינוּ, לְעוֹלָם וָעֶד תִּשְׁכּוֹן. תִּתְגַּדַּל וְתִתְקַדַּשׁ בְּתוֹךְ יְרוּשָׁלַיִם עִירְךָ, לְדוֹר וָדוֹר וּלְנֵצַח נְצָחִים. וְעֵינֵינוּ תִרְאֶינָה מַלְכוּתֶךָ, כַּדָּבָר הָאָמוּר בְּשִׁירֵי עֻזֶּךָ, עַל יְדֵי דָוִד מְשִׁיחַ צִדְקֶךָ.

Congregation and Leader: ▲יִמְלֹךְ יהוה לְעוֹלָם, אֱלֹהַיִךְ צִיּוֹן לְדֹר וָדֹר, הַלְלוּיָהּ.

Leader: לְדוֹר וָדוֹר נַגִּיד גָּדְלֶךָ וּלְנֵצַח נְצָחִים קְדֻשָּׁתְךָ נַקְדִּישׁ, וְשִׁבְחֲךָ אֱלֹהֵינוּ מִפִּינוּ לֹא יָמוּשׁ לְעוֹלָם וָעֶד, כִּי אֵל מֶלֶךְ גָּדוֹל וְקָדוֹשׁ אָתָּה. בָּרוּךְ אַתָּה יהוה, *הָאֵל הַקָּדוֹשׁ.

---

*On שַׁבַּת שׁוּבָה, end the blessing:

הַמֶּלֶךְ הַקָּדוֹשׁ.

Continue with ישמח משה overleaf.:

Faithful are You to revive the dead. Blessed are You, Lord, who revives the dead.

When saying the *Amidah* silently, go to "You are holy" overleaf.

KEDUSHAH

During the Leader's repetition, the following is said standing, with feet together, rising on the toes at the words indicated by ▲:

Congregation then Leader: נְקַדֵּשׁ We will sanctify Your name on earth, as they sanctify it in the highest heavens, as is written by Your prophet, "And they [the angels] call to one another saying:

Congregation and Leader: ▲Holy, ▲holy, ▲holy is the Lord of Hosts: the whole world is filled with His glory."

Congregation then Leader: Then with a sound of mighty noise, majestic and strong, they make their voice heard, raising themselves toward the Seraphim, and facing them say: "Blessed…

Congregation and Leader: "▲Blessed is the Lord's glory from His place."

Congregation then Leader: Reveal Yourself from Your place, O our King, and reign over us, for we are waiting for You. When will You reign in Zion? May it be soon in our days, and may You dwell there for ever and all time. May You be exalted and sanctified in the midst of Jerusalem, Your city, from generation to generation for evermore. May our eyes see Your kingdom, as is said in the songs of Your splendour, written by David your righteous anointed one:

Congregation and Leader: "▲The Lord shall reign for ever. He is your God, Zion, from generation to generation, Halleluyah!"

Leader: From generation to generation we will declare Your greatness, and we will proclaim Your holiness for evermore. Your praise, our God, shall never leave our mouth, for You, God, are a great and holy King. Blessed are You, Lord, *the holy God.

---

*On the Shabbat of Penitence, end the blessing:

the holy King.

Continue with "Moses rejoiced" overleaf.

קְדוּשָּׁה *Kedushah*: As on weekdays, the core of the *Kedushah* are the two lines said by the angels in the mystic visions of Isaiah ("Holy, holy, holy") and Ezekiel ("Blessed is the Lord's glory from His place"), together with a line from Psalms ("The Lord shall reign for ever"). The connecting passages, however, are longer than on weekdays.

The *Kedushah* is the supremely mystical moment in the prayers, and it may have had its origin in mystical circles in ancient times. So holy is it that in Israel until the era of the Geonim it was said

קדושת השם

אַתָּה קָדוֹשׁ וְשִׁמְךָ קָדוֹשׁ, וּקְדוֹשִׁים בְּכָל־יוֹם יְהַלְלוּךָ סֶּלָה. בָּרוּךְ אַתָּה יהוה, *הָאֵל הַקָּדוֹשׁ.

On שַׁבָּת שׁוּבָה, end the blessing:

*הַמֶּלֶךְ הַקָּדוֹשׁ.

קדושת היום

יִשְׂמַח מֹשֶׁה בְּמַתְּנַת חֶלְקוֹ, כִּי עֶבֶד נֶאֱמָן קָרָאתָ לּוֹ. כְּלִיל תִּפְאֶרֶת בְּרֹאשׁוֹ נָתַתָּ, בְּעָמְדוֹ לְפָנֶיךָ עַל הַר־סִינָי. וּשְׁנֵי לוּחוֹת אֲבָנִים הוֹרִיד בְּיָדוֹ, וְכָתוּב בָּהֶם שְׁמִירַת שַׁבָּת. וְכֵן כָּתוּב בְּתוֹרָתֶךָ,

וְשָׁמְרוּ בְנֵי־יִשְׂרָאֵל אֶת־הַשַּׁבָּת, לַעֲשׂוֹת אֶת־הַשַּׁבָּת לְדֹרֹתָם בְּרִית עוֹלָם. בֵּינִי וּבֵין בְּנֵי יִשְׂרָאֵל אוֹת הִיא לְעֹלָם, כִּי־שֵׁשֶׁת יָמִים עָשָׂה יהוה אֶת־הַשָּׁמַיִם וְאֶת־הָאָרֶץ, וּבַיּוֹם הַשְּׁבִיעִי שָׁבַת וַיִּנָּפַשׁ.

וְלֹא נְתַתּוֹ יהוה אֱלֹהֵינוּ לְגוֹיֵי הָאֲרָצוֹת, וְלֹא הִנְחַלְתּוֹ מַלְכֵּנוּ לְעוֹבְדֵי פְסִילִים, וְגַם בִּמְנוּחָתוֹ לֹא יִשְׁכְּנוּ עֲרֵלִים, כִּי לְיִשְׂרָאֵל עַמְּךָ נְתַתּוֹ בְּאַהֲבָה, לְזֶרַע יַעֲקֹב אֲשֶׁר בָּם בָּחָרְתָּ. עַם מְקַדְּשֵׁי שְׁבִיעִי, כֻּלָּם יִשְׂבְּעוּ וְיִתְעַנְּגוּ מִטּוּבֶךָ, וּבַשְּׁבִיעִי רָצִיתָ בּוֹ וְקִדַּשְׁתּוֹ, חֶמְדַּת יָמִים אוֹתוֹ קָרָאתָ, זֵכֶר לְמַעֲשֵׂה בְרֵאשִׁית.

אֱלֹהֵינוּ וֵאלֹהֵי אֲבוֹתֵינוּ, רְצֵה בִמְנוּחָתֵנוּ, קַדְּשֵׁנוּ בְּמִצְוֹתֶיךָ,

---

only once a week, on Shabbat morning. In Babylon, however, it was said at every Reader's repetition of the *Amidah*. During its recital we stand with our feet together, rising on our toes at key words, as if we were angels, striving upward.

יִשְׂמַח מֹשֶׁה *Moses rejoiced*: As explained in the commentary for Friday night, the central blessings of the Shabbat evening, morning and afternoon services are different, forming a three-movement structure. This can be understood in three ways: 1. in terms of Jewish faith in creation, revelation and redemption; 2. in terms of eras: Shabbat past, present and future; and 3. as

HOLINESS

אַתָּה You are holy and Your name is holy, and holy ones praise You daily, Selah! Blessed are You, LORD, *the holy GOD.

*On the Shabbat of Penitence, end the blessing:
the holy King.

HOLINESS OF THE DAY

יִשְׂמַח Moses rejoiced at the gift of his portion when You called him "faithful servant". A crown of glory You placed on his head when he stood before You on Mount Sinai. He brought down in his hands two tablets of stone on which was engraved the observance of the Sabbath. So it is written in your Torah:

וְשָׁמְרוּ The children of Israel must keep the Sabbath, observing the Sabbath in every generation as an everlasting covenant. It is a sign between Me and the children of Israel for ever, for in six days GOD made the heavens and the earth, but on the seventh day He ceased work and refreshed Himself.

וְלֹא You, O LORD our GOD, did not give it to the other nations of the world, nor did You, our King, give it as a heritage to those who worship idols. In its rest the uncircumcised do not dwell, for You gave it in love to Israel Your people, to the descendants of Jacob whom You chose. May the people who sanctify the seventh day all find satisfaction and delight in Your goodness, for You favoured the seventh day and made it holy, calling it the most cherished of days, a remembrance of the act of creation.

אֱלֹהֵינוּ Our GOD and GOD of our ancestors, find favour in our rest. Make us holy through Your commandments and grant us our share

---

the three parts of a wedding: betrothal, marriage (marked by *simchah*, rejoicing), and *yichud*, the coming together of bride and groom. The morning blessing fits all three patterns. It speaks about revelation – Moses bringing down the tablets of stone from Mount Sinai; about time present – the Israelites "observing the Sabbath throughout their generations"; and it speaks of joy – "Moses rejoiced".

וְלֹא נְתַתּוֹ *You...did not give it to the other nations of the world*: Creation is universal; so is redemption, the time when "GOD will be Sovereign over all the earth". Revelation, however, is particular – the unique covenant of love between GOD and His people – hence the emphasis on the special nature of the bond between Shabbat and the Jewish people.

וְתֵן חֶלְקֵנוּ בְּתוֹרָתֶךָ, שַׂבְּעֵנוּ מִטּוּבֶךָ, וְשַׂמְּחֵנוּ בִּישׁוּעָתֶךָ, וְטַהֵר לִבֵּנוּ לְעָבְדְּךָ בֶּאֱמֶת. וְהַנְחִילֵנוּ יהוה אֱלֹהֵינוּ בְּאַהֲבָה וּבְרָצוֹן שַׁבַּת קָדְשֶׁךָ. וְיָנוּחוּ בָהּ יִשְׂרָאֵל מְקַדְּשֵׁי שְׁמֶךָ. בָּרוּךְ אַתָּה יהוה, מְקַדֵּשׁ הַשַּׁבָּת.

עבודה

רְצֵה יהוה אֱלֹהֵינוּ בְּעַמְּךָ יִשְׂרָאֵל וּבִתְפִלָּתָם, וְהָשֵׁב אֶת־הָעֲבוֹדָה לִדְבִיר בֵּיתֶךָ. וְאִשֵּׁי יִשְׂרָאֵל וּתְפִלָּתָם בְּאַהֲבָה תְקַבֵּל בְּרָצוֹן, וּתְהִי לְרָצוֹן תָּמִיד עֲבוֹדַת יִשְׂרָאֵל עַמֶּךָ.

On רֹאשׁ חֹדֶשׁ and חוֹל הַמּוֹעֵד, say:

אֱלֹהֵינוּ וֵאלֹהֵי אֲבוֹתֵינוּ, יַעֲלֶה, וְיָבֹא, וְיַגִּיעַ, וְיֵרָאֶה, וְיֵרָצֶה, וְיִשָּׁמַע, וְיִפָּקֵד, וְיִזָּכֵר זִכְרוֹנֵנוּ וּפִקְדוֹנֵנוּ, וְזִכְרוֹן אֲבוֹתֵינוּ, וְזִכְרוֹן מָשִׁיחַ בֶּן דָּוִד עַבְדֶּךָ, וְזִכְרוֹן יְרוּשָׁלַיִם עִיר קָדְשֶׁךָ, וְזִכְרוֹן כָּל־עַמְּךָ בֵּית יִשְׂרָאֵל לְפָנֶיךָ, לִפְלֵיטָה וּלְטוֹבָה, וּלְחֵן וּלְחֶסֶד וּלְרַחֲמִים, וּלְחַיִּים וּלְשָׁלוֹם בְּיוֹם

On רֹאשׁ חֹדֶשׁ:	On פֶּסַח:	On סֻכּוֹת:
רֹאשׁ הַחֹדֶשׁ	חַג הַמַּצּוֹת	חַג הַסֻּכּוֹת

הַזֶּה. זָכְרֵנוּ יהוה אֱלֹהֵינוּ בּוֹ לְטוֹבָה, וּפָקְדֵנוּ בוֹ לִבְרָכָה, וְהוֹשִׁיעֵנוּ בוֹ לְחַיִּים. וּבִדְבַר יְשׁוּעָה וְרַחֲמִים, חוּס וְחָנֵּנוּ וְרַחֵם עָלֵינוּ וְהוֹשִׁיעֵנוּ, כִּי אֵלֶיךָ עֵינֵינוּ, כִּי אֵל מֶלֶךְ חַנּוּן וְרַחוּם אָתָּה.

וְתֶחֱזֶינָה עֵינֵינוּ בְּשׁוּבְךָ לְצִיּוֹן בְּרַחֲמִים. בָּרוּךְ אַתָּה יהוה, הַמַּחֲזִיר שְׁכִינָתוֹ לְצִיּוֹן.

הודאה

▽ Bow at the first five words.

▽**מוֹדִים** אֲנַחְנוּ לָךְ, שָׁאַתָּה הוּא יהוה אֱלֹהֵינוּ וֵאלֹהֵי אֲבוֹתֵינוּ לְעוֹלָם וָעֶד. צוּר חַיֵּינוּ, מָגֵן יִשְׁעֵנוּ אַתָּה הוּא לְדוֹר וָדוֹר.

During the Leader's repetition, the Congregation says quietly:

▽**מוֹדִים** אֲנַחְנוּ לָךְ, שָׁאַתָּה הוּא יהוה אֱלֹהֵינוּ וֵאלֹהֵי אֲבוֹתֵינוּ,

in Your Torah. Satisfy us with Your goodness, grant us joy in Your salvation, and purify our hearts to serve You in truth. In love and favour, Lord our God, grant us as our heritage Your holy Sabbath, so that Israel who sanctify Your name may find rest on it. Blessed are You, Lord, who sanctifies the Sabbath.

TEMPLE SERVICE

רְצֵה Find favour, Lord our God, in Your people Israel and their prayer. Restore the service to Your most holy house, and accept in love and favour the fire-offerings of Israel and their prayer. May the service of Your people Israel always find favour with You.

On Rosh Chodesh and the Intermediate Days of Festivals, say:

אֱלֹהֵינוּ Our God and God of our ancestors, may there rise, come, reach, appear, be favoured, heard, regarded and remembered before You, our recollection and remembrance, as well as the remembrance of our ancestors, and of the Messiah son of David Your servant, and of Jerusalem Your holy city, and of all Your people the House of Israel – for deliverance and well-being, grace, lovingkindness and compassion, life and peace, on this day of:

On Rosh Chodesh, say:	On Pesach, say:	On Sukkot, say:
Rosh Chodesh.	the Festival of Matzot.	the Festival of Sukkot.

On it remember us, Lord our God, for good, recollect us for blessing, and deliver us for life. In accord with Your promise of salvation and compassion, spare us and be gracious to us, have compassion on us and deliver us, for our eyes are turned to You because You, God, are a gracious and compassionate King.

וְתֶחֱזֶינָה And may our eyes witness Your return to Zion in compassion. Blessed are You, Lord, who restores His Presence to Zion.

THANKSGIVING

▽ Bow at the first nine words.

מוֹדִים▽ We give thanks to You, for You are the Lord our God and God of our ancestors for ever and all time. You are the Rock of our lives, Shield of our salvation from generation to

During the Leader's repetition, the Congregation says quietly:

מוֹדִים▽ We give thanks to You, for You are the Lord our God and God of our ancestors,

נוֹדֶה לְּךָ וּנְסַפֵּר תְּהִלָּתֶךָ עַל חַיֵּינוּ הַמְּסוּרִים בְּיָדֶךָ, וְעַל נִשְׁמוֹתֵינוּ הַפְּקוּדוֹת לָךְ, וְעַל נִסֶּיךָ שֶׁבְּכָל־יוֹם עִמָּנוּ, וְעַל נִפְלְאוֹתֶיךָ וְטוֹבוֹתֶיךָ שֶׁבְּכָל־עֵת, עֶרֶב וָבֹקֶר וְצָהֳרָיִם. הַטּוֹב כִּי לֹא־כָלוּ רַחֲמֶיךָ, וְהַמְרַחֵם כִּי לֹא־תַמּוּ חֲסָדֶיךָ, מֵעוֹלָם קִוִּינוּ לָךְ.

אֱלֹהֵי כָל־בָּשָׂר, יוֹצְרֵנוּ, יוֹצֵר בְּרֵאשִׁית. בְּרָכוֹת וְהוֹדָאוֹת לְשִׁמְךָ הַגָּדוֹל וְהַקָּדוֹשׁ, עַל שֶׁהֶחֱיִיתָנוּ וְקִיַּמְתָּנוּ. כֵּן תְּחַיֵּנוּ וּתְקַיְּמֵנוּ, וְתֶאֱסוֹף גָּלֻיּוֹתֵינוּ לְחַצְרוֹת קָדְשֶׁךָ, לִשְׁמוֹר חֻקֶּיךָ וְלַעֲשׂוֹת רְצוֹנֶךָ, וּלְעָבְדְּךָ בְּלֵבָב שָׁלֵם, עַל שֶׁאֲנַחְנוּ מוֹדִים לָךְ. בָּרוּךְ אֵל הַהוֹדָאוֹת.

On שַׁבַּת חֲנֻכָּה, say:

עַל הַנִּסִּים, וְעַל הַפֻּרְקָן, וְעַל הַגְּבוּרוֹת, וְעַל הַתְּשׁוּעוֹת, וְעַל הַמִּלְחָמוֹת, שֶׁעָשִׂיתָ לַאֲבוֹתֵינוּ בַּיָּמִים הָהֵם בַּזְּמַן הַזֶּה.

בִּימֵי מַתִּתְיָהוּ בֶּן־יוֹחָנָן כֹּהֵן גָּדוֹל חַשְׁמוֹנַאי וּבָנָיו, כְּשֶׁעָמְדָה מַלְכוּת יָוָן הָרְשָׁעָה עַל־עַמְּךָ יִשְׂרָאֵל, לְהַשְׁכִּיחָם תּוֹרָתֶךָ, וּלְהַעֲבִירָם מֵחֻקֵּי רְצוֹנֶךָ. וְאַתָּה בְּרַחֲמֶיךָ הָרַבִּים, עָמַדְתָּ לָהֶם בְּעֵת צָרָתָם, רַבְתָּ אֶת־רִיבָם, דַּנְתָּ אֶת־דִּינָם, נָקַמְתָּ אֶת־נִקְמָתָם. מָסַרְתָּ גִבּוֹרִים בְּיַד חַלָּשִׁים, וְרַבִּים בְּיַד מְעַטִּים, וּטְמֵאִים בְּיַד טְהוֹרִים, וּרְשָׁעִים בְּיַד צַדִּיקִים, וְזֵדִים בְּיַד עוֹסְקֵי תוֹרָתֶךָ. וּלְךָ עָשִׂיתָ שֵׁם גָּדוֹל וְקָדוֹשׁ בְּעוֹלָמֶךָ, וּלְעַמְּךָ יִשְׂרָאֵל עָשִׂיתָ תְּשׁוּעָה גְדוֹלָה וּפֻרְקָן כְּהַיּוֹם הַזֶּה. וְאַחַר כֵּן בָּאוּ בָנֶיךָ לִדְבִיר בֵּיתֶךָ, וּפִנּוּ אֶת־הֵיכָלֶךָ, וְטִהֲרוּ אֶת־מִקְדָּשֶׁךָ, וְהִדְלִיקוּ נֵרוֹת בְּחַצְרוֹת קָדְשֶׁךָ, וְקָבְעוּ שְׁמוֹנַת יְמֵי חֲנֻכָּה אֵלּוּ, לְהוֹדוֹת וּלְהַלֵּל לְשִׁמְךָ הַגָּדוֹל.

וְעַל כֻּלָּם יִתְבָּרַךְ וְיִתְרוֹמַם שִׁמְךָ מַלְכֵּנוּ תָּמִיד לְעוֹלָם וָעֶד.

generation. We will thank You and declare Your praise for our lives which are entrusted into Your hand; our souls which are placed in Your charge; for Your miracles which are with us every day; and for Your wonders and favours at all times, evening, morning and midday. You are good – for Your compassion never fails. You are compassionate – for Your lovingkindnesses never cease. We have always placed our hope in You.

God of all flesh, who formed us and formed the universe. Blessings and thanks are due to Your great and holy name for giving us life and sustaining us. May You continue to give us life and sustain us; and may You gather our exiles to Your holy courts, to keep Your decrees, do Your will and serve You with a perfect heart, for it is for us to give You thanks. Blessed be God to whom thanksgiving is due.

On Shabbat Chanukah, say:

עַל הַנִּסִּים [We thank You also] for the miracles, the redemption, the mighty deeds, and the victories in battle which You performed for our ancestors in those days at this time.

בִּימֵי In the days of Mattityahu, son of Yochanan the High Priest, the Hasmonean, and his sons, the wicked Greek kingdom rose up against Your people Israel to make them forget Your Torah and to force them to transgress the statutes of Your will. It was then that You in Your great compassion stood by them in the time of their distress. You championed their cause, judged their claim, and avenged their wrong. You delivered the strong into the hands of the weak, the many into the hands of the few, the impure into the hands of the pure, the wicked into the hands of the righteous, and the arrogant into the hands of those who were engaged in the study of Your Torah. You made for Yourself great and holy renown in Your world, and for Your people Israel You performed a great salvation and redemption on this day. Your children then entered the holiest part of Your house, cleansed Your Temple, purified Your sanctuary, kindled lights in Your holy courts, and designated these eight days of Chanukah for giving thanks and praise to Your great name.

וְעַל For all these things may Your name be blessed and exalted, our King, continually, for ever and all time.

On שַׁבַּת שׁוּבָה, add:

וּכְתוֹב לְחַיִּים טוֹבִים כָּל־בְּנֵי בְרִיתֶךָ.

וְכֹל הַחַיִּים יוֹדְוּךָ סֶּלָה, וִיהַלְלוּ אֶת־שִׁמְךָ בֶּאֱמֶת, הָאֵל יְשׁוּעָתֵנוּ וְעֶזְרָתֵנוּ סֶלָה. ▾בָּרוּךְ אַתָּה יהוה, הַטּוֹב שִׁמְךָ וּלְךָ נָאֶה לְהוֹדוֹת.

During the repetition of the עֲמִידָה, the Leader says the following:

אֱלֹהֵינוּ וֵאלֹהֵי אֲבוֹתֵינוּ, בָּרְכֵנוּ בַבְּרָכָה הַמְשֻׁלֶּשֶׁת, בַּתּוֹרָה, הַכְּתוּבָה עַל יְדֵי מֹשֶׁה עַבְדֶּךָ, הָאֲמוּרָה מִפִּי אַהֲרֹן וּבָנָיו כֹּהֲנִים, עַם קְדוֹשֶׁךָ, כָּאָמוּר.

יְבָרֶכְךָ יהוה, וְיִשְׁמְרֶךָ. (Cong.: כֵּן יְהִי רָצוֹן)

יָאֵר יהוה פָּנָיו אֵלֶיךָ וִיחֻנֶּךָּ. (Cong.: כֵּן יְהִי רָצוֹן)

יִשָּׂא יהוה פָּנָיו אֵלֶיךָ וְיָשֵׂם לְךָ שָׁלוֹם. (Cong.: כֵּן יְהִי רָצוֹן)

ברכת שלום

שִׂים שָׁלוֹם, טוֹבָה, וּבְרָכָה, חֵן, וָחֶסֶד וְרַחֲמִים עָלֵינוּ וְעַל כָּל־יִשְׂרָאֵל עַמֶּךָ. בָּרְכֵנוּ אָבִינוּ, כֻּלָּנוּ כְּאֶחָד בְּאוֹר פָּנֶיךָ, כִּי בְאוֹר פָּנֶיךָ נָתַתָּ לָּנוּ, יהוה אֱלֹהֵינוּ, תּוֹרַת חַיִּים וְאַהֲבַת חֶסֶד, וּצְדָקָה, וּבְרָכָה, וְרַחֲמִים, וְחַיִּים, וְשָׁלוֹם. וְטוֹב בְּעֵינֶיךָ לְבָרֵךְ אֶת־עַמְּךָ יִשְׂרָאֵל, בְּכָל־עֵת וּבְכָל־שָׁעָה בִּשְׁלוֹמֶךָ. *בָּרוּךְ אַתָּה יהוה, הַמְבָרֵךְ אֶת עַמּוֹ יִשְׂרָאֵל בַּשָּׁלוֹם.

*On שַׁבַּת שׁוּבָה, substitute the following:

בְּסֵפֶר חַיִּים בְּרָכָה וְשָׁלוֹם, וּפַרְנָסָה טוֹבָה, נִזָּכֵר וְנִכָּתֵב לְפָנֶיךָ, אֲנַחְנוּ וְכָל־עַמְּךָ בֵּית יִשְׂרָאֵל, לְחַיִּים טוֹבִים וּלְשָׁלוֹם. בָּרוּךְ אַתָּה יהוה, עֹשֵׂה הַשָּׁלוֹם.

The Leader's Repetition ends at this point.

אֱלֹהַי, נְצוֹר לְשׁוֹנִי מֵרָע, וּשְׂפָתַי מִדַּבֵּר מִרְמָה, וְלִמְקַלְלַי נַפְשִׁי תִדּוֹם, וְנַפְשִׁי כֶּעָפָר לַכֹּל תִּהְיֶה. פְּתַח לִבִּי בְּתוֹרָתֶךָ,

On the Shabbat of Penitence, add:
And write, for a good life, all the children of Your covenant.

Let all that lives thank You, Selah! and praise Your name in truth, God, our Saviour and Help, Selah! ▾Blessed are You, Lord, whose name is "the Good" and to whom thanks is due.

During the repetition of the *Amidah*, the Leader says the following:
אֱלֹהֵינוּ Our God and God of our fathers, bless us with the threefold blessing in the Torah, written by the hand of Moses Your servant and pronounced by Aaron and his sons the priests, Your holy people, as it is said:
May the Lord bless you and protect you. (Cong.: May it be Your will.)
May the Lord make His face shine on you and be gracious to you. (Cong.: May it be Your will.)
May the Lord turn His face towards you, and give you peace. (Cong.: May it be Your will.)

PEACE

שִׂים Grant peace, goodness and blessing, grace, lovingkindness and compassion to us and all Israel Your people. Bless us, our Father, all as one, with the light of Your face, for by the light of Your face You have given us, Lord our God, the Torah of life and love of kindness, righteousness, blessing, compassion, life and peace. May it be good in Your eyes to bless Your people Israel at every time, in every hour, with Your peace. *Blessed are You, Lord, who blesses His people Israel with peace.

*On the Shabbat of Penitence, substitute the following::
In the book of life, blessing, peace and prosperity, may we and all Your people the house of Israel be remembered and written before You for a good life, and for peace. Blessed are You, Lord, who makes peace.

The Leader's repetition ends at this point.

אֱלֹהַי My God, guard my tongue from evil and my lips from deceitful speech. To those who curse me, let my soul be silent; may my soul be to all like the dust. Open my heart to Your Torah and

וּבְמִצְוֹתֶיךָ תִּרְדּוֹף נַפְשִׁי. וְכָל הַחוֹשְׁבִים עָלַי רָעָה, מְהֵרָה הָפֵר עֲצָתָם וְקַלְקֵל מַחֲשַׁבְתָּם. עֲשֵׂה לְמַעַן שְׁמֶךָ, עֲשֵׂה לְמַעַן יְמִינֶךָ, עֲשֵׂה לְמַעַן קְדֻשָּׁתֶךָ, עֲשֵׂה לְמַעַן תּוֹרָתֶךָ. לְמַעַן יֵחָלְצוּן יְדִידֶיךָ, הוֹשִׁיעָה יְמִינְךָ וַעֲנֵנִי. יִהְיוּ לְרָצוֹן אִמְרֵי־פִי וְהֶגְיוֹן לִבִּי לְפָנֶיךָ, יהוה צוּרִי וְגוֹאֲלִי.

Bow, take three steps back, then bow, first left, then right, then centre, while saying:

עֹשֶׂה שָׁלוֹם בִּמְרוֹמָיו, הוּא יַעֲשֶׂה שָׁלוֹם עָלֵינוּ, וְעַל־כָּל־יִשְׂרָאֵל, וְאִמְרוּ אָמֵן.

יְהִי רָצוֹן מִלְּפָנֶיךָ יהוה אֱלֹהֵינוּ וֵאלֹהֵי אֲבוֹתֵינוּ, שֶׁיִּבָּנֶה בֵּית הַמִּקְדָּשׁ בִּמְהֵרָה בְיָמֵינוּ, וְתֵן חֶלְקֵנוּ בְּתוֹרָתֶךָ. וְשָׁם נַעֲבָדְךָ בְּיִרְאָה, כִּימֵי עוֹלָם וּכְשָׁנִים קַדְמוֹנִיּוֹת. וְעָרְבָה לַיהוה מִנְחַת יְהוּדָה וִירוּשָׁלָיִם, כִּימֵי עוֹלָם וּכְשָׁנִים קַדְמוֹנִיּוֹת.

When praying with a מִנְיָן, the עֲמִידָה is repeated aloud by the Leader page 390.

On שַׁבָּת which is also ראש חֹדֶשׁ, יום טוב, חול הַמּוֹעֵד and חֲנֻכָּה, הַלֵּל on page 618, is said next.

On other days, the Leader says קַדִּישׁ תִּתְקַבַּל.

קדיש תתקבל

Leader:

יִתְגַּדַּל וְיִתְקַדַּשׁ שְׁמֵהּ רַבָּא. (Cong. אָמֵן) בְּעָלְמָא דִּי־בְרָא כִרְעוּתֵהּ. וְיַמְלִיךְ מַלְכוּתֵהּ, בְּחַיֵּיכוֹן וּבְיוֹמֵיכוֹן וּבְחַיֵּי דְכָל־בֵּית יִשְׂרָאֵל, בַּעֲגָלָא וּבִזְמַן קָרִיב. וְאִמְרוּ אָמֵן. (Cong. אָמֵן)

All:

יְהֵא שְׁמֵהּ רַבָּא מְבָרַךְ לְעָלַם וּלְעָלְמֵי עָלְמַיָּא.

Leader:

יִתְבָּרַךְ וְיִשְׁתַּבַּח וְיִתְפָּאַר וְיִתְרוֹמַם וְיִתְנַשֵּׂא וְיִתְהַדַּר וְיִתְעַלֶּה וְיִתְהַלָּל שְׁמֵהּ דְּקֻדְשָׁא בְּרִיךְ הוּא (Cong. בְּרִיךְ הוּא) לְעֵלָּא (On שַׁבָּת שׁוּבָה add לְעֵלָּא) מִן־כָּל־בִּרְכָתָא וְשִׁירָתָא

let my soul pursue Your commandments. As for all who plan evil against me, swiftly thwart their counsel and frustrate their plans. Act for the sake of Your name; act for the sake of Your right hand; act for the sake of Your holiness; act for the sake of Your Torah. That Your beloved ones may be delivered, save with Your right hand and answer me. May the words of my mouth and the meditation of my heart find favour before You, LORD, my Rock and Redeemer.

Bow, take three steps back, then bow, first left, then right, then centre, while saying:

May He who makes peace in His high places, make peace for us and all Israel – and say: Amen.

יְהִי May it be Your will, LORD our GOD and GOD of our ancestors, that the Temple be rebuilt speedily in our days, and grant us a share in Your Torah. And there we will serve You with reverence, as in the days of old and as in former years. Then the offering of Judah and Jerusalem will be pleasing to the LORD as in the days of old and as in former years.

When praying with a *minyan*, the *Amidah* is repeated aloud by the Leader on page 391.

On Shabbat which is also Rosh Chodesh, Festivals and their Intermediate Days, and Chanukah, *Hallel* on page 619, is said next.

On other days, the Leader says full *Kaddish*

FULL KADDISH

Leader:

יִתְגַּדַּל Magnified and sanctified may His great name be, in the world He created by His will. May He establish His kingdom in your lifetime and in your days, and in the lifetime of all the House of Israel, swiftly and soon – and say: Amen.

All:

May His great name be blessed for ever and all time.

Leader:

Blessed and praised, glorified and exalted, raised and honoured, uplifted and lauded be the name of the Holy One, blessed be He, (between

תֻּשְׁבְּחָתָא וְנֶחֱמָתָא, דַּאֲמִירָן בְּעָלְמָא. וְאִמְרוּ אָמֵן. (Cong. אָמֵן)

תִּתְקַבַּל צְלוֹתְהוֹן וּבָעוּתְהוֹן דְּכָל־יִשְׂרָאֵל קֳדָם אֲבוּהוֹן דִּי בִשְׁמַיָּא. וְאִמְרוּ אָמֵן. (Cong. אָמֵן)

יְהֵא שְׁלָמָא רַבָּא מִן־שְׁמַיָּא, וְחַיִּים עָלֵינוּ וְעַל־כָּל־יִשְׂרָאֵל. וְאִמְרוּ אָמֵן. (Cong. אָמֵן)

Take three steps back and bow, first left, then right, then centre, while saying:

עֹשֶׂה שָׁלוֹם בִּמְרוֹמָיו, הוּא יַעֲשֶׂה שָׁלוֹם עָלֵינוּ, וְעַל־כָּל־יִשְׂרָאֵל. וְאִמְרוּ אָמֵן. (Cong. אָמֵן)

Some congregations say the Psalm for the Day (weekdays page 144 ff, שַׁבָּת page 152) and additional psalms at this point. קדיש יָתוֹם is then said. Others say them later.

Other congregations say these psalms later or earlier in the service.

סדר קריאת התורה לשבת ויום טוב

אֵין־כָּמוֹךָ בָאֱלֹהִים | אֲדֹנָי, וְאֵין כְּמַעֲשֶׂיךָ. מַלְכוּתְךָ מַלְכוּת כָּל־עֹלָמִים, וּמֶמְשַׁלְתְּךָ בְּכָל־דּוֹר וָדֹר. יהוה מֶלֶךְ, יהוה מָלָךְ, יהוה | יִמְלֹךְ לְעֹלָם וָעֶד. יהוה עֹז לְעַמּוֹ יִתֵּן, יהוה | יְבָרֵךְ אֶת־עַמּוֹ בַשָּׁלוֹם.

אַב הָרַחֲמִים, הֵיטִיבָה בִרְצוֹנְךָ אֶת־צִיּוֹן, תִּבְנֶה חוֹמוֹת יְרוּשָׁלָיִם. כִּי בְךָ לְבַד בָּטָחְנוּ, מֶלֶךְ אֵל רָם וְנִשָּׂא, אֲדוֹן עוֹלָמִים.

READING OF THE TORAH

Since the revelation at Mount Sinai, the Jewish people has been a nation defined by book: the Torah. The Mosaic books are more than sacred literature, they are the written constitution of the house of Israel as a nation under the sovereignty of God, the basis of its collective memory, the record of its covenant with God, the template of its existence as "a kingdom of priests and a holy nation", and the detailed specification of the task it is called on to perform, to construct a society on the basis of justice and compassion and the inalienable dignity of the human person as the image of God. Just as the Torah is central to Jewish life, so the reading of the Torah is central to the synagogue service.

Rosh Hashanah and Yom Kippur add 'well') beyond any blessing, song, praise and consolation uttered in the world – and say: Amen.

May the prayers and pleas of all Israel be accepted by their Father in heaven – and say: Amen.

May there be great peace from heaven, and life for us and all Israel – and say: Amen.

Take three steps back and bow, first left, then right, then centre, while saying:

May He who makes peace in His high places, make peace for us and all Israel – and say: Amen.

Some congregations say the Psalm for the Day (weekdays page 145 ff, Shabbat page 153) and additional psalms at this point. The Mourner's *Kaddish* is then said. Others say them later. Other congregations say these psalms earlier or later in the service.

ORDER OF THE READING OF THE TORAH ON SHABBAT AND FESTIVALS

אֵין־כָּמְוֹךָ There is none like You among the heavenly powers, LORD, and there are no works like Yours. Your kingdom is an eternal kingdom, and Your dominion is for all generations. The LORD is King, the LORD was King, the LORD shall be King for ever and all time. The LORD will give strength to His people; the LORD will bless His people with peace.

Father of compassion, favour Zion with Your goodness; rebuild the walls of Jerusalem. For we trust in You alone, King, GOD, high and exalted, Master of worlds.

The Tanach records several key moments in Jewish history when national rededication was accompanied by a public reading of the Torah, most famously in the days of King Josiah (II Kings 23) and Ezra (Nehemiah 8). According to tradition, Moses ordained that the Torah be read regularly and publicly, a long reading on Shabbat morning and shorter readings on Mondays and Thursdays. Ezra, reinstituting this practice, added the reading on Shabbat afternoon. Thus from its earliest days the synagogue was a place of study as well as prayer. During the Second Temple period and later eras, the reading was accompanied by verse-by-verse translation into the vernacular, mainly Aramaic. Over the course of time, the act of taking the Torah from, and returning it to, the Ark became ceremonial moments in their own right.

אֵין־כָּמְוֹךָ *There is none like You among the heavenly powers*: A collection of verses

The Ark is opened. All stand.

וַיְהִי בִּנְסֹעַ הָאָרֹן וַיֹּאמֶר מֹשֶׁה, קוּמָה יהוה וְיָפֻצוּ אֹיְבֶיךָ וְיָנֻסוּ מְשַׂנְאֶיךָ מִפָּנֶיךָ. כִּי מִצִּיּוֹן תֵּצֵא תוֹרָה, וּדְבַר יהוה מִירוּשָׁלָיִם. בָּרוּךְ שֶׁנָּתַן תּוֹרָה לְעַמּוֹ יִשְׂרָאֵל בִּקְדֻשָּׁתוֹ.

On a יוֹם טוֹב, except when it falls on שַׁבָּת, say the following verse three times:

יהוה, יהוה, אֵל, רַחוּם, וְחַנּוּן, אֶרֶךְ אַפַּיִם, וְרַב־חֶסֶד, וֶאֱמֶת, נֹצֵר חֶסֶד לָאֲלָפִים, נֹשֵׂא עָוֹן, וָפֶשַׁע, וְחַטָּאָה, וְנַקֵּה.

Insert appropriate phrase/s in brackets.

רִבּוֹן הָעוֹלָם. מַלֵּא מִשְׁאֲלוֹת לִבִּי לְטוֹבָה. וְהָפֵק רְצוֹנִי, וְתֵן שְׁאֵלָתִי, לִי עַבְדְּךָ (פלוני בֶּן אֲמָתְךָ פלונית / פלונית בַּת אֲמָתְךָ פלונית) וְזַכֵּנִי (וְאֶת אִשְׁתִּי / וְאֶת־בַּעְלִי), (וּבָנַי וּבְנוֹתַי), לַעֲשׂוֹת רְצוֹנְךָ בְּלֵבָב שָׁלֵם. וּמַלְּטֵנוּ מִיֵּצֶר הָרָע, וְתֵן חֶלְקֵנוּ בְּתוֹרָתֶךָ. וְזַכֵּנוּ כְּדֵי שֶׁתִּשְׁרֶה שְׁכִינָתְךָ עָלֵינוּ, וְהוֹפַע עָלֵינוּ רוּחַ חָכְמָה וּבִינָה, רוּחַ עֵצָה וּגְבוּרָה, רוּחַ דַּעַת וְיִרְאַת יהוה. וְכֵן יְהִי רָצוֹן מִלְּפָנֶיךָ, יהוה אֱלֹהֵינוּ וֵאלֹהֵי אֲבוֹתֵינוּ, שֶׁאֶזְכֶּה לַעֲשׂוֹת מַעֲשִׂים טוֹבִים בְּעֵינֶיךָ, וְלָלֶכֶת בְּדַרְכֵי יְשָׁרִים לְפָנֶיךָ. וְקַדְּשֵׁנוּ בְּמִצְוֹתֶיךָ כְּדֵי שֶׁנִּזְכֶּה לְחַיִּים טוֹבִים וַאֲרֻכִּים לְחַיֵּי הָעוֹלָם הַבָּא. וְתִשְׁמְרֵנוּ מִמַּעֲשִׂים רָעִים, וּמִשָּׁעוֹת רָעוֹת הַמִּתְרַגְּשׁוֹת לָבֹא לָעוֹלָם. וְהַבּוֹטֵחַ בַּיהוה חֶסֶד יְסוֹבְבֶנּוּ, אָמֵן.

יִהְיוּ לְרָצוֹן אִמְרֵי־פִי, וְהֶגְיוֹן לִבִּי לְפָנֶיךָ, יהוה צוּרִי וְגוֹאֲלִי.

The following verse is said three times:

וַאֲנִי תְפִלָּתִי לְךָ יהוה עֵת רָצוֹן, אֱלֹהִים בְּרָב־חַסְדֶּךָ, עֲנֵנִי בֶּאֱמֶת יִשְׁעֶךָ.

---

and phrases from the Book of Psalms.

Whenever the Ark set out – A description of the Ark during the journeys of the Israelites in the wilderness. The parallel verse, "When it came to rest", is recited when the Torah is returned to the Ark. Thus the taking of the Torah scroll from the Ark and its return recall the Ark of the covenant which accompanied the Israelites in the days of Moses.

כִּי מִצִּיּוֹן תֵּצֵא תוֹרָה *For the Torah shall come forth from Zion*: Part of Isaiah's famous vision (2:2–4) of the end of days.

The Ark is opened. All stand.

וַיְהִי בִּנְסֹעַ Whenever the Ark set out, Moses would say, "Arise, LORD, and may Your enemies be scattered; may those who hate You flee before You." For the Torah shall come forth from Zion, and the word of the LORD from Jerusalem. Blessed be He who in His holiness gave the Torah to His people Israel.

On a Festival, except when it falls on Shabbat, say the following verse three times:

יהוה The LORD, the LORD, compassionate and gracious, slow to anger, abounding in love and truth, extending love to a thousand generations, forgiving iniquity, rebellion and sin, and absolving [the guilty who repent].

Insert appropriate phrase/s in brackets.

רִבּוֹן הָעוֹלָם Master of the Universe, fulfil my heart's requests for good. Satisfy my desire, and grant the request of Your servant (name), son/daughter of (mother's name), and enable me (and my wife/husband, and my son/s /daughter/s) to do Your will with a perfect heart. Deliver me from the evil impulse. Grant us a share in Your Torah, and make us worthy that Your Presence may rest on us. Confer on us a spirit of wisdom and understanding, a spirit of counsel and strength, a spirit of knowledge and reverence for the LORD. So too may it be Your will, LORD our GOD and GOD of our ancestors, that I be worthy to do deeds that are good in Your sight, and to walk before You in the ways of the upright. Make us holy through Your commandments so that we may be worthy of a long and good life, and of the World to Come. Guard us from evil deeds and bad times that threaten to bring turmoil to the world. May kindness surround one who trusts in the LORD. Amen.

May the words of my mouth and the meditation of my heart find favour before You, LORD, my Rock and Redeemer.

The following verse is said three times:

וַאֲנִי As for me, may my prayer come to You, LORD, at a time of favour. O GOD, in Your great love, answer me with Your faithful salvation.

רִבּוֹן הָעוֹלָם *Master of the Universe*: A personal prayer for the welfare of the family, which first appeared in the prayer book of Rabbi Nathan Hannover in 1662.

In some congregations, the following is said:

זוהר פרשת ויקהל

בְּרִיךְ שְׁמֵהּ דְּמָרֵא עָלְמָא, בְּרִיךְ כִּתְרָךְ וְאַתְרָךְ. יְהֵא רְעוּתָךְ עִם עַמָּךְ יִשְׂרָאֵל לְעָלַם, וּפֻרְקַן יְמִינָךְ אַחֲזִי לְעַמָּךְ בְּבֵית מַקְדְּשָׁךְ, וּלְאַמְטוּיֵי לָנָא מִטּוּב נְהוֹרָךְ, וּלְקַבֵּל צְלוֹתָנָא בְּרַחֲמִין. יְהֵא רַעֲוָא קֳדָמָךְ, דְּתוֹרִיךְ לָן חַיִּין בְּטִיבוּתָא, וְלֶהֱוֵי אֲנָא פְקִידָא בְּגוֹ צַדִּיקַיָּא, לְמִרְחַם עָלַי וּלְמִנְטַר יָתִי וְיַת כָּל־דִּי לִי, וְדִי לְעַמָּךְ יִשְׂרָאֵל. אַנְתְּ הוּא זָן לְכֹלָּא וּמְפַרְנֵס לְכֹלָּא, אַנְתְּ הוּא שַׁלִּיט עַל כֹּלָּא. אַנְתְּ הוּא דְּשַׁלִּיט עַל מַלְכַיָּא, וּמַלְכוּתָא דִּי־לָךְ הִיא. אֲנָא עַבְדָּא דְקֻדְשָׁא בְּרִיךְ הוּא, דְּסָגִידְנָא קַמֵּהּ וּמִקַּמָּא דִּיקַר אוֹרַיְתֵהּ בְּכָל־עִדָּן וְעִדָּן. לָא עַל אֱנָשׁ רָחִיצְנָא, וְלָא עַל בַּר אֱלָהִין סָמִיכְנָא, אֶלָּא בֶּאֱלָהָא דִשְׁמַיָּא, דְּהוּא אֱלָהָא קְשׁוֹט, וְאוֹרַיְתֵהּ קְשׁוֹט, וּנְבִיאוֹהִי קְשׁוֹט, וּמַסְגֵּא לְמֶעְבַּד טַבְוָן וּקְשׁוֹט. בֵּהּ אֲנָא רָחֵץ, וְלִשְׁמֵהּ קַדִּישָׁא יַקִּירָא אֲנָא אֵמַר תֻּשְׁבְּחָן. ◂ יְהֵא רַעֲוָא קֳדָמָךְ, דְּתִפְתַּח לִבִּי בְּאוֹרַיְתָא, וְתַשְׁלִים מִשְׁאֲלִין דְּלִבִּי, וְלִבָּא דְכָל־עַמָּךְ יִשְׂרָאֵל, לְטַב וּלְחַיִּין וְלִשְׁלָם.

The סֵפֶר תּוֹרָה is handed to the Leader, who holds it on his right and says:

Leader then Congregation:

שְׁמַע יִשְׂרָאֵל יהוה אֱלֹהֵינוּ יהוה אֶחָד.

Leader then Congregation:

אֶחָד אֱלֹהֵינוּ גָּדוֹל אֲדוֹנֵנוּ, קָדוֹשׁ (On הושענה רבה וְנוֹרָא) **שְׁמוֹ.**

The Leader turns to face the Ark, bows and says:

גַּדְּלוּ לַיהוה אִתִּי וּנְרוֹמְמָה שְׁמוֹ יַחְדָּו.

The Ark is closed.

The Leader carries the סֵפֶר תּוֹרָה to the reading desk, while all sing:

לְךָ יהוה הַגְּדֻלָּה וְהַגְּבוּרָה וְהַתִּפְאֶרֶת וְהַנֵּצַח וְהַהוֹד כִּי כֹל בַּשָּׁמַיִם וּבָאָרֶץ, לְךָ יהוה הַמַּמְלָכָה וְהַמִּתְנַשֵּׂא לְכֹל לְרֹאשׁ. רוֹמְמוּ יהוה אֱלֹהֵינוּ, וְהִשְׁתַּחֲווּ לַהֲדֹם רַגְלָיו, קָדוֹשׁ הוּא. רוֹמְמוּ יהוה אֱלֹהֵינוּ, וְהִשְׁתַּחֲווּ לְהַר קָדְשׁוֹ, כִּי קָדוֹשׁ יהוה אֱלֹהֵינוּ.

בְּרִיךְ שְׁמֵהּ *Blessed is the name*: This passage, from the mystical text, the Zohar, is prefaced in its original context with the words: "Rabbi Shimon said: When the scroll of the Torah is taken out to be read in public, the Gates of Compassion are opened, and love is aroused on high. Therefore one should say (at this time):..."

In some congregations, the following is said:

ZOHAR, PARSHAT VAYAKHEL

בְּרִיךְ שְׁמֵהּ Blessed is the name of the Master of the Universe. Blessed is Your crown and Your place. May Your favour always be with Your people Israel. Show Your people the salvation of Your right hand in Your Temple. Grant us the gift of Your good light, and accept our prayers in mercy. May it be Your Will to prolong our life in goodness. May I be counted among the righteous, so that You will have compassion on me and protect me and all that is mine and all that is Your people Israel's. You feed all; You sustain all; You rule over all; You rule over kings, for sovereignty is Yours. I am a servant of the Holy One, blessed be He, before whom and before whose glorious Torah I bow at all times. Not in man do I trust, nor on any angel do I rely, but on the God of heaven who is the God of truth, whose Torah is truth, whose prophets speak truth, and who abounds in acts of love and truth. In Him I trust, and to His holy and glorious name I offer praises. → May it be Your will to open my heart to the Torah, and to fulfil the wishes of my heart and of the hearts of all Your people Israel for good, for life, and for peace.

The Torah scroll is handed to the Leader, who holds it on his right and says:

Leader then Congregation:

Listen, Israel, the Lord is our God, the Lord is One.

Leader then Congregation:

One is our God; great is our Master; holy
(On Hoshana Rabba: and awesome) **is His name.**

The Leader turns to face the Ark, bows and says:

Magnify the Lord with me, and let us exalt His name together.

The Ark is closed.

The Leader carries the Torah scroll to the reading desk, while all sing:

לְךָ Yours, Lord, are the greatness and the power, the glory, majesty and splendour, for everything in heaven and earth is Yours. Yours, Lord, is the kingdom; You are exalted as head over all. Exalt the Lord our God and bow to His footstool; He is holy. Exalt the Lord our God, and bow at His holy mountain, for holy is the Lord our God.

Blessed is the name then follows. The custom of reciting it has its origins in the circle of mystics in Tzefat associated with Rabbi Isaac Luria.

— LAWS FOR A PERSON CALLED TO THE TORAH

1. One who is called to the Torah (an *oleh*) should go to where it is being read by the shortest route (after the reading he returns by a longer route). He should be wearing a *tallit*. If he is not, he may borrow one for this purpose.

2. Before making the blessings, he will be shown the place in the scroll from which the reading will take place. It is the custom to kiss this place (usually with a corner of the *tallit*) before making the blessing. While making the blessing, he should hold the handles of the scroll. He should say the blessings in a loud and clear voice so that the congrega-

עַל הַכֹּל, יִתְגַּדַּל וְיִתְקַדַּשׁ וְיִשְׁתַּבַּח וְיִתְפָּאַר וְיִתְרוֹמַם וְיִתְנַשֵּׂא שְׁמוֹ שֶׁל־מֶלֶךְ מַלְכֵי הַמְּלָכִים הַקָּדוֹשׁ בָּרוּךְ הוּא, בָּעוֹלָמוֹת שֶׁבָּרָא, הָעוֹלָם הַזֶּה וְהָעוֹלָם הַבָּא, כִּרְצוֹנוֹ, וְכִרְצוֹן יְרֵאָיו, וְכִרְצוֹן כָּל־בֵּית יִשְׂרָאֵל. צוּר הָעוֹלָמִים, אֲדוֹן כָּל־הַבְּרִיּוֹת, אֱלוֹהַּ כָּל־הַנְּפָשׁוֹת, הַיּוֹשֵׁב בְּמֶרְחֲבֵי מָרוֹם, הַשּׁוֹכֵן בִּשְׁמֵי שְׁמֵי קֶדֶם. קְדֻשָּׁתוֹ עַל־הַחַיּוֹת, וּקְדֻשָּׁתוֹ עַל־כִּסֵּא הַכָּבוֹד. וּבְכֵן יִתְקַדַּשׁ שִׁמְךָ בָּנוּ יהוה אֱלֹהֵינוּ לְעֵינֵי כָּל־חָי. וְנֹאמַר לְפָנָיו שִׁיר חָדָשׁ, כַּכָּתוּב, שִׁירוּ לֵאלֹהִים זַמְּרוּ שְׁמוֹ, סֹלּוּ לָרֹכֵב בָּעֲרָבוֹת בְּיָהּ שְׁמוֹ, וְעִלְזוּ לְפָנָיו. וְנִרְאֵהוּ עַיִן בְּעַיִן בְּשׁוּבוֹ אֶל־נָוֵהוּ, כַּכָּתוּב, כִּי עַיִן בְּעַיִן יִרְאוּ בְּשׁוּב יהוה צִיּוֹן. וְנֶאֱמַר, וְנִגְלָה כְּבוֹד יהוה, וְרָאוּ כָל־בָּשָׂר יַחְדָּו כִּי פִּי יהוה דִּבֵּר.

אַב הָרַחֲמִים הוּא יְרַחֵם עַם עֲמוּסִים, וְיִזְכֹּר בְּרִית אֵיתָנִים, וְיַצִּיל נַפְשׁוֹתֵינוּ מִן־הַשָּׁעוֹת הָרָעוֹת, וְיִגְעַר בְּיֵצֶר הָרָע מִן הַנְּשׂוּאִים, וְיָחֹן אוֹתָנוּ לִפְלֵיטַת עוֹלָמִים, וִימַלֵּא מִשְׁאֲלוֹתֵינוּ בְּמִדָּה טוֹבָה יְשׁוּעָה וְרַחֲמִים.

The סֵפֶר תּוֹרָה is placed on the reading desk. The Leader says:

וְיַעֲזֹר וְיָגֵן וְיוֹשִׁיעַ לְכֹל הַחוֹסִים בּוֹ, וְנֹאמַר אָמֵן. הַכֹּל הָבוּ גֹדֶל לֵאלֹהֵינוּ וּתְנוּ כָבוֹד לַתּוֹרָה.

A כֹּהֵן, if present, is called up to the reading thus:

כֹּהֵן קְרַב, יַעֲמֹד (פלוני בֶּן פלוני) הַכֹּהֵן.

If no כֹּהֵן is present, a לֵוִי or יִשְׂרָאֵל is called up thus:

אֵין כַּאן כֹּהֵן, יַעֲמֹד (פלוני בֶּן פלוני הלוי/ישראל) בִּמְקוֹם כֹּהֵן.

בָּרוּךְ שֶׁנָּתַן תּוֹרָה לְעַמּוֹ יִשְׂרָאֵל בִּקְדֻשָּׁתוֹ.

All:

וְאַתֶּם הַדְּבֵקִים בַּיהוה אֱלֹהֵיכֶם, חַיִּים כֻּלְּכֶם הַיּוֹם.

---

tion will be able to hear the words and make the appropriate responses.

3. After saying "Bless the LORD, the blessed One", the Congregation respond, "Bless the LORD, the blessed One, for ever and all time." The *oleh* repeats this response, then makes the blessing "who has chosen us". There should be no interruption between the blessing and the beginning of the reading.

4. While the portion is being read, the *oleh* should, quietly and inaudibly, say the words along with the reader.

5. When the reading is over, it is a custom to kiss the scroll at the point where the reading ended, and roll it closed. The *oleh* then says the blessing, "who has given us the Torah of truth".

6. It is our custom that the *oleh* remains at the reading desk until the end of the next Torah portion.

עַל הַכֹּל Over all may the name of the Supreme King of kings, the Holy One blessed be He, be magnified and sanctified, praised and glorified, exalted and extolled, in the worlds that He has created – this world and the World to Come – in accordance with His will, and the will of those who fear Him, and the will of the whole house of Israel. He is the Rock of worlds, LORD of all creatures, GOD of all souls, who dwells in the spacious heights and inhabits the high heavens of old. His holiness is over the Chayot and over the throne of glory. Therefore may Your name, LORD our GOD, be sanctified among us in the sight of all that lives. Let us sing before Him a new song, as it is written: "Sing to GOD, chant praises to His name, extol Him who rides the clouds – the LORD is His name – and exult before Him". And may we see Him eye to eye when He returns to His abode as it is written: "For they shall see eye to eye when the LORD returns to Zion". And it is said: "Then will the glory of the LORD be revealed, and all mankind together shall see that the mouth of the LORD has spoken".

אַב הָרַחֲמִים Father of mercy, have compassion on the people always borne by Him. May He remember the covenant with the mighty (patriarchs), and deliver us from evil times. May He reproach the evil instinct in the people borne by Him, and graciously grant that we be an eternal remnant. May He fulfil in good measure our requests for salvation and compassion.

The Torah scroll is placed on the reading desk. The Leader says:

וְיַעֲזוֹר May He help, shield and save all who seek refuge in Him, and let us say, Amen. Let us all render greatness to our GOD and give honour to the Torah.

A Cohen, if present, is called up to the reading thus:

Let the Cohen come forward. Arise (Hebrew name), the Cohen.

If no Cohen is present, a Levi or Yisrael is called up thus:

As there is no Cohen, arise (Hebrew name) in place of a Cohen.

Blessed is He who, in His holiness, gave the Torah to His people Israel.

All:

You who cling to the LORD your GOD are all alive today.

---

7. No conversation should take place while the Torah is being read. No one should leave the synagogue during the reading or the recitation of the blessings.

ASCENT TO THE TORAH

The original custom was that each of those called to the Torah read his own portion. Not everyone was able to do this, so the practice developed of entrusting the reading to one with expertise (commonly, though ungrammatically, known as the *ba'al kore*), "so as not to shame those who do not know how to read" their own portions. Instead, they say the blessings before and after the portion, and recite the text silently along with the Reader.

The Reader shows the עוֹלֶה (the person called to the reading) the section to be read. The עוֹלֶה touches the scroll at that place with the צִיצִית of his טַלִּית, which he then kisses. Bow when saying ברכו את and the first ברוך. Holding the handles of the scroll, he says:

בָּרְכוּ אֶת יהוה הַמְבֹרָךְ.

The Congregation responds:

בָּרוּךְ יהוה הַמְבֹרָךְ לְעוֹלָם וָעֶד.

The עוֹלֶה continues:

בָּרוּךְ יהוה הַמְבֹרָךְ לְעוֹלָם וָעֶד.

בָּרוּךְ אַתָּה יהוה אֱלֹהֵינוּ מֶלֶךְ הָעוֹלָם, אֲשֶׁר־בָּחַר בָּנוּ מִכָּל־הָעַמִּים, וְנָתַן לָנוּ אֶת־תּוֹרָתוֹ. בָּרוּךְ אַתָּה יהוה, נוֹתֵן הַתּוֹרָה.

After the reading, the עוֹלֶה says:

בָּרוּךְ אַתָּה יהוה אֱלֹהֵינוּ מֶלֶךְ הָעוֹלָם, אֲשֶׁר נָתַן־לָנוּ תּוֹרַת־אֱמֶת, וְחַיֵּי עוֹלָם נָטַע בְּתוֹכֵנוּ. בָּרוּךְ אַתָּה יהוה, נוֹתֵן הַתּוֹרָה.

One who has survived a situation of danger (safe arrival after a hazardous journey, release from captivity, or recovery from serious illness) says:

בָּרוּךְ אַתָּה יהוה אֱלֹהֵינוּ מֶלֶךְ הָעוֹלָם, הַגּוֹמֵל לְחַיָּבִים טוֹבוֹת, שֶׁגְּמָלַנִי כָּל־טוֹב.

The Congregation responds:

אָמֵן. מִי שֶׁגְּמָלְךָ כָּל־טוֹב, הוּא יִגְמָלְךָ כָּל־טוֹב, סֶלָה.

בָּרְכוּ *Bless the Lord*: An invitation to the congregation to join in blessing God, similar to the one that precedes communal prayer in the morning and evening services. *Who has chosen us from all peoples* – this ancient blessing, to be said before Torah study as well as before the public reading of the Torah, makes it clear that chosenness is not a right but a responsibility. *Who has given us the Torah of truth* – an act of affirmation following the reading. The blessing, simply but beautifully, expresses the thought that in reading, studying and observing the word of the Eternal, we touch eternity.

הַגּוֹמֵל *Who bestows good on the unworthy*: This blessing, known as *HaGomel* ("who bestows"), is mentioned in the Talmud (*Berachot* 54b). It is to be said after the

The Reader shows the *oleh* (the person called to the Torah) the section to be read. The *oleh* touches the scroll at that place with the *tzitzit* of his *tallit*, which he then kisses. Bow when saying *Bar'chu et* and the first *Baruch*. Holding the handles of the scroll, he says:

Bar'chu et Adonai haM'vorach.

Bless the Lord, the blessed One.

The Congregation responds:

Baruch Adonai haM'vorach le-olam va-ed.

Bless the Lord, the blessed One, for ever and all time.

The *oleh* continues:

Baruch Adonai haM'vorach le-olam va-ed.

Baruch atah Adonai, Eloheinu Melech ha-olam, asher bachar banu mikol ha-amim, venatan lanu et Torato, baruch atah Adonai, noten haTorah.

Bless the Lord, the blessed One, for ever and all time.

Blessed are You, Lord our God, King of the Universe, who has chosen us from all peoples and has given us His Torah. Blessed are You, Lord, Giver of the Torah.

After the reading, the *oleh* says:

Baruch atah Adonai, Eloheinu Melech ha-olam, asher natan lanu Torat emet, v'chayei olam nata b'tochenu, baruch atah Adonai, noten haTorah.

Blessed are You, Lord our God, King of the Universe, who has given us the Torah of truth, planting everlasting life in our midst. Blessed are You, Lord, Giver of the Torah.

One who has survived a situation of danger (safe arrival after a hazardous journey, release from captivity, or recovery from serious illness) says:

Baruch atah Adonai, Eloheinu Melech ha-olam, hagomel l'chayavim tovot, sheg'malani kol tov.

Blessed are You, Lord our God, King of the Universe, who bestows good on the unworthy, who has bestowed on me much good.

The Congregation responds:

Amen. May He who bestowed much good on you
continue to bestow on you much good, Selah.

After a בַּר מִצְוָה has finished the תּוֹרָה blessing, his father says aloud:

בָּרוּךְ שֶׁפְּטָרַנִי מֵעָנְשׁוֹ שֶׁל זֶה.

Special מִי שֶׁבֵּרַךְ and memorial prayers may be said at this point. See page 922.

After קְרִיאַת הַתּוֹרָה, the Leader says חֲצִי קַדִּישׁ.

Leader:

יִתְגַּדַּל וְיִתְקַדַּשׁ שְׁמֵהּ רַבָּא. (Cong. אָמֵן) בְּעָלְמָא דִּי־בְרָא כִרְעוּתֵהּ. וְיַמְלִיךְ מַלְכוּתֵהּ, בְּחַיֵּיכוֹן וּבְיוֹמֵיכוֹן וּבְחַיֵּי דְּכָל־בֵּית יִשְׂרָאֵל, בַּעֲגָלָא וּבִזְמַן קָרִיב. וְאִמְרוּ אָמֵן.

All:

יְהֵא שְׁמֵהּ רַבָּא מְבָרַךְ לְעָלַם וּלְעָלְמֵי עָלְמַיָּא.

Leader:

יִתְבָּרַךְ וְיִשְׁתַּבַּח וְיִתְפָּאַר וְיִתְרוֹמַם וְיִתְנַשֵּׂא וְיִתְהַדָּר וְיִתְעַלֶּה וְיִתְהַלָּל שְׁמֵהּ דְּקֻדְשָׁא בְּרִיךְ הוּא (Cong. בְּרִיךְ הוּא) לְעֵלָּא (On שַׁבַּת שׁוּבָה add לְעֵלָּא) מִן־כָּל־בִּרְכָתָא וְשִׁירָתָא תֻּשְׁבְּחָתָא וְנֶחֱמָתָא, דַּאֲמִירָן בְּעָלְמָא. וְאִמְרוּ אָמֵן. (Cong. אָמֵן)

After the reading, the סֵפֶר תּוֹרָה is lifted, and the Congregation says:

וְזֹאת הַתּוֹרָה אֲשֶׁר־שָׂם מֹשֶׁה לִפְנֵי בְּנֵי יִשְׂרָאֵל, עַל־פִּי יהוה בְּיַד־מֹשֶׁה.

When the סֵפֶר תּוֹרָה has been tied and covered, the person about to read the הַפְטָרָה says:

בָּרוּךְ אַתָּה יהוה אֱלֹהֵינוּ מֶלֶךְ הָעוֹלָם, אֲשֶׁר בָּחַר בִּנְבִיאִים טוֹבִים, וְרָצָה בְדִבְרֵיהֶם הַנֶּאֱמָרִים בֶּאֱמֶת, בָּרוּךְ אַתָּה יהוה, הַבּוֹחֵר בַּתּוֹרָה וּבְמֹשֶׁה עַבְדּוֹ, וּבְיִשְׂרָאֵל עַמּוֹ, וּבִנְבִיאֵי הָאֱמֶת וָצֶדֶק.

---

following four circumstances: 1. release from captivity; 2. recovery from a potentially life-threatening illness; 3. a dangerous journey; and 4. a sea-crossing (nowadays, many also say it after an air flight). It is said in the presence of a *minyan* (at least ten adult males), usually, though not necessarily, at the time of the reading of

After a *Bar Mitzvah* boy has finished the Torah blessing, his father says aloud:

Blessed is He who has released me from the responsibility for this boy.

Special blessings and memorial prayers may be said at this point. See page 922.

After the Torah reading, the Leader says half-*Kaddish*.

Leader:

יִתְגַּדַּל Magnified and sanctified may His great name be, in the world He created by His will. May He establish His kingdom in your lifetime and in your days, and in the lifetime of all the House of Israel, swiftly and soon – and say: Amen.

All:

May His great name be blessed for ever and all time.

Leader:

Blessed and praised, glorified and exalted, raised and honoured, uplifted and lauded be the name of the Holy One, blessed be He, (between Rosh Hashanah and Yom Kippur add 'well') beyond any blessing, song, praise and consolation uttered in the world – and say: Amen.

After the reading, the Torah scroll is lifted, and the Congregation says:

וְזֹאת This is the Torah that Moses placed before the children of Israel, at the LORD's commandment, by the hand of Moses.

When the Torah scroll has been tied and covered, the person about to read the *Haftarah* says:

בָּרוּךְ Blessed are You, LORD our GOD, King of the Universe, who chose good prophets and was pleased with their words, spoken in truth. Blessed are You, LORD, who chose the Torah, His servant Moses, His people Israel, and the prophets of truth and righteousness.

---

the Torah, and within three days of the event. *Who bestows good on the unworthy* – reminiscent of Jacob's prayer (Genesis 32:11), "I am unworthy of all the kindness and faithfulness You have shown Your servant".

בָּרוּךְ שֶׁפְּטָרַנִי *Who has released me from the responsibility for this child*: Until a boy reaches the age of thirteen (twelve for girls), the parents are responsible for his or her deeds. This blessing expresses the parents' gratitude for having lived to see their child reach the age of responsibility.

וְזֹאת הַתּוֹרָה *This is the Torah.* The raising (*hagbahah*) and rolling (*gelilah*) of the Torah – ancient customs regarded as

After the הַפְטָרָה, its Reader says the following blessings:

בָּרוּךְ אַתָּה יהוה אֱלֹהֵינוּ מֶלֶךְ הָעוֹלָם, צוּר כָּל־הָעוֹלָמִים, צַדִּיק בְּכָל־הַדּוֹרוֹת, הָאֵל הַנֶּאֱמָן הָאוֹמֵר וְעוֹשֶׂה, הַמְדַבֵּר וּמְקַיֵּם, שֶׁכָּל־דְּבָרָיו אֱמֶת וָצֶדֶק. נֶאֱמָן אַתָּה הוּא יהוה אֱלֹהֵינוּ, וְנֶאֱמָנִים דְּבָרֶיךָ, וְדָבָר אֶחָד מִדְּבָרֶיךָ אָחוֹר לֹא־יָשׁוּב רֵיקָם, כִּי אֵל מֶלֶךְ נֶאֱמָן וְרַחֲמָן אָתָּה. בָּרוּךְ אַתָּה יהוה. הָאֵל הַנֶּאֱמָן בְּכָל־דְּבָרָיו.

רַחֵם עַל־צִיּוֹן כִּי הִיא בֵּית חַיֵּינוּ, וְלַעֲלוּבַת נֶפֶשׁ תּוֹשִׁיעַ בִּמְהֵרָה בְיָמֵינוּ. בָּרוּךְ אַתָּה יהוה, מְשַׂמֵּחַ צִיּוֹן בְּבָנֶיהָ.

שַׂמְּחֵנוּ יהוה אֱלֹהֵינוּ בְּאֵלִיָּהוּ הַנָּבִיא עַבְדֶּךָ, וּבְמַלְכוּת בֵּית דָּוִד מְשִׁיחֶךָ, בִּמְהֵרָה יָבֹא וְיָגֵל לִבֵּנוּ, עַל־כִּסְאוֹ לֹא־יֵשֶׁב זָר וְלֹא יִנְחֲלוּ עוֹד אֲחֵרִים אֶת־כְּבוֹדוֹ, כִּי בְשֵׁם קָדְשְׁךָ נִשְׁבַּעְתָּ לּוֹ, שֶׁלֹּא יִכְבֶּה נֵרוֹ לְעוֹלָם וָעֶד. בָּרוּךְ אַתָּה יהוה, מָגֵן דָּוִד.

On שַׁבָּת, including שַׁבַּת חוֹל הַמּוֹעֵד פֶּסַח, say:

עַל־הַתּוֹרָה, וְעַל־הָעֲבוֹדָה, וְעַל־הַנְּבִיאִים, וְעַל־יוֹם הַשַּׁבָּת הַזֶּה, שֶׁנָּתַתָּ־לָּנוּ יהוה אֱלֹהֵינוּ, לִקְדֻשָּׁה וְלִמְנוּחָה, לְכָבוֹד וּלְתִפְאָרֶת. עַל־הַכֹּל יהוה אֱלֹהֵינוּ, אֲנַחְנוּ מוֹדִים לָךְ, וּמְבָרְכִים אוֹתָךְ, יִתְבָּרַךְ שִׁמְךָ בְּפִי כָּל־חַי תָּמִיד לְעוֹלָם וָעֶד. בָּרוּךְ אַתָּה יהוה, מְקַדֵּשׁ הַשַּׁבָּת.

---

high honours are accompanied by a reaffirmation of the holiness of the Torah as God's word, "at the Lord's commandment, by the hand of Moses" (the declaration is an amalgam of Deuteronomy 4:44 and Numbers 9:23).

THE HAFTARAH

The reading of a passage from the prophetic works (the second of the three parts of Tanach) dates back, in origin, to the period of the Second Temple. The word *haftarah* means "conclusion" of the

After the *Haftarah*, its Reader says the following blessings:

בָּרוּךְ Blessed are You, LORD our GOD, King of the Universe, Rock of all worlds, righteous for all generations, the faithful GOD who says and does, speaks and fulfils, all of whose words are truth and righteousness. You are faithful, LORD our GOD, and faithful are Your words, not one of which returns unfulfilled, for You, GOD, are a faithful and compassionate King. Blessed are You, LORD, faithful in all His words.

רַחֵם Have compassion on Zion for it is the source of our life, and save the one grieved in spirit swiftly in our days. Blessed are You, LORD, who makes Zion rejoice in her children.

שַׂמְּחֵנוּ Grant us joy, LORD our GOD, through Elijah the prophet Your servant, and through the kingdom of the house of David Your anointed – may he soon come and make our hearts glad. May no stranger sit on his throne, and may others not continue to inherit his glory, for You promised him by Your holy name that his light would never be extinguished. Blessed are You, LORD, Shield of David.

On Shabbat, including the Intermediate Shabbat of Pesach, say:

עַל־הַתּוֹרָה For the Torah, for Divine worship, for the prophets, and for this Sabbath day which You, LORD our GOD, have given us for holiness and rest, honour and glory – for all these we thank and bless You, LORD our GOD, and may Your name be blessed by the mouth of all that lives, continually, for ever and all time. Blessed are You, LORD, who sanctifies the Sabbath.

Torah reading. The person who reads the *haftarah* is first called to the Torah (*maftir* – a re-reading of the last verses of the weekly Torah portion) to emphasise the connection between the Mosaic and prophetic books. The *haftarah* is usually connected, verbally or thematically, with the Torah reading. Some *haftarot*, however, are related to the time of the year, such as the readings for the New Moon when it falls on a Shabbat, or before and after the Tishah B'Av. The blessing before the reading emphasises our faith in the truth of the words of the prophets. The four blessings afterwards speak of: 1. our faith in GOD's promises, through the prophets; 2. our hope for the restoration of Zion; 3. a prayer for the return of the Davidic monarchy (there are traces here of a polemic against rival claims to sovereignty, such as that of the Hasmonean kings of the Second Temple period, who were not from the house of David); and 4. a hymn of praise to the day: Shabbat or Festival.

On יוֹם טוֹב and on שַׁבַּת חוֹל הַמּוֹעֵד סֻכּוֹת, say (adding on שַׁבָּת the words in brackets):

עַל־הַתּוֹרָה, וְעַל־הָעֲבוֹדָה, וְעַל־הַנְּבִיאִים, וְעַל־יוֹם (הַשַּׁבָּת הַזֶּה וְעַל־יוֹם)

On פֶּסַח:	On שָׁבוּעוֹת:	On סֻכּוֹת:	On שְׁמִינִי עֲצֶרֶת and שִׂמְחַת תּוֹרָה:
חַג הַמַּצּוֹת	חַג הַשָּׁבוּעוֹת	חַג הַסֻּכּוֹת	הַשְּׁמִינִי חַג הָעֲצֶרֶת

הַזֶּה, שֶׁנָּתַתָּ לָּנוּ יהוה אֱלֹהֵינוּ, (לִקְדֻשָּׁה וְלִמְנוּחָה) לְשָׂשׂוֹן וּלְשִׂמְחָה, לְכָבוֹד וּלְתִפְאָרֶת. עַל־הַכֹּל יהוה אֱלֹהֵינוּ, אֲנַחְנוּ מוֹדִים לָךְ, וּמְבָרְכִים אוֹתָךְ, יִתְבָּרַךְ שִׁמְךָ בְּפִי כָּל־חַי תָּמִיד לְעוֹלָם וָעֶד. בָּרוּךְ אַתָּה, יהוה. מְקַדֵּשׁ (הַשַּׁבָּת וְ) יִשְׂרָאֵל וְהַזְּמַנִּים.

The following three paragraphs are not said on a יוֹם טוֹב occurring on a weekday:

יְקוּם פֻּרְקָן מִן־שְׁמַיָּא, חִנָּא וְחִסְדָּא וְרַחֲמֵי, וְחַיֵּי אֲרִיכֵי, וּמְזוֹנֵי רְוִיחֵי, וְסִיַּעְתָּא דִי־שְׁמַיָּא, וּבַרְיוּת גּוּפָא, וּנְהוֹרָא מַעַלְיָא, זַרְעָא חַיָּא וְקַיָּמָא, זַרְעָא דִּי לָא־יִפְסֻק וְדִי לָא־יִבְטֻל מִפִּתְגָּמֵי אוֹרַיְתָא. לְמָרָנָן וְרַבָּנָן חֲבוּרָתָא קַדִּישָׁתָא דִּי בְּאַרְעָא דְיִ־יִשְׂרָאֵל דִּי בְּבָבֶל, וְדִי בְּכָל אַרְעָת גָּלְוָתָנָא, לְרֵישֵׁי כַלֵּי, וּלְרֵישֵׁי גָלְוָתָא וּלְרֵישֵׁי מְתִיבָתָא, וּלְדַיָּנֵי דִי־בָבָא, לְכָל־תַּלְמִידֵיהוֹן, וּלְכָל־תַּלְמִידֵי תַלְמִידֵיהוֹן, וּלְכָל־מָן דִּי עָסְקִין בְּאוֹרַיְתָא. מַלְכָּא דִי עָלְמָא יְבָרֵךְ יָתְהוֹן, יַפִּישׁ חַיֵּיהוֹן, וְיַסְגֵּא יוֹמֵיהוֹן, וְיִתֵּן אַרְכָה לִשְׁנֵיהוֹן, וְיִתְפָּרְקוּן וְיִשְׁתֵּזְבוּן מִן כָּל־עָקָא וּמִן כָּל־מַרְעִין בִּישִׁין. ← מָרָן דִּי בִשְׁמַיָּא יְהֵא בְסַעְדְּהוֹן, כָּל־זְמַן וְעִדָּן. וְנֹאמַר אָמֵן.

Special Prayers: A series of five prayers for leaders and leadership of various kinds: 1. the religious and lay leaders of Babylonian Jewry; 2. and by extension those of other communities; and 3. those who work for the benefit of the community; 4. the Head of State and government; and 5. the State of Israel. As Lord Jakobovits pointed out, they date from different centuries and places of origin,

On a Festival and on the Intermediate Shabbat of Sukkot, say (adding on Shabbat the words in brackets):

For the Torah, for Divine worship, for the prophets, (for this Sabbath day) and for this day of

On Pesach, say:	On Shavuot, say:	On Sukkot, say:	On Shmini Atzeret and Simchat Torah, say:
the Festival of Matzot	the Festival of Shavuot	the Festival of Sukkot	the Festival of Shmini Atzeret

which You, LORD our GOD, have given Us (for holiness and rest,) for joy and gladness, honour and glory – for all these we thank and bless You, LORD our GOD, and may Your name be blessed by the mouth of all that lives, continually, for ever and all time. Blessed are You, LORD, who sanctifies (the Sabbath,) Israel and the festivals.

The following three paragraphs are not said on Festivals occurring on a weekday:

יְקוּם פֻּרְקָן May deliverance arise from heaven, bringing grace, love and compassion, long life, ample sustenance and heavenly help, physical health and enlightenment of mind, living and thriving children who will neither interrupt nor cease from the words of the Torah – to our masters and teachers of the holy communities in the land of Israel, Babylon and all the lands of our dispersion; to the leaders of assemblies and the leaders of communities in exile; to the heads of academies and to the judges in the gates; to all their disciples and their disciples' disciples, and to all who occupy themselves in study of the Torah. May the King of the Universe bless them, prolonging their lives, increasing their days, and adding to their years. May they be redeemed and delivered from all distress and illness. ✦ May our Master in heaven be their help at all times and seasons; and let us say, Amen.

---

they use three languages, Aramaic, Hebrew and the vernacular, and thus "mirror more faithfully than any other part of the Siddur the diversity and versatility of the Jewish experience".

יְקוּם פֻּרְקָן *May deliverance arise:* A prayer for the religious and lay leadership of Babylonian Jewry, dating from a period – the Talmudic and Gaonic eras – when it was a major centre of Jewish life. The phrase "and all the lands of our dispersion" was added to make the prayer relevant to other centres. The next two blessings – one in Aramaic and based on the previous prayer, the other in Hebrew – are for all those who work for and sustain the congregation.

The following two paragraphs are said only when praying with a מִנְיָן:

יְקוּם פֻּרְקָן מִן־שְׁמַיָּא, חִנָּא וְחִסְדָּא וְרַחֲמֵי, וְחַיֵּי אֲרִיכֵי, וּמְזוֹנֵי רְוִיחֵי, וְסִיַּעְתָּא דִי־שְׁמַיָּא, וּבַרְיוּת גּוּפָא, וּנְהוֹרָא מַעַלְיָא, זַרְעָא חַיָּא וְקַיָּמָא, זַרְעָא דִי לָא־יִפְסֻק וְדִי לָא־יִבְטֻל מִפִּתְגָּמֵי אוֹרַיְתָא. לְכָל־קְהָלָא קַדִּישָׁא הָדֵין, רַבְרְבַיָּא עִם זְעֵרַיָּא, טַפְלָא וּנְשַׁיָּא, מַלְכָּא דִי עָלְמָא יְבָרֵךְ יָתְכוֹן, יַפִּישׁ חַיֵּיכוֹן, וְיַסְגֵּא יוֹמֵיכוֹן, וְיִתֵּן אַרְכָא לִשְׁנֵיכוֹן, וְתִתְפָּרְקוּן וְתִשְׁתֵּיזְבוּן מִן כָּל־עָקָא וּמִן כָּל־מַרְעִין בִּישִׁין. ◂ מָרָן דִּי בִשְׁמַיָּא יְהֵא בְסַעְדְּכוֹן, כָּל־זְמַן וְעִדָּן. וְנֹאמַר אָמֵן.

מִי שֶׁבֵּרַךְ אֲבוֹתֵינוּ אַבְרָהָם יִצְחָק וְיַעֲקֹב, הוּא יְבָרֵךְ אֶת־כָּל־הַקָּהָל הַקָּדוֹשׁ הַזֶּה, עִם כָּל־קְהִלּוֹת הַקֹּדֶשׁ, הֵם, וּנְשֵׁיהֶם, וּבְנֵיהֶם, וּבְנוֹתֵיהֶם, וְכָל אֲשֶׁר לָהֶם. וּמִי שֶׁמְּיַחֲדִים בָּתֵּי כְנֵסִיּוֹת לִתְפִלָּה, וּמִי שֶׁבָּאִים בְּתוֹכָם לְהִתְפַּלֵּל, וּמִי שֶׁנּוֹתְנִים נֵר לַמָּאוֹר, וְיַיִן לְקִדּוּשׁ וּלְהַבְדָּלָה, וּפַת לָאוֹרְחִים, וּצְדָקָה לָעֲנִיִּים, ◂ וְכָל־מִי שֶׁעוֹסְקִים בְּצָרְכֵי צִבּוּר בֶּאֱמוּנָה, הַקָּדוֹשׁ בָּרוּךְ הוּא יְשַׁלֵּם שְׂכָרָם, וְיָסִיר מֵהֶם כָּל־מַחֲלָה, וְיִרְפָּא לְכָל־גּוּפָם, וְיִסְלַח לְכָל־עֲוֹנָם, וְיִשְׁלַח בְּרָכָה וְהַצְלָחָה בְּכָל־מַעֲשֵׂה יְדֵיהֶם, עִם כָּל־יִשְׂרָאֵל אֲחֵיהֶם. וְנֹאמַר אָמֵן.

תפלה לשלום המלכות

The סֵפֶר תּוֹרָה is held while the following two prayers are said. All stand.

הַנּוֹתֵן תְּשׁוּעָה לַמְּלָכִים וּמֶמְשָׁלָה לַנְּסִיכִים, מַלְכוּתוֹ מַלְכוּת כָּל־עוֹלָמִים. הוּא יְבָרֵךְ

OUR SOVEREIGN LORD, KING CHARLES,
OUR GRACIOUS QUEEN CONSORT CAMILLA,
THE PRINCE AND PRINCESS OF WALES,*
AND ALL THE ROYAL FAMILY.

*In Scotland, say the Duke and Duchess of Rothesay

The following two paragraphs are said only when praying with a *minyan*:

יְקוּם פֻּרְקָן May deliverance arise from heaven, bringing grace, love and compassion, long life, ample sustenance and heavenly help, physical health and enlightenment of mind, living and thriving children who will neither interrupt nor cease from the words of the Torah – to all this holy congregation, great and small, women and children. May the King of the Universe bless you, prolonging your lives, increasing your days, and adding to your years. May you be redeemed and delivered from all distress and illness. ➔ May our Master in heaven be your help at all times and seasons; and let us say, Amen.

מִי שֶׁבֵּרַךְ May He who blessed our fathers, Abraham, Isaac and Jacob, bless all this holy congregation, together with all other holy congregations: them and all that is theirs. May He bless those who unite to form synagogues for prayer and those who come there to pray; those who provide lamps for light and wine for *Kiddush* and *Havdalah*, food for visitors and charity for the poor, ➔ and all who faithfully occupy themselves with the needs of the community. May the Holy One, blessed be He, give them their reward; may He remove from them all illness, grant them complete healing, and forgive all their sins. May He send blessing and success to all the work of their hands, together with all Israel their brethren; and let us say, Amen.

PRAYER FOR THE ROYAL FAMILY

The Torah scroll is held while the following two prayers are said. All stand.

הַנּוֹתֵן He who gives salvation to kings and dominion to princes, whose kingdom is an everlasting kingdom – may He bless

OUR SOVEREIGN LORD, KING CHARLES,
OUR GRACIOUS QUEEN CONSORT CAMILLA,
THE PRINCE AND PRINCESS OF WALES,*
AND ALL THE ROYAL FAMILY.

*In Scotland, say the Duke and Duchess of Rothesay

PRAYER FOR THE ROYAL FAMILY
This prayer echoes the instruction of Jeremiah (29:7) to those dispersed at the time of the Babylonian exile (sixth century BCE): "Seek the peace of the city to which I have carried you in exile. Pray to

מֶלֶךְ מַלְכֵי הַמְּלָכִים בְּרַחֲמָיו, יְחַיֵּיהוּ, וְיִשְׁמְרֵהוּ, וּמִכָּל־צָרָה וְיָגוֹן יַצִּילֵהוּ. וִיבָרֵךְ וְיִשְׁמֹר אֶת צְבָא הַמֶּלֶךְ. וְיִתֵּן בְּלִבּוֹ וּבְלֵב כָּל־יוֹעֲצָיו, רוּחַ חָכְמָה וּבִינָה, לְהַחֲזִיק שְׁלוֹם הַמַּלְכוּת, וְשַׁלְוַת עַמּוֹ, וְלַעֲשׂוֹת חֶסֶד וֶאֱמֶת עִם־כָּל־יִשְׂרָאֵל. בְּיָמָיו, וּבְיָמֵינוּ, יִפְרֹשׂ אָבִינוּ שֶׁבַּשָּׁמַיִם סֻכַּת שָׁלוֹם עַל־כָּל־יוֹשְׁבֵי תֵבֵל, וּבָא לְצִיּוֹן גּוֹאֵל. וְנֹאמַר אָמֵן.

תפלה לשלום מדינת ישראל וחיילי צה"ל

מִי שֶׁבֵּרַךְ אֲבוֹתֵינוּ אַבְרָהָם יִצְחָק וְיַעֲקֹב, הוּא יְבָרֵךְ אֶת־מְדִינַת יִשְׂרָאֵל, רָאשֶׁיהָ, וְיוֹעֲצֶיהָ, עַל הָאֲדָמָה אֲשֶׁר נִשְׁבַּע לַאֲבוֹתֵינוּ לָתֵת לָנוּ. תֵּן בְּלִבָּם אַהֲבָתְךָ, וְיִרְאָתְךָ, לְסַעֲדָהּ בְּמִשְׁפָּט וּבִצְדָקָה, וְנִזְכֶּה בְּיָמֵינוּ לְדִבְרֵי עֲבָדֶיךָ הַנְּבִיאִים, כִּי מִצִּיּוֹן תֵּצֵא תוֹרָה, וּדְבַר יהוה מִירוּשָׁלָיִם. אָבִינוּ שֶׁבַּשָּׁמַיִם, פְּקוֹד נָא אֶת חַיָּלֵי צְבָא הַהֲגָנָּה לְיִשְׂרָאֵל וְאַנְשֵׁי כּוֹחוֹת הַבִּטָּחוֹן מְגִנֵּי אֶרֶץ קָדְשֵׁנוּ, שָׁמְרֵם מִכָּל־צָרָה וְצוּקָה, וּשְׁלַח בְּרָכָה, וְהַצְלָחָה, בְּכָל־מַעֲשֵׂה יְדֵיהֶם. שִׂים שָׁלוֹם בָּאָרֶץ, וְשִׂמְחַת עוֹלָם עַל־כָּל־יוֹשְׁבֶיהָ, וְשָׁב יַעֲקֹב וְשָׁקַט וְשַׁאֲנַן וְאֵין מַחֲרִיד. וּפְרוֹשׂ סֻכַּת שְׁלוֹמְךָ עַל־כָּל־יוֹשְׁבֵי תֵבֵל אַרְצֶךָ, וְכֵן יְהִי רָצוֹן. וְנֹאמַר אָמֵן.

---

the Lord for it, because in its peace, you shall find peace." In the first century CE, Rabbi Chanina, the deputy High Priest, taught: "Pray for the welfare of the government, for were it not for fear of it, people would swallow one another alive" (*Avot* 3:2). In the third century CE, Mar Samuel of Nahardea ruled that "The law of the land is law". Loyalty to country, its Head of State, government and laws is fundamental to Judaism, as is active citizenship and contribution to the common good.

מִי שֶׁבֵּרַךְ *Prayer for the State of Israel*: Introduced after the birth of the modern State of Israel in 1948. The words, "For out of Zion shall go forth the Law", re-

May the supreme King of kings in His mercy preserve the King in life, guard him and deliver him from all trouble and sorrow. May He bless and protect his Majesty's Armed Forces. May He put a spirit of wisdom and understanding into his heart and into the hearts of all his counsellors, that they may uphold the peace of the realm, advance the welfare of the nation, and deal kindly and justly with all the House of Israel. In his days and in ours may our Heavenly Father spread the tabernacle of peace over all the dwellers on earth; and may the redeemer come to Zion; and let us say Amen.

PRAYER FOR THE WELFARE OF THE STATE OF ISRAEL AND ITS DEFENCE FORCES

מִי שֶׁבֵּרַךְ May He who blessed our fathers, Abraham, Isaac and Jacob, bless the State of Israel, its leaders and advisors in the land which He swore unto our fathers to give us. Put into their hearts the love and fear of You to uphold it with justice and righteousness, and may we be worthy in our days to witness the fulfilment of the words of Your servants, the prophets: "For out of Zion shall go forth the Law and the word of the Lord from Jerusalem". Heavenly Father: Remember the Israel Defence Forces, and all security personnel, guardians of our Holy Land. Protect them from all distress and anguish, and send blessing and success to all the work of their hands. Grant peace in Your Holy land and everlasting happiness to all its inhabitants, so that Jacob shall again have peace and tranquillity, with none to make him afraid. Spread the tabernacle of Your peace over all the dwellers on earth. May this be Your will; and let us say, Amen.

---

mind us of those that follow in the next verse in the book of Isaiah: "He will judge between the nations and will settle disputes for many peoples. They will beat their swords into ploughshares and their spears into pruning hooks. Nation will not take up sword against nation, nor will they train for war any more" (Isaiah 2:4). The prophets of Israel were the first in history to see peace as an ideal, and uppermost in our prayers for Israel is the hope for peace.

ברכת החודש

On the שַׁבָּת before רֹאשׁ חֹדֶשׁ, the following is said by the Congregation, and repeated by the Leader:

יְהִי רָצוֹן מִלְּפָנֶיךָ, יהוה אֱלֹהֵינוּ וֵאלֹהֵי אֲבוֹתֵינוּ, שֶׁתְּחַדֵּשׁ עָלֵינוּ אֶת־הַחֹדֶשׁ הַזֶּה לְטוֹבָה וְלִבְרָכָה. וְתִתֶּן־לָנוּ חַיִּים אֲרֻכִּים, חַיִּים שֶׁל־שָׁלוֹם, חַיִּים שֶׁל־טוֹבָה, חַיִּים שֶׁל־בְּרָכָה, חַיִּים שֶׁל־פַּרְנָסָה, חַיִּים שֶׁל־חִלּוּץ עֲצָמוֹת, חַיִּים שֶׁיֵּשׁ בָּהֶם יִרְאַת שָׁמַיִם וְיִרְאַת חֵטְא, חַיִּים שֶׁאֵין בָּהֶם בּוּשָׁה וּכְלִמָּה, חַיִּים שֶׁל־עֹשֶׁר וְכָבוֹד, חַיִּים שֶׁתְּהֵא בָנוּ אַהֲבַת תּוֹרָה וְיִרְאַת שָׁמַיִם, חַיִּים שֶׁיְּמָּלְאוּ מִשְׁאֲלוֹת לִבֵּנוּ לְטוֹבָה. אָמֵן, סֶלָה.

Leader holding the ספר תורה says:

מִי שֶׁעָשָׂה נִסִּים לַאֲבוֹתֵינוּ, וְגָאַל אוֹתָם מֵעַבְדוּת לְחֵרוּת, הוּא יִגְאַל אוֹתָנוּ בְּקָרוֹב, וִיקַבֵּץ נִדָּחֵינוּ מֵאַרְבַּע כַּנְפוֹת הָאָרֶץ, חֲבֵרִים כָּל־יִשְׂרָאֵל. וְנֹאמַר אָמֵן.

Leader, then Congregation (A list of Hebrew days and months in on page 1053.):

רֹאשׁ חֹדֶשׁ (the Hebrew month) יִהְיֶה בַּיּוֹם (the Hebrew day/s) הַבָּא עָלֵינוּ וְעַל כָּל־יִשְׂרָאֵל לְטוֹבָה.

Congregation respond, then Leader repeats::

יְחַדְּשֵׁהוּ הַקָּדוֹשׁ בָּרוּךְ הוּא עָלֵינוּ וְעַל כָּל־עַמּוֹ בֵּית יִשְׂרָאֵל, לְחַיִּים וּלְשָׁלוֹם, לְשָׂשׂוֹן וּלְשִׂמְחָה, לִישׁוּעָה וּלְנֶחָמָה. וְנֹאמַר אָמֵן.

BLESSING OF THE NEW MOON
Originally the New Moon was determined by the *Sanhedrin* on the basis of eye-witness testimony. Since this could not be precisely predicted in advance, the decision of the court had to be communicated to the Jewish communities in Israel and elsewhere. At first

BLESSING THE NEW MONTH

On the Shabbat before Rosh Chodesh, the following is said by the Congregation, and repeated by the Leader:

יְהִי רָצוֹן May it be Your will, LORD our GOD and GOD of our fathers, to renew for us this coming month for good and blessing. Grant us long life, a life of peace, a life of goodness, a life of blessing, a life of sustenance, a life of physical health, a life marked by reverence for heaven and dread of sin, a life without shame or disgrace, a life of wealth and honour, a life in which we have love for the Torah and reverence for heaven, a life in which our heart's desires are fulfilled for good. Amen, Selah.

Leader holding the Sefer Torah says:

מִי שֶׁעָשָׂה May He who performed miracles for our ancestors and redeemed them from slavery to freedom, redeem us soon, and gather in our dispersed people from the four quarters of the earth, so that all Israel may be united in friendship, and let us say, Amen.

Leader, then Congregation (A list of Hebrew days and months is on page 1053):

The new month of (the Hebrew month) will occur on (the Hebrew day/s). May it come to us and all Israel for good.

Congregation respond, then Leader repeats:

May the Holy One, blessed be He, renew this new month for us and for all His people, the house of Israel, for life and peace, gladness and joy, salvation and consolation; and let us say, Amen.

---

this was done by lighting fire signals on hill-tops. Later it was done by messengers, and in the fourth century, when much of the Jewish population had been forced to leave Israel, Hillel II ordained that the new moon be determined by astronomical calculation. Our ceremony, though of a later date, recalls the earlier custom.

יְהִי רָצוֹן *May it be Your will*: A prayer based on the meditation of the third-century scholar, Rav. *So that all Israel may be united in friendship* – a beautiful phrase derived from the rabbinic interpretation of Psalm 122:3, "Jerusalem built as a city joined together", as "a city that turns all Israel into friends" (*Yerushalmi Chagigah* 3:6).

Many congregations say the following only on the שַׁבָּת before שָׁבוּעוֹת and the שַׁבָּת before תִּשְׁעָה בְּאָב:

אַב הָרַחֲמִים, שׁוֹכֵן מְרוֹמִים, בְּרַחֲמָיו הָעֲצוּמִים הוּא יִפְקוֹד בְּרַחֲמִים, הַחֲסִידִים וְהַיְשָׁרִים וְהַתְּמִימִים, קְהִלּוֹת הַקֹּדֶשׁ שֶׁמָּסְרוּ נַפְשָׁם עַל קְדֻשַּׁת הַשֵּׁם, הַנֶּאֱהָבִים וְהַנְּעִימִים בְּחַיֵּיהֶם, וּבְמוֹתָם לֹא נִפְרָדוּ. מִנְּשָׁרִים קַלּוּ, וּמֵאֲרָיוֹת גָּבֵרוּ, לַעֲשׂוֹת רְצוֹן קוֹנָם וְחֵפֶץ צוּרָם. יִזְכְּרֵם אֱלֹהֵינוּ לְטוֹבָה, עִם שְׁאָר צַדִּיקֵי עוֹלָם, וְיִנְקוֹם נִקְמַת דַּם עֲבָדָיו הַשָּׁפוּךְ, כַּכָּתוּב בְּתוֹרַת מֹשֶׁה אִישׁ הָאֱלֹהִים, הַרְנִינוּ גוֹיִם עַמּוֹ כִּי דַם־עֲבָדָיו יִקּוֹם, וְנָקָם יָשִׁיב לְצָרָיו, וְכִפֶּר אַדְמָתוֹ עַמּוֹ. וְעַל יְדֵי עֲבָדֶיךָ הַנְּבִיאִים כָּתוּב לֵאמֹר, וְנִקֵּיתִי דָּמָם לֹא נִקֵּיתִי, וַיהוה שֹׁכֵן בְּצִיּוֹן. וּבְכִתְבֵי הַקֹּדֶשׁ נֶאֱמַר, לָמָּה יֹאמְרוּ הַגּוֹיִם, אַיֵּה אֱלֹהֵיהֶם, יִוָּדַע בַּגּוֹיִם לְעֵינֵינוּ, נִקְמַת דַּם עֲבָדֶיךָ הַשָּׁפוּךְ. ‹ וְאוֹמֵר, כִּי דֹרֵשׁ דָּמִים אוֹתָם זָכָר, לֹא שָׁכַח צַעֲקַת עֲנָוִים. וְאוֹמֵר, יָדִין בַּגּוֹיִם מָלֵא גְוִיּוֹת, מָחַץ רֹאשׁ עַל אֶרֶץ רַבָּה. מִנַּחַל בַּדֶּרֶךְ יִשְׁתֶּה, עַל־כֵּן יָרִים רֹאשׁ.

אשרי

אַשְׁרֵי יוֹשְׁבֵי בֵיתֶךָ, עוֹד יְהַלְלוּךָ סֶּלָה.
אַשְׁרֵי הָעָם שֶׁכָּכָה לּוֹ, אַשְׁרֵי הָעָם שֶׁיהוה אֱלֹהָיו.

תהלים קמה

תְּהִלָּה לְדָוִד,

אֲרוֹמִמְךָ אֱלוֹהַי הַמֶּלֶךְ, וַאֲבָרְכָה שִׁמְךָ לְעוֹלָם וָעֶד.
בְּכָל יוֹם אֲבָרְכֶךָּ, וַאֲהַלְלָה שִׁמְךָ לְעוֹלָם וָעֶד.
גָּדוֹל יהוה וּמְהֻלָּל מְאֹד, וְלִגְדֻלָּתוֹ אֵין חֵקֶר.
דּוֹר לְדוֹר יְשַׁבַּח מַעֲשֶׂיךָ, וּגְבוּרֹתֶיךָ יַגִּידוּ.
הֲדַר כְּבוֹד הוֹדֶךָ, וְדִבְרֵי נִפְלְאֹתֶיךָ אָשִׂיחָה.

אַב הָרַחֲמִים *Father of compassion*: A prayer, written in profound grief, dating from one of the darkest moments in medieval Jewish history, the massacre of Jews during the First Crusade (1096–99). It came to serve also for the victims of

Many congregations say the following only on the Shabbat before Shavuot and the Shabbat before the Ninth of Av:

אַב הָרַחֲמִים Father of compassion, who dwells on high: may He remember in His compassion the pious, the upright and the blameless – holy communities who sacrificed their lives for the sanctification of God's name. Lovely and pleasant in their lives, in death they were not parted. They were swifter than eagles and stronger than lions to do the will of their Maker and the desire of their Creator. O our God, remember them for good with the other righteous of the world, and may He exact retribution for the shed blood of His servants, as it is written in the Torah of Moses, the man of God: "O nations, acclaim His people, for He will avenge the blood of His servants, wreak vengeance on His foes, and make clean His people's land". And by Your servants, the prophets, it is written: "I shall cleanse their blood which I have not yet cleansed, says the Lord who dwells in Zion". And in the Holy Writings it says: "Why should the nations say: Where is their God? Before our eyes, may those nations know that You avenge the shed blood of Your servants". ➔ And it also says: "For the Avenger of blood remembers them and does not forget the cry of the afflicted". And it further says: "He will execute judgement among the nations, heaping up the dead, crushing rulers far and wide. From the brook by the wayside he will drink, then he will hold his head high".

ASHREI

אַשְׁרֵי Happy are those who dwell in Your House;
they shall continue to praise You, Selah!
Happy are the people for whom this is so;
happy are the people whose God is the Lord.

PSALM 145

A song of praise by David.

I will exalt You, my God, the King,
and bless Your name for ever and all time.
Every day I will bless You,
and praise Your name for ever and all time.
God is great and greatly to be praised;
His greatness is unfathomable.
One generation will praise Your works to the next,
and tell of Your mighty deeds.
On the glorious splendour of Your majesty I will meditate,
and on the acts of Your wonders.

וֶעֱזוּז נוֹרְאוֹתֶיךָ יֹאמֵרוּ, וּגְדֻלָּתְךָ אֲסַפְּרֶנָּה.
זֵכֶר רַב־טוּבְךָ יַבִּיעוּ, וְצִדְקָתְךָ יְרַנֵּנוּ.
חַנּוּן וְרַחוּם יהוה, אֶרֶךְ אַפַּיִם וּגְדָל־חָסֶד.
טוֹב יהוה לַכֹּל, וְרַחֲמָיו עַל כָּל מַעֲשָׂיו.
יוֹדוּךָ יהוה כָּל מַעֲשֶׂיךָ, וַחֲסִידֶיךָ יְבָרְכוּכָה.
כְּבוֹד מַלְכוּתְךָ יֹאמֵרוּ, וּגְבוּרָתְךָ יְדַבֵּרוּ.
לְהוֹדִיעַ לִבְנֵי הָאָדָם גְּבוּרֹתָיו, וּכְבוֹד הֲדַר מַלְכוּתוֹ.
מַלְכוּתְךָ מַלְכוּת כָּל עֹלָמִים, וּמֶמְשַׁלְתְּךָ בְּכָל דּוֹר וָדֹר.
סוֹמֵךְ יהוה לְכָל הַנֹּפְלִים, וְזוֹקֵף לְכָל הַכְּפוּפִים.
עֵינֵי כֹל אֵלֶיךָ יְשַׂבֵּרוּ, וְאַתָּה נוֹתֵן לָהֶם אֶת אָכְלָם בְּעִתּוֹ.
פּוֹתֵחַ אֶת יָדֶךָ, וּמַשְׂבִּיעַ לְכָל־חַי רָצוֹן.
צַדִּיק יהוה בְּכָל דְּרָכָיו, וְחָסִיד בְּכָל מַעֲשָׂיו.
קָרוֹב יהוה לְכָל קֹרְאָיו, לְכֹל אֲשֶׁר יִקְרָאֻהוּ בֶאֱמֶת.
רְצוֹן יְרֵאָיו יַעֲשֶׂה, וְאֶת שַׁוְעָתָם יִשְׁמַע, וְיוֹשִׁיעֵם.
שׁוֹמֵר יהוה אֶת כָּל אֹהֲבָיו, וְאֵת כָּל־הָרְשָׁעִים יַשְׁמִיד.
◄ תְּהִלַּת יהוה יְדַבֶּר פִּי, וִיבָרֵךְ כָּל־בָּשָׂר שֵׁם קָדְשׁוֹ לְעוֹלָם וָעֶד.
וַאֲנַחְנוּ נְבָרֵךְ יָהּ, מֵעַתָּה וְעַד־עוֹלָם, הַלְלוּיָהּ.

The Leader takes the סֵפֶר תּוֹרָה. The Ark is opened. All stand. The Leader says:

יְהַלְלוּ אֶת־שֵׁם יהוה, כִּי נִשְׂגָּב שְׁמוֹ לְבַדּוֹ.

Congregation:

הוֹדוֹ עַל אֶרֶץ וְשָׁמָיִם. וַיָּרֶם קֶרֶן לְעַמּוֹ,
תְּהִלָּה לְכָל־חֲסִידָיו, לִבְנֵי יִשְׂרָאֵל עַם קְרֹבוֹ, הַלְלוּיָהּ.

---

other tragedies and pogroms, and for the victims of the Holocaust. Our custom is to say it on two special moments of the Jewish year: the Shabbat before Shavuot (as an anniversary of the massacre of Rhineland Jewish communities in 1096), and before Tishah B'Av, on which we mourn the destruction of the two Temples and the victims of those and later persecutions.

They shall talk of the power of Your awesome deeds,
and I will tell of Your greatness.
They shall recite the record of Your great goodness,
and sing with joy of Your righteousness.
The LORD is gracious and compassionate,
slow to anger and great in lovingkindness.
The LORD is good to all,
and His compassion extends to all His works.
All Your works shall thank You, LORD,
and Your devoted ones shall bless You.
They shall talk of the glory of Your kingship,
and speak of Your might,
To make known to mankind His mighty deeds
and the glorious majesty of His kingship.
Your kingdom is an everlasting kingdom,
and Your reign is for all generations.
The LORD supports all who fall,
and raises all who are bowed down.
All raise their eyes to You in hope,
and You give them their food in due season.
You open Your hand,
and satisfy every living thing with Your favour.
The LORD is righteous in all His ways,
and kind in all He does.
The LORD is close to all who call on Him,
to all who call on Him in truth.
He fulfils the will of those who revere Him;
He hears their cry and saves them.
The LORD guards all who love Him,
but all the wicked He will destroy.
→ My mouth shall speak the praise of the LORD,
and all creatures shall bless His holy name for ever and all time.
We will bless the LORD now and for ever. Halleluyah!

The Leader takes the Torah scroll. The Ark is opened. All stand. The Leader says:

יְהַלְלוּ Let them praise the name of the LORD, for His name alone is sublime.

Congregation:

הוֹדוֹ His majesty is above earth and heaven. He has raised the horn of His people, for the glory of all His devoted ones, the children of Israel, the people close to Him. Halleluyah!

As the סֵפֶר תּוֹרָה is returned to the Ark, the following is said on שַׁבָּת:

תהלים כט

מִזְמוֹר לְדָוִד, הָבוּ לַיהוה בְּנֵי אֵלִים, הָבוּ לַיהוה כָּבוֹד וָעֹז. הָבוּ לַיהוה כְּבוֹד שְׁמוֹ, הִשְׁתַּחֲווּ לַיהוה בְּהַדְרַת־קֹדֶשׁ. קוֹל יהוה עַל הַמָּיִם, אֵל־הַכָּבוֹד הִרְעִים, יהוה עַל־מַיִם רַבִּים. קוֹל־יהוה בַּכֹּחַ, קוֹל יהוה בֶּהָדָר. קוֹל יהוה שֹׁבֵר אֲרָזִים, וַיְשַׁבֵּר יהוה אֶת־אַרְזֵי הַלְּבָנוֹן. וַיַּרְקִידֵם כְּמוֹ־עֵגֶל, לְבָנוֹן וְשִׂרְיוֹן כְּמוֹ בֶן־רְאֵמִים. קוֹל־יהוה חֹצֵב לַהֲבוֹת אֵשׁ. קוֹל יהוה יָחִיל מִדְבָּר, יָחִיל יהוה מִדְבַּר קָדֵשׁ. קוֹל יהוה יְחוֹלֵל אַיָּלוֹת, וַיֶּחֱשֹׂף יְעָרוֹת, וּבְהֵיכָלוֹ, כֻּלּוֹ אֹמֵר כָּבוֹד. יהוה לַמַּבּוּל יָשָׁב, וַיֵּשֶׁב יהוה מֶלֶךְ לְעוֹלָם. יהוה, עֹז לְעַמּוֹ יִתֵּן, יהוה יְבָרֵךְ אֶת עַמּוֹ בַשָּׁלוֹם.

On יוֹם טוֹב occurring on a weekday, say (תהלים כד):

לְדָוִד מִזְמוֹר, לַיהוה הָאָרֶץ וּמְלוֹאָהּ, תֵּבֵל וְיֹשְׁבֵי בָהּ. כִּי־הוּא עַל יַמִּים יְסָדָהּ, וְעַל נְהָרוֹת יְכוֹנְנֶהָ. מִי־יַעֲלֶה בְהַר יהוה, וּמִי־יָקוּם בִּמְקוֹם קָדְשׁוֹ. נְקִי כַפַּיִם וּבַר לֵבָב, אֲשֶׁר לֹא־נָשָׂא לַשָּׁוְא נַפְשִׁי וְלֹא נִשְׁבַּע לְמִרְמָה. יִשָּׂא בְרָכָה מֵאֵת יהוה, וּצְדָקָה מֵאֱלֹהֵי יִשְׁעוֹ. זֶה דּוֹר דֹּרְשָׁיו, מְבַקְשֵׁי פָנֶיךָ, יַעֲקֹב, סֶלָה. שְׂאוּ שְׁעָרִים רָאשֵׁיכֶם, וְהִנָּשְׂאוּ פִּתְחֵי עוֹלָם, וְיָבוֹא מֶלֶךְ הַכָּבוֹד. מִי זֶה מֶלֶךְ הַכָּבוֹד, יהוה עִזּוּז וְגִבּוֹר, יהוה גִּבּוֹר מִלְחָמָה. שְׂאוּ שְׁעָרִים רָאשֵׁיכֶם, וּשְׂאוּ פִּתְחֵי עוֹלָם, וְיָבֹא מֶלֶךְ הַכָּבוֹד. מִי הוּא זֶה מֶלֶךְ הַכָּבוֹד, יהוה צְבָאוֹת הוּא מֶלֶךְ הַכָּבוֹד, סֶלָה.

RETURN OF THE TORAH TO THE ARK

A ceremony parallel to that accompanying the taking out of the scroll(s).

מִזְמוֹר לְדָוִד *A psalm of David*: Psalm 29, with its sevenfold reference to "the LORD's voice" that makes the world tremble, was

As the Torah scroll is returned to the Ark, the following is said on Shabbat:

PSALM 29

מִזְמוֹר לְדָוִד A psalm of David. Render to the LORD, you angelic powers, render to the LORD glory and might. Render to the LORD the glory due to His name. Bow to the LORD in the beauty of holiness. The LORD's voice echoes over the waters; the GOD of glory thunders; the LORD is over the mighty waters. The LORD's voice in power, the LORD's voice in beauty, the LORD's voice breaks cedars, the LORD shatters the cedars of Lebanon. He makes Lebanon skip like a calf, Sirion like a young wild ox. The LORD's voice cleaves flames of fire. The LORD's voice makes the desert quake; the LORD shakes the desert of Kadesh. The LORD's voice makes hinds calve and strips the forests bare, and in His Temple all say: "Glory!" The LORD sat enthroned at the Flood; the LORD sits enthroned as King for ever. The LORD will give strength to His people; the LORD will bless His people with peace.

On a Festival occurring on a weekday, say (PSALM 24):

מִזְמוֹר לְדָוִד A psalm of David. The earth is the LORD's and all it contains, the world and all who live in it. For He founded it on the seas, and established it on the streams. Who may climb the mountain of the LORD? Who may stand in His holy place? He who has clean hands and a pure heart, who has not taken My name in vain, or sworn deceitfully. He shall receive blessing from the LORD, and just reward from GOD, his salvation. This is a generation of those who seek Him, the descendants of Jacob who seek Your presence, Selah! Lift up your heads, O gates; be uplifted, eternal doors, so that the King of glory may enter. Who is the King of glory? It is the LORD, strong and mighty, the LORD mighty in battle. Lift up your heads, O gates; be uplifted, eternal doors, that the King of glory may enter. Who is he, the King of glory? The LORD of hosts, He is the King of glory, Selah!

---

traditionally associated with the giving of the Torah at Mount Sinai, accompanied by thunder and lighting, when the mountain "trembled violently" (Exodus 19:18–19).

As the סֵפֶר תּוֹרָה is being placed in the Ark, the Leader and Congregation say:

וּבְנֻחֹה יֹאמַר, שׁוּבָה יהוה רִבְבוֹת אַלְפֵי יִשְׂרָאֵל. קוּמָה יהוה לִמְנוּחָתֶךָ, אַתָּה וַאֲרוֹן עֻזֶּךָ. כֹּהֲנֶיךָ יִלְבְּשׁוּ צֶדֶק, וַחֲסִידֶיךָ יְרַנֵּנוּ. בַּעֲבוּר דָּוִד עַבְדֶּךָ אַל־תָּשֵׁב פְּנֵי מְשִׁיחֶךָ. כִּי לֶקַח טוֹב נָתַתִּי לָכֶם, תּוֹרָתִי אַל־תַּעֲזֹבוּ. ◂ עֵץ־חַיִּים הִיא לַמַּחֲזִיקִים בָּהּ, וְתֹמְכֶיהָ מְאֻשָּׁר. דְּרָכֶיהָ דַרְכֵי־נֹעַם, וְכָל־נְתִיבוֹתֶיהָ שָׁלוֹם. הֲשִׁיבֵנוּ יהוה אֵלֶיךָ וְנָשׁוּבָה, חַדֵּשׁ יָמֵינוּ כְּקֶדֶם.

The Ark is closed.

The Leader says חֲצִי קַדִּישׁ.

Leader:

יִתְגַּדַּל וְיִתְקַדַּשׁ שְׁמֵהּ רַבָּא. (Cong. אָמֵן) בְּעָלְמָא דִּי־בְרָא כִרְעוּתֵהּ. וְיַמְלִיךְ מַלְכוּתֵהּ, בְּחַיֵּיכוֹן וּבְיוֹמֵיכוֹן וּבְחַיֵּי דְּכָל־בֵּית יִשְׂרָאֵל, בַּעֲגָלָא וּבִזְמַן קָרִיב. וְאִמְרוּ אָמֵן.

All:

יְהֵא שְׁמֵהּ רַבָּא מְבָרַךְ לְעָלַם וּלְעָלְמֵי עָלְמַיָּא. יִתְבָּרַךְ

Leader:

יִתְבָּרַךְ וְיִשְׁתַּבַּח וְיִתְפָּאַר וְיִתְרוֹמַם וְיִתְנַשֵּׂא וְיִתְהַדַּר וְיִתְעַלֶּה וְיִתְהַלָּל שְׁמֵהּ דְּקֻדְשָׁא בְּרִיךְ הוּא (Cong. בְּרִיךְ הוּא) לְעֵלָּא (On שַׁבַּת שׁוּבָה add לְעֵלָּא) מִן־כָּל־בִּרְכָתָא וְשִׁירָתָא תֻּשְׁבְּחָתָא וְנֶחֱמָתָא, דַּאֲמִירָן בְּעָלְמָא. וְאִמְרוּ אָמֵן. (Cong. אָמֵן)

וּבְנֻחֹה יֹאמַר *When the Ark came to rest*: The verse (Numbers 10:36) describing the moments in the wilderness years when the Israelites encamped. As at the opening of the Ark, a ceremony in the present recalls the ancient past, when the Israelites carried the Ark, containing the Tablets, with them on all their journeys. Hence the poignancy of the last line, taken from the Book of Lamentations, "Renew our days as of old". In Judaism – the world's oldest monotheistic faith – the new is old, and the old is new. The symbol of this constant renewal is the Torah, the word of the One who is beyond time.

As the Torah scroll is being placed in the Ark, the Leader and Congregation say:

וּבְנֻחֹה When the Ark came to rest, Moses would say: "Return, O LORD, to the myriad thousands of Israel." Advance, LORD, to Your resting place, You and Your mighty Ark. Your priests are clothed in righteousness, and Your devoted ones sing for joy. For the sake of Your servant David, do not reject Your anointed one. For I give you good instruction; do not forsake My Torah. ➔ It is a tree of life to those who grasp it, and those who uphold it are happy. Its ways are ways of pleasantness, and all its paths are peace. Turn us back, O LORD, to You, and we will return. Renew our days as of old.

The Ark is closed.

The Leader says half-*Kaddish*.

Leader:

יִתְגַּדַּל Magnified and sanctified may His great name be, in the world He created by His will. May He establish His kingdom in your lifetime and in your days, and in the lifetime of all the House of Israel, swiftly and soon – and say: Amen.

All:

May His great name be blessed for ever and all time.

Leader:

Blessed and praised, glorified and exalted, raised and honoured, uplifted and lauded be the name of the Holy One, blessed be He, (between Rosh Hashanah and Yom Kippur add 'well') beyond any blessing, song, praise and consolation uttered in the world – and say: Amen.

THE ADDITIONAL SERVICE

On Shabbat, festivals and New Moons, an extra sacrifice, *Musaf*, was brought in addition to the regular daily morning and afternoon offerings. The *Musaf Amidah* corresponds to that sacrifice. Through it we ask GOD, in the absence of the Temple and its rites, to accept our prayer in place of sacrifice in the spirit of the words of Hosea (14:3), "Receive us graciously that we may offer (the words of) our lips as the sacrifices of bulls". The Hebrew word for sacrifice, *korban*, derives from the root *k-r-b* meaning "to come, or bring close". The act of coming close to GOD involves sacrifice in the deepest sense of the word: surrendering something of ourselves to One greater than ourselves, the Author and ultimate Owner of all. Prayer-as-sacrifice means not asking GOD to do our will, but pledging ourselves to do His will. It is the supreme act of acknowledging our dependency on GOD.

תפילת מוסף לשבת

On a יום טוב, including שַׁבָּת חול הַמּוֹעֵד, turn to page 670.

עמידה

The following prayer, until קַדְמוֹנִיּוֹת, on page 448, is said standing with feet together.

The עֲמִידָה is first said silently; then, if there is a מִנְיָן, it is repeated aloud by the Leader.

Take three steps back, then forward. At the points indicated by ▾, bend the knees at the first word, bow at the second, and stand straight before God's name.

אֲדֹנָי, שְׂפָתַי תִּפְתָּח, וּפִי יַגִּיד תְּהִלָּתֶךָ.

אבות

▾**בָּרוּךְ** אַתָּה יהוה אֱלֹהֵינוּ וֵאלֹהֵי אֲבוֹתֵינוּ, אֱלֹהֵי אַבְרָהָם, אֱלֹהֵי יִצְחָק, וֵאלֹהֵי יַעֲקֹב, הָאֵל הַגָּדוֹל הַגִּבּוֹר וְהַנּוֹרָא, אֵל עֶלְיוֹן, גּוֹמֵל חֲסָדִים טוֹבִים וְקוֹנֵה הַכֹּל, וְזוֹכֵר חַסְדֵי אָבוֹת, וּמֵבִיא גוֹאֵל לִבְנֵי בְנֵיהֶם, לְמַעַן שְׁמוֹ בְּאַהֲבָה.

On שַׁבָּת שׁוּבָה, add:

זָכְרֵנוּ לַחַיִּים, מֶלֶךְ חָפֵץ בַּחַיִּים, וְכָתְבֵנוּ בְּסֵפֶר הַחַיִּים, לְמַעַנְךָ אֱלֹהִים חַיִּים.

מֶלֶךְ עוֹזֵר וּמוֹשִׁיעַ וּמָגֵן. ▾בָּרוּךְ אַתָּה יהוה, מָגֵן אַבְרָהָם.

גבורות

אַתָּה גִּבּוֹר לְעוֹלָם אֲדֹנָי, מְחַיֵּה מֵתִים אַתָּה, רַב לְהוֹשִׁיעַ.

From after שְׁמִינִי עֲצֶרֶת until מוּסָף on the first day of פֶּסַח, add:

מַשִּׁיב הָרְוּחַ וּמוֹרִיד הַגֶּשֶׁם.

מְכַלְכֵּל חַיִּים בְּחֶסֶד, מְחַיֵּה מֵתִים בְּרַחֲמִים רַבִּים, סוֹמֵךְ נוֹפְלִים, וְרוֹפֵא חוֹלִים, וּמַתִּיר אֲסוּרִים, וּמְקַיֵּם אֱמוּנָתוֹ לִישֵׁנֵי עָפָר. מִי כָמְוֹךָ בַּעַל גְּבוּרוֹת, וּמִי דוֹמֶה לָּךְ, מֶלֶךְ מֵמִית וּמְחַיֶּה וּמַצְמִיחַ יְשׁוּעָה.

On שַׁבָּת שׁוּבָה, add:

מִי כָמְוֹךָ אַב הָרַחֲמִים, זוֹכֵר יְצוּרָיו לַחַיִּים בְּרַחֲמִים.

ADDITIONAL SERVICE FOR SHABBAT

On Festivals, including the Shabbat of the Intermediate Days of a Festival, turn to page 671.

AMIDAH: THE STANDING PRAYER

The following prayer, until "in former years", on page 449, is said standing with feet together.

The *Amidah* is first said silently; then, if there is a *minyan*, it is repeated aloud by the Leader.

Take three steps back, then forward. At the points indicated by ▾, bend the knees at the first word, bow at the second, and stand straight before God's name.

O Lord, open my lips, so that my mouth may declare Your praise.

PATRIARCHS

▾בָּרוּךְ Blessed are You, Lord our God and God of our Fathers, God of Abraham, God of Isaac and God of Jacob; the great, mighty and awesome God, God Most High, who bestows acts of lovingkindness and creates all, who remembers the lovingkindness of the Fathers and will bring a Redeemer to their children's children for the sake of His name, in love.

On the Shabbat of Penitence, add:

Remember us for life, O King who desires life, and write us in the book of life – for Your sake, O God of life.

King, Helper, Saviour, Shield: ▾Blessed are You, Lord, Shield of Abraham.

DIVINE MIGHT

אַתָּה You are eternally mighty, Lord. You give life to the dead and have great power to save.

From after Shemini Atzeret until *Musaf* on the first day of Pesach, add:

He makes the wind blow and the rain fall.

He sustains the living with lovingkindness, and with great compassion revives the dead. He supports the fallen, heals the sick, sets captives free, and keeps His faith with those who sleep in the dust. Who is like You, Master of might, and to whom can You be compared, O King who brings death and gives life, and makes salvation grow?

On the Shabbat of Penitence, add:

Who is like You, compassionate Father, who remembers His creatures in compassion, for life?

וְנֶאֱמָן אַתָּה לְהַחֲיוֹת מֵתִים. בָּרוּךְ אַתָּה יהוה, מְחַיֵּה הַמֵּתִים.

When saying the עֲמִידָה silently, go to אַתָּה קָדוֹשׁ on page 438.

קדושה

During the Leader's repetition, the following is said standing, with feet together, rising on the toes at the words indicated by ▲.

Congregation then Leader: **נְעָרִיצְךָ** וְנַקְדִּישְׁךָ כְּסוֹד שִׂיחַ שַׂרְפֵי קֹדֶשׁ, הַמַּקְדִּישִׁים שִׁמְךָ בַּקֹּדֶשׁ, כַּכָּתוּב עַל יַד נְבִיאֶךָ, וְקָרָא זֶה אֶל־זֶה וְאָמַר,

Congregation and Leader: ▲קָדוֹשׁ ▲קָדוֹשׁ ▲קָדוֹשׁ יהוה צְבָאוֹת, מְלֹא כָל־הָאָרֶץ כְּבוֹדוֹ.

Congregation then Leader: כְּבוֹדוֹ מָלֵא עוֹלָם, מְשָׁרְתָיו שׁוֹאֲלִים זֶה לָזֶה, אַיֵּה מְקוֹם כְּבוֹדוֹ, לְעֻמָּתָם בָּרוּךְ יֹאמֵרוּ,

Congregation and Leader: ▲בָּרוּךְ כְּבוֹד־יהוה, מִמְּקוֹמוֹ.

Congregation then Leader: מִמְּקוֹמוֹ הוּא יִפֶן בְּרַחֲמִים, וְיָחֹן עַם הַמְיַחֲדִים שְׁמוֹ, עֶרֶב וָבֹקֶר בְּכָל־יוֹם תָּמִיד, פַּעֲמַיִם בְּאַהֲבָה שְׁמַע אוֹמְרִים.

Congregation and Leader: שְׁמַע יִשְׂרָאֵל, יהוה אֱלֹהֵינוּ, יהוה אֶחָד.

Congregation then Leader: אֶחָד הוּא אֱלֹהֵינוּ, הוּא אָבִינוּ, הוּא מַלְכֵּנוּ, הוּא מוֹשִׁיעֵנוּ, וְהוּא יַשְׁמִיעֵנוּ בְּרַחֲמָיו שֵׁנִית, לְעֵינֵי כָּל־חָי, לִהְיוֹת לָכֶם לֵאלֹהִים,

Congregation and Leader: אֲנִי יהוה אֱלֹהֵיכֶם.

Leader: וּבְדִבְרֵי קָדְשְׁךָ כָּתוּב לֵאמֹר,

Congregation and Leader: ▲יִמְלֹךְ יהוה לְעוֹלָם, אֱלֹהַיִךְ צִיּוֹן לְדֹר וָדֹר, הַלְלוּיָהּ.

Leader: לְדוֹר וָדוֹר נַגִּיד גָּדְלֶךָ וּלְנֵצַח נְצָחִים קְדֻשָּׁתְךָ נַקְדִּישׁ, וְשִׁבְחֲךָ אֱלֹהֵינוּ מִפִּינוּ לֹא יָמוּשׁ לְעוֹלָם וָעֶד, כִּי אֵל מֶלֶךְ גָּדוֹל וְקָדוֹשׁ אָתָּה. בָּרוּךְ אַתָּה יהוה, *הָאֵל הַקָּדוֹשׁ.

---

*On שַׁבַּת שׁוּבָה, end the blessing:

הַמֶּלֶךְ הַקָּדוֹשׁ.

Faithful are You to revive the dead. Blessed are You, LORD, who revives the dead.

When saying the *Amidah* silently, go to "You are holy" on page 439.

KEDUSHAH

During the Leader's repetition, the following is said standing, with feet together, rising on the toes at the words indicated by ▲:

Congregation then Leader: נְקַדֵּשׁ We will revere and sanctify You with the words uttered by the holy Seraphim who sanctify Your name in the sanctuary; as is written by Your prophet: "They call out to one another, saying:

Congregation and Leader: ▲Holy, ▲holy, ▲holy is the LORD of Hosts: the whole world is filled with His glory."

Congregation then Leader: His glory fills the universe. His ministering angels ask each other, "Where is the place of His glory?" Those facing them reply "Blessed –

Congregation and Leader: "▲Blessed is the LORD's glory from His place."

Congregation then Leader: From His place may He turn with compassion and be gracious to the people who proclaim the unity of His name, evening and morning, every day, continually, twice each day reciting in love the *Shema*:

Congregation and Leader: "Listen, Israel, the LORD is our GOD, the LORD is One."

Congregation then Leader: He is our GOD, He is our Father, He is our King, He is our Saviour – and He, in His compassion, will let us hear a second time in the presence of all that lives, His promise to be "Your GOD".

Congregation and Leader: "I am the LORD your GOD."

Leader: And in Your Holy Writings it is written:

Congregation and Leader: "▲The LORD shall reign forever. He is your GOD, Zion, from generation to generation, Halleluyah!"

Leader: From generation to generation we will declare Your greatness, and we will proclaim Your holiness for evermore. Your praise, our GOD, shall never leave our mouth, for You, GOD, are a great and holy King. Blessed are You, LORD, *the holy GOD.

---

*On the Shabbat of Penitence, end the blessing:
the holy King.

When saying the עֲמִידָה silently, continue here:

קדושת השם

אַתָּה קָדוֹשׁ וְשִׁמְךָ קָדוֹשׁ, וּקְדוֹשִׁים בְּכָל־יוֹם יְהַלְלְוּךָ סֶּלָה. בָּרוּךְ אַתָּה יהוה, *הָאֵל הַקָּדוֹשׁ.

On שַׁבַּת שׁוּבָה, end the blessing:

*הַמֶּלֶךְ הַקָּדוֹשׁ.

On שַׁבָּת which is also רֹאשׁ חֹדֶשׁ, turn to אַתָּה יָצַרְתָּ on page 440.

קדושת היום

תִּכַּנְתָּ שַׁבָּת רָצִיתָ קָרְבְּנוֹתֶיהָ, צִוִּיתָ פֵּרוּשֶׁיהָ עִם סִדּוּרֵי נְסָכֶיהָ, מְעַנְּגֶיהָ לְעוֹלָם כָּבוֹד יִנְחָלוּ, טוֹעֲמֶיהָ חַיִּים זָכוּ, וְגַם הָאוֹהֲבִים דְּבָרֶיהָ גְּדֻלָּה בָּחָרוּ, אָז מִסִּינַי נִצְטַוּוּ עָלֶיהָ, וַתְּצַוֵּנוּ יהוה אֱלֹהֵינוּ, לְהַקְרִיב בָּהּ קָרְבַּן מוּסַף שַׁבָּת כָּרָאוּי. יְהִי רָצוֹן מִלְּפָנֶיךָ, יהוה אֱלֹהֵינוּ וֵאלֹהֵי אֲבוֹתֵינוּ, שֶׁתַּעֲלֵנוּ בְשִׂמְחָה לְאַרְצֵנוּ, וְתִטָּעֵנוּ בִּגְבוּלֵנוּ, וְשָׁם נַעֲשֶׂה לְפָנֶיךָ אֶת־קָרְבְּנוֹת חוֹבוֹתֵינוּ, תְּמִידִים כְּסִדְרָם וּמוּסָפִים כְּהִלְכָתָם. וְאֶת־מוּסַף יוֹם הַשַּׁבָּת הַזֶּה נַעֲשֶׂה וְנַקְרִיב לְפָנֶיךָ בְּאַהֲבָה, כְּמִצְוַת רְצוֹנֶךָ, כְּמוֹ שֶׁכָּתַבְתָּ עָלֵינוּ בְּתוֹרָתֶךָ, עַל־יְדֵי מֹשֶׁה עַבְדֶּךָ, מִפִּי כְבוֹדֶךָ כָּאָמוּר,

וּבְיוֹם הַשַּׁבָּת שְׁנֵי־כְבָשִׂים בְּנֵי־שָׁנָה, תְּמִימִם, וּשְׁנֵי עֶשְׂרֹנִים סֹלֶת מִנְחָה בְּלוּלָה בַשֶּׁמֶן וְנִסְכּוֹ. עֹלַת שַׁבַּת בְּשַׁבַּתּוֹ, עַל־עֹלַת הַתָּמִיד וְנִסְכָּהּ.

יִשְׂמְחוּ בְמַלְכוּתְךָ שׁוֹמְרֵי שַׁבָּת וְקוֹרְאֵי עֹנֶג, עַם מְקַדְּשֵׁי

קְדוּשָּׁה *Kedushah*: As with all forms of the *Kedushah*, the central verses are the praises of the angels as described in the mystical visions of Isaiah and Ezekiel. The surrounding verses are different in *Musaf* to those of the other *Amidot*, most notably by the inclusion of the first verse of the *Shema*. According to Rabbi Amram Gaon (ninth century) this originated at a time of persecution when Jews were

When saying the *Amidah* silently, continue here:

HOLINESS

אַתָּה You are holy and Your name is holy, and holy ones praise You daily, Selah! Blessed are You, LORD, *the holy GOD.

*On the Shabbat of Penitence, end the blessing:
the holy King.

On a Shabbat which is also Rosh Chodesh, turn to, "You formed Your world" on page 441.

HOLINESS OF THE DAY

תִּכַּנְתָּ שַׁבָּת You instituted the Sabbath, You favoured its offerings. You commanded its specific laws along with the order of its libations. Those who delight in it inherit eternal glory, those who relish it merit life, and those who love its teachings have chosen greatness. Even before Sinai they were commanded about it. Then You, LORD our GOD, commanded us to offer on it the additional offering of the Sabbath in the proper way. May it be Your will, LORD our GOD and GOD of our ancestors, to lead us back in joy to our land and to plant us within our borders. There we will prepare for you our obligatory offerings: the regular daily offerings in their order, and the additional offerings according to their laws. And the additional offering of this Sabbath day we will prepare and offer before You in love, in accord with Your will's commandment, as You wrote for us in Your Torah through Your servant Moses, by Your own word, as it is said:

וּבְיוֹם הַשַּׁבָּת "On the Sabbath day, make an offering of two lambs a year old, without blemish, together with two-tenths of an ephah of fine flour mixed with oil as a meal-offering, and its appropriate libation. This is the burnt-offering for every Sabbath, in addition to the regular daily burnt-offering and its libation."

יִשְׂמְחוּ Those who keep the Sabbath and call it a delight shall rejoice in Your kingship. The people who sanctify the seventh day shall all be

---

forbidden to publicly declare their faith. They then incorporated the first verse into the *Musaf Amidah*, where it remains to this day.

תִּכַּנְתָּ שַׁבָּת *You instituted the Sabbath*: The central blessing of the *Amidah* focuses on the biblical passage describing the additional Sabbath sacrifice (Numbers

שְׁבִיעִי, כֻּלָּם יִשְׂבְּעוּ וְיִתְעַנְּגוּ מִטּוּבֶךָ, וּבַשְּׁבִיעִי רָצִיתָ בּוֹ וְקִדַּשְׁתּוֹ, חֶמְדַּת יָמִים אוֹתוֹ קָרָאתָ, זֵכֶר לְמַעֲשֵׂה בְרֵאשִׁית.

אֱלֹהֵינוּ וֵאלֹהֵי אֲבוֹתֵינוּ, רְצֵה בִמְנוּחָתֵנוּ, קַדְּשֵׁנוּ בְּמִצְוֹתֶיךָ, וְתֵן חֶלְקֵנוּ בְּתוֹרָתֶךָ, שַׂבְּעֵנוּ מִטּוּבֶךָ, וְשַׂמְּחֵנוּ בִּישׁוּעָתֶךָ, וְטַהֵר לִבֵּנוּ לְעָבְדְּךָ בֶּאֱמֶת, וְהַנְחִילֵנוּ יהוה אֱלֹהֵינוּ בְּאַהֲבָה וּבְרָצוֹן שַׁבַּת קָדְשֶׁךָ, וְיָנוּחוּ בָהּ יִשְׂרָאֵל מְקַדְּשֵׁי שְׁמֶךָ. בָּרוּךְ אַתָּה יהוה, מְקַדֵּשׁ הַשַּׁבָּת.

Continue with רְצֵה on page 442.

On שַׁבַּת רֹאשׁ חֹדֶשׁ, say:

אַתָּה יָצַרְתָּ עוֹלָמְךָ מִקֶּדֶם, כִּלִּיתָ מְלַאכְתְּךָ בַּיּוֹם הַשְּׁבִיעִי, אָהַבְתָּ אוֹתָנוּ וְרָצִיתָ בָּנוּ, וְרוֹמַמְתָּנוּ מִכָּל־הַלְּשׁוֹנוֹת, וְקִדַּשְׁתָּנוּ בְּמִצְוֹתֶיךָ, וְקֵרַבְתָּנוּ מַלְכֵּנוּ לַעֲבוֹדָתֶךָ, וְשִׁמְךָ הַגָּדוֹל וְהַקָּדוֹשׁ עָלֵינוּ קָרָאתָ. וַתִּתֶּן־לָנוּ יהוה אֱלֹהֵינוּ בְּאַהֲבָה, שַׁבָּתוֹת לִמְנוּחָה וְרָאשֵׁי חֳדָשִׁים לְכַפָּרָה. וּלְפִי שֶׁחָטָאנוּ לְפָנֶיךָ אֲנַחְנוּ וַאֲבוֹתֵינוּ, חָרְבָה עִירֵנוּ, וְשָׁמֵם בֵּית מִקְדָּשֵׁנוּ, וְגָלָה יְקָרֵנוּ, וְנֻטַּל כָּבוֹד מִבֵּית חַיֵּינוּ, וְאֵין אֲנַחְנוּ יְכוֹלִים לַעֲשׂוֹת חוֹבוֹתֵינוּ בְּבֵית בְּחִירָתֶךָ, בַּבַּיִת הַגָּדוֹל וְהַקָּדוֹשׁ שֶׁנִּקְרָא שִׁמְךָ עָלָיו, מִפְּנֵי הַיָּד שֶׁנִּשְׁתַּלְּחָה בְּמִקְדָּשֶׁךָ. יְהִי רָצוֹן מִלְּפָנֶיךָ יהוה אֱלֹהֵינוּ וֵאלֹהֵי אֲבוֹתֵינוּ, שֶׁתַּעֲלֵנוּ בְשִׂמְחָה לְאַרְצֵנוּ, וְתִטָּעֵנוּ בִּגְבוּלֵנוּ, וְשָׁם נַעֲשֶׂה לְפָנֶיךָ אֶת־קָרְבְּנוֹת חוֹבוֹתֵינוּ, תְּמִידִים כְּסִדְרָם, וּמוּסָפִים כְּהִלְכָתָם. וְאֶת־מוּסְפֵי יוֹם הַשַּׁבָּת הַזֶּה וְיוֹם רֹאשׁ הַחֹדֶשׁ הַזֶּה נַעֲשֶׂה וְנַקְרִיב לְפָנֶיךָ בְּאַהֲבָה, כְּמִצְוַת רְצוֹנֶךָ, כְּמוֹ שֶׁכָּתַבְתָּ עָלֵינוּ בְּתוֹרָתֶךָ, עַל־יְדֵי מֹשֶׁה עַבְדֶּךָ, מִפִּי כְבוֹדֶךָ כָּאָמוּר,

---

28:9–10). Surrounding it are two prayers. The first, "You instituted the Sabbath", opens with an acrostic: the initial letters of the first twenty-two words spell out the

satisfied and take delight in Your goodness, for You favoured the seventh day and declared it holy. You called it "most desirable of days" in remembrance of Creation.

אֱלֹהֵינוּ Our God and God of our ancestors, find favour in our rest. Make us holy through Your commandments and grant us our share in Your Torah. Satisfy us with Your goodness, grant us joy in Your salvation, and purify our hearts to serve You in truth. In love and favour, Lord our God, grant us as our heritage Your holy Sabbath, so that Israel who sanctify Your name may find rest on it. Blessed are You, Lord, who sanctifies the Sabbath.

Continue with "Find favour" on page 443.

On Shabbat which is also Rosh Chodesh, say:

אַתָּה יָצַרְתָּ Long ago You formed Your world, completing Your work on the seventh day. You loved us. You favoured us, raising us above all languages. You made us holy through Your commandments, brought us near, O our King, to Your service, and called us by Your great and holy name. You also gave us in love, Lord our God, Sabbaths for rest and New Moons for atonement. But because we and our ancestors sinned against You, our city was laid waste, our sanctuary made desolate, our splendour exiled, and the glory gone from our house of life. We can no longer fulfill our obligations in Your chosen house, the great and holy Temple called by Your name, because of the hand stretched out against Your sanctuary. May it be Your will, Lord our God and God of our ancestors, to lead us back in joy to our land, and to plant us within our borders. There we will prepare for You our obligatory offerings: the regular daily offerings in their order, and the additional offerings according to their laws. And the additional offerings of this Sabbath day, and of this New Moon day, we will prepare and offer before You in love, in accord with Your will's commandment, as You wrote for us in Your Torah through Your servant Moses, by Your own word, as it is said:

Hebrew alphabet in reverse. It continues with a prayer for the return of Jews to Israel and the restoration of the Temple service. The second, "Those who keep the Sabbath and call it a delight", speaks of the joyous nature of the day of rest.

וּבְיוֹם הַשַּׁבָּת שְׁנֵי־כְבָשִׂים בְּנֵי־שָׁנָה, תְּמִימִם, וּשְׁנֵי עֶשְׂרֹנִים סֹלֶת מִנְחָה בְּלוּלָה בַשֶּׁמֶן וְנִסְכּוֹ. עֹלַת שַׁבַּת בְּשַׁבַּתּוֹ, עַל־עֹלַת הַתָּמִיד וְנִסְכָּהּ.

וּבְרָאשֵׁי חָדְשֵׁיכֶם תַּקְרִיבוּ עֹלָה לַיהוה, פָּרִים בְּנֵי־בָקָר שְׁנַיִם, וְאַיִל אֶחָד, כְּבָשִׂים בְּנֵי־שָׁנָה שִׁבְעָה, תְּמִימִם. וּמִנְחָתָם וְנִסְכֵּיהֶם כִּמְדֻבָּר, שְׁלֹשָׁה עֶשְׂרֹנִים לַפָּר, וּשְׁנֵי עֶשְׂרֹנִים לָאָיִל, וְעִשָּׂרוֹן לַכֶּבֶשׂ, וְיַיִן כְּנִסְכּוֹ, וְשָׂעִיר לְכַפֵּר, וּשְׁנֵי תְמִידִים כְּהִלְכָתָם.

יִשְׂמְחוּ בְמַלְכוּתְךָ שׁוֹמְרֵי שַׁבָּת וְקוֹרְאֵי עֹנֶג, עַם מְקַדְּשֵׁי שְׁבִיעִי, כֻּלָּם יִשְׂבְּעוּ וְיִתְעַנְּגוּ מִטּוּבֶךָ, וּבַשְּׁבִיעִי רָצִיתָ בּוֹ וְקִדַּשְׁתּוֹ, חֶמְדַּת יָמִים אוֹתוֹ קָרָאתָ, זֵכֶר לְמַעֲשֵׂה בְרֵאשִׁית.

אֱלֹהֵינוּ וֵאלֹהֵי אֲבוֹתֵינוּ רְצֵה בִמְנוּחָתֵנוּ, וְחַדֵּשׁ עָלֵינוּ בְּיוֹם הַשַּׁבָּת הַזֶּה אֶת־הַחֹדֶשׁ הַזֶּה לְטוֹבָה וְלִבְרָכָה, לְשָׂשׂוֹן וּלְשִׂמְחָה, לִישׁוּעָה וּלְנֶחָמָה, לְפַרְנָסָה וּלְכַלְכָּלָה, לְחַיִּים וּלְשָׁלוֹם, לִמְחִילַת חֵטְא וְלִסְלִיחַת עָוֹן.

From חֶשְׁוָן to אֲדָר שֵׁנִי in a Jewish leap year (see page 1037), add: וּלְכַפָּרַת פָּשַׁע

כִּי בְעַמְּךָ יִשְׂרָאֵל בָּחַרְתָּ מִכָּל־הָאֻמּוֹת, וְשַׁבַּת קָדְשְׁךָ לָהֶם הוֹדָעְתָּ, וְחֻקֵּי רָאשֵׁי חֳדָשִׁים לָהֶם קָבָעְתָּ. בָּרוּךְ אַתָּה יהוה, מְקַדֵּשׁ הַשַּׁבָּת וְיִשְׂרָאֵל וְרָאשֵׁי חֳדָשִׁים.

עבודה

רְצֵה יהוה אֱלֹהֵינוּ בְּעַמְּךָ יִשְׂרָאֵל וּבִתְפִלָּתָם, וְהָשֵׁב אֶת־הָעֲבוֹדָה לִדְבִיר בֵּיתֶךָ. וְאִשֵּׁי יִשְׂרָאֵל וּתְפִלָּתָם בְּאַהֲבָה תְקַבֵּל בְּרָצוֹן, וּתְהִי לְרָצוֹן תָּמִיד עֲבוֹדַת יִשְׂרָאֵל עַמֶּךָ.

וְתֶחֱזֶינָה עֵינֵינוּ בְּשׁוּבְךָ לְצִיּוֹן בְּרַחֲמִים. בָּרוּךְ אַתָּה יהוה, הַמַּחֲזִיר שְׁכִינָתוֹ לְצִיּוֹן.

"On the Sabbath day, make an offering of two lambs a year old, without blemish, together with two-tenths of an ephah of fine flour mixed with oil as a meal-offering, and its appropriate libation. This is the burnt-offering for every Sabbath, in addition to the regular daily burnt-offering and its libation."

"And on your new moons, present as a burnt-offering to the LORD two young bulls, one ram, and seven yearling lambs without blemish." And their meal-offerings and wine-libations as ordained: three-tenths of an ephah for each bull, two-tenths of an ephah for the ram, one-tenth of an ephah for each lamb, wine for the libations, a male goat for atonement, and two regular daily offerings according to their law.

Those who keep the Sabbath and call it a delight shall rejoice in Your kingship. The people who sanctify the seventh day shall all be satisfied and take delight in Your goodness, for You favoured the seventh day and declared it holy. You called it "most desirable of days" in remembrance of Creation.

Our GOD and GOD of our ancestors, find favour in our rest, and on this Sabbath day renew for us the coming month for good and blessing, joy and gladness, deliverance and consolation, sustenance and support, life and peace, pardon of sin and forgiveness of iniquity.

From Cheshvan to Adar II in a Jewish leap year (see page 1037), add:
"and atonement of transgression".

For You have chosen Your people Israel from all nations; You have made known to them Your holy Sabbath, and instituted for them rules for the New Moon. Blessed are You, LORD, who sanctifies the Sabbath, Israel and the New Moons.

TEMPLE SERVICE

רְצֵה Find favour, LORD our GOD, in Your people Israel and their prayer. Restore the service to Your most holy house, and accept in love and favour the fire-offerings of Israel and their prayer. May the service of Your people Israel always find favour with You.

וְתֶחֱזֶינָה And may our eyes witness Your return to Zion in compassion. Blessed are You, LORD, who restores His Presence to Zion.

הודאה

▽ Bow at the first five words.

▽**מוֹדִים** אֲנַחְנוּ לָךְ, שָׁאַתָּה הוּא יהוה אֱלֹהֵינוּ וֵאלֹהֵי אֲבוֹתֵינוּ לְעוֹלָם וָעֶד. צוּר חַיֵּינוּ, מָגֵן יִשְׁעֵנוּ אַתָּה הוּא לְדוֹר וָדוֹר. נוֹדֶה לְּךָ וּנְסַפֵּר תְּהִלָּתֶךָ עַל חַיֵּינוּ הַמְּסוּרִים בְּיָדֶךָ, וְעַל נִשְׁמוֹתֵינוּ הַפְּקוּדוֹת לָךְ, וְעַל נִסֶּיךָ שֶׁבְּכָל־יוֹם עִמָּנוּ, וְעַל נִפְלְאוֹתֶיךָ וְטוֹבוֹתֶיךָ שֶׁבְּכָל־עֵת, עֶרֶב וָבֹקֶר וְצָהֳרָיִם. הַטּוֹב כִּי לֹא־כָלוּ רַחֲמֶיךָ, וְהַמְרַחֵם כִּי לֹא־תַמּוּ חֲסָדֶיךָ, מֵעוֹלָם קִוִּינוּ לָךְ.

During the Leader's repetition, the Congregation says quietly:

▽**מוֹדִים** אֲנַחְנוּ לָךְ, שָׁאַתָּה הוּא יהוה אֱלֹהֵינוּ וֵאלֹהֵי אֲבוֹתֵינוּ, אֱלֹהֵי כָל־בָּשָׂר, יוֹצְרֵנוּ, יוֹצֵר בְּרֵאשִׁית. בְּרָכוֹת וְהוֹדָאוֹת לְשִׁמְךָ הַגָּדוֹל וְהַקָּדוֹשׁ, עַל שֶׁהֶחֱיִיתָנוּ וְקִיַּמְתָּנוּ. כֵּן תְּחַיֵּנוּ וּתְקַיְּמֵנוּ, וְתֶאֱסֹף גָּלֻיּוֹתֵינוּ לְחַצְרוֹת קָדְשֶׁךָ, לִשְׁמוֹר חֻקֶּיךָ וְלַעֲשׂוֹת רְצוֹנֶךָ, וּלְעָבְדְּךָ בְּלֵבָב שָׁלֵם, עַל שֶׁאֲנַחְנוּ מוֹדִים לָךְ. בָּרוּךְ אֵל הַהוֹדָאוֹת.

On חֲנֻכָּה, say:

עַל הַנִּסִּים, וְעַל הַפֻּרְקָן, וְעַל הַגְּבוּרוֹת, וְעַל הַתְּשׁוּעוֹת, וְעַל הַמִּלְחָמוֹת, שֶׁעָשִׂיתָ לַאֲבוֹתֵינוּ בַּיָּמִים הָהֵם בַּזְּמַן הַזֶּה.

בִּימֵי מַתִּתְיָהוּ בֶּן־יוֹחָנָן כֹּהֵן גָּדוֹל חַשְׁמוֹנַאי וּבָנָיו, כְּשֶׁעָמְדָה מַלְכוּת יָוָן הָרְשָׁעָה עַל־עַמְּךָ יִשְׂרָאֵל, לְהַשְׁכִּיחָם תּוֹרָתֶךָ, וּלְהַעֲבִירָם מֵחֻקֵּי רְצוֹנֶךָ. וְאַתָּה בְּרַחֲמֶיךָ הָרַבִּים, עָמַדְתָּ לָהֶם בְּעֵת צָרָתָם, רַבְתָּ אֶת־רִיבָם, דַּנְתָּ אֶת־דִּינָם, נָקַמְתָּ אֶת־נִקְמָתָם. מָסַרְתָּ גִּבּוֹרִים בְּיַד חַלָּשִׁים, וְרַבִּים בְּיַד מְעַטִּים, וּטְמֵאִים בְּיַד טְהוֹרִים, וּרְשָׁעִים בְּיַד צַדִּיקִים, וְזֵדִים בְּיַד עוֹסְקֵי תוֹרָתֶךָ. וּלְךָ עָשִׂיתָ שֵׁם גָּדוֹל וְקָדוֹשׁ בְּעוֹלָמֶךָ, וּלְעַמְּךָ יִשְׂרָאֵל עָשִׂיתָ תְּשׁוּעָה גְדוֹלָה וּפֻרְקָן כְּהַיּוֹם הַזֶּה. וְאַחַר כֵּן

THANKSGIVING

▽ Bow at the first nine words.

מוֹדִים▽ We give thanks to You, for You are the LORD our GOD and GOD of our ancestors for ever and all time. You are the Rock of our lives, Shield of our salvation from generation to generation. We will thank You and declare Your praise for our lives, which are entrusted into Your hand; our souls, which are placed in Your charge; for Your miracles which are with us every day; and for Your wonders and favours at all times, evening, morning and midday. You are good – for Your compassion never fails. You are compassionate – for Your lovingkindnesses never cease. We have always placed our hope in You.

During the Leader's repetition, the Congregation says quietly:

מוֹדִים▽ We give thanks to You, for You are the LORD our GOD and GOD of our ancestors, GOD of all flesh, who formed us and formed the universe. Blessings and thanks are due to Your great and holy name for giving us life and sustaining us. May You continue to give us life and sustain us; and may You gather our exiles to Your holy courts, to keep Your decrees, do Your will and serve You with a perfect heart, for it is for us to give You thanks. Blessed be GOD to whom thanksgiving is due.

On Chanukah, say:

עַל הַנִּסִּים [We thank You also] for the miracles, the redemption, the mighty deeds, and the victories in battle which You performed for our ancestors in those days at this time.

בִּימֵי In the days of Mattityahu, son of Yochanan the High Priest, the Hasmonean, and his sons, the wicked Greek kingdom rose up against Your people Israel to make them forget Your Torah and to force them to transgress the statutes of Your will. It was then that You in Your great compassion stood by them in the time of their distress. You championed their cause, judged their claim, and avenged their wrong. You delivered the strong into the hands of the weak, the many into the hands of the few, the impure into the hands of the pure, the wicked into the hands of the righteous, and the arrogant into the hands of those who were engaged in the study

בָּאוּ בָנֶיךָ לִדְבִיר בֵּיתֶךָ, וּפִנּוּ אֶת־הֵיכָלֶךָ, וְטִהֲרוּ אֶת־מִקְדָּשֶׁךָ, וְהִדְלִיקוּ נֵרוֹת בְּחַצְרוֹת קָדְשֶׁךָ, וְקָבְעוּ שְׁמוֹנַת יְמֵי חֲנֻכָּה אֵלּוּ, לְהוֹדוֹת וּלְהַלֵּל לְשִׁמְךָ הַגָּדוֹל.

וְעַל כֻּלָּם יִתְבָּרַךְ וְיִתְרוֹמַם שִׁמְךָ מַלְכֵּנוּ תָּמִיד לְעוֹלָם וָעֶד.

On שַׁבַּת שׁוּבָה, add:

וּכְתוֹב לְחַיִּים טוֹבִים כָּל־בְּנֵי בְרִיתֶךָ.

וְכֹל הַחַיִּים יוֹדוּךָ סֶּלָה, וִיהַלְלוּ אֶת־שִׁמְךָ בֶּאֱמֶת, הָאֵל יְשׁוּעָתֵנוּ וְעֶזְרָתֵנוּ סֶלָה. ▾בָּרוּךְ אַתָּה יהוה, הַטּוֹב שִׁמְךָ וּלְךָ נָאֶה לְהוֹדוֹת.

During the repetition of the עֲמִידָה, the Leader says the following:

אֱלֹהֵינוּ וֵאלֹהֵי אֲבוֹתֵינוּ, בָּרְכֵנוּ בַבְּרָכָה הַמְשֻׁלֶּשֶׁת, בַּתּוֹרָה, הַכְּתוּבָה עַל יְדֵי מֹשֶׁה עַבְדֶּךָ, הָאֲמוּרָה מִפִּי אַהֲרֹן וּבָנָיו כֹּהֲנִים, עַם קְדוֹשֶׁךָ, כָּאָמוּר.

יְבָרֶכְךָ יהוה, וְיִשְׁמְרֶךָ. (Cong.: כֵּן יְהִי רָצוֹן)

יָאֵר יהוה פָּנָיו אֵלֶיךָ וִיחֻנֶּךָּ. (Cong.: כֵּן יְהִי רָצוֹן)

יִשָּׂא יהוה פָּנָיו אֵלֶיךָ וְיָשֵׂם לְךָ שָׁלוֹם. (Cong.: כֵּן יְהִי רָצוֹן)

ברכת שלום

שִׂים שָׁלוֹם, טוֹבָה, וּבְרָכָה, חֵן, וָחֶסֶד וְרַחֲמִים עָלֵינוּ וְעַל כָּל־יִשְׂרָאֵל עַמֶּךָ. בָּרְכֵנוּ אָבִינוּ, כֻּלָּנוּ כְּאֶחָד בְּאוֹר פָּנֶיךָ, כִּי בְאוֹר פָּנֶיךָ נָתַתָּ לָּנוּ, יהוה אֱלֹהֵינוּ, תּוֹרַת חַיִּים וְאַהֲבַת חֶסֶד, וּצְדָקָה, וּבְרָכָה, וְרַחֲמִים, וְחַיִּים, וְשָׁלוֹם. וְטוֹב בְּעֵינֶיךָ לְבָרֵךְ אֶת־עַמְּךָ יִשְׂרָאֵל, בְּכָל־עֵת וּבְכָל־שָׁעָה בִּשְׁלוֹמֶךָ.

of Your Torah. You made for Yourself great and holy renown in Your world, and for Your people Israel You performed a great salvation and redemption on this day. Your children then entered the holiest part of Your house, cleansed Your Temple, purified Your sanctuary, kindled lights in Your holy courts, and designated these eight days of Chanukah for giving thanks and praise to Your great name.

וְעַל For all these things may Your name be blessed and exalted, our King, continually, for ever and all time.

On the Shabbat of Penitence, add:

And write, for a good life, all the children of Your covenant.

Let all that lives thank You, Selah! and praise Your name in truth, God, our Saviour and Help, Selah! ▾Blessed are You, Lord, whose name is "the Good" and to whom thanks is due.

During the repetition of the *Amidah*, the Leader says the following:

אֱלֹהֵינוּ Our God and God of our fathers, bless us with the threefold blessing in the Torah, written by the hand of Moses Your servant and pronounced by Aaron and his sons the priests, Your holy people, as it is said:

May the Lord bless you and protect you. (Cong.: May it be Your will.)

May the Lord make His face shine on you and be gracious to you. (Cong.: May it be Your will.)

May the Lord turn His face towards you, and give you peace. (Cong.: May it be Your will.)

PEACE

שִׂים Grant peace, goodness and blessing, grace, lovingkindness and compassion to us and all Israel Your people. Bless us, our Father, all as one, with the light of Your face, for by the light of Your face You have given us, Lord our God, the Torah of life and love of kindness, righteousness, blessing, compassion, life and peace. May it be good in Your eyes to bless Your people Israel at every time, in every hour,

*בָּרוּךְ אַתָּה יהוה, הַמְבָרֵךְ אֶת עַמּוֹ יִשְׂרָאֵל בַּשָּׁלוֹם.

---

*On שַׁבַּת שׁוּבָה, substitute the following:

בְּסֵפֶר חַיִּים בְּרָכָה וְשָׁלוֹם, וּפַרְנָסָה טוֹבָה, נִזָּכֵר וְנִכָּתֵב לְפָנֶיךָ, אֲנַחְנוּ וְכָל־עַמְּךָ בֵּית יִשְׂרָאֵל, לְחַיִּים טוֹבִים וּלְשָׁלוֹם. בָּרוּךְ אַתָּה יהוה, עֹשֵׂה הַשָּׁלוֹם.

The Leader's repetition ends at this point.

אֱלֹהַי, נְצוֹר לְשׁוֹנִי מֵרָע, וּשְׂפָתַי מִדַּבֵּר מִרְמָה, וְלִמְקַלְלַי נַפְשִׁי תִדּוֹם, וְנַפְשִׁי כֶּעָפָר לַכֹּל תִּהְיֶה. פְּתַח לִבִּי בְּתוֹרָתֶךָ, וּבְמִצְוֹתֶיךָ תִּרְדּוֹף נַפְשִׁי. וְכֹל הַחוֹשְׁבִים עָלַי רָעָה, מְהֵרָה הָפֵר עֲצָתָם וְקַלְקֵל מַחֲשַׁבְתָּם. עֲשֵׂה לְמַעַן שְׁמֶךָ, עֲשֵׂה לְמַעַן יְמִינֶךָ, עֲשֵׂה לְמַעַן קְדֻשָּׁתֶךָ, עֲשֵׂה לְמַעַן תּוֹרָתֶךָ. לְמַעַן יֵחָלְצוּן יְדִידֶיךָ, הוֹשִׁיעָה יְמִינְךָ וַעֲנֵנִי. יִהְיוּ לְרָצוֹן אִמְרֵי־פִי וְהֶגְיוֹן לִבִּי לְפָנֶיךָ, יהוה צוּרִי וְגוֹאֲלִי.

Bow, take three steps back, then bow, first left, then right, then centre, while saying:

עֹשֶׂה שָׁלוֹם בִּמְרוֹמָיו, הוּא יַעֲשֶׂה שָׁלוֹם עָלֵינוּ, וְעַל־כָּל־יִשְׂרָאֵל, וְאִמְרוּ אָמֵן.

יְהִי רָצוֹן מִלְּפָנֶיךָ יהוה אֱלֹהֵינוּ וֵאלֹהֵי אֲבוֹתֵינוּ, שֶׁיִּבָּנֶה בֵּית הַמִּקְדָּשׁ בִּמְהֵרָה בְיָמֵינוּ, וְתֵן חֶלְקֵנוּ בְּתוֹרָתֶךָ. וְשָׁם נַעֲבָדְךָ בְּיִרְאָה, כִּימֵי עוֹלָם וּכְשָׁנִים קַדְמוֹנִיּוֹת. וְעָרְבָה לַיהוה מִנְחַת יְהוּדָה וִירוּשָׁלָיִם, כִּימֵי עוֹלָם וּכְשָׁנִים קַדְמוֹנִיּוֹת.

When praying with a מִנְיָן, the עֲמִידָה is repeated aloud by the Leader on page 434.

קדיש תתקבל

Leader:

יִתְגַּדַּל וְיִתְקַדַּשׁ שְׁמֵהּ רַבָּא. (Cong. אָמֵן) בְּעָלְמָא דִּי־בְרָא כִרְעוּתֵהּ. וְיַמְלִיךְ מַלְכוּתֵהּ, בְּחַיֵּיכוֹן וּבְיוֹמֵיכוֹן וּבְחַיֵּי דְּכָל־

with Your peace. *Blessed are You, LORD, who blesses His people Israel with peace.

---

*On the Shabbat of Penitence, substitute the following:

In the book of life, blessing, peace and prosperity, may we and all Your people the house of Israel be remembered and written before You for a good life, and for peace. Blessed are You, LORD, who makes peace.

The Leader's repetition ends at this point.

אֱלֹהַי My GOD, guard my tongue from evil and my lips from deceitful speech. To those who curse me, let my soul be silent; may my soul be to all like the dust. Open my heart to Your Torah and let my soul pursue Your commandments. As for all who plan evil against me, swiftly thwart their counsel and frustrate their plans. Act for the sake of Your name; act for the sake of Your right hand; act for the sake of Your holiness; act for the sake of Your Torah. That Your beloved ones may be delivered, save with Your right hand and answer me. May the words of my mouth and the meditation of my heart find favour before You, LORD, my Rock and Redeemer.

Bow, take three steps back, then bow, first left, then right, then centre, while saying:

May He who makes peace in His high places, make peace for us and all Israel – and say: Amen.

יְהִי May it be Your will, LORD our GOD and GOD of our ancestors, that the Temple be rebuilt speedily in our days, and grant us a share in Your Torah. And there we will serve You with reverence, as in the days of old and as in former years. Then the offering of Judah and Jerusalem will be pleasing to the LORD as in the days of old and as in former years.

When praying with a *minyan*, the *Amidah* is repeated aloud by the Leader on page 435.

FULL KADDISH

Leader:

יִתְגַּדַּל Magnified and sanctified may His great name be, in the world He created by His will. May He establish His kingdom in your lifetime

בֵּית יִשְׂרָאֵל, בַּעֲגָלָא וּבִזְמַן קָרִיב. וְאִמְרוּ אָמֵן. (Cong. אָמֵן)

All:

יְהֵא שְׁמֵהּ רַבָּא מְבָרַךְ לְעָלַם וּלְעָלְמֵי עָלְמַיָּא.

Leader:

יִתְבָּרַךְ וְיִשְׁתַּבַּח וְיִתְפָּאַר וְיִתְרוֹמַם וְיִתְנַשֵּׂא וְיִתְהַדַּר וְיִתְעַלֶּה וְיִתְהַלָּל שְׁמֵהּ דְּקֻדְשָׁא בְּרִיךְ הוּא (Cong. בְּרִיךְ הוּא) לְעֵלָּא (On שַׁבַּת שׁוּבָה add לְעֵלָּא) מִן־כָּל־בִּרְכָתָא וְשִׁירָתָא תֻּשְׁבְּחָתָא וְנֶחֱמָתָא, דַּאֲמִירָן בְּעָלְמָא. וְאִמְרוּ אָמֵן. (Cong. אָמֵן)

תִּתְקַבַּל צְלוֹתְהוֹן וּבָעוּתְהוֹן דְּכָל־יִשְׂרָאֵל קֳדָם אֲבוּהוֹן דִּי בִשְׁמַיָּא. וְאִמְרוּ אָמֵן. (Cong. אָמֵן)

יְהֵא שְׁלָמָא רַבָּא מִן־שְׁמַיָּא, וְחַיִּים עָלֵינוּ וְעַל־כָּל־יִשְׂרָאֵל. וְאִמְרוּ אָמֵן. (Cong. אָמֵן)

Bow, take three steps back, then bow, first left, then right, then centre, while saying:

עֹשֶׂה שָׁלוֹם בִּמְרוֹמָיו, הוּא יַעֲשֶׂה שָׁלוֹם עָלֵינוּ, וְעַל־כָּל־יִשְׂרָאֵל. וְאִמְרוּ אָמֵן. (Cong. אָמֵן)

אין כאלהינו

אֵין כֵּאלֹהֵינוּ, אֵין כַּאדוֹנֵינוּ, אֵין כְּמַלְכֵּנוּ, אֵין כְּמוֹשִׁיעֵנוּ. מִי כֵאלֹהֵינוּ, מִי כַאדוֹנֵינוּ, מִי כְמַלְכֵּנוּ, מִי כְמוֹשִׁיעֵנוּ. נוֹדֶה לֵאלֹהֵינוּ, נוֹדֶה לַאדוֹנֵינוּ, נוֹדֶה לְמַלְכֵּנוּ, נוֹדֶה לְמוֹשִׁיעֵנוּ. בָּרוּךְ אֱלֹהֵינוּ, בָּרוּךְ אֲדוֹנֵינוּ, בָּרוּךְ מַלְכֵּנוּ, בָּרוּךְ מוֹשִׁיעֵנוּ. אַתָּה הוּא אֱלֹהֵינוּ, אַתָּה הוּא אֲדוֹנֵינוּ, אַתָּה הוּא מַלְכֵּנוּ, אַתָּה הוּא מוֹשִׁיעֵנוּ. אַתָּה הוּא שֶׁהִקְטִירוּ אֲבוֹתֵינוּ לְפָנֶיךָ אֶת־קְטֹרֶת הַסַּמִּים.

and in your days, and in the lifetime of all the House of Israel, swiftly and soon – and say: Amen.

All:

May His great name be blessed for ever and all time.

Leader:

Blessed and praised, glorified and exalted, raised and honoured, uplifted and lauded be the name of the Holy One, blessed be He, (between Rosh Hashanah and Yom Kippur add 'well') beyond any blessing, song, praise and consolation uttered in the world – and say: Amen.

May the prayers and pleas of all Israel be accepted by their Father in heaven – and say: Amen.

May there be great peace from heaven, and life for us and all Israel – and say: Amen.

Bow, take three steps back, then bow, first left, then right, then centre, while saying:

May He who makes peace in His high places, make peace for us and all Israel – and say: Amen.

EIN KELOHEYNU

אֵין כֵּאלֹהֵינוּ There is none like our God, none like our Lord, none like our King, none like our Saviour. Who is like our God? Like our Lord? Like our King? Like our Saviour? We will thank our God, thank our Lord, thank our King, thank our Saviour. Blessed is our God, blessed our Lord, blessed our King, blessed our Saviour. You are our God, You are our Lord, You are our King, You are our Saviour. You are He to whom our ancestors offered the fragrant incense.

אֵין כֵּאלֹהֵינוּ *There is none like our God*: This paragraph, usually sung in the synagogue, is a poetic introduction to the reading of the passage about the incense offering in the Temple. The initial letters of the first three lines spell Amen; the first words of the next two are "Blessed are You". Thus the poem is also a way of re-affirming the preceding prayers, a coded coda to the service as a whole.

תלמוד בבלי מסכת כריתות ו:א׳

פִּטּוּם הַקְּטֹרֶת, הַצֳּרִי, וְהַצִּפֹּרֶן, הַחֶלְבְּנָה, וְהַלְּבוֹנָה, מִשְׁקַל שִׁבְעִים שִׁבְעִים מָנֶה, מוֹר, וּקְצִיעָה, שִׁבֹּלֶת נֵרְדְּ, וְכַרְכֹּם, מִשְׁקַל שִׁשָּׁה עָשָׂר שִׁשָּׁה עָשָׂר מָנֶה, הַקֹּשְׁטְ שְׁנֵים עָשָׂר, וְקִלּוּפָה שְׁלֹשָׁה, וְקִנָּמוֹן תִּשְׁעָה. בֹּרִית כַּרְשִׁינָה תִּשְׁעָה קַבִּין, יֵין קַפְרִיסִין סְאִין תְּלָתָא וְקַבִּין תְּלָתָא, וְאִם אֵין לוֹ יֵין קַפְרִיסִין, מֵבִיא חֲמַר חִוַּרְיָן עַתִּיק, מֶלַח סְדוֹמִית רֹבַע הַקָּב, מַעֲלֶה עָשָׁן כָּל־שֶׁהוּא. רַבִּי נָתָן אוֹמֵר, אַף כִּפַּת הַיַּרְדֵּן כָּל־שֶׁהוּא. וְאִם נָתַן בָּהּ דְּבַשׁ פְּסָלָהּ. אִם חִסֵּר אַחַת מִכָּל סַמָּנֶיהָ, חַיָּב מִיתָה. רַבָּן שִׁמְעוֹן בֶּן גַּמְלִיאֵל אוֹמֵר, הַצֳּרִי אֵינוֹ אֶלָּא שְׂרָף הַנּוֹטֵף מֵעֲצֵי הַקְּטָף. בֹּרִית כַּרְשִׁינָה שֶׁשָּׁפִין בָּהּ אֶת הַצִּפֹּרֶן כְּדֵי שֶׁתְּהֵא נָאָה, יֵין קַפְרִיסִין שֶׁשּׁוֹרִין בּוֹ אֶת הַצִּפֹּרֶן כְּדֵי שֶׁתְּהֵא עַזָּה. וַהֲלֹא מֵי רַגְלַיִם יָפִין לָהּ, אֶלָּא שֶׁאֵין מַכְנִיסִין מֵי רַגְלַיִם בַּמִּקְדָּשׁ, מִפְּנֵי הַכָּבוֹד.

משנה תמיד ז:ד

הַשִּׁיר שֶׁהַלְוִיִּם הָיוּ אוֹמְרִים בְּבֵית הַמִּקְדָּשׁ. בַּיּוֹם הָרִאשׁוֹן הָיוּ אוֹמְרִים, לַיהוה הָאָרֶץ וּמְלוֹאָהּ, תֵּבֵל וְיֹשְׁבֵי בָהּ. בַּשֵּׁנִי הָיוּ אוֹמְרִים, גָּדוֹל יהוה וּמְהֻלָּל מְאֹד, בְּעִיר אֱלֹהֵינוּ הַר־קָדְשׁוֹ. בַּשְּׁלִישִׁי הָיוּ אוֹמְרִים, אֱלֹהִים נִצָּב בַּעֲדַת־אֵל, בְּקֶרֶב אֱלֹהִים יִשְׁפֹּט. בָּרְבִיעִי הָיוּ אוֹמְרִים, אֵל נְקָמוֹת יהוה, אֵל נְקָמוֹת הוֹפִיעַ. בַּחֲמִישִׁי הָיוּ אוֹמְרִים, הַרְנִינוּ לֵאלֹהִים עוּזֵּנוּ, הָרִיעוּ לֵאלֹהֵי יַעֲקֹב. בַּשִּׁשִּׁי הָיוּ אוֹמְרִים, יהוה מָלָךְ גֵּאוּת לָבֵשׁ, לָבֵשׁ יהוה עֹז הִתְאַזָּר,

---

פִּטּוּם הַקְּטֹרֶת *The incense mixture:* This paragraph is a Talmudic passage (*Keritot* 6a) describing the composition of the incense, burned in the Temple every morning and evening (Exodus 30:7–9).

BABYLONIAN TALMUD, KERITOT 6A

פִּטּוּם הַקְּטֹרֶת The incense mixture consisted of balsam, onycha, galbanum and frankincense, each weighing seventy manehs; myrrh, cassia, spikenard and saffron, each weighing sixteen manehs; twelve manehs of costus, three of aromatic bark; nine of cinnamon; nine kabs of Carsina lye; three seahs and three kabs of Cyprus wine. If Cyprus wine was not available, old white wine might be used. A quarter of a kab of Sodom salt, and a minute amount of a smoke-raising herb. Rabbi Nathan says: Also a minute amount of Jordan amber. If one added honey to the mixture, he rendered it unfit for sacred use. If he omitted any one of its ingredients, he is guilty of a capital offence. Rabban Shimon ben Gamliel says: "Balsam" refers to the sap that drips from the balsam tree. The Carsina lye was used for bleaching the onycha to improve it. The Cyprus wine was used to soak the onycha in it to make it pungent. Though urine is suitable for this purpose, it is not brought into the Temple out of respect.

MISHNAH, TAMID 7:4

הַשִּׁיר These were the Psalms which the Levites used to recite in the Temple: On the first day of the week they used to say: "The earth is the LORD's and all it contains, the world and all who live in it." On the second day they used to say: "Great is the LORD and greatly to be praised in the city of GOD, on His holy mountain." On the third day they used to say: "GOD stands in the Divine assembly. Among the judges He delivers judgement." On the fourth day they used to say: "GOD of retribution, LORD, GOD of retribution, appear." On the fifth day they used to say: "Sing for joy to GOD, our strength. Shout aloud to the GOD of Jacob." On the sixth day they used to say: "The LORD reigns: He is robed in majesty; the LORD is robed, girded with strength; the world is firmly established; it cannot be moved." On the

---

הַשִּׁיר שֶׁהַלְוִיִּם הָיוּ אוֹמְרִים בְּבֵית הַמִּקְדָּשׁ *These were the Psalms which the Levites used to recite in the Temple:* Each day of the week, after the regular offerings in the Temple, the Levites would sing a particular psalm, signaling that each day has its own character, its own tasks, its own tonality in the symphony of time. We still say these psalms, usually at the end of the service. In this way, a further connection is made between our prayers and the Temple service.

אַף־תִּכּוֹן תֵּבֵל בַּל־תִּמּוֹט. בַּשַּׁבָּת הָיוּ אוֹמְרִים, מִזְמוֹר שִׁיר לְיוֹם הַשַּׁבָּת. מִזְמוֹר שִׁיר לֶעָתִיד לָבֹא, לְיוֹם שֶׁכֻּלּוֹ שַׁבָּת וּמְנוּחָה לְחַיֵּי הָעוֹלָמִים.

תלמוד בבלי מסכת ברכות סד:א׳

אָמַר רַבִּי אֶלְעָזָר אָמַר רַבִּי חֲנִינָא, תַּלְמִידֵי חֲכָמִים מַרְבִּים שָׁלוֹם בָּעוֹלָם, שֶׁנֶּאֱמַר, וְכָל בָּנַיִךְ לִמּוּדֵי יהוה, וְרַב שְׁלוֹם בָּנָיִךְ, אַל תִּקְרֵי בָּנָיִךְ אֶלָּא בּוֹנָיִךְ. שָׁלוֹם רָב לְאֹהֲבֵי תוֹרָתֶךָ, וְאֵין לָמוֹ מִכְשׁוֹל. יְהִי שָׁלוֹם בְּחֵילֵךְ, שַׁלְוָה בְּאַרְמְנוֹתָיִךְ. לְמַעַן אַחַי וְרֵעָי, אֲדַבְּרָה נָּא שָׁלוֹם בָּךְ. לְמַעַן בֵּית יהוה אֱלֹהֵינוּ, אֲבַקְשָׁה טוֹב לָךְ. ◂ יהוה עֹז לְעַמּוֹ יִתֵּן, יהוה יְבָרֵךְ אֶת עַמּוֹ בַשָּׁלוֹם.

Some congregations say קַדִּישׁ דְּרַבָּנָן on page 34.

עלינו

Stand while saying עָלֵינוּ. Bow at ▾.

עָלֵינוּ לְשַׁבֵּחַ לַאֲדוֹן הַכֹּל, לָתֵת גְּדֻלָּה לְיוֹצֵר בְּרֵאשִׁית, שֶׁלֹּא עָשָׂנוּ כְּגוֹיֵי הָאֲרָצוֹת, וְלֹא שָׂמָנוּ כְּמִשְׁפְּחוֹת הָאֲדָמָה. שֶׁלֹּא שָׂם חֶלְקֵנוּ כָּהֶם, וְגוֹרָלֵנוּ כְּכָל־הֲמוֹנָם. ▾וַאֲנַחְנוּ כּוֹרְעִים וּמִשְׁתַּחֲוִים וּמוֹדִים, לִפְנֵי מֶלֶךְ מַלְכֵי הַמְּלָכִים הַקָּדוֹשׁ בָּרוּךְ הוּא. שֶׁהוּא נוֹטֶה שָׁמַיִם וְיוֹסֵד אָרֶץ, וּמוֹשַׁב יְקָרוֹ בַּשָּׁמַיִם מִמַּעַל, וּשְׁכִינַת עֻזּוֹ בְּגָבְהֵי מְרוֹמִים. הוּא אֱלֹהֵינוּ, אֵין עוֹד. אֱמֶת מַלְכֵּנוּ, אֶפֶס זוּלָתוֹ, כַּכָּתוּב בְּתוֹרָתוֹ, וְיָדַעְתָּ הַיּוֹם וַהֲשֵׁבֹתָ אֶל־לְבָבֶךָ, כִּי יהוה הוּא הָאֱלֹהִים בַּשָּׁמַיִם מִמַּעַל וְעַל־הָאָרֶץ מִתָּחַת, אֵין עוֹד.

עַל־כֵּן נְקַוֶּה לְּךָ יהוה אֱלֹהֵינוּ לִרְאוֹת מְהֵרָה בְּתִפְאֶרֶת עֻזֶּךָ, לְהַעֲבִיר גִּלּוּלִים מִן הָאָרֶץ, וְהָאֱלִילִים כָּרוֹת יִכָּרֵתוּן, לְתַקֵּן עוֹלָם בְּמַלְכוּת שַׁדַּי. וְכָל־בְּנֵי בָשָׂר יִקְרְאוּ בִשְׁמֶךָ, לְהַפְנוֹת אֵלֶיךָ כָּל־רִשְׁעֵי אָרֶץ. יַכִּירוּ וְיֵדְעוּ כָּל־יוֹשְׁבֵי תֵבֵל, כִּי לְךָ תִּכְרַע כָּל־בֶּרֶךְ, תִּשָּׁבַע כָּל־לָשׁוֹן. לְפָנֶיךָ יהוה אֱלֹהֵינוּ יִכְרְעוּ וְיִפֹּלוּ, וְלִכְבוֹד שִׁמְךָ יְקָר יִתֵּנוּ. וִיקַבְּלוּ כֻלָּם אֶת־עוֹל

Sabbath they used to say: "A psalm, a song for the Sabbath day" – [meaning] a psalm and song for the time to come, for the day which will be entirely Sabbath and rest for life everlasting.

BABYLONIAN TALMUD, BERACHOT 64A

Rabbi Eleazar said in the name of Rabbi Chanina: The disciples of the Sages increase peace in the world, as it is said, "And all your children shall be taught of the LORD, and great shall be the peace of your children [*banayich*]". Read not *banayich*, "your children", but *bonayich*, "your builders". Those who love Your Torah have great peace; there is no stumbling block for them. May there be peace within your ramparts, prosperity in your palaces. For the sake of my brothers and friends, I shall say, "Peace be within you". For the sake of the house of the LORD our GOD, I will seek your good. ➔ May the LORD grant strength to His people; may the LORD bless His people with peace.

Some congregations say the Rabbis' *Kaddish* on page 35.

ALEINU

Stand while saying *Aleinu*. Bow at ▼.

עָלֵינוּ It is our duty to praise the Master of all, and ascribe greatness to the Author of creation, who has not made us like the nations of the lands nor placed us like the families of the earth; who has not made our portion like theirs, nor our destiny like all their multitudes. Therefore ▼we bow in worship and thank the Supreme King of kings, the Holy One, blessed be He, who extends the heavens and establishes the earth, whose throne of glory is in the heavens above, and whose power's presence is in the highest of heights. He is our GOD; there is no other. Truly He is our King, there is none else, as it is written in His Torah, "You shall know and take to heart this day that the LORD is GOD, in heaven above and on earth below. There is no other."

Therefore we place our hope in You, LORD our GOD, that we may soon see the glory of Your power, when You will remove abominations from the earth, and idols will be utterly destroyed, when the world will be perfected under the sovereignty of the Almighty, when all humanity will call on Your name, and the earth's wicked will all turn to You. All the world's inhabitants will realise and know that to You every knee must bow and every tongue swear loyalty. Before You, LORD our GOD, they will kneel and bow down and give honour to

מַלְכוּתֶךָ, וְתִמְלֹךְ עֲלֵיהֶם מְהֵרָה לְעוֹלָם וָעֶד. כִּי הַמַּלְכוּת שֶׁלְּךָ הִיא וּלְעוֹלְמֵי עַד תִּמְלוֹךְ בְּכָבוֹד, כַּכָּתוּב בְּתוֹרָתֶךָ, יהוה יִמְלֹךְ לְעוֹלָם וָעֶד. ← וְנֶאֱמַר, וְהָיָה יהוה לְמֶלֶךְ עַל־כָּל־הָאָרֶץ, בַּיּוֹם הַהוּא יִהְיֶה יהוה אֶחָד וּשְׁמוֹ אֶחָד.

Some congregations add:

אַל תִּירָא מִפַּחַד פִּתְאֹם, וּמִשֹּׁאַת רְשָׁעִים כִּי תָבֹא. עֻצוּ עֵצָה וְתֻפָר, דַּבְּרוּ דָבָר וְלֹא יָקוּם, כִּי עִמָּנוּ אֵל. וְעַד זִקְנָה אֲנִי הוּא, וְעַד שֵׂיבָה אֲנִי אֶסְבֹּל, אֲנִי עָשִׂיתִי וַאֲנִי אֶשָּׂא, וַאֲנִי אֶסְבֹּל וַאֲמַלֵּט.

קדיש יתום

The transliteration can be found at the end of the Siddur.

Mourner:

יִתְגַּדַּל וְיִתְקַדַּשׁ שְׁמֵהּ רַבָּא. (Cong. אָמֵן) בְּעָלְמָא דִּי־בְרָא כִרְעוּתֵהּ. וְיַמְלִיךְ מַלְכוּתֵהּ, בְּחַיֵּיכוֹן וּבְיוֹמֵיכוֹן וּבְחַיֵּי דִי־כָל־בֵּית יִשְׂרָאֵל, בַּעֲגָלָא וּבִזְמַן קָרִיב. וְאִמְרוּ אָמֵן. (Cong. אָמֵן)

All:

יְהֵא שְׁמֵהּ רַבָּא מְבָרַךְ לְעָלַם וּלְעָלְמֵי עָלְמַיָּא.

Mourner:

יִתְבָּרַךְ וְיִשְׁתַּבַּח וְיִתְפָּאַר וְיִתְרוֹמַם וְיִתְנַשֵּׂא וְיִתְהַדָּר וְיִתְעַלֶּה וְיִתְהַלָּל שְׁמֵהּ דְּקֻדְשָׁא בְּרִיךְ הוּא (Cong. בְּרִיךְ הוּא) לְעֵלָּא (On שַׁבַּת שׁוּבָה add לְעֵלָּא) מִן־כָּל־בִּרְכָתָא וְשִׁירָתָא תֻּשְׁבְּחָתָא וְנֶחֱמָתָא, דַּאֲמִירָן בְּעָלְמָא. וְאִמְרוּ אָמֵן. (Cong. אָמֵן)

יְהֵא שְׁלָמָא רַבָּא מִן־שְׁמַיָּא, וְחַיִּים עָלֵינוּ וְעַל־כָּל־יִשְׂרָאֵל. וְאִמְרוּ אָמֵן. (Cong. אָמֵן)

Bow, take three steps back, then bow, first left, then right, then centre, while saying:

עֹשֶׂה שָׁלוֹם בִּמְרוֹמָיו, הוּא יַעֲשֶׂה שָׁלוֹם עָלֵינוּ, וְעַל־כָּל־יִשְׂרָאֵל. וְאִמְרוּ אָמֵן. (Cong. אָמֵן)

Your glorious name. They will all accept the yoke of Your kingdom, and You will reign over them soon and for ever. For the kingdom is Yours, and to all eternity You will reign in glory, as it is written in Your Torah: "The LORD will reign for ever and ever." ➔ And it is said: "Then the LORD shall be King over all the earth: on that day the LORD shall be One and His name One."

Some congregations add:

Have no fear of sudden terror or of the ruin that overtakes the wicked. Devise your strategy, but it will be thwarted; propose your plan, but it will not stand, for GOD is with us. When you grow old, I will still be the same. When your hair turns grey, I will still carry you. I made you, I will bear you, I will carry you, and I will rescue you.

MOURNER'S KADDISH

The transliteration can be found at the end of the Siddur.

Mourner:

יִתְגַּדַּל Magnified and sanctified may His great name be, in the world He created by His will. May He establish His kingdom in your lifetime and in your days, and in the lifetime of all the House of Israel, swiftly and soon – and say: Amen.

All:

May His great name be blessed for ever and all time.

Mourner:

Blessed and praised, glorified and exalted, raised and honoured, uplifted and lauded be the name of the Holy One, blessed be He, (between Rosh Hashanah and Yom Kippur add 'well') beyond any blessing, song, praise and consolation uttered in the world – and say: Amen.

May there be great peace from heaven, and life for us and all Israel – and say: Amen.

Bow, take three steps back, then bow, first left, then right, then centre, while saying:

May He who makes peace in His high places, make peace for us and all Israel – and say: Amen.

שיר הכבוד

The Ark is opened. All stand. The following hymn is sung in alternate verses by the Leader and Congregation.

אַנְעִים זְמִירוֹת וְשִׁירִים אֶאֱרוֹג, כִּי אֵלֶיךָ נַפְשִׁי תַעֲרוֹג.
נַפְשִׁי חִמְּדָה בְּצֵל יָדֶךָ, לָדַעַת כָּל רָז סוֹדֶךָ.

מִדֵּי דַבְּרִי בִּכְבוֹדֶךָ, הוֹמֶה לִבִּי אֶל דּוֹדֶיךָ.
עַל כֵּן אֲדַבֵּר בְּךָ נִכְבָּדוֹת, וְשִׁמְךָ אֲכַבֵּד בְּשִׁירֵי יְדִידוֹת.

אֲסַפְּרָה כְבוֹדְךָ וְלֹא רְאִיתִיךָ, אֲדַמְּךָ אֲכַנְּךָ וְלֹא יְדַעְתִּיךָ.
בְּיַד נְבִיאֶךָ בְּסוֹד עֲבָדֶיךָ, דִּמִּיתָ הֲדַר כְּבוֹד הוֹדֶךָ.

גְּדֻלָּתְךָ וּגְבוּרָתֶךָ, כִּנּוּ לְתֹקֶף פְּעֻלָּתֶךָ.
דִּמּוּ אוֹתְךָ וְלֹא כְּפִי יֶשְׁךָ, וַיְשַׁוּוּךָ לְפִי מַעֲשֶׂיךָ.

הִמְשִׁילוּךָ בְּרֹב חֶזְיוֹנוֹת, הִנְּךָ אֶחָד בְּכָל דִּמְיוֹנוֹת.
וַיֶּחֱזוּ בְךָ זִקְנָה וּבַחֲרוּת, וּשְׂעַר רֹאשְׁךָ בְּשֵׂיבָה וְשַׁחֲרוּת.

זִקְנָה בְּיוֹם דִּין וּבַחֲרוּת בְּיוֹם קְרָב, כְּאִישׁ מִלְחָמוֹת יָדָיו לוֹ רָב.
חָבַשׁ כּוֹבַע יְשׁוּעָה בְּרֹאשׁוֹ, הוֹשִׁיעָה לּוֹ יְמִינוֹ וּזְרוֹעַ קָדְשׁוֹ.

אַנְעִים זְמִירוֹת *Song of Glory*: Attributed to either Rabbi Judah he-Chassid (d. 1217) or his father Rabbi Samuel, this hymn is structured as an alphabetical acrostic, with a (non-acrostic) four-line introduction and a three-line conclusion, followed by biblical verses. The poem, with great grace and depth, speaks about the limits of language in describing the experience of God. On the one hand, God – Infinite, eternal, invisible – is beyond the reach of language. On the other, we can only address Him in and through language. Hence the various literary forms – metaphor, image, mystic vision – used by the prophets and poets and their successors to indicate, through words, that which lies beyond words. The images are many, but God is one.

In some communities the hymn is said each day. Many authorities, however, held that it was too sublime to be said daily, and limited its recital to Shabbat and festivals.

בְּצֵל יָדֶךָ *The shelter of Your hand:* An image of intimacy and protection (see Isaiah 49:2, 51:16; Song of Songs 2:3).

אֲדַמְּךָ אֲכַנְּךָ וְלֹא יְדַעְתִּיךָ *Imagine and describe You, though I have not known You* – The finite cannot truly know the

SONG OF GLORY

The Ark is opened. All stand. The following hymn is sung in alternate verses by the Leader and Congregation.

אַנְעִים זְמִירוֹת I will sing sweet psalms and I will weave songs,
to You for whom my soul longs.
My soul yearns for the shelter of Your hand,
that all Your mystic secrets I might understand.

Whenever I speak of Your glory above,
my heart is yearning for Your love.
So Your glories I will proclaim,
and in songs of love give honour to Your name.

I will tell of Your glory though I have not seen You,
imagine and describe You, though I have not known You.
By the hand of Your prophets, through Your servants' mystery,
You gave a glimpse of Your wondrous majesty.

Recounting Your grandeur and Your glory,
of Your great deeds they told the story.
They depicted You, though not as You are,
but as You do: Your acts, Your power.

They represented You in many visions;
through them all You are One without divisions.
They saw You, now old, then young,
Your head with grey, with black hair hung.

Age on the day of judgement, yet on the day of war,
a young warrior with mighty hands they saw.
Triumph like a helmet He wore on his head;
His right hand and holy arm to victory have led.

Infinite; physical beings cannot fully understand the One who is non-physical.

הִנְּךָ אֶחָד בְּכָל דִּמְיוֹנוֹת *Through them all You are One without divisions:* Literally, "You are One through all the images", a preface to the following verses, which give examples of this theme.

זִקְנָה בְּיוֹם דִּין *Age on the day of judgement*: A reference to the mystical vision in Daniel (7:9) of God sitting on the throne of judgement, "The hair of his head was white as wool".

וּבַחֲרוּת בְּיוֹם קְרָב *Yet on the day of war*: From the vision of Zechariah (14:3).

טַלְלֵי אוֹרוֹת רֹאשׁוֹ נִמְלָא, קְוֻצּוֹתָיו רְסִיסֵי לָיְלָה.
יִתְפָּאֵר בִּי כִּי חָפֵץ בִּי, וְהוּא יִהְיֶה לִּי לַעֲטֶרֶת צְבִי.

כֶּתֶם טָהוֹר פָּז דְּמוּת רֹאשׁוֹ, וְחַק עַל מֵצַח כְּבוֹד שֵׁם קָדְשׁוֹ.
לְחֵן וּלְכָבוֹד צְבִי תִפְאָרָה, אֻמָּתוֹ לוֹ עִטְּרָה עֲטָרָה.

מַחְלְפוֹת רֹאשׁוֹ כְּבִימֵי בְחֻרוֹת, קְוֻצּוֹתָיו תַּלְתַּלִּים שְׁחוֹרוֹת.
נְוֵה הַצֶּדֶק צְבִי תִפְאַרְתּוֹ, יַעֲלֶה נָּא עַל רֹאשׁ שִׂמְחָתוֹ.

סְגֻלָּתוֹ, תְּהִי בְיָדוֹ עֲטֶרֶת, וּצְנִיף מְלוּכָה צְבִי תִפְאֶרֶת.
עֲמוּסִים נְשָׂאָם עֲטֶרֶת עִנְּדָם. מֵאֲשֶׁר יָקְרוּ בְעֵינָיו כִּבְּדָם.

פְּאֵרוֹ עָלַי וּפְאֵרִי עָלָיו, וְקָרוֹב אֵלַי בְּקָרְאִי אֵלָיו.
צַח וְאָדוֹם לִלְבוּשׁוֹ אָדוֹם, פּוּרָה בְדָרְכוֹ בְּבוֹאוֹ מֵאֱדוֹם.

קֶשֶׁר תְּפִלִּין הֶרְאָה לֶעָנָו, תְּמוּנַת יהוה לְנֶגֶד עֵינָיו.
רוֹצֶה בְעַמּוֹ עֲנָוִים יְפָאֵר, יוֹשֵׁב תְּהִלּוֹת בָּם לְהִתְפָּאֵר.

רֹאשׁ דְּבָרְךָ אֱמֶת קוֹרֵא מֵרֹאשׁ, דּוֹר וָדוֹר עַם דּוֹרֶשְׁךָ דְּרוֹשׁ.
שִׁית הֲמוֹן שִׁירַי, נָא עָלֶיךָ, וְרִנָּתִי תִּקְרַב אֵלֶיךָ.

תְּהִלָּתִי, תְּהִי לְרֹאשְׁךָ עֲטֶרֶת, וּתְפִלָּתִי תִּכּוֹן קְטֹרֶת.
תִּיקַר שִׁירַת רָשׁ בְּעֵינֶיךָ, כַּשִּׁיר יוּשַׁר עַל קָרְבָּנֶיךָ.

בִּרְכָתִי תַעֲלֶה לְרֹאשׁ מַשְׁבִּיר, מְחוֹלֵל וּמוֹלִיד צַדִּיק כַּבִּיר.
וּבְבִרְכָתִי תְנַעֲנַע לִי רֹאשׁ, וְאוֹתָהּ קַח לְךָ כִּבְשָׂמִים רֹאשׁ.

טַלְלֵי אוֹרוֹת *Dew-drops of light*: This phrase together with the following images are drawn from Isaiah and The Song of Songs.

פְּאֵרוֹ עָלַי וּפְאֵרִי עָלָיו *His glory is on me; my glory is on Him*: A reference to the daring metaphor of the Sages (*Berachot* 6a), that just as the children of Israel wear *tefillin* (an emblem of glory) proclaiming the oneness of God, so too, God, as it were, wears *tefillin* proclaiming the uniqueness of Israel ("Who is like Your people Israel, a nation unique on earth?") – hence the later phrase that *"He showed the tefillin-knot to Moses"*, a reference to Exodus 33:23, "You will see My back". *Tefillin* symbolise the bond of love between God and His people.

בְּבוֹאוֹ מֵאֱדוֹם *When He comes from Edom*: An image of judgement at the end of days, taken from Isaiah 63:1–2. By invoking some of the most dramatic images of God in the Bible and rabbinic literature, the poet tells us that they are not to be

His curls are filled with dew-drops of light,
His locks with fragments of the night.
He will glory in me, for He delights in me;
My diadem of beauty He shall be.

His head is like pure beaten gold;
Engraved on His brow, His sacred name behold.
For grace and glory, beauty and renown,
His people have adorned Him with a crown.

Like a youth's, His hair in locks unfurls;
Its black tresses flowing in curls.
Jerusalem, His splendour, is the dwelling place of right
– may He prize it as His highest delight.

Like a crown in His hand may His treasured people be,
a turban of beauty and of majesty.
He bore them, carried them, with a crown He adorned them.
They were precious in His sight, and He honoured them.

His glory is on me; my glory is on Him.
He is near to me when I call to Him.
He is bright and rosy; red will be His dress,
when He comes from Edom, treading the winepress.

He showed the *tefillin*-knot to Moses, humble, wise,
when the LORD's likeness was before his eyes.
He delights in His people; the humble He does raise –
He glories in them; He sits enthroned upon their praise.

Your first word, Your call to every age, is true:
O seek the people who seek You.
My many songs please take and hear
and may my hymn of joy to You come near.

May my praise be a crown for Your head,
and like incense before You, the prayers I have said.
May a poor man's song be precious in Your eyes,
like a song sung over sacrifice.

To the One who sustains all, may my blessing take flight:
Creator, Life-giver, GOD of right and might.
And when I offer blessing, to me Your head incline:
accepting it as spice, fragrant and fine.

יֶעֱרַב נָא שִׂיחִי עָלֶיךָ, כִּי נַפְשִׁי תַעֲרוֹג אֵלֶיךָ.

The Ark is closed.

All:

לְךָ יהוה הַגְּדֻלָּה וְהַגְּבוּרָה וְהַתִּפְאֶרֶת וְהַנֵּצַח וְהַהוֹד, כִּי כֹל בַּשָּׁמַיִם וּבָאָרֶץ, לְךָ יהוה הַמַּמְלָכָה וְהַמִּתְנַשֵּׂא לְכֹל לְרֹאשׁ.
מִי יְמַלֵּל גְּבוּרוֹת יהוה, יַשְׁמִיעַ כָּל תְּהִלָּתוֹ.

קדיש יתום

The transliteration can be found at the end of the Siddur.

Mourner:

יִתְגַּדַּל וְיִתְקַדַּשׁ שְׁמֵהּ רַבָּא. (Cong. אָמֵן) בְּעָלְמָא דִּי־בְרָא כִרְעוּתֵהּ. וְיַמְלִיךְ מַלְכוּתֵהּ, בְּחַיֵּיכוֹן וּבְיוֹמֵיכוֹן וּבְחַיֵּי דִי־כָל־בֵּית יִשְׂרָאֵל, בַּעֲגָלָא וּבִזְמַן קָרִיב. וְאִמְרוּ אָמֵן. (Cong. אָמֵן)

All:

יְהֵא שְׁמֵהּ רַבָּא מְבָרַךְ לְעָלַם וּלְעָלְמֵי עָלְמַיָּא.

Mourner:

יִתְבָּרַךְ וְיִשְׁתַּבַּח וְיִתְפָּאַר וְיִתְרוֹמַם וְיִתְנַשֵּׂא וְיִתְהַדַּר וְיִתְעַלֶּה וְיִתְהַלָּל שְׁמֵהּ דְּקֻדְשָׁא בְּרִיךְ הוּא (Cong. בְּרִיךְ הוּא) לְעֵלָּא (On שַׁבַּת שׁוּבָה add לְעֵלָּא) מִן־כָּל־בִּרְכָתָא וְשִׁירָתָא תֻּשְׁבְּחָתָא וְנֶחֱמָתָא, דַּאֲמִירָן בְּעָלְמָא. וְאִמְרוּ אָמֵן. (Cong. אָמֵן)

יְהֵא שְׁלָמָא רַבָּא מִן־שְׁמַיָּא, וְחַיִּים עָלֵינוּ וְעַל־כָּל־יִשְׂרָאֵל. וְאִמְרוּ אָמֵן. (Cong. אָמֵן)

Bow, take three steps back, then bow, first left, then right, then centre, while saying:

עֹשֶׂה שָׁלוֹם בִּמְרוֹמָיו, הוּא יַעֲשֶׂה שָׁלוֹם עָלֵינוּ, וְעַל־כָּל־יִשְׂרָאֵל. וְאִמְרוּ אָמֵן. (Cong. אָמֵן)

May my prayer be to You sweet song.
For You my soul will always long.

The Ark is closed.

All:

Yours, LORD, are the greatness and the power, the glory, the majesty and splendour, for everything in heaven and earth is Yours. Yours, O LORD, is the kingdom; You are exalted as head over all.
Who can tell of the LORD's mighty acts of the LORD and make all His praise be heard?

MOURNER'S KADDISH

The transliteration can be found at the end of the Siddur.

Mourner:

יִתְגַּדַּל Magnified and sanctified may His great name be, in the world He created by His will. May He establish His kingdom in your lifetime and in your days, and in the lifetime of all the House of Israel, swiftly and soon – and say: Amen.

All:

May His great name be blessed for ever and all time.

Mourner:

Blessed and praised, glorified and exalted, raised and honoured, uplifted and lauded be the name of the Holy One, blessed be He, (between Rosh Hashanah and Yom Kippur add 'well') beyond any blessing, song, praise and consolation uttered in the world – and say: Amen.

May there be great peace from heaven, and life for us and all Israel – and say: Amen.

Bow, take three steps back, then bow, first left, then right, then centre, while saying:

May He who makes peace in His high places, make peace for us and all Israel – and say: Amen.

---

understood literally – poetry, metaphor and imagery are ways in which prophets and mystics intimate what lies beyond the sayable.

כִּי נַפְשִׁי תַעֲרוֹג אֵלֶיךָ *For You my soul will always long*: The poet brings the song to an end by referring back to the line with which it began.

Many congregations say the Psalm for the Day (weekdays page 144 ff, שַׁבָּת page 152) and additional psalms at this point. קַדִּישׁ יָתוֹם is then said.

אדון עולם

אֲדוֹן עוֹלָם אֲשֶׁר מָלַךְ, בְּטֶרֶם כָּל־יְצִיר נִבְרָא.
לְעֵת נַעֲשָׂה בְחֶפְצוֹ כֹּל, אֲזַי מֶלֶךְ שְׁמוֹ נִקְרָא.
וְאַחֲרֵי כִּכְלוֹת הַכֹּל, לְבַדּוֹ יִמְלוֹךְ נוֹרָא.
וְהוּא הָיָה וְהוּא הֹוֶה, וְהוּא יִהְיֶה בְּתִפְאָרָה.
וְהוּא אֶחָד וְאֵין שֵׁנִי, לְהַמְשִׁיל לוֹ לְהַחְבִּירָה.
בְּלִי רֵאשִׁית בְּלִי תַכְלִית, וְלוֹ הָעֹז וְהַמִּשְׂרָה.
וְהוּא אֵלִי וְחַי גֹּאֲלִי, וְצוּר חֶבְלִי בְּעֵת צָרָה.
וְהוּא נִסִּי וּמָנוֹס לִי, מְנָת כּוֹסִי בְּיוֹם אֶקְרָא.
בְּיָדוֹ אַפְקִיד רוּחִי, בְּעֵת אִישַׁן וְאָעִירָה.
וְעִם־רוּחִי גְּוִיָּתִי, יהוה לִי וְלֹא אִירָא.

קידושא רבא לשבת

שמות לא:טז–יז

וְשָׁמְרוּ בְנֵי־יִשְׂרָאֵל אֶת־הַשַּׁבָּת, לַעֲשׂוֹת אֶת־הַשַּׁבָּת לְדֹרֹתָם בְּרִית עוֹלָם. בֵּינִי וּבֵין בְּנֵי יִשְׂרָאֵל אוֹת הִיא לְעֹלָם, כִּי־שֵׁשֶׁת יָמִים עָשָׂה יהוה אֶת־הַשָּׁמַיִם וְאֶת־הָאָרֶץ, וּבַיּוֹם הַשְּׁבִיעִי שָׁבַת וַיִּנָּפַשׁ.

SHABBAT MORNING KIDDUSH
The *Kiddush* of Shabbat morning is known as *Kiddusha Rabba*, "the great *Kiddush*", despite or possibly because of its brevity: essentially it involves only the blessing over wine. Over the course of time, biblical readings were added. The two we say according to our custom refer, respectively, to the two essential elements of the Shabbat. The first is about the day as a memorial of creation, the second – taken from the Exodus text of the Ten Commandments – is about the Shabbat as a memory of the exodus from

Some congregations say the Psalm for the Day (weekdays page 145 ff, Shabbat page 153) and additional psalms at this point. The Mourner's *Kaddish* is then said.

ADON OLAM

אֲדוֹן עוֹלָם Lord of the universe, who reigned
before the birth of any thing –
When by His will all things were made
then was His name proclaimed King.
And when all things shall cease to be
He alone will reign in awe.
He was, He is, and He shall be
glorious for evermore.
He is One, there is none else,
alone, unique, beyond compare;
Without beginning, without end,
His might, His rule are everywhere.
He is my God; my Redeemer lives.
He is the Rock on whom I rely –
My banner and my safe retreat,
my cup, my portion when I cry.
Into His hand my soul I place,
when I awake and when I sleep.
God is with me, I shall not fear;
body and soul from harm will He keep.

KIDDUSH FOR SHABBAT MORNING

EXODUS 31:16–17

וְשָׁמְרוּ The children of Israel must keep the Sabbath, observing the Sabbath in every generation as an everlasting covenant. It is a sign between Me and the children of Israel for ever, for in six days God made the heavens and the earth, but on the seventh day He ceased work and refreshed Himself.

Egypt. The Israelites were to create a society in which, one day in seven, everyone, even a slave, was free: the antithesis of Egypt. Often the *Kiddush* is said communally in the synagogue, as well as at home.

שמות כ:ח–יא

זָכוֹר אֶת יוֹם הַשַּׁבָּת לְקַדְּשׁוֹ. שֵׁשֶׁת יָמִים תַּעֲבֹד וְעָשִׂיתָ כָּל מְלַאכְתֶּךָ. וְיוֹם הַשְּׁבִיעִי שַׁבָּת לַיהוה אֱלֹהֶיךָ, לֹא תַעֲשֶׂה כָל מְלָאכָה, אַתָּה וּבִנְךָ וּבִתֶּךָ עַבְדְּךָ וַאֲמָתְךָ וּבְהֶמְתֶּךָ, וְגֵרְךָ אֲשֶׁר בִּשְׁעָרֶיךָ. כִּי שֵׁשֶׁת יָמִים עָשָׂה יהוה אֶת הַשָּׁמַיִם וְאֶת הָאָרֶץ אֶת הַיָּם וְאֶת כָּל אֲשֶׁר בָּם, וַיָּנַח בַּיּוֹם הַשְּׁבִיעִי.

עַל כֵּן בֵּרַךְ יהוה אֶת יוֹם הַשַּׁבָּת וַיְקַדְּשֵׁהוּ.

When saying קִדּוּשׁ for others, add:

סַבְרִי מָרָנָן וְרַבָּנָן וְרַבּוֹתַי.

If making קִדּוּשׁ on wine or grape juice, say:

בָּרוּךְ אַתָּה יהוה אֱלֹהֵינוּ מֶלֶךְ הָעוֹלָם, בּוֹרֵא פְּרִי הַגָּפֶן.

If making קִדּוּשׁ on any other drink, say:

בָּרוּךְ אַתָּה יהוה אֱלֹהֵינוּ מֶלֶךְ הָעוֹלָם, שֶׁהַכֹּל נִהְיֶה בִּדְבָרוֹ.

Immediately after washing hands before the meal, say:

בָּרוּךְ אַתָּה יהוה אֱלֹהֵינוּ מֶלֶךְ הָעוֹלָם, אֲשֶׁר קִדְּשָׁנוּ בְּמִצְוֹתָיו, וְצִוָּנוּ עַל נְטִילַת יָדָיִם.

After washing hands, one should not speak until one has eaten some of the חַלָּה, the שַׁבָּת bread.

Holding both loaves, the one making the blessing says:

בָּרוּךְ אַתָּה יהוה אֱלֹהֵינוּ מֶלֶךְ הָעוֹלָם, הַמּוֹצִיא לֶחֶם מִן הָאָרֶץ.

A piece of the bread should be given to all present.

A SHABBAT MEDITATION

The Hassidic master, Rabbi Levi Yitzhak of Berditchev, was once looking out of his window watching people rushing across the town square. He leaned out and asked one, "Why are you running?" The man replied, "I'm running to make a living." The rabbi replied, "Are you so

EXODUS 20:8–11

זָכוֹר Remember the Sabbath day to keep it holy. Six days you shall labour and do all your work, but the seventh day is a Sabbath of the LORD your GOD; on it you shall not do any work – you, your son or daughter, your male or female slave, or your cattle, or the stranger within your gates. For in six days the LORD made heaven and earth and sea and all that is in them, and rested on the seventh day;

עַל כֵּן therefore the LORD blessed the Sabbath day and declared it holy.

When saying *Kiddush* for others, add:

Please pay attention, my teachers, rabbis and friends.

If making *Kiddush* on wine or grape juice, say:

בָּרוּךְ Blessed are You, LORD our GOD, King of the Universe, who creates the fruit of the vine.

If making *Kiddush* on any other drink, say:

בָּרוּךְ Blessed are You, LORD our GOD, King of the Universe, by whose word all things came to be.

Immediately after washing hands before the meal, say:

בָּרוּךְ Blessed are You, LORD our GOD, King of the Universe, who has made us holy through His commandments, and has commanded us about washing hands.

After washing hands, one should not speak until one has eaten some of the *challah*, the Shabbat bread.

Holding both loaves, the one making the blessing says:

בָּרוּךְ Blessed are You, LORD our GOD, King of the Universe, who brings forth bread from the earth.

A piece of the bread should be given to all present.

---

sure that your livelihood is running away from you and you have to rush to catch it up? Perhaps it's running towards you, and all you have to do is stand still and let it catch up with you."

Still today, in our busy, modern world, Shabbat is the day we stand still and let our blessings catch up with us. Without it, we can be so busy making a living that we hardly have time to live. We risk making the journey while missing the view. On Shabbat we cease striving for what we do not have, and thank GOD for what we have.

זמירות ליום שבת

יום זה מכבד

יוֹם זֶה מְכֻבָּד מִכָּל יָמִים,
כִּי בוֹ שָׁבַת צוּר עוֹלָמִים.

שֵׁשֶׁת יָמִים תַּעֲשֶׂה מְלַאכְתֶּךָ,
וְיוֹם הַשְּׁבִיעִי לֵאלֹהֶיךָ,
שַׁבָּת לֹא תַעֲשֶׂה בוֹ מְלָאכָה,
כִּי כֹל עָשָׂה שֵׁשֶׁת יָמִים.

יוֹם זֶה מְכֻבָּד מִכָּל יָמִים, כִּי בוֹ שָׁבַת צוּר עוֹלָמִים.

רִאשׁוֹן הוּא לְמִקְרָאֵי קֹדֶשׁ,
יוֹם שַׁבָּתוֹן יוֹם שַׁבַּת קֹדֶשׁ,
עַל כֵּן כָּל אִישׁ בְּיֵינוֹ יְקַדֵּשׁ,
עַל שְׁתֵּי לֶחֶם יִבְצְעוּ תְמִימִים.

יוֹם זֶה מְכֻבָּד מִכָּל יָמִים, כִּי בוֹ שָׁבַת צוּר עוֹלָמִים.

אֱכוֹל מַשְׁמַנִּים שְׁתֵה מַמְתַּקִּים,
כִּי אֵל יִתֵּן לְכָל בּוֹ דְבֵקִים,
בֶּגֶד לִלְבּוֹשׁ לֶחֶם חֻקִּים,
בָּשָׂר וְדָגִים וְכָל מַטְעַמִּים.

יוֹם זֶה מְכֻבָּד מִכָּל יָמִים, כִּי בוֹ שָׁבַת צוּר עוֹלָמִים.

לֹא תֶחְסַר כֹּל בּוֹ וְאָכַלְתָּ,
וְשָׂבָעְתָּ, וּבֵרַכְתָּ,
אֶת יהוה אֱלֹהֶיךָ אֲשֶׁר אָהַבְתָּ,
כִּי בֵרַכְךָ מִכָּל הָעַמִּים.

יוֹם זֶה מְכֻבָּד מִכָּל יָמִים, כִּי בוֹ שָׁבַת צוּר עוֹלָמִים.

SHABBAT DAY ZEMIROT

YOM ZEH MECHUBAD

יוֹם זֶה מְכֻבָּד This day is honoured above all others,
For on it He who formed worlds found rest.

שֵׁשֶׁת For six days, do your work
But the seventh day is God's:
On the Sabbath you shall do no work,
For in six days He made all.
This day is honoured above all others,
for on it He who formed worlds found rest.

רִאשׁוֹן Foremost among sacred days
Is this day of rest, this holy Sabbath.
So let each say *Kiddush* over wine,
And break bread over two complete loaves.
This day is honoured above all others,
for on it He who formed worlds found rest.

אֱכוֹל Eat choice food, drink sweet wine,
For God will give to those who cleave to Him
Clothes to wear, due portions of bread,
Meat and fish, and all tasty foods.
This day is honoured above all others,
for on it He who formed worlds found rest.

לֹא תֶחְסַר On it you shall lack nothing – so eat,
Be satisfied and bless
The Lord, whom you love,
For He has blessed you from all peoples.
This day is honoured above all others,
for on it He who formed worlds found rest.

יוֹם זֶה מְכֻבָּד *Yom Zeh Mechubad*: The initial letters of the five verses spell out the name Israel: other than this we do not know the identity of the composer. The theme is the honour due to Shabbat, in the food we eat and the clothes

הַשָּׁמַיִם מְסַפְּרִים כְּבוֹדוֹ,
וְגַם הָאָרֶץ מָלְאָה חַסְדּוֹ,
רְאוּ כִּי כָל אֵלֶּה עָשְׂתָה יָדוֹ,
כִּי הוּא הַצּוּר פָּעֳלוֹ תָמִים.
יוֹם זֶה מְכֻבָּד מִכָּל יָמִים, כִּי בוֹ שָׁבַת צוּר עוֹלָמִים.

מנוחה ושמחה

מְנוּחָה וְשִׂמְחָה אוֹר לַיְּהוּדִים,
יוֹם שַׁבָּתוֹן יוֹם מַחֲמַדִּים,
שׁוֹמְרָיו וְזוֹכְרָיו הֵמָּה מְעִידִים,
כִּי לְשִׁשָּׁה כֹּל בְּרוּאִים וְעוֹמְדִים.

שְׁמֵי שָׁמַיִם אֶרֶץ וְיַמִּים,
כָּל צְבָא מָרוֹם גְּבוֹהִים וְרָמִים,
תַּנִּין וְאָדָם וְחַיַּת רְאֵמִים,
כִּי בְּיָהּ יהוה צוּר עוֹלָמִים.

הוּא אֲשֶׁר דִּבֶּר לְעַם סְגֻלָּתוֹ,
שָׁמוֹר לְקַדְּשׁוֹ מִבּוֹאוֹ וְעַד צֵאתוֹ,
שַׁבַּת קֹדֶשׁ יוֹם חֶמְדָּתוֹ,
כִּי בוֹ שָׁבַת אֵל מִכָּל מְלַאכְתּוֹ.

בְּמִצְוַת שַׁבָּת אֵל יַחֲלִיצָךְ,
קוּם קְרָא אֵלָיו יָחִישׁ לְאַמְּצָךְ,
נִשְׁמַת כָּל חַי וְגַם נַעֲרִיצָךְ,
אֱכוֹל בְּשִׂמְחָה כִּי כְבָר רָצָךְ.

---

we wear. *Foremost* [literally "first"] *among sacred days*: Though the Shabbat is distinct from the festivals, it is placed first in the list of holy days in Leviticus 23. *And*

הַשָּׁמַיִם The heavens declare His glory
And the earth is full of His lovingkindness.
See all these things His hand has made
For He is the Rock, His work is perfect.

This day is honoured above all others,
for on it He who formed worlds found rest.

MENUCHAH VE-SIMCHAH

מְנוּחָה וְשִׂמְחָה Rest and joy, light for all Jews,
Is the Sabbath day, day of delights;
Those who keep and recall it bear witness
That in six days all creation was made.

שְׁמֵי שָׁמַיִם The highest heavens, land and seas,
The hosts of heaven, high and sublime;
Sea monsters, humans and all wild beasts,
Were created by LORD GOD, He who formed worlds.

הוּא It was He who spoke to His treasured people:
"Keep it to make it holy from beginning to end".
The holy Sabbath is His day of delight,
For on it GOD rested from all His work.

בְּמִצְוַת Through the Shabbat commandment GOD will give you strength,
Rise, pray to Him, and He will invigorate you.
Recite the *Nishmat* prayer, and the *Kedushah*,
Then eat with joy, for He is pleased with you.

---

break bread over two complete loaves: The Hebrew is ambiguous, and could mean: "The upright break bread over two loaves".

מְנוּחָה וְשִׂמְחָה *Menuchah ve-Simcha*: This song first appeared in print in 1545; author unknown. The word *menuchah*, "rest", has a range of meanings, including peace of mind, quiet, repose, ease, contentment, tranquillity and serenity. Used of Shabbat, it describes the positive corollary to the cessation of work. According to the midrash, at the end of the sixth day of creation, when everything physical had been made, GOD looked to see what the world still lacked. He saw that it lacked *menuchah*, and that is what GOD made on the seventh day.

בְּמִשְׁנֶה לֶחֶם וְקִדּוּשׁ רַבָּה,
בְּרֹב מַטְעַמִּים וְרְוּחַ נְדִיבָה,
יִזְכּוּ לְרַב טוּב הַמִּתְעַנְּגִים בָּהּ,
בְּבִיאַת גּוֹאֵל לְחַיֵּי הָעוֹלָם הַבָּא.

ברוך אל עליון

בָּרוּךְ אֵל עֶלְיוֹן אֲשֶׁר נָתַן מְנוּחָה,
לְנַפְשֵׁנוּ פִדְיוֹן מִשֵּׁאת וַאֲנָחָה,
וְהוּא יִדְרוֹשׁ לְצִיּוֹן עִיר הַנִּדָּחָה,
עַד אָנָה תּוּגְיוֹן נֶפֶשׁ נֶאֱנָחָה.
הַשּׁוֹמֵר שַׁבָּת, הַבֵּן עִם הַבַּת, לָאֵל יֵרָצוּ כְּמִנְחָה עַל מַחֲבַת.

רוֹכֵב בָּעֲרָבוֹת מֶלֶךְ עוֹלָמִים,
אֶת עַמּוֹ לִשְׁבּוֹת אִזֵּן בַּנְּעִימִים,
בְּמַאֲכָלֵי עֲרֵבוֹת בְּמִינֵי מַטְעַמִּים,
בְּמַלְבּוּשֵׁי כָבוֹד זֶבַח מִשְׁפָּחָה.
הַשּׁוֹמֵר שַׁבָּת, הַבֵּן עִם הַבַּת, לָאֵל יֵרָצוּ כְּמִנְחָה עַל מַחֲבַת.

וְאַשְׁרֵי כָּל חוֹכֶה לְתַשְׁלוּמֵי כֵפֶל,
מֵאֵת כָּל סוֹכֶה שׁוֹכֵן בָּעֲרָפֶל,
נַחֲלָה לוֹ יִזְכֶּה בָּהָר וּבַשָּׁפֶל,
נַחֲלָה וּמְנוּחָה כַּשֶּׁמֶשׁ לוֹ זָרְחָה.
הַשּׁוֹמֵר שַׁבָּת, הַבֵּן עִם הַבַּת, לָאֵל יֵרָצוּ כְּמִנְחָה עַל מַחֲבַת.

כָּל שׁוֹמֵר שַׁבָּת כַּדָּת מֵחַלְּלוֹ,
הֵן הֶכְשַׁר חִבַּת קֹדֶשׁ גּוֹרָלוֹ,
וְאִם יָצָא חוֹבַת הַיּוֹם אַשְׁרֵי לוֹ,
אֶל אֵל אָדוֹן מְחוֹלְלוֹ מִנְחָה הִיא שְׁלוּחָה.
הַשּׁוֹמֵר שַׁבָּת, הַבֵּן עִם הַבַּת, לָאֵל יֵרָצוּ כְּמִנְחָה עַל מַחֲבַת.

בְּמִשְׁנֶה With twin loaves, and wine for the *Kiddush*,
With many delicacies and a willing spirit;
Those who delight in it shall merit great reward:
The coming of the Redeemer, and life in the World to Come.

BARUCH EL ELYON

בָּרוּךְ Blessed is God Most High who has given us rest,
To relieve our souls from distress and pain.
May He seek the good of Zion, the outcast city.
How long must she grieve, her spirits downcast?

All who keep the Sabbath, man and woman alike,
find favour like an offering made to God.

רוֹכֵב He who rides the heavens, King of worlds,
Gently told His people to rest,
With tasty food and delicacies of all kinds,
With elegant dress, as at a family feast.

All who keep the Sabbath, man and woman alike,
find favour like an offering made to God.

וְאַשְׁרֵי Happy are all who await a double reward
From the One who sees all, though He dwells in dense dark.
He will grant him a heritage in hill and valley,
A heritage and resting place like (Jacob) on whom the sun shone.

All who keep the Sabbath, man and woman alike,
find favour like an offering made to God.

כָּל Whoever keeps the Sabbath fully, not profaning it,
Shows that he is worthy; holy is his lot.
Happy is he who fulfills the day's duty;
It is like a gift presented to God who fashioned him.

All who keep the Sabbath, man and woman alike,
find favour like an offering made to God.

בָּרוּךְ אֵל עֶלְיוֹן *Baruch El Elyon*: A hymn of praise to those who keep Shabbat. The author, Rabbi Barukh ben Shmuel, who lived in Mayence in the late twelfth and early thirteenth century, was a member of the group of Talmudic scholars known

חֶמְדַּת הַיָּמִים קְרָאוֹ אֵלִי צוּר,
וְאַשְׁרֵי לִתְמִימִים אִם יִהְיֶה נָצוּר,
כֶּתֶר הִלּוּמִים. עַל רֹאשָׁם יָצוּר,
צוּר הָעוֹלָמִים רוּחוֹ בָּם נָחָה.
הַשּׁוֹמֵר שַׁבָּת, הַבֵּן עִם הַבַּת, לָאֵל יֵרָצוּ כְּמִנְחָה עַל מַחֲבַת.

זָכוֹר אֶת יוֹם הַשַּׁבָּת לְקַדְּשׁוֹ,
קַרְנוֹ כִּי גָבְהָה נֵזֶר עַל רֹאשׁוֹ,
עַל כֵּן יִתֵּן הָאָדָם לְנַפְשׁוֹ,
עֹנֶג וְגַם שִׂמְחָה בָּהֶם לְמָשְׁחָה.
הַשּׁוֹמֵר שַׁבָּת, הַבֵּן עִם הַבַּת, לָאֵל יֵרָצוּ כְּמִנְחָה עַל מַחֲבַת.

קֹדֶשׁ הִיא לָכֶם שַׁבָּת הַמַּלְכָּה,
אֶל תּוֹךְ בָּתֵּיכֶם לְהָנִיחַ בְּרָכָה,
בְּכָל מוֹשְׁבוֹתֵיכֶם לֹא תַעֲשׂוּ מְלָאכָה,
בְּנֵיכֶם וּבְנוֹתֵיכֶם עֶבֶד וְגַם שִׁפְחָה.
הַשּׁוֹמֵר שַׁבָּת, הַבֵּן עִם הַבַּת, לָאֵל יֵרָצוּ כְּמִנְחָה עַל מַחֲבַת.

בִּרְכַּת הַמָּזוֹן can be found on page 756.

---

as the Tosafists. Mayence had been the scene of a massacre of Jews by Crusaders in 1096. The memory of this haunts the first stanza in which the poet speaks with great poignancy about Jewish suffering, asking, "How long must she [the Jewish people] grieve?" Throughout the song we sense how Shabbat brought blessed relief to an otherwise afflicted people.

A SHABBAT MEDITATION

There have been many utopias in history: dreams of an ideal world, a perfected planet, a humanity at peace with itself. None has ever been realised. The word "utopia" means "no place", that which does not exist. Only one utopia has ever been achieved. Its name is Shabbat.

The ideal of Judaism is the messianic age, a world without weapons or war, injustice or strife. All the prophets, said Maimonides, longed for this time, yet none lived to see it nor have we reached it yet. How then do we keep faith with a dream so long deferred? The answer is Shabbat. The seventh day – when all hierarchies are suspended, when we cease to strive, renouncing our technical mastery over nature and seeing it instead in all its wondrous beauty – is our rehearsal

חֶמְדַּת The Rock, my God, called it "Beloved of days".
Happy are the faithful if it is kept intact.
He will set on their head a close-fitting crown.
On them the rock of eternity will make His spirit rest.

All who keep the Sabbath, man and woman alike,
find favour like an offering made to God.

זָכוֹר He who remembers the Sabbath day to keep it holy
Will gain high honour like a diadem on his head.
Therefore let each give to his soul
Delight and joy with which to be exalted.

All who keep the Sabbath, man and woman alike,
find favour like an offering made to God.

קַדְּשׁ Let her be holy to you – Sabbath the queen –
Placing a blessing in your home.
In all your dwellings, do no work,
Nor your sons and daughters, your servant or maid.

All who keep the Sabbath, man and woman alike,
find favour like an offering made to God.

Grace after Meals can be found on page 757.

---

for the messianic age. It is a glimpse of the destination in the midst of the journey. It is utopia now.

Shabbat sustains each of Judaism's great institutions. In the synagogue we re-engage with the community, sharing our prayers and joys. Hearing and studying the Torah portion of the week, we travel back to join our ancestors at Sinai, when God spoke and gave us His written word, His marriage contract with the Jewish people. At home we spend time – sacrosanct, undisturbed – with family and friends, sheltered under God's tabernacle of peace.

Shabbat is where a restless people rested and renewed itself. In ages of oppression, it reminded Jews they were free. At times of hardship, it meant rest from physical exhaustion. In ages of tension, it brings release from psychological fatigue and stress. Judah Halevi once said that on Shabbat the poorest Jew is freer than the greatest king. In political terms it was the day on which Jews, often oppressed by the world outside, relinquished their burdens and breathed free air.

Within the cycle of the week it creates a rhythm of action and reflection, doing and being. Without that pause Jews might never have continued the journey. Shabbat is the holy time of a people that found truth in time: our foretaste of a world at peace under the sovereignty of God.

תפילת מנחה לשבת ויום טוב

אשרי

אַשְׁרֵי יוֹשְׁבֵי בֵיתֶךָ, עוֹד יְהַלְלוּךָ סֶּלָה.
אַשְׁרֵי הָעָם שֶׁכָּכָה לּוֹ, אַשְׁרֵי הָעָם שֶׁיהוה אֱלֹהָיו.

תהלים קמה

תְּהִלָּה לְדָוִד,
אֲרוֹמִמְךָ אֱלוֹהַי הַמֶּלֶךְ, וַאֲבָרְכָה שִׁמְךָ לְעוֹלָם וָעֶד.
בְּכָל יוֹם אֲבָרְכֶךָּ, וַאֲהַלְלָה שִׁמְךָ לְעוֹלָם וָעֶד.
גָּדוֹל יהוה וּמְהֻלָּל מְאֹד, וְלִגְדֻלָּתוֹ אֵין חֵקֶר.
דּוֹר לְדוֹר יְשַׁבַּח מַעֲשֶׂיךָ, וּגְבוּרֹתֶיךָ יַגִּידוּ.
הֲדַר כְּבוֹד הוֹדֶךָ, וְדִבְרֵי נִפְלְאוֹתֶיךָ אָשִׂיחָה.
וֶעֱזוּז נוֹרְאוֹתֶיךָ יֹאמֵרוּ, וּגְדוּלָּתְךָ אֲסַפְּרֶנָּה.
זֵכֶר רַב־טוּבְךָ יַבִּיעוּ, וְצִדְקָתְךָ יְרַנֵּנוּ.
חַנּוּן וְרַחוּם יהוה, אֶרֶךְ אַפַּיִם וּגְדָל־חָסֶד.
טוֹב יהוה לַכֹּל, וְרַחֲמָיו עַל כָּל מַעֲשָׂיו.
יוֹדוּךָ יהוה כָּל מַעֲשֶׂיךָ, וַחֲסִידֶיךָ יְבָרְכוּכָה.
כְּבוֹד מַלְכוּתְךָ יֹאמֵרוּ, וּגְבוּרָתְךָ יְדַבֵּרוּ.
לְהוֹדִיעַ לִבְנֵי הָאָדָם גְּבוּרֹתָיו, וּכְבוֹד הֲדַר מַלְכוּתוֹ.
מַלְכוּתְךָ מַלְכוּת כָּל עֹלָמִים, וּמֶמְשַׁלְתְּךָ בְּכָל דּוֹר וָדֹר.
סוֹמֵךְ יהוה לְכָל הַנֹּפְלִים, וְזוֹקֵף לְכָל הַכְּפוּפִים.

אַשְׁרֵי *Happy are those*: As on weekdays, the Afternoon Service begins with *Ashrei* as a prelude to prayer. The addition of two verses from other psalms at the beginning and one at the end mean that the prayer, as we say it, begins with the word *Ashrei*, the first word of the first psalm, and ends with *Halleluyah*, the last word of the last psalm. It thus stands, in miniature, for the Book of Psalms as a whole.

AFTERNOON SERVICE FOR SHABBAT AND FESTIVALS

ASHREI

אַשְׁרֵי Happy are those who dwell in Your House;
they shall continue to praise You, Selah!
Happy are the people for whom this is so;
happy are the people whose God is the Lord.

PSALM 145

A song of praise by David.

I will exalt You, my God, the King,
and bless Your name for ever and all time.
Every day I will bless You,
and praise Your name for ever and all time.
God is great and greatly to be praised;
His greatness is unfathomable.
One generation will praise Your works to the next,
and tell of Your mighty deeds.
On the glorious splendour of Your majesty I will meditate,
and on the acts of Your wonders.
They shall talk of the power of Your awesome deeds,
and I will tell of Your greatness.
They shall recite the record of Your great goodness,
and sing with joy of Your righteousness.
The Lord is gracious and compassionate,
slow to anger and great in lovingkindness.
The Lord is good to all,
and His compassion extends to all His works.
All Your works shall thank You, Lord,
and Your devoted ones shall bless You.
They shall talk of the glory of Your kingship,
and speak of Your might.
To make known to mankind His mighty deeds
and the glorious majesty of His kingship.
Your kingdom is an everlasting kingdom,
and Your reign is for all generations.
The Lord supports all who fall,
and raises all who are bowed down.

עֵינֵי כֹל אֵלֶיךָ יְשַׂבֵּרוּ, וְאַתָּה נוֹתֵן לָהֶם אֶת אָכְלָם בְּעִתּוֹ.
פּוֹתֵחַ אֶת יָדֶךָ, וּמַשְׂבִּיעַ לְכָל־חַי רָצוֹן.
צַדִּיק יהוה בְּכָל דְּרָכָיו, וְחָסִיד בְּכָל מַעֲשָׂיו.
קָרוֹב יהוה לְכָל קֹרְאָיו, לְכֹל אֲשֶׁר יִקְרָאֻהוּ בֶאֱמֶת.
רְצוֹן יְרֵאָיו יַעֲשֶׂה, וְאֶת שַׁוְעָתָם יִשְׁמַע, וְיוֹשִׁיעֵם.
שׁוֹמֵר יהוה אֶת כָּל אֹהֲבָיו, וְאֵת כָּל־הָרְשָׁעִים יַשְׁמִיד.
← תְּהִלַּת יהוה יְדַבֶּר פִּי, וִיבָרֵךְ כָּל־בָּשָׂר שֵׁם קָדְשׁוֹ לְעוֹלָם וָעֶד.
וַאֲנַחְנוּ נְבָרֵךְ יָהּ, מֵעַתָּה וְעַד־עוֹלָם, הַלְלוּיָהּ.

The words in bold type are said aloud together by the Leader and Congregation.

וּבָא לְצִיּוֹן גּוֹאֵל, וּלְשָׁבֵי פֶשַׁע בְּיַעֲקֹב נְאֻם יהוה. וַאֲנִי, זֹאת בְּרִיתִי אוֹתָם, אָמַר יהוה, רוּחִי אֲשֶׁר עָלֶיךָ, וּדְבָרַי אֲשֶׁר שַׂמְתִּי בְּפִיךָ, לֹא יָמוּשׁוּ מִפִּיךָ וּמִפִּי זַרְעֲךָ וּמִפִּי זֶרַע זַרְעֲךָ, אָמַר יהוה, מֵעַתָּה וְעַד עוֹלָם, ← וְאַתָּה קָדוֹשׁ יוֹשֵׁב תְּהִלּוֹת יִשְׂרָאֵל. וְקָרָא זֶה אֶל־זֶה וְאָמַר, **קָדוֹשׁ, קָדוֹשׁ, קָדוֹשׁ יהוה צְבָאוֹת, מְלֹא כָל הָאָרֶץ כְּבוֹדוֹ.** וּמְקַבְּלִין דֵּין מִן דֵּין וְאָמְרִין, קַדִּישׁ בִּשְׁמֵי מְרוֹמָא עִלָּאָה בֵּית שְׁכִינְתֵּהּ, קַדִּישׁ עַל אַרְעָא עוֹבַד גְּבוּרְתֵּהּ, קַדִּישׁ לְעָלַם וּלְעָלְמֵי עָלְמַיָּא, יהוה צְבָאוֹת, מַלְיָא כָל־אַרְעָא זִיו יְקָרֵהּ. ← וַתִּשָּׂאֵנִי רוּחַ, וָאֶשְׁמַע אַחֲרַי קוֹל רַעַשׁ גָּדוֹל, **בָּרוּךְ כְּבוֹד יהוה מִמְּקוֹמוֹ.** וּנְטָלַתְנִי רוּחָא, וְשִׁמְעֵת בַּתְרַי קָל זִיעַ סַגִּיא דִּמְשַׁבְּחִין וְאָמְרִין, בְּרִיךְ יְקָרָא דַיָי מֵאֲתַר

וּבָא לְצִיּוֹן גּוֹאֵל *A redeemer will come to Zion*: The proper place for this prayer, as on weekdays, is in the morning service. However, since the Shabbat morning prayers are already long, it was moved to the afternoon. Another possibility is that, since it was usually said after a period of study, it may testify to the custom of com-

All raise their eyes to You in hope,
and You give them their food in due season.
You open Your hand,
and satisfy every living thing with Your favour.
The LORD is righteous in all His ways,
and kind in all He does.
The LORD is close to all who call on Him,
to all who call on Him in truth.
He fulfils the will of those who revere Him;
He hears their cry and saves them.
The LORD guards all who love Him,
but all the wicked He will destroy.
→ My mouth shall speak the praise of the LORD,
and all creatures shall bless His holy name for ever and all time.
We will bless the LORD now and for ever. Halleluyah!

The words in bold type are said aloud together by the Leader and Congregation.

וּבָא לְצִיּוֹן גּוֹאֵל "A redeemer will come to Zion, to those in Jacob who repent of their sins," declares the LORD. "As for Me, this is My covenant with them," says the LORD. "My spirit, that is on you, and My words I have placed in your mouth will not depart from your mouth, or from the mouth of your children, or from the mouth of their descendants from this time on and forever," says the LORD. → You are the Holy One, enthroned on the praises of Israel. And (the angels) call to one another, saying, "**Holy, holy, holy is the LORD of hosts. The whole earth is full of His glory.**" And they receive permission from one another, saying: "Holy in the highest heavens, home of His presence; holy on earth, the work of His strength; holy for ever and all time is the LORD of hosts; the whole earth is full of His radiant glory." Then a wind lifted me up and I heard behind me the sound of a great noise, saying, "**Blessed is the LORD's glory from His place.**" → Then a wind lifted me up and I heard behind me the sound of a great tempest of those who uttered praise, saying, "Blessed is the LORD's glory from the place of the home

---

munal study before the afternoon prayer. The passage is composed of the following elements: 1. two consecutive verses from Isaiah about redemption; 2. the *Kedushah*,

בֵּית שְׁכִינְתֵּהּ. **יהוה יִמְלֹךְ לְעֹלָם וָעֶד.** יהוה מַלְכוּתֵהּ קָאֵם לְעָלַם וּלְעָלְמֵי עָלְמַיָּא.

יהוה אֱלֹהֵי אַבְרָהָם יִצְחָק וְיִשְׂרָאֵל אֲבוֹתֵינוּ, שָׁמְרָה זֹּאת לְעוֹלָם, לְיֵצֶר מַחְשְׁבוֹת לְבַב עַמֶּךָ, וְהָכֵן לְבָבָם אֵלֶיךָ. וְהוּא רַחוּם, יְכַפֵּר עָוֹן וְלֹא יַשְׁחִית, וְהִרְבָּה לְהָשִׁיב אַפּוֹ, וְלֹא יָעִיר כָּל־חֲמָתוֹ. כִּי אַתָּה אֲדֹנָי טוֹב וְסַלָּח, וְרַב חֶסֶד לְכָל־קוֹרְאֶיךָ. צִדְקָתְךָ צֶדֶק לְעוֹלָם, וְתוֹרָתְךָ אֱמֶת. תִּתֵּן אֱמֶת לְיַעֲקֹב, חֶסֶד לְאַבְרָהָם, אֲשֶׁר נִשְׁבַּעְתָּ לַאֲבוֹתֵינוּ מִימֵי קֶדֶם. בָּרוּךְ אֲדֹנָי יוֹם יוֹם יַעֲמָס־לָנוּ, הָאֵל יְשׁוּעָתֵנוּ סֶלָה. יהוה צְבָאוֹת עִמָּנוּ, מִשְׂגָּב לָנוּ אֱלֹהֵי יַעֲקֹב סֶלָה. יהוה צְבָאוֹת, אַשְׁרֵי אָדָם בֹּטֵחַ בָּךְ. יהוה הוֹשִׁיעָה, הַמֶּלֶךְ יַעֲנֵנוּ בְיוֹם קָרְאֵנוּ.

בָּרוּךְ אֱלֹהֵינוּ שֶׁבְּרָאָנוּ לִכְבוֹדוֹ, וְהִבְדִּילָנוּ מִן הַתּוֹעִים, וְנָתַן לָנוּ תּוֹרַת אֱמֶת, וְחַיֵּי עוֹלָם נָטַע בְּתוֹכֵנוּ. הוּא יִפְתַּח לִבֵּנוּ בְּתוֹרָתוֹ, וְיָשֵׂם בְּלִבֵּנוּ אַהֲבָתוֹ וְיִרְאָתוֹ וְלַעֲשׂוֹת רְצוֹנוֹ וּלְעָבְדוֹ בְּלֵבָב שָׁלֵם, לְמַעַן לֹא נִיגַע לָרִיק, וְלֹא נֵלֵד לַבֶּהָלָה.

יְהִי רָצוֹן מִלְּפָנֶיךָ יהוה אֱלֹהֵינוּ וֵאלֹהֵי אֲבוֹתֵינוּ, שֶׁנִּשְׁמֹר חֻקֶּיךָ בָּעוֹלָם הַזֶּה, וְנִזְכֶּה וְנִחְיֶה וְנִרְאֶה וְנִירַשׁ טוֹבָה וּבְרָכָה לִשְׁנֵי יְמוֹת הַמָּשִׁיחַ וּלְחַיֵּי הָעוֹלָם הַבָּא. לְמַעַן יְזַמֶּרְךָ כָבוֹד וְלֹא יִדֹּם, יהוה אֱלֹהַי לְעוֹלָם אוֹדֶךָּ. ◄ בָּרוּךְ הַגֶּבֶר אֲשֶׁר יִבְטַח בַּיהוה, וְהָיָה יהוה מִבְטַחוֹ. בִּטְחוּ בַיהוה עֲדֵי־עַד, כִּי בְּיָהּ יהוה צוּר עוֹלָמִים. וְיִבְטְחוּ בְךָ יוֹדְעֵי שְׁמֶךָ, כִּי לֹא עָזַבְתָּ דֹרְשֶׁיךָ, יהוה. יהוה חָפֵץ לְמַעַן צִדְקוֹ, יַגְדִּיל תּוֹרָה וְיַאְדִּיר.

of His Presence." **The Lord shall reign for ever and all time**. The Lord's kingdom is established for ever and all time.

Lord, God of Abraham, Isaac and Israel, our ancestors, may You keep this for ever so that it forms the thoughts in Your people's heart, and directs their heart towards You. He is compassionate. He forgives iniquity and does not destroy. Repeatedly He suppresses His anger, not rousing His full wrath. For You, my Lord, are good and forgiving, abundantly kind to all who call on You. Your righteousness is eternally righteous, and Your Torah is truth. Grant truth to Jacob, lovingkindness to Abraham, as You promised our ancestors in ancient times. Blessed is the Lord who day after day bears our burden, for God is our salvation, Selah! The Lord of hosts is with us; the God of Jacob is our refuge, Selah! Lord of hosts, happy is the one who trusts in You. Lord, save. May the King answer us on the day we call.

Blessed is our God who created us for His glory, separating us from those who go astray; who gave us the Torah of truth, planting within us eternal life. May He open our heart to His Torah, imbuing our heart with the love and awe of Him, that we may do His will and serve Him with a perfect heart, so that we neither toil in vain nor give birth to confusion.

May it be Your will, O Lord our God and God of our ancestors, that we keep Your laws in this world, and thus be worthy to live, see and inherit goodness and blessing in the Messianic Age and in the life of the World to Come, so that my soul may sing to You and not be silent. Lord, my God, for ever I will thank You. → Blessed is the man who trusts in the Lord, whose trust is in the Lord alone. Trust in the Lord for evermore, for God the Lord is an everlasting Rock. Those who know Your name trust in You, for You, Lord, do not forsake those who seek You. The Lord desired, for the sake of Israel's merit, to make the Torah great and glorious.

---

together with an Aramaic translation; 3. a collection of verses about faithfulness to God; 4. a blessing thanking God for the Torah and praying for the ability to fulfil the commandments; 5. a further collection of verses, about trust in God.

The Leader says חֲצִי קַדִּישׁ.

Leader:

יִתְגַּדַּל וְיִתְקַדַּשׁ שְׁמֵהּ רַבָּא. (Cong. אָמֵן) בְּעָלְמָא דִּי־בְרָא כִרְעוּתֵהּ. וְיַמְלִיךְ מַלְכוּתֵהּ, בְּחַיֵּיכוֹן וּבְיוֹמֵיכוֹן וּבְחַיֵּי דְכָל־בֵּית יִשְׂרָאֵל, בַּעֲגָלָא וּבִזְמַן קָרִיב. וְאִמְרוּ אָמֵן.

All:

יְהֵא שְׁמֵהּ רַבָּא מְבָרַךְ לְעָלַם וּלְעָלְמֵי עָלְמַיָּא.

Leader:

יִתְבָּרַךְ וְיִשְׁתַּבַּח וְיִתְפָּאַר וְיִתְרוֹמַם וְיִתְנַשֵּׂא וְיִתְהַדָּר וְיִתְעַלֶּה וְיִתְהַלָּל שְׁמֵהּ דְּקֻדְשָׁא בְּרִיךְ הוּא (Cong. בְּרִיךְ הוּא) לְעֵלָּא (On שַׁבַּת שׁוּבָה add לְעֵלָּא) מִן־כָּל־בִּרְכָתָא וְשִׁירָתָא תֻּשְׁבְּחָתָא וְנֶחֱמָתָא, דַּאֲמִירָן בְּעָלְמָא. וְאִמְרוּ אָמֵן. (Cong. אָמֵן)

On שַׁבָּת, continue below. On יוֹם טוֹב falling on weekdays, say the appropriate עֲמִידָה on page 646.

וַאֲנִי תְפִלָּתִי לְךָ יהוה עֵת רָצוֹן, אֱלֹהִים בְּרָב־חַסְדֶּךָ, עֲנֵנִי בֶּאֱמֶת יִשְׁעֶךָ.

קריאת התורה

The Ark is opened and the Congregation stands. All say:

וַיְהִי בִּנְסֹעַ הָאָרֹן, וַיֹּאמֶר מֹשֶׁה, קוּמָה יהוה וְיָפֻצוּ אֹיְבֶיךָ, וְיָנֻסוּ מְשַׂנְאֶיךָ מִפָּנֶיךָ. כִּי מִצִּיּוֹן תֵּצֵא תוֹרָה, וּדְבַר יהוה מִירוּשָׁלָיִם. בָּרוּךְ שֶׁנָּתַן תּוֹרָה לְעַמּוֹ יִשְׂרָאֵל בִּקְדֻשָּׁתוֹ.

וַאֲנִי תְפִלָּתִי לְךָ *As for me, may my prayer come to You*: The presence of this verse prior to the reading of the Torah on Shabbat afternoon may be a reminder of the saying of the Sages that the afternoon prayer is a "time of favour" because El-

The Leader says half-*Kaddish*.

Leader:

יִתְגַּדַּל Magnified and sanctified may His great name be, in the world He created by His will. May He establish His kingdom in your lifetime and in your days, and in the lifetime of all the House of Israel, swiftly and soon – and say: Amen.

All:

May His great name be blessed for ever and all time.

Leader:

Blessed and praised, glorified and exalted, raised and honoured, uplifted and lauded be the name of the Holy One, blessed be He, (on the Shabbat of Penitence add 'well') beyond any blessing, song, praise and consolation uttered in the world – and say: Amen.

On Shabbat, continue below. On Festivals falling on weekdays, say the appropriate *Amidah* on page 647.

וַאֲנִי As for me, may my prayer come to You, God, at a time of favour. Lord, in Your great love, answer me with Your sure salvation.

READING OF THE TORAH

The Ark is opened and the Congregation stands. All say:

וַיְהִי בִּנְסֹעַ Whenever the Ark set out, Moses would say, "Arise, Lord, and may Your enemies be scattered. May those who hate You flee before You." For the Torah shall come forth from Zion, and the word of the Lord from Jerusalem. Blessed is He who in His Holiness gave the Torah to His people Israel.

---

ijah's prayer at Mount Carmel (1 Kings 18:36) was answered in the afternoon.

READING OF THE TORAH

The custom of reading the opening section of the coming week's Torah portion on Shabbat afternoon is undoubtedly of ancient origin. It is ttributed in the Talmud to Ezra after the return of Jews from Babylon.

The סֵפֶר תּוֹרָה is handed to the Leader, who holds it on his right, bows toward the Ark, and says:

גַּדְּלוּ לַיהוה אִתִּי, וּנְרוֹמְמָה שְׁמוֹ יַחְדָּו.

The Ark is closed.

All:

לְךָ יהוה הַגְּדֻלָּה וְהַגְּבוּרָה וְהַתִּפְאֶרֶת וְהַנֵּצַח וְהַהוֹד, כִּי כֹל בַּשָּׁמַיִם וּבָאָרֶץ, לְךָ יהוה הַמַּמְלָכָה וְהַמִּתְנַשֵּׂא לְכֹל לְרֹאשׁ. רוֹמְמוּ יהוה אֱלֹהֵינוּ וְהִשְׁתַּחֲווּ לַהֲדֹם רַגְלָיו, קָדוֹשׁ הוּא. רוֹמְמוּ יהוה אֱלֹהֵינוּ וְהִשְׁתַּחֲווּ לְהַר קָדְשׁוֹ, כִּי קָדוֹשׁ יהוה אֱלֹהֵינוּ.

אַב הָרַחֲמִים הוּא יְרַחֵם עַם עֲמוּסִים, וְיִזְכֹּר בְּרִית אֵיתָנִים, וְיַצִּיל נַפְשׁוֹתֵינוּ מִן־הַשָּׁעוֹת הָרָעוֹת, וְיִגְעַר בְּיֵצֶר הָרַע מִן הַנְּשׂוּאִים, וְיָחֹן אוֹתָנוּ לִפְלֵיטַת עוֹלָמִים, וִימַלֵּא מִשְׁאֲלוֹתֵינוּ בְּמִדָּה טוֹבָה יְשׁוּעָה וְרַחֲמִים.

The סֵפֶר תּוֹרָה is placed on the reading desk and is prepared for reading.
A mourner, during the week of שִׁבְעָה, may not read the תּוֹרָה (unless he is the only person capable of so doing), nor may he be called to the reading of the תּוֹרָה.

The Leader says:

וְתִגָּלֶה וְתֵרָאֶה מַלְכוּתוֹ עָלֵינוּ בִּזְמַן קָרוֹב, וְיָחֹן פְּלֵטָתֵנוּ וּפְלֵטַת עַמּוֹ בֵּית יִשְׂרָאֵל לְחֵן וּלְחֶסֶד וּלְרַחֲמִים וּלְרָצוֹן. וְנֹאמַר אָמֵן. הַכֹּל הָבוּ גֹדֶל לֵאלֹהֵינוּ וּתְנוּ כָבוֹד לַתּוֹרָה.

A כֹּהֵן, if present, is called up to the reading thus:

כֹּהֵן קְרָב, יַעֲמֹד (פלוני בֶּן פלוני) הַכֹּהֵן.

If no כֹּהֵן is present, a לֵוִי or יִשְׂרָאֵל is called up thus:

אֵין כָּאן כֹּהֵן, יַעֲמֹד (פלוני בֶּן פלוני הלוי/ישראל) בִּמְקוֹם כֹּהֵן.

בָּרוּךְ שֶׁנָּתַן תּוֹרָה לְעַמּוֹ יִשְׂרָאֵל בִּקְדֻשָּׁתוֹ.

All:

וְאַתֶּם הַדְּבֵקִים בַּיהוה אֱלֹהֵיכֶם, חַיִּים כֻּלְּכֶם הַיּוֹם.

The Torah scroll is handed to the Leader, who holds it on his right, bows toward the Ark, and says:

Magnify the LORD with me, and let us exalt His name together.

The Ark is closed.

All:

לְךָ Yours, LORD, are the greatness and the power, the glory and the majesty and splendour, for everything in heaven and earth is Yours. Yours, LORD, is the kingdom; You are exalted as head over all. Exalt the LORD our GOD and bow to His footstool; He is holy. Exalt the LORD our GOD, and bow at His holy mountain, for holy is the LORD our GOD.

אַב הָרַחֲמִים May the Father of compassion have compassion on the people borne by Him. May He remember the covenant with the mighty [patriarchs], and deliver us from evil times. May He reproach the evil instinct in the people carried by Him, and graciously grant that we be an everlasting remnant. May He fulfil in good measure our requests for salvation and compassion.

The Torah scroll is placed on the reading desk and is prepared for reading.

A mourner, during the week of *shivah*, may not read the Torah (unless he is the only person capable of so doing), nor may he be called to the reading of the Torah.

The Leader says:

וְתִגָּלֶה May His kingship over us be soon revealed and made manifest. May He be gracious to our surviving remnant, the remnant of His people the house of Israel in grace, lovingkindness, compassion and favour, and let us say Amen. Let us all render greatness to our GOD and give honour to the Torah.

A Cohen, if present, is called up to the reading thus:

Let the Cohen come forward. Arise (Hebrew name), the Cohen.

If no Cohen is present, a Levi or Yisrael is called up thus:

As there is no Cohen, arise (Hebrew name) in place of a Cohen.

Blessed is He who, in His holiness, gave the Torah to His people Israel.

All:

You who cling to the LORD your GOD are all alive today.

The appropriate תּוֹרָה portions are to be found from page 846.

The reader shows the עוֹלֶה (the person called to the reading) the section to be read. The עוֹלֶה touches the scroll at that place with the צִיצִת of his טַלִּית, which he then kisses. Bow when saying ברכו את and the first ברוך. Holding the handles of the scroll, he says:

בָּרְכוּ אֶת יהוה הַמְבֹרָךְ.

The Congregation responds:

בָּרוּךְ יהוה הַמְבֹרָךְ לְעוֹלָם וָעֶד.

The עוֹלֶה continues:

בָּרוּךְ יהוה הַמְבֹרָךְ לְעוֹלָם וָעֶד.

בָּרוּךְ אַתָּה יהוה אֱלֹהֵינוּ מֶלֶךְ הָעוֹלָם, אֲשֶׁר־בָּחַר בָּנוּ מִכָּל־הָעַמִּים, וְנָתַן לָנוּ אֶת־תּוֹרָתוֹ. בָּרוּךְ אַתָּה יהוה, נוֹתֵן הַתּוֹרָה.

After the reading, the עוֹלֶה says:

בָּרוּךְ אַתָּה יהוה אֱלֹהֵינוּ מֶלֶךְ הָעוֹלָם, אֲשֶׁר נָתַן־לָנוּ תּוֹרַת־אֱמֶת, וְחַיֵּי עוֹלָם נָטַע בְּתוֹכֵנוּ. בָּרוּךְ אַתָּה יהוה, נוֹתֵן הַתּוֹרָה.

One who has survived a situation of danger (safe arrival after a hazardous journey, release from captivity, or recovery from serious illness) says:

בָּרוּךְ אַתָּה יהוה אֱלֹהֵינוּ מֶלֶךְ הָעוֹלָם, הַגּוֹמֵל לְחַיָּבִים טוֹבוֹת, שֶׁגְּמָלַנִי כָּל־טוֹב.

The Congregation responds:

אָמֵן. מִי שֶׁגְּמָלְךָ כָּל־טוֹב, הוּא יִגְמָלְךָ כָּל־טוֹב, סֶלָה.

Special מִי שֶׁבֵּרַךְ and memorial prayers may be said at this point. See page 922.

The appropriate Torah portions are to be found from page 846.

The reader shows the *oleh* (the person called to the Torah) the section to be read. The *oleh* touches the scroll at that place with the *tzitzit* of his *tallit,* which he then kisses. Bow when saying *Bar'chu et* and the first *Baruch* Holding the handles of the scroll, he says:

Bar'chu et Adonai haM'vorach.

Bless the LORD, the blessed One.

The Congregation responds:

Baruch Adonai haM'vorach le-olam va-ed.

Bless the LORD, the blessed One, for ever and all time.

The *oleh* continues:

Baruch Adonai haM'vorach le-olam va-ed.

Baruch atah Adonai, Eloheinu Melech ha-olam, asher bachar banu mikol ha-amim, venatan lanu et Torato, baruch atah Adonai, noten haTorah.

Bless the LORD, the blessed One, for ever and all time.

Blessed are You, LORD our GOD, King of the Universe, who has chosen us from all peoples and has given us His Torah. Blessed are You, LORD, Giver of the Torah.

After the reading, the *oleh* says:

Baruch atah Adonai, Eloheinu Melech ha-olam, asher natan lanu Torat emet, v'chayei olam nata b'tochenu, baruch atah Adonai, noten haTorah.

Blessed are You, LORD our GOD, King of the Universe, who has given us the Torah of truth, planting everlasting life in our midst. Blessed are You, LORD, Giver of the Torah.

One who has survived a situation of danger (safe arrival after a hazardous journey, release from captivity, or recovery from serious illness) says:

Baruch atah Adonai, Eloheinu Melech ha-olam, hagomel l'chayavim tovot, sheg'malani kol tov.

Blessed are You, LORD our GOD, King of the Universe, who bestows good on the unworthy, who has bestowed on me much good.

The Congregation responds:

Amen. May He who bestowed much good on you
continue to bestow on you much good, Selah.

Special blessings and memorial prayers may be said at this point. See page 922.

After the reading, the סֵפֶר תּוֹרָה is lifted, and the Congregation says:

וְזֹאת הַתּוֹרָה אֲשֶׁר־שָׂם מֹשֶׁה לִפְנֵי בְּנֵי יִשְׂרָאֵל, עַל־פִּי יהוה בְּיַד־מֹשֶׁה.

תהלים צב

מִזְמוֹר שִׁיר לְיוֹם הַשַּׁבָּת. טוֹב לְהֹדוֹת לַיהוה, וּלְזַמֵּר לְשִׁמְךָ עֶלְיוֹן. לְהַגִּיד בַּבֹּקֶר חַסְדֶּךָ, וֶאֱמוּנָתְךָ בַּלֵּילוֹת. עֲלֵי־עָשׂוֹר וַעֲלֵי־נָבֶל, עֲלֵי הִגָּיוֹן בְּכִנּוֹר. כִּי שִׂמַּחְתַּנִי יהוה בְּפָעֳלֶךָ, בְּמַעֲשֵׂי יָדֶיךָ אֲרַנֵּן. מַה־גָּדְלוּ מַעֲשֶׂיךָ יהוה, מְאֹד עָמְקוּ מַחְשְׁבֹתֶיךָ. אִישׁ בַּעַר לֹא יֵדָע, וּכְסִיל לֹא־יָבִין אֶת־זֹאת. בִּפְרֹחַ רְשָׁעִים כְּמוֹ־עֵשֶׂב, וַיָּצִיצוּ כָּל־פֹּעֲלֵי אָוֶן, לְהִשָּׁמְדָם עֲדֵי־עַד. וְאַתָּה מָרוֹם לְעֹלָם יהוה. כִּי־הִנֵּה אֹיְבֶיךָ יהוה, כִּי־הִנֵּה אֹיְבֶיךָ יֹאבֵדוּ, יִתְפָּרְדוּ כָּל־פֹּעֲלֵי אָוֶן. וַתָּרֶם כִּרְאֵים קַרְנִי, בַּלֹּתִי בְּשֶׁמֶן רַעֲנָן. וַתַּבֵּט עֵינִי בְּשׁוּרָי, בַּקָּמִים עָלַי מְרֵעִים, תִּשְׁמַעְנָה אָזְנָי. צַדִּיק כַּתָּמָר יִפְרָח, כְּאֶרֶז בַּלְּבָנוֹן יִשְׂגֶּה. שְׁתוּלִים בְּבֵית יהוה, בְּחַצְרוֹת אֱלֹהֵינוּ יַפְרִיחוּ. עוֹד יְנוּבוּן בְּשֵׂיבָה, דְּשֵׁנִים וְרַעֲנַנִּים יִהְיוּ. לְהַגִּיד כִּי־יָשָׁר יהוה, צוּרִי, וְלֹא עַוְלָתָה בּוֹ.

The Leader takes the סֵפֶר תּוֹרָה and says:

יְהַלְלוּ אֶת־שֵׁם יהוה, כִּי נִשְׂגָּב שְׁמוֹ לְבַדּוֹ.

Congregation:

הוֹדוֹ עַל אֶרֶץ וְשָׁמָיִם. וַיָּרֶם קֶרֶן לְעַמּוֹ,
תְּהִלָּה לְכָל־חֲסִידָיו, לִבְנֵי יִשְׂרָאֵל עַם קְרֹבוֹ, הַלְלוּיָהּ.

While the סֵפֶר תּוֹרָה is returned to the Ark, say:

תהלים כד

לְדָוִד מִזְמוֹר, לַיהוה הָאָרֶץ וּמְלוֹאָהּ, תֵּבֵל וְיֹשְׁבֵי בָהּ. כִּי־הוּא עַל יַמִּים יְסָדָהּ, וְעַל נְהָרוֹת יְכוֹנְנֶהָ. מִי־יַעֲלֶה בְהַר יהוה, וּמִי־יָקוּם בִּמְקוֹם קָדְשׁוֹ. נְקִי כַפַּיִם וּבַר לֵבָב, אֲשֶׁר

After the reading, the Torah scroll is lifted, and the Congregation says:

וְזֹאת This is the Torah that Moses placed before the children of Israel, at the LORD's commandment, by the hand of Moses.

PSALM 92

מִזְמוֹר A Psalm. A Song for the Sabbath Day. It is good to thank the LORD and sing psalms to Your name, Most High – to tell of Your lovingkindness in the morning and Your faithfulness at night, to the music of the ten-stringed lyre and the melody of the harp. For You have made me rejoice by Your work, O LORD; I sing for joy at the deeds of Your hands. How great are Your deeds, LORD, and how very deep are Your thoughts. A boor cannot know, nor can a fool understand, that though the wicked spring up like grass and all evildoers flourish, it is only that they may be destroyed for ever. But You, LORD, are eternally exalted. For behold Your enemies, LORD, behold Your enemies will perish; all evildoers will be scattered. You have raised my pride like that of a wild ox; I am anointed with fresh oil. My eyes shall look in triumph on my adversaries, my ears shall hear the downfall of the wicked who rise against me. The righteous will flourish like a palm tree and grow tall like a cedar in Lebanon. Planted in the LORD's house, blossoming in our GOD's courtyards, they will still bear fruit in old age, and stay vigorous and fresh, proclaiming that the LORD is upright: He is my Rock, in whom there is no wrong.

The Leader takes the Torah scroll and says:

יְהַלְלוּ Let them praise the name of the LORD, for His name alone is sublime.

Congregation:

הוֹדוֹ His majesty is above earth and heaven. He has raised the horn of His people, for the glory of all His devoted ones, the children of Israel, the people close to Him. Halleluyah!

While the Torah scroll is returned to the Ark, say:

PSALM 24

לְדָוִד A psalm of David. The earth is the LORD's and all it contains, the world and all who live in it. For He founded it on the seas and established it on the streams. Who may climb the mountain of the LORD?

לֹא־נָשָׂא לַשָּׁוְא נַפְשִׁי וְלֹא נִשְׁבַּע לְמִרְמָה. יִשָּׂא בְרָכָה מֵאֵת יהוה, וּצְדָקָה מֵאֱלֹהֵי יִשְׁעוֹ. זֶה דּוֹר דֹּרְשָׁיו, מְבַקְשֵׁי פָנֶיךָ, יַעֲקֹב, סֶלָה. שְׂאוּ שְׁעָרִים רָאשֵׁיכֶם, וְהִנָּשְׂאוּ פִּתְחֵי עוֹלָם, וְיָבוֹא מֶלֶךְ הַכָּבוֹד. מִי זֶה מֶלֶךְ הַכָּבוֹד, יהוה עִזּוּז וְגִבּוֹר, יהוה גִּבּוֹר מִלְחָמָה. שְׂאוּ שְׁעָרִים רָאשֵׁיכֶם, וּשְׂאוּ פִּתְחֵי עוֹלָם, וְיָבֹא מֶלֶךְ הַכָּבוֹד. מִי הוּא זֶה מֶלֶךְ הַכָּבוֹד, יהוה צְבָאוֹת הוּא מֶלֶךְ הַכָּבוֹד, סֶלָה.

While the סֵפֶר תּוֹרָה is placed into the Ark, say:

וּבְנֻחֹה יֹאמַר, שׁוּבָה יהוה רִבְבוֹת אַלְפֵי יִשְׂרָאֵל. קוּמָה יהוה לִמְנוּחָתֶךָ, אַתָּה וַאֲרוֹן עֻזֶּךָ. כֹּהֲנֶיךָ יִלְבְּשׁוּ צֶדֶק, וַחֲסִידֶיךָ יְרַנֵּנוּ. בַּעֲבוּר דָּוִד עַבְדֶּךָ אַל־תָּשֵׁב פְּנֵי מְשִׁיחֶךָ. כִּי לֶקַח טוֹב נָתַתִּי לָכֶם, תּוֹרָתִי אַל־תַּעֲזֹבוּ. עֵץ־חַיִּים הִיא לַמַּחֲזִיקִים בָּהּ, וְתֹמְכֶיהָ מְאֻשָּׁר. דְּרָכֶיהָ דַרְכֵי־נֹעַם, וְכָל־נְתִיבוֹתֶיהָ שָׁלוֹם. ← הֲשִׁיבֵנוּ יהוה אֵלֶיךָ וְנָשׁוּבָה, חַדֵּשׁ יָמֵינוּ כְּקֶדֶם.

The Ark is closed.

The Leader says חֲצִי קַדִּישׁ.

Leader:

יִתְגַּדַּל וְיִתְקַדַּשׁ שְׁמֵהּ רַבָּא. (Cong. אָמֵן) בְּעָלְמָא דִּי־בְרָא כִרְעוּתֵהּ. וְיַמְלִיךְ מַלְכוּתֵהּ, בְּחַיֵּיכוֹן וּבְיוֹמֵיכוֹן וּבְחַיֵּי דְּכָל־בֵּית יִשְׂרָאֵל, בַּעֲגָלָא וּבִזְמַן קָרִיב. וְאִמְרוּ אָמֵן.

All:

יְהֵא שְׁמֵהּ רַבָּא מְבָרַךְ לְעָלַם וּלְעָלְמֵי עָלְמַיָּא.

Leader:

יִתְבָּרַךְ וְיִשְׁתַּבַּח וְיִתְפָּאַר וְיִתְרוֹמַם וְיִתְנַשֵּׂא וְיִתְהַדַּר וְיִתְעַלֶּה וְיִתְהַלָּל שְׁמֵהּ דְּקֻדְשָׁא בְּרִיךְ הוּא (Cong. בְּרִיךְ הוּא)

Who may stand in His holy place? He who has clean hands and a pure heart, who has not taken My name in vain, or sworn deceitfully. He shall receive blessing from the LORD, and just reward from GOD, his salvation. This is a generation of those who seek Him, the descendants of Jacob who seek Your presence, Selah! Lift up your heads, O gates; be uplifted, eternal doors, so that the King of glory may enter. Who is the King of glory? It is the LORD, strong and mighty, the LORD mighty in battle. Lift up your heads, O gates; be uplifted, eternal doors, so that the King of glory may enter. Who is he, the King of glory? The LORD of hosts, He is the King of glory, Selah!

While the Torah scroll is placed into the Ark, say:

וּבְנֻחֹה When the Ark came to rest, Moses would say: "Return, O LORD, to the myriad thousands of Israel." Advance, LORD, to Your resting place, You and Your mighty Ark. Your priests are clothed in righteousness, and Your devoted ones sing in joy. For the sake of Your servant David, do not reject Your anointed one. For I give you good instruction; do not forsake My Torah. ➔ It is a tree of life to those who grasp it, and those who uphold it are happy. Its ways are ways of pleasantness, and all its paths are peace. Turn us back, O LORD, to You, and we will return. Renew our days as of old.

The Ark is closed.

The Leader says half-*Kaddish*.

Leader:

יִתְגַּדַּל Magnified and sanctified may His great name be, in the world He created by His will. May He establish His kingdom in your lifetime and in your days, and in the lifetime of all the House of Israel, swiftly and soon – and say: Amen.

All:

May His great name be blessed for ever and all time.

Leader:

Blessed and praised, glorified and exalted, raised and honoured, uplifted and lauded be the name of the Holy One, blessed be He, (between

לְעֵלָּא (On שַׁבַּת שׁוּבָה add לְעֵלָּא) מִן־כָּל־בִּרְכָתָא וְשִׁירָתָא תֻּשְׁבְּחָתָא וְנֶחֱמָתָא, דַּאֲמִירָן בְּעָלְמָא. וְאִמְרוּ אָמֵן. (Cong. אָמֵן)

עמידה

On יום טוב, say the appropriate עֲמִידָה on page 646.

The following prayer, until קַדְמוֹנִיּוֹת, on page 504, is said standing with feet together.

The עֲמִידָה is first said silently; then, if there is a מִנְיָן, it is repeated aloud by the Leader.

Take three steps back, then forward. At the points indicated by ▾, bend the knees at the first word, bow at the second, and stand straight before God's name.

אֲדֹנָי, שְׂפָתַי תִּפְתָּח, וּפִי יַגִּיד תְּהִלָּתֶךָ.

אבות

▾**בָּרוּךְ** אַתָּה יהוה אֱלֹהֵינוּ וֵאלֹהֵי אֲבוֹתֵינוּ, אֱלֹהֵי אַבְרָהָם, אֱלֹהֵי יִצְחָק, וֵאלֹהֵי יַעֲקֹב, הָאֵל הַגָּדוֹל הַגִּבּוֹר וְהַנּוֹרָא, אֵל עֶלְיוֹן, גּוֹמֵל חֲסָדִים טוֹבִים וְקוֹנֵה הַכֹּל, וְזוֹכֵר חַסְדֵי אָבוֹת, וּמֵבִיא גוֹאֵל לִבְנֵי בְנֵיהֶם, לְמַעַן שְׁמוֹ בְּאַהֲבָה.

On שַׁבַּת שׁוּבָה, add:

זָכְרֵנוּ לְחַיִּים, מֶלֶךְ חָפֵץ בַּחַיִּים, וְכָתְבֵנוּ בְּסֵפֶר הַחַיִּים, לְמַעַנְךָ אֱלֹהִים חַיִּים.

מֶלֶךְ עוֹזֵר וּמוֹשִׁיעַ וּמָגֵן. ▾בָּרוּךְ אַתָּה יהוה, מָגֵן אַבְרָהָם.

גבורות

אַתָּה גִּבּוֹר לְעוֹלָם אֲדֹנָי, מְחַיֵּה מֵתִים אַתָּה, רַב לְהוֹשִׁיעַ.

From after שִׂמְחַת תּוֹרָה until פֶּסַח, add:

מַשִּׁיב הָרוּחַ וּמוֹרִיד הַגֶּשֶׁם.

מְכַלְכֵּל חַיִּים בְּחֶסֶד, מְחַיֵּה מֵתִים בְּרַחֲמִים רַבִּים, סוֹמֵךְ נוֹפְלִים, וְרוֹפֵא חוֹלִים, וּמַתִּיר אֲסוּרִים, וּמְקַיֵּם אֱמוּנָתוֹ לִישֵׁנֵי עָפָר. מִי כָמוֹךָ בַּעַל גְּבוּרוֹת, וּמִי דּוֹמֶה לָּךְ, מֶלֶךְ מֵמִית וּמְחַיֶּה וּמַצְמִיחַ יְשׁוּעָה.

Rosh Hashanah and Yom Kippur add 'well') beyond any blessing, song, praise and consolation uttered in the world – and say: Amen.

AMIDAH: THE STANDING PRAYER

On Festivals, say the appropriate *Amidah* on page 647.

The following prayer, until "in former years", on page 505, is said standing with feet together.

The *Amidah* is first said silently; then, if there is a *minyan*, it is repeated aloud by the Leader.

Take three steps back, then forward. At the points indicated by ▾, bend the knees at the first word, bow at the second, and stand straight before GOD's name.

O LORD, open my lips, so that my mouth may declare Your praise.

PATRIARCHS

▾בָּרוּךְ Blessed are You, LORD our GOD and GOD of our Fathers, GOD of Abraham, GOD of Isaac and GOD of Jacob; the great, mighty and awesome GOD, GOD Most High, who bestows acts of lovingkindness and creates all, who remembers the lovingkindness of the Fathers and will bring a Redeemer to their children's children for the sake of His name, in love.

On the Shabbat of Penitence, add:

Remember us for life, O King who desires life, and write us in the book of life – for Your sake, O GOD of life.

King, Helper, Saviour, Shield: ▾Blessed are You, LORD, Shield of Abraham.

DIVINE MIGHT

אַתָּה You are eternally mighty, LORD. You give life to the dead and have great power to save.

From after Simchat Torah until Pesach, add:

He makes the wind blow and the rain fall.

He sustains the living with lovingkindness, and with great compassion revives the dead. He supports the fallen, heals the sick, sets captives free, and keeps His faith with those who sleep in the dust. Who is like You, Master of might, and to whom can You be compared, O King, who brings death and gives life and makes salvation grow?

On שַׁבָּת שׁוּבָה, add:

מִי כָמְוֹךָ אַב הָרַחֲמִים, זוֹכֵר יְצוּרָיו לַחַיִּים בְּרַחֲמִים.

וְנֶאֱמָן אַתָּה לְהַחֲיוֹת מֵתִים. בָּרוּךְ אַתָּה יהוה, מְחַיֵּה הַמֵּתִים.

When saying the עֲמִידָה silently, go to אַתָּה קָדוֹשׁ on page 496.

קדושה

During the Leader's repetition, the following is said standing, with feet together, rising on the toes at the words indicated by ▲.

Congregation then Leader: נְקַדֵּשׁ אֶת־שִׁמְךָ בָּעוֹלָם, כְּשֵׁם שֶׁמַּקְדִּישִׁים אוֹתוֹ בִּשְׁמֵי מָרוֹם, כַּכָּתוּב עַל יַד נְבִיאֶךָ, וְקָרָא זֶה אֶל־זֶה וְאָמַר.

Congregation and Leader: ▲קָדוֹשׁ ▲קָדוֹשׁ ▲קָדוֹשׁ יהוה צְבָאוֹת, מְלֹא כָל־הָאָרֶץ כְּבוֹדוֹ.

Leader: לְעֻמָּתָם בָּרוּךְ יֹאמֵרוּ.

Congregation and Leader: ▲בָּרוּךְ כְּבוֹד־יהוה, מִמְּקוֹמוֹ.

Leader: וּבְדִבְרֵי קָדְשְׁךָ כָּתוּב לֵאמֹר.

Congregation and Leader: ▲יִמְלֹךְ יהוה לְעוֹלָם, אֱלֹהַיִךְ צִיּוֹן לְדֹר וָדֹר, הַלְלוּיָהּ.

Leader: לְדוֹר וָדוֹר נַגִּיד גָּדְלֶךָ וּלְנֵצַח נְצָחִים קְדֻשָּׁתְךָ נַקְדִּישׁ, וְשִׁבְחֲךָ אֱלֹהֵינוּ מִפִּינוּ לֹא יָמוּשׁ לְעוֹלָם וָעֶד, כִּי אֵל מֶלֶךְ גָּדוֹל וְקָדוֹשׁ אָתָּה. בָּרוּךְ אַתָּה יהוה, *הָאֵל הַקָּדוֹשׁ.

*On שַׁבָּת שׁוּבָה, end the blessing:

הַמֶּלֶךְ הַקָּדוֹשׁ.

On the Shabbat of Penitence, add:

Who is like You, compassionate Father, who remembers His creatures in compassion for life?

Faithful are You to revive the dead. Blessed are You, LORD, who revives the dead.

When saying the *Amidah* silently, go to "You are holy" on page 497.

KEDUSHAH

During the Leader's repetition, the following is said standing, with feet together, rising on the toes at the words indicated by ▲:

Congregation then Leader: נְקַדֵּשׁ We will sanctify Your name on earth, as they sanctify it in the highest heavens, as is written by Your prophet, "And they [the angels] call to one another saying:

Congregation and Leader: ▲Holy, ▲holy, ▲holy is the LORD of Hosts: the whole world is filled with His glory."

Leader: Those facing them say: "Blessed – "

Congregation and Leader: ▲Blessed is the LORD's glory from His place."

Leader: And in Your Holy Writings it is written thus:

Congregation and Leader: ▲The LORD shall reign forever. He is your GOD, Zion, from generation to generation, Halleluyah!"

Leader: From generation to generation we will declare Your greatness, and we will proclaim Your holiness for evermore. Your praise, our GOD, shall never leave our mouth, for You, GOD, are a great and holy King. Blessed are You, LORD, *the holy GOD.

*On the Shabbat of Penitence, end the blessing:

the holy King.

נְקַדֵּשׁ *We will sanctify*: Rabbi Israel Meir ha-Cohen, the "Chafetz Chayim", used to say: Just as the angels were created to sing GOD's praises in heaven, so were the Jewish people created to sing His praises on earth.

When saying the עֲמִידָה silently, continue here.

קדושת השם

אַתָּה קָדוֹשׁ וְשִׁמְךָ קָדוֹשׁ, וּקְדוֹשִׁים בְּכָל־יוֹם יְהַלְלוּךָ סֶּלָה. בָּרוּךְ אַתָּה יהוה, *הָאֵל הַקָּדוֹשׁ.

On שַׁבַּת שׁוּבָה, end the blessing:
*הַמֶּלֶךְ הַקָּדוֹשׁ.

קדושת היום

אַתָּה אֶחָד וְשִׁמְךָ אֶחָד, וּמִי כְּעַמְּךָ יִשְׂרָאֵל גּוֹי אֶחָד בָּאָרֶץ, תִּפְאֶרֶת גְּדֻלָּה, וַעֲטֶרֶת יְשׁוּעָה, יוֹם מְנוּחָה וּקְדֻשָּׁה לְעַמְּךָ נָתָתָּ, אַבְרָהָם יָגֵל, יִצְחָק יְרַנֵּן, יַעֲקֹב וּבָנָיו יָנוּחוּ בוֹ, מְנוּחַת אַהֲבָה וּנְדָבָה, מְנוּחַת אֱמֶת וֶאֱמוּנָה, מְנוּחַת שָׁלוֹם וְשַׁלְוָה וְהַשְׁקֵט וָבֶטַח, מְנוּחָה שְׁלֵמָה שָׁאַתָּה רוֹצֶה בָּהּ, יַכִּירוּ בָנֶיךָ וְיֵדְעוּ כִּי מֵאִתְּךָ הִיא מְנוּחָתָם, וְעַל מְנוּחָתָם יַקְדִּישׁוּ אֶת שְׁמֶךָ.

אֱלֹהֵינוּ וֵאלֹהֵי אֲבוֹתֵינוּ, רְצֵה בִמְנוּחָתֵנוּ, קַדְּשֵׁנוּ בְּמִצְוֹתֶיךָ, וְתֵן חֶלְקֵנוּ בְּתוֹרָתֶךָ, שַׂבְּעֵנוּ מִטּוּבֶךָ, וְשַׂמְּחֵנוּ בִּישׁוּעָתֶךָ, וְטַהֵר לִבֵּנוּ לְעָבְדְּךָ בֶּאֱמֶת. וְהַנְחִילֵנוּ יהוה אֱלֹהֵינוּ בְּאַהֲבָה וּבְרָצוֹן שַׁבַּת קָדְשֶׁךָ. וְיָנוּחוּ בָהּ יִשְׂרָאֵל מְקַדְּשֵׁי שְׁמֶךָ. בָּרוּךְ אַתָּה יהוה, מְקַדֵּשׁ הַשַּׁבָּת.

אַתָּה אֶחָד וְשִׁמְךָ אֶחָד *You are One, Your name is One*: As mentioned before, Shabbat is unique in that the central section of the evening, morning and afternoon *Amidah* prayers is different on each occasion. There are three related explanations: 1. the prayers chart the movement from creation to revelation to redemption; 2. they speak of past, present and future; and 3. they describe the three stages of a wedding: betrothal, rejoicing and *yichud*, the coming together of bride and groom. The afternoon prayer fits this pattern closely. It speaks of redemption and the future, when "God shall be One and His name One", and of *yichud*, when the Oneness of God joins the uniqueness of the Jewish people in perfect union. A

When saying the *Amidah* silently, continue here.

HOLINESS

אַתָּה You are holy and Your name is holy, and holy ones praise You daily, Selah! Blessed are You, LORD, *the holy GOD.

---

*On the Shabbat of Penitence, end the blessing:
the holy King.

HOLINESS OF THE DAY

אַתָּה You are One, Your name is One; and who is like Your people Israel, a nation unique on earth? Splendour of greatness and a crown of salvation is the day of rest and holiness You have given Your people. Abraham will rejoice, Isaac sing for joy, Jacob and his children find rest in it – a rest of love and generosity, a rest of truth and faith, a rest of peace and tranquillity, calm and trust; a complete rest in which You find favour. May Your children recognise and know that their rest comes from You, and that by their rest they sanctify Your name.

אֱלֹהֵינוּ Our GOD and GOD of our ancestors, find favour in our rest. Make us holy through Your commandments and grant us our share in Your Torah. Satisfy us with Your goodness, grant us joy in Your salvation, and purify our hearts to serve You in truth. In love and favour, LORD our GOD, grant us as our heritage Your holy Sabbath, so that Israel who sanctify Your name may find rest on it. Blessed are You, LORD, who sanctifies the Sabbath.

Midrash teaches: "GOD, Israel and the Sabbath all testify to one another; GOD and Israel testify to the holiness of the Sabbath; Israel and the Sabbath testify to the creative and redemptive power of GOD; GOD and the Sabbath testify to the uniqueness of Israel."

תִּפְאֶרֶת גְּדֻלָּה *Splendour of greatness*: As the day reaches its greatest intensity, the emphasis shifts to the experiential quality of the day itself. The word *menuchah*, "rest, serenity", appears seven times in this one paragraph, together with an idyllic description of a world at peace with itself: "a rest of love and generosity, a rest of truth and faith, a rest of peace and tranquillity, calm and trust". *Abraham will rejoice* – a reference to the future, when the patriarchs will rejoice that their descendants have found peace and "the day that is wholly Sabbath".

עבודה

רְצֵה יהוה אֱלֹהֵינוּ בְּעַמְּךָ יִשְׂרָאֵל וּבִתְפִלָּתָם, וְהָשֵׁב אֶת־הָעֲבוֹדָה לִדְבִיר בֵּיתֶךָ. וְאִשֵּׁי יִשְׂרָאֵל וּתְפִלָּתָם בְּאַהֲבָה תְקַבֵּל בְּרָצוֹן, וּתְהִי לְרָצוֹן תָּמִיד עֲבוֹדַת יִשְׂרָאֵל עַמֶּךָ.

On רֹאשׁ חֹדֶשׁ and חוֹל הַמּוֹעֵד, say:

אֱלֹהֵינוּ וֵאלֹהֵי אֲבוֹתֵינוּ, יַעֲלֶה, וְיָבֹא, וְיַגִּיעַ, וְיֵרָאֶה, וְיֵרָצֶה, וְיִשָּׁמַע, וְיִפָּקֵד, וְיִזָּכֵר זִכְרוֹנֵנוּ וּפִקְדוֹנֵנוּ, וְזִכְרוֹן אֲבוֹתֵינוּ, וְזִכְרוֹן מָשִׁיחַ בֶּן דָּוִד עַבְדֶּךָ, וְזִכְרוֹן יְרוּשָׁלַיִם עִיר קָדְשֶׁךָ, וְזִכְרוֹן כָּל־עַמְּךָ בֵּית יִשְׂרָאֵל לְפָנֶיךָ, לִפְלֵיטָה וּלְטוֹבָה, וּלְחֵן וּלְחֶסֶד וּלְרַחֲמִים, וּלְחַיִּים וּלְשָׁלוֹם בְּיוֹם

On רֹאשׁ חֹדֶשׁ:	On פֶּסַח:	On סֻכּוֹת:
רֹאשׁ הַחֹדֶשׁ	חַג הַמַּצּוֹת	חַג הַסֻּכּוֹת

הַזֶּה. זָכְרֵנוּ יהוה אֱלֹהֵינוּ בּוֹ לְטוֹבָה, וּפָקְדֵנוּ בוֹ לִבְרָכָה, וְהוֹשִׁיעֵנוּ בוֹ לְחַיִּים. וּבִדְבַר יְשׁוּעָה וְרַחֲמִים, חוּס וְחָנֵּנוּ וְרַחֵם עָלֵינוּ וְהוֹשִׁיעֵנוּ, כִּי אֵלֶיךָ עֵינֵינוּ, כִּי אֵל מֶלֶךְ חַנּוּן וְרַחוּם אָתָּה.

וְתֶחֱזֶינָה עֵינֵינוּ בְּשׁוּבְךָ לְצִיּוֹן בְּרַחֲמִים. בָּרוּךְ אַתָּה יהוה, הַמַּחֲזִיר שְׁכִינָתוֹ לְצִיּוֹן.

הודאה

▽ Bow at the first five words.

▽**מוֹדִים** אֲנַחְנוּ לָךְ, שָׁאַתָּה הוּא יהוה אֱלֹהֵינוּ וֵאלֹהֵי אֲבוֹתֵינוּ לְעוֹלָם וָעֶד. צוּר חַיֵּינוּ, מָגֵן יִשְׁעֵנוּ אַתָּה הוּא לְדוֹר וָדוֹר. נוֹדֶה לְּךָ וּנְסַפֵּר תְּהִלָּתֶךָ עַל חַיֵּינוּ הַמְּסוּרִים בְּיָדֶךָ, וְעַל נִשְׁמוֹתֵינוּ הַפְּקוּדוֹת לָךְ, וְעַל

During the Leader's repetition, the Congregation says quietly:

▽**מוֹדִים** אֲנַחְנוּ לָךְ, שָׁאַתָּה הוּא יהוה אֱלֹהֵינוּ וֵאלֹהֵי אֲבוֹתֵינוּ, אֱלֹהֵי כָל־בָּשָׂר, יוֹצְרֵנוּ, יוֹצֵר בְּרֵאשִׁית. בְּרָכוֹת וְהוֹדָאוֹת לְשִׁמְךָ הַגָּדוֹל וְהַקָּדוֹשׁ, עַל

TEMPLE SERVICE

רְצֵה Find favour, LORD our GOD, in Your people Israel and their prayer. Restore the service to Your most holy house, and accept in love and favour the fire-offerings of Israel and their prayer. May the service of Your people Israel always find favour with You.

On Rosh Chodesh and the Intermediate Days of Festivals, say:

אֱלֹהֵינוּ Our GOD and GOD of our ancestors, may there rise, come, reach, appear, be favoured, heard, regarded and remembered before You, our recollection and remembrance, as well as the remembrance of our ancestors, and of the Messiah son of David Your servant, and of Jerusalem Your holy city, and of all Your people the House of Israel – for deliverance and well-being, grace, lovingkindness and compassion, life and peace, on this day of:

On Rosh Chodesh, say:	On Pesach, say:	On Sukkot, say:
Rosh Chodesh.	the Festival of Matzot.	the Festival of Sukkot.

On it remember us, LORD our GOD, for good, recollect us for blessing, and deliver us for life. In accord with Your promise of salvation and compassion, spare us and be gracious to us, have compassion on us and deliver us, for our eyes are turned to You because You, GOD, are a gracious and compassionate King.

וְתֶחֱזֶינָה And may our eyes witness Your return to Zion in compassion. Blessed are You, LORD, who restores His Presence to Zion.

THANKSGIVING

▽ Bow at the first nine words.

מוֹדִים▽ We give thanks to You, for You are the LORD our GOD and GOD of our ancestors for ever and all time. You are the Rock of our lives, Shield of our salvation from generation to generation. We will thank You and declare Your praise for our lives which are entrusted into Your hand; our souls which are placed in Your

During the Leader's repetition, the Congregation says quietly:

מוֹדִים▽ We give thanks to You, for You are the LORD our GOD and GOD of our ancestors, GOD of all flesh, who formed us and formed the universe. Blessings and thanks are due to Your great and holy name for giving us life and sustain-

נִסֶּיךָ שֶׁבְּכָל־יוֹם עִמָּנוּ, וְעַל נִפְלְאוֹתֶיךָ וְטוֹבוֹתֶיךָ שֶׁבְּכָל־עֵת, עֶרֶב וָבֹקֶר וְצָהֳרָיִם. הַטּוֹב כִּי לֹא־כָלוּ רַחֲמֶיךָ, וְהַמְרַחֵם כִּי לֹא־תַמּוּ חֲסָדֶיךָ, מֵעוֹלָם קִוִּינוּ לָךְ.

שֶׁהֶחֱיִיתָנוּ וְקִיַּמְתָּנוּ. כֵּן תְּחַיֵּנוּ וּתְקַיְּמֵנוּ, וְתֶאֱסֹף גָּלֻיּוֹתֵינוּ לְחַצְרוֹת קָדְשֶׁךָ, לִשְׁמוֹר חֻקֶּיךָ וְלַעֲשׂוֹת רְצוֹנֶךָ, וּלְעָבְדְךָ בְּלֵבָב שָׁלֵם, עַל שֶׁאֲנַחְנוּ מוֹדִים לָךְ. בָּרוּךְ אֵל הַהוֹדָאוֹת.

On שַׁבַּת חֲנֻכָּה, say:

עַל הַנִּסִּים, וְעַל הַפֻּרְקָן, וְעַל הַגְּבוּרוֹת, וְעַל הַתְּשׁוּעוֹת, וְעַל הַמִּלְחָמוֹת, שֶׁעָשִׂיתָ לַאֲבוֹתֵינוּ בַּיָּמִים הָהֵם בַּזְּמַן הַזֶּה.

בִּימֵי מַתִּתְיָהוּ בֶּן־יוֹחָנָן כֹּהֵן גָּדוֹל חַשְׁמוֹנַאי וּבָנָיו, כְּשֶׁעָמְדָה מַלְכוּת יָוָן הָרְשָׁעָה עַל־עַמְּךָ יִשְׂרָאֵל, לְהַשְׁכִּיחָם תּוֹרָתֶךָ, וּלְהַעֲבִירָם מֵחֻקֵּי רְצוֹנֶךָ. וְאַתָּה בְּרַחֲמֶיךָ הָרַבִּים, עָמַדְתָּ לָהֶם בְּעֵת צָרָתָם, רַבְתָּ אֶת־רִיבָם, דַּנְתָּ אֶת־דִּינָם, נָקַמְתָּ אֶת־נִקְמָתָם. מָסַרְתָּ גִבּוֹרִים בְּיַד חַלָּשִׁים, וְרַבִּים בְּיַד מְעַטִּים, וּטְמֵאִים בְּיַד טְהוֹרִים, וּרְשָׁעִים בְּיַד צַדִּיקִים, וְזֵדִים בְּיַד עוֹסְקֵי תוֹרָתֶךָ. וּלְךָ עָשִׂיתָ שֵׁם גָּדוֹל וְקָדוֹשׁ בְּעוֹלָמֶךָ, וּלְעַמְּךָ יִשְׂרָאֵל עָשִׂיתָ תְּשׁוּעָה גְדוֹלָה וּפֻרְקָן כְּהַיּוֹם הַזֶּה. וְאַחַר כֵּן בָּאוּ בָנֶיךָ לִדְבִיר בֵּיתֶךָ, וּפִנּוּ אֶת־הֵיכָלֶךָ, וְטִהֲרוּ אֶת־מִקְדָּשֶׁךָ, וְהִדְלִיקוּ נֵרוֹת בְּחַצְרוֹת קָדְשֶׁךָ, וְקָבְעוּ שְׁמוֹנַת יְמֵי חֲנֻכָּה אֵלּוּ, לְהוֹדוֹת וּלְהַלֵּל לְשִׁמְךָ הַגָּדוֹל.

וְעַל כֻּלָּם יִתְבָּרַךְ וְיִתְרוֹמַם שִׁמְךָ מַלְכֵּנוּ תָּמִיד לְעוֹלָם וָעֶד.

On שַׁבַּת שׁוּבָה, add:

וּכְתוֹב לְחַיִּים טוֹבִים כָּל־בְּנֵי בְרִיתֶךָ.

---

charge; for Your miracles which are with us every day; and for Your wonders and favours at all times, evening, morning and midday. You are good – for Your compassion never fails. You are compassionate – for Your loving-kindnesses never cease. We have always placed our hope in You.

ing us. May You continue to give us life and sustain us; and may You gather our exiles to Your holy courts, to keep Your decrees, do Your will and serve You with a perfect heart, for it is for us to give You thanks. Blessed be God to whom thanksgiving is due.

On Shabbat Chanukah, say:

עַל הַנִּסִּים [We thank You also] for the miracles, the redemption, the mighty deeds, and the victories in battle which You performed for our ancestors in those days at this time.

בִּימֵי In the days of Mattityahu, son of Yochanan the High Priest, the Hasmonean, and his sons, the wicked Greek kingdom rose up against Your people Israel to make them forget Your Torah and to force them to transgress the statutes of Your will. It was then that You in Your great compassion stood by them in the time of their distress. You championed their cause, judged their claim, and avenged their wrong. You delivered the strong into the hands of the weak, the many into the hands of the few, the impure into the hands of the pure, the wicked into the hands of the righteous, and the arrogant into the hands of those who were engaged in the study of Your Torah. You made for Yourself great and holy renown in Your world, and for Your people Israel You performed a great salvation and redemption on this day. Your children then entered the holiest part of Your house, cleansed Your Temple, purified Your sanctuary, kindled lights in Your holy courts, and designated these eight days of Chanukah for giving thanks and praise to Your great name.

וְעַל For all these things may Your name be blessed and exalted, our King, continually, for ever and all time.

On the Shabbat of Penitence, add:

And write, for a good life, all the children of Your covenant.

וְכֹל הַחַיִּים יוֹדְוּךָ סֶּלָה, וִיהַלְלוּ אֶת־שִׁמְךָ בֶּאֱמֶת, הָאֵל יְשׁוּעָתֵנוּ וְעֶזְרָתֵנוּ סֶלָה. ▾בָּרוּךְ אַתָּה יהוה, הַטּוֹב שִׁמְךָ וּלְךָ נָאֶה לְהוֹדוֹת.

שלום

שָׁלוֹם רָב עַל יִשְׂרָאֵל עַמְּךָ תָּשִׂים לְעוֹלָם, כִּי אַתָּה הוּא מֶלֶךְ אָדוֹן לְכָל הַשָּׁלוֹם. וְטוֹב בְּעֵינֶיךָ לְבָרֵךְ אֶת עַמְּךָ יִשְׂרָאֵל בְּכָל עֵת וּבְכָל שָׁעָה בִּשְׁלוֹמֶךָ. *בָּרוּךְ אַתָּה יהוה, הַמְבָרֵךְ אֶת עַמּוֹ יִשְׂרָאֵל בַּשָּׁלוֹם.

---

*On שַׁבַּת שׁוּבָה, substitute the following:

בְּסֵפֶר חַיִּים בְּרָכָה וְשָׁלוֹם, וּפַרְנָסָה טוֹבָה, נִזָּכֵר וְנִכָּתֵב לְפָנֶיךָ, אֲנַחְנוּ וְכָל־עַמְּךָ בֵּית יִשְׂרָאֵל, לְחַיִּים טוֹבִים וּלְשָׁלוֹם. בָּרוּךְ אַתָּה יהוה, עֹשֵׂה הַשָּׁלוֹם.

The Leader's repetition ends at this point.

אֱלֹהַי, נְצוֹר לְשׁוֹנִי מֵרָע, וּשְׂפָתַי מִדַּבֵּר מִרְמָה, וְלִמְקַלְלַי נַפְשִׁי תִדּוֹם, וְנַפְשִׁי כֶּעָפָר לַכֹּל תִּהְיֶה. פְּתַח לִבִּי בְּתוֹרָתֶךָ, וּבְמִצְוֹתֶיךָ תִּרְדּוֹף נַפְשִׁי. וְכֹל הַחוֹשְׁבִים עָלַי רָעָה, מְהֵרָה הָפֵר עֲצָתָם וְקַלְקֵל מַחֲשַׁבְתָּם. עֲשֵׂה לְמַעַן שְׁמֶךָ, עֲשֵׂה לְמַעַן יְמִינֶךָ, עֲשֵׂה לְמַעַן קְדֻשָּׁתֶךָ, עֲשֵׂה לְמַעַן תּוֹרָתֶךָ. לְמַעַן יֵחָלְצוּן יְדִידֶיךָ, הוֹשִׁיעָה יְמִינְךָ וַעֲנֵנִי. יִהְיוּ לְרָצוֹן אִמְרֵי־פִי וְהֶגְיוֹן לִבִּי לְפָנֶיךָ, יהוה צוּרִי וְגוֹאֲלִי.

Bow, take three steps back, then bow, first left, then right, then centre, while saying:

עֹשֶׂה שָׁלוֹם בִּמְרוֹמָיו, הוּא יַעֲשֶׂה שָׁלוֹם עָלֵינוּ, וְעַל־כָּל־יִשְׂרָאֵל, וְאִמְרוּ אָמֵן.

יְהִי רָצוֹן מִלְּפָנֶיךָ יהוה אֱלֹהֵינוּ וֵאלֹהֵי אֲבוֹתֵינוּ, שֶׁיִּבָּנֶה בֵּית הַמִּקְדָּשׁ בִּמְהֵרָה בְיָמֵינוּ, וְתֵן חֶלְקֵנוּ בְּתוֹרָתֶךָ. וְשָׁם נַעֲבָדְךָ

Let all that lives thank You, Selah! and praise Your name in truth, God, our Saviour and Help, Selah! ▼Blessed are You, Lord, whose name is "the Good" and to whom thanks is due.

PEACE

שָׁלוֹם Grant great peace to Your people Israel for ever, for You are the sovereign Lord of all peace; and may it be good in Your eyes to bless Your people Israel at every time, at every hour, with Your peace.*Blessed are You, Lord, who blesses His people Israel with peace.

---

*On the Shabbat of Penitence, substitute the following:

In the book of life, blessing, peace and prosperity, may we and all Your people the house of Israel be remembered and written before You for a good life and for peace. Blessed are You, Lord, who makes peace.

The Leader's repetition ends at this point.

אֱלֹהַי My God, guard my tongue from evil and my lips from deceitful speech. To those who curse me, let my soul be silent; may my soul be to all like the dust. Open my heart to Your Torah and let my soul pursue Your commandments. As for all who plan evil against me, swiftly thwart their counsel and frustrate their plans. Act for the sake of Your name; act for the sake of Your right hand; act for the sake of Your holiness; act for the sake of Your Torah. That Your beloved ones may be delivered, save with Your right hand and answer me. May the words of my mouth and the meditation of my heart find favour before You, Lord, my Rock and Redeemer.

Bow, take three steps back, then bow, first left, then right, then centre, while saying:

May He who makes peace in His high places, make peace for us and all Israel – and say: Amen.

יְהִי May it be Your will, Lord our God and God of our ancestors, that the Temple be rebuilt speedily in our days, and grant us a share in Your Torah. And there we will serve You with reverence, as in the

בִּירָאָה, כִּימֵי עוֹלָם וּכְשָׁנִים קַדְמֹנִיּוֹת. וְעָרְבָה לַיהוה מִנְחַת יְהוּדָה וִירוּשָׁלָםִ, כִּימֵי עוֹלָם וּכְשָׁנִים קַדְמֹנִיּוֹת.

The following prayer, צִדְקָתְךָ is omitted: 1. On רֹאשׁ חֹדֶשׁ and the preceding afternoon, during the whole month of נִיסָן, on the afternoon before לַ״ג בָּעֹמֶר and יוֹם יְרוּשָׁלַיִם, during the first eight days of סִיוָן, on תִּשְׁעָה בְּאָב and the preceding afternoon, on ט״ו בְּאָב, from the Shabbat after יוֹם כִּפּוּר until two days after שִׂמְחַת תּוֹרָה, on חֲנֻכָּה and the preceding afternoon, on ט״ו בִּשְׁבָט, on the afternoon before פּוּרִים, the 15th of אֲדָר and אֲדָר רִאשׁוֹן in a Jewish leap year. 2. In the presence of a bridegroom during the six days following the Wedding.

צִדְקָתְךָ צֶדֶק לְעוֹלָם, וְתוֹרָתְךָ אֱמֶת. וְצִדְקָתְךָ אֱלֹהִים עַד מָרוֹם, אֲשֶׁר עָשִׂיתָ גְדֹלוֹת, אֱלֹהִים, מִי כָמוֹךָ. צִדְקָתְךָ כְּהַרְרֵי אֵל, מִשְׁפָּטֶיךָ תְּהוֹם רַבָּה, אָדָם וּבְהֵמָה תוֹשִׁיעַ יהוה.

קדיש תתקבל

Leader:

יִתְגַּדַּל וְיִתְקַדַּשׁ שְׁמֵהּ רַבָּא. (Cong. אָמֵן) בְּעָלְמָא דִּי־בְרָא כִרְעוּתֵהּ. וְיַמְלִיךְ מַלְכוּתֵהּ, בְּחַיֵּיכוֹן וּבְיוֹמֵיכוֹן וּבְחַיֵּי דִי־כָל־בֵּית יִשְׂרָאֵל, בַּעֲגָלָא וּבִזְמַן קָרִיב. וְאִמְרוּ אָמֵן. (Cong. אָמֵן)

All:

יְהֵא שְׁמֵהּ רַבָּא מְבָרַךְ לְעָלַם וּלְעָלְמֵי עָלְמַיָּא.

Leader:

יִתְבָּרַךְ וְיִשְׁתַּבַּח וְיִתְפָּאַר וְיִתְרוֹמַם וְיִתְנַשֵּׂא וְיִתְהַדַּר וְיִתְעַלֶּה וְיִתְהַלַּל שְׁמֵהּ דִּי־קֻדְשָׁא בְּרִיךְ הוּא (Cong. בְּרִיךְ הוּא) לְעֵלָּא (On שַׁבַּת שׁוּבָה add לְעֵלָּא) מִן־כָּל־בִּרְכָתָא וְשִׁירָתָא תֻּשְׁבְּחָתָא וְנֶחֱמָתָא, דִּי־אֲמִירָן בְּעָלְמָא. וְאִמְרוּ אָמֵן. (Cong. אָמֵן)

צִדְקָתְךָ צֶדֶק לְעוֹלָם *Your righteousness is an everlasting righteousness*: Three verses vindicating God's justice. Their recitation at this point in the prayers dates

days of old and as in former years. Then the offering of Judah and Jerusalem will be pleasing to the LORD as in the days of old and as in former years.

The following prayer, *Tzidkat'cha* is omitted: 1. On Rosh Chodesh and the preceding afternoon, during the whole month of *Nisan*, on the afternoon before Lag BaOmer and Yom Yerushalayim, during the first eight days of Sivan, on the Ninth of Av and the preceding afternoon, on the 15th of Av, from the Shabbat after Yom Kippur until two days after Simchat Torah, on Chanukah and the preceding afternoon, on the 15th of Shevat, on the afternoon before Purim, the 15th of Adar and Adar Rishon in a Jewish leap year. 2. In the presence of a bridegroom during the six days following the Wedding.

צִדְקָתְךָ Your righteousness is an everlasting righteousness, and Your Torah is truth. Your righteousness, O GOD, reaches to the highest heights, for You have done great things. O GOD, who is like You? Your righteousness is like the mighty mountains; Your judgements like the great depths. O LORD, You save both man and beast.

FULL KADDISH

Leader:

יִתְגַּדַּל Magnified and sanctified may His great name be, in the world He created by His will. May He establish His kingdom in your lifetime and in your days, and in the lifetime of all the House of Israel, swiftly and soon – and say: Amen.

All:

May His great name be blessed for ever and all time.

Leader:

Blessed and praised, glorified and exalted, raised and honoured, uplifted and lauded be the name of the Holy One, blessed be He, (between Rosh Hashanah and Yom Kippur add 'well') beyond any blessing, song, praise and consolation uttered in the world – and say: Amen.

---

back to the period of the Geonim, who explained them by reference to Joseph, Moses and David who, according to tradition, died on Shabbat afternoon. Like words we say at a funeral, they are an acceptance of loss as GOD's just decree. Because of these sad associations, the verses are not said at celebratory times of the year when *Tachanun* is not said.

תִּתְקַבַּל צְלוֹתְהוֹן וּבָעוּתְהוֹן דְּכָל־יִשְׂרָאֵל קֳדָם אֲבוּהוֹן דִּי בִשְׁמַיָּא. וְאִמְרוּ אָמֵן. (Cong. אָמֵן)

יְהֵא שְׁלָמָא רַבָּא מִן־שְׁמַיָּא, וְחַיִּים עָלֵינוּ וְעַל־כָּל־יִשְׂרָאֵל. וְאִמְרוּ אָמֵן. (Cong. אָמֵן)

Bow, take three steps back, then bow, first left, then right, then centre, while saying:

עֹשֶׂה שָׁלוֹם בִּמְרוֹמָיו, הוּא יַעֲשֶׂה שָׁלוֹם עָלֵינוּ, וְעַל־כָּל־יִשְׂרָאֵל. וְאִמְרוּ אָמֵן. (Cong. אָמֵן)

The following psalms are read from the שַׁבָּת after שִׂמְחַת תּוֹרָה until the שַׁבָּת before פֶּסַח, when the first part of the הַגָּדָה שֶׁל פֶּסַח is read instead.

תהלים קד

בָּרְכִי נַפְשִׁי אֶת־יהוה, יהוה אֱלֹהַי גָּדַלְתָּ מְּאֹד, הוֹד וְהָדָר לָבָשְׁתָּ. עֹטֶה אוֹר כַּשַּׂלְמָה, נוֹטֶה שָׁמַיִם כַּיְרִיעָה. הַמְקָרֶה בַמַּיִם עֲלִיּוֹתָיו, הַשָּׂם־עָבִים רְכוּבוֹ, הַמְהַלֵּךְ עַל־כַּנְפֵי־רוּחַ. עֹשֶׂה מַלְאָכָיו רוּחוֹת, מְשָׁרְתָיו אֵשׁ לֹהֵט. יָסַד אֶרֶץ עַל־מְכוֹנֶיהָ, בַּל־תִּמּוֹט עוֹלָם וָעֶד. תְּהוֹם כַּלְּבוּשׁ כִּסִּיתוֹ, עַל־הָרִים יַעַמְדוּ מָיִם. מִן־גַּעֲרָתְךָ יְנוּסוּן, מִן־קוֹל רַעַמְךָ יֵחָפֵזוּן. יַעֲלוּ הָרִים, יֵרְדוּ בְקָעוֹת, אֶל־מְקוֹם זֶה יָסַדְתָּ לָהֶם. גְּבוּל־שַׂמְתָּ בַּל־יַעֲבֹרוּן, בַּל־יְשׁוּבוּן לְכַסּוֹת הָאָרֶץ. הַמְשַׁלֵּחַ מַעְיָנִים בַּנְּחָלִים, בֵּין הָרִים יְהַלֵּכוּן. יַשְׁקוּ כָּל־חַיְתוֹ שָׂדָי, יִשְׁבְּרוּ פְרָאִים צְמָאָם. עֲלֵיהֶם עוֹף־הַשָּׁמַיִם יִשְׁכּוֹן, מִבֵּין עֳפָאיִם יִתְּנוּ־קוֹל. מַשְׁקֶה הָרִים מֵעֲלִיּוֹתָיו, מִפְּרִי מַעֲשֶׂיךָ תִּשְׂבַּע הָאָרֶץ. מַצְמִיחַ חָצִיר לַבְּהֵמָה, וְעֵשֶׂב לַעֲבֹדַת הָאָדָם, לְהוֹצִיא לֶחֶם מִן־הָאָרֶץ. וְיַיִן יְשַׂמַּח

SHABBAT AFTERNOON PSALMS

Between afternoon and evening services, customs varied. Some communities recited *Ethics of the Fathers* throughout the year; others between Pesach and Shavuot. Our custom is to do so between Pesach and the Shabbat before Rosh Hashanah. Between Shabbat Bereishit and the week before Pesach we recite Psalm 104 and the fifteen psalms known as "Songs of Ascents". The connection between Shabbat Bereishit and Psalm 104 is that

May the prayers and pleas of all Israel be accepted by their Father in heaven – and say: Amen.

May there be great peace from heaven, and life for us and all Israel – and say: Amen.

Bow, take three steps back, then bow, first left, then right, then centre, while saying:

May He who makes peace in His high places, make peace for us and all Israel – and say: Amen.

The following psalms are read from the Shabbat after Simchat Torah until the Shabbat before Pesach, when the first part of the Pesach Haggadah is read instead.

PSALM 104

בָּרְכִי נַפְשִׁי Bless the LORD, my soul. LORD, my GOD, You are very great, clothed in majesty and splendour, wrapped in a robe of light. You have spread out the heavens like a tent. He has laid the beams of His lofts in the waters. He makes the clouds His chariot, riding on the wings of the wind. He makes the winds His messengers, flames of fire His ministers. He has fixed the earth on its foundations so that it will never be shaken. You covered it with the deep like a cloak; the waters stood above the mountains. At Your rebuke they fled; at the sound of Your thunder they rushed away, flowing over the hills, pouring down into the valleys to the place You appointed for them. You fixed a boundary they were not to pass, so that they would never cover the earth again. He makes springs flow in the valleys; they make their way between the hills, giving drink to all the beasts of the field; the wild donkeys quench their thirst. The birds of the sky dwell beside them, singing among the foliage. He waters the mountains from His lofts: the earth is sated with the fruit of Your work. He makes grass grow for the cattle, and plants for the use of man, that he may produce bread

---

both are about creation. In general, the saying of these psalms during the winter months accords with the tradition that creation took place in the month of Tishrei, while the exodus took place in Nisan. The winter months therefore correspond to the period through which GOD was known through creation rather than redemption (the exodus) and revelation (the giving of the Torah at Mount Sinai).

Psalm 104. With the first chapter of Genesis and chapters 38–41 of the Book of Job, this psalm is one of the supreme celebrations of creation in *Tanach*. Note

לְבַב־אֱנוֹשׁ, לְהַצְהִיל פָּנִים מִשָּׁמֶן, וְלֶחֶם לְבַב־אֱנוֹשׁ יִסְעָד. יִשְׂבְּעוּ עֲצֵי יהוה, אַרְזֵי לְבָנוֹן אֲשֶׁר נָטָע. אֲשֶׁר־שָׁם צִפֳּרִים יְקַנֵּנוּ, חֲסִידָה בְּרוֹשִׁים בֵּיתָהּ. הָרִים הַגְּבֹהִים לַיְּעֵלִים, סְלָעִים מַחְסֶה לַשְׁפַנִּים. עָשָׂה יָרֵחַ לְמוֹעֲדִים, שֶׁמֶשׁ יָדַע מְבוֹאוֹ. תָּשֶׁת חֹשֶׁךְ וִיהִי לָיְלָה, בּוֹ תִרְמֹשׂ כָּל־חַיְתוֹ־יָעַר. הַכְּפִירִים שֹׁאֲגִים לַטָּרֶף, וּלְבַקֵּשׁ מֵאֵל אָכְלָם. תִּזְרַח הַשֶּׁמֶשׁ יֵאָסֵפוּן, וְאֶל־מְעוֹנֹתָם יִרְבָּצוּן. יֵצֵא אָדָם לְפָעֳלוֹ, וְלַעֲבֹדָתוֹ עֲדֵי־עָרֶב. מָה־רַבּוּ מַעֲשֶׂיךָ יהוה, כֻּלָּם בְּחָכְמָה עָשִׂיתָ, מָלְאָה הָאָרֶץ קִנְיָנֶךָ. זֶה הַיָּם, גָּדוֹל וּרְחַב יָדָיִם, שָׁם רֶמֶשׂ וְאֵין מִסְפָּר, חַיּוֹת קְטַנּוֹת עִם־גְּדֹלוֹת. שָׁם אֳנִיּוֹת יְהַלֵּכוּן, לִוְיָתָן זֶה יָצַרְתָּ לְשַׂחֶק־בּוֹ. כֻּלָּם אֵלֶיךָ יְשַׂבֵּרוּן, לָתֵת אָכְלָם בְּעִתּוֹ. תִּתֵּן לָהֶם, יִלְקֹטוּן, תִּפְתַּח יָדְךָ, יִשְׂבְּעוּן טוֹב. תַּסְתִּיר פָּנֶיךָ יִבָּהֵלוּן, תֹּסֵף רוּחָם יִגְוָעוּן, וְאֶל־עֲפָרָם יְשׁוּבוּן. תְּשַׁלַּח רוּחֲךָ יִבָּרֵאוּן, וּתְחַדֵּשׁ פְּנֵי אֲדָמָה. יְהִי כְבוֹד יהוה לְעוֹלָם, יִשְׂמַח יהוה בְּמַעֲשָׂיו. הַמַּבִּיט לָאָרֶץ וַתִּרְעָד, יִגַּע בֶּהָרִים וְיֶעֱשָׁנוּ. אָשִׁירָה לַיהוה בְּחַיָּי, אֲזַמְּרָה לֵאלֹהַי בְּעוֹדִי. יֶעֱרַב עָלָיו שִׂיחִי, אָנֹכִי אֶשְׂמַח בַּיהוה. יִתַּמּוּ חַטָּאִים מִן־הָאָרֶץ, וּרְשָׁעִים עוֹד אֵינָם, בָּרְכִי נַפְשִׁי אֶת־יהוה, הַלְלוּיָהּ.

תהלים קכ

שִׁיר הַמַּעֲלוֹת, אֶל־יהוה בַּצָּרָתָה לִּי, קָרָאתִי וַיַּעֲנֵנִי. יהוה הַצִּילָה נַפְשִׁי מִשְּׂפַת־שֶׁקֶר, מִלָּשׁוֹן רְמִיָּה. מַה־יִּתֵּן לְךָ,

---

the profound difference between these religious texts and scientific cosmologies. They speak in poetry, not prose; they express wonder rather than causal explanation; and they testify to the goodness of the world and its Creator rather than to blind, indifferent forces. The account in Psalm 104 is consistent with that of Genesis 1, though it is structured differently because the Psalmist wishes to emphasise the beauty and grandeur of creation rather than the order in which it

from the earth, wine to cheer the heart of man, oil to make the face shine, and bread to sustain man's heart. The trees of the LORD drink their fill, the cedars of Lebanon which He planted. There birds build their nests; the stork makes its home in the cypresses. High hills are for the wild goats; crags are shelter for the badgers. He made the moon to mark the seasons, and makes the sun know when to set. You bring darkness and it is night; then all the beasts of the forests stir. The young lions roar for prey, seeking their food from GOD. When the sun rises, they slink away and seek rest in their lairs. Man goes out to his work and his labour until evening. How many are Your works, LORD; You made them all with wisdom; the earth is full of Your creations. There is the vast, immeasurable sea with its countless swarming creatures, living things great and small. There ships sail. There is Leviathan You formed to sport there. All of them look to You in hope, to give them their food when it is due. What you give them they gather up. When You open Your hand, they are sated with good. When You hide Your face, they are dismayed. When You take away their breath, they die and return to dust. When You send back Your breath, they are created, giving new life to the earth. May the glory of the LORD be for ever; may the LORD rejoice in His works. When He looks at the earth, it trembles. When He touches the mountains, they pour forth smoke. I will sing to the LORD as long as I live; I will sing psalms to my GOD all my life. May my meditation be pleasing to Him; I shall rejoice in the LORD. May sinners vanish from the earth, and the wicked be no more. Bless the LORD, my soul. Halleluyah!

PSALM 120

A song of ascents. I called to the LORD in my distress and He answered me. "LORD, save my soul from lying lips, from a deceitful tongue."

---

emerged. What emerges above all – signalled by both beginning and end, "Bless the LORD, my soul" – is the sense of the Psalmist that despite the vastness of the universe and the infinity of its Creator, He is close. He hears prayer. He attends to the human voice. This is the song of one at home in the world, awed by its beauty, trusting in the graciousness of existence as GOD's gift.

Psalms 120–134. A sequence of fifteen psalms, all bearing the heading "A song of ascents". The meaning of this phrase

וּמַה־יֹּסִיף לָךְ, לָשׁוֹן רְמִיָּה. חִצֵּי גִבּוֹר שְׁנוּנִים, עִם גַּחֲלֵי רְתָמִים. אוֹיָה לִי כִּי־גַרְתִּי מֶשֶׁךְ, שָׁכַנְתִּי עִם־אָהֳלֵי קֵדָר. רַבַּת שָׁכְנָה־לָּהּ נַפְשִׁי, עִם שׂוֹנֵא שָׁלוֹם. אֲנִי־שָׁלוֹם, וְכִי אֲדַבֵּר, הֵמָּה לַמִּלְחָמָה.

תהלים קכא

שִׁיר לַמַּעֲלוֹת, אֶשָּׂא עֵינַי אֶל־הֶהָרִים, מֵאַיִן יָבֹא עֶזְרִי. עֶזְרִי מֵעִם יהוה, עֹשֵׂה שָׁמַיִם וָאָרֶץ. אַל־יִתֵּן לַמּוֹט רַגְלֶךָ, אַל־יָנוּם שֹׁמְרֶךָ. הִנֵּה לֹא יָנוּם וְלֹא יִישָׁן, שׁוֹמֵר יִשְׂרָאֵל. יהוה שֹׁמְרֶךָ, יהוה צִלְּךָ עַל־יַד יְמִינֶךָ. יוֹמָם הַשֶּׁמֶשׁ לֹא־יַכֶּכָּה וְיָרֵחַ בַּלָּיְלָה. יהוה יִשְׁמָרְךָ מִכָּל־רָע, יִשְׁמֹר אֶת־נַפְשֶׁךָ. יהוה יִשְׁמָר־צֵאתְךָ וּבוֹאֶךָ, מֵעַתָּה וְעַד־עוֹלָם.

תהלים קכב

שִׁיר הַמַּעֲלוֹת, לְדָוִד, שָׂמַחְתִּי בְּאֹמְרִים לִי, בֵּית יהוה נֵלֵךְ. עֹמְדוֹת הָיוּ רַגְלֵינוּ, בִּשְׁעָרַיִךְ יְרוּשָׁלָםִ. יְרוּשָׁלַםִ הַבְּנוּיָה, כְּעִיר שֶׁחֻבְּרָה־לָּהּ יַחְדָּו. שֶׁשָּׁם עָלוּ שְׁבָטִים, שִׁבְטֵי־יָהּ עֵדוּת לְיִשְׂרָאֵל, לְהֹדוֹת לְשֵׁם יהוה. כִּי שָׁמָּה יָשְׁבוּ כִסְאוֹת לְמִשְׁפָּט, כִּסְאוֹת לְבֵית דָּוִד. שַׁאֲלוּ שְׁלוֹם יְרוּשָׁלָםִ, יִשְׁלָיוּ אֹהֲבָיִךְ. יְהִי־שָׁלוֹם בְּחֵילֵךְ, שַׁלְוָה בְּאַרְמְנוֹתָיִךְ. לְמַעַן־אַחַי וְרֵעָי, אֲדַבְּרָה־נָּא שָׁלוֹם בָּךְ. לְמַעַן בֵּית־יהוה אֱלֹהֵינוּ, אֲבַקְשָׁה טוֹב לָךְ.

---

is debated. Some relate it to the fifteen steps in the Temple between the men's and women's courtyards, on which the Levites would stand and sing. Others suggest that they were songs sung by the exiles returning from Babylon to Israel (ascending to the holy land). Radak argues that they were said by pilgrims on the three Pilgrimage festivals on their ascent to Jerusalem. Meiri argues that it is a musical direction, meaning a song begun softly and continued with ever-increasing volume. Others speculate that it may be a reference to the particular poetical style in which these psalms are written, in which a repeated phrase serves as a rung on which the poem ascends towards its final theme.

What will a deceitful tongue profit you? What will you gain? Only a warrior's sharp arrows, and hot coals of broom-wood. Woe to me that I dwell in Meshech, that I live among the tents of Kedar. I have lived too long among those who hate peace. I am for peace, but whenever I speak of it, they are for war.

PSALM 121

A song of ascents. I lift my eyes up to the hills; from where will my help come? My help comes from the LORD, Maker of heaven and earth. He will not let your foot stumble; He who guards you does not slumber. See: the Guardian of Israel neither slumbers nor sleeps. The LORD is your Guardian; the LORD is your Shade at your right hand. The sun will not strike you by day, nor the moon by night. The LORD will guard you from all harm; He will guard your life. The LORD will guard your going and coming, now and for evermore.

PSALM 122

A song of ascents. Of David. I rejoiced when they said to me, "Let us go to the house of the LORD." Our feet stood within your gates, Jerusalem: Jerusalem built as a city joined together. There the tribes went up, the tribes of the LORD – as a testimony to Israel – to give thanks to the name of the LORD. For there the thrones of justice are set, the thrones of the house of David. Pray for the peace of Jerusalem: "May those who love you prosper. May there be peace within your ramparts, tranquillity in your citadels." For the sake of my brothers and my friends, I shall say, "Peace be within you." For the sake of the house of the LORD our GOD, I shall seek your good.

Psalm 120. Meshech: Descendants of Noah's son Japhet (Genesis 10:2) who lived near the Caspian Sea. *Kedar* – descendants of Ishmael (Genesis 25:12–13; 1 Chronicles 1:29), a generic term for Arab tribes in the north of the Arabian peninsula. Though both were remote from Israel, they figure in the psalm as examples of warlike peoples.

Psalm 121. One of the great expressions of trust in GOD's protection, often recited in times of trouble. The Hebrew root *sh-m-r*, "guard, protect", appears six times in this short psalm.

Psalm 122. A song sung by pilgrims on the way to Jerusalem. The Hebrew is shot through with alliterations on the *sh* sound – as in ***sha'alu shalom Yerushalayim yish-***

תהלים קכג

שִׁיר הַמַּעֲלוֹת, אֵלֶיךָ נָשָׂאתִי אֶת־עֵינַי, הַיֹּשְׁבִי בַּשָּׁמָיִם. הִנֵּה כְעֵינֵי עֲבָדִים אֶל־יַד אֲדוֹנֵיהֶם, כְּעֵינֵי שִׁפְחָה אֶל־יַד גְּבִרְתָּהּ, כֵּן עֵינֵינוּ אֶל־יהוה אֱלֹהֵינוּ, עַד שֶׁיְּחָנֵּנוּ. חָנֵּנוּ יהוה חָנֵּנוּ, כִּי־רַב שָׂבַעְנוּ בוּז. רַבַּת שָׂבְעָה־לָּהּ נַפְשֵׁנוּ הַלַּעַג הַשַּׁאֲנַנִּים, הַבּוּז לִגְאֵי־יוֹנִים.

תהלים קכד

שִׁיר הַמַּעֲלוֹת, לְדָוִד, לוּלֵי יהוה שֶׁהָיָה לָנוּ, יֹאמַר־נָא יִשְׂרָאֵל. לוּלֵי יהוה שֶׁהָיָה לָנוּ, בְּקוּם עָלֵינוּ אָדָם. אֲזַי חַיִּים בְּלָעוּנוּ, בַּחֲרוֹת אַפָּם בָּנוּ. אֲזַי הַמַּיִם שְׁטָפוּנוּ, נַחְלָה עָבַר עַל־נַפְשֵׁנוּ. אֲזַי עָבַר עַל־נַפְשֵׁנוּ, הַמַּיִם הַזֵּידוֹנִים. בָּרוּךְ יהוה, שֶׁלֹּא נְתָנָנוּ טֶרֶף לְשִׁנֵּיהֶם. נַפְשֵׁנוּ כְּצִפּוֹר נִמְלְטָה מִפַּח יוֹקְשִׁים, הַפַּח נִשְׁבָּר וַאֲנַחְנוּ נִמְלָטְנוּ. עֶזְרֵנוּ בְּשֵׁם יהוה, עֹשֵׂה שָׁמַיִם וָאָרֶץ.

תהלים קכה

שִׁיר הַמַּעֲלוֹת, הַבֹּטְחִים בַּיהוה, כְּהַר־צִיּוֹן לֹא־יִמּוֹט לְעוֹלָם יֵשֵׁב. יְרוּשָׁלַיִם, הָרִים סָבִיב לָהּ, וַיהוה סָבִיב לְעַמּוֹ, מֵעַתָּה וְעַד־עוֹלָם. כִּי לֹא יָנוּחַ שֵׁבֶט הָרֶשַׁע עַל גּוֹרַל הַצַּדִּיקִים, לְמַעַן לֹא־יִשְׁלְחוּ הַצַּדִּיקִים, בְּעַוְלָתָה יְדֵיהֶם. הֵיטִיבָה יהוה לַטּוֹבִים, וְלִישָׁרִים בְּלִבּוֹתָם. וְהַמַּטִּים עֲקַלְקַלּוֹתָם יוֹלִיכֵם יהוה אֶת־פֹּעֲלֵי הָאָוֶן, שָׁלוֹם עַל־יִשְׂרָאֵל.

תהלים קכו

שִׁיר הַמַּעֲלוֹת, בְּשׁוּב יהוה אֶת־שִׁיבַת צִיּוֹן הָיִינוּ כְּחֹלְמִים. אָז יִמָּלֵא שְׂחוֹק פִּינוּ, וּלְשׁוֹנֵנוּ רִנָּה, אָז יֹאמְרוּ בַגּוֹיִם,

---

layu – echoing the sound of the second half of the name "Jerusalem", *shalayim*, related to *shalom*, "peace". Here, literary style mirrors substance: the gentle, soothing sounds evoke Jerusalem at peace.

Psalm 124. A psalm of thanksgiving for

PSALM 123

A song of ascents. To You, enthroned in heaven, I lift my eyes. As the eyes of slaves turn to their master's hand, or the eyes of a slave-girl to the hand of her mistress, so our eyes are turned to the LORD our GOD, awaiting His favour. Show us favour, LORD, show us favour, for we have suffered more than enough contempt. Too long have we suffered the scorn of the complacent, the contempt of arrogant men.

PSALM 124

A song of ascents. Of David. Had the LORD not been on our side – let Israel say it – had the LORD not been on our side when men rose up against us, they would have swallowed us alive when their anger raged against us. The waters would have engulfed us; the torrent would have swept over us; over us would have swept the raging waters. Blessed be the LORD who did not leave us as a prey for their teeth. We escaped like a bird from the fowler's trap; the trap broke and we escaped. Our help is in the name of the LORD, Maker of heaven and earth.

PSALM 125

A song of ascents. Those who trust in the LORD are like Mount Zion that cannot be moved, that stands firm for ever. As hills surround Jerusalem so the LORD surrounds His people, now and evermore. The sceptre of the wicked shall not rest on the land allotted to the righteous, so that the righteous shall not set their hand to wrongdoing. Do good, LORD, to those who are good, to those who are upright in heart. As for those who turn aside to crooked ways, may the LORD make them go the way of evildoers. Peace be on Israel!

PSALM 126

A song of ascents. When the LORD brought back the exiles of Zion we

---

deliverance, using – as often in Psalms – a rapid succession of different images: the people have been in danger of being swallowed, swept away as if in a flood, a prey to the enemy's teeth, captured in a hunter's trap. The images do not coalesce into a single metaphor. Rather, they combine to express a mood; in this case, the sense of sudden release from danger.

Psalm 125. A prayer expressing trust in GOD, likening Divine protection to the hills that surround Jerusalem. The final phrase, "Peace be on Israel", became popular in later times and is found as part of the mosaic in the Byzantine synagogue of Jericho (sixth century CE).

Psalm 126. The psalm sung as the song

הִגְדִּיל יהוה לַעֲשׂוֹת עִם־אֵלֶּה. הִגְדִּיל יהוה לַעֲשׂוֹת עִמָּנוּ, הָיִינוּ שְׂמֵחִים. שׁוּבָה יהוה אֶת־שְׁבִיתֵנוּ, כַּאֲפִיקִים בַּנֶּגֶב. הַזֹּרְעִים בְּדִמְעָה בְּרִנָּה יִקְצֹרוּ. הָלוֹךְ יֵלֵךְ וּבָכֹה נֹשֵׂא מֶשֶׁךְ־הַזָּרַע, בֹּא־יָבוֹא בְרִנָּה נֹשֵׂא אֲלֻמֹּתָיו.

תהלים קכז

שִׁיר הַמַּעֲלוֹת, לִשְׁלֹמֹה, אִם־יהוה לֹא יִבְנֶה בַיִת, שָׁוְא עָמְלוּ בוֹנָיו בּוֹ, אִם־יהוה לֹא־יִשְׁמָר־עִיר, שָׁוְא שָׁקַד שׁוֹמֵר. שָׁוְא לָכֶם מַשְׁכִּימֵי קוּם מְאַחֲרֵי־שֶׁבֶת, אֹכְלֵי לֶחֶם הָעֲצָבִים, כֵּן יִתֵּן לִידִידוֹ שֵׁנָא. הִנֵּה נַחֲלַת יהוה בָּנִים, שָׂכָר פְּרִי הַבָּטֶן. כְּחִצִּים בְּיַד־גִּבּוֹר כֵּן בְּנֵי הַנְּעוּרִים. אַשְׁרֵי הַגֶּבֶר אֲשֶׁר מִלֵּא אֶת־אַשְׁפָּתוֹ מֵהֶם, לֹא יֵבֹשׁוּ, כִּי־יְדַבְּרוּ אֶת־אוֹיְבִים בַּשָּׁעַר.

תהלים קכח

שִׁיר הַמַּעֲלוֹת, אַשְׁרֵי כָּל־יְרֵא יהוה, הַהֹלֵךְ בִּדְרָכָיו. יְגִיעַ כַּפֶּיךָ כִּי תֹאכֵל, אַשְׁרֶיךָ וְטוֹב לָךְ. אֶשְׁתְּךָ כְּגֶפֶן פֹּרִיָּה בְּיַרְכְּתֵי בֵיתֶךָ, בָּנֶיךָ כִּשְׁתִלֵי זֵיתִים, סָבִיב לְשֻׁלְחָנֶךָ. הִנֵּה כִי־כֵן יְבֹרַךְ גָּבֶר יְרֵא יהוה. יְבָרֶכְךָ יהוה מִצִּיּוֹן, וּרְאֵה בְּטוּב יְרוּשָׁלָיִם, כֹּל יְמֵי חַיֶּיךָ. וּרְאֵה־בָנִים לְבָנֶיךָ, שָׁלוֹם עַל־יִשְׂרָאֵל.

תהלים קכט

שִׁיר הַמַּעֲלוֹת, רַבַּת צְרָרוּנִי מִנְּעוּרָי יֹאמַר־נָא יִשְׂרָאֵל. רַבַּת צְרָרוּנִי מִנְּעוּרָי, גַּם לֹא יָכְלוּ־לִי. עַל־גַּבִּי חָרְשׁוּ חֹרְשִׁים, הֶאֱרִיכוּ לְמַעֲנִיתָם. יהוה צַדִּיק, קִצֵּץ עֲבוֹת

---

preceding Grace after Meals on Shabbat and festivals. Its interpretation is difficult because of the change of tenses from past (verses 1–3) to future (4–6). It may be entirely future-oriented, anticipating the ingathering of exiles and the restoration of national sovereignty, or it may be that the Psalmist prays for the future return

were like people who dream. Then were our mouths filled with laughter, and our tongues with songs of joy. Then was it said among the nations, "The LORD has done great things for them". The LORD did do great things for us and we rejoiced. Bring back our exiles, LORD, like streams in a dry land. May those who sowed in tears, reap in joy. May one who goes out weeping, carrying a bag of seed, come back with songs of joy, carrying his sheaves.

PSALM 127

A song of ascents. Of Solomon. Unless the LORD builds the house, its builders labour in vain. Unless the LORD guards the city, in vain does the guard keep watch. In vain do you rise early and go late to rest, toiling for the bread you eat. He provides for His loved ones while they sleep. Children are a heritage from the LORD; the fruit of the womb, His reward. Like arrows in the hand of a warrior are the sons of one's youth. Happy is the man who fills his quiver with them; they shall not be put to shame when they contend with the enemy at the gate.

PSALM 128

A song of ascents. Happy are all who fear the LORD, who walk in His ways. When you eat the fruit of your labour, happy and fortunate are you. Your wife shall be like a fruitful vine within your house; your sons like olive saplings around your table. So shall the man who fears the LORD be blessed. May the LORD bless you from Zion; may you see the good of Jerusalem all the days of your life; and may you live to see your children's children. Peace be on Israel!

PSALM 129

A song of ascents. Often since I was young I have been attacked – let Israel now say – often since I was young I have been attacked, but never have my attackers prevailed. Ploughmen ploughed across my

---

of Jews to Zion by recalling events in the past. The current state of the people is compared in the last two verses to grain before the spring: though now it seems buried in the earth, it will eventually grow and yield a rich harvest.

Psalm 130. A penitential psalm, recited during the Ten Days of Repentance. *From the depths* – a graphic phrase, signalling closeness to despair or death, used in only one other Psalm, 69. *With You there is forgiveness* – the Psalmist makes the powerful, paradoxical point that GOD is to be

רְשָׁעִים. יֵבֹשׁוּ וְיִסֹּגוּ אָחוֹר כֹּל שֹׂנְאֵי צִיּוֹן. יִהְיוּ כַּחֲצִיר גַּגּוֹת שֶׁקַּדְמַת שָׁלַף יָבֵשׁ. שֶׁלֹּא מִלֵּא כַפּוֹ קוֹצֵר, וְחִצְנוֹ מְעַמֵּר. וְלֹא אָמְרוּ הָעֹבְרִים, בִּרְכַּת יהוה אֲלֵיכֶם, בֵּרַכְנוּ אֶתְכֶם בְּשֵׁם יהוה.

תהלים קל

שִׁיר הַמַּעֲלוֹת, מִמַּעֲמַקִּים קְרָאתִיךָ יהוה. אֲדֹנָי שִׁמְעָה בְקוֹלִי, תִּהְיֶינָה אָזְנֶיךָ קַשֻּׁבוֹת לְקוֹל תַּחֲנוּנָי. אִם עֲוֹנוֹת תִּשְׁמָר־יָהּ, אֲדֹנָי מִי יַעֲמֹד. כִּי עִמְּךָ הַסְּלִיחָה, לְמַעַן תִּוָּרֵא. קִוִּיתִי יהוה קִוְּתָה נַפְשִׁי, וְלִדְבָרוֹ הוֹחָלְתִּי. נַפְשִׁי לַיהוה, מִשֹּׁמְרִים לַבֹּקֶר, שֹׁמְרִים לַבֹּקֶר. יַחֵל יִשְׂרָאֵל אֶל יהוה, כִּי־עִם־יהוה הַחֶסֶד, וְהַרְבֵּה עִמּוֹ פְדוּת. וְהוּא יִפְדֶּה אֶת יִשְׂרָאֵל, מִכֹּל עֲוֹנוֹתָיו.

תהלים קלא

שִׁיר הַמַּעֲלוֹת, לְדָוִד, יהוה לֹא־גָבַהּ לִבִּי, וְלֹא־רָמוּ עֵינַי, וְלֹא־הִלַּכְתִּי בִּגְדֹלוֹת וּבְנִפְלָאוֹת מִמֶּנִּי. אִם־לֹא שִׁוִּיתִי וְדוֹמַמְתִּי נַפְשִׁי, כְּגָמֻל עֲלֵי אִמּוֹ, כַּגָּמֻל עָלַי נַפְשִׁי. יַחֵל יִשְׂרָאֵל אֶל־יהוה, מֵעַתָּה וְעַד־עוֹלָם.

תהלים קלב

שִׁיר הַמַּעֲלוֹת, זְכוֹר־יהוה לְדָוִד, אֵת כָּל־עֻנּוֹתוֹ. אֲשֶׁר נִשְׁבַּע לַיהוה, נָדַר לַאֲבִיר יַעֲקֹב. אִם־אָבֹא בְּאֹהֶל בֵּיתִי, אִם־אֶעֱלֶה עַל־עֶרֶשׂ יְצוּעָי. אִם־אֶתֵּן שְׁנַת לְעֵינָי, לְעַפְעַפַּי תְּנוּמָה. עַד־אֶמְצָא מָקוֹם לַיהוה, מִשְׁכָּנוֹת לַאֲבִיר יַעֲקֹב. הִנֵּה־שְׁמַעֲנוּהָ בְאֶפְרָתָה, מְצָאנוּהָ בִּשְׂדֵי־יָעַר.

---

held in awe not because He punishes but because He forgives.

Psalm 132. A psalm about the Temple and its priests. The first five verses describe David's determination to build a house

back, making long furrows. But the LORD is just; He has cut the bonds of the wicked. Let all who hate Zion be driven back in shame. Let them be like the grass on roofs that fades before it can be pulled up. It will never fill a reaper's hand nor yield an armful for the gatherer of sheaves. No passersby will say to them: "The LORD's blessing be upon you. We bless you in the name of the LORD."

PSALM 130

A song of ascents. From the depths I have called to You, O LORD. LORD, hear my voice; let Your ears be attentive to my plea. If You, LORD, should keep account of sins, who could stand? But with You there is forgiveness, that You may be held in awe. I wait for the LORD, my soul waits, and in His word I put my hope. My soul waits for the LORD more than watchmen wait for the morning, more than watchmen wait for the morning. Israel, put your hope in the LORD, for with the LORD there is lovingkindness, and great is His power to redeem. It is He who will redeem Israel from all their sins.

PSALM 131

A song of ascents. Of David. LORD, my heart is not proud, nor are my eyes haughty. I do not busy myself with great affairs or with things beyond me. But I have made my soul still and quiet, like a weaned child with its mother; like a weaned child is my soul within me. Israel, put your hope in the LORD, now and for evermore.

PSALM 132

A song of ascents. LORD, remember David and all the hardship he endured. He swore an oath to the LORD and made a vow to the Mighty One of Jacob: "I will not enter my house, nor go to bed; I will not give sleep to my eyes or slumber to my eyelids, until I find a place for the LORD, a dwelling for the Mighty One of Jacob." We heard of it in Efrat,

---

for GOD: "Here I am living in a house of cedar, while the Ark of the LORD is housed in a tent" (II Samuel 7:2). Verses 10–12 describe GOD's promise to David that the monarchy would be an eternal gift to his descendants: "Your family and

נָבוֹאָה לְמִשְׁכְּנוֹתָיו, נִשְׁתַּחֲוֶה לַהֲדֹם רַגְלָיו. קוּמָה יהוה לִמְנוּחָתֶךָ, אַתָּה וַאֲרוֹן עֻזֶּךָ. כֹּהֲנֶיךָ יִלְבְּשׁוּ־צֶדֶק, וַחֲסִידֶיךָ יְרַנֵּנוּ. בַּעֲבוּר דָּוִד עַבְדֶּךָ, אַל־תָּשֵׁב פְּנֵי מְשִׁיחֶךָ. נִשְׁבַּע יהוה לְדָוִד, אֱמֶת לֹא־יָשׁוּב מִמֶּנָּה, מִפְּרִי בִטְנְךָ אָשִׁית לְכִסֵּא־לָךְ. אִם־יִשְׁמְרוּ בָנֶיךָ בְּרִיתִי, וְעֵדֹתִי זוֹ אֲלַמְּדֵם, גַּם־בְּנֵיהֶם עֲדֵי־עַד, יֵשְׁבוּ לְכִסֵּא־לָךְ. כִּי־בָחַר יהוה בְּצִיּוֹן, אִוָּהּ לְמוֹשָׁב לוֹ. זֹאת־מְנוּחָתִי עֲדֵי־עַד, פֹּה אֵשֵׁב כִּי אִוִּתִיהָ. צֵידָהּ בָּרֵךְ אֲבָרֵךְ, אֶבְיוֹנֶיהָ אַשְׂבִּיעַ לָחֶם. וְכֹהֲנֶיהָ אַלְבִּישׁ יֶשַׁע, וַחֲסִידֶיהָ רַנֵּן יְרַנֵּנוּ. שָׁם אַצְמִיחַ קֶרֶן לְדָוִד, עָרַכְתִּי נֵר לִמְשִׁיחִי. אוֹיְבָיו אַלְבִּישׁ בֹּשֶׁת, וְעָלָיו יָצִיץ נִזְרוֹ.

תהלים קלג

שִׁיר הַמַּעֲלוֹת, לְדָוִד, הִנֵּה מַה־טּוֹב וּמַה־נָּעִים, שֶׁבֶת אַחִים גַּם־יָחַד. כַּשֶּׁמֶן הַטּוֹב עַל־הָרֹאשׁ יֹרֵד עַל־הַזָּקָן, זְקַן אַהֲרֹן שֶׁיֹּרֵד עַל־פִּי מִדּוֹתָיו. כְּטַל־חֶרְמוֹן שֶׁיֹּרֵד עַל־הַרְרֵי צִיּוֹן, כִּי שָׁם צִוָּה יהוה אֶת־הַבְּרָכָה, חַיִּים עַד־הָעוֹלָם.

תהלים קלד

שִׁיר הַמַּעֲלוֹת, הִנֵּה בָּרְכוּ אֶת־יהוה כָּל־עַבְדֵי יהוה, הָעֹמְדִים בְּבֵית־יהוה בַּלֵּילוֹת. שְׂאוּ־יְדֵכֶם קֹדֶשׁ, וּבָרְכוּ אֶת־יהוה. יְבָרֶכְךָ יהוה מִצִּיּוֹן, עֹשֵׂה שָׁמַיִם וָאָרֶץ.

In many congregations, קַדִּישׁ יָתוֹם on page 522 is said at this point.

---

your kingdom will be established for ever in My sight; your throne will endure for all time" (II Samuel 7:16).

Psalm 133. A short poem on the blessing of harmony between brothers – possibly a reference to the divided kingdom, Israel in the north, Judah in the south, with a hope for their reunification. When Aaron was ordained as High Priest, anointing oil was poured over his head (Exodus 29:7). Mount Hermon, in

we found it in the fields of Yaar. Let us enter His dwelling, worship at His footstool. Advance, LORD, to Your resting place, You and Your mighty Ark. Your priests are robed in righteousness; Your devoted ones sing for joy. For the sake of Your servant David, do not reject Your anointed one. The LORD swore to David a firm oath that He will not revoke: "One of your own descendants I will set upon your throne. If your sons keep My covenant and My decrees that I teach them, then their sons shall sit upon your throne for all time." For the LORD has chosen Zion; He desired it for His home. This is My resting place for all time; here I will dwell, for that is My desire. I will amply bless its store of food; its poor I will satisfy with bread. I will clothe its priests with salvation; its loyal ones shall sing for joy. There I will make David's dynasty flourish; I will prepare a lamp for My anointed one. I will clothe his enemies with shame, but on him will be a shining crown.

PSALM 133

A song of ascents. Of David. How good and pleasant it is when brothers dwell together. It is like fragrant oil on the head, running down onto the beard, Aaron's beard, that runs down over the collar of his robes. It is like the dew of Hermon that falls on the mountains of Zion. There the LORD bestows His blessing, life for evermore.

PSALM 134

A song of ascents. Come, bless the LORD, all you servants of the LORD, who nightly stand in the house of the LORD. Lift up your hands toward the sanctuary and bless the LORD. May the LORD, Maker of heaven and earth, bless you from Zion!

In many congregations, the Mourner's *Kaddish* on page 523 is said at this point.

---

the north, was the highest mountain in Israel. Both images, of oil on the priest's head and dew on the mountain, are metaphors of plenitude.

Psalm 134. The last of the Psalms of Ascents brings the sequence to a close by calling on the people to bless GOD, and GOD to bless the people. The juxtaposition in the last verse, of "heaven

עלינו

Stand while saying עָלֵינוּ. Bow at ▼.

עָלֵינוּ לְשַׁבֵּחַ לַאֲדוֹן הַכֹּל, לָתֵת גְּדֻלָּה לְיוֹצֵר בְּרֵאשִׁית, שֶׁלֹּא עָשָׂנוּ כְּגוֹיֵי הָאֲרָצוֹת, וְלֹא שָׂמָנוּ כְּמִשְׁפְּחוֹת הָאֲדָמָה. שֶׁלֹּא שָׂם חֶלְקֵנוּ כָּהֶם, וְגוֹרָלֵנוּ כְּכָל־הֲמוֹנָם. ▼וַאֲנַחְנוּ כּוֹרְעִים וּמִשְׁתַּחֲוִים וּמוֹדִים, לִפְנֵי מֶלֶךְ מַלְכֵי הַמְּלָכִים הַקָּדוֹשׁ בָּרוּךְ הוּא. שֶׁהוּא נוֹטֶה שָׁמַיִם וְיוֹסֵד אָרֶץ, וּמוֹשַׁב יְקָרוֹ בַּשָּׁמַיִם מִמַּעַל, וּשְׁכִינַת עֻזּוֹ בְּגָבְהֵי מְרוֹמִים. הוּא אֱלֹהֵינוּ, אֵין עוֹד. אֱמֶת מַלְכֵּנוּ, אֶפֶס זוּלָתוֹ, כַּכָּתוּב בְּתוֹרָתוֹ, וְיָדַעְתָּ הַיּוֹם וַהֲשֵׁבֹתָ אֶל־לְבָבֶךָ, כִּי יהוה הוּא הָאֱלֹהִים בַּשָּׁמַיִם מִמַּעַל וְעַל־הָאָרֶץ מִתָּחַת, אֵין עוֹד.

עַל־כֵּן נְקַוֶּה לְּךָ יהוה אֱלֹהֵינוּ לִרְאוֹת מְהֵרָה בְּתִפְאֶרֶת עֻזֶּךָ, לְהַעֲבִיר גִּלּוּלִים מִן הָאָרֶץ, וְהָאֱלִילִים כָּרוֹת יִכָּרֵתוּן, לְתַקֵּן עוֹלָם בְּמַלְכוּת שַׁדַּי. וְכָל־בְּנֵי בָשָׂר יִקְרְאוּ בִשְׁמֶךָ, לְהַפְנוֹת אֵלֶיךָ כָּל־רִשְׁעֵי אָרֶץ. יַכִּירוּ וְיֵדְעוּ כָּל־יוֹשְׁבֵי תֵבֵל, כִּי לְךָ תִּכְרַע כָּל־בֶּרֶךְ, תִּשָּׁבַע כָּל־לָשׁוֹן. לְפָנֶיךָ יהוה אֱלֹהֵינוּ יִכְרְעוּ וְיִפֹּלוּ, וְלִכְבוֹד שִׁמְךָ יְקָר יִתֵּנוּ. וִיקַבְּלוּ כֻלָּם אֶת־עוֹל מַלְכוּתֶךָ, וְתִמְלֹךְ עֲלֵיהֶם מְהֵרָה לְעוֹלָם וָעֶד. כִּי הַמַּלְכוּת שֶׁלְּךָ הִיא וּלְעוֹלְמֵי עַד תִּמְלוֹךְ בְּכָבוֹד, כַּכָּתוּב בְּתוֹרָתֶךָ, יהוה יִמְלֹךְ לְעוֹלָם וָעֶד. ← וְנֶאֱמַר, וְהָיָה יהוה לְמֶלֶךְ עַל־כָּל־הָאָרֶץ, בַּיּוֹם הַהוּא יִהְיֶה יהוה אֶחָד וּשְׁמוֹ אֶחָד.

Some congregations add:

אַל תִּירָא מִפַּחַד פִּתְאֹם, וּמִשֹּׁאַת רְשָׁעִים כִּי תָבֹא. עֻצוּ עֵצָה וְתֻפָר, דַּבְּרוּ דָבָר וְלֹא יָקוּם, כִּי עִמָּנוּ אֵל. וְעַד זִקְנָה אֲנִי הוּא, וְעַד שֵׂיבָה אֲנִי אֶסְבֹּל, אֲנִי עָשִׂיתִי וַאֲנִי אֶשָּׂא, וַאֲנִי אֶסְבֹּל וַאֲמַלֵּט.

ALEINU

Stand while saying *Aleinu*. Bow at ▾.

עָלֵינוּ It is our duty to praise the Master of all, and ascribe greatness to the Author of creation, who has not made us like the nations of the lands nor placed us like the families of the earth; who has not made our portion like theirs, nor our destiny like all their multitudes. Therefore ▾we bow in worship and thank the Supreme King of kings, the Holy One, blessed be He, who extends the heavens and establishes the earth, whose throne of glory is in the heavens above, and whose power's presence is in the highest of heights. He is our God; there is no other. Truly He is our King, there is none else, as it is written in His Torah, "You shall know and take to heart this day that the Lord is God, in heaven above and on earth below. There is no other."

Therefore we place our hope in You, Lord our God, that we may soon see the glory of Your power, when You will remove abominations from the earth, and idols will be utterly destroyed; when the world will be perfected under the sovereignty of the Almighty; when all humanity will call on Your name, and the earth's wicked will all turn to You. All the world's inhabitants will realise and know that to You every knee must bow and every tongue swear loyalty. Before You, Lord our God, they will kneel and bow down and give honour to Your glorious name. They will all accept the yoke of Your kingdom, and You will reign over them soon and for ever. For the kingdom is Yours, and to all eternity You will reign in glory, as it is written in Your Torah: "The Lord will reign for ever and ever." → And it is said: "Then the Lord shall be King over all the earth: on that day the Lord shall be One and His name One."

Some congregations add:

Have no fear of sudden terror or of the ruin that overtakes the wicked. Devise your strategy, but it will be thwarted; propose your plan, but it will not stand, for God is with us. When you grow old, I will still be the same. When your hair turns grey, I will still carry you. I made you, I will bear you, I will carry you, and I will rescue you.

קדיש יתום

The transliteration can be found at the end of the Siddur.

Mourner:

יִתְגַּדַּל וְיִתְקַדַּשׁ שְׁמֵהּ רַבָּא. (Cong. אָמֵן) בְּעָלְמָא דִּי־בְרָא
כִרְעוּתֵהּ. וְיַמְלִיךְ מַלְכוּתֵהּ, בְּחַיֵּיכוֹן וּבְיוֹמֵיכוֹן וּבְחַיֵּי דְכָל־
בֵּית יִשְׂרָאֵל, בַּעֲגָלָא וּבִזְמַן קָרִיב. וְאִמְרוּ אָמֵן. (Cong. אָמֵן)

All:

יְהֵא שְׁמֵהּ רַבָּא מְבָרַךְ לְעָלַם וּלְעָלְמֵי עָלְמַיָּא.

Mourner:

יִתְבָּרַךְ וְיִשְׁתַּבַּח וְיִתְפָּאַר וְיִתְרוֹמַם וְיִתְנַשֵּׂא וְיִתְהַדַּר
וְיִתְעַלֶּה וְיִתְהַלָּל שְׁמֵהּ דְּקֻדְשָׁא בְּרִיךְ הוּא (Cong. בְּרִיךְ הוּא)
לְעֵלָּא (On שַׁבַּת שׁוּבָה add לְעֵלָּא) מִן־כָּל־בִּרְכָתָא וְשִׁירָתָא
תֻּשְׁבְּחָתָא וְנֶחֱמָתָא, דַּאֲמִירָן בְּעָלְמָא. וְאִמְרוּ אָמֵן.
(Cong. אָמֵן)

יְהֵא שְׁלָמָא רַבָּא מִן־שְׁמַיָּא, וְחַיִּים עָלֵינוּ וְעַל־כָּל־יִשְׂרָאֵל.
וְאִמְרוּ אָמֵן. (Cong. אָמֵן)

Bow, take three steps back, then bow, first left, then right, then centre, while saying:

עֹשֶׂה שָׁלוֹם בִּמְרוֹמָיו, הוּא יַעֲשֶׂה שָׁלוֹם עָלֵינוּ, וְעַל־כָּל־
יִשְׂרָאֵל. וְאִמְרוּ אָמֵן. (Cong. אָמֵן)

---

and earth" and Zion, encapsulates the two dimensions of Judaism – the universal and the particular. God is everywhere, but it is in Zion that His presence is most apparent.

ETHICS OF THE FATHERS
Ethics of the Fathers is the name given to the tractate of the Mishnah which gathers together many of the ethical teachings of the Sages. The word *Avot* may mean "fundamental principles", however it is more likely to mean "the Fathers" of the oral tradition, the teachers of the Mishnah and their predecessors. To the five chapters of the Mishnah was added a sixth, not itself part of the Mishnah but a later addition, similar in style and content. The need for

MOURNER'S KADDISH

The transliteration can be found at the end of the Siddur.

Mourner:

יִתְגַּדַּל Magnified and sanctified may His great name be, in the world He created by His will. May He establish His kingdom in your lifetime and in your days, and in the lifetime of all the House of Israel, swiftly and soon – and say: Amen.

All:

May His great name be blessed for ever and all time.

Mourner:

Blessed and praised, glorified and exalted, raised and honoured, uplifted and lauded be the name of the Holy One, blessed be He, (between Rosh Hashanah and Yom Kippur add 'well') beyond any blessing, song, praise and consolation uttered in the world – and say: Amen.

May there be great peace from heaven, and life for us and all Israel – and say: Amen.

Bow, take three steps back, then bow, first left, then right, then centre, while saying:

May He who makes peace in His high places, make peace for us and all Israel – and say: Amen.

---

such an addition arose in circles where the custom was to study one chapter each week during the six Shabbatot between Pesach and Shavuot. It is our custom, however, to study *Avot* from Pesach until the Shabbat before Rosh Hashanah.

The tractate begins by tracing the unbroken continuity of the Oral Law from Moses to the Sages. Interestingly, the Sages traced their provenance to the prophets rather than the priests, who go unmentioned in the chain of succession.

The tractate ranges widely over matters of belief and conduct, but its primary concern is to set out values and virtues of a life dedicated to the study and practice of Torah. Its style is aphoristic; its statements brief, epigrammatic, and at times even cryptic. The first two chapters are organised chronologically; chapters three and four are collections of sayings; chapter five records teachings whose common feature is that they are associated with numerical lists; and the sixth is a paean of praise to the life of Torah and the virtues it requires.

No finer account exists of the way of life epitomised by the Sages, which was quiet, scholarly, profoundly driven by a

פרקי אבות

One of the following chapters is read each שַׁבָּת after פֶּסַח until the שַׁבָּת before רֹאשׁ הַשָּׁנָה. On the last three שַׁבָּתוֹת before רֹאשׁ הַשָּׁנָה, two chapters are read.

פרק ראשון

כׇּל־יִשְׂרָאֵל יֵשׁ לָהֶם חֵלֶק לָעוֹלָם הַבָּא, שֶׁנֶּאֱמַר, וְעַמֵּךְ כֻּלָּם צַדִּיקִים, לְעוֹלָם יִירְשׁוּ אָרֶץ, נֵצֶר מַטָּעַי, מַעֲשֵׂה יָדַי לְהִתְפָּאֵר.

א מֹשֶׁה קִבֵּל תּוֹרָה מִסִּינַי, וּמְסָרָהּ לִיהוֹשֻׁעַ, וִיהוֹשֻׁעַ
לִזְקֵנִים, וּזְקֵנִים לִנְבִיאִים, וּנְבִיאִים מְסָרוּהָ לְאַנְשֵׁי
כְנֶסֶת הַגְּדוֹלָה. הֵם אָמְרוּ שְׁלֹשָׁה דְבָרִים, הֱווּ מְתוּנִים
בַּדִּין, וְהַעֲמִידוּ תַלְמִידִים הַרְבֵּה, וַעֲשׂוּ סְיָג לַתּוֹרָה.
ב שִׁמְעוֹן הַצַּדִּיק הָיָה מִשְּׁיָרֵי כְנֶסֶת הַגְּדוֹלָה. הוּא הָיָה
אוֹמֵר, עַל־שְׁלֹשָׁה דְבָרִים הָעוֹלָם עוֹמֵד, עַל הַתּוֹרָה,
וְעַל הָעֲבוֹדָה, וְעַל גְּמִילוּת חֲסָדִים. ג אַנְטִיגְנוֹס אִישׁ
שׂוֹכוֹ קִבֵּל מִשִּׁמְעוֹן הַצַּדִּיק. הוּא הָיָה אוֹמֵר, אַל־תִּהְיוּ
כַּעֲבָדִים הַמְשַׁמְּשִׁין אֶת־הָרַב עַל־מְנָת לְקַבֵּל פְּרָס, אֶלָּא
הֱווּ כַּעֲבָדִים הַמְשַׁמְּשִׁין אֶת־הָרַב שֶׁלֹּא עַל־מְנָת לְקַבֵּל
פְּרָס, וִיהִי מוֹרָא שָׁמַיִם עֲלֵיכֶם. ד יוֹסֵי בֶּן־יוֹעֶזֶר אִישׁ
צְרֵדָה וְיוֹסֵי בֶּן־יוֹחָנָן אִישׁ יְרוּשָׁלַיִם קִבְּלוּ מֵהֶם. יוֹסֵי בֶּן־
יוֹעֶזֶר אִישׁ צְרֵדָה אוֹמֵר, יְהִי בֵיתְךָ בֵּית וַעַד לַחֲכָמִים,
וֶהֱוֵה מִתְאַבֵּק בַּעֲפַר רַגְלֵיהֶם, וֶהֱוֵה שׁוֹתֶה בַצָּמָא אֶת־
דִּבְרֵיהֶם. ה יוֹסֵי בֶּן־יוֹחָנָן אִישׁ יְרוּשָׁלַיִם אוֹמֵר, יְהִי בֵיתְךָ
פָּתוּחַ לִרְוָחָה, וְיִהְיוּ עֲנִיִּים בְּנֵי בֵיתֶךָ, וְאַל־תַּרְבֶּה שִׂיחָה
עִם הָאִשָּׁה. בְּאִשְׁתּוֹ אָמְרוּ, קַל וָחֹמֶר בְּאֵשֶׁת חֲבֵרוֹ. מִכָּאן
אָמְרוּ חֲכָמִים, כׇּל־הַמַּרְבֶּה שִׂיחָה עִם הָאִשָּׁה גּוֹרֵם רָעָה
לְעַצְמוֹ, וּבוֹטֵל מִדִּבְרֵי תוֹרָה, וְסוֹפוֹ יוֹרֵשׁ גֵּיהִנֹּם. ו יְהוֹשֻׁעַ

ETHICS OF THE FATHERS

One of the following chapters is read each Shabbat after Pesach until the Shabbat before Rosh Hashanah. On the last three Shabbatot before Rosh Hashanah, two chapters are read.

CHAPTER I

All Israel have a share in the World to Come, as it is said, "Your people are all righteous; they shall inherit the land forever; they are a shoot of My own planting, a work of My own hands, that I may be glorified". 1. Moses received the Torah at Sinai and handed it on to Yehoshua; Yehoshua to the elders; the elders to the prophets; and the prophets handed it on to the men of the Great Assembly. They (the men of the Great Assembly) said three things: Be careful in judgement; raise up many disciples; and make a fence for the Torah. 2. Simon the Just was one of the last survivors of the Great Assembly. He used to say: On three things the world stands: on the Torah, on Divine worship, and on acts of lovingkindness. 3. Antigonos of Sokho received (the Torah tradition) from Simon the Just. He used to say: Do not be like servants who serve their master on condition of receiving a reward, but be like servants who serve their master not on condition of receiving a reward; and let the fear of Heaven be upon you. 4. Yose ben Yoezer of Zeredah and Yose ben Yochanan of Jerusalem received (the tradition) from them. Yose ben Yoezer of Zeredah used to say: Let your house be a meeting place for Sages; sit in the dust at their feet, and with thirst, drink in their words. 5. Yose ben Yochanan of Jerusalem used to say: Let your house be open wide; let the poor join the members of your household; and do not gossip inordinately with women. This was said about one's own wife; all the more so does it apply to another man's wife. Hence the Sages say: a man who talks too much with a woman brings trouble on himself, neglects the study of Torah, and in the end will inherit Gehinnom. 6. Yehoshua ben Perachyah and Nittai the Arbelite received (the tradition) from them. Yehoshua ben Perachyah

---

sense of justice and integrity, sceptical of politics and politicians, and dedicated to the life of the mind and to the spiritual drama of study as the highest connection between the mind of man and the will of God.

בֶּן־פְּרַחְיָה וְנִתַּי הָאַרְבֵּלִי קִבְּלוּ מֵהֶם. יְהוֹשֻׁעַ בֶּן־פְּרַחְיָה
אוֹמֵר, עֲשֵׂה לְךָ רַב, וּקְנֵה לְךָ חָבֵר, וֶהֱוֵה דָן אֶת־כָּל־
הָאָדָם לְכַף זְכוּת. ז נִתַּי הָאַרְבֵּלִי אוֹמֵר, הַרְחֵק מִשָּׁכֵן רָע,
וְאַל־תִּתְחַבֵּר לָרָשָׁע, וְאַל־תִּתְיָאֵשׁ מִן־הַפֻּרְעָנוּת. ח יְהוּדָה
בֶּן־טַבַּאי וְשִׁמְעוֹן בֶּן־שָׁטַח קִבְּלוּ מֵהֶם. יְהוּדָה בֶּן־טַבַּאי
אוֹמֵר, אַל־תַּעַשׂ עַצְמְךָ כְּעוֹרְכֵי הַדַּיָּנִים, וּכְשֶׁיִּהְיוּ בַּעֲלֵי
הַדִּין עוֹמְדִים לְפָנֶיךָ, יִהְיוּ בְעֵינֶיךָ כִּרְשָׁעִים, וּכְשֶׁנִּפְטָרִים
מִלְּפָנֶיךָ, יִהְיוּ בְעֵינֶיךָ כְּזַכָּאִין, כְּשֶׁקִּבְּלוּ עֲלֵיהֶם אֶת־הַדִּין.
ט שִׁמְעוֹן בֶּן־שָׁטַח אוֹמֵר, הֱוֵה מַרְבֶּה לַחֲקוֹר אֶת הָעֵדִים,
וֶהֱוֵה זָהִיר בִּדְבָרֶיךָ, שֶׁמָּא מִתּוֹכָם יִלְמְדוּ לְשַׁקֵּר.
י שְׁמַעְיָה וְאַבְטַלְיוֹן קִבְּלוּ מֵהֶם. שְׁמַעְיָה אוֹמֵר, אֱהוֹב
אֶת־הַמְּלָאכָה, וּשְׂנָא אֶת־הָרַבָּנוּת, וְאַל־תִּתְוַדַּע לָרָשׁוּת.
יא אַבְטַלְיוֹן אוֹמֵר, חֲכָמִים, הִזָּהֲרוּ בְּדִבְרֵיכֶם, שֶׁמָּא
תָחוֹבוּ חוֹבַת גָּלוּת וְתִגְלוּ לִמְקוֹם מַיִם הָרָעִים, וְיִשְׁתּוּ
הַתַּלְמִידִים הַבָּאִים אַחֲרֵיכֶם וְיָמוּתוּ, וְנִמְצָא שֵׁם שָׁמַיִם
מִתְחַלֵּל. יב הִלֵּל וְשַׁמַּאי קִבְּלוּ מֵהֶם. הִלֵּל אוֹמֵר, הֱוֵה
מִתַּלְמִידָיו שֶׁל־אַהֲרֹן, אוֹהֵב שָׁלוֹם וְרוֹדֵף שָׁלוֹם, אוֹהֵב
אֶת־הַבְּרִיּוֹת וּמְקָרְבָן לַתּוֹרָה. יג הוּא הָיָה אוֹמֵר, נְגַד שְׁמָא
אֲבַד שְׁמֵהּ, וּדְלָא מוֹסִיף יָסֵף, וּדְלָא יָלֵף קְטָלָא חַיָּב,
וּדְאִשְׁתַּמַּשׁ בְּתָגָא חֳלָף. יד הוּא הָיָה אוֹמֵר, אִם אֵין אֲנִי לִי,
מִי לִי, וּכְשֶׁאֲנִי לְעַצְמִי, מָה אֲנִי, וְאִם לֹא עַכְשָׁו, אֵימָתָי.
טו שַׁמַּאי אוֹמֵר, עֲשֵׂה תוֹרָתְךָ קֶבַע, אֱמוֹר מְעַט וַעֲשֵׂה
הַרְבֵּה, וֶהֱוֵה מְקַבֵּל אֶת־כָּל־הָאָדָם בְּסֵבֶר פָּנִים יָפוֹת.

Chapter 1

1:1. *The elders*: Leaders of the people in the days of the Judges (see Judges 2:7). *Men of the Great Assembly* – a council of the Sages convened by Ezra or shortly thereafter, during the Second Temple period.

used to say: Get yourself a teacher, acquire a companion, and give everyone the benefit of the doubt. 7. Nittai the Arbelite used to say: Keep far from a bad neighbour, do not associate with a bad person, and do not despair of Divine retribution. 8. Judah ben Tabbai and Simon ben Shatach received (the tradition) from them. Judah ben Tabbai used to say: (When sitting as a judge) do not act as an advocate; when the parties to a lawsuit appear before you, regard them both as guilty; but when they leave you, having accepted the verdict, regard them both as innocent. 9. Simon ben Shatach used to say: Examine the witnesses thoroughly, and be careful in your words, lest through them they learn how to lie. 10. Shemayah and Avtalyon received (the tradition) from them. Shemayah used to say: Love work, hate public office, and do not become too intimate with the ruling power. 11. Avtalyon used to say: Sages, be careful in what you say, lest you incur the penalty of exile and find yourself banished to a place of evil waters, where your disciples who follow you may drink from them and die, with the result that the name of Heaven will be profaned. 12. Hillel and Shammai received (the tradition) from them. Hillel said: Be among the disciples of Aaron, loving peace and pursuing peace, loving people and drawing them close to the Torah. 13. He used to say: A name made great is a name destroyed. He who does not increase (his knowledge) loses it. He who does not study deserves to die, and he who makes worldly use of the crown (of Torah) passes away. 14. He used to say: If I am not for myself, who will be for me? And if I am only for myself, what am I? And if not now, when? 15. Shammai used to say: Make your Torah study a fixed habit. Say little and do much; and greet everyone cheerfully. 16. Rabban Gamliel used to say: Get yourself a teacher, avoid doubt,

---

Make a fence – Rabbinic enactments designed to safeguard Torah observance.

1:8. *Do not act as an advocate*: A judge must maintain strict neutrality. While the case is being heard, the judge must exercise proper scepticism. Once the verdict has been delivered and accepted, there must be no ill-will on either side.

1:13. *A name made great*: Those who take pride in fame will eventually lose it. *He who does not study* – life is learning, and learning is life. *He who makes worldly use of the crown* – Torah scholarship must

טז רַבָּן גַּמְלִיאֵל אוֹמֵר, עֲשֵׂה לְךָ רַב, וְהִסְתַּלֵּק מִן הַסָּפֵק, וְאַל־תַּרְבֶּה לְעַשֵּׂר אוּמָדוֹת. יז שִׁמְעוֹן בְּנוֹ אוֹמֵר, כָּל־יָמַי גָּדַלְתִּי בֵּין הַחֲכָמִים, וְלֹא מָצָאתִי לַגּוּף טוֹב מִשְּׁתִיקָה. וְלֹא הַמִּדְרָשׁ עִקָּר, אֶלָּא הַמַּעֲשֶׂה. וְכָל־הַמַּרְבֶּה דְבָרִים מֵבִיא חֵטְא. יח רַבָּן שִׁמְעוֹן בֶּן־גַּמְלִיאֵל אוֹמֵר, עַל־שְׁלֹשָׁה דְבָרִים הָעוֹלָם קַיָּם, עַל־הָאֱמֶת וְעַל־הַדִּין וְעַל־הַשָּׁלוֹם, שֶׁנֶּאֱמַר, אֱמֶת וּמִשְׁפַּט שָׁלוֹם שִׁפְטוּ בְּשַׁעֲרֵיכֶם.

רַבִּי חֲנַנְיָא בֶּן־עֲקַשְׁיָא אוֹמֵר, רָצָה הַקָּדוֹשׁ בָּרוּךְ הוּא לְזַכּוֹת אֶת־יִשְׂרָאֵל, לְפִיכָךְ הִרְבָּה לָהֶם תּוֹרָה וּמִצְוֹת, שֶׁנֶּאֱמַר, יהוה חָפֵץ לְמַעַן צִדְקוֹ, יַגְדִּיל תּוֹרָה וְיַאְדִּיר.

In many congregations, קַדִּישׁ דְּרַבָּנָן on page 34
is said at this point, then עָלֵינוּ on page 520.

פרק שני

כָּל־יִשְׂרָאֵל יֵשׁ לָהֶם חֵלֶק לָעוֹלָם הַבָּא, שֶׁנֶּאֱמַר, וְעַמֵּךְ כֻּלָּם צַדִּיקִים, לְעוֹלָם יִירְשׁוּ אָרֶץ, נֵצֶר מַטָּעַי, מַעֲשֵׂה יָדַי לְהִתְפָּאֵר.

א רַבִּי אוֹמֵר, אֵיזוֹ הִיא דֶרֶךְ יְשָׁרָה שֶׁיָּבוֹר לוֹ הָאָדָם, כָּל־שֶׁהִיא תִפְאֶרֶת לְעוֹשֶׂהָ וְתִפְאֶרֶת לוֹ מִן הָאָדָם. וֶהֱוֵה זָהִיר בְּמִצְוָה קַלָּה כְּבַחֲמוּרָה, שֶׁאֵין אַתָּה יוֹדֵעַ מַתַּן שְׂכָרָן שֶׁל־מִצְוֹת. וֶהֱוֵה מְחַשֵּׁב הֶפְסֵד מִצְוָה כְּנֶגֶד שְׂכָרָהּ, וּשְׂכַר עֲבֵרָה כְּנֶגֶד הֶפְסֵדָהּ. הִסְתַּכֵּל בִּשְׁלֹשָׁה דְבָרִים, וְאֵין אַתָּה בָא לִידֵי עֲבֵרָה, דַּע מַה־לְּמַעְלָה מִמְּךָ, עַיִן רוֹאָה,

---

never be used for personal advantage. It is for us to honour the Torah, and not use the Torah to honour ourselves.

1:14. *If I am not for myself*: A succinct summary of Judaism's philosophy of personal responsibility combined with social responsibility. *If not now* – a moment of opportunity, unseized, may never come again.

1:16: *Get yourself a teacher*: As with Yeho-

and do not make a habit of giving tithes by guessing. 17. Simon, his son, used to say: All my life I grew up among Sages and I found that nothing is better for a person than silence. Not learning but doing is the main thing; and one who talks too much causes sin. 18. Rabban Simon ben Gamliel used to say: On three things does the world stand – on truth, justice and peace, as it is said, "Administer truth and the judgement of peace in your gates".

Rabbi Chananya ben Akashya said: The Holy One, blessed be He, wanted to confer merit on Israel. That is why He gave them a copious Torah and many commandments, as it is said, "It pleased the Lord, for the sake of [Israel's] righteousness, to make the Torah great and glorious."

In many congregations, the Rabbis' *Kaddish* on page 35
is said at this point, then "It is our duty" on page 521.

CHAPTER 2

All Israel have a share in the World to Come, as it is said, "Your people are all righteous; they shall inherit the land forever; they are a shoot of My own planting, a work of My own hands, that I may be glorified".
1. Rabbi [Judah the Prince] said: What is the right path a person should choose for himself? Whatever is honourable to one who chooses it and honourable in the eyes of others. Be as meticulous in the observance of a minor *mitzvah* as a major one, for you do not know the reward for each *mitzvah*. Against the loss that fulfilling a *mitzvah* may entail, reckon its reward, and against the benefit a transgression may bring, reckon the loss it involves. Reflect on three things and you will not fall into transgression: know what is above you – a seeing eye, a

---

shua ben Perachyah's teaching (above, 1:6), the emphasis is on the choice of one particular teacher as primary mentor and role model. Scholarship depends on discipleship. *Avoid doubt* – keep away from situations in which you are called on to make a decision when the facts are unclear.

Rabbi Chananya ben Akashya: This paragraph is not part of the *Pirkei Avot* but a liturgical addition. According to Maimonides, its implication is that "It is a fundamental principle of Jewish faith that if a person fulfils even one of the 613 commands fully and properly, without ulterior motive but simply for its own sake and out of love, he merits a share in the World to Come. Therefore Rabbi Chananya teaches that there are so many commands that it is impossible that a person should not have fulfilled at

וְאֹזֶן שׁוֹמַעַת, וְכָל מַעֲשֶׂיךָ בַּסֵּפֶר נִכְתָּבִים. ב רַבָּן גַּמְלִיאֵל בְּנוֹ שֶׁל־רַבִּי יְהוּדָה הַנָּשִׂיא אוֹמֵר, יָפֶה תַּלְמוּד תּוֹרָה עִם דֶּרֶךְ אֶרֶץ, שֶׁיְּגִיעַת שְׁנֵיהֶם מַשְׁכַּחַת עָוֹן. וְכָל־תּוֹרָה שֶׁאֵין עִמָּהּ מְלָאכָה, סוֹפָהּ בְּטֵלָה וְגוֹרֶרֶת עָוֹן. וְכָל־הָעוֹסְקִים עִם־הַצִּבּוּר, יִהְיוּ עוֹסְקִים עִמָּהֶם לְשֵׁם שָׁמַיִם, שֶׁזְּכוּת אֲבוֹתָם מְסַיַּעְתָּם, וְצִדְקָתָם עוֹמֶדֶת לָעַד. וְאַתֶּם, מַעֲלֶה אֲנִי עֲלֵיכֶם שָׂכָר הַרְבֵּה כְּאִלּוּ עֲשִׂיתֶם. ג הֱווּ זְהִירִים בָּרָשׁוּת, שֶׁאֵין מְקָרְבִים לוֹ לְאָדָם אֶלָּא לְצֹרֶךְ עַצְמָם, נִרְאִים כְּאוֹהֲבִים בִּשְׁעַת הֲנָאָתָם, וְאֵין עוֹמְדִים לוֹ לְאָדָם בִּשְׁעַת דָּחְקוֹ. ד הוּא הָיָה אוֹמֵר, עֲשֵׂה רְצוֹנוֹ כִּרְצוֹנֶךָ, כְּדֵי שֶׁיַּעֲשֶׂה רְצוֹנְךָ כִּרְצוֹנוֹ. בַּטֵּל רְצוֹנְךָ מִפְּנֵי רְצוֹנוֹ, כְּדֵי שֶׁיְּבַטֵּל רְצוֹן אֲחֵרִים מִפְּנֵי רְצוֹנֶךָ. ה הִלֵּל אוֹמֵר, אַל־תִּפְרוֹשׁ מִן־הַצִּבּוּר, וְאַל־תַּאֲמִן בְּעַצְמְךָ עַד יוֹם מוֹתְךָ, וְאַל־תָּדִין אֶת־חֲבֵרְךָ עַד שֶׁתַּגִּיעַ לִמְקוֹמוֹ, וְאַל־תֹּאמַר דָּבָר שֶׁאִי אֶפְשַׁר לִשְׁמוֹעַ, שֶׁסּוֹפוֹ לְהִשָּׁמַע. וְאַל־תֹּאמַר לִכְשֶׁאֶפָּנֶה אֶשְׁנֶה, שֶׁמָּא לֹא תִפָּנֶה. ו הוּא הָיָה אוֹמֵר, אֵין בּוּר יְרֵא חֵטְא, וְלֹא עַם הָאָרֶץ חָסִיד, וְלֹא הַבַּיְשָׁן לָמֵד, וְלֹא הַקַּפְּדָן מְלַמֵּד, וְלֹא כָּל הַמַּרְבֶּה בִסְחוֹרָה מַחְכִּים, וּבִמְקוֹם שֶׁאֵין אֲנָשִׁים הִשְׁתַּדֵּל לִהְיוֹת אִישׁ. ז אַף הוּא רָאָה גֻּלְגֹּלֶת אַחַת שֶׁצָּפָה עַל־פְּנֵי הַמָּיִם. אָמַר לָהּ, עַל דַּאֲטֵיפְתְּ אַטִיפוּךְ, וְסוֹף מְטַיְּפָיִךְ יְטוּפוּן. ח הוּא הָיָה אוֹמֵר, מַרְבֶּה בָשָׂר, מַרְבֶּה רִמָּה. מַרְבֶּה נְכָסִים, מַרְבֶּה

---

least one in the course of a lifetime, and thereby merits eternal life." The statement of Rabbi Chananya thus complements the teaching recited at the beginning, that "All Israel have a share in the World to Come."

hearing ear, and a book in which all your deeds are written. 2. Rabban Gamliel, son of Rabbi Judah the Prince, said: It is good to combine Torah study with a worldly occupation, for the effort involved in both makes one forget sin. Torah study without an occupation will in the end fail and lead to sin. And all who work for the community should do so for the sake of Heaven, for their ancestral merit will support them and their righteousness endures for ever. And as for you (GOD will say), I count you worthy of great reward as though you yourselves had accomplished it all. 3. Be wary in your dealings with the ruling power, for they only befriend a man when it serves their needs. When it is to their advantage, they appear as friends, but they do not stand by a person in his hour of need. 4. He used to say: Do His will as if it were yours, so that He may do your will as if it were His. Set aside your will for the sake of His, that He may set aside the will of others before yours. 5. Hillel said: Do not separate yourself from the community. Do not be sure of yourself until the day you die. Do not judge your fellow until you have stood in his place. Do not say anything that cannot be understood (at once) in the hope that it will eventually be understood. And do not say, I will study when I have the time, for you may never have the time. 6. He used to say: An uncouth person cannot be sin-fearing, nor can an ignoramus be pious. A shy person cannot learn, nor can an impatient one teach. A person over-occupied in business does not always become wise. In a place where there are no worthy people, strive to be worthy. 7. Seeing a skull floating on the water, he said: "Because you drowned others, they drowned you, and those who drowned you will themselves eventually be drowned." 8. He used to say: The more flesh, the more worms. The more possessions, the more worries. The more wives, the more witchcraft. The more maidservants, the more lewdness. The more menservants, the more

---

Chapter 2
The chapter continues the chronological sequence of the previous chapter, beginning with Rabbi (Judah the Prince) and his son, Rabban Gamliel, before reverting to the teachings of earlier Sages, beginning with Hillel.

2:5. *Do not say anything that cannot be understood*: Alternative translation: "Do not say of anything you have been una-

דְאָגָה. מַרְבֶּה נָשִׁים, מַרְבֶּה כְשָׁפִים. מַרְבֶּה שְׁפָחוֹת,
מַרְבֶּה זִמָּה. מַרְבֶּה עֲבָדִים, מַרְבֶּה גָזֵל. מַרְבֶּה תוֹרָה,
מַרְבֶּה חַיִּים. מַרְבֶּה יְשִׁיבָה, מַרְבֶּה חָכְמָה. מַרְבֶּה עֵצָה,
מַרְבֶּה תְבוּנָה. מַרְבֶּה צְדָקָה, מַרְבֶּה שָׁלוֹם. קָנָה שֵׁם טוֹב,
קָנָה לְעַצְמוֹ. קָנָה לוֹ דִבְרֵי תוֹרָה, קָנָה לוֹ חַיֵּי הָעוֹלָם הַבָּא.
ט רַבָּן יוֹחָנָן בֶּן־זַכַּאי קִבֵּל מֵהִלֵּל וּמִשַּׁמַּאי. הוּא הָיָה אוֹמֵר,
אִם לָמַדְתָּ תוֹרָה הַרְבֵּה, אַל־תַּחֲזִיק טוֹבָה לְעַצְמְךָ, כִּי לְכָךְ
נוֹצָרְתָּ. י חֲמִשָּׁה תַלְמִידִים הָיוּ לוֹ לְרַבָּן יוֹחָנָן בֶּן־זַכַּאי,
וְאֵלּוּ הֵן, רַבִּי אֱלִיעֶזֶר בֶּן־הוֹרְקְנוֹס, רַבִּי יְהוֹשֻׁעַ בֶּן־חֲנַנְיָה,
רַבִּי יוֹסֵי הַכֹּהֵן, רַבִּי שִׁמְעוֹן בֶּן־נְתַנְאֵל, וְרַבִּי אֶלְעָזָר בֶּן־
עֲרָךְ. יא הוּא הָיָה מוֹנֶה שִׁבְחָם, אֱלִיעֶזֶר בֶּן־הוֹרְקְנוֹס, בּוֹר
סוּד שֶׁאֵינוֹ מְאַבֵּד טִפָּה. יְהוֹשֻׁעַ בֶּן־חֲנַנְיָה, אַשְׁרֵי יוֹלַדְתּוֹ.
יוֹסֵי הַכֹּהֵן, חָסִיד. שִׁמְעוֹן בֶּן־נְתַנְאֵל, יְרֵא חֵטְא. אֶלְעָזָר
בֶּן־עֲרָךְ, כְּמַעְיָן הַמִּתְגַּבֵּר. יב הוּא הָיָה אוֹמֵר, אִם יִהְיוּ כָּל־
חַכְמֵי יִשְׂרָאֵל בְּכַף מֹאזְנַיִם, וֶאֱלִיעֶזֶר בֶּן־הוֹרְקְנוֹס בְּכַף
שְׁנִיָּה, מַכְרִיעַ אֶת־כֻּלָּם. אַבָּא שָׁאוּל אוֹמֵר מִשְּׁמוֹ, אִם
יִהְיוּ כָּל־חַכְמֵי יִשְׂרָאֵל בְּכַף מֹאזְנַיִם, וֶאֱלִיעֶזֶר בֶּן־הוֹרְקְנוֹס
אַף עִמָּהֶם, וְאֶלְעָזָר בֶּן־עֲרָךְ בְּכַף שְׁנִיָּה, מַכְרִיעַ אֶת־כֻּלָּם.
יג אָמַר לָהֶם, צְאוּ וּרְאוּ אֵיזוֹ הִיא דֶרֶךְ טוֹבָה שֶׁיִּדְבַּק בָּהּ
הָאָדָם. רַבִּי אֱלִיעֶזֶר אוֹמֵר, עַיִן טוֹבָה. רַבִּי יְהוֹשֻׁעַ אוֹמֵר,
חָבֵר טוֹב. רַבִּי יוֹסֵי אוֹמֵר, שָׁכֵן טוֹב. רַבִּי שִׁמְעוֹן אוֹמֵר,
הָרוֹאֶה אֶת־הַנּוֹלָד. רַבִּי אֶלְעָזָר אוֹמֵר, לֵב טוֹב. אָמַר לָהֶם,
רוֹאֶה אֲנִי אֶת־דִּבְרֵי אֶלְעָזָר בֶּן־עֲרָךְ מִדִּבְרֵיכֶם, שֶׁבִּכְלַל
דְּבָרָיו דִּבְרֵיכֶם. יד אָמַר לָהֶם, צְאוּ וּרְאוּ אֵיזוֹ הִיא דֶרֶךְ
רָעָה שֶׁיִּתְרַחֵק מִמֶּנָּה הָאָדָם. רַבִּי אֱלִיעֶזֶר אוֹמֵר, עַיִן רָעָה.

robbery. The more Torah, the more life. The more study, the more wisdom. The more counsel, the more understanding. The more charity, the more peace. Whoever acquires a good name acquires something for himself. Whoever acquires for himself words of Torah acquires for himself life in the World to Come. 9. Rabban Yochanan ben Zakkai received (the tradition) from Hillel and Shammai. He used to say: If you have learnt much Torah, take no special credit for yourself, for it was for this that you were created. 10. Rabban Yochanan ben Zakkai had five (pre-eminent) disciples, namely Rabbi Eliezer ben Hyrcanus, Rabbi Yehoshua ben Chananya, Rabbi Yose the Priest, Rabbi Simon ben Netanel and Rabbi Elazar ben Arach. 11. He used to recount their praise: Eliezer ben Hyrcanus: a plastered well that never loses a drop. Yehoshua ben Chananya: happy the one who gave him birth. Yose the Priest: a pious man. Shimon ben Netanel: a man who fears sin. Elazar ben Arach: an ever-flowing spring. 12. He used to say: If all the Sages of Israel were in one scale of a balance and Eliezer ben Hyrcanus in the other, he would outweigh them all. However, Abba Saul said in his name: If all the Sages of Israel, including Eliezer ben Hyrcanus, were in one scale of a balance, and Elazar ben Arach in the other, he would outweigh them all. 13. He said to them: Go and see which is the right way to which one should cling. Rabbi Eliezer said: a good eye (generosity of spirit). Rabbi Yehoshua said: a good companion. Rabbi Yose said: a good neighbour. Rabbi Shimon said: one who considers the consequences. Rabbi Elazar said: a good heart. Then he said to them: I prefer the answer of Elazar ben Arach, for his view includes all of yours. 14. He said to them: Go and see which is the wrong way one should avoid. Rabbi Eliezer said: an evil eye (envy). Rabbi Yehoshua said: an evil companion. Rabbi Yose said: an evil neighbour. Rabbi Shimon said: one who borrows and does not repay, for borrowing from a person is like borrowing from God, as it is said, "The wicked

---

ble to understand that it is unintelligible. Eventually – through repeated study and fellowship – you will find that you can understand it."

2:7. *A skull floating on the water*: The principle of measure for measure. This is one half of the basic ethic of Judaism. The first is the principle of altruism: Do

רַבִּי יְהוֹשֻׁעַ אוֹמֵר, חָבֵר רָע. רַבִּי יוֹסֵי אוֹמֵר, שָׁכֵן רָע. רַבִּי שִׁמְעוֹן אוֹמֵר, הַלֹּוֶה וְאֵינוֹ מְשַׁלֵּם. אֶחָד הַלֹּוֶה מִן־הָאָדָם כְּלֹוֶה מִן־הַמָּקוֹם. שֶׁנֶּאֱמַר, לֹוֶה רָשָׁע וְלֹא יְשַׁלֵּם, וְצַדִּיק חוֹנֵן וְנוֹתֵן. רַבִּי אֶלְעָזָר אוֹמֵר, לֵב רָע. אָמַר לָהֶם, רוֹאֶה אֲנִי אֶת־דִּבְרֵי אֶלְעָזָר בֶּן־עֲרָךְ מִדִּבְרֵיכֶם, שֶׁבִּכְלַל דְּבָרָיו דִּבְרֵיכֶם.
טו הֵם אָמְרוּ שְׁלֹשָׁה דְבָרִים. רַבִּי אֱלִיעֶזֶר אוֹמֵר, יְהִי כְבוֹד חֲבֵרְךָ חָבִיב עָלֶיךָ כְּשֶׁלָּךְ, וְאַל־תְּהִי נוֹחַ לִכְעוֹס, וְשׁוּב יוֹם אֶחָד לִפְנֵי מִיתָתְךָ, וֶהֱוֵה מִתְחַמֵּם כְּנֶגֶד אוּרָן שֶׁל־חֲכָמִים, וֶהֱוֵה זָהִיר בְּגַחַלְתָּן שֶׁלֹּא תִכָּוֶה, שֶׁנְּשִׁיכָתָן נְשִׁיכַת שׁוּעָל, וַעֲקִיצָתָן עֲקִיצַת עַקְרָב, וּלְחִישָׁתָן לְחִישַׁת שָׂרָף, וְכָל־דִּבְרֵיהֶם כְּגַחֲלֵי אֵשׁ.
טז רַבִּי יְהוֹשֻׁעַ אוֹמֵר, עַיִן הָרַע, וְיֵצֶר הָרָע, וְשִׂנְאַת הַבְּרִיּוֹת מוֹצִיאִים אֶת־הָאָדָם מִן־הָעוֹלָם.
יז רַבִּי יוֹסֵי אוֹמֵר, יְהִי מָמוֹן חֲבֵרְךָ חָבִיב עָלֶיךָ כְּשֶׁלָּךְ, וְהַתְקֵן עַצְמְךָ לִלְמוֹד תּוֹרָה, שֶׁאֵינָהּ יְרֻשָּׁה לָךְ, וְכָל־מַעֲשֶׂיךָ יִהְיוּ לְשֵׁם שָׁמָיִם.
יח רַבִּי שִׁמְעוֹן אוֹמֵר, הֱוֵה זָהִיר בִּקְרִיאַת שְׁמַע וּבִתְפִלָּה, וּכְשֶׁאַתָּה מִתְפַּלֵּל, אַל־תַּעַשׂ תְּפִלָּתְךָ קֶבַע, אֶלָּא רַחֲמִים וְתַחֲנוּנִים לִפְנֵי הַמָּקוֹם, שֶׁנֶּאֱמַר, כִּי־חַנּוּן וְרַחוּם הוּא אֶרֶךְ אַפַּיִם וְרַב־חֶסֶד וְנִחָם עַל־הָרָעָה. וְאַל־תְּהִי רָשָׁע בִּפְנֵי עַצְמֶךָ.
יט רַבִּי אֶלְעָזָר אוֹמֵר, הֱוֵה שָׁקוּד לִלְמוֹד תּוֹרָה, וְדַע מַה־שֶּׁתָּשִׁיב לְאֶפִּיקוּרוֹס. וְדַע לִפְנֵי מִי אַתָּה עָמֵל, וּמִי הוּא בַּעַל מְלַאכְתְּךָ, שֶׁיְּשַׁלֶּם־לְךָ שְׂכַר פְּעֻלָּתֶךָ.
כ רַבִּי טַרְפוֹן אוֹמֵר, הַיּוֹם קָצֵר, וְהַמְּלָאכָה מְרֻבָּה, וְהַפּוֹעֲלִים עֲצֵלִים, וְהַשָּׂכָר הַרְבֵּה, וּבַעַל הַבַּיִת דּוֹחֵק.
כא הוּא הָיָה אוֹמֵר, לֹא עָלֶיךָ הַמְּלָאכָה לִגְמוֹר, וְלֹא־אַתָּה בֶן־חוֹרִין לְהִבָּטֵל מִמֶּנָּה. אִם

borrows and does not repay, but the Righteous One is gracious and repays". Rabbi Elazar said: an evil heart. Then he said to them: I prefer the answer of Elazar ben Arach, for his view includes all of yours. 15. Each of the disciples said three things. Rabbi Eliezer said: Let the honour of your fellow be as precious to you as your own. Do not be easily provoked to anger. Repent one day before you die. (He also said:) Warm yourself by the fire of the Sages, but be careful of their glowing coals lest you be burnt; for their bite is the bite of a fox, their sting is the sting of a scorpion, their hiss is the hiss of a serpent, and all their words are like fiery coals. 16. Rabbi Yehoshua said: The evil eye (envy), the evil impulse, and hatred of humankind drive a person out of the world. 17. Rabbi Yose said: Let the property of your fellow be as precious to you as your own. Prepare yourself to study Torah, for it does not come to you as an inheritance. And let all your deeds be for the sake of Heaven. 18. Rabbi Shimon said: Be meticulous in reciting the *Shema* and the (*Amidah*) prayer. When you pray, do not do so as a fixed routine, but as a plea for mercy and grace before God, as it is said, "For He is gracious and compassionate, slow to anger, abounding in kindness, and renouncing punishment". Do not be evil in your own eyes. 19. Rabbi Elazar said: Be diligent in the study of Torah. Know how to answer a heretic. Know for whom you labour and who is your Employer who will pay you the reward of your work. 20. Rabbi Tarfon said: The day is short, the task is great, the labourers are lazy, the reward is much, and the Master insistent. 21. He used to say: It is not for you to complete the task, but neither are you free to stand aside from it. If you have studied much Torah, you will be given great reward, for

---

not do to others what you would not wish them to do to you. The second is the principle of retributive justice: As you do to others, so shall others do to you.

2:10–11. *Rabban Yochanan ben Zakkai*: Rabban Yochanan was able to raise distinguished disciples because "he used to recount their praise". A great teacher is one who recognises the distinctive potential of each student, and by praise and encouragement brings them to fruition.

2:16. *Rabbi Yehoshua said*: Life is shortened by negative emotions. This has been confirmed by many medical studies.

לָמַדְתָּ תּוֹרָה הַרְבֵּה, נוֹתְנִים לְךָ שָׂכָר הַרְבֵּה, וְנֶאֱמָן הוּא בַּעַל מְלַאכְתְּךָ, שֶׁיְּשַׁלֶּם־לְךָ שְׂכַר פְּעֻלָּתֶךָ. וְדַע שֶׁמַּתַּן שְׂכָרָם שֶׁל־צַדִּיקִים לֶעָתִיד לָבוֹא.

רַבִּי חֲנַנְיָא בֶּן־עֲקַשְׁיָא אוֹמֵר, רָצָה הַקָּדוֹשׁ בָּרוּךְ הוּא לְזַכּוֹת אֶת־יִשְׂרָאֵל, לְפִיכָךְ הִרְבָּה לָהֶם תּוֹרָה וּמִצְוֹת, שֶׁנֶּאֱמַר, יהוה חָפֵץ לְמַעַן צִדְקוֹ, יַגְדִּיל תּוֹרָה וְיַאְדִּיר.

In many congregations, קַדִּישׁ דְּרַבָּנָן on page 34
is said at this point, then עָלֵינוּ on page 520.

פרק שלישי

כָּל־יִשְׂרָאֵל יֵשׁ לָהֶם חֵלֶק לָעוֹלָם הַבָּא, שֶׁנֶּאֱמַר, וְעַמֵּךְ כֻּלָּם צַדִּיקִים, לְעוֹלָם יִירְשׁוּ אָרֶץ, נֵצֶר מַטָּעַי, מַעֲשֵׂה יָדַי לְהִתְפָּאֵר.

א עֲקַבְיָא בֶּן־מַהֲלַלְאֵל אוֹמֵר, הִסְתַּכֵּל בִּשְׁלֹשָׁה דְבָרִים
וְאֵין אַתָּה בָא לִידֵי עֲבֵרָה, דַּע מֵאַיִן בָּאתָ, וּלְאָן אַתָּה
הוֹלֵךְ, וְלִפְנֵי מִי אַתָּה עָתִיד לִתֵּן דִּין וְחֶשְׁבּוֹן. מֵאַיִן בָּאתָ,
מִטִּפָּה סְרוּחָה. וּלְאָן אַתָּה הוֹלֵךְ, לִמְקוֹם עָפָר רִמָּה
וְתוֹלֵעָה. וְלִפְנֵי מִי אַתָּה עָתִיד לִתֵּן דִּין וְחֶשְׁבּוֹן, לִפְנֵי
מֶלֶךְ מַלְכֵי הַמְּלָכִים הַקָּדוֹשׁ בָּרוּךְ הוּא. ב רַבִּי חֲנִינָא
סְגַן הַכֹּהֲנִים אוֹמֵר, הֱוֵה מִתְפַּלֵּל בִּשְׁלוֹמָהּ שֶׁל־מַלְכוּת,
שֶׁאִלְמָלֵא מוֹרָאָהּ, אִישׁ אֶת־רֵעֵהוּ חַיִּים בְּלָעוֹ. ג רַבִּי
חֲנַנְיָא בֶּן־תְּרַדְיוֹן אוֹמֵר, שְׁנַיִם שֶׁיּוֹשְׁבִים וְאֵין בֵּינֵיהֶם

2:17. *Prepare yourself to study Torah*: Though Torah is described as "the heritage of the congregation of Jacob", it does not pass automatically from one generation to the next. Only those who labour for it, acquire it. *Let all your deeds be for the sake of heaven* – even those that are not specifically religious acts.

2:21. *It is not for you to complete the task*: The task of creating a society built on justice and compassion, freedom and respect for human dignity, cannot be achieved by one generation alone. It is a continuous struggle, in which each of us has a part to play; hence the idea of the covenant as a challenge extending over time, in which we build on the achievements of our an-

your Employer will faithfully reward your work. Know, though, that the reward of the righteous is granted in the time to come.

Rabbi Chananya ben Akashya said: The Holy One, blessed be He, wanted to confer merit on Israel. That is why He gave them a copious Torah and many commandments, as it is said, "It pleased the LORD, for the sake of [Israel's] righteousness, to make the Torah great and glorious".

In many congregations, the Rabbis' *Kaddish* on page 35
is said at this point, then "It is our duty" on page 521.

CHAPTER 3

All Israel have a share in the World to Come, as it is said, "Your people are all righteous; they shall inherit the land forever; they are a shoot of My own planting, a work of My own hands, that I may be glorified". 1. Akavya ben Mahalalel said: Reflect on three things and you will avoid transgression: Know where you came from, where you are going, and before whom you will have to give an account and reckoning. "Where you came from" – from a putrid drop. "Where you are going" – to a place of dust, worms and maggots. "And before whom you will have to give an account and reckoning" – before the Supreme King of kings, the Holy One, blessed be He. 2. Rabbi Chanina, the deputy High Priest, said: Pray for the welfare of the government, for were it not for fear of it, people would swallow one another alive. 3. Rabbi Chananya ben Teradyon said: When two people sit together and no words of Torah pass between them, they are regarded as a company of scoffers, as it is said, "He does not sit in the company of scoffers". But when two people sit together and words of Torah do pass between them, the Divine Presence rests with them, as it is said, "Then those who feared the LORD talked together, and the LORD listened

---

cestors and hand on our ideals to those who will come after us.

Chapter 3

3:1. *Akavya ben Mahalalel*: Considered as physical beings, we come from dust and to the dust we return. Only in matters of the spirit do we touch the wings of eternity.

3:2. *Rabbi Chanina, the deputy High Priest*: An anticipation, by some sixteen centuries, of the argument of Thomas Hobbes' political classic, *The Leviathan*. Without a centralised power, charged

דִּבְרֵי תוֹרָה, הֲרֵי זֶה מוֹשַׁב לֵצִים, שֶׁנֶּאֱמַר, וּבְמוֹשַׁב לֵצִים לֹא יָשָׁב. אֲבָל שְׁנַיִם שֶׁיּוֹשְׁבִים וְיֵשׁ בֵּינֵיהֶם דִּבְרֵי תוֹרָה, שְׁכִינָה שְׁרוּיָה בֵינֵיהֶם, שֶׁנֶּאֱמַר, אָז נִדְבְּרוּ יִרְאֵי יהוה אִישׁ אֶל־רֵעֵהוּ, וַיַּקְשֵׁב יהוה וַיִּשְׁמָע, וַיִּכָּתֵב סֵפֶר זִכָּרוֹן לְפָנָיו, לְיִרְאֵי יהוה וּלְחֹשְׁבֵי שְׁמוֹ. אֵין לִי אֶלָּא שְׁנַיִם, מִנַּיִן אֲפִלּוּ אֶחָד שֶׁיּוֹשֵׁב וְעוֹסֵק בַּתּוֹרָה, שֶׁהַקָּדוֹשׁ בָּרוּךְ הוּא קוֹבֵעַ לוֹ שָׂכָר, שֶׁנֶּאֱמַר, יֵשֵׁב בָּדָד וְיִדֹּם, כִּי נָטַל עָלָיו.

ד רַבִּי שִׁמְעוֹן אוֹמֵר, שְׁלֹשָׁה שֶׁאָכְלוּ עַל שֻׁלְחָן אֶחָד וְלֹא אָמְרוּ עָלָיו דִּבְרֵי תוֹרָה, כְּאִלּוּ אָכְלוּ מִזִּבְחֵי מֵתִים, שֶׁנֶּאֱמַר, כִּי כָּל־שֻׁלְחָנוֹת מָלְאוּ קִיא צֹאָה, בְּלִי מָקוֹם, אֲבָל שְׁלֹשָׁה שֶׁאָכְלוּ עַל שֻׁלְחָן אֶחָד וְאָמְרוּ עָלָיו דִּבְרֵי תוֹרָה, כְּאִלּוּ אָכְלוּ מִשֻּׁלְחָנוֹ שֶׁל־מָקוֹם, שֶׁנֶּאֱמַר, וַיְדַבֵּר אֵלַי, זֶה הַשֻּׁלְחָן אֲשֶׁר לִפְנֵי יהוה. ה רַבִּי חֲנִינָא בֶּן־חֲכִינַאי אוֹמֵר, הַנֵּעוֹר בַּלַּיְלָה, וְהַמְהַלֵּךְ בַּדֶּרֶךְ יְחִידִי, וּמְפַנֶּה לִבּוֹ לְבַטָּלָה, הֲרֵי זֶה מִתְחַיֵּב בְּנַפְשׁוֹ. ו רַבִּי נְחוּנְיָא בֶּן־הַקָּנָה אוֹמֵר, כָּל־הַמְקַבֵּל עָלָיו עֹל תּוֹרָה, מַעֲבִירִים מִמֶּנּוּ עֹל מַלְכוּת וְעֹל דֶּרֶךְ אֶרֶץ, וְכָל־הַפּוֹרֵק מִמֶּנּוּ עֹל תּוֹרָה, נוֹתְנִים עָלָיו עֹל מַלְכוּת וְעֹל דֶּרֶךְ אֶרֶץ. ז רַבִּי חֲלַפְתָּא בֶּן־דּוֹסָא אִישׁ כְּפַר חֲנַנְיָה אוֹמֵר, עֲשָׂרָה שֶׁיּוֹשְׁבִים וְעוֹסְקִים בַּתּוֹרָה, שְׁכִינָה שְׁרוּיָה בֵינֵיהֶם, שֶׁנֶּאֱמַר, אֱלֹהִים נִצָּב בַּעֲדַת־אֵל. וּמִנַּיִן אֲפִלּוּ חֲמִשָּׁה, שֶׁנֶּאֱמַר, וַאֲגֻדָּתוֹ עַל־אֶרֶץ יְסָדָהּ. וּמִנַּיִן אֲפִלּוּ שְׁלֹשָׁה, שֶׁנֶּאֱמַר, בְּקֶרֶב אֱלֹהִים יִשְׁפֹּט. וּמִנַּיִן אֲפִלּוּ שְׁנַיִם, שֶׁנֶּאֱמַר, אָז נִדְבְּרוּ יִרְאֵי יהוה אִישׁ אֶל־רֵעֵהוּ וַיַּקְשֵׁב יהוה וַיִּשְׁמָע. וּמִנַּיִן אֲפִלּוּ אֶחָד, שֶׁנֶּאֱמַר, בְּכָל־הַמָּקוֹם אֲשֶׁר אַזְכִּיר אֶת־שְׁמִי, אָבוֹא אֵלֶיךָ

and heard, and a scroll of remembrance was written before Him concerning those who feared the LORD and cherished His name". This verse tells me about two people; from where can I learn that even one person who sits alone and studies Torah, the Holy One, blessed be He, grants him a reward? From the verse, "Though he sits alone and meditates quietly, He will grant him a reward". 4. Rabbi Shimon said: Three who eat at one table, and do not speak words of Torah, are as if they had eaten of sacrifices of dead idols, as it is said, "For all the tables are full of vomit and filth, when GOD is absent". However, three who eat at one table and speak words of Torah, it is as if they had eaten at GOD's table, as it is said, "And He spoke to me: This is the table before the LORD". 5. Rabbi Chanina ben Chachinai said: One who stays awake at night, travels alone, or turns his mind to idle thoughts, endangers his soul. 6. Rabbi Nechunya ben ha-Kanah said: One who takes on himself the yoke of Torah will be spared the yoke of government and the yoke of worldly responsibilities, but one who throws off the yoke of the Torah will bear the yoke of government and the yoke of worldly responsibilities. 7. Rabbi Chalafta ben Dosa of Kfar Chananya said: When ten people sit together and study Torah, the Divine Presence rests among them, as it is said, "GOD stands in the Divine assembly". How do we know that the same applies to five? From the verse, "He has founded His group on the earth". And how do we know that it applies even to three? From the verse, "He judges among the judges". How do we know that the same applies even to two? From the verse, "Then those who feared the LORD talked together, and the LORD listened and heard". And how do we know that it applies even to one? From the verse, "In every place where I cause My name to be mentioned, I will come to you and bless you". 8. Rabbi Elazar of Bartota said: Give Him what is His, for you and yours are

---

with the authority of enforcing the rule of law, society would degenerate into a "war of every man against every man" in which life would be "solitary, poor, nasty, brutish, and short".

3:3 *Rabbi Chananya ben Teradyon*: A restatement of the argument of Psalm 1: "Happy is the man who does not…sit in the seat of mockers. But his delight is in the law of the LORD, and on his Torah he

וּבֵרַכְתִּיךָ. ח רַבִּי אֶלְעָזָר אִישׁ בַּרְתּוֹתָא אוֹמֵר, תֶּן־לוֹ מִשֶּׁלּוֹ,
שֶׁאַתָּה וְשֶׁלְּךָ שֶׁלּוֹ, וְכֵן בְּדָוִד הוּא אוֹמֵר, כִּי־מִמְּךָ הַכֹּל,
וּמִיָּדְךָ נָתַנּוּ לָךְ. ט רַבִּי יַעֲקֹב אוֹמֵר, הַמְהַלֵּךְ בַּדֶּרֶךְ וְשׁוֹנֶה,
וּמַפְסִיק מִמִּשְׁנָתוֹ, וְאוֹמֵר, מַה־נָּאֶה אִילָן זֶה, מַה־נָּאֶה
נִיר־זֶה, מַעֲלֶה עָלָיו הַכָּתוּב כְּאִלּוּ מִתְחַיֵּב בְּנַפְשׁוֹ. י רַבִּי
דוֹסְתַּי בַּר־יַנַּי מִשּׁוּם רַבִּי מֵאִיר אוֹמֵר, כָּל הַשּׁוֹכֵחַ דָּבָר
אֶחָד מִמִּשְׁנָתוֹ, מַעֲלֶה עָלָיו הַכָּתוּב כְּאִלּוּ מִתְחַיֵּב בְּנַפְשׁוֹ,
שֶׁנֶּאֱמַר, רַק הִשָּׁמֶר לְךָ, וּשְׁמֹר נַפְשְׁךָ מְאֹד, פֶּן־תִּשְׁכַּח
אֶת־הַדְּבָרִים אֲשֶׁר־רָאוּ עֵינֶיךָ. יָכוֹל אֲפִלּוּ תָקְפָה עָלָיו
מִשְׁנָתוֹ, תַּלְמוּד לוֹמַר, וּפֶן־יָסוּרוּ מִלְּבָבְךָ כֹּל יְמֵי חַיֶּיךָ, הָא
אֵינוֹ מִתְחַיֵּב בְּנַפְשׁוֹ עַד־שֶׁיֵּשֵׁב וִיסִירֵם מִלִּבּוֹ. יא רַבִּי חֲנִינָא
בֶּן־דּוֹסָא אוֹמֵר, כֹּל שֶׁיִּרְאַת חֶטְאוֹ קוֹדֶמֶת לְחָכְמָתוֹ,
חָכְמָתוֹ מִתְקַיֶּמֶת, וְכֹל שֶׁחָכְמָתוֹ קוֹדֶמֶת לְיִרְאַת חֶטְאוֹ,
אֵין חָכְמָתוֹ מִתְקַיֶּמֶת. יב הוּא הָיָה אוֹמֵר, כֹּל שֶׁמַּעֲשָׂיו
מְרֻבִּים מֵחָכְמָתוֹ, חָכְמָתוֹ מִתְקַיֶּמֶת, וְכֹל שֶׁחָכְמָתוֹ מְרֻבָּה
מִמַּעֲשָׂיו, אֵין חָכְמָתוֹ מִתְקַיֶּמֶת. יג הוּא הָיָה אוֹמֵר, כֹּל
שֶׁרְוּחַ הַבְּרִיּוֹת נוֹחָה הֵימֶנּוּ, רְוּחַ הַמָּקוֹם נוֹחָה הֵימֶנּוּ, וְכֹל
שֶׁאֵין רְוּחַ הַבְּרִיּוֹת נוֹחָה הֵימֶנּוּ, אֵין רְוּחַ הַמָּקוֹם נוֹחָה
הֵימֶנּוּ. יד רַבִּי דוֹסָא בֶּן־הָרְכִּינַס אוֹמֵר, שֵׁנָה שֶׁל־שַׁחֲרִית,
וְיַיִן שֶׁל־צָהֳרַיִם, וְשִׂיחַת הַיְלָדִים, וִישִׁיבַת בָּתֵּי כְנֵסִיּוֹת
שֶׁל־עַמֵּי הָאָרֶץ, מוֹצִיאִים אֶת־הָאָדָם מִן־הָעוֹלָם. טו רַבִּי
אֶלְעָזָר הַמּוֹדָעִי אוֹמֵר, הַמְחַלֵּל אֶת הַקֳּדָשִׁים, וְהַמְבַזֶּה
אֶת־הַמּוֹעֲדוֹת, וְהַמַּלְבִּין פְּנֵי חֲבֵרוֹ בָּרַבִּים, וְהַמֵּפֵר בְּרִיתוֹ
שֶׁל־אַבְרָהָם אָבִינוּ, וְהַמְגַלֶּה פָנִים בַּתּוֹרָה שֶׁלֹּא כַהֲלָכָה,
אַף עַל פִּי שֶׁיֵּשׁ בְּיָדוֹ תּוֹרָה וּמַעֲשִׂים טוֹבִים, אֵין לוֹ חֵלֶק

His. This was also said by David: "For all things come from You, and we have given You only what is Yours". 9. Rabbi Jacob said: One who is reviewing his Torah study while walking on the way, and interrupts his study to say, "What a beautiful tree" or "What a beautiful field", is regarded by Scripture as if he had endangered his soul. 10. Rabbi Dostai ben Yannai said in the name of Rabbi Meir: One who forgets even one thing of his Torah learning, Scripture regards him as if he had endangered his soul, for it is said, "Only take heed and guard your soul very carefully so that you do not forget the things that your eyes saw". One might think that this applies even to one who finds his studies too hard to remember. Therefore the verse adds, "Lest they be removed from your heart all the days of your life". Thus, one does not endanger his soul unless he deliberately removes teachings from his heart. 11. Rabbi Chanina ben Dosa said: For one who puts fear of sin before wisdom, wisdom endures. For one who puts wisdom before fear of sin, wisdom does not endure. 12. He also used to say: For one whose good deeds exceed his wisdom, wisdom endures. For one whose wisdom exceeds his good deeds, wisdom does not endure. 13. He also used to say: In one in whom people delight, God delights. In one in whom people do not delight, God does not delight. 14. Rabbi Dosa ben Harkinas said: Sleeping late in the morning, drinking wine at midday, chattering with children and sitting in gatherings of the ignorant – these drive a person from the world. 15. Rabbi Elazar of Modin said: One who desecrates sacred things, despises the festivals, shames his fellow in public, nullifies the covenant of our father Abraham, or attributes meanings to the Torah contrary to normative

---

meditates day and night." Sharing words of Torah at the table transforms a physical act into a spiritual one, and those present into a learning fellowship.

3:5 *Endangers his soul*: Literally, "is mortally guilty". The Sages used this phrase to emphasise serious spiritual danger, rather than to suggest that an individual has committed a capital crime.

3:7 *Ten, five*: "Assembly" signifies ten as in the case of the spies who brought back an evil report about the land (Numbers 14:27). "Band" (*agudah*) refers to that which can be held together in the five

לָעוֹלָם הַבָּא. טז רַבִּי יִשְׁמָעֵאל אוֹמֵר, הֱוֵה קַל לְרֹאשׁ,
וְנוֹחַ לְתִשְׁחֹרֶת, וֶהֱוֵה מְקַבֵּל אֶת־כׇּל־הָאָדָם בְּשִׂמְחָה.
יז רַבִּי עֲקִיבָא אוֹמֵר, שְׂחוֹק וְקַלּוּת רֹאשׁ מַרְגִּילִין אֶת־
הָאָדָם לְעֶרְוָה. מַסֹּרֶת סְיָג לַתּוֹרָה, מַעְשְׂרוֹת סְיָג לָעֹשֶׁר,
נְדָרִים סְיָג לַפְּרִישׁוּת, סְיָג לַחׇכְמָה שְׁתִיקָה. יח הוּא הָיָה
אוֹמֵר, חָבִיב אָדָם שֶׁנִּבְרָא בְצֶלֶם, חִבָּה יְתֵרָה נוֹדַעַת לוֹ
שֶׁנִּבְרָא בְּצֶלֶם אֱלֹהִים, שֶׁנֶּאֱמַר, כִּי בְּצֶלֶם אֱלֹהִים עָשָׂה
אֶת־הָאָדָם. חֲבִיבִים יִשְׂרָאֵל, שֶׁנִּקְרְאוּ בָנִים לַמָּקוֹם, חִבָּה
יְתֵרָה נוֹדַעַת לָהֶם שֶׁנִּקְרְאוּ בָנִים לַמָּקוֹם, שֶׁנֶּאֱמַר, בָּנִים
אַתֶּם לַיהוה אֱלֹהֵיכֶם. חֲבִיבִים יִשְׂרָאֵל, שֶׁנִּתַּן לָהֶם כְּלִי
חֶמְדָּה, חִבָּה יְתֵרָה נוֹדַעַת לָהֶם, שֶׁנִּתַּן לָהֶם כְּלִי חֶמְדָּה
שֶׁבּוֹ נִבְרָא הָעוֹלָם, שֶׁנֶּאֱמַר, כִּי לֶקַח טוֹב נָתַתִּי לָכֶם,
תּוֹרָתִי אַל־תַּעֲזֹבוּ. יט הַכֹּל צָפוּי, וְהָרְשׁוּת נְתוּנָה. וּבְטוֹב
הָעוֹלָם נָדוֹן, וְהַכֹּל לְפִי רֹב הַמַּעֲשֶׂה. כ הוּא הָיָה אוֹמֵר,
הַכֹּל נָתוּן בְּעֵרָבוֹן, וּמְצוּדָה פְרוּסָה עַל־כׇּל־הַחַיִּים. הֶחָנוּת
פְּתוּחָה, וְהַחֶנְוָנִי מַקִּיף, וְהַפִּנְקָס פָּתוּחַ, וְהַיָּד כּוֹתֶבֶת, וְכׇל
הָרוֹצֶה לִלְווֹת יָבוֹא וְיִלְוֶה. וְהַגַּבָּאִים מַחֲזִירִים תָּדִיר בְּכׇל־
יוֹם וְנִפְרָעִים מִן־הָאָדָם, מִדַּעְתּוֹ וְשֶׁלֹּא מִדַּעְתּוֹ, וְיֵשׁ לָהֶם
עַל מַה שֶּׁיִּסְמֹכוּ. וְהַדִּין דִּין אֱמֶת, וְהַכֹּל מְתֻקָּן לִסְעוּדָה.
כא רַבִּי אֶלְעָזָר בֶּן־עֲזַרְיָה אוֹמֵר, אִם אֵין תּוֹרָה, אֵין דֶּרֶךְ
אֶרֶץ, אִם אֵין דֶּרֶךְ אֶרֶץ, אֵין תּוֹרָה. אִם אֵין חׇכְמָה, אֵין

---

fingers of one hand: hence it signifies five.

3:9 *One who is reviewing his Torah study*: Judaism is a religion of the ear rather than the eye. Pagans *saw* the gods in the phenomena of nature; in Judaism, God cannot be seen, but *heard*. Hence one of the key words of the Bible is *Shema*, "listen, hear". One who gives priority to sight over sound has started to stray from the path of Jewish values.

3:15 *One who…nullifies the covenant of our*

law, even though he has to his credit Torah and good deeds, has no share in the World to Come. 16. Rabbi Ishmael said: Be yielding to a superior, pleasing to the young, and receive everyone cheerfully. 17. Rabbi Akiva said: Mocking and frivolity lead to immorality. The oral tradition (Massorah) is a fence protecting the Torah; tithes are a fence protecting wealth; vows are a fence protecting abstinence. The fence protecting wisdom is silence. 18. He used to say: Beloved is man, for he was created in the image of God. As a gesture of special love, it was made known to him that he was created in the image of God, as it is said, "For in the image of God He made man". Beloved are Israel for they are called God's children. As a gesture of special love, it was made known to them that they are called God's children, as it is said, "You are the children of the Lord your God". Beloved are Israel, for they were given a precious vessel (the Torah). As a gesture of special love, it was made known to them that they were given the precious vessel through which the world was created, as it is said, "I have given you good instruction; do not forsake My Torah". 19. All is foreseen, yet freedom of choice is given. The world is judged with goodness, but all depends on the majority of one's deeds. 20. He used to say: All is given on collateral, and a net is spread over all the living. The shop is open, the shopkeeper extends credit, the ledger is open, and the hand records. Whoever wishes to borrow may come and borrow. The collectors regularly make their daily rounds and collect payment from a person, whether he realises it or not. They have (a record) on which they can rely; the judgement is just; and all is prepared for the banquet. 21. Rabbi Elazar ben Azariah said: If there is no Torah, there is no respect; if there is no respect, there is no Torah. If there is no wisdom,

---

father Abraham: The reference is to those who, under the influence of Hellenism, tried to remove the mark of circumcision. *Who...attributes meanings to the Torah contrary to normative law* – for instance, giving an allegorical meaning to commandments, arguing that they are not laws to be practised, but rather philosophical statements to be contemplated.

3:19. *All is foreseen*: This is the standard translation, according to which Rabbi Akiva sets out the paradox between Divine foreknowledge and human free will. God knows in advance what we will do, but this

יִרְאָה, אִם אֵין יִרְאָה, אֵין חָכְמָה. אִם אֵין דַּעַת, אֵין בִּינָה, אִם אֵין בִּינָה, אֵין דַּעַת. אִם אֵין קֶמַח, אֵין תּוֹרָה, אִם אֵין תּוֹרָה, אֵין קֶמַח. כב הוּא הָיָה אוֹמֵר, כֹּל שֶׁחָכְמָתוֹ מְרֻבָּה מִמַּעֲשָׂיו, לְמָה הוּא דוֹמֶה, לְאִילָן שֶׁעֲנָפָיו מְרֻבִּים וְשָׁרָשָׁיו מֻעָטִים, וְהָרוּחַ בָּאָה וְעוֹקַרְתּוֹ וְהוֹפַכְתּוֹ עַל פָּנָיו, שֶׁנֶּאֱמַר, וְהָיָה כְּעַרְעָר בָּעֲרָבָה, וְלֹא יִרְאֶה כִּי־יָבוֹא טוֹב, וְשָׁכַן חֲרֵרִים בַּמִּדְבָּר, אֶרֶץ מְלֵחָה וְלֹא תֵשֵׁב. אֲבָל כֹּל שֶׁמַּעֲשָׂיו מְרֻבִּים מֵחָכְמָתוֹ, לְמָה הוּא דוֹמֶה, לְאִילָן שֶׁעֲנָפָיו מֻעָטִים וְשָׁרָשָׁיו מְרֻבִּים, שֶׁאֲפִלּוּ כָּל־הָרוּחוֹת שֶׁבָּעוֹלָם בָּאוֹת וְנוֹשְׁבוֹת בּוֹ, אֵין מְזִיזִים אוֹתוֹ מִמְּקוֹמוֹ, שֶׁנֶּאֱמַר, וְהָיָה כְּעֵץ שָׁתוּל עַל־מַיִם, וְעַל־יוּבַל יְשַׁלַּח שָׁרָשָׁיו, וְלֹא יִרְאֶה כִּי־יָבֹא חֹם, וְהָיָה עָלֵהוּ רַעֲנָן, וּבִשְׁנַת בַּצֹּרֶת לֹא יִדְאָג, וְלֹא יָמִישׁ מֵעֲשׂוֹת פֶּרִי. כג רַבִּי אֱלְעָזָר בֶּן חִסְמָא אוֹמֵר, קִנִּין וּפִתְחֵי נִדָּה הֵן הֵן גּוּפֵי הֲלָכוֹת, תְּקוּפוֹת וְגִמַטְרִיָּאוֹת, פַּרְפְּרָאוֹת לַחָכְמָה.

רַבִּי חֲנַנְיָא בֶּן־עֲקַשְׁיָא אוֹמֵר, רָצָה הַקָּדוֹשׁ בָּרוּךְ הוּא לְזַכּוֹת אֶת־יִשְׂרָאֵל, לְפִיכָךְ הִרְבָּה לָהֶם תּוֹרָה וּמִצְוֹת, שֶׁנֶּאֱמַר, יהוה חָפֵץ לְמַעַן צִדְקוֹ, יַגְדִּיל תּוֹרָה וְיַאְדִּיר.

In many congregations, קַדִּישׁ דְּרַבָּנָן on page 34
is said at this point, then עָלֵינוּ on page 520.

פרק רביעי

כָּל־יִשְׂרָאֵל יֵשׁ לָהֶם חֵלֶק לָעוֹלָם הַבָּא, שֶׁנֶּאֱמַר, וְעַמֵּךְ כֻּלָּם צַדִּיקִים, לְעוֹלָם יִירְשׁוּ אָרֶץ, נֵצֶר מַטָּעַי, מַעֲשֵׂה יָדַי לְהִתְפָּאֵר.

א בֶּן־זוֹמָא אוֹמֵר, אֵיזֶהוּ חָכָם, הַלּוֹמֵד מִכָּל־אָדָם, שֶׁנֶּאֱמַר, מִכָּל־מְלַמְּדַי הִשְׂכַּלְתִּי. אֵיזֶהוּ גִבּוֹר, הַכּוֹבֵשׁ אֶת־יִצְרוֹ,

there is no reverence; if there is no reverence, there is no wisdom. If there is no knowledge, there is no understanding; if there is no understanding, there is no knowledge. If there is no flour (sustenance), there is no Torah; if there is no Torah, there is no flour. 22. He used to say: To what may one whose wisdom exceeds his deeds be compared? To a tree with many branches but few roots. When a wind comes, it uproots and overturns it, as it is said, "He shall be like a juniper tree in the desert, which does not sense the coming of good: it is set in the scorched places of the wilderness in a barren, uninhabited land". To what may one whose deeds exceed his wisdom be compared? To a tree with few branches but many roots. Even if all the winds of the world come and blow against it, they cannot dislodge it from its place, as it is said, "He shall be like a tree planted by waters, sending forth its roots by a stream: it does not sense the coming of heat; its leaves are ever fresh; it has no care in a year of drought; it does not cease to bear fruit". 23. Rabbi Elazar Chisma said: The laws of bird offerings and the calculation of menstrual periods are essential laws; astronomy and mathematics are adjuncts to wisdom.

Rabbi Chananya ben Akashya said: The Holy One, blessed be He, wanted to confer merit on Israel. That is why He gave them a copious Torah and many commandments, as it is said, "It pleased the Lord, for the sake of [Israel's] righteousness, to make the Torah great and glorious".

In many congregations, the Rabbis' *Kaddish* on page 35
is said at this point, then "It is our duty" on page 521.

CHAPTER 4

All Israel have a share in the World to Come, as it is said, "Your people are all righteous; they shall inherit the land forever; they are a shoot of My own planting, a work of My own hands, that I may be glorified".
1. Ben Zoma said: Who is wise? One who learns from everyone, as it is said, "From all my teachers I gained wisdom". Who is strong? One

---

does not negate our freedom to choose. An alternative translation is: "All is *seen*, yet freedom of choice is given." According to this, Rabbi Akiva is not speaking about divine *fore*knowledge. He is teaching that, though we are free to choose, we cannot

שֶׁנֶּאֱמַר, טוֹב אֶרֶךְ אַפַּיִם מִגִּבּוֹר, וּמֹשֵׁל בְּרוּחוֹ מִלֹּכֵד
עִיר. אֵיזֶהוּ עָשִׁיר, הַשָּׂמֵחַ בְּחֶלְקוֹ, שֶׁנֶּאֱמַר, יְגִיעַ כַּפֶּיךָ
כִּי תֹאכֵל אַשְׁרֶיךָ וְטוֹב לָךְ. אַשְׁרֶיךָ בָּעוֹלָם הַזֶּה, וְטוֹב לָךְ
לָעוֹלָם הַבָּא. אֵיזֶהוּ מְכֻבָּד, הַמְכַבֵּד אֶת־הַבְּרִיּוֹת, שֶׁנֶּאֱמַר,
כִּי מְכַבְּדַי אֲכַבֵּד, וּבֹזַי יֵקָלּוּ. ב בֶּן־עַזַּאי אוֹמֵר, הֱוֵה רָץ
לְמִצְוָה קַלָּה, וּבוֹרֵחַ מִן־הָעֲבֵרָה, שֶׁמִּצְוָה גּוֹרֶרֶת מִצְוָה,
וַעֲבֵרָה גוֹרֶרֶת עֲבֵרָה, שֶׁשְּׂכַר מִצְוָה מִצְוָה, וּשְׂכַר עֲבֵרָה
עֲבֵרָה. ג הוּא הָיָה אוֹמֵר, אַל־תְּהִי בָז לְכָל־אָדָם, וְאַל־תְּהִי
מַפְלִיג לְכָל־דָּבָר, שֶׁאֵין לְךָ אָדָם שֶׁאֵין לוֹ שָׁעָה, וְאֵין לְךָ
דָּבָר שֶׁאֵין לוֹ מָקוֹם. ד רַבִּי לְוִיטַס אִישׁ יַבְנֶה אוֹמֵר, מְאֹד
מְאֹד הֱוֵה שְׁפַל רוּחַ, שֶׁתִּקְוַת אֱנוֹשׁ רִמָּה. ה רַבִּי יוֹחָנָן בֶּן־
בְּרוֹקָא אוֹמֵר, כָּל־הַמְחַלֵּל שֵׁם שָׁמַיִם בַּסֵּתֶר, נִפְרָעִים
מִמֶּנּוּ בַּגָּלוּי. אֶחָד בְּשׁוֹגֵג וְאֶחָד בְּמֵזִיד בְּחִלּוּל הַשֵּׁם. ו רַבִּי
יִשְׁמָעֵאל בְּנוֹ אוֹמֵר, הַלּוֹמֵד עַל־מְנָת לְלַמֵּד, מַסְפִּיקִים
בְּיָדוֹ לִלְמוֹד וּלְלַמֵּד, וְהַלּוֹמֵד עַל־מְנָת לַעֲשׂוֹת, מַסְפִּיקִים
בְּיָדוֹ לִלְמוֹד וּלְלַמֵּד, לִשְׁמוֹר וְלַעֲשׂוֹת. ז רַבִּי צָדוֹק אוֹמֵר,
אַל־תִּפְרוֹשׁ מִן־הַצִּבּוּר, וְאַל־תַּעַשׂ עַצְמְךָ כְּעוֹרְכֵי הַדִּינִים,
וְאַל־תַּעֲשֶׂהָ עֲטָרָה לְהִתְגַּדֶּל־בָּהּ, וְלֹא קַרְדֹּם לַחְפָּר בָּהּ.
וְכָךְ הָיָה הִלֵּל אוֹמֵר, וּדְאִשְׁתַּמַּשׁ בְּתָגָא חֲלָף. הָא לָמַדְתָּ,
כָּל־הַנֶּהֱנֶה מִדִּבְרֵי תוֹרָה, נוֹטֵל חַיָּיו מִן־הָעוֹלָם. ח רַבִּי יוֹסֵי
אוֹמֵר, כָּל־הַמְכַבֵּד אֶת־הַתּוֹרָה, גּוּפוֹ מְכֻבָּד עַל־הַבְּרִיּוֹת,
וְכָל־הַמְחַלֵּל אֶת־הַתּוֹרָה, גּוּפוֹ מְחֻלָּל עַל־הַבְּרִיּוֹת. ט רַבִּי

---

escape responsibility for the consequences of our choice, because God sees all.

3:20 *All is given on collateral*: An extended metaphor on life under Divine justice. Because we are not punished immediately for our misdeeds, we may come to think that bad behaviour has no consequences. The reality is, however, that God is merely extending credit. He keeps

who masters his evil impulse, as it is said, "He who is slow to anger is better than the mighty, and he who rules over his spirit is better than he who conquers a city". Who is rich? One who rejoices in what he has, as it is said, "When you eat from the labour of your hands, you will be happy and all will be well with you". "You will be happy" – in this world, "and all will be well with you" – in the World to Come. Who is honoured? One who honours others, as it is said, "Those who honour Me, I will honour; but those who scorn Me will be despised". 2. Ben Azzai said: Run to do even a minor *mitzvah*, and flee from sin, for one *mitzvah* leads to another, and one sin leads to another – for the reward of a *mitzvah* is another *mitzvah*, and the recompense of a sin is another sin. 3. He used to say: Despise no one and disdain nothing, for there is no one who does not have his hour and there is nothing that does not have its place. 4. Rabbi Levitas of Yavneh said: Have extreme humility of spirit, for the end of mortal man is the worm [the grave]. 5. Rabbi Yochanan ben Berokah said: Whoever profanes GOD's name in secret will be punished in public. Profaning the name is the same whether done inadvertently or deliberately. 6. Rabbi Ishmael his son said: One who learns in order to teach will be given the opportunity to learn and teach. One who learns in order to do will be given the opportunity to learn, teach, keep and do. 7. Rabbi Zadok said: Do not separate yourself from the community. [When sitting as a judge] do not act as a lawyer. Do not use [the Torah] as a crown for self-glorification, or as a spade with which to dig. Likewise Hillel used to say: One who makes worldly use of the crown [of the Torah] shall fade away. From this you learn that one who seeks personal benefit from the words of Torah risks destroying his life. 8. Rabbi Yose said: One who honours the Torah will be honoured by mankind. One who disgraces the Torah will be disgraced by mankind. 9. Rabbi Ishmael his son said: One who avoids serving as a judge spares himself enmity,

---

a record of our deeds, and ultimately we will have to pay the price. *The banquet* refers to the World to Come.

Chapter 4

4:1. *Ben Zoma said*: Truth, argues Ben Zoma, is often the reverse of conventional wisdom. Who is wise? Not one who teaches, but one who is always will-

יִשְׁמָעֵאל בְּנוֹ אוֹמֵר, הַחוֹשֵׂךְ עַצְמוֹ מִן־הַדִּין, פּוֹרֵק מִמֶּנּוּ
אֵיבָה וְגָזֵל וּשְׁבוּעַת שָׁוְא. וְהַגַּס לִבּוֹ בְּהוֹרָאָה, שׁוֹטֶה
רָשָׁע וְגַס רוּחַ. י הוּא הָיָה אוֹמֵר, אַל־תְּהִי דָן יְחִידִי שֶׁאֵין
דָּן יְחִידִי אֶלָּא אֶחָד. וְאַל־תֹּאמַר, קַבְּלוּ דַעְתִּי, שֶׁהֵם
רַשָּׁאִים וְלֹא אָתָּה. יא רַבִּי יוֹנָתָן אוֹמֵר, כָּל־הַמְקַיֵּם אֶת־
הַתּוֹרָה מֵעֹנִי, סוֹפוֹ לְקַיְּמָהּ מֵעֹשֶׁר, וְכָל הַמְבַטֵּל אֶת־
הַתּוֹרָה מֵעֹשֶׁר, סוֹפוֹ לְבַטְּלָהּ מֵעֹנִי. יב רַבִּי מֵאִיר אוֹמֵר,
הֱוֵה מְמַעֵט בְּעֵסֶק, וַעֲסֹק בַּתּוֹרָה, וֶהֱוֵה שְׁפַל־רוּחַ בִּפְנֵי
כָל־אָדָם, וְאִם־בָּטַלְתָּ מִן־הַתּוֹרָה, יֶשׁ־לְךָ בְּטֵלִים הַרְבֵּה
כְּנֶגְדֶּךָ, וְאִם־עָמַלְתָּ בַּתּוֹרָה, יֶשׁ־לוֹ שָׂכָר הַרְבֵּה לִתֶּן־
לָךְ. יג רַבִּי אֱלִיעֶזֶר בֶּן־יַעֲקֹב אוֹמֵר, הָעוֹשֶׂה מִצְוָה אַחַת
קוֹנֶה לּוֹ פְּרַקְלִיט אֶחָד, וְהָעוֹבֵר עֲבֵרָה אַחַת, קוֹנֶה לוֹ
קַטֵּיגוֹר אֶחָד. תְּשׁוּבָה וּמַעֲשִׂים טוֹבִים כִּתְרִיס בִּפְנֵי
הַפֻּרְעָנוּת. יד רַבִּי יוֹחָנָן הַסַּנְדְּלָר אוֹמֵר, כָּל־כְּנֵסִיָּה שֶׁהִיא
לְשֵׁם שָׁמַיִם, סוֹפָהּ לְהִתְקַיֵּם, וְשֶׁאֵינָהּ לְשֵׁם שָׁמַיִם, אֵין
סוֹפָהּ לְהִתְקַיֵּם. טו רַבִּי אֶלְעָזָר בֶּן־שַׁמּוּעַ אוֹמֵר. יְהִי כְבוֹד
תַּלְמִידְךָ חָבִיב עָלֶיךָ כְּשֶׁלָּךְ וּכְבוֹד חֲבֵרְךָ כְּמוֹרָא רַבָּךְ
וּמוֹרָא רַבָּךְ כְּמוֹרָא שָׁמָיִם. טז רַבִּי יְהוּדָה אוֹמֵר, הֱוֵה
זָהִיר בְּתַלְמוּד, שֶׁשִּׁגְגַת תַּלְמוּד עוֹלָה זָדוֹן. יז רַבִּי שִׁמְעוֹן
אוֹמֵר, שְׁלֹשָׁה כְתָרִים הֵן, כֶּתֶר תּוֹרָה, וְכֶתֶר כְּהֻנָּה, וְכֶתֶר
מַלְכוּת, וְכֶתֶר שֵׁם טוֹב עוֹלֶה עַל גַּבֵּיהֶן. יח רַבִּי נְהוֹרַאי

---

ing to learn. Who is strong? Not one who can defeat his enemies but one who can defeat his own worst impulses (*Avot de-Rabbi Nathan* adds: Who is strong? One who turns an enemy into a friend). Who is rich? Not one who has everything he wants, but one who enjoys what he has. The greatest honours are not those we receive but those we give.

4:6. *One who learns in order to teach*: The best way to learn is to teach. The best way to teach is to practise what we preach.

robbery and false swearing. One who is over-confident in giving decisions is foolish, wicked and arrogant. 10. He used to say: Do not act as a judge alone, for none may judge alone except the One. Do not say "Accept my view"; for they are permitted, not you. 11. Rabbi Yonatan said: Whoever keeps the Torah when poor will eventually keep it in wealth. Whoever neglects the Torah when wealthy will eventually neglect it in poverty. 12. Rabbi Meir said: Limit your business activities and occupy yourself with Torah. Have humility before everyone. If you neglect the Torah, you will have many excuses to neglect it, but if you labour in the Torah, He has great reward to give you. 13. Rabbi Eliezer ben Jacob said: One who performs a single *mitzvah* acquires for himself an advocate. One who commits a single transgression acquires for himself an accuser. Repentance and good deeds are a shield against punishment. 14. Rabbi Yochanan the sandal maker said: Every gathering that meets for the sake of heaven will have an enduring effect. One that is not for the sake of heaven will not have an enduring effect. 15. Rabbi Elazar ben Shammua said: Let your student's honour be as precious to you as your own; let your colleague's honour be like the reverence due to your teacher; and let the reverence you have for your teacher be like the reverence due to Heaven. 16. Rabbi Judah said: Be careful when you study, for an inadvertent error in study is tantamount to an intentional sin. 17. Rabbi Simeon said: There are three crowns: the crown of Torah, the crown of priesthood, and the crown of kingship – but the crown of a good name surpasses them all. 18. Rabbi Nehorai said: Exile yourself to a place of Torah, and do

---

4:8. *One who honours the Torah*: No one wins honour by betraying his or her faith.

4:9. *Spares himself enmity, robbery and false swearing*: *Enmity* of the litigants; *robbery*, if the judge gives an incorrect verdict in a civil case, with the result that money is wrongfully transferred from one party to the other; *false swearing*, if the judge requires one of the litigants to take an oath, and he then testifies falsely.

4:10. *Do not say "Accept my view"*: If your colleagues disagree, do not compel them to agree with you. They have the right to accept your view if your arguments are compelling; you do not have the right to put pressure on them to do so.

4:12. *Have humility before everyone*: Not just those who are greater than you. Behave towards everyone as if they were your superior. Greatness is humility, and humility is greatness.

אוֹמֵר, הֱוֵה גוֹלֶה לִמְקוֹם תּוֹרָה, וְאַל־תֹּאמַר שֶׁהִיא תָבוֹא
אַחֲרֶיךָ שֶׁחֲבֵרֶיךָ, יְקַיְּמוּהָ בְיָדֶךָ. וְאֶל־בִּינָתְךָ אַל תִּשָּׁעֵן.
יט רַבִּי יַנַּאי אוֹמֵר, אֵין בְּיָדֵינוּ לֹא מִשַּׁלְוַת הָרְשָׁעִים וְאַף
לֹא מִיִּסּוּרֵי הַצַּדִּיקִים. כ רַבִּי מַתִּתְיָא בֶן־חָרָשׁ אוֹמֵר, הֱוֵה
מַקְדִּים בִּשְׁלוֹם כָּל־אָדָם, וֶהֱוֵה זָנָב לָאֲרָיוֹת, וְאַל־תְּהִי
רֹאשׁ לַשְּׁעָלִים. כא רַבִּי יַעֲקֹב אוֹמֵר, הָעוֹלָם הַזֶּה דּוֹמֶה
לִפְרוֹזְדוֹר בִּפְנֵי הָעוֹלָם הַבָּא, הַתְקֵן עַצְמְךָ בַּפְּרוֹזְדוֹר,
כְּדֵי שֶׁתִּכָּנֵס לַטְּרַקְלִין. כב הוּא הָיָה אוֹמֵר, יָפָה שָׁעָה
אַחַת בִּתְשׁוּבָה וּמַעֲשִׂים טוֹבִים בָּעוֹלָם הַזֶּה מִכָּל־חַיֵּי
הָעוֹלָם הַבָּא, וְיָפָה שָׁעָה אַחַת שֶׁל־קוֹרַת רוּחַ בָּעוֹלָם
הַבָּא מִכָּל־חַיֵּי הָעוֹלָם הַזֶּה. כג רַבִּי שִׁמְעוֹן בֶּן־אֶלְעָזָר
אוֹמֵר, אַל־תְּרַצֶּה אֶת־חֲבֵרְךָ בִּשְׁעַת כַּעֲסוֹ, וְאַל־תְּנַחֲמֶנּוּ
בְּשָׁעָה שֶׁמֵּתוֹ מֻטָּל לְפָנָיו, וְאַל־תִּשְׁאַל לוֹ בִּשְׁעַת נִדְרוֹ,
וְאַל־תִּשְׁתַּדֵּל לִרְאוֹתוֹ בִּשְׁעַת קַלְקָלָתוֹ. כד שְׁמוּאֵל הַקָּטָן
אוֹמֵר, בִּנְפֹל אוֹיִבְךָ אַל־תִּשְׂמָח, וּבִכָּשְׁלוֹ אַל־יָגֵל לִבֶּךָ. פֶּן־
יִרְאֶה יהוה וְרַע בְּעֵינָיו, וְהֵשִׁיב מֵעָלָיו אַפּוֹ. כה אֱלִישָׁע בֶּן־
אֲבוּיָה אוֹמֵר, הַלּוֹמֵד יֶלֶד, לְמָה הוּא דוֹמֶה, לִדְיוֹ כְתוּבָה
עַל־נְיָר חָדָשׁ. וְהַלּוֹמֵד זָקֵן, לְמָה הוּא דוֹמֶה, לִדְיוֹ כְתוּבָה
עַל־נְיָר מָחוּק. כו רַבִּי יוֹסֵי בַּר יְהוּדָה אִישׁ כְּפַר הַבַּבְלִי
אוֹמֵר, הַלּוֹמֵד מִן־הַקְּטַנִּים, לְמָה הוּא דוֹמֶה, לְאוֹכֵל
עֲנָבִים קֵהוֹת, וְשׁוֹתֶה יַיִן מִגִּתּוֹ. וְהַלּוֹמֵד מִן־הַזְּקֵנִים, לְמָה
הוּא דוֹמֶה, לְאוֹכֵל עֲנָבִים בְּשׁוּלוֹת, וְשׁוֹתֶה יַיִן יָשָׁן. כז רַבִּי
מֵאִיר אוֹמֵר, אַל־תִּסְתַּכֵּל בְּקַנְקַן, אֶלָּא בְמַה שֶּׁיֵּשׁ בּוֹ, יֵשׁ
קַנְקַן חָדָשׁ מָלֵא יָשָׁן, וְיָשָׁן שֶׁאֲפִלּוּ חָדָשׁ אֵין בּוֹ. כח רַבִּי

4:17. *There are three crowns*: The Judaic principle of the separation of powers. Kingship is the crown of government; priesthood, the crown of religious worship; and Torah is the crown of Jewish study and education. The Sages were

not assume that it will come after you, for your fellow students will ensure that it will remain with you. Do not rely on your own understanding. 19. Rabbi Yannai said: It is not in our power to explain either the peace of the wicked or the suffering of the righteous. 20. Rabbi Matitya ben Cheresh said: Be first in greeting everyone. Be a tail to lions rather than a head to foxes. 21. Rabbi Jacob said: This world is like an antechamber before the World to Come. Prepare yourself in the antechamber so that you may enter the banqueting hall. 22. He used to say: Better one hour of repentance and good deeds in this world than all the life in the World to Come. Better one hour of bliss in the World to Come than the whole life of this world. 23. Rabbi Simeon ben Elazar said: Do not try to placate your fellow in his hour of anger. Do not try to comfort him while his dead lies before him. Do not question him about his vow at the time he is making it. Do not try to see him in his hour of disgrace. 24. Samuel the Younger used to quote: "If your enemy falls, do not rejoice; if he stumbles, let not your heart be glad; lest the Lord see it and be displeased, and divert His wrath from him to you". 25. Elisha ben Abuya said: When you learn as a child, what is it like? Like ink written on clean paper. When you learn in old age, what is it like? Like ink written on blotted paper. 26. Rabbi Yose bar Judah of Kfar Bavli said: When you learn from the young, what is it like? Like eating unripe grapes or drinking wine straight from the vat. When you learn from the old, what is it like? Like eating ripe grapes and drinking old wine. 27. Rabbi Meir said: Do not look at the container but at what it contains, for a new flask may contain old wine, and an old flask may not contain anything, even new wine. 28. Rabbi Elazar ha-Kappar said: Envy, lust, and the seeking of honour,

---

critical of the Hasmonean kings, some of whom appointed themselves as High Priests, thus breaching the separation of the crowns of kingship and priesthood. *The crown of a good name* – alternative translation, "But the crown of a good name must accompany them all." Unlike the other crowns, which exist in virtue of office or accomplishment, a good name is won by the individual him or herself, regardless of office or accomplishment, by the integrity and grace with which he or she relates to others.

4:18. *Exile yourself to a place of Torah*: Be prepared to travel to a centre of Torah study where there are outstanding teachers and scholars. Torah is learned not

אֶלְעָזָר הַקַּפָּר אוֹמֵר, הַקִּנְאָה וְהַתַּאֲוָה וְהַכָּבוֹד מוֹצִיאִים
אֶת־הָאָדָם מִן הָעוֹלָם. כט הוּא הָיָה אוֹמֵר, הַיִּלּוֹדִים לָמוּת,
וְהַמֵּתִים לְהֵחָיוֹת, וְהַחַיִּים לִדּוֹן, לֵידַע וּלְהוֹדִיעַ וּלְהִוָּדַע
שֶׁהוּא אֵל, הוּא הַיּוֹצֵר, הוּא הַבּוֹרֵא, הוּא הַמֵּבִין, הוּא
הַדַּיָּן, הוּא הָעֵד, הוּא בַּעַל דִּין, הוּא עָתִיד לָדוּן. בָּרוּךְ
הוּא, שֶׁאֵין לְפָנָיו לֹא עַוְלָה, וְלֹא שִׁכְחָה, וְלֹא מַשּׂוֹא פָנִים,
וְלֹא מִקַּח שֹׁחַד, וְדַע שֶׁהַכֹּל לְפִי הַחֶשְׁבּוֹן. וְאַל־יַבְטִיחֲךָ
יִצְרְךָ שֶׁהַשְּׁאוֹל בֵּית מָנוֹס לָךְ, שֶׁעַל כָּרְחֲךָ אַתָּה נוֹצָר,
וְעַל כָּרְחֲךָ אַתָּה נוֹלָד, וְעַל כָּרְחֲךָ אַתָּה חַי, וְעַל כָּרְחֲךָ
אַתָּה מֵת, וְעַל כָּרְחֲךָ אַתָּה עָתִיד לִתֵּן דִּין וְחֶשְׁבּוֹן לִפְנֵי
מֶלֶךְ מַלְכֵי הַמְּלָכִים, הַקָּדוֹשׁ בָּרוּךְ הוּא.

רַבִּי חֲנַנְיָא בֶּן־עֲקַשְׁיָא אוֹמֵר, רָצָה הַקָּדוֹשׁ בָּרוּךְ הוּא לְזַכּוֹת אֶת־יִשְׂרָאֵל, לְפִיכָךְ הִרְבָּה לָהֶם תּוֹרָה וּמִצְוֹת, שֶׁנֶּאֱמַר, יהוה חָפֵץ לְמַעַן צִדְקוֹ, יַגְדִּיל תּוֹרָה וְיַאְדִּיר.

In many congregations, קַדִּישׁ דְּרַבָּנָן on page 34
is said at this point, then עָלֵינוּ on page 520.

פרק חמישי

כָּל־יִשְׂרָאֵל יֵשׁ לָהֶם חֵלֶק לָעוֹלָם הַבָּא, שֶׁנֶּאֱמַר, וְעַמֵּךְ כֻּלָּם צַדִּיקִים, לְעוֹלָם יִירְשׁוּ אָרֶץ, נֵצֶר מַטָּעַי, מַעֲשֵׂה יָדַי לְהִתְפָּאֵר.

א בַּעֲשָׂרָה מַאֲמָרוֹת נִבְרָא הָעוֹלָם, וּמַה־תַּלְמוּד לוֹמַר,
וַהֲלֹא בְּמַאֲמָר אֶחָד יָכוֹל לְהִבָּרְאוֹת, אֶלָּא לְהִפָּרַע מִן־
הָרְשָׁעִים, שֶׁמְּאַבְּדִים אֶת־הָעוֹלָם שֶׁנִּבְרָא בַּעֲשָׂרָה
מַאֲמָרוֹת, וְלִתֵּן שָׂכָר טוֹב לַצַּדִּיקִים, שֶׁמְּקַיְּמִים אֶת־
הָעוֹלָם שֶׁנִּבְרָא בַּעֲשָׂרָה מַאֲמָרוֹת. ב עֲשָׂרָה דוֹרוֹת מֵאָדָם
וְעַד נֹחַ, לְהוֹדִיעַ כַּמָּה אֶרֶךְ אַפַּיִם לְפָנָיו, שֶׁכָּל־הַדּוֹרוֹת
הָיוּ מַכְעִיסִים לְפָנָיו, עַד שֶׁהֵבִיא עֲלֵיהֶם אֶת־מֵי הַמַּבּוּל.

drive a person out of the world. 29. He used to say: Those who are born will one day die, those who die will live again, and the living will be judged. It is for us to know, make known, and confirm that He is God, He is the Maker; He is the Creator; He is the Discerner; He is the Judge; He is the Witness; He is the Plaintiff; and He will deliver the judgement. Blessed is He before whom there is no unrighteousness, no forgetfulness, no favouritism and no taking of bribes; and know that all is according to a strict reckoning. Do not let your evil impulse persuade you that the grave is, for you, a place of refuge: for without your consent you were formed, without your consent you were born, without your consent you live, without your consent you will die, and without your consent you will in the future have to give an account and reckoning before the Supreme King of kings, the Holy One, blessed be He.

Rabbi Chananya ben Akashya said: The Holy One, blessed be He, wanted to confer merit on Israel. That is why He gave them a copious Torah and many commandments, as it is said, "It pleased the Lord, for the sake of [Israel's] righteousness, to make the Torah great and glorious".

In many congregations, the Rabbis' *Kaddish* on page 35
is said at this point, then "It is our duty" on page 521.

CHAPTER 5

All Israel have a share in the World to Come, as it is said, "Your people are all righteous; they shall inherit the land forever; they are a shoot of My own planting, a work of My own hands, that I may be glorified".
1. By ten acts of speech the world was created. What does this teach us? Could not the world have been created by a single act of speech? It is to exact punishment from the wicked who destroy a world created by ten acts of speech, and richly to reward the righteous who

---

only from books but also, and essentially, from people, their conduct, and the fellowship of argument.

4:19. *It is not in our power to explain*: Seen from beneath, a Turkish carpet looks like a meaningless tangle of threads. Only when we view it from the other side do we see its intricately designed pattern. So it is with the justice of events. On earth, we seem to see the righteous suffer and the wicked prosper. Only from the other side – Heaven – is it possible to see the

ג עֲשָׂרָה דוֹרוֹת מִנֹּחַ וְעַד אַבְרָהָם, לְהוֹדִיעַ כַּמָּה אֶרֶךְ אַפַּיִם לְפָנָיו, שֶׁכָּל־הַדּוֹרוֹת הָיוּ מַכְעִיסִים לְפָנָיו, עַד שֶׁבָּא אַבְרָהָם אָבִינוּ וְקִבֵּל שְׂכַר כֻּלָּם. ד עֲשָׂרָה נִסְיוֹנוֹת נִתְנַסָּה אַבְרָהָם אָבִינוּ וְעָמַד בְּכֻלָּם, לְהוֹדִיעַ כַּמָּה חִבָּתוֹ שֶׁל־אַבְרָהָם אָבִינוּ. ה עֲשָׂרָה נִסִּים נַעֲשׂוּ לַאֲבוֹתֵינוּ בְּמִצְרַיִם וַעֲשָׂרָה עַל הַיָּם. ו עֶשֶׂר מַכּוֹת הֵבִיא הַקָּדוֹשׁ בָּרוּךְ הוּא עַל הַמִּצְרִיִּים בְּמִצְרַיִם וְעֶשֶׂר עַל הַיָּם. ז עֲשָׂרָה נִסְיוֹנוֹת נִסּוּ אֲבוֹתֵינוּ אֶת־הַקָּדוֹשׁ בָּרוּךְ הוּא, בַּמִּדְבָּר. שֶׁנֶּאֱמַר, וַיְנַסּוּ אֹתִי זֶה עֶשֶׂר פְּעָמִים וְלֹא שָׁמְעוּ בְּקוֹלִי. ח עֲשָׂרָה נִסִּים נַעֲשׂוּ לַאֲבוֹתֵינוּ בְּבֵית הַמִּקְדָּשׁ, לֹא הִפִּילָה אִשָּׁה מֵרֵיחַ בְּשַׂר הַקֹּדֶשׁ, וְלֹא הִסְרִיחַ בְּשַׂר הַקֹּדֶשׁ מֵעוֹלָם, וְלֹא נִרְאָה זְבוּב בְּבֵית הַמִּטְבְּחַיִם, וְלֹא אֵרַע קֶרִי לְכֹהֵן גָּדוֹל בְּיוֹם הַכִּפֻּרִים, וְלֹא כִבּוּ הַגְּשָׁמִים אֵשׁ שֶׁל־עֲצֵי הַמַּעֲרָכָה, וְלֹא נִצְּחָה הָרוּחַ אֶת־עַמּוּד הֶעָשָׁן, וְלֹא נִמְצָא פְסוּל בָּעֹמֶר, וּבִשְׁתֵּי הַלֶּחֶם, וּבְלֶחֶם הַפָּנִים, עֹמְדִים צְפוּפִים, וּמִשְׁתַּחֲוִים רְוָחִים, וְלֹא הִזִּיק נָחָשׁ וְעַקְרָב בִּירוּשָׁלַיִם מֵעוֹלָם, וְלֹא אָמַר אָדָם לַחֲבֵרוֹ, צַר לִי הַמָּקוֹם שֶׁאָלִין בִּירוּשָׁלָיִם. ט עֲשָׂרָה דְבָרִים נִבְרְאוּ בְּעֶרֶב שַׁבָּת בֵּין הַשְּׁמָשׁוֹת, וְאֵלּוּ הֵן, פִּי הָאָרֶץ, פִּי הַבְּאֵר, פִּי הָאָתוֹן, הַקֶּשֶׁת, וְהַמָּן, וְהַמַּטֶּה, וְהַשָּׁמִיר, הַכְּתָב, וְהַמִּכְתָּב,

---

logic, the pattern; but that is a vantage point we cannot attain in this life.

4:20. *Be a tail to lions*: The great seek the company of those greater than themselves.

4:23. *Do not try to placate*: There is a time and a place for everything, especially speech. The right word at the wrong time makes matters worse.

Chapter 5

Unlike the previous chapters, where the emphasis was placed on the authors as well as their teachings, most of the passages in this final chapter of *Avot*, are pre-

sustain the world created by ten acts of speech. 2. There were ten generations from Adam to Noah, to make known how patient God is, for all those generations increasingly provoked Him until He brought on them the waters of the Flood. 3. There were ten generations from Noah to Abraham, to make known how patient God is, for all those generations increasingly provoked Him until Abraham our father came and received the reward which could have been theirs. 4. Abraham our father was tested with ten trials and he withstood all of them, to make known how deep was our father Abraham's love of God. 5. Ten miracles were performed for our ancestors in Egypt, and ten at the Sea. 6. The Holy One, blessed be He, brought ten plagues against the Egyptians in Egypt, and ten at the Sea. 7. With ten trials our ancestors tried the patience of the Holy One, blessed be He, in the wilderness, as it is written, "They have tested Me these ten times, and did not listen to My voice". 8. Ten miracles were performed for our ancestors in the Temple: (1) No woman miscarried from the aroma of the sacrificial meat; (2) the sacrificial meat never became putrid; (3) no fly was seen in the slaughterhouse; (4) the High Priest never suffered ritual pollution on the Day of Atonement; (5) rain never extinguished the fire of the wood-pile on the altar; (6) the wind never blew away the column of smoke that rose from the altar; (7) no defect was ever found in the Omer, the Two Loaves, or the Showbread; (8) the people stood crowded together, yet there was ample space when they prostrated themselves; (9) no serpent or scorpion ever harmed anyone in Jerusalem; and (10) no one ever said to his fellow, "There is no room for me to stay overnight in Jerusalem." 9. Ten things were created on the eve of the Sabbath at twilight. They were: (1) the

---

sented anonymously. They begin with a series of numerical lists.

5:1. *By ten acts of speech*: The word וַיֹּאמֶר, "and He said", appears ten times in Genesis chapter 1.

5:4. *Ten trials*: Such as the commandment to leave his father's house; being forced by famine to go to Egypt; and the binding of Isaac. There are different midrashic traditions as to the precise enumeration.

5:7. *With ten trials our ancestors tried the patience*: Such as their rebellion at the Reed Sea; their complaints about the food and water; the Golden Calf; the report of the spies; and other provocations.

וְהַלֻּחוֹת. וְיֵשׁ אוֹמְרִים, אַף הַמַּזִּיקִין, וּקְבוּרָתוֹ שֶׁל־מֹשֶׁה,
וְאֵילוֹ שֶׁל־אַבְרָהָם אָבִינוּ. וְיֵשׁ אוֹמְרִים, אַף צְבַת בִּצְבַת
עֲשׂוּיָה. י שִׁבְעָה דְבָרִים בְּגֹלֶם, וְשִׁבְעָה בְּחָכָם. חָכָם אֵינוֹ
מְדַבֵּר לִפְנֵי מִי שֶׁגָּדוֹל מִמֶּנּוּ בְּחָכְמָה, וְאֵינוֹ נִכְנָס לְתוֹךְ
דִּבְרֵי חֲבֵרוֹ, וְאֵינוֹ נִבְהָל לְהָשִׁיב, שׁוֹאֵל כָּעִנְיָן, וּמֵשִׁיב
כַּהֲלָכָה, וְאוֹמֵר עַל־רִאשׁוֹן רִאשׁוֹן, וְעַל־אַחֲרוֹן אַחֲרוֹן, וְעַל
מַה־שֶּׁלֹּא שָׁמַע אוֹמֵר, לֹא שָׁמַעְתִּי, וּמוֹדֶה עַל הָאֱמֶת.
וְחִלּוּפֵיהֶם בְּגֹלֶם. יא שִׁבְעָה מִינֵי פֻרְעָנִיּוֹת בָּאִים לָעוֹלָם
עַל שִׁבְעָה גוּפֵי עֲבֵרָה, מִקְצָתָם מְעַשְּׂרִים וּמִקְצָתָם אֵינָם
מְעַשְּׂרִים, רָעָב שֶׁל־בַּצֹּרֶת בָּאָה, מִקְצָתָם רְעֵבִים וּמִקְצָתָם
שְׂבֵעִים, גָּמְרוּ שֶׁלֹּא לְעַשֵּׂר, רָעָב שֶׁל־מְהוּמָה וְשֶׁל־בַּצֹּרֶת
בָּא, וְשֶׁלֹּא לִטּוֹל אֶת־הַחַלָּה, רָעָב שֶׁל־כְּלָיָה בָּא. דֶּבֶר בָּא
לָעוֹלָם עַל־מִיתוֹת הָאֲמוּרוֹת בַּתּוֹרָה שֶׁלֹּא נִמְסְרוּ לְבֵית
דִּין, וְעַל פֵּרוֹת שְׁבִיעִית, חֶרֶב בָּאָה לָעוֹלָם עַל־עִנּוּי הַדִּין,
וְעַל־עִוּוּת הַדִּין, וְעַל־הַמּוֹרִים בַּתּוֹרָה שֶׁלֹּא כַהֲלָכָה, חַיָּה
רָעָה בָּאָה לָעוֹלָם עַל־שְׁבוּעַת שָׁוְא, וְעַל־חִלּוּל הַשֵּׁם,
גָּלוּת בָּאָה לָעוֹלָם עַל־עֲבוֹדַת אֱלִילִים, וְעַל־גִּלּוּי עֲרָיוֹת,
וְעַל־שְׁפִיכוּת דָּמִים, וְעַל־שְׁמִטַּת הָאָרֶץ. יב בְּאַרְבָּעָה
פְרָקִים הַדֶּבֶר מִתְרַבֶּה, בָּרְבִיעִית, וּבַשְּׁבִיעִית, וּבְמוֹצָאֵי
שְׁבִיעִית, וּבְמוֹצָאֵי הֶחָג שֶׁבְּכָל־שָׁנָה וְשָׁנָה. בָּרְבִיעִית
מִפְּנֵי מַעְשַׂר עָנִי שֶׁבַּשְּׁלִישִׁית, בַּשְּׁבִיעִית, מִפְּנֵי מַעְשַׂר

5:9. *Ten things were created*: Miraculous events which involved temporary suspension of natural or scientific law. The Mishnah teaches that these events were programmed into nature at the outset. In general, Judaism emphasises the law-like structure of the physical universe, as in Ecclesiastes' saying, "There is nothing new under the sun." *On the eve of the Sabbath at twilight* – between the six days of nature, and the seventh, which belongs to the One who transcends nature.

mouth of the earth; (2) the mouth of the well; (3) the mouth of [Balaam's] ass; (4) the rainbow; (5) the manna; (6) the staff; (7) the Shamir; (8) the writing [on the Tablets]; (9) the inscription; and (10) the Tablets. Some say: also the demons, Moses' burial place, and the ram of our father Abraham. And some say: also tongs made with tongs. 10. Seven traits characterise an uncultured person, and seven a Sage. A Sage: (1) does not speak before one who is wiser than he; (2) does not interrupt the words of his fellow; (3) does not answer impetuously; (4) asks relevant questions and gives appropriate answers; (5) deals with first things first, and last things last; (6) about something he has not heard he says, "I have not heard"; and (7) he acknowledges the truth. The opposites of these characterise an uncultured person. 11. Seven types of punishment come into the world for seven kinds of transgression: (1) If some tithe and others do not, a famine caused by drought occurs, so that some go hungry while others have sufficient. (2) If all decide not to tithe, a famine comes through tumult (of war) as well as drought. (3) If they also decide not to set apart challah, a fatal famine ensues. (4) Pestilence comes to the world for crimes that, according to the Torah, carry the death penalty, but are not the preserve of a human tribunal, and also for violation of the laws relating to produce of the seventh year. (5) The sword comes to the world for delay of justice, the perversion of justice, and for those who give a legal decision in violation of normative Torah law. (6) Wild beasts come to the world because of perjury and the desecration of God's name. (7) Exile comes to the world for idolatry, sexual immorality and bloodshed, and for violating the sabbatical year of the land. 12. At four periods (of the seven-year sabbatical cycle) pestilence increases: in the fourth year, the seventh year, the year following the sabbatical year, and annually at the conclusion of the Festival of Sukkot. In the fourth

---

The mouth of the earth, which opened to swallow Korach; *the mouth of the well,* which accompanied the Israelites on their journey through the wilderness; *the mouth of [Balaam's] ass,* which spoke (Numbers 22:28); *the rainbow,* which appeared after the Flood; *the manna,* which descended as "bread from heaven"; *the staff,* with which Moses performed signs and wonders; *the Shamir,* the miraculous worm which, according to tradition, split the stones from which the Temple

עָנִי שֶׁבַּשִּׁשִּׁית, בְּמוֹצָאֵי שְׁבִיעִית, מִפְּנֵי פֵּרוֹת שְׁבִיעִית,
בְּמוֹצָאֵי הֶחָג שֶׁבְּכָל־שָׁנָה וְשָׁנָה, מִפְּנֵי גֶזֶל מַתְּנוֹת עֲנִיִּים.
יג אַרְבַּע מִדּוֹת בָּאָדָם. הָאוֹמֵר, שֶׁלִּי שֶׁלִּי וְשֶׁלְּךָ שֶׁלָּךְ, זוֹ
מִדָּה בֵינוֹנִית, וְיֵשׁ אוֹמְרִים, זוֹ מִדַּת סְדוֹם. שֶׁלִּי שֶׁלָּךְ
וְשֶׁלְּךָ שֶׁלִּי, עַם הָאָרֶץ. שֶׁלִּי שֶׁלָּךְ וְשֶׁלְּךָ שֶׁלָּךְ, חָסִיד.
שֶׁלְּךָ שֶׁלִּי וְשֶׁלִּי שֶׁלִּי, רָשָׁע. יד אַרְבַּע מִדּוֹת בְּדֵעוֹת, נוֹחַ
לִכְעוֹס וְנוֹחַ לִרְצוֹת, יָצָא הֶפְסֵדוֹ בִּשְׂכָרוֹ. קָשֶׁה לִכְעוֹס
וְקָשֶׁה לִרְצוֹת, יָצָא שְׂכָרוֹ בְּהֶפְסֵדוֹ. קָשֶׁה לִכְעוֹס וְנוֹחַ
לִרְצוֹת, חָסִיד. נוֹחַ לִכְעוֹס וְקָשֶׁה לִרְצוֹת, רָשָׁע. טו אַרְבַּע
מִדּוֹת בְּתַלְמִידִים, מָהִיר לִשְׁמוֹעַ, וּמָהִיר לְאַבֵּד, יָצָא
שְׂכָרוֹ בְּהֶפְסֵדוֹ. קָשֶׁה לִשְׁמוֹעַ וְקָשֶׁה לְאַבֵּד, יָצָא הֶפְסֵדוֹ
בִּשְׂכָרוֹ. מָהִיר לִשְׁמוֹעַ וְקָשֶׁה לְאַבֵּד, זוֹ חֵלֶק טוֹב. קָשֶׁה
לִשְׁמוֹעַ וּמָהִיר לְאַבֵּד, זוֹ חֵלֶק רָע. טז אַרְבַּע מִדּוֹת בְּנוֹתְנֵי
צְדָקָה, הָרוֹצֶה שֶׁיִּתֵּן וְלֹא יִתְּנוּ אֲחֵרִים, עֵינוֹ רָעָה בְּשֶׁל־
אֲחֵרִים. יִתְּנוּ אֲחֵרִים וְהוּא לֹא יִתֵּן, עֵינוֹ רָעָה בְּשֶׁלּוֹ. יִתֵּן
וְיִתְּנוּ אֲחֵרִים, חָסִיד. לֹא יִתֵּן וְלֹא יִתְּנוּ אֲחֵרִים, רָשָׁע.
יז אַרְבַּע מִדּוֹת בְּהוֹלְכֵי בֵית הַמִּדְרָשׁ, הוֹלֵךְ וְאֵינוֹ עוֹשֶׂה,
שְׂכַר הֲלִיכָה בְּיָדוֹ. עוֹשֶׂה וְאֵינוֹ הוֹלֵךְ, שְׂכַר מַעֲשֶׂה בְּיָדוֹ.
הוֹלֵךְ וְעוֹשֶׂה, חָסִיד. לֹא הוֹלֵךְ וְלֹא עוֹשֶׂה, רָשָׁע. יח אַרְבַּע
מִדּוֹת בְּיוֹשְׁבִים לִפְנֵי חֲכָמִים, סְפוֹג, וּמַשְׁפֵּךְ, מְשַׁמֶּרֶת,
וְנָפָה. סְפוֹג, שֶׁהוּא סוֹפֵג אֶת־הַכֹּל. וּמַשְׁפֵּךְ, שֶׁמַּכְנִיס
בְּזוֹ וּמוֹצִיא בְזוֹ. מְשַׁמֶּרֶת, שֶׁמּוֹצִיאָה אֶת־הַיַּיִן וְקוֹלֶטֶת

---

was made; *the writing [on the Tablets]*, which could be seen from both sides; *the inscription* of the Tablets and *the Tablets* themselves, hewn and inscribed by God. *Some say, also tongs made with tongs* – the infinite regress – what held the first implement forged by fire, if not another implement forged by fire?

year, [pestilence increases] because of neglect of the tithe for the poor in the third year; in the seventh year, because of neglect of the tithe for the poor in the sixth year; in the year following the sabbatical year, because of the violation of the laws of the seventh-year produce; and at the conclusion of the Festival of Sukkot, for robbing the poor of their gifts. 13. There are four types of human character: (1) One who says, "What is mine is mine, and what is yours is yours", is an average person, though some say this is a Sodom type. (2) One who says, "What is mine is yours and what is yours is mine", is an ignoramus. (3) One who says, "What is mine is yours and what is yours is yours", is pious. (4) One who says, "What is yours is mine and what is mine is mine", is wicked. 14. There are four types of temperament: (1) One who is easily angered and easily pacified – his loss is cancelled by his gain. (2) One who is hard to anger and hard to pacify – his gain is cancelled by his loss. (3) One who is hard to anger and easily pacified is pious. (4) One who is easily angered and hard to pacify is wicked. 15. There are four types of student: (1) One who learns quickly and forgets quickly – his gain is cancelled by his loss. (2) One who learns slowly and forgets slowly – his loss is cancelled by his gain. (3) One who learns quickly and forgets slowly – his is a happy lot. (4) One who learns slowly and forgets quickly – his is a sad lot. 16. There are four types of donor to charity: (1) One who wishes to give but does not want others to give, begrudges others. (2) One who wants others to give, but does not himself give, begrudges himself. (3) One who gives and wants others to give is pious. (4) One who does not himself give and does not want others to give is wicked. 17. There are four types among those who attend the House of Study: (1) One who goes but does not practice (what he learns) receives a reward for going. (2) One who practices but does not go receives a reward for practising. (3) One who goes and also practices is pious. (4) One who neither goes nor practices is wicked. 18. There are four types among those who sit before the Sages: the sponge, the funnel, the strainer and the sieve. The sponge absorbs everything. The funnel takes in at one end and lets out at the other. The strainer lets out the wine and retains the sedi-

אֶת־הַשְּׁמָרִים. וְנָפָה, שֶׁמּוֹצִיאָה אֶת־הַקֶּמַח וְקוֹלֶטֶת
אֶת־הַסֹּלֶת. יט כָּל־אַהֲבָה שֶׁהִיא־תְלוּיָה בְדָבָר, בָּטֵל דָּבָר,
בְּטֵלָה אַהֲבָה. וְשֶׁאֵינָהּ תְּלוּיָה בְדָבָר, אֵינָהּ בְּטֵלָה לְעוֹלָם.
אֵיזוֹ הִיא אַהֲבָה שֶׁהִיא־תְלוּיָה בְדָבָר, זוֹ אַהֲבַת אַמְנוֹן
וְתָמָר. וְשֶׁאֵינָהּ תְּלוּיָה בְדָבָר, זוֹ אַהֲבַת דָּוִד וִיהוֹנָתָן. כ כָּל
מַחֲלֹקֶת שֶׁהִיא לְשֵׁם שָׁמַיִם, סוֹפָהּ לְהִתְקַיֵּם, וְשֶׁאֵינָהּ
לְשֵׁם שָׁמַיִם, אֵין סוֹפָהּ לְהִתְקַיֵּם. אֵיזוֹ הִיא מַחֲלֹקֶת
שֶׁהִיא לְשֵׁם שָׁמַיִם, זוֹ מַחֲלֹקֶת הִלֵּל וְשַׁמַּאי. וְשֶׁאֵינָהּ
לְשֵׁם שָׁמַיִם, זוֹ מַחֲלֹקֶת קֹרַח וְכָל־עֲדָתוֹ. כא כָּל־הַמְזַכֶּה
אֶת־הָרַבִּים, אֵין חֵטְא בָּא עַל יָדוֹ, וְכָל־הַמַּחֲטִיא אֶת־
הָרַבִּים, אֵין מַסְפִּיקִים בְּיָדוֹ לַעֲשׂוֹת תְּשׁוּבָה. מֹשֶׁה זָכָה
וְזִכָּה אֶת־הָרַבִּים, זְכוּת הָרַבִּים תָּלוּי בוֹ, שֶׁנֶּאֱמַר, צִדְקַת
יהוה עָשָׂה, וּמִשְׁפָּטָיו עִם־יִשְׂרָאֵל. יָרָבְעָם בֶּן־נְבָט חָטָא
וְהֶחֱטִיא אֶת־הָרַבִּים, חֵטְא הָרַבִּים תָּלוּי בוֹ, שֶׁנֶּאֱמַר, עַל
חַטֹּאות יָרָבְעָם אֲשֶׁר חָטָא, וַאֲשֶׁר הֶחֱטִיא אֶת־יִשְׂרָאֵל.
כב כָּל־מִי שֶׁיֶּשׁ־בּוֹ שְׁלֹשָׁה דְבָרִים הַלָּלוּ, הוּא מִתַּלְמִידָיו
שֶׁל־אַבְרָהָם אָבִינוּ, וּשְׁלֹשָׁה דְבָרִים אֲחֵרִים, הוּא
מִתַּלְמִידָיו שֶׁל־בִּלְעָם הָרָשָׁע. עַיִן טוֹבָה, וְרוּחַ נְמוּכָה,
וְנֶפֶשׁ שְׁפָלָה, מִתַּלְמִידָיו שֶׁל־אַבְרָהָם אָבִינוּ. עַיִן רָעָה,
וְרוּחַ גְּבוֹהָה, וְנֶפֶשׁ רְחָבָה, מִתַּלְמִידָיו שֶׁל־בִּלְעָם הָרָשָׁע.
מַה בֵּין תַּלְמִידָיו שֶׁל־אַבְרָהָם אָבִינוּ לְתַלְמִידָיו שֶׁל־
בִּלְעָם הָרָשָׁע, תַּלְמִידָיו שֶׁל־אַבְרָהָם אָבִינוּ אוֹכְלִים
בָּעוֹלָם הַזֶּה, וְנוֹחֲלִים הָעוֹלָם הַבָּא, שֶׁנֶּאֱמַר, לְהַנְחִיל

5:11. *Seven types of punishment*: As heirs to the prophetic tradition, the Sages sought to understand national calamities as Divine punishment, measure for measure, for national failings, religious, ethical or social. Thus the appropriate response

ment. The sifter allows the flour dust to pass through and retains the fine flour. 19. If love depends on a specific cause, when the cause ends, so does the love. If love does not depend on a specific cause, then it never ends. What is an example of love depending on a specific cause? The love of Amnon for Tamar. What is an example of love not dependent on a specific cause? The love of David and Jonathan. 20. Any dispute for the sake of Heaven will have enduring value, but any dispute not for the sake of Heaven will not have enduring value. What is an example of a dispute for the sake of heaven? The dispute between Hillel and Shammai. What is an example of one not for the sake of heaven? The dispute of Korach and all his company. 21. One who brings merit to the many will not be the cause of sin. One who causes the many to sin will be denied the means to repent. Moses attained merit and brought merit to the many; therefore the merit of the many was attributed to him, as it is said, "He carried out the LORD's righteousness and His ordinances with Israel". Jeroboam, son of Nebat, sinned and caused the many to sin; therefore the sin of the many was attributed to him, as it is said, "For the sins of Jeroboam that he committed and that he caused Israel to commit". 22. Whoever possesses these three traits is one of the disciples of our father Abraham; whoever possesses the three opposite traits is one of the disciples of the wicked Balaam. A generous eye, a modest demeanour and a humble soul are the traits of the disciples of our father Abraham. An evil eye, an arrogant demeanour and an insatiable soul are attributes of the disciples of the wicked Balaam. What is the difference between our father Abraham's disciples and those of the wicked Balaam? Our father Abraham's disciples enjoy this world and inherit the World to Come, as it is said, "That I may cause those who love me to inherit substance and so that I may fill their treasures". The wicked Balaam's disciples inherit Gehinnom and go down to the pit of destruction, as

---

to tragedy was collective penitence and rededication of the nation to the principles on which it was founded.

5:12. *Robbing the poor of their gifts*: The gleanings of the harvest, the corners of the field, and forgotten sheaves. These were to be left for the poor at harvest time; hence the connection with Sukkot, the harvest festival.

אֹהֲבַי יֵשׁ, וְאֹצְרֹתֵיהֶם אֲמַלֵּא. תַּלְמִידָיו שֶׁל־בִּלְעָם הָרָשָׁע יוֹרְשִׁים גֵּיהִנֹּם, וְיוֹרְדִים לִבְאֵר שַׁחַת, שֶׁנֶּאֱמַר, וְאַתָּה אֱלֹהִים תּוֹרִדֵם לִבְאֵר שַׁחַת, אַנְשֵׁי דָמִים וּמִרְמָה לֹא־יֶחֱצוּ יְמֵיהֶם, וַאֲנִי אֶבְטַח־בָּךְ. כג יְהוּדָה בֶן־תֵּימָא אוֹמֵר, הֱוֵה עַז כַּנָּמֵר, וְקַל כַּנֶּשֶׁר, רָץ כַּצְּבִי, וְגִבּוֹר כָּאֲרִי לַעֲשׂוֹת רְצוֹן אָבִיךָ שֶׁבַּשָּׁמָיִם. הוּא הָיָה אוֹמֵר, עַז פָּנִים לְגֵיהִנֹּם, וּבֹשֶׁת פָּנִים לְגַן עֵדֶן. יְהִי רָצוֹן מִלְּפָנֶיךָ יהוה אֱלֹהֵינוּ וֵאלֹהֵי אֲבוֹתֵינוּ שֶׁיִּבָּנֶה בֵּית הַמִּקְדָּשׁ בִּמְהֵרָה בְיָמֵינוּ. וְתֵן חֶלְקֵנוּ בְּתוֹרָתֶךָ. כד הוּא הָיָה אוֹמֵר, בֶּן־חָמֵשׁ שָׁנִים לַמִּקְרָא, בֶּן־עֶשֶׂר שָׁנִים לַמִּשְׁנָה, בֶּן־שְׁלֹשׁ עֶשְׂרֵה לַמִּצְוֹת, בֶּן־חֲמֵשׁ עֶשְׂרֵה לַתַּלְמוּד, בֶּן־שְׁמֹנֶה עֶשְׂרֵה לַחֻפָּה, בֶּן־עֶשְׂרִים לִרְדּוֹף, בֶּן־שְׁלֹשִׁים לַכֹּחַ, בֶּן־אַרְבָּעִים לַבִּינָה, בֶּן־חֲמִשִּׁים לָעֵצָה, בֶּן־שִׁשִּׁים לַזִּקְנָה, בֶּן־שִׁבְעִים לַשֵּׂיבָה, בֶּן־שְׁמוֹנִים לַגְּבוּרָה, בֶּן־תִּשְׁעִים לָשׁוּחַ, בֶּן־מֵאָה כְּאִלּוּ מֵת וְעָבַר וּבָטֵל מִן הָעוֹלָם. כה בֶּן־בַּג בַּג אוֹמֵר, הֲפָךְ בַּהּ וַהֲפָךְ בַּהּ, דְּכֹלָּא בַהּ, וּבַהּ תֶּחֱזֵי, וְסִיב וּבְלֵה בַהּ, וּמִנַּהּ לָא תְזוּעַ, שֶׁאֵין לְךָ מִדָּה טוֹבָה הֵימֶנָּה. כו בֶּן־הֵא הֵא אוֹמֵר, לְפוּם צַעֲרָא אַגְרָא.

רַבִּי חֲנַנְיָא בֶּן־עֲקַשְׁיָא אוֹמֵר, רָצָה הַקָּדוֹשׁ בָּרוּךְ הוּא לְזַכּוֹת אֶת־יִשְׂרָאֵל, לְפִיכָךְ הִרְבָּה לָהֶם תּוֹרָה וּמִצְוֹת, שֶׁנֶּאֱמַר, יהוה חָפֵץ לְמַעַן צִדְקוֹ, יַגְדִּיל תּוֹרָה וְיַאְדִּיר.

In many congregations, קַדִּישׁ דְּרַבָּנָן on page 34
is said at this point, then עָלֵינוּ on page 520.

פרק ששי

כָּל־יִשְׂרָאֵל יֵשׁ לָהֶם חֵלֶק לָעוֹלָם הַבָּא, שֶׁנֶּאֱמַר, וְעַמֵּךְ כֻּלָּם צַדִּיקִים, לְעוֹלָם יִירְשׁוּ אָרֶץ, נֵצֶר מַטָּעַי, מַעֲשֵׂה יָדַי

it is said, "But You, GOD, will bring them down to the pit of destruction; bloodthirsty and deceitful men shall not live out half their days; but I trust in You". 23. Judah ben Tema said: Be strong as a leopard, light as an eagle, swift as a gazelle, and brave as a lion, to do the will of your Father in heaven. He used to say: The shameless go to Gehinnom; those who have a sense of shame are destined for the Garden of Eden. May it be Your will, O LORD our GOD and GOD of our ancestors that the Temple be speedily rebuilt in our days; and grant us our portion in Your Torah. 24. He used to say: Five years old is the age to begin studying Scripture; ten for Mishnah; thirteen for the obligation of the commandments; fifteen for the study of Talmud; eighteen for marriage; twenty for seeking a livelihood; thirty for full strength; forty for understanding; fifty for giving counsel; sixty for old age; seventy for ripe old age; eighty for exceptional strength; and ninety for a bent back; at a hundred, one is as if he were dead and had left and gone from the world. 25. Ben Bag-Bag said: Turn it [the Torah] over and over, for everything is in it. Reflect on it, grow old and grey in it and do not stir from it, for there is no better portion for you than this. 26. Ben He-He said: According to the effort is the reward.

Rabbi Chananya ben Akashya said: The Holy One, blessed be He, wanted to confer merit on Israel. That is why He gave them a copious Torah and many commandments, as it is said, "It pleased the LORD, for the sake of [Israel's] righteousness, to make the Torah great and glorious".

In many congregations, the Rabbis' *Kaddish* on page 35 is said at this point, then "It is our duty" on page 521.

CHAPTER 6

All Israel have a share in the World to Come, as it is said, "Your people

---

5:13. *Some say this is a Sodom type*: The sin of Sodom, according to Ezekiel 16:49, was that "they did not help the poor and needy". Insisting on property rights, they frowned on charity. *An ignoramus* – this, according to some scholars, is a critique of the property-sharing communes associated with the Essenes.

5:20. *Any dispute for the sake of Heaven* is an argument for the sake of truth. *Any dispute not for the sake of Heaven* is an argument for the sake of victory. In an ar-

לְהִתְפָּאֵר. שָׁנוּ חֲכָמִים בִּלְשׁוֹן הַמִּשְׁנָה. בָּרוּךְ שֶׁבָּחַר בָּהֶם וּבְמִשְׁנָתָם.

א רַבִּי מֵאִיר אוֹמֵר, כָּל הָעוֹסֵק בַּתּוֹרָה לִשְׁמָהּ זוֹכֶה לִדְבָרִים הַרְבֵּה, וְלֹא עוֹד, אֶלָּא שֶׁכָּל־הָעוֹלָם כֻּלּוֹ כְּדַי הוּא לוֹ. נִקְרָא רֵעַ, אָהוּב. אוֹהֵב אֶת־הַמָּקוֹם, אוֹהֵב אֶת־הַבְּרִיּוֹת, וּמַלְבַּשְׁתּוֹ עֲנָוָה וְיִרְאָה, וּמַכְשַׁרְתּוֹ לִהְיוֹת צַדִּיק, חָסִיד, יָשָׁר, וְנֶאֱמָן, וּמְרַחַקְתּוֹ מִן־הַחֵטְא, וּמְקָרַבְתּוֹ לִידֵי זְכוּת. וְנֶהֱנִים מִמֶּנּוּ עֵצָה וְתוּשִׁיָּה, בִּינָה וּגְבוּרָה, שֶׁנֶּאֱמַר, לִי עֵצָה וְתוּשִׁיָּה, אֲנִי בִינָה, לִי גְבוּרָה. וְנוֹתֶנֶת לוֹ מַלְכוּת, וּמֶמְשָׁלָה, וְחִקּוּר דִּין, וּמְגַלִּים לוֹ רָזֵי תוֹרָה, וְנַעֲשֶׂה כְּמַעְיָן שֶׁאֵינוֹ פוֹסֵק, וּכְנָהָר שֶׁמִּתְגַּבֵּר, וְהוֹלֵךְ וְהֹוֶה צָנוּעַ, וְאֶרֶךְ רוּחַ, וּמוֹחֵל עַל־עֶלְבּוֹנוֹ. וּמְגַדַּלְתּוֹ וּמְרוֹמַמְתּוֹ עַל כָּל־הַמַּעֲשִׂים. ב אָמַר רַבִּי יְהוֹשֻׁעַ בֶּן־לֵוִי, בְּכָל־יוֹם וָיוֹם בַּת־קוֹל יוֹצֵאת מֵהַר חוֹרֵב, וּמַכְרֶזֶת וְאוֹמֶרֶת, אוֹי לָהֶם לַבְּרִיּוֹת, מֵעֶלְבּוֹנָהּ שֶׁל־תּוֹרָה. שֶׁכָּל־מִי שֶׁאֵינוֹ עוֹסֵק בַּתּוֹרָה נִקְרָא נָזוּף, שֶׁנֶּאֱמַר, נֶזֶם זָהָב בְּאַף חֲזִיר, אִשָּׁה יָפָה וְסָרַת טָעַם. וְאוֹמֵר, וְהַלֻּחֹת מַעֲשֵׂה אֱלֹהִים הֵמָּה וְהַמִּכְתָּב מִכְתַּב אֱלֹהִים הוּא חָרוּת עַל־הַלֻּחֹת. אַל־תִּקְרָא חָרוּת אֶלָּא חֵרוּת, שֶׁאֵין לְךָ בֶּן־חוֹרִין אֶלָּא מִי שֶׁעוֹסֵק בְּתַלְמוּד תּוֹרָה. וְכָל־מִי שֶׁעוֹסֵק בְּתַלְמוּד תּוֹרָה הֲרֵי זֶה מִתְעַלֶּה, שֶׁנֶּאֱמַר, וּמִמַּתָּנָה נַחֲלִיאֵל, וּמִנַּחֲלִיאֵל בָּמוֹת. ג הַלּוֹמֵד מֵחֲבֵרוֹ פֶּרֶק אֶחָד, אוֹ הֲלָכָה אַחַת, אוֹ פָּסוּק אֶחָד, אוֹ דִבּוּר אֶחָד, אוֹ

---

gument for the sake of heaven, both sides win; one because his views are accepted, the other because he has learned something new. To be defeated by the truth is the only defeat that is also a victory, for by it we grow. "Just as I received reward for the exposition", said Rabbi Shimon ha-Amsoni, "so I will receive reward for the retraction." In an argument for the sake of victory, both sides lose, even the vic-

are all righteous; they shall inherit the land forever; they are a shoot of My own planting, a work of My own hands, that I may be glorified". The Sages taught the following in the style of the Mishnah – blessed be He who chose them and their teaching.

1. Rabbi Meir said: Whoever engages in Torah study for its own sake merits many things; moreover, the whole world is worthwhile for his sake alone. He is called friend, beloved, a lover of God and a lover of mankind. (The Torah) clothes him with humility and reverence. It prepares him to be righteous, pious, upright and faithful. It keeps him far from sin and near to virtue. People benefit from his advice and wisdom, understanding and courage, as it is said, "Mine are counsel and wisdom; I am understanding, courage is mine". It gives him sovereignty, dominion and discerning judgement. To him the secrets of the Torah are revealed. He becomes like a never-failing fountain, like a river that never runs dry. He becomes modest and patient; he forgives insults. It makes him great, exalting him above all things. 2. Rabbi Yehoshua ben Levi said: Every day a heavenly voice resounds from Mount Horeb, proclaiming and saying: "Woe to mankind for their contempt of the Torah!" For whoever does not occupy himself with the Torah is called reprehensible, as it is said, "Like a gold ring in the snout of a pig is a beautiful woman bereft of sense". It also says, "The tablets were the work of God, and the writing was the writing of God, engraved (*charut*) on the tablets". Read not *charut* ("engraved") but *cherut* ("freedom"), for the only person who is truly free is one who occupies himself with Torah study; and whoever occupies himself with Torah study will be exalted, as it is said, "And from Mattanah to Nachaliel, and from Nachaliel to Bamot". 3. Whoever learns from

---

tor, for in diminishing the other, he has diminished himself.

5:23. *May it be Your will*: This passage originally marked the end of the chapter, and of the tractate, hence its formulaic character.

Chapter 6

This chapter, as the text explains, is not part of the Tractate *Avot*, but is a later compilation. It is known as *The Chapter of R. Meir*, because of its first speaker, or *The Chapter of the Acquisition of Torah*, because of its central theme. Like Chapter 119 of the Book of Psalms, it is a poetic ex-

אֲפִילוּ אוֹת אַחַת, צָרִיךְ לִנְהָג בּוֹ כָּבוֹד. שֶׁכֵּן מָצִינוּ בְּדָוִד מֶלֶךְ יִשְׂרָאֵל, שֶׁלֹּא לָמַד מֵאֲחִיתֹפֶל אֶלָּא שְׁנֵי דְבָרִים בִּלְבָד, קְרָאוֹ רַבּוֹ, אַלּוּפוֹ, וּמְיֻדָּעוֹ, שֶׁנֶּאֱמַר, וְאַתָּה אֱנוֹשׁ כְּעֶרְכִּי, אַלּוּפִי וּמְיֻדָּעִי. וַהֲלֹא דְבָרִים קַל וָחוֹמֶר, וּמַה דָּוִד מֶלֶךְ יִשְׂרָאֵל, שֶׁלֹּא לָמַד מֵאֲחִיתֹפֶל אֶלָּא שְׁנֵי דְבָרִים בִּלְבָד, קְרָאוֹ רַבּוֹ אַלּוּפוֹ וּמְיֻדָּעוֹ הַלּוֹמֵד מֵחֲבֵרוֹ פֶּרֶק אֶחָד, אוֹ הֲלָכָה אַחַת, אוֹ פָּסוּק אֶחָד, אוֹ דִבּוּר אֶחָד, אוֹ אֲפִילוּ אוֹת אַחַת, עַל־אַחַת כַּמָּה וְכַמָּה שֶׁצָּרִיךְ לִנְהָג בּוֹ כָּבוֹד. וְאֵין כָּבוֹד אֶלָּא תוֹרָה, שֶׁנֶּאֱמַר, כָּבוֹד חֲכָמִים יִנְחָלוּ, וּתְמִימִים יִנְחֲלוּ טוֹב, וְאֵין טוֹב אֶלָּא תוֹרָה, שֶׁנֶּאֱמַר, כִּי לֶקַח טוֹב נָתַתִּי לָכֶם, תּוֹרָתִי אַל־תַּעֲזֹבוּ. ד כַּךְ הִיא דַּרְכָּהּ שֶׁל־תּוֹרָה, פַּת בַּמֶּלַח תֹּאכֵל, וּמַיִם בִּמְשׂוּרָה תִּשְׁתֶּה, וְעַל הָאָרֶץ תִּישָׁן, וְחַיֵּי צַעַר תִּחְיֶה, וּבַתּוֹרָה אַתָּה עָמֵל, אִם־אַתָּה עֹשֶׂה כֵּן, אַשְׁרֶיךָ וְטוֹב לָךְ. אַשְׁרֶיךָ בָּעוֹלָם הַזֶּה, וְטוֹב לָךְ לָעוֹלָם הַבָּא. ה אַל־תְּבַקֵּשׁ גְּדֻלָּה לְעַצְמְךָ, וְאַל־תַּחְמוֹד כָּבוֹד, יוֹתֵר מִלִּמּוּדְךָ עֲשֵׂה. וְאַל־תִּתְאַוֶּה לְשֻׁלְחָנָם שֶׁל־מְלָכִים, שֶׁשֻּׁלְחָנְךָ גָּדוֹל מִשֻּׁלְחָנָם, וְכִתְרְךָ גָּדוֹל מִכִּתְרָם, וְנֶאֱמָן הוּא בַּעַל מְלַאכְתְּךָ, שֶׁיְּשַׁלֶּם לְךָ שְׂכַר פְּעֻלָּתֶךָ. ו גְּדוֹלָה תוֹרָה יוֹתֵר מִן־הַכְּהֻנָּה וּמִן־הַמַּלְכוּת, שֶׁהַמַּלְכוּת נִקְנֵית בִּשְׁלֹשִׁים מַעֲלוֹת, וְהַכְּהֻנָּה בְּעֶשְׂרִים וְאַרְבַּע, וְהַתּוֹרָה נִקְנֵית בְּאַרְבָּעִים וּשְׁמוֹנָה דְבָרִים, וְאֵלּוּ הֵן, בְּתַלְמוּד, בִּשְׁמִיעַת הָאֹזֶן, בַּעֲרִיכַת שְׂפָתַיִם, בְּבִינַת הַלֵּב, בְּשִׂכּוּל הַלֵּב, בְּאֵימָה, בְּיִרְאָה, בַּעֲנָוָה, בְּשִׂמְחָה, בְּשִׁמּוּשׁ חֲכָמִים, בְּדִבּוּק חֲבֵרִים, בְּפִלְפּוּל הַתַּלְמִידִים, בְּיִשּׁוּב, בְּמִקְרָא, וּבְמִשְׁנָה, בְּמִעוּט

someone else a single chapter, a single law, a single verse, a single word, even a single letter, must treat him with honour, for so we find in the case of David, king of Israel, who learned only two things from Achitophel, yet he called him his teacher, his guide, and his close friend, for so it says, "But it is you, my equal, my guide, my close friend". The following inference can be derived: If David, king of Israel, who learned only two things from Achitophel, called him his teacher, guide and close friend, how much more must one who learns from someone else a chapter, a law, a verse, a word or even a single letter, treat him with honour! And honour is due only to Torah, as it is written, "The wise shall inherit honour", and "The wholehearted shall attain good", and "good" signifies Torah, as it is said, "I have given you good instruction; do not forsake My Torah". 4. This is the way of Torah: Eat bread with salt, drink water by measure, sleep on the ground, live a life of hardship, but toil in the Torah! If you do so, "You will be happy and it will be well with you": "You will be happy" in this world, "and it shall be well with you" in the World to Come. 5. Do not seek greatness for yourself, and do not long for honour. Let your deeds exceed your learning. Do not crave the table of kings, for your table is greater than theirs, your crown is greater than their crown, and your Employer can be relied upon to pay you your labour's reward. 6. The Torah is greater than priesthood and kingship, for kingship is acquired with thirty attainments, and priesthood is endowed with twenty-four gifts, but the Torah is acquired by forty-eight virtues. They are: study, attentive listening, well-ordered speech, intuitive understanding, a discerning mind, awe, reverence, humility, joy, serving the wise, association with colleagues, debate with students, serenity, knowledge of Scripture and Mishnah; minimising time spent on business, worldly

pression of the love of a people for a book, the Book of Books, and a quintessential declaration of rabbinic faith.

6:2. *The only person who is truly free*: Hebrew distinguishes two kinds of freedom, *chofesh* and *cherut*. *Chofesh* is negative liberty, the absence of coercion, while *cherut* is positive liberty, the freedom that honours the freedom of others. Positive freedom requires habits of self-restraint; hence it belongs only to those who have internalised the teachings of Torah. "*From Mattanah to Nachaliel, and from Nachaliel to Bamot*", reading the phrase as, "From the gift of Torah

סְחוֹרָה, בְּמִעוּט דֶּרֶךְ אֶרֶץ, בְּמִעוּט תַּעֲנוּג, בְּמִעוּט שֵׁנָה, בְּמִעוּט שִׂיחָה, בְּמִעוּט שְׂחוֹק, בְּאֹרֶךְ אַפַּיִם, בְּלֵב־טוֹב, בֶּאֱמוּנַת חֲכָמִים, בְּקַבָּלַת הַיִּסּוּרִים, הַמַּכִּיר אֶת־מְקוֹמוֹ, וְהַשָּׂמֵחַ בְּחֶלְקוֹ, וְהָעוֹשֶׂה סְיָג לִדְבָרָיו, וְאֵינוֹ מַחֲזִיק טוֹבָה לְעַצְמוֹ, אָהוּב, אוֹהֵב אֶת־הַמָּקוֹם, אוֹהֵב אֶת־הַבְּרִיּוֹת, אוֹהֵב אֶת־הַצְּדָקוֹת, אוֹהֵב אֶת־הַמֵּישָׁרִים, אוֹהֵב אֶת־הַתּוֹכָחוֹת, וּמִתְרַחֵק מִן־הַכָּבוֹד, וְלֹא־מֵגִיס לִבּוֹ בְּתַלְמוּדוֹ, וְאֵינוֹ שָׂמֵחַ בְּהוֹרָאָה, נוֹשֵׂא בְעֹל עִם־חֲבֵרוֹ, וּמַכְרִיעוֹ לְכַף זְכוּת, וּמַעֲמִידוֹ עַל־הָאֱמֶת, וּמַעֲמִידוֹ עַל־הַשָּׁלוֹם, וּמִתְיַשֵּׁב לִבּוֹ בְּתַלְמוּדוֹ, שׁוֹאֵל וּמֵשִׁיב, שׁוֹמֵעַ וּמוֹסִיף, הַלּוֹמֵד עַל־מְנָת לְלַמֵּד, וְהַלּוֹמֵד עַל־מְנָת לַעֲשׂוֹת, הַמַּחְכִּים אֶת־רַבּוֹ, וְהַמְכַוֵּן אֶת־שְׁמוּעָתוֹ, וְהָאוֹמֵר דָּבָר בְּשֵׁם אוֹמְרוֹ. הָא לָמַדְתָּ, כָּל־הָאוֹמֵר דָּבָר בְּשֵׁם אוֹמְרוֹ, מֵבִיא גְאֻלָּה לָעוֹלָם, שֶׁנֶּאֱמַר, וַתֹּאמֶר אֶסְתֵּר לַמֶּלֶךְ בְּשֵׁם מָרְדֳּכָי. ז גְּדוֹלָה תוֹרָה, שֶׁהִיא נוֹתֶנֶת חַיִּים לְעוֹשֶׂיהָ בָּעוֹלָם הַזֶּה וּבָעוֹלָם הַבָּא, שֶׁנֶּאֱמַר, כִּי־חַיִּים הֵם לְמֹצְאֵיהֶם, וּלְכָל־בְּשָׂרוֹ מַרְפֵּא. וְאוֹמֵר, רִפְאוּת תְּהִי לְשָׁרֶּךָ, וְשִׁקּוּי לְעַצְמוֹתֶיךָ. וְאוֹמֵר, עֵץ־חַיִּים הִיא לַמַּחֲזִיקִים בָּהּ וְתֹמְכֶיהָ מְאֻשָּׁר. וְאוֹמֵר, כִּי לִוְיַת חֵן הֵם לְרֹאשֶׁךָ, וַעֲנָקִים לְגַרְגְּרֹתֶךָ. וְאוֹמֵר, תִּתֵּן לְרֹאשְׁךָ לִוְיַת־חֵן, עֲטֶרֶת תִּפְאֶרֶת תְּמַגְּנֶךָּ. וְאוֹמֵר, כִּי־בִי יִרְבּוּ יָמֶיךָ, וְיוֹסִיפוּ לְךָ שְׁנוֹת חַיִּים. וְאוֹמֵר, אֹרֶךְ יָמִים בִּימִינָהּ, בִּשְׂמֹאולָהּ עֹשֶׁר וְכָבוֹד. וְאוֹמֵר, כִּי אֹרֶךְ יָמִים וּשְׁנוֹת חַיִּים, וְשָׁלוֹם יוֹסִיפוּ לָךְ. ח רַבִּי שִׁמְעוֹן בֶּן־יְהוּדָה מִשּׁוּם רַבִּי שִׁמְעוֹן בֶּן־יוֹחַי אוֹמֵר, הַנּוֹי, וְהַכֹּחַ, וְהָעֹשֶׁר, וְהַכָּבוֹד, וְהַחָכְמָה, הַזִּקְנָה, וְהַשֵּׂיבָה, וְהַבָּנִים,

matters, pleasure, sleep, small talk or laughter; patience, a kindly heart, faith in the Sages, and acceptance of suffering; knowing one's place, being happy with one's lot, restraining one's words, and claiming no credit for oneself; being loved, loving God, loving mankind and loving righteousness, justice and admonishment; shunning honours, avoiding arrogance in one's learning or delight in giving decisions; sharing someone else's burden, giving him the benefit of the doubt, guiding him to truth and peace; concentrating on one's study, asking and answering questions, listening and adding to one's knowledge; learning in order to teach, learning in order to do, making one's teacher wiser, being precise in one's studies, and reporting a saying in the name of the one who said it. For you have learned: Whoever reports a saying in the name of the one who said it brings deliverance to the world, as it is said, "And Esther told the king in the name of Mordechai". 7. Great is Torah for it gives life to its practitioners in both this world and the World to Come, as it is said, "For they are life to those that find them, and healing to all their flesh"; and it says, "It shall be healing for your body and marrow for your bones"; and it says, "It is a tree of life to those who grasp it, and those who support it shall be happy"; and it says, "They shall be a garland of grace on your head, and pendants for your neck"; and it says, "It will adorn your head with a garland of grace, and bestow on you a crown of glory"; and it says, "Through me shall your days increase, and years of life shall be added to you"; and it says, "At its right hand is length of days; in its left, riches and honour"; and it says, "For length of days and years of life and peace shall they add to you". 8. Rabbi Shimon ben Judah said in the name of Rabbi Shimon ben Yochai: Beauty, strength, wealth, honour, wisdom, old age, grey hair, and children are fitting for the righteous

---

6:6. *Whoever reports a saying in the name of the one who said it*: There is a fundamental difference between "wisdom" (*chochmah*) and Torah. Wisdom, which includes science (the universe as God's work) and the humanities (the human person as God's image) is the truth we discover. Torah is the truth we inherit. In the case of wisdom, says Maimonides, we "accept the truth whoever says it". In the case of Torah, however, what matters is the authentic chain of transmission. Hence it is essential to know "the name of the one who said" a particular Torah teaching.

נָאֶה לַצַּדִּיקִים וְנָאֶה לָעוֹלָם, שֶׁנֶּאֱמַר, עֲטֶרֶת תִּפְאֶרֶת
שֵׂיבָה, בְּדֶרֶךְ צְדָקָה תִּמָּצֵא. וְאוֹמֵר, תִּפְאֶרֶת בַּחוּרִים
כֹּחָם, וַהֲדַר זְקֵנִים שֵׂיבָה. וְאוֹמֵר, עֲטֶרֶת חֲכָמִים עָשְׁרָם.
וְאוֹמֵר, עֲטֶרֶת זְקֵנִים בְּנֵי בָנִים, וְתִפְאֶרֶת בָּנִים אֲבוֹתָם.
וְאוֹמֵר, וְחָפְרָה הַלְּבָנָה וּבוֹשָׁה הַחַמָּה, כִּי־מָלַךְ יהוה
צְבָאוֹת בְּהַר צִיּוֹן וּבִירוּשָׁלַיִם, וְנֶגֶד זְקֵנָיו כָּבוֹד. רַבִּי
שִׁמְעוֹן בֶּן־מְנַסְיָא אוֹמֵר, אֵלּוּ שֶׁבַע מִדּוֹת, שֶׁמָּנוּ חֲכָמִים
לַצַּדִּיקִים, כֻּלָּם נִתְקַיְּמוּ בְּרַבִּי וּבְבָנָיו. ט אָמַר רַבִּי יוֹסֵי בֶּן־
קִסְמָא, פַּעַם אַחַת הָיִיתִי מְהַלֵּךְ בַּדֶּרֶךְ, וּפָגַע בִּי אָדָם
אֶחָד. וְנָתַן־לִי שָׁלוֹם, וְהֶחֱזַרְתִּי לוֹ שָׁלוֹם. אָמַר לִי, רַבִּי,
מֵאֵיזֶה מָקוֹם אָתָּה, אָמַרְתִּי לוֹ, מֵעִיר גְּדוֹלָה שֶׁל־חֲכָמִים
וְשֶׁל־סוֹפְרִים אָנִי. אָמַר לִי, רַבִּי רְצוֹנְךָ שֶׁתָּדוּר עִמָּנוּ
בִּמְקוֹמֵנוּ, וַאֲנִי אֶתֵּן לְךָ אֶלֶף אֲלָפִים דִּינְרֵי זָהָב וַאֲבָנִים
טוֹבוֹת וּמַרְגָּלִיּוֹת. אָמַרְתִּי לוֹ, אִם אַתָּה נוֹתֵן לִי כָּל־כֶּסֶף
וְזָהָב וַאֲבָנִים טוֹבוֹת וּמַרְגָּלִיּוֹת שֶׁבָּעוֹלָם, אֵינִי דָר אֶלָּא
בִּמְקוֹם תּוֹרָה. וְכֵן כָּתוּב בְּסֵפֶר תְּהִלִּים עַל־יְדֵי דָוִד מֶלֶךְ
יִשְׂרָאֵל, טוֹב לִי תוֹרַת פִּיךָ מֵאַלְפֵי זָהָב וָכָסֶף. וְלֹא עוֹד
אֶלָּא שֶׁבִּשְׁעַת פְּטִירָתוֹ שֶׁל־אָדָם אֵין מְלַוִּין לוֹ לְאָדָם לֹא
כֶּסֶף וְלֹא זָהָב וְלֹא אֲבָנִים טוֹבוֹת וּמַרְגָּלִיּוֹת, אֶלָּא תּוֹרָה
וּמַעֲשִׂים טוֹבִים בִּלְבָד, שֶׁנֶּאֱמַר, בְּהִתְהַלֶּכְךָ תַּנְחֶה אֹתָךְ
בְּשָׁכְבְּךָ תִּשְׁמוֹר עָלֶיךָ, וַהֲקִיצוֹתָ הִיא תְשִׂיחֶךָ. בְּהִתְהַלֶּכְךָ
תַּנְחֶה אֹתָךְ, בָּעוֹלָם הַזֶּה, בְּשָׁכְבְּךָ תִּשְׁמוֹר עָלֶיךָ, בַּקָּבֶר.
וַהֲקִיצוֹתָ הִיא תְשִׂיחֶךָ לָעוֹלָם הַבָּא. וְאוֹמֵר, לִי הַכֶּסֶף וְלִי
הַזָּהָב, נְאֻם יהוה צְבָאוֹת. י חֲמִשָּׁה קִנְיָנִים קָנָה לוֹ הַקָּדוֹשׁ
בָּרוּךְ הוּא בְּעוֹלָמוֹ, וְאֵלּוּ הֵן, תּוֹרָה קִנְיָן אֶחָד, שָׁמַיִם

and for the world, as it is said: "Grey hair is a crown of glory; it is attained by the way of righteousness"; and it says, "The glory of the young is their strength; the majesty of the old is their grey hair"; and it says, "The crown of the wise is their wealth"; and it says, "Grandchildren are the crown of their elders; the glory of children is their parents"; and it says, "Then the moon shall be ashamed and the sun shall be abashed, for the LORD of hosts will reign on Mount Zion and in Jerusalem, and glory shall be before His elders". Rabbi Shimon ben Menasya said: These seven qualities which the Sages attributed to the righteous were all present in Rabbi [Judah the Prince] and his sons. 9. Rabbi Yose ben Kisma said: Once I was walking along the road when a man met and greeted me, and I returned his greeting. He said to me, "Rabbi, where do you come from?" I replied, "I come from a great city of Sages and scribes." He said to me, "Rabbi, if you are willing to live with us in our place I will give you a million gold dinars, as well as precious stones and pearls." I replied, "Were you to give me all the silver and gold and precious stones and pearls in the world, I would not live anywhere except in a place of Torah, for so it is written in the Book of Psalms by David, king of Israel, 'I prefer the Torah of your mouth to thousands of gold and silver pieces'. Furthermore, when a person departs from this world, neither silver nor gold nor precious stones nor pearls accompany him, but only Torah and good deeds, as it is said, 'When you walk, it will lead you; when you lie down, it will watch over you; and when you awake, it will talk with you'. 'When you walk, it will lead you' – in this world; 'when you lie down, it will watch over you' – in the grave; 'and when you awake, it will talk with you' – in the World to Come. And it says, 'Mine is the silver, and Mine is the gold, says the LORD of hosts'." 10. Five possessions did the Holy One,

---

6:9 *Rabbi Jose ben Kisma*: A fascinating vignette about true and false values. A stranger approaches Jose ben Kisma, struck by his distinguished appearance, and makes him a grandiloquent offer which the rabbi refuses. We are told nothing about the context of this exchange but we recognise immediately the perennial temptation it expresses. From time immemorial, people have been drawn to places of affluence and luxury. Yet their glitter is false, their lure seductive, their culture corrupting. Choose, rather, the company of Sages, whose values bespeak eternity,

וָאָרֶץ קִנְיָן אֶחָד, אַבְרָהָם קִנְיָן אֶחָד, יִשְׂרָאֵל קִנְיָן אֶחָד, בֵּית הַמִּקְדָּשׁ קִנְיָן אֶחָד. תּוֹרָה מִנַּיִן, דִּכְתִיב, יהוה קָנָנִי רֵאשִׁית דַּרְכּוֹ, קֶדֶם מִפְעָלָיו מֵאָז. שָׁמַיִם וָאָרֶץ מִנַּיִן, דִּכְתִיב, כֹּה אָמַר יהוה, הַשָּׁמַיִם כִּסְאִי, וְהָאָרֶץ הֲדֹם רַגְלָי, אֵיזֶה בַיִת אֲשֶׁר תִּבְנוּ־לִי, וְאֵיזֶה מָקוֹם מְנוּחָתִי, וְאוֹמֵר, מָה רַבּוּ מַעֲשֶׂיךָ יהוה, כֻּלָּם בְּחָכְמָה עָשִׂיתָ, מָלְאָה הָאָרֶץ קִנְיָנֶךָ. אַבְרָהָם מִנַּיִן, דִּכְתִיב, וַיְבָרְכֵהוּ וַיֹּאמַר, בָּרוּךְ אַבְרָם לְאֵל עֶלְיוֹן, קֹנֵה שָׁמַיִם וָאָרֶץ. יִשְׂרָאֵל מִנַּיִן, דִּכְתִיב, עַד־יַעֲבֹר עַמְּךָ יהוה, עַד־יַעֲבֹר עַם־זוּ קָנִיתָ, וְאוֹמֵר, לִקְדוֹשִׁים אֲשֶׁר־בָּאָרֶץ הֵמָּה, וְאַדִּירֵי כָּל־חֶפְצִי בָם. בֵּית הַמִּקְדָּשׁ מִנַּיִן, דִּכְתִיב, מָכוֹן לְשִׁבְתְּךָ פָּעַלְתָּ יהוה, מִקְּדָשׁ אֲדֹנָי כּוֹנְנוּ יָדֶיךָ, וְאוֹמֵר, וַיְבִיאֵם אֶל־גְּבוּל קָדְשׁוֹ, הַר־זֶה קָנְתָה יְמִינוֹ. יא כָּל מַה־שֶּׁבָּרָא הַקָּדוֹשׁ בָּרוּךְ הוּא בְּעוֹלָמוֹ לֹא בְרָאוֹ אֶלָּא לִכְבוֹדוֹ, שֶׁנֶּאֱמַר, כֹּל הַנִּקְרָא בִשְׁמִי וְלִכְבוֹדִי בְּרָאתִיו, יְצַרְתִּיו אַף עֲשִׂיתִיו, וְאוֹמֵר, יהוה | יִמְלֹךְ לְעֹלָם וָעֶד.

רַבִּי חֲנַנְיָא בֶּן־עֲקַשְׁיָא אוֹמֵר, רָצָה הַקָּדוֹשׁ בָּרוּךְ הוּא לְזַכּוֹת אֶת־יִשְׂרָאֵל, לְפִיכָךְ הִרְבָּה לָהֶם תּוֹרָה וּמִצְוֹת, שֶׁנֶּאֱמַר, יהוה חָפֵץ לְמַעַן צִדְקוֹ, יַגְדִּיל תּוֹרָה וְיַאְדִּיר.

In many congregations, קַדִּישׁ דְּרַבָּנָן on page 34
is said at this point, then עָלֵינוּ on page 520.

for we are shaped by those among whom we live, and we are measured not by what we own but by how we live.

6:10 *Five possessions*: All that exists is God's, for without Him nothing would exist. The emphasis here is on the five ways in which we come to know God through phenomena peculiarly associated with His activity within space and time. The first is Torah, God's word to humanity, His self-revelation, without which we would know little, perhaps nothing, of His nature and will. The second is creation: the universe in its vastness and majesty. The third is Abraham,

blessed be He, declare as His own in His world, and they are: the Torah, heaven and earth, Abraham, Israel and the Temple. How do we know this about the Torah? Because it is written, "The LORD created me at the beginning of His way, as the first of His works in days of old". How do we know it about heaven and earth? Because it is written, "So says the LORD: the heaven is My throne, and the earth is My footstool; what house can you build for Me, and where is the place for My rest?"; and it also says, "How many are Your works, O LORD! You made them all in wisdom; the earth is full of Your possessions". How do we know it about Abraham? Because it is written, "And He blessed him and said, Blessed be Abram of GOD the Most High, owner of heaven and earth". How do we know it about Israel? Because it is written, "Until Your people pass over, O LORD, until this people You acquired pass over"; and it also says, "As for the holy ones who are on earth and for the mighty, all My delight is in them". How do we know it about the Temple? Because it is written, "Your dwelling place which You, LORD, have made; the Temple, O LORD, which Your hands established"; and it also says, "He brought them to His holy realm, the mountain His right hand had acquired". 11. All that the Holy One, blessed be He, created in His world, He created solely for His glory, as it is said, "All that is called by My name, it is for My glory that I created it, formed it and made it"; and it also says, "The LORD shall reign for ever and ever".

Rabbi Chananya ben Akashya said: The Holy One, blessed be He, wanted to confer merit on Israel. That is why He gave them a copious Torah and many commandments, as it is said, "It pleased the LORD, for the sake of [Israel's] righteousness, to make the Torah great and glorious".

In many congregations, the Rabbis' *Kaddish* on page 35
is said at this point, then "It is our duty" on page 521.

---

the one who, responding to GOD's call, left his home and land to travel to an unknown destination and there begin to create a new kind of life. The fourth is Israel, the Jewish people, whose history has consistently defied the usual laws that govern the fate of nations. The fifth is the Temple in Jerusalem, earthly home of the Divine presence. What each of these has in common is that they point to something beyond themselves: they are "signals of transcendence", witnesses to the One who called them into being and lit them with the light of His love.

זמירות לסעודה שלישית

תהלים כג

מִזְמוֹר לְדָוִד, יהוה רֹעִי לֹא אֶחְסָר. בִּנְאוֹת דֶּשֶׁא יַרְבִּיצֵנִי, עַל־מֵי מְנוּחֹת יְנַהֲלֵנִי. נַפְשִׁי יְשׁוֹבֵב, יַנְחֵנִי בְמַעְגְּלֵי־צֶדֶק לְמַעַן שְׁמוֹ. גַּם כִּי־אֵלֵךְ בְּגֵיא צַלְמָוֶת, לֹא־אִירָא רָע כִּי־אַתָּה עִמָּדִי, שִׁבְטְךָ וּמִשְׁעַנְתֶּךָ הֵמָּה יְנַחֲמֻנִי. תַּעֲרֹךְ לְפָנַי שֻׁלְחָן נֶגֶד צֹרְרָי, דִּשַּׁנְתָּ בַשֶּׁמֶן רֹאשִׁי, כּוֹסִי רְוָיָה. אַךְ טוֹב וָחֶסֶד יִרְדְּפוּנִי כָּל־יְמֵי חַיָּי, וְשַׁבְתִּי בְּבֵית יהוה לְאֹרֶךְ יָמִים.

(Mattanah) one reaches the heritage of God (Nachaliel), and from there to the heights (Bamot)".

6:3. *Even a single letter*: Such as the correct text of a verse, which may depend on a single letter. *David and Achitophel* – the poignancy of this passage is that it was Achitophel who urged King David's son Absolom to rebel against him (II Samuel 16). He was therefore a traitor against the king. However, the Sages had a tradition that Psalm 55 was composed by David during Absolom's rebellion, and understood the following verses as referring to Achitophel: "If an enemy were insulting me, I could endure it…But it is you, a man like myself, my companion, my close friend, with whom I once enjoyed sweet fellowship as we walked with the throng at the house of God."

6:6 *Kingship is acquired with thirty attainments*, set out in Mishnah, *Sanhedrin* 2:2–5. *Priesthood is endowed with twenty-four gifts*, derived from Numbers 18:8–32.

THE THIRD SHABBAT MEAL

One of the ways in which Shabbat is honoured is by eating a third meal, *Seudah shlishit*: on weekdays, in Talmudic times, only two meals were eaten. The third meal – often, especially in summer, eaten communally – is a time of great spiritual intensity. The special atmosphere of Shabbat here reaches its climax. We have passed through the Shabbat of creation, the theme of Friday night, and the Shabbat of revelation, the mood of Shabbat

ZEMIROT FOR THE THIRD SHABBAT MEAL

PSALM 23

A psalm of David. The LORD is my shepherd, I shall not want. He makes me lie down in green pastures. He leads me beside the still waters. He refreshes my soul. He guides me in the paths of righteousness for His name's sake. Though I walk through the valley of the shadow of death, I will fear no evil, for You are with me; Your rod and Your staff, they comfort me. You set a table before me in the presence of my enemies; You anoint my head with oil; my cup is filled to overflowing. May goodness and kindness follow me all the days of my life, and may I live in the house of the LORD for evermore.

---

morning. We now enter the Shabbat of redemption, the distantly glimpsed future of a world in which GOD's sovereignty will be recognised by all, and life on earth will recover the harmonies it once had at the dawn of time.

Something of that serenity suffuses the third meal as the sun sinks low on the horizon, sending its slanting rays through the leaves and etching the landscape with red gold. The melodies of the third meal are more meditative, and the words of Torah at the table more inward and profound. Yet there is also the knowledge that this charmed moment is the end of something, and the workday week, with its tensions and hazards, is about to begin. The Hassidim in particular seek to draw out these closing moments as long as possible, as if one could make time itself slow to a standstill. This is a time of spiritual longing, as we reluctantly prepare to leave the world-that-ought-to-be for the testing reality of the world-that-is.

Psalm 23: One of the most sublime passages in all religious literature: a poetic masterpiece – a mere 57 words long – of trust in GOD's gentle care. In the first half, the psalmist sees himself as a sheep of GOD's flock, vulnerable yet safe under the shepherd's protective eye. The tone of serenity is conveyed by a series of pastoral images: "green pastures", "still waters", and *ma'aglei tzedek*, "right (i.e. safe) paths".

The mood then quickens. The psalmist speaks of "the valley of the shadow of death" (or "a valley of deep darkness"), perhaps a crevice in the rocks where the

ידיד נפש

יְדִיד נֶפֶשׁ אָב הָרַחֲמָן, מְשֹׁךְ עַבְדְּךָ אֶל רְצוֹנֶךָ,
יָרוּץ עַבְדְּךָ כְּמוֹ אַיָּל, יִשְׁתַּחֲוֶה אֶל מוּל הֲדָרֶךָ,
יֶעֱרַב לוֹ יְדִידוּתֶיךָ, מִנֹּפֶת צוּף וְכָל טָעַם.

הָדוּר, נָאֶה זִיו, הָעוֹלָם, נַפְשִׁי חוֹלַת אַהֲבָתֶךָ,
אָנָּא, אֵל נָא, רְפָא נָא לָהּ, בְּהַרְאוֹת לָהּ נֹעַם זִיוֶךָ,
אָז תִּתְחַזֵּק וְתִתְרַפֵּא, וְהָיְתָה לָּהּ שִׂמְחַת עוֹלָם.

וָתִיק, יֶהֱמוּ נָא רַחֲמֶיךָ, וְחוּסָה נָּא עַל בֵּן אֲהוּבֶךָ,
כִּי זֶה כַּמֶּה נִכְסֹף נִכְסַפְתִּי, לִרְאוֹת בְּתִפְאֶרֶת עֻזֶּךָ,
אֵלֶּה חָמְדָה לִבִּי, וְחוּסָה נָּא וְאַל תִּתְעַלָּם.

הִגָּלֶה נָא, וּפְרֹשׂ חֲבִיבִי עָלַי, אֶת סֻכַּת שְׁלוֹמֶךָ,
תָּאִיר אֶרֶץ מִכְּבוֹדֶךָ, נָגִילָה וְנִשְׂמְחָה בָךְ.
מַהֵר, אֱהֹב, כִּי בָא מוֹעֵד, וְחָנֵּנוּ כִּימֵי עוֹלָם.

---

sun cannot penetrate and where there may be danger from predators. At this point, the psalm shifts from third to second person as the author turns directly to God, uttering in six simple Hebrew words one of the great declarations of faith: "I will fear no evil, for You are with me."

The metaphor then changes. Now the psalmist is a guest at God's table, his cup of wine filled to overflowing, his head anointed with oil (oil was placed on the heads of honoured guests at banquets: see Ecclesiastes 9:8; Psalm 92:11). Though his enemies are close, they can do him no harm for he is under his host's protection. The last line delivers the unexpected denouement: the place where the poet experiences these rich feelings of safety is the Temple, "the house of the Lord".

YEDID NEFESH

י Beloved of the soul, Father of compassion,
draw Your servant close to Your will.
Like a deer will Your servant run
and fall prostrate before Your beauty.
To him Your love is sweeter
than honey from the comb, than any taste.

ה Glorious, beautiful, radiance of the world,
my soul is sick with love for You.
Please, God, heal her now
by showing her Your tender radiance.
Then she will recover her strength and be healed,
and have everlasting joy.

ו Ancient of days, let Your mercy be aroused
and have pity on Your beloved child.
How long have I yearned
to see the glory of Your strength.
These things my heart passionately desires –
have pity; do not hide Yourself.

ה Reveal Yourself, my beloved, and spread over me
the tabernacle of Your peace.
Let the earth shine with Your glory,
let us be overjoyed and rejoice in You.
Hurry, beloved, for the appointed time has come,
and be gracious to us as in the times of old.

Said here, towards the end of Shabbat, the psalm has particular force. Often Jews were all too conscious of the dangers that lay ahead as they left the refuge of

תפילת מעריב למוצאי שבת

In some congregations, the following two psalms are said before מַעֲרִיב at the end of שַׁבָּת.

תהלים קמד

לְדָוִד, בָּרוּךְ יהוה צוּרִי, הַמְלַמֵּד יָדַי לַקְרָב, אֶצְבְּעוֹתַי לַמִּלְחָמָה. חַסְדִּי וּמְצוּדָתִי מִשְׂגַּבִּי וּמְפַלְטִי־לִי מָגִנִּי וּבוֹ חָסִיתִי, הָרוֹדֵד עַמִּי תַחְתָּי. יהוה מָה־אָדָם וַתֵּדָעֵהוּ, בֶּן־אֱנוֹשׁ וַתְּחַשְּׁבֵהוּ. אָדָם לַהֶבֶל דָּמָה, יָמָיו כְּצֵל עוֹבֵר. יהוה הַט־שָׁמֶיךָ וְתֵרֵד, גַּע בֶּהָרִים וְיֶעֱשָׁנוּ. בְּרוֹק בָּרָק וּתְפִיצֵם, שְׁלַח חִצֶּיךָ וּתְהֻמֵּם. שְׁלַח יָדֶיךָ מִמָּרוֹם, פְּצֵנִי וְהַצִּילֵנִי מִמַּיִם רַבִּים, מִיַּד בְּנֵי־נֵכָר. אֲשֶׁר־פִּיהֶם דִּבֶּר־שָׁוְא, וִימִינָם יְמִין שָׁקֶר. אֱלֹהִים שִׁיר חָדָשׁ אָשִׁירָה לָּךְ, בְּנֵבֶל עָשׂוֹר אֲזַמְּרָה־לָּךְ. הַנּוֹתֵן תְּשׁוּעָה לַמְּלָכִים, הַפּוֹצֶה אֶת־דָּוִד עַבְדּוֹ מֵחֶרֶב רָעָה. פְּצֵנִי וְהַצִּילֵנִי מִיַּד בְּנֵי־נֵכָר אֲשֶׁר־פִּיהֶם דִּבֶּר־שָׁוְא וִימִינָם יְמִין שָׁקֶר. אֲשֶׁר בָּנֵינוּ כִּנְטִעִים, מְגֻדָּלִים בִּנְעוּרֵיהֶם, בְּנוֹתֵינוּ כְזָוִיֹּת, מְחֻטָּבוֹת תַּבְנִית הֵיכָל. מְזָוֵינוּ מְלֵאִים, מְפִיקִים מִזַּן אֶל־זַן, צֹאונֵנוּ מַאֲלִיפוֹת מְרֻבָּבוֹת בְּחוּצוֹתֵינוּ. אַלּוּפֵינוּ מְסֻבָּלִים אֵין פֶּרֶץ וְאֵין יוֹצֵאת, וְאֵין צְוָחָה בִּרְחֹבֹתֵינוּ. אַשְׁרֵי הָעָם שֶׁכָּכָה לּוֹ, אַשְׁרֵי הָעָם שֶׁיהוה אֱלֹהָיו.

CONCLUSION OF SHABBAT

The end of Shabbat is one of the most intense Jewish experiences of time. According to rabbinic tradition, Adam and Eve, created on the sixth day, sinned and were sentenced to exile from the Garden of Eden. God granted them stay of sentence, allowing them to spend one day, Shabbat itself, in the garden. During that day, say the Sages, the sun did not set. As Shabbat came to an end, and darkness began to fall, the first human beings prepared to leave paradise and enter the world outside with its conflicts and challenges, hazards and fears. Assuring them that He would be with

SERVICE FOR THE CONCLUSION OF SHABBAT

In some congregations, the following two psalms are said before the Evening Service at the end of Shabbat.

PSALM 144

לְדָוִד Of David. Blessed is the LORD, my Rock, who trains my hands for war, my fingers for battle. He is my Benefactor, my Fortress, my Stronghold and my Refuge, my Shield in whom I trust, He who subdues nations under me. LORD, what is man that You care for him, what are mortals that You think of them? Man is no more than a breath, his days like a fleeting shadow. LORD, part Your heavens and come down; touch the mountains so that they pour forth smoke. Flash forth lightning and scatter them; shoot Your arrows and panic them. Reach out Your hand from on high; deliver me and rescue me from the mighty waters, from the hands of strangers, whose every word is worthless, whose right hands are raised in falsehood. To You, GOD, I will sing a new song; to You I will play music on a ten-stringed harp. He who gives salvation to kings, who saved His servant David from the cruel sword: may He deliver me and rescue me from the hands of strangers, whose every word is worthless, whose right hands are raised in falsehood. Then our sons will be like saplings, well-nurtured in their youth. Our daughters will be like pillars carved for a palace. Our barns will be filled with every kind of provision. Our sheep will increase by thousands, even tens of thousands in our fields. Our oxen will draw heavy loads. There will be no breach in the walls, no going into captivity, no cries of distress in our streets. Happy are the people for whom this is so; happy are the people whose GOD is the LORD.

---

them, GOD gave them a gift, the ability to make light: hence our custom of making a blessing over light in the *Havdalah* service.

The story is a parable of Jewish spirituality. Shabbat is our weekly return to the harmony and serenity of the Garden of Eden. As the day ends we, like Adam and Eve, prepare to re-engage with the world – a world often fraught with dangers. We pray to GOD to be with us in the days ahead, to protect us from harm, and to bless the work of our hands.

לְדָוִד *Psalm 144*: As the arrival of Shabbat is greeted with Psalms, so is its departure.

תהלים סז

לַמְנַצֵּחַ בִּנְגִינֹת מִזְמוֹר שִׁיר. אֱלֹהִים יְחָנֵּנוּ וִיבָרְכֵנוּ, יָאֵר פָּנָיו אִתָּנוּ סֶלָה. לָדַעַת בָּאָרֶץ דַּרְכֶּךָ, בְּכָל־גּוֹיִם יְשׁוּעָתֶךָ. יוֹדוּךָ עַמִּים אֱלֹהִים, יוֹדוּךָ עַמִּים כֻּלָּם. יִשְׂמְחוּ וִירַנְּנוּ לְאֻמִּים, כִּי־תִשְׁפֹּט עַמִּים מִישֹׁר, וּלְאֻמִּים בָּאָרֶץ תַּנְחֵם סֶלָה. יוֹדוּךָ עַמִּים אֱלֹהִים, יוֹדוּךָ עַמִּים כֻּלָּם. אֶרֶץ נָתְנָה יְבוּלָהּ, יְבָרְכֵנוּ אֱלֹהִים אֱלֹהֵינוּ. יְבָרְכֵנוּ אֱלֹהִים, וְיִירְאוּ אוֹתוֹ כָּל־אַפְסֵי־אָרֶץ.

Turn to page 202 for מַעֲרִיב and after the עֲמִידָה, continue here.

If a יום טוב occurs during the week before the coming Shabbat, the Leader says קַדִּישׁ תִּתְקַבַּל on page 586 and the service continues with וְיִתֶּן־לְךָ on page 588. On תִּשְׁעָה בְּאָב, the service then continues with the reading of מְגִלַּת אֵיכָה. This is followed by וְאַתָּה קָדוֹשׁ on page 582. On פּוּרִים, it continues with the reading of מְגִלַּת אֶסְתֵּר. This is followed by וְאַתָּה קָדוֹשׁ.

The Leader says חֲצִי קַדִּישׁ.

Leader:

יִתְגַּדַּל וְיִתְקַדַּשׁ שְׁמֵהּ רַבָּא. (Cong. אָמֵן) בְּעָלְמָא דִּי־בְרָא כִרְעוּתֵהּ. וְיַמְלִיךְ מַלְכוּתֵהּ, בְּחַיֵּיכוֹן וּבְיוֹמֵיכוֹן וּבְחַיֵּי דְּכָל־בֵּית יִשְׂרָאֵל, בַּעֲגָלָא וּבִזְמַן קָרִיב. וְאִמְרוּ אָמֵן. (Cong. אָמֵן)

All:

יְהֵא שְׁמֵהּ רַבָּא מְבָרַךְ לְעָלַם וּלְעָלְמֵי עָלְמַיָּא.

Leader:

יִתְבָּרַךְ וְיִשְׁתַּבַּח וְיִתְפָּאַר וְיִתְרוֹמַם וְיִתְנַשֵּׂא וְיִתְהַדַּר וְיִתְעַלֶּה וְיִתְהַלַּל שְׁמֵהּ דְּקֻדְשָׁא בְּרִיךְ הוּא (Cong. בְּרִיךְ הוּא) לְעֵלָּא (Between רֹאשׁ הַשָּׁנָה and יוֹם כִּפּוּר add לְעֵלָּא) מִן־כָּל־בִּרְכָתָא

Psalm 144 speaks with confidence about facing the battles that may lie ahead, and the blessings, human and material, that come from hard work. This is the song of a people who, trusting in God, face the future without fear.

לַמְנַצֵּחַ *Psalm 67*: A psalm of thanksgiv-

PSALM 67

לַמְנַצֵּח For the director of music. With stringed instruments. A psalm. A song. May God be gracious to us and bless us. May He make His face shine on us, Selah. Then will Your way be known on earth, Your salvation among all the nations. Let the peoples praise You, God; let all peoples praise You. Let nations rejoice and sing for joy, for You judge the peoples with equity, and guide the nations of the earth, Selah. Let the peoples praise You, God; let all peoples praise You. The earth has yielded its harvest. May God, our God, bless us. God will bless us, and all the ends of the earth will fear Him.

Turn to page 203 for the Evening Service and after the *Amidah*, continue here.
If a Festival occurs on a weekday during the week before the coming Shabbat, the Leader says full *Kaddish* on page 587, and the service continues with "May God give you" on page 589. On the Ninth of Av, the service then continues with the reading of the Book of Lamentations. This is followed by "You are the holy One" on page 583. On Purim, it continues with the reading of the Book of Esther. This is followed by "You are the holy One".

The Leader says half-*Kaddish*.

Leader:

יִתְגַּדַּל Magnified and sanctified may His great name be, in the world He created by His will. May He establish His kingdom in your lifetime and in your days, and in the lifetime of all the House of Israel, swiftly and soon – and say: Amen.

All:

May His great name be blessed for ever and all time.

Leader:

Blessed and praised, glorified and exalted, raised and honoured, uplifted and lauded be the name of the Holy One, blessed be He, (between

---

ing whose key phrase is "the earth has yielded its harvest". The second verse uses language reminiscent of the Priestly blessings. The word "earth" appears four times in a variety of senses, suggesting that when we do God's will on earth, the earth yields its blessings with the result that God is recognised by all nations of the earth. As we prepare to meet the time that recalls Adam's exile from Eden, we do so in a spirit directly opposite to the mood that prevailed then. Then it was said: "Cursed be the ground because of you." Now we pray for it to be blessed.

וְשִׁירָתָא תֻּשְׁבְּחָתָא וְנֶחֱמָתָא, דַּאֲמִירָן בְּעָלְמָא, וְאִמְרוּ אָמֵן. (Cong. אָמֵן)

In a house of mourning during the week of שִׁבְעָה, omit this verse and continue with יֹשֵׁב בְּסֵתֶר below.

וִיהִי נֹעַם אֲדֹנָי אֱלֹהֵינוּ עָלֵינוּ, וּמַעֲשֵׂה יָדֵינוּ כּוֹנְנָה עָלֵינוּ, וּמַעֲשֵׂה יָדֵינוּ כּוֹנְנֵהוּ.

תהלים צא

יֹשֵׁב בְּסֵתֶר עֶלְיוֹן, בְּצֵל שַׁדַּי יִתְלוֹנָן. אֹמַר לַיהוה מַחְסִי וּמְצוּדָתִי, אֱלֹהַי אֶבְטַח־בּוֹ. כִּי הוּא יַצִּילְךָ מִפַּח יָקוּשׁ, מִדֶּבֶר הַוּוֹת. בְּאֶבְרָתוֹ יָסֶךְ לָךְ, וְתַחַת כְּנָפָיו תֶּחְסֶה, צִנָּה וְסֹחֵרָה אֲמִתּוֹ. לֹא־תִירָא מִפַּחַד לָיְלָה, מֵחֵץ יָעוּף יוֹמָם. מִדֶּבֶר בָּאֹפֶל יַהֲלֹךְ, מִקֶּטֶב יָשׁוּד צָהֳרָיִם. יִפֹּל מִצִּדְּךָ אֶלֶף, וּרְבָבָה מִימִינֶךָ, אֵלֶיךָ לֹא יִגָּשׁ. רַק בְּעֵינֶיךָ תַבִּיט, וְשִׁלֻּמַת רְשָׁעִים תִּרְאֶה. כִּי־אַתָּה יהוה מַחְסִי, עֶלְיוֹן שַׂמְתָּ מְעוֹנֶךָ. לֹא־תְאֻנֶּה אֵלֶיךָ רָעָה, וְנֶגַע לֹא־יִקְרַב בְּאָהֳלֶךָ. כִּי מַלְאָכָיו יְצַוֶּה־לָּךְ, לִשְׁמָרְךָ בְּכָל־דְּרָכֶיךָ. עַל־כַּפַּיִם יִשָּׂאוּנְךָ, פֶּן תִּגֹּף בָּאֶבֶן רַגְלֶךָ. עַל־שַׁחַל וָפֶתֶן תִּדְרֹךְ, תִּרְמֹס כְּפִיר וְתַנִּין. כִּי בִי חָשַׁק וַאֲפַלְּטֵהוּ, אֲשַׂגְּבֵהוּ כִּי־יָדַע שְׁמִי. יִקְרָאֵנִי וְאֶעֱנֵהוּ, עִמּוֹ אָנֹכִי בְצָרָה, אֲחַלְּצֵהוּ וַאֲכַבְּדֵהוּ. ◄ אֹרֶךְ יָמִים אַשְׂבִּיעֵהוּ, וְאַרְאֵהוּ בִּישׁוּעָתִי. אֹרֶךְ יָמִים אַשְׂבִּיעֵהוּ, וְאַרְאֵהוּ בִּישׁוּעָתִי.

The words in bold type are said aloud together by the Leader and Congregation.

◄ וְאַתָּה קָדוֹשׁ יוֹשֵׁב תְּהִלּוֹת יִשְׂרָאֵל. וְקָרָא זֶה אֶל־זֶה

וִיהִי נֹעַם *May the pleasantness of the* L*ORD*: Psalm 91 which follows immediately is known as the Psalm of Blessing and is the most famous of prayers for deliverance from harm. It is said at the end of Shabbat as a prayer for GOD's protection against the dangers that may lie ahead in the coming week. It is prefaced by the last verse of the previous psalm. According to tradition, this was the blessing Moses gave to those who had helped build the sanctuary, adding: "May the Divine presence rest in the work of your hands". Said here at the begin-

Rosh Hashanah and Yom Kippur add 'well') beyond any blessing, song, praise and consolation uttered in the world – and say: Amen.

In a house of mourning during the week of *shivah*, omit this verse and continue with Psalm 91 below.

וִיהִי נֹעַם May the pleasantness of the LORD our GOD be upon us. Establish for us the work of our hands, O establish the work of our hands.

PSALM 91

יֹשֵׁב בְּסֵתֶר He who lives in the shelter of the Most High dwells in the shadow of the Almighty. I say of the LORD, my Refuge and Stronghold, my GOD in whom I trust, that He will save you from the fowler's snare and the deadly pestilence. With His pinions He will cover you, and beneath His wings you will find shelter; His faithfulness is an encircling shield. You need not fear terror by night, nor the arrow that flies by day; not the pestilence that stalks in darkness, nor the plague that ravages at noon. A thousand may fall at your side, ten thousand at your right hand, but it will not come near you. You will only look with your eyes and see the punishment of the wicked. Because you said "The LORD is my refuge", taking the Most High as your shelter, no harm will befall you, no plague come near your tent, for He will command His angels about you, to guard you in all your ways. They will lift you in their hands, lest your foot stumble on a stone. You will tread on lions and vipers, you will trample on young lions and snakes. [GOD says:] "Because he loves Me, I will rescue him; I will protect him, because he acknowledges My name. When he calls on Me, I will answer him, I will be with him in distress, I will deliver him and bring him honour. ➜ With long life I will satisfy him, and show him My salvation. With long life I will satisfy him, and show him My salvation."

The words in bold type are said aloud together by the Leader and Congregation.

וְאַתָּה קָדוֹשׁ ➜ You are the Holy One, enthroned on the praises of Israel.

---

ning of the workday week, it is a prayer that GOD may send His blessings for our labours.

This and the following section are not said in a week in which a Festival falls, because we do not then face a full working week, and because the merit of the coming Festival itself is an augury of Divine protection.

וְאַתָּה קָדוֹשׁ *You are the Holy One*: This prayer, with its parallels in the weekday morning and Shabbat afternoon services, was usually associated with periods of

וְאָמַר, **קָדוֹשׁ, קָדוֹשׁ, קָדוֹשׁ יהוה צְבָאוֹת, מְלֹא כָל הָאָרֶץ כְּבוֹדוֹ.** וּמְקַבְּלִין דֵּין מִן דֵּין וְאָמְרִין, קַדִּישׁ בִּשְׁמֵי מְרוֹמָא עִלָּאָה בֵּית שְׁכִינְתֵּהּ, קַדִּישׁ עַל אַרְעָא עוֹבַד גְּבוּרְתֵּהּ, קַדִּישׁ לְעָלַם וּלְעָלְמֵי עָלְמַיָּא, יהוה צְבָאוֹת, מַלְיָא כָל־אַרְעָא זִיו יְקָרֵהּ. ← וַתִּשָּׂאֵנִי רוּחַ, וָאֶשְׁמַע אַחֲרַי קוֹל רַעַשׁ גָּדוֹל, **בָּרוּךְ כְּבוֹד יהוה מִמְּקוֹמוֹ.** וּנְטָלַתְנִי רוּחָא, וּשְׁמַעִית בַּתְרַי קָל זִיעַ סַגִּיא דִּמְשַׁבְּחִין וְאָמְרִין, בְּרִיךְ יְקָרָא דַיי מֵאֲתַר בֵּית שְׁכִינְתֵּהּ. **יהוה יִמְלֹךְ לְעֹלָם וָעֶד.** יהוה מַלְכוּתֵהּ קָאֵם לְעָלַם וּלְעָלְמֵי עָלְמַיָּא. יהוה אֱלֹהֵי אַבְרָהָם יִצְחָק וְיִשְׂרָאֵל אֲבוֹתֵינוּ, שָׁמְרָה זֹּאת לְעוֹלָם, לְיֵצֶר מַחְשְׁבוֹת לְבַב עַמֶּךָ, וְהָכֵן לְבָבָם אֵלֶיךָ. וְהוּא רַחוּם, יְכַפֵּר עָוֹן וְלֹא יַשְׁחִית, וְהִרְבָּה לְהָשִׁיב אַפּוֹ, וְלֹא יָעִיר כָּל־חֲמָתוֹ. כִּי אַתָּה אֲדֹנָי טוֹב וְסַלָּח, וְרַב חֶסֶד לְכָל־קֹרְאֶיךָ. צִדְקָתְךָ צֶדֶק לְעוֹלָם, וְתוֹרָתְךָ אֱמֶת. תִּתֵּן אֱמֶת לְיַעֲקֹב, חֶסֶד לְאַבְרָהָם, אֲשֶׁר נִשְׁבַּעְתָּ לַאֲבֹתֵינוּ מִימֵי קֶדֶם. בָּרוּךְ אֲדֹנָי יוֹם יוֹם יַעֲמָס־לָנוּ, הָאֵל יְשׁוּעָתֵנוּ סֶלָה. יהוה צְבָאוֹת עִמָּנוּ, מִשְׂגָּב לָנוּ אֱלֹהֵי יַעֲקֹב סֶלָה. יהוה צְבָאוֹת, אַשְׁרֵי אָדָם בֹּטֵחַ בָּךְ. יהוה הוֹשִׁיעָה, הַמֶּלֶךְ יַעֲנֵנוּ בְיוֹם קָרְאֵנוּ. בָּרוּךְ אֱלֹהֵינוּ שֶׁבְּרָאָנוּ לִכְבוֹדוֹ, וְהִבְדִּילָנוּ מִן הַתּוֹעִים, וְנָתַן לָנוּ תּוֹרַת אֱמֶת, וְחַיֵּי עוֹלָם נָטַע בְּתוֹכֵנוּ. הוּא יִפְתַּח לִבֵּנוּ בְּתוֹרָתוֹ, וְיָשֵׂם בְּלִבֵּנוּ אַהֲבָתוֹ וְיִרְאָתוֹ וְלַעֲשׂוֹת רְצוֹנוֹ וּלְעָבְדוֹ בְּלֵבָב שָׁלֵם, לְמַעַן לֹא נִיגַע לָרִיק, וְלֹא נֵלֵד לַבֶּהָלָה. יְהִי רָצוֹן מִלְּפָנֶיךָ יהוה אֱלֹהֵינוּ וֵאלֹהֵי אֲבוֹתֵינוּ, שֶׁנִּשְׁמֹר חֻקֶּיךָ בָּעוֹלָם הַזֶּה, וְנִזְכֶּה וְנִחְיֶה וְנִרְאֶה וְנִירַשׁ טוֹבָה וּבְרָכָה לִשְׁנֵי יְמוֹת הַמָּשִׁיחַ וּלְחַיֵּי הָעוֹלָם הַבָּא. לְמַעַן יְזַמֶּרְךָ כָבוֹד וְלֹא יִדֹּם, יהוה אֱלֹהַי לְעוֹלָם

And (the angels) call to one another, saying, "**Holy, holy, holy is the Lord of hosts. The whole earth is full of His glory.**" And they receive permission from one another, saying: "Holy in the highest heavens, home of His presence; holy on earth, the work of His strength; holy for ever and all time is the Lord of hosts; the whole earth is full of His radiant glory." ➔ Then a wind lifted me up and I heard behind me the sound of a great noise, saying, "**Blessed is the Lord's glory from His place.**" Then a wind lifted me up and I heard behind me the sound of a great tempest of those who uttered praise, saying, "Blessed is the Lord's glory from the place of the home of His Presence." **The Lord shall reign for ever and all time.** The Lord's kingdom is established for ever and all time. Lord, God of Abraham, Isaac and Israel, our ancestors, may You keep this for ever so that it forms the thoughts in Your people's heart, and directs their heart towards You. He is compassionate. He forgives iniquity and does not destroy. Repeatedly He suppresses His anger, not rousing His full wrath. For You, my Lord, are good and forgiving, abundantly kind to all who call on You. Your righteousness is eternally righteous, and Your Torah is truth. Grant truth to Jacob, lovingkindness to Abraham, as You promised our ancestors in ancient times. Blessed is the Lord who day after day bears our burden, for God is our salvation, Selah! The Lord of hosts is with us; the God of Jacob is our refuge, Selah! Lord of hosts, happy is the one who trusts in You. Lord, save. May the King answer us on the day we call. Blessed is our God who created us for His glory, separating us from those who go astray; who gave us the Torah of truth, planting within us eternal life. May He open our heart to His Torah, imbuing our heart with the love and awe of Him, that we may do His will and serve Him with a perfect heart, so that we neither toil in vain nor give birth to confusion. May it be Your will, O Lord our God and God of our ancestors, that we keep Your laws in this world, and thus be worthy to live, see and inherit goodness and blessing in the messianic age and in the life of the World to Come, so that my soul may sing to You and not be silent. Lord, my God, for ever I will

communal study. Its presence here may hark back to a time when it was customary to dedicate time to a period of study at the end of the Shabbat.

אוֹדֶךָּ. בָּרוּךְ הַגֶּבֶר אֲשֶׁר יִבְטַח בַּיהוה, וְהָיָה יהוה מִבְטַחוֹ.
בִּטְחוּ בַיהוה עֲדֵי־עַד, כִּי בְּיָהּ יהוה צוּר עוֹלָמִים. וְיִבְטְחוּ
בְךָ יוֹדְעֵי שְׁמֶךָ, כִּי לֹא עָזַבְתָּ דֹרְשֶׁיךָ, יהוה. ← יהוה חָפֵץ
לְמַעַן צִדְקוֹ, יַגְדִּיל תּוֹרָה וְיַאְדִּיר.

The Leader says קַדִּישׁ תִּתְקַבַּל.

קדיש תתקבל

Leader:

יִתְגַּדַּל וְיִתְקַדַּשׁ שְׁמֵהּ רַבָּא. (Cong. אָמֵן) בְּעָלְמָא דִּי־בְרָא
כִרְעוּתֵהּ. וְיַמְלִיךְ מַלְכוּתֵהּ, בְּחַיֵּיכוֹן וּבְיוֹמֵיכוֹן וּבְחַיֵּי דִי־כָל־
בֵּית יִשְׂרָאֵל, בַּעֲגָלָא וּבִזְמַן קָרִיב. וְאִמְרוּ אָמֵן. (Cong. אָמֵן)

All:

יְהֵא שְׁמֵהּ רַבָּא מְבָרַךְ לְעָלַם וּלְעָלְמֵי עָלְמַיָּא.

Leader:

יִתְבָּרַךְ וְיִשְׁתַּבַּח וְיִתְפָּאַר וְיִתְרוֹמַם וְיִתְנַשֵּׂא וְיִתְהַדַּר
וְיִתְעַלֶּה וְיִתְהַלָּל שְׁמֵהּ דִּי־קֻדְשָׁא בְּרִיךְ הוּא (Cong. בְּרִיךְ הוּא)
לְעֵלָּא (Between רֹאשׁ הַשָּׁנָה and יוֹם כִּפּוּר add לְעֵלָּא) מִן־כָּל־בִּרְכָתָא
וְשִׁירָתָא תֻּשְׁבְּחָתָא וְנֶחֱמָתָא, דִּי־אֲמִירָן בְּעָלְמָא. וְאִמְרוּ
אָמֵן. (Cong. אָמֵן)

The following line is not said on פּוּרִים and תִּשְׁעָה בְּאָב:

תִּתְקַבַּל צְלוֹתְהוֹן וּבָעוּתְהוֹן דִּי־כָל־יִשְׂרָאֵל קֳדָם אֲבוּהוֹן
דִּי בִשְׁמַיָּא. וְאִמְרוּ אָמֵן. (Cong. אָמֵן)

יְהֵא שְׁלָמָא רַבָּא מִן־שְׁמַיָּא, וְחַיִּים עָלֵינוּ וְעַל־כָּל־יִשְׂרָאֵל.
וְאִמְרוּ אָמֵן. (Cong. אָמֵן)

Bow, take three steps back, then bow, first left, then right, then centre, while saying:

עֹשֶׂה שָׁלוֹם בִּמְרוֹמָיו, הוּא יַעֲשֶׂה שָׁלוֹם עָלֵינוּ, וְעַל־כָּל־
יִשְׂרָאֵל. וְאִמְרוּ אָמֵן. (Cong. אָמֵן)

thank You. Blessed is the man who trusts in the LORD, whose trust is in the LORD alone. Trust in the LORD for evermore, for GOD the LORD is an everlasting Rock. Those who know Your name trust in You, for You, LORD, do not forsake those who seek You. ➔ The LORD desired, for the sake of Israel's merit, to make the Torah great and glorious.

The Leader says full *Kaddish*.

FULL KADDISH

Leader:

יִתְגַּדַּל Magnified and sanctified may His great name be, in the world He created by His will. May He establish His kingdom in your lifetime and in your days, and in the lifetime of all the House of Israel, swiftly and soon – and say: Amen.

All:

May His great name be blessed for ever and all time.

Leader:

Blessed and praised, glorified and exalted, raised and honoured, uplifted and lauded be the name of the Holy One, blessed be He, (between Rosh Hashanah and Yom Kippur add 'well') beyond any blessing, song, praise and consolation uttered in the world – and say: Amen.

The following line is not said on Purim and the Ninth of Av:

May the prayers and pleas of all Israel be accepted by their Father in heaven – and say: Amen.

May there be great peace from heaven, and life for us and all Israel – and say: Amen.

Bow, take three steps back, then bow, first left, then right, then centre, while saying:

May He who makes peace in His high places, make peace for us and all Israel – and say: Amen.

Between פֶּסַח and שָׁבֻעוֹת, the עֹמֶר is counted here on page 238.

On חֲנֻכָּה, the lights are lit at this point on page 732.

If תִּשְׁעָה בְּאָב falls on Saturday night, the following prayers are omitted. Turn to עָלֵינוּ on page 598.

פסוקי ברכה

וְיִתֶּן־לְךָ הָאֱלֹהִים מִטַּל הַשָּׁמַיִם וּמִשְׁמַנֵּי הָאָרֶץ, וְרֹב דָּגָן וְתִירֹשׁ. יַעַבְדוּךָ עַמִּים, וְיִשְׁתַּחֲווּ לְךָ לְאֻמִּים, הֱוֵה גְבִיר לְאַחֶיךָ, וְיִשְׁתַּחֲווּ לְךָ בְּנֵי אִמֶּךָ, אֹרְרֶיךָ אָרוּר, וּמְבָרְכֶיךָ בָּרוּךְ. וְאֵל שַׁדַּי יְבָרֵךְ אֹתְךָ וְיַפְרְךָ וְיַרְבֶּךָ, וְהָיִיתָ לִקְהַל עַמִּים. וְיִתֶּן־לְךָ אֶת־בִּרְכַּת אַבְרָהָם, לְךָ וּלְזַרְעֲךָ אִתָּךְ, לְרִשְׁתְּךָ אֶת־אֶרֶץ מְגֻרֶיךָ, אֲשֶׁר־נָתַן אֱלֹהִים לְאַבְרָהָם. מֵאֵל אָבִיךָ וְיַעְזְרֶךָּ, וְאֵת שַׁדַּי וִיבָרְכֶךָּ, בִּרְכֹת שָׁמַיִם מֵעָל, בִּרְכֹת תְּהוֹם רֹבֶצֶת תָּחַת, בִּרְכֹת שָׁדַיִם וָרָחַם. בִּרְכֹת אָבִיךָ גָּבְרוּ עַל־בִּרְכֹת הוֹרַי, עַד־תַּאֲוַת גִּבְעֹת עוֹלָם, תִּהְיֶיןָ לְרֹאשׁ יוֹסֵף, וּלְקָדְקֹד נְזִיר אֶחָיו. וַאֲהֵבְךָ וּבֵרַכְךָ וְהִרְבֶּךָ, וּבֵרַךְ פְּרִי־בִטְנְךָ וּפְרִי־אַדְמָתֶךָ, דְּגָנְךָ וְתִירֹשְׁךָ וְיִצְהָרֶךָ, שְׁגַר אֲלָפֶיךָ וְעַשְׁתְּרֹת צֹאנֶךָ, עַל הָאֲדָמָה אֲשֶׁר־נִשְׁבַּע לַאֲבֹתֶיךָ לָתֶת לָךְ. בָּרוּךְ תִּהְיֶה מִכָּל־הָעַמִּים, לֹא־יִהְיֶה בְךָ עָקָר וַעֲקָרָה, וּבִבְהֶמְתֶּךָ. וְהֵסִיר יהוה מִמְּךָ כָּל־חֹלִי, וְכָל־מַדְוֵי מִצְרַיִם הָרָעִים אֲשֶׁר יָדַעְתָּ, לֹא יְשִׂימָם בָּךְ, וּנְתָנָם בְּכָל־שֹׂנְאֶיךָ.

הַמַּלְאָךְ הַגֹּאֵל אֹתִי מִכָּל־רָע יְבָרֵךְ אֶת־הַנְּעָרִים וְיִקָּרֵא בָהֶם שְׁמִי, וְשֵׁם אֲבֹתַי אַבְרָהָם וְיִצְחָק, וְיִדְגּוּ לָרֹב בְּקֶרֶב

פְּסוּקֵי בְּרָכָה *Biblical Verses of Blessing.* Setting out on a journey is a time to seek blessing and Divine protection through the challenges that lie ahead, hence this long series of verses from Tanach, including many of the blessings recorded

Between Pesach and Shavuot, the *Omer* is counted here on page 239.
On Chanukah, the lights are lit at this point on page 733.
If the Ninth of Av falls on Saturday night, the following prayers are omitted. Turn to "It is our duty" on page 599.

BIBLICAL VERSES OF BLESSING

וְיִתֶּן־לְךָ May God give you dew from heaven and the richness of the earth, and corn and wine in plenty. May peoples serve you and nations bow down to you. Be lord over your brothers, and may your mother's sons bow down to you. A curse on those who curse you, but a blessing on those who bless you. May God Almighty bless you; may He make you fruitful and numerous until you become an assembly of peoples. May He give you and your descendants the blessing of Abraham, that you may possess the land where you are now staying, the land God gave to Abraham. This comes from the God of your father – may He help you – and from the Almighty – may He bless you with blessings of the heaven above and the blessings of the deep that lies below, the blessings of breast and womb. The blessings of your father surpass the blessings of my fathers to the bounds of the endless hills. May they rest on the head of Joseph, on the brow of the prince among his brothers. He will love you and bless you and increase your numbers. He will bless the fruit of your womb and the fruit of your land: your corn, your wine and oil, the calves of your herds and the lambs of your flocks, in the land He swore to your fathers to give you. You will be blessed more than any other people. None of your men or women will be childless, nor any of your livestock without young. The Lord will keep you free from any disease. He will not inflict on you the terrible diseases you knew in Egypt, but He will inflict them on those who hate you.

הַמַּלְאָךְ May the angel who rescued me from all harm, bless these boys. May they be called by my name and the names of my fathers Abraham and Isaac, and may they increase greatly on the earth. The Lord your

---

in the Mosaic books. They are clustered around the themes of blessing, redemption and salvation; rescue and transformation; peace and consolation. Together they emphasise that time is a journey and we are about to begin the next stage,

הָאָרֶץ. יהוה אֱלֹהֵיכֶם הִרְבָּה אֶתְכֶם, וְהִנְּכֶם הַיּוֹם כְּכוֹכְבֵי הַשָּׁמַיִם לָרֹב. יהוה אֱלֹהֵי אֲבוֹתֵיכֶם יֹסֵף עֲלֵיכֶם כָּכֶם אֶלֶף פְּעָמִים, וִיבָרֵךְ אֶתְכֶם כַּאֲשֶׁר דִּבֶּר לָכֶם. בָּרוּךְ אַתָּה בָּעִיר, וּבָרוּךְ אַתָּה בַּשָּׂדֶה. בָּרוּךְ אַתָּה בְּבֹאֶךָ, וּבָרוּךְ אַתָּה בְּצֵאתֶךָ. בָּרוּךְ טַנְאֲךָ וּמִשְׁאַרְתֶּךָ. בָּרוּךְ פְּרִי־בִטְנְךָ וּפְרִי־אַדְמָתֶךָ וּפְרִי־בְהֶמְתֶּךָ, שְׁגַר אֲלָפֶיךָ וְעַשְׁתְּרוֹת צֹאנֶךָ. יְצַו יהוה אִתְּךָ אֶת־הַבְּרָכָה בַּאֲסָמֶיךָ וּבְכֹל מִשְׁלַח יָדֶךָ, וּבֵרַכְךָ בָּאָרֶץ אֲשֶׁר־יהוה אֱלֹהֶיךָ נֹתֵן לָךְ. יִפְתַּח יהוה לְךָ אֶת־אוֹצָרוֹ הַטּוֹב, אֶת־הַשָּׁמַיִם, לָתֵת מְטַר־אַרְצְךָ בְּעִתּוֹ, וּלְבָרֵךְ אֵת כָּל־מַעֲשֵׂה יָדֶךָ, וְהִלְוִיתָ גּוֹיִם רַבִּים, וְאַתָּה לֹא תִלְוֶה. כִּי־יהוה אֱלֹהֶיךָ בֵּרַכְךָ כַּאֲשֶׁר דִּבֶּר לָךְ, וְהַעֲבַטְתָּ גּוֹיִם רַבִּים, וְאַתָּה לֹא תַעֲבֹט, וּמָשַׁלְתָּ בְּגוֹיִם רַבִּים, וּבְךָ לֹא יִמְשֹׁלוּ. אַשְׁרֶיךָ יִשְׂרָאֵל, מִי כָמוֹךָ, עַם נוֹשַׁע בַּיהוה, מָגֵן עֶזְרֶךָ, וַאֲשֶׁר־חֶרֶב גַּאֲוָתֶךָ, וְיִכָּחֲשׁוּ אֹיְבֶיךָ לָךְ, וְאַתָּה עַל־בָּמוֹתֵימוֹ תִדְרֹךְ.

גאולה

מָחִיתִי כָעָב פְּשָׁעֶיךָ וְכֶעָנָן חַטֹּאותֶיךָ, שׁוּבָה אֵלַי כִּי גְאַלְתִּיךָ. רָנּוּ שָׁמַיִם, כִּי־עָשָׂה יהוה, הָרִיעוּ תַּחְתִּיּוֹת אָרֶץ, פִּצְחוּ הָרִים רִנָּה, יַעַר וְכָל־עֵץ בּוֹ, כִּי־גָאַל יהוה יַעֲקֹב וּבְיִשְׂרָאֵל יִתְפָּאָר. גֹּאֲלֵנוּ יהוה צְבָאוֹת שְׁמוֹ, קְדוֹשׁ יִשְׂרָאֵל.

ישועה

יִשְׂרָאֵל נוֹשַׁע בַּיהוה תְּשׁוּעַת עוֹלָמִים, לֹא־תֵבֹשׁוּ וְלֹא־תִכָּלְמוּ עַד־עוֹלְמֵי עַד. וַאֲכַלְתֶּם אָכוֹל וְשָׂבוֹעַ, וְהִלַּלְתֶּם אֶת־שֵׁם יהוה אֱלֹהֵיכֶם אֲשֶׁר־עָשָׂה עִמָּכֶם לְהַפְלִיא,

God has increased your numbers so that today you are as many as the stars in the sky. May the Lord, God of your fathers, increase you a thousand times, and bless you as He promised you. You will be blessed in the city, and blessed in the field. You will be blessed when you come in, and blessed when you go out. Your basket and your kneading trough will be blessed. The fruit of your womb will be blessed, and the crops of your land, and the young of your livestock, the calves of your herds and the lambs of your flocks. The Lord will send a blessing on your barns, and on everything you put your hand to. The Lord your God will bless you in the land He is giving you. The Lord will open for you the heavens, the storehouse of His bounty, to send rain on your land in season, and to bless all the work of your hands. You will lend to many nations but will borrow from none. For the Lord your God will bless you as He has promised: you will lend to many nations but will borrow from none. You will rule over many nations, but none will rule over you. Happy are you, Israel! Who is like you, a people saved by the Lord? He is your Shield and Helper and your glorious Sword. Your enemies will cower before you, and you will tread on their high places.

REDEMPTION

מָחִיתִי I have wiped away your transgressions like a cloud, your sins like the morning mist. Return to Me for I have redeemed you. Sing for joy, O heavens, for the Lord has done this; shout aloud, you depths of the earth; burst into song, you mountains, you forests and all your trees, for the Lord has redeemed Jacob, and will glory in Israel. Our Redeemer, Lord of hosts is His name, is the Holy One of Israel.

SALVATION

יִשְׂרָאֵל Israel is saved by the Lord with everlasting salvation. You will never be ashamed or disgraced to time everlasting. You will eat your fill and praise the name of the Lord your God, who has worked wonders for you. Never again shall My people be shamed. Then you will know

---

confident in the knowledge that God is with us. They begin with the blessings of Isaac to Jacob, Jacob to Joseph and his brothers, and Moses' closing addresses to the Israelites in the book of Deuteronomy.

וְלֹא־יֵבֹשׁוּ עַמִּי לְעוֹלָם. וִידַעְתֶּם כִּי בְקֶרֶב יִשְׂרָאֵל אָנִי, וַאֲנִי יהוה אֱלֹהֵיכֶם, וְאֵין עוֹד, וְלֹא־יֵבֹשׁוּ עַמִּי לְעוֹלָם. כִּי־בְשִׂמְחָה תֵצֵאוּ וּבְשָׁלוֹם תּוּבָלוּן, הֶהָרִים וְהַגְּבָעוֹת יִפְצְחוּ לִפְנֵיכֶם רִנָּה, וְכָל־עֲצֵי הַשָּׂדֶה יִמְחֲאוּ־כָף. הִנֵּה אֵל יְשׁוּעָתִי, אֶבְטַח וְלֹא אֶפְחָד, כִּי עָזִּי וְזִמְרָת יָהּ יהוה, וַיְהִי־לִי לִישׁוּעָה. וּשְׁאַבְתֶּם מַיִם בְּשָׂשׂוֹן, מִמַּעַיְנֵי הַיְשׁוּעָה. וַאֲמַרְתֶּם בַּיּוֹם הַהוּא, הוֹדוּ לַיהוה קִרְאוּ בִשְׁמוֹ, הוֹדִיעוּ בָעַמִּים עֲלִילֹתָיו, הַזְכִּירוּ כִּי נִשְׂגָּב שְׁמוֹ. זַמְּרוּ יהוה כִּי גֵאוּת עָשָׂה, מוּדַעַת זֹאת בְּכָל הָאָרֶץ. צַהֲלִי וָרֹנִּי יוֹשֶׁבֶת צִיּוֹן, כִּי־גָדוֹל בְּקִרְבֵּךְ קְדוֹשׁ יִשְׂרָאֵל. וְאָמַר בַּיּוֹם הַהוּא, הִנֵּה אֱלֹהֵינוּ זֶה, קִוִּינוּ לוֹ וְיוֹשִׁיעֵנוּ, זֶה יהוה קִוִּינוּ לוֹ, נָגִילָה וְנִשְׂמְחָה בִּישׁוּעָתוֹ.

דעת השם

בֵּית יַעֲקֹב, לְכוּ וְנֵלְכָה בְּאוֹר יהוה. וְהָיָה אֱמוּנַת עִתֶּיךָ חֹסֶן יְשׁוּעֹת חָכְמַת וָדָעַת, יִרְאַת יהוה הִיא אוֹצָרוֹ. וַיְהִי דָוִד לְכָל־דְּרָכָיו מַשְׂכִּיל, וַיהוה עִמּוֹ.

פדיום

פָּדָה בְשָׁלוֹם נַפְשִׁי מִקְּרָב־לִי, כִּי־בְרַבִּים הָיוּ עִמָּדִי. וַיֹּאמֶר הָעָם אֶל־שָׁאוּל, הֲיוֹנָתָן יָמוּת אֲשֶׁר עָשָׂה הַיְשׁוּעָה הַגְּדוֹלָה הַזֹּאת בְּיִשְׂרָאֵל, חָלִילָה, חַי־יהוה, אִם־יִפֹּל מִשַּׂעֲרַת רֹאשׁוֹ אַרְצָה, כִּי־עִם־אֱלֹהִים עָשָׂה הַיּוֹם הַזֶּה, וַיִּפְדּוּ הָעָם אֶת־יוֹנָתָן וְלֹא־מֵת. וּפְדוּיֵי יהוה יְשֻׁבוּן, וּבָאוּ צִיּוֹן בְּרִנָּה, וְשִׂמְחַת עוֹלָם עַל־רֹאשָׁם, שָׂשׂוֹן וְשִׂמְחָה יַשִּׂיגוּ וְנָסוּ יָגוֹן וַאֲנָחָה.

that I am in the midst of Israel, that I am the LORD your GOD, and there is no other. Never again will My people be shamed. You will go out in joy and be led out in peace. The mountains and hills will burst into song before you, and all the trees of the field will clap their hands. Behold, GOD is my salvation. I will trust and not be afraid. The LORD, the LORD, is my strength and my song. He has become my salvation. With joy you will draw water from the springs of salvation. On that day you will say, "Thank the LORD, proclaim His name, make His deeds known among the nations." Declare that His name is exalted. Sing to the LORD, for He has done glorious things; let this be known throughout the world. Shout aloud and sing for joy, you who dwell in Zion, for great in your midst is the Holy One of Israel. On that day they will say, "See, this is our GOD; we set our hope in Him and He saved us. This is the LORD in whom we hoped; let us rejoice and be glad in His salvation."

KNOWLEDGE OF GOD

בֵּית Come, house of Jacob: let us walk in the light of the LORD. He will be the sure foundation of your times; a rich store of salvation, wisdom and knowledge – the fear of the LORD is a person's treasure. In everything he did, David was successful, for the LORD was with him.

RESCUE

פָּדָה He redeemed my soul in peace from the battle waged against me, for the sake of the many who were with me. The people said to Saul, "Shall Jonathan die – he who has brought about this great deliverance in Israel? Heaven forbid! As surely as the LORD lives, not a hair of his head shall fall to the ground, for he did this today with GOD's help." So the people rescued Jonathan and he did not die. Those redeemed by the LORD shall return; they will enter Zion singing; everlasting joy will crown their heads. Gladness and joy will overtake them, and sorrow and sighing will flee away.

פָּדָה *He redeemed my soul in peace*: There now follow three verses on the theme of redemption, three on transformation of fortune from bad to good, and three on peace. These three verses, according to the Talmud (*Berachot* 55b), should be said to banish fear of misfortune.

הפוך צרה

הָפַכְתָּ מִסְפְּדִי לְמָחוֹל לִי, פִּתַּחְתָּ שַׂקִּי, וַתְּאַזְּרֵנִי שִׂמְחָה. וְלֹא־אָבָה יהוה אֱלֹהֶיךָ לִשְׁמוֹעַ אֶל־בִּלְעָם, וַיַּהֲפֹךְ יהוה אֱלֹהֶיךָ לְּךָ אֶת־הַקְּלָלָה לִבְרָכָה, כִּי אֲהֵבְךָ יהוה אֱלֹהֶיךָ. אָז תִּשְׂמַח בְּתוּלָה בְּמָחוֹל, וּבַחוּרִים וּזְקֵנִים יַחְדָּו, וְהָפַכְתִּי אֶבְלָם לְשָׂשׂוֹן, וְנִחַמְתִּים וְשִׂמַּחְתִּים מִיגוֹנָם.

שלום

בּוֹרֵא נִיב שְׂפָתָיִם, שָׁלוֹם שָׁלוֹם לָרָחוֹק וְלַקָּרוֹב, אָמַר יהוה וּרְפָאתִיו. וְרוּחַ לָבְשָׁה אֶת־עֲמָשַׂי, רֹאשׁ הַשָּׁלִישִׁים, לְךָ דָוִיד וְעִמְּךָ בֶן־יִשַׁי שָׁלוֹם, שָׁלוֹם לְךָ, וְשָׁלוֹם לְעֹזְרֶךָ כִּי עֲזָרְךָ אֱלֹהֶיךָ וַיְקַבְּלֵם דָּוִיד וַיִּתְּנֵם בְּרָאשֵׁי הַגְּדוּד. וַאֲמַרְתֶּם, כֹּה לֶחָי, וְאַתָּה שָׁלוֹם וּבֵיתְךָ שָׁלוֹם וְכֹל אֲשֶׁר־לְךָ שָׁלוֹם. יהוה עֹז לְעַמּוֹ יִתֵּן, יהוה יְבָרֵךְ אֶת עַמּוֹ בַשָּׁלוֹם.

תלמוד בבלי מגילה לא:א'

אָמַר רַבִּי יוֹחָנָן, בְּכָל־מָקוֹם שֶׁאַתָּה מוֹצֵא גְּדֻלָּתוֹ שֶׁל־הַקָּדוֹשׁ בָּרוּךְ הוּא, שָׁם אַתָּה מוֹצֵא עַנְוְתָנוּתוֹ. דָּבָר זֶה כָּתוּב בַּתּוֹרָה, וְשָׁנוּי בַּנְּבִיאִים, וּמְשֻׁלָּשׁ בַּכְּתוּבִים. כָּתוּב בַּתּוֹרָה, כִּי יהוה אֱלֹהֵיכֶם הוּא אֱלֹהֵי הָאֱלֹהִים וַאֲדֹנֵי הָאֲדֹנִים, הָאֵל הַגָּדֹל הַגִּבֹּר וְהַנּוֹרָא אֲשֶׁר לֹא־יִשָּׂא פָנִים וְלֹא יִקַּח שֹׁחַד. וּכְתִיב בַּתְרֵהּ, עֹשֶׂה מִשְׁפַּט יָתוֹם וְאַלְמָנָה, וְאֹהֵב גֵּר לָתֶת לוֹ לֶחֶם וְשִׂמְלָה. שָׁנוּי בַּנְּבִיאִים, דִּכְתִיב, כִּי כֹה אָמַר רָם וְנִשָּׂא שֹׁכֵן עַד וְקָדוֹשׁ שְׁמוֹ, מָרוֹם וְקָדוֹשׁ אֶשְׁכּוֹן, וְאֶת־דַּכָּא וּשְׁפַל־רוּחַ, לְהַחֲיוֹת רוּחַ שְׁפָלִים וּלְהַחֲיוֹת לֵב נִדְכָּאִים. מְשֻׁלָּשׁ בַּכְּתוּבִים, דִּכְתִיב, שִׁירוּ לֵאלֹהִים, זַמְּרוּ שְׁמוֹ, סֹלּוּ לָרֹכֵב בָּעֲרָבוֹת,

TRANSFORMATION OF SUFFERING INTO JOY

הָפַכְתָּ You have turned my sorrow into dancing. You have removed my sackcloth and clothed me with joy. The LORD your GOD refused to listen to Balaam; instead the LORD your GOD turned the curse into a blessing, for the LORD your GOD loves you. Then maidens will dance and be glad; so too will young men and old together; I will turn their mourning into gladness; I will give them comfort and joy instead of sorrow.

PEACE

בּוֹרֵא I create the speech of lips: Peace, peace to those far and near, says the LORD, and I will heal them. Then the spirit came upon Amasai, chief of the captains, and he said: "We are yours, David! We are with you, son of Jesse! Peace, peace to you, and peace to those who help you; for your GOD will help you." Then David received them and made them leaders of his troop. And you shall say: "To life! Peace be to you, peace to your household, and peace to all that is yours!" The LORD will give strength to His people; the LORD will bless His people with peace.

BABYLONIAN TALMUD, MEGILLAH 31A

אָמַר Rabbi Yochanan said: Wherever you find the greatness of the Holy One, blessed be He, there you find His humility. This is written in the Torah, repeated in the Prophets, and stated a third time in the Writings. It is written in the Torah: "For the LORD your GOD is GOD of gods and LORD of lords, the great, mighty and awe-inspiring GOD, who shows no favoritism and accepts no bribe." Immediately afterwards it is written, "He upholds the cause of the orphan and widow, and loves the stranger, giving him food and clothing." It is repeated in the Prophets, as it says: "So says the High and Exalted One, who lives for ever and whose name is Holy: I live in a high and holy place, but also with the contrite and lowly in spirit, to revive the spirit of

---

אָמַר רַבִּי יוֹחָנָן *Rabbi Yochanan said*: A magnificent passage from the Talmud (*Megillah* 31a) telling us to learn from GOD that greatness is humility, and humility greatness. The Creator of all cares for all; the power of powers cares for the powerless. The deeper our compassion, the higher we stand.

בְּיָהּ שְׁמוֹ, וְעִלְזוּ לְפָנָיו. וּכְתִיב בַּתְרֵהּ, אֲבִי יְתוֹמִים וְדַיַּן אַלְמָנוֹת, אֱלֹהִים בִּמְעוֹן קָדְשׁוֹ. יְהִי יהוה אֱלֹהֵינוּ עִמָּנוּ כַּאֲשֶׁר הָיָה עִם־אֲבֹתֵינוּ, אַל־יַעַזְבֵנוּ וְאַל־יִטְּשֵׁנוּ. וְאַתֶּם הַדְּבֵקִים בַּיהוה אֱלֹהֵיכֶם, חַיִּים כֻּלְּכֶם הַיּוֹם. כִּי־נִחַם יהוה צִיּוֹן, נִחַם כָּל־חָרְבֹתֶיהָ, וַיָּשֶׂם מִדְבָּרָהּ כְּעֵדֶן וְעַרְבָתָהּ כְּגַן־יהוה, שָׂשׂוֹן וְשִׂמְחָה יִמָּצֵא בָהּ, תּוֹדָה וְקוֹל זִמְרָה. יהוה חָפֵץ לְמַעַן צִדְקוֹ, יַגְדִּיל תּוֹרָה וְיַאְדִּיר.

תהלים קכח

שִׁיר הַמַּעֲלוֹת, אַשְׁרֵי כָּל־יְרֵא יהוה, הַהֹלֵךְ בִּדְרָכָיו. יְגִיעַ כַּפֶּיךָ כִּי תֹאכֵל, אַשְׁרֶיךָ וְטוֹב לָךְ. אֶשְׁתְּךָ כְּגֶפֶן פֹּרִיָּה בְּיַרְכְּתֵי בֵיתֶךָ, בָּנֶיךָ כִּשְׁתִלֵי זֵיתִים, סָבִיב לְשֻׁלְחָנֶךָ. הִנֵּה כִי־כֵן יְבֹרַךְ גָּבֶר יְרֵא יהוה. ◂ יְבָרֶכְךָ יהוה מִצִּיּוֹן, וּרְאֵה בְּטוּב יְרוּשָׁלָיִם, כֹּל יְמֵי חַיֶּיךָ. וּרְאֵה־בָנִים לְבָנֶיךָ, שָׁלוֹם עַל־יִשְׂרָאֵל.

הבדלה

At the end of a יום טוב falling on a weekday, the blessings for the spices and the flame are omitted. At the end of יום כפור, the blessing for the flame is added.

The Leader takes the cup of wine in his right hand, and says:

בָּרוּךְ אַתָּה יהוה אֱלֹהֵינוּ מֶלֶךְ הָעוֹלָם, בּוֹרֵא פְּרִי הַגָּפֶן.

Putting down the cup, he takes the spice box and says:

בָּרוּךְ אַתָּה יהוה אֱלֹהֵינוּ מֶלֶךְ הָעוֹלָם, בּוֹרֵא מִינֵי בְשָׂמִים.

The blessing over the הַבְדָּלָה candle is recited, following which fingers are held up to the flame to see the reflected light.

בָּרוּךְ אַתָּה יהוה אֱלֹהֵינוּ מֶלֶךְ הָעוֹלָם, בּוֹרֵא מְאוֹרֵי הָאֵשׁ.

שִׁיר הַמַּעֲלוֹת *Psalm 128.* The biblical readings at the end of the service conclude with Psalm 128: a song of praise to the virtues of work.

הַבְדָּלָה *Havdalah*: Just as *Kiddush* is said in the synagogue as well as in the home, so is *Havdalah*. The introductory verses said at home are not recited in the synagogue.

the lowly, and to revive the heart of the contrite." It is stated a third time in the Writings: "Sing to God, make music for His name, extol Him who rides the clouds – God is His name – and exult before Him." Immediately afterwards it is written: "Father of the fatherless and Judge of widows is God in His holy habitation." May the Lord our God be with us, as He was with our ancestors. May He never abandon us or forsake us. You who cleave to the Lord your God are all alive this day. For the Lord will comfort Zion, He will comfort all her ruins; He will make her wilderness like Eden, and her desert like a garden of the Lord. Joy and gladness will be found there, thanksgiving and the sound of singing. It pleased the Lord for the sake of (Israel's) righteousness to make the Torah great and glorious.

PSALM 128

שִׁיר הַמַּעֲלוֹת A song of ascents. Happy are all who fear the Lord, who walk in His ways. When you eat the fruit of your labour, happy and fortunate are you. Your wife shall be like a fruitful vine within your house; your sons like olive saplings around your table. So shall the man who fears the Lord be blessed. ➔ May the Lord bless you from Zion; may you see the good of Jerusalem all the days of your life; and may you live to see your children's children. Peace be on Israel!

HAVDALAH

At the end of a Festival falling on a weekday, the blessings for the spices and the flame are omitted. At the end of Yom Kippur, the blessing for the flame is added.

The Leader takes the cup of wine in his right hand, and says:

Blessed are You, Lord our God, King of the Universe, who creates the fruit of the vine.

Putting down the cup, he takes the spice box and says:

Blessed are You, Lord our God, King of the Universe, who creates the various spices.

The blessing over the *Havdalah* candle is recited, following which fingers are held up to the flame to see the reflected light.

Blessed are You, Lord our God, King of the Universe, who creates the lights of fire.

He lifts the cup of wine in his right hand, and says:

בָּרוּךְ אַתָּה יהוה אֱלֹהֵינוּ מֶלֶךְ הָעוֹלָם, הַמַּבְדִּיל בֵּין קֹדֶשׁ לְחוֹל, בֵּין אוֹר לְחֹשֶׁךְ, בֵּין יִשְׂרָאֵל לָעַמִּים, בֵּין יוֹם הַשְּׁבִיעִי לְשֵׁשֶׁת יְמֵי הַמַּעֲשֶׂה. בָּרוּךְ אַתָּה יהוה, הַמַּבְדִּיל בֵּין־קֹדֶשׁ לְחוֹל.

עלינו

Stand while saying עָלֵינוּ. Bow at ▾.

עָלֵינוּ לְשַׁבֵּחַ לַאֲדוֹן הַכֹּל, לָתֵת גְּדֻלָּה לְיוֹצֵר בְּרֵאשִׁית, שֶׁלֹּא עָשָׂנוּ כְּגוֹיֵי הָאֲרָצוֹת, וְלֹא שָׂמָנוּ כְּמִשְׁפְּחוֹת הָאֲדָמָה. שֶׁלֹּא שָׂם חֶלְקֵנוּ כָּהֶם, וְגֹרָלֵנוּ כְּכָל־הֲמוֹנָם. ▾וַאֲנַחְנוּ כּוֹרְעִים וּמִשְׁתַּחֲוִים וּמוֹדִים, לִפְנֵי מֶלֶךְ מַלְכֵי הַמְּלָכִים הַקָּדוֹשׁ בָּרוּךְ הוּא. שֶׁהוּא נוֹטֶה שָׁמַיִם וְיוֹסֵד אָרֶץ, וּמוֹשַׁב יְקָרוֹ בַּשָּׁמַיִם מִמַּעַל, וּשְׁכִינַת עֻזּוֹ בְּגָבְהֵי מְרוֹמִים. הוּא אֱלֹהֵינוּ, אֵין עוֹד. אֱמֶת מַלְכֵּנוּ, אֶפֶס זוּלָתוֹ, כַּכָּתוּב בְּתוֹרָתוֹ, וְיָדַעְתָּ הַיּוֹם וַהֲשֵׁבֹתָ אֶל־לְבָבֶךָ, כִּי יהוה הוּא הָאֱלֹהִים בַּשָּׁמַיִם מִמַּעַל וְעַל־הָאָרֶץ מִתָּחַת, אֵין עוֹד.

עַל־כֵּן נְקַוֶּה לְּךָ יהוה אֱלֹהֵינוּ לִרְאוֹת מְהֵרָה בְּתִפְאֶרֶת עֻזֶּךָ, לְהַעֲבִיר גִּלּוּלִים מִן הָאָרֶץ, וְהָאֱלִילִים כָּרוֹת יִכָּרֵתוּן, לְתַקֵּן עוֹלָם בְּמַלְכוּת שַׁדַּי. וְכָל־בְּנֵי בָשָׂר יִקְרְאוּ בִשְׁמֶךָ, לְהַפְנוֹת אֵלֶיךָ כָּל־רִשְׁעֵי אָרֶץ. יַכִּירוּ וְיֵדְעוּ כָּל־יוֹשְׁבֵי תֵבֵל, כִּי לְךָ תִּכְרַע כָּל־בֶּרֶךְ, תִּשָּׁבַע כָּל־לָשׁוֹן. לְפָנֶיךָ יהוה אֱלֹהֵינוּ יִכְרְעוּ וְיִפֹּלוּ, וְלִכְבוֹד שִׁמְךָ יְקָר יִתֵּנוּ. וִיקַבְּלוּ כֻלָּם אֶת־עוֹל מַלְכוּתֶךָ, וְתִמְלֹךְ עֲלֵיהֶם מְהֵרָה לְעוֹלָם וָעֶד. כִּי הַמַּלְכוּת שֶׁלְּךָ הִיא וּלְעוֹלְמֵי עַד תִּמְלוֹךְ בְּכָבוֹד, כַּכָּתוּב בְּתוֹרָתֶךָ,

He lifts the cup of wine in his right hand, and says:

בָּרוּךְ Blessed are You, LORD our GOD, King of the Universe, who distinguishes between sacred and secular, between light and darkness, between Israel and the nations, between the seventh day and the six days of work. Blessed are You, LORD, who distinguishes between sacred and secular.

ALEINU

Stand while saying *Aleinu*. Bow at ▾.

עָלֵינוּ It is our duty to praise the Master of all, and ascribe greatness to the Author of creation, who has not made us like the nations of the lands nor placed us like the families of the earth; who has not made our portion like theirs, nor our destiny like all their multitudes. Therefore ▾we bow in worship and thank the Supreme King of kings, the Holy One, blessed be He, who extends the heavens and establishes the earth, whose throne of glory is in the heavens above, and whose power's presence is in the highest of heights. He is our GOD; there is no other. Truly He is our King, there is none else, as it is written in His Torah: "You shall know and take to heart this day that the LORD is GOD, in heaven above and on earth below. There is no other."

Therefore we place our hope in You, LORD our GOD, that we may soon see the glory of Your power, when You will remove abominations from the earth, and idols will be utterly destroyed, when the world will be perfected under the sovereignty of the Almighty, when all humanity will call on Your name, and the earth's wicked will all turn to You. All the world's inhabitants will realise and know that to You every knee must bow and every tongue swear loyalty. Before You, LORD our GOD, they will kneel and bow down and give honour to Your glorious name. They will all accept the yoke of Your kingdom, and You will reign over them soon and for ever. For the kingdom is Yours, and to all eternity You will reign in glory, as it is written in Your

יהוה יִמְלֹךְ לְעֹלָם וָעֶד. ◄ וְנֶאֱמַר, וְהָיָה יהוה לְמֶלֶךְ עַל־כָּל־הָאָרֶץ, בַּיּוֹם הַהוּא יִהְיֶה יהוה אֶחָד וּשְׁמוֹ אֶחָד.

Some congregations add:

אַל תִּירָא מִפַּחַד פִּתְאֹם, וּמִשֹּׁאַת רְשָׁעִים כִּי תָבֹא. עֻצוּ עֵצָה וְתֻפָר, דַּבְּרוּ דָבָר וְלֹא יָקוּם, כִּי עִמָּנוּ אֵל. וְעַד זִקְנָה אֲנִי הוּא, וְעַד שֵׂיבָה אֲנִי אֶסְבֹּל, אֲנִי עָשִׂיתִי וַאֲנִי אֶשָּׂא, וַאֲנִי אֶסְבֹּל וַאֲמַלֵּט.

קדיש יתום

The transliteration can be found at the end of the Siddur.

Mourner:

יִתְגַּדַּל וְיִתְקַדַּשׁ שְׁמֵהּ רַבָּא. (Cong. אָמֵן) בְּעָלְמָא דִּי־בְרָא כִרְעוּתֵהּ. וְיַמְלִיךְ מַלְכוּתֵהּ, בְּחַיֵּיכוֹן וּבְיוֹמֵיכוֹן וּבְחַיֵּי דְכָל־בֵּית יִשְׂרָאֵל, בַּעֲגָלָא וּבִזְמַן קָרִיב. וְאִמְרוּ אָמֵן. (Cong. אָמֵן)

All:

יְהֵא שְׁמֵהּ רַבָּא מְבָרַךְ לְעָלַם וּלְעָלְמֵי עָלְמַיָּא.

Mourner:

יִתְבָּרַךְ וְיִשְׁתַּבַּח וְיִתְפָּאַר וְיִתְרוֹמַם וְיִתְנַשֵּׂא וְיִתְהַדַּר וְיִתְעַלֶּה וְיִתְהַלָּל שְׁמֵהּ דְּקֻדְשָׁא בְּרִיךְ הוּא (Cong. בְּרִיךְ הוּא) לְעֵלָּא (Between רֹאשׁ הַשָּׁנָה and יוֹם כִּפּוּר add לְעֵלָּא) מִן־כָּל־בִּרְכָתָא וְשִׁירָתָא תֻּשְׁבְּחָתָא וְנֶחֱמָתָא, דַּאֲמִירָן בְּעָלְמָא. וְאִמְרוּ אָמֵן. (Cong. אָמֵן)

יְהֵא שְׁלָמָא רַבָּא מִן־שְׁמַיָּא, וְחַיִּים עָלֵינוּ וְעַל־כָּל־יִשְׂרָאֵל. וְאִמְרוּ אָמֵן. (Cong. אָמֵן)

Bow, take three steps back, then bow, first left, then right, then centre, while saying:

עֹשֶׂה שָׁלוֹם בִּמְרוֹמָיו, הוּא יַעֲשֶׂה שָׁלוֹם עָלֵינוּ, וְעַל־כָּל־יִשְׂרָאֵל. וְאִמְרוּ אָמֵן. (Cong. אָמֵן)

Torah: "The LORD will reign for ever and ever." ➔ And it is said: "Then the LORD shall be King over all the earth: on that day the LORD shall be One and His name One."

Some congregations add:

Have no fear of sudden terror or of the ruin that overtakes the wicked. Devise your strategy, but it will be thwarted; propose your plan, but it will not stand, for GOD is with us. When you grow old, I will still be the same. When your hair turns grey, I will still carry you. I made you, I will bear you, I will carry you, and I will rescue you.

MOURNER'S KADDISH

The transliteration can be found at the end of the Siddur.

Mourner:

יִתְגַּדַּל Magnified and sanctified may His great name be, in the world He created by His will. May He establish His kingdom in your lifetime and in your days, and in the lifetime of all the House of Israel, swiftly and soon – and say: Amen.

All:

May His great name be blessed for ever and all time.

Mourner:

Blessed and praised, glorified and exalted, raised and honoured, uplifted and lauded be the name of the Holy One, blessed be He, (between Rosh Hashanah and Yom Kippur add 'well') beyond any blessing, song, praise and consolation uttered in the world – and say: Amen.

May there be great peace from heaven, and life for us and all Israel – and say: Amen.

Bow, take three steps back, then bow, first left, then right, then centre, while saying:

May He who makes peace in His high places, make peace for us and all Israel – and say: Amen.

From the second day of רֹאשׁ חֹדֶשׁ אֱלוּל, until and including שְׁמִינִי עֲצֶרֶת,
the following psalm is said every evening and morning.

תהלים כז

לְדָוִד, יהוה אוֹרִי וְיִשְׁעִי, מִמִּי אִירָא, יהוה מָעוֹז חַיַּי, מִמִּי אֶפְחָד. בִּקְרֹב עָלַי מְרֵעִים לֶאֱכֹל אֶת בְּשָׂרִי, צָרַי וְאֹיְבַי לִי, הֵמָּה כָשְׁלוּ וְנָפָלוּ. אִם תַּחֲנֶה עָלַי מַחֲנֶה, לֹא יִירָא לִבִּי, אִם תָּקוּם עָלַי מִלְחָמָה, בְּזֹאת אֲנִי בוֹטֵחַ. אַחַת שָׁאַלְתִּי מֵאֵת יהוה, אוֹתָהּ אֲבַקֵּשׁ, שִׁבְתִּי בְּבֵית יהוה כָּל יְמֵי חַיַּי, לַחֲזוֹת בְּנֹעַם יהוה, וּלְבַקֵּר בְּהֵיכָלוֹ. כִּי יִצְפְּנֵנִי בְּסֻכֹּה בְּיוֹם רָעָה, יַסְתִּרֵנִי בְּסֵתֶר אָהֳלוֹ, בְּצוּר יְרוֹמְמֵנִי. וְעַתָּה יָרוּם רֹאשִׁי עַל אֹיְבַי סְבִיבוֹתַי, וְאֶזְבְּחָה בְאָהֳלוֹ זִבְחֵי תְרוּעָה, אָשִׁירָה וַאֲזַמְּרָה לַיהוה. שְׁמַע יהוה קוֹלִי אֶקְרָא, וְחָנֵּנִי וַעֲנֵנִי. לְךָ אָמַר לִבִּי בַּקְּשׁוּ פָנָי, אֶת פָּנֶיךָ יהוה אֲבַקֵּשׁ. אַל תַּסְתֵּר פָּנֶיךָ מִמֶּנִּי, אַל תַּט בְּאַף עַבְדֶּךָ, עֶזְרָתִי הָיִיתָ, אַל תִּטְּשֵׁנִי וְאַל תַּעַזְבֵנִי, אֱלֹהֵי יִשְׁעִי. כִּי אָבִי וְאִמִּי עֲזָבוּנִי, וַיהוה יַאַסְפֵנִי. הוֹרֵנִי יהוה דַּרְכֶּךָ, וּנְחֵנִי בְּאֹרַח מִישׁוֹר, לְמַעַן שׁוֹרְרָי. אַל תִּתְּנֵנִי בְּנֶפֶשׁ צָרָי, כִּי קָמוּ בִי עֵדֵי שֶׁקֶר, וִיפֵחַ חָמָס. ◄ לוּלֵא הֶאֱמַנְתִּי לִרְאוֹת בְּטוּב יהוה בְּאֶרֶץ חַיִּים. קַוֵּה אֶל יהוה, חֲזַק וְיַאֲמֵץ לִבֶּךָ, וְקַוֵּה אֶל יהוה.

קַדִּישׁ יָתוֹם is on page 600.

סדר קדוש לבנה

קִדּוּשׁ לְבָנָה, the Blessing of the New Moon, is said between the third day and the middle day of each month. If possible, it should be said at the end of שַׁבָּת, when the moon is visible, and in the presence of a מִנְיָן.

תהלים קמח

הַלְלוּיָהּ, הַלְלוּ אֶת־יהוה מִן־הַשָּׁמַיִם, הַלְלוּהוּ בַּמְּרוֹמִים. הַלְלוּהוּ כָל־מַלְאָכָיו, הַלְלוּהוּ כָּל־צְבָאָיו. הַלְלוּהוּ שֶׁמֶשׁ

From the second day of Rosh Chodesh Ellul, until and including Shemini Atzeret, the following psalm is said every evening and morning.

PSALM 27

לְדָוִד A psalm of David. The LORD is my light and my salvation – whom then shall I fear? The LORD is the stronghold of my life – of whom shall I be afraid? When evil men close in on me to devour my flesh, it is they, my enemies and foes, who stumble and fall. Should an army besiege me, my heart would not fear. Should war break out against me, still I would be confident. One thing I ask of the LORD, only this do I seek: to live in the house of the LORD all the days of my life, to gaze on the beauty of the LORD and worship in His Temple. For He will keep me safe in His pavilion on the day of trouble. He will hide me under the cover of His tent. He will set me high upon a rock. Now my head is high above my enemies who surround me. I will sacrifice in His tent with shouts of joy. I will sing and chant praises to the LORD. LORD, hear my voice when I call. Be gracious to me and answer me. On Your behalf my heart says, "Seek My face." Your face, LORD, will I seek. Do not hide Your face from me. Do not turn Your servant away in anger. You have been my help. Do not reject or forsake me, GOD, my Saviour. Were my father and my mother to forsake me, the LORD would take me in. Teach me Your way, LORD, and lead me on a level path, because of my oppressors. Do not abandon me to the will of my foes, for false witnesses have risen against me, breathing violence. ➔ Were it not for my faith that I shall see the LORD's goodness in the land of the living... Hope in the LORD. Be strong and of good courage, and hope in the LORD!

Mourner's *Kaddish* is on page 601.

BLESSING OF THE NEW MOON

Kiddush Levanah, the Blessing of the New Moon, is said between the third day and the middle day of each month. If possible, it should be said at the end of Shabbat, when the moon is visible, and in the presence of a *minyan*.

PSALM 148:1–6

הַלְלוּיָהּ Halleluyah! Praise the LORD from the heavens, praise Him in the heights. Praise Him, all His angels, praise Him, all His hosts. Praise

וְיָרֵחַ, הַלְלוּהוּ כָּל־כּוֹכְבֵי אוֹר. הַלְלוּהוּ שְׁמֵי הַשָּׁמָיִם, וְהַמַּיִם אֲשֶׁר מֵעַל הַשָּׁמָיִם. יְהַלְלוּ אֶת־שֵׁם יהוה, כִּי הוּא צִוָּה וְנִבְרָאוּ. וַיַּעֲמִידֵם לָעַד לְעוֹלָם, חָק־נָתַן וְלֹא יַעֲבוֹר.

Look at the moon, then say:

בָּרוּךְ אַתָּה יהוה, אֱלֹהֵינוּ מֶלֶךְ הָעוֹלָם, אֲשֶׁר בְּמַאֲמָרוֹ בָּרָא שְׁחָקִים, וּבְרוּחַ פִּיו כָּל־צְבָאָם. חֹק וּזְמַן נָתַן לָהֶם שֶׁלֹּא יְשַׁנּוּ אֶת תַּפְקִידָם. שָׂשִׂים וּשְׂמֵחִים לַעֲשׂוֹת רְצוֹן קוֹנָם, פּוֹעֵל אֱמֶת שֶׁפְּעֻלָּתוֹ אֱמֶת. וְלַלְּבָנָה אָמַר שֶׁתִּתְחַדֵּשׁ עֲטֶרֶת תִּפְאֶרֶת לַעֲמוּסֵי בָטֶן, שֶׁהֵם עֲתִידִים לְהִתְחַדֵּשׁ כְּמוֹתָהּ, וּלְפָאֵר לְיוֹצְרָם עַל שֵׁם כְּבוֹד מַלְכוּתוֹ. בָּרוּךְ אַתָּה יהוה, מְחַדֵּשׁ חֳדָשִׁים.

The following five passages are each said three times:

בָּרוּךְ יוֹצְרֵךְ, בָּרוּךְ עוֹשֵׂךְ, בָּרוּךְ קוֹנֵךְ, בָּרוּךְ בּוֹרְאֵךְ.

Rise on your toes for this verse.

כְּשֵׁם שֶׁאֲנִי רוֹקֵד כְּנֶגְדֵּךְ וְאֵינִי יָכוֹל לִנְגֹּעַ בָּךְ כָּךְ לֹא יוּכְלוּ כָּל־אוֹיְבַי לִנְגֹּעַ בִּי לְרָעָה.

תִּפֹּל עֲלֵיהֶם אֵימָתָה וָפַחַד, בִּגְדֹל זְרוֹעֲךָ יִדְּמוּ כָּאָבֶן.

כָּאָבֶן יִדְּמוּ זְרוֹעֲךָ בִּגְדֹל וָפַחַד אֵימָתָה עֲלֵיהֶם תִּפֹּל.

דָּוִד מֶלֶךְ יִשְׂרָאֵל חַי וְקַיָּם.

Turn to three people and say to each:

שָׁלוֹם עֲלֵיכֶם.

They respond:

עֲלֵיכֶם שָׁלוֹם.

Say three times:

סִמָּן טוֹב וּמַזָּל טוֹב יְהֵא לָנוּ וּלְכָל־יִשְׂרָאֵל. אָמֵן.

Him, sun and moon, praise Him, all shining stars. Praise Him, highest heavens and the waters above the heavens. Let them praise the name of the LORD, for He commanded and they were created. He established them for ever and all time, issuing a decree that will never change.

Look at the moon, then say:

בָּרוּךְ Blessed are You, LORD our GOD, King of the Universe who by His word created the heavens, and by His breath all their host. He set for them laws and times, so that they should not deviate from their appointed task. They are joyous and glad to perform the will of their Owner, the Worker of truth whose work is truth. To the moon He said that it should renew itself as a crown of beauty for those He carried from the womb [Israel], for they are destined to be renewed like it, and to praise their Creator for the sake of His glorious majesty. Blessed are You, LORD, who renews the months

The following five passages are each said three times:

Blessed is He who formed you. Blessed is He who made you. Blessed is He who owns you. Blessed is He who created you.

Rise on your toes for this verse.

Just as I leap toward you but cannot touch you, so may none of my enemies be able to touch me to do me harm.

May fear and dread fall upon them; by the power of Your arm may they be still as stone.

May they be still as stone through the power of Your arm, when dread and fear fall upon them.

David, king of Israel, lives and endures.

Turn to three people and say to each:

Peace upon you.

They respond:

Upon you, peace.

Say three times:

May it be a good sign and a good omen
for us and all Israel. Amen.

שיר השירים ב:ח–ט

קוֹל דּוֹדִי הִנֵּה זֶה בָּא. מְדַלֵּג עַל הֶהָרִים. מְקַפֵּץ עַל הַגְּבָעוֹת. דּוֹמֶה דוֹדִי לִצְבִי אוֹ לְעֹפֶר הָאַיָּלִים. הִנֵּה זֶה עוֹמֵד אַחַר כָּתְלֵנוּ, מַשְׁגִּיחַ מִן הַחַלֹּנוֹת, מֵצִיץ מִן הַחֲרַכִּים.

תהלים קכא

שִׁיר לַמַּעֲלוֹת, אֶשָּׂא עֵינַי אֶל־הֶהָרִים, מֵאַיִן יָבֹא עֶזְרִי. עֶזְרִי מֵעִם יהוה, עֹשֵׂה שָׁמַיִם וָאָרֶץ. אַל־יִתֵּן לַמּוֹט רַגְלֶךָ, אַל־יָנוּם שֹׁמְרֶךָ. הִנֵּה לֹא יָנוּם וְלֹא יִישָׁן, שׁוֹמֵר יִשְׂרָאֵל. יהוה שֹׁמְרֶךָ, יהוה צִלְּךָ עַל־יַד יְמִינֶךָ. יוֹמָם הַשֶּׁמֶשׁ לֹא־יַכֶּכָּה וְיָרֵחַ בַּלָּיְלָה. יהוה יִשְׁמָרְךָ מִכָּל־רָע, יִשְׁמֹר אֶת־נַפְשֶׁךָ. יהוה יִשְׁמָר־צֵאתְךָ וּבוֹאֶךָ, מֵעַתָּה וְעַד־עוֹלָם.

תהלים קנ

הַלְלוּיָהּ,
הַלְלוּ־אֵל בְּקָדְשׁוֹ, הַלְלוּהוּ בִּרְקִיעַ עֻזּוֹ.
הַלְלוּהוּ בִגְבוּרֹתָיו, הַלְלוּהוּ כְּרֹב גֻּדְלוֹ.
הַלְלוּהוּ בְּתֵקַע שׁוֹפָר, הַלְלוּהוּ בְּנֵבֶל וְכִנּוֹר.
הַלְלוּהוּ בְתֹף וּמָחוֹל, הַלְלוּהוּ בְּמִנִּים וְעֻגָב.
הַלְלוּהוּ בְצִלְצְלֵי־שָׁמַע, הַלְלוּהוּ בְּצִלְצְלֵי־תְרוּעָה.
כֹּל הַנְּשָׁמָה תְּהַלֵּל יָהּ, הַלְלוּיָהּ.
כֹּל הַנְּשָׁמָה תְּהַלֵּל יָהּ, הַלְלוּיָהּ.

סנהדרין מב

תָּנָא דְבֵי רַבִּי יִשְׁמָעֵאל, אִלְמָלֵי לֹא זָכוּ יִשְׂרָאֵל אֶלָּא לְהַקְבִּיל פְּנֵי אֲבִיהֶם שֶׁבַּשָּׁמַיִם פַּעַם אַחַת בַּחֹדֶשׁ, דַּיָּם. אָמַר אַבַּיֵּי, הִלְכָּךְ צָרִיךְ לְמֵימְרָא מְעֻמָּד. מִי זֹאת עֹלָה מִן־הַמִּדְבָּר מִתְרַפֶּקֶת עַל דּוֹדָהּ. וִיהִי רָצוֹן מִלְּפָנֶיךָ יהוה אֱלֹהַי וֵאלֹהֵי אֲבוֹתַי, לְמַלֹּאת פְּגִימַת הַלְּבָנָה, וְלֹא יִהְיֶה

SONG OF SONGS 2:8–9

קוֹל Hark! My beloved! Here he comes, leaping over the mountains, bounding over the hills. My beloved is like a gazelle, like a young deer. There he stands outside our wall, peering in through the windows, gazing through the lattice.

PSALM 121

שִׁיר לַמַּעֲלוֹת A song of ascents. I lift my eyes up to the hills; from where will my help come? My help comes from the Lord, Maker of heaven and earth. He will not let your foot stumble; He who guards you does not slumber. See: the guardian of Israel neither slumbers nor sleeps. The Lord is your Guardian; the Lord is your Shade at your right hand. The sun will not strike you by day, nor the moon by night. The Lord will guard you from all harm; He will guard your life. The Lord will guard your going and coming, now and for evermore.

PSALM 150

הַלְלוּיָהּ Halleluyah!

Praise God in His holy place; praise Him in the heavens of His power.

Praise Him for His mighty deeds; praise Him for His surpassing greatness.

Praise Him with blasts of the ram's horn; praise Him with the harp and lyre.

Praise Him with timbrel and dance; praise Him with strings and flute.

Praise Him with clashing cymbals; praise Him with resounding cymbals.

Let all that breathes praise the Lord. Halleluyah!

Let all that breathes praise the Lord. Halleluyah!

BABYLONIAN TALMUD, SANHEDRIN 42

תָּנָא In the academy of Rabbi Ishmael it was taught: Were the people of Israel privileged to greet the presence of their heavenly Father only once a month, it would have been sufficient for them. Abaye said: Therefore it [the blessing of the moon] should be said standing.

בָּהּ שׁוּם מִעוּט, וִיהִי אוֹר הַלְּבָנָה כְּאוֹר הַחַמָּה, וּכְאוֹר שִׁבְעַת יְמֵי בְרֵאשִׁית כְּמוֹ שֶׁהָיְתָה קֹדֶם מִעוּטָהּ, שֶׁנֶּאֱמַר, אֶת־שְׁנֵי הַמְּאֹרֹת הַגְּדֹלִים. וְיִתְקַיֵּם בָּנוּ מִקְרָא שֶׁכָּתוּב, וּבִקְשׁוּ אֶת יהוה אֱלֹהֵיהֶם, וְאֵת דָּוִד מַלְכָּם. אָמֵן.

תהלים סז

לַמְנַצֵּחַ בִּנְגִינֹת מִזְמוֹר שִׁיר. אֱלֹהִים יְחָנֵּנוּ וִיבָרְכֵנוּ, יָאֵר פָּנָיו אִתָּנוּ סֶלָה. לָדַעַת בָּאָרֶץ דַּרְכֶּךָ, בְּכָל־גּוֹיִם יְשׁוּעָתֶךָ. יוֹדוּךָ עַמִּים אֱלֹהִים, יוֹדוּךָ עַמִּים כֻּלָּם. יִשְׂמְחוּ וִירַנְּנוּ לְאֻמִּים, כִּי־תִשְׁפֹּט עַמִּים מִישֹׁר, וּלְאֻמִּים בָּאָרֶץ תַּנְחֵם סֶלָה. יוֹדוּךָ עַמִּים אֱלֹהִים, יוֹדוּךָ עַמִּים כֻּלָּם. אֶרֶץ נָתְנָה יְבוּלָהּ, יְבָרְכֵנוּ אֱלֹהִים אֱלֹהֵינוּ. יְבָרְכֵנוּ אֱלֹהִים, וְיִירְאוּ אוֹתוֹ כָּל־אַפְסֵי־אָרֶץ.

סדר הבדלה בבית

At the end of a יום טוב and יום כפור falling on a weekday, the first paragraph and the blessings for the spices are omitted.

At the end of יום טוב, the blessing for the flame is omitted.

A cup of wine is taken in the right hand and the following is said.

הִנֵּה אֵל יְשׁוּעָתִי אֶבְטַח וְלֹא אֶפְחָד, כִּי עָזִּי וְזִמְרָת יָהּ יהוה, וַיְהִי־לִי לִישׁוּעָה. וּשְׁאַבְתֶּם מַיִם בְּשָׂשׂוֹן, מִמַּעַיְנֵי

HAVDALAH

Havdalah is to the end of Shabbat what *Kiddush* is at the beginning: the marking of a transition from secular to holy time and vice versa. It is our way of fulfilling the commandment to "Remember the Sabbath day", understood by the Sages to mean: "Remember it at the beginning and at the end" – in both cases over a cup of wine.

Its deeper meaning recalls the moment at which Adam and Eve, exiled from Eden because of their sin, prepared to enter, for the first time, the world outside, with its darkness and dangers. As a gift, God showed them how to make light. Hence the light of *Havdalah*.

This profound parable is the reverse of the Greek myth of Prometheus – who

Who is this coming up from the desert, leaning on her beloved? May it be Your will, LORD my GOD and GOD of my ancestors, to make good the deficiency of the moon, so that it is no longer in its diminished state. May the light of the moon be like the light of the sun and like the light of the seven days of creation as it was before it was diminished, as it says, "The two great luminaries". And may there be fulfilled for us the verse: "They shall seek the LORD their GOD, and David their king". Amen.

PSALM 67

לַמְנַצֵּחַ For the leader. With stringed instruments. A psalm. A song. May GOD be gracious to us and bless us. May He make His face shine upon us, Selah, that Your ways be known on earth, Your salvation among all nations. May peoples praise You, GOD; may all the peoples praise You. May the nations rejoice and sing for joy, for You judge the peoples justly, and guide the nations of the earth, Selah. May peoples praise You, GOD; may all the peoples praise You. The earth has yielded its produce; GOD, our GOD, will bless us. May GOD bless us, and all the ends of the earth fear Him.

HAVDALAH SERVICE AT HOME

At the end of a Festival and Yom Kippur falling on a weekday, the first paragraph and the blessings for the spices are omitted.

At the end of a Festival, the blessing for the flame is ommited.

A cup of wine is taken in the right hand and the following is said.

הִנֵּה Behold, GOD is my salvation. I will trust and not be afraid. The LORD, the LORD, is my strength and my song. He has become my

---

stole fire from the gods and was sentenced to everlasting torment. Judaism taught that GOD wants and blesses human creativity. Day 8, for humans, was the counterpart to Day 1 for GOD. Just as GOD began creation by making light, so He taught humans how to make light – inviting them to become "His partners in the work of creation."

One of the key verbs in Genesis 1 is *b-d-l*, "to separate, distinguish, divide" – the root of the word *Havdalah*. It appears five times in the chapter. By inviting human beings to engage in *Havdalah* at the

הַיְשׁוּעָה. לַיהוה הַיְשׁוּעָה, עַל־עַמְּךָ בִרְכָתֶךָ סֶּלָה. יהוה צְבָאוֹת עִמָּנוּ, מִשְׂגָּב־לָנוּ אֱלֹהֵי יַעֲקֹב סֶלָה. לַיְּהוּדִים הָיְתָה אוֹרָה וְשִׂמְחָה, וְשָׂשׂוֹן וִיקָר, כֵּן תִּהְיֶה לָּנוּ. כּוֹס יְשׁוּעוֹת אֶשָּׂא, וּבְשֵׁם יהוה אֶקְרָא.

בָּרוּךְ אַתָּה יהוה אֱלֹהֵינוּ מֶלֶךְ הָעוֹלָם, בּוֹרֵא פְּרִי הַגָּפֶן.

Putting down the cup, the spice box is taken and the following said:

בָּרוּךְ אַתָּה יהוה אֱלֹהֵינוּ מֶלֶךְ הָעוֹלָם, בּוֹרֵא מִינֵי בְשָׂמִים.

Smell the spices and put the spice box down. The blessing over the הַבְדָּלָה candle is recited, following which fingers are held up to the flame to see the reflected light.

בָּרוּךְ אַתָּה יהוה אֱלֹהֵינוּ מֶלֶךְ הָעוֹלָם, בּוֹרֵא מְאוֹרֵי הָאֵשׁ.

The cup of wine is again taken in the right hand and the following is said:

בָּרוּךְ אַתָּה יהוה אֱלֹהֵינוּ מֶלֶךְ הָעוֹלָם, הַמַּבְדִּיל בֵּין קֹדֶשׁ לְחוֹל, בֵּין אוֹר לְחֹשֶׁךְ, בֵּין יִשְׂרָאֵל לָעַמִּים, בֵּין יוֹם הַשְּׁבִיעִי לְשֵׁשֶׁת יְמֵי הַמַּעֲשֶׂה. בָּרוּךְ אַתָּה יהוה, הַמַּבְדִּיל בֵּין־קֹדֶשׁ לְחוֹל.

---

end of Shabbat, God invites us to create worlds. Creation involves the ability to make distinctions, to rescue order from chaos, to respect the integrity of creation. *Havdalah* is thus not only a human blessing over the end of the day of rest, but as it were a Divine blessing over the days of work. The Creator invites us to be creative – but always and only in a way that respects differences and distinctions, the laws of nature and the moral law. The message of *Havdalah* is: if we respect the integrity of boundaries, we can turn chaos into order, darkness into light.

The order of *Havdalah* is: 1. preliminary verses from Isaiah and Psalms; 2. the blessing over wine; 3. spices, to refresh us after the loss of the "extra soul" we had on Shabbat; 4. a blessing over lights; 5. the *Havdalah* blessing itself, for the ability to recognise, and the responsibility to honour, boundaries.

salvation. With joy you will draw water from the springs of salvation. Salvation is the LORD's; on Your people is Your blessing, Selah. The LORD of hosts is with us, the GOD of Jacob is our Stronghold, Selah. For the Jews there was light and gladness, joy and honour – so may it be for us. I will lift the cup of salvation and call on the name of the LORD.

בָּרוּךְ Blessed are You, LORD our GOD, King of the Universe, who creates the fruit of the vine.

Putting down the cup, the spice box is taken and the following said:

בָּרוּךְ Blessed are You, LORD our GOD, King of the Universe, who creates the various spices.

Smell the spices and put the spice box down. The blessing over the *Havdalah* candle is recited, following which fingers are held up to the flame to see the reflected light.

בָּרוּךְ Blessed are You, LORD our GOD, King of the Universe, who creates the lights of fire.

The cup of wine is again taken in the right hand and the following is said:

בָּרוּךְ Blessed are You, LORD our GOD, King of the Universe, who distinguishes between sacred and secular, between light and darkness, between Israel and the nations, between the seventh day and the six days of work. Blessed are You, LORD, who distinguishes between sacred and secular.

LAWS OF HAVDALAH

1. Our custom is to slightly overfill the wineglass, in keeping with the phrase from Psalm 23, "my cup is filled to overflowing".
2. The light used for *Havdalah* should have several wicks so that the flames of each merge. Failing this, two candles may be used, their flames brought together to form one while we say the blessing.
3. While saying the blessing over light, it is a custom to lift our hands toward the flame, bending our fingers inward, so that we use the light while making a blessing over it, and so that we see both its light and the shadow it casts.
4. At the end of *Havdalah*, the one who has made the blessing drinks most of the wine. The custom is to pour some of the remainder into a saucer and extinguish the flame of the *Havdalah* candle in it.

המבדיל

הַמַּבְדִּיל בֵּין קֹדֶשׁ לְחוֹל, חַטֹּאתֵינוּ הוּא יִמְחֹל,
זַרְעֵנוּ וְכַסְפֵּנוּ יַרְבֶּה כַּחוֹל, וְכַכּוֹכָבִים בַּלָּיְלָה.
יוֹם פָּנָה כְּצֵל תֹּמֶר, אֶקְרָא לָאֵל עָלַי גֹּמֵר,
אָמַר שׁוֹמֵר, אָתָא בֹקֶר וְגַם־לָיְלָה.
צִדְקָתְךָ כְּהַר תָּבוֹר, עַל־חֲטָאַי עָבוֹר תַּעֲבוֹר,
כְּיוֹם אֶתְמוֹל כִּי יַעֲבוֹר, וְאַשְׁמוּרָה בַלָּיְלָה.
חָלְפָה עוֹנַת מִנְחָתִי, מִי יִתֵּן מְנוּחָתִי,
יָגַעְתִּי בְאַנְחָתִי, אַשְׂחֶה בְכָל־לָיְלָה.
קוֹלִי שְׁמַעְ בַּל יֻנְטַל, פְּתַח לִי שַׁעַר הַמְנֻטָּל,
שֶׁרֹּאשִׁי נִמְלָא טָל, קְוֻצּוֹתַי רְסִיסֵי לָיְלָה.
הֵעָתֵר נוֹרָא וְאָיוֹם, אֲשַׁוֵּעַ תְּנָה פִדְיוֹם,
בְּנֶשֶׁף בְּעֶרֶב יוֹם, בְּאִישׁוֹן לָיְלָה.
קְרָאתִיךָ יָהּ הוֹשִׁיעֵנִי, אֹרַח חַיִּים תּוֹדִיעֵנִי,
מִדַּלָּה תְבַצְּעֵנִי, מִיּוֹם עַד לָיְלָה.
טַהֵר טִנּוּף מַעֲשַׂי, פֶּן יֹאמְרוּ מַכְעִיסַי,
אַיֵּה נָא אֱלוֹהַּ עֹשָׂי, נֹתֵן זְמִירוֹת בַּלָּיְלָה.
נַחְנוּ בְיָדְךָ כַּחֹמֶר, סְלַח נָא עַל קַל וָחֹמֶר,
יוֹם לְיוֹם יַבִּיעַ אֹמֶר, וְלַיְלָה לְּלָיְלָה.
הַמַּבְדִּיל בֵּין קֹדֶשׁ לְחוֹל, חַטֹּאתֵינוּ הוּא יִמְחֹל,
זַרְעֵנוּ וְכַסְפֵּנוּ יַרְבֶּה כַּחוֹל, וְכַכּוֹכָבִים בַּלָּיְלָה.

הַמַּבְדִּיל *Hamavdil.* As we welcomed the arrival of Shabbat in song, so we bid our farewell to it in song. This beautiful hymn, originally part of the *Ne'ilah* service on Yom Kippur, was composed by Isaac ibn Chayat (1030–1089).

HAMAVDIL

הַמַּבְדִּיל He who distinguishes between sacred and secular, may He forgive our sins. May He multiply our offspring and wealth like the sand, and like the stars at night.

יוֹם The day has passed like a palm tree's shadow; I call on God to fulfil what the watchman said: "Morning comes, though now it is night."

צִדְקָתְךָ Your righteousness is as high as Mount Tabor. May You pass high over my sins. Let them be like yesterday when it is past, or like a watch in the night.

חָלְפָה The time of offerings has passed. Would that I might rest. I am weary with my sigh, drenched with tears each night.

קוֹלִי Hear my voice; let it not be cast aside. Open for me the lofty gate. My head is filled with the dew of dawn, my hair with raindrops of the night.

הֵעָתֵר Heed my prayer, revered and awesome God. When I cry, grant me deliverance at twilight, as the day fades, or in the darkness of the night.

קְרָאתִיךָ I call to You, Lord: Save me. Make known to me the path of life. Rescue me from misery before day turns to night.

טַהֵר Cleanse the defilement of my deeds, lest those who torment me say, "Where is the God who made me, who gives cause for songs in the night?"

נַחְנוּ We are in Your hands like clay: please forgive our sins, light and grave. Day speaks Your word to day, and night its knowledge to night.

הַמַּבְדִּיל He who distinguishes between sacred and secular, may He forgive our sins. May He multiply our offspring and wealth like the sand, and like the stars at night.

תפילות לחגים וראש חודש

Services for Festivals and New Moon

סדר נטילת לולב

On סֻכּוֹת, except on שַׁבָּת, the לוּלָב and אֶתרוֹג are taken before הַלֵּל.

Many say the following meditation:

הֲרֵינִי מוּכָן וּמְזֻמָּן, לְקַיֵּם מִצְוַת בּוֹרְאִי, שֶׁצִּוָּנוּ בְּתוֹרָתוֹ, וּלְקַחְתֶּם לָכֶם בַּיּוֹם הָרִאשׁוֹן, פְּרִי עֵץ הָדָר, כַּפֹּת תְּמָרִים, וַעֲנַף עֵץ־עָבֹת, וְעַרְבֵי־נָחַל. וּבְנַעֲנוּעִי אוֹתָם יַשְׁפִּיעַ עָלַי שֶׁפַע בְּרָכוֹת, וּמַחֲשָׁבוֹת קְדוֹשׁוֹת, שֶׁהוּא אֱלֹהֵי הָאֱלֹהִים, וַאֲדוֹנֵי הָאֲדוֹנִים, שַׁלִּיט בְּמַטָּה וּבְמַעַל, וּמַלְכוּתוֹ בַּכּוֹל מָשָׁלָה. וּתְהֵא חֲשׁוּבָה מִצְוַת אַרְבָּעָה מִינִים, כְּאִלּוּ קִיַּמְתִּיהָ בְּכָל־פְּרָטֶיהָ וְדִקְדּוּקֶיהָ, וִיהִי נֹעַם אֲדֹנָי אֱלֹהֵינוּ עָלֵינוּ, וּמַעֲשֵׂה יָדֵינוּ כּוֹנְנָה עָלֵינוּ, וּמַעֲשֵׂה יָדֵינוּ כּוֹנְנֵהוּ. בָּרוּךְ יהוה לְעוֹלָם, אָמֵן, וְאָמֵן.

The לוּלָב is taken in the right hand, with the הֲדַסִּים leaves on the right, עֲרָבוֹת leaves on the left. The אֶתרוֹג is taken in the left hand, with its pointed end toward the floor. Then say the following blessing:

בָּרוּךְ אַתָּה יהוה אֱלֹהֵינוּ מֶלֶךְ הָעוֹלָם, אֲשֶׁר קִדְּשָׁנוּ בְּמִצְוֹתָיו וְצִוָּנוּ עַל־נְטִילַת לוּלָב.

On the first day the לוּלָב is taken, add:

בָּרוּךְ אַתָּה יהוה אֱלֹהֵינוּ מֶלֶךְ הָעוֹלָם, שֶׁהֶחֱיָנוּ וְקִיְּמָנוּ וְהִגִּיעָנוּ לַזְּמַן הַזֶּה.

Invert the אֶתרוֹג, so that its pointed end is facing up. Face the front of the synagogue and wave the לוּלָב and אֶתרוֹג in the following sequence: ahead; right; back; left; up; down. Continue to hold the לוּלָב and אֶתרוֹג during הַלֵּל.

MEDITATION AND BLESSING ON TAKING THE LULAV

Meditations before fulfilling commandments are a way of focusing our attention on the specific religious character of the act we are about to perform. They are a conscious declaration of *kavannah,* sacred intent. This meditation first appeared in Rabbi Nathan Hannover's *Sha'arei Zion*, published in Prague, 1662.

MEDITATION AND BLESSING ON TAKING THE LULAV

On Sukkot, except on Shabbat, the *lulav* and *etrog* are taken before *Hallel*.

Many say the following meditation:

הֲרֵינִי I am ready and prepared to fulfil the commandment of my Creator, who commanded us in His Torah: "On the first day you shall take fruit of the citrus tree, branches of palm trees, leafy branches and willows of the brook." As I wave them may a stream of blessings flow down on me, together with holy thoughts – that He is the God of gods and the Lord of lords, governing below and above, whose rule extends over all. May my observance of the commandment of the Four Species be considered as though I fulfilled it in all its particulars and details. May the pleasantness of the Lord our God be upon us. Establish for us the work of our hands, O establish the work of our hands. Blessed be the Lord for ever. Amen and Amen.

The *lulav* is taken in the right hand, with the myrtle leaves on the right, willow leaves on the left. The *etrog* is taken in the left hand, with its pointed end toward the floor. Then say the following blessing:

בָּרוּךְ Blessed are You, Lord our God, King of the Universe, who has made us holy through His commandments, and has commanded us about taking the *lulav*.

On the first day the *lulav* is taken, add:

בָּרוּךְ Blessed are You, Lord our God, King of the Universe, who has given us life, sustained us and brought us to this time.

Invert the *etrog*, so that its pointed end is facing up. Face the front of the synagogue and wave the *lulav* and *etrog* in the following sequence: ahead; right; back; left; up; down. Continue to hold the *lulav* and *etrog* during *Hallel*.

The *lulav*, *etrog*, myrtle and willow leaves bear witness to the power of rain to give life to the earth and its produce. We offer them to God in the hope that He will continue to send rain in the coming year. The meditation speaks of the commandment in spiritual terms: just as we, on earth, dedicate this act to heaven, so may heaven grant a downward flow of God's blessings to earth.

סדר הלל

הַלֵּל is said on רֹאשׁ חֹדֶשׁ, פֶּסַח, שָׁבֻעוֹת, סֻכּוֹת and חֲנֻכָּה.

On יוֹם הָעַצְמָאוּת and יוֹם יְרוּשָׁלַיִם, there are varying customs: some say it with, some without, the opening and concluding blessings.

On חוֹל הַמּוֹעֵד (except the first day חוֹל הַמּוֹעֵד פֶּסַח, or the second day if the first is שַׁבָּת), the תְּפִלִּין are removed before הַלֵּל; on רֹאשׁ חֹדֶשׁ and the first day חוֹל הַמּוֹעֵד פֶּסַח, or the second day if the first is שַׁבָּת, they are removed before מוּסָף.

Mourners during the week of שִׁבְעָה do not say הַלֵּל.

בָּרוּךְ אַתָּה יהוה אֱלֹהֵינוּ מֶלֶךְ הָעוֹלָם, אֲשֶׁר קִדְּשָׁנוּ בְּמִצְוֹתָיו וְצִוָּנוּ לִקְרֹא אֶת־הַהַלֵּל.

תהלים קיג

הַלְלוּיָהּ, הַלְלוּ עַבְדֵי יהוה, הַלְלוּ אֶת־שֵׁם יהוה. יְהִי שֵׁם יהוה מְבֹרָךְ, מֵעַתָּה וְעַד־עוֹלָם. מִמִּזְרַח־שֶׁמֶשׁ עַד־מְבוֹאוֹ, מְהֻלָּל שֵׁם יהוה. רָם עַל־כָּל־גּוֹיִם יהוה, עַל־הַשָּׁמַיִם כְּבוֹדוֹ. מִי כַּיהוה אֱלֹהֵינוּ, הַמַּגְבִּיהִי לָשָׁבֶת. הַמַּשְׁפִּילִי לִרְאוֹת, בַּשָּׁמַיִם וּבָאָרֶץ. ← מְקִימִי מֵעָפָר דָּל, מֵאַשְׁפֹּת יָרִים אֶבְיוֹן. לְהוֹשִׁיבִי עִם־נְדִיבִים, עִם נְדִיבֵי עַמּוֹ. מוֹשִׁיבִי עֲקֶרֶת הַבַּיִת, אֵם־הַבָּנִים שְׂמֵחָה, הַלְלוּיָהּ.

תהלים קיד

בְּצֵאת יִשְׂרָאֵל מִמִּצְרָיִם, בֵּית יַעֲקֹב מֵעַם לֹעֵז. הָיְתָה יְהוּדָה לְקָדְשׁוֹ, יִשְׂרָאֵל מַמְשְׁלוֹתָיו. הַיָּם רָאָה וַיָּנֹס,

---

Psalms 113–118 – known as the Egyptian *Hallel* because of the reference in the second paragraph to the exodus from Egypt – are among the earliest prayers written to be recited in the Temple on days of national celebration. They were sung as accompaniment to the Pesach sacrifice, and early rabbinic sources suggest that they were said on the pilgrimage festivals: Pesach, Shavuot and Sukkot.

By the Talmudic era, a shortened form (known as "half-*Hallel*") was in use for New Moons and the last six days of Pesach. The full *Hallel* was not said on Rosh Chodesh, because it is not a full festival, and on the last days of Pesach because the main event of the exodus took place on the first day, and because the miracle of the seventh day, the division of the Reed Sea, involved suffering for the Egyptians. According to the Talmud, when the angels wished to sing a Song at the Sea, God refused, saying: "Shall you sing a song while My creatures are drowning in the sea?"

HALLEL

Hallel is said on Rosh Chodesh, Pesach, Shavuot, Sukkot and Chanukah.
On Yom Ha'Atzma'ut and Yom Yerushalayim, there are varying customs:
some say it with, some without, the opening and concluding blessings.
On the Intermediate Days of Festivals (except the first Intermediate Day of Pesach, or the second day if the first is Shabbat) the *tefillin* are removed before *Hallel*; on Rosh Chodesh and the first Intermediate Day of Pesach, or the second day if the first is Shabbat, they are removed before *Musaf*.
Mourners during the week of *shivah* do not say *Hallel*.

בָּרוּךְ Blessed are You, LORD our GOD, King of the Universe, who has made us holy through His commandments and has commanded us to recite the *Hallel*.

PSALM 113

הַלְלוּיָהּ Halleluyah! Servants of the LORD, give praise; praise the name of the LORD. Blessed be the name of the LORD now and for evermore. From the rising of the sun to its setting, may the LORD's name be praised. High is the LORD above all nations; His glory is above the heavens. Who is like the LORD our GOD, who sits enthroned so high, yet turns so low to see the heavens and the earth? → He raises the poor from the dust and the needy from the refuse heap, giving them a place alongside princes, the princes of His people. He makes the woman in a childless house a happy mother of children. Halleluyah!

PSALM 114

בְּצֵאת When Israel came out of Egypt, the house of Jacob from a people of foreign tongue, Judah became His sanctuary, Israel His domin-

---

Because of its association with the miracles of Jewish history, *Hallel* is not said on Rosh Hashanah and Yom Kippur, which are not days of celebration, but rather judgement.

מְקִימִי מֵעָפָר דָּל *He raises the poor from the dust*: A verse reminiscent of Hannah's prayer after the birth of her child (I Samuel 2:8). The religions of the ancient world were deeply conservative, designed to vindicate and perpetuate hierarchies of power. Judaism, believing that human dignity is the prerogative of everyone, was an ongoing protest against such inequalities. GOD's greatness is evident in the fact that He can lift the poor and the needy to a place of honour alongside princes.

בְּצֵאת יִשְׂרָאֵל מִמִּצְרָיִם *When Israel came out of Egypt*: A lyrical account of how nature itself trembled and rejoiced at the exodus, when the supreme Power intervened to rescue the powerless.

הַיַּרְדֵּן יִסֹּב לְאָחוֹר. הֶהָרִים רָקְדוּ כְאֵילִים, גְּבָעוֹת כִּבְנֵי־צֹאן. מַה־לְּךָ הַיָּם כִּי תָנוּס, הַיַּרְדֵּן תִּסֹּב לְאָחוֹר. הֶהָרִים תִּרְקְדוּ כְאֵילִים, גְּבָעוֹת כִּבְנֵי־צֹאן. ◂ מִלִּפְנֵי אָדוֹן חְוּלִי אָרֶץ, מִלִּפְנֵי אֱלוֹהַּ יַעֲקֹב. הַהֹפְכִי הַצּוּר אֲגַם־מָיִם, חַלָּמִישׁ לְמַעְיְנוֹ־מָיִם.

On רֹאשׁ חֹדֶשׁ (except on חֲנֻכָּה) and the last six days of פֶּסַח, omit the following paragraph (תהלים קטו:א–יא):

לֹא לָנוּ יהוה לֹא לָנוּ, כִּי לְשִׁמְךָ תֵּן כָּבוֹד, עַל־חַסְדְּךָ עַל־אֲמִתֶּךָ. לָמָּה יֹאמְרוּ הַגּוֹיִם, אַיֵּה־נָא אֱלֹהֵיהֶם. וֵאלֹהֵינוּ בַשָּׁמָיִם, כֹּל אֲשֶׁר־חָפֵץ עָשָׂה. עֲצַבֵּיהֶם כֶּסֶף וְזָהָב, מַעֲשֵׂה יְדֵי אָדָם. פֶּה־לָהֶם וְלֹא יְדַבֵּרוּ, עֵינַיִם לָהֶם וְלֹא יִרְאוּ. אָזְנַיִם לָהֶם וְלֹא יִשְׁמָעוּ, אַף לָהֶם וְלֹא יְרִיחוּן. יְדֵיהֶם וְלֹא יְמִישׁוּן, רַגְלֵיהֶם וְלֹא יְהַלֵּכוּ, לֹא־יֶהְגּוּ בִּגְרוֹנָם. כְּמוֹהֶם יִהְיוּ עֹשֵׂיהֶם, כֹּל אֲשֶׁר־בֹּטֵחַ בָּהֶם. ◂ יִשְׂרָאֵל בְּטַח בַּיהוה, עֶזְרָם וּמָגִנָּם הוּא. בֵּית אַהֲרֹן בִּטְחוּ בַיהוה, עֶזְרָם וּמָגִנָּם הוּא. יִרְאֵי יהוה בִּטְחוּ בַיהוה, עֶזְרָם וּמָגִנָּם הוּא.

תהלים קטו:יב–יח

יהוה זְכָרָנוּ יְבָרֵךְ, יְבָרֵךְ אֶת־בֵּית יִשְׂרָאֵל, יְבָרֵךְ אֶת־בֵּית אַהֲרֹן. יְבָרֵךְ יִרְאֵי יהוה, הַקְּטַנִּים עִם־הַגְּדֹלִים. יֹסֵף יהוה עֲלֵיכֶם, עֲלֵיכֶם וְעַל־בְּנֵיכֶם. בְּרוּכִים אַתֶּם לַיהוה, עֹשֵׂה שָׁמַיִם וָאָרֶץ. ◂ הַשָּׁמַיִם שָׁמַיִם לַיהוה, וְהָאָרֶץ נָתַן לִבְנֵי־

כְּמוֹהֶם יִהְיוּ עֹשֵׂיהֶם *Those who make them become like them*: Worshipping impersonal objects or forces eventually dehumanises a culture and those who are part of it. Whether what is worshipped is an icon, a ruler, a race or a political ideology, the final outcome is the sacrifice of human lives on the altar of high, yet imperfect, ideals. Idolatry is the worship of the part instead of the whole, one aspect of the universe in place of the Creator of all who transcends all.

יִרְאֵי ה׳ *You who fear the Lord*: This may

ion. The sea saw and fled; the Jordan turned back. The mountains skipped like rams, the hills like lambs. Why was it, sea, that you fled? Jordan, why did you turn back? Why, mountains, did you skip like rams, and you, hills, like lambs? ➛ It was at the presence of the LORD, Creator of the earth, at the presence of the GOD of Jacob, who turned the rock into a pool of water, flint into a flowing spring.

On Rosh Chodesh (except on Chanukah) and the last six days of Pesach, omit the following paragraph (PSALM 115:1–11):

לֹא לָנוּ Not to us, LORD, not to us, but to Your name give glory, for Your love, for Your faithfulness. Why should the nations say, "Where now is their GOD?" Our GOD is in heaven; whatever He wills He does. Their idols are silver and gold, made by human hands. They have mouths but cannot speak; eyes but cannot see. They have ears but cannot hear; noses but cannot smell. They have hands but cannot feel; feet but cannot walk. No sound comes from their throat. Those who make them become like them; so will all who trust in them.

➛ Israel, trust in the LORD – He is their Help and Shield. House of Aaron, trust in the LORD – He is their Help and their Shield. You who fear the LORD, trust in the LORD – He is their Help and Shield.

PSALM 115

יהוה זְכָרָנוּ The LORD remembers us and will bless us. He will bless the house of Israel. He will bless the house of Aaron. He will bless those who fear the LORD, small and great alike. May the LORD give you increase: you and your children. May you be blessed by the LORD, Maker of heaven and earth. ➛ The heavens are the LORD's, but the earth He has given over to mankind. It is not the dead who praise the LORD,

---

refer to converts to Judaism (Rashi), or GOD-fearers among the nations (Ibn Ezra).

וְהָאָרֶץ נָתַן לִבְנֵי־אָדָם *But the earth He has given over to mankind*: "Given over" rather than "given": placed in the guardianship of mankind. We do not own the earth; we hold it in trust from GOD and there are conditions to that trust, namely that we respect the earth's integrity and the dignity of the human person; in short, that we honour GOD's laws.

אָדָם. לֹא־הַמֵּתִים יְהַלְלוּ־יָהּ, וְלֹא כָּל־יֹרְדֵי דוּמָה. וַאֲנַחְנוּ נְבָרֵךְ יָהּ, מֵעַתָּה וְעַד־עוֹלָם, הַלְלוּיָהּ.

On רֹאשׁ חֹדֶשׁ (except on חֲנֻכָּה) and the last six days of פֶּסַח, omit the following paragraph (תהלים קטז:א–יא):

אָהַבְתִּי, כִּי־יִשְׁמַע יהוה, אֶת־קוֹלִי תַּחֲנוּנָי. כִּי־הִטָּה אָזְנוֹ לִי, וּבְיָמַי אֶקְרָא. אֲפָפוּנִי חֶבְלֵי־מָוֶת, וּמְצָרֵי שְׁאוֹל מְצָאוּנִי, צָרָה וְיָגוֹן אֶמְצָא. וּבְשֵׁם־יהוה אֶקְרָא, אָנָּה יהוה מַלְּטָה נַפְשִׁי. חַנּוּן יהוה וְצַדִּיק, וֵאלֹהֵינוּ מְרַחֵם. שֹׁמֵר פְּתָאִים יהוה, דַּלֹּתִי וְלִי יְהוֹשִׁיעַ. שׁוּבִי נַפְשִׁי לִמְנוּחָיְכִי, כִּי יהוה גָּמַל עָלָיְכִי. כִּי חִלַּצְתָּ נַפְשִׁי מִמָּוֶת, אֶת־עֵינִי מִן־דִּמְעָה, אֶת־רַגְלִי מִדֶּחִי. ◄ אֶתְהַלֵּךְ לִפְנֵי יהוה, בְּאַרְצוֹת הַחַיִּים. הֶאֱמַנְתִּי כִּי אֲדַבֵּר, אֲנִי עָנִיתִי מְאֹד. אֲנִי אָמַרְתִּי בְחָפְזִי, כָּל־הָאָדָם כֹּזֵב.

תהלים קטז:יב–יט

מָה־אָשִׁיב לַיהוה, כָּל־תַּגְמוּלוֹהִי עָלָי. כּוֹס־יְשׁוּעוֹת אֶשָּׂא, וּבְשֵׁם יהוה אֶקְרָא. נְדָרַי לַיהוה אֲשַׁלֵּם, נֶגְדָה־נָּא לְכָל־עַמּוֹ. יָקָר בְּעֵינֵי יהוה, הַמָּוְתָה לַחֲסִידָיו. אָנָּה יהוה כִּי־אֲנִי עַבְדֶּךָ, אֲנִי עַבְדְּךָ, בֶּן־אֲמָתֶךָ, פִּתַּחְתָּ לְמוֹסֵרָי. ◄ לְךָ־

אָהַבְתִּי *I love the* L*ORD*: This and the next paragraph form a single psalm. The Psalmist turns from the collective to the individual. GOD has saved him from crisis and he gives public voice to his thanks. This prayer was included in *Hallel* because it spoke to the many among the pilgrims to Jerusalem who had vowed to bring thanksgiving offerings, as is clear from the next paragraph. The juxtaposition of the individual and the collective is a significant feature of biblical texts generally. The Hebrew prophets and poets never saw the nation as an abstraction and the people an amorphous mass. The individual never loses his or her significance even in the presence of vast gatherings. *Even when I said rashly, "All men are liars"* – the commentators relate this to King David who, when forced to flee from Saul, felt betrayed by everyone. Alternatively: "Even when I was fleeing for my life, I knew that those [who preached despair] were false" (Radak).

מָה־אָשִׁיב *How can I repay?* A rhetorical question: we can never repay GOD's kindnesses to us. All that we have is His.

nor those who go down to the silent grave. But we will bless the LORD, now and forever. Halleluyah!

On Rosh Chodesh (except on Chanukah) and the last six days of Pesach, omit the following paragraph (PSALM 116:1–11).

אָהַבְתִּי I love the LORD, for He hears my voice, my pleas. He turns His ear to me whenever I call. The bonds of death encompassed me, the anguish of the grave came upon me, I was overcome by trouble and sorrow. Then I called on the name of the LORD: "LORD, I pray, save my life." Gracious is the LORD, and righteous; our GOD is full of compassion. The LORD protects the simple-hearted. When I was brought low, He saved me. My soul, be at peace once more, for the LORD has been good to you. For You have rescued me from death, my eyes from weeping, my feet from stumbling. ➝ I shall walk in the presence of the LORD in the land of the living. I had faith, even when I said, "I am greatly afflicted", even when I said rashly, "All men are liars."

PSALM 116:12–19

מָה־אָשִׁיב How can I repay the LORD for all His goodness to me? I will lift the cup of salvation and call on the name of the LORD. I will fulfil my vows to the LORD in the presence of all His people. Grievous in the LORD's sight is the death of His devoted ones. Truly, LORD, I am Your servant, I am Your servant, the son of Your maidservant. You set

---

The very fact that we exist is due to His creative love. All we can do is express our thanks.

כּוֹס־יְשׁוּעוֹת אֶשָּׂא *I will lift the cup of salvation*: A reference to the wine libation accompanying a thanksgiving offering (Rashi). Alternatively, I will hold a feast of thanksgiving at which I will raise a glass of wine in thanks to GOD. *Grievous in the LORD's sight is the death of His devoted ones* – this is Rashi's understanding of the text; others translate it as "Precious in the LORD's sight". GOD does not wish His devoted ones to die. As the previous two paragraphs have made clear, GOD is the GOD of life; only idolatrous cultures worship death.

בֶּן־אֲמָתֶךָ *The son of Your maidservant*: Serving You comes naturally because my mother did likewise (Radak). A father teaches us "the discipline of thought as well as the discipline of action"; a mother teaches us the "living experience" of the commandments, their "flavour, scent and warmth". From her we learn "to feel the presence of the Almighty". "The fathers knew much about the Shabbat; the mothers lived the Shabbat, experienced her

אֶזְבַּח זֶבַח תּוֹדָה, וּבְשֵׁם יהוה אֶקְרָא. נְדָרַי לַיהוה אֲשַׁלֵּם, נֶגְדָה־נָּא לְכָל־עַמּוֹ. בְּחַצְרוֹת בֵּית יהוה. בְּתוֹכֵכִי יְרוּשָׁלָיִם, הַלְלוּיָהּ.

תהלים קיז

← הַלְלוּ אֶת־יהוה, כָּל־גּוֹיִם, שַׁבְּחוּהוּ כָּל־הָאֻמִּים. כִּי גָבַר עָלֵינוּ חַסְדּוֹ, וֶאֱמֶת־יהוה לְעוֹלָם, הַלְלוּיָהּ.

The following verses are chanted by the Leader.

At the end of each verse, the Congregation responds, הוֹדוּ לַיהוה כִּי־טוֹב, כִּי לְעוֹלָם חַסְדּוֹ.

On סֻכּוֹת, the לוּלָב and אֶתְרוֹג are waved at each verse in the following sequence: ahead; right; back; left; up; down. They are not waved when saying God's name. The Leader waves only for the first two verses

תהלים קיח

הוֹדוּ לַיהוה כִּי־טוֹב, כִּי לְעוֹלָם חַסְדּוֹ.

יֹאמַר־נָא יִשְׂרָאֵל, כִּי לְעוֹלָם חַסְדּוֹ.

יֹאמְרוּ־נָא בֵית־אַהֲרֹן, כִּי לְעוֹלָם חַסְדּוֹ.

יֹאמְרוּ־נָא יִרְאֵי יהוה, כִּי לְעוֹלָם חַסְדּוֹ.

מִן־הַמֵּצַר קָרָאתִי יָּהּ, עָנָנִי בַמֶּרְחַבְיָהּ. יהוה לִי לֹא אִירָא, מַה־יַּעֲשֶׂה לִי אָדָם. יהוה לִי בְּעֹזְרָי, וַאֲנִי אֶרְאֶה בְשֹׂנְאָי. טוֹב לַחֲסוֹת בַּיהוה, מִבְּטֹחַ בָּאָדָם. טוֹב לַחֲסוֹת בַּיהוה, מִבְּטֹחַ בִּנְדִיבִים. כָּל־גּוֹיִם סְבָבוּנִי, בְּשֵׁם יהוה כִּי אֲמִילַם. סַבּוּנִי גַם־סְבָבוּנִי, בְּשֵׁם יהוה כִּי אֲמִילַם. סַבּוּנִי כִדְבֹרִים דֹּעֲכוּ כְּאֵשׁ קוֹצִים, בְּשֵׁם יהוה כִּי אֲמִילַם. דָּחֹה דְחִיתַנִי

---

presence, and perceived her beauty and splendour" (Rav Joseph Soloveitchik).

הַלְלוּ אֶת־ה׳, כָּל־גּוֹיִם *Praise the Lord, all nations*: The shortest of all the psalms, a mere two verses. The Psalmist speaks of the universal significance of Israel's history. It is not Israel alone, but all the nations, who will see in the story of this people, something beyond mere history. "The Jew is the emblem of eternity. He whom neither slaughter nor torture of

me free me from my chains. ❖ To You I shall bring a thanksgiving-offering and call on the LORD by name. I will fulfil my vows to the LORD in the presence of all His people, in the courts of the house of the LORD, in your midst, Jerusalem. Halleluyah.

PSALM 117

הַלְלוּ ❖ Praise the LORD, all nations; acclaim Him, all you peoples; for His lovingkindness to us is strong, and the LORD's faithfulness is everlasting. Halleluyah.

The following verses are chanted by the Leader.
At the end of each verse, the Congregation responds, "Thank the LORD..."
On Sukkot, the *lulav* and *etrog* are waved at each verse in the following sequence: ahead; right; back; left; up; down. They are not waved when saying GOD's name. The Leader waves only for the first two verses

PSALM 118

הוֹדוּ Thank the LORD for He is good,	His lovingkindness is for ever.
Let Israel say	His lovingkindness is for ever.
Let the house of Aaron say	His lovingkindness is for ever.
Let those who fear the LORD say	His lovingkindness is for ever.

מִן־הַמֵּצַר In my distress I called on the LORD. The LORD answered me and set me free. The LORD is with me; I will not be afraid. What can man do to me? The LORD is with me. He is my Helper. I will see the downfall of my enemies. It is better to take refuge in the LORD than to trust in man. It is better to take refuge in the LORD than to trust in princes. The nations all surrounded me, but in the LORD's name I drove them off. They surrounded me on every side, but in the LORD's

---

thousands of years could destroy, he who neither fire nor sword nor inquisition was able to wipe off the face of the earth, he who was the first to produce the oracles of GOD, who has been for so long the guardian of prophecy and transmitted it to the rest of the world – such a nation cannot be destroyed. The Jew is everlasting as eternity itself" (Tolstoy).

הוֹדוּ לַה׳ כִּי־טוֹב *Thank the LORD for He is good*: This verse was first recited by King David when he brought the ark to Jerusalem (I Chronicles 16:34).

מִן־הַמֵּצַר *In my distress...set me free*: The terms mean, respectively, "straights, confined space" and "broad space, expanse". The Psalmist writes that he felt

לִנְפֹּל, וַיהוה עֲזָרָנִי. עָזִּי וְזִמְרָת יָהּ, וַיְהִי־לִי לִישׁוּעָה. קוֹל רִנָּה וִישׁוּעָה בְּאָהֳלֵי צַדִּיקִים, יְמִין יהוה עֹשָׂה חָיִל. יְמִין יהוה רוֹמֵמָה, יְמִין יהוה עֹשָׂה חָיִל. לֹא־אָמוּת כִּי־אֶחְיֶה, וַאֲסַפֵּר מַעֲשֵׂי יָהּ. יַסֹּר יִסְּרַנִּי יָּהּ, וְלַמָּוֶת לֹא נְתָנָנִי. פִּתְחוּ־לִי שַׁעֲרֵי־צֶדֶק, אָבֹא־בָם אוֹדֶה יָהּ. זֶה־הַשַּׁעַר לַיהוה, צַדִּיקִים יָבֹאוּ בוֹ.

אוֹדְךָ כִּי עֲנִיתָנִי, וַתְּהִי־לִי לִישׁוּעָה.
אוֹדְךָ כִּי עֲנִיתָנִי, וַתְּהִי־לִי לִישׁוּעָה.

אֶבֶן מָאֲסוּ הַבּוֹנִים, הָיְתָה לְרֹאשׁ פִּנָּה.
אֶבֶן מָאֲסוּ הַבּוֹנִים, הָיְתָה לְרֹאשׁ פִּנָּה.

מֵאֵת יהוה הָיְתָה זֹּאת, הִיא נִפְלָאת בְּעֵינֵינוּ.
מֵאֵת יהוה הָיְתָה זֹּאת, הִיא נִפְלָאת בְּעֵינֵינוּ.

← זֶה־הַיּוֹם עָשָׂה יהוה, נָגִילָה וְנִשְׂמְחָה בוֹ.
זֶה־הַיּוֹם עָשָׂה יהוה, נָגִילָה וְנִשְׂמְחָה בוֹ.

Leader followed by Congregation.

On סֻכּוֹת, the לוּלָב and אֶתרוֹג are waved while saying אָנָּא יהוה הוֹשִׁיעָה נָּא, in the following sequence: ahead; right; back; left; up; down. They are not waved when saying God's name.

אָנָּא יהוה הוֹשִׁיעָה נָּא.	**אָנָּא יהוה הוֹשִׁיעָה נָּא.**
אָנָּא יהוה הַצְלִיחָה נָא.	**אָנָּא יהוה הַצְלִיחָה נָא.**

פִּתְחוּ־לִי *Open for me the gates of righteousness*: A reference to the gates of the Temple.

אוֹדְךָ *I will thank You*: This and the next eight verses, the last of Psalm 118, are repeated. Litany – a prayer in which the Leader says a verse or phrase and the

hemmed in by enemies; his eventual victory brings a sense of spaciousness and freedom.

עָזִּי וְזִמְרָת יָהּ *The Lord is my strength and my song*: a quotation from the Song at the Sea (Exodus 15:2); it also appears in Isaiah 12:2.

name I drove them off. They surrounded me like bees, they attacked me as fire attacks brushwood, but in the LORD's name I drove them off. They thrust so hard against me, I nearly fell, but the LORD came to my help. The LORD is my strength and my song; He has become my salvation. Sounds of song and salvation resound in the tents of the righteous: "The LORD's right hand has done mighty deeds. The LORD's right hand is lifted high. The LORD's right hand has done mighty deeds." I will not die but live, and tell what the LORD has done. The LORD has chastened me severely, but He has not given me over to death. Open for me the gates of righteousness that I may enter them and thank the LORD. This is the gateway to the LORD; through it, the righteous shall enter.

אוֹדְךָ I will thank You, for You answered me, and became my salvation.
I will thank You, for You answered me, and became my salvation.

The stone the builders rejected has become the main cornerstone.
The stone the builders rejected has become the main cornerstone.

This is the LORD's doing. It is wondrous in our eyes.
This is the LORD's doing. It is wondrous in our eyes.

→ This is the day the LORD has made. Let us rejoice and be glad in it.
This is the day the LORD has made. Let us rejoice and be glad in it.

Leader followed by Congregation.

On Sukkot, the *lulav* and *etrog* are waved while saying "LORD, please save us", in the following sequence: ahead; right; back; left; up; down. They are not waved when saying GOD's name.

אָנָּא LORD, please, save us. LORD, please, save us.

LORD, please, grant us success. LORD, please, grant us success.

Congregation respond – was an aspect of worship in the Temple, and is developed most fully in the *hakafot*, processions around the synagogue, on Sukkot.

אֶבֶן מָאֲסוּ *The stone the builders rejected*: This is a reference to the people of Israel. Two of the first references to Israel in non-Jewish sources – the Merneptah stele (Egypt, thirteenth century BCE) and the Mesha stele (Moab, ninth century BCE) – both declare that Israel has been destroyed. Israel is the people that outlives its obituaries.

בָּרוּךְ הַבָּא בְּשֵׁם יהוה, בֵּרַכְנוּכֶם מִבֵּית יהוה.

בָּרוּךְ הַבָּא בְּשֵׁם יהוה, בֵּרַכְנוּכֶם מִבֵּית יהוה.

אֵל יהוה וַיָּאֶר־לָנוּ, אִסְרוּ־חַג בַּעֲבֹתִים עַד־קַרְנוֹת הַמִּזְבֵּחַ.

אֵל יהוה וַיָּאֶר־לָנוּ, אִסְרוּ־חַג בַּעֲבֹתִים עַד־קַרְנוֹת הַמִּזְבֵּחַ.

אֵלִי אַתָּה וְאוֹדֶךָּ, אֱלֹהַי אֲרוֹמְמֶךָּ.

אֵלִי אַתָּה וְאוֹדֶךָּ, אֱלֹהַי אֲרוֹמְמֶךָּ.

On סֻכּוֹת, the לוּלָב and אֶתְרוֹג are waved while saying הוֹדוּ לַיהוה, in the following sequence: ahead; right; back; left; up; down. They are not waved when saying God's name.

הוֹדוּ לַיהוה כִּי־טוֹב, כִּי לְעוֹלָם חַסְדּוֹ.

הוֹדוּ לַיהוה כִּי־טוֹב, כִּי לְעוֹלָם חַסְדּוֹ.

יְהַלְלוּךָ יהוה אֱלֹהֵינוּ כָּל־מַעֲשֶׂיךָ, וַחֲסִידֶיךָ צַדִּיקִים עוֹשֵׂי רְצוֹנֶךָ, וְכָל עַמְּךָ בֵּית יִשְׂרָאֵל בְּרִנָּה יוֹדוּ וִיבָרְכוּ וִישַׁבְּחוּ וִיפָאֲרוּ וִירוֹמְמוּ וְיַעֲרִיצוּ וְיַקְדִּישׁוּ וְיַמְלִיכוּ אֶת־שִׁמְךָ מַלְכֵּנוּ, ← כִּי לְךָ טוֹב לְהוֹדוֹת וּלְשִׁמְךָ נָאֶה לְזַמֵּר, כִּי מֵעוֹלָם וְעַד עוֹלָם אַתָּה אֵל. בָּרוּךְ אַתָּה יהוה, מֶלֶךְ מְהֻלָּל בַּתִּשְׁבָּחוֹת.

On רֹאשׁ חֹדֶשׁ and חוֹל הַמּוֹעֵד, say קַדִּישׁ תִּתְקַבַּל on page 138 and the service continues with קְרִיאַת הַתּוֹרָה on page 120.

On שַׁבָּת and יוֹם טוֹב, the service continues with קַדִּישׁ תִּתְקַבַּל on page 402.

On weekday חֲנֻכָּה, יוֹם הָעַצְמָאוּת and יוֹם יְרוּשָׁלַיִם, the service continues with חֲצִי קַדִּישׁ on page 118.

בָּרוּךְ הַבָּא *Blessed is one who comes*: A blessing made by the priests to those who come to worship in the Temple (Rashi, Radak). One of the tasks of the priests was to bless the people who came in pilgrimage to the Temple to make their offerings.

אֵל יהוה *The Lord is God*: This verse gives us the response of the people to the blessing of the priests, affirming that the offering they bring is dedicated to God.

אִסְרוּ־חַג בַּעֲבֹתִים *Bind the festival offering with thick cords*: Alternatively, "Order the festival procession with boughs, up to the horns of the altar", a reference to the pro-

בָּרוּךְ Blessed is one who comes in the name of the LORD; we bless you from the house of the LORD.

Blessed is one who comes in the name of the LORD; we bless you from the house of the LORD.

The LORD is GOD; He has given us light. Bind the festival offering with thick cords [and bring it] to the horns of the altar.

The LORD is GOD; He has given us light. Bind the festival offering with thick cords [and bring it] to the horns of the altar.

You are my GOD and I will thank You; You are my GOD, I will exalt You.

You are my GOD and I will thank You; You are my GOD, I will exalt You.

On Sukkot, the *lulav* and *etrog* are waved while saying "Thank the LORD..." in the following sequence: ahead; right; back; left; up; down. They are not waved when saying GOD's name.

Thank the LORD for He is good, His lovingkindness is for ever.

Thank the LORD for He is good, His lovingkindness is for ever.

יְהַלְלוּךָ All Your works will praise You, LORD our GOD, and Your devoted ones – the righteous who do Your will, together with all Your people the house of Israel – will joyously thank, bless, praise, glorify, exalt, revere, sanctify, and proclaim the sovereignty of Your name, our King. ➔ For it is good to thank You and fitting to sing psalms to Your name, for from eternity to eternity You are GOD. Blessed are You, LORD, King who is extolled with praises.

On Rosh Chodesh and the Intermediate Days of Festivals, say full *Kaddish* on page 139 and the service continues with the Reading of the Law on page 121.

On Shabbat and a Festival, the service continues with full *Kaddish* on page 403.

On weekday Chanukah, Yom Ha'Atzma'ut and Yom Yerushalayim, the service continues with half-*Kaddish* on page 119.

---

cession around the altar, with a *lulav*, on Sukkot (*Sukkah* 45a).

אֵלִי אַתָּה *You are my GOD*: The words of one who is bringing the offering. *And I will thank You* – alternatively, "I will acknowledge You". These are words of dedication, meaning: This offering I bring is an expression of thanks and acknowledgement to GOD for all His kindnesses to me.

יְהַלְלוּךָ *All Your works will praise You*: A concluding benediction, as at the end of the Verses of Praise.

תפילת מוסף לראש חודש

The תְּפִלִּין are now removed.

עמידה

The following prayer, until קַדְמוֹנִיּוֹת, on page 640, is said standing with feet together.

The עֲמִידָה is first said silently; then, if there is a מִנְיָן, it is repeated aloud by the Leader.

Take three steps back, then forward. At the points indicated by ▾, bend the knees at the first word, bow at the second, and stand straight before GOD's name.

אֲדֹנָי, שְׂפָתַי תִּפְתָּח, וּפִי יַגִּיד תְּהִלָּתֶךָ.

אבות

▾בָּרוּךְ אַתָּה יהוה אֱלֹהֵינוּ וֵאלֹהֵי אֲבוֹתֵינוּ, אֱלֹהֵי אַבְרָהָם, אֱלֹהֵי יִצְחָק, וֵאלֹהֵי יַעֲקֹב, הָאֵל הַגָּדוֹל הַגִּבּוֹר וְהַנּוֹרָא, אֵל עֶלְיוֹן, גּוֹמֵל חֲסָדִים טוֹבִים וְקוֹנֵה הַכֹּל, וְזוֹכֵר חַסְדֵי אָבוֹת, וּמֵבִיא גוֹאֵל לִבְנֵי בְנֵיהֶם, לְמַעַן שְׁמוֹ בְּאַהֲבָה. מֶלֶךְ עוֹזֵר וּמוֹשִׁיעַ וּמָגֵן. ▾בָּרוּךְ אַתָּה יהוה, מָגֵן אַבְרָהָם.

גבורות

אַתָּה גִּבּוֹר לְעוֹלָם אֲדֹנָי, מְחַיֵּה מֵתִים אַתָּה, רַב לְהוֹשִׁיעַ.

From after שִׂמְחַת תּוֹרָה until פֶּסַח, add:

מַשִּׁיב הָרוּחַ וּמוֹרִיד הַגָּשֶׁם.

ADDITIONAL SERVICE FOR THE NEW MOON

The New Moon, like the New Year, is understood in Judaism as a time of renewal and rededication, in which we pray for forgiveness and atonement and seek to begin again. In Temple times a special offering was brought, of which the *Musaf* prayer is a memory. The central blessing of the *Amidah* begins with a brief statement of the nature of the day, followed by a prayer for the restoration of

ADDITIONAL SERVICE FOR THE NEW MOON

The *tefillin* are now removed.

AMIDAH: THE STANDING PRAYER

The following prayer, until "in former years", on page 641, is said standing with feet together.

The *Amidah* is first said silently; then, if there is a *minyan*, it is repeated aloud by the Leader.

Take three steps back, then forward. At the points indicated by ▾, bend the knees at the first word, bow at the second, and stand straight before GOD's name.

O LORD, open my lips, so that my mouth may declare Your praise.

PATRIARCHS

▾בָּרוּךְ▾ Blessed are You, LORD our GOD and GOD of our Fathers, GOD of Abraham, GOD of Isaac and GOD of Jacob; the great, mighty and awesome GOD, GOD Most High, who bestows acts of lovingkindness and creates all, who remembers the lovingkindness of the Fathers and will bring a Redeemer to their children's children for the sake of His name, in love. King, Helper, Saviour, Shield: ▾Blessed are You, LORD, Shield of Abraham.

DIVINE MIGHT

אַתָּה You are eternally mighty, LORD. You give life to the dead and have great power to save.

From after Simchat Torah until Pesach, add:
He makes the wind blow and the rain fall.

---

the Temple and its sacrifices, a biblical passage describing the New Moon offering, and a prayer that the new month be blessed for good.

A midrashic tradition associates the New Moon with Jewish women, as a tribute to their faithfulness and to their generosity in providing gifts for the construction of the Tabernacle. From the first month of the second year after the Exodus, the day the Tabernacle was dedicated, it became a women's festival.

מְכַלְכֵּל חַיִּים בְּחֶסֶד, מְחַיֵּה מֵתִים בְּרַחֲמִים רַבִּים, סוֹמֵךְ נוֹפְלִים, וְרוֹפֵא חוֹלִים, וּמַתִּיר אֲסוּרִים, וּמְקַיֵּם אֱמוּנָתוֹ לִישֵׁנֵי עָפָר. מִי כָמְוֹךָ בַּעַל גְּבוּרוֹת, וּמִי דּוֹמֶה לָּךְ, מֶלֶךְ מֵמִית וּמְחַיֶּה וּמַצְמִיחַ יְשׁוּעָה. וְנֶאֱמָן אַתָּה לְהַחֲיוֹת מֵתִים. בָּרוּךְ אַתָּה יהוה, מְחַיֵּה הַמֵּתִים.

When saying the עֲמִידָה silently, go to אַתָּה קָדוֹשׁ overleaf.

קדושה

During the Leader's repetition, the following is said standing, with feet together, rising on the toes at the words indicated by ▲.

Congregation then Leader: **נְקַדֵּשׁ** אֶת־שִׁמְךָ בָּעוֹלָם, כְּשֵׁם שֶׁמַּקְדִּישִׁים אוֹתוֹ בִּשְׁמֵי מָרוֹם, כַּכָּתוּב עַל יַד נְבִיאֶךָ, וְקָרָא זֶה אֶל־זֶה וְאָמַר.

Congregation and Leader: ▲קָדוֹשׁ ▲קָדוֹשׁ ▲קָדוֹשׁ יהוה צְבָאוֹת, מְלֹא כָל־הָאָרֶץ כְּבוֹדוֹ.

Leader: לְעֻמָּתָם בָּרוּךְ יֹאמֵרוּ.

Congregation and Leader: ▲בָּרוּךְ כְּבוֹד־יהוה, מִמְּקוֹמוֹ.

Leader: וּבְדִבְרֵי קָדְשְׁךָ כָּתוּב לֵאמֹר.

Congregation and Leader: ▲יִמְלֹךְ יהוה לְעוֹלָם, אֱלֹהַיִךְ צִיּוֹן לְדֹר וָדֹר, הַלְלוּיָהּ.

Leader: לְדוֹר וָדוֹר נַגִּיד גָּדְלֶךָ וּלְנֵצַח נְצָחִים קְדֻשָּׁתְךָ נַקְדִּישׁ, וְשִׁבְחֲךָ אֱלֹהֵינוּ מִפִּינוּ לֹא יָמוּשׁ לְעוֹלָם וָעֶד, כִּי אֵל מֶלֶךְ גָּדוֹל וְקָדוֹשׁ אָתָּה. בָּרוּךְ אַתָּה יהוה, הָאֵל הַקָּדוֹשׁ.

He sustains the living with lovingkindness, and with great compassion revives the dead. He supports the fallen, heals the sick, sets captives free, and keeps His faith with those who sleep in the dust. Who is like You, Master of might, and to whom can You be compared, O King who brings death and gives life, and makes salvation grow? Faithful are You to revive the dead. Blessed are You, LORD, who revives the dead.

When saying the *Amidah* silently, go to "You are holy" overleaf.

KEDUSHAH

During the Leader's repetition, the following is said standing, with feet together, rising on the toes at the words indicated by ▲.

Congregation then Leader — נְקַדֵּשׁ We will sanctify Your name on earth, as they sanctify it in the highest heavens, as is written by Your prophet, "And they [the angels] call to one another saying:

Congregation and Leader — ▲Holy, ▲holy, ▲holy is the LORD of Hosts: the whole world is filled with His glory."

Leader — Those facing them say: "Blessed – "

Congregation and Leader — "▲Blessed is the LORD's glory from His place."

Leader — And in Your Holy Writings it is written thus:

Congregation and Leader — "▲The LORD shall reign forever. He is your GOD, Zion, from generation to generation, Halleluyah!"

Leader — From generation to generation we will declare Your greatness, and we will proclaim Your holiness for evermore. Your praise, our GOD, shall never leave our mouth, for You, GOD, are a great and holy King. Blessed are You, LORD, the holy GOD.

רָאשֵׁי חֳדָשִׁים *You have given New Moons to Your people*: The Jewish people is compared to the moon because, whereas the sun shines with its own light, the moon shines with reflected light. So too with Israel: the light with which we shine comes not from ourselves but from GOD, of whose glory we are but a reflection (Sforno).

When saying the עֲמִידָה silently, continue here:

קדושת השם

אַתָּה קָדוֹשׁ וְשִׁמְךָ קָדוֹשׁ, וּקְדוֹשִׁים בְּכָל־יוֹם יְהַלְלְוּךָ סֶּלָה. בָּרוּךְ אַתָּה יהוה, הָאֵל הַקָּדוֹשׁ.

קדושת היום

רָאשֵׁי חֳדָשִׁים לְעַמְּךָ נָתַתָּ, זְמַן כַּפָּרָה לְכָל־תּוֹלְדוֹתָם, בִּהְיוֹתָם מַקְרִיבִים לְפָנֶיךָ זִבְחֵי רָצוֹן, וּשְׂעִירֵי חַטָּאת לְכַפֵּר בַּעֲדָם. זִכָּרוֹן לְכֻלָּם יִהְיוּ, וּתְשׁוּעַת נַפְשָׁם מִיַּד שׂוֹנֵא. מִזְבֵּחַ חָדָשׁ בְּצִיּוֹן תָּכִין, וְעוֹלַת רֹאשׁ חֹדֶשׁ נַעֲלֶה עָלָיו, וּשְׂעִירֵי עִזִּים נַעֲשֶׂה בְרָצוֹן. וּבַעֲבוֹדַת בֵּית הַמִּקְדָּשׁ נִשְׂמַח כֻּלָּנוּ, וּבְשִׁירֵי דָוִד עַבְדְּךָ הַנִּשְׁמָעִים בְּעִירֶךָ, הָאֲמוּרִים לִפְנֵי מִזְבְּחֶךָ. אַהֲבַת עוֹלָם תָּבִיא לָהֶם, וּבְרִית אָבוֹת לַבָּנִים תִּזְכּוֹר. וַהֲבִיאֵנוּ לְצִיּוֹן עִירְךָ בְּרִנָּה, וְלִירוּשָׁלַיִם בֵּית מִקְדָּשְׁךָ בְּשִׂמְחַת עוֹלָם. וְשָׁם נַעֲשֶׂה לְפָנֶיךָ אֶת־קָרְבְּנוֹת חוֹבוֹתֵינוּ, תְּמִידִים כְּסִדְרָם, וּמוּסָפִים כְּהִלְכָתָם, וְאֶת־מוּסַף יוֹם רֹאשׁ הַחֹדֶשׁ הַזֶּה נַעֲשֶׂה וְנַקְרִיב לְפָנֶיךָ בְּאַהֲבָה כְּמִצְוַת רְצוֹנֶךָ, כְּמוֹ שֶׁכָּתַבְתָּ עָלֵינוּ בְּתוֹרָתֶךָ, עַל־יְדֵי מֹשֶׁה עַבְדֶּךָ, מִפִּי כְבוֹדֶךָ, כָּאָמוּר.

וּבְרָאשֵׁי חָדְשֵׁיכֶם תַּקְרִיבוּ עֹלָה לַיהוה, פָּרִים בְּנֵי בָקָר שְׁנַיִם, וְאַיִל אֶחָד, כְּבָשִׂים בְּנֵי שָׁנָה שִׁבְעָה תְּמִימִם. וּמִנְחָתָם וְנִסְכֵּיהֶם כִּמְדֻבָּר, שְׁלֹשָׁה עֶשְׂרֹנִים לַפָּר, וּשְׁנֵי עֶשְׂרֹנִים לָאָיִל, וְעִשָּׂרוֹן לַכֶּבֶשׂ וְיַיִן כְּנִסְכּוֹ, וְשָׂעִיר לְכַפֵּר, וּשְׁנֵי תְמִידִים כְּהִלְכָתָם.

אֱלֹהֵינוּ וֵאלֹהֵי אֲבוֹתֵינוּ, חַדֵּשׁ עָלֵינוּ אֶת־הַחֹדֶשׁ הַזֶּה לְטוֹבָה וְלִבְרָכָה, לְשָׂשׂוֹן וּלְשִׂמְחָה, לִישׁוּעָה וּלְנֶחָמָה, לְפַרְנָסָה וּלְכַלְכָּלָה, לְחַיִּים וּלְשָׁלוֹם, לִמְחִילַת חֵטְא וְלִסְלִיחַת עָוֹן,

When saying the *Amidah* silently, continue here:

HOLINESS

אַתָּה קָדוֹשׁ You are holy and Your name is holy, and holy ones praise You daily, Selah! Blessed are You, LORD, the holy GOD.

HOLINESS OF THE DAY

רָאשֵׁי חֳדָשִׁים You have given New Moons to Your people as a time of atonement for all their offspring. They would bring You offerings of goodwill, and goats as sin-offerings for atonement. It served as a remembrance for them all, and a deliverance of their lives from the hand of the enemy. May You establish a new altar in Zion, and may we offer on it the New Moon burnt-offering, and prepare goats in favour. May we all rejoice in the Temple service, and may the songs of David Your servant, be heard in Your city, chanted before Your altar. Bestow on them everlasting love, and remember the covenant of the fathers for their children. Bring us back, with song, to Zion Your city, and to Jerusalem Your sanctuary with everlasting joy. There we will prepare for You our obligatory offerings: the regular daily offerings in their order, and the additional offerings according to their law. The additional offering of this New Moon day we will prepare and offer to You with love according to Your will's commandment, as You have written for us in Your Torah by Your own word, through Your servant Moses, as it is said:

וּבְרָאשֵׁי "On your new moons, present as a burnt-offering to the LORD, two young bulls, one ram, and seven yearling lambs without blemish." And their meal-offerings and wine-libations as ordained: three-tenths of an ephah for each bull, two-tenths of an ephah for the ram, one-tenth of an ephah for each lamb, wine for the libations, a male goat for atonement, and two regular daily offerings according to their law.

אֱלֹהֵינוּ O GOD and GOD of our ancestors, renew for us the coming month for good and blessing, joy and gladness, deliverance and consolation, sustenance and support, life and peace, pardon of sin and forgiveness of iniquity,

---

וּלְכַפָּרַת פָּשַׁע *And atonement for transgression*: There are six months from Tishrei (Rosh Hashanah, the beginning of the year) to Nisan (the first of months: Exodus 12:2), hence the six double expressions of blessing. In a leap year there are seven months before Nisan, hence a seventh expression is added from Tishrei to Nisan.

From חֶשְׁוָן to אֲדָר שֵׁנִי in a Jewish leap year (see page 1037), add:

וּלְכַפָּרַת פָּשַׁע.

כִּי בְעַמְּךָ יִשְׂרָאֵל בָּחַרְתָּ מִכָּל־הָאֻמּוֹת, וְחֻקֵּי רָאשֵׁי חֳדָשִׁים לָהֶם קָבָעְתָּ. בָּרוּךְ אַתָּה יהוה, מְקַדֵּשׁ יִשְׂרָאֵל וְרָאשֵׁי חֳדָשִׁים.

עבודה

רְצֵה יהוה אֱלֹהֵינוּ בְּעַמְּךָ יִשְׂרָאֵל וּבִתְפִלָּתָם, וְהָשֵׁב אֶת־הָעֲבוֹדָה לִדְבִיר בֵּיתֶךָ. וְאִשֵּׁי יִשְׂרָאֵל וּתְפִלָּתָם בְּאַהֲבָה תְקַבֵּל בְּרָצוֹן, וּתְהִי לְרָצוֹן תָּמִיד עֲבוֹדַת יִשְׂרָאֵל עַמֶּךָ.

וְתֶחֱזֶינָה עֵינֵינוּ בְּשׁוּבְךָ לְצִיּוֹן בְּרַחֲמִים. בָּרוּךְ אַתָּה יהוה, הַמַּחֲזִיר שְׁכִינָתוֹ לְצִיּוֹן.

הודאה

▽ Bow at the first five words.

▽**מוֹדִים** אֲנַחְנוּ לָךְ, שָׁאַתָּה הוּא יהוה אֱלֹהֵינוּ וֵאלֹהֵי אֲבוֹתֵינוּ לְעוֹלָם וָעֶד. צוּר חַיֵּינוּ, מָגֵן יִשְׁעֵנוּ אַתָּה הוּא לְדוֹר וָדוֹר. נוֹדֶה לְּךָ וּנְסַפֵּר תְּהִלָּתֶךָ עַל חַיֵּינוּ הַמְּסוּרִים בְּיָדֶךָ, וְעַל נִשְׁמוֹתֵינוּ הַפְּקוּדוֹת לָךְ, וְעַל נִסֶּיךָ שֶׁבְּכָל־יוֹם עִמָּנוּ, וְעַל נִפְלְאוֹתֶיךָ וְטוֹבוֹתֶיךָ שֶׁבְּכָל־עֵת, עֶרֶב וָבֹקֶר וְצָהֳרָיִם. הַטּוֹב כִּי לֹא־כָלוּ רַחֲמֶיךָ, וְהַמְרַחֵם כִּי לֹא־תַמּוּ חֲסָדֶיךָ, מֵעוֹלָם קִוִּינוּ לָךְ.

During the Leader's repetition, the Congregation says quietly:

▽**מוֹדִים** אֲנַחְנוּ לָךְ, שָׁאַתָּה הוּא יהוה אֱלֹהֵינוּ וֵאלֹהֵי אֲבוֹתֵינוּ, אֱלֹהֵי כָל־בָּשָׂר, יוֹצְרֵנוּ, יוֹצֵר בְּרֵאשִׁית. בְּרָכוֹת וְהוֹדָאוֹת לְשִׁמְךָ הַגָּדוֹל וְהַקָּדוֹשׁ, עַל שֶׁהֶחֱיִיתָנוּ וְקִיַּמְתָּנוּ. כֵּן תְּחַיֵּנוּ וּתְקַיְּמֵנוּ, וְתֶאֱסוֹף גָּלֻיּוֹתֵינוּ לְחַצְרוֹת קָדְשֶׁךָ, לִשְׁמוֹר חֻקֶּיךָ וְלַעֲשׂוֹת רְצוֹנֶךָ, וּלְעָבְדְּךָ בְּלֵבָב שָׁלֵם, עַל שֶׁאֲנַחְנוּ מוֹדִים לָךְ. בָּרוּךְ אֵל הַהוֹדָאוֹת.

From Cheshvan to Adar II in a Jewish leap year (see page 1037), add:
and atonement of transgression.

For You have chosen Your people Israel from all nations, and have instituted for them rules for the New Moon. Blessed are You, LORD, who sanctifies Israel and the New Moons.

TEMPLE SERVICE

רְצֵה Find favour, LORD our GOD, in Your people Israel and their prayer. Restore the service to Your most holy house, and accept in love and favour the fire-offerings of Israel and their prayer. May the service of Your people Israel always find favour with You.

וְתֶחֱזֶינָה And may our eyes witness Your return to Zion in compassion. Blessed are You, LORD, who restores His Presence to Zion.

THANKSGIVING

▽ Bow at the first nine words.

מוֹדִים▽ We give thanks to You, for You are the LORD our GOD and GOD of our ancestors for ever and all time. You are the Rock of our lives, Shield of our salvation from generation to generation. We will thank You and declare Your praise for our lives, which are entrusted into Your hand; our souls, which are placed in Your charge; for Your miracles which are with us every day; and for Your wonders and favours at all times, evening, morning and midday. You are good – for Your compassion never fails. You are compassionate – for Your loving-kindnesses never cease. We have always placed our hope in You.

During the Leader's repetition, the Congregation says quietly:

מוֹדִים▽ We give thanks to You, for You are the LORD our GOD and GOD of our ancestors, GOD of all flesh, who formed us and formed the universe. Blessings and thanks are due to Your great and holy name for giving us life and sustaining us. May You continue to give us life and sustain us; and may You gather our exiles to Your holy courts, to keep Your decrees, do Your will and serve You with a perfect heart, for it is for us to give You thanks. Blessed be GOD to whom thanksgiving is due.

On חֲנֻכָּה, say:

עַל הַנִּסִּים, וְעַל הַפֻּרְקָן, וְעַל הַגְּבוּרוֹת, וְעַל הַתְּשׁוּעוֹת, וְעַל הַמִּלְחָמוֹת, שֶׁעָשִׂיתָ לַאֲבוֹתֵינוּ בַּיָּמִים הָהֵם בַּזְּמַן הַזֶּה.

בִּימֵי מַתִּתְיָהוּ בֶּן־יוֹחָנָן כֹּהֵן גָּדוֹל חַשְׁמוֹנַאי וּבָנָיו, כְּשֶׁעָמְדָה מַלְכוּת יָוָן הָרְשָׁעָה עַל־עַמְּךָ יִשְׂרָאֵל, לְהַשְׁכִּיחָם תּוֹרָתֶךָ, וּלְהַעֲבִירָם מֵחֻקֵּי רְצוֹנֶךָ. וְאַתָּה בְּרַחֲמֶיךָ הָרַבִּים, עָמַדְתָּ לָהֶם בְּעֵת צָרָתָם, רַבְתָּ אֶת־רִיבָם, דַּנְתָּ אֶת־דִּינָם, נָקַמְתָּ אֶת־נִקְמָתָם. מָסַרְתָּ גִבּוֹרִים בְּיַד חַלָּשִׁים, וְרַבִּים בְּיַד מְעַטִּים, וּטְמֵאִים בְּיַד טְהוֹרִים, וּרְשָׁעִים בְּיַד צַדִּיקִים, וְזֵדִים בְּיַד עוֹסְקֵי תוֹרָתֶךָ. וּלְךָ עָשִׂיתָ שֵׁם גָּדוֹל וְקָדוֹשׁ בְּעוֹלָמֶךָ, וּלְעַמְּךָ יִשְׂרָאֵל עָשִׂיתָ תְּשׁוּעָה גְדוֹלָה וּפֻרְקָן כְּהַיּוֹם הַזֶּה. וְאַחַר כֵּן בָּאוּ בָנֶיךָ לִדְבִיר בֵּיתֶךָ, וּפִנּוּ אֶת־הֵיכָלֶךָ, וְטִהֲרוּ אֶת־מִקְדָּשֶׁךָ, וְהִדְלִיקוּ נֵרוֹת בְּחַצְרוֹת קָדְשֶׁךָ, וְקָבְעוּ שְׁמוֹנַת יְמֵי חֲנֻכָּה אֵלּוּ, לְהוֹדוֹת וּלְהַלֵּל לְשִׁמְךָ הַגָּדוֹל.

וְעַל כֻּלָּם יִתְבָּרַךְ וְיִתְרוֹמַם שִׁמְךָ מַלְכֵּנוּ תָּמִיד לְעוֹלָם וָעֶד. וְכֹל הַחַיִּים יוֹדוּךָ סֶּלָה, וִיהַלְלוּ אֶת־שִׁמְךָ בֶּאֱמֶת, הָאֵל יְשׁוּעָתֵנוּ וְעֶזְרָתֵנוּ סֶלָה. ▾בָּרוּךְ אַתָּה יהוה, הַטּוֹב שִׁמְךָ וּלְךָ נָאֶה לְהוֹדוֹת.

During the repetition of the עֲמִידָה, the Leader says the following, except at in a house of mourning during the week of שִׁבְעָה:

אֱלֹהֵינוּ וֵאלֹהֵי אֲבוֹתֵינוּ, בָּרְכֵנוּ בַּבְּרָכָה הַמְשֻׁלֶּשֶׁת, בַּתּוֹרָה, הַכְּתוּבָה עַל יְדֵי מֹשֶׁה עַבְדֶּךָ, הָאֲמוּרָה מִפִּי אַהֲרֹן וּבָנָיו כֹּהֲנִים, עַם קְדוֹשֶׁךָ, כָּאָמוּר.

יְבָרֶכְךָ יהוה, וְיִשְׁמְרֶךָ. (Cong.: כֵּן יְהִי רָצוֹן)

יָאֵר יהוה פָּנָיו אֵלֶיךָ וִיחֻנֶּךָּ. (Cong.: כֵּן יְהִי רָצוֹן)

יִשָּׂא יהוה פָּנָיו אֵלֶיךָ וְיָשֵׂם לְךָ שָׁלוֹם. (Cong.: כֵּן יְהִי רָצוֹן)

On Chanukah, say:

עַל הַנִּסִּים [We thank You also] for the miracles, the redemption, the mighty deeds, and the victories in battle which You performed for our ancestors in those days at this time.

בִּימֵי In the days of Mattityahu, son of Yochanan the High Priest, the Hasmonean, and his sons, the wicked Greek kingdom rose up against Your people Israel to make them forget Your Torah and to force them to transgress the statutes of Your will. It was then that You in Your great compassion stood by them in the time of their distress. You championed their cause, judged their claim, and avenged their wrong. You delivered the strong into the hands of the weak, the many into the hands of the few, the impure into the hands of the pure, the wicked into the hands of the righteous, and the arrogant into the hands of those who were engaged in the study of Your Torah. You made for Yourself great and holy renown in Your world, and for Your people Israel You performed a great salvation and redemption on this day. Your children then entered the holiest part of Your house, cleansed Your Temple, purified Your sanctuary, kindled lights in Your holy courts, and designated these eight days of Chanukah for giving thanks and praise to Your great name.

וְעַל For all these things may Your name be blessed and exalted, our King, continually, for ever and all time. Let all that lives thank You, Selah! and praise Your name in truth, God, our Saviour and Help, Selah! ▼Blessed are You, Lord, whose name is "the Good" and to whom thanks are due.

During the repetition of the *Amidah*, the Leader says the following, except in a house of mourning during the week of *shivah*:

אֱלֹהֵינוּ Our God and God of our fathers, bless us with the threefold blessing in the Torah, written by the hand of Moses Your servant and pronounced by Aaron and his sons the priests, Your holy people, as it is said:

May the Lord bless you and protect you. (Cong.: May it be Your will.)

May the Lord make His face shine on you and be gracious to you. (Cong.: May it be Your will.)

May the Lord turn His face towards you, and give you peace. (Cong.: May it be Your will.)

ברכת שלום

שִׂים שָׁלוֹם, טוֹבָה, וּבְרָכָה, חֵן, וָחֶסֶד וְרַחֲמִים עָלֵינוּ וְעַל כָּל־יִשְׂרָאֵל עַמֶּךָ. בָּרְכֵנוּ אָבִינוּ, כֻּלָּנוּ כְּאֶחָד בְּאוֹר פָּנֶיךָ, כִּי בְאוֹר פָּנֶיךָ נָתַתָּ לָּנוּ, יהוה אֱלֹהֵינוּ, תּוֹרַת חַיִּים וְאַהֲבַת חֶסֶד, וּצְדָקָה, וּבְרָכָה, וְרַחֲמִים, וְחַיִּים, וְשָׁלוֹם. וְטוֹב בְּעֵינֶיךָ לְבָרֵךְ אֶת־עַמְּךָ יִשְׂרָאֵל, בְּכָל־עֵת וּבְכָל־שָׁעָה בִּשְׁלוֹמֶךָ. בָּרוּךְ אַתָּה יהוה, הַמְבָרֵךְ אֶת עַמּוֹ יִשְׂרָאֵל בַּשָּׁלוֹם.

The Leader's repetition ends at this point.

אֱלֹהַי, נְצֹר לְשׁוֹנִי מֵרָע, וּשְׂפָתַי מִדַּבֵּר מִרְמָה, וְלִמְקַלְלַי נַפְשִׁי תִדֹּם, וְנַפְשִׁי כֶּעָפָר לַכֹּל תִּהְיֶה. פְּתַח לִבִּי בְּתוֹרָתֶךָ, וּבְמִצְוֹתֶיךָ תִּרְדֹּף נַפְשִׁי. וְכָל הַחוֹשְׁבִים עָלַי רָעָה, מְהֵרָה הָפֵר עֲצָתָם וְקַלְקֵל מַחֲשַׁבְתָּם. עֲשֵׂה לְמַעַן שְׁמֶךָ, עֲשֵׂה לְמַעַן יְמִינֶךָ, עֲשֵׂה לְמַעַן קְדֻשָּׁתֶךָ, עֲשֵׂה לְמַעַן תּוֹרָתֶךָ. לְמַעַן יֵחָלְצוּן יְדִידֶיךָ, הוֹשִׁיעָה יְמִינְךָ וַעֲנֵנִי. יִהְיוּ לְרָצוֹן אִמְרֵי־פִי וְהֶגְיוֹן לִבִּי לְפָנֶיךָ, יהוה צוּרִי וְגוֹאֲלִי.

Bow, take three steps back, then bow, first left, then right, then centre, while saying:

עֹשֶׂה שָׁלוֹם בִּמְרוֹמָיו, הוּא יַעֲשֶׂה שָׁלוֹם עָלֵינוּ, וְעַל־כָּל־יִשְׂרָאֵל, וְאִמְרוּ אָמֵן.

יְהִי רָצוֹן מִלְּפָנֶיךָ יהוה אֱלֹהֵינוּ וֵאלֹהֵי אֲבוֹתֵינוּ, שֶׁיִּבָּנֶה בֵּית הַמִּקְדָּשׁ בִּמְהֵרָה בְיָמֵינוּ, וְתֵן חֶלְקֵנוּ בְּתוֹרָתֶךָ. וְשָׁם נַעֲבָדְךָ בְּיִרְאָה, כִּימֵי עוֹלָם וּכְשָׁנִים קַדְמוֹנִיּוֹת. וְעָרְבָה לַיהוה מִנְחַת יְהוּדָה וִירוּשָׁלָםִ, כִּימֵי עוֹלָם וּכְשָׁנִים קַדְמוֹנִיּוֹת.

When praying with a מִנְיָן, the עֲמִידָה is repeated aloud by the Leader.

The weekday service continues with קַדִּישׁ תִּתְקַבַּל on page 138.

PEACE

שִׂים Grant peace, goodness and blessing, grace, lovingkindness and compassion to us and all Israel Your people. Bless us, our Father, all as one, with the light of Your face, for by the light of Your face You have given us, LORD our GOD, the Torah of life and love of kindness, righteousness, blessing, compassion, life and peace. May it be good in Your eyes to bless Your people Israel at every time, in every hour, with Your peace. Blessed are You, LORD, who blesses His people Israel with peace.

The Leader's repetition ends at this point.

אֱלֹהַי My GOD, guard my tongue from evil and my lips from deceitful speech. To those who curse me, let my soul be silent; may my soul be to all like the dust. Open my heart to Your Torah and let my Soul pursue Your commandments. As for all who plan evil against me, swiftly thwart their counsel and frustrate their plans. Act for the sake of Your name; act for the sake of Your right hand; act for the sake of Your holiness; act for the sake of Your Torah. That Your beloved ones may be delivered, save with Your right hand and answer me. May the words of my mouth and the meditation of my heart find favour before You, LORD, my Rock and Redeemer.

Bow, take three steps back, then bow, first left, then right, then centre, while saying:

May He who makes peace in His high places, make peace for us and all Israel – and say: Amen.

יְהִי May it be Your will, LORD our GOD and GOD of our ancestors, that the Temple be rebuilt speedily in our days, and grant us a share in Your Torah. And there we will serve You with reverence, as in the days of old and as in former years. Then the offering of Judah and Jerusalem will be pleasing to the LORD as in the days of old and as in former years.

When praying with a *minyan*, the *Amidah* is repeated aloud by the Leader.

The weekday service continues with full *Kaddish* on page 139.

בדיקת חמץ

On the night before פֶּסַח, a search for חָמֵץ such as breadcrumbs, products containing leaven, and grain alcohol, is made in the house. The custom is to do so at night by the light of a candle. If פֶּסַח falls on Saturday night, the search is made on Thursday night. Those who plan to be away on פֶּסַח conduct the search the night before their departure, but without making a blessing. Before the search, make the following blessing:

בָּרוּךְ אַתָּה יהוה אֱלֹהֵינוּ מֶלֶךְ הָעוֹלָם, אֲשֶׁר קִדְּשָׁנוּ בְּמִצְוֹתָיו, וְצִוָּנוּ עַל בִּעוּר חָמֵץ.

After the search, say:

כָּל־חֲמִירָא וַחֲמִיעָא דְּאִכָּא בִרְשׁוּתִי דְּלָא חֲמִתֵּהּ וּדְלָא בִעַרְתֵּהּ לִבְטִל וְלֶהֱוֵא כְּעַפְרָא דְאַרְעָא.

On the following morning after burning the חָמֵץ, make the following declaration:

כָּל־חֲמִירָא וַחֲמִיעָא דְּאִכָּא בִרְשׁוּתִי, דַּחֲמִתֵּהּ וּדְלָא חֲמִתֵּהּ, דְּבִעַרְתֵּהּ וּדְלָא בִעַרְתֵּהּ, לִבְטִל וְלֶהֱוֵא כְּעַפְרָא דְאַרְעָא.

ערוב תבשילין

It is not permitted to cook for שַׁבָּת when a יום טוב falls on Thursday or Friday unless an עֵרוּב תַּבְשִׁילִין has been made prior to the יום טוב. This is done by taking a loaf or piece of matzah together with a boiled egg, or a piece of cooked fish or meat to be used on שַׁבָּת. While holding them, say the following:

בָּרוּךְ אַתָּה יהוה אֱלֹהֵינוּ מֶלֶךְ הָעוֹלָם, אֲשֶׁר קִדְּשָׁנוּ בְּמִצְוֹתָיו, וְצִוָּנוּ עַל מִצְוַת עֵרוּב.

בְּדֵין עֵרוּבָא יְהֵא שְׁרֵא לָנָא לְמֵיפָא וּלְבַשָּׁלָא וּלְאַטְמָנָא וּלְאַדְלָקָא שְׁרָגָא, וּלְמֶעְבַּד כָּל־צָרְכָּנָא, מִיּוֹמָא טָבָא לְשַׁבְּתָא, לָנוּ וּלְכָל־הַדָּרִים בָּעִיר הַזֹּאת.

SEARCH FOR CHAMETZ
On Pesach, not only is it forbidden to eat leavened products, it is also forbidden to have them in our possession (Exodus 12:19; 13:7). For that reason, a search was instituted on the night before the festival. All leaven is to be removed (usually destroyed by burning) the next morning. The blessing said prior to the search refers to the removal, since the search is a means to that end. The two declarations – one made at night after the search, the other in the morning after the removal – constitute a legal nullification and renunciation of ownership of any remaining *chametz*.

SEARCH FOR CHAMETZ

On the night before Pesach, a search for *chametz*, such as breadcrumbs, products containing leaven and grain alcohol, is made in the house. The custom is to do so at night by the light of a candle. If Pesach falls on Saturday night, the search is made on Thursday night. Those who plan to be away on Pesach should conduct the search the night before their departure, but without making a blessing. Before the search, make the following blessing:

בָּרוּךְ Blessed are You, LORD our GOD, King of the Universe, who has made us holy through His commandments, and has commanded us about the removal of leaven.

After the search, say:

כָּל־חֲמִירָא May all *chametz* or leaven that is in my possession which I have not seen or removed be annulled and deemed like the dust of the earth.

On the following morning after burning the *chametz*, make the following declaration:

כָּל־חֲמִירָא May all *chametz* or leaven that is in my possession, whether I have seen it or not, whether I have removed it or not, be annulled and deemed like the dust of the earth.

ERUV TAVSHILIN

It is not permitted to cook for Shabbat when a festival falls on Thursday or Friday unless an *Eruv Tavshilin* has been made prior to the festival. This is done by taking a loaf or piece of matzah together with a boiled egg, or a piece of cooked fish or meat to be used on Shabbat. While holding them, say the following:

בָּרוּךְ Blessed are You, LORD our GOD, King of the Universe, who has made us holy through His commandments, and has commanded us about the *mitzvah* of *Eruv*.

בְּדֵין By means of this *Eruv*, may we be permitted to bake, cook, insulate, light the Sabbath lights, and prepare during the festival all we need for the Sabbath – we and all Jews who live in this town.

ERUV TAVSHILIN
Though food may be prepared on a festival for the day itself, it may not be prepared for a subsequent weekday. When a festival falls on Thursday or Friday, cooking on the festival for the Shabbat is permitted only when an *Eruv* has been made before the festival begins. The *Eruv*, consisting of a loaf of bread or piece of matzah, together with an item of cooked food, represents a symbolic preparation of food for Shabbat prior to the festival, and serves as a reminder of the law that no cooking is permitted on a festival for a weekday.

הדלקת נרות של יום טוב

It is a tradition to give צְדָקָה before kindling the יום טוב lights.
Meditation before lighting the יום טוב candles.
On Friday, add the words in brackets.

רִבּוֹן הָעוֹלָמִים, הִנֵּה בָאתִי לְהַדְלִיק אֶת הַנֵּרוֹת (לִכְבוֹד הַשַּׁבָּת וְ) לִכְבוֹד *הָרֶגֶל.

*on עֶרֶב רֹאשׁ הַשָּׁנָה substitute:
יוֹם הַזִּכָּרוֹן הַזֶּה
on עֶרֶב יוֹם כִּפּוּר substitute:
יוֹם הַכִּפּוּרִים

וּבִזְכוּת מִצְוָה זוֹ, תַּשְׁפִּיעַ עָלַי וְעַל בְּנֵי בֵיתִי, שֶׁפַע הַחַיִּים שֶׁתְּחָנֵּנוּ וּתְבָרְכֵנוּ בְּרֹב בְּרָכוֹת, וְתַשְׁכֵּן שְׁכִינָתְךָ בְּתוֹכֵנוּ.

Add the words in brackets if you have children.

אַב הָרַחֲמִים, אָנָּא מְשֹׁךְ חַסְדְּךָ עָלַי וְעַל קְרוֹבַי הָאֲהוּבִים (וְזַכֵּנִי לְגַדֵּל בָּנַי וּבְנוֹתַי) לָלֶכֶת בְּדַרְכֵי יְשָׁרִים לְפָנֶיךָ, דְּבֵקִים בַּתּוֹרָה, וּבְמַעֲשִׂים טוֹבִים. הַרְחֵק מֵעָלֵינוּ כָּל חֶרְפָּה, תּוּגָה, וְיָגוֹן, וְשִׂים שָׁלוֹם אוֹרָה וְשִׂמְחָה בִּמְעוֹנֵנוּ, כִּי עִמְּךָ מְקוֹר חַיִּים, בְּאוֹרְךָ נִרְאֶה־אוֹר, אָמֵן.

On פֶּסַח, שָׁבֻעוֹת and סֻכּוֹת, cover your eyes with your hands after lighting the candles, and say (on Friday add the words in brackets):

בָּרוּךְ אַתָּה יהוה אֱלֹהֵינוּ מֶלֶךְ הָעוֹלָם, אֲשֶׁר קִדְּשָׁנוּ בְּמִצְוֹתָיו, וְצִוָּנוּ לְהַדְלִיק נֵר שֶׁל (שַׁבָּת וְ) יוֹם טוֹב.

On יוֹם כִּפּוּר, cover your eyes with your hands after lighting the candles and say (on Friday add the words in brackets):

בָּרוּךְ אַתָּה יהוה אֱלֹהֵינוּ מֶלֶךְ הָעוֹלָם, אֲשֶׁר קִדְּשָׁנוּ בְּמִצְוֹתָיו, וְצִוָּנוּ לְהַדְלִיק נֵר שֶׁל (שַׁבָּת וְ) יוֹם הַכִּיפּוּרִים.

The following blessing is not said on the last two evenings of פֶּסַח.

בָּרוּךְ אַתָּה יהוה אֱלֹהֵינוּ מֶלֶךְ הָעוֹלָם, שֶׁהֶחֱיָנוּ וְקִיְּמָנוּ וְהִגִּיעָנוּ לַזְּמַן הַזֶּה.

LIGHTING THE FESTIVAL CANDLES

It Is a tradition to give charity before kindling the festival lights.
Meditation before lighting the festival candles.
On Friday, add the words in brackets.

רִבּוֹן הָעוֹלָמִים Master of the Universe: I am about to fulfil the commandment of lighting lights (in honour of the Sabbath and) in honour of the *festival.

*On the eve of Rosh Hashanah substitute:
Day of Memorial
On the eve of Yom Kippur substitute:
Yom Kippur

May You, in the merit of this commandment, bestow on me and my family a full life. Be gracious to us. May You bless us with many blessings, and cause Your Presence to dwell among us.

Add the words in brackets if you have children.

אַב Compassionate Father, extend Your lovingkindness to me and my loved ones (and grant me the privilege of raising my children) so that they walk before You in the ways of the upright, holding fast to Your Torah and to good deeds. Keep far from us any shame, grief and sorrow. Set peace, light and joy in our home, for with You is the source of life; in Your light, we see light. Amen.

On Pesach, Shavuot and Sukkot, cover your eyes with your hands after lighting the candles, and say (on Friday add the words in brackets):

בָּרוּךְ Blessed are You, Lord our God, King of the Universe, who has made us holy through His commandments, and has commanded us to light (the Sabbath light and) the festival light.

On Yom Kippur, cover your eyes with your hands after lighting the candles, and say (on Friday add the words in brackets):

בָּרוּךְ Blessed are You, Lord our God, King of the Universe, who has made us holy through His commandments, and has commanded us to light (the Sabbath light and) the light of the Day of Atonement.

The following blessing is not said on the last two evenings of Pesach.

בָּרוּךְ Blessed are You, Lord our God, King of the Universe, who has given us life, sustained us, and brought us to this time.

סדר התפילה לרגלים

On עֶרֶב יוֹם טוֹב, the מִנְחָה Service is said on page 170. When יוֹם טוֹב falls on שַׁבָּת, and on שַׁבָּת חוֹל הַמּוֹעֵד, the מַעֲרִיב Service begins with מִזְמוֹר שִׁיר, on page 270. When יוֹם טוֹב or חוֹל הַמּוֹעֵד falls on a weekday, the מַעֲרִיב Service begins with בָּרְכוּ, on page 274. The following עֲמִידָה is said at שַׁחֲרִית, מִנְחָה and מַעֲרִיב of שִׂמְחַת תּוֹרָה and שְׁמִינִי עֲצֶרֶת, סֻכּוֹת, שָׁבֻעוֹת, פֶּסַח, but not on חוֹל הַמּוֹעֵד.

עמידה

The following prayer, until קַדְמוֹנִיּוֹת on page 660, is said standing with feet together. The עֲמִידָה is first said silently; then, if there is a מִנְיָן, it is repeated aloud by the Leader except at מַעֲרִיב. Take three steps back, then forward. At the points indicated by ▾, bend the knees at the first word, bow at the second, and stand straight before God's name.

אֲדֹנָי שְׂפָתַי תִּפְתָּח, וּפִי יַגִּיד תְּהִלָּתֶךָ.

אבות

▾**בָּרוּךְ** אַתָּה יהוה אֱלֹהֵינוּ וֵאלֹהֵי אֲבוֹתֵינוּ, אֱלֹהֵי אַבְרָהָם, אֱלֹהֵי יִצְחָק, וֵאלֹהֵי יַעֲקֹב, הָאֵל הַגָּדוֹל הַגִּבּוֹר וְהַנּוֹרָא, אֵל עֶלְיוֹן, גּוֹמֵל חֲסָדִים טוֹבִים וְקוֹנֵה הַכֹּל, וְזוֹכֵר חַסְדֵי אָבוֹת, וּמֵבִיא גּוֹאֵל לִבְנֵי בְנֵיהֶם, לְמַעַן שְׁמוֹ בְּאַהֲבָה. מֶלֶךְ עוֹזֵר וּמוֹשִׁיעַ וּמָגֵן. ▾בָּרוּךְ אַתָּה יהוה, מָגֵן אַבְרָהָם.

גבורות

אַתָּה גִּבּוֹר לְעוֹלָם אֲדֹנָי, מְחַיֵּה מֵתִים אַתָּה, רַב לְהוֹשִׁיעַ.

From שְׁמִינִי עֲצֶרֶת of מִנְחָה until, and including, שַׁחֲרִית on the first day of פֶּסַח, add:

מַשִּׁיב הָרוּחַ וּמוֹרִיד הַגֶּשֶׁם.

מְכַלְכֵּל חַיִּים בְּחֶסֶד, מְחַיֵּה מֵתִים בְּרַחֲמִים רַבִּים, סוֹמֵךְ נוֹפְלִים, וְרוֹפֵא חוֹלִים, וּמַתִּיר אֲסוּרִים, וּמְקַיֵּם אֱמוּנָתוֹ לִישֵׁנֵי עָפָר. מִי כָמוֹךָ בַּעַל גְּבוּרוֹת, וּמִי דּוֹמֶה לָּךְ, מֶלֶךְ מֵמִית וּמְחַיֶּה וּמַצְמִיחַ יְשׁוּעָה. וְנֶאֱמָן אַתָּה לְהַחֲיוֹת מֵתִים. בָּרוּךְ אַתָּה יהוה, מְחַיֵּה הַמֵּתִים.

SERVICE FOR FESTIVALS

On the eve of Festivals, the Afternoon Service is said on page 171. When a Festival falls on Shabbat, and on the Intermediate Shabbat of a Festival, the Evening Service begins with "A Psalm, a Song for the Sabbath Day", on page 271. When a Festival or one of its Intermediate Days falls on a weekday, the Evening Service begins with, "Bless" on page 275. The following *Amidah* is said at the Morning, Afternoon and Evening Services of Pesach, Shavuot, Sukkot, Shemini Atzeret and Simchat Torah, but not on the Intermediate Days of festivals.

AMIDAH: THE STANDING PRAYER

The following prayer, until "former years" on page 661, is said standing with feet together. The *Amidah* is first said silently; then, if there is a *minyan*, it is repeated aloud by the Leader, except at the Evening Service. Take three steps back, then forward. At the points indicated by ▾, bend the knees at the first word, bow at the second, and stand straight before God's name.

O Lord, open my lips, so that my mouth may declare Your praise.

PATRIARCHS

▾בָּרוּךְ Blessed are You, Lord our God and God of our Fathers, God of Abraham, God of Isaac and God of Jacob; the great, mighty and awesome God, God Most High, who bestows acts of lovingkindness and creates all, who remembers the lovingkindness of the Fathers and will bring a Redeemer to their children's children for the sake of His name, in love. King, Helper, Saviour, Shield: ▾Blessed are You, Lord, Shield of Abraham.

DIVINE MIGHT

אַתָּה You are eternally mighty, Lord. You give life to the dead and have great power to save.

From the Afternoon Service of Shemini Atzeret until, and including, the Morning Service on the first day of Pesach, add:
He makes the wind blow and the rain fall.

He sustains the living with lovingkindness, and with great compassion revives the dead. He supports the fallen, heals the sick, sets captives free, and keeps His faith with those who sleep in the dust. Who is like You, Master of might, and to whom can You be compared, O King who brings death and gives life, and makes salvation grow? Faithful are You to revive the dead. Blessed are You, Lord, who revives the dead.

When saying the עֲמִידָה silently, continue with אַתָּה קָדוֹשׁ overleaf.

During the repetition of the עֲמִידָה at מִנְחָה, turn to the קְדוּשָּׁה overleaf.

At שַׁחֲרִית, the קְדוּשָּׁה is as follows:

קדושה לשחרית

During the Leader's repetition, the following is said standing, with feet together, rising on the toes at the words indicated by ▲.

Congregation then Leader: נְקַדֵּשׁ אֶת־שִׁמְךָ בָּעוֹלָם, כְּשֵׁם שֶׁמַּקְדִּישִׁים אוֹתוֹ בִּשְׁמֵי מָרוֹם, כַּכָּתוּב עַל יַד נְבִיאֶךָ, וְקָרָא זֶה אֶל־זֶה וְאָמַר.

Congregation and Leader: ▲קָדוֹשׁ ▲קָדוֹשׁ ▲קָדוֹשׁ יהוה צְבָאוֹת, מְלֹא כָל־הָאָרֶץ כְּבוֹדוֹ.

Congregation then Leader: אָז בְּקוֹל רַעַשׁ גָּדוֹל אַדִּיר וְחָזָק מַשְׁמִיעִים קוֹל, מִתְנַשְּׂאִים לְעֻמַּת שְׂרָפִים, לְעֻמָּתָם בָּרוּךְ יֹאמֵרוּ.

Congregation and Leader: ▲בָּרוּךְ כְּבוֹד יהוה, מִמְּקוֹמוֹ

Congregation then Leader: מִמְּקוֹמְךָ מַלְכֵּנוּ תוֹפִיעַ, וְתִמְלֹךְ עָלֵינוּ, כִּי מְחַכִּים אֲנַחְנוּ לָךְ. מָתַי תִּמְלֹךְ בְּצִיּוֹן, בְּקָרוֹב בְּיָמֵינוּ, לְעוֹלָם וָעֶד תִּשְׁכּוֹן. תִּתְגַּדַּל וְתִתְקַדַּשׁ בְּתוֹךְ יְרוּשָׁלַיִם עִירְךָ, לְדוֹר וָדוֹר וּלְנֵצַח נְצָחִים. וְעֵינֵינוּ תִרְאֶינָה מַלְכוּתֶךָ, כַּדָּבָר הָאָמוּר בְּשִׁירֵי עֻזֶּךָ, עַל יְדֵי דָוִד מְשִׁיחַ צִדְקֶךָ.

Congregation and Leader: ▲יִמְלֹךְ יהוה לְעוֹלָם, אֱלֹהַיִךְ צִיּוֹן לְדֹר וָדֹר, הַלְלוּיָהּ.

Leader: לְדוֹר וָדוֹר נַגִּיד גָּדְלֶךָ וּלְנֵצַח נְצָחִים קְדֻשָּׁתְךָ נַקְדִּישׁ, וְשִׁבְחֲךָ אֱלֹהֵינוּ מִפִּינוּ לֹא יָמוּשׁ לְעוֹלָם וָעֶד, כִּי אֵל מֶלֶךְ גָּדוֹל וְקָדוֹשׁ אָתָּה. בָּרוּךְ אַתָּה יהוה, הָאֵל הַקָּדוֹשׁ.

The repetition continues with אַתָּה בְחַרְתָּנוּ overleaf.

When saying the *Amidah* silently, continue with "You are holy" overleaf.

During the repetition of the *Amidah* at the Afternoon Service, turn to the *Kedushah* overleaf.

At the Morning Service, the *Kedushah* is as follows:

KEDUSHAH FOR THE MORNING SERVICE

During the Leader's repetition, the following is said standing, with feet together, rising on the toes at the words indicated by ▲.

Congregation then Leader: נְקַדֵּשׁ We will sanctify Your name on earth, as they sanctify it in the highest heavens, as is written by Your prophet, "And they (the angels) call to one another saying:

Congregation and Leader: ▲Holy, ▲holy, ▲holy is the LORD of Hosts: the whole world is filled with His glory."

Congregation then Leader: Then with a sound of mighty noise, majestic and strong, they make their voice heard, raising themselves toward the Seraphim, and facing them say:

Congregation and Leader: "▲Blessed is the LORD's glory from His place."

Congregation then Leader: Reveal Yourself from Your place, O our King, and reign over us, for we are waiting for You. When will You reign in Zion? May it be soon in our days, and may You dwell there for ever and all time. May You be exalted and sanctified in the midst of Jerusalem, Your city, from generation to generation for evermore. May our eyes see Your kingdom, as is said in the songs of Your splendour, written by David your righteous anointed one:

Congregation and Leader: "▲The LORD shall reign forever. He is your GOD, Zion, from generation to generation, Halleluyah!"

Leader: From generation to generation we will declare Your greatness, and we will proclaim Your holiness for evermore. Your praise, our GOD, shall never leave our mouth, for You, GOD, are a great and holy King. Blessed are You, LORD, the holy GOD.

The repetition continues with "You have chosen us" overleaf.

At מִנְחָה, the קְדוּשָׁה is as follows:

קדושה למנחה

During the Leader's repetition, the following is said standing, with feet together, rising on the toes at the words indicated by ▲.

Congregation then Leader: **נְקַדֵּשׁ** אֶת־שִׁמְךָ בָּעוֹלָם, כְּשֵׁם שֶׁמַּקְדִּישִׁים אוֹתוֹ בִּשְׁמֵי מָרוֹם, כַּכָּתוּב עַל יַד נְבִיאֶךָ, וְקָרָא זֶה אֶל־זֶה וְאָמַר.

Congregation and Leader: ▲קָדוֹשׁ ▲קָדוֹשׁ ▲קָדוֹשׁ יהוה צְבָאוֹת, מְלֹא כָל־הָאָרֶץ כְּבוֹדוֹ.

Leader: לְעֻמָּתָם בָּרוּךְ יֹאמֵרוּ

Congregation and Leader: ▲בָּרוּךְ כְּבוֹד יהוה, מִמְּקוֹמוֹ

Leader: וּבְדִבְרֵי קָדְשְׁךָ כָּתוּב לֵאמֹר.

Congregation and Leader: ▲יִמְלֹךְ יהוה לְעוֹלָם, אֱלֹהַיִךְ צִיּוֹן לְדֹר וָדֹר, הַלְלוּיָהּ.

Leader: לְדוֹר וָדוֹר נַגִּיד גָּדְלֶךָ וּלְנֵצַח נְצָחִים קְדֻשָּׁתְךָ נַקְדִּישׁ, וְשִׁבְחֲךָ אֱלֹהֵינוּ מִפִּינוּ לֹא יָמוּשׁ לְעוֹלָם וָעֶד, כִּי אֵל מֶלֶךְ גָּדוֹל וְקָדוֹשׁ אָתָּה. בָּרוּךְ אַתָּה יהוה, הָאֵל הַקָּדוֹשׁ.

The repetition continues with אַתָּה בְחַרְתָּנוּ, below.
When saying the עֲמִידָה silently, continue here:

קדושת השם

אַתָּה קָדוֹשׁ וְשִׁמְךָ קָדוֹשׁ, וּקְדוֹשִׁים בְּכָל־יוֹם יְהַלְלוּךָ סֶּלָה. בָּרוּךְ אַתָּה יהוה, הָאֵל הַקָּדוֹשׁ.

קדושת היום

אַתָּה בְחַרְתָּנוּ מִכָּל־הָעַמִּים, אָהַבְתָּ אוֹתָנוּ, וְרָצִיתָ בָּנוּ, וְרוֹמַמְתָּנוּ מִכָּל הַלְּשׁוֹנוֹת, וְקִדַּשְׁתָּנוּ בְּמִצְוֹתֶיךָ, וְקֵרַבְתָּנוּ מַלְכֵּנוּ לַעֲבוֹדָתֶךָ, וְשִׁמְךָ הַגָּדוֹל וְהַקָּדוֹשׁ עָלֵינוּ קָרָאתָ.

At the Afternoon Service, the *Kedushah* is as follows:

KEDUSHAH FOR THE AFTERNOON SERVICE

During the Leader's repetition, the following is said standing, with feet together, rising on the toes at the words indicated by ▲.

Congregation then Leader: **נְקַדֵּשׁ** We will sanctify Your name on earth, as they sanctify it in the highest heavens, as is written by Your prophet, "And they (the angels) call to one another saying:

Congregation and Leader: ▲Holy, ▲holy, ▲holy is the LORD of Hosts: the whole world is filled with His glory."

Leader: Those facing them say: "Blessed – "

Congregation and Leader: "▲Blessed is the LORD's glory from His place."

Leader: And in Your Holy Writings it is written thus:

Congregation and Leader: "▲The LORD shall reign forever. He is your GOD, Zion, from generation to generation, Halleluyah!"

Leader: From generation to generation we will declare Your greatness, and we will proclaim Your holiness for evermore. Your praise, our GOD, shall never leave our mouth, for You, GOD, are a great and holy King. Blessed are You, LORD, the holy GOD.

The repetition continues with "You have chosen us", below.
When saying the *Amidah* silently, continue here:

HOLINESS

אַתָּה קָדוֹשׁ You are holy and Your name is holy, and holy ones praise You daily, Selah! Blessed are You, LORD, the holy GOD.

HOLINESS OF THE DAY

אַתָּה בְחַרְתָּנוּ You have chosen us from among all peoples. You have loved and favoured us. You have raised us above all tongues. You have made us holy through Your commandments. You have brought us near, our King, to Your service, and have called us by Your great and holy name.

THE FESTIVAL SERVICE
As on Shabbat, the festival *Amidah* consists of seven blessings, of which the central one speaks of the holiness of the day.

On Saturday night add:

וַתּוֹדִיעֵנוּ יהוה אֱלֹהֵינוּ אֶת־מִשְׁפְּטֵי צִדְקֶךָ, וַתְּלַמְּדֵנוּ לַעֲשׂוֹת חֻקֵּי רְצוֹנֶךָ. וַתִּתֶּן־לָנוּ יהוה אֱלֹהֵינוּ מִשְׁפָּטִים יְשָׁרִים וְתוֹרוֹת אֱמֶת חֻקִּים וּמִצְוֹת טוֹבִים. וַתַּנְחִילֵנוּ זְמַנֵּי שָׂשׂוֹן וּמוֹעֲדֵי קֹדֶשׁ וְחַגֵּי נְדָבָה. וַתּוֹרִישֵׁנוּ קְדֻשַּׁת שַׁבָּת וּכְבוֹד מוֹעֵד וַחֲגִיגַת הָרֶגֶל. וַתַּבְדֵּל יהוה אֱלֹהֵינוּ בֵּין קֹדֶשׁ לְחוֹל, בֵּין אוֹר לְחֹשֶׁךְ, בֵּין יִשְׂרָאֵל לָעַמִּים, בֵּין יוֹם הַשְּׁבִיעִי לְשֵׁשֶׁת יְמֵי הַמַּעֲשֶׂה. בֵּין קְדֻשַּׁת שַׁבָּת לִקְדֻשַּׁת יוֹם טוֹב הִבְדַּלְתָּ, וְאֶת־יוֹם הַשְּׁבִיעִי מִשֵּׁשֶׁת יְמֵי הַמַּעֲשֶׂה קִדַּשְׁתָּ, הִבְדַּלְתָּ וְקִדַּשְׁתָּ אֶת־עַמְּךָ יִשְׂרָאֵל בִּקְדֻשָּׁתֶךָ.

On שַׁבָּת, add the words in brackets:

וַתִּתֶּן־לָנוּ יהוה אֱלֹהֵינוּ בְּאַהֲבָה (שַׁבָּתוֹת לִמְנוּחָה וּ) מוֹעֲדִים לְשִׂמְחָה חַגִּים וּזְמַנִּים לְשָׂשׂוֹן, אֶת־יוֹם (הַשַּׁבָּת הַזֶּה וְאֶת־יוֹם)

On פֶּסַח:	On שָׁבֻעוֹת:	On סֻכּוֹת:	On שְׁמִינִי עֲצֶרֶת and שִׂמְחַת תּוֹרָה:
חַג הַמַּצּוֹת הַזֶּה, זְמַן חֵרוּתֵנוּ	חַג הַשָּׁבֻעוֹת הַזֶּה, זְמַן מַתַּן תּוֹרָתֵנוּ	חַג הַסֻּכּוֹת הַזֶּה, זְמַן שִׂמְחָתֵנוּ	הַשְּׁמִינִי חַג הָעֲצֶרֶת הַזֶּה, זְמַן שִׂמְחָתֵנוּ

(בְּאַהֲבָה) מִקְרָא קֹדֶשׁ, זֵכֶר לִיצִיאַת מִצְרָיִם.

אֱלֹהֵינוּ וֵאלֹהֵי אֲבוֹתֵינוּ, יַעֲלֶה, וְיָבֹא, וְיַגִּיעַ, וְיֵרָאֶה, וְיֵרָצֶה, וְיִשָּׁמַע, וְיִפָּקֵד, וְיִזָּכֵר זִכְרוֹנֵנוּ וּפִקְדוֹנֵנוּ, וְזִכְרוֹן

אַתָּה בְחַרְתָּנוּ *You have chosen us*: Unlike Shabbat, which recalls pre-history (creation) and the end of history (ultimate redemption), the festivals recall specific moments *within* history: on Pesach, the exodus from Egypt; on Shavuot, the giving of the Torah at Mount Sinai; and on Sukkot, the forty years of wandering in

On Saturday night, add:

וַתּוֹדִיעֵנוּ You have made known to us, LORD our GOD, Your righteous laws, and have taught us to perform Your will's decrees. You have given us, LORD our GOD, just laws and true teachings, good precepts and commandments. You have given us as our heritage seasons of joy, holy festivals, and occasions for presenting our freewill offerings. You have given us as our heritage the holiness of the Sabbath, the glory of the festival, and the festive offerings of the pilgrimage days. You have distinguished, LORD our GOD, between sacred and secular, between light and darkness, between Israel and the nations, between the seventh day and the six days of work. You have distinguished between the holiness of the Sabbath and the holiness of the festival, and have made the seventh day holy above the six days of work. You have distinguished and sanctified Your people Israel with Your holiness.

On Shabbat, add the words in brackets:

וַתִּתֶּן־לָנוּ And You, LORD our GOD, have given us in love (Sabbaths for rest and) festivals for rejoicing, holy days and seasons for joy, (this Sabbath day and) this day of:

On Pesach:	On Shavuot:	On Sukkot:	On Shemini Atzeret and Simchat Torah:
the festival of Matzot, the time of our freedom	the festival of Shavuot, the time of the giving of our Torah	the festival of Sukkot, our time of rejoicing	the festival of eighth day, Shemini Atzeret, our time of rejoicing

(with love), a holy assembly in memory of the Exodus from Egypt.

אֱלֹהֵינוּ Our GOD and GOD of our ancestors, may there rise, come, reach, appear, be favoured, heard, regarded and remembered before You, our recollection and remembrance, as well as the remembrance

---

the wilderness. Hence the reference to the Divine choice of Israel as the people who, through their singular history, bear witness to the role of GOD in history.

The names of the festivals. The connection between Passover, "the festival of Matzot (unleavened bread)" and "the time of our freedom" is self-evident. It

אֲבוֹתֵינוּ, וְזִכְרוֹן מָשִׁיחַ בֶּן דָּוִד עַבְדֶּךָ, וְזִכְרוֹן יְרוּשָׁלַיִם עִיר קָדְשֶׁךָ, וְזִכְרוֹן כָּל־עַמְּךָ בֵּית יִשְׂרָאֵל לְפָנֶיךָ, לִפְלֵיטָה וּלְטוֹבָה וּלְחֵן וּלְחֶסֶד וּלְרַחֲמִים, וּלְחַיִּים וּלְשָׁלוֹם בְּיוֹם

On פֶּסַח:	On שָׁבֻעוֹת:	On סֻכּוֹת:	On שְׁמִינִי עֲצֶרֶת and שִׂמְחַת תּוֹרָה:
חַג הַמַּצּוֹת	חַג הַשָּׁבֻעוֹת	חַג הַסֻּכּוֹת	הַשְּׁמִינִי חַג הָעֲצֶרֶת

הַזֶּה. זָכְרֵנוּ יהוה אֱלֹהֵינוּ בּוֹ לְטוֹבָה, וּפָקְדֵנוּ בוֹ לִבְרָכָה, וְהוֹשִׁיעֵנוּ בוֹ לְחַיִּים, וּבִדְבַר יְשׁוּעָה וְרַחֲמִים, חוּס וְחָנֵּנוּ וְרַחֵם עָלֵינוּ וְהוֹשִׁיעֵנוּ, כִּי אֵלֶיךָ עֵינֵינוּ, כִּי אֵל מֶלֶךְ חַנּוּן וְרַחוּם אָתָּה.

On שַׁבָּת, add the words in brackets:

וְהַשִּׂיאֵנוּ יהוה אֱלֹהֵינוּ אֶת־בִּרְכַּת מוֹעֲדֶיךָ לְחַיִּים וּלְשָׁלוֹם, לְשִׂמְחָה וּלְשָׂשׂוֹן, כַּאֲשֶׁר רָצִיתָ וְאָמַרְתָּ לְבָרְכֵנוּ. (אֱלֹהֵינוּ וֵאלֹהֵי אֲבוֹתֵינוּ רְצֵה בִמְנוּחָתֵנוּ) קַדְּשֵׁנוּ בְּמִצְוֹתֶיךָ וְתֵן חֶלְקֵנוּ בְּתוֹרָתֶךָ, שַׂבְּעֵנוּ מִטּוּבֶךָ וְשַׂמְּחֵנוּ בִּישׁוּעָתֶךָ, וְטַהֵר לִבֵּנוּ לְעָבְדְּךָ בֶּאֱמֶת, וְהַנְחִילֵנוּ יהוה אֱלֹהֵינוּ (בְּאַהֲבָה וּבְרָצוֹן) בְּשִׂמְחָה וּבְשָׂשׂוֹן (שַׁבַּת וּ) מוֹעֲדֵי קָדְשֶׁךָ, וְיִשְׂמְחוּ בְךָ יִשְׂרָאֵל מְקַדְּשֵׁי שְׁמֶךָ. בָּרוּךְ אַתָּה יהוה, מְקַדֵּשׁ (הַשַּׁבָּת וְ) יִשְׂרָאֵל וְהַזְּמַנִּים.

---

recalls liberation from Egypt and slavery. The connection between Shavuot and the giving of the Torah is not explicit in the Torah but is part of the Oral tradition as well as calculation of dates by the Sages (*Shabbat* 86–88). Because of this, the date of Shavuot became a subject of controversy in the Second Temple period and immediately thereafter among sects such as the Sadducees, who did not accept the authority of the Oral tradition. Sukkot is called "our time of rejoicing" because the word "rejoice" is mentioned three times in the Torah in connection with Sukkot (Leviticus 23:40, Deuteronomy 16:14, 15) – more than any other festival.

of our ancestors, and of the Messiah son of David Your servant, and of Jerusalem Your Holy city, and of all Your people the House of Israel – for deliverance and well-being, grace, kindness and compassion, life and peace, on this day of:

On Pesach:	On Shavuot:	On Sukkot:	On Shemini Atzeret and Simchat Torah:
the festival of Matzot.	the festival of Shavuot.	the festival of Sukkot.	the festival of Shemini Atzeret.

On it remember us, LORD our GOD, for good, recollect us for blessing, and deliver us for life. In accord with Your promise of salvation and compassion, spare us and be gracious to us, have compassion on us and deliver us, for our eyes are turned to You because You, GOD, are a gracious and compassionate King.

On Shabbat, add the words in brackets.

וְהַשִּׂיאֵנוּ Bestow on us, LORD our GOD, the blessings of Your festivals for good life and peace, joy and gladness, as You desired and promised to bless us. (Our GOD and GOD of our fathers, find favour in our rest.) Make us holy through Your commandments and grant us a share in Your Torah. Satisfy us with Your goodness, gladden us with Your salvation, and purify our hearts to serve You in truth. Grant us as our heritage, LORD our GOD (with love and favour,) with joy and gladness, Your holy (Sabbath and) festivals, and may Israel, who sanctify Your name, rejoice in You. Blessed are You, LORD, who sanctifies (the Sabbath and) Israel and the festive seasons.

Shmini Atzeret, while it shares in the joy of Sukkot, is, in some respects, a festival in its own right and is therefore referred to as such.

מְקַדֵּשׁ *Who sanctifies [the Sabbath and] Israel and the festive seasons*: The precise order of the words is significant. It was the Israelites who were charged with determining the monthly and yearly calendar on which the festivals depend: hence the sanctity of the people of Israel is prior to that of the festivals. Shabbat, however, was determined by GOD on the seventh day of creation: hence its sanctity precedes the other two.

עבודה

רְצֵה יהוה אֱלֹהֵינוּ בְּעַמְּךָ יִשְׂרָאֵל וּבִתְפִלָּתָם, וְהָשֵׁב אֶת־הָעֲבוֹדָה לִדְבִיר בֵּיתֶךָ. וְאִשֵּׁי יִשְׂרָאֵל וּתְפִלָּתָם בְּאַהֲבָה תְקַבֵּל בְּרָצוֹן, וּתְהִי לְרָצוֹן תָּמִיד עֲבוֹדַת יִשְׂרָאֵל עַמֶּךָ.

וְתֶחֱזֶינָה עֵינֵינוּ בְּשׁוּבְךָ לְצִיּוֹן בְּרַחֲמִים. בָּרוּךְ אַתָּה יהוה, הַמַּחֲזִיר שְׁכִינָתוֹ לְצִיּוֹן.

הודאה

▽ Bow at the first five words.

▽**מוֹדִים** אֲנַחְנוּ לָךְ, שָׁאַתָּה הוּא יהוה אֱלֹהֵינוּ וֵאלֹהֵי אֲבוֹתֵינוּ לְעוֹלָם וָעֶד. צוּר חַיֵּינוּ, מָגֵן יִשְׁעֵנוּ אַתָּה הוּא לְדוֹר וָדוֹר. נוֹדֶה לְּךָ וּנְסַפֵּר תְּהִלָּתֶךָ עַל חַיֵּינוּ הַמְּסוּרִים בְּיָדֶךָ, וְעַל נִשְׁמוֹתֵינוּ הַפְּקוּדוֹת לָךְ, וְעַל נִסֶּיךָ שֶׁבְּכָל־יוֹם עִמָּנוּ, וְעַל נִפְלְאוֹתֶיךָ וְטוֹבוֹתֶיךָ שֶׁבְּכָל־עֵת, עֶרֶב וָבֹקֶר וְצָהֳרָיִם. הַטּוֹב כִּי לֹא־כָלוּ רַחֲמֶיךָ, וְהַמְרַחֵם כִּי לֹא־תַמּוּ חֲסָדֶיךָ, מֵעוֹלָם קִוִּינוּ לָךְ.

During the Leader's repetition, the Congregation says quietly:

▽**מוֹדִים** אֲנַחְנוּ לָךְ, שָׁאַתָּה הוּא יהוה אֱלֹהֵינוּ וֵאלֹהֵי אֲבוֹתֵינוּ, אֱלֹהֵי כָל־בָּשָׂר, יוֹצְרֵנוּ, יוֹצֵר בְּרֵאשִׁית. בְּרָכוֹת וְהוֹדָאוֹת לְשִׁמְךָ הַגָּדוֹל וְהַקָּדוֹשׁ, עַל שֶׁהֶחֱיִיתָנוּ וְקִיַּמְתָּנוּ. כֵּן תְּחַיֵּנוּ וּתְקַיְּמֵנוּ, וְתֶאֱסוֹף גָּלֻיּוֹתֵינוּ לְחַצְרוֹת קָדְשֶׁךָ, לִשְׁמוֹר חֻקֶּיךָ וְלַעֲשׂוֹת רְצוֹנֶךָ, וּלְעָבְדְּךָ בְּלֵבָב שָׁלֵם, עַל שֶׁאֲנַחְנוּ מוֹדִים לָךְ. בָּרוּךְ אֵל הַהוֹדָאוֹת.

וְעַל כֻּלָּם יִתְבָּרַךְ וְיִתְרוֹמַם שִׁמְךָ מַלְכֵּנוּ תָּמִיד לְעוֹלָם וָעֶד. וְכֹל הַחַיִּים יוֹדוּךָ סֶּלָה, וִיהַלְלוּ אֶת־שִׁמְךָ בֶּאֱמֶת, הָאֵל יְשׁוּעָתֵנוּ וְעֶזְרָתֵנוּ סֶלָה. ▼בָּרוּךְ אַתָּה יהוה, הַטּוֹב שִׁמְךָ וּלְךָ נָאֶה לְהוֹדוֹת.

TEMPLE SERVICE

רְצֵה Find favour, LORD our GOD, in Your people Israel and their prayer. Restore the service to Your most holy house, and accept in love and favour the fire-offerings of Israel and their prayer. May the service of Your people Israel always find favour with You.

וְתֶחֱזֶינָה And may our eyes witness Your return to Zion in compassion. Blessed are You, LORD, who restores His Presence to Zion.

THANKSGIVING

▽ Bow at the first nine words.

מוֹדִים▽ We give thanks to You, for You are the LORD our GOD and GOD of our ancestors for ever and all time. You are the Rock of our lives, Shield of our salvation from generation to generation. We will thank You and declare Your praise for our lives, which are entrusted into Your hand; our souls, which are placed in Your charge; for Your miracles which are with us every day; and for Your wonders and favours at all times, evening, morning and midday. You are good – for Your compassion never fails. You are compassionate – for Your lovingkindnesses never cease. We have always placed our hope in You.

During the Leader's repetition, the Congregation says quietly:

מוֹדִים▽ We give thanks to You, for You are the LORD our GOD and GOD of our ancestors, GOD of all flesh, who formed us and formed the universe. Blessings and thanks are due to Your great and holy name for giving us life and sustaining us. May You continue to give us life and sustain us; and may You gather our exiles to Your holy courts, to keep Your decrees, do Your will and serve You with a perfect heart, for it is for us to give You thanks. Blessed be GOD to whom thanksgiving is due.

וְעַל For all these things may Your name be blessed and exalted, our King, continually, for ever and all time. Let all that lives thank You, Selah! and praise Your name in truth, GOD, our Saviour and Help, Selah! ▼Blessed are You, LORD, whose name is "the Good" and to whom thanks are due.

At the repetition of the שַׁחֲרִית עֲמִידָה by the Leader, the following is said:

אֱלֹהֵינוּ וֵאלֹהֵי אֲבוֹתֵינוּ, בָּרְכֵנוּ בַּבְּרָכָה הַמְשֻׁלֶּשֶׁת, בַּתּוֹרָה הַכְּתוּבָה עַל יְדֵי מֹשֶׁה עַבְדֶּךָ, הָאֲמוּרָה מִפִּי אַהֲרֹן וּבָנָיו כֹּהֲנִים, עַם קְדוֹשֶׁךָ, כָּאָמוּר.

יְבָרֶכְךָ יהוה, וְיִשְׁמְרֶךָ. (Cong.: כֵּן יְהִי רָצוֹן)

יָאֵר יהוה פָּנָיו אֵלֶיךָ וִיחֻנֶּךָּ. (Cong.: כֵּן יְהִי רָצוֹן)

יִשָּׂא יהוה פָּנָיו אֵלֶיךָ וְיָשֵׂם לְךָ שָׁלוֹם. (Cong.: כֵּן יְהִי רָצוֹן)

ברכת שלום

At שַׁחֲרִית, say:

שִׂים שָׁלוֹם, טוֹבָה, וּבְרָכָה, חֵן, וָחֶסֶד וְרַחֲמִים עָלֵינוּ וְעַל כָּל־יִשְׂרָאֵל עַמֶּךָ. בָּרְכֵנוּ אָבִינוּ, כֻּלָּנוּ כְּאֶחָד בְּאוֹר פָּנֶיךָ, כִּי בְאוֹר פָּנֶיךָ נָתַתָּ לָּנוּ, יהוה אֱלֹהֵינוּ, תּוֹרַת חַיִּים וְאַהֲבַת חֶסֶד, וּצְדָקָה, וּבְרָכָה, וְרַחֲמִים, וְחַיִּים, וְשָׁלוֹם. וְטוֹב בְּעֵינֶיךָ לְבָרֵךְ אֶת־עַמְּךָ יִשְׂרָאֵל, בְּכָל־עֵת וּבְכָל־שָׁעָה בִּשְׁלוֹמֶךָ. בָּרוּךְ אַתָּה יהוה, הַמְבָרֵךְ אֶת עַמּוֹ יִשְׂרָאֵל בַּשָּׁלוֹם.

At מִנְחָה and מַעֲרִיב, say:

שָׁלוֹם רָב עַל יִשְׂרָאֵל עַמְּךָ תָּשִׂים לְעוֹלָם, כִּי אַתָּה הוּא מֶלֶךְ אָדוֹן לְכָל הַשָּׁלוֹם. וְטוֹב בְּעֵינֶיךָ לְבָרֵךְ אֶת עַמְּךָ יִשְׂרָאֵל בְּכָל עֵת וּבְכָל שָׁעָה בִּשְׁלוֹמֶךָ. בָּרוּךְ אַתָּה יהוה, הַמְבָרֵךְ אֶת עַמּוֹ יִשְׂרָאֵל בַּשָּׁלוֹם.

The Leader's Repetition ends at this point.

אֱלֹהַי, נְצוֹר לְשׁוֹנִי מֵרָע, וּשְׂפָתַי מִדַּבֵּר מִרְמָה, וְלִמְקַלְלַי נַפְשִׁי תִדּוֹם, וְנַפְשִׁי כֶּעָפָר לַכֹּל תִּהְיֶה. פְּתַח לִבִּי בְּתוֹרָתֶךָ, וּבְמִצְוֹתֶיךָ תִּרְדּוֹף נַפְשִׁי. וְכֹל הַחוֹשְׁבִים עָלַי רָעָה, מְהֵרָה הָפֵר עֲצָתָם וְקַלְקֵל מַחֲשַׁבְתָּם. עֲשֵׂה לְמַעַן שְׁמֶךָ, עֲשֵׂה לְמַעַן יְמִינֶךָ, עֲשֵׂה לְמַעַן קְדֻשָּׁתֶךָ, עֲשֵׂה לְמַעַן

At the repetition of the morning *Amidah* by the Leader, the following is said:

אֱלֹהֵינוּ Our God and God of our fathers, bless us with the threefold blessing in the Torah, written by the hand of Moses Your servant and pronounced by Aaron and his sons the priests, Your holy people, as it is said:

May the Lord bless you and protect you. (Cong.: May it be Your will.)

May the Lord make His face shine on you and be gracious to you. (Cong.: May it be Your will.)

May the Lord turn His face towards you, and give you peace. (Cong.: May it be Your will.)

PEACE

At the Morning Service, say:

שִׂים Grant peace, goodness and blessing, grace, lovingkindness and compassion to us and all Israel Your people. Bless us, our Father, all as one, with the light of Your face, for by the light of Your face You have given us, Lord our God, the Torah of life and love of kindness, righteousness, blessing, compassion, life and peace. May it be good in Your eyes to bless Your people Israel at every time, in every hour, With Your peace. Blessed are You, Lord, who blesses His people Israel with peace.

At the Afternoon and Evening Services, say:

שָׁלוֹם Grant great peace to Your people Israel for ever, for You are the sovereign Lord of all peace; and may it be good in Your eyes to bless Your people Israel at every time, at every hour, with Your peace. Blessed are You, O God, who blesses His people Israel with peace.

The Leader's repetition ends at this point.

אֱלֹהַי My God, guard my tongue from evil and my lips from deceitful speech. To those who curse me, let my soul be silent; may my soul be to all like the dust. Open my heart to Your Torah and let my soul pursue Your commandments. As for all who plan evil against me, swiftly thwart their counsel and frustrate their plans. Act for the sake of Your name; act for the sake of Your right hand; act for the sake of Your holiness; act for the sake of Your Torah.

תּוֹרָתֶךָ. לְמַעַן יֵחָלְצוּן יְדִידֶיךָ, הוֹשִׁיעָה יְמִינְךָ וַעֲנֵנִי. יִהְיוּ לְרָצוֹן אִמְרֵי־פִי וְהֶגְיוֹן לִבִּי לְפָנֶיךָ, יהוה צוּרִי וְגוֹאֲלִי.

Bow, take three steps back, then bow, first left, then right, then centre, while saying:

עֹשֶׂה שָׁלוֹם בִּמְרוֹמָיו, הוּא יַעֲשֶׂה שָׁלוֹם עָלֵינוּ, וְעַל־כָּל־יִשְׂרָאֵל. וְאִמְרוּ אָמֵן.

יְהִי רָצוֹן מִלְּפָנֶיךָ יהוה אֱלֹהֵינוּ וֵאלֹהֵי אֲבוֹתֵינוּ, שֶׁיִּבָּנֶה בֵּית הַמִּקְדָּשׁ בִּמְהֵרָה בְיָמֵינוּ, וְתֵן חֶלְקֵנוּ בְּתוֹרָתֶךָ. וְשָׁם נַעֲבָדְךָ בְּיִרְאָה, כִּימֵי עוֹלָם וּכְשָׁנִים קַדְמוֹנִיּוֹת. וְעָרְבָה לַיהוה מִנְחַת יְהוּדָה וִירוּשָׁלָיִם, כִּימֵי עוֹלָם וּכְשָׁנִים קַדְמוֹנִיּוֹת.

In שַׁחֲרִית and מִנְחָה, when praying with a מִנְיָן,
the עֲמִידָה is repeated aloud by the Leader.

סדר קידוש לרגלים

The following קִדּוּשׁ is said on the evenings of
שִׂמְחַת תּוֹרָה and שְׁמִינִי עֲצֶרֶת ,סֻכּוֹת ,שָׁבֻעוֹת ,פֶּסַח:

When יוֹם טוֹב falls on שַׁבָּת, begin here.

Quietly וַיְהִי־עֶרֶב וַיְהִי בֹקֶר

יוֹם הַשִּׁשִּׁי. וַיְכֻלּוּ הַשָּׁמַיִם וְהָאָרֶץ וְכָל־צְבָאָם. וַיְכַל אֱלֹהִים בַּיּוֹם הַשְּׁבִיעִי מְלַאכְתּוֹ אֲשֶׁר עָשָׂה, וַיִּשְׁבֹּת בַּיּוֹם הַשְּׁבִיעִי מִכָּל־מְלַאכְתּוֹ אֲשֶׁר עָשָׂה. וַיְבָרֶךְ אֱלֹהִים אֶת־יוֹם הַשְּׁבִיעִי וַיְקַדֵּשׁ אֹתוֹ, כִּי בוֹ שָׁבַת מִכָּל־מְלַאכְתּוֹ אֲשֶׁר־בָּרָא אֱלֹהִים לַעֲשׂוֹת.

When saying קִדּוּשׁ for others, add:

סַבְרִי מָרָנָן וְרַבָּנָן וְרַבּוֹתַי.

בָּרוּךְ אַתָּה יהוה אֱלֹהֵינוּ מֶלֶךְ הָעוֹלָם, בּוֹרֵא פְּרִי הַגָּפֶן.

On שַׁבָּת, add the words in brackets.

בָּרוּךְ אַתָּה יהוה אֱלֹהֵינוּ מֶלֶךְ הָעוֹלָם, אֲשֶׁר בָּחַר בָּנוּ

KIDDUSH FOR FESTIVALS
As in the *Amidah*, the emphasis on the idea of the chosen people signifies that it was through the epic events of Israel's

That Your beloved ones may be delivered, save with Your right hand and answer me. May the words of my mouth and the meditation of my heart find favour before You, LORD, my Rock and Redeemer.

Bow, take three steps back, then bow, first left, then right, then centre, while saying:

May He who makes peace in His high places, make peace for us and all Israel – and say: Amen.

יְהִי May it be Your will, LORD our GOD and GOD of our ancestors, that the Temple be rebuilt speedily in our days, and grant us a share in Your Torah. And there we will serve You with reverence, as in the days of old and as in former years. Then the offering of Judah and Jerusalem will be pleasing to the LORD as in the days of old and as in former years.

In the Morning and Afternoon Services, when praying with a *minyan*, the *Amidah* is repeated aloud by the Leader.

KIDDUSH FOR FESTIVAL EVENINGS

The following *Kiddush* is said on the evenings of Pesach, Shavuot, Sukkot, Shemini Atzeret and Simchat Torah:

When the Festival falls on Shabbat, begin here:

Quietly: And it was evening, and it was morning,

יוֹם הַשִּׁשִּׁי the sixth day. Then the heavens and the earth were completed, and all their array. With the seventh day, GOD completed the work He had done. He ceased on the seventh day from all the work He had done. GOD blessed the seventh day and declared it holy, because on it He ceased from all His work He had created to do.

When saying *Kiddush* for others, add:

Please pay attention, my teachers, rabbis and friends.

בָּרוּךְ Blessed are You, LORD our GOD, King of the Universe, who creates the fruit of the vine.

On Shabbat, add the words in brackets.

בָּרוּךְ Blessed are You, LORD our GOD, King of the Universe, who has chosen us from among all peoples, raised us above all tongues, and made us holy through His commandments. You have given us, LORD

history recalled on the festivals – the exodus, the giving of the Torah, and the forty years of wandering in the wilderness – that GOD was made manifest in history.

מִכָּל־עָם, וְרוֹמְמָנוּ מִכָּל־לָשׁוֹן, וְקִדְּשָׁנוּ בְּמִצְוֹתָיו. וַתִּתֶּן־לָנוּ יהוה אֱלֹהֵינוּ בְּאַהֲבָה (שַׁבָּתוֹת לִמְנוּחָה וּ) מוֹעֲדִים לְשִׂמְחָה חַגִּים וּזְמַנִּים לְשָׂשׂוֹן, אֶת־יוֹם (הַשַּׁבָּת הַזֶּה וְאֶת־יוֹם)

On פֶּסַח:	On שָׁבֻעוֹת:	On סֻכּוֹת:	On שְׁמִינִי עֲצֶרֶת and שִׂמְחַת תּוֹרָה:
חַג הַמַּצּוֹת הַזֶּה, זְמַן חֵרוּתֵנוּ	חַג הַשָּׁבֻעוֹת הַזֶּה, זְמַן מַתַּן תּוֹרָתֵנוּ	חַג הַסֻּכּוֹת הַזֶּה, זְמַן שִׂמְחָתֵנוּ	הַשְּׁמִינִי חַג הָעֲצֶרֶת הַזֶּה, זְמַן שִׂמְחָתֵנוּ

(בְּאַהֲבָה) מִקְרָא קֹדֶשׁ, זֵכֶר לִיצִיאַת מִצְרָיִם. כִּי בָנוּ בָחַרְתָּ וְאוֹתָנוּ קִדַּשְׁתָּ מִכָּל־הָעַמִּים, (וְשַׁבָּת) וּמוֹעֲדֵי קָדְשֶׁךָ (בְּאַהֲבָה וּבְרָצוֹן) בְּשִׂמְחָה וּבְשָׂשׂוֹן הִנְחַלְתָּנוּ. בָּרוּךְ אַתָּה יהוה, מְקַדֵּשׁ (הַשַּׁבָּת וְ) יִשְׂרָאֵל וְהַזְּמַנִּים.

On Saturday night, the following הַבְדָּלָה is added:

בָּרוּךְ אַתָּה יהוה אֱלֹהֵינוּ מֶלֶךְ הָעוֹלָם, בּוֹרֵא מְאוֹרֵי הָאֵשׁ. בָּרוּךְ אַתָּה יהוה אֱלֹהֵינוּ מֶלֶךְ הָעוֹלָם, הַמַּבְדִּיל בֵּין קֹדֶשׁ לְחוֹל, בֵּין אוֹר לְחֹשֶׁךְ, בֵּין יִשְׂרָאֵל לָעַמִּים, בֵּין יוֹם הַשְּׁבִיעִי לְשֵׁשֶׁת יְמֵי הַמַּעֲשֶׂה. בֵּין קְדֻשַּׁת שַׁבָּת לִקְדֻשַּׁת יוֹם טוֹב הִבְדַּלְתָּ, וְאֶת יוֹם הַשְּׁבִיעִי מִשֵּׁשֶׁת יְמֵי הַמַּעֲשֶׂה קִדַּשְׁתָּ, הִבְדַּלְתָּ וְקִדַּשְׁתָּ אֶת עַמְּךָ יִשְׂרָאֵל בִּקְדֻשָּׁתֶךָ. בָּרוּךְ אַתָּה יהוה, הַמַּבְדִּיל בֵּין־קֹדֶשׁ לְקֹדֶשׁ.

On סֻכּוֹת, say the following blessing. On the first night it is said before the blessing שֶׁהֶחֱיָנוּ; on the second night, after it.

בָּרוּךְ אַתָּה יהוה אֱלֹהֵינוּ מֶלֶךְ הָעוֹלָם, אֲשֶׁר קִדְּשָׁנוּ בְּמִצְוֹתָיו וְצִוָּנוּ לֵישֵׁב בַּסֻּכָּה.

The following blessing is omitted on the last two nights of פֶּסַח:

בָּרוּךְ אַתָּה יהוה אֱלֹהֵינוּ מֶלֶךְ הָעוֹלָם, שֶׁהֶחֱיָנוּ וְקִיְּמָנוּ וְהִגִּיעָנוּ לַזְּמַן הַזֶּה.

Blessings in the Sukkah: The blessing "who has commanded us" is said throughout the seven days of the festival whenever we eat in the *Sukkah*. The bless-

our GOD, in love (Sabbaths for rest), festivals for rejoicing, holy days and seasons for joy, this day of:

On Pesach:	On Shavuot:	On Sukkot:	On Shemini Atzeret and Simchat Torah:
the festival of Matzot, the time of our freedom	the festival of Shavuot, the time of the giving of our Torah	the festival of Sukkot, our time of rejoicing	the festival of eighth day, Shemini Atzeret, our time of rejoicing

(with love), a holy assembly in memory of the exodus from Egypt. For You have chosen us and sanctified us above all peoples, and given us as our heritage (Your holy Sabbath in love and favour and) Your holy festivals for joy and gladness. Blessed are you, LORD, who sanctifies (the Sabbath,) Israel and the festivals.

On Saturday night, the following *Havdalah* is added:

בָּרוּךְ Blessed are You, LORD our GOD, King of the Universe, who creates the lights of fire.

Blessed are You, LORD our GOD, King of the Universe, who distinguishes between sacred and secular, between light and darkness, between Israel and the nations, between the seventh day and the six days of work. You have made a distinction between the holiness of the Sabbath and the holiness of festivals, and have sanctified the seventh day above the six days of work. You have distinguished and sanctified your people Israel with your holiness. Blessed are You, LORD, who distinguishes between holy and holy.

On Sukkot, say the following blessing. On the first night it is said before the blessing "who has given us life"; on the second night, after it.

בָּרוּךְ Blessed are You, LORD our GOD, King of the Universe, who has made us holy though His commandments, and has commanded us to dwell in the *Sukkah*.

The following blessing is omitted on the last two nights of Pesach:

בָּרוּךְ Blessed are You, LORD our GOD, King of the Universe, who has given us life, sustained us, and brought us to this time.

---

ing "who has given us life" refers to two things: 1. the holiness of the day itself, and 2. the first act of sitting in the *Sukkah*. On the first night, "who has given us life" is said last so that it can refer to both. On the second night, it no longer refers to sitting in the *sukkah* since this is not the first time we have done so. Thus it is said immediately after *Kiddush*, since it only refers to the holiness of the day.

It is customary for all present to drink of the wine.

All then wash their hands, saying, immediately after the washing:

בָּרוּךְ אַתָּה יהוה אֱלֹהֵינוּ מֶלֶךְ הָעוֹלָם, אֲשֶׁר קִדְּשָׁנוּ בְּמִצְוֹתָיו וְצִוָּנוּ עַל נְטִילַת יָדָיִם.

After washing hands, one should not speak until one has eaten some of the חַלָּה.

Holding both loaves (on פֶּסַח, two מַצּוֹת), the person making the blessing says:

בָּרוּךְ אַתָּה יהוה אֱלֹהֵינוּ מֶלֶךְ הָעוֹלָם, הַמּוֹצִיא לֶחֶם מִן הָאָרֶץ.

Some of the bread or מַצָּה should be given to each person present.

סדר חג הסכות

To be said in the סֻכָּה on the first night of סֻכּוֹת, before קִדּוּשׁ.

יְהִי רָצוֹן מִלְּפָנֶיךָ, יהוה אֱלֹהַי וֵאלֹהֵי אֲבוֹתַי, שֶׁתַּשְׁרֶה שְׁכִינָתְךָ בֵּינֵינוּ, וְתִפְרוֹשׂ עָלֵינוּ סֻכַּת שְׁלוֹמֶךָ, בִּזְכוּת מִצְוַת סֻכָּה שֶׁאֲנַחְנוּ מְקַיְּמִים, לְיַחֵד שֵׁם קֻדְשָׁא בְּרִיךְ הוּא בִּדְחִילוּ וּרְחִימוּ, וּלְהַקִּיף אוֹתָנוּ מִזִּיו כְּבוֹדְךָ הַקָּדוֹשׁ וְהַטָּהוֹר, נָטוּי עַל רָאשֵׁינוּ מִלְמַעְלָה כְּנֶשֶׁר יָעִיר קִנּוֹ, וּמִשָּׁם תַּשְׁפִּיעַ שֶׁפַע הַחַיִּים לְעַבְדְּךָ (פלוני בֶּן אֲמָתְךָ פלונית / פלונית בַּת אֲמָתְךָ פלונית). וּבִזְכוּת צֵאתִי מִבֵּיתִי הַחוּצָה, וְדֶרֶךְ מִצְוֹתֶיךָ אָרוּצָה, יֵחָשֵׁב־לִי זֹאת כְּאִלּוּ הִרְחַקְתִּי נְדוֹד. וְהֶרֶב כַּבְּסֵנִי מֵעֲוֹנִי, וּמֵחַטָּאתִי טַהֲרֵנִי. תְּחַיֵּנִי אֲדֹנָי, תַּשְׁפִּיעַ לִי רֹב בְּרָכוֹת, וְלָרְעֵבִים, גַּם צְמֵאִים, תֵּן לַחְמָם, וּמֵימָם נֶאֱמָנִים. וְתִתֶּן־לִי זְכוּת לָשֶׁבֶת וְלַחֲסוֹת בְּסֵתֶר צֵל כְּנָפֶיךָ, בְּעֵת פְּטִירָתִי מִן־הָעוֹלָם. וְתֵיטִיב לָנוּ הַחֲתִימָה. וּתְזַכֵּנוּ לֵישֵׁב יָמִים רַבִּים עַל הָאֲדָמָה, אַדְמַת קֹדֶשׁ. בָּרוּךְ יהוה לְעוֹלָם, אָמֵן וְאָמֵן.

MEDITATION IN THE SUKKAH
Meditations before the fulfilment of commandments are especially important when an essential component of the commandment is its symbolic content (for example, *tzitzit* serves as a reminder of the entire life of commandments, and *tefillin* reminds us of the bond of love be-

It is customary for all present to drink of the wine.

All then wash their hands, saying, immediately after the washing:

בָּרוּךְ Blessed are You, LORD our GOD, King of the Universe, who has made us holy through His commandments, and has commanded us about washing hands.

After washing hands, one should not speak until one has eaten some of the *challah*.

Holding both loaves (on Pesach, two Matzot), the person making the blessing says:

בָּרוּךְ Blessed are You, LORD our GOD, King of the Universe, who brings forth bread from the earth.

Some of the bread or Matzah should be given to each person present.

MEDITATION IN THE SUKKAH

To be said in the *Sukkah* on the first night of Sukkot, before *Kiddush*:

יְהִי May it be Your will, LORD my GOD and GOD of my ancestors, to let Your presence rest among us. Spread over us Your shelter of peace through the merit of the commandment of the *Sukkah* that we are now fulfilling, acknowledging in love and reverence the unity of Your holy and blessed name. Encircle us with the pure and holy radiance of Your glory, set over our heads as an eagle hovers over its nest. Send forth a rich stream of life on Your servant/handmaid (name), the child of (mother's name). May the merit of leaving my house to live outside – eagerly pursuing the path of Your commandments – be accounted to me as though I had wandered far for Your sake. Wash me thoroughly from my iniquity, and cleanse me from my sin. Keep me in life, LORD, and bestow on me abounding blessings; and to the hungry and thirsty, give bread and water unfailingly. Help me to be worthy to find refuge under the sheltering shadow of Your wings when I leave this world. Inscribe us for good life and grant us the privilege to live many days on the land, the holy land, in service to and reverence of You. Blessed is the LORD for ever. Amen and Amen.

---

tween us and GOD). The Torah explicitly mentions the symbolism of the *Sukkah*: "So that your descendants will know that I made the Israelites live in booths (*Sukkot*) when I brought them out of Egypt; I am the LORD your GOD" (Leviticus 23:43). The meditation, said in the first night of *Sukkot*, emphasises the nature of the *Sukkah* as a symbol of GOD's protective presence.

הזכרת נשמות

On the eighth day of פֶּסַח, the second day of שָׁבֻעוֹת,
שְׁמִינִי עֲצֶרֶת and יוֹם כִּפּוּר, the following is said:

יהוה מָה־אָדָם וַתֵּדָעֵהוּ, בֶּן־אֱנוֹשׁ וַתְּחַשְּׁבֵהוּ. אָדָם לַהֶבֶל דָּמָה, יָמָיו כְּצֵל עוֹבֵר. בַּבֹּקֶר יָצִיץ וְחָלָף, לָעֶרֶב יְמוֹלֵל וְיָבֵשׁ. לִמְנוֹת יָמֵינוּ כֵּן הוֹדַע, וְנָבִא לְבַב חָכְמָה. שְׁמָר־תָּם וּרְאֵה יָשָׁר, כִּי אַחֲרִית לְאִישׁ שָׁלוֹם. אַךְ־אֱלֹהִים יִפְדֶּה־נַפְשִׁי מִיַּד שְׁאוֹל, כִּי יִקָּחֵנִי סֶלָה. כָּלָה שְׁאֵרִי וּלְבָבִי צוּר לְבָבִי וְחֶלְקִי אֱלֹהִים לְעוֹלָם. וְיָשֹׁב הֶעָפָר עַל־הָאָרֶץ כְּשֶׁהָיָה, וְהָרְוּחַ תָּשׁוּב אֶל־הָאֱלֹהִים אֲשֶׁר נְתָנָהּ. אֲנִי בְּצֶדֶק אֶחֱזֶה פָנֶיךָ, אֶשְׂבְּעָה בְהָקִיץ תְּמוּנָתֶךָ.

For one's father:

יִזְכּוֹר אֱלֹהִים נִשְׁמַת אָבִי מוֹרִי (add full Hebrew name) שֶׁהָלַךְ לְעוֹלָמוֹ, אָנָּא תְּהִי נַפְשׁוֹ צְרוּרָה בִּצְרוֹר הַחַיִּים, וּתְהִי מְנוּחָתוֹ כָּבוֹד, שֹׂבַע שְׂמָחוֹת אֶת־פָּנֶיךָ, נְעִימוֹת בִּימִינְךָ נֶצַח, אָמֵן.

For one's mother:

יִזְכּוֹר אֱלֹהִים נִשְׁמַת אִמִּי מוֹרָתִי (add full Hebrew name) שֶׁהָלְכָה לְעוֹלָמָהּ, אָנָּא תְּהִי נַפְשָׁהּ צְרוּרָה בִּצְרוֹר הַחַיִּים, וּתְהִי מְנוּחָתָהּ כָּבוֹד, שֹׂבַע שְׂמָחוֹת אֶת־פָּנֶיךָ, נְעִימוֹת בִּימִינְךָ נֶצַח, אָמֵן.

YIZKOR: MEMORIAL SERVICE FOR THE DEAD

From the eleventh century onward it has become customary to pray, at key moments in the year, for the souls of the departed. At first, this prayer was said only on Yom Kippur, but it was soon extended to the last days of the other festivals: the eighth day of Pesach, the second of Shavuot, and the day of Shemini Atzeret.

Remembrance is fundamental to Judaism. The word *zachor*, "remember", in one or other of its forms, appears no fewer than 169 times in the Hebrew Bible. The past is not lost: we remain connected to it to the extent that we remember it, honour it, and keep faith with it. We are its

YIZKOR: MEMORIAL SERVICE FOR THE DEAD

On the eighth day of Pesach, the second day of Shavuot,
Yom Kippur and Shemini Atzeret, the following is said:

יהוה LORD, what is man that You care for him, a mortal that You notice him? Man is like a fleeting breath, his days like a passing shadow. In the morning he flourishes and grows; in the evening he withers and dries up. Teach us to number our days, that we may get a heart of wisdom. Mark the blameless, note the upright, for the end of such a person is peace. GOD will redeem my soul from the grave, for He will receive me, Selah. My flesh and my heart may fail, but GOD is the strength of my heart and my portion for ever. The dust returns to the earth as it was, but the spirit returns to GOD who gave it. Then I, in righteousness, will see Your face, and be blessed with a vision of You when I awake.

For one's father:

יִזְכּוֹר May GOD remember the soul of my revered father (add name) who has gone to his everlasting home. May his soul be bound in the bond of life. May his rest be with honour, fullness of joy in Your presence, and bliss at Your right hand for evermore. Amen.

For one's mother:

יִזְכּוֹר May GOD remember the soul of my revered mother (add name) who has gone to her everlasting home. May her soul be bound in the bond of life. May her rest be with honour, fullness of joy in Your presence, and bliss at Your right hand for evermore. Amen.

---

heirs – our lives are part of a story that began long before we were born and will continue long after we physically cease to be. Above all, GOD remembers – as we say in every *Amidah*, He "remembers the kindness of the Fathers". For Him, there is no forgetting.

At *Yizkor*, our memory reaches out to that of GOD. We ask Him to remember those of our family who are no longer here. We ask Him to look on the good we do; it is a custom to donate a sum to *tzedakah* at this time and attribute it to the souls of the departed ones, for it is because of their influence on us that we are in the synagogue; that we pray, and that we try to do good in this life. A connection is thus made between the dead and the living. We remember them; with GOD's help, their virtues live on in us. That is as much of immortality as we can know in the land of the living.

It is a custom at *Yizkor* also to remember the Jewish martyrs including

אַב הָרַחֲמִים, אֲשֶׁר בְּיָדְךָ נַפְשׁוֹת הַחַיִּים וְהַמֵּתִים, תַּנְחוּמֶיךָ יְשַׁעַשְׁעוּ נַפְשֵׁנוּ בְּזָכְרֵנוּ (בַּיּוֹם הַקָּדוֹשׁ הַזֶּה) אֶת־קְרוֹבֵינוּ הָאֲהוּבִים וְהַנִּכְבָּדִים, אֲשֶׁר הָלְכוּ לִמְנוּחָתָם. אֶת־הוֹרֵינוּ הַיְקָרִים, עֲטֶרֶת רֹאשֵׁנוּ וְתִפְאַרְתֵּנוּ, אֲשֶׁר כָּל־מְגַמָּתָם לְהַדְרִיכֵנוּ בְּדֶרֶךְ הַטּוֹב וְהַיֹּשֶׁר, לְלַמְּדֵנוּ חֻקֶּיךָ וּמִצְוֹתֶיךָ, וּלְהוֹרוֹתֵנוּ עֲשׂוֹת צְדָקָה וְאַהֲבַת חֶסֶד. אָנָּא יהוה, אַמְּצֵנוּ לִשְׁמוֹר אֶת פְּקוּדָּתָם כָּל עוֹד נִשְׁמָתֵנוּ בְּקִרְבֵּנוּ, וְנַפְשָׁם תָּנְוּחַ בְּאֶרֶץ הַחַיִּים, לַחֲזוֹת בְּנוֹעַמְךָ וּלְהִתְעַנֵּג מִטּוּבֶךָ.

וְעַתָּה, הָאֵל הַטּוֹב וְהַמֵּטִיב, מַה־נֹּאמַר וּמַה־נְּדַבֵּר, צָרְכֵינוּ מְרֻבִּים, וְדַעְתֵּנוּ קְצָרָה. בֹּשֶׁת פָּנִים כִּסָּתְנוּ, מִדֵּי עֲלוֹת עַל־לִבֵּנוּ זֵכֶר כָּל־הַטּוֹבָה שֶׁגְּמַלְתָּ עָלֵינוּ. אָנָּא פְּנֵה הַיּוֹם בְּחֶסֶד וּבְרַחֲמִים אֶל תְּפִלַּת עֲבָדֶיךָ, הַשּׁוֹפְכִים אֶת־נַפְשָׁם לְפָנֶיךָ. אָנָּא חַסְדְּךָ, מֵאִתָּנוּ אַל־יָמוּשׁ. הַטְרִיפֵנוּ לֶחֶם חֻקֵּנוּ, וְאַל־תַּצְרִיכֵנוּ לִידֵי מַתְּנַת בָּשָׂר וָדָם. הָסֵר מֵעָלֵינוּ כָּל־דְּאָגָה וְתוּגָה, כָּל־צָרָה וָפַחַד, כָּל־חֶרְפָּה וָבוּז. בְּיִרְאָתְךָ הַטְּהוֹרָה תְּחַזְּקֵנוּ, וּבְתוֹרָתְךָ הַתְּמִימָה תְּאַמְּצֵנוּ. זַכֵּנוּ לְגַדֵּל אֶת־בָּנֵינוּ וּבְנוֹתֵינוּ, לִשְׁמוֹר מִצְוֹתֶיךָ, וְלַעֲשׂוֹת רְצוֹנְךָ, כָּל־יְמֵי חַיֵּיהֶם. אַל נָא, אַל תַּעֲלֵנוּ בַּחֲצִי יָמֵינוּ, וּנְמַלֵּא בְשָׁלוֹם אֶת מִסְפַּר יָמֵינוּ. יָדַעְנוּ, אַף יָדַעְנוּ, כִּי חָדַל כֹּחֵנוּ, וְטִפָּחוֹת נָתַתָּ יָמֵינוּ. עָזְרֵנוּ אֱלֹהֵי יִשְׁעֵנוּ, לְהִתְנַהֵג בֶּאֱמֶת וּבִתְמִים, יְמֵי שְׁנֵי חַיֵּי מְגוּרֵנוּ. וְכַאֲשֶׁר יַגִּיעַ קִצֵּנוּ לְהִפָּרֵד מִן הָעוֹלָם, הֱיֵה אַתָּה עִמָּנוּ, וְנִשְׁמוֹתֵינוּ תִּהְיֶינָה צְרוּרוֹת בִּצְרוֹר הַחַיִּים, עִם נִשְׁמוֹת אֲבוֹתֵינוּ, וְנִשְׁמוֹת הַצַּדִּיקִים הָעוֹמְדִים לְפָנֶיךָ. אָמֵן, וְאָמֵן.

אַב הָרַחֲמִים Father of compassion, in whose hands are the souls of the living and the dead, may Your consolations hearten us as we remember (on this holy day) our beloved and honoured relatives who have gone to their eternal rest. We think of our cherished parents, the crown of our head and our glory, whose desire it was to guide us in the path of good and right, to teach us Your laws and commandments, and to instruct us to act justly and to love kindness. Please, Lord, grant us the strength to remain faithful to their charge while the breath of life is within us, and may their souls find rest in the land of everlasting life, seeing Your beauty and delighting in Your goodness.

וְעַתָּה And now, God, You who are good and do good, what shall we say? What words shall we speak? Our needs are so many; our knowledge is so slender. Confusion covers us when we call to mind all the goodness You have bestowed on us. Please turn, this day, in love and compassion to the prayer of Your servants who pour out their soul before You. May Your love never leave us. Grant us our sustenance so that we will not need the gifts of others. Remove from us care and sorrow, distress and fear, humiliation and shame. Strengthen us in our pure reverence for You, and invigorate us through Your perfect Torah. Help us be worthy to bring up our children to keep Your commandments and do Your will all the days of their life. Please, God, do not take us away in the midst of our days. Let us complete in peace the number of our years. We surely know how frail is our strength, and how short – mere handbreadths – is the life you have given us. Help us, God of our salvation, to act in truth and integrity during the years of our stay on earth. And when our end and our departure from this world draw near, be with us, so that our souls may be bound in the bond of life with the souls of our parents and of the righteous who are ever with You. Amen and Amen.

---

the victims of the Holocaust, for we are the guardians of their memory. The dead cannot be brought back to life, but we can act in such a way as to ensure that they did not die in vain by showing that the faith for which they died still lives. To the *Yizkor* prayer itself have been added a series of biblical verses on life and death, together with a prayer that we may act in such a way as to honour the memory of those, especially our parents, who are no longer here.

תפלת מוסף לרגלים

To be said on שְׁמִינִי עֲצֶרֶת ,סֻכּוֹת ,שָׁבֻעוֹת ,פֶּסַח,
חוֹל הַמּוֹעֵד and שִׂמְחַת תּוֹרָה.

On the first day of פֶּסַח , the Leader begins the repetition of the עֲמִידָה
with תְּפִלַּת טַל, page 696; on שְׁמִינִי עֲצֶרֶת with תְּפִלַּת גֶּשֶׁם, page 702.

On the first weekday of חוֹל הַמּוֹעֵד פֶּסַח, the תְּפִלִּין are now removed.

עמידה

The following prayer, until קַדְמוֹנִיּוֹת, on page 690, is said standing with feet together.
The עֲמִידָה is first said silently; then, if there is a מִנְיָן, it is repeated aloud by the Leader.
Take three steps back, then forward. At the points indicated by ▾, Bend the knees
at the first word, bow at the second, and stand straight before GOD's name.

אֲדֹנָי שְׂפָתַי תִּפְתָּח, וּפִי יַגִּיד תְּהִלָּתֶךָ.

אבות

▾**בָּרוּךְ** אַתָּה יהוה אֱלֹהֵינוּ וֵאלֹהֵי אֲבוֹתֵינוּ, אֱלֹהֵי אַבְרָהָם, אֱלֹהֵי יִצְחָק, וֵאלֹהֵי יַעֲקֹב, הָאֵל הַגָּדוֹל הַגִּבּוֹר וְהַנּוֹרָא, אֵל עֶלְיוֹן, גּוֹמֵל חֲסָדִים טוֹבִים וְקוֹנֵה הַכֹּל, וְזוֹכֵר חַסְדֵי אָבוֹת, וּמֵבִיא גּוֹאֵל לִבְנֵי בְנֵיהֶם, לְמַעַן שְׁמוֹ בְּאַהֲבָה. מֶלֶךְ עוֹזֵר וּמוֹשִׁיעַ וּמָגֵן. ▾בָּרוּךְ אַתָּה יהוה, מָגֵן אַבְרָהָם.

גבורות

אַתָּה גִּבּוֹר לְעוֹלָם אֲדֹנָי, מְחַיֵּה מֵתִים אַתָּה, רַב לְהוֹשִׁיעַ.

On שִׂמְחַת תּוֹרָה and the first day of פֶּסַח, add:

מַשִּׁיב הָרוּחַ וּמוֹרִיד הַגָּשֶׁם.

מְכַלְכֵּל חַיִּים בְּחֶסֶד, מְחַיֵּה מֵתִים בְּרַחֲמִים רַבִּים, סוֹמֵךְ נוֹפְלִים, וְרוֹפֵא חוֹלִים, וּמַתִּיר אֲסוּרִים, וּמְקַיֵּם אֱמוּנָתוֹ לִישֵׁנֵי עָפָר. מִי כָמוֹךָ בַּעַל גְּבוּרוֹת, וּמִי דּוֹמֶה לָּךְ, מֶלֶךְ מֵמִית וּמְחַיֶּה וּמַצְמִיחַ יְשׁוּעָה. וְנֶאֱמָן אַתָּה לְהַחֲיוֹת מֵתִים. בָּרוּךְ אַתָּה יהוה, מְחַיֵּה הַמֵּתִים.

ADDITIONAL SERVICE FOR FESTIVALS

To be said on Pesach, Shavuot, Sukkot, Shemini Atzeret,
Simchat Torah and the Intermediate Days of Festivals.

On the first day of Pesach, the Leader begins the repetition of the *Amidah* with the Prayer for Dew on page 697; on Shemini Atzeret with the Prayer for Rain on page 703.

On the first weekday Intermediate Day of Pesach, the *tefillin* are now removed.

AMIDAH: THE STANDING PRAYER

The following prayer, until "in former years", on page 691, is said standing with feet together.

The *Amidah* is first said silently; then, if there is a *minyan*, it is repeated aloud by the Leader.

Take three steps back, then forward. At the points indicated by ▾, bend the knees at the first word, bow at the second, and stand straight before God's name.

O Lord, open my lips, so that my mouth may declare Your praise.

PATRIARCHS

▾בָּרוּךְ Blessed are You, Lord our God and God of our Fathers, God of Abraham, God of Isaac and God of Jacob; the great, mighty and awesome God, God Most High, who bestows acts of lovingkindness and creates all, who remembers the lovingkindness of the Fathers and will bring a Redeemer to their children's children for the sake of His name, in love. King, Helper, Saviour, Shield: ▾Blessed are You, Lord, Shield of Abraham.

DIVINE MIGHT

אַתָּה You are eternally mighty, Lord. You give life to the dead and have great power to save.

On Simchat Torah and the first day of Pesach, add:
He makes the wind blow and the rain fall.

He sustains the living with lovingkindness, and with great compassion revives the dead. He supports the fallen, heals the sick, sets captives free, and keeps His faith with those who sleep in the dust. Who is like You, Master of might, and to whom can You be compared, O King who brings death and gives life, and makes salvation grow? Faithful are You to revive the dead. Blessed are You, Lord, who revives the dead.

When saying the עֲמִידָה silently, go to אַתָּה קָדוֹשׁ overleaf.

קדושה

On שַׁבָּת חוֹל הַמּוֹעֵד turn to the קְדוּשָּׁה overleaf. On a יוֹם טוֹב, חוֹל הַמּוֹעֵד and הוֹשַׁעְנָא רַבָּה, during the Leader's repetition, the following is said standing, with feet together, rising on the toes at the words indicated by ▲.

Congregation then Leader: נַעֲרִיצְךָ וְנַקְדִּישְׁךָ כְּסוֹד שִׂיחַ שַׂרְפֵי קֹדֶשׁ, הַמַּקְדִּישִׁים שִׁמְךָ בַּקֹּדֶשׁ, כַּכָּתוּב עַל יַד נְבִיאֶךָ, וְקָרָא זֶה אֶל־זֶה וְאָמַר,

Congregation and Leader: ▲קָדוֹשׁ ▲קָדוֹשׁ ▲קָדוֹשׁ יהוה צְבָאוֹת, מְלֹא כָל־הָאָרֶץ כְּבוֹדוֹ.

Congregation then Leader: כְּבוֹדוֹ מָלֵא עוֹלָם, מְשָׁרְתָיו שׁוֹאֲלִים זֶה לָזֶה, אַיֵּה מְקוֹם כְּבוֹדוֹ, לְעֻמָּתָם בָּרוּךְ יֹאמֵרוּ,

Congregation and Leader: ▲בָּרוּךְ כְּבוֹד יהוה, מִמְּקוֹמוֹ

Congregation then Leader: מִמְּקוֹמוֹ הוּא יִפֶן בְּרַחֲמִים, וְיָחֹן עַם הַמְיַחֲדִים שְׁמוֹ, עֶרֶב וָבֹקֶר בְּכָל־יוֹם תָּמִיד, פַּעֲמַיִם בְּאַהֲבָה שְׁמַע אוֹמְרִים.

Congregation and Leader: שְׁמַע יִשְׂרָאֵל, יהוה אֱלֹהֵינוּ, יהוה אֶחָד.

Congregation then Leader: אֶחָד הוּא אֱלֹהֵינוּ, הוּא אָבִינוּ, הוּא מַלְכֵּנוּ, הוּא מוֹשִׁיעֵנוּ, וְהוּא יַשְׁמִיעֵנוּ בְּרַחֲמָיו שֵׁנִית, לְעֵינֵי כָּל־חָי, לִהְיוֹת לָכֶם לֵאלֹהִים,

Congregation and Leader: אֲנִי יהוה אֱלֹהֵיכֶם.

Congregation then Leader: אַדִּיר אַדִּירֵנוּ, יהוה אֲדוֹנֵנוּ, מָה אַדִּיר שִׁמְךָ בְּכָל־הָאָרֶץ. וְהָיָה יהוה לְמֶלֶךְ עַל־כָּל־הָאָרֶץ, בַּיּוֹם הַהוּא יִהְיֶה יהוה אֶחָד וּשְׁמוֹ אֶחָד.

Leader: וּבְדִבְרֵי קָדְשְׁךָ כָּתוּב לֵאמֹר,

Congregation and Leader: ▲יִמְלֹךְ יהוה לְעוֹלָם, אֱלֹהַיִךְ צִיּוֹן לְדֹר וָדֹר, הַלְלוּיָהּ.

Leader: לְדוֹר וָדוֹר נַגִּיד גָּדְלֶךָ וּלְנֵצַח נְצָחִים קְדֻשָּׁתְךָ נַקְדִּישׁ, וְשִׁבְחֲךָ אֱלֹהֵינוּ מִפִּינוּ לֹא יָמוּשׁ לְעוֹלָם וָעֶד, כִּי אֵל מֶלֶךְ גָּדוֹל וְקָדוֹשׁ אָתָּה. בָּרוּךְ אַתָּה יהוה, הָאֵל הַקָּדוֹשׁ.

The repetition continues with אַתָּה בְחַרְתָּנוּ overleaf.

When saying the *Amidah* silently, go to "You are holy" overleaf.

KEDUSHAH

On Intermediate Days, turn to the *Kedushah* overleaf. On a Festival the Intermediate Shabbat of a Festival and Hoshana Rabba, during the Leader's repetition, the following is said standing, with feet together, rising on the toes at the words indicated by ▲.

Congregation then Leader: נַעֲרִיצְךָ We will revere and sanctify You with the words uttered by the holy Seraphim who sanctify Your name in the sanctuary; as is written by Your prophet: "They call out to one another, saying:

Congregation and Leader: "▲Holy, ▲holy, ▲holy is the LORD of Hosts: the whole world is filled with His glory."

Congregation then Leader: His glory fills the universe. His ministering angels ask each other, "Where is the place of His glory?" Those facing them reply "Blessed –

Cong. and Leader: "▲Blessed is the LORD's glory from His place."

Congregation then Leader: From His place may He turn with compassion and be gracious to the people who proclaim the unity of His name, morning and evening, every day, continually, twice each day reciting in love the *Shema*:

Cong. and Leader: "Listen, Israel, the LORD is our GOD, the LORD is one."

Congregation then Leader: He is our GOD, He is our Father, He is our King, He is our Saviour – and He, in His compassion, will let us hear a second time in the presence of all that lives, His promise to be "Your GOD".

Cong. and Leader: "I am the LORD your GOD."

Congregation then Leader: Glorious is our glorious One, LORD our Master, and glorious is your name throughout the earth. Then the LORD shall be King over all the earth: on that day the LORD shall be One and His name One.

Leader: And in Your Holy Writings it is written:

Congregation and Leader: "▲The LORD shall reign forever. He is your GOD, Zion, from generation to generation, Halleluyah!"

Leader: From generation to generation we will declare Your greatness, and we will proclaim Your holiness for evermore. Your praise, our GOD, shall never leave our mouth, for You, GOD, are a great and holy King. Blessed are You, LORD, the holy GOD.

The repetition continues with "You have chosen us" overleaf.

קדושה לחול המועד

During the Leader's repetition, the following is said standing, with feet together, rising on the toes at the words indicated by ▲.

Congregation then Leader: נְקַדֵּשׁ אֶת־שִׁמְךָ בָּעוֹלָם, כְּשֵׁם שֶׁמַּקְדִּישִׁים אוֹתוֹ בִּשְׁמֵי מָרוֹם, כַּכָּתוּב עַל יַד נְבִיאֶךָ, וְקָרָא זֶה אֶל־זֶה וְאָמַר.

Congregation and Leader: ▲קָדוֹשׁ ▲קָדוֹשׁ ▲קָדוֹשׁ יהוה צְבָאוֹת, מְלֹא כָל־הָאָרֶץ כְּבוֹדוֹ.

Leader: לְעֻמָּתָם בָּרוּךְ יֹאמֵרוּ

Congregation and Leader: ▲בָּרוּךְ כְּבוֹד יהוה, מִמְּקוֹמוֹ

Leader: וּבְדִבְרֵי קָדְשְׁךָ כָּתוּב לֵאמֹר.

Congregation and Leader: ▲יִמְלֹךְ יהוה לְעוֹלָם, אֱלֹהַיִךְ צִיּוֹן לְדֹר וָדֹר, הַלְלוּיָהּ.

Leader: לְדוֹר וָדוֹר נַגִּיד גָּדְלֶךָ וּלְנֵצַח נְצָחִים קְדֻשָּׁתְךָ נַקְדִּישׁ, וְשִׁבְחֲךָ אֱלֹהֵינוּ מִפִּינוּ לֹא יָמוּשׁ לְעוֹלָם וָעֶד, כִּי אֵל מֶלֶךְ גָּדוֹל וְקָדוֹשׁ אָתָּה. בָּרוּךְ אַתָּה יהוה, הָאֵל הַקָּדוֹשׁ.

The repetition continues with אַתָּה בְחַרְתָּנוּ, below.
When saying the עֲמִידָה silently, continue here:

קדושת השם

אַתָּה קָדוֹשׁ וְשִׁמְךָ קָדוֹשׁ, וּקְדוֹשִׁים בְּכָל־יוֹם יְהַלְלוּךָ סֶּלָה. בָּרוּךְ אַתָּה יהוה, הָאֵל הַקָּדוֹשׁ.

קדושת היום

אַתָּה בְחַרְתָּנוּ מִכָּל־הָעַמִּים, אָהַבְתָּ אוֹתָנוּ, וְרָצִיתָ בָּנוּ, וְרוֹמַמְתָּנוּ מִכָּל הַלְּשׁוֹנוֹת, וְקִדַּשְׁתָּנוּ בְּמִצְוֹתֶיךָ, וְקֵרַבְתָּנוּ מַלְכֵּנוּ לַעֲבוֹדָתֶךָ, וְשִׁמְךָ הַגָּדוֹל וְהַקָּדוֹשׁ עָלֵינוּ קָרָאתָ.

KEDUSHAH FOR CHOL HAMOED

During the Leader's repetition, the following is said standing, with feet together, rising on the toes at the words indicated by ▲.

Congregation then Leader: **נְקַדֵּשׁ** We will sanctify Your name on earth, as they sanctify it in the highest heavens, as is written by Your prophet, "And they (the angels) call to one another saying:

Congregation and Leader: ▲Holy, ▲holy, ▲holy is the LORD of Hosts: the whole world is filled with His glory."

Leader: Those facing them say: "Blessed – "

Congregation and Leader: "▲Blessed is the LORD's glory from His place."

Leader: And in Your Holy Writings it is written thus:

Congregation and Leader: "▲The LORD shall reign forever. He is your GOD, Zion, from generation to generation, Halleluyah!"

Leader: From generation to generation we will declare Your greatness, and we will proclaim Your holiness for evermore. Your praise, our GOD, shall never leave our mouth, for You, GOD, are a great and holy King. Blessed are You, LORD, the holy GOD.

The repetition continues with "You have chosen us", below.
When saying the *Amidah* silently, continue here:

HOLINESS

אַתָּה קָדוֹשׁ You are holy and Your name is holy, and holy ones praise You daily, Selah! Blessed are You, LORD, the holy GOD.

HOLINESS OF THE DAY

אַתָּה בְחַרְתָּנוּ You have chosen us from among all peoples. You have loved and favoured us. You have raised us above all tongues. You have made us holy through Your commandments. You have brought us near, our King, to Your service, and have called us by Your great and holy name.

ADDITIONAL SERVICE FOR FESTIVALS
The *Musaf* on festivals, like that of Shabbat, corresponds to the additional sacrifice brought on these days. The *Amidah* follows the normal form for prayers on

On שַׁבָּת add the words in brackets.

וַתִּתֶּן־לָנוּ יהוה אֱלֹהֵינוּ בְּאַהֲבָה (שַׁבָּתוֹת לִמְנוּחָה וּ) מוֹעֲדִים לְשִׂמְחָה חַגִּים וּזְמַנִּים לְשָׂשׂוֹן, אֶת־יוֹם (הַשַּׁבָּת הַזֶּה וְאֶת־יוֹם)

On פֶּסַח:	On שָׁבֻעוֹת:	On סֻכּוֹת:	On שְׁמִינִי עֲצֶרֶת and שִׂמְחַת תּוֹרָה:
חַג הַמַּצּוֹת הַזֶּה, זְמַן חֵרוּתֵנוּ	חַג הַשָּׁבֻעוֹת הַזֶּה, זְמַן מַתַּן תּוֹרָתֵנוּ	חַג הַסֻּכּוֹת הַזֶּה, זְמַן שִׂמְחָתֵנוּ	הַשְּׁמִינִי חַג הָעֲצֶרֶת הַזֶּה, זְמַן שִׂמְחָתֵנוּ

(בְּאַהֲבָה) מִקְרָא קֹדֶשׁ, זֵכֶר לִיצִיאַת מִצְרָיִם.

וּמִפְּנֵי חֲטָאֵינוּ גָּלִינוּ מֵאַרְצֵנוּ, וְנִתְרַחַקְנוּ מֵעַל אַדְמָתֵנוּ. וְאֵין אֲנַחְנוּ יְכוֹלִים לַעֲלוֹת וְלֵרָאוֹת וּלְהִשְׁתַּחֲוֹת לְפָנֶיךָ, וְלַעֲשׂוֹת חוֹבוֹתֵינוּ בְּבֵית בְּחִירָתֶךָ, בַּבַּיִת הַגָּדוֹל וְהַקָּדוֹשׁ שֶׁנִּקְרָא שִׁמְךָ עָלָיו, מִפְּנֵי הַיָּד שֶׁנִּשְׁתַּלְּחָה בְּמִקְדָּשֶׁךָ. יְהִי רָצוֹן מִלְּפָנֶיךָ יהוה אֱלֹהֵינוּ וֵאלֹהֵי אֲבוֹתֵינוּ, מֶלֶךְ רַחֲמָן, שֶׁתָּשׁוּב וּתְרַחֵם עָלֵינוּ וְעַל־מִקְדָּשְׁךָ בְּרַחֲמֶיךָ הָרַבִּים, וְתִבְנֵהוּ מְהֵרָה וּתְגַדֵּל כְּבוֹדוֹ. אָבִינוּ מַלְכֵּנוּ, גַּלֵּה כְּבוֹד מַלְכוּתְךָ עָלֵינוּ מְהֵרָה, וְהוֹפַע וְהִנָּשֵׂא עָלֵינוּ לְעֵינֵי כָּל־חָי. וְקָרֵב פְּזוּרֵינוּ מִבֵּין הַגּוֹיִם, וּנְפוּצוֹתֵינוּ כַּנֵּס מִיַּרְכְּתֵי אָרֶץ. וַהֲבִיאֵנוּ לְצִיּוֹן עִירְךָ בְּרִנָּה, וְלִירוּשָׁלַיִם בֵּית מִקְדָּשְׁךָ בְּשִׂמְחַת עוֹלָם. וְשָׁם נַעֲשֶׂה לְפָנֶיךָ אֶת־קָרְבְּנוֹת חוֹבוֹתֵינוּ,

---

holy days: the first and last three *Amidah* blessings are the same as on other days of the year; the middle blessing is specific to the "holiness of the day". On festivals, special emphasis is placed on rejoicing, mentioned in the Torah (Deuteronomy 16:11–15) in connection with festivals.

וּמִפְּנֵי חֲטָאֵינוּ *But because of our sins we were exiled from our land*: The concept of exile is emphasised on the festivals

On Shabbat, add the words in brackets.

וַתִּתֶּן־לָנוּ And You, LORD our GOD, have given us in love (Sabbaths for rest and) festivals for rejoicing, holy days and seasons for joy, (this Sabbath day and) this day of:

On Pesach:	On Shavuot:	On Sukkot:	On Shemini Atzeret and Simchat Torah:
The festival of Matzot, the time of our freedom.	The festival of Shavuot, the time of the giving of our Torah.	The festival of Sukkot, our time of rejoicing.	The festival of eighth day, Shemini Atzeret, our time of rejoicing.

(with love), a holy assembly in memory of the exodus from Egypt.

וּמִפְּנֵי חֲטָאֵינוּ But because of our sins we were exiled from our land and driven far from our country. We cannot go up to appear and bow before You, and to perform our duties in Your chosen house, the great and holy Temple that was called by Your name, because of the hand stretched out against Your sanctuary. May it be Your will, LORD our GOD and GOD of our ancestors, merciful King, that You in Your abounding compassion may once more have mercy on us and on Your sanctuary, rebuilding it swiftly and adding to its glory. Our Father, our King, reveal the glory of Your kingdom to us swiftly. Appear and be exalted over us in the sight of all that lives. Bring back our scattered ones from among the nations, and gather our dispersed people from the ends of the earth. Lead us to Zion, Your city, in jubilation, and to Jerusalem, home of Your Temple, with everlasting joy. There we will prepare for You our obligatory offerings: the regular daily offerings in

---

for two reasons: 1. The three pilgrimage festivals were occasions when people throughout the land went to Jerusalem to take part in the Temple celebrations. They are thus times in which we feel, most acutely, the absence of the Temple. 2. The festivals testify to the presence of GOD in history. Exile is the opposite. Not only is exile physical and geographical dispersion, it is also metaphysical: the "hiding of the face" of GOD (Deuteronomy 31:18). The prayers for forgiveness, return to the land, the rebuilding of the Temple, and the re-appearance of GOD in history, are thus intimately connected, and are most intensely felt on these days when we recall GOD's deliverances and saving acts in Israel's past.

תְּמִידִים כְּסִדְרָם, וּמוּסָפִים כְּהִלְכָתָם. וְאֶת־מוּסַף יוֹם (הַשַּׁבָּת הַזֶּה וְאֶת־מוּסַף יוֹם)

On פֶּסַח:	On שָׁבֻעוֹת:	On סֻכּוֹת:	On שְׁמִינִי עֲצֶרֶת and שִׂמְחַת תּוֹרָה:
חַג הַמַּצּוֹת	חַג הַשָּׁבֻעוֹת	חַג הַסֻּכּוֹת	הַשְּׁמִינִי חַג הָעֲצֶרֶת

הַזֶּה. נַעֲשֶׂה וְנַקְרִיב לְפָנֶיךָ בְּאַהֲבָה כְּמִצְוַת רְצוֹנֶךָ, כְּמוֹ שֶׁכָּתַבְתָּ עָלֵינוּ בְּתוֹרָתֶךָ, עַל־יְדֵי מֹשֶׁה עַבְדֶּךָ, מִפִּי כְבוֹדֶךָ כָּאָמוּר,

---

On שַׁבָּת, say:

וּבְיוֹם הַשַּׁבָּת שְׁנֵי־כְבָשִׂים בְּנֵי־שָׁנָה תְּמִימִם, וּשְׁנֵי עֶשְׂרֹנִים סֹלֶת מִנְחָה בְּלוּלָה בַשֶּׁמֶן וְנִסְכּוֹ, עֹלַת שַׁבַּת בְּשַׁבַּתּוֹ, עַל־עֹלַת הַתָּמִיד וְנִסְכָּהּ.

On the first two days of פֶּסַח, say:

וּבַחֹדֶשׁ הָרִאשׁוֹן בְּאַרְבָּעָה עָשָׂר יוֹם לַחֹדֶשׁ, פֶּסַח לַיהוה. וּבַחֲמִשָּׁה עָשָׂר יוֹם לַחֹדֶשׁ הַזֶּה, חָג, שִׁבְעַת יָמִים מַצּוֹת יֵאָכֵל. בַּיּוֹם הָרִאשׁוֹן מִקְרָא־קֹדֶשׁ, כָּל־מְלֶאכֶת עֲבֹדָה לֹא תַעֲשׂוּ. וְהִקְרַבְתֶּם אִשֶּׁה עֹלָה לַיהוה, פָּרִים בְּנֵי־בָקָר שְׁנַיִם, וְאַיִל אֶחָד, וְשִׁבְעָה כְבָשִׂים בְּנֵי שָׁנָה, תְּמִימִם יִהְיוּ לָכֶם. וּמִנְחָתָם וְנִסְכֵּיהֶם כִּמְדֻבָּר, שְׁלֹשָׁה עֶשְׂרֹנִים לַפָּר, וּשְׁנֵי עֶשְׂרֹנִים לָאַיִל, וְעִשָּׂרוֹן לַכֶּבֶשׂ, וְיַיִן כְּנִסְכּוֹ. וְשָׂעִיר לְכַפֵּר, וּשְׁנֵי תְמִידִים כְּהִלְכָתָם.

On the last six days of פֶּסַח, say:

וְהִקְרַבְתֶּם אִשֶּׁה עֹלָה לַיהוה, פָּרִים בְּנֵי־בָקָר שְׁנַיִם, וְאַיִל אֶחָד, וְשִׁבְעָה כְבָשִׂים בְּנֵי שָׁנָה, תְּמִימִם יִהְיוּ לָכֶם. וּמִנְחָתָם וְנִסְכֵּיהֶם כִּמְדֻבָּר, שְׁלֹשָׁה עֶשְׂרֹנִים לַפָּר, וּשְׁנֵי עֶשְׂרֹנִים לָאַיִל, וְעִשָּׂרוֹן לַכֶּבֶשׂ, וְיַיִן כְּנִסְכּוֹ. וְשָׂעִיר לְכַפֵּר, וּשְׁנֵי תְמִידִים כְּהִלְכָתָם.

their order and the additional offerings according to their law. And the additional offering(s of this Sabbath day and) of this day of:

On Pesach:	On Shavuot:	On Sukkot:	On Shemini Atzeret and Simchat Torah:
the festival of Matzot	the festival of Shavuot	the festival of Sukkot	the festival of Shemini Atzeret

we will prepare and offer before You in love, in accord with Your will's commandment, as You wrote for us in your Torah through Your servant Moses, by Your own word, as it is said:

On Shabbat, say:

וּבְיוֹם הַשַּׁבָּת On the Sabbath day, make an offering of two lambs a year old, without blemish, together with two-tenths of an ephah of fine flour mixed with oil as a meal-offering, and its appropriate libation. This is the burnt-offering for every Sabbath, in addition to the regular daily burnt-offering and its libation.

On the first two days of Pesach, say:

וּבַחֹדֶשׁ הָרִאשׁוֹן On the fourteenth day of the first month there shall be a Passover offering to the LORD. And on the fifteenth day of this month there shall be a festival: seven days unleavened bread shall be eaten. On the first day there shall be a sacred assembly: you shall do no laborious work. And you shall bring an offering consumed by fire, a burnt-offering to the LORD: two young bullocks, one ram, and seven yearling male lambs; they shall be to you unblemished. And their meal-offerings and wine-libations as ordained: three-tenths of an ephah for each bull, two-tenths of an ephah for the ram, one-tenth of an ephah for each lamb, wine for the libations, a male goat for atonement, and two regular daily offerings according to their law.

On the last six days of Pesach, say:

וְהִקְרַבְתֶּם And you shall bring an offering consumed by fire, a burnt-offering to the LORD: two young bullocks, one ram, and seven yearling male lambs; they shall be to you unblemished. And their meal-offerings and wine-libations as ordained: three-tenths of an ephah for each bull, two-tenths of an ephah for the ram, one-tenth of an ephah for each lamb, wine for the libations, a male goat for atonement, and two regular daily offerings according to their law.

On שָׁבֻעוֹת, say:

וּבְיוֹם הַבִּכּוּרִים, בְּהַקְרִיבְכֶם מִנְחָה חֲדָשָׁה לַיהוה, בְּשָׁבֻעֹתֵיכֶם, מִקְרָא־קֹדֶשׁ יִהְיֶה לָכֶם, כָּל־מְלֶאכֶת עֲבֹדָה לֹא תַעֲשׂוּ. וְהִקְרַבְתֶּם עוֹלָה לְרֵיחַ נִיחֹחַ לַיהוה, פָּרִים בְּנֵי־בָקָר שְׁנַיִם, אַיִל אֶחָד, שִׁבְעָה כְבָשִׂים בְּנֵי שָׁנָה. וּמִנְחָתָם וְנִסְכֵּיהֶם כִּמְדֻבָּר, שְׁלֹשָׁה עֶשְׂרֹנִים לַפָּר, וּשְׁנֵי עֶשְׂרֹנִים לָאָיִל, וְעִשָּׂרוֹן לַכֶּבֶשׂ, וְיַיִן כְּנִסְכּוֹ. וְשָׂעִיר לְכַפֵּר, וּשְׁנֵי תְמִידִים כְּהִלְכָתָם.

On the first two days of סֻכּוֹת, say:

וּבַחֲמִשָּׁה עָשָׂר יוֹם לַחֹדֶשׁ הַשְּׁבִיעִי, מִקְרָא־קֹדֶשׁ יִהְיֶה לָכֶם, כָּל־מְלֶאכֶת עֲבֹדָה לֹא תַעֲשׂוּ, וְחַגֹּתֶם חַג לַיהוה שִׁבְעַת יָמִים. וְהִקְרַבְתֶּם עוֹלָה אִשֵּׁה רֵיחַ נִיחֹחַ לַיהוה, פָּרִים בְּנֵי־בָקָר שְׁלֹשָׁה־עָשָׂר, אֵילִם שְׁנָיִם, כְּבָשִׂים בְּנֵי־שָׁנָה אַרְבָּעָה עָשָׂר, תְּמִימִם יִהְיוּ. וּמִנְחָתָם וְנִסְכֵּיהֶם כִּמְדֻבָּר, שְׁלֹשָׁה עֶשְׂרֹנִים לַפָּר, וּשְׁנֵי עֶשְׂרֹנִים לָאָיִל, וְעִשָּׂרוֹן לַכֶּבֶשׂ, וְיַיִן כְּנִסְכּוֹ. וְשָׂעִיר לְכַפֵּר, וּשְׁנֵי תְמִידִים כְּהִלְכָתָם.

On the first day of חוֹל הַמּוֹעֵד סֻכּוֹת, say:

וּבַיּוֹם הַשֵּׁנִי, פָּרִים בְּנֵי־בָקָר שְׁנֵים עָשָׂר, אֵילִם שְׁנָיִם, כְּבָשִׂים בְּנֵי־שָׁנָה אַרְבָּעָה עָשָׂר, תְּמִימִם. וּמִנְחָתָם וְנִסְכֵּיהֶם כִּמְדֻבָּר, שְׁלֹשָׁה עֶשְׂרֹנִים לַפָּר, וּשְׁנֵי עֶשְׂרֹנִים לָאָיִל, וְעִשָּׂרוֹן לַכֶּבֶשׂ, וְיַיִן כְּנִסְכּוֹ. וְשָׂעִיר לְכַפֵּר, וּשְׁנֵי תְמִידִים כְּהִלְכָתָם. וּבַיּוֹם הַשְּׁלִישִׁי, פָּרִים עַשְׁתֵּי־עָשָׂר, אֵילִם שְׁנָיִם, כְּבָשִׂים בְּנֵי־שָׁנָה אַרְבָּעָה עָשָׂר, תְּמִימִם. וּמִנְחָתָם וְנִסְכֵּיהֶם כִּמְדֻבָּר, שְׁלֹשָׁה עֶשְׂרֹנִים לַפָּר, וּשְׁנֵי עֶשְׂרֹנִים לָאָיִל, וְעִשָּׂרוֹן לַכֶּבֶשׂ, וְיַיִן כְּנִסְכּוֹ. וְשָׂעִיר לְכַפֵּר, וּשְׁנֵי תְמִידִים כְּהִלְכָתָם.

On the second day of חוֹל הַמּוֹעֵד סֻכּוֹת, say:

וּבַיּוֹם הַשְּׁלִישִׁי, פָּרִים עַשְׁתֵּי־עָשָׂר, אֵילִם שְׁנָיִם, כְּבָשִׂים בְּנֵי־שָׁנָה אַרְבָּעָה עָשָׂר, תְּמִימִם. וּמִנְחָתָם וְנִסְכֵּיהֶם כִּמְדֻבָּר, שְׁלֹשָׁה עֶשְׂרֹנִים לַפָּר, וּשְׁנֵי עֶשְׂרֹנִים לָאָיִל, וְעִשָּׂרוֹן לַכֶּבֶשׂ, וְיַיִן כְּנִסְכּוֹ. וְשָׂעִיר לְכַפֵּר, וּשְׁנֵי תְמִידִים כְּהִלְכָתָם. וּבַיּוֹם

On Shavuot, say:

וּבְיוֹם הַבִּכּוּרִים On the day of the first fruits, when you bring an offering of new grain to the LORD, on your Festival of Weeks, there shall be a sacred assembly: you shall do no laborious work. You shall offer a burnt-offering of pleasing aroma to the LORD: two young bullocks, one ram, and seven yearling male lambs. And their meal-offerings and wine-libations as ordained: three-tenths of an ephah for each bull, two-tenths of an ephah for the ram, one-tenth of an ephah for each lamb, wine for the libations, a male goat for atonement, and two regular daily offerings according to their law.

On the first two days of Sukkot, say:

וּבַחֲמִשָּׁה עָשָׂר On the fifteenth day of the seventh month you shall hold a sacred assembly. You shall do no laborious work, and you shall celebrate a festival to the LORD for seven days. You shall offer a burnt-offering, a fire-offering of pleasing aroma to the LORD: thirteen young bullocks, two rams, and fourteen yearling male lambs; they shall be without blemish. And their meal-offerings and wine-libations as ordained: three-tenths of an ephah for each bull, two-tenths of an ephah for the ram, one-tenth of an ephah for each lamb, wine for the libations, a male goat for atonement, and two regular daily offerings according to their law.

On the first Intermediate Day of Sukkot, say:

וּבַיּוֹם הַשֵּׁנִי On the second day you shall offer twelve young bullocks, two rams, fourteen yearling male lambs without blemish. And their meal-offerings and wine-libations as ordained: three-tenths of an ephah for each bull, two-tenths of an ephah for the ram, one-tenth of an ephah for each lamb, wine for the libations, a male goat for atonement, and two regular daily offerings according to their law. On the third day you shall offer eleven young bullocks, two rams, fourteen yearling male lambs without blemish. And their meal-offerings and wine-libations as ordained: three-tenths of an ephah for each bull, two-tenths of an ephah for the ram, one-tenth of an ephah for each lamb, wine for the libations, a male goat for atonement, and two regular daily offerings according to their law.

On the second Intermediate Day of Sukkot, say:

וּבַיּוֹם הַשְּׁלִישִׁי On the third day you shall offer eleven bullocks, two rams, fourteen yearling male lambs without blemish. And their meal-offerings and wine-libations as ordained: three-tenths of an ephah for each bull, two-tenths of an ephah for the ram, one-tenth of an ephah for each lamb, wine for the libations, a male goat for atonement, and two regular daily offerings according to their law. On the fourth day

הָרְבִיעִי, פָּרִים עֲשָׂרָה, אֵילִם שְׁנָיִם, כְּבָשִׂים בְּנֵי־שָׁנָה אַרְבָּעָה עָשָׂר, תְּמִימִם. וּמִנְחָתָם וְנִסְכֵּיהֶם כִּמְדֻבָּר, שְׁלֹשָׁה עֶשְׂרֹנִים לַפָּר, וּשְׁנֵי עֶשְׂרֹנִים לָאָיִל, וְעִשָּׂרוֹן לַכֶּבֶשׂ, וְיַיִן כְּנִסְכּוֹ. וְשָׂעִיר לְכַפֵּר, וּשְׁנֵי תְמִידִים כְּהִלְכָתָם.

On the third day of חוֹל הַמּוֹעֵד סֻכּוֹת, say:

וּבַיּוֹם הָרְבִיעִי, פָּרִים עֲשָׂרָה, אֵילִם שְׁנָיִם, כְּבָשִׂים בְּנֵי־שָׁנָה אַרְבָּעָה עָשָׂר, תְּמִימִם. וּמִנְחָתָם וְנִסְכֵּיהֶם כִּמְדֻבָּר, שְׁלֹשָׁה עֶשְׂרֹנִים לַפָּר, וּשְׁנֵי עֶשְׂרֹנִים לָאָיִל, וְעִשָּׂרוֹן לַכֶּבֶשׂ, וְיַיִן כְּנִסְכּוֹ. וְשָׂעִיר לְכַפֵּר, וּשְׁנֵי תְמִידִים כְּהִלְכָתָם. וּבַיּוֹם הַחֲמִישִׁי, פָּרִים תִּשְׁעָה, אֵילִם שְׁנָיִם, כְּבָשִׂים בְּנֵי־שָׁנָה אַרְבָּעָה עָשָׂר, תְּמִימִם. וּמִנְחָתָם וְנִסְכֵּיהֶם כִּמְדֻבָּר, שְׁלֹשָׁה עֶשְׂרֹנִים לַפָּר, וּשְׁנֵי עֶשְׂרֹנִים לָאָיִל, וְעִשָּׂרוֹן לַכֶּבֶשׂ, וְיַיִן כְּנִסְכּוֹ. וְשָׂעִיר לְכַפֵּר, וּשְׁנֵי תְמִידִים כְּהִלְכָתָם.

On the fourth day of חוֹל הַמּוֹעֵד סֻכּוֹת, say:

וּבַיּוֹם הַחֲמִישִׁי, פָּרִים תִּשְׁעָה, אֵילִם שְׁנָיִם, כְּבָשִׂים בְּנֵי־שָׁנָה אַרְבָּעָה עָשָׂר, תְּמִימִם. וּמִנְחָתָם וְנִסְכֵּיהֶם כִּמְדֻבָּר, שְׁלֹשָׁה עֶשְׂרֹנִים לַפָּר, וּשְׁנֵי עֶשְׂרֹנִים לָאָיִל, וְעִשָּׂרוֹן לַכֶּבֶשׂ, וְיַיִן כְּנִסְכּוֹ. וְשָׂעִיר לְכַפֵּר, וּשְׁנֵי תְמִידִים כְּהִלְכָתָם. וּבַיּוֹם הַשִּׁשִּׁי, פָּרִים שְׁמֹנָה, אֵילִם שְׁנָיִם, כְּבָשִׂים בְּנֵי־שָׁנָה אַרְבָּעָה עָשָׂר, תְּמִימִם. וּמִנְחָתָם וְנִסְכֵּיהֶם כִּמְדֻבָּר, שְׁלֹשָׁה עֶשְׂרֹנִים לַפָּר, וּשְׁנֵי עֶשְׂרֹנִים לָאָיִל, וְעִשָּׂרוֹן לַכֶּבֶשׂ, וְיַיִן כְּנִסְכּוֹ. וְשָׂעִיר לְכַפֵּר, וּשְׁנֵי תְמִידִים כְּהִלְכָתָם.

On הוֹשַׁעְנָא רַבָּה, say:

וּבַיּוֹם הַשִּׁשִּׁי, פָּרִים שְׁמֹנָה, אֵילִם שְׁנָיִם, כְּבָשִׂים בְּנֵי־שָׁנָה אַרְבָּעָה עָשָׂר, תְּמִימִם. וּמִנְחָתָם וְנִסְכֵּיהֶם כִּמְדֻבָּר, שְׁלֹשָׁה עֶשְׂרֹנִים לַפָּר, וּשְׁנֵי עֶשְׂרֹנִים לָאָיִל, וְעִשָּׂרוֹן לַכֶּבֶשׂ, וְיַיִן כְּנִסְכּוֹ. וְשָׂעִיר לְכַפֵּר, וּשְׁנֵי תְמִידִים כְּהִלְכָתָם. וּבַיּוֹם הַשְּׁבִיעִי, פָּרִים שִׁבְעָה, אֵילִם שְׁנָיִם, כְּבָשִׂים בְּנֵי־שָׁנָה אַרְבָּעָה עָשָׂר, תְּמִימִם.

you shall offer ten bullocks, two rams, fourteen yearling male lambs without blemish. And their meal-offerings and wine-libations as ordained: three-tenths of an ephah for each bull, two-tenths of an ephah for the ram, one-tenth of an ephah for each lamb, wine for the libations, a male goat for atonement, and two regular daily offerings according to their law.

On the third Intermediate Day of Sukkot, say:

וּבַיּוֹם הָרְבִיעִי On the fourth day you shall offer ten bullocks, two rams, fourteen yearling male lambs without blemish. And their meal-offerings and wine-libations as ordained: three-tenths of an ephah for each bull, two-tenths of an ephah for the ram, one-tenth of an ephah for each lamb, wine for the libations, a male goat for atonement, and two regular daily offerings according to their law. On the fifth day you shall offer nine bullocks, two rams, fourteen yearling male lambs without blemish. And their meal-offerings and wine-libations as ordained: three-tenths of an ephah for each bull, two-tenths of an ephah for the ram, one-tenth of an ephah for each lamb, wine for the libations, a male goat for atonement, and two regular daily offerings according to their law.

On the fourth Intermediate Day of Sukkot, say.

וּבַיּוֹם הַחֲמִישִׁי On the fifth day you shall offer nine bullocks, two rams, fourteen yearling male lambs without blemish. And their meal-offerings and wine-libations as ordained: three-tenths of an ephah for each bull, two-tenths of an ephah for the ram, one-tenth of an ephah for each lamb, wine for the libations, a male goat for atonement, and two regular daily offerings according to their law. On the sixth day you shall offer eight bullocks, two rams, fourteen yearling male lambs without blemish. And their meal-offerings and wine-libations as ordained: three-tenths of an ephah for each bull, two-tenths of an ephah for the ram, one-tenth of an ephah for each lamb, wine for the libations, a male goat for atonement, and two regular daily offerings according to their law.

On Hoshana Rabba, say:

וּבַיּוֹם הַשִּׁשִּׁי On the sixth day you shall offer eight bullocks, two rams, fourteen yearling male lambs without blemish. And their meal-offerings and wine-libations as ordained: three-tenths of an ephah for each bull, two-tenths of an ephah for the ram, one-tenth of an ephah for each lamb, wine for the libations, a male goat for atonement, and two regular daily offerings according to their law. On the seventh day you shall offer seven bullocks, two rams, fourteen yearling male

וּמִנְחָתָם וְנִסְכֵּיהֶם כִּמְדֻבָּר, שְׁלֹשָׁה עֶשְׂרֹנִים לַפָּר, וּשְׁנֵי עֶשְׂרֹנִים לָאָיִל, וְעִשָּׂרוֹן לַכֶּבֶשׂ, וְיַיִן כְּנִסְכּוֹ. וְשָׂעִיר לְכַפֵּר, וּשְׁנֵי תְמִידִים כְּהִלְכָתָם.

On שִׂמְחַת תּוֹרָה and שְׁמִינִי עֲצֶרֶת say:

בַּיּוֹם הַשְּׁמִינִי, עֲצֶרֶת תִּהְיֶה לָכֶם, כָּל־מְלֶאכֶת עֲבֹדָה לֹא תַעֲשׂוּ. וְהִקְרַבְתֶּם עֹלָה אִשֵּׁה רֵיחַ נִיחֹחַ לַיהוה, פַּר אֶחָד, אַיִל אֶחָד, כְּבָשִׂים בְּנֵי־שָׁנָה שִׁבְעָה, תְּמִימִם. וּמִנְחָתָם וְנִסְכֵּיהֶם כִּמְדֻבָּר, שְׁלֹשָׁה עֶשְׂרֹנִים לַפָּר, וּשְׁנֵי עֶשְׂרֹנִים לָאָיִל, וְעִשָּׂרוֹן לַכֶּבֶשׂ, וְיַיִן כְּנִסְכּוֹ. וְשָׂעִיר לְכַפֵּר, וּשְׁנֵי תְמִידִים כְּהִלְכָתָם.

On שַׁבָּת, say:

יִשְׂמְחוּ בְמַלְכוּתְךָ שׁוֹמְרֵי שַׁבָּת וְקוֹרְאֵי עֹנֶג, עַם מְקַדְּשֵׁי שְׁבִיעִי, כֻּלָּם יִשְׂבְּעוּ וְיִתְעַנְּגוּ מִטּוּבֶךָ, וְהַשְּׁבִיעִי רָצִיתָ בּוֹ וְקִדַּשְׁתּוֹ, חֶמְדַּת יָמִים אוֹתוֹ קָרָאתָ, זֵכֶר לְמַעֲשֵׂה בְרֵאשִׁית.

אֱלֹהֵינוּ וֵאלֹהֵי אֲבוֹתֵינוּ, מֶלֶךְ רַחֲמָן רַחֵם עָלֵינוּ, טוֹב וּמֵטִיב הִדָּרֶשׁ־לָנוּ, שׁוּבָה אֵלֵינוּ בַּהֲמוֹן רַחֲמֶיךָ, בִּגְלַל אָבוֹת שֶׁעָשׂוּ רְצוֹנֶךָ. בְּנֵה בֵיתְךָ כְּבַתְּחִלָּה, וְכוֹנֵן מִקְדָּשְׁךָ עַל־מְכוֹנוֹ, וְהַרְאֵנוּ בְּבִנְיָנוֹ, וְשַׂמְּחֵנוּ בְּתִקּוּנוֹ. וְהָשֵׁב כֹּהֲנִים לַעֲבוֹדָתָם, וּלְוִיִּם לְשִׁירָם וּלְזִמְרָם, וְהָשֵׁב יִשְׂרָאֵל לִנְוֵיהֶם. וְשָׁם נַעֲלֶה וְנֵרָאֶה וְנִשְׁתַּחֲוֶה לְפָנֶיךָ, בְּשָׁלֹשׁ פַּעֲמֵי רְגָלֵינוּ, כַּכָּתוּב בְּתוֹרָתֶךָ, שָׁלוֹשׁ פְּעָמִים בַּשָּׁנָה, יֵרָאֶה כָל־זְכוּרְךָ אֶת־פְּנֵי יהוה אֱלֹהֶיךָ, בַּמָּקוֹם אֲשֶׁר יִבְחָר, בְּחַג הַמַּצּוֹת, וּבְחַג הַשָּׁבֻעוֹת, וּבְחַג הַסֻּכּוֹת, וְלֹא יֵרָאֶה אֶת־פְּנֵי יהוה רֵיקָם. אִישׁ כְּמַתְּנַת יָדוֹ, כְּבִרְכַּת יהוה אֱלֹהֶיךָ, אֲשֶׁר נָתַן־לָךְ.

On שַׁבָּת, add the words in brackets:

וְהַשִּׂיאֵנוּ יהוה אֱלֹהֵינוּ אֶת־בִּרְכַּת מוֹעֲדֶיךָ לְחַיִּים וּלְשָׁלוֹם, לְשִׂמְחָה וּלְשָׂשׂוֹן, כַּאֲשֶׁר רָצִיתָ וְאָמַרְתָּ לְבָרְכֵנוּ.

lambs without blemish. And their meal-offerings and wine-libations as ordained: three-tenths of an ephah for each bull, two-tenths of an ephah for the ram, one-tenth of an ephah for each lamb, wine for the libations, a male goat for atonement, and two regular daily offerings according to their law.

On Shemini Atzeret and Simchat Torah, say:

בַּיּוֹם הַשְּׁמִינִי On the eighth day you shall hold an assembly; you shall do no laborious work. And you shall offer a burnt-offering, a fire-offering of pleasing odour to the LORD: one bullock, one ram, seven yearling male lambs without blemish. And their meal-offerings and wine-libations as ordained: three-tenths of an ephah for each bull, two-tenths of an ephah for the ram, one-tenth of an ephah for each lamb, wine for the libations, a male goat for atonement, and two regular daily offerings according to their law.

On Shabbat, say:

יִשְׂמְחוּ Those who keep the Sabbath and call it a delight shall rejoice in Your kingship. The people who sanctify the seventh day shall all be satisfied and take delight in Your goodness, for You favoured the seventh day and declared it holy. You called it "most desirable of days" in remembrance of Creation.

אֱלֹהֵינוּ Our GOD and GOD of our ancestors, merciful King, have compassion upon us. You who are good and do good, respond to our call. Return to us in Your abounding mercy for the sake of our fathers who did Your will. Rebuild Your Temple as at the beginning, and establish Your sanctuary on its site. Let us witness its rebuilding and gladden us by its restoration. Bring the priests back to their service, the Levites to their song and music, and the Israelites to their homes. There we will go up and appear and bow before You on the three pilgrimage festivals, as is written in Your Torah: "Three times in the year all your males shall appear before the LORD your GOD at the place He will choose: on Pesach, Shavuot and Sukkot. They shall not appear before the LORD empty-handed. Each shall bring such a gift as he can in proportion to the blessing that the LORD your GOD grants you."

On Shabbat, add the words in brackets:

וְהַשִּׂיאֵנוּ Bestow on us, LORD our GOD, the blessing of Your festivals for life and peace, joy and gladness, as You desired and promised to

(אֱלֹהֵינוּ וֵאלֹהֵי אֲבוֹתֵינוּ רְצֵה בִמְנוּחָתֵנוּ) קַדְּשֵׁנוּ בְּמִצְוֹתֶיךָ וְתֵן חֶלְקֵנוּ בְּתוֹרָתֶךָ, שַׂבְּעֵנוּ מִטּוּבֶךָ וְשַׂמְּחֵנוּ בִּישׁוּעָתֶךָ, וְטַהֵר לִבֵּנוּ לְעָבְדְּךָ בֶּאֱמֶת, וְהַנְחִילֵנוּ יהוה אֱלֹהֵינוּ (בְּאַהֲבָה וּבְרָצוֹן) בְּשִׂמְחָה וּבְשָׂשׂוֹן (שַׁבָּת וּ) מוֹעֲדֵי קָדְשֶׁךָ, וְיִשְׂמְחוּ בְךָ יִשְׂרָאֵל מְקַדְּשֵׁי שְׁמֶךָ. בָּרוּךְ אַתָּה יהוה, מְקַדֵּשׁ (הַשַּׁבָּת וְ) יִשְׂרָאֵל וְהַזְּמַנִּים.

עבודה

רְצֵה יהוה אֱלֹהֵינוּ בְּעַמְּךָ יִשְׂרָאֵל וּבִתְפִלָּתָם, וְהָשֵׁב אֶת־הָעֲבוֹדָה לִדְבִיר בֵּיתֶךָ. וְאִשֵּׁי יִשְׂרָאֵל וּתְפִלָּתָם בְּאַהֲבָה תְקַבֵּל בְּרָצוֹן, וּתְהִי לְרָצוֹן תָּמִיד עֲבוֹדַת יִשְׂרָאֵל עַמֶּךָ.

During the Leader's repetition – except on שִׂמְחַת תּוֹרָה, שַׁבָּת and חוֹל הַמּוֹעֵד – בִּרְכַּת כֹּהֲנִים is said at this point: turn to page 690.
On שַׁבָּת, שִׂמְחַת תּוֹרָה and חוֹל הַמּוֹעֵד, or if no כֹּהֵן is present, continue:

וְתֶחֱזֶינָה עֵינֵינוּ בְּשׁוּבְךָ לְצִיּוֹן בְּרַחֲמִים. בָּרוּךְ אַתָּה יהוה, הַמַּחֲזִיר שְׁכִינָתוֹ לְצִיּוֹן.

הודאה

▽ Bow at the first five words.

▽**מוֹדִים** אֲנַחְנוּ לָךְ, שָׁאַתָּה הוּא יהוה אֱלֹהֵינוּ וֵאלֹהֵי אֲבוֹתֵינוּ לְעוֹלָם וָעֶד. צוּר חַיֵּינוּ, מָגֵן יִשְׁעֵנוּ אַתָּה הוּא לְדוֹר וָדוֹר. נוֹדֶה לְּךָ וּנְסַפֵּר תְּהִלָּתֶךָ עַל חַיֵּינוּ הַמְּסוּרִים בְּיָדֶךָ, וְעַל נִשְׁמוֹתֵינוּ הַפְּקוּדוֹת לָךְ, וְעַל נִסֶּיךָ שֶׁבְּכָל־יוֹם עִמָּנוּ, וְעַל נִפְלְאוֹתֶיךָ וְטוֹבוֹתֶיךָ שֶׁבְּכָל־עֵת, עֶרֶב וָבֹקֶר וְצָהֳרָיִם. הַטּוֹב

During the Leader's repetition, the Congregation says quietly:

▽**מוֹדִים** אֲנַחְנוּ לָךְ, שָׁאַתָּה הוּא יהוה אֱלֹהֵינוּ וֵאלֹהֵי אֲבוֹתֵינוּ, אֱלֹהֵי כָל־בָּשָׂר, יוֹצְרֵנוּ, יוֹצֵר בְּרֵאשִׁית. בְּרָכוֹת וְהוֹדָאוֹת לְשִׁמְךָ הַגָּדוֹל וְהַקָּדוֹשׁ, עַל שֶׁהֶחֱיִיתָנוּ וְקִיַּמְתָּנוּ. כֵּן תְּחַיֵּנוּ וּתְקַיְּמֵנוּ, וְתֶאֱסֹף גָּלֻיּוֹתֵינוּ לְחַצְרוֹת קָדְשֶׁךָ,

bless us. (Our God and God of our ancestors, be pleased with our rest.) Make us holy through Your commandments and grant us a share in Your Torah; satisfy us with Your goodness, gladden us with Your salvation, and purify our hearts to serve You in truth. And grant us a heritage, Lord our God, (with love and favour,) with joy and gladness Your holy (Sabbath and) festivals. May Israel, who sanctify Your name, rejoice in You. Blessed are You, Lord, who sanctifies (the Sabbath and) Israel, and the festive seasons.

TEMPLE SERVICE

רְצֵה Find favour, Lord our God, in Your people Israel and their prayer. Restore the service to Your most holy house, and accept in love and favour the fire-offerings of Israel and their prayer. May the service of Your people Israel always find favour with You.

During the Leader's repetition – except on Shabbat, Simchat Torah and the Intermediate Days of Festivals – the Priestly Blessing is said at this point: turn to page 691.
On Shabbat, Simchat Torah, Intermediate Days, or if no Cohen is present, continue:

וְתֶחֱזֶינָה And may our eyes witness Your return to Zion in compassion. Blessed are You, Lord, who restores His Presence to Zion.

THANKSGIVING

▽ Bow at the first nine words.

מוֹדִים▽ We give thanks to You, for You are the Lord our God and God of our ancestors for ever and all time. You are the Rock of our lives, Shield of our salvation from generation to generation. We will thank You and declare Your praise for our lives, which are entrusted into Your hand; our souls, which are placed in Your charge; for Your miracles which are with us every day; and for Your wonders and favours at all times, evening, morning and midday. You are good –

During the Leader's repetition, the Congregation says quietly:

מוֹדִים▽ We give thanks to You, for You are the Lord our God and God of our ancestors, God of all flesh, who formed us and formed the universe. Blessings and thanks are due to Your great and holy name for giving us life and sustaining us. May You continue to give us life and sustain us; and may You gather our exiles to Your holy courts, to keep Your

כִּי לֹא־כָלוּ רַחֲמֶיךָ, וְהַמְרַחֵם כִּי לֹא־תַמּוּ חֲסָדֶיךָ, מֵעוֹלָם קִוִּינוּ לָךְ.

לִשְׁמוֹר חֻקֶּיךָ וְלַעֲשׂוֹת רְצוֹנֶךָ, וּלְעָבְדְּךָ בְּלֵבָב שָׁלֵם, עַל שֶׁאֲנַחְנוּ מוֹדִים לָךְ. בָּרוּךְ אֵל הַהוֹדָאוֹת.

וְעַל כֻּלָּם יִתְבָּרַךְ וְיִתְרוֹמַם שִׁמְךָ מַלְכֵּנוּ תָּמִיד לְעוֹלָם וָעֶד. וְכֹל הַחַיִּים יוֹדוּךָ סֶּלָה, וִיהַלְלוּ אֶת־שִׁמְךָ בֶּאֱמֶת, הָאֵל יְשׁוּעָתֵנוּ וְעֶזְרָתֵנוּ סֶלָה. ▾בָּרוּךְ אַתָּה יהוה, הַטּוֹב שִׁמְךָ וּלְךָ נָאֶה לְהוֹדוֹת.

During the Leader's repetition on שְׂמְחַת תּוֹרָה, שַׁבָּת or חוֹל הַמּוֹעֵד, or if no כֹּהֵן is present, the Leader says:

אֱלֹהֵינוּ וֵאלֹהֵי אֲבוֹתֵינוּ, בָּרְכֵנוּ בַבְּרָכָה הַמְשֻׁלֶּשֶׁת, בַּתּוֹרָה הַכְּתוּבָה עַל יְדֵי מֹשֶׁה עַבְדֶּךָ, הָאֲמוּרָה מִפִּי אַהֲרֹן וּבָנָיו, כֹּהֲנִים עַם קְדוֹשֶׁךָ, כָּאָמוּר.

יְבָרֶכְךָ יהוה, וְיִשְׁמְרֶךָ. (Cong.: כֵּן יְהִי רָצוֹן)

יָאֵר יהוה פָּנָיו אֵלֶיךָ וִיחֻנֶּךָּ. (Cong.: כֵּן יְהִי רָצוֹן)

יִשָּׂא יהוה פָּנָיו אֵלֶיךָ וְיָשֵׂם לְךָ שָׁלוֹם. (Cong.: כֵּן יְהִי רָצוֹן)

ברכת שלום

שִׂים שָׁלוֹם, טוֹבָה, וּבְרָכָה, חֵן, וָחֶסֶד וְרַחֲמִים עָלֵינוּ וְעַל כָּל־יִשְׂרָאֵל עַמֶּךָ. בָּרְכֵנוּ אָבִינוּ, כֻּלָּנוּ כְּאֶחָד בְּאוֹר פָּנֶיךָ, כִּי בְאוֹר פָּנֶיךָ נָתַתָּ לָנוּ, יהוה אֱלֹהֵינוּ, תּוֹרַת חַיִּים וְאַהֲבַת חֶסֶד, וּצְדָקָה, וּבְרָכָה, וְרַחֲמִים, וְחַיִּים, וְשָׁלוֹם. וְטוֹב בְּעֵינֶיךָ לְבָרֵךְ אֶת־עַמְּךָ יִשְׂרָאֵל, בְּכָל־עֵת וּבְכָל־שָׁעָה בִּשְׁלוֹמֶךָ. בָּרוּךְ אַתָּה יהוה, הַמְבָרֵךְ אֶת עַמּוֹ יִשְׂרָאֵל בַּשָּׁלוֹם.

The Leader's repetition ends at this point.

On חוֹל הַמּוֹעֵד פֶּסַח, the Leader continues with קַדִּישׁ תִּתְקַבַּל, page 138.

On שְׁמִינִי עֲצֶרֶת, שָׁבֻעוֹת, שַׁבָּת חוֹל הַמּוֹעֵד פֶּסַח including and שִׂמְחַת תּוֹרָה, the Leader continues with קַדִּישׁ תִּתְקַבַּל, page 448.

On סֻכּוֹת and הוֹשַׁעְנָא רַבָּא, the Leader's repetition ends here. Continue with הוֹשַׁעְנוֹת, page 708 ff.

for Your compassion never fails. You are compassionate – for Your lovingkindnesses never cease. We have always placed our hope in You.

decrees, do Your will and serve You with a perfect heart, for it is for us to give You thanks. Blessed be God to whom thanksgiving is due.

וְעַל For all these things may Your name be blessed and exalted, our King, continually, for ever and all time. Let all that lives thank You, Selah! and praise Your name in truth, God, our Saviour and Help, Selah! ▾Blessed are You, Lord, whose name is "the Good" and to whom thanks are due.

During the Leader's repetition on Shabbat, Simchat Torah or the Intermediate Days of Festivals, or if no Cohen is present, the Leader says:

אֱלֹהֵינוּ Our God and God of our fathers, bless us with the threefold blessing in the Torah, written by the hand of Moses Your servant and pronounced by Aaron and his sons the priests, Your holy people, as it is said:

May the Lord bless you and protect you. (Cong.: May it be Your will.)

May the Lord make His face shine on you and be gracious to you. (Cong.: May it be Your will.)

May the Lord turn His face towards you, and give you peace. (Cong.: May it be Your will.)

PEACE

שִׂים Grant peace, goodness and blessing, grace, lovingkindness and compassion to us and all Israel Your people. Bless us, our Father, all as one, with the light of Your face, for by the light of Your face You have given us, Lord our God, the Torah of life and love of kindness, righteousness, blessing, compassion, life and peace. May it be good in Your eyes to bless Your people Israel at every time, in every hour, with Your peace. Blessed are You, Lord, who blesses His people Israel with peace.

The Leader's repetition ends at this point.

On the Intermediate Days of Pesach, the Leader continues with full *Kaddish*, page 139.
On Pesach, including the Intermediate Shabbat, Shavuot, Shemini Atzeret and Simchat Torah, the Leader continues with full *Kaddish*, page 449.
On Sukkot and Hoshana Rabba, the Leader's repetition ends here. Continue with Hoshanot, page 708.

אֱלֹהַי, נְצֹר לְשׁוֹנִי מֵרָע, וּשְׂפָתַי מִדַּבֵּר מִרְמָה, וְלִמְקַלְלַי נַפְשִׁי תִדֹּם, וְנַפְשִׁי כֶּעָפָר לַכֹּל תִּהְיֶה. פְּתַח לִבִּי בְּתוֹרָתֶךָ, וּבְמִצְוֹתֶיךָ תִּרְדֹּף נַפְשִׁי. וְכָל הַחוֹשְׁבִים עָלַי רָעָה, מְהֵרָה הָפֵר עֲצָתָם וְקַלְקֵל מַחֲשַׁבְתָּם. עֲשֵׂה לְמַעַן שְׁמֶךָ, עֲשֵׂה לְמַעַן יְמִינֶךָ, עֲשֵׂה לְמַעַן קְדֻשָּׁתֶךָ, עֲשֵׂה לְמַעַן תּוֹרָתֶךָ. לְמַעַן יֵחָלְצוּן יְדִידֶיךָ, הוֹשִׁיעָה יְמִינְךָ וַעֲנֵנִי. יִהְיוּ לְרָצוֹן אִמְרֵי־פִי וְהֶגְיוֹן לִבִּי לְפָנֶיךָ, יהוה צוּרִי וְגוֹאֲלִי.

Bow, take three steps back, then bow, first left, then right, then centre, while saying:

עֹשֶׂה שָׁלוֹם בִּמְרוֹמָיו, הוּא יַעֲשֶׂה שָׁלוֹם עָלֵינוּ, וְעַל־כָּל־יִשְׂרָאֵל. וְאִמְרוּ אָמֵן.

יְהִי רָצוֹן מִלְּפָנֶיךָ יהוה אֱלֹהֵינוּ וֵאלֹהֵי אֲבוֹתֵינוּ, שֶׁיִּבָּנֶה בֵּית הַמִּקְדָּשׁ בִּמְהֵרָה בְיָמֵינוּ, וְתֵן חֶלְקֵנוּ בְּתוֹרָתֶךָ. וְשָׁם נַעֲבָדְךָ בְּיִרְאָה, כִּימֵי עוֹלָם וּכְשָׁנִים קַדְמוֹנִיּוֹת. וְעָרְבָה לַיהוה מִנְחַת יְהוּדָה וִירוּשָׁלָיִם, כִּימֵי עוֹלָם וּכְשָׁנִים קַדְמוֹנִיּוֹת.

סדר נשיאת כפים / ברכת כהנים

On יוֹם טוֹב, except on שַׁבָּת and שִׂמְחַת תּוֹרָה, the following בִּרְכַּת כֹּהֲנִים is added during the Leader's repetition of מוּסָף, after יִשְׂרָאֵל עַמֶּךָ, on page 686. The כֹּהֲנִים stand in front of the Ark. Those sitting between where the כֹּהֲנִים stand and the Ark come forward at this point so that they are in front of the כֹּהֲנִים when the blessings are said.

Congregation and Leader:

וְתֶעֱרַב לְפָנֶיךָ עֲתִירָתֵנוּ כְּעוֹלָה וּכְקָרְבָּן. אָנָּא, רַחוּם, בְּרַחֲמֶיךָ הָרַבִּים הָשֵׁב שְׁכִינָתְךָ לְצִיּוֹן עִירֶךָ, וְסֵדֶר הָעֲבוֹדָה לִירוּשָׁלָיִם. וְתֶחֱזֶינָה עֵינֵינוּ בְּשׁוּבְךָ לְצִיּוֹן בְּרַחֲמִים, וְשָׁם נַעֲבָדְךָ בְּיִרְאָה, כִּימֵי עוֹלָם וּכְשָׁנִים קַדְמוֹנִיּוֹת.

THE PRIESTLY BLESSING
The Priestly Blessing is unique among our prayers: not only is it ordained by the Torah itself, but so is its precise wording (Numbers 6:24–26). It are therefore our most ancient prayer. The blessing is beau-

אֱלֹהַי My God, guard my tongue from evil and my lips from deceitful speech. To those who curse me, let my soul be silent; may my soul be to all like the dust. Open my heart to Your Torah and let my soul pursue Your commandments. As for all who plan evil against me, swiftly thwart their counsel and frustrate their plans. Act for the sake of Your name; act for the sake of Your right hand; act for the sake of Your holiness; act for the sake of Your Torah. That Your beloved ones may be delivered, save with Your right hand and answer me. May the words of my mouth and the meditation of my heart find favour before You, Lord, my Rock and Redeemer.

Bow, take three steps back, then bow, first left, then right, then centre, while saying:

May He who makes peace in His high places, make peace for us and all Israel – and say: Amen.

יְהִי May it be Your will, Lord our God and God of our ancestors, that the Temple be rebuilt speedily in our days, and grant us a share in Your Torah. And there we will serve You with reverence, as in the days of old and as in former years. Then the offering of Judah and Jerusalem will be pleasing to the Lord as in the days of old and as in former years.

THE ORDER OF THE PRIESTLY BLESSING

On Festivals, except on Shabbat and Simchat Torah, the following Order of the Priestly Blessing is added during the Leader's repetition of *Musaf*, after "find favour with You", on page 687. The Cohanim stand in front of the Ark. Those sitting between where the Cohanim stand and the Ark come forward at this point so that they are in front of the Cohanim when the blessings are said.

Congregation and Leader:

וְתֶעֱרַב May our entreaty be as pleasing to You as a burnt-offering and sacrifice. Please, Compassionate One, in Your abounding mercy restore Your Presence to Zion, Your city, and the order of the Temple service to Jerusalem. May our eyes witness Your return in compassion to Zion, that there we may serve You with reverence as in the days of old and as in former years.

---

tifully constructed. It grows in length: the first line has three words; the second, five; and the third, seven. In each, God's holiest name is the second word of the blessing. The threefold blessing ascends thematically: the first is for material blessing,

Leader only:

בָּרוּךְ אַתָּה יהוה, שֶׁאוֹתְךָ לְבַדְּךָ בְּיִרְאָה נַעֲבוֹד.

הודאה

▽ Bow at the first five words.

▽**מוֹדִים** אֲנַחְנוּ לָךְ, שָׁאַתָּה הוּא יהוה אֱלֹהֵינוּ וֵאלֹהֵי אֲבוֹתֵינוּ לְעוֹלָם וָעֶד. צוּר חַיֵּינוּ, מָגֵן יִשְׁעֵנוּ אַתָּה הוּא לְדוֹר וָדוֹר. נוֹדֶה לְּךָ וּנְסַפֵּר תְּהִלָּתֶךָ עַל חַיֵּינוּ הַמְּסוּרִים בְּיָדֶךָ, וְעַל נִשְׁמוֹתֵינוּ הַפְּקוּדוֹת לָךְ, וְעַל נִסֶּיךָ שֶׁבְּכָל־יוֹם עִמָּנוּ, וְעַל נִפְלְאוֹתֶיךָ וְטוֹבוֹתֶיךָ שֶׁבְּכָל־עֵת, עֶרֶב וָבֹקֶר וְצָהֳרָיִם. הַטּוֹב כִּי לֹא־כָלוּ רַחֲמֶיךָ, וְהַמְרַחֵם כִּי לֹא־תַמּוּ חֲסָדֶיךָ, מֵעוֹלָם קִוִּינוּ לָךְ.

During the Leader's repetition, the Congregation says quietly:

▽**מוֹדִים** אֲנַחְנוּ לָךְ, שָׁאַתָּה הוּא יהוה אֱלֹהֵינוּ וֵאלֹהֵי אֲבוֹתֵינוּ, אֱלֹהֵי כָל־בָּשָׂר, יוֹצְרֵנוּ, יוֹצֵר בְּרֵאשִׁית. בְּרָכוֹת וְהוֹדָאוֹת לְשִׁמְךָ הַגָּדוֹל וְהַקָּדוֹשׁ, עַל שֶׁהֶחֱיִיתָנוּ וְקִיַּמְתָּנוּ. כֵּן תְּחַיֵּנוּ וּתְקַיְּמֵנוּ, וְתֶאֱסוֹף גָּלֻיּוֹתֵינוּ לְחַצְרוֹת קָדְשֶׁךָ, לִשְׁמוֹר חֻקֶּיךָ וְלַעֲשׂוֹת רְצוֹנֶךָ, וּלְעָבְדְּךָ בְּלֵבָב שָׁלֵם, עַל שֶׁאֲנַחְנוּ מוֹדִים לָךְ. בָּרוּךְ אֵל הַהוֹדָאוֹת.

וְעַל כֻּלָּם יִתְבָּרַךְ וְיִתְרוֹמַם שִׁמְךָ מַלְכֵּנוּ תָּמִיד לְעוֹלָם וָעֶד. וְכֹל הַחַיִּים יוֹדוּךָ סֶּלָה, וִיהַלְלוּ אֶת־שִׁמְךָ בֶּאֱמֶת, הָאֵל יְשׁוּעָתֵנוּ וְעֶזְרָתֵנוּ סֶלָה. ▼בָּרוּךְ אַתָּה יהוה, הַטּוֹב שִׁמְךָ וּלְךָ נָאֶה לְהוֹדוֹת.

The Leader then says the following quietly:

אֱלֹהֵינוּ וֵאלֹהֵי אֲבוֹתֵינוּ, בָּרְכֵנוּ בַבְּרָכָה הַמְשֻׁלֶּשֶׁת, בַּתּוֹרָה הַכְּתוּבָה עַל־יְדֵי מֹשֶׁה עַבְדֶּךָ, הָאֲמוּרָה מִפִּי אַהֲרֹן וּבָנָיו,

the second for spiritual blessing, the third for peace, without which no blessings can be enjoyed.

The Torah is careful to state: "So they (the Cohanim) shall place My name on the Israelites and I will bless them" (Numbers 6:27). Thus it is not the Cohanim who bless the people, but

Leader only:

Blessed are You, Lord, for You alone do we serve with reverence.

THANKSGIVING

▽ Bow at the first nine words.

מוֹדִים▽ We give thanks to You, for You are the Lord our God and God of our ancestors for ever and all time. You are the Rock of our lives, Shield of our salvation from generation to generation. We will thank You and declare Your praise for our lives, which are entrusted into Your hand; our souls, which are placed in Your charge; for Your miracles which are with us every day; and for Your wonders and favours at all times, evening, morning and midday. You are good – for Your compassion never fails. You are compassionate – for Your lovingkindnesses never cease. We have always placed our hope in You.

During the Leader's repetition, the Congregation says quietly:

מוֹדִים▽ We give thanks to You, for You are the Lord our God and God of our ancestors, God of all flesh, who formed us and formed the universe. Blessings and thanks are due to Your great and holy name for giving us life and sustaining us. May You continue to give us life and sustain us; and may You gather our exiles to Your holy courts, to keep Your decrees, do Your will and serve You with a perfect heart, for it is for us to give You thanks. Blessed be God to whom thanksgiving is due.

וְעַל For all these things may Your name be blessed and exalted, our King, continually, for ever and all time. Let all that lives thank You, Selah! and praise Your name in truth, God, our Saviour and Help, Selah! ▼Blessed are You, Lord, whose name is "the Good" and to whom thanks are due.

The Leader then says the following quietly:

Our God and God of our fathers, bless us with the three-fold blessing in the Torah, written by the hand of Moses Your servant and pronounced by Aaron and his sons:

God. The priests – whose entire life was dedicated to Divine service – were holy vehicles through which Divine blessing flowed. In Temple times, the Cohanim blessed the people daily. That remains the custom in Israel. Outside Israel, our custom is that the Priestly Blessing is said only on Festivals, for only then do we experience some of the joy that those who live in God's land feel every day.

Leader, who should not be a כֹּהֵן, says aloud:

כֹּהֲנִים

Congregation:

עַם קְדוֹשֶׁךָ כָּאָמוּר,

The כֹּהֲנִים say the following blessing in unison:

בָּרוּךְ אַתָּה יהוה, אֱלֹהֵינוּ מֶלֶךְ הָעוֹלָם, אֲשֶׁר קִדְּשָׁנוּ בִּקְדֻשָּׁתוֹ שֶׁל אַהֲרֹן, וְצִוָּנוּ לְבָרֵךְ אֶת־עַמּוֹ יִשְׂרָאֵל בְּאַהֲבָה.

Leader, followed by the כֹּהֲנִים, say the following, word by word.
One should not look at the כֹּהֲנִים while the blessings are being said.

יְבָרֶכְךָ יהוה וְיִשְׁמְרֶךָ. (Cong.: אָמֵן)

יָאֵר יהוה פָּנָיו אֵלֶיךָ וִיחֻנֶּךָּ. (Cong.: אָמֵן)

יִשָּׂא יהוה פָּנָיו אֵלֶיךָ וְיָשֵׂם לְךָ שָׁלוֹם. (Cong.: אָמֵן סֶלָה)

The Congregation say:

אַדִּיר בַּמָּרוֹם, שׁוֹכֵן בִּגְבוּרָה, אַתָּה שָׁלוֹם וְשִׁמְךָ שָׁלוֹם. יְהִי רָצוֹן שֶׁתָּשִׂים עָלֵינוּ וְעַל־כָּל־עַמְּךָ בֵּית יִשְׂרָאֵל חַיִּים וּבְרָכָה לְמִשְׁמֶרֶת שָׁלוֹם.

ברכת שלום

שִׂים שָׁלוֹם, טוֹבָה, וּבְרָכָה, חֵן, וָחֶסֶד וְרַחֲמִים עָלֵינוּ וְעַל כָּל־יִשְׂרָאֵל עַמֶּךָ. בָּרְכֵנוּ אָבִינוּ, כֻּלָּנוּ כְּאֶחָד בְּאוֹר פָּנֶיךָ, כִּי בְאוֹר פָּנֶיךָ נָתַתָּ לָּנוּ, יהוה אֱלֹהֵינוּ, תּוֹרַת חַיִּים וְאַהֲבַת חֶסֶד, וּצְדָקָה, וּבְרָכָה, וְרַחֲמִים, וְחַיִּים, וְשָׁלוֹם. וְטוֹב בְּעֵינֶיךָ לְבָרֵךְ אֶת־עַמְּךָ יִשְׂרָאֵל, בְּכָל־עֵת וּבְכָל־שָׁעָה בִּשְׁלוֹמֶךָ. בָּרוּךְ אַתָּה יהוה, הַמְבָרֵךְ אֶת עַמּוֹ יִשְׂרָאֵל בַּשָּׁלוֹם.

The Leader's repetition ends at this point.

The Service continues as indicated on page 688.

During the Leader's repetition of the *Amidah*, and prior to the Priestly Blessings, the Cohanim wash their hands in water poured from a special vessel by the Levites. They remove their shoes. When the Leader reaches "Find favour", they ascend to stand in front of the Ark. They cover their head and upper body with the *tallit*, and raise their arms and hands during the blessing in

Leader, who should not be a Cohen, says aloud:

the priests,

Congregation:

Your holy people, as it is said:

The Cohanim say the following blessing in unison:

בָּרוּךְ Blessed are You, LORD our GOD, King of the Universe, who has made us holy with His commandments, and has commanded us to bless His people Israel with love.

Leader, followed by the Cohanim, say the following, word by word.
One should not look at the Cohanim while the blessings are being said.

יְבָרֶכְךָ May the LORD bless you and protect you. (Cong.: Amen)

יָאֵר May the LORD make His face shine on you and be gracious to you. (Cong.: Amen)

יִשָּׂא May the LORD turn His face toward you, and give you peace. (Cong.: Amen, Selah)

The Congregation say:

אַדִּיר Majestic One on high who dwells in power. You are Peace and Your name is Peace. May it be Your will to bestow on us and on Your people the house of Israel, life and blessing as a safeguard for peace.

PEACE

שִׂים Grant peace, goodness and blessing, grace, lovingkindness and compassion to us and all Israel Your people. Bless us, our Father, all as one, with the light of Your face, for by the light of Your face You have given us, LORD our GOD, the Torah of life and love of kindness, righteousness, blessing, compassion, life and peace. May it be good in Your eyes to bless Your people Israel at every time, in every hour, with Your peace. Blessed are You, LORD, who blesses His people Israel with peace.

The Leader's repetition ends at this point.
The Service continues as indicated on page 689.

---

a special manner. During the blessings, which they repeat word for word after the Leader, all other members of the congregation should be in front of them: those sitting behind should move forward at this time. Their faces should be turned toward the Cohanim, but they should not look at them while the blessings are being said. *Majestic One on high* – a prayer by the congregation, echoing three times the last word of the Priestly Blessing: peace.

תפילת טל

On the first day of פֶּסַח, at the repetition of the מוּסָף עֲמִידָה, the Ark is opened. All stand.

Leader:

אֲדֹנָי שְׂפָתַי תִּפְתָּח, וּפִי יַגִּיד תְּהִלָּתֶךָ.

אבות

בָּרוּךְ אַתָּה יהוה אֱלֹהֵינוּ וֵאלֹהֵי אֲבוֹתֵינוּ, אֱלֹהֵי אַבְרָהָם, אֱלֹהֵי יִצְחָק, וֵאלֹהֵי יַעֲקֹב, הָאֵל הַגָּדוֹל הַגִּבּוֹר וְהַנּוֹרָא, אֵל עֶלְיוֹן, גּוֹמֵל חֲסָדִים טוֹבִים וְקוֹנֵה הַכֹּל, וְזוֹכֵר חַסְדֵי אָבוֹת, וּמֵבִיא גוֹאֵל לִבְנֵי בְנֵיהֶם, לְמַעַן שְׁמוֹ בְּאַהֲבָה. מֶלֶךְ עוֹזֵר וּמוֹשִׁיעַ וּמָגֵן.

בְּדַעְתּוֹ אַבִּיעָה חִידוֹת,
בְּעַם זוּ בְּזוֹ בְּטַל לְהַחֲדוֹת.
טַל גֵּיא וּדְשָׁאֶיהָ לַחֲדוֹת,
דָּצִים בְּצִלּוֹ לְהַחֲדוֹת.
אוֹת יַלְדוּת טַל לְהָגֵן לְתוֹלָדוֹת.
בָּרוּךְ אַתָּה יהוה, מָגֵן אַבְרָהָם.

אַתָּה גִּבּוֹר לְעוֹלָם אֲדֹנָי, מְחַיֵּה מֵתִים אַתָּה, רַב לְהוֹשִׁיעַ.

PRAYER FOR DEW

Pesach, the "festival of spring", marks the end of the rainy season. Accordingly, on the first day at *Musaf*, we stop saying, "He makes the wind blow and the rain fall" in the second paragraph of the *Amidah*. The Sephardi and Israeli custom is to say instead, "who causes the dew to fall"; we do not have this custom. Nonetheless, to mark the transition, we recite a special liturgical poem (*piyyut*).

Its author is the greatest of Jewry's liturgical poets, Eleazar Kalir. Despite his genius and the sheer number of his compositions (many previously unknown works of his were discovered in the Cairo Genizah), we remain uncertain as to when and where he lived. The most

PRAYER FOR DEW

On the first day of Pesach, at the repetition of the *Musaf Amidah*, the Ark is opened. All stand.

Leader:
O LORD, open my lips, so that my mouth may declare Your praise.

PATRIARCHS

▾**בָּרוּךְ** Blessed are You, LORD our GOD and GOD of our Fathers, GOD of Abraham, GOD of Isaac and GOD of Jacob; the great, mighty and awesome GOD, GOD Most High, who bestows acts of lovingkindness and creates all, who remembers the lovingkindness of the Fathers and will bring a Redeemer to their children's children for the sake of His name, in love. King, Helper, Saviour, Shield:

בְּדַעְתּוֹ With His consent I will speak of hidden things,
That for this people, by this prayer, there may be joy in dew,
May the valley and its vegetation be renewed through dew,
Springing up under His shade anew,
Sign of regeneration, shield of future generations – dew.
▾Blessed are You, LORD, Shield of Abraham.

אַתָּה You are eternally mighty, O LORD. You give life to the dead and have great power to save.

---

likely hypothesis is that he lived in Israel in the sixth century. His compositions are full of allusions to rabbinic traditions; he coined many new words, and his style – intricate, erudite, full of wordplay and subtle acrostics – influenced many later liturgical poets.

בְּדַעְתּוֹ *With His consent*: The preamble to the prayer involves an untranslatable play on the similar-sounding words *chidot* ("hidden things"), *lehachadot* ("have joy"), and *lachadot* ("be as new": an Aramaic form of the Hebrew *chadash*). The fourth line is a complex allusion to a wedding. It uses two words that appear together in the last of the seven marriage blessings (*ditzah* and *chedvah*). The word "shade" (meaning both cloud and Divine protection) may also be an allusion to the bridal canopy. Thus Kalir, through complex verbal resonances, strikes a mood of joy as if spring were the wedding of heaven and earth.

תְּהוֹמוֹת הֲדוֹם לִרְסִיסוֹ כְּסוּפִים,
וְכָל־נְאוֹת דֶּשֶׁא לוֹ נִכְסָפִים.
טַל זִכְרוּ גְּבוּרוֹת מוּסִיפִים,
חָקוּק בְּגִישַׁת מוּסָפִים,
טַל לְהַחֲיוֹת בּוֹ נְקוּקֵי סְעִיפִים.

אֱלֹהֵינוּ וֵאלֹהֵי אֲבוֹתֵינוּ,

טַל תֵּן לִרְצוֹת אַרְצָךְ,
שִׁיתֵנוּ בְרָכָה בְּדִיצָךְ,
רֹב דָּגָן וְתִירוֹשׁ בְּהַפְרִיצָךְ,
קוֹמֵם עִיר בָּהּ חֶפְצָךְ,
בְּטַל.

טַל צַוֵּה שָׁנָה טוֹבָה וּמְעֻטֶּרֶת,
פְּרִי הָאָרֶץ לְגָאוֹן וּלְתִפְאֶרֶת,
עִיר כַּסֻּכָּה נוֹתֶרֶת,
שִׂימָהּ בְּיָדְךָ עֲטֶרֶת,
בְּטַל.

טַל נוֹפֵף עֲלֵי אֶרֶץ בְּרוּכָה,
מִמֶּגֶד שָׁמַיִם שַׂבְּעֵנוּ בְרָכָה,
לְהָאִיר מִתּוֹךְ חֲשֵׁכָה,
כַּנָּה אַחֲרֶיךָ מְשׁוּכָה,
בְּטַל.

טַל יַעֲסִיס צוּף הָרִים,
טְעֵם בִּמְאוֹדֶיךָ מֻבְחָרִים,

תְּהוֹמוֹת The depths of the earth yearn for drops of dew;
All the green pastures long for them.
The mention of dew adds to His might,
Inscribed as we approach in the *Musaf* prayer.
Dew – to revive those (buried) in the clefts of the rocks.

Our God and God of our fathers.

טַל Dew – Grant it to favour Your land.
In Your jubilation, set us as a blessing.
Increase for us our corn and wine.
Establish the city in which You delight –
With dew.

טַל Dew – Decree it for a good and resplendent year.
May the fruit of the earth be fine and fair.
As for the city now deserted like a hut,
Place it in Your hand like a crown –
With dew.

טַל Dew – May it drop gently on the blessed land.
Satisfy us with a blessing of the rich gifts of heaven.
Send light in the midst of darkness
To the stock (Israel) who are drawn to You –
With dew.

טַל Dew – Let it sweeten the mountain streams;
Let the chosen ones taste Your magnanimity.

תְּהוֹמוֹת *The depths of the earth*: A meditation on the fact that dew (and rain) are mentioned in the second paragraph of the *Amidah*, known as *Gevurot*, "Divine might", whose dominant theme is the resurrection of the dead. Just as at the end of time God will revive the dead ("those buried in the clefts of the rocks"), so does dew now revive the earth and makes it green again. *The mention of dew adds to His might* – an ambiguous phrase which also means, "Dew is mentioned in (the second paragraph of the *Amidah* known as) 'His might'."

טַל *Dew – grant it to favour Your land*: The six verses of the poem begin and end with the word "Dew", and the whole is con-

חֲנוּנֶיךָ חַלֵּץ מִמַּסְגְּרִים,
זִמְרָה נַנְעִים וְקוֹל נָרִים,
בְּטַל.

טַל וְשׁוֹבַע מַלֵּא אֲסָמֵינוּ,
הֲכָעֵת תְּחַדֵּשׁ יָמֵינוּ,
דּוֹד כְּעֶרְכְּךָ הַעֲמֵד שְׁמֵנוּ,
גַּן רָוֶה שִׂימֵנוּ,
בְּטַל.

טַל בּוֹ תְּבָרֵךְ מָזוֹן,
בְּמַשְׁמַנֵּינוּ אַל יְהִי רָזוֹן,
אֲיֻמָּה אֲשֶׁר הִסַּעְתָּ כַּצֹּאן,
אָנָּא תָּפֵק לָהּ רָצוֹן,
בְּטַל.

Leader:

שָׁאַתָּה הוּא יהוה אֱלֹהֵינוּ,
מַשִּׁיב הָרוּחַ וּמוֹרִיד הַטָּל.

Congregation then Leader, responsively:

לִבְרָכָה וְלֹא לִקְלָלָה. (Cong.: אָמֵן)
לְחַיִּים וְלֹא לְמָוֶת. (Cong.: אָמֵן)
לְשֹׂבַע וְלֹא לְרָזוֹן. (Cong.: אָמֵן)

The Ark is closed. The Leader continues with מְכַלְכֵּל חַיִּים, on page 670.

structed as a reverse alphabetical acrostic, the last two letters (*bet* and *aleph*) each being allocated two lines. The poem deftly intertwines the themes of nature (spring, renewal) and history (asking God to bring His people back from the winter

Free Your beloved ones from captivity.
Then sweetly we will raise our voices and sing –
With dew.

טַל Dew – May it fill our granaries to overflowing.
Would that now You might renew our days.
Beloved! Let our name endure as Yours.
Make us like a well-watered garden –
With dew.

טַל Dew – With it bless our food.
In our fertile lands may there be no scarcity.
The nation You once led like a flock,
On her please, we pray, bestow Your favour –
With dew.

Leader:

For You, Lord our God,
make the wind blow and the dew fall.

Congregation then Leader, responsively:

For blessing, and not for curse. (Cong.: Amen)

For life, and not for death. (Cong.: Amen)

For plenty, and not for scarcity. (Cong.: Amen)

The Ark is closed. The Leader continues with "He sustains the living" on page 671.

---

of exile to a spring of national renewal). *To the stock* – the root or stem of a vine, a metaphor for Israel (see Psalm 80:16 and commentaries thereto). By comparing Israel to a plant, the poet can extend the metaphor of dew to the fortunes of the nation. *Let our name endure as Yours* – just as God is eternal, so may be the people who carry His name ("Then all the peoples on earth will see that you are called by the name of the Lord", Deuteronomy 28:10). *In our fertile lands* – literally, "In our fat places may there be no leanness".

For blessing, and not for curse: In this rousing three-line climax (paralleled in the prayer for rain), Reader and Congregation join in fervent prayer that the forces of nature, under the care of the Maker of nature, should bring blessing to the land and its people.

תפילת גשם

On שְׁמִינִי עֲצֶרֶת at the repetition of the מוּסָף עֲמִידָה, the Ark is opened. All stand.

Leader:

אֲדֹנָי שְׂפָתַי תִּפְתָּח, וּפִי יַגִּיד תְּהִלָּתֶךָ.

אבות

בָּרוּךְ אַתָּה יהוה אֱלֹהֵינוּ וֵאלֹהֵי אֲבוֹתֵינוּ, אֱלֹהֵי אַבְרָהָם, אֱלֹהֵי יִצְחָק, וֵאלֹהֵי יַעֲקֹב, הָאֵל הַגָּדוֹל הַגִּבּוֹר וְהַנּוֹרָא, אֵל עֶלְיוֹן, גּוֹמֵל חֲסָדִים טוֹבִים וְקוֹנֵה הַכֹּל, וְזוֹכֵר חַסְדֵי אָבוֹת, וּמֵבִיא גוֹאֵל לִבְנֵי בְנֵיהֶם, לְמַעַן שְׁמוֹ בְּאַהֲבָה. מֶלֶךְ עוֹזֵר וּמוֹשִׁיעַ וּמָגֵן.

אַף־בְּרִי אֻתַּת שֵׁם שַׂר מָטָר,
לְהַעֲבִיב וּלְהַעֲנִין לְהָרִיק וּלְהַמְטַר,
מַיִם אִבִּים בָּם גֵּיא לַעֲטַר,
לְבַל יֵעָצְרוּ בְּנִשְׁיוֹן שְׁטַר,
אֱמוּנִים גְּנוֹן בָּם שׁוֹאֲלֵי מָטָר.
בָּרוּךְ אַתָּה יהוה, מָגֵן אַבְרָהָם.

אַתָּה גִּבּוֹר לְעוֹלָם אֲדֹנָי, מְחַיֵּה מֵתִים אַתָּה, רַב לְהוֹשִׁיעַ.

יַטְרִיחַ לְפַלֵּג מִפֶּלֶג גֶּשֶׁם,
לְמוֹגֵג פְּנֵי נֶשִׁי בְּצַחוֹת לֶשֶׁם,
מַיִם לְאַדְּרָךְ כִּנִּיתָ בְּרֶשֶׁם,

PRAYER FOR RAIN
"On the festival (of Sukkot) the rainfall of the world is judged" (Mishnah, *Rosh Hashanah* 1:2). Israel is peculiarly dependent on rain, as Moses told the Israelites: "The land you are crossing the Jordan to take possession of is a land of mountains and valleys that drinks rain from heaven. It is a land the LORD your GOD cares for; the eyes of the LORD your GOD are continually on it from the beginning of the year to its end" (Deuteronomy 11:11–12). Sukkot is the festival closest to the start of the rainy season. In theory, the prayer for rain should be said at the beginning of Sukkot, but since rain-

PRAYER FOR RAIN

On Shemini Atzeret at the repetition of the *Musaf Amidah*, the Ark is opened. All stand.

Leader:

O LORD, open my lips, so that my mouth may declare Your praise.

PATRIARCHS

▼בָּרוּךְ Blessed are You, LORD our GOD and GOD of our Fathers, GOD of Abraham, GOD of Isaac and GOD of Jacob; the great, mighty and awesome GOD, GOD Most High, who bestows acts of lovingkindness and creates all, who remembers the lovingkindness of the Fathers and will bring a Redeemer to their children's children for the sake of His name, in love. King, Helper, Saviour, Shield:

אַף־בְּרִי Af-bri is the name of the angel of rain,
Who overcasts (the sky), forms clouds and precipitates them,
making them rain
Water to crown the valley with green.
May rain not be withheld from us because of our unpaid debts.
May the merit of the faithful Patriarchs protect their offspring
who pray for rain.
▼Blessed are You, LORD, Shield of Abraham.

אַתָּה You are eternally mighty, O LORD. You give life to the dead and have great power to save.

יַטְרִיחַ May He make him apportion due portions of rain,
Moistening the earth with drops pure as opal.
In the Torah You symbolised Your might by water.

---

fall would interfere with the command to eat in the *Sukkah*, it was deferred to Shemini Atzeret. The liturgical poem that precedes the prayer was, like that for dew, composed by Eleazar Kalir. The initial letter of each line spells out an alphabetical acrostic, and each line ends with the word "water". The six verses enumerate events related to water in six lives: those of the patriarchs Abraham, Isaac and Jacob, the leaders of the Israelites in the wilderness, Moses and Aaron, and the people of Israel as a whole.

אַף־בְּרִי *Af-bri is the name of the angel of rain*: Job 37:11 reads: "Even when it is clear [*af-bri*] He gives the dense clouds their load, and the clouds spread His mist abroad". Rashi interprets the phrase *Af-bri* as "the angel of rain", a person-

לְהַרְגִּיעַ בְּרַעֲפָם לִנְפוּחֵי נֶשֶׁם,
לְהַחֲיוֹת מַזְכִּירִים גְּבוּרוֹת הַגֶּשֶׁם.

אֱלֹהֵינוּ וֵאלֹהֵי אֲבוֹתֵינוּ,

זְכוֹר אָב נִמְשַׁךְ אַחֲרֶיךָ כַּמַּיִם,
בֵּרַכְתּוֹ כְּעֵץ שָׁתוּל עַל פַּלְגֵי מַיִם,
גְּנַנְתּוֹ, הִצַּלְתּוֹ מֵאֵשׁ וּמִמַּיִם,
דְּרַשְׁתּוֹ בְּזָרְעוֹ עַל כָּל־מַיִם.

Congregation:

בַּעֲבוּרוֹ אַל תִּמְנַע מַיִם.

זְכוֹר הַנּוֹלָד בִּבְשׂוֹרַת יֻקַּח נָא מְעַט מַיִם,
וְשַׂחְתָּ לְהוֹרוֹ לְשָׁחֲטוֹ,
לִשְׁפֹּךְ דָּמוֹ כַּמַּיִם,
זְהֵר גַּם הוּא לִשְׁפֹּךְ לֵב כַּמַּיִם,
חָפַר וּמָצָא בְּאֵרוֹת מַיִם.

Congregation:

בְּצִדְקוֹ חֹן חַשְׁרַת מַיִם.

זְכוֹר טָעַן מַקְלוֹ וְעָבַר יַרְדֵּן מַיִם,
יִחַד לֵב וְגָל אֶבֶן מִפִּי בְּאֵר מַיִם,
כְּנֶאֱבַק לוֹ שַׂר בָּלוּל מֵאֵשׁ וּמִמַּיִם,
לָכֵן הִבְטַחְתּוֹ הֱיוֹת עִמּוֹ בָּאֵשׁ וּבַמָּיִם.

Congregation:

בַּעֲבוּרוֹ אַל תִּמְנַע מַיִם.

גְּנַנְתּוֹ, הִצַּלְתּוֹ מֵאֵשׁ וּמִמַּיִם *You shielded him and rescued him from fire and water*: According to rabbinic tradition, Abraham was cast into a fiery furnace by

ification of the two aspects of rain. At times it is fierce-like anger (*af*); at others it is gentle, healing (*bri*) the earth's thirst.

Its drops refresh those in whom was breathed the breath of life,
Reviving those who make mention of the powers of rain.

Our God and God of our fathers.

זְכוֹר Remember the Patriarch (Abraham) who followed You like water.
You blessed him like a tree planted beside streams of water.
You shielded him and rescued him from fire and water.
You sought him because he sowed (righteousness) by all waters.

Congregation:

For his sake do not withhold water.

זְכוֹר Remember (Isaac) whose birth was foretold when (Abraham said) "Let there be brought some water."
You told his father to offer him, to shed his blood like water.
(Isaac), too, cared and poured out his soul like water.
When he dug, he discovered wells of water.

Congregation:

For his righteousness' sake grant abundant water.

זְכוֹר Remember (Jacob) who carried his staff and crossed the Jordan's water.
With steadfast heart he rolled away the stone from the well of water.
He wrestled with an angel composed of fire and water,
So You promised to be with him through fire and water.

Congregation:

For his sake do not withhold water.

Nimrod and was saved by God. Satan created a river to block Abraham's way on his journey to the binding of Isaac. Abraham walked undaunted into the water; when it came up to his neck, God rebuked Satan and the river vanished. *Remember (Isaac) whose birth was foretold* when the three angels visited Abraham, and he urged them to stay, rest, eat and drink water. *When he dug* – Isaac re-opened the wells Abraham had dug, which had been stopped up by the Philistines (Genesis 26:17–22).

וְגַל אֶבֶן מִפִּי בְּאֵר מַיִם *He rolled away the stone from the well of water*: When Jacob arrived at Haran and saw Rachel coming to water the sheep, Jacob removed the stone covering the well (Genesis 29:10). *An angel composed of fire and water* – the Talmud Yerushalmi (*Rosh Hashanah* 2:4) describes the angel with whom Jacob wrestled as "half water, half fire". *They said: "He drew water for us"* – the daughters of Jethro said this about Moses (Exodus 2:19). *He struck the rock* – the reference is to Exodus 17:6, shortly after

זְכוֹר מָשׁוּי בְּתֵבַת גֹּמֶא מִן הַמַּיִם,
נָמוּ דָּלֹה דָלָה וְהִשְׁקָה צֹּאן מַיִם,
סְגוּלֶיךָ עֵת צָמְאוּ לַמַּיִם,
עַל הַסֶּלַע הָךְ וַיֵּצְאוּ מָיִם.

Congregation:

בְּצִדְקוֹ חוֹן חַשְׁרַת מָיִם.

זְכוֹר פְּקִיד שָׁתוֹת טוֹבֵל חָמֵשׁ טְבִילוֹת בַּמַּיִם,
צוֹעֶה וּמַרְחִיץ כַּפָּיו בְּקִדּוּשׁ מַיִם,
קוֹרֵא וּמַזֶּה טָהֳרַת מַיִם,
רֻחַק מֵעַם פַּחַז כַּמָּיִם.

Congregation:

בַּעֲבוּרוֹ אַל תִּמְנַע מָיִם.

זְכוֹר שְׁנֵים עָשָׂר שְׁבָטִים שֶׁהֶעֱבַרְתָּ בְּגִזְרַת מַיִם,
שֶׁהִמְתַּקְתָּ לָמוֹ מְרִירוּת מַיִם,
תּוֹלְדוֹתָם נִשְׁפַּךְ דָּמָם עָלֶיךָ כַּמַּיִם,
תֵּפֶן כִּי נַפְשֵׁנוּ אָפְפוּ מָיִם.

Congregation:

בְּצִדְקָם חוֹן חַשְׁרַת מָיִם.

Leader:

שָׁאַתָּה הוּא יהוה אֱלֹהֵינוּ,
מַשִּׁיב הָרוּחַ וּמוֹרִיד הַגָּשֶׁם.

Congregation then Leader, responsively:

לִבְרָכָה וְלֹא לִקְלָלָה. (Cong.: אָמֵן)
לְחַיִּים וְלֹא לְמָוֶת. (Cong.: אָמֵן)
לְשֹׂבַע וְלֹא לְרָזוֹן. (Cong.: אָמֵן)

The Ark is closed. The Leader continues with מְכַלְכֵּל חַיִּים, on page 670.

זְכוֹר Remember (Moses) who in a reed basket was drawn out of the water.
They said: "He drew water for us, and gave the flock water."
When Your treasured people thirsted for water,
He struck the rock and out gushed water.

Congregation:

For his righteousness' sake grant abundant water.

זְכוֹר Remember (Aaron), chief officer of the Temple, who immersed five times in water.
He went and washed his hands in the sanctifying water.
He called out and sprinkled blood, purifying the people as if with water.
He kept apart from the people who were as unruly as water.

Congregation:

For his sake do not withhold water.

זְכוֹר Remember the twelve tribes You brought through the divided water,
For whom You sweetened the bitterness of the water.
For Your sake their descendants' blood was spilled like water.
Turn to us, for troubles engulf our souls like water.

Congregation:

For their righteousness' sake grant abundant water.

Leader:

For You, Lord our God,
make the wind blow and the rain fall.

Congregation then Leader, responsively:

For blessing, and not for curse. (Cong.: Amen)

For life, and not for death. (Cong.: Amen)

For plenty, and not for scarcity. (Cong.: Amen)

The Ark is closed. The Leader continues with "He sustains the living" on page 671.

---

the crossing of the Reed Sea (and not to the later episode, Numbers 20, when God instructed Moses to speak to the rock). *Who immersed five times in water* – as part of the rites of the Day of Atonement.

סדר הושענות

הוֹשַׁעְנוֹת are said after the repetition of the מוּסָף עֲמִידָה on every day of סֻכּוֹת.

On weekdays, the Ark is opened and a סֵפֶר תּוֹרָה is taken to the בִּימָה. Members of the Congregation who have a לוּלָב and אֶתְרוֹג make a circuit around the בִּימָה and recite הוֹשַׁעְנוֹת. Mourners do not participate in the circuit.

At the conclusion of the הוֹשַׁעְנוֹת, the סֵפֶר תּוֹרָה is returned to the Ark, which is then closed.

On שַׁבָּת, turn to page 712. On הוֹשַׁעְנָא רַבָּה, turn to page 715.

On sixth day	On fifth day	On fourth day	On third day	On second day	On first day	If first day סֻכּוֹת falls on
הוֹשַׁעְנוֹת לַשַּׁבָּת	אֵל לְמוֹשָׁעוֹת	אוֹם אֲנִי חוֹמָה	אֶעֱרוֹךְ שׁוּעִי	אֶבֶן שְׁתִיָּה	לְמַעַן אֲמִתָּךְ	Monday
אָדוֹן הַמּוֹשִׁיעַ	הוֹשַׁעְנוֹת לַשַּׁבָּת	אֵל לְמוֹשָׁעוֹת	אֶעֱרוֹךְ שׁוּעִי	אֶבֶן שְׁתִיָּה	לְמַעַן אֲמִתָּךְ	Tuesday
אָדוֹן הַמּוֹשִׁיעַ	אֵל לְמוֹשָׁעוֹת	אֶעֱרוֹךְ שׁוּעִי	הוֹשַׁעְנוֹת לַשַּׁבָּת	אֶבֶן שְׁתִיָּה	לְמַעַן אֲמִתָּךְ	Thursday
אָדוֹן הַמּוֹשִׁיעַ	אֵל לְמוֹשָׁעוֹת	אֶבֶן שְׁתִיָּה	אֶעֱרוֹךְ שׁוּעִי	לְמַעַן אֲמִתָּךְ	הוֹשַׁעְנוֹת לַשַּׁבָּת	שַׁבָּת

Leader then Congregation:

הוֹשַׁע נָא, לְמַעַנְךָ אֱלֹהֵינוּ, הוֹשַׁע נָא.

Leader then Congregation:

הוֹשַׁע נָא, לְמַעַנְךָ בּוֹרְאֵנוּ, הוֹשַׁע נָא.

Leader then Congregation:

הוֹשַׁע נָא, לְמַעַנְךָ גּוֹאֲלֵנוּ, הוֹשַׁע נָא.

Leader then Congregation:

הוֹשַׁע נָא, לְמַעַנְךָ דּוֹרְשֵׁנוּ, הוֹשַׁע נָא.

הוֹשַׁע נָא.

לְמַעַן אֲמִתָּךְ. לְמַעַן בְּרִיתָךְ. לְמַעַן גָּדְלָךְ וְתִפְאַרְתָּךְ. לְמַעַן דָּתָךְ. לְמַעַן הוֹדָךְ. לְמַעַן וִעוּדָךְ. לְמַעַן זִכְרָךְ. לְמַעַן חַסְדָּךְ.

לְמַֽעַן טוּבָךְ. לְמַֽעַן יִחוּדָךְ. לְמַֽעַן כְּבוֹדָךְ. לְמַֽעַן לִמּוּדָךְ. לְמַֽעַן מַלְכוּתָךְ. לְמַֽעַן נִצְחָךְ. לְמַֽעַן סוֹדָךְ. לְמַֽעַן עֻזָּךְ. לְמַֽעַן פְּאֵרָךְ. לְמַֽעַן צִדְקָתָךְ. לְמַֽעַן קְדֻשָּׁתָךְ. לְמַֽעַן רַחֲמֶֽיךָ הָרַבִּים. לְמַֽעַן שְׁכִינָתָךְ. לְמַֽעַן תְּהִלָּתָךְ. הוֹשַֽׁע נָא.

Continue with אֲנִי וָהוֹ on page 711.

הוֹשַֽׁע נָא.

אֶֽבֶן שְׁתִיָּה. בֵּית הַבְּחִירָה. גֹּֽרֶן אָרְנָן. דְּבִיר הַמֻּצְנָע. הַר הַמּוֹרִיָּה. וְהַר יֵרָאֶה. זְבוּל תִּפְאַרְתֶּֽךָ. חָנָה דָוִד. טוּב הַלְּבָנוֹן. יְפֵה נוֹף מְשׂוֹשׂ כָּל הָאָֽרֶץ. כְּלִֽילַת יֹֽפִי. לִינַת הַצֶּֽדֶק. מָכוֹן לְשִׁבְתֶּֽךָ. נָוֶה שַׁאֲנָן. סֻכַּת שָׁלֵם. עֲלִיַּת שְׁבָטִים. פִּנַּת יִקְרַת. צִיּוֹן הַמְצֻיֶּֽנֶת. קֹֽדֶשׁ הַקֳּדָשִׁים. רָצוּף אַהֲבָה. שְׁכִינַת כְּבוֹדֶֽךָ. תֵּל תַּלְפִּיּוֹת. הוֹשַֽׁע נָא.

Continue with אֲנִי וָהוֹ on page 711.

הוֹשַֽׁע נָא.

אֶעֱרוֹךְ שׁוּעִי. בְּבֵית שַׁוְעִי. גִּלִּֽיתִי בַצּוֹם פִּשְׁעִי. דְּרַשְׁתִּֽיךָ בּוֹ לְהוֹשִׁיעִי. הַקְשִֽׁיבָה לְקוֹל שַׁוְעִי. וְקוּמָה וְהוֹשִׁיעִי. זְכוֹר וְרַחֵם מוֹשִׁיעִי. חַי כֵּן תְּשַׁעְשְׁעִי. טוֹב בְּאֶֽנֶק שְׁעִי. יָחִישׁ מוֹשִׁיעִי. כַּלֵּה מַרְשִׁיעִי. לְבַל עוֹד תַּרְשִׁיעִי. מַהֵר אֱלֹהֵי יִשְׁעִי. נֶֽצַח לְהוֹשִׁיעִי. שָׂא נָא עֲוֹן רִשְׁעִי. עֲבוֹר עַל פִּשְׁעִי. פְּנֵה נָא לְהוֹשִׁיעִי. צוּר צַדִּיק מוֹשִׁיעִי. קַבֵּל נָא שַׁוְעִי. רוֹמֵם קֶֽרֶן יִשְׁעִי. שַׁדַּי מוֹשִׁיעִי. תּוֹפִֽיעַ וְתוֹשִׁיעִי. הוֹשַֽׁע נָא.

Continue with אֲנִי וָהוֹ on page 711.

הוֹשַֽׁע נָא.

אוֹם אֲנִי חוֹמָה. בָּרָה כַּחַמָּה. גּוֹלָה וְסוּרָה. דָּמְתָה לְתָמָר. הַהֲרוּגָה עָלֶֽיךָ. וְנֶחֱשֶֽׁבֶת כְּצֹאן טִבְחָה. זְרוּיָה

בֵּין מַכְעִיסֶיהָ. חֲבוּקָה וּדְבוּקָה בָּךְ. טוֹעֶנֶת עֻלָּךְ. יְחִידָה לְיַחֲדָךְ. כְּבוּשָׁה בַּגּוֹלָה. לוֹמֶדֶת יִרְאָתָךְ. מְרוּטַת לֶחִי. נְתוּנָה לְמַכִּים. סוֹבֶלֶת סִבְלָךְ. עֲנִיָּה סֹעֲרָה. פְּדוּיַת טוֹבִיָּה. צֹאן קָדָשִׁים. קְהִלּוֹת יַעֲקֹב. רְשׁוּמִים בִּשְׁמֶךָ. שׁוֹאֲגִים הוֹשַׁע נָא. תְּמוּכִים עָלֶיךָ. הוֹשַׁע נָא.

Continue with אֲנִי וָהוֹ on page 711.

הוֹשַׁע נָא.

אֵל לְמוֹשָׁעוֹת. בְּאַרְבַּע שְׁבֻעוֹת. גָּשִׁים בְּשַׁוְעוֹת. דּוֹפְקֵי עֶרֶךְ שׁוּעוֹת. הוֹגֵי שַׁעֲשֻׁעוֹת. וְחִידֹתָם מִשְׁתַּעְשְׁעוֹת. זֹעֲקִים לְהַשְׁעוֹת. חוֹכֵי יְשׁוּעוֹת. טְפוּלִים בָּךְ שְׁעוֹת. יוֹדְעֵי בִּין שָׁעוֹת. כּוֹרְעֶיךָ בְּשַׁוְעוֹת. לְהָבִין שְׁמוּעוֹת. מִפִּיךָ נִשְׁמָעוֹת. נוֹתֵן תְּשׁוּעוֹת. סְפוּרוֹת מַשְׁמָעוֹת. עֵדוּת מַשְׁמִיעוֹת. פּוֹעֵל יְשׁוּעוֹת. צַדִּיק נוֹשָׁעוֹת. קִרְיַת תְּשׁוּעוֹת. רֶגֶשׁ תְּשֻׁאוֹת. שָׁלֹשׁ שָׁעוֹת. תָּחִישׁ לִתְשׁוּעוֹת. הוֹשַׁע נָא.

Continue with אֲנִי וָהוֹ on page 711.

הוֹשַׁע נָא.

אָדוֹן הַמּוֹשִׁיעַ. בִּלְתְּךָ אֵין לְהוֹשִׁיעַ. גִּבּוֹר וְרַב לְהוֹשִׁיעַ. דַּלּוֹתִי וְלִי יְהוֹשִׁיעַ. הָאֵל הַמּוֹשִׁיעַ. וּמַצִּיל וּמוֹשִׁיעַ. זוֹעֲקֶיךָ תּוֹשִׁיעַ. חוֹכֶיךָ הוֹשִׁיעַ. טְלָאֶיךָ תַּשְׂבִּיעַ. יְבוּל לְהַשְׁפִּיעַ. כָּל שִׂיחַ תַּדְשֵׁא וְתוֹשִׁיעַ. לְגֵיא בַּל תַּרְשִׁיעַ. מְגָדִים תַּמְתִּיק וְתוֹשִׁיעַ. נְשִׂיאִים לְהַסִּיעַ. שְׂעִירִים לְהָנִיעַ. עֲנָנִים מִלְּהַמְנִיעַ. פּוֹתֵחַ יָד וּמַשְׂבִּיעַ. צְמֵאֶיךָ תַּשְׂבִּיעַ. קוֹרְאֶיךָ תּוֹשִׁיעַ. רְחוּמֶיךָ תּוֹשִׁיעַ. שׁוֹחֲרֶיךָ הוֹשִׁיעַ. תְּמִימֶיךָ תּוֹשִׁיעַ. הוֹשַׁע נָא.

Continue with אֲנִי וָהוֹ on page 711.

אֲנִי וָהוֹ הוֹשִׁיעָה נָּא.

כְּהוֹשַֽׁעְתָּ אֵלִים בְּלוּד עִמָּךְ,
בְּצֵאתְךָ לְיֵֽשַׁע עַמָּךְ, כֵּן הוֹשַֽׁע נָא.
כְּהוֹשַֽׁעְתָּ גּוֹי וֵאלֹהִים,
דְּרוּשִׁים לְיֵֽשַׁע אֱלֹהִים, כֵּן הוֹשַֽׁע נָא.
כְּהוֹשַֽׁעְתָּ הֲמוֹן צְבָאוֹת,
וְעִמָּם מַלְאֲכֵי צְבָאוֹת, כֵּן הוֹשַֽׁע נָא.
כְּהוֹשַֽׁעְתָּ זַכִּים מִבֵּית עֲבָדִים,
חַנּוּן בְּיָדָם מַעֲבִידִים, כֵּן הוֹשַֽׁע נָא.
כְּהוֹשַֽׁעְתָּ טְבוּעִים בְּצוּל גְּזָרִים,
יְקָרְךָ עִמָּם מַעֲבִירִים כֵּן הוֹשַֽׁע נָא.
כְּהוֹשַֽׁעְתָּ כַּנָּה מְשׁוֹרֶֽרֶת וַיּֽוֹשַׁע,
לְגוֹחָהּ מְצֻיֶּֽנֶת וַיִּוָּֽשַׁע, כֵּן הוֹשַֽׁע נָא.
כְּהוֹשַֽׁעְתָּ מַאֲמַר וְהוֹצֵאתִי אֶתְכֶם,
נָקוּב וְהוּצֵאתִי אִתְּכֶם, כֵּן הוֹשַֽׁע נָא.
כְּהוֹשַֽׁעְתָּ סוֹבְבֵי מִזְבֵּֽחַ,
עוֹמְסֵי עֲרָבָה לְהַקִּיף מִזְבֵּֽחַ, כֵּן הוֹשַֽׁע נָא.
כְּהוֹשַֽׁעְתָּ פִּלְאֵי אָרוֹן כְּהֻפְשַׁע,
צִעֵר פְּלֶֽשֶׁת בַּחֲרוֹן אַף וְנוֹשַׁע, כֵּן הוֹשַֽׁע נָא.
כְּהוֹשַֽׁעְתָּ קְהִלּוֹת בָּבֶֽלָה שִׁלַּֽחְתָּ,
רַחוּם לְמַעֲנָם שֻׁלַּֽחְתָּ, כֵּן הוֹשַֽׁע נָא.
כְּהוֹשַֽׁעְתָּ שְׁבוּת שִׁבְטֵי יַעֲקֹב,
תָּשׁוּב וְתָשִׁיב שְׁבוּת אָהֳלֵי יַעֲקֹב, וְהוֹשִֽׁיעָה נָּא.
כְּהוֹשַֽׁעְתָּ שׁוֹמְרֵי מִצְוֹת, וְחוֹכֵי יְשׁוּעוֹת,
אֵל לְמוֹשָׁעוֹת, וְהוֹשִֽׁיעָה נָּא.

אֲנִי וָהוֹ הוֹשִֽׁיעָה נָּא.

The סֵֽפֶר תּוֹרָה is returned to the Ark

הוֹשִׁיעָה אֶת עַמֶּךָ, וּבָרֵךְ אֶת נַחֲלָתֶךָ, וּרְעֵם וְנַשְּׂאֵם עַד הָעוֹלָם. וְיִהְיוּ דְבָרַי אֵלֶּה אֲשֶׁר הִתְחַנַּנְתִּי לִפְנֵי יהוה, קְרֹבִים אֶל יהוה אֱלֹהֵינוּ יוֹמָם וָלָיְלָה, לַעֲשׂוֹת מִשְׁפַּט עַבְדּוֹ וּמִשְׁפַּט עַמּוֹ יִשְׂרָאֵל, דְּבַר יוֹם בְּיוֹמוֹ. לְמַעַן דַּעַת כָּל עַמֵּי הָאָרֶץ, כִּי יהוה הוּא הָאֱלֹהִים, אֵין עוֹד.

The Ark is closed and the Leader continues the Service with קַדִּישׁ תִּתְקַבַּל on page 448.

הושענות לשבת

The Ark is opened but no סֵפֶר תּוֹרָה is taken out.

The Congregation does not walk round the בִּימָה.

Leader then Congregation:

הוֹשַׁע נָא, לְמַעַנְךָ אֱלֹהֵינוּ, הוֹשַׁע נָא.

Leader then Congregation:

הוֹשַׁע נָא, לְמַעַנְךָ בּוֹרְאֵנוּ, הוֹשַׁע נָא.

Leader then Congregation:

הוֹשַׁע נָא, לְמַעַנְךָ גּוֹאֲלֵנוּ, הוֹשַׁע נָא.

Leader then Congregation:

הוֹשַׁע נָא, לְמַעַנְךָ דּוֹרְשֵׁנוּ, הוֹשַׁע נָא.

הוֹשַׁע נָא.

אוֹם נְצוּרָה כְּבָבַת. בּוֹנֶנֶת בְּדָת נֶפֶשׁ מְשִׁיבַת. גּוֹמֶרֶת הִלְכוֹת שַׁבָּת. דּוֹרֶשֶׁת מַשְׂאַת שַׁבָּת. הַקּוֹבַעַת אַלְפַּיִם תְּחוּם שַׁבָּת. וּמְשִׁיבַת רֶגֶל מִשַּׁבָּת. זָכוֹר וְשָׁמוֹר מְקַיֶּמֶת בְּשַׁבָּת. חָשָׁה לְמַהֵר בִּיאַת שַׁבָּת. טוֹרַחַת כֹּל מִשִּׁשָּׁה לַשַּׁבָּת. יוֹשֶׁבֶת וּמַמְתֶּנֶת עַד כְּלוֹת שַׁבָּת. כָּבוֹד וָעֹנֶג קוֹרְאָה לַשַּׁבָּת. לְבוּשׁ וּכְסוּת מַחֲלֶפֶת בַּשַּׁבָּת. מַאֲכָל וּמִשְׁתֶּה מְכִינָה לַשַּׁבָּת. נֹעַם מְגָדִים מְנַעֶמֶת לַשַּׁבָּת.

סְעוּדוֹת שָׁלֹשׁ מְקַיֶּמֶת בַּשַּׁבָּת. עַל שְׁתֵּי כִכָּרוֹת בּוֹצַעַת בַּשַּׁבָּת. פּוֹרֶטֶת אַרְבַּע רְשֻׁיּוֹת בַּשַּׁבָּת. צִוּוּי הַדְלָקַת נֵר מַדְלֶקֶת בַּשַּׁבָּת. קִדּוּשׁ הַיּוֹם מְקַדֶּשֶׁת בַּשַּׁבָּת. רֶנֶן שֶׁבַע מְפַלֶּלֶת בַּשַּׁבָּת. שִׁבְעָה בַדָּת קוֹרְאָה בַּשַּׁבָּת. תַּנְחִילֶנָּה לְיוֹם שֶׁכֻּלּוֹ שַׁבָּת. הוֹשַׁע נָא.

אֲנִי וָהוּ הוֹשִׁיעָה נָּא.

כְּהוֹשַׁעְתָּ אָדָם יְצִיר כַּפֶּיךָ לְגוֹנְנָה,
בְּשַׁבַּת קֹדֶשׁ הִמְצֵאתוֹ כֹּפֶר וַחֲנִינָה, כֵּן הוֹשַׁע נָא.
כְּהוֹשַׁעְתָּ גּוֹי מְצֻיָּן מְקַוִּים חֹפֶשׁ,
דֵּעָה כִּוְּנוּ לָבוֹר שְׁבִיעִי לְנֹפֶשׁ, כֵּן הוֹשַׁע נָא.
כְּהוֹשַׁעְתָּ הָעָם נִהַגְתָּ כַּצֹּאן לְהַנְחוֹת,
וְחֹק שַׂמְתָּ בְּמָרָה עַל מֵי מְנוּחוֹת, כֵּן הוֹשַׁע נָא.
כְּהוֹשַׁעְתָּ זְבוּדֶיךָ בְּמִדְבַּר סִין בְּמַחֲנֶה,
חָכְמוּ וְלָקְטוּ בַּשִּׁשִּׁי לֶחֶם מִשְׁנֶה, כֵּן הוֹשַׁע נָא.
כְּהוֹשַׁעְתָּ טְפוּלֶיךָ הוֹרוּ הֲכָנָה בְּמַדָּעַם,
יִשַּׁר כֹּחָם וְהוֹדָה לָמוֹ רוֹעָם, כֵּן הוֹשַׁע נָא.
כְּהוֹשַׁעְתָּ כֻּלְכְּלוּ בְּעֹנֶג מָן הַמִּשְׁמָר,
לֹא הָפַךְ עֵינוֹ וְרֵיחוֹ לֹא נָמָר, כֵּן הוֹשַׁע נָא.
כְּהוֹשַׁעְתָּ מִשְׁפְּטֵי מַשְׂאוֹת שַׁבָּת גָּמֳרוּ,
נָחוּ וְשָׁבְתוּ רְשֻׁיּוֹת וּתְחוּמִים שָׁמָרוּ, כֵּן הוֹשַׁע נָא.
כְּהוֹשַׁעְתָּ סִינַי הָשְׁמְעוּ בְּדִבּוּר רְבִיעִי,
עִנְיַן זָכוֹר וְשָׁמוֹר לְקַדֵּשׁ שְׁבִיעִי, כֵּן הוֹשַׁע נָא.
כְּהוֹשַׁעְתָּ פְּקֻדוּ יְרִיחוֹ שֶׁבַע לְהַקֵּף,
צָרוּ עַד רִדְתָּהּ בַּשַּׁבָּת לְתַקֵּף, כֵּן הוֹשַׁע נָא.

כְּהוֹשַׁעְתָּ קְהֶלֶת וְעַמּוֹ בְּבֵית עוֹלָמִים,
רְצוּפְךָ בְּחָגְגָם שִׁבְעָה וּשְׁבְעָה יָמִים, כֵּן הוֹשַׁע נָא.
כְּהוֹשַׁעְתָּ שָׁבִים עוֹלֵי גוֹלָה לְפִדְיוֹם,
תּוֹרָתְךָ בְּקָרְאָם בֶּחָג יוֹם יוֹם, כֵּן הוֹשַׁע נָא.
כְּהוֹשַׁעְתָּ מְשַׂמְּחֶיךָ בְּבִנְיַן שֵׁנִי הַמְחֻדָּשׁ,
נוֹטְלִין לוּלָב כָּל שִׁבְעָה בַּמִּקְדָּשׁ, כֵּן הוֹשַׁע נָא.
כְּהוֹשַׁעְתָּ חִבּוּט עֲרָבָה שַׁבָּת מַדְחִים,
מֻרְבִּיּוֹת מוֹצָא לִיסוֹד מִזְבֵּחַ מַנִּיחִים, כֵּן הוֹשַׁע נָא.
כְּהוֹשַׁעְתָּ בְּרַכּוֹת וַאֲרוּכוֹת וּגְבוֹהוֹת מְעַלְּסִים,
בִּפְטִירָתָן יֹפִי לְךָ מִזְבֵּחַ מְקַלְּסִים, כֵּן הוֹשַׁע נָא.
כְּהוֹשַׁעְתָּ מוֹדִים וּמְיַחֲלִים וְלֹא מְשַׁנִּים,
כֻּלָּנוּ אָנוּ לְיָהּ וְעֵינֵינוּ לְיָהּ שׁוֹנִים, כֵּן הוֹשַׁע נָא.
כְּהוֹשַׁעְתָּ יֶקֶב מַחְצָבֶיךָ סוֹבְבִים בְּרַעֲנָנָה,
רוֹנְנִים אֲנִי וָהוּ הוֹשִׁיעָה נָּא, כֵּן הוֹשַׁע נָא.
כְּהוֹשַׁעְתָּ חֵיל זְרִיזִים מְשָׁרְתִים בִּמְנוּחָה,
קָרְבַּן שַׁבָּת כָּפוּל עוֹלָה וּמִנְחָה, כֵּן הוֹשַׁע נָא.
כְּהוֹשַׁעְתָּ לְוִיֶּיךָ עַל דּוּכָנָם לְהַרְבָּת,
אוֹמְרִים מִזְמוֹר שִׁיר לְיוֹם הַשַּׁבָּת, כֵּן הוֹשַׁע נָא.
כְּהוֹשַׁעְתָּ נְחוּמֶיךָ בְּמִצְוֹתֶיךָ תָּמִיד יִשְׁתַּעְשְׁעוּן,
וּרְצֵם וְהַחֲלִיצֵם בְּשׁוּבָה וָנַחַת יִוָּשֵׁעוּן, כֵּן הוֹשַׁע נָא.
כְּהוֹשַׁעְתָּ שְׁבוּת שִׁבְטֵי יַעֲקֹב,
תָּשׁוּב וְתָשִׁיב שְׁבוּת אָהֳלֵי יַעֲקֹב, וְהוֹשִׁיעָה נָּא.
כְּהוֹשַׁעְתָּ שׁוֹמְרֵי מִצְוֹת,
וְחוֹכֵי יְשׁוּעוֹת אֵל לְמוֹשָׁעוֹת, וְהוֹשִׁיעָה נָּא.

אֲנִי וָהוּ הוֹשִׁיעָה נָּא.

הוֹשִֽׁיעָה אֶת עַמֶּךָ, וּבָרֵךְ אֶת נַחֲלָתֶךָ, וּרְעֵם וְנַשְּׂאֵם עַד הָעוֹלָם. וְיִהְיוּ דְבָרַי אֵלֶּה אֲשֶׁר הִתְחַנַּנְתִּי לִפְנֵי יהוה, קְרֹבִים אֶל יהוה אֱלֹהֵינוּ יוֹמָם וָלָֽיְלָה, לַעֲשׂוֹת מִשְׁפַּט עַבְדּוֹ וּמִשְׁפַּט עַמּוֹ יִשְׂרָאֵל, דְּבַר יוֹם בְּיוֹמוֹ. לְמַֽעַן דַּֽעַת כָּל עַמֵּי הָאָֽרֶץ, כִּי יהוה הוּא הָאֱלֹהִים, אֵין עוֹד.

The Ark is closed and the Leader continues the Service with קַדִּישׁ תִּתְקַבַּל on page 448.

הושענות להושענא רבה

It is the custom to leave the Ark open until the end of הוֹשַׁעְנוֹת.

Seven סִפְרֵי תּוֹרָה are held on the בִּימָה. Members of the Congregation who have a לוּלָב and אֶתְרוֹג circle the בִּימָה seven times whilst הוֹשַׁעְנוֹת are read. After they have finished walking around the בִּימָה once, they say כִּי אָמַֽרְתִּי and immediately proceed to make another circuit, saying אֶֽבֶן שְׁתִיָּה, etc. One סֵֽפֶר תּוֹרָה is returned to the Ark after each of the first six circuits, following which אֲנִי וָהוֹ is said on on page 719.

Leader then Congregation:

הוֹשַׁע נָא, לְמַֽעַנְךָ אֱלֹהֵֽינוּ, הוֹשַֽׁע נָא.

Leader then Congregation:

הוֹשַׁע נָא, לְמַֽעַנְךָ בּוֹרְאֵֽנוּ, הוֹשַֽׁע נָא.

Leader then Congregation:

הוֹשַׁע נָא, לְמַֽעַנְךָ גּוֹאֲלֵֽנוּ, הוֹשַֽׁע נָא.

Leader then Congregation:

הוֹשַׁע נָא, לְמַֽעַנְךָ דּוֹרְשֵֽׁנוּ, הוֹשַֽׁע נָא.

הוֹשַֽׁע נָא.

לְמַֽעַן אֲמִתָּךְ. לְמַֽעַן בְּרִיתָךְ. לְמַֽעַן גָּדְלָךְ וְתִפְאַרְתָּךְ. לְמַֽעַן דָּתָךְ. לְמַֽעַן הוֹדָךְ. לְמַֽעַן וִעוּדָךְ. לְמַֽעַן זִכְרָךְ. לְמַֽעַן חַסְדָּךְ. לְמַֽעַן טוּבָךְ. לְמַֽעַן יִחוּדָךְ. לְמַֽעַן כְּבוֹדָךְ. לְמַֽעַן לִמּוּדָךְ. לְמַֽעַן מַלְכוּתָךְ. לְמַֽעַן נִצְחָךְ. לְמַֽעַן סוֹדָךְ. לְמַֽעַן עֻזָּךְ.

לְמַעַן פְּאֵרָךְ. לְמַעַן צִדְקָתָךְ. לְמַעַן קְדֻשָּׁתָךְ. לְמַעַן רַחֲמֶיךָ הָרַבִּים. לְמַעַן שְׁכִינָתָךְ. לְמַעַן תְּהִלָּתָךְ. הוֹשַׁע נָא.

After circling the בִּימָה the 1st time, say:

כִּי אָמַרְתִּי עוֹלָם חֶסֶד יִבָּנֶה.

One סֵפֶר תּוֹרָה is returned to the Ark.

הוֹשַׁע נָא.

אֶבֶן שְׁתִיָּה. בֵּית הַבְּחִירָה. גֹּרֶן אָרְנָן. דְּבִיר הַמֻּצְנָע. הַר הַמּוֹרִיָּה. וְהַר יֵרָאֶה. זְבוּל תִּפְאַרְתֶּךָ. חָנָה דָוִד. טוֹב הַלְּבָנוֹן. יְפֵה נוֹף מְשׂוֹשׂ כָּל הָאָרֶץ. כְּלִילַת יֹפִי. לִינַת הַצֶּדֶק. מָכוֹן לְשִׁבְתֶּךָ. נָוֶה שַׁאֲנָן. סֻכַּת שָׁלֵם. עֲלִיַּת שְׁבָטִים. פִּנַּת יִקְרַת. צִיּוֹן הַמְצֻיֶּנֶת. קֹדֶשׁ הַקֳּדָשִׁים. רָצוּף אַהֲבָה. שְׁכִינַת כְּבוֹדֶךָ. תֵּל תַּלְפִּיּוֹת. הוֹשַׁע נָא.

After circling the בִּימָה the 2nd time, say:

לְךָ זְרוֹעַ עִם גְּבוּרָה, תָּעֹז יָדְךָ תָּרוּם יְמִינֶךָ.

One סֵפֶר תּוֹרָה is returned to the Ark.

הוֹשַׁע נָא.

אוֹם אֲנִי חוֹמָה. בָּרָה כַּחַמָּה. גּוֹלָה וְסוּרָה. דָּמְתָה לְתָמָר. הַהֲרוּגָה עָלֶיךָ. וְנֶחְשֶׁבֶת כְּצֹאן טִבְחָה. זְרוּיָה בֵּין מַכְעִיסֶיהָ. חֲבוּקָה וּדְבוּקָה בָּךְ. טוֹעֶנֶת עֻלָּךְ. יְחִידָה לְיַחֲדָךְ. כְּבוּשָׁה בַּגּוֹלָה. לוֹמֶדֶת יִרְאָתָךְ. מְרוּטַת לֶחִי. נְתוּנָה לְמַכִּים. סוֹבֶלֶת סִבְלָךְ. עֲנִיָּה סֹעֲרָה. פְּדוּיַת טוֹבִיָּה. צֹאן קָדָשִׁים. קְהִלּוֹת יַעֲקֹב. רְשׁוּמִים בִּשְׁמֶךָ. שׁוֹאֲגִים הוֹשַׁע נָא. תְּמוּכִים עָלֶיךָ. הוֹשַׁע נָא.

After circling the בִּימָה the 3rd time, say:

תִּתֵּן אֱמֶת לְיַעֲקֹב, חֶסֶד לְאַבְרָהָם.

One סֵפֶר תּוֹרָה is returned to the Ark.

הוֹשַׁע נָא.

אָדוֹן הַמּוֹשִׁיעַ. בִּלְתְּךָ אֵין לְהוֹשִׁיעַ. גִּבּוֹר וְרַב לְהוֹשִׁיעַ. דַּלּוֹתִי וְלִי יְהוֹשִׁיעַ. הָאֵל הַמּוֹשִׁיעַ. וּמַצִּיל וּמוֹשִׁיעַ. זוֹעֲקֶיךָ תּוֹשִׁיעַ. חוֹכֶיךָ הוֹשִׁיעַ. טְלָאֶיךָ תַּשְׂבִּיעַ. יְבוּל לְהַשְׁפִּיעַ. כָּל שִׂיחַ תַּדְשֵׁא וְתוֹשִׁיעַ. לְגֵיא בַּל תַּרְשִׁיעַ. מְגָדִים תַּמְתִּיק וְתוֹשִׁיעַ. נְשִׂיאִים לְהַסִּיעַ. שְׂעִירִים לְהָנִיעַ. עֲנָנִים מִלְּהַמְנִיעַ. פּוֹתֵחַ יָד וּמַשְׂבִּיעַ. צְמֵאֶיךָ תַּשְׂבִּיעַ. קוֹרְאֶיךָ תּוֹשִׁיעַ. רְחוּמֶיךָ תּוֹשִׁיעַ. שׁוֹחֲרֶיךָ הוֹשִׁיעַ. תְּמִימֶיךָ תּוֹשִׁיעַ. הוֹשַׁע נָא.

After circling the בִּימָה the 4th time, say:

נְעִמוֹת בִּימִינְךָ נֶצַח.

One סֵפֶר תּוֹרָה is returned to the Ark.

הוֹשַׁע נָא.

אָדָם וּבְהֵמָה. בָּשָׂר וְרוּחַ וּנְשָׁמָה. גִּיד וְעֶצֶם וְקָרְמָה. דְּמוּת וְצֶלֶם וְרִקְמָה. הוֹד לַהֶבֶל דָּמָה. וְנִמְשַׁל כַּבְּהֵמוֹת נִדְמָה. זִיו וְתֹאַר וְקוֹמָה. חִדּוּשׁ פְּנֵי אֲדָמָה. טִיעַת עֲצֵי נְשַׁמָּה. יְקָבִים וְקָמָה. כְּרָמִים וְשִׁקְמָה. לְתֵבֵל הַמְסֻיָּמָה. מִטְרוֹת עֹז לְסַמְּמָה. נְשִׁיָּה לְקַיְּמָה. שִׂיחִים לְקוֹמְמָה. עֲדָנִים לְעָצְמָה. פְּרָחִים לְהַעֲצִימָה. צְמָחִים לְגָשְׁמָה. קָרִים לְזָרְמָה. רְבִיבִים לְשַׁלְּמָה. שְׁתִיָּה לְרוֹמְמָה. תְּלוּיָה עַל בְּלִימָה. הוֹשַׁע נָא.

After circling the בִּימָה the 5th time, say:

יהוה אֲדֹנֵינוּ מָה אַדִּיר שִׁמְךָ בְּכָל־הָאָרֶץ,
אֲשֶׁר תְּנָה הוֹדְךָ עַל הַשָּׁמָיִם.

One סֵפֶר תּוֹרָה is returned to the Ark.

הוֹשַׁע נָא.

אֲדָמָה מֵאֶרֶר. בְּהֵמָה מִמְּשַׁכֶּלֶת. גֹּרֶן מִגָּזָם. דָּגָן מִדַּלֶּקֶת. הוֹן מִמְּאֵרָה. וְאֹכֶל מִמְּהוּמָה. זַיִת מִנֶּשֶׁל. חִטָּה מֵחָגָב. טֶרֶף מִגּוֹבַי. יֶקֶב מִיֶּלֶק. כֶּרֶם מִתּוֹלַעַת. לֶקֶשׁ מֵאַרְבֶּה. מֶגֶד מִצְּלָצַל. נֶפֶשׁ מִבֶּהָלָה. שֹׂבַע מִסָּלְעָם. עֲדָרִים מִדַּלּוּת. פֵּרוֹת מִשִּׁדָּפוֹן. צֹאן מִצְּמִיתוּת. קָצִיר מִקְּלָלָה. רֹב מֵרָזוֹן. שִׁבֹּלֶת מִצִּנָּמוֹן. תְּבוּאָה מֵחָסִיל. הוֹשַׁע נָא.

After circling the בִּימָה the 6th time, say:

צַדִּיק יהוה בְּכָל־דְּרָכָיו, וְחָסִיד בְּכָל־מַעֲשָׂיו.

One סֵפֶר תּוֹרָה is returned to the Ark.

הוֹשַׁע נָא.

לְמַעַן אֵיתָן הַנִּזְרָק בְּלַהַב אֵשׁ.
לְמַעַן בֵּן הַנֶּעֱקַד עַל עֵצִים וָאֵשׁ.
לְמַעַן גִּבּוֹר הַנֶּאֱבַק עִם שַׂר אֵשׁ.
לְמַעַן דְּגָלִים נָחִיתָ בֶּעָנָן וְאוֹר אֵשׁ.
לְמַעַן הָעֲלָה לַמָּרוֹם וְנִתְעַלָּה כְּמַלְאֲכֵי אֵשׁ.
לְמַעַן וְהוּא לָךְ כְּסֶגֶן בְּאֶרְאֶלֵּי אֵשׁ.
לְמַעַן זֶבֶד דִּבְּרוֹת הַנְּתוּנוֹת מֵאֵשׁ.
לְמַעַן חִפּוּי יְרִיעוֹת וַעֲנַן אֵשׁ.
לְמַעַן טֶכֶס הַר יָרַדְתָּ עָלָיו בָּאֵשׁ.
לְמַעַן יְדִידוּת בַּיִת אֲשֶׁר אָהַבְתָּ מִשְּׁמֵי אֵשׁ.
לְמַעַן כָּמַהּ עַד שָׁקְעָה הָאֵשׁ.
לְמַעַן לָקַח מַחְתַּת אֵשׁ וְהֵסִיר חֲרוֹן אֵשׁ.
לְמַעַן מְקַנֵּא קִנְאָה גְדוֹלָה בָּאֵשׁ.
לְמַעַן נָף יָדוֹ וְיָרְדוּ אַבְנֵי אֵשׁ.
לְמַעַן שָׂם טְלֵה חָלָב כְּלִיל אֵשׁ.

לְמַעַן עָמַד בַּגֹּרֶן וְנִתְרַצָּה בָאֵשׁ.
לְמַעַן פִּלֵּל בָּעֲזָרָה וְיָרְדָה הָאֵשׁ.
לְמַעַן צִיר עָלָה וְנִתְעַלָּה בְּרֶכֶב וְסוּסֵי אֵשׁ.
לְמַעַן קְדוֹשִׁים מֻשְׁלָכִים בָּאֵשׁ.
לְמַעַן רִבּוֹ רִבְבָן חָז וְנַהֲרֵי אֵשׁ.
לְמַעַן שִׁמְמוֹת עִירְךָ הַשְּׂרוּפָה בָאֵשׁ.
לְמַעַן תּוֹלְדוֹת אַלּוּפֵי יְהוּדָה תָּשִׂים כְּכִיּוֹר אֵשׁ.

הוֹשַׁע נָא.

After circling the בִּימָה the 7th time, say:

לְךָ יהוה הַגְּדֻלָּה וְהַגְּבוּרָה וְהַתִּפְאֶרֶת וְהַנֵּצַח וְהַהוֹד כִּי כֹל בַּשָּׁמַיִם וּבָאָרֶץ, לְךָ יהוה הַמַּמְלָכָה וְהַמִּתְנַשֵּׂא לְכֹל לְרֹאשׁ. וְהָיָה יהוה לְמֶלֶךְ עַל־כָּל־הָאָרֶץ, בַּיּוֹם הַהוּא יִהְיֶה יהוה אֶחָד וּשְׁמוֹ אֶחָד. וּבְתוֹרָתְךָ כָּתוּב לֵאמֹר, שְׁמַע יִשְׂרָאֵל יהוה אֱלֹהֵינוּ יהוה אֶחָד. בָּרוּךְ שֵׁם כְּבוֹד מַלְכוּתוֹ לְעוֹלָם וָעֶד.

אֲנִי וָהוּ הוֹשִׁיעָה נָּא.

כְּהוֹשַׁעְתָּ אֵלִים בְּלוּד עִמָּךְ,
בְּצֵאתְךָ לְיֵשַׁע עַמָּךְ, כֵּן הוֹשַׁע נָא.
כְּהוֹשַׁעְתָּ גּוֹי וֵאלֹהִים,
דְּרוּשִׁים לְיֵשַׁע אֱלֹהִים, כֵּן הוֹשַׁע נָא.
כְּהוֹשַׁעְתָּ הֲמוֹן צְבָאוֹת,
וְעִמָּם מַלְאֲכֵי צְבָאוֹת, כֵּן הוֹשַׁע נָא.
כְּהוֹשַׁעְתָּ זַכִּים מִבֵּית עֲבָדִים,
חַנּוּן בְּיָדָם מַעֲבִידִים, כֵּן הוֹשַׁע נָא.
כְּהוֹשַׁעְתָּ טְבוּעִים בְּצוּל גְּזָרִים,
יְקָרְךָ עִמָּם מַעֲבִירִים כֵּן הוֹשַׁע נָא.

כְּהוֹשַֽׁעְתָּ כַּנָּה מְשׁוֹרֶֽרֶת וַיִּֽוָּשַׁע,
לְגוֹחָה מְצֻיֶּֽנֶת וַיִּוָּֽשַׁע, כֵּן הוֹשַׁע נָא.
כְּהוֹשַֽׁעְתָּ מַאֲמַר וְהוֹצֵאתִי אֶתְכֶם,
נָקוּב וְהוּצֵאתִי אִתְּכֶם, כֵּן הוֹשַׁע נָא.
כְּהוֹשַֽׁעְתָּ סוֹבְבֵי מִזְבֵּֽחַ,
עוֹמְסֵי עֲרָבָה לְהַקִּיף מִזְבֵּֽחַ, כֵּן הוֹשַׁע נָא.
כְּהוֹשַֽׁעְתָּ פִּלְאֵי אָרוֹן כְּהֻפְשַׁע,
צִעֵר פְּלֶֽשֶׁת בַּחֲרוֹן אַף וְנוֹשַׁע, כֵּן הוֹשַׁע נָא.
כְּהוֹשַֽׁעְתָּ קְהִלּוֹת בָּבֶֽלָה שִׁלַּֽחְתָּ,
רַחוּם לְמַֽעֲנָם שֻׁלַּֽחְתָּ, כֵּן הוֹשַׁע נָא.
כְּהוֹשַֽׁעְתָּ שְׁבוּת שִׁבְטֵי יַעֲקֹב,
תָּשׁוּב וְתָשִׁיב שְׁבוּת אָהֳלֵי יַעֲקֹב, וְהוֹשִֽׁיעָה נָּא.
כְּהוֹשַֽׁעְתָּ שׁוֹמְרֵי מִצְוֹת, וְחוֹכֵי יְשׁוּעוֹת,
אֵל לְמוֹשָׁעוֹת, וְהוֹשִֽׁיעָה נָּא.

אֲנִי וָהוֹ הוֹשִֽׁיעָה נָּא.

תִּתְּנֵֽנוּ לְשֵׁם וְלִתְהִלָּה. תְּשִׁיבֵֽנוּ אֶל הַחֶֽבֶל וְאֶל הַנַּחֲלָה. תְּרוֹמְמֵֽנוּ לְמַֽעְלָה לְמַֽעְלָה. תְּקַבְּצֵֽנוּ לְבֵית הַתְּפִלָּה. תַּצִּיבֵֽנוּ כְּעֵץ עַל פַּלְגֵי מַֽיִם שְׁתוּלָה. תִּפְדֵּֽנוּ מִכָּל־נֶֽגַע וּמַחֲלָה. תְּעַטְּרֵֽנוּ בְּאַהֲבָה כְלוּלָה. תְּשַׂמְּחֵֽנוּ בְּבֵית הַתְּפִלָּה. תְּנַהֲלֵֽנוּ עַל מֵי מְנוּחוֹת סֶֽלָה. תְּמַלְּאֵֽנוּ חָכְמָה וְשִׂכְלָה. תַּלְבִּישֵֽׁנוּ עֹז וּגְדֻלָּה. תַּכְתִּירֵֽנוּ בְּכֶֽתֶר כְּלוּלָה. תְּיַשְּׁרֵֽנוּ בְּאֹֽרַח סְלוּלָה. תִּטָּעֵֽנוּ בְּיֹֽשֶׁר מְסִלָּה. תְּחָנֵּֽנוּ בְּרַחֲמִים וּבְחֶמְלָה. תַּזְכִּירֵֽנוּ בְּמִי זֹאת עוֹלָה. תּוֹשִׁיעֵֽנוּ לְקֵץ הַגְּאֻלָּה. תְּהַדְּרֵֽנוּ בְּזִיו הֲמֻלָּה. תַּדְבִּיקֵֽנוּ כְּאֵזוֹר חֲתוּלָה. תְּגַדְּלֵֽנוּ בְּיָד הַגְּדוֹלָה. תְּבִיאֵֽנוּ לְבֵיתְךָ בְּרִנָּה וְצָהֳלָה. תְּאַדְּרֵֽנוּ בְּיֶֽשַׁע וְגִילָה. תְּאַמְּצֵֽנוּ בְּרֽוּחַ וְהַצָּלָה. תְּלַבְּבֵֽנוּ בְּבִנְיַן עִירְךָ כְּבַתְּחִלָּה. תְּעוֹרְרֵֽנוּ לְצִיּוֹן

בְּשִׁכְלוּלָהּ. תְּזַכֵּנוּ בְּנִבְנְתָה הָעִיר עַל תִּלָּהּ. תַּרְבִּיצֵנוּ בְּשָׂשׂוֹן וְגִילָה. תְּחַזְּקֵנוּ אֱלֹהֵי יַעֲקֹב סֶלָה. הוֹשַׁע נָא.

Leader then Congregation:

אָנָּא הוֹשִׁיעָה נָּא.

אָנָּא אֱזוֹן חִין תְּאֵבֵי יִשְׁעָךְ,
בְּעַרְבֵי נַחַל לְשַׁעְשְׁעָךְ, וְהוֹשִׁיעָה נָּא.
אָנָּא גְּאַל כַּנַּת נִטְעָךְ,
דּוּמָה בְּטַאטְאָךְ, וְהוֹשִׁיעָה נָּא.
אָנָּא הַבֵּט לַבְּרִית טִבְעָךְ,
וּמַחֲשַׁכֵּי אֶרֶץ בְּהַטְבִּיעָךְ, וְהוֹשִׁיעָה נָּא.
אָנָּא זְכָר לָנוּ אָב יִדְעָךְ,
חַסְדְּךָ לָמוֹ בְּהוֹדִיעָךְ, וְהוֹשִׁיעָה נָּא.
אָנָּא טְהוֹרֵי לֵב בְּהַפְלִיאָךְ,
יִוָּדַע כִּי הוּא פִלְאָךְ, וְהוֹשִׁיעָה נָּא.
אָנָּא כַּבִּיר כֹּחַ תֶּן לָנוּ יִשְׁעָךְ,
לַאֲבוֹתֵינוּ כְּהִשָּׁבְעָךְ, וְהוֹשִׁיעָה נָּא.
אָנָּא מַלֵּא מִשְׁאֲלוֹת עַם מְשַׁוְּעָךְ,
נֶעֱקַד בְּהַר מוֹר כְּמוֹ שִׁוְּעָךְ, וְהוֹשִׁיעָה נָּא.
אָנָּא סַגֵּב אֶשְׁלֵי נִטְעָךְ,
עֲרִיצִים בַּהֲנִיעָךְ, וְהוֹשִׁיעָה נָּא.
אָנָּא פְּתַח לָנוּ אוֹצְרוֹת רִבְעָךְ,
צִיָּה מֵהֶם בְּהַרְבִּיעָךְ, וְהוֹשִׁיעָה נָּא.
אָנָּא קוֹרְאֶיךָ אֶרֶץ בְּרוֹעֲעָךְ,
רְעֵם בְּטוּב מִרְעָךְ, וְהוֹשִׁיעָה נָּא.
אָנָּא שְׁעָרֶיךָ תַּעַל מִמְּשׁוֹאָךְ,
תֵּל תַּלְפִּיּוֹת בְּהַשִּׂיאָךְ, וְהוֹשִׁיעָה נָּא.

Leader then Congregation:

אָנָּא אֵל נָא, הוֹשַׁע נָא וְהוֹשִׁיעָה נָּא.

אֵל נָא תָּעִינוּ כְּשֶׂה אוֹבֵד,
שְׁמֵנוּ מִסִּפְרְךָ אַל תְּאַבֵּד, הוֹשַׁע נָא וְהוֹשִׁיעָה נָּא.
אֵל נָא רְעֵה אֶת־צֹאן הַהֲרֵגָה,
קְצוּפָה וְעָלֶיךָ הֲרוּגָה, הוֹשַׁע נָא וְהוֹשִׁיעָה נָּא.
אֵל נָא צֹאנְךָ וְצֹאן מַרְעִיתֶךָ,
פְּעֻלָּתְךָ וְרַעְיָתֶךָ, הוֹשַׁע נָא וְהוֹשִׁיעָה נָּא.
אֵל נָא עֲנִיֵּי הַצֹּאן,
שִׂיחָם עֲנֵה בְּעֵת רָצוֹן, הוֹשַׁע נָא וְהוֹשִׁיעָה נָּא.
אֵל נָא נוֹשְׂאֵי לְךָ עַיִן,
מִתְקוֹמְמֶיךָ יִהְיוּ כְּאַיִן, הוֹשַׁע נָא וְהוֹשִׁיעָה נָּא.
אֵל נָא לִמְנַסְּכֵי לְךָ מַיִם,
כְּמִמַּעַיְנֵי הַיְשׁוּעָה יִשְׁאֲבוּן מַיִם,
הוֹשַׁע נָא וְהוֹשִׁיעָה נָּא.
אֵל נָא יַעֲלוּ לְצִיּוֹן מוֹשִׁיעִים,
טְפוּלִים בְּךָ וּבְשִׁמְךָ נוֹשָׁעִים,
הוֹשַׁע נָא וְהוֹשִׁיעָה נָּא.
אֵל נָא חֲמוּץ בְּגָדִים,
זְעוֹם לְנַעֵר כָּל־בּוֹגְדִים, הוֹשַׁע נָא וְהוֹשִׁיעָה נָּא.
אֵל נָא וְזָכוֹר תִּזְכּוֹר,
הַנְּכוּרִים בְּלֶתֶךָ וָכוֹר, הוֹשַׁע נָא וְהוֹשִׁיעָה נָּא.
אֵל נָא דּוֹרְשֶׁיךָ בְּעַנְפֵי עֲרָבוֹת,
גַּעְיָם שְׁעֵה מֵעֲרָבוֹת, הוֹשַׁע נָא וְהוֹשִׁיעָה נָּא.
אֵל נָא בָּרֵךְ בְּעִטּוּר שָׁנָה,
אֲמָרֵי רְצֵה בְּפִלּוּלֵי בְּיוֹם הוֹשַׁע נָא,
הוֹשַׁע נָא וְהוֹשִׁיעָה נָּא.

Leader then Congregation:

אָנָּא אֵל נָא, הוֹשַׁע נָא וְהוֹשִׁיעָה נָּא, אָבִינוּ אָתָּה.

לְמַעַן תָּמִים בְּדוֹרוֹתָיו, הַנִּמְלָט בְּרוֹב צִדְקוֹתָיו,
מֻצָּל מִשֶּׁטֶף בְּבֹא מַבּוּל מַיִם. לְאוֹם אֲנִי חוֹמָה,
הוֹשַׁע נָא וְהוֹשִׁיעָה נָּא, אָבִינוּ אָתָּה.
לְמַעַן שָׁלֵם בְּכָל־מַעֲשִׂים, הַמְנֻסֶּה בַּעֲשָׂרָה נִסִּים,
כְּשֶׁר מַלְאָכִים נָם יֻקַּח נָא מְעַט מַיִם. לְבָרָה כַּחַמָּה,
הוֹשַׁע נָא וְהוֹשִׁיעָה נָּא, אָבִינוּ אָתָּה.
לְמַעַן רַךְ וְיָחִיד נֶחֱנַט פְּרִי לְמֵאָה,
זָעַק אַיֵּה הַשֶּׂה לְעוֹלָה, בִּשְּׂרוּהוּ עֲבָדָיו מָצָאנוּ מַיִם.
לְגוֹלָה וְסוּרָה, הוֹשַׁע נָא וְהוֹשִׁיעָה נָּא, אָבִינוּ אָתָּה.
לְמַעַן קִדֵּם שְׂאֵת בְּרָכָה, הַנִּשְׂטָם וּלְשִׁמְךָ חִכָּה,
מְיַחֵם בְּמַקְלוֹת בְּשִׁקְתוֹת הַמַּיִם. לְדָמְתָה לְתָמָר,
הוֹשַׁע נָא וְהוֹשִׁיעָה נָּא, אָבִינוּ אָתָּה.
לְמַעַן צַדַּק הֱיוֹת לְךָ לְכֹהֵן, כֶּחָתָן פְּאֵר יְכַהֵן,
מְנֻסֶּה בְּמַסָּה בְּמֵי מְרִיבַת מַיִם. לְהָהָר הַטּוֹב,
הוֹשַׁע נָא וְהוֹשִׁיעָה נָּא, אָבִינוּ אָתָּה.
לְמַעַן פְּאַר הֱיוֹת גְּבִיר לְאֶחָיו, יְהוּדָה אֲשֶׁר גָּבַר בְּאֶחָיו,
מִסְפַּר רֹבַע מִדָּלְיָו יִזַּל מַיִם. לֹא לָנוּ כִּי אִם לְמַעַנְךָ,
הוֹשַׁע נָא וְהוֹשִׁיעָה נָּא, אָבִינוּ אָתָּה.
לְמַעַן עָנָו מִכֹּל וְנֶאֱמָן, אֲשֶׁר בְּצִדְקוֹ כִּלְכֵּל הַמָּן,
מָשׁוּךְ לְגוֹאֵל וּמָשׁוּי מִמַּיִם. לְזֹאת הַנִּשְׁקָפָה,
הוֹשַׁע נָא וְהוֹשִׁיעָה נָּא, אָבִינוּ אָתָּה.
לְמַעַן שַׂמְתּוֹ כְּמַלְאֲכֵי מְרוֹמִים, הַלּוֹבֵשׁ אוּרִים וְתֻמִּים,
מְצֻוֶּה לָבוֹא בַּמִּקְדָּשׁ בְּקִדּוּשׁ יָדַיִם
וְרַגְלַיִם וּרְחִיצַת מַיִם. לְחוֹלַת אַהֲבָה,
הוֹשַׁע נָא וְהוֹשִׁיעָה נָּא, אָבִינוּ אָתָּה.

לְמַעַן נְבִיאָה מְחוֹלַת מַחֲנַיִם, לְכִמְהֵי לֵב הוּשְׁמָה
עֵינַיִם, לְרַגְלָהּ רָצָה עֲלוֹת וָרֶדֶת בְּאֵר מַיִם. לְטוֹבוּ
אֹהָלָיו, הוֹשַׁע נָא וְהוֹשִׁיעָה נָּא, אָבִינוּ אָתָּה.
לְמַעַן מְשָׁרֵת לֹא מָשׁ מֵאֹהֶל, וְרוּחַ הַקֹּדֶשׁ עָלָיו אֹהֵל,
בְּעָבְרוֹ בַּיַּרְדֵּן נִכְרְתוּ הַמַּיִם. לְיָפָה וּבָרָה,
הוֹשַׁע נָא וְהוֹשִׁיעָה נָּא, אָבִינוּ אָתָּה.
לְמַעַן לָמַד רְאוֹת לְטוֹבָה אוֹת, זָעַק אַיֵּה נִפְלָאוֹת,
מִצָּה טַל מִגִּזָּה מְלֹא הַסֵּפֶל מַיִם. לְכַלַּת לְבָנוֹן,
הוֹשַׁע נָא וְהוֹשִׁיעָה נָּא, אָבִינוּ אָתָּה.
לְמַעַן כְּלוּלֵי עֲשׂוֹת מִלְחַמְתֶּךָ,
אֲשֶׁר בְּיָדָם תַּתָּה יְשׁוּעָתֶךָ,
צְרוּפֵי מִגּוֹי בְּלָקְקָם בְּיָדָם מַיִם.
לְלֹא בָגְדוּ בָךְ, הוֹשַׁע נָא וְהוֹשִׁיעָה נָּא, אָבִינוּ אָתָּה.
לְמַעַן יָחִיד צוֹרְרִים דָּשׁ, אֲשֶׁר מֵרֶחֶם לְנָזִיר הֻקְדָּשׁ,
מִמַּכְתֵּשׁ לֶחִי הִבְקַעְתָּ לוֹ מַיִם. לְמַעַן שֵׁם קָדְשֶׁךָ,
הוֹשַׁע נָא וְהוֹשִׁיעָה נָּא, אָבִינוּ אָתָּה.
לְמַעַן טוֹב הוֹלֵךְ וְגָדֵל, אֲשֶׁר מֵעֹשֶׁק עֵדָה חִדֵּל,
בְּשׁוּב עָם מֵחֵטְא צָו שְׁאָב מַיִם. לְנָאוָה כִּירוּשָׁלָיִם,
הוֹשַׁע נָא וְהוֹשִׁיעָה נָּא, אָבִינוּ אָתָּה.
לְמַעַן חַיָּךְ מְכַרְכֵּר בְּשִׁיר, הַמְלַמֵּד תּוֹרָה בְּכָל־כְּלֵי שִׁיר,
מְנַסֵּךְ לְפָנֶיךָ כְּתָאֵב שְׁתוֹת מַיִם. לְשָׂמוּ בְךָ סִבְרָם,
הוֹשַׁע נָא וְהוֹשִׁיעָה נָּא, אָבִינוּ אָתָּה.
לְמַעַן זָךְ עָלָה בִסְעָרָה, הַמְקַנֵּא וּמֵשִׁיב עֶבְרָה,
לְפִלּוּלוֹ יָרְדָה אֵשׁ וְלִחֲכָה עָפָר וּמַיִם. לְעֵינֶיהָ בְּרֵכוֹת,
הוֹשַׁע נָא וְהוֹשִׁיעָה נָּא, אָבִינוּ אָתָּה.
לְמַעַן וְשֵׁרֵת בֶּאֱמֶת לְרַבּוֹ, פִּי שְׁנַיִם בְּרוּחוֹ נֶאֱצַל בּוֹ,

בְּקַחְתּוֹ מְנַגֵּן נִתְמַלְּאוּ גֵּבִים מַיִם. לְפָצוּ מִי כָמְכָה,
הוֹשַׁע נָא וְהוֹשִׁיעָה נָּא, אָבִינוּ אָתָּה.
לְמַעַן הַרְהֵר עֲשׂוֹת רְצוֹנֶךָ, הַמַּכְרִיז תְּשׁוּבָה לְצֹאנֶךָ,
אָז בְּבוֹא מְחָרֵף סָתַם עֵינוֹת מַיִם. לְצִיּוֹן מִכְלַל יֹפִי,
הוֹשַׁע נָא וְהוֹשִׁיעָה נָּא, אָבִינוּ אָתָּה.
לְמַעַן דְּרָשְׁוּךָ בְּתוֹךְ הַגּוֹלָה, וְסוֹדְךָ לָמוֹ נִגְלָה,
בְּלִי לְהִתְגָּאֵל דָּרְשׁוּ זֵרְעוֹנִים וּמַיִם. לְקוֹרְאֶיךָ בַּצָּר,
הוֹשַׁע נָא וְהוֹשִׁיעָה נָּא, אָבִינוּ אָתָּה.
לְמַעַן גָּמַר חָכְמָה וּבִינָה, סוֹפֵר מָהִיר מְפַלֵּשׂ אֲמָנָה,
מַחְכְּמֵנוּ אֲמָרִים הַמְּשׁוּלִים בְּרַחֲבֵי מַיִם. לְרַבָּתִי עָם,
הוֹשַׁע נָא וְהוֹשִׁיעָה נָּא, אָבִינוּ אָתָּה.
לְמַעַן בָּאֵי לְךָ הַיּוֹם בְּכָל־לֵב,
שׁוֹפְכִים לְךָ שִׂיחַ בְּלֹא לֵב וָלֵב,
שׁוֹאֲלִים מִמְּךָ עוֹז מִטְרוֹת מַיִם.
לְשׁוֹרְרוּ בַיָּם, הוֹשַׁע נָא וְהוֹשִׁיעָה נָּא, אָבִינוּ אָתָּה.
לְמַעַן אוֹמְרֵי יִגְדַּל שְׁמֶךָ, וְהֵם נַחֲלָתְךָ וְעַמֶּךָ,
צְמֵאִים לְיֶשְׁעֲךָ, כְּאֶרֶץ עֲיֵפָה לַמַּיִם.
לְתָרְתָּ לָמוֹ מְנוּחָה,
הוֹשַׁע נָא וְהוֹשִׁיעָה נָּא, אָבִינוּ אָתָּה.

Leader then Congregation:

הוֹשַׁע נָא, אֵל נָא, אָנָּא הוֹשִׁיעָה נָּא.
הוֹשַׁע נָא, סְלַח נָא, וְהַצְלִיחָה נָא, וְהוֹשִׁיעֵנוּ אֵל מָעֻזֵּנוּ.

Put the לוּלָב and אֶתרוֹג down and pick up the הוֹשַׁעְנוֹת.

תַּעֲנֶה אֱמוּנִים שׁוֹפְכִים לְךָ
לֵב כַּמַּיִם, וְהוֹשִׁיעָה נָּא,
לְמַעַן בָּא בָאֵשׁ וּבַמַּיִם, וְהַצְלִיחָה נָא,

גָּזַר וְנָם יֻקַּח נָא מְעַט מַיִם, וְהוֹשִׁיעֵנוּ אֵל מָעֻזֵּנוּ.
תַּעֲנֶה דְגָלִים גָּזוּ גִזְרֵי מַיִם, וְהוֹשִׁיעָה נָּא,
לְמַעַן הַנֶּעֱקַד בְּשַׁעַר הַשָּׁמַיִם, וְהַצְלִיחָה נָא,
וְשָׁב וְחָפַר בְּאֵרוֹת מַיִם, וְהוֹשִׁיעֵנוּ אֵל מָעֻזֵּנוּ.
תַּעֲנֶה זַכִּים חוֹנִים עֲלֵי מַיִם, וְהוֹשִׁיעָה נָּא,
לְמַעַן חָלָק מְפַצֵּל מַקְלוֹת
בְּשִׁקְתוֹת הַמַּיִם, וְהַצְלִיחָה נָא,
טָעַן וְגָל אֶבֶן מִבְּאֵר מַיִם, וְהוֹשִׁיעֵנוּ אֵל מָעֻזֵּנוּ.
תַּעֲנֶה יְדִידִים נוֹחֲלֵי דָת
מְשׁוּלַת מַיִם, וְהוֹשִׁיעָה נָּא,
לְמַעַן כָּרוּ בְּמִשְׁעֲנוֹתָם מַיִם, וְהַצְלִיחָה נָא,
לְהָכִין לָמוֹ וּלְצֶאֱצָאֵימוֹ מַיִם, וְהוֹשִׁיעֵנוּ אֵל מָעֻזֵּנוּ.
תַּעֲנֶה מִתְחַנְּנִים כְּבִישִׁימוֹן
עֲלֵי מַיִם, וְהוֹשִׁיעָה נָּא,
לְמַעַן נֶאֱמַן בַּיִת מַסְפִּיק
לָעָם מַיִם, וְהַצְלִיחָה נָא,
סֶלַע הָךְ וַיָּזוּבוּ מַיִם, וְהוֹשִׁיעֵנוּ אֵל מָעֻזֵּנוּ.
תַּעֲנֶה עוֹנִים עֲלִי בְאֵר מַיִם, וְהוֹשִׁיעָה נָּא,
לְמַעַן פָּקַד בְּמֵי מְרִיבַת מַיִם, וְהַצְלִיחָה נָא,
צְמֵאִים לְהַשְׁקוֹת מַיִם, וְהוֹשִׁיעֵנוּ אֵל מָעֻזֵּנוּ.
תַּעֲנֶה קְדוֹשִׁים מְנַסְּכִים לְךָ מַיִם, וְהוֹשִׁיעָה נָּא,
לְמַעַן רֹאשׁ מְשׁוֹרְרִים כְּתָאַב
שְׁתוֹת מַיִם, וְהַצְלִיחָה נָא,
שָׁב וְנָסַךְ לְךָ מַיִם, וְהוֹשִׁיעֵנוּ אֵל מָעֻזֵּנוּ.
תַּעֲנֶה שׁוֹאֲלִים בְּרִבּוּעַ אֶשְׁלֵי מַיִם, וְהוֹשִׁיעָה נָּא,
לְמַעַן תֵּל תַּלְפִּיּוֹת בֵּית מוֹצָא מַיִם, וְהַצְלִיחָה נָא,
תִּפְתַּח אֶרֶץ וְתַרְעִיף שָׁמַיִם, וְהוֹשִׁיעֵנוּ אֵל מָעֻזֵּנוּ.

Leader then Congregation:

רַחֶם נָא קְהַל עֲדַת יְשׁוּרוּן, סְלַח וּמְחַל עֲוֹנָם,
וְהוֹשִׁיעֵנוּ אֱלֹהֵי יִשְׁעֵנוּ.

אָז כְּעֵינֵי עֲבָדִים אֶל יַד אֲדוֹנִים, בָּאנוּ לְפָנֶיךָ נְדוֹנִים,
וְהוֹשִׁיעֵנוּ אֱלֹהֵי יִשְׁעֵנוּ.
גֵּאֶה אֲדוֹנֵי הָאֲדוֹנִים, נִתְגָּרוּ בָנוּ מְדָנִים,
דָּשׁוּנוּ וּבְעָלוּנוּ זוּלָתְךָ אֲדוֹנִים,
וְהוֹשִׁיעֵנוּ אֱלֹהֵי יִשְׁעֵנוּ.
הֵן גַּשְׁנוּ הַיּוֹם בְּתַחֲנוּן, עָדֶיךָ רַחוּם וְחַנּוּן,
וְסִפַּרְנוּ נִפְלְאוֹתֶיךָ בְּשִׁנּוּן, וְהוֹשִׁיעֵנוּ אֱלֹהֵי יִשְׁעֵנוּ.
זָבַת חָלָב וּדְבָשׁ, נָא אַל תִּיבָשׁ,
חַשְׁרַת מַיִם כְּאֵבֶה תֶּחְבָּשׁ, וְהוֹשִׁיעֵנוּ אֱלֹהֵי יִשְׁעֵנוּ.
טְעֵנוּ בַּשְּׁמֵנָה, בְּיַד שִׁבְעָה וּשְׁמוֹנָה,
יָשָׁר צַדִּיק אֵל אֱמוּנָה, וְהוֹשִׁיעֵנוּ אֱלֹהֵי יִשְׁעֵנוּ.
כָּרַתָּ בְּרִית לָאָרֶץ, עוֹד כָּל־יְמֵי הָאָרֶץ,
לְבִלְתִּי פְּרָץ בָּהּ פֶּרֶץ, וְהוֹשִׁיעֵנוּ אֱלֹהֵי יִשְׁעֵנוּ.
מִתְחַנְּנִים עֲלֵי מַיִם, בַּעֲרָבִים עַל יִבְלֵי מַיִם, נָא זְכָר
לָמוֹ נִסּוּךְ הַמַּיִם, וְהוֹשִׁיעֵנוּ אֱלֹהֵי יִשְׁעֵנוּ.
שִׂיחִים בְּדֶרֶךְ מַטָּעָתָם,
עוֹמְסִים בְּשַׁוְעָתָם עֲנֵם בְּקוֹל פְּגִיעָתָם, וְהוֹשִׁיעֵנוּ
אֱלֹהֵי יִשְׁעֵנוּ.
פּוֹעֵל יְשׁוּעוֹת, פְּנֵה לְפִלּוּלָם שְׁעוֹת,
צַדְּקֵם אֵל לְמוֹשָׁעוֹת, וְהוֹשִׁיעֵנוּ אֱלֹהֵי יִשְׁעֵנוּ.
קוֹל רִגְשָׁם תְּשַׁע, תִּפְתַּח אֶרֶץ וְיִפְרוּ יֶשַׁע,
רַב לְהוֹשִׁיעַ וְלֹא חָפֵץ רֶשַׁע, וְהוֹשִׁיעֵנוּ אֱלֹהֵי יִשְׁעֵנוּ.

Leader then Congregation:

שַׁעֲרֵי שָׁמַיִם פְּתַח, וְאוֹצָרְךָ הַטּוֹב לָנוּ תִפְתַּח,
תּוֹשִׁיעֵנוּ וְרִיב אַל תִּמְתַּח, וְהוֹשִׁיעֵנוּ אֱלֹהֵי יִשְׁעֵנוּ.

Leader then Congregation:

קוֹל מְבַשֵּׂר מְבַשֵּׂר וְאוֹמֵר,

אֹמֶץ יֶשְׁעֲךָ בָּא, קוֹל דּוֹדִי הִנֵּה זֶה בָּא, מְבַשֵּׂר וְאוֹמֵר.
בָּא בְּרִבְבוֹת כִּתִּים, לַעֲמוֹד עַל הַר הַזֵּיתִים, מְבַשֵּׂר וְאוֹמֵר.
גִּשְׁתּוֹ בַּשּׁוֹפָר לִתְקַע, תַּחְתָּיו הַר יִבָּקַע, מְבַשֵּׂר וְאוֹמֵר.
דָּפַק וְהֵצִיץ וְזָרַח, וּמָשׁ חֲצִי הָהָר מִמִּזְרָח, מְבַשֵּׂר וְאוֹמֵר.
הֵקִים מִלּוּל נְאֻמוֹ, וּבָא הוּא וְכָל קְדוֹשָׁיו עִמּוֹ, מְבַשֵּׂר וְאוֹמֵר.
וּלְכָל־בָּאֵי הָעוֹלָם, בַּת־קוֹל יִשָּׁמַע בָּעוֹלָם, מְבַשֵּׂר וְאוֹמֵר.
זֶרַע עֲמוּסֵי רַחְמוֹ, נוֹלְדוּ כְּיֶלֶד מִמְּעֵי אִמּוֹ, מְבַשֵּׂר וְאוֹמֵר.
חָלָה וְיָלְדָה מִי זֹאת, מִי שָׁמַע כָּזֹאת, מְבַשֵּׂר וְאוֹמֵר.
טָהוֹר פָּעַל כָּל־אֵלֶּה, מִי רָאָה כָּאֵלֶּה, מְבַשֵּׂר וְאוֹמֵר.
יֶשַׁע וּזְמַן הוּחַד, הֲיוּחַל אֶרֶץ בְּיוֹם אֶחָד, מְבַשֵּׂר וְאוֹמֵר.
כַּבִּיר רוֹם וָתַחַת, אִם יִוָּלֵד גּוֹי פַּעַם אֶחָת, מְבַשֵּׂר וְאוֹמֵר.
לְעֵת יִגְאַל עַמּוֹ נָאוֹר, וְהָיָה לְעֵת עֶרֶב יִהְיֶה אוֹר, מְבַשֵּׂר וְאוֹמֵר.
מוֹשִׁיעִים יַעֲלוּ לְהַר צִיּוֹן, כִּי חָלָה גַּם יָלְדָה צִיּוֹן, מְבַשֵּׂר וְאוֹמֵר.
נִשְׁמַע בְּכָל־גְּבוּלֵךְ, הַרְחִיבִי מְקוֹם אָהֳלֵךְ, מְבַשֵּׂר וְאוֹמֵר.
שִׂימִי עַד דַּמֶּשֶׂק מִשְׁכְּנוֹתַיִךְ, קַבְּלִי בָנַיִךְ וּבְנוֹתַיִךְ, מְבַשֵּׂר וְאוֹמֵר.
עִלְזִי חֲבַצֶּלֶת הַשָּׁרוֹן, כִּי קָמוּ יְשֵׁנֵי חֶבְרוֹן, מְבַשֵּׂר וְאוֹמֵר.
פְּנוּ אֵלַי וְהִוָּשְׁעוּ, הַיּוֹם אִם בְּקוֹלִי תִשְׁמָעוּ, מְבַשֵּׂר וְאוֹמֵר.
צָמַח אִישׁ צֶמַח שְׁמוֹ, הוּא דָוִד בְּעַצְמוֹ, מְבַשֵּׂר וְאוֹמֵר.
קוּמוּ כְּפוּשֵׁי עָפָר, הָקִיצוּ וְרַנְּנוּ שׁוֹכְנֵי עָפָר, מְבַשֵּׂר וְאוֹמֵר.
רַבָּתִי עָם בְּהַמְלִיכוֹ, מִגְדּוֹל יְשׁוּעוֹת מַלְכּוֹ, מְבַשֵּׂר וְאוֹמֵר.
שֵׁם רְשָׁעִים לְהַאֲבִיד, עֹשֶׂה חֶסֶד לִמְשִׁיחוֹ לְדָוִד, מְבַשֵּׂר וְאוֹמֵר.
תְּנָה יְשׁוּעוֹת לְעַם עוֹלָם, לְדָוִד וּלְזַרְעוֹ עַד עוֹלָם, מְבַשֵּׂר וְאוֹמֵר.

Leader and Congregation say:

קוֹל מְבַשֵּׂר מְבַשֵּׂר וְאוֹמֵר.

קוֹל מְבַשֵּׂר מְבַשֵּׂר וְאוֹמֵר.

קוֹל מְבַשֵּׂר מְבַשֵּׂר וְאוֹמֵר.

Beat the הוֹשַׁעְנוֹת against a chair or the floor five times, after which the following is said:

הוֹשִׁיעָה אֶת עַמֶּךָ, וּבָרֵךְ אֶת נַחֲלָתֶךָ, וּרְעֵם וְנַשְּׂאֵם עַד הָעוֹלָם. וְיִהְיוּ דְבָרַי אֵלֶּה אֲשֶׁר הִתְחַנַּנְתִּי לִפְנֵי יהוה, קְרֹבִים אֶל יהוה אֱלֹהֵינוּ יוֹמָם וָלָיְלָה, לַעֲשׂוֹת מִשְׁפַּט עַבְדּוֹ וּמִשְׁפַּט עַמּוֹ יִשְׂרָאֵל, דְּבַר יוֹם בְּיוֹמוֹ. לְמַעַן דַּעַת כָּל עַמֵּי הָאָרֶץ, כִּי יהוה הוּא הָאֱלֹהִים, אֵין עוֹד.

The final סֵפֶר תּוֹרָה is returned to the Ark, which is then closed.

יְהִי רָצוֹן מִלְּפָנֶיךָ יהוה אֱלֹהֵינוּ וֵאלֹהֵי אֲבוֹתֵינוּ, הַבּוֹחֵר בִּנְבִיאִים טוֹבִים וּבְמִנְהֲגֵיהֶם הַטּוֹבִים, שֶׁתְּקַבֵּל בְּרַחֲמִים וּבְרָצוֹן אֶת תְּפִלָּתֵנוּ וְהַקָּפוֹתֵינוּ, וּזְכָר לָנוּ זְכוּת שִׁבְעַת תְּמִימֶיךָ, וְתָסִיר מְחִצַּת הַבַּרְזֶל הַמַּפְסֶקֶת בֵּינֵינוּ וּבֵינֶיךָ, וְתַאֲזִין שַׁוְעָתֵנוּ, וְתֵיטִיב לָנוּ הַחֲתִימָה, תּוֹלֶה אֶרֶץ עַל בְּלִימָה. וְחָתְמֵנוּ בְּסֵפֶר חַיִּים טוֹבִים. וְהַיּוֹם הַזֶּה תִּתֵּן בִּשְׁכִינַת עֻזֶּךָ חָמֵשׁ גְּבוּרוֹת מְמֻתָּקוֹת עַל יְדֵי חֲבִיטַת עֲרָבָה מִנְהַג נְבִיאֶיךָ הַקְּדוֹשִׁים. וְתִתְעוֹרֵר הָאַהֲבָה בֵּינֵיהֶם, וּתְנַשְּׁקֵנוּ מִנְּשִׁיקוֹת פִּיךָ, מְמַתֶּקֶת כָּל־הַגְּבוּרוֹת וְכָל־הַדִּינִין, וְתָאִיר לִשְׁכִינַת עֻזֶּךָ בְּשֵׁם יוּ״ד הֵ״א וָא״ו שֶׁהוּא טַל אוֹרוֹת טַלֶּךָ, וּמִשָּׁם תַּשְׁפִּיעַ שֶׁפַע לְעַבְדְּךָ הַמִּתְפַּלֵּל לְפָנֶיךָ, שֶׁתַּאֲרִיךְ יָמָיו וְתִמְחַל לוֹ חֲטָאָיו וַעֲוֹנוֹתָיו וּפְשָׁעָיו, וְתִפְשֹׁט יְמִינְךָ וְיָדְךָ לְקַבְּלוֹ בִּתְשׁוּבָה שְׁלֵמָה לְפָנֶיךָ, וְאוֹצָרְךָ הַטּוֹב תִּפְתַּח לְהַשְׂבִּיעַ מַיִם נֶפֶשׁ שׁוֹקֵקָה, כְּמוֹ שֶׁכָּתוּב, יִפְתַּח יהוה לְךָ אֶת־אוֹצָרוֹ הַטּוֹב אֶת־הַשָּׁמַיִם, לָתֵת מְטַר אַרְצְךָ בְּעִתּוֹ וּלְבָרֵךְ אֵת כָּל־מַעֲשֵׂה יָדֶךָ. אָמֵן.

The Leader continues with קַדִּישׁ תִּתְקַבַּל on page 448.

קידושא רבא לשלש רגלים

On שַׁבָּת, add the following paragraph:

וְשָׁמְרוּ בְנֵי־יִשְׂרָאֵל אֶת־הַשַּׁבָּת, לַעֲשׂוֹת אֶת־הַשַּׁבָּת לְדֹרֹתָם בְּרִית עוֹלָם. בֵּינִי וּבֵין בְּנֵי יִשְׂרָאֵל אוֹת הִיא לְעֹלָם, כִּי־שֵׁשֶׁת יָמִים עָשָׂה יהוה אֶת־הַשָּׁמַיִם וְאֶת־הָאָרֶץ, וּבַיּוֹם הַשְּׁבִיעִי שָׁבַת וַיִּנָּפַשׁ.

אֵלֶּה מוֹעֲדֵי יהוה מִקְרָאֵי קֹדֶשׁ אֲשֶׁר־תִּקְרְאוּ אֹתָם בְּמוֹעֲדָם. וַיְדַבֵּר מֹשֶׁה אֶת־מוֹעֲדֵי יהוה, אֶל־בְּנֵי יִשְׂרָאֵל.

When saying קִדּוּשׁ for others, add:

סַבְרִי מָרָנָן וְרַבָּנָן וְרַבּוֹתַי.

בָּרוּךְ אַתָּה יהוה אֱלֹהֵינוּ מֶלֶךְ הָעוֹלָם, בּוֹרֵא פְּרִי הַגָּפֶן.

If you are making קִדּוּשׁ on any other drink, say:

בָּרוּךְ אַתָּה יהוה אֱלֹהֵינוּ מֶלֶךְ הָעוֹלָם, שֶׁהַכֹּל נִהְיֶה בִּדְבָרוֹ.

In a סֻכָּה, say:

בָּרוּךְ אַתָּה יהוה אֱלֹהֵינוּ מֶלֶךְ הָעוֹלָם, אֲשֶׁר קִדְּשָׁנוּ בְּמִצְוֹתָיו וְצִוָּנוּ לֵישֵׁב בַּסֻּכָּה.

Immediately after washing hands before the meal, say:

בָּרוּךְ אַתָּה יהוה אֱלֹהֵינוּ מֶלֶךְ הָעוֹלָם, אֲשֶׁר קִדְּשָׁנוּ בְּמִצְוֹתָיו וְצִוָּנוּ עַל נְטִילַת יָדָיִם.

After washing hands, one should not speak until one has eaten some חַלָּה (or מַצָּה on פֶּסַח). Holding both loaves or מַצּוֹת, the person making the blessing says:

בָּרוּךְ אַתָּה יהוה אֱלֹהֵינוּ מֶלֶךְ הָעוֹלָם, הַמּוֹצִיא לֶחֶם מִן הָאָרֶץ.

A piece of the חַלָּה or מַצָּה should be given to all present.

KIDDUSH FOR FESTIVAL MORNINGS

On Shabbat, add the following paragraph:

וְשָׁמְרוּ The children of Israel must keep the Sabbath, observing the Sabbath in every generation as an everlasting covenant. It is a sign between Me and the children of Israel for ever, for in six days God made the heavens and the earth, but on the seventh day He ceased work and refreshed Himself.

אֵלֶּה These are the appointed times of the Lord, sacred assemblies, which you shall announce in their due season. Thus Moses announced the Lord's appointed seasons to the children of Israel.

When saying *Kiddush* for others, add:

Please pay attention, my teachers, rabbis and friends.

בָּרוּךְ Blessed are You, Lord our God, King of the Universe, who creates the fruit of the vine.

If you are making *Kiddush* on any other drink, say:

בָּרוּךְ Blessed are You, Lord our God, King of the Universe, by whose word all things came to be.

In a *Sukkah*, say:

בָּרוּךְ Blessed are You, Lord our God, King of the Universe, who has made us holy through His commandments and has commanded us to dwell in the *Sukkah*.

Immediately after washing hands before the meal, say:

בָּרוּךְ Blessed are You, Lord our God, King of the Universe, who has made us holy through His commandments, and has commanded us about washing hands.

After washing hands, one should not speak until one has eaten some *challah* (or matzah on Pesach). Holding both loaves or Matzot, the person making the blessing says:

בָּרוּךְ Blessed are You, Lord our God, King of the Universe, who brings forth bread from the earth.

A piece of the *challah* or Matzah should be given to all present.

סדר לחנוכה

On each of the eight nights of חֲנֻכָּה, the lights of the מְנוֹרָה are lit: one on the first night, two on the second, and so on. On the first night, the rightmost branch of the מְנוֹרָה is used; on each subsequent night, an additional light is added to the left. Each night, the new light is lit first, then the others, moving rightwards. If possible, the מְנוֹרָה should be displayed near a window so that it is visible from the street.

The lights are lit using a separate candle (known as the שַׁמָּשׁ). The lighting should be carried out as soon as possible after nightfall. On Friday night, it must be done before the beginning of שַׁבָּת. Before lighting the מְנוֹרָה lights, say:

בָּרוּךְ אַתָּה יהוה אֱלֹהֵינוּ מֶלֶךְ הָעוֹלָם, אֲשֶׁר קִדְּשָׁנוּ בְּמִצְוֹתָיו, וְצִוָּנוּ לְהַדְלִיק נֵר שֶׁל חֲנֻכָּה.

בָּרוּךְ אַתָּה יהוה אֱלֹהֵינוּ מֶלֶךְ הָעוֹלָם, שֶׁעָשָׂה נִסִּים לַאֲבוֹתֵינוּ, בַּיָּמִים הָהֵם בַּזְּמַן הַזֶּה.

On the first night, add:

בָּרוּךְ אַתָּה יהוה אֱלֹהֵינוּ מֶלֶךְ הָעוֹלָם, שֶׁהֶחֱיָנוּ וְקִיְּמָנוּ וְהִגִּיעָנוּ לַזְּמַן הַזֶּה.

After lighting the first light, say:

הַנֵּרוֹת הַלָּלוּ אֲנַחְנוּ מַדְלִיקִין עַל הַנִּסִּים וְעַל הַתְּשׁוּעוֹת וְעַל הַנִּפְלָאוֹת, שֶׁעָשִׂיתָ לַאֲבוֹתֵינוּ עַל־יְדֵי כֹּהֲנֶיךָ

CHANUKAH

After the conquests of Alexander the Great, Israel came under the rule of Greece, in the third century BCE under the Ptolemies, based in Egypt; then in the second century BCE under the Seleucids, based in Syria. Beginning in 175 BCE, one of the Seleucid rulers, Antiochus Epiphanes, decided to embark on a campaign of enforced Hellenisation of the Jews in Israel. A gymnasium was built at the foot of the Temple Mount. Temple funds were diverted to Greek athletic and cultural events. Eventually in 167 BCE, the public practice of Judaism was forbidden and a statue of Zeus erected in the Temple. Many Jews went to their death as martyrs rather than abandon their faith.

A group of pious Jews, led by an elderly priest, Mattityahu, and his sons, most famously Judah, known as the Maccabee, rose in revolt. Over the next three years they fought a successful campaign, driving the Greek forces out of Jerusalem and rededicating the desecrated Temple. Chanukah is the anniversary of that ceremony of rededication, celebrating not only the military victory and the restoration of Jewish self-government, but also the spiritual victory of Jewish faith

SERVICE FOR CHANUKAH

On each of the eight nights of Chanukah, the lights of the *menorah* are lit: one on the first night, two on the second, and so on. On the first night, the rightmost branch of the *menorah* is used; on each subsequent night, an additional light is added to the left. Each night, the new light is lit first, then the others, moving rightwards. If possible, the *menorah* should be displayed near a window so that it is visible from the street.

The lights are lit using a separate candle (known as the *shamash*). The lighting should be carried out as soon as possible after nightfall. On Friday night, it must be done before the beginning of Shabbat. Before lighting the *menorah* lights, say:

בָּרוּךְ Blessed are You, LORD our GOD, King of the Universe, who has made us holy through His commandments, and has commanded us to light the Chanukah lights.

בָּרוּךְ Blessed are You, LORD our GOD, King of the Universe, who performed miracles for our ancestors in those days, at this time.

On the first night, add:

בָּרוּךְ Blessed are You, LORD our GOD, King of the Universe, who has given us life, sustained us, and brought us to this time.

After lighting the first light, say:

הַנֵּרוֹת הַלָּלוּ We light these lights because of the miracles, deliverances and wonders You performed for our ancestors through Your holy priests. Throughout the eight days of Chanukah these lights are

---

over enforced assimilation. Shortly afterward, it was decided to hold an annual eight-day celebration in memory of those events, together with the recitation of *Hallel*.

One incident came to hold immense symbolic significance: the fact that among the debris of the Temple, a single cruse of oil was found, its seal intact, with which the *menorah* – the Temple candelabrum – could be lit. The oil that would normally have lasted for one day burned for eight, the full period of the rededication ceremony. Even after the Temple was destroyed more than two centuries later by the Romans, the Chanukah lights bore witness to the fact that after the worst desecration, something pure remains, lighting a way to the future. The Chanukah lights became one of the great symbols of Jewish hope.

They are lit at home, at nightfall or soon thereafter, preferably in a position where they can be seen by passers-by. Our custom is to light one candle (or olive-oil lamp) on the first night; two on the second; and so on. The first candle is placed at the right of the *menorah*; on each night, the first light to be lit is the left-most.

הַנֵּרוֹת הַלָּלוּ *We light these lights*: A hymn about the holiness of the lights and why

הַקְּדוֹשִׁים. וְכָל־שְׁמֹנַת יְמֵי חֲנֻכָּה, הַנֵּרוֹת הַלָּלוּ קֹדֶשׁ הֵם. וְאֵין לָנוּ רְשׁוּת לְהִשְׁתַּמֵּשׁ בָּהֶם, אֶלָּא לִרְאוֹתָם בִּלְבַד, כְּדֵי לְהוֹדוֹת לְשִׁמְךָ עַל־נִסֶּיךָ וְעַל־יְשׁוּעָתֶךָ וְעַל־נִפְלְאוֹתֶיךָ.

In the Synagogue, the following psalm is said:

תהלים ל

מִזְמוֹר שִׁיר חֲנֻכַּת הַבַּיִת לְדָוִד. אֲרוֹמִמְךָ יהוה כִּי דִלִּיתָנִי, וְלֹא־שִׂמַּחְתָּ אֹיְבַי לִי. יהוה אֱלֹהָי, שִׁוַּעְתִּי אֵלֶיךָ וַתִּרְפָּאֵנִי. יהוה הֶעֱלִיתָ מִן־שְׁאוֹל נַפְשִׁי, חִיִּיתַנִי מִיָּרְדִי־בוֹר. זַמְּרוּ לַיהוה חֲסִידָיו, וְהוֹדוּ לְזֵכֶר קָדְשׁוֹ. כִּי רֶגַע בְּאַפּוֹ, חַיִּים בִּרְצוֹנוֹ, בָּעֶרֶב יָלִין בֶּכִי וְלַבֹּקֶר רִנָּה. וַאֲנִי אָמַרְתִּי בְשַׁלְוִי, בַּל אֶמּוֹט לְעוֹלָם. יהוה בִּרְצוֹנְךָ הֶעֱמַדְתָּה לְהַרְרִי עֹז, הִסְתַּרְתָּ פָנֶיךָ הָיִיתִי נִבְהָל. אֵלֶיךָ יהוה אֶקְרָא, וְאֶל־אֲדֹנָי אֶתְחַנָּן. מַה־בֶּצַע בְּדָמִי, בְּרִדְתִּי אֶל שָׁחַת, הֲיוֹדְךָ עָפָר, הֲיַגִּיד אֲמִתֶּךָ. שְׁמַע־יהוה וְחָנֵּנִי, יהוה הֱיֵה עֹזֵר לִי. הָפַכְתָּ מִסְפְּדִי לְמָחוֹל לִי, פִּתַּחְתָּ שַׂקִּי, וַתְּאַזְּרֵנִי שִׂמְחָה. לְמַעַן יְזַמֶּרְךָ כָבוֹד וְלֹא יִדֹּם, יהוה אֱלֹהַי לְעוֹלָם אוֹדֶךָּ.

מעוז צור

מָעוֹז צוּר יְשׁוּעָתִי לְךָ נָאֶה לְשַׁבֵּחַ,
תִּכּוֹן בֵּית תְּפִלָּתִי וְשָׁם תּוֹדָה נְזַבֵּחַ,
לְעֵת תָּכִין מַטְבֵּחַ מִצָּר הַמְנַבֵּחַ,
אָז אֶגְמוֹר בְּשִׁיר מִזְמוֹר חֲנֻכַּת הַמִּזְבֵּחַ.

---

we light them. The text is known from the rabbinic tractate, *Sofrim*, though it has undergone some changes in the intervening centuries. *We are not permitted to make any other use of them* – unlike Shabbat lights, those of Chanukah are not lit for the sake of the light they give, but rather are lit in order to "publicise the miracle". A separate light or candle, the *shamash*, is used to light the others, and is placed slightly higher, so that if we benefit from the light, it is from the *shamash*, and not those that form part of the *mitzvah* itself.

holy and we are not permitted to make any other use of them, except to look at them that we may offer thanks to Your name for Your miracles, Your deliverances and Your wonders.

In the Synagogue, the following psalm is said:

PSALM 30

מִזְמוֹר A psalm of David. A song for the dedication of the House. I will exalt You, LORD, for You have lifted me up, and not let my enemies rejoice over me. LORD, my GOD, I cried to You for help and You healed me. LORD, You lifted my soul from the grave; You spared me from going down to the pit. Sing to the LORD, you His devoted ones, and give thanks to His holy name. For His anger is for a moment, but His favour for a lifetime. At night there may be weeping, but in the morning there is joy. When I felt secure, I said, "I shall never be shaken." LORD, when You favoured me, You made me stand firm as a mountain, but when You hid Your face, I was terrified. To You, LORD, I called; I pleaded with my LORD: "What gain would there be if I died and went down to the grave? Can dust thank You? Can it declare Your truth? Hear, LORD, and be gracious to me; LORD, be my help." You have turned my sorrow into dancing. You have removed my sackcloth and clothed me with joy, so that my soul may sing to You and not be silent. LORD my GOD, for ever I will thank You.

MAOZ TZUR

מָעוֹז צוּר Refuge, Rock of my salvation: to You it is a delight to give praise.
Restore my house of prayer, so that there I may offer You thanksgiving.
When You silence the loud-mouthed foe,
Then will I complete, with song and psalm, the altar's dedication.

מָעוֹז צוּר *Refuge, Rock of my salvation*: Composed in Germany in the thirteenth century. The first letters of the verses spell out the name Mordechai; other than this we cannot identify the author. The first verse recalls the rededication of the Temple and looks forward to its future restoration. The next four describe, sequentially, four crises and deliverances of Jewish history – slavery in Egypt, the

רָעוֹת שָׂבְעָה נַפְשִׁי בְּיָגוֹן כֹּחִי כָּלָה,
חַיַּי מֵרְרוּ בְקוֹשִׁי בְּשִׁעְבּוּד מַלְכוּת עֶגְלָה,
וּבְיָדוֹ הַגְּדוֹלָה הוֹצִיא אֶת־הַסְּגֻלָּה,
חֵיל פַּרְעֹה וְכָל־זַרְעוֹ יָרְדוּ כְּאֶבֶן מְצוּלָה.

דְּבִיר קָדְשׁוֹ הֱבִיאַנִי וְגַם שָׁם לֹא שָׁקַטְתִּי,
וּבָא נוֹגֵשׂ וְהִגְלַנִי כִּי זָרִים עָבַדְתִּי,
וְיֵין רַעַל מָסַכְתִּי כִּמְעַט שֶׁעָבַרְתִּי,
קֵץ בָּבֶל, זְרֻבָּבֶל, לְקֵץ שִׁבְעִים נוֹשַׁעְתִּי.

כְּרוֹת קוֹמַת בְּרוֹשׁ בִּקֵּשׁ אֲגָגִי בֶּן־הַמְּדָתָא,
וְנִהְיְתָה לוֹ לְמוֹקֵשׁ וְגַאֲוָתוֹ נִשְׁבָּתָה,
רֹאשׁ יְמִינִי נִשֵּׂאתָ וְאוֹיֵב שְׁמוֹ מָחִיתָ,
רוֹב בָּנָיו וְקִנְיָנָיו עַל הָעֵץ תָּלִיתָ.

יְוָנִים נִקְבְּצוּ עָלַי אֲזַי בִּימֵי חַשְׁמַנִּים,
וּפָרְצוּ חוֹמוֹת מִגְדָּלַי וְטִמְּאוּ כָּל הַשְּׁמָנִים,
וּמִנּוֹתַר קַנְקַנִּים נַעֲשָׂה נֵס לַשּׁוֹשַׁנִּים,
בְּנֵי בִינָה יְמֵי שְׁמוֹנָה קָבְעוּ שִׁיר וּרְנָנִים.

Some add:

חֲשׂוֹף זְרוֹעַ קָדְשֶׁךָ וְקָרֵב יוֹם הַיְשׁוּעָה,
נְקוֹם נִקְמַת עֲבָדֶיךָ מִמַּלְכוּת הָרְשָׁעָה,
כִּי אָרְכָה הַשָּׁעָה וְאֵין קֵץ לִימֵי רָעָה,
דְּחֵה אַדְמוֹן בְּצֵל צַלְמוֹן וְהָקֵם רוֹעִים שִׁבְעָה.

Babylonian exile, Purim, and Chanukah itself. The last verse, missing from some manuscripts, may have been a later addition; alternatively it may have been part of the original text, but was censored by the non-Jewish authorities.

רָעוֹת Troubles sated my soul; my strength was spent with sorrow.
They embittered my life with hardship, when I was enslaved under Egyptian rule.
But GOD with His great power brought out His treasured people,
While Pharaoh's host and followers sank like a stone in the deep.

דְּבִיר He brought me to His holy abode, but even there I found no rest.
The oppressor came and exiled me, because I had served strange gods.
I had drunk poisoned wine. I almost perished.
Then Babylon fell, Zerubbabel came: within seventy years I was saved.

כְּרוֹת The Agagite, son of Hammedatha, sought to cut down the tall fir tree,
But it became a trap to him, and his arrogance was brought to an end.
You raised the head of the Benjaminite, and the enemy's name You blotted out.
His many sons and his household You hanged on the gallows.

יְוָנִים Then the Greeks gathered against me, in the days of the Hasmoneans.
They broke down the walls of my towers, and defiled all the oils.
But from the last remaining flask a miracle was wrought for Your beloved.
Therefore the Sages ordained these eight days for song and praise.

Some add:

חֲשׂוֹף Bare Your holy arm, and hasten the time of salvation.
Take retribution against the evil nation on behalf of Your servants,
For deliverance has been too long delayed; there seems no end to the evil days.
Thrust the enemy into the darkness of death, and establish for us the seven Shepherds.

סדר לפורים

Before reading the מְגִלָּה, the person who is to read says the following blessings. While they are being said, the Congregation stands.

בָּרוּךְ אַתָּה יהוה אֱלֹהֵינוּ מֶלֶךְ הָעוֹלָם, אֲשֶׁר קִדְּשָׁנוּ בְּמִצְוֹתָיו, וְצִוָּנוּ עַל מִקְרָא מְגִלָּה.

בָּרוּךְ אַתָּה יהוה אֱלֹהֵינוּ מֶלֶךְ הָעוֹלָם, שֶׁעָשָׂה נִסִּים לַאֲבוֹתֵינוּ, בַּיָּמִים הָהֵם בַּזְּמַן הַזֶּה.

בָּרוּךְ אַתָּה יהוה אֱלֹהֵינוּ מֶלֶךְ הָעוֹלָם, שֶׁהֶחֱיָנוּ וְקִיְּמָנוּ וְהִגִּיעָנוּ לַזְּמַן הַזֶּה.

After the מְגִלָּה reading – though only if a מִנְיָן is present – say:

בָּרוּךְ אַתָּה יהוה אֱלֹהֵינוּ מֶלֶךְ הָעוֹלָם, הָרָב אֶת־רִיבֵנוּ, וְהַדָּן אֶת־דִּינֵנוּ, וְהַנּוֹקֵם אֶת נִקְמָתֵנוּ, וְהַמְשַׁלֵּם גְּמוּל לְכָל־אוֹיְבֵי נַפְשֵׁנוּ, וְהַנִּפְרָע לָנוּ מִצָּרֵינוּ. בָּרוּךְ אַתָּה יהוה, הַנִּפְרָע לְעַמּוֹ יִשְׂרָאֵל מִכָּל־צָרֵיהֶם, הָאֵל הַמּוֹשִׁיעַ.

The following is said after the night reading of the מְגִלָּה:

אֲשֶׁר הֵנִיא עֲצַת גּוֹיִם, וַיָּפֶר מַחְשְׁבוֹת עֲרוּמִים.
בְּקוּם עָלֵינוּ אָדָם רָשָׁע, נֵצֶר זָדוֹן מִזֶּרַע עֲמָלֵק.
גָּאָה בְעָשְׁרוֹ, וְכָרָה לוֹ בּוֹר, וּגְדֻלָּתוֹ יָקְשָׁה לּוֹ לָכֶד.
דִּמָּה בְנַפְשׁוֹ לִלְכֹּד, וְנִלְכַּד, בִּקֵּשׁ לְהַשְׁמִיד, וְנִשְׁמַד מְהֵרָה.
הָמָן הוֹדִיעַ אֵיבַת אֲבוֹתָיו, וְעוֹרֵר שִׂנְאַת אַחִים לַבָּנִים.
וְלֹא זָכַר רַחֲמֵי שָׁאוּל, כִּי־בְחֶמְלָתוֹ עַל־אֲגָג נוֹלַד אוֹיֵב.
זָמַם רָשָׁע לְהַכְרִית צַדִּיק, וְנִלְכַּד טָמֵא, בִּידֵי טָהוֹר.
חֶסֶד גָּבַר עַל־שִׁגְגַת אָב, וְרָשָׁע הוֹסִיף חֵטְא עַל־חֲטָאָיו.
טָמַן בְּלִבּוֹ מַחְשְׁבוֹת עֲרוּמָיו, וַיִּתְמַכֵּר לַעֲשׂוֹת רָעָה.

PURIM
Purim is the annual remembrance and celebration of the events described in the Book of Esther. During the reign of Achashverosh of Persia, one of his senior officials, Haman, conspired to "destroy,

SERVICE FOR PURIM

Before reading the *Megillah*, the person who is to read says the following three blessings. While they are being said, the Congregation stands.

בָּרוּךְ Blessed are You, LORD our GOD, King of the Universe, who has made us holy through His commandments, and has commanded us about reading the *Megillah*.

בָּרוּךְ Blessed are You, LORD our GOD, King of the Universe, who performed miracles for our ancestors in those days at this time.

בָּרוּךְ Blessed are You, LORD our GOD, King of the Universe, who has given us life, sustained us, and brought us to this time.

After the *Megillah* reading – though only if a *minyan* is present – say:

בָּרוּךְ Blessed are You, LORD our GOD, King of the Universe who pleads our cause, judges our claim, avenges our wrong, brings retribution to our enemies, and punishes our foes. Blessed are You, LORD, who on behalf of His people Israel, exacts punishment from all their foes, the GOD who brings salvation.

The following is said after the night reading of the *Megillah*:

אֲשֶׁר הֵנִיא (GOD) frustrated the plan of the nations,
Thwarted the intentions of the crafty.
An evil man rose up against us,
An arrogant branch of Amalek's tree,
Haughty, rich, he dug his own pit.
His hubris became his own snare.
He was trapped in the trap he set for others.
Seeking to destroy, he was destroyed.
Haman shared his ancestors' hate,
And stirred against children the hostility of brothers.
He did not remember Saul's act of mercy,
his pity for Agag, through which a new enemy was born.
The wicked planned to cut off the righteous,
but the impure were defeated by the pure.
(Mordechai's) goodness overcame the father's (Saul's) error,
but the evil (Haman) piled sin upon sin.
He hid in his heart his cunning schemes,
intent on his evildoing.

יָדוֹ שָׁלַח בִּקְדוֹשֵׁי אֵל, כַּסְפּוֹ נָתַן לְהַכְרִית זִכְרָם.
כִּרְאוֹת מָרְדְּכַי, כִּי־יָצָא קֶצֶף, וְדָתֵי הָמָן נִתְּנוּ בְשׁוּשָׁן.
לָבַשׁ שַׂק וְקָשַׁר מִסְפֵּד, וְגָזַר צוֹם, וַיֵּשֶׁב עַל־הָאֵפֶר.
מִי זֶה יַעֲמֹד לְכַפֵּר שְׁגָגָה, וְלִמְחֹל חַטַּאת עֲוֹן אֲבוֹתֵינוּ.
נֵץ פָּרַח מִלּוּלָב, הֵן הֲדַסָּה עָמְדָה לְעוֹרֵר יְשֵׁנִים.
סָרִיסֶיהָ הִבְהִילוּ לְהָמָן, לְהַשְׁקוֹתוֹ יֵין חֲמַת תַּנִּינִים.
עָמַד בְּעָשְׁרוֹ, וְנָפַל בְּרִשְׁעוֹ, עָשָׂה לוֹ עֵץ, וְנִתְלָה עָלָיו.
פִּיהֶם פָּתְחוּ, כָּל־יוֹשְׁבֵי תֵבֵל, כִּי פוּר הָמָן נֶהְפַּךְ לְפוּרֵנוּ.
צַדִּיק נֶחֱלַץ מִיַּד רָשָׁע, אוֹיֵב נִתַּן תַּחַת נַפְשׁוֹ.
קִיְּמוּ עֲלֵיהֶם, לַעֲשׂוֹת פּוּרִים, וְלִשְׂמֹחַ בְּכָל־שָׁנָה וְשָׁנָה.
רָאִיתָ אֶת־תְּפִלַּת מָרְדְּכַי וְאֶסְתֵּר, הָמָן וּבָנָיו עַל־הָעֵץ תָּלִיתָ.

The following is said after both night and morning readings of the מְגִלָּה:

שׁוֹשַׁנַּת יַעֲקֹב צָהֲלָה וְשָׂמֵחָה, בִּרְאוֹתָם יַחַד תְּכֵלֶת מָרְדְּכָי. תְּשׁוּעָתָם הָיִיתָ לָנֶצַח, וְתִקְוָתָם בְּכָל־דּוֹר וָדוֹר. לְהוֹדִיעַ, שֶׁכָּל־קֹוֶיךָ לֹא יֵבֹשׁוּ, וְלֹא יִכָּלְמוּ לָנֶצַח כָּל־הַחוֹסִים בָּךְ. אָרוּר הָמָן, אֲשֶׁר בִּקֵּשׁ לְאַבְּדִי, בָּרוּךְ מָרְדְּכַי הַיְּהוּדִי. אֲרוּרָה זֶרֶשׁ, אֵשֶׁת מַפְחִידִי, בְּרוּכָה אֶסְתֵּר מְגִנָּה בַּעֲדִי, וְגַם חַרְבוֹנָה זָכוּר לַטּוֹב.

After the night reading, מַעֲרִיב continues with וְאַתָּה קָדוֹשׁ to וַיַּאְדִּיר, pages 582 (on Saturday evening, begin with וִיהִי נֹעַם, page 582). The Leader then continues with קַדִּישׁ תִּתְקַבַּל page 586 (omitting the line תִּתְקַבַּל). On Saturday evening, continue with וְיִתֶּן־לְךָ, on page 588, עָלֵינוּ, on page 598, and קַדִּישׁ יָתוֹם, on page 600.

In the morning, continue with אַשְׁרֵי, on page 132.

---

kill and annihilate all the Jews, young and old, women and children, on a single day" – the day chosen by the lottery (*pur*) that gives the festival its name. The Jews were saved by a combination of the defiance of Mordechai and the plea of his cousin Esther, who had been taken into the royal harem and was a favourite of the king. Haman's plan was thwarted, and he and his sons were hanged on the gallows they had prepared for Mordechai.

He stretched out his hand against GOD's holy ones;
he spent his wealth to destroy every memory of them.
When Mordechai saw the wrath go forth,
and Haman's decrees issued in Shushan,
he put on sackcloth, wrapped himself in mourning,
decreed a fast and sat on ashes.
"Who will arise to atone for error,
and find forgiveness for our ancestors' sins?"
A flower blossomed from the palm tree;
Hadassah arose to wake those who slept.
Her servants hastened Haman to come,
to serve him wine with the venom of serpents.
He had risen by his wealth, but fell by his evil.
He made the very gallows by which he was hanged.
All the inhabitants of the world were amazed
When Haman's ploy (*pur*) became our joy (*Purim*).
The righteous was saved from evil hands,
the perpetrator suffered the fate of his intended victim.
They undertook to celebrate Purim,
and to rejoice on it year after year.
You heeded the prayer of Mordechai and Esther;
and Haman and his sons were hanged on the gallows.

The following is said after both night and morning readings of the *Megillah*:

שׁוֹשַׁנַּת יַעֲקֹב The lily of Jacob rejoiced and was glad,
When, together, they saw Mordechai robed in royal blue.
You have been their eternal salvation, their hope in every generation;
To make known that all who hope in You will not be put to shame,
All who trust in You will never be humiliated.
Cursed be Haman who sought to destroy me.
Blessed be Mordechai the Yehudi.
Cursed be Zeresh, wife of him who terrified me.
Blessed be Esther (whose actions saved) me.
And may Harbonah, too, be remembered for good.

After the night reading, the Evening Service continues with "You are Holy" to "great and glorious" on page 583 (on Saturday evening, begin with "May the pleasantness" on page 583). The Leader then continues with *Kaddish* on page 587 (omitting the line "May the prayers and pleas"). On Saturday evening, continue with "May GOD give you" on page 589, "It is our duty" on page 599, and Mourner's *Kaddish* on page 601.

In the morning, continue with "Happy are those" on page 133.

יום העצמאות

There are different customs as far as Order of Service is concerned. Synagogues should follow their normal custom. In most communities, in שַׁחֲרִית, הַלֵּל is said. After it, the Leader says חֲצִי קַדִּישׁ. No תַּחֲנוּן is recited. The following is read to the tune of a הַפְטָרָה, without blessings.

ישעיהו י:לב–יב:ו

לב עוֹד הַיּוֹם בְּנֹב לַעֲמֹד יְנֹפֵף יָדוֹ הַר בֵּית▽־צִיּוֹן גִּבְעַת
יְרוּשָׁלָ͏ִם׃ לג הִנֵּה הָאָדוֹן יְהוָה צְבָאוֹת מְסָעֵף פֻּארָה
בְּמַעֲרָצָה וְרָמֵי הַקּוֹמָה גְּדוּעִים וְהַגְּבֹהִים יִשְׁפָּלוּ׃ לד וְנִקַּף
סִבְכֵי הַיַּעַר בַּבַּרְזֶל וְהַלְּבָנוֹן בְּאַדִּיר יִפּוֹל׃ יא א וְיָצָא חֹטֶר
מִגֵּזַע יִשָׁי וְנֵצֶר מִשָּׁרָשָׁיו יִפְרֶה׃ ב וְנָחָה עָלָיו רוּחַ יְהוָה
רוּחַ חָכְמָה וּבִינָה רוּחַ עֵצָה וּגְבוּרָה רוּחַ דַּעַת וְיִרְאַת
יְהוָה׃ ג וַהֲרִיחוֹ בְּיִרְאַת יְהוָה וְלֹא־לְמַרְאֵה עֵינָיו יִשְׁפּוֹט
וְלֹא־לְמִשְׁמַע אָזְנָיו יוֹכִיחַ׃ ד וְשָׁפַט בְּצֶדֶק דַּלִּים וְהוֹכִיחַ
בְּמִישׁוֹר לְעַנְוֵי־אָרֶץ וְהִכָּה־אֶרֶץ בְּשֵׁבֶט פִּיו וּבְרוּחַ שְׂפָתָיו
יָמִית רָשָׁע׃ ה וְהָיָה צֶדֶק אֵזוֹר מָתְנָיו וְהָאֱמוּנָה אֵזוֹר
חֲלָצָיו׃ ו וְגָר זְאֵב עִם־כֶּבֶשׂ וְנָמֵר עִם־גְּדִי יִרְבָּץ וְעֵגֶל וּכְפִיר
וּמְרִיא יַחְדָּו וְנַעַר קָטֹן נֹהֵג בָּם׃ ז וּפָרָה וָדֹב תִּרְעֶינָה יַחְדָּו
יִרְבְּצוּ יַלְדֵיהֶן וְאַרְיֵה כַּבָּקָר יֹאכַל־תֶּבֶן׃ ח וְשִׁעֲשַׁע יוֹנֵק
עַל־חֻר פָּתֶן וְעַל מְאוּרַת צִפְעוֹנִי גָּמוּל יָדוֹ הָדָה׃ ט לֹא־
יָרֵעוּ וְלֹא־יַשְׁחִיתוּ בְּכָל־הַר קָדְשִׁי כִּי־מָלְאָה הָאָרֶץ דֵּעָה
אֶת־יְהוָה כַּמַּיִם לַיָּם מְכַסִּים׃ י וְהָיָה בַּיּוֹם הַהוּא שֹׁרֶשׁ יִשַׁי
אֲשֶׁר עֹמֵד לְנֵס עַמִּים אֵלָיו גּוֹיִם יִדְרֹשׁוּ וְהָיְתָה מְנֻחָתוֹ
כָּבוֹד׃ יא וְהָיָה ׀ בַּיּוֹם הַהוּא יוֹסִיף אֲדֹנָי ׀ שֵׁנִית יָדוֹ לִקְנוֹת

▽ בַּת

YOM HA'ATZMA'UT – ISRAEL INDEPENDENCE DAY

There are different customs as far as Order of Service is concerned. Synagogues should follow their normal custom. In most communities, in the Morning Service, *Hallel* is said. After it, the Leader says half-*Kaddish*. No *Tachanun* is recited. The following is read to the tune of a *Haftarah*, without blessings.

ISAIAH 10:32–12:6

עוֹד הַיּוֹם This day he will halt at Nob; he will wave his hand, mount of the daughter of Zion, hill of Jerusalem. See, the sovereign LORD of hosts will lop off the boughs with an axe. The tall trees will be felled, the lofty ones laid low. He will cut down the forest thickets with an axe. Lebanon will fall before the Mighty One. A shoot will grow from the stump of Jesse; from his roots a branch will bear fruit. The spirit of the LORD will rest on him – a spirit of wisdom and understanding, a spirit of counsel and power, a spirit of knowledge and the fear of the LORD, and he will delight in the fear of the LORD. He will not judge by what his eyes see, or decide by what his ears hear; with justice he will judge the poor, and with equity defend humble in the land. He will strike the earth with the rod of his mouth; with the breath of his lips he will slay the wicked. Justice will be his belt and faithfulness the sash around his waist. The wolf will live with the lamb, the leopard will lie down with the kid, the calf and the lion and the yearling together; and a little child will lead them. The cow will graze with the bear, their young will lie down together, and the lion will eat straw like the ox. An infant will play near the cobra's hole, and a young child put his hand into the viper's nest. They will neither harm nor destroy on all My holy mountain, for the earth will be full of the knowledge of the LORD as the waters cover the sea. On that day the stock of Jesse will stand as a banner for the peoples; nations will rally to him, and his place of rest will be glorious. On that day the LORD will reach out His hand a second time to reclaim the remnant that is left of His people from Assyria, Lower Egypt, Pathros, Cush, Elam, Shinar, Hamath

אֶת־שְׁאָר עַמּוֹ אֲשֶׁר יִשָּׁאֵר מֵאַשּׁוּר וּמִמִּצְרַיִם וּמִפַּתְרוֹס
וּמִכּוּשׁ וּמֵעֵילָם וּמִשִּׁנְעָר וּמֵחֲמָת וּמֵאִיֵּי הַיָּם: יב וְנָשָׂא נֵס
לַגּוֹיִם וְאָסַף נִדְחֵי יִשְׂרָאֵל וּנְפֻצוֹת יְהוּדָה יְקַבֵּץ מֵאַרְבַּע
כַּנְפוֹת הָאָרֶץ: יג וְסָרָה קִנְאַת אֶפְרַיִם וְצֹרְרֵי יְהוּדָה יִכָּרֵתוּ
אֶפְרַיִם לֹא־יְקַנֵּא אֶת־יְהוּדָה וִיהוּדָה לֹא־יָצֹר אֶת־אֶפְרָיִם:
יד וְעָפוּ בְכָתֵף פְּלִשְׁתִּים יָמָּה יַחְדָּו יָבֹזּוּ אֶת־בְּנֵי־קֶדֶם אֱדוֹם
וּמוֹאָב מִשְׁלוֹחַ יָדָם וּבְנֵי עַמּוֹן מִשְׁמַעְתָּם: טו וְהֶחֱרִים
יְהוָה אֵת לְשׁוֹן יָם־מִצְרַיִם וְהֵנִיף יָדוֹ עַל־הַנָּהָר בַּעְיָם רוּחוֹ
וְהִכָּהוּ לְשִׁבְעָה נְחָלִים וְהִדְרִיךְ בַּנְּעָלִים: טז וְהָיְתָה מְסִלָּה
לִשְׁאָר עַמּוֹ אֲשֶׁר יִשָּׁאֵר מֵאַשּׁוּר כַּאֲשֶׁר הָיְתָה לְיִשְׂרָאֵל
בְּיוֹם עֲלֹתוֹ מֵאֶרֶץ מִצְרָיִם: יב א וְאָמַרְתָּ בַּיּוֹם הַהוּא אוֹדְךָ
יְהוָה כִּי אָנַפְתָּ בִּי יָשֹׁב אַפְּךָ וּתְנַחֲמֵנִי: ב הִנֵּה אֵל יְשׁוּעָתִי
אֶבְטַח וְלֹא אֶפְחָד כִּי עָזִּי וְזִמְרָת יָהּ יְהוָה וַיְהִי־לִי לִישׁוּעָה:
ג וּשְׁאַבְתֶּם־מַיִם בְּשָׂשׂוֹן מִמַּעַיְנֵי הַיְשׁוּעָה: ד וַאֲמַרְתֶּם
בַּיּוֹם הַהוּא הוֹדוּ לַיהוָה קִרְאוּ בִשְׁמוֹ הוֹדִיעוּ בָעַמִּים
עֲלִילֹתָיו הַזְכִּירוּ כִּי נִשְׂגָּב שְׁמוֹ: ה זַמְּרוּ יְהוָה כִּי גֵאוּת
עָשָׂה מידעת▽ זֹאת בְּכָל־הָאָרֶץ: ו צַהֲלִי וָרֹנִּי יוֹשֶׁבֶת צִיּוֹן
כִּי־גָדוֹל בְּקִרְבֵּךְ קְדוֹשׁ יִשְׂרָאֵל:

▽ מוּדַעַת

יום ירושלים

No תַּחֲנוּן is said on the previous afternoon. מַעֲרִיב is said as usual.
The עֹמֶר is counted (43rd day). At the end of the service, psalms of celebration are said.
In שַׁחֲרִית, תַּחֲנוּן is not said. After the Leader's repetition of the עֲמִידָה, הַלֵּל is said.

and the islands of the sea. He will raise a banner for the nations and gather the exiles of Israel; He will assemble the scattered people of Judah from the four quarters of the earth. Ephraim's jealousy will vanish, and Judah's harassment will end. Ephraim will not be jealous of Judah, nor will Judah be hostile toward Ephraim. They will swoop down on the slopes of Philistia to the west; together they will plunder the people to the east. Edom and Moab will be subject to them, and the Ammonites shall obey them. The LORD will dry up the gulf of the Egyptian sea; with a scorching wind He will sweep his hand over the Euphrates River. He will break it up into seven streams so that people can cross over in sandals. There will be a highway for the remnant of His people that is left from Assyria, as there was for Israel when they came up from Egypt. In that day you will say: "I will praise You, O LORD. Although You were angry with me, Your anger has turned away and You have comforted me. Surely GOD is my salvation; I will trust and not be afraid. The LORD, the LORD, is my strength and my song; He has become my salvation." With joy you will draw water from the wells of salvation. In that day you will say: "Give thanks to the LORD, call on His name; make known among the nations what He has done, and proclaim that His name is exalted. Sing to the LORD, for He has done glorious things; let this be known to all the world. Shout aloud and sing for joy, people of Zion, for great is the Holy One of Israel among you."

YOM YERUSHALAYIM – JERUSALEM DAY

No *Tachanun* is said on the previous afternoon. The Evening Service is said as usual. The *Omer* is counted (43rd day). At the end of the service, psalms of celebration are said.

In the morning, *Tachanun* is not said. After the Leader's repetition of the *Amidah*, *Hallel* is said.

סדר קדוש ראש השנה

When רֹאשׁ הַשָּׁנָה falls on שַׁבָּת, in the home begin here:

Quietly וַיְהִי־עֶרֶב וַיְהִי בֹקֶר

יוֹם הַשִּׁשִּׁי. וַיְכֻלּוּ הַשָּׁמַיִם וְהָאָרֶץ וְכׇל־צְבָאָם. וַיְכַל אֱלֹהִים בַּיּוֹם הַשְּׁבִיעִי מְלַאכְתּוֹ אֲשֶׁר עָשָׂה, וַיִּשְׁבֹּת בַּיּוֹם הַשְּׁבִיעִי מִכׇּל־מְלַאכְתּוֹ אֲשֶׁר עָשָׂה. וַיְבָרֶךְ אֱלֹהִים אֶת־יוֹם הַשְּׁבִיעִי וַיְקַדֵּשׁ אֹתוֹ, כִּי בוֹ שָׁבַת מִכׇּל־מְלַאכְתּוֹ אֲשֶׁר־בָּרָא אֱלֹהִים לַעֲשׂוֹת.

When saying קִדּוּשׁ for others, add:

סַבְרִי מָרָנָן וְרַבָּנָן וְרַבּוֹתַי.

בָּרוּךְ אַתָּה יהוה אֱלֹהֵינוּ מֶלֶךְ הָעוֹלָם, בּוֹרֵא פְּרִי הַגָּפֶן.

On שַׁבָּת, add the words in brackets.

בָּרוּךְ אַתָּה יהוה אֱלֹהֵינוּ מֶלֶךְ הָעוֹלָם, אֲשֶׁר בָּחַר בָּנוּ מִכׇּל־עָם, וְרוֹמְמָנוּ מִכׇּל־לָשׁוֹן, וְקִדְּשָׁנוּ בְּמִצְוֺתָיו. וַתִּתֶּן לָנוּ יהוה אֱלֹהֵינוּ בְּאַהֲבָה אֶת יוֹם (הַשַּׁבָּת הַזֶּה וְאֶת יוֹם) הַזִּכָּרוֹן הַזֶּה, יוֹם (זִכְרוֹן) תְּרוּעָה (בְּאַהֲבָה) מִקְרָא קֹדֶשׁ, זֵכֶר לִיצִיאַת מִצְרָיִם. כִּי בָנוּ בָחַרְתָּ וְאוֹתָנוּ קִדַּשְׁתָּ מִכׇּל־הָעַמִּים, וּדְבָרְךָ אֱמֶת וְקַיָּם לָעַד. בָּרוּךְ אַתָּה יהוה, מֶלֶךְ עַל כׇּל־הָאָרֶץ, מְקַדֵּשׁ (הַשַּׁבָּת וְ) יִשְׂרָאֵל וְיוֹם הַזִּכָּרוֹן.

On Saturday Night the following הַבְדָּלָה is added:

בָּרוּךְ אַתָּה יהוה אֱלֹהֵינוּ מֶלֶךְ הָעוֹלָם, בּוֹרֵא מְאוֹרֵי הָאֵשׁ.

בָּרוּךְ אַתָּה יהוה אֱלֹהֵינוּ מֶלֶךְ הָעוֹלָם, הַמַּבְדִּיל בֵּין קֹדֶשׁ לְחוֹל, בֵּין אוֹר לְחֹשֶׁךְ, בֵּין יִשְׂרָאֵל לָעַמִּים, בֵּין יוֹם הַשְּׁבִיעִי לְשֵׁשֶׁת יְמֵי הַמַּעֲשֶׂה. בֵּין קְדֻשַּׁת שַׁבָּת לִקְדֻשַּׁת יוֹם טוֹב הִבְדַּלְתָּ, וְאֶת יוֹם הַשְּׁבִיעִי מִשֵּׁשֶׁת יְמֵי הַמַּעֲשֶׂה קִדַּשְׁתָּ, הִבְדַּלְתָּ וְקִדַּשְׁתָּ אֶת עַמְּךָ יִשְׂרָאֵל בִּקְדֻשָּׁתֶךָ. בָּרוּךְ אַתָּה יהוה, הַמַּבְדִּיל בֵּין־קֹדֶשׁ לְקֹדֶשׁ.

KIDDUSH FOR ROSH HASHANAH EVENING

When Rosh Hashanah falls on Shabbat, in the home begin here:

Quietly: And it was evening, and it was morning,

יוֹם הַשִּׁשִּׁי the sixth day. Then the heavens and the earth were completed, and all their array. With the seventh day, God completed the work He had done. He ceased on the seventh day from all the work He had done. God blessed the seventh day and declared it holy, because on it He ceased from all His work He had created to do.

When saying *Kiddush* for others, add:

Please pay attention, my teachers, rabbis and friends.

בָּרוּךְ Blessed are You, Lord our God, King of the Universe, who creates the fruit of the vine.

On Shabbat, add the words in brackets.

בָּרוּךְ Blessed are You, Lord our God, King of the Universe, who has chosen us from among all peoples, raised us above all tongues, and made us holy through His commandments. You have given us, Lord our God, in love (this Sabbath day and), this Day of Memorial, a day of (remembrance) blowing the shofar (in love), a sacred assembly, in memory of the Exodus from Egypt. For You have chosen us and sanctified us above all peoples, and Your word is truth and endures forever. Blessed are You, Lord, King over all the earth, who sanctifies (the Sabbath and) Israel and the Day of Memorial.

On Saturday night, the following *Havdalah* is added:

בָּרוּךְ Blessed are You, Lord our God, King of the Universe, who creates the lights of fire.

Blessed are You, Lord our God, King of the Universe, who distinguishes between sacred and secular, between light and darkness, between Israel and the nations, between the seventh day and the six days of work. You have made a distinction between the holiness of the Sabbath and the holiness of festivals, and have sanctified the seventh day above the six days of work. You have distinguished and sanctified your people Israel with your holiness. Blessed are You, Lord, who distinguishes between holy and holy.

בָּרוּךְ אַתָּה יהוה אֱלֹהֵינוּ מֶלֶךְ הָעוֹלָם, שֶׁהֶחֱיָנוּ וְקִיְּמָנוּ וְהִגִּיעָנוּ לַזְּמַן הַזֶּה.

Following קִדּוּשׁ and הַמּוֹצִיא, an apple is dipped in honey and the following is said:

בָּרוּךְ אַתָּה יהוה אֱלֹהֵינוּ מֶלֶךְ הָעוֹלָם, בּוֹרֵא פְּרִי הָעֵץ.

After eating some of the apple and honey, say:

יְהִי רָצוֹן מִלְּפָנֶיךָ, יהוה אֱלֹהֵינוּ וֵאלֹהֵי אֲבוֹתֵינוּ, שֶׁתְּחַדֵּשׁ עָלֵינוּ שָׁנָה טוֹבָה וּמְתוּקָה.

סדר קידושא רבא לראש השנה

On שַׁבָּת, add the following paragraph:

וְשָׁמְרוּ בְנֵי־יִשְׂרָאֵל אֶת־הַשַּׁבָּת, לַעֲשׂוֹת אֶת־הַשַּׁבָּת לְדֹרֹתָם בְּרִית עוֹלָם. בֵּינִי וּבֵין בְּנֵי יִשְׂרָאֵל אוֹת הִיא לְעוֹלָם, כִּי־שֵׁשֶׁת יָמִים עָשָׂה יהוה אֶת־הַשָּׁמַיִם וְאֶת־הָאָרֶץ, וּבַיּוֹם הַשְּׁבִיעִי שָׁבַת וַיִּנָּפַשׁ.

תִּקְעוּ בַחֹדֶשׁ שׁוֹפָר בַּכֶּסֶה לְיוֹם חַגֵּנוּ. כִּי חֹק לְיִשְׂרָאֵל הוּא, מִשְׁפָּט לֵאלֹהֵי יַעֲקֹב.

When saying קִדּוּשׁ for others, add:

סַבְרִי מָרָנָן וְרַבָּנָן וְרַבּוֹתַי.

בָּרוּךְ אַתָּה יהוה אֱלֹהֵינוּ מֶלֶךְ הָעוֹלָם, בּוֹרֵא פְּרִי הַגָּפֶן.

Apple and honey: The custom of eating symbolic foods at the start of a New Year is based on the Talmudic statement that "omens have significance" (*Horayot* 12a). Customs vary from community to community. The most widespread is to eat an apple dipped in honey as a sign of a "sweet New Year". Others eat carrots, leeks, beets, dates, gourds, pomegranates, fish, or the head of a sheep. Each custom has its own symbolism and associated prayer.

In Judaism, the beginning of something contains within it the potentiality of the whole, hence what we experience on the

בָּרוּךְ Blessed are You, LORD our GOD, King of the Universe, who has given us life, sustained us, and brought us to this time.

Following *Kiddush* and the Blessing over Bread,
an apple is dipped in honey and the following is said:

בָּרוּךְ Blessed are You, LORD our GOD, King of the Universe, who creates the fruit of the tree.

After eating some of the apple and honey, say:

יְהִי May it be Your will, LORD our GOD and GOD of our ancestors, to renew for us a happy and sweet year.

KIDDUSH FOR ROSH HASHANAH MORNING

On Shabbat, add the following paragraph:

וְשָׁמְרוּ The children of Israel must keep the Sabbath, observing the Sabbath in every generation as an everlasting covenant. It is a sign between Me and the children of Israel for ever, for in six days GOD made the heavens and the earth, but on the seventh day He ceased work and refreshed Himself.

תִּקְעוּ Blow the shofar on the New Moon, on our festival when the moon is hidden. For it is a statute for Israel, an ordinance of the GOD of Jacob.

When saying *Kiddush* for others, add:

Please pay attention, my teachers, rabbis and friends.

בָּרוּךְ Blessed are You, LORD our GOD, King of the Universe, who creates the fruit of the vine.

first day of the year is a token of the days that are to come. Tasting the sweetness of the apple and honey, we pray that the rest of the year, too, will bring sweetness.

Commentators note that our prayers on Rosh Hashanah speak of exalted things: GOD's sovereignty over the Universe and His judgement of our lives. We do not pray for material blessings; rather we do so, obliquely and gently, at the table while eating symbolic food. The custom mitigates the severity of the day and serves as a reminder that all we enjoy comes to us from GOD.

סדר תשליך

On the first day of רֹאשׁ הַשָּׁנָה (or, if that day is שַׁבָּת, on the second day), it is customary, in the afternoon, to go to the banks of a river, or of any stretch of water, and say the following:

מיכה ז

מִי אֵל כָּמְוֹךָ נֹשֵׂא עָוֹן וְעֹבֵר עַל־פֶּשַׁע לִשְׁאֵרִית נַחֲלָתוֹ, לֹא־הֶחֱזִיק לָעַד אַפּוֹ, כִּי־חָפֵץ חֶסֶד הוּא. יָשׁוּב יְרַחֲמֵנוּ יִכְבֹּשׁ עֲוֹנֹתֵינוּ, וְתַשְׁלִיךְ בִּמְצֻלוֹת יָם כָּל־חַטֹּאתָם. תִּתֵּן אֱמֶת לְיַעֲקֹב, חֶסֶד לְאַבְרָהָם, אֲשֶׁר־נִשְׁבַּעְתָּ לַאֲבֹתֵינוּ מִימֵי קֶדֶם.

תהלים קל

שִׁיר הַמַּעֲלוֹת, מִמַּעֲמַקִּים קְרָאתִיךָ יהוה. אֲדֹנָי שִׁמְעָה בְקוֹלִי, תִּהְיֶינָה אָזְנֶיךָ קַשֻּׁבוֹת לְקוֹל תַּחֲנוּנָי. אִם עֲוֹנוֹת תִּשְׁמָר־יָהּ, אֲדֹנָי מִי יַעֲמֹד. כִּי עִמְּךָ הַסְּלִיחָה, לְמַעַן תִּוָּרֵא. קִוִּיתִי יהוה קִוְּתָה נַפְשִׁי, וְלִדְבָרוֹ הוֹחָלְתִּי. נַפְשִׁי לַיהוה, מִשֹּׁמְרִים לַבֹּקֶר, שֹׁמְרִים לַבֹּקֶר. יַחֵל יִשְׂרָאֵל אֶל יהוה, כִּי־עִם־יהוה הַחֶסֶד, וְהַרְבֵּה עִמּוֹ פְדוּת. וְהוּא יִפְדֶּה אֶת יִשְׂרָאֵל, מִכֹּל עֲוֹנוֹתָיו.

TASHLICH: THE CASTING

It is a custom, on the afternoon of the first day of Rosh Hashanah (or second, if the first is Shabbat) to go to the shore of the sea, the bank of a river, or other running stream of water, as a symbolic enactment of the words of the prophet Micah: "He will cast (*tashlich*) into the depths of the sea all their sins" (7:19).

The first mention of the custom is in Sefer Maharil of Rabbi Jacob Moellin (d. 1425). Various explanations have been given. Rabbi Moellin himself relates the custom to a midrashic tradition about the binding of Isaac (on Rosh Hashanah, according to the Talmud, we blow the ram's horn in memory of the ram Abraham offered as a sacrifice in place of his son). On the journey, the Accuser placed a river in his way. Abraham was undeterred and walked straight through. Thus, as with the blowing of the shofar, we ask God to forgive us in the merit of Abraham.

TASHLICH

On the first day of the New Year (or, if that day is Shabbat, on the second day), it is customary, in the afternoon, to go to the banks of a river, or of any stretch of water, and say the following:

MICHAH 7

מִי אֵל כָּמְוֹךָ Who is a God like You, who pardons iniquity and forgives the transgression of the remnant of His heritage? He does stay angry for ever, but delights in lovingkindness. He will again have compassion on us, suppress our iniquities, and cast into the depths of the sea all their sins. Grant truth to Jacob, kindness to Abraham, as You promised our fathers in days long ago.

PSALM 130

שִׁיר הַמַּעֲלוֹת A song of ascents. From the depths I have called to You, O Lord. Lord, hear my voice; let Your ears be attentive to my plea. If You, Lord, should keep account of sins, who could stand? But with You there is forgiveness, that You may be held in awe. I wait for the Lord, my soul waits; and in His word I put my hope. My soul waits for the Lord more than watchmen wait for the morning, more than watchmen wait for the morning. Israel, put your hope in the Lord, for with the Lord there is unfailing love, and great is His power to redeem. It is He who will redeem Israel from all their sins.

Water, too, is a symbol of Torah – of the knowledge that leads to virtue and peace: "They will neither harm nor destroy on all My holy mountain, for the earth will be full of the knowledge of the Lord as the waters cover the sea" (Isaiah 11:9).

Rivers are a symbol of tears (Avot de-Rabbi Nathan 31) and thus a sign of repentance and remorse. "By the rivers of Babylon, there we sat and wept as we remembered Zion" (Psalm 137:1). Flowing water is also a symbol of time, mortality and the shortness of life: "One generation goes, another comes…All streams flow into the sea, yet the sea is never full". Consciousness of mortality is a fundamental theme of Rosh Hashanah ("Write us in the Book of Life").

Some have the custom to shake the hems of their clothing, in accordance with Nehemiah 5:13, "Also I shook out my lap, and said: So may God shake out…" (*Machzor Oholei Yaakov*).

ברכות

Blessings

סדר סעודה וברכותיה

On washing hands before eating bread:

בָּרוּךְ אַתָּה יהוה אֱלֹהֵינוּ מֶלֶךְ הָעוֹלָם, אֲשֶׁר קִדְּשָׁנוּ בְּמִצְוֹתָיו, וְצִוָּנוּ עַל נְטִילַת יָדָיִם.

Before eating bread:

בָּרוּךְ אַתָּה יהוה אֱלֹהֵינוּ מֶלֶךְ הָעוֹלָם, הַמּוֹצִיא לֶחֶם מִן הָאָרֶץ.

Before eating food, other than bread, made from the five species of grain: wheat, barley, rye, oats and spelt:

בָּרוּךְ אַתָּה יהוה אֱלֹהֵינוּ מֶלֶךְ הָעוֹלָם, בּוֹרֵא מִינֵי מְזוֹנוֹת.

Before drinking wine or grape juice:

בָּרוּךְ אַתָּה יהוה אֱלֹהֵינוּ מֶלֶךְ הָעוֹלָם, בּוֹרֵא פְּרִי הַגָּפֶן.

Before eating fruit that grows on trees:

בָּרוּךְ אַתָּה יהוה אֱלֹהֵינוּ מֶלֶךְ הָעוֹלָם, בּוֹרֵא פְּרִי הָעֵץ.

BLESSINGS ON VARIOUS OCCASIONS

LAWS OF WASHING HANDS AND THE BLESSING OVER BREAD

1. Before eating bread, it is necessary to wash one's hands. Water should be poured over the hands from a vessel (not directly from a tap). Many people keep a special vessel for this purpose. The rim of the vessel should not be cracked or chipped. The vessel should contain enough water to pour liberally over the hands up to the wrist. The custom is to pour water first over the right hand, then the left.
2. The blessing is made *after* washing the hands but before drying them.
3. Between the blessing over washing and the blessing over bread, one must be silent. Since the former is a preparation for the latter, there should be no interruption between them. One may, however, answer Amen to someone else's blessing.
4. The bread should be held while saying a blessing over it. It is a custom to dip the bread in salt, except on Rosh Hashanah (and some say, Sukkot), when it is dipped in honey instead. Some people sprinkle salt over the bread instead.

BLESSINGS OVER FOOD OR DRINK

On washing hands before eating bread:

Blessed are You, Lord our God, King of the Universe, who has made us holy through His commandments, and has commanded us about washing hands.

Before eating bread:

Blessed are You, Lord our God, King of the Universe, who brings forth bread from the earth.

Before eating food, other than bread, made from the five species of grain: wheat, barley, rye, oats and spelt:

Blessed are You, the Lord our God, King of the Universe, who creates the various kinds of nourishment.

Before drinking wine or grape juice:

Blessed are You, Lord our God, King of the Universe, who creates fruit of the vine.

Before eating fruit that grows on trees:

Blessed are You, Lord our God, King of the Universe, who creates fruit of the tree.

Washing hands. The rule of washing hands before eating bread represents the idea that the act of eating – a physical necessity – should be transformed into a religious ceremony: as if the home were a miniature sanctuary, the table an altar, and the food a sacrifice dedicated to God (this is the reason we dip the bread over which we make a blessing in salt, in memory of the offerings in the Temple to which salt was added: Leviticus 2:13).

Blessing over bread and other foods. According to the Sages, "It is forbidden to take enjoyment from the world without making a blessing and whoever does so is as if he made secular use of holy things" (*Berachot* 35b). The universe belongs to God, and thus is sacred. Before we may make use of it we must first redeem it; that is, we must offer something else in its place, namely the blessing, by which we acknowledge that all we enjoy derives from God. This articulated gratitude is a profound gesture of the soul. To rejoice in what one has, and see it as the gift of God, is true wealth, Ben Zoma taught (*Avot* 4:1).

Before eating fruit for the first time in a season:

בָּרוּךְ אַתָּה יהוה אֱלֹהֵינוּ מֶלֶךְ הָעוֹלָם, שֶׁהֶחֱיָנוּ וְקִיְּמָנוּ וְהִגִּיעָנוּ לַזְּמַן הַזֶּה.

Before eating vegetables or fruit that grows on plants or bushes:

בָּרוּךְ אַתָּה יהוה אֱלֹהֵינוּ מֶלֶךְ הָעוֹלָם, בּוֹרֵא פְּרִי הָאֲדָמָה.

Before eating other food or drinking other liquids:

בָּרוּךְ אַתָּה יהוה אֱלֹהֵינוּ מֶלֶךְ הָעוֹלָם, שֶׁהַכֹּל נִהְיֶה בִּדְבָרוֹ.

ברכת המזון

On יום טוב, שַׁבָּת and festive occasions, say (תהלים קכו):

שִׁיר הַמַּעֲלוֹת, בְּשׁוּב יהוה אֶת־שִׁיבַת צִיּוֹן הָיִינוּ כְּחֹלְמִים. אָז יִמָּלֵא שְׂחוֹק פִּינוּ, וּלְשׁוֹנֵנוּ רִנָּה, אָז יֹאמְרוּ בַגּוֹיִם, הִגְדִּיל יהוה לַעֲשׂוֹת עִם־אֵלֶּה. הִגְדִּיל יהוה לַעֲשׂוֹת עִמָּנוּ, הָיִינוּ שְׂמֵחִים. שׁוּבָה יהוה אֶת־שְׁבִיתֵנוּ, כַּאֲפִיקִים בַּנֶּגֶב. הַזֹּרְעִים בְּדִמְעָה בְּרִנָּה יִקְצֹרוּ. הָלוֹךְ יֵלֵךְ וּבָכֹה נֹשֵׂא מֶשֶׁךְ־הַזָּרַע, בֹּא־יָבוֹא בְרִנָּה נֹשֵׂא אֲלֻמֹּתָיו.

תְּהִלַּת יהוה יְדַבֶּר פִּי, וִיבָרֵךְ כָּל־בָּשָׂר שֵׁם קָדְשׁוֹ לְעוֹלָם וָעֶד. וַאֲנַחְנוּ נְבָרֵךְ יָהּ, מֵעַתָּה וְעַד־עוֹלָם, הַלְלוּיָהּ. הוֹדוּ לַיהוה כִּי־טוֹב, כִּי לְעוֹלָם חַסְדּוֹ. מִי יְמַלֵּל גְּבוּרוֹת יהוה, יַשְׁמִיעַ כָּל־תְּהִלָּתוֹ.

שֶׁהֶחֱיָנוּ *Who has given us life, sustained us, and brought us to this time*: This blessing, said over new fruit, is also said on buying a new house, wearing new clothes, hearing good news, and performing seasonal commandments. It turns our attention from the immediate cause of pleasure to life itself and to our safe passage through the hazards of time.

GRACE AFTER MEALS

Grace after Meals is specifically mandated by the Torah itself: "You shall eat and be satisfied and bless the LORD your GOD" (Deuteronomy 8:10). Thanksgiving, Moses taught the Israelites, is central to Jewish life, "lest your heart grow haughty and you forget the LORD your GOD…and you say to yourselves, 'My own power and

Before eating fruit for the first time in a season:

Blessed are You, LORD our GOD, King of the Universe who has given us life, sustained us, and brought us to this time.

Before eating vegetables or fruit that grows on plants or bushes:

Blessed are You, LORD our GOD, King of the Universe, who creates fruit of the ground.

Before eating other food or drinking other liquids:

Blessed are You, LORD our GOD, King of the Universe, by whose word all things came to be.

GRACE AFTER MEALS

On Shabbat, Festivals and festive occasions, say (PSALM 126):

שִׁיר הַמַּעֲלוֹת A song of ascents. When the LORD brought back the exiles of Zion we were like people who dream. Then were our mouths filled with laughter, and our tongues with songs of joy. Then was it said among the nations, "The LORD has done great things for them". The LORD did do great things for us and we rejoiced. Bring back our exiles, LORD, like streams in a dry land. May those who sowed in tears, reap in joy. May one who goes out weeping, carrying a bag of seed, come back with songs of joy, carrying his sheaves.

תְּהִלַּת My mouth shall speak the praise of GOD, and all creatures shall bless His holy name for ever and all time. We will bless GOD now and for ever. Halleluyah! Thank the LORD for He is good: His lovingkindness is for ever. Who can tell of the LORD's mighty acts and make all His praise be heard?

the might of my own hand have won this wealth for me' (ibid, vv. 14–17)." Bereft of a sense of gratitude and of a power higher than humans, nations like individuals eventually decay.

The original form of Grace consisted of three blessings, which move sequentially from the universal to the particular. In the first, we thank GOD for sustaining the world and all that lives. The second is national: we thank GOD for the land of Israel as well as for the other blessings of Jewish life: the covenant and its sign, circumcision, and the Torah. The third turns to Jerusalem. The fourth paragraph is a later addition: according to

זימון

For the special Grace said at a wedding meal or during the wedding week, see page 792.

For the special Grace said at a בְּרִית מִילָה see page 804.

In the house of a mourner when there are three or more men, see page 770.

When three or more men say Grace together, the following is said (when there is a מִנְיָן present, add the bracketed words):

When three or more women say Grace with no men present, they substitute חֲבֵרוֹתַי with רַבּוֹתַי:

Leader:

רַבּוֹתַי נְבָרֵךְ.

Others:

יְהִי שֵׁם יהוה מְבֹרָךְ מֵעַתָּה וְעַד־עוֹלָם.

Leader:

יְהִי שֵׁם יהוה מְבֹרָךְ מֵעַתָּה וְעַד־עוֹלָם.

בִּרְשׁוּת רַבּוֹתַי, נְבָרֵךְ (אֱלֹהֵינוּ) שֶׁאָכַלְנוּ מִשֶּׁלּוֹ.

Others*:

בָּרוּךְ (אֱלֹהֵינוּ) שֶׁאָכַלְנוּ מִשֶּׁלּוֹ וּבְטוּבוֹ חָיִינוּ.

---

*People present who have not taken part in the meal say:

בָּרוּךְ (אֱלֹהֵינוּ) וּמְבֹרָךְ שְׁמוֹ תָּמִיד לְעוֹלָם וָעֶד.

Leader:

בָּרוּךְ (אֱלֹהֵינוּ) שֶׁאָכַלְנוּ מִשֶּׁלּוֹ וּבְטוּבוֹ חָיִינוּ.

בָּרוּךְ הוּא וּבָרוּךְ שְׁמוֹ.

---

the Talmud (*Berachot* 48b), it was added after the Bar Kochba rebellion, c. 135 CE. Over the course of time, it has expanded considerably.

Zimmun. A meal at which there are three adult males requires a formal invitation, *zimmun*, to say Grace. The Talmud derives this from the verse, "Magnify the Lord with me; let us exalt His name together" (Psalm 34:4). A slightly longer version is used when at least ten are present.

ZIMMUN / INVITATION

For the special Grace said at a wedding meal or during the wedding week, see page 793.

For the special Grace said at a circumcision feast, see page 805.

In the house of a mourner when there are three or more men, see page 771.

When three or more men say Grace together, the following is said (when there is a *minyan* present, add the bracketed words)

When three or more women say Grace with no men present, they substitute *Rabotai* with *Chaveirotai*:

Leader:

Friends, let us say grace.

Others:

May the name of the LORD be blessed from now and for ever.

Leader:

May the name of the LORD be blessed from now and for ever. With your permission, let us bless the One (our GOD) from whose food we have eaten.

Others*:

Blessed be the One (our GOD) from whose food we have eaten, and by whose goodness we live.

---

*People present who have not taken part in the meal say:

Blessed be the One whose name is continually blessed for ever and all time.

Leader:

Blessed be the One (our GOD) from whose food we have eaten, and by whose goodness we live. All Blessed be He, and blessed be His name.

The act of inviting those present to join in the act of praise is similar to the recitation of *Bar'chu*, with which morning and evening services begin. It emphasises the essentially communal nature of prayer in Judaism. In addition to the regular *zimmun* here, there are special forms of *zimmun* for: 1. a wedding meal; 2. a meal after a circumcision; and 3. a meal in a house of mourning.

ברכת הזן

בָּרוּךְ אַתָּה יהוה אֱלֹהֵֽינוּ מֶֽלֶךְ הָעוֹלָם, הַזָּן אֶת־הָעוֹלָם כֻּלּוֹ, בְּטוּבוֹ, בְּחֵן בְּחֶֽסֶד וּבְרַחֲמִים, הוּא נוֹתֵן לֶֽחֶם לְכָל־בָּשָׂר, כִּי לְעוֹלָם חַסְדּוֹ. וּבְטוּבוֹ הַגָּדוֹל, תָּמִיד לֹא־חָֽסַר לָֽנוּ, וְאַל יֶחְסַר־לָֽנוּ מָזוֹן לְעוֹלָם וָעֶד. בַּעֲבוּר שְׁמוֹ הַגָּדוֹל, כִּי הוּא זָן וּמְפַרְנֵס לַכֹּל, וּמֵטִיב לַכֹּל, וּמֵכִין מָזוֹן לְכָל־בְּרִיּוֹתָיו אֲשֶׁר בָּרָא. בָּרוּךְ אַתָּה יהוה, הַזָּן אֶת־הַכֹּל.

ברכת הארץ

נוֹדֶה לְּךָ יהוה אֱלֹהֵֽינוּ, עַל שֶׁהִנְחַֽלְתָּ לַאֲבוֹתֵֽינוּ אֶֽרֶץ חֶמְדָּה טוֹבָה וּרְחָבָה. וְעַל שֶׁהוֹצֵאתָֽנוּ יהוה אֱלֹהֵֽינוּ מֵאֶֽרֶץ מִצְרַֽיִם, וּפְדִיתָֽנוּ מִבֵּית עֲבָדִים, וְעַל בְּרִיתְךָ שֶׁחָתַֽמְתָּ בִּבְשָׂרֵֽנוּ, וְעַל תּוֹרָתְךָ שֶׁלִּמַּדְתָּֽנוּ, וְעַל חֻקֶּֽיךָ שֶׁהוֹדַעְתָּֽנוּ, וְעַל חַיִּים חֵן וָחֶֽסֶד שֶׁחוֹנַנְתָּֽנוּ, וְעַל אֲכִילַת מָזוֹן שָׁאַתָּה זָן וּמְפַרְנֵס אוֹתָֽנוּ תָּמִיד, בְּכָל־יוֹם וּבְכָל־עֵת וּבְכָל־שָׁעָה.

On חֲנֻכָּה and פּוּרִים, say:

עַל הַנִּסִּים, וְעַל הַפֻּרְקָן, וְעַל הַגְּבוּרוֹת, וְעַל הַתְּשׁוּעוֹת, וְעַל הַמִּלְחָמוֹת, שֶׁעָשִֽׂיתָ לַאֲבוֹתֵֽינוּ בַּיָּמִים הָהֵם בַּזְּמַן הַזֶּה.

On חֲנֻכָּה, say:

בִּימֵי מַתִּתְיָֽהוּ בֶּן־יוֹחָנָן כֹּהֵן גָּדוֹל חַשְׁמוֹנַאי וּבָנָיו, כְּשֶׁעָמְדָה מַלְכוּת יָוָן הָרְשָׁעָה עַל־עַמְּךָ יִשְׂרָאֵל, לְהַשְׁכִּיחָם תּוֹרָתֶֽךָ, וּלְהַעֲבִירָם מֵחֻקֵּי רְצוֹנֶֽךָ. וְאַתָּה בְּרַחֲמֶֽיךָ הָרַבִּים, עָמַֽדְתָּ לָהֶם בְּעֵת צָרָתָם, רַֽבְתָּ אֶת־רִיבָם, דַּֽנְתָּ אֶת־דִּינָם, נָקַֽמְתָּ אֶת־נִקְמָתָם. מָסַֽרְתָּ גִבּוֹרִים בְּיַד חַלָּשִׁים, וְרַבִּים בְּיַד מְעַטִּים, וּטְמֵאִים בְּיַד טְהוֹרִים, וּרְשָׁעִים בְּיַד צַדִּיקִים, וְזֵדִים בְּיַד עוֹסְקֵי תוֹרָתֶֽךָ. וּלְךָ עָשִֽׂיתָ שֵׁם גָּדוֹל וְקָדוֹשׁ בְּעוֹלָמֶֽךָ, וּלְעַמְּךָ יִשְׂרָאֵל עָשִֽׂיתָ תְּשׁוּעָה גְדוֹלָה וּפֻרְקָן כְּהַיּוֹם הַזֶּה. וְאַחַר כֵּן בָּֽאוּ בָנֶֽיךָ לִדְבִיר בֵּיתֶֽךָ, וּפִנּוּ אֶת־הֵיכָלֶֽךָ, וְטִהֲרוּ אֶת־מִקְדָּשֶֽׁךָ,

BLESSING OF NOURISHMENT

בָּרוּךְ Blessed are You, Lord our God, King of the Universe, who in His goodness feeds the whole world with grace, kindness and compassion. He gives food to all living things, for His kindness is for ever. Because of His continual great goodness, we have never lacked food, nor may we ever lack it, for the sake of His great name. For He is God who feeds and sustains all, does good to all, and prepares food for all creatures He has created. Blessed are You, Lord, who feeds all.

BLESSING OF LAND

נוֹדֶה We thank You, Lord our God, for having granted as a heritage to our ancestors a desirable, good and spacious land; for bringing us out, Lord our God, from the land of Egypt, freeing us from the house of slavery; for Your covenant which You sealed in our flesh; for Your Torah which You taught us; for Your laws which You made known to us; for the life, grace and kindness You have bestowed on us; and for the food by which You continually feed and sustain us, every day, every season, every hour.

On Chanukah and Purim, say:

עַל הַנִּסִּים [We thank You also] for the miracles, the redemption, the mighty deeds, and the victories in battle which You performed for our ancestors in those days at this time.

On Chanukah, say:

בִּימֵי In the days of Mattityahu, son of Yochanan the High Priest, the Hasmonean, and his sons, the wicked Greek kingdom rose up against Your people Israel to make them forget Your Torah and to force them to transgress the statutes of Your will. It was then that You in Your great compassion stood by them in the time of their distress. You championed their cause, judged their claim, and avenged their wrong. You delivered the strong into the hands of the weak, the many into the hands of the few, the impure into the hands of the pure, the wicked into the hands of the righteous, and the arrogant into the hands of those who were

---

נוֹדֶה *We thank*: After thanking God for the land, the paragraph goes on to add thanks for God's other kindnesses to Israel: the exodus from Egypt, the covenant and its sign, circumcision, the giving of the Torah and the commandments. On

וְהִדְלִיקוּ נֵרוֹת בְּחַצְרוֹת קָדְשֶׁךָ, וְקָבְעוּ שְׁמוֹנַת יְמֵי חֲנֻכָּה אֵלּוּ, לְהוֹדוֹת וּלְהַלֵּל לְשִׁמְךָ הַגָּדוֹל.

On פּוּרִים, say:

בִּימֵי מָרְדְּכַי וְאֶסְתֵּר בְּשׁוּשַׁן הַבִּירָה, כְּשֶׁעָמַד עֲלֵיהֶם הָמָן הָרָשָׁע, בִּקֵּשׁ לְהַשְׁמִיד לַהֲרֹג וּלְאַבֵּד אֶת־כָּל־הַיְּהוּדִים, מִנַּעַר וְעַד זָקֵן, טַף וְנָשִׁים בְּיוֹם אֶחָד, בִּשְׁלוֹשָׁה־עָשָׂר לְחֹדֶשׁ שְׁנֵים־עָשָׂר, הוּא־חֹדֶשׁ אֲדָר, וּשְׁלָלָם לָבוֹז. וְאַתָּה בְּרַחֲמֶיךָ הָרַבִּים הֵפַרְתָּ אֶת־עֲצָתוֹ, וְקִלְקַלְתָּ אֶת־מַחֲשַׁבְתּוֹ, וַהֲשֵׁבוֹתָ גְּמוּלוֹ בְּרֹאשׁוֹ, וְתָלוּ אוֹתוֹ וְאֶת־בָּנָיו עַל־הָעֵץ.

וְעַל הַכֹּל יהוה אֱלֹהֵינוּ אֲנַחְנוּ מוֹדִים לָךְ, וּמְבָרְכִים אוֹתָךְ, יִתְבָּרַךְ שִׁמְךָ בְּפִי כָּל־חַי תָּמִיד לְעוֹלָם וָעֶד. כַּכָּתוּב, וְאָכַלְתָּ וְשָׂבָעְתָּ, וּבֵרַכְתָּ אֶת־יהוה אֱלֹהֶיךָ, עַל־הָאָרֶץ הַטֹּבָה אֲשֶׁר־נָתַן לָךְ. בָּרוּךְ אַתָּה יהוה, עַל־הָאָרֶץ וְעַל־הַמָּזוֹן.

ברכת ירושלים

רַחֵם יהוה אֱלֹהֵינוּ עַל־יִשְׂרָאֵל עַמֶּךָ, וְעַל־יְרוּשָׁלַיִם עִירֶךָ, וְעַל־צִיּוֹן מִשְׁכַּן כְּבוֹדֶךָ, וְעַל־מַלְכוּת בֵּית דָּוִד מְשִׁיחֶךָ, וְעַל־הַבַּיִת הַגָּדוֹל וְהַקָּדוֹשׁ שֶׁנִּקְרָא שִׁמְךָ עָלָיו. אֱלֹהֵינוּ אָבִינוּ רְעֵנוּ זוּנֵנוּ פַּרְנְסֵנוּ וְכַלְכְּלֵנוּ וְהַרְוִיחֵנוּ, וְהַרְוַח־לָנוּ יהוה אֱלֹהֵינוּ מְהֵרָה מִכָּל־צָרוֹתֵינוּ. וְנָא אַל־תַּצְרִיכֵנוּ יהוה אֱלֹהֵינוּ, לֹא לִידֵי מַתְּנַת בָּשָׂר־וָדָם, וְלֹא לִידֵי הַלְוָאָתָם, כִּי אִם לְיָדְךָ הַמְּלֵאָה הַפְּתוּחָה הַקְּדוֹשָׁה וְהָרְחָבָה, שֶׁלֹּא נֵבוֹשׁ וְלֹא נִכָּלֵם לְעוֹלָם וָעֶד.

Chanukah and Purim, *Al Hanissim* is said here, as it is in the *Amidah* in the parallel paragraph of "Thanks" (*Modim*).

Jerusalem. The third blessing speaks of Jerusalem, home of God's glory, as well as the Davidic monarchy and the Temple, for the restoration of which we pray. As is often the case in the Siddur, Jerusalem is associated with the Divine attribute

engaged in the study of Your Torah. You made for Yourself great and holy renown in Your world, and for Your people Israel You performed a great salvation and redemption on this day. Your children then entered the holiest part of Your house, cleansed Your Temple, purified Your sanctuary, kindled lights in Your holy courts, and designated these eight days of Chanukah for giving thanks and praise to Your great name.

On Purim, say:

בִּימֵי In the days of Mordechai and Esther, in Shushan the capital, the wicked Haman rose up against them and sought to destroy, slay and exterminate all the Jews, young and old, children and women, on one day, the thirteenth day of the twelfth month, which is the month of Adar, and to plunder their possessions. Then You in Your great compassion thwarted his counsel, frustrated his plans, and caused his scheme to recoil on his own head, so that they hanged him and his sons on the gallows.

וְעַל הַכֹּל For all this, LORD our GOD, we thank and bless You. May Your name be blessed continually by the mouth of all that lives, for ever and all time – for so it is written: "You will eat and be satisfied, then you shall bless the LORD your GOD for the good land He has given you." Blessed are You, LORD, for the land and for the food.

BLESSING FOR JERUSALEM

רַחֵם Have compassion, LORD our GOD, on Israel Your people, on Jerusalem Your city, on Zion the dwelling place of Your glory, on the royal house of David Your anointed, and on the great and holy house that bears Your name. Our GOD, our Father, tend us, feed us, sustain us, support us and relieve us. Quickly relieve us, LORD our GOD, from all our troubles. Please, O LORD our GOD, do not make us dependent on the gifts or loans of other people, but only on Your full, open, holy and generous hand so that we may suffer neither shame nor humiliation for ever and all time.

---

of compassion, reflecting the words of Zechariah: "Therefore, this is what the LORD says: I will return to Jerusalem with compassion, and there My house will be rebuilt" (1:16). According to tradition, the Divine presence never left Jerusalem, even when the city lay in ruins.

Who in His compassion will rebuild Jerusalem. Amen – the unusual appearance of the word Amen in this passage (normally we do not say it after our own blessings) signals that this was originally the end of Grace, Amen signalling the end of a sequence of blessings.

On שַׁבָּת, say:

רְצֵה וְהַחֲלִיצֵנוּ יהוה אֱלֹהֵינוּ בְּמִצְוֹתֶיךָ, וּבְמִצְוַת יוֹם הַשְּׁבִיעִי הַשַּׁבָּת הַגָּדוֹל וְהַקָּדוֹשׁ הַזֶּה, כִּי יוֹם זֶה גָּדוֹל וְקָדוֹשׁ הוּא לְפָנֶיךָ, לִשְׁבׇּת־בּוֹ וְלָנוּחַ בּוֹ בְּאַהֲבָה כְּמִצְוַת רְצוֹנֶךָ, בִּרְצוֹנְךָ הָנִיחַ לָנוּ יהוה אֱלֹהֵינוּ, שֶׁלֹּא תְהִי צָרָה וְיָגוֹן וַאֲנָחָה בְּיוֹם מְנוּחָתֵנוּ, וְהַרְאֵנוּ יהוה אֱלֹהֵינוּ בְּנֶחָמַת צִיּוֹן עִירֶךָ, וּבְבִנְיַן יְרוּשָׁלַיִם עִיר קׇדְשֶׁךָ, כִּי אַתָּה הוּא בַּעַל הַיְשׁוּעוֹת וּבַעַל הַנֶּחָמוֹת.

On רֹאשׁ חֹדֶשׁ, יוֹם טוֹב and חגים, say:

אֱלֹהֵינוּ וֵאלֹהֵי אֲבוֹתֵינוּ, יַעֲלֶה, וְיָבֹא, וְיַגִּיעַ, וְיֵרָאֶה, וְיֵרָצֶה, וְיִשָּׁמַע, וְיִפָּקֵד, וְיִזָּכֵר זִכְרוֹנֵנוּ וּפִקְדּוֹנֵנוּ, וְזִכְרוֹן אֲבוֹתֵינוּ, וְזִכְרוֹן מָשִׁיחַ בֶּן דָּוִד עַבְדֶּךָ, וְזִכְרוֹן יְרוּשָׁלַיִם עִיר קׇדְשֶׁךָ, וְזִכְרוֹן כׇּל־עַמְּךָ בֵּית יִשְׂרָאֵל לְפָנֶיךָ, לִפְלֵיטָה וּלְטוֹבָה, וּלְחֵן וּלְחֶסֶד וּלְרַחֲמִים, וּלְחַיִּים וּלְשָׁלוֹם בְּיוֹם

On רֹאשׁ חֹדֶשׁ:
רֹאשׁ הַחֹדֶשׁ

On פֶּסַח:
חַג הַמַּצּוֹת

On שָׁבֻעוֹת:
חַג הַשָּׁבֻעוֹת

On רֹאשׁ הַשָּׁנָה:
הַזִּכָּרוֹן

On סֻכּוֹת:
חַג הַסֻּכּוֹת

On שִׂמְחַת תּוֹרָה and שְׁמִינִי עֲצֶרֶת:
הַשְּׁמִינִי חַג הָעֲצֶרֶת

הַזֶּה. זׇכְרֵנוּ יהוה אֱלֹהֵינוּ בּוֹ לְטוֹבָה, וּפׇקְדֵנוּ בוֹ לִבְרָכָה, וְהוֹשִׁיעֵנוּ בוֹ לְחַיִּים. וּבִדְבַר יְשׁוּעָה וְרַחֲמִים, חוּס וְחׇנֵּנוּ וְרַחֵם עָלֵינוּ וְהוֹשִׁיעֵנוּ, כִּי אֵלֶיךָ עֵינֵינוּ, כִּי אֵל מֶלֶךְ חַנּוּן וְרַחוּם אָתָּה.

In the house of a mourner, נַחֵם on page 772 is substituted for the next two paragraphs:

וּבְנֵה יְרוּשָׁלַיִם עִיר הַקֹּדֶשׁ בִּמְהֵרָה בְיָמֵינוּ. בָּרוּךְ אַתָּה יהוה, בּוֹנֶה בְרַחֲמָיו יְרוּשָׁלָיִם. אָמֵן.

ברכת הטוב ומטיב

בָּרוּךְ אַתָּה יהוה אֱלֹהֵינוּ מֶלֶךְ הָעוֹלָם, הָאֵל אָבִינוּ מַלְכֵּנוּ אַדִּירֵנוּ בּוֹרְאֵנוּ גּוֹאֲלֵנוּ יוֹצְרֵנוּ קְדוֹשֵׁנוּ קְדוֹשׁ יַעֲקֹב, רוֹעֵנוּ

בָּרוּךְ *Blessed*: A later addition, dated by the Talmud (*Berachot* 48b) to the period following the Bar Kochba rebellion when, after a long delay, the Romans gave per-

On Shabbat, say:

רְצֵה Favour and strengthen us, Lord our God, through Your commandments, especially through the commandment of the seventh day, this great and holy Sabbath. For it is, for You, a great and holy day. On it we cease work and rest in love in accord with Your will's commandment. May it be Your will, Lord our God, to grant us rest without distress, grief, or lament on our day of rest. May You show us the consolation of Zion Your city, and the rebuilding of Jerusalem Your holy city, for You are the Master of salvation and consolation.

On Rosh Chodesh and Festivals, say:

אֱלֹהֵינוּ Our God and God of our ancestors, may there rise, come, reach, appear, be favoured, heard, regarded and remembered before You, our recollection and remembrance, as well as the remembrance of our ancestors, and of the Messiah son of David Your servant, and of Jerusalem Your holy city, and of all Your people the House of Israel – for deliverance and well-being, grace, lovingkindness and compassion, life and peace, on this day of:

On Rosh Chodesh:	On Pesach:	On Shavuot:	On Rosh Hashanah:
Rosh Chodesh.	the Festival of Matzot.	the Festival of Shavuot.	the Day of Memorial.

On Sukkot:	On Shemini Atzeret and Simchat Torah:
the Festival of Sukkot.	the Festival of Shemini Atzeret.

On it remember us, Lord our God, for good; recollect us for blessing, and deliver us for life. In accord with Your promise of salvation and compassion, spare us and be gracious to us; have compassion on us and deliver us, for our eyes are turned to You because You, God, are a gracious and compassionate King.

In the house of a mourner, "Comfort" on page 773 is substituted for the next two paragraphs:

וּבְנֵה And may Jerusalem the holy city be rebuilt soon, in our time. Blessed are You, Lord, who in His compassion will rebuild Jerusalem. Amen.

BLESSING OF GOD'S GOODNESS

בָּרוּךְ Blessed are You, Lord our God, King of the Universe – God our father, our King, our Sovereign, our Creator, our Redeemer, our

רוֹעֵה יִשְׂרָאֵל, הַמֶּלֶךְ הַטּוֹב וְהַמֵּטִיב לַכֹּל, שֶׁבְּכָל־יוֹם וָיוֹם הוּא הֵטִיב, הוּא מֵטִיב, הוּא יֵטִיב לָנוּ. הוּא גְמָלָנוּ הוּא גוֹמְלֵנוּ הוּא יִגְמְלֵנוּ לָעַד, לְחֵן לְחֶסֶד וּלְרַחֲמִים וּלְרֶוַח הַצָּלָה וְהַצְלָחָה, בְּרָכָה וִישׁוּעָה. נֶחָמָה פַּרְנָסָה וְכַלְכָּלָה וְרַחֲמִים וְחַיִּים וְשָׁלוֹם וְכָל־טוֹב, וּמִכָּל־טוּב אַל־יְחַסְּרֵנוּ.

בקשות נוספות

הָרַחֲמָן הוּא יִמְלוֹךְ עָלֵינוּ לְעוֹלָם וָעֶד. הָרַחֲמָן הוּא יִתְבָּרַךְ בַּשָּׁמַיִם וּבָאָרֶץ. הָרַחֲמָן הוּא יִשְׁתַּבַּח לְדוֹר־דּוֹרִים, וְיִתְפָּאַר בָּנוּ לָנֶצַח נְצָחִים, וְיִתְהַדַּר בָּנוּ לָעַד וּלְעוֹלְמֵי עוֹלָמִים. הָרַחֲמָן הוּא יְפַרְנְסֵנוּ בְּכָבוֹד. הָרַחֲמָן הוּא יִשְׁבּוֹר עֻלֵּנוּ מֵעַל צַוָּארֵנוּ, וְהוּא יוֹלִיכֵנוּ קוֹמְמִיּוּת לְאַרְצֵנוּ. הָרַחֲמָן הוּא יִשְׁלַח בְּרָכָה מְרֻבָּה בַּבַּיִת הַזֶּה, וְעַל שֻׁלְחָן זֶה שֶׁאָכַלְנוּ עָלָיו. הָרַחֲמָן הוּא יִשְׁלַח לָנוּ אֶת־אֵלִיָּהוּ הַנָּבִיא זָכוּר לַטּוֹב, וִיבַשֶּׂר־לָנוּ בְּשׂוֹרוֹת טוֹבוֹת יְשׁוּעוֹת וְנֶחָמוֹת.

הָרַחֲמָן הוּא יְבָרֵךְ

When eating at one's own table, say (include the words in brackets that apply):

אוֹתִי (וְאֶת־אִשְׁתִּי / וְאֶת־בַּעְלִי / וְאֶת־אָבִי מוֹרִי / וְאֶת־אִמִּי מוֹרָתִי / וְאֶת־זַרְעִי) וְאֶת־כָּל־אֲשֶׁר לִי.

A guest at someone else's table says (include the words in brackets that apply):

אֶת־בַּעַל הַבַּיִת הַזֶּה, אוֹתוֹ (וְאֶת אִשְׁתּוֹ בַּעֲלַת הַבַּיִת הַזֶּה / וְאֶת זַרְעוֹ) וְאֶת־כָּל־אֲשֶׁר לוֹ.

mission to the Jews to bury their dead. The failure of the Bar Kochba rebellion was one of the low points of Jewish history. According to the Roman historian Dio, 580,000 Jews died in the fighting and many others by starvation. Nine hundred and eighty-five towns, villages and settlements were destroyed. Jerusalem was levelled to the ground and rebuilt as a Roman city, Aelia Capitolina. The fact that the Sages were able to salvage a fragment of consolation from the fact that the dead were not denied the dignity of burial is testimony to an extraordinary ability to sur-

Maker, our Holy One, the Holy One of Jacob. He is our Shepherd, Israel's Shepherd, the good King who does good to all. Every day He has done, is doing, and will do good to us. He has acted, is acting, and will act kindly toward us, granting us grace, kindness and compassion, relief and rescue, prosperity, blessing, redemption and comfort, sustenance and support, compassion, life, peace and all good things. Of all that is good, may He never let us lack.

ADDITIONAL REQUESTS

הָרַחֲמָן May the Compassionate One reign over us for ever and all time. May the Compassionate One be blessed in heaven and on earth. May the Compassionate One be praised from generation to generation, be glorified by us to all eternity, and honoured among us for ever and all time. May the Compassionate One grant us an honourable livelihood. May the Compassionate One break the yoke from our neck and lead us upright to our land. May the Compassionate One send many blessings to this house and this table at which we have eaten. May the Compassionate One send us Elijah the prophet – may he be remembered for good – to bring us good tidings of salvation and consolation.

הָרַחֲמָן May the Compassionate One bless –

When eating at one's own table, say (include the words in brackets that apply):

me, (my wife/husband, / my father, my teacher / my mother, my teacher/ my children,) and all that is mine.

A guest at someone else's table says (include the words in brackets that apply):

my hosts, (their children, and all that is theirs)

---

vive catastrophe and preserve the lineaments of hope. The passage is built around threefold references to God's kingship, goodness and bestowal of kindness.

הָרַחֲמָן *May the Compassionate One*: A series of additional prayers, dating from the Geonic period. The oldest is the one in which a guest invokes blessings on the hosts and their family. This is immediately preceded by a prayer that Elijah may come and announce the coming of the Messiah. The juxtaposition is striking: we bring redemption by acts of hospitality. This, according to the Sages, is how Abraham and Sarah brought monotheism to the world. They would provide hospitality to strangers. When the meal was over, and the guests would begin to thank them, Abraham would reply, "Thank the One from whom all we have enjoyed has come."

A child at his/her parents' table says (include the words in brackets if in parents' home):

אֶת־אָבִי מוֹרִי (בַּעַל הַבַּיִת הַזֶּה), וְאֶת־אִמִּי מוֹרָתִי (בַּעֲלַת הַבַּיִת הַזֶּה), אוֹתָם וְאֶת־בֵּיתָם וְאֶת־זַרְעָם וְאֶת־כָּל־אֲשֶׁר לָהֶם.

A parent at his/her son's table says (include the words in brackets that apply):

אֶת־בְּנִי בַּעַל הַבַּיִת הַזֶּה (וְאֶת אִשְׁתּוֹ בַּעֲלַת הַבַּיִת הַזֶּה/וְאֶת זַרְעוֹ).

A parent at his/her daughter's table says (include the words in brackets that apply):

וְאֶת בִּתִּי בַּעֲלַת הַבַּיִת הַזֶּה (וְאֶת בַּעֲלָהּ בַּעַל הַבַּיִת הַזֶּה / וְאֶת זַרְעָהּ).

אוֹתָנוּ וְאֶת־כָּל־אֲשֶׁר לָנוּ, כְּמוֹ שֶׁנִּתְבָּרְכוּ אֲבוֹתֵינוּ אַבְרָהָם יִצְחָק וְיַעֲקֹב בַּכֹּל מִכֹּל כֹּל, כֵּן יְבָרֵךְ אוֹתָנוּ כֻּלָּנוּ יַחַד בִּבְרָכָה שְׁלֵמָה, וְנֹאמַר, אָמֵן.

בַּמָּרוֹם יְלַמְּדוּ עֲלֵיהֶם וְעָלֵינוּ זְכוּת, שֶׁתְּהִי לְמִשְׁמֶרֶת שָׁלוֹם. וְנִשָּׂא בְרָכָה מֵאֵת יהוה, וּצְדָקָה מֵאֱלֹהֵי יִשְׁעֵנוּ, וְנִמְצָא־חֵן וְשֵׂכֶל־טוֹב בְּעֵינֵי אֱלֹהִים וְאָדָם.

On שַׁבָּת, add:

הָרַחֲמָן הוּא יַנְחִילֵנוּ יוֹם שֶׁכֻּלּוֹ שַׁבָּת וּמְנוּחָה לְחַיֵּי הָעוֹלָמִים.

On רֹאשׁ חֹדֶשׁ, add:

הָרַחֲמָן הוּא יְחַדֵּשׁ עָלֵינוּ אֶת־הַחֹדֶשׁ הַזֶּה לְטוֹבָה וְלִבְרָכָה.

On יוֹם טוֹב, add:

הָרַחֲמָן הוּא יַנְחִילֵנוּ יוֹם שֶׁכֻּלּוֹ טוֹב.

On רֹאשׁ הַשָּׁנָה, add:

הָרַחֲמָן הוּא יְחַדֵּשׁ עָלֵינוּ אֶת־הַשָּׁנָה הַזֹּאת לְטוֹבָה וְלִבְרָכָה.

On חוֹל הַמּוֹעֵד סֻכּוֹת, add:

הָרַחֲמָן הוּא יָקִים לָנוּ אֶת־סֻכַּת דָּוִד הַנּוֹפֶלֶת.

הָרַחֲמָן הוּא יְזַכֵּנוּ לִימוֹת הַמָּשִׁיחַ וּלְחַיֵּי הָעוֹלָם הַבָּא.

A child at his/her parents' table says (include the words in brackets if in parents' home):

my father, my teacher, (master of this house,) and my mother, my teacher, (mistress of this house,) them, their household, their children, and all that is theirs

A parent at his/her son's table says (include the words in brackets that apply):

my son, master of this house, (his wife, mistress of this house / their children)

A parent at his/her daughter's table says (include the words in brackets that apply):

My daughter, the mistress of this house, (her husband master of this house, / their children)

אוֹתָנוּ – together with us and all that is ours, just as our forefathers Abraham, Isaac and Jacob were blessed in all, from all, with all, so may He bless all of us together with a complete blessing, and let us say: Amen.

בַּמָּרוֹם On high, may grace be invoked for them and for us, as a safeguard of peace. May we receive a blessing from the Lord and a just reward from the God of our salvation, and may we find grace and good favour in the eyes of God and man.

On Shabbat, add:

הָרַחֲמָן May the Compassionate One let us inherit the time that will be entirely Shabbat and rest for life everlasting.

On Rosh Chodesh, add:

הָרַחֲמָן May the Compassionate One renew this month for us for good and blessing.

On Festivals, add:

הָרַחֲמָן May the Compassionate One let us inherit the day that is all good.

On Rosh Hashanah, add:

הָרַחֲמָן May the Compassionate One renew for us this year for good and blessing.

On the Intermediate Days of Sukkot, add:

הָרַחֲמָן May the Compassionate One restore for us the fallen Tabernacle of David.

הָרַחֲמָן May the Compassionate One make us worthy of the Messianic Age and life in the World to Come.

On weekdays:

מַגְדִּיל

On רֹאשׁ חֹדֶשׁ and חוֹל הַמּוֹעֵד ,יוֹם טוֹב ,שַׁבָּת:

מִגְדּוֹל

יְשׁוּעוֹת מַלְכּוֹ וְעֹשֶׂה חֶסֶד לִמְשִׁיחוֹ לְדָוִד וּלְזַרְעוֹ עַד־עוֹלָם. עֹשֶׂה שָׁלוֹם בִּמְרוֹמָיו, הוּא יַעֲשֶׂה שָׁלוֹם עָלֵינוּ וְעַל־כָּל־יִשְׂרָאֵל. וְאִמְרוּ, אָמֵן.

יְראוּ אֶת־יהוה קְדֹשָׁיו, כִּי אֵין מַחְסוֹר לִירֵאָיו. כְּפִירִים רָשׁוּ וְרָעֵבוּ, וְדֹרְשֵׁי יהוה לֹא־יַחְסְרוּ כָל־טוֹב. הוֹדוּ לַיהוה כִּי־טוֹב, כִּי לְעוֹלָם חַסְדּוֹ. פּוֹתֵחַ אֶת יָדֶךָ, וּמַשְׂבִּיעַ לְכָל־חַי רָצוֹן. בָּרוּךְ הַגֶּבֶר אֲשֶׁר יִבְטַח בַּיהוה, וְהָיָה יהוה מִבְטַחוֹ. נַעַר הָיִיתִי גַּם־זָקַנְתִּי, וְלֹא־רָאִיתִי צַדִּיק נֶעֱזָב, וְזַרְעוֹ מְבַקֶּשׁ־לָחֶם. יהוה עֹז לְעַמּוֹ יִתֵּן, יהוה יְבָרֵךְ אֶת־עַמּוֹ בַשָּׁלוֹם.

ברכת המזון בבית האבל

Leader:

רַבּוֹתַי נְבָרֵךְ.

Others:

יְהִי שֵׁם יהוה מְבֹרָךְ מֵעַתָּה וְעַד־עוֹלָם.

נַעַר הָיִיתִי *Once I was young*: The standard translation of this verse (Psalm 37:5) is "I was young and now am old and I have not seen the righteous forsaken or his children searching for bread". I have translated it here according to the fine insight of the late Rav Joseph Soloveitchik, who argued that the verb *ra'iti* should be understood in the sense in which it appears in the Book of Esther, when Esther, pleading on behalf of Jewry, says: "For *how can I watch* the evil that shall come unto my people? Or *how can I watch* the destruction of my kindred?" (8:6). The

On weekdays:

He gives great –

On Shabbat, Festivals and their Intermediate Days and Rosh Chodesh:

He is a tower of –

salvation to His king, showing kindness to His anointed, to David and his descendants for ever. He who makes peace in His high places, may He make peace for us and all Israel, and let us say: Amen.

יְראוּ Fear the Lord, you His holy ones; those who fear Him lack nothing. Young lions may grow weak and hungry, but those who seek the Lord lack no good thing. Thank the Lord for He is good: His loving-kindness is for ever. You open Your hand and satisfy the desire of every living thing. Blessed is the person who trusts in the Lord, whose trust is in the Lord alone. Once I was young, and now I am old, yet I have never watched a righteous man forsaken or his children begging for bread. The Lord will give His people strength. The Lord will bless His people with peace.

GRACE AFTER MEALS IN A HOUSE OF MOURNING

Leader:

Friends, let us say grace.

Others:

May the name of the Lord be blessed from now and for ever.

---

verb there means "stand as a passive witness to". Taken in this sense, Psalm 37:5 should be understood as, "When the righteous was forsaken or his children forced to search for bread, I never merely stood and watched." Understood thus, it is a warning against being a mere bystander while other people suffer. It thus brings the Grace to a symmetrical close: It began by speaking of God's goodness in feeding the hungry and ends with an injunction for us to do likewise. This too is part of "walking in God's ways".

Leader:

יְהִי שֵׁם יהוה מְבֹרָךְ מֵעַתָּה וְעַד־עוֹלָם.
בִּרְשׁוּת רַבּוֹתַי, נְבָרֵךְ מְנַחֵם אֲבֵלִים שֶׁאָכַלְנוּ מִשֶּׁלּוֹ.

Others*:

בָּרוּךְ מְנַחֵם אֲבֵלִים שֶׁאָכַלְנוּ מִשֶּׁלּוֹ וּבְטוּבוֹ חָיִינוּ.

---

*People present who have not taken part in the meal say:

בָּרוּךְ מְנַחֵם אֲבֵלִים וּמְבֹרָךְ שְׁמוֹ תָּמִיד לְעוֹלָם וָעֶד.

Leader:

בָּרוּךְ מְנַחֵם אֲבֵלִים שֶׁאָכַלְנוּ מִשֶּׁלּוֹ וּבְטוּבוֹ חָיִינוּ.
בָּרוּךְ הוּא וּבָרוּךְ שְׁמוֹ.

Continue with בִּרְכַּת הַמָּזוֹן on page 760 until וּבְנֵה יְרוּשָׁלַיִם on page 764. Then say:

נַחֵם יהוה אֱלֹהֵינוּ אֶת־אֲבֵלֵי יְרוּשָׁלַיִם וְאֶת־הָאֲבֵלִים הַמִּתְאַבְּלִים בָּאֵבֶל הַזֶּה. נַחֲמֵם מֵאֶבְלָם וְשַׂמְּחֵם מִיגוֹנָם, כָּאָמוּר, כְּאִישׁ אֲשֶׁר אִמּוֹ תְּנַחֲמֶנּוּ, כֵּן אָנֹכִי אֲנַחֶמְכֶם וּבִירוּשָׁלַיִם תְּנֻחָמוּ. בָּרוּךְ אַתָּה יהוה, מְנַחֵם צִיּוֹן בְּבִנְיַן יְרוּשָׁלָיִם.

בָּרוּךְ אַתָּה יהוה אֱלֹהֵינוּ מֶלֶךְ הָעוֹלָם, הָאֵל אָבִינוּ מַלְכֵּנוּ אַדִּירֵנוּ בּוֹרְאֵנוּ גּוֹאֲלֵנוּ יוֹצְרֵנוּ קְדוֹשֵׁנוּ קְדוֹשׁ יַעֲקֹב, רוֹעֵנוּ רוֹעֵה יִשְׂרָאֵל, הַמֶּלֶךְ הַחַי, הַטּוֹב וְהַמֵּטִיב. אֵל אֱמֶת, דַּיַּן אֱמֶת, שׁוֹפֵט צֶדֶק, וְלֹקֵחַ נְפָשׁוֹת בְּמִשְׁפָּט, וְשַׁלִּיט בְּעוֹלָמוֹ לַעֲשׂוֹת בּוֹ כִּרְצוֹנוֹ. כִּי כָל־דְּרָכָיו מִשְׁפָּט, וַאֲנַחְנוּ עַמּוֹ וַעֲבָדָיו. וְעַל הַכֹּל אֲנַחְנוּ חַיָּבִים לְהוֹדוֹת לוֹ וּלְבָרְכוֹ. גּוֹדֵר פְּרָצוֹת בְּיִשְׂרָאֵל, הוּא יִגְדּוֹר אֶת־הַפִּרְצָה הַזֹּאת, מֵעָלֵינוּ לְחַיִּים וּלְשָׁלוֹם, הוּא יִגְמְלֵנוּ לָעַד. חֵן וָחֶסֶד וְרַחֲמִים וְכָל־טוֹב, וּמִכָּל־טוּב אַל־יְחַסְּרֵנוּ.

Continue with הָרַחֲמָן הוּא יִמְלוֹךְ on page 766.

Leader:

May the name of the LORD be blessed from now and for ever. With your permission, let us bless the One who comforts mourners from whose food we have eaten.

Others*:

Blessed be the One who comforts mourners, from whose food we have eaten, and by whose goodness we live.

---

*People present who have not taken part in the meal say:

Blessed be the One who comforts mourners, whose name is continually blessed for ever and all time.

Leader:

Blessed be the One who comforts mourners, from whose food we have eaten, and by whose goodness we live.

All Blessed be He, and blessed be His name.

Continue with Grace After Meals on page 761 until "And may Jerusalem" on page 765. Then say:

נַחֵם Comfort, O LORD our GOD, the mourners of Jerusalem and those who mourn here. Grant them consolation in their mourning and gladness in their grief, as it is said, "As a mother comforts her son, so will I comfort you, and in Jerusalem you shall find comfort." Blessed are You, LORD, who brings comfort to Zion through the rebuilding of Jerusalem.

בָּרוּךְ Blessed are You, LORD our GOD, King of the Universe – GOD our Father, our King, our Creator, our Redeemer, our Holy One, the Holy One of Jacob, our living King who is good and does good, the true GOD, the true Judge, who judges righteously and takes back souls in judgement. He rules the world according to His will, for all His ways are just, and we are his people and his servants. For everything, we are dutybound to acknowledge and bless Him. May He who repairs the breaches in Israel, repair this breach in us and grant us life and peace. May He always bestow on us grace, kindness, compassion and all good things. Of all that is good, may He never let us lack.

Continue with "May the Compassionate One" on page 767.

ברכת המזון בקצרה

In emergencies only, the following shortened form may be used on weekdays.

בָּרוּךְ אַתָּה יהוה אֱלֹהֵינוּ מֶלֶךְ הָעוֹלָם, הַזָּן אֶת־הָעוֹלָם כֻּלּוֹ, בְּטוּבוֹ בְּחֵן בְּחֶסֶד וּבְרַחֲמִים, הוּא נוֹתֵן לֶחֶם לְכָל־בָּשָׂר, כִּי לְעוֹלָם חַסְדּוֹ. וּבְטוּבוֹ הַגָּדוֹל, תָּמִיד לֹא־חָסַר לָנוּ וְאַל־יֶחְסַר לָנוּ, מָזוֹן לְעוֹלָם וָעֶד. בַּעֲבוּר שְׁמוֹ הַגָּדוֹל, כִּי הוּא זָן וּמְפַרְנֵס לַכֹּל, וּמֵטִיב לַכֹּל, וּמֵכִין מָזוֹן לְכָל־בְּרִיּוֹתָיו אֲשֶׁר בָּרָא. בָּרוּךְ אַתָּה יהוה, הַזָּן אֶת־הַכֹּל.

נוֹדֶה לְךָ יהוה אֱלֹהֵינוּ, עַל שֶׁהִנְחַלְתָּ לַאֲבוֹתֵינוּ אֶרֶץ חֶמְדָּה טוֹבָה וּרְחָבָה, בְּרִית וְתוֹרָה, וְלֶחֶם לָשׂוֹבַע. בָּרוּךְ אַתָּה יהוה, עַל־הָאָרֶץ וְעַל־הַמָּזוֹן.

רַחֵם יהוה אֱלֹהֵינוּ עַל־יִשְׂרָאֵל עַמֶּךָ, וְעַל־מַלְכוּת בֵּית דָּוִד מְשִׁיחֶךָ, וְתַגְדִּל מְהֵרָה כְּבוֹד הַבַּיִת, וְתְנַחֲמֵנוּ בְּכִפְלַיִם. בָּרוּךְ אַתָּה יהוה, בּוֹנֵה בְּרַחֲמָיו יְרוּשָׁלָיִם. אָמֵן.

בָּרוּךְ אַתָּה יהוה אֱלֹהֵינוּ, הָאֵל אָבִינוּ מַלְכֵּנוּ הַמֶּלֶךְ הַטּוֹב וְהַמֵּטִיב לַכֹּל, הוּא הֵטִיב, הוּא מֵטִיב, הוּא יֵטִיב לָנוּ. וִיזַכֵּנוּ לִימוֹת הַמָּשִׁיחַ וּלְחַיֵּי הָעוֹלָם הַבָּא. עֹשֶׂה שָׁלוֹם בִּמְרוֹמָיו, הוּא יַעֲשֶׂה שָׁלוֹם עָלֵינוּ, וְעַל־כָּל־יִשְׂרָאֵל. וְאִמְרוּ אָמֵן.

THE SHORTER FORM OF GRACE
This abridged Grace is to be said only in emergencies and not to be taken as a regular substitute for the longer form. The Talmud (*Berachot* 16a) mentions a shorter form to be said during working hours by employees, though the ruling of the Shulchan Aruch is that this is no longer a permissible option. The Siddur of Rabbi Amram Gaon includes a shorter form for use by mourners (ed. Frumkin, vol. 2, p. 207). Other abridged forms are found in *Kol Bo* and Rabbi Aaron of Lunel's *Orchot Chayim*.

SHORTER FORM OF GRACE

In emergencies only, the following shortened form may be used on weekdays.

בָּרוּךְ Blessed are You, LORD our GOD, King of the Universe, who in His goodness feeds the whole world with grace, kindness and compassion. He gives food to all living things, for His kindness is for ever. Because of His continual great goodness, we have never lacked food, nor may we ever lack it, for the sake of His great name. For He is GOD who feeds and sustains all, does good to all, and prepares food for all creatures He has created. Blessed are You, LORD, who feeds all.

נוֹדֶה We thank You, LORD our GOD, for having granted as a heritage to our ancestors a desirable, good and spacious land; for the covenant and the Torah; and for the food You have given us in plenty. Blessed are You, LORD, for the land and for the food.

רַחֵם Have compassion, LORD our GOD, on Israel Your people and on the royal house of David Your anointed. May you soon make great the glory of the Temple, granting us a double consolation. Blessed are You, LORD, who in His compassion will rebuild Jerusalem. Amen.

בָּרוּךְ Blessed are You, LORD our GOD – GOD our Father and King, the good King who does good to all, who has acted, is acting, and will act kindly toward us. May the Compassionate One make us worthy of the Messianic Age and life in the World to Come. He who makes peace in His high places, may He make peace for us and all Israel, and let us say: Amen.

The current text is based on a version by Rabbi Naftali ben David Zechariah Mendel which first appeared in Venice, 1603, and won the approval of Rabbi Joel Sirkes (*Bayit Chadash* to *Tur* 1:192) and Rabbi Judah Ashkenzai (*Be'er Hetev* to *Orach Chayim* 192:1). It appeared, with slight emendations, in the Siddur *Avodat Yisrael* of Rabbi Isaac Seligman Baer. It preserves the essential four-blessing structure of the full form, together with all the elements deemed mandatory. It is not used on Shabbat or festivals.

Granting us a double consolation: The restoration of the Davidic monarchy and the rebuilding of the Temple.

סדר הברכות

ברכה אחרונה, מעין שלש

בָּרוּךְ אַתָּה יהוה אֱלֹהֵינוּ מֶלֶךְ הָעוֹלָם,

After grapes, figs, olives, pomegranates or dates:	After wine or grape juice:	After grain products, but not bread or מַצָּה:	After grain products, but not bread or מַצָּה, and wine or grape juice:
			עַל הַמִּחְיָה
עַל הָעֵץ	**עַל הַגֶּפֶן**	**עַל הַמִּחְיָה**	וְעַל הַכַּלְכָּלָה
וְעַל פְּרִי	וְעַל פְּרִי	וְעַל	**עַל הַגֶּפֶן**
הָעֵץ,	הַגֶּפֶן,	הַכַּלְכָּלָה,	וְעַל פְּרִי הַגֶּפֶן,

וְעַל תְּנוּבַת הַשָּׂדֶה, וְעַל אֶרֶץ חֶמְדָּה טוֹבָה וּרְחָבָה, שֶׁרָצִיתָ וְהִנְחַלְתָּ לַאֲבוֹתֵינוּ, לֶאֱכוֹל מִפִּרְיָהּ וְלִשְׂבּוֹעַ מִטּוּבָהּ. רַחֵם יהוה אֱלֹהֵינוּ עַל יִשְׂרָאֵל עַמֶּךָ, וְעַל יְרוּשָׁלַיִם עִירֶךָ, וְעַל צִיּוֹן מִשְׁכַּן כְּבוֹדֶךָ, וְעַל מִזְבְּחֶךָ וְעַל הֵיכָלֶךָ. וּבְנֵה יְרוּשָׁלַיִם עִיר הַקֹּדֶשׁ בִּמְהֵרָה בְיָמֵינוּ, וְהַעֲלֵנוּ לְתוֹכָהּ, וְשַׂמְּחֵנוּ בְּבִנְיָנָהּ, וְנֹאכַל מִפִּרְיָהּ, וְנִשְׂבַּע מִטּוּבָהּ, וּנְבָרֶכְךָ עָלֶיהָ בִּקְדֻשָּׁה וּבְטָהֳרָה.

On שַׁבָּת, add:

וּרְצֵה וְהַחֲלִיצֵנוּ בְּיוֹם הַשַּׁבָּת הַזֶּה.

On רֹאשׁ חֹדֶשׁ, add:

וְזָכְרֵנוּ לְטוֹבָה בְּיוֹם רֹאשׁ הַחֹדֶשׁ הַזֶּה.

On פֶּסַח, add:

וְשַׂמְּחֵנוּ בְּיוֹם חַג הַמַּצּוֹת הַזֶּה.

On שָׁבֻעוֹת, add:

וְשַׂמְּחֵנוּ בְּיוֹם חַג הַשָּׁבֻעוֹת הַזֶּה.

On סֻכּוֹת, add:

וְשַׂמְּחֵנוּ בְּיוֹם חַג הַסֻּכּוֹת הַזֶּה.

BLESSINGS

BLESSING AFTER FOOD, AL HAMICHYAH

בָּרוּךְ Blessed are you, LORD our GOD, King of the Universe,

After grain products, but not bread or Matzah, and wine or grape juice:	After grain products, but not bread or Matzah:	After wine or grape juice:	After grapes, figs, olives, pomegranates or dates:
for the nourishment and sustenance and **for the vine** and the fruit of the vine.	**for the nourishment** and sustenance	**for the vine** and the fruit of the vine	**for the tree** and the fruit of the tree

and for the produce of the field; for the desirable, good and spacious land that you willingly gave as heritage to our ancestors, that they might eat of its fruit and be satisfied with its goodness. Have compassion, LORD our GOD, on Israel Your people, on Jerusalem, Your city, on Zion the home of Your glory, on Your altar and Your Temple. May You rebuild Jerusalem, the holy city swiftly in our time, and may You bring us back there, rejoicing in its rebuilding, eating from its fruit, satisfied by its goodness, and blessing You for it in holiness and purity.

On Shabbat, add:

וּרְצֵה Be pleased to refresh us on this Sabbath Day.

On Rosh Chodesh, add:

וְזָכְרֵנוּ Remember us for good on this day of the New Moon.

On Pesach, add:

וְשַׂמְּחֵנוּ Grant us joy on this Festival of Matzot.

On Shavuot, add:

וְשַׂמְּחֵנוּ Grant us joy on this Festival of Shavuot.

On Sukkot, add:

וְשַׂמְּחֵנוּ Grant us joy on this Festival of Sukkot.

עַל הַמִּחְיָה *A blessing after other food or drink*: Known as the "three-in-one" blessing, this prayer summarises the first three paragraphs of the Grace after Meals. It is said after consuming any of the "seven kinds" of produce for which

On שְׂמִחַת תּוֹרָה and שְׁמִינִי עֲצֶרֶת, add:

וְשַׂמְּחֵנוּ בְּיוֹם הַשְּׁמִינִי חַג הָעֲצֶרֶת הַזֶּה.

On רֹאשׁ הַשָּׁנָה, add:

וְזָכְרֵנוּ לְטוֹבָה בְּיוֹם הַזִּכָּרוֹן הַזֶּה.

כִּי אַתָּה יהוה טוֹב וּמֵטִיב לַכֹּל, וְנוֹדֶה לְּךָ עַל הָאָרֶץ

After grapes, figs, olives, pomegranates or dates:	After wine or grape juice:	After grain products, but not bread or מַצָּה:	After grain products, but not bread or מַצָּה, and wine or grape juice:
וְעַל הַפֵּרוֹת.** בָּרוּךְ אַתָּה יהוה. עַל הָאָרֶץ וְעַל הַפֵּרוֹת**.	**וְעַל פְּרִי הַגָּפֶן*.** בָּרוּךְ אַתָּה יהוה, עַל הָאָרֶץ וְעַל פְּרִי הַגָּפֶן*.	**וְעַל הַמִּחְיָה.** בָּרוּךְ אַתָּה יהוה. עַל הָאָרֶץ וְעַל הַמִּחְיָה.	**וְעַל הַמִּחְיָה וְעַל פְּרִי הַגָּפֶן*.** בָּרוּךְ אַתָּה יהוה. עַל הָאָרֶץ וְעַל הַמִּחְיָה וְעַל פְּרִי הַגָּפֶן*.

*If the wine is from Israel, then substitute גַּפְנָהּ for הַגָּפֶן.

**If the fruit is from Israel, then substitute פֵּרוֹתֶיהָ for הַפֵּרוֹת.

ברכה אחרונה, בורא נפשות

After food or drink that does not require Grace after Meals or the above Grace – such as vegetables, beverages, or fruit other than grapes, figs, olives, pomegranates or dates – say:

בָּרוּךְ אַתָּה יהוה אֱלֹהֵינוּ מֶלֶךְ הָעוֹלָם, בּוֹרֵא נְפָשׁוֹת רַבּוֹת וְחֶסְרוֹנָן, עַל־כָּל־מַה שֶּׁבָּרָאתָ לְהַחֲיוֹת בָּהֶם נֶפֶשׁ כָּל־חָי. בָּרוּךְ חֵי הָעוֹלָמִים.

Israel is praised in the Torah (Deuteronomy 8:8) other than bread or Matzah, namely: 1. food made from wheat, barley, rye, oats or spelt; 2. grape wine or juice; or 3. grapes, figs, pomegranates, olives or dates.

On Shemini Atzeret and Simchat Torah, add:

וְשַׂמְּחֵנוּ Grant us joy on this festival of Shemini Atzeret.

On Rosh Hashanah, add:

וְזָכְרֵנוּ Remember as for good on this day of remembrance.

כִּי For You, God, are good and do good to all and we thank you for the land

After grain products, but not bread or Matzah, and wine or grape juice:	After grain products, but not bread or Matzah:	After wine or grape juice:	After grapes, figs, olives, pomegranates or dates:
and for the nourishment and for the fruit of the vine. Blessed are You, Lord, for the land and for the nourishment and the fruit of the vine.	**and for the nourishment.** Blessed are You, Lord, for the land and for the nourishment.	**and for the fruit of the vine.** Blessed are You, Lord, for the land and for the fruit of the vine.	**and for the fruit.** Blessed are You, Lord, for the land and for the fruit.

BLESSING AFTER FOOD, BOREH NEFASHOT

After food or drink that does not require Grace after Meals or the above Grace – such as vegetables, beverages, or fruit other than grapes, figs, olives, pomegranates or dates – say:

בָּרוּךְ Blessed are You, Lord our God, King of the Universe, who creates the many forms of life and their needs. For all You have created to sustain the life of all that lives, blessed be He, the life of worlds.

Blessings on various occasions. These blessings, many of which are to be said on encountering dramatic or sublime phenomena of nature, synthesise aesthetic sense with spiritual sensibility. The Judaic mind moves instinctively from nature to its Creator, a movement that is evident throughout the Book of Psalms and many of the prophetic and wisdom texts.

Blessings over commandments: Most commandments, except those "between man

ברכות הריח

On smelling fragrant shrubs or trees, such as roses or myrtles:

בָּרוּךְ אַתָּה יהוה אֱלֹהֵינוּ מֶלֶךְ הָעוֹלָם, בּוֹרֵא עֲצֵי בְשָׂמִים.

On smelling fragrant herbs or grasses, such as coriander:

בָּרוּךְ אַתָּה יהוה אֱלֹהֵינוּ מֶלֶךְ הָעוֹלָם, בּוֹרֵא עִשְּׂבֵי בְשָׂמִים.

On smelling fragrant spices or perfumes:

בָּרוּךְ אַתָּה יהוה אֱלֹהֵינוּ מֶלֶךְ הָעוֹלָם, בּוֹרֵא מִינֵי בְשָׂמִים

On smelling fragrant fruits, such as etrog, lemon or nutmeg:

בָּרוּךְ אַתָּה יהוה אֱלֹהֵינוּ מֶלֶךְ הָעוֹלָם, הַנּוֹתֵן רֵיחַ טוֹב בַּפֵּרוֹת.

ברכות שונות

On fixing a מְזוּזָה to the doorpost:

בָּרוּךְ אַתָּה יהוה אֱלֹהֵינוּ מֶלֶךְ הָעוֹלָם, אֲשֶׁר קִדְּשָׁנוּ בְּמִצְוֹתָיו, וְצִוָּנוּ לִקְבּוֹעַ מְזוּזָה.

On taking חַלָּה:

בָּרוּךְ אַתָּה יהוה אֱלֹהֵינוּ מֶלֶךְ הָעוֹלָם, אֲשֶׁר קִדְּשָׁנוּ בְּמִצְוֹתָיו, וְצִוָּנוּ לְהַפְרִישׁ חַלָּה מִן הָעִסָּה.

On eating seasonal fruit for the first time in the year; buying or wearing a new garment of significant value (e.g. a dress or suit); entering a new home for the first time; or hearing personal good news:

בָּרוּךְ אַתָּה יהוה אֱלֹהֵינוּ מֶלֶךְ הָעוֹלָם, שֶׁהֶחֱיָנוּ וְקִיְּמָנוּ וְהִגִּיעָנוּ לַזְּמַן הַזֶּה.

On hearing good news from which others as well as oneself will benefit:

בָּרוּךְ אַתָּה יהוה אֱלֹהֵינוּ מֶלֶךְ הָעוֹלָם, הַטּוֹב וְהַמֵּטִיב.

---

and man", require a blessing prior to their performance. The blessing is, in effect, the declaration of an intention to fulfil the commandment, an expression of *kavannah,* sacred intent. There are two basic formulae, "Who has commanded us *to*..." and "Who has commanded us *about*..." The most common explanation – though there

BLESSINGS OVER FRAGRANCES

On smelling fragrant shrubs or trees, such as roses or myrtles:

Blessed are You, LORD our GOD, King of the Universe, who creates fragrant trees.

On smelling fragrant herbs or grasses, such as coriander:

Blessed are You, LORD our GOD, King of the Universe, who creates fragrant plants.

On smelling fragrant spices or perfumes:

Blessed are You, LORD our GOD, King of the Universe, who creates the various spices.

On smelling fragrant fruits, such as etrog, lemon or nutmeg:

Blessed are You, LORD our GOD, King of the Universe, who gives pleasant fragrance to fruits.

BLESSINGS ON VARIOUS OCCASIONS

On fixing a *mezuzah* to the doorpost:

Blessed are You, LORD our GOD, King of the Universe, who has made us holy through His commandment, and has commanded us to affix the *mezuzah*.

On taking *challah*:

Blessed are You, LORD our GOD, King of the Universe, who has made us holy through His commandment, and has commanded us to set aside *challah* from the dough.

On eating seasonal fruit for the first time in the year; buying or wearing a new garment of significant value (e.g. a dress or suit); entering a new home for the first time; or hearing personal good news:

Blessed are You, LORD our GOD, King of the Universe who has given us life, sustained us, and brought us to this day.

On hearing good news from which others as well as oneself will benefit:

Blessed are You, LORD our GOD, King of the Universe, who is good and does good.

---

are exceptions – is that the former is used when fulfilling a commandment which I personally am obligated to do, while the latter relates to fulfilling a commandment on behalf of others (as when a *mohel* circumcises a child on behalf of its parents).

On hearing bad news, and recited by a mourner before the קְרִיעָה (ritual tearing of the garment):

בָּרוּךְ אַתָּה יהוה אֱלֹהֵינוּ מֶלֶךְ הָעוֹלָם, דַּיַּן הָאֱמֶת.

On seeing the wonders of Nature, such as lightning:

בָּרוּךְ אַתָּה יהוה אֱלֹהֵינוּ מֶלֶךְ הָעוֹלָם, עוֹשֶׂה מַעֲשֵׂה בְרֵאשִׁית.

On hearing thunder or experiencing a hurricane:

בָּרוּךְ אַתָּה יהוה אֱלֹהֵינוּ מֶלֶךְ הָעוֹלָם, שֶׁכֹּחוֹ וּגְבוּרָתוֹ מָלֵא עוֹלָם.

On seeing a rainbow:

בָּרוּךְ אַתָּה יהוה אֱלֹהֵינוּ מֶלֶךְ הָעוֹלָם, זוֹכֵר הַבְּרִית, וְנֶאֱמָן בִּבְרִיתוֹ, וְקַיָּם בְּמַאֲמָרוֹ.

On seeing the ocean:

בָּרוּךְ אַתָּה יהוה אֱלֹהֵינוּ מֶלֶךְ הָעוֹלָם, שֶׁעָשָׂה אֶת־הַיָּם הַגָּדוֹל.

On seeing trees blossoming the first time in the year:

בָּרוּךְ אַתָּה יהוה אֱלֹהֵינוּ מֶלֶךְ הָעוֹלָם, שֶׁלֹּא חִסַּר בְּעוֹלָמוֹ דָּבָר, וּבָרָא בוֹ בְּרִיּוֹת טוֹבוֹת וְאִילָנוֹת טוֹבִים, לְהַנּוֹת בָּהֶם בְּנֵי אָדָם.

On seeing an outstanding תּוֹרָה scholar:

בָּרוּךְ אַתָּה יהוה אֱלֹהֵינוּ מֶלֶךְ הָעוֹלָם, שֶׁחָלַק מֵחָכְמָתוֹ לִירֵאָיו.

On seeing an outstanding secular scholar:

בָּרוּךְ אַתָּה יהוה אֱלֹהֵינוּ מֶלֶךְ הָעוֹלָם, שֶׁנָּתַן מֵחָכְמָתוֹ לְבָשָׂר וָדָם.

On seeing a Monarch or Head of State:

בָּרוּךְ אַתָּה יהוה אֱלֹהֵינוּ מֶלֶךְ הָעוֹלָם, שֶׁנָּתַן מִכְּבוֹדוֹ לְבָשָׂר וָדָם.

On hearing bad news, and recited by a mourner before the ritual tearing of the garment:

Blessed are You, LORD our GOD, King of the Universe, the true Judge.

On seeing the wonders of Nature, such as lightning:

Blessed are You, LORD our GOD, King of the Universe, Author of creation.

On hearing thunder or experiencing a hurricane:

Blessed are You, LORD our GOD, King of the Universe, whose power and might fill the world.

On seeing a rainbow:

Blessed are You, LORD our GOD, King of the Universe, who remembers the covenant, is faithful to the covenant, and fulfils His word.

On seeing the ocean:

Blessed are You, LORD our GOD, King of the Universe, who has made the great sea.

On seeing trees blossoming for the first time in the year:

Blessed are You, LORD our GOD, King of the Universe, who has withheld nothing from His world, but has created in it beautiful creatures and trees for human beings to enjoy.

On seeing an outstanding Torah scholar:

Blessed are You, LORD our GOD, King of the Universe, who has shared of His wisdom with those who revere Him.

On seeing an outstanding secular scholar:

Blessed are You, LORD our GOD, King of the Universe, who has given of His wisdom with human beings.

On seeing a Monarch or Head of State:

Blessed are You, LORD our GOD, King of the Universe, who has given of His glory to human beings.

סדר תפלת הדרך

יְהִי רָצוֹן מִלְּפָנֶיךָ יהוה אֱלֹהֵינוּ וֵאלֹהֵי אֲבוֹתֵינוּ שֶׁתּוֹלִיכֵנוּ לְשָׁלוֹם, וְתַצְעִידֵנוּ לְשָׁלוֹם, וְתַסְמְכֵנוּ לְשָׁלוֹם, וְתַנְחֵנוּ אֶל־מְחוֹז חֶפְצֵנוּ לְחַיִּים וּלְשִׂמְחָה וּלְשָׁלוֹם, וְתַצִּילֵנוּ מִכַּף כָּל־אוֹיֵב וְאוֹרֵב וְאָסוֹן בַּדֶּרֶךְ, וּמִכָּל־מִינֵי פֻּרְעָנִיּוֹת הַמִּתְרַגְּשׁוֹת לָבוֹא לָעוֹלָם, וְתִשְׁלַח בְּרָכָה בְּמַעֲשֵׂה יָדֵינוּ, וְתִתְּנֵנוּ לְחֵן וּלְחֶסֶד וּלְרַחֲמִים בְּעֵינֶיךָ וּבְעֵינֵי כָל־רוֹאֵינוּ, וְתִשְׁמַע קוֹל תַּחֲנוּנֵינוּ, כִּי אֵל שׁוֹמֵעַ תְּפִלָּה וְתַחֲנוּן אָתָּה. בָּרוּךְ אַתָּה יהוה, שׁוֹמֵעַ תְּפִלָּה.

וְיַעֲקֹב הָלַךְ לְדַרְכּוֹ, וַיִּפְגְּעוּ־בוֹ מַלְאֲכֵי אֱלֹהִים. וַיֹּאמֶר יַעֲקֹב כַּאֲשֶׁר רָאָם מַחֲנֵה אֱלֹהִים זֶה, וַיִּקְרָא שֵׁם־הַמָּקוֹם הַהוּא מַחֲנָיִם. הִנֵּה אָנֹכִי שֹׁלֵחַ מַלְאָךְ לְפָנֶיךָ לִשְׁמָרְךָ בַּדָּרֶךְ, וְלַהֲבִיאֲךָ אֶל־הַמָּקוֹם אֲשֶׁר הֲכִנֹתִי. יְבָרֶכְךָ יהוה, וְיִשְׁמְרֶךָ. יָאֵר יהוה פָּנָיו אֵלֶיךָ וִיחֻנֶּךָּ. יִשָּׂא יהוה פָּנָיו אֵלֶיךָ וְיָשֵׂם לְךָ שָׁלוֹם.

When travelling by sea, some say:

יוֹרְדֵי הַיָּם בָּאֳנִיּוֹת עֹשֵׂי מְלָאכָה בְּמַיִם רַבִּים. הֵמָּה רָאוּ מַעֲשֵׂי יהוה וְנִפְלְאוֹתָיו בִּמְצוּלָה. וַיֹּאמֶר וַיַּעֲמֵד רוּחַ סְעָרָה וַתְּרוֹמֵם גַּלָּיו. יַעֲלוּ שָׁמַיִם יֵרְדוּ תְהוֹמוֹת נַפְשָׁם בְּרָעָה תִתְמוֹגָג. יָחוֹגּוּ וְיָנוּעוּ כַּשִּׁכּוֹר וְכָל־חָכְמָתָם תִּתְבַּלָּע. וַיִּצְעֲקוּ אֶל־יהוה בַּצַּר לָהֶם וּמִמְּצוּקֹתֵיהֶם יוֹצִיאֵם. יָקֵם סְעָרָה לִדְמָמָה וַיֶּחֱשׁוּ גַּלֵּיהֶם. וַיִּשְׂמְחוּ כִי־יִשְׁתֹּקוּ וַיַּנְחֵם אֶל־מְחוֹז חֶפְצָם. יוֹדוּ לַיהוה חַסְדּוֹ וְנִפְלְאוֹתָיו לִבְנֵי אָדָם.

When travelling by air, some say:

כִּי־אֶרְאֶה שָׁמֶיךָ מַעֲשֵׂי אֶצְבְּעֹתֶיךָ יָרֵחַ וְכוֹכָבִים אֲשֶׁר כּוֹנָנְתָּה. מָה־אֱנוֹשׁ כִּי־תִזְכְּרֶנּוּ וּבֶן־אָדָם כִּי תִפְקְדֶנּוּ. אִם־אֶסַּק שָׁמַיִם שָׁם אָתָּה וְאַצִּיעָה שְּׁאוֹל הִנֶּךָּ. אֶשָּׂא כַנְפֵי־שָׁחַר אֶשְׁכְּנָה בְּאַחֲרִית יָם. גַּם־שָׁם יָדְךָ תַנְחֵנִי וְתֹאחֲזֵנִי יְמִינֶךָ.

וִיהִי נֹעַם אֲדֹנָי אֱלֹהֵינוּ עָלֵינוּ, וּמַעֲשֵׂה יָדֵינוּ כּוֹנְנָה עָלֵינוּ, וּמַעֲשֵׂה יָדֵינוּ כּוֹנְנֵהוּ.

Many people also say תהלים צא on page 582.

THE TRAVELLERS' PRAYER

יְהִי רָצוֹן May it be Your will, LORD our GOD and GOD of our fathers, to lead us to peace, to direct our steps to peace, to guide us to peace, and to let us reach our desired destination in life, joy and peace. Rescue us from any enemy, ambush and danger on the way, and from all afflictions that trouble the world. Send blessing to the work of our hands, and let us find grace, kindness and compassion from You and from all who see us. Hear our pleas, for You are a GOD who hears prayer and pleas. Blessed are You, LORD, who listens to prayer.

וְיַעֲקֹב And Jacob went on his way and angels of GOD met him. When he saw them, Jacob said, "This is GOD's camp" and he named the place Machanaim [two camps]. Behold I am sending an angel before you to guard you on the way and to bring you to the place I have made ready. May the LORD bless you and keep you. May the LORD make His face shine upon you. May the LORD turn His face to you and give you peace.

When travelling by sea, some say:

יוֹרְדֵי הַיָּם Those who go to sea in ships, plying their trade on the wide ocean – they have seen the works of the LORD and His wonders in the deep. At His commandment, the storm-wind rose and lifted the waves high. They were carried up to the skies, then plunged down into the depths; their courage dissolved in the peril. They reeled and staggered like drunkards; all their skill was to no avail. Then they cried to the LORD in their distress, and He brought them out from their straits. He turned the storm to a murmur, and the waves were stilled. They rejoiced when all was quiet, and He guided them to their desired destination. Let them give thanks to the LORD for His kindness, and for His wonders to mankind.

When travelling by air, some say:

כִּי־אֶרְאֶה When I look up at Your heavens, the work of Your fingers, at the moon and the stars You set in place: what is man that You should be mindful of him, or the son of man that You should care for him? If I climb to heaven, You are there; if I make my bed in the underworld, You are there. If I rise on the wings of the dawn, if I settle on the far side of the sea, even there Your hand will guide me, Your right hand will hold me fast.

וִיהִי נֹעַם May the pleasantness of the LORD our GOD be upon us. Establish for us the work of our hands, O establish the work of our hands.

Many people also say Psalm 91 on page 583.

THE TRAVELLERS' PRAYER

At most times in history, travel has been associated with danger. The Talmud (*Berachot* 29b) contains a prayer to be said on journeys on which our present prayer is based. Over time, further verses relating to safekeeping on the way have been added, together with Psalm 91 whose theme is protection from danger.

סדר אירוסין ונישואין

As the bride enters:

בָּרוּךְ הַבָּא בְּשֵׁם יהוה, בֵּרַכְנוּכֶם מִבֵּית יהוה.

If the bride circles the bridegroom, any of the following may be sung:

וְאֵרַשְׂתִּיךְ לִי לְעוֹלָם. וְאֵרַשְׂתִּיךְ לִי בְּצֶדֶק וּבְמִשְׁפָּט וּבְחֶסֶד וּבְרַחֲמִים. וְאֵרַשְׂתִּיךְ לִי בֶּאֱמוּנָה, וְיָדַעַתְּ אֶת־יהוה.

משלי לא:י–לא

אֵשֶׁת חַיִל מִי יִמְצָא, וְרָחֹק מִפְּנִינִים מִכְרָהּ.
בָּטַח בָּהּ לֵב בַּעְלָהּ, וְשָׁלָל לֹא יֶחְסָר.
גְּמָלַתְהוּ טוֹב וְלֹא רָע, כֹּל יְמֵי חַיֶּיהָ.
דָּרְשָׁה צֶמֶר וּפִשְׁתִּים, וַתַּעַשׂ בְּחֵפֶץ כַּפֶּיהָ.
הָיְתָה כָּאֳנִיּוֹת סוֹחֵר, מִמֶּרְחָק תָּבִיא לַחְמָהּ.
וַתָּקָם בְּעוֹד לַיְלָה, וַתִּתֵּן טֶרֶף לְבֵיתָהּ, וְחֹק לְנַעֲרֹתֶיהָ.
זָמְמָה שָׂדֶה וַתִּקָּחֵהוּ, מִפְּרִי כַפֶּיהָ נָטְעָה כָּרֶם.
חָגְרָה בְעוֹז מָתְנֶיהָ, וַתְּאַמֵּץ זְרוֹעֹתֶיהָ.
טָעֲמָה כִּי־טוֹב סַחְרָהּ, לֹא־יִכְבֶּה בַלַּיְלָה נֵרָהּ.
יָדֶיהָ שִׁלְּחָה בַכִּישׁוֹר, וְכַפֶּיהָ תָּמְכוּ פָלֶךְ.
כַּפָּהּ פָּרְשָׂה לֶעָנִי, וְיָדֶיהָ שִׁלְּחָה לָאֶבְיוֹן.
לֹא־תִירָא לְבֵיתָהּ מִשָּׁלֶג, כִּי כָל־בֵּיתָהּ לָבֻשׁ שָׁנִים.
מַרְבַדִּים עָשְׂתָה־לָּהּ, שֵׁשׁ וְאַרְגָּמָן לְבוּשָׁהּ.
נוֹדָע בַּשְּׁעָרִים בַּעְלָהּ, בְּשִׁבְתּוֹ עִם־זִקְנֵי־אָרֶץ.
סָדִין עָשְׂתָה וַתִּמְכֹּר, וַחֲגוֹר נָתְנָה לַכְּנַעֲנִי.
עֹז וְהָדָר לְבוּשָׁהּ, וַתִּשְׂחַק לְיוֹם אַחֲרוֹן.

MARRIAGE SERVICE

"The LORD GOD said: It is not good for man to be alone, I will make a partner suited to him…That is why a man leaves his father and mother and attaches himself to his wife, and they become one flesh" (Genesis 2:18, 24). Marriage is one of the supreme institutions of Judaism, the first

MARRIAGE SERVICE

As the bride enters:

בָּרוּךְ הַבָּא Blessed is one who comes in the name of the LORD. We bless you from the house of the LORD.

If the bride circles the bridegroom, any of the following may be sung:

וְאֵרַשְׂתִּיךְ I will betroth you to Me for ever; I will betroth you to Me in righteousness and justice; love and compassion; I will betroth you to Me in faithfulness; and you shall know the LORD.

PROVERBS 31:10–31.

אֵשֶׁת חַיִל A woman of strength, who can find? Her worth is far beyond pearls.
Her husband's heart trusts in her, and he has no lack of gain.
She brings him good, not harm, all the days of her life.
She seeks wool and linen, and works with willing hands.
She is like a ship laden with merchandise, bringing her food from afar.
She rises while it is still night, providing food for her household, portions for her maids.
She considers a field and buys it; from her earnings she plants a vineyard.
She girds herself with strength, and braces her arms for her tasks.
She sees that her business goes well; her lamp does not go out at night.
She holds the distaff in her hand, and grasps the spindle with her palms.
She reaches out her palm to the poor, and extends her hand to the needy.
She has no fear for her family when it snows, for all her household is clothed in crimson wool.
She makes elegant coverings; her clothing is fine linen and purple wool.
Her husband is well known in the gates, where he sits with the elders of the land.
She makes linen garments and sells them, and supplies merchants with sashes.
She is clothed with strength and dignity; she can laugh at the days to come.

---

mentioned in the Bible, and the one spoken of by the prophets in their deepest moments as the most compelling metaphor for GOD's relationship with His people. In marriage, the bridegroom and bride pledge themselves to one another in a bond of loyalty and love, each respecting the integrity of the other while joining their destinies to achieve together what neither could achieve alone. The very word *chayyim*, "life", in Hebrew is plural, as if to suggest that life, at its fullest, is to be shared. Marriage is the moralisation of passion, love translated into a covenant of mutual responsibility through which, by sharing our vulnerabilities, we redeem our solitude and discover strength.

פִּיהָ פָּתְחָה בְחָכְמָה, וְתוֹרַת־חֶסֶד עַל־לְשׁוֹנָהּ.
צוֹפִיָּה הֲלִיכוֹת בֵּיתָהּ, וְלֶחֶם עַצְלוּת לֹא תֹאכֵל.
קָמוּ בָנֶיהָ וַיְאַשְּׁרוּהָ, בַּעְלָהּ וַיְהַלְלָהּ.
רַבּוֹת בָּנוֹת עָשׂוּ חָיִל, וְאַתְּ עָלִית עַל־כֻּלָּנָה.
שֶׁקֶר הַחֵן וְהֶבֶל הַיֹּפִי, אִשָּׁה יִרְאַת־יהוה הִיא תִתְהַלָּל.
תְּנוּ־לָהּ מִפְּרִי יָדֶיהָ, וִיהַלְלוּהָ בַשְּׁעָרִים מַעֲשֶׂיהָ.

מי אדיר

מִי אַדִּיר עַל־הַכֹּל, מִי בָּרוּךְ עַל־הַכֹּל, מִי גָּדוֹל עַל־הַכֹּל, הוּא יְבָרֵךְ הֶחָתָן וְהַכַּלָּה.

At this point, it is customary for words of blessing to be addressed to the couple.

ברכות אירוסין

The officiant takes a cup of wine and says:

בָּרוּךְ אַתָּה יהוה אֱלֹהֵינוּ מֶלֶךְ הָעוֹלָם, בּוֹרֵא פְּרִי הַגָּפֶן.

בָּרוּךְ אַתָּה יהוה אֱלֹהֵינוּ מֶלֶךְ הָעוֹלָם, אֲשֶׁר קִדְּשָׁנוּ בְּמִצְוֹתָיו, וְצִוָּנוּ עַל הָעֲרָיוֹת, וְאָסַר לָנוּ אֶת־הָאֲרוּסוֹת, וְהִתִּיר לָנוּ אֶת־הַנְּשׂוּאוֹת לָנוּ עַל יְדֵי חֻפָּה וְקִדּוּשִׁין. בָּרוּךְ אַתָּה יהוה, מְקַדֵּשׁ עַמּוֹ יִשְׂרָאֵל עַל־יְדֵי חֻפָּה וְקִדּוּשִׁין.

The bride and bridegroom both drink from the wine. The bridegroom takes the ring and, holding it ready to be placed on the forefinger of the bride's right hand, says:

הֲרֵי אַתְּ מְקֻדֶּשֶׁת לִי, בְּטַבַּעַת זוֹ, כְּדַת מֹשֶׁה וְיִשְׂרָאֵל.

He then places the ring on the forefinger of the bride's right hand. The כְּתֻבָּה (marriage contract) is then read. A second cup of wine is taken, and over it, the שֶׁבַע בְּרָכוֹת are said.

מִי אַדִּיר *He who is majestic over all*: We begin by asking God Himself to bless the bridegroom and bride.

בָּרוּךְ *Blessed are You*: Marriage originally took the form of two distinct moments. The first, *Erusin* or *Kiddushin*, "betrothal", joined the couple in a mutual pledge. Bride and groom then returned to their respective families. A year or so later, the bride would be brought under the bridal canopy to the groom and they would begin their life together. This was called *Nissu'in*, and was accompanied by its own blessings. During the upheavals of Jewish life in the early Middle Ages, the two ceremonies were brought together. Each involves blessings said over a cup of wine,

She opens her mouth with wisdom, and the law of kindness is on her tongue.
She watches over the ways of her household, and never eats the bread of idleness.
Her children rise and call her happy; her husband also praises her:
"Many women have excelled, but you surpass them all."
Charm is deceptive and beauty vain: it is the GOD-fearing woman who deserves praise.
Give her the reward she has earned; let her deeds bring her praise in the gates.

INVOCATION OF GOD'S BLESSING

מִי אַדִּיר He who is majestic over all, He who is blessed over all, He who is great over all, May He bless the bridegroom and the bride.

At this point, it is customary for words of blessing to be addressed to the couple.

BLESSINGS OF BETROTHAL

The officiant takes a cup of wine and says:

בָּרוּךְ Blessed are You, LORD our GOD, King of the Universe, who creates the fruit of the vine.

בָּרוּךְ Blessed are You, LORD our GOD, King of the Universe, who has made us holy through His commandments, and has commanded us concerning forbidden unions, forbidding us those who are betrothed, permitting us those who are wedded to us through the rite of the canopy and sacred covenant of marriage. Blessed are You, LORD, who sanctifies His people Israel by the rite of the canopy and sacred covenant of marriage.

The bride and bridegroom both drink from the wine. The bridegroom takes the ring and, holding it ready to be placed on the forefinger of the bride's right hand, says:

הֲרֵי Behold you are consecrated to me by this ring in accordance with the law of Moses and of Israel.

He then places the ring on the forefinger of the bride's right hand. The *Ketubah* (marriage contract) is then read. A second cup of wine is taken, and over it, the "Seven Blessings" are said:

---

and nowadays they are separated by the reading of the marriage contract. The betrothal blessing spells out the fact that both ceremonies must be observed for the marriage to be complete.

הֲרֵי *Behold you are consecrated to me*: The declaration accompanying the giving of the ring by the groom to the bride. The use of the word "consecration" in the context of marriage signals the sacred

שבע ברכות לנישואין

בָּרוּךְ אַתָּה יהוה אֱלֹהֵינוּ מֶלֶךְ הָעוֹלָם, בּוֹרֵא פְּרִי הַגָּפֶן.

בָּרוּךְ אַתָּה יהוה אֱלֹהֵינוּ מֶלֶךְ הָעוֹלָם, שֶׁהַכֹּל בָּרָא לִכְבוֹדוֹ.

בָּרוּךְ אַתָּה יהוה אֱלֹהֵינוּ מֶלֶךְ הָעוֹלָם, יוֹצֵר הָאָדָם.

בָּרוּךְ אַתָּה יהוה אֱלֹהֵינוּ מֶלֶךְ הָעוֹלָם, אֲשֶׁר יָצַר אֶת־הָאָדָם בְּצַלְמוֹ, בְּצֶלֶם דְּמוּת תַּבְנִיתוֹ, וְהִתְקִין לוֹ מִמֶּנּוּ בִּנְיַן עֲדֵי־עַד. בָּרוּךְ אַתָּה יהוה, יוֹצֵר הָאָדָם.

שׂוֹשׂ תָּשִׂישׂ וְתָגֵל הָעֲקָרָה, בְּקִבּוּץ בָּנֶיהָ לְתוֹכָהּ בְּשִׂמְחָה. בָּרוּךְ אַתָּה יהוה, מְשַׂמֵּחַ צִיּוֹן בְּבָנֶיהָ.

שַׂמֵּחַ תְּשַׂמַּח רֵעִים הָאֲהוּבִים, כְּשַׂמֵּחֲךָ יְצִירְךָ בְּגַן עֵדֶן מִקֶּדֶם. בָּרוּךְ אַתָּה יהוה, מְשַׂמֵּחַ חָתָן וְכַלָּה.

בָּרוּךְ אַתָּה יהוה אֱלֹהֵינוּ מֶלֶךְ הָעוֹלָם, אֲשֶׁר בָּרָא שָׂשׂוֹן וְשִׂמְחָה, חָתָן וְכַלָּה, גִּילָה, רִנָּה, דִּיצָה וְחֶדְוָה, אַהֲבָה וְאַחֲוָה, וְשָׁלוֹם וְרֵעוּת. מְהֵרָה יהוה אֱלֹהֵינוּ יִשָּׁמַע בְּעָרֵי יְהוּדָה וּבְחוּצוֹת יְרוּשָׁלָיִם, קוֹל שָׂשׂוֹן וְקוֹל שִׂמְחָה, קוֹל חָתָן וְקוֹל כַּלָּה, קוֹל מִצְהֲלוֹת חֲתָנִים מֵחֻפָּתָם, וּנְעָרִים מִמִּשְׁתֵּה נְגִינָתָם. בָּרוּךְ אַתָּה יהוה, מְשַׂמֵּחַ חָתָן עִם הַכַּלָּה.

The bride and bridegroom both drink from the wine.

---

nature of the bond between the partners. *The law of Moses and of Israel* – the bridegroom undertakes to honour his obligations according to both biblical (Moses) and rabbinic (Israel) law.

The marriage contract. Read in its original Aramaic, it spells out the duty of a Jewish husband to his wife, to "work for, honour, support and maintain" her, and to meet all financial obligations arising out of the marriage. The *Ketubah* dates back more than two thousand years, and was intended to secure the bride's legal rights within the marriage. It is made binding by the bridegroom raising an

THE SEVEN BLESSINGS OF MARRIAGE

בָּרוּךְ Blessed are You, LORD our GOD, King of the Universe, who creates the fruit of the vine.

בָּרוּךְ Blessed are You, LORD our GOD, King of the Universe, who has created all for His glory.

בָּרוּךְ Blessed are You, LORD our GOD, King of the Universe, Creator of mankind.

בָּרוּךְ Blessed are You, LORD our GOD, King of the Universe, who made humanity in His image, the image of His likeness, and out of His very self formed a building for eternity. Blessed are You, LORD, Creator of mankind.

שׂוֹשׂ Bring great happiness and joy to one who was barren [Zion], as her children return to her in joy. Blessed are You, LORD, who gladdens Zion through her children.

שַׂמֵּחַ Bring great joy to these loving friends, as You gave joy to Your creations in the Garden of Eden. Blessed are You, LORD, who gives joy to the bridegroom and bride.

בָּרוּךְ Blessed are You, LORD our GOD, King of the Universe, who created joy and gladness, bridegroom and bride, happiness and jubilation, cheer and delight, love, fellowship, peace and friendship. Soon, LORD our GOD, may there be heard in the cities of Judah, and in the streets of Jerusalem, the sounds of joy and gladness, the sounds of the bridegroom and bride, the joyous sounds of bridegrooms from their wedding canopy and of young people at their feasts of song. Blessed are You, LORD, who makes the bridegroom rejoice with the bride.

The bride and bridegroom both drink from the wine.

---

object, usually a handkerchief, in the presence of two witnesses, who sign the document. These witnesses sign the document, which is also usually signed by the bridegroom.

The Seven Blessings. These blessings, accompanying the second stage of the marriage, date back to early rabbinic times. After the blessing over wine, the remaining six benedictions move sequentially from the universal to the particular. The second praises GOD as Creator of all. The third speaks of His creation of man. The fourth alludes to the second chapter of Genesis in which GOD, seeing that the

The bridegroom breaks a glass. Some say the following beforehand:

אִם־אֶשְׁכָּחֵךְ יְרוּשָׁלָםִ תִּשְׁכַּח יְמִינִי. תִּדְבַּק־לְשׁוֹנִי לְחִכִּי אִם־לֹא אֶזְכְּרֵכִי אִם־לֹא אַעֲלֶה אֶת יְרוּשָׁלַםִ עַל רֹאשׁ שִׂמְחָתִי.

The officiant pronounces the blessing:

יְבָרֶכְךָ יהוה וְיִשְׁמְרֶךָ. יָאֵר יהוה פָּנָיו אֵלֶיךָ וִיחֻנֶּךָּ. יִשָּׂא יהוה פָּנָיו אֵלֶיךָ, וְיָשֵׂם לְךָ שָׁלוֹם.

In some congregations, תהלים קנ on page 52 is said at this point.

סדר ברכת המזון לנישואין

Leader:

רַבּוֹתַי נְבָרֵךְ.

Others:

יְהִי שֵׁם יהוה מְבֹרָךְ מֵעַתָּה וְעַד־עוֹלָם.

Leader:

יְהִי שֵׁם יהוה מְבֹרָךְ מֵעַתָּה וְעַד־עוֹלָם.

דְּוַי הָסֵר וְגַם חָרוֹן, וְאָז אִלֵּם בְּשִׁיר יָרוֹן, נְחֵנוּ בְּמַעְגְּלֵי צֶדֶק, שְׁעֵה בִּרְכַּת בְּנֵי יְשֻׁרוּן. בִּרְשׁוּת רַבּוֹתַי, נְבָרֵךְ אֱלֹהֵינוּ שֶׁהַשִּׂמְחָה בִּמְעוֹנוֹ, וְשֶׁאָכַלְנוּ מִשֶּׁלּוֹ.

---

man was alone, formed "out of His very self" a partner so that they could become "a building for eternity" through their descendants. The fifth movingly speaks about the Jewish people (Zion) as a whole, renewed through this marriage of her children. The sixth prays that the bride and groom should find joy together and bring joy to God. The seventh and longest brings all of these themes together, invoking the words of the prophet Jeremiah (33:10–11) that in the future there will be heard "the sounds of joy and gladness, the sounds of bridegroom and bride".

Breaking the glass: An ancient custom, reminding us that while the Temple remains unbuilt, our joy cannot be complete. It has become a custom to preface this by reciting the verse from Psalm 137, "If I forget you, O Jerusalem", said by the exiles in Babylon after the destruction of the First Temple.

Grace after the Wedding Feast: The special invocation, with its phrase "in whose dwelling place is joy", is mentioned in the Talmud (*Ketubot* 8a). *Banish grief and anger* – a poem written by the tenth-century

The bridegroom breaks a glass. Some say the following beforehand:

אִם־אֶשְׁכָּחֵךְ If I forget you, O Jerusalem, may my right hand forget its skill. May my tongue cling to the roof of my mouth. If I do not remember you, If I do not set Jerusalem above my highest joy.

The officiant pronounces the blessing:

יְבָרֶכְךָ May the Lord bless you and protect you. May the Lord make His face shine on you and be gracious to you. May the Lord turn His face toward you and give you peace.

In some congregations, Psalm 150 on page 53 is said at this point.

GRACE AFTER THE WEDDING FEAST

Leader:

Friends, let us say grace.

Others:

May the name of the Lord be blessed from now and for ever.

Leader:

May the name of the Lord be blessed from now and for ever. Banish grief and anger. Let even the mute celebrate in song. Guide us in the paths of righteousness. Hear the blessing of the children of Yeshurun. With permission of those present, let us bless our God, in whose dwelling place is joy, from whose food we have eaten.

---

linguist and poet, Dunash ben Labrat. The initial letters of the four phrases spell out his name.

LAWS OF GRACE AFTER A WEDDING AND FOR THE NEXT SIX DAYS

1. The special Grace is said at the meal after the wedding and for the next six days. The "seven blessings" are said after grace if: (1) a *minyan* is present; (2) the meal is held in honour of the bride and groom; and (3) at least one of those making up the *minyan* has not been present at a previous meal in honour of this married couple (this requirement does not apply on Shabbat or Festivals).

2. The person who says Grace does so over a cup of wine. He also says the last of the seven blessings ("who creates the fruit of the vine"), holding the same cup of wine.

3. A second cup of wine is poured before the other six blessings, which may be distributed to others (but not to the bridegroom) to say. Each holds the second cup while saying the blessing.

4. After the seventh blessing, the person who said Grace drinks from the first cup. Wine from the two cups is then mixed and poured into two cups, one of which is then given to the bridegroom, the other to the bride, to drink.

Others:

בָּרוּךְ אֱלֹהֵינוּ שֶׁהַשִּׂמְחָה בִּמְעוֹנוֹ,
וְשֶׁאָכַלְנוּ מִשֶּׁלּוֹ, וּבְטוּבוֹ חָיִינוּ.

Leader:

בָּרוּךְ אֱלֹהֵינוּ שֶׁהַשִּׂמְחָה בִּמְעוֹנוֹ,
וְשֶׁאָכַלְנוּ מִשֶּׁלּוֹ, וּבְטוּבוֹ חָיִינוּ.
בָּרוּךְ הוּא וּבָרוּךְ שְׁמוֹ.

Continue with בִּרְכַּת הַמָּזוֹן on page 760, at the end of which, say the שֶׁבַע בְּרָכוֹת:

בָּרוּךְ אַתָּה יהוה אֱלֹהֵינוּ מֶלֶךְ הָעוֹלָם, שֶׁהַכֹּל בָּרָא לִכְבוֹדוֹ.

בָּרוּךְ אַתָּה יהוה אֱלֹהֵינוּ מֶלֶךְ הָעוֹלָם, יוֹצֵר הָאָדָם.

בָּרוּךְ אַתָּה יהוה אֱלֹהֵינוּ מֶלֶךְ הָעוֹלָם, אֲשֶׁר יָצַר אֶת־הָאָדָם בְּצַלְמוֹ, בְּצֶלֶם דְּמוּת תַּבְנִיתוֹ, וְהִתְקִין לוֹ מִמֶּנּוּ בִּנְיַן עֲדֵי־עַד. בָּרוּךְ אַתָּה יהוה, יוֹצֵר הָאָדָם.

שׂוֹשׂ תָּשִׂישׂ וְתָגֵל הָעֲקָרָה, בְּקִבּוּץ בָּנֶיהָ לְתוֹכָהּ בְּשִׂמְחָה. בָּרוּךְ אַתָּה יהוה, מְשַׂמֵּחַ צִיּוֹן בְּבָנֶיהָ.

שַׂמֵּחַ תְּשַׂמַּח רֵעִים הָאֲהוּבִים, כְּשַׂמֵּחֲךָ יְצִירְךָ בְּגַן עֵדֶן מִקֶּדֶם. בָּרוּךְ אַתָּה יהוה, מְשַׂמֵּחַ חָתָן וְכַלָּה.

בָּרוּךְ אַתָּה יהוה אֱלֹהֵינוּ מֶלֶךְ הָעוֹלָם, אֲשֶׁר בָּרָא שָׂשׂוֹן וְשִׂמְחָה, חָתָן וְכַלָּה, גִּילָה, רִנָּה, דִּיצָה וְחֶדְוָה, אַהֲבָה וְאַחֲוָה, וְשָׁלוֹם וְרֵעוּת. מְהֵרָה יהוה אֱלֹהֵינוּ יִשָּׁמַע בְּעָרֵי יְהוּדָה וּבְחוּצוֹת יְרוּשָׁלָיִם, קוֹל שָׂשׂוֹן וְקוֹל שִׂמְחָה, קוֹל חָתָן וְקוֹל כַּלָּה, קוֹל מִצְהֲלוֹת חֲתָנִים מֵחֻפָּתָם, וּנְעָרִים מִמִּשְׁתֵּה נְגִינָתָם. בָּרוּךְ אַתָּה יהוה, מְשַׂמֵּחַ חָתָן עִם הַכַּלָּה.

בָּרוּךְ אַתָּה יהוה אֱלֹהֵינוּ מֶלֶךְ הָעוֹלָם, בּוֹרֵא פְּרִי הַגָּפֶן.

Others:

Blessed be our God in whose dwelling place
is joy, from whose food we have eaten.

Leader:

Blessed be our God in whose dwelling place is joy,
from whose food we have eaten.
All Blessed be He, and blessed be His name.

Continue with Grace After Meals on page 761, at the end of which say the Seven Blessings:

בָּרוּךְ Blessed are You, Lord our God, King of the Universe, who has created all for His glory.

בָּרוּךְ Blessed are You, Lord our God, King of the Universe, Creator of mankind.

בָּרוּךְ Blessed are You, Lord our God, King of the Universe, who made humanity in His image, the image of His likeness, and out of His very self formed a building for eternity. Blessed are You, Lord, Creator of mankind.

שׂוֹשׂ Bring great happiness and joy to one who was barren [Zion], as her children return to her in joy. Blessed are You, Lord, who gladdens Zion through her children.

שַׂמֵּחַ Bring great joy to these loving friends, as You gave joy to Your creations in the Garden of Eden. Blessed are You, Lord, who gives joy to the bridegroom and bride.

בָּרוּךְ Blessed are You, Lord our God, King of the Universe, who created joy and gladness, bridegroom and bride, happiness and jubilation, cheer and delight, love, fellowship, peace and friendship. Soon, Lord our God, may there be heard in the cities of Judah, and in the streets of Jerusalem, the sounds of joy and gladness, the sounds of the bridegroom and bride, the joyous sounds of bridegrooms from their wedding canopy and of young people at their feasts of song. Blessed are You, Lord, who makes the bridegroom rejoice with the bride.

בָּרוּךְ Blessed are You, Lord our God, King of the Universe, who creates the fruit of the vine.

סדר חנכת הבית

תהלים ל

מִזְמוֹר שִׁיר חֲנֻכַּת הַבַּיִת לְדָוִד. אֲרוֹמִמְךָ יהוה כִּי דִלִּיתָנִי, וְלֹא־שִׂמַּחְתָּ אֹיְבַי לִי. יהוה אֱלֹהָי, שִׁוַּעְתִּי אֵלֶיךָ וַתִּרְפָּאֵנִי. יהוה, הֶעֱלִיתָ מִן־שְׁאוֹל נַפְשִׁי, חִיִּיתַנִי מִיָּרְדִי־בוֹר. זַמְּרוּ לַיהוה חֲסִידָיו, וְהוֹדוּ לְזֵכֶר קָדְשׁוֹ. כִּי רֶגַע בְּאַפּוֹ, חַיִּים בִּרְצוֹנוֹ, בָּעֶרֶב יָלִין בֶּכִי וְלַבֹּקֶר רִנָּה. וַאֲנִי אָמַרְתִּי בְשַׁלְוִי, בַּל אֶמּוֹט לְעוֹלָם. יהוה בִּרְצוֹנְךָ הֶעֱמַדְתָּה לְהַרְרִי עֹז, הִסְתַּרְתָּ פָנֶיךָ הָיִיתִי נִבְהָל. אֵלֶיךָ יהוה אֶקְרָא, וְאֶל־אֲדֹנָי אֶתְחַנָּן. מַה־בֶּצַע בְּדָמִי, בְּרִדְתִּי אֶל שָׁחַת, הֲיוֹדְךָ עָפָר, הֲיַגִּיד אֲמִתֶּךָ. שְׁמַע־יהוה וְחָנֵּנִי, יהוה הֱיֵה עֹזֵר לִי. הָפַכְתָּ מִסְפְּדִי לְמָחוֹל לִי, פִּתַּחְתָּ שַׂקִּי, וַתְּאַזְּרֵנִי שִׂמְחָה. לְמַעַן יְזַמֶּרְךָ כָבוֹד וְלֹא יִדֹּם, יהוה אֱלֹהַי לְעוֹלָם אוֹדֶךָּ.

תהלים טו

מִזְמוֹר לְדָוִד, יהוה מִי־יָגוּר בְּאָהֳלֶךָ, מִי־יִשְׁכֹּן בְּהַר קָדְשֶׁךָ. הוֹלֵךְ תָּמִים וּפֹעֵל צֶדֶק, וְדֹבֵר אֱמֶת בִּלְבָבוֹ. לֹא־רָגַל עַל־לְשֹׁנוֹ, לֹא־עָשָׂה לְרֵעֵהוּ רָעָה, וְחֶרְפָּה לֹא־נָשָׂא עַל־קְרֹבוֹ. נִבְזֶה בְּעֵינָיו נִמְאָס, וְאֶת־יִרְאֵי יהוה יְכַבֵּד, נִשְׁבַּע לְהָרַע וְלֹא יָמִר. כַּסְפּוֹ לֹא־נָתַן בְּנֶשֶׁךְ, וְשֹׁחַד עַל־נָקִי לֹא־לָקָח, עֹשֵׂה אֵלֶּה, לֹא יִמּוֹט לְעוֹלָם.

SERVICE AT THE CONSECRATION OF A HOUSE

The Torah mentions the dedication of a house: "The officials shall say to the troops: Has anyone built a new house and not dedicated it? Let him go home, or he may die in battle and someone else may dedicate it" (Deuteronomy 20:5). There are also descriptions of the consecration of the altar (Numbers 8) and of the Temple (1 Kings 8).

No formal ceremony for the conse-

SERVICE AT THE CONSECRATION OF A HOUSE

PSALM 30

מִזְמוֹר A psalm of David. A song for the dedication of the House. I will exalt You, LORD, for You have lifted me up, and not let my enemies rejoice over me. LORD, my GOD, I cried to You for help and You healed me. LORD, You lifted my soul from the grave; You spared me from going down to the pit. Sing to LORD, you His devoted ones, and give thanks to His holy name. For His anger is for a moment, but His favour is for a lifetime. At night there may be weeping, but in the morning there is joy. When I felt secure, I said, "I shall never be shaken." O LORD, when You favoured me, You made me stand firm as a mountain, but when You hid Your face, I was terrified. To You, LORD, I called; to my LORD I cried for mercy: "What gain would there be if I died and went down to the grave? Can dust thank You? Can it declare Your truth? Hear, LORD, and be gracious to me; O LORD, be my help." You have turned my sorrow into dancing; You have removed my sackcloth and clothed me with joy, so that my soul may sing to You and not be silent. O LORD my GOD, for ever I will thank You.

PSALM 15

מִזְמוֹר A Psalm of David. LORD, who may dwell in Your tent? Who may live on Your holy mountain? One who walks in integrity, does what is right, and speaks the truth from his heart; who has no malice on his tongue, does no wrong to his fellow, nor casts a slur on his neighbour; who scorns those who are vile, but honours those who fear the LORD; who keeps his oath even when it hurts; who does not demand interest on his loans and never takes a bribe against the innocent. One who does these things will never be shaken.

---

cration of a house is mentioned in the early rabbinic literature, other than saying *Shehecheyanu* ("Who has given us life, sustained us, and brought us to this day") and the blessing on fixing the *mezuzah*. The current ceremony is part of longstanding Anglo-Jewish custom. A service for the consecration of a house was com-

רִבּוֹן הָעוֹלָם הַשְׁקִיפָה מִמְּעוֹן קָדְשְׁךָ וְקַבֵּל בְּרַחֲמִים וּבְרָצוֹן אֶת־תְּפִלַּת בָּנֶיךָ וְתַחֲנוּנָם, אֲשֶׁר הִתְאַסְּפוּ פֹּה לַחֲנֹךְ אֶת־הַבַּיִת הַזֶּה וּלְהַקְרִיב לְפָנֶיךָ אֶת־תּוֹדָתָם עַל כָּל־הַחֶסֶד וְהָאֱמֶת אֲשֶׁר עָשִׂיתָ אִתָּם. אָנָּא חַסְדְּךָ מֵאִתָּם אַל יָמוּשׁ, וּבְרִית שְׁלוֹמְךָ אַל תָּמוּט. הָגֵן בְּעַד בֵּית מְגוּרָם, לֹא תְאֻנֶּה אֵלָיו רָעָה, וְנֶגַע וְצַעַר לֹא יִקְרַב אֵלָיו, וְלֹא יִשָּׁמַע קוֹל צְוָחָה בְּחוֹמוֹתָיו. זַכֵּה אֶת־בְּנֵי הַבַּיִת לָשֶׁבֶת בְּמִשְׁכָּנָם בְּאַחֲוָה וְרֵעוּת, לְאַהֲבָה וּלְיִרְאָה אוֹתְךָ וּלְדָבְקָה בָךְ, וְלַהֲגוֹת בְּתוֹרָתְךָ וּלְקַיֵּם מִצְוֹתֶיהָ.

Where appropriate, add the words in brackets:

הָרֵק בִּרְכוֹתֶיךָ עַל בַּעַל הַבַּיִת, בָּרֵךְ יהוה חֵילוֹ וּפֹעַל יָדָיו תִּרְצֶה. הַרְחִיקֵהוּ מִידֵי עֲבֵרָה וְעָוֹן, וִיהִי נוֹעַמְךָ עָלָיו, וּמַעֲשֵׂה יָדֵינוּ כּוֹנְנֵהוּ. יְהִי נָא חַסְדְּךָ אֶת אִשְׁתּוֹ צוֹפִיָּה הֲלִיכוֹת בֵּיתָהּ, וְתֵדַע כִּי אִשָּׁה יִרְאַת יהוה הִיא תִתְהַלָּל. (הוֹפַע עַל בְּנֵיהֶם וּבְנוֹתֵיהֶם רוּחַ חָכְמָה וּבִינָה, הַדְרִיכֵם בִּנְתִיב מִצְוֹתֶיךָ, וְכָל רוֹאֵיהֶם יַכִּירוּם כִּי הֵם זֶרַע בֵּרַךְ יהוה, בְּרוּכִים בַּתּוֹרָה וּבְיִרְאָה). שָׁמְרֵם מִכָּל־רָע, שְׁמוֹר אֶת נַפְשָׁם, וִיקֻיַּם בָּהֶם, בָּרוּךְ אַתָּה בְּבוֹאֶךָ, וּבָרוּךְ אַתָּה בְּצֵאתֶךָ. וְכַאֲשֶׁר זָכִינוּ לַעֲשׂוֹת חִנּוּךְ הַבַּיִת עַתָּה, כֵּן נִזְכֶּה גַם יַחַד לִרְאוֹת חֲנֻכַּת הַבַּיִת הַגָּדוֹל וְהַקָּדוֹשׁ בִּירוּשָׁלַיִם עִירְךָ, קִרְיַת מוֹעֲדֵינוּ, בִּמְהֵרָה בְיָמֵינוּ, אָמֵן.

---

piled by Chief Rabbi Solomon Hirschell; another was compiled by Chief Rabbi Dr Hermann Adler, which is the basis of the present text.

Where appropriate, the ceremony should begin with the fixing of *mezuzot* with the appropriate blessing, together with *Shehecheyanu* (page 780).

Psalm 30 is then recited because of its superscription, "A song for the dedication of the House". Psalm 15 speaks of the qualities required for "dwelling in the tent" of God – "tent" being understood by the Sages (as in "How beautiful are your tents, Jacob") as a metaphor for the Jewish home.

רִבּוֹן הָעוֹלָם Master of the Universe, look down from Your holy dwelling place, and in compassion and favour accept the prayer and plea of Your children, who are gathered here to consecrate this house, and to offer You their thanksgiving for all the kindness and truth You have shown them. Please do let not Your kindness depart, nor Your covenant of Your peace be removed from them. Shield this their home so that no evil befalls it. May illness and sadness never come near it, nor the sound of sorrow be heard within its walls. May the members of this household live together in this home in fellowship and friendship. May they love and revere You, hold fast to You, meditating in Your Torah, and living faithfully by its commandments.

Where appropriate, add the words in brackets:

הָרֵק Bestow Your blessings on the owners of this house. Bless what they own and find favour in what they do. Keep them far from sin and transgression. May Your tender love be upon them, and establish the work of their hands. May Your kindness be with her who watches over the affairs of her household, knowing that it is the God-fearing woman who deserves praise. (Bestow on their children a spirit of wisdom and understanding. Lead them in the path of Your commandments, so that all who see them recognise that they are children blessed by the Lord, knowing Your Torah and revering You.) Protect them from all evil; protect their lives. May this Your promise be fulfilled in them: "You will be blessed when you come in, and blessed when you go out." And as we have been able to consecrate this house, so together may we witness the consecration of Your great and holy Temple in Jerusalem, city of our sacred assemblies, swiftly in our days. Amen.

רִבּוֹן הָעוֹלָם *Master of the Universe*: A prayer of thanksgiving, followed by prayers for the welfare of those who will live in the house. The sanctity of the home is fundamental to Judaism. It is where we celebrate the love between husband and wife – which is symbolic of the love between God and Israel. It is where, with God's blessing, parents pass on their faith and teachings to their children. It is where we practice hospitality, said by the Sages to be even greater than receiving the Divine presence. And it is where we create *Shalom bayit*, "peace in the home", from which, we believe, flows peace to the world (See Maimonides, Laws of Chanukah 4:14).

סדר ברית מילה

When the baby is brought in, all stand and say:

בָּרוּךְ הַבָּא.

The father of the child says:

הִנְנִי מוּכָן לְקַיֵּם מִצְוַת עֲשֵׂה שֶׁצִּוָּנוּ הַבּוֹרֵא יִתְבָּרַךְ, לָמוּל אֶת בְּנִי. כַּכָּתוּב בַּתּוֹרָה, וּבֶן־שְׁמֹנַת יָמִים יִמּוֹל לָכֶם כָּל־זָכָר לְדֹרֹתֵיכֶם.

The baby is placed on a seat, and the מוֹהֵל says:

זֶה הַכִּסֵּא שֶׁל אֵלִיָּהוּ, זָכוּר לַטּוֹב. לִישׁוּעָתְךָ קִוִּיתִי יהוה. שִׂבַּרְתִּי לִישׁוּעָתְךָ יהוה, וּמִצְוֹתֶיךָ עָשִׂיתִי. שִׂבַּרְתִּי לִישׁוּעָתְךָ יהוה. שָׂשׂ אָנֹכִי עַל־אִמְרָתֶךָ, כְּמוֹצֵא שָׁלָל רָב. שָׁלוֹם רָב לְאֹהֲבֵי תוֹרָתֶךָ, וְאֵין לָמוֹ מִכְשׁוֹל. אַשְׁרֵי, תִּבְחַר וּתְקָרֵב, יִשְׁכֹּן חֲצֵרֶיךָ,

All respond:

נִשְׂבְּעָה בְּטוּב בֵּיתֶךָ, קְדֹשׁ הֵיכָלֶךָ.

The baby is placed on the knees of the סַנְדָּק, and the מוֹהֵל says:

בָּרוּךְ אַתָּה יהוה אֱלֹהֵינוּ מֶלֶךְ הָעוֹלָם, אֲשֶׁר קִדְּשָׁנוּ בְּמִצְוֹתָיו, וְצִוָּנוּ עַל הַמִּילָה.

SERVICE AT A CIRCUMCISION

Since the days of Abraham (Genesis 17:4–14), circumcision has been the sign, for Jewish males, of the covenant between God and His people. Despite the fact that the law was restated by Moses (Leviticus 12:3), it remains known as the "Covenant of Abraham". The ceremony – always performed on the eighth day, even on Shabbat, unless there are medical reasons for delay – marks the entry of the child into the covenant of Jewish fate and destiny. The duty of circumcision devolves, in principle, on the father of the child; in practice it is performed only by a qualified *mohel.*

הִנְנִי *I am here ready to perform the positive commandment*: The father acknowledges his responsibility to fulfil the commandment. *This is the throne of Elijah* – according to tradition, the prophet Elijah is present at every circumcision, as guardian of the child.

SERVICE AT A CIRCUMCISION

When the baby is brought in, all stand and say:

Blessed is he who comes.

The father of the child says:

הִנְנִי I am here ready to perform the positive commandment to circumcise my son, as the Creator, blessed be He, has commanded us, as is written in the Torah, "Throughout your generations, every male child among you who is eight days old must be circumcised."

The baby is placed on a seat, and the *mohel* says:

זֶה הַכִּסֵּא This is the throne of Elijah, may he be remembered for good. For Your salvation I wait, O Lord. I await Your deliverance, Lord, and I observe Your commandments. I await Your deliverance, Lord. I rejoice in Your word like one who finds much spoil. Those who love Your Torah have great peace, and there is no stumbling block before them. Happy are those You choose and bring near to dwell in Your courts.

All respond:

May we be sated with the goodness of Your house, Your holy Temple.

The baby is placed on the knees of the *sandek*, and the *mohel* says:

בָּרוּךְ Blessed are You, Lord our God, King of the Universe, who has made us holy through His commandments, and has commanded us concerning circumcision.

בָּרוּךְ *Blessed are You*: There are three blessings to be said at a circumcision: 1. *Who has commanded us concerning circumcision* – a blessing over the commandment itself, the "about" formula signalling that the *mohel* is performing the commandment on behalf of the father; 2. *To bring (our son) into the covenant of Abraham, our father* – a separate blessing, referring not to the circumcision itself, but what it is a sign of – namely entry into the life of the covenant, under the sheltering wings of the Divine presence (*Aruch HaShulchan*); 3. *Who made the beloved one [Isaac] holy from the womb* – a blessing of acknowledgement. Isaac was the first child to have a circumcision at the age of eight days. He was consecrated before birth, Abraham having been told that it would be Isaac who would continue the covenant (Genesis 17:19–21).

Immediately after the circumcision, the father says:

בָּרוּךְ אַתָּה יהוה אֱלֹהֵינוּ מֶלֶךְ הָעוֹלָם, אֲשֶׁר קִדְּשָׁנוּ בְּמִצְוֹתָיו, וְצִוָּנוּ לְהַכְנִיסוֹ בִּבְרִיתוֹ שֶׁל אַבְרָהָם אָבִינוּ.

All respond:

אָמֵן. כְּשֵׁם שֶׁנִּכְנַס לַבְּרִית, כֵּן יִכָּנֵס לְתוֹרָה וּלְחֻפָּה וּלְמַעֲשִׂים טוֹבִים.

After the circumcision has been completed, the מוֹהֵל takes a cup of wine and says:

בָּרוּךְ אַתָּה יהוה אֱלֹהֵינוּ מֶלֶךְ הָעוֹלָם, בּוֹרֵא פְּרִי הַגָּפֶן.

בָּרוּךְ אַתָּה יהוה אֱלֹהֵינוּ מֶלֶךְ הָעוֹלָם, אֲשֶׁר קִדֵּשׁ יְדִיד מִבֶּטֶן, וְחוֹק בִּשְׁאֵרוֹ שָׂם, וְצֶאֱצָאָיו חָתַם בְּאוֹת בְּרִית קֹדֶשׁ. עַל כֵּן בִּשְׂכַר זֹאת, אֵל חַי, חֶלְקֵנוּ, צוּרֵנוּ, צַוֵּה לְהַצִּיל יְדִידוּת שְׁאֵרֵנוּ מִשַּׁחַת. לְמַעַן בְּרִיתוֹ אֲשֶׁר שָׂם בִּבְשָׂרֵנוּ. בָּרוּךְ אַתָּה יהוה, כּוֹרֵת הַבְּרִית.

אֱלֹהֵינוּ וֵאלֹהֵי אֲבוֹתֵינוּ, קַיֵּם אֶת־הַיֶּלֶד הַזֶּה לְאָבִיו וּלְאִמּוֹ, וְיִקָּרֵא שְׁמוֹ, בְּיִשְׂרָאֵל (פלוני בֶּן פלוני) יִשְׂמַח הָאָב בְּיוֹצֵא חֲלָצָיו, וְתָגֵל אִמּוֹ בִּפְרִי בִטְנָהּ. כַּכָּתוּב, יִשְׂמַח אָבִיךָ וְאִמֶּךָ, וְתָגֵל יוֹלַדְתֶּךָ. וְנֶאֱמַר, וָאֶעֱבֹר עָלַיִךְ וָאֶרְאֵךְ מִתְבּוֹסֶסֶת בְּדָמָיִךְ, וָאֹמַר לָךְ בְּדָמַיִךְ חֲיִי, וָאֹמַר לָךְ בְּדָמַיִךְ חֲיִי.

וְנֶאֱמַר, זָכַר לְעוֹלָם בְּרִיתוֹ, דָּבָר צִוָּה לְאֶלֶף דּוֹר. אֲשֶׁר כָּרַת אֶת־אַבְרָהָם, וּשְׁבוּעָתוֹ לְיִשְׂחָק. וַיַּעֲמִידֶהָ לְיַעֲקֹב לְחֹק, לְיִשְׂרָאֵל בְּרִית עוֹלָם. וְנֶאֱמַר, וַיָּמָל אַבְרָהָם אֶת־יִצְחָק בְּנוֹ, בֶּן־שְׁמוֹנַת יָמִים, כַּאֲשֶׁר צִוָּה אֹתוֹ אֱלֹהִים. הוֹדוּ לַיהוה כִּי־טוֹב, כִּי לְעוֹלָם חַסְדּוֹ. הוֹדוּ לַיהוה כִּי־

כְּשֵׁם שֶׁנִּכְנַס לַבְּרִית *Just as he has entered into the covenant*: Mentioned already in early rabbinic sources as the response of those present. The three phrases refer to the duties of a parent to a child: 1. to teach him Torah; 2. to ensure that he marries;

Immediately after the circumcision, the father says:

בָּרוּךְ Blessed are You, LORD our GOD, King of the Universe, who has made us holy through His commandments, and has commanded us to bring (our son) into the covenant of Abraham, our father.

All respond:

Just as he has entered into the covenant, so may he enter into Torah, marriage and good deeds.

After the circumcision has been completed, the *mohel* takes a cup of wine and says:

בָּרוּךְ Blessed are You, LORD our GOD, King of the Universe, who creates the fruit of the vine.

בָּרוּךְ Blessed are You, LORD our GOD, King of the Universe, who made the beloved one [Isaac] holy from the womb, marked the decree of circumcision in his flesh, and gave his descendants the seal and sign of the holy covenant. As a reward for this, may the living GOD, our portion, our Rock, order deliverance from destruction for the beloved of our flesh, for the sake of His covenant that He has set in our flesh. Blessed are You, LORD, who establishes the covenant.

אֱלֹהֵינוּ Our GOD and GOD of our fathers, preserve this child to his father and mother, and let his name be called in Israel…the son of…. May the father rejoice in the issue of his body, and the mother be glad with the fruit of her womb, as is written, "May your father and mother rejoice, and she who bore you be glad." And it is said, "Then I passed by you and saw you downtrodden in your blood, and I said to you: In your blood, live; and I said to you: In your blood, live."

וְנֶאֱמַר And it is said, "He remembered His covenant for ever; the word He ordained for a thousand generations; the covenant He made with Abraham and gave on oath to Isaac, confirming it as a statute for Jacob, an everlasting covenant for Israel." And it is said, "And Abraham circumcised his son Isaac at the age of eight days, as GOD had commanded him." Thank the LORD for He is good; for His love endures

---

and 3. to train him to do good deeds, as the Torah says in the case of Abraham: "For I have singled him out so that he may instruct his children and his posterity to keep the way of the LORD by doing what is just and right" (Genesis 18:19).

טוֹב, כִּי לְעוֹלָם חַסְדּוֹ. זֶה הַקָּטָן (פלוני בֶּן פלוני) גָּדוֹל יִהְיֶה. כְּשֵׁם שֶׁנִּכְנַס לַבְּרִית, כֵּן יִכָּנֵס לְתוֹרָה, וּלְחֻפָּה, וּלְמַעֲשִׂים טוֹבִים.

The סַנְדֵּק also drinks some of the wine; some drops are given to the baby; the cup of blessing is then sent to the mother, who also drinks from it.

סדר ברכת המזון לברית מילה

When there is a מִנְיָן present, add the bracketed words:

Leader:

רַבּוֹתַי נְבָרֵךְ.

Others, then Leader:

יְהִי שֵׁם יהוה מְבֹרָךְ מֵעַתָּה וְעַד־עוֹלָם.

Leader:

יְהִי שֵׁם יהוה מְבֹרָךְ מֵעַתָּה וְעַד־עוֹלָם.
נוֹדֶה לְשִׁמְךָ בְּתוֹךְ אֱמוּנַי, בְּרוּכִים אַתֶּם לַיהוה.

Others:

נוֹדֶה לְשִׁמְךָ בְּתוֹךְ אֱמוּנַי, בְּרוּכִים אַתֶּם לַיהוה.

Leader:

בִּרְשׁוּת אֵל אָיוֹם וְנוֹרָא, מִשְׂגָּב לְעִתּוֹת בַּצָּרָה,
אֵל נֶאְזָר בִּגְבוּרָה, אַדִּיר בַּמָּרוֹם יהוה.

Others:

נוֹדֶה לְשִׁמְךָ בְּתוֹךְ אֱמוּנַי, בְּרוּכִים אַתֶּם לַיהוה.

GRACE AFTER THE MEAL FOLLOWING A CIRCUMCISION
נוֹדֶה לְשִׁמְךָ בְּתוֹךְ אֱמוּנַי *We give thanks to Your name among the faithful*: A highly stylised form of the invitation to say Grace, asking permission respectively from God, the Torah, Cohanim and Levites, and the assembled company, dating from the Mid-

for ever. May this child.... the son of.... become great. Just as he has entered into the covenant, so may he enter into Torah, marriage and good deeds.

The *sandek* also drinks some of the wine; some drops are given to the baby; the cup of blessing is then sent to the mother, who also drinks from it.

GRACE AFTER THE MEAL FOLLOWING A CIRCUMCISION

When there is a *minyan* present, add the bracketed words:

Leader:

Friends, let us say grace.

Others, then Leader:

May the name of the LORD be blessed from now and for ever.

Leader:

May the name of the LORD be blessed from now and for ever.
We give thanks to Your name among the faithful. Blessed are you to the LORD.

Others:

We give thanks to Your name among the faithful. Blessed are you to the LORD.

Leader:

With permission of GOD, awesome and revered, a refuge in times of trouble, Almighty, girded with strength – majestic on high, the LORD.

Others:

We give thanks to Your name among the faithful. Blessed are you to the LORD.

dle Ages. Originally said at other festive occasions, it has come, over the course of time, to be associated specifically with the celebration of a circumcision.

Leader:

בִּרְשׁוּת הַתּוֹרָה הַקְּדוֹשָׁה, טְהוֹרָה הִיא וְגַם פְּרוּשָׁה,
צִוָּה לָנוּ מוֹרָשָׁה, מֹשֶׁה עֶבֶד יהוה.

Others:

נוֹדֶה לְשִׁמְךָ בְּתוֹךְ אֱמוּנָי, בְּרוּכִים אַתֶּם לַיהוה.

Leader:

בִּרְשׁוּת הַכֹּהֲנִים הַלְוִיִּם. אֶקְרָא לֵאלֹהֵי הָעִבְרִיִּים,
אֲהוֹדֶנּוּ בְּכָל אִיִּים, אֲבָרְכָה אֶת־יהוה.

Others:

נוֹדֶה לְשִׁמְךָ בְּתוֹךְ אֱמוּנָי, בְּרוּכִים אַתֶּם לַיהוה.

Leader:

בִּרְשׁוּת מָרָנָן וְרַבָּנָן וְרַבּוֹתַי, אֶפְתְּחָה בְּשִׁיר פִּי וּשְׂפָתַי,
וְתֹאמַרְנָה עַצְמוֹתַי, בָּרוּךְ הַבָּא בְּשֵׁם יהוה.

Others:

נוֹדֶה לְשִׁמְךָ בְּתוֹךְ אֱמוּנָי, בְּרוּכִים אַתֶּם לַיהוה.

The Leader continues:

בִּרְשׁוּת רַבּוֹתַי,
נְבָרֵךְ (אֱלֹהֵינוּ) שֶׁאָכַלְנוּ מִשֶּׁלּוֹ.

Others:

בָּרוּךְ (אֱלֹהֵינוּ) שֶׁאָכַלְנוּ מִשֶּׁלּוֹ. וּבְטוּבוֹ חָיִינוּ.

Leader:

בָּרוּךְ (אֱלֹהֵינוּ) שֶׁאָכַלְנוּ מִשֶּׁלּוֹ. וּבְטוּבוֹ חָיִינוּ.
בָּרוּךְ הוּא וּבָרוּךְ שְׁמוֹ.

Continue with בִּרְכַּת הַמָּזוֹן on page 760 until בְּעֵינֵי אֱלֹהִים וְאָדָם on page 768. Then say:

Someone other than the father says:

הָרַחֲמָן הוּא יְבָרֵךְ אֲבִי הַיֶּלֶד וְאִמּוֹ, וְיִזְכּוּ לְגַדְּלוֹ וּלְחַנְּכוֹ

הָרַחֲמָן *May the Compassionate One*: A series of special blessings for: 1. the parents of the child; 2. the *sandek*; 3. the child; and 4. the *mohel*. The fifth and sixth are prayers for the coming of the Messiah, and for Elijah, who is believed to be

Leader:

With permission of the holy Torah, pure and clear, given to us as a heritage by Moses the servant of the Lord.

Others:

We give thanks to Your name among the faithful. Blessed are you to the Lord.

Leader:

With permission of the priests, the Levites, I call upon the God of the Hebrews, declaring His glory to the furthest isles, and offering blessings to the Lord.

Others:

We give thanks to Your name among the faithful. Blessed are you to the Lord.

Leader:

With the permission of the rabbis, teachers and friends, I open my lips with song, saying from my innermost being: "Blessed is he that comes in the name of the Lord."

Others:

We give thanks to Your name among the faithful. Blessed are you to the Lord.

The Leader continues:

With your permission, let us bless Him (our God) from whose food we have eaten.

Others:

Blessed be He (our God) from whose food we have eaten, and through whose goodness we live.

Leader:

Blessed be He (our God) from whose food we have eaten, and through whose goodness we live. Blessed be He, and blessed be His name.

Continue with Grace After Meals on page 761 until "in the sight of God and man" on page 769. Then say:

Someone other than the father says:

הָרַחֲמָן May the Compassionate One bless the father and mother of this child. May they be worthy to raise him, educate him, and train

וְלְחַכְּמוֹ, מִיּוֹם הַשְּׁמִינִי וָהָלְאָה יֵרָצֶה דָמוֹ, וִיהִי יהוה אֱלֹהָיו עִמּוֹ.

Someone other than the סַנְדָּק says:

הָרַחֲמָן הוּא יְבָרֵךְ בַּעַל בְּרִית הַמִּילָה, אֲשֶׁר שָׂשׂ לַעֲשׂוֹת צֶדֶק בְּגִילָה, וִישַׁלֵּם פָּעֳלוֹ וּמַשְׂכֻּרְתּוֹ כְּפוּלָה, וְיִתְּנֵהוּ לְמַעְלָה לְמָעְלָה.

הָרַחֲמָן הוּא יְבָרֵךְ רַךְ הַנִּמּוֹל לִשְׁמוֹנָה, וְיִהְיוּ יָדָיו וְלִבּוֹ לָאֵל אֱמוּנָה, וְיִזְכֶּה לִרְאוֹת פְּנֵי הַשְּׁכִינָה, שָׁלֹשׁ פְּעָמִים בַּשָּׁנָה.

Someone other than the מוֹהֵל says:

הָרַחֲמָן הוּא יְבָרֵךְ הַמָּל בְּשַׂר הָעָרְלָה, וּפָרַע וּמָצַץ דְּמֵי הַמִּילָה, אִישׁ הַיָּרֵא וְרַךְ הַלֵּבָב עֲבוֹדָתוֹ פְּסוּלָה, אִם־שְׁלָשׁ־אֵלֶּה לֹא יַעֲשֶׂה לָהּ.

הָרַחֲמָן הוּא יִשְׁלַח לָנוּ מְשִׁיחוֹ הוֹלֵךְ תָּמִים, בִּזְכוּת חֲתְנֵי מוּלוֹת דָּמִים, לְבַשֵּׂר בְּשׂוֹרוֹת טוֹבוֹת וְנִחוּמִים, לְעַם אֶחָד מְפֻזָּר וּמְפֹרָד בֵּין הָעַמִּים.

הָרַחֲמָן הוּא יִשְׁלַח לָנוּ כֹּהֵן צֶדֶק אֲשֶׁר לֻקַּח לְעֵילוֹם, עַד הוּכַן כִּסְאוֹ כַּשֶּׁמֶשׁ וְיַהֲלוֹם, וַיָּלֶט פָּנָיו בְּאַדַּרְתּוֹ וַיִּגְלוֹם, בְּרִיתִי הָיְתָה אִתּוֹ הַחַיִּים וְהַשָּׁלוֹם.

הָרַחֲמָן הוּא יְזַכֵּנוּ לִימוֹת הַמָּשִׁיחַ וּלְחַיֵּי הָעוֹלָם הַבָּא.

On weekdays:

מַגְדִּיל

On שַׁבָּת, יוֹם טוֹב, חוֹל הַמּוֹעֵד and רֹאשׁ חֹדֶשׁ:

מִגְדּוֹל

יְשׁוּעוֹת מַלְכּוֹ וְעֹשֶׂה חֶסֶד לִמְשִׁיחוֹ לְדָוִד וּלְזַרְעוֹ עַד־

him in wisdom. From this eighth day onward may his blood be accepted, and may the LORD his GOD be with him always.

Someone other than the *sandek* says:

הָרַחֲמָן May the Compassionate One bless him (the *sandek*) who assisted in the covenant of circumcision and rejoiced to do this pious deed. May GOD doubly reward him for his deed, exalting him ever higher.

הָרַחֲמָן May the Compassionate One bless the tender child, circumcised on his eighth day. May his heart and hands be firm with GOD, and may he be worthy to witness the Divine Presence three times a year.

Someone other than the *mohel* says:

הָרַחֲמָן May the Compassionate One bless him who performed the circumcision, and fulfilled every part of the precept. The service of the faint-hearted would not be acceptable if he failed to perform the three essentials of the precept.

הָרַחֲמָן May the Compassionate One send us His anointed, blameless in life, through the merit of this child groomed by the blood of circumcision, to proclaim good news and consolations to the unique people scattered and dispersed among the nations.

הָרַחֲמָן May the Compassionate One send us the righteous priest, who was taken into hiding, until a throne, bright as the sun, radiant as a diamond, is prepared for him; the prophet who covered his face with his mantle and wrapped himself in it when GOD declared: My covenant is with him for life and peace.

הָרַחֲמָן May the Compassionate One make us worthy of the Messianic Age and life in the World to Come.

On weekdays:

He gives great –

On Shabbat, Festivals and their Intermediate Days, and Rosh Chodesh:

He is a tower of –

salvation to His king, showing kindness to His anointed, to David and

---

present at the circumcision. The author has left his name, Abraham, in an acrostic formed by the initial letters of the fourth word in the first five blessings.

עוֹלָם. עֹשֶׂה שָׁלוֹם בִּמְרוֹמָיו, הוּא יַעֲשֶׂה שָׁלוֹם עָלֵינוּ וְעַל־כָּל־יִשְׂרָאֵל. וְאִמְרוּ, אָמֵן.

יְראוּ אֶת־יהוה קְדֹשָׁיו, כִּי אֵין מַחְסוֹר לִירֵאָיו. כְּפִירִים רָשׁוּ וְרָעֵבוּ, וְדֹרְשֵׁי יהוה לֹא־יַחְסְרוּ כָל־טוֹב. הוֹדוּ לַיהוה כִּי־טוֹב, כִּי לְעוֹלָם חַסְדּוֹ. פּוֹתֵחַ אֶת יָדֶךָ, וּמַשְׂבִּיעַ לְכָל־חַי רָצוֹן. בָּרוּךְ הַגֶּבֶר אֲשֶׁר יִבְטַח בַּיהוה, וְהָיָה יהוה מִבְטַחוֹ. נַעַר הָיִיתִי גַּם־זָקַנְתִּי, וְלֹא־רָאִיתִי צַדִּיק נֶעֱזָב, וְזַרְעוֹ מְבַקֶּשׁ־לָחֶם. יהוה עֹז לְעַמּוֹ יִתֵּן, יהוה יְבָרֵךְ אֶת־עַמּוֹ בַשָּׁלוֹם.

סדר פדיון הבן

A firstborn child, if a male, must be redeemed on the 31st day of his birth – unless the father is a כֹּהֵן or לֵוִי, or the mother is a daughter of a כֹּהֵן or a לֵוִי.

If the 31st day falls on שַׁבָּת or יוֹם טוֹב, the ceremony is postponed to the following weekday.

The father, presenting his child to the כֹּהֵן, declares:

זֶה, בְּנִי בְכוֹרִי, הוּא פֶּטֶר רֶחֶם לְאִמּוֹ. וְהַקָּדוֹשׁ בָּרוּךְ הוּא צִוָּה לִפְדּוֹתוֹ. שֶׁנֶּאֱמַר, וּפְדוּיָו מִבֶּן־חֹדֶשׁ תִּפְדֶּה, בְּעֶרְכְּךָ, כֶּסֶף חֲמֵשֶׁת שְׁקָלִים, בְּשֶׁקֶל הַקֹּדֶשׁ עֶשְׂרִים גֵּרָה הוּא. וְנֶאֱמַר, קַדֶּשׁ־לִי כָל־בְּכוֹר, פֶּטֶר כָּל־רֶחֶם בִּבְנֵי יִשְׂרָאֵל, בָּאָדָם וּבַבְּהֵמָה לִי הוּא.

SERVICE FOR THE REDEMPTION OF THE FIRSTBORN
According to the Torah, firstborn males originally carried a special sanctity. Their lives spared during the last of the ten plagues, the firstborns were to become God's special ministers, who would dedicate themselves to His service. (The supreme biblical example is Samuel, dedicated to God by his mother Hannah, I Samuel 1:11). After the sin of the Golden Calf, that responsibility was transferred to the Levites, the only tribe that did not take part in the sin (Numbers 3:11–13). In memory of the earlier sanctity, however, the Torah prescribes a cere-

his descendants for ever. He who makes peace in His high places, may He make peace for us and all Israel, and let us say: Amen.

יְראוּ Fear the Lord, you His holy ones; those who fear Him lack nothing. Young lions may grow weak and hungry, but those who seek the Lord lack no good thing. Thank the Lord for He is good: His loving-kindness is for ever. You open Your hand and satisfy the desire of every living thing. Blessed is the person who trusts in the Lord, whose trust is in the Lord alone. Once I was young, and now I am old, yet I have never watched a righteous man forsaken or his children begging for bread. The Lord will give His people strength. The Lord will bless His people with peace.

SERVICE FOR THE REDEMPTION OF THE FIRSTBORN

A firstborn child, if a male, must be redeemed on the 31st day of his birth – unless the father is a Cohen or Levi, or the mother is a daughter of a Cohen or a Levite.

If the 31st day falls on Shabbat or a Festival, the ceremony is postponed to the following weekday.

The father, presenting his child to the Cohen, declares:

זֶה This is my firstborn son, the first issue of his mother's womb. The Holy One, blessed be He, has commanded us to redeem him, as is said, "Those who are to be redeemed, you must redeem from the age of one month, at the fixed price of five shekels of silver by the sacred standard, which is twenty gerahs to the shekel." And it is also stated, "Consecrate to Me every firstborn; the first of every womb among the people of Israel, whether of man or beast, belongs to Me."

---

mony of redemption, in which the father of the child makes a monetary offering (see Laws, below) to a Cohen, symbolically exchanging it for his son. The substance of the ceremony has not changed since biblical times, though its wording is first mentioned in the Talmud.

LAWS OF REDEMPTION OF THE FIRSTBORN

1. The ceremony is performed only if: (1) the child is male; (2) he is the firstborn of its mother, (3) the birth was normal, i.e. not by Caesarian section; (4) the father is neither a Cohen nor a Levi, nor the mother a daughter of a Cohen or Levi.

The כֹּהֵן asks:

מַאי בָּעֵית טְפֵי, לִתֵּן לִי בִּנְךָ בְּכוֹרְךָ שֶׁהוּא פֶּטֶר רֶחֶם לְאִמּוֹ, אוֹ בָּעֵית לִפְדּוֹתוֹ בְּעַד חָמֵשׁ סְלָעִים כִּדְמִחֻיַּבְתְּ מִדְּאוֹרַיְתָא.

The father replies:

חָפֵץ אֲנִי לִפְדּוֹת אֶת־בְּנִי, וְהֵילָךְ דְּמֵי פִדְיוֹנוֹ כִּדְמִחֻיַּבְנָא מִדְּאוֹרַיְתָא.

Taking the redemption money, the father says:

בָּרוּךְ אַתָּה יהוה אֱלֹהֵינוּ מֶלֶךְ הָעוֹלָם, אֲשֶׁר קִדְּשָׁנוּ בְּמִצְוֹתָיו, וְצִוָּנוּ עַל פִּדְיוֹן הַבֵּן.

בָּרוּךְ אַתָּה יהוה אֱלֹהֵינוּ מֶלֶךְ הָעוֹלָם, שֶׁהֶחֱיָנוּ וְקִיְּמָנוּ וְהִגִּיעָנוּ לַזְּמַן הַזֶּה.

The redemption money is given to the כֹּהֵן who,
holding it above the child's head, says:

זֶה תַּחַת זֶה. זֶה חִלּוּף זֶה. זֶה מָחוּל עַל־זֶה. וְיִכָּנֵס זֶה הַבֵּן לְחַיִּים, לַתּוֹרָה וּלְיִרְאַת שָׁמַיִם. יְהִי רָצוֹן שֶׁכְּשֵׁם שֶׁנִּכְנַס לַפִּדְיוֹן כֵּן יִכָּנֵס לְתוֹרָה וּלְחֻפָּה וּלְמַעֲשִׂים טוֹבִים. אָמֵן.

Placing his right hand on the head of the child, the כֹּהֵן blesses him as follows:

יְשִׂמְךָ אֱלֹהִים כְּאֶפְרַיִם וְכִמְנַשֶּׁה. יְבָרֶכְךָ יהוה וְיִשְׁמְרֶךָ. יָאֵר יהוה פָּנָיו אֵלֶיךָ וִיחֻנֶּךָּ. יִשָּׂא יהוה פָּנָיו אֵלֶיךָ, וְיָשֵׂם לְךָ שָׁלוֹם. יהוה שׁוֹמְרֶךָ, יהוה צִלְּךָ עַל־יַד יְמִינֶךָ. כִּי אֹרֶךְ יָמִים וּשְׁנוֹת חַיִּים וְשָׁלוֹם יוֹסִיפוּ לָךְ. יהוה יִשְׁמָרְךָ מִכָּל־רָע, יִשְׁמוֹר אֶת־נַפְשֶׁךָ. אָמֵן.

---

2. The ceremony is performed on the 31st day after the birth. It takes place during the day, not at night, except if the 31st day is Shabbat, in which case it is performed after Shabbat has ended, on Saturday night. The ceremony should be performed even if, for medical reasons, circumcision has not yet taken place.

3. It is a custom to use five silver coins for the ceremony, each of a shekel weight (117

The Cohen asks:

מַאי Which do you prefer: to give me your firstborn son, the first birth of his mother, or to redeem him for five selas as you are bound to do according to the Torah?

The father replies:

חָפֵץ I wish to redeem my son. I present you with the cost of his redemption which I am bound to give according to the Torah.

Taking the redemption money, the father says:

בָּרוּךְ Blessed are You, LORD our GOD, King of the Universe, who has made us holy through His commandments, and has commanded us concerning the redemption of a son.

בָּרוּךְ Blessed are You, LORD our GOD, King of the Universe who has given us life, sustained us, and brought us to this time.

The redemption money is given to the Cohen who,
holding it above the child's head, says:

זֶה This is instead of that, this in exchange for that, this in redemption for that. May this child enter into life, Torah and the fear of Heaven. May it be Your will that just as he has entered into redemption, so may he enter into Torah, marriage and good deeds.

Placing his right hand on the head of the child, the Cohen blesses him as follows:

יְשִׂמְךָ May GOD make you like Ephraim and Manasseh. May the LORD bless you and protect you. May the LORD make His face shine on you and be gracious to you. May the LORD turn His face toward you and grant you peace. The LORD is your Guardian; the LORD is your protection at your right hand. For length of days, years of life, and peace He will increase for you. The LORD will guard you against all harm. He will guard your life. Amen.

---

grams). If these are unavailable, a silver object of equivalent value may be used.

מַאי בָּעֵית טְפֵי *Which do you prefer*: A notional question. In fact, the father has no choice but to redeem the child. The question is asked to ensure that the father understands the nature of the ceremony. The present text is in Aramaic, but it can be said in any language. *This is instead of that* – a symbolic exchange, similar to the *Kapparot*, the "atonements" ceremony performed immediately prior to the Day of Atonement.

סדר תפלה ליולדת

On entering the synagogue, say:

וַאֲנִי בְּרֹב חַסְדְּךָ אָבוֹא בֵיתֶךָ, אֶשְׁתַּחֲוֶה אֶל־הֵיכַל קָדְשְׁךָ בְּיִרְאָתֶךָ.

תהלים קטז

אָהַבְתִּי, כִּי־יִשְׁמַע יהוה, אֶת־קוֹלִי תַּחֲנוּנָי. כִּי־הִטָּה אָזְנוֹ לִי, וּבְיָמַי אֶקְרָא. אֲפָפוּנִי חֶבְלֵי־מָוֶת, וּמְצָרֵי שְׁאוֹל מְצָאוּנִי, צָרָה וְיָגוֹן אֶמְצָא. וּבְשֵׁם־יהוה אֶקְרָא, אָנָּה יהוה מַלְּטָה נַפְשִׁי. חַנּוּן יהוה וְצַדִּיק, וֵאלֹהֵינוּ מְרַחֵם. שֹׁמֵר פְּתָאִים יהוה, דַּלֹּתִי וְלִי יְהוֹשִׁיעַ. שׁוּבִי נַפְשִׁי לִמְנוּחָיְכִי, כִּי יהוה גָּמַל עָלָיְכִי. כִּי חִלַּצְתָּ נַפְשִׁי מִמָּוֶת, אֶת־עֵינִי מִן־דִּמְעָה, אֶת־רַגְלִי מִדֶּחִי. אֶתְהַלֵּךְ לִפְנֵי יהוה, בְּאַרְצוֹת הַחַיִּים. הֶאֱמַנְתִּי כִּי אֲדַבֵּר, אֲנִי עָנִיתִי מְאֹד. אֲנִי אָמַרְתִּי בְחָפְזִי, כָּל־הָאָדָם כֹּזֵב.

מָה־אָשִׁיב לַיהוה כָּל־תַּגְמוּלוֹהִי עָלָי. לְךָ־אֶזְבַּח זֶבַח תּוֹדָה וּבְשֵׁם יהוה אֶקְרָא. נְדָרַי לַיהוה אֲשַׁלֵּם נֶגְדָה־נָּא לְכָל־עַמּוֹ. בְּחַצְרוֹת בֵּית יהוה בְּתוֹכֵכִי יְרוּשָׁלָיִם. הַלְלוּיָהּ.

The following blessing is then said:

בָּרוּךְ אַתָּה יהוה אֱלֹהֵינוּ מֶלֶךְ הָעוֹלָם, הַגּוֹמֵל לְחַיָּבִים טוֹבוֹת, שֶׁגְּמָלַנִי כָּל־טוֹב.

Those present respond:

אָמֵן. מִי שֶׁגְּמָלֵךְ כָּל־טוֹב, הוּא יִגְמְלֵךְ כָּל־טוֹב, סֶלָה.

PRAYER OF THANKSGIVING FOR WOMEN AFTER RECOVERY FROM CHILDBIRTH

On entering the synagogue, say:

וַאֲנִי As for me, by Your great love, I will come into Your house. I will bow down toward Your holy Temple in awe of You.

PSALM 116

אָהַבְתִּי I love the LORD, for He hears my voice, my pleas; for He turns His ear to me whenever I call. The bonds of death encompassed me; the anguish of the grave came upon me; I was overcome by trouble and sorrow. Then I called on the name of the LORD: "LORD, I pray, save my life." Gracious is the LORD and righteous; our GOD is full of compassion. The LORD protects the simple-hearted; when I was brought low, He saved me. My soul, be at peace once more, for the LORD has been good to you. For You have rescued me from death, my eyes from weeping, my feet from stumbling. I shall walk in the presence of the LORD in the land of the living.

מָה־אָשִׁיב How can I repay the LORD for all His goodness to me? I will lift up the cup of salvation and call on the name of the LORD. To You I shall bring a thanks-offering and call on the LORD by name. I will fulfil my vows to the LORD in the presence of all His people, in the courts of the house of the LORD, in your midst, O Jerusalem. Halleluyah.

The following blessing is then said:

בָּרוּךְ Blessed are You, LORD our GOD, King of the Universe, who bestows good things on the unworthy, who has bestowed on me much good.

Those present respond:

אָמֵן May He who bestowed much good on you, continue to bestow on you much good. Selah.

PRAYER OF THANKSGIVING FOR WOMEN AFTER RECOVERY FROM CHILDBIRTH
In Temple times, mothers would offer a sacrifice after the birth of a child (Leviticus 12:6–8). No record exists of a formal prayer offered on such occasions: there may have been no fixed text. Hannah's

אָנָּא הָאֵל הַגָּדוֹל הַגִּבּוֹר וְהַנּוֹרָא, בְּרֹב חַסְדְּךָ אָבוֹא בֵיתֶךָ לִזְבּוֹחַ לְךָ זֶבַח תּוֹדָה עַל־כׇּל־הַטּוֹבוֹת אֲשֶׁר גָּמַלְתָּ עָלָי. אֲפָפוּנִי חֲבָלִים וְצִירִים אֲחָזוּנִי, בַּצַּר־לִי קָרָאתִי אֵלֶיךָ וַתִּשְׁמַע מֵהֵיכָלְךָ קוֹלִי וְהָיִיתָ בְּעֶזְרִי, רִפֵּאתָ לְכׇל־תַּחֲלוּאַי עִטַּרְתַּנִי חֶסֶד וְרַחֲמִים. עַד־הֵנָּה עֲזָרוּנִי רַחֲמֶיךָ, אָנָּא אַל־תִּטְּשֵׁנִי לָנֶצַח, הוֹאֵל אֱלוֹהַּ וּבָרֵךְ אֶת־אֲמָתֶךָ, חַזְּקֵנִי וְאַמְּצֵנִי אוֹתִי וְאֶת־בַּעְלִי וּנְגַדֵּל אֶת־הַיֶּלֶד אֲשֶׁר יֻלַּד לָנוּ, לְיִרְאָתֶךָ וּלְעָבְדְּךָ בֶּאֱמֶת, וְלָלֶכֶת אֹרַח מֵישָׁרִים. שְׁמוֹר אֶת־הַיֶּלֶד הָרַךְ בְּכׇל־דְּרָכָיו, חָנֵּנוּ דֵּעָה בִּינָה וְהַשְׂכֵּל, וְתֵן חֶלְקוֹ בְּתוֹרָתֶךָ, וִיקַדֵּשׁ אֶת שִׁמְךָ הַגָּדוֹל, וְהָיָה לְמֵשִׁיב נֶפֶשׁ לָנוּ בִּימֵי שֵׂיבָתֵנוּ. וַאֲנִי תְפִלָּתִי לְךָ יהוה עֵת רָצוֹן, אֱלֹהִים בְּרׇב־חַסְדֶּךָ, עֲנֵנִי בֶּאֱמֶת יִשְׁעֶךָ. אָמֵן.

If a baby is brought to the synagogue, the Rabbi says the following blessings over him/her:

יְבָרֶכְךָ יהוה וְיִשְׁמְרֶךָ. יָאֵר יהוה פָּנָיו אֵלֶיךָ וִיחֻנֶּךָּ. יִשָּׂא יהוה פָּנָיו אֵלֶיךָ, וְיָשֵׂם לְךָ שָׁלוֹם.

סדר זבד הבת

The mother or father says:

יוֹנָתִי בְּחַגְוֵי הַסֶּלַע בְּסֵתֶר הַמַּדְרֵגָה, הַרְאִינִי אֶת־מַרְאַיִךְ הַשְׁמִיעִינִי אֶת־קוֹלֵךְ, כִּי־קוֹלֵךְ עָרֵב וּמַרְאֵיךְ נָאוֶה.

---

prayer after the birth of Samuel (1 Samuel 2:1–10) is, however, a powerful example of a such song of thanksgiving. The above prayer is composed of the following elements: 1. a prayer on entry to the synagogue; 2. verses of thanksgiving from *Hallel*; 3. the blessing "Who bestows good things" (*HaGomel*) together with the congregational response; and 4. prayers for recovery from the pains of birth, and for success in raising the child.

ZEVED HABAT

There has long been a custom among Sephardim – increasingly adopted by Ashkenazim – to mark the birth of a

אָנָּא O great, mighty and revered God. By Your great love I now come into Your house, to offer You a thanksgiving-offering for all the good You have bestowed on me. Travail beset me, pains seized me. In my distress I cried to You, and from Your habitation You heard my voice and helped me. You healed all my sickness, and crowned me with kindness and compassion. Until now Your mercy has helped me. I pray to You, God, never forsake me. Bestow Your blessing upon Your handmaid. Strengthen and support me together with my husband, that we may raise the child that has been born to us, to revere You and serve You in truth, and to walk in the path of righteousness. Protect our tender child in all his/her ways. Favour him/her with knowledge, understanding and discernment, and let his/her portion be in Your Torah, so that he/she may sanctify Your great name, and become a comfort to us as grow old. As for me, may my prayer come to You, Lord, at a time of favour. O God, in Your great love, answer me with Your faithful salvation.

If a baby is brought to the synagogue, the Rabbi says the following blessings over him/her:

יְבָרֶכְךָ May the Lord bless you and protect you. May the Lord make His face shine on you and be gracious to you. May the Lord turn His face toward you and grant you peace.

HOME CEREMONY ON THE BIRTH OF A DAUGHTER

The mother or father says:

יוֹנָתִי My dove in the clefts of the rock, in the hiding places of the mountain side, show me your face, let me hear your voice; for your voice is sweet, and your face is lovely.

---

daughter with a special ceremony known as *Zeved Habat* ("the gift of a daughter"), during which the baby is named and blessed. We give expression to our thanks to God for the miracle of a new life, and pray that His blessings should accompany her through the course of her life. If food is served at the ceremony, the meal has religious significance (*seudat mitzvah*), and should be accompanied by words of Torah.

יוֹנָתִי *My dove in the clefts of the rock*: Song of Songs 2:14. *There is one alone* – Song of

If this is their first daughter, they add:

אַחַת הִיא יוֹנָתִי תַמָּתִי, אַחַת הִיא לְאִמָּהּ בָּרָה הִיא לְיוֹלַדְתָּהּ, רָאוּהָ בָנוֹת וַיְאַשְּׁרוּהָ, מְלָכוֹת וּפִילַגְשִׁים וַיְהַלְלוּהָ.

The Rabbi or officiant says:

מִי שֶׁבֵּרַךְ אֲבוֹתֵינוּ אַבְרָהָם יִצְחָק וְיַעֲקֹב מֹשֶׁה וְאַהֲרֹן דָּוִד וּשְׁלֹמֹה שָׂרָה רִבְקָה רָחֵל וְלֵאָה, הוּא יְבָרֵךְ אֶת הָאִשָּׁה הַיּוֹלֶדֶת (פלונית בַּת פלונית)

If the baby has already been named in the synagogue:

עִם בִּתָּהּ (שֵׁם הַיַּלְדָּה) הַנּוֹלְדָה לָהּ בְּמַזָּל טוֹב.

If the baby has not been named in the synagogue:

עִם בִּתָּהּ הַנּוֹלְדָה לָהּ בְּמַזָּל טוֹב, וְיִקָּרֵא שְׁמָהּ בְּיִשְׂרָאֵל (שֵׁם הַיַּלְדָּה).

אָנָּא בָּרֵךְ אֶת אָבִיהָ וְאֶת אִמָּהּ, וְיִזְכּוּ לְגַדְּלָהּ לְתוֹרָה וּלְחֻפָּה וּלְמַעֲשִׂים טוֹבִים וְנֹאמַר אָמֵן.

The parents bless the child:

יְשִׂמֵךְ אֱלֹהִים כְּשָׂרָה רִבְקָה רָחֵל וְלֵאָה. יְבָרְכֵךְ יהוה וְיִשְׁמְרֵךְ. יָאֵר יהוה פָּנָיו אֵלַיִךְ וִיחֻנֵּךְ. יִשָּׂא יהוה פָּנָיו אֵלַיִךְ, וְיָשֵׂם לָךְ שָׁלוֹם.

וִיהִי רָצוֹן מִלִּפְנֵי אָבִינוּ שֶׁבַּשָּׁמַיִם שֶׁיִּתֵּן בְּלִבֵּךְ אַהֲבָתוֹ וְיִרְאָתוֹ, וְתִהְיֶה יִרְאַת יהוה עַל פָּנַיִךְ כָּל יָמַיִךְ שֶׁלֹּא תֶחֱטָאִי, וִיהִי חֶשְׁקֵךְ בַּתּוֹרָה וּבַמִּצְוֹת. עֵינַיִךְ לְנֹכַח יַבִּיטוּ,

---

Songs 6:9. *May God make you like* – the traditional blessing given by parents to daughters. *May the Lord bless you* – the Priestly Blessing (Numbers 6:24–26).

וִיהִי רָצוֹן *May it be the will*: Taken from a traditional blessing given by parents to children on the eve of Yom Kippur. *May God before whom my fathers* – the

If this is their first daughter, they add:

אַחַת There is one alone, my dove, my perfect one, her mother's only child, the favourite of the one who bore her. Maidens see her and called her blessed; queens and concubines praise her.

The Rabbi or officiant says:

מִי שֶׁבֵּרַךְ He who blessed our ancestors, Abraham, Isaac and Jacob, Moses, Aaron, David and Solomon, Sarah, Rebecca, Rachel and Leah – may He bless (the name of the mother), daughter of (the name of the mother's mother) who has given birth.

If the baby has already been named in the synagogue:

and her newborn daughter, (the girl's name), born in favour.

If the baby has not been named in the synagogue:

and her newborn daughter, born in favour, whose name in Israel shall be called (the girl's name).

Bless, we pray to You, her parents that they may have the merit to raise her to the Torah, to the marriage canopy and to good deeds; and let us say, Amen.

The parents bless the child:

יְשִׂמֵךְ May God make you like Sarah, Rebecca, Rachel and Leah. May the Lord bless you and protect you. May the Lord make His face shine on you and be gracious to you. May the Lord turn His face toward you and give you peace.

וִיהִי רָצוֹן May it be the will of our Father in heaven, that He set in your heart the love and awe of Him all your days, so that you do not come to sin. May your desire be for the Torah and the commandments. May your eyes look straight before you; may your mouth speak wisdom and your heart meditate in awe; may your hands be occupied

---

blessing given by Jacob to the children of Joseph (Genesis 48:15–16), the only instance in the Torah of a grandparent blessing grandchildren. *Our sister* – the blessing given to Rebecca by her family (Genesis 24:60).

פִּיךְ יְדַבֵּר חָכְמוֹת וְלִבֵּךְ יֶהְגֶּה אֵימוֹת, יָדַיִךְ יַעַסְקוּ בְּמִצְוֹת וְרַגְלַיִךְ יָרוּצוּ לַעֲשׂוֹת רְצוֹן אָבִיךְ שֶׁבַּשָּׁמָיִם.

If grandparents are present, they say the following blessing:

הָאֱלֹהִים אֲשֶׁר הִתְהַלְּכוּ אֲבֹתַי לְפָנָיו אַבְרָהָם וְיִצְחָק הָאֱלֹהִים הָרֹעֶה אֹתִי מֵעוֹדִי עַד־הַיּוֹם הַזֶּה. הַמַּלְאָךְ הַגֹּאֵל אֹתִי מִכָּל־רָע יְבָרֵךְ אֶת־הַנְּעָרִים וְיִקָּרֵא בָהֶם שְׁמִי וְשֵׁם אֲבֹתַי אַבְרָהָם וְיִצְחָק וְיִדְגּוּ לָרֹב בְּקֶרֶב הָאָרֶץ.

All say:

אֲחֹתֵנוּ אַתְּ הֲיִי לְאַלְפֵי רְבָבָה.

תפלת החולה

תהלים כג

מִזְמוֹר לְדָוִד, יהוה רֹעִי לֹא אֶחְסָר. בִּנְאוֹת דֶּשֶׁא יַרְבִּיצֵנִי, עַל־מֵי מְנוּחוֹת יְנַהֲלֵנִי. נַפְשִׁי יְשׁוֹבֵב, יַנְחֵנִי בְמַעְגְּלֵי־צֶדֶק לְמַעַן שְׁמוֹ. גַּם כִּי־אֵלֵךְ בְּגֵיא צַלְמָוֶת, לֹא־אִירָא רָע כִּי־אַתָּה עִמָּדִי, שִׁבְטְךָ וּמִשְׁעַנְתֶּךָ הֵמָּה יְנַחֲמֻנִי. תַּעֲרֹךְ לְפָנַי שֻׁלְחָן נֶגֶד צֹרְרָי, דִּשַּׁנְתָּ בַשֶּׁמֶן רֹאשִׁי, כּוֹסִי רְוָיָה. אַךְ טוֹב וָחֶסֶד יִרְדְּפוּנִי כָּל־יְמֵי חַיָּי, וְשַׁבְתִּי בְּבֵית יהוה לְאֹרֶךְ יָמִים.

תהלים קג

לְדָוִד, בָּרְכִי נַפְשִׁי אֶת־יהוה, וְכָל־קְרָבַי אֶת־שֵׁם קָדְשׁוֹ. בָּרְכִי נַפְשִׁי אֶת־יהוה, וְאַל־תִּשְׁכְּחִי כָּל־גְּמוּלָיו. הַסֹּלֵחַ לְכָל־עֲוֺנֵכִי, הָרֹפֵא לְכָל־תַּחֲלוּאָיְכִי. הַגּוֹאֵל מִשַּׁחַת חַיָּיְכִי, הַמְעַטְּרֵכִי חֶסֶד וְרַחֲמִים. הַמַּשְׂבִּיעַ בַּטּוֹב עֶדְיֵךְ, תִּתְחַדֵּשׁ

PRAYER FOR RECOVERY FROM ILLNESS
Since the birth of faith, people have turned to God "who heals the broken-hearted and binds up their wounds" for strength and recovery in times of sick-

with the commandments and may your feet run to do the will of your Father in heaven.

If grandparents are present, they say the following blessing:

הָאֱלֹהִים May God before whom my fathers Abraham and Isaac walked – God who has been my Shepherd all my life to this day, the Angel who has rescued me from all harm – may He bless the children. May they be called by my name and the names of my fathers Abraham and Isaac, and may they increase greatly on earth.

All say:

Our sister, may you grow to become thousands of myriads.

PRAYER FOR RECOVERY FROM ILLNESS

PSALM 23

מִזְמוֹר לְדָוִד A psalm of David. The Lord is my Shepherd, I shall not want. He makes me lie down in green pastures, He leads me beside the still waters. He refreshes my soul; He guides me in the paths of righteousness for His name's sake. Though I walk through the valley of the shadow of death, I will fear no evil, for You are with me; Your rod and Your staff, they comfort me. You set a table before me in the presence of my enemies, You anoint my head with oil; my cup is filled to overflowing. May goodness and kindness follow me all the days of my life, and may I live in the house of the Lord for evermore.

PSALM 103

לְדָוִד A Psalm of David. Bless the Lord, my soul; with all my being I bless His holy name. Bless the Lord, my soul, and forget none of His benefits. He forgives all your sins. He heals all your ills. He redeems your life from the pit. He crowns you with love and compassion. He satisfies your soul with good things, so that your youth is renewed like

---

ness. Many of the psalms are supreme examples of such prayers. There is a deep connection, still not fully understood by medical science, between "healing of the spirit and healing of the body". Prayer, said the Sages, is not a substi-

כַּנֶּשֶׁר נְעוּרָיְכִי. עֹשֵׂה צְדָקוֹת יהוה, וּמִשְׁפָּטִים לְכָל־עֲשׁוּקִים. יוֹדִיעַ דְּרָכָיו לְמֹשֶׁה, לִבְנֵי יִשְׂרָאֵל עֲלִילוֹתָיו. רַחוּם וְחַנּוּן יהוה, אֶרֶךְ אַפַּיִם וְרַב־חָסֶד. לֹא־לָנֶצַח יָרִיב, וְלֹא לְעוֹלָם יִטּוֹר. לֹא כַחֲטָאֵינוּ עָשָׂה לָנוּ, וְלֹא כַעֲוֹנֹתֵינוּ גָּמַל עָלֵינוּ. כִּי כִגְבֹהַּ שָׁמַיִם עַל־הָאָרֶץ, גָּבַר חַסְדּוֹ עַל־יְרֵאָיו. כִּרְחֹק מִזְרָח מִמַּעֲרָב, הִרְחִיק מִמֶּנּוּ אֶת־פְּשָׁעֵינוּ. כְּרַחֵם אָב עַל־בָּנִים, רִחַם יהוה עַל־יְרֵאָיו. כִּי הוּא יָדַע יִצְרֵנוּ, זָכוּר כִּי־עָפָר אֲנָחְנוּ. אֱנוֹשׁ כֶּחָצִיר יָמָיו, כְּצִיץ הַשָּׂדֶה כֵּן יָצִיץ. כִּי רוּחַ עָבְרָה־בּוֹ וְאֵינֶנּוּ, וְלֹא־יַכִּירֶנּוּ עוֹד מְקוֹמוֹ. וְחֶסֶד יהוה מֵעוֹלָם וְעַד־עוֹלָם עַל־יְרֵאָיו, וְצִדְקָתוֹ לִבְנֵי בָנִים. לְשֹׁמְרֵי בְרִיתוֹ, וּלְזֹכְרֵי פִקֻּדָיו לַעֲשׂוֹתָם. יהוה בַּשָּׁמַיִם הֵכִין כִּסְאוֹ, וּמַלְכוּתוֹ בַּכֹּל מָשָׁלָה. בָּרְכוּ יהוה מַלְאָכָיו, גִּבֹּרֵי כֹחַ עֹשֵׂי דְבָרוֹ, לִשְׁמֹעַ בְּקוֹל דְּבָרוֹ. בָּרְכוּ יהוה כָּל־צְבָאָיו, מְשָׁרְתָיו עֹשֵׂי רְצוֹנוֹ. בָּרְכוּ יהוה כָּל־מַעֲשָׂיו, בְּכָל־מְקֹמוֹת מֶמְשַׁלְתּוֹ, בָּרְכִי נַפְשִׁי אֶת־יהוה.

תהלים קלט

לַמְנַצֵּחַ לְדָוִד מִזְמוֹר, יהוה חֲקַרְתַּנִי וַתֵּדָע. אַתָּה יָדַעְתָּ שִׁבְתִּי וְקוּמִי, בַּנְתָּה לְרֵעִי מֵרָחוֹק. אָרְחִי וְרִבְעִי זֵרִיתָ, וְכָל־דְּרָכַי הִסְכַּנְתָּה. כִּי אֵין מִלָּה בִּלְשׁוֹנִי, הֵן יהוה יָדַעְתָּ כֻלָּהּ. אָחוֹר וָקֶדֶם צַרְתָּנִי, וַתָּשֶׁת עָלַי כַּפֶּכָה. פְּלִיאָה דַעַת מִמֶּנִּי, נִשְׂגְּבָה לֹא־אוּכַל לָהּ. אָנָה אֵלֵךְ מֵרוּחֶךָ, וְאָנָה מִפָּנֶיךָ אֶבְרָח. אִם־אֶסַּק שָׁמַיִם שָׁם אָתָּה, וְאַצִּיעָה שְּׁאוֹל הִנֶּךָּ. אֶשָּׂא כַנְפֵי־שָׁחַר, אֶשְׁכְּנָה בְּאַחֲרִית יָם. גַּם־שָׁם יָדְךָ

---

tute for medicine, but neither is medicine a substitute for prayer: both have their part to play in the healing process. Prayer gives strength, as does the knowledge that God is close to all who call on Him in truth. The above passages consist

the eagle's. The LORD is righteous in all He does; He brings justice to all the oppressed. He made known His ways to Moses, His deeds to the people of Israel. The LORD is compassionate and gracious, slow to anger, abounding in love. He will not always accuse or nurse His anger for ever. He has not treated us as our sins deserve, or repaid us according to our misdeeds. For as high as the heavens are above the earth, so great is His love for those who fear Him. As far as the east is from the west, so far has He has removed our transgressions from us. As a father has compassion on his children, so the LORD has compassion on those who fear Him. For He knows how we are formed; He remembers that we are dust. As for man, his days are like grass; like a flower of the field he flourishes. For a wind passes over it and it is gone, and its place knows it no more. But the kindness of the LORD is for all eternity to those who fear Him; His righteousness is with their children's children – with those who keep His covenant, and remember to obey His precepts. The LORD has established His throne in heaven, and His kingdom rules over all. Bless the LORD, you His angels, mighty in power, who do His bidding, who obey His word. Bless the LORD, all you His host, the ministers who do His will. Bless the LORD, all His works, everywhere in His dominion. Bless the LORD, my soul.

PSALM 139

לַמְנַצֵּחַ To the Chief Musician. A psalm of David. O LORD, You have examined me and You know me. You know when I sit and when I rise; You understand my thoughts from afar. You encompass my going out and lying down. You are familiar with all my ways. Before a word is on my tongue, You, LORD, know it all. You keep close guard behind and before me. You have laid Your hand upon me. Knowledge so wonderful is beyond me; so high, it is above my reach. Where can I escape from Your spirit? Where can I flee from Your presence? If I climb to heaven, You are there; if I make my bed in the underworld, You are there. If I rise on the wings of the dawn, if I settle on the far side of the

---

of three psalms long associated with deliverance from harm, together with two prayers, one for healing, the other for forgiveness, since, our tradition tells us, illness is a time for self-examination and rededication.

תַּנְחֵנִי, וְתֹאחֲזֵנִי יְמִינֶךָ. וָאֹמַר אַךְ־חֹשֶׁךְ יְשׁוּפֵנִי, וְלַיְלָה אוֹר בַּעֲדֵנִי. גַּם־חֹשֶׁךְ לֹא־יַחְשִׁיךְ מִמֶּךָּ, וְלַיְלָה כַּיּוֹם יָאִיר, כַּחֲשֵׁיכָה כָּאוֹרָה. כִּי־אַתָּה קָנִיתָ כִלְיֹתָי, תְּסֻכֵּנִי בְּבֶטֶן אִמִּי. אוֹדְךָ עַל כִּי נוֹרָאוֹת נִפְלֵיתִי, נִפְלָאִים מַעֲשֶׂיךָ וְנַפְשִׁי יֹדַעַת מְאֹד. לֹא־נִכְחַד עָצְמִי מִמֶּךָּ אֲשֶׁר־עֻשֵּׂיתִי בַסֵּתֶר, רֻקַּמְתִּי בְּתַחְתִּיּוֹת אָרֶץ. גָּלְמִי רָאוּ עֵינֶיךָ, וְעַל־סִפְרְךָ כֻּלָּם יִכָּתֵבוּ, יָמִים יֻצָּרוּ וְלוֹ אֶחָד בָּהֶם. וְלִי מַה־יָּקְרוּ רֵעֶיךָ אֵל, מֶה עָצְמוּ רָאשֵׁיהֶם. אֶסְפְּרֵם מֵחוֹל יִרְבּוּן, הֱקִיצֹתִי וְעוֹדִי עִמָּךְ. אִם־תִּקְטֹל, אֱלוֹהַּ, רָשָׁע, וְאַנְשֵׁי דָמִים סוּרוּ מֶנִּי. אֲשֶׁר יֹמְרוּךָ לִמְזִמָּה, נָשֻׂא לַשָּׁוְא עָרֶיךָ. הֲלוֹא־מְשַׂנְאֶיךָ יהוה, אֶשְׂנָא, וּבִתְקוֹמְמֶיךָ אֶתְקוֹטָט. תַּכְלִית שִׂנְאָה שְׂנֵאתִים, לְאוֹיְבִים הָיוּ לִי. חָקְרֵנִי אֵל וְדַע לְבָבִי, בְּחָנֵנִי וְדַע שַׂרְעַפָּי. וּרְאֵה אִם־דֶּרֶךְ־עֹצֶב בִּי, וּנְחֵנִי בְּדֶרֶךְ עוֹלָם.

תהלים קב

תְּפִלָּה לְעָנִי כִי־יַעֲטֹף, וְלִפְנֵי יהוה יִשְׁפֹּךְ שִׂיחוֹ. יהוה שִׁמְעָה תְפִלָּתִי, וְשַׁוְעָתִי אֵלֶיךָ תָבוֹא. אַל־תַּסְתֵּר פָּנֶיךָ מִמֶּנִּי בְּיוֹם צַר־לִי, הַטֵּה־אֵלַי אָזְנֶךָ בְּיוֹם אֶקְרָא מַהֵר עֲנֵנִי. אָנָּא יהוה רוֹפֵא כָל בָּשָׂר, רַחֵם עָלַי, וּסְעָדֵנִי בְּחַסְדְּךָ הַגָּדוֹל עַל עֶרֶשׂ דְּוָי, כִּי אֻמְלַל אָנִי. שְׁלַח לִי תְּרוּפָה וּתְעָלָה, בְּתוֹךְ שְׁאָר חוֹלֵי בָנֶיךָ. רְפָה אֶת־מַכְאֹבִי, וְחַדֵּשׁ כְּנֶשֶׁר נְעוּרָי. תֵּן בִּינָה לָרוֹפֵא, וְיִגְהֶה מִמֶּנִּי מְזוֹרִי, וַאֲרוּכָתִי מְהֵרָה תִצְמָח. שְׁמַע תְּפִלָּתִי, וְהוֹסֵף יָמִים עַל יָמַי, וַאֲכַלֶּה שְׁנוֹתַי בַּנְּעִימִים, לְמַעַן אוּכַל לַעֲבוֹד עֲבוֹדָתֶךָ, וְלִשְׁמוֹר פִּקּוּדֶיךָ בְּלֵב שָׁלֵם. הֲבִינֵנִי וְאֵדְעָה, כִּי לְשָׁלוֹמִי מַר־לִי מָר. וְאַל־אֶמְאַס אֶת־מוּסָרְךָ, וּבְתוֹכַחְתְּךָ אַל־אָקוּץ.

sea, even there Your hand will guide me, Your right hand will hold me fast. Were I to say, "Surely the darkness will hide me, and light become night around me", to You the darkness would not be dark; night is light as day; to You dark and light are one. For You created my innermost being; You knitted me together in my mother's womb. I praise You because I am awesomely, wondrously made; wonderful are Your works; I know that full well. My frame was not hidden from You when I was formed in the secret place, woven in the depths of the earth. Your eyes saw my unformed body. All the days ordained for me were written in Your book before one of them came to be. How precious to me are Your thoughts, God, how vast in number they are. Were I to count them, they would outnumber the grains of the sand. I awake and I am still with You. God, if only You would slay the wicked – away from me, you bloodthirsty men. They speak of You with evil intent; Your adversaries misuse Your name. Do I not hate those who hate You, Lord, and loathe those who rise up against You? I have nothing but hatred for them; I count them my enemies. Search me, God, and know my heart; test me and know my innermost thoughts. See if there is grief in the way I follow, and lead me in the everlasting way.

PSALM 102

תְּפִלָּה לְעָנִי A prayer of one who is afflicted, when he is faint, and pours out his anguish before the Lord. Lord, hear my prayer and let my cry come before You. Do not hide Your face from me in my day of distress. Turn Your ear toward me; answer me swiftly on the day I call. Please, Lord, Healer of all flesh, have pity on me, and support me on my sick bed, in Your great love, for I am weak. Send relief and healing to me and to the others of Your children who are sick. Heal my pain and renew my youth as the eagle's. Grant wisdom to the physician that he may cure my illness, so that my healing may spring up swiftly. Hear my prayer, prolong my life, and let me complete my years in happiness, so that I may be able to serve You and keep Your precepts with a perfect heart. Grant me the understanding to know that this bitter trial has come upon me for my welfare. Let me not reject Your discipline or spurn Your rebuke.

אֱלוֹהַּ סְלִיחוֹת, חַנּוּן וְרַחוּם אֶרֶךְ אַפַּיִם וְרַב־חֶסֶד, מוֹדֶה אֲנִי לְפָנֶיךָ בְּלֵב נִשְׁבָּר וְנִדְכֶּה, כִּי חָטָאתִי וְהָרַע בְּעֵינֶיךָ עָשִׂיתִי. הִנֵּה נִחַמְתִּי עַל רָעָתִי, וְאָשׁוּב בִּתְשׁוּבָה שְׁלֵמָה לְפָנֶיךָ. עָזְרֵנִי אֱלֹהֵי יִשְׁעִי, וְלֹא אָשׁוּב לְכִסְלָה, וְאֶתְהַלֵּךְ לְפָנֶיךָ בֶּאֱמֶת וּבְתָמִים. שַׂמֵּחַ נֶפֶשׁ עַבְדֶּךָ, כִּי־אֵלֶיךָ יהוה, נַפְשִׁי אֶשָּׂא. רְפָאֵנִי יהוה וְאֵרָפֵא, הוֹשִׁיעֵנִי וְאִוָּשֵׁעָה, כִּי תְהִלָּתִי אָתָּה. אָמֵן, וְאָמֵן.

תפלה לעומד מחליו

Read Psalms 23 and 103 on page 820. Then continue with:

אָנָּא הָאֵל הַגָּדוֹל הַגִּבּוֹר וְהַנּוֹרָא, בְּרֹב חַסְדְּךָ אָבוֹא לְפָנֶיךָ לְהוֹדוֹת לְךָ עַל כָּל הַטּוֹבוֹת אֲשֶׁר גָּמַלְתָּ עָלָי. מִן הַמֵּצַר קְרָאתִיךָ וַתַּעֲנֵנִי, מֵעֶרֶשׂ דְּוַי שִׁוַּעְתִּי אֵלֶיךָ, וַתִּשְׁמַע אֶת־קוֹלִי תַּחֲנוּנָי. יַסֹּר יִסְּרַנִּי יָּהּ, וְלַמָּוֶת לֹא נְתָנָנִי. בְּאַהֲבָתְךָ וּבְחֶמְלָתְךָ, הֶעֱלִיתָ מִן שְׁאוֹל נַפְשִׁי. כִּי רֶגַע בְּאַפְּךָ, חַיִּים בִּרְצוֹנְךָ, בָּעֶרֶב יָלִין בֶּכִי וְלַבֹּקֶר רִנָּה. חַי חַי הוּא יוֹדֶךָ, כָּמוֹנִי הַיּוֹם. וְנַפְשִׁי אֲשֶׁר פָּדִיתָ, תְּסַפֵּר נִפְלְאוֹתֶיךָ לִבְנֵי אָדָם. בָּרוּךְ אַתָּה, רוֹפֵא נֶאֱמָן לְכָל־בָּשָׂר.

אֵל רַחוּם וְחַנּוּן, הַגּוֹמֵל לְחַיָּבִים טוֹבוֹת, קָטֹנְתִּי מִכֹּל הַחֲסָדִים, אֲשֶׁר עָשִׂיתָ עִמָּדִי עַד הֵנָּה. אָנָּא טַהֵר לְבָבִי, וְזַכֵּנִי לָלֶכֶת בְּדֶרֶךְ יְשָׁרִים לְפָנֶיךָ, וּמְשֹׁךְ עֶזְרְךָ לְעַבְדֶּךָ. חַזְּקֵנִי וְאַמְּצֵנִי מֵרִפְיוֹן, וּבְחִלּוּץ עֲצָמוֹת תְּבָרְכֵנִי. הַרְחֵק

THANKSGIVING PRAYER AFTER RECOVERY FROM ILLNESS

No less important than prayer *for* recovery is thanksgiving *after* recovery. There are many psalms which share this theme; two are suggested here, together with a

אֱלוֹהַּ סְלִיחוֹת God of forgiveness, gracious and compassionate, slow to anger, abounding in love, I acknowledge before You with a broken and contrite heart that I have sinned and done evil in Your sight. I hereby repent of my evil and turn to You in complete repentance. Help me, God of my salvation, that I may not turn to folly again, but instead walk before You in truth and integrity. Gladden Your servant's heart, for to You, Lord, I lift up my soul. Heal me, Lord, and I will be healed, save me and I will be saved, for You are my glory. Amen and Amen!

THANKSGIVING PRAYERS AFTER RECOVERY FROM ILLNESS

Read Psalms 23 and 103 on page 821. Then continue with:

אָנָּא O great, mighty and awesome God: By Your great love I come before You to offer thanks for all the good You have bestowed on me. In my distress I called to You and You answered me; from my sick bed I cried to You, and You heard my voice and my pleas. You chastened me severely, Lord, but You did not hand me over to death. In Your love and compassion You lifted my soul from the grave. For Your anger is for a moment, Your favour for a lifetime. At night there may be weeping, but in the morning there is joy. The living, only the living, praise You as I do this day. My soul which You have redeemed shall tell of Your wonders to the children of men. Blessed are You, the faithful Healer of all flesh.

אֵל רַחוּם O God, compassionate and gracious, who grants favours to the undeserving: I am not worthy of all the kindness You have shown to me until now. Purify, please, my heart that I may be worthy to walk before You in the way of the upright. Extend Your help to Your servant. Grant me the strength and resolution to overcome my weakness, and bless me with physical health. Keep sorrow and grief far from me;

---

thanksgiving prayer. If it is felt that the illness was potentially life-threatening, the *HaGomel* blessing (on page 124) should be said on the first occasion one is able to attend the synagogue, either weekday, Shabbat or Festival.

מֵעָלַי כָּל צָרָה וְתוּגָה, שָׁמְרֵנִי מִכָּל רָע, וּבַעֲצָתְךָ תַנְחֵנִי. וְזָרְחָה לִי תָּמִיד שֶׁמֶשׁ צְדָקָה, וּמַרְפֵּה בִּכְנָפֶיהָ. יִהְיוּ לְרָצוֹן אִמְרֵי־פִי וְהֶגְיוֹן לִבִּי לְפָנֶיךָ, יהוה צוּרִי וְגוֹאֲלִי. אָמֵן.

וידוי שכיב מרע

The following confession is said by one near death. He or she should be told: "Do not fear. Many confessed their sins, and then recovered. Everyone who does confess has reward in the World to Come" (Proverbs 28:13).

מוֹדֶה אֲנִי לְפָנֶיךָ, יהוה אֱלֹהַי וֵאלֹהֵי אֲבוֹתַי, שֶׁרְפוּאָתִי וּמִיתָתִי בְּיָדֶךָ. יְהִי רָצוֹן מִלְּפָנֶיךָ, שֶׁתִּרְפָּאֵנִי רְפוּאָה שְׁלֵמָה, וְאִם הַמָּוֶת כָּלֶה וְנֶחֱרָץ מֵעִמְּךָ, אֶקָּחֶנּוּ מִיָּדְךָ בְּאַהֲבָה. וּתְהִי מִיתָתִי כַפָּרָה עַל כָּל חֲטָאִים וַעֲוֹנוֹת וּפְשָׁעִים שֶׁחָטָאתִי וְשֶׁעָוִיתִי וְשֶׁפָּשַׁעְתִּי לְפָנֶיךָ. וְתַשְׁפִּיעַ לִי מֵרַב טוּב הַצָּפוּן לַצַּדִּיקִים, וְתוֹדִיעֵנִי אֹרַח חַיִּים, שֹׂבַע שְׂמָחוֹת אֶת־פָּנֶיךָ, נְעִימוֹת בִּימִינְךָ נֶצַח.

אֲבִי יְתוֹמִים, וְדַיַּן אַלְמָנוֹת, הָגֵן בְּעַד קְרוֹבַי הַיְקָרִים, אֲשֶׁר נַפְשִׁי קְשׁוּרָה בְּנַפְשָׁם. בְּיָדְךָ אַפְקִיד רוּחִי, פָּדִיתָה אוֹתִי יהוה אֵל אֱמֶת. אָמֵן, וְאָמֵן.

When the end is approaching, the following should be said:

Three times:

יהוה מֶלֶךְ, יהוה מָלָךְ, יהוה יִמְלֹךְ לְעוֹלָם וָעֶד.

Three times:

בָּרוּךְ שֵׁם כְּבוֹד מַלְכוּתוֹ לְעוֹלָם וָעֶד.

CONFESSION ON A DEATH BED "One who confesses and renounces his sins finds mercy" (Proverbs 28:13). "When a person is sick and close to death, he or

protect me from all harm, and guide me with Your counsel. May the sun of righteousness shine for me, bringing healing in its wings. May the words of my mouth and the meditation of my heart find favour before You, O Lord, my Rock and my Redeemer. Amen.

CONFESSION ON A DEATH BED

The following confession is said by one near death. He or she should be told: "Do not fear. Many confessed their sins, and then recovered. Everyone who does confess has reward in the World to Come" (Proverbs 28:13).

מוֹדֶה אֲנִי I acknowledge before You, Lord my God and God of my ancestors, that my cure and my death are in Your hands. May it be Your will to send me a perfect healing. Yet if my death is fully determined by You, I accept it in love at Your hand. May my death be an atonement for all the sins, iniquities and transgressions I have committed before You. Grant me of the great happiness that is stored up for the righteous. Make known to me the path of life, in Your presence is fullness of joy; at Your right hand bliss for evermore.

אֲבִי יְתוֹמִים Father of the fatherless and defender of the widow, protect my cherished family, whose souls are bound with mine. Into Your hand I entrust my spirit. May You redeem me, Lord, God of truth. Amen and Amen.

When the end is approaching, the following should be said:

Three times:

The Lord is King, the Lord was King,
and the Lord will be King for ever and ever.

Three times:

Blessed be the name of His glorious kingdom
for ever and ever.

---

she is told: make a confession" (*Shabbat* 32a). These prayers are supreme testimonies of faith, as the human soul reaches upward to the world of souls.

Seven times:

יהוה הוּא הָאֱלֹהִים.

Once:

שְׁמַע יִשְׂרָאֵל יהוה אֱלֹהֵינוּ יהוה אֶחָד.

תפילה קודם הלוית המת

תהלים כג

מִזְמוֹר לְדָוִד, יהוה רֹעִי לֹא אֶחְסָר. בִּנְאוֹת דֶּשֶׁא יַרְבִּיצֵנִי, עַל־מֵי מְנֻחוֹת יְנַהֲלֵנִי. נַפְשִׁי יְשׁוֹבֵב, יַנְחֵנִי בְמַעְגְּלֵי־צֶדֶק לְמַעַן שְׁמוֹ. גַּם כִּי־אֵלֵךְ בְּגֵיא צַלְמָוֶת, לֹא־אִירָא רָע כִּי־אַתָּה עִמָּדִי, שִׁבְטְךָ וּמִשְׁעַנְתֶּךָ הֵמָּה יְנַחֲמֻנִי. תַּעֲרֹךְ לְפָנַי שֻׁלְחָן נֶגֶד צֹרְרָי, דִּשַּׁנְתָּ בַשֶּׁמֶן רֹאשִׁי, כּוֹסִי רְוָיָה. אַךְ טוֹב וָחֶסֶד יִרְדְּפוּנִי כָּל־יְמֵי חַיָּי, וְשַׁבְתִּי בְּבֵית יהוה לְאֹרֶךְ יָמִים.

תהלים קל

שִׁיר הַמַּעֲלוֹת, מִמַּעֲמַקִּים קְרָאתִיךָ יהוה. אֲדֹנָי שִׁמְעָה בְקוֹלִי, תִּהְיֶינָה אָזְנֶיךָ קַשֻּׁבוֹת לְקוֹל תַּחֲנוּנָי. אִם עֲוֹנוֹת תִּשְׁמָר־יָהּ, אֲדֹנָי מִי יַעֲמֹד. כִּי עִמְּךָ הַסְּלִיחָה, לְמַעַן תִּוָּרֵא. קִוִּיתִי יהוה קִוְּתָה נַפְשִׁי, וְלִדְבָרוֹ הוֹחָלְתִּי. נַפְשִׁי לַיהוה, מִשֹּׁמְרִים לַבֹּקֶר, שֹׁמְרִים לַבֹּקֶר. יַחֵל יִשְׂרָאֵל אֶל יהוה,

---

HOME SERVICE PRIOR TO A FUNERAL

At times of bereavement and loss, prayer makes grief articulate. Ancient words, inspired, hallowed by time, words that have given comfort to many before us, help us as we struggle in the midst of intense emotion. Each loss, like each life, is unique; yet death itself is part of the human condition, and when it happens to those close to us, God extends to us His embrace of comfort through the words of His prophets and poets. These prayers, from Psalm 90, Isaiah 55, and other biblical passages, re-

Seven times:

The Lord, He is God.

Once:

Listen, Israel, the Lord is our God, the Lord is One.

HOME SERVICE PRIOR TO A FUNERAL

PSALM 23

לְדָוִד A psalm of David. The Lord is my Shepherd, I shall not want. He makes me lie down in green pastures, He leads me beside the still waters. He refreshes my soul; He guides me in the paths of righteousness for His name's sake. Though I walk through the valley of the shadow of death, I will fear no evil, for You are with me; Your rod and Your staff, they comfort me. You set a table before me in the presence of my enemies, You anoint my head with oil, my cup is filled to overflowing. May goodness and kindness follow me all the days of my life, and may I live in the house of the Lord for evermore.

PSALM 130

A song of ascents. From the depths I have called to You, O Lord. Lord, hear my voice; let Your ears be attentive to my plea. If You, Lord, should keep account of sins, who could stand? But with You there is forgiveness, that You may be held in awe. I wait for the Lord, my soul waits, and in His word I put my hope. My soul waits for the Lord more than watchmen wait for the morning, more than watchmen wait for the morning. Israel, put your hope in the Lord, for with

---

mind us of the brevity of our lives on earth, but they also tell us with absolute faith that death is not an end but rather a beginning. "The dust returns to the earth as it was, but the spirit returns to God who gave it" (Ecclesiastes 12:7). After these biblical readings, and others specific to men and women, we say the moving prayer for the dead, *God, full of compassion,* asking God to shelter the soul of the one we have lost, under the shadow of His wings, binding it in the bonds of eternal life.

כִּי־עִם־יהוה הַחֶסֶד, וְהַרְבֵּה עִמּוֹ פְדוּת. וְהוּא יִפְדֶּה אֶת יִשְׂרָאֵל, מִכֹּל עֲוֹנוֹתָיו.

אֲדֹנָי מָעוֹן אַתָּה הָיִיתָ לָּנוּ בְּדֹר וָדֹר, בְּטֶרֶם הָרִים יֻלָּדוּ, וַתְּחוֹלֵל אֶרֶץ וְתֵבֵל וּמֵעוֹלָם עַד־עוֹלָם, אַתָּה אֵל. תָּשֵׁב אֱנוֹשׁ עַד־דַּכָּא, וַתֹּאמֶר, שׁוּבוּ בְנֵי־אָדָם. כִּי אֶלֶף שָׁנִים בְּעֵינֶיךָ כְּיוֹם אֶתְמוֹל כִּי יַעֲבֹר, וְאַשְׁמוּרָה בַלָּיְלָה. יְמֵי שְׁנוֹתֵינוּ בָהֶם שִׁבְעִים שָׁנָה, וְאִם בִּגְבוּרֹת שְׁמוֹנִים שָׁנָה, וְרָהְבָּם עָמָל וָאָוֶן, כִּי גָז חִישׁ וַנָּעֻפָה. לִמְנוֹת יָמֵינוּ כֵּן הוֹדַע, וְנָבִא לְבַב חָכְמָה.

דִּרְשׁוּ יהוה בְּהִמָּצְאוֹ, קְרָאֻהוּ בִּהְיוֹתוֹ קָרוֹב. יַעֲזֹב רָשָׁע דַּרְכּוֹ, וְאִישׁ אָוֶן מַחְשְׁבֹתָיו, וְיָשֹׁב אֶל־יהוה וִירַחֲמֵהוּ, וְאֶל־אֱלֹהֵינוּ כִּי־יַרְבֶּה לִסְלוֹחַ. כִּי לֹא מַחְשְׁבוֹתַי מַחְשְׁבוֹתֵיכֶם, וְלֹא דַרְכֵיכֶם דְּרָכָי, נְאֻם יהוה. כִּי גָבְהוּ שָׁמַיִם מֵאָרֶץ, כֵּן גָּבְהוּ דְרָכַי מִדַּרְכֵיכֶם, וּמַחְשְׁבֹתַי מִמַּחְשְׁבֹתֵיכֶם.

אֱנוֹשׁ כֶּחָצִיר יָמָיו כְּצִיץ הַשָּׂדֶה כֵּן יָצִיץ. כִּי רוּחַ עָבְרָה־בּוֹ וְאֵינֶנּוּ, וְלֹא־יַכִּירֶנּוּ עוֹד מְקוֹמוֹ. וְחֶסֶד יהוה מֵעוֹלָם וְעַד־עוֹלָם עַל־יְרֵאָיו, וְצִדְקָתוֹ לִבְנֵי בָנִים. בְּאֹרַח צְדָקָה חַיִּים וְדֶרֶךְ נְתִיבָה אַל־מָוֶת. וְיָשֹׁב הֶעָפָר עַל הָאָרֶץ כְּשֶׁהָיָה, וְהָרוּחַ תָּשׁוּב אֶל הָאֱלֹהִים אֲשֶׁר נְתָנָהּ. מִי לִי בַשָּׁמָיִם, וְעִמְּךָ לֹא־חָפַצְתִּי בָאָרֶץ. כָּלָה שְׁאֵרִי וּלְבָבִי צוּר־לְבָבִי, וְחֶלְקִי אֱלֹהִים לְעוֹלָם. מַה־יָּקָר חַסְדְּךָ אֱלֹהִים, וּבְנֵי אָדָם בְּצֵל כְּנָפֶיךָ יֶחֱסָיוּן. כִּי עִמְּךָ מְקוֹר חַיִּים, בְּאוֹרְךָ נִרְאֶה־אוֹר.

PRAYER IN A HOUSE OF MOURNING
Psalm 49. Repentance is part of the process of mourning (Maimonides). Confronted with an awareness of our mortality, we begin to rethink our priorities, knowing that what occupy our energies and thoughts much of the time are often matters of relatively minor significance

the LORD there is lovingkindness, and great is His power to redeem. It is He who will redeem Israel from all their sins.

אֲדֹנָי LORD, You have been our shelter in every generation. Before the mountains were born, before You brought forth the earth and the world, from everlasting to everlasting You are GOD. You turn men back to dust, saying, "Return, you children of men." For a thousand years in Your sight are like yesterday when it has passed, like a watch in the night. The span of our life is seventy years, or if we are strong, eighty years; but the best of them is trouble and sorrow; for they quickly pass, and we fly away. Teach us rightly to number our days, that we may gain a heart of wisdom.

דִּרְשׁוּ Seek the LORD while He may be found; call on Him while He is near. Let the wicked abandon his way, and the evil man his thoughts; and let him return to the LORD, and He will have mercy on him; to our GOD, for He will freely forgive. "For My thoughts are not your thoughts, nor are your ways My ways", says the LORD. As the heavens are high above the earth, so are My ways high above your ways, and My thoughts above your thoughts.

אֱנוֹשׁ As for man, his days are like grass; like a flower of the field he flourishes. For a wind passes over it and it is gone, and its place knows it no more. But the kindness of the LORD is for all eternity to those who fear Him; His righteousness is with their children's children. In the way of righteousness there is life; in that path there is no death. The dust returns to the earth as it was, but the spirit returns to GOD who gave it. Whom have I in heaven but You? And having You, I desire nothing else on earth. My flesh and my heart may fail, but GOD is the strength of my heart and my portion for ever. How precious is Your unfailing love, O LORD; mortals seek refuge under the shadow of Your wings. For with You is the fountain of life; in Your light, we see light.

---

when weighed against the fullness of eternity and the brevity of our lives on earth. Psalm 49 is a most powerful expression of this idea. What lives on after us is not our wealth but the ideals for which we live and the good we do.

Psalm 16. On days when *Tachanun* is not said, we recite this psalm, quite differ-

For a child, turn to page 836.

For a man, say:

מִי־יַעֲלֶה בְהַר יהוה, וּמִי־יָקוּם בִּמְקוֹם קָדְשׁוֹ. נְקִי כַפַּיִם וּבַר לֵבָב, אֲשֶׁר לֹא־נָשָׂא לַשָּׁוְא נַפְשִׁי וְלֹא נִשְׁבַּע לְמִרְמָה. יִשָּׂא בְרָכָה מֵאֵת יהוה, וּצְדָקָה מֵאֱלֹהֵי יִשְׁעוֹ. סוֹף דָּבָר הַכֹּל נִשְׁמָע, אֶת־הָאֱלֹהִים יְרָא, וְאֶת־מִצְוֹתָיו שְׁמוֹר, כִּי זֶה כָּל־הָאָדָם. הַיּוֹם קָצֵר, וְהַמְּלָאכָה מְרֻבָּה, וְהַפּוֹעֲלִים עֲצֵלִים, וְהַשָּׂכָר הַרְבֵּה, וּבַעַל הַבַּיִת דּוֹחֵק. לֹא עָלֶיךָ הַמְּלָאכָה לִגְמוֹר, וְלֹא־אַתָּה בֶן־חוֹרִין לְהִבָּטֵל מִמֶּנָּה. נֶאֱמָן הוּא בַּעַל מְלַאכְתְּךָ, שֶׁיְּשַׁלֶּם לְךָ שְׂכַר פְּעֻלָּתֶךָ. וְדַע שֶׁמַּתַּן שְׂכָרָם שֶׁל־צַדִּיקִים לֶעָתִיד לָבוֹא.

For a woman, say (add words in brackets according to circumstances):

אֵשֶׁת חַיִל מִי יִמְצָא, וְרָחֹק מִפְּנִינִים מִכְרָהּ. (בָּטַח בָּהּ לֵב בַּעְלָהּ, וְשָׁלָל לֹא יֶחְסָר. גְּמָלַתְהוּ טוֹב וְלֹא רָע, כֹּל יְמֵי חַיֶּיהָ.) כַּפָּהּ פָּרְשָׂה לֶעָנִי, וְיָדֶיהָ שִׁלְּחָה לָאֶבְיוֹן. עֹז וְהָדָר לְבוּשָׁהּ, וַתִּשְׂחַק לְיוֹם אַחֲרוֹן. פִּיהָ פָּתְחָה בְחָכְמָה, וְתוֹרַת־חֶסֶד עַל־לְשׁוֹנָהּ. (צוֹפִיָּה הֲלִיכוֹת בֵּיתָהּ, וְלֶחֶם עַצְלוּת לֹא תֹאכֵל. קָמוּ בָנֶיהָ וַיְאַשְּׁרוּהָ, בַּעְלָהּ וַיְהַלְלָהּ. רַבּוֹת בָּנוֹת עָשׂוּ חָיִל, וְאַתְּ עָלִית עַל־כֻּלָּנָה.) תְּנוּ־לָהּ מִפְּרִי יָדֶיהָ, וִיהַלְלוּהָ בַשְּׁעָרִים מַעֲשֶׂיהָ. יְשַׁלֵּם יהוה פָּעֳלֵךְ, וּתְהִי מַשְׂכֻּרְתֵּךְ שְׁלֵמָה מֵעִם יהוה אֱלֹהֵי יִשְׂרָאֵל, אֲשֶׁר בָּאת לַחֲסוֹת תַּחַת כְּנָפָיו.

אֵל מָלֵא רַחֲמִים שׁוֹכֵן בַּמְּרוֹמִים, אֱלוֹהַּ סְלִיחוֹת חַנּוּן וְרַחוּם אֶרֶךְ אַפַּיִם וְרַב חֶסֶד, הַמְצֵא כַּפָּרַת פֶּשַׁע וְהַקְרָבַת יֶשַׁע וּמְנוּחָה נְכוֹנָה, תַּחַת כַּנְפֵי הַשְּׁכִינָה, בְּמַעֲלוֹת קְדוֹשִׁים וּטְהוֹרִים כְּזֹהַר הָרָקִיעַ מַזְהִירִים, אֶת נִשְׁמַת

---

ent in mood from Psalm 49. The psalm reflects that, despite our loss, we are here, alive, and with much for which to thank God. This is a poem of re-affirmation.

אֵל מָלֵא *God, full of compassion*: Prayers for the deceased, with slight variations, have been part of the liturgy since the massacre of Jews throughout Europe and

For a child, turn to page 837.

For a man, say:

Who may climb the mountain of the LORD? Who may stand in His holy place? He who has clean hands and a pure heart, who has not taken My name in vain or not sworn deceitfully. He shall receive blessing from the LORD and a just reward from GOD, his Deliverer. The last word, when all is heard: Revere GOD and keep His commandments, for this is the whole duty of man. The day is short, the task is great; the labourers are lazy, the reward is much, and the Master insistent. It is not for you to complete the task, but neither are you free to stand aside from it. Your Employer will faithfully reward your work. Know though that the reward of the righteous is granted in the time to come.

For a woman, say (add words in brackets according to circumstances):

A woman of strength, who can find? Her worth is far beyond pearls. (Her husband's heart trusts in her, and he has no lack of gain. She brings him good, not harm, all the days of her life.) She reaches out her palm to the poor, and extends her hand to the needy. She is clothed with strength and dignity; she can laugh at the days to come. She opens her mouth with wisdom, and the law of kindness is on her tongue. (She watches over the affairs of her household, and never eats the bread of idleness. Her children rise and call her happy; her husband also praises her: "Many women have excelled, but you surpass them all.") Give her the reward she has earned; let her deeds bring her praise in the gates. May the LORD repay your deeds. May you have a full reward from the LORD GOD of Israel, under whose wings you have sought refuge.

אֵל מָלֵא GOD, full of compassion, who dwells on high, GOD of forgiveness, who is gracious and compassionate, slow to anger and abounding in kindness, may He grant pardon of transgression, nearness of salvation, and perfect rest beneath the wings of the Divine Presence, in the exalted places among the holy and pure, who shine as the brightness of heaven, to

the Levant during the First Crusade at the end of the eleventh century. This version includes a prayer for the mourners, and ends with some of the greatest of all verses of consolation, by the prophet Isaiah.

For a male, say:

(פלוני בֶּן פלוני) שֶׁהָלַךְ לְעוֹלָמוֹ. אָנָּא בַּעַל הָרַחֲמִים, זָכְרָה לוֹ לְטוֹבָה כָּל זְכִיּוֹתָיו וְצִדְקוֹתָיו בְּאַרְצוֹת הַחַיִּים, וּפְתַח לוֹ שַׁעֲרֵי צֶדֶק וְאוֹרָה, שַׁעֲרֵי חֶמְלָה וַחֲנִינָה, בְּסֵתֶר כְּנָפֶיךָ תַּסְתִּירֵהוּ לְעוֹלָמִים, וּצְרוֹר בִּצְרוֹר הַחַיִּים אֶת נִשְׁמָתוֹ, יהוה הוּא נַחֲלָתוֹ, וְיָנוּחַ בְּשָׁלוֹם עַל מִשְׁכָּבוֹ.

For a female, say:

(פלונית בַּת פלוני) שֶׁהָלְכָה לְעוֹלָמָהּ. אָנָּא בַּעַל הָרַחֲמִים, זָכְרָה לָהּ לְטוֹבָה כָּל זְכִיּוֹתֶיהָ וְצִדְקוֹתֶיהָ בְּאַרְצוֹת הַחַיִּים, וּפְתַח לָהּ שַׁעֲרֵי צֶדֶק וְאוֹרָה, שַׁעֲרֵי חֶמְלָה וַחֲנִינָה, בְּסֵתֶר כְּנָפֶיךָ תַּסְתִּירֶהָ לְעוֹלָמִים, וּצְרוֹר בִּצְרוֹר הַחַיִּים אֶת נִשְׁמָתָהּ, יהוה הוּא נַחֲלָתָהּ, וְתָנוּחַ בְּשָׁלוֹם עַל מִשְׁכָּבָהּ.

וְנֹאמַר, אָמֵן.

For a child, say:

אֵל מָלֵא רַחֲמִים שׁוֹכֵן בַּמְּרוֹמִים, הַמְצֵא מְנוּחָה נְכוֹנָה תַּחַת כַּנְפֵי הַשְּׁכִינָה, בְּמַעֲלוֹת קְדוֹשִׁים וּטְהוֹרִים כְּזֹהַר הָרָקִיעַ מַזְהִירִים, אֶת נִשְׁמַת

For a boy, add:

הַיֶּלֶד (פלוני בֶּן פלוני) שֶׁהָלַךְ לְעוֹלָמוֹ. אָנָּא בַּעַל הָרַחֲמִים הַסְתִּירֵהוּ בְּסֵתֶר כְּנָפֶיךָ לְעוֹלָמִים, וּצְרוֹר בִּצְרוֹר הַחַיִּים אֶת נִשְׁמָתוֹ, יהוה הוּא נַחֲלָתוֹ, וְיָנוּחַ בְּשָׁלוֹם עַל מִשְׁכָּבוֹ.

For a girl, add:

הַיַּלְדָּה (פלונית בַּת פלוני) שֶׁהָלְכָה לְעוֹלָמָהּ. אָנָּא בַּעַל הָרַחֲמִים הַסְתִּירֶהָ בְּסֵתֶר כְּנָפֶיךָ לְעוֹלָמִים, וּצְרוֹר בִּצְרוֹר הַחַיִּים אֶת נִשְׁמָתָהּ, יהוה הוּא נַחֲלָתָהּ, וְתָנוּחַ בְּשָׁלוֹם עַל מִשְׁכָּבָהּ.

וְנֹאמַר, אָמֵן.

For a male, say:
who has gone to his eternal home. We pray to You, LORD of compassion: remember to him with favour all the worthy and righteous deeds which he did on earth. Open for him the gates of righteousness and light, the gates of pity and grace. Shelter him for evermore under the cover of Your wings; and let his soul be bound in the bonds of life. The LORD is his heritage; may he rest in peace.

For a female, say:
who has gone to her eternal home. We pray to You, LORD of compassion: remember to her with favour all the worthy and righteous deeds which she did on earth. Open for her the gates of righteousness and light, the gates of pity and grace. Shelter her for evermore under the cover of Your wings; and let her soul be bound in the bonds of life. The LORD is her heritage; may she rest in peace.

And let us say, Amen.

For a child, say:

אֵל מָלֵא GOD, full of compassion, who dwells on high, may He grant perfect rest beneath the wings of the Divine Presence, in the exalted places among the holy and pure, who shine as the brightness of the sky, to the child

For a boy, add:
who has gone to his eternal rest. We beg You, O LORD of compassion, shelter his soul for evermore under the cover of Your wings; and let his soul be bound up in the bond of life. The LORD is his portion; may he rest in peace, who has gone to his eternal rest.

For a girl, add:
who has gone to her eternal rest. We beg You, O LORD of compassion, shelter her soul for evermore under the cover of Your wings; and let her soul be bound up in the bond of life. The LORD is her portion; may she rest in peace, who has gone to her eternal rest.

And let us say, Amen.

תפילה בבית האבל

After the regular service, the following תהלים מט is read in the בֵּית אָבֵל during the שִׁבְעָה week. On those days on which תַּחֲנוּן is not said, תהלים טז is substituted.

תהלים מט

לַמְנַצֵּחַ לִבְנֵי קֹרַח מִזְמוֹר. שִׁמְעוּ־זֹאת כָּל־הָעַמִּים, הַאֲזִינוּ כָּל־יֹשְׁבֵי חָלֶד. גַּם־בְּנֵי אָדָם, גַּם־בְּנֵי־אִישׁ, יַחַד עָשִׁיר וְאֶבְיוֹן. פִּי יְדַבֵּר חָכְמוֹת, וְהָגוּת לִבִּי תְבוּנוֹת. אַטֶּה לְמָשָׁל אָזְנִי, אֶפְתַּח בְּכִנּוֹר חִידָתִי. לָמָּה אִירָא בִּימֵי רָע, עֲוֹן עֲקֵבַי יְסֻבֵּנִי. הַבֹּטְחִים עַל־חֵילָם, וּבְרֹב עָשְׁרָם יִתְהַלָּלוּ. אָח לֹא־פָדֹה יִפְדֶּה אִישׁ, לֹא יִתֵּן לֵאלֹהִים כָּפְרוֹ. וְיֵקַר פִּדְיוֹן נַפְשָׁם, וְחָדַל לְעוֹלָם. וִיחִי־עוֹד לָנֶצַח, לֹא יִרְאֶה הַשָּׁחַת. כִּי יִרְאֶה חֲכָמִים יָמוּתוּ, יַחַד כְּסִיל וָבַעַר יֹאבֵדוּ, וְעָזְבוּ לַאֲחֵרִים חֵילָם. קִרְבָּם בָּתֵּימוֹ לְעוֹלָם, מִשְׁכְּנֹתָם לְדוֹר וָדֹר, קָרְאוּ בִשְׁמוֹתָם עֲלֵי אֲדָמוֹת. וְאָדָם בִּיקָר בַּל־יָלִין, נִמְשַׁל כַּבְּהֵמוֹת נִדְמוּ. זֶה דַרְכָּם, כֵּסֶל לָמוֹ, וְאַחֲרֵיהֶם בְּפִיהֶם יִרְצוּ, סֶלָה. כַּצֹּאן לִשְׁאוֹל שַׁתּוּ, מָוֶת יִרְעֵם, וַיִּרְדּוּ בָם יְשָׁרִים לַבֹּקֶר, וְצוּרָם לְבַלּוֹת שְׁאוֹל מִזְּבֻל לוֹ. אַךְ־אֱלֹהִים יִפְדֶּה־נַפְשִׁי מִיַּד שְׁאוֹל, כִּי יִקָּחֵנִי סֶלָה. אַל־תִּירָא כִּי יַעֲשִׁר אִישׁ, כִּי־יִרְבֶּה כְּבוֹד בֵּיתוֹ. כִּי לֹא בְמוֹתוֹ יִקַּח הַכֹּל, לֹא־יֵרֵד אַחֲרָיו כְּבוֹדוֹ. כִּי נַפְשׁוֹ בְּחַיָּיו יְבָרֵךְ, וְיוֹדֻךָ כִּי־תֵיטִיב לָךְ. תָּבוֹא עַד־דּוֹר אֲבוֹתָיו, עַד־נֵצַח לֹא יִרְאוּ־אוֹר. אָדָם בִּיקָר וְלֹא יָבִין, נִמְשַׁל כַּבְּהֵמוֹת נִדְמוּ.

On those days on which תַּחֲנוּן is not said, substitute:

תהלים טז

מִכְתָּם לְדָוִד, שָׁמְרֵנִי אֵל כִּי־חָסִיתִי בָךְ. אָמַרְתְּ לַיהוה, אֲדֹנָי אָתָּה, טוֹבָתִי בַּל־עָלֶיךָ. לִקְדוֹשִׁים אֲשֶׁר־בָּאָרֶץ הֵמָּה,

PRAYER IN A HOUSE OF MOURNING

After the regular service, the following Psalm 49 is read in a house of mourning during the *shivah* week. On those days on which *Tachanun* is not said, Psalm 16 is substituted.

PSALM 49

לַמְנַצֵּחַ For the director of music. Of the sons of Korach. A sacred song. Hear this, all you peoples. Listen, all inhabitants of the World, low and high, rich and poor alike. My mouth will speak words of wisdom; the utterance of my heart will give understanding. I listen with care to a parable; I expound my mystery to the music of the harp. Why should I fear when evil days come, when the wickedness of my foes surrounds me, trusting in their wealth, boasting of their great riches? No man can redeem his brother or pay God the price of his release, for the ransom of a life is costly; no payment is ever enough that would let him live for ever, never seeing the grave. For all can see that wise men die, that the foolish and senseless all perish and leave their wealth to others. They think their houses will remain for ever, their dwellings for all generations; they give their names to their estates. But man, despite his splendour, does not endure; he is like the beasts that perish. Such is the fate of the foolish and their followers who approve their words, Selah. Like sheep they are destined for the grave: death will be their shepherd. The upright will rule over them in the morning. Their forms will decay in the grave, far from their mansions. But God will redeem my life from the grave; He will surely take me to Himself, Selah. Do not be overawed when a man grows rich, when the glory of his house increases, for he will take nothing with him when he dies; his wealth will not descend with him. Though while he lived he counted himself blessed – men always praise you when you prosper – he will join the generation of his ancestors who will never again see the light. A man who, despite his splendour, lacks understanding is like the beasts that perish.

On those days on which *Tachanun* is not said, substitute:

PSALM 16

מִכְתָּם לְדָוִד Protect me, God, for in You I have found refuge. I have said to the Lord: You are my Lord: from You alone comes the good I

וְאַדִּירֵי כָּל־חֶפְצִי־בָם. יִרְבּוּ עַצְּבוֹתָם אַחֵר מָהָרוּ, בַּל־אַסִּיךְ נִסְכֵּיהֶם מִדָּם, וּבַל־אֶשָּׂא אֶת־שְׁמוֹתָם עַל־שְׂפָתָי. יהוה, מְנָת־חֶלְקִי וְכוֹסִי, אַתָּה תּוֹמִיךְ גּוֹרָלִי. חֲבָלִים נָפְלוּ־לִי בַּנְּעִמִים, אַף־נַחֲלָת שָׁפְרָה עָלָי. אֲבָרֵךְ אֶת־יהוה אֲשֶׁר יְעָצָנִי, אַף־לֵילוֹת יִסְּרוּנִי כִלְיוֹתָי. שִׁוִּיתִי יהוה לְנֶגְדִּי תָמִיד, כִּי מִימִינִי בַּל־אֶמּוֹט. לָכֵן שָׂמַח לִבִּי וַיָּגֶל כְּבוֹדִי, אַף־בְּשָׂרִי יִשְׁכֹּן לָבֶטַח. כִּי לֹא־תַעֲזֹב נַפְשִׁי לִשְׁאוֹל, לֹא־תִתֵּן חֲסִידְךָ לִרְאוֹת שָׁחַת. תּוֹדִיעֵנִי אֹרַח חַיִּים, שֹׂבַע שְׂמָחוֹת אֶת־פָּנֶיךָ, נְעִמוֹת בִּימִינְךָ נֶצַח.

אזכרה

אָנָּא יהוה מֶלֶךְ מָלֵא רַחֲמִים, אֱלֹהֵי הָרוּחוֹת לְכָל־בָּשָׂר, אֲשֶׁר בְּיָדְךָ נַפְשׁוֹת הַחַיִּים וְהַמֵּתִים, אָנָּא קַבֵּל בְּחַסְדְּךָ הַגָּדוֹל אֶת־נִשְׁמַת

For a man, say:

(פלוני בֶּן פלוני) אֲשֶׁר נֶאֱסַף אֶל עַמּוֹ. חוּס וַחֲמוֹל עָלָיו, סְלַח וּמְחַל לְכָל־פְּשָׁעָיו, כִּי אָדָם אֵין צַדִּיק בָּאָרֶץ אֲשֶׁר יַעֲשֶׂה־טּוֹב וְלֹא יֶחֱטָא. זְכוֹר לוֹ צִדְקָתוֹ אֲשֶׁר עָשָׂה, וִיהִי שְׂכָרוֹ אִתּוֹ, וּפְעֻלָּתוֹ לְפָנָיו. אָנָּא הַסְתֵּר אֶת־נִשְׁמָתוֹ בְּצֵל כְּנָפֶיךָ, הוֹדִיעֵהוּ אֹרַח חַיִּים, שֹׂבַע שְׂמָחוֹת אֶת־פָּנֶיךָ נְעִימוֹת בִּימִינְךָ נֶצַח, וְתַשְׁפִּיעַ לוֹ מֵרַב טוּב הַצָּפוּן לַצַּדִּיקִים.

For a woman, say:

(פלונית בַּת פלוני) אֲשֶׁר נֶאֶסְפָה אֶל עַמָּהּ. חוּס וַחֲמוֹל עָלֶיהָ, סְלַח וּמְחַל לְכָל־פְּשָׁעֶיהָ, כִּי אָדָם אֵין צַדִּיק בָּאָרֶץ אֲשֶׁר יַעֲשֶׂה־טּוֹב וְלֹא יֶחֱטָא. זְכוֹר לָהּ צִדְקָתָהּ אֲשֶׁר עָשְׂתָה, וִיהִי שְׂכָרָהּ אִתָּהּ, וּפְעֻלָּתָהּ לְפָנֶיהָ. אָנָּא הַסְתֵּר אֶת־נִשְׁמָתָהּ בְּצֵל

enjoy. All my delight is in the holy ones, the mighty in the land. Those who run after other gods multiply their sorrows. I shall never offer them libations of blood, nor will their names pass my lips. The LORD is my allotted portion and my cup: You direct my fate. The lines have fallen for me in pleasant places; I am well content with my inheritance. I will bless the LORD who has guided me; at night my innermost being admonishes me. I have set the LORD before me at all times. He is at my right hand: I shall not be shaken. Therefore my heart is glad, my spirit rejoices, and my body rests secure. For You will not abandon me to the grave, nor let Your faithful one see the pit. You will teach me the path of life. In Your presence is fullness of joy; at Your right hand, bliss for evermore.

MEMORIAL PRAYER

O LORD and King, full of compassion, GOD of the spirits of all flesh, in whose hand are the souls of the living and the dead, receive, we pray You, in Your great love the soul of

For a man, say:

(name of person) who has been gathered to his people. Have mercy on him, pardon all his transgressions, for there is no one so righteous on earth as to have done only good and never sinned. Remember the righteousness that he did, and let his reward be with him, his recompense before him. O shelter his soul in the shadow of Your wings. Make known to him the path of life. In Your presence is fullness of joy, at Your right hand bliss for evermore. Bestow upon him the great goodness that is stored up for the righteous.

For a woman, say:

(name of person) who has been gathered to her people. Have mercy on her, pardon all her transgressions, for there is no one so righteous on earth as to have done only good and never sinned. Remember the righteousness that she did, and let her reward be with her, her recompense before her. O shelter her soul in the shadow of Your wings. Make known to her the path of life. In Your presence is full-

כְּנָפֶיךָ, הוֹדִיעֶהָ אֹרַח חַיִּים, שֹׂבַע שְׂמָחוֹת אֶת־פָּנֶיךָ נְעִימוֹת בִּימִינְךָ נֶצַח, וְתַשְׁפִּיעַ לָהּ מֵרַב טוּב הַצָּפוּן לַצַּדִּיקִים.

For a boy, say:

(פלוני בֶּן פלוני) אֲשֶׁר נֶאֱסַף אֶל עַמּוֹ. זְכוֹר לוֹ צִדְקָתוֹ אֲשֶׁר עָשָׂה, וִיהִי שְׂכָרוֹ אִתּוֹ, וּפְעֻלָּתוֹ לְפָנָיו. אָנָּא הַסְתֵּר אֶת־נִשְׁמָתוֹ בְּצֵל כְּנָפֶיךָ, הוֹדִיעֵהוּ אֹרַח חַיִּים, שֹׂבַע שְׂמָחוֹת אֶת־פָּנֶיךָ נְעִימוֹת בִּימִינְךָ נֶצַח, וְתַשְׁפִּיעַ לוֹ מֵרַב טוּב הַצָּפוּן לַצַּדִּיקִים.

For a girl, say:

(פלונית בַּת פלוני) אֲשֶׁר נֶאֶסְפָה אֶל עַמָּהּ. זְכוֹר לָהּ צִדְקָתָהּ אֲשֶׁר עָשְׂתָה, וִיהִי שְׂכָרָהּ אִתָּהּ, וּפְעֻלָּתָהּ לְפָנֶיהָ. אָנָּא הַסְתֵּר אֶת־נִשְׁמָתָהּ בְּצֵל כְּנָפֶיךָ, הוֹדִיעֶהָ אֹרַח חַיִּים, שֹׂבַע שְׂמָחוֹת אֶת־פָּנֶיךָ נְעִימוֹת בִּימִינְךָ נֶצַח, וְתַשְׁפִּיעַ לָהּ מֵרַב טוּב הַצָּפוּן לַצַּדִּיקִים.

כְּמוֹ שֶׁכָּתוּב, מָה רַב טוּבְךָ אֲשֶׁר־צָפַנְתָּ לִּירֵאֶיךָ פָּעַלְתָּ לַחוֹסִים בָּךְ, נֶגֶד בְּנֵי אָדָם.

אָנָּא יהוה הָרוֹפֵא לִשְׁבוּרֵי לֵב, וּמְחַבֵּשׁ לְעַצְּבוֹתָם, שַׁלֵּם נִחוּמִים לָאֲבֵלִים.

For a young boy, add:

וּתְהִי פְּטִירַת הַיֶּלֶד הַזֶּה קֵץ לְכָל־צָרָה וְצוּקָה לְאָבִיו וּלְאִמּוֹ.

For a young girl, add:

וּתְהִי פְּטִירַת הַיַּלְדָּה הַזֹּאת קֵץ לְכָל־צָרָה וְצוּקָה לְאָבִיהָ וּלְאִמָּהּ.

If the mourners have children, add the words in brackets:

חַזְּקֵם וְאַמְּצֵם בְּיוֹם אֶבְלָם וִיגוֹנָם, וְזָכְרֵם (וּבְנֵי בֵיתָם) לְחַיִּים טוֹבִים וַאֲרֻכִּים. תֵּן בְּלִבָּם יִרְאָתְךָ וְאַהֲבָתְךָ לְעָבְדְךָ בְּלֵבָב שָׁלֵם, וּתְהִי אַחֲרִיתָם שָׁלוֹם, אָמֵן.

כְּאִישׁ אֲשֶׁר אִמּוֹ תְּנַחֲמֶנּוּ, כֵּן אָנֹכִי אֲנַחֶמְכֶם, וּבִירוּשָׁלַיִם

ness of joy, at Your right hand bliss for evermore. Bestow upon her the great goodness that is stored up for the righteous,

For a boy, say:

(name of child) who has been gathered to his people. O shelter his soul in the shadow of Your wings. Make known to him the path of life. In Your presence is fullness of joy, at Your right hand bliss for evermore. Bestow upon him the great goodness that is stored up for the righteous,

For a girl, say:

(name of child) who has been gathered to her people. O shelter her soul in the shadow of Your wings. Make known to her the path of life. In Your presence is fullness of joy, at Your right hand bliss for evermore. Bestow upon her the great goodness that is stored up for the righteous,

---

as it is written, "How great is Your goodness which You have stored up for those who revere You, which You bestow on those that trust in You before the children of men."

אָנָּא May the Lord who heals the broken-hearted and binds up their wounds, grant consolation to the mourners.

For a young boy, add:

May the death of this boy mark the end of all anguish and sorrow for his parents.

For a young girl, add:

May the death of this girl mark the end of all anguish and sorrow for her parents.

If the mourners have children, add the words in brackets:

Strengthen and support them in the day of their sadness and grief; and remember them (and their children) for a long and good life. Put into their hearts love and reverence for You, so that they may serve You with a perfect heart; and let their end be peace. Amen.

כְּאִישׁ As a mother comforts her son, so will I comfort you; and in Jerusalem you shall find comfort. Your sun shall no more set, your

תְּנוּחָמוּ. לֹא־יָבוֹא עוֹד שִׁמְשֵׁךְ, וִירֵחֵךְ לֹא יֵאָסֵף. כִּי יהוה יִהְיֶה־לָּךְ לְאוֹר עוֹלָם. וְשָׁלְמוּ יְמֵי אֶבְלֵךְ. בִּלַּע הַמָּוֶת לָנֶצַח, וּמָחָה יהוה אֱלֹהִים דִּמְעָה מֵעַל כָּל־פָּנִים, וְחֶרְפַּת עַמּוֹ יָסִיר מֵעַל כָּל־הָאָרֶץ, כִּי יהוה דִּבֵּר.

קדיש יתום

The transliteration can be found at the end of the Siddur.

Mourner:

יִתְגַּדַּל וְיִתְקַדַּשׁ שְׁמֵהּ רַבָּא. (Cong. אָמֵן) בְּעָלְמָא דִּי־בְרָא כִרְעוּתֵהּ. וְיַמְלִיךְ מַלְכוּתֵהּ, בְּחַיֵּיכוֹן וּבְיוֹמֵיכוֹן וּבְחַיֵּי דִי־כָל־בֵּית יִשְׂרָאֵל, בַּעֲגָלָא וּבִזְמַן קָרִיב. וְאִמְרוּ אָמֵן. (Cong. אָמֵן)

All:

יְהֵא שְׁמֵהּ רַבָּא מְבָרַךְ לְעָלַם וּלְעָלְמֵי עָלְמַיָּא.

Mourner:

יִתְבָּרַךְ וְיִשְׁתַּבַּח וְיִתְפָּאַר וְיִתְרוֹמַם וְיִתְנַשֵּׂא וְיִתְהַדַּר וְיִתְעַלֶּה וְיִתְהַלָּל שְׁמֵהּ דְּקֻדְשָׁא בְּרִיךְ הוּא (Cong. בְּרִיךְ הוּא) לְעֵלָּא (Between רֹאשׁ הַשָּׁנָה and יוֹם כִּפּוּר add לְעֵלָּא) מִן־כָּל־בִּרְכָתָא וְשִׁירָתָא תֻּשְׁבְּחָתָא וְנֶחֱמָתָא, דַּאֲמִירָן בְּעָלְמָא. וְאִמְרוּ אָמֵן. (Cong. אָמֵן)

יְהֵא שְׁלָמָא רַבָּא מִן־שְׁמַיָּא, וְחַיִּים עָלֵינוּ וְעַל־כָּל־יִשְׂרָאֵל. וְאִמְרוּ אָמֵן. (Cong. אָמֵן)

Bow, take three steps back, then bow, first left, then right, then centre, while saying:

עֹשֶׂה שָׁלוֹם בִּמְרוֹמָיו, הוּא יַעֲשֶׂה שָׁלוֹם עָלֵינוּ, וְעַל־כָּל־יִשְׂרָאֵל, וְאִמְרוּ אָמֵן. (Cong. אָמֵן)

moon shall no more withdraw itself, for the LORD shall be your everlasting light, and your days of mourning shall be ended. He will destroy death for ever; and the LORD GOD will wipe away the tears from all faces, and remove the reproach of His people from the whole earth; for the LORD has spoken it.

MOURNER'S KADDISH

The transliteration can be found at the end of the Siddur.

Mourner:

יִתְגַּדַּל Magnified and sanctified may His great name be, in the world He created by His will. May He establish His kingdom in your lifetime and in your days, and in the lifetime of all the House of Israel, swiftly and soon – and say: Amen.

All:

May His great name be blessed for ever and all time.

Mourner:

Blessed and praised, glorified and exalted, raised and honoured, uplifted and lauded be the name of the Holy One, blessed be He, (between Rosh Hashanah and Yom Kippur add 'well') beyond any blessing, song, praise and consolation uttered in the world – and say: Amen.

May there be great peace from heaven, and life for us and all Israel – and say: Amen.

Bow, take three steps back, then bow, first left, then right, then centre, while saying:

May He who makes peace in His high places, make peace for us and all Israel – and say: Amen.

TORAH READINGS

FOR SHABBAT מִנְחָה, AND ON MONDAY AND THURSDAY MORNINGS AT שַׁחֲרִית.

פרשת בראשית

פרק א א בְּרֵאשִׁ֖ית בָּרָ֣א אֱלֹהִ֑ים אֵ֥ת הַשָּׁמַ֖יִם וְאֵ֥ת הָאָֽרֶץ׃
ב וְהָאָ֗רֶץ הָיְתָ֥ה תֹ֙הוּ֙ וָבֹ֔הוּ וְחֹ֖שֶׁךְ עַל־פְּנֵ֣י תְה֑וֹם וְר֣וּחַ אֱלֹהִ֔ים
מְרַחֶ֖פֶת עַל־פְּנֵ֥י הַמָּֽיִם׃ ג וַיֹּ֥אמֶר אֱלֹהִ֖ים יְהִ֣י א֑וֹר וַֽיְהִי־אֽוֹר׃
ד וַיַּ֧רְא אֱלֹהִ֛ים אֶת־הָא֖וֹר כִּי־ט֑וֹב וַיַּבְדֵּ֣ל אֱלֹהִ֔ים בֵּ֥ין הָא֖וֹר
וּבֵ֥ין הַחֹֽשֶׁךְ׃ ה וַיִּקְרָ֨א אֱלֹהִ֤ים ׀ לָאוֹר֙ י֔וֹם וְלַחֹ֖שֶׁךְ קָ֣רָא לָ֑יְלָה
וַֽיְהִי־עֶ֥רֶב וַֽיְהִי־בֹ֖קֶר י֥וֹם אֶחָֽד׃ [לוי] פ ו וַיֹּ֣אמֶר אֱלֹהִ֔ים יְהִ֥י
רָקִ֖יעַ בְּת֣וֹךְ הַמָּ֑יִם וִיהִ֣י מַבְדִּ֔יל בֵּ֥ין מַ֖יִם לָמָֽיִם׃ ז וַיַּ֣עַשׂ אֱלֹהִים֮
אֶת־הָרָקִיעַ֒ וַיַּבְדֵּ֗ל בֵּ֤ין הַמַּ֙יִם֙ אֲשֶׁר֙ מִתַּ֣חַת לָרָקִ֔יעַ וּבֵ֣ין
הַמַּ֔יִם אֲשֶׁ֖ר מֵעַ֣ל לָרָקִ֑יעַ וַֽיְהִי־כֵֽן׃ ח וַיִּקְרָ֧א אֱלֹהִ֛ים לָֽרָקִ֖יעַ
שָׁמָ֑יִם וַֽיְהִי־עֶ֥רֶב וַֽיְהִי־בֹ֖קֶר י֥וֹם שֵׁנִֽי׃ פ [ישראל] ט וַיֹּ֣אמֶר
אֱלֹהִ֗ים יִקָּו֨וּ הַמַּ֜יִם מִתַּ֤חַת הַשָּׁמַ֙יִם֙ אֶל־מָק֣וֹם אֶחָ֔ד וְתֵרָאֶ֖ה
הַיַּבָּשָׁ֑ה וַֽיְהִי־כֵֽן׃ י וַיִּקְרָ֨א אֱלֹהִ֤ים ׀ לַיַּבָּשָׁה֙ אֶ֔רֶץ וּלְמִקְוֵ֥ה
הַמַּ֖יִם קָרָ֣א יַמִּ֑ים וַיַּ֥רְא אֱלֹהִ֖ים כִּי־טֽוֹב׃ יא וַיֹּ֣אמֶר אֱלֹהִ֗ים
תַּֽדְשֵׁ֤א הָאָ֙רֶץ֙ דֶּ֔שֶׁא עֵ֚שֶׂב מַזְרִ֣יעַ זֶ֔רַע עֵ֣ץ פְּרִ֞י עֹ֤שֶׂה פְּרִי֙
לְמִינ֔וֹ אֲשֶׁ֥ר זַרְעוֹ־ב֖וֹ עַל־הָאָ֑רֶץ וַֽיְהִי־כֵֽן׃ יב וַתּוֹצֵ֨א הָאָ֜רֶץ
דֶּ֠שֶׁא עֵ֣שֶׂב מַזְרִ֤יעַ זֶ֙רַע֙ לְמִינֵ֔הוּ וְעֵ֧ץ עֹֽשֶׂה־פְּרִ֛י אֲשֶׁ֥ר זַרְעוֹ־
ב֖וֹ לְמִינֵ֑הוּ וַיַּ֥רְא אֱלֹהִ֖ים כִּי־טֽוֹב׃ יג וַֽיְהִי־עֶ֥רֶב וַֽיְהִי־בֹ֖קֶר י֥וֹם
שְׁלִישִֽׁי׃

פרשת נח

פרק ו ט אֵלֶּה תּוֹלְדֹת נֹחַ נֹחַ אִישׁ צַדִּיק תָּמִים הָיָה בְּדֹרֹתָיו אֶת־
הָאֱלֹהִים הִתְהַלֶּךְ־נֹחַ׃ י וַיּוֹלֶד נֹחַ שְׁלֹשָׁה בָנִים אֶת־שֵׁם אֶת־
חָם וְאֶת־יָפֶת׃ יא וַתִּשָּׁחֵת הָאָרֶץ לִפְנֵי הָאֱלֹהִים וַתִּמָּלֵא
הָאָרֶץ חָמָס׃ יב וַיַּרְא אֱלֹהִים אֶת־הָאָרֶץ וְהִנֵּה נִשְׁחָתָה
כִּי־הִשְׁחִית כָּל־בָּשָׂר אֶת־דַּרְכּוֹ עַל־הָאָרֶץ׃ ס יג וַיֹּאמֶר
אֱלֹהִים לְנֹחַ קֵץ כָּל־בָּשָׂר בָּא לְפָנַי כִּי־מָלְאָה הָאָרֶץ חָמָס
מִפְּנֵיהֶם וְהִנְנִי מַשְׁחִיתָם אֶת־הָאָרֶץ׃ יד עֲשֵׂה לְךָ תֵּבַת
עֲצֵי־גֹפֶר קִנִּים תַּעֲשֶׂה אֶת־הַתֵּבָה וְכָפַרְתָּ אֹתָהּ מִבַּיִת
וּמִחוּץ בַּכֹּפֶר׃ טו וְזֶה אֲשֶׁר תַּעֲשֶׂה אֹתָהּ שְׁלֹשׁ מֵאוֹת אַמָּה
אֹרֶךְ הַתֵּבָה חֲמִשִּׁים אַמָּה רָחְבָּהּ וּשְׁלֹשִׁים אַמָּה קוֹמָתָהּ׃
טז צֹהַר ׀ תַּעֲשֶׂה לַתֵּבָה וְאֶל־אַמָּה תְּכַלֶּנָּה מִלְמַעְלָה וּפֶתַח
הַתֵּבָה בְּצִדָּהּ תָּשִׂים תַּחְתִּיִּם שְׁנִיִּם וּשְׁלִשִׁים תַּעֲשֶׂהָ׃
[לוי] יז וַאֲנִי הִנְנִי מֵבִיא אֶת־הַמַּבּוּל מַיִם עַל־הָאָרֶץ לְשַׁחֵת
כָּל־בָּשָׂר אֲשֶׁר־בּוֹ רוּחַ חַיִּים מִתַּחַת הַשָּׁמָיִם כֹּל אֲשֶׁר־בָּאָרֶץ
יִגְוָע׃ יח וַהֲקִמֹתִי אֶת־בְּרִיתִי אִתָּךְ וּבָאתָ אֶל־הַתֵּבָה אַתָּה
וּבָנֶיךָ וְאִשְׁתְּךָ וּנְשֵׁי־בָנֶיךָ אִתָּךְ׃ יט וּמִכָּל־הָחַי מִכָּל־בָּשָׂר
שְׁנַיִם מִכֹּל תָּבִיא אֶל־הַתֵּבָה לְהַחֲיֹת אִתָּךְ זָכָר וּנְקֵבָה יִהְיוּ׃
[ישראל] כ מֵהָעוֹף לְמִינֵהוּ וּמִן־הַבְּהֵמָה לְמִינָהּ מִכֹּל רֶמֶשׂ
הָאֲדָמָה לְמִינֵהוּ שְׁנַיִם מִכֹּל יָבֹאוּ אֵלֶיךָ לְהַחֲיוֹת׃ כא וְאַתָּה
קַח־לְךָ מִכָּל־מַאֲכָל אֲשֶׁר יֵאָכֵל וְאָסַפְתָּ אֵלֶיךָ וְהָיָה לְךָ וְלָהֶם
לְאָכְלָה׃ כב וַיַּעַשׂ נֹחַ כְּכֹל אֲשֶׁר צִוָּה אֹתוֹ אֱלֹהִים כֵּן עָשָׂה׃

פרשת לך לך

פרק יב א וַיֹּאמֶר יְהוָה אֶל־אַבְרָם לֶךְ־לְךָ מֵאַרְצְךָ וּמִמּוֹלַדְתְּךָ
וּמִבֵּית אָבִיךָ אֶל־הָאָרֶץ אֲשֶׁר אַרְאֶךָּ׃ ב וְאֶעֶשְׂךָ לְגוֹי גָּדוֹל

וַאֲבָרֶכְךָ וַאֲגַדְּלָה שְׁמֶךָ וֶהְיֵה בְּרָכָה׃ ג וַאֲבָרְכָה מְבָרְכֶיךָ
וּמְקַלֶּלְךָ אָאֹר וְנִבְרְכוּ בְךָ כֹּל מִשְׁפְּחֹת הָאֲדָמָה׃ [לוי] ד וַיֵּלֶךְ
אַבְרָם כַּאֲשֶׁר דִּבֶּר אֵלָיו יְהֹוָה וַיֵּלֶךְ אִתּוֹ לוֹט וְאַבְרָם בֶּן־
חָמֵשׁ שָׁנִים וְשִׁבְעִים שָׁנָה בְּצֵאתוֹ מֵחָרָן׃ ה וַיִּקַּח אַבְרָם
אֶת־שָׂרַי אִשְׁתּוֹ וְאֶת־לוֹט בֶּן־אָחִיו וְאֶת־כָּל־רְכוּשָׁם אֲשֶׁר
רָכָשׁוּ וְאֶת־הַנֶּפֶשׁ אֲשֶׁר־עָשׂוּ בְחָרָן וַיֵּצְאוּ לָלֶכֶת אַרְצָה
כְּנַעַן וַיָּבֹאוּ אַרְצָה כְּנָעַן׃ ו וַיַּעֲבֹר אַבְרָם בָּאָרֶץ עַד מְקוֹם
שְׁכֶם עַד אֵלוֹן מוֹרֶה וְהַכְּנַעֲנִי אָז בָּאָרֶץ׃ ז וַיֵּרָא יְהֹוָה
אֶל־אַבְרָם וַיֹּאמֶר לְזַרְעֲךָ אֶתֵּן אֶת־הָאָרֶץ הַזֹּאת וַיִּבֶן שָׁם
מִזְבֵּחַ לַיהֹוָה הַנִּרְאֶה אֵלָיו׃ ח וַיַּעְתֵּק מִשָּׁם הָהָרָה מִקֶּדֶם
לְבֵית־אֵל וַיֵּט אָהֳלֹה בֵּית־אֵל מִיָּם וְהָעַי מִקֶּדֶם וַיִּבֶן־שָׁם
מִזְבֵּחַ לַיהֹוָה וַיִּקְרָא בְּשֵׁם יְהֹוָה׃ ט וַיִּסַּע אַבְרָם הָלוֹךְ וְנָסוֹעַ
הַנֶּגְבָּה׃ פ [ישראל] י וַיְהִי רָעָב בָּאָרֶץ וַיֵּרֶד אַבְרָם מִצְרַיְמָה
לָגוּר שָׁם כִּי־כָבֵד הָרָעָב בָּאָרֶץ׃ יא וַיְהִי כַּאֲשֶׁר הִקְרִיב לָבוֹא
מִצְרָיְמָה וַיֹּאמֶר אֶל־שָׂרַי אִשְׁתּוֹ הִנֵּה־נָא יָדַעְתִּי כִּי אִשָּׁה
יְפַת־מַרְאֶה אָתְּ׃ יב וְהָיָה כִּי־יִרְאוּ אֹתָךְ הַמִּצְרִים וְאָמְרוּ
אִשְׁתּוֹ זֹאת וְהָרְגוּ אֹתִי וְאֹתָךְ יְחַיּוּ׃ יג אִמְרִי־נָא אֲחֹתִי אָתְּ
לְמַעַן יִיטַב־לִי בַעֲבוּרֵךְ וְחָיְתָה נַפְשִׁי בִּגְלָלֵךְ׃

פרשת וירא

פרק יח א וַיֵּרָא אֵלָיו יְהֹוָה בְּאֵלֹנֵי מַמְרֵא וְהוּא יֹשֵׁב פֶּתַח־
הָאֹהֶל כְּחֹם הַיּוֹם׃ ב וַיִּשָּׂא עֵינָיו וַיַּרְא וְהִנֵּה שְׁלֹשָׁה אֲנָשִׁים
נִצָּבִים עָלָיו וַיַּרְא וַיָּרָץ לִקְרָאתָם מִפֶּתַח הָאֹהֶל וַיִּשְׁתַּחוּ
אָרְצָה׃ ג וַיֹּאמַר אֲדֹנָי אִם־נָא מָצָאתִי חֵן בְּעֵינֶיךָ אַל־נָא
תַעֲבֹר מֵעַל עַבְדֶּךָ׃ ד יֻקַּח־נָא מְעַט־מַיִם וְרַחֲצוּ רַגְלֵיכֶם
וְהִשָּׁעֲנוּ תַּחַת הָעֵץ׃ ה וְאֶקְחָה פַת־לֶחֶם וְסַעֲדוּ לִבְּכֶם אַחַר

תַּֽעֲבֹ֔רוּ כִּֽי־עַל־כֵּ֥ן עֲבַרְתֶּ֖ם עַֽל־עַבְדְּכֶ֑ם וַיֹּ֣אמְר֔וּ כֵּ֥ן תַּעֲשֶׂ֖ה
כַּאֲשֶׁ֥ר דִּבַּֽרְתָּ׃ [לוי] ו וַיְמַהֵ֧ר אַבְרָהָ֛ם הָאֹ֖הֱלָה אֶל־שָׂרָ֑ה
וַיֹּ֗אמֶר מַהֲרִ֞י שְׁלֹ֤שׁ סְאִים֙ קֶ֣מַח סֹ֔לֶת ל֖וּשִׁי וַעֲשִׂ֥י עֻגֽוֹת׃
ז וְאֶל־הַבָּקָ֖ר רָ֣ץ אַבְרָהָ֑ם וַיִּקַּ֨ח בֶּן־בָּקָ֜ר רַ֤ךְ וָטוֹב֙ וַיִּתֵּ֣ן אֶל־
הַנַּ֔עַר וַיְמַהֵ֖ר לַעֲשׂ֥וֹת אֹתֽוֹ׃ ח וַיִּקַּ֨ח חֶמְאָ֜ה וְחָלָ֗ב וּבֶן־הַבָּקָר֙
אֲשֶׁ֣ר עָשָׂ֔ה וַיִּתֵּ֖ן לִפְנֵיהֶ֑ם וְהֽוּא־עֹמֵ֧ד עֲלֵיהֶ֛ם תַּ֥חַת הָעֵ֖ץ
וַיֹּאכֵֽלוּ׃ [ישראל] ט וַיֹּאמְר֣וּ אֵלָ֔יו אַיֵּ֖ה שָׂרָ֣ה אִשְׁתֶּ֑ךָ וַיֹּ֖אמֶר
הִנֵּ֥ה בָאֹֽהֶל׃ י וַיֹּ֗אמֶר שׁ֣וֹב אָשׁ֤וּב אֵלֶ֙יךָ֙ כָּעֵ֣ת חַיָּ֔ה וְהִנֵּה־בֵ֖ן
לְשָׂרָ֣ה אִשְׁתֶּ֑ךָ וְשָׂרָ֥ה שֹׁמַ֛עַת פֶּ֥תַח הָאֹ֖הֶל וְה֥וּא אַחֲרָֽיו׃
יא וְאַבְרָהָ֤ם וְשָׂרָה֙ זְקֵנִ֔ים בָּאִ֖ים בַּיָּמִ֑ים חָדַל֙ לִהְי֣וֹת לְשָׂרָ֔ה
אֹ֖רַח כַּנָּשִֽׁים׃ יב וַתִּצְחַ֥ק שָׂרָ֖ה בְּקִרְבָּ֣הּ לֵאמֹ֑ר אַחֲרֵ֤י בְלֹתִי֙
הָֽיְתָה־לִּ֣י עֶדְנָ֔ה וַֽאדֹנִ֖י זָקֵֽן׃ יג וַיֹּ֥אמֶר יְהוָ֖ה אֶל־אַבְרָהָ֑ם
לָ֣מָּה זֶּה֩ צָחֲקָ֨ה שָׂרָ֜ה לֵאמֹ֗ר הַאַ֥ף אֻמְנָ֛ם אֵלֵ֖ד וַאֲנִ֥י זָקַֽנְתִּי׃
יד הֲיִפָּלֵ֥א מֵיְהוָ֖ה דָּבָ֑ר לַמּוֹעֵ֞ד אָשׁ֥וּב אֵלֶ֛יךָ כָּעֵ֥ת חַיָּ֖ה וּלְשָׂרָ֥ה
בֵֽן׃

פרשת חיי שרה

פרק כג א וַיִּֽהְיוּ֙ חַיֵּ֣י שָׂרָ֔ה מֵאָ֥ה שָׁנָ֛ה וְעֶשְׂרִ֥ים שָׁנָ֖ה וְשֶׁ֣בַע
שָׁנִ֑ים שְׁנֵ֖י חַיֵּ֥י שָׂרָֽה׃ ב וַתָּ֣מָת שָׂרָ֗ה בְּקִרְיַ֥ת אַרְבַּ֛ע הִ֥וא
חֶבְר֖וֹן בְּאֶ֣רֶץ כְּנָ֑עַן וַיָּבֹא֙ אַבְרָהָ֔ם לִסְפֹּ֥ד לְשָׂרָ֖ה וְלִבְכֹּתָֽהּ׃
ג וַיָּ֙קָם֙ אַבְרָהָ֔ם מֵעַ֖ל פְּנֵ֣י מֵת֑וֹ וַיְדַבֵּ֥ר אֶל־בְּנֵי־חֵ֖ת לֵאמֹֽר׃
ד גֵּר־וְתוֹשָׁ֥ב אָנֹכִ֖י עִמָּכֶ֑ם תְּנ֨וּ לִ֤י אֲחֻזַּת־קֶ֙בֶר֙ עִמָּכֶ֔ם
וְאֶקְבְּרָ֥ה מֵתִ֖י מִלְּפָנָֽי׃ ה וַיַּעֲנ֧וּ בְנֵי־חֵ֛ת אֶת־אַבְרָהָ֖ם לֵאמֹ֥ר
לֽוֹ׃ ו שְׁמָעֵ֣נוּ ׀ אֲדֹנִ֗י נְשִׂ֨יא אֱלֹהִ֤ים אַתָּה֙ בְּתוֹכֵ֔נוּ בְּמִבְחַ֣ר
קְבָרֵ֔ינוּ קְבֹ֖ר אֶת־מֵתֶ֑ךָ אִ֣ישׁ מִמֶּ֗נּוּ אֶת־קִבְר֛וֹ לֹֽא־יִכְלֶ֥ה
מִמְּךָ֖ מִקְּבֹ֥ר מֵתֶֽךָ׃ ז וַיָּ֧קָם אַבְרָהָ֛ם וַיִּשְׁתַּ֥חוּ לְעַם־הָאָ֖רֶץ

לִבְנֵי־חֵת׃ [לוי] ח וַיְדַבֵּר אִתָּם לֵאמֹר אִם־יֵשׁ אֶת־נַפְשְׁכֶם
לִקְבֹּר אֶת־מֵתִי מִלְּפָנַי שְׁמָעוּנִי וּפִגְעוּ־לִי בְּעֶפְרוֹן בֶּן־צֹחַר׃
ט וְיִתֶּן־לִי אֶת־מְעָרַת הַמַּכְפֵּלָה אֲשֶׁר־לוֹ אֲשֶׁר בִּקְצֵה שָׂדֵהוּ
בְּכֶסֶף מָלֵא יִתְּנֶנָּה לִּי בְּתוֹכְכֶם לַאֲחֻזַּת־קָבֶר׃ י וְעֶפְרוֹן יֹשֵׁב
בְּתוֹךְ בְּנֵי־חֵת וַיַּעַן עֶפְרוֹן הַחִתִּי אֶת־אַבְרָהָם בְּאָזְנֵי בְנֵי־חֵת
לְכֹל בָּאֵי שַׁעַר־עִירוֹ לֵאמֹר׃ יא לֹא־אֲדֹנִי שְׁמָעֵנִי הַשָּׂדֶה
נָתַתִּי לָךְ וְהַמְּעָרָה אֲשֶׁר־בּוֹ לְךָ נְתַתִּיהָ לְעֵינֵי בְנֵי־עַמִּי
נְתַתִּיהָ לָּךְ קְבֹר מֵתֶךָ׃ יב וַיִּשְׁתַּחוּ אַבְרָהָם לִפְנֵי עַם־הָאָרֶץ׃
[ישראל] יג וַיְדַבֵּר אֶל־עֶפְרוֹן בְּאָזְנֵי עַם־הָאָרֶץ לֵאמֹר אַךְ אִם־
אַתָּה לוּ שְׁמָעֵנִי נָתַתִּי כֶּסֶף הַשָּׂדֶה קַח מִמֶּנִּי וְאֶקְבְּרָה אֶת־
מֵתִי שָׁמָּה׃ יד וַיַּעַן עֶפְרוֹן אֶת־אַבְרָהָם לֵאמֹר לוֹ׃ טו אֲדֹנִי
שְׁמָעֵנִי אֶרֶץ אַרְבַּע מֵאֹת שֶׁקֶל־כֶּסֶף בֵּינִי וּבֵינְךָ מַה־הִוא
וְאֶת־מֵתְךָ קְבֹר׃ טז וַיִּשְׁמַע אַבְרָהָם אֶל־עֶפְרוֹן וַיִּשְׁקֹל
אַבְרָהָם לְעֶפְרֹן אֶת־הַכֶּסֶף אֲשֶׁר דִּבֶּר בְּאָזְנֵי בְנֵי־חֵת אַרְבַּע
מֵאוֹת שֶׁקֶל כֶּסֶף עֹבֵר לַסֹּחֵר׃

פרשת תולדות

פרק כה יט וְאֵלֶּה תּוֹלְדֹת יִצְחָק בֶּן־אַבְרָהָם אַבְרָהָם הוֹלִיד
אֶת־יִצְחָק׃ כ וַיְהִי יִצְחָק בֶּן־אַרְבָּעִים שָׁנָה בְּקַחְתּוֹ אֶת־
רִבְקָה בַּת־בְּתוּאֵל הָאֲרַמִּי מִפַּדַּן אֲרָם אֲחוֹת לָבָן הָאֲרַמִּי
לוֹ לְאִשָּׁה׃ כא וַיֶּעְתַּר יִצְחָק לַיהוָה לְנֹכַח אִשְׁתּוֹ כִּי עֲקָרָה
הִוא וַיֵּעָתֶר לוֹ יְהוָה וַתַּהַר רִבְקָה אִשְׁתּוֹ׃ כב וַיִּתְרֹצֲצוּ
הַבָּנִים בְּקִרְבָּהּ וַתֹּאמֶר אִם־כֵּן לָמָּה זֶּה אָנֹכִי וַתֵּלֶךְ לִדְרֹשׁ
אֶת־יְהוָה׃ [לוי] כג וַיֹּאמֶר יְהוָה לָהּ שְׁנֵי גיים▽ בְּבִטְנֵךְ וּשְׁנֵי
לְאֻמִּים מִמֵּעַיִךְ יִפָּרֵדוּ וּלְאֹם מִלְאֹם יֶאֱמָץ וְרַב יַעֲבֹד
צָעִיר׃ כד וַיִּמְלְאוּ יָמֶיהָ לָלֶדֶת וְהִנֵּה תוֹמִם בְּבִטְנָהּ׃ כה וַיֵּצֵא

▽ גּוֹיִם

הָרִאשׁוֹן אַדְמוֹנִי כֻּלּוֹ כְּאַדֶּרֶת שֵׂעָר וַיִּקְרְאוּ שְׁמוֹ עֵשָׂו׃
כו וְאַחֲרֵי־כֵן יָצָא אָחִיו וְיָדוֹ אֹחֶזֶת בַּעֲקֵב עֵשָׂו וַיִּקְרָא שְׁמוֹ
יַעֲקֹב וְיִצְחָק בֶּן־שִׁשִּׁים שָׁנָה בְּלֶדֶת אֹתָם׃ [ישראל] כז וַיִּגְדְּלוּ
הַנְּעָרִים וַיְהִי עֵשָׂו אִישׁ יֹדֵעַ צַיִד אִישׁ שָׂדֶה וְיַעֲקֹב אִישׁ תָּם
יֹשֵׁב אֹהָלִים׃ כח וַיֶּאֱהַב יִצְחָק אֶת־עֵשָׂו כִּי־צַיִד בְּפִיו וְרִבְקָה
אֹהֶבֶת אֶת־יַעֲקֹב׃ כט וַיָּזֶד יַעֲקֹב נָזִיד וַיָּבֹא עֵשָׂו מִן־הַשָּׂדֶה
וְהוּא עָיֵף׃ ל וַיֹּאמֶר עֵשָׂו אֶל־יַעֲקֹב הַלְעִיטֵנִי נָא מִן־הָאָדֹם
הָאָדֹם הַזֶּה כִּי עָיֵף אָנֹכִי עַל־כֵּן קָרָא־שְׁמוֹ אֱדוֹם׃ לא וַיֹּאמֶר
יַעֲקֹב מִכְרָה כַיּוֹם אֶת־בְּכֹרָתְךָ לִי׃ לב וַיֹּאמֶר עֵשָׂו הִנֵּה אָנֹכִי
הוֹלֵךְ לָמוּת וְלָמָּה־זֶּה לִי בְּכֹרָה׃ לג וַיֹּאמֶר יַעֲקֹב הִשָּׁבְעָה
לִּי כַּיּוֹם וַיִּשָּׁבַע לוֹ וַיִּמְכֹּר אֶת־בְּכֹרָתוֹ לְיַעֲקֹב׃ לד וְיַעֲקֹב נָתַן
לְעֵשָׂו לֶחֶם וּנְזִיד עֲדָשִׁים וַיֹּאכַל וַיֵּשְׁתְּ וַיָּקָם וַיֵּלַךְ וַיִּבֶז עֵשָׂו
אֶת־הַבְּכֹרָה׃ פ פרק כו א וַיְהִי רָעָב בָּאָרֶץ מִלְּבַד הָרָעָב
הָרִאשׁוֹן אֲשֶׁר הָיָה בִּימֵי אַבְרָהָם וַיֵּלֶךְ יִצְחָק אֶל־אֲבִימֶלֶךְ
מֶלֶךְ־פְּלִשְׁתִּים גְּרָרָה׃ ב וַיֵּרָא אֵלָיו יְהוָה וַיֹּאמֶר אַל־תֵּרֵד
מִצְרָיְמָה שְׁכֹן בָּאָרֶץ אֲשֶׁר אֹמַר אֵלֶיךָ׃ ג גּוּר בָּאָרֶץ הַזֹּאת
וְאֶהְיֶה עִמְּךָ וַאֲבָרְכֶךָּ כִּי־לְךָ וּלְזַרְעֲךָ אֶתֵּן אֶת־כָּל־הָאֲרָצֹת
הָאֵל וַהֲקִמֹתִי אֶת־הַשְּׁבֻעָה אֲשֶׁר נִשְׁבַּעְתִּי לְאַבְרָהָם אָבִיךָ׃
ד וְהִרְבֵּיתִי אֶת־זַרְעֲךָ כְּכוֹכְבֵי הַשָּׁמַיִם וְנָתַתִּי לְזַרְעֲךָ אֵת
כָּל־הָאֲרָצֹת הָאֵל וְהִתְבָּרְכוּ בְזַרְעֲךָ כֹּל גּוֹיֵי הָאָרֶץ׃ ה עֵקֶב
אֲשֶׁר־שָׁמַע אַבְרָהָם בְּקֹלִי וַיִּשְׁמֹר מִשְׁמַרְתִּי מִצְוֹתַי חֻקּוֹתַי
וְתוֹרֹתָי׃

פרשת ויצא

פרק כח י וַיֵּצֵא יַעֲקֹב מִבְּאֵר שָׁבַע וַיֵּלֶךְ חָרָנָה׃ יא וַיִּפְגַּע
בַּמָּקוֹם וַיָּלֶן שָׁם כִּי־בָא הַשֶּׁמֶשׁ וַיִּקַּח מֵאַבְנֵי הַמָּקוֹם וַיָּשֶׂם
מְרַאֲשֹׁתָיו וַיִּשְׁכַּב בַּמָּקוֹם הַהוּא׃ יב וַיַּחֲלֹם וְהִנֵּה סֻלָּם

מֻצָּ֣ב אַ֔רְצָה וְרֹאשׁ֖וֹ מַגִּ֣יעַ הַשָּׁמָ֑יְמָה וְהִנֵּה֙ מַלְאֲכֵ֣י אֱלֹהִ֔ים
עֹלִ֥ים וְיֹרְדִ֖ים בּֽוֹ׃ [לוי] יג וְהִנֵּ֨ה יְהֹוָ֜ה נִצָּ֣ב עָלָיו֮ וַיֹּאמַר֒ אֲנִ֣י
יְהֹוָ֗ה אֱלֹהֵי֙ אַבְרָהָ֣ם אָבִ֔יךָ וֵאלֹהֵ֖י יִצְחָ֑ק הָאָ֗רֶץ אֲשֶׁ֤ר אַתָּה֙
שֹׁכֵ֣ב עָלֶ֔יהָ לְךָ֥ אֶתְּנֶ֖נָּה וּלְזַרְעֶֽךָ׃ יד וְהָיָ֤ה זַרְעֲךָ֙ כַּעֲפַ֣ר הָאָ֔רֶץ
וּפָרַצְתָּ֛ יָ֥מָּה וָקֵ֖דְמָה וְצָפֹ֣נָה וָנֶ֑גְבָּה וְנִבְרְכ֥וּ בְךָ֛ כָּל־מִשְׁפְּחֹ֥ת
הָאֲדָמָ֖ה וּבְזַרְעֶֽךָ׃ טו וְהִנֵּ֨ה אָנֹכִ֜י עִמָּ֗ךְ וּשְׁמַרְתִּ֙יךָ֙ בְּכֹ֣ל אֲשֶׁר־
תֵּלֵ֔ךְ וַהֲשִׁ֣בֹתִ֔יךָ אֶל־הָאֲדָמָ֖ה הַזֹּ֑את כִּ֚י לֹ֣א אֶֽעֱזָבְךָ֔ עַ֚ד אֲשֶׁ֣ר
אִם־עָשִׂ֔יתִי אֵ֥ת אֲשֶׁר־דִּבַּ֖רְתִּי לָֽךְ׃ טז וַיִּיקַ֣ץ יַעֲקֹב֮ מִשְּׁנָתוֹ֒
וַיֹּ֕אמֶר אָכֵן֙ יֵ֣שׁ יְהֹוָ֔ה בַּמָּק֖וֹם הַזֶּ֑ה וְאָנֹכִ֖י לֹ֥א יָדָֽעְתִּי׃ יז וַיִּירָא֙
וַיֹּאמַ֔ר מַה־נּוֹרָ֖א הַמָּק֣וֹם הַזֶּ֑ה אֵ֣ין זֶ֗ה כִּ֚י אִם־בֵּ֣ית אֱלֹהִ֔ים
וְזֶ֖ה שַׁ֥עַר הַשָּׁמָֽיִם׃ [ישראל] יח וַיַּשְׁכֵּ֨ם יַעֲקֹ֜ב בַּבֹּ֗קֶר וַיִּקַּ֤ח
אֶת־הָאֶ֙בֶן֙ אֲשֶׁר־שָׂ֣ם מְרַאֲשֹׁתָ֔יו וַיָּ֥שֶׂם אֹתָ֖הּ מַצֵּבָ֑ה וַיִּצֹ֥ק
שֶׁ֖מֶן עַל־רֹאשָֽׁהּ׃ יט וַיִּקְרָ֛א אֶת־שֵֽׁם־הַמָּק֥וֹם הַה֖וּא בֵּֽית־אֵ֑ל
וְאוּלָ֛ם ל֥וּז שֵׁם־הָעִ֖יר לָרִאשֹׁנָֽה׃ כ וַיִּדַּ֥ר יַעֲקֹ֖ב נֶ֣דֶר לֵאמֹ֑ר
אִם־יִהְיֶ֨ה אֱלֹהִ֜ים עִמָּדִ֗י וּשְׁמָרַ֙נִי֙ בַּדֶּ֤רֶךְ הַזֶּה֙ אֲשֶׁ֣ר אָנֹכִ֣י
הוֹלֵ֔ךְ וְנָֽתַן־לִ֥י לֶ֛חֶם לֶאֱכֹ֖ל וּבֶ֥גֶד לִלְבֹּֽשׁ׃ כא וְשַׁבְתִּ֥י בְשָׁל֖וֹם
אֶל־בֵּ֣ית אָבִ֑י וְהָיָ֧ה יְהֹוָ֛ה לִ֖י לֵאלֹהִֽים׃ כב וְהָאֶ֣בֶן הַזֹּ֗את
אֲשֶׁר־שַׂ֙מְתִּי֙ מַצֵּבָ֔ה יִהְיֶ֖ה בֵּ֣ית אֱלֹהִ֑ים וְכֹל֙ אֲשֶׁ֣ר תִּתֶּן־לִ֔י
עַשֵּׂ֖ר אֲעַשְּׂרֶ֥נּוּ לָֽךְ׃

פרשת וישלח

פרק לב ד וַיִּשְׁלַ֨ח יַעֲקֹ֤ב מַלְאָכִים֙ לְפָנָ֔יו אֶל־עֵשָׂ֖ו אָחִ֑יו אַ֥רְצָה
שֵׂעִ֖יר שְׂדֵ֥ה אֱדֽוֹם׃ ה וַיְצַ֤ו אֹתָם֙ לֵאמֹ֔ר כֹּ֣ה תֹאמְר֔וּן לַאדֹנִ֖י
לְעֵשָׂ֑ו כֹּ֤ה אָמַר֙ עַבְדְּךָ֣ יַעֲקֹ֔ב עִם־לָבָ֣ן גַּ֔רְתִּי וָאֵחַ֖ר עַד־עָֽתָּה׃
ו וַיְהִי־לִי֙ שׁ֣וֹר וַחֲמ֔וֹר צֹ֖אן וְעֶ֣בֶד וְשִׁפְחָ֑ה וָֽאֶשְׁלְחָה֙ לְהַגִּ֣יד
לַֽאדֹנִ֔י לִמְצֹא־חֵ֖ן בְּעֵינֶֽיךָ׃ [לוי] ז וַיָּשֻׁ֙בוּ֙ הַמַּלְאָכִ֔ים אֶל־

יַעֲקֹב לֵאמֹר בָּאנוּ אֶל־אָחִיךָ אֶל־עֵשָׂו וְגַם הֹלֵךְ לִקְרָאתְךָ
וְאַרְבַּע־מֵאוֹת אִישׁ עִמּוֹ: ח וַיִּירָא יַעֲקֹב מְאֹד וַיֵּצֶר לוֹ וַיַּחַץ
אֶת־הָעָם אֲשֶׁר־אִתּוֹ וְאֶת־הַצֹּאן וְאֶת־הַבָּקָר וְהַגְּמַלִּים
לִשְׁנֵי מַחֲנוֹת: ט וַיֹּאמֶר אִם־יָבוֹא עֵשָׂו אֶל־הַמַּחֲנֶה הָאַחַת
וְהִכָּהוּ וְהָיָה הַמַּחֲנֶה הַנִּשְׁאָר לִפְלֵיטָה: [ישראל] י וַיֹּאמֶר
יַעֲקֹב אֱלֹהֵי אָבִי אַבְרָהָם וֵאלֹהֵי אָבִי יִצְחָק יְהוָה הָאֹמֵר
אֵלַי שׁוּב לְאַרְצְךָ וּלְמוֹלַדְתְּךָ וְאֵיטִיבָה עִמָּךְ: יא קָטֹנְתִּי
מִכֹּל הַחֲסָדִים וּמִכָּל־הָאֱמֶת אֲשֶׁר עָשִׂיתָ אֶת־עַבְדֶּךָ כִּי
בְמַקְלִי עָבַרְתִּי אֶת־הַיַּרְדֵּן הַזֶּה וְעַתָּה הָיִיתִי לִשְׁנֵי מַחֲנוֹת:
יב הַצִּילֵנִי נָא מִיַּד אָחִי מִיַּד עֵשָׂו כִּי־יָרֵא אָנֹכִי אֹתוֹ פֶּן־יָבוֹא
וְהִכַּנִי אֵם עַל־בָּנִים: יג וְאַתָּה אָמַרְתָּ הֵיטֵב אֵיטִיב עִמָּךְ
וְשַׂמְתִּי אֶת־זַרְעֲךָ כְּחוֹל הַיָּם אֲשֶׁר לֹא־יִסָּפֵר מֵרֹב:

פרשת וישב

פרק לז א וַיֵּשֶׁב יַעֲקֹב בְּאֶרֶץ מְגוּרֵי אָבִיו בְּאֶרֶץ כְּנָעַן: ב אֵלֶּה |
תֹּלְדוֹת יַעֲקֹב יוֹסֵף בֶּן־שְׁבַע־עֶשְׂרֵה שָׁנָה הָיָה רֹעֶה אֶת־
אֶחָיו בַּצֹּאן וְהוּא נַעַר אֶת־בְּנֵי בִלְהָה וְאֶת־בְּנֵי זִלְפָּה נְשֵׁי
אָבִיו וַיָּבֵא יוֹסֵף אֶת־דִּבָּתָם רָעָה אֶל־אֲבִיהֶם: ג וְיִשְׂרָאֵל
אָהַב אֶת־יוֹסֵף מִכָּל־בָּנָיו כִּי־בֶן־זְקֻנִים הוּא לוֹ וְעָשָׂה לוֹ
כְּתֹנֶת פַּסִּים: [לוי] ד וַיִּרְאוּ אֶחָיו כִּי־אֹתוֹ אָהַב אֲבִיהֶם
מִכָּל־אֶחָיו וַיִּשְׂנְאוּ אֹתוֹ וְלֹא יָכְלוּ דַּבְּרוֹ לְשָׁלֹם: ה וַיַּחֲלֹם
יוֹסֵף חֲלוֹם וַיַּגֵּד לְאֶחָיו וַיּוֹסִפוּ עוֹד שְׂנֹא אֹתוֹ: ו וַיֹּאמֶר
אֲלֵיהֶם שִׁמְעוּ־נָא הַחֲלוֹם הַזֶּה אֲשֶׁר חָלָמְתִּי: ז וְהִנֵּה
אֲנַחְנוּ מְאַלְּמִים אֲלֻמִּים בְּתוֹךְ הַשָּׂדֶה וְהִנֵּה קָמָה אֲלֻמָּתִי
וְגַם־נִצָּבָה וְהִנֵּה תְסֻבֶּינָה אֲלֻמֹּתֵיכֶם וַתִּשְׁתַּחֲוֶיןָ לַאֲלֻמָּתִי:
[ישראל] ח וַיֹּאמְרוּ לוֹ אֶחָיו הֲמָלֹךְ תִּמְלֹךְ עָלֵינוּ אִם־מָשׁוֹל

תִּמְשֹׁל בָּנוּ וַיּוֹסִפוּ עוֹד שְׂנֹא אֹתוֹ עַל־חֲלֹמֹתָיו וְעַל־דְּבָרָיו׃
ט וַיַּחֲלֹם עוֹד חֲלוֹם אַחֵר וַיְסַפֵּר אֹתוֹ לְאֶחָיו וַיֹּאמֶר הִנֵּה
חָלַמְתִּי חֲלוֹם עוֹד וְהִנֵּה הַשֶּׁמֶשׁ וְהַיָּרֵחַ וְאַחַד עָשָׂר כּוֹכָבִים
מִשְׁתַּחֲוִים לִי׃ י וַיְסַפֵּר אֶל־אָבִיו וְאֶל־אֶחָיו וַיִּגְעַר־בּוֹ אָבִיו
וַיֹּאמֶר לוֹ מָה הַחֲלוֹם הַזֶּה אֲשֶׁר חָלָמְתָּ הֲבוֹא נָבוֹא אֲנִי
וְאִמְּךָ וְאַחֶיךָ לְהִשְׁתַּחֲוֹת לְךָ אָרְצָה׃ יא וַיְקַנְאוּ־בוֹ אֶחָיו
וְאָבִיו שָׁמַר אֶת־הַדָּבָר׃

פרשת מקץ

פרק מא א וַיְהִי מִקֵּץ שְׁנָתַיִם יָמִים וּפַרְעֹה חֹלֵם וְהִנֵּה
עֹמֵד עַל־הַיְאֹר׃ ב וְהִנֵּה מִן־הַיְאֹר עֹלֹת שֶׁבַע פָּרוֹת יְפוֹת
מַרְאֶה וּבְרִיאֹת בָּשָׂר וַתִּרְעֶינָה בָּאָחוּ׃ ג וְהִנֵּה שֶׁבַע פָּרוֹת
אֲחֵרוֹת עֹלוֹת אַחֲרֵיהֶן מִן־הַיְאֹר רָעוֹת מַרְאֶה וְדַקּוֹת
בָּשָׂר וַתַּעֲמֹדְנָה אֵצֶל הַפָּרוֹת עַל־שְׂפַת הַיְאֹר׃ ד וַתֹּאכַלְנָה
הַפָּרוֹת רָעוֹת הַמַּרְאֶה וְדַקֹּת הַבָּשָׂר אֵת שֶׁבַע הַפָּרוֹת
יְפֹת הַמַּרְאֶה וְהַבְּרִיאֹת וַיִּיקַץ פַּרְעֹה׃ [לוי] ה וַיִּישָׁן וַיַּחֲלֹם
שֵׁנִית וְהִנֵּה | שֶׁבַע שִׁבֳּלִים עֹלוֹת בְּקָנֶה אֶחָד בְּרִיאוֹת
וְטֹבוֹת׃ ו וְהִנֵּה שֶׁבַע שִׁבֳּלִים דַּקּוֹת וּשְׁדוּפֹת קָדִים צֹמְחוֹת
אַחֲרֵיהֶן׃ ז וַתִּבְלַעְנָה הַשִּׁבֳּלִים הַדַּקּוֹת אֵת שֶׁבַע הַשִּׁבֳּלִים
הַבְּרִיאוֹת וְהַמְּלֵאוֹת וַיִּיקַץ פַּרְעֹה וְהִנֵּה חֲלוֹם׃ [ישראל] ח וַיְהִי
בַבֹּקֶר וַתִּפָּעֶם רוּחוֹ וַיִּשְׁלַח וַיִּקְרָא אֶת־כָּל־חַרְטֻמֵּי מִצְרַיִם
וְאֶת־כָּל־חֲכָמֶיהָ וַיְסַפֵּר פַּרְעֹה לָהֶם אֶת־חֲלֹמוֹ וְאֵין־פּוֹתֵר
אוֹתָם לְפַרְעֹה׃ ט וַיְדַבֵּר שַׂר הַמַּשְׁקִים אֶת־פַּרְעֹה לֵאמֹר
אֶת־חֲטָאַי אֲנִי מַזְכִּיר הַיּוֹם׃ י פַּרְעֹה קָצַף עַל־עֲבָדָיו וַיִּתֵּן
אֹתִי בְּמִשְׁמַר בֵּית שַׂר הַטַּבָּחִים אֹתִי וְאֵת שַׂר הָאֹפִים׃
יא וַנַּחַלְמָה חֲלוֹם בְּלַיְלָה אֶחָד אֲנִי וָהוּא אִישׁ כְּפִתְרוֹן
חֲלֹמוֹ חָלָמְנוּ׃ יב וְשָׁם אִתָּנוּ נַעַר עִבְרִי עֶבֶד לְשַׂר הַטַּבָּחִים

וַנְּסַפֶּר־לוֹ֙ וַיִּפְתָּר־לָ֖נוּ אֶת־חֲלֹמֹתֵ֑ינוּ אִ֥ישׁ כַּחֲלֹמ֖וֹ פָּתָֽר׃
יג וַיְהִ֛י כַּאֲשֶׁ֥ר פָּֽתַר־לָ֖נוּ כֵּ֣ן הָיָ֑ה אֹתִ֛י הֵשִׁ֥יב עַל־כַּנִּ֖י וְאֹת֥וֹ
תָלָֽה׃ יד וַיִּשְׁלַ֤ח פַּרְעֹה֙ וַיִּקְרָ֣א אֶת־יוֹסֵ֔ף וַיְרִיצֻ֖הוּ מִן־הַבּ֑וֹר
וַיְגַלַּח֙ וַיְחַלֵּ֣ף שִׂמְלֹתָ֔יו וַיָּבֹ֖א אֶל־פַּרְעֹֽה׃

פרשת ויגש

פרק מד יח וַיִּגַּ֨שׁ אֵלָ֜יו יְהוּדָ֗ה וַיֹּאמֶר֮ בִּ֣י אֲדֹנִי֒ יְדַבֶּר־נָ֨א עַבְדְּךָ֤
דָבָר֙ בְּאָזְנֵ֣י אֲדֹנִ֔י וְאַל־יִ֥חַר אַפְּךָ֖ בְּעַבְדֶּ֑ךָ כִּ֥י כָמ֖וֹךָ כְּפַרְעֹֽה׃
יט אֲדֹנִ֣י שָׁאַ֔ל אֶת־עֲבָדָ֖יו לֵאמֹ֑ר הֲיֵשׁ־לָכֶ֥ם אָ֖ב אוֹ־אָֽח׃
כ וַנֹּ֙אמֶר֙ אֶל־אֲדֹנִ֔י יֶשׁ־לָ֙נוּ֙ אָ֣ב זָקֵ֔ן וְיֶ֥לֶד זְקֻנִ֖ים קָטָ֑ן וְאָחִ֣יו
מֵ֗ת וַיִּוָּתֵ֨ר ה֧וּא לְבַדּ֛וֹ לְאִמּ֖וֹ וְאָבִ֥יו אֲהֵבֽוֹ׃ [לוי] כא וַתֹּ֙אמֶר֙
אֶל־עֲבָדֶ֔יךָ הוֹרִדֻ֖הוּ אֵלָ֑י וְאָשִׂ֥ימָה עֵינִ֖י עָלָֽיו׃ כב וַנֹּ֙אמֶר֙
אֶל־אֲדֹנִ֔י לֹא־יוּכַ֥ל הַנַּ֖עַר לַעֲזֹ֣ב אֶת־אָבִ֑יו וְעָזַ֥ב אֶת־אָבִ֖יו
וָמֵֽת׃ כג וַתֹּ֙אמֶר֙ אֶל־עֲבָדֶ֔יךָ אִם־לֹ֥א יֵרֵ֛ד אֲחִיכֶ֥ם הַקָּטֹ֖ן
אִתְּכֶ֑ם לֹ֥א תֹסִפ֖וּן לִרְא֥וֹת פָּנָֽי׃ כד וַיְהִי֙ כִּ֣י עָלִ֔ינוּ אֶל־עַבְדְּךָ֖
אָבִ֑י וַנַּ֨גֶּד־ל֔וֹ אֵ֖ת דִּבְרֵ֥י אֲדֹנִֽי׃ [ישראל] כה וַיֹּ֖אמֶר אָבִ֑ינוּ שֻׁ֖בוּ
שִׁבְרוּ־לָ֥נוּ מְעַט־אֹֽכֶל׃ כו וַנֹּ֕אמֶר לֹ֥א נוּכַ֖ל לָרֶ֑דֶת אִם־יֵשׁ֩
אָחִ֨ינוּ הַקָּטֹ֤ן אִתָּ֙נוּ֙ וְיָרַ֔דְנוּ כִּי־לֹ֣א נוּכַ֗ל לִרְאוֹת֙ פְּנֵ֣י הָאִ֔ישׁ
וְאָחִ֥ינוּ הַקָּטֹ֖ן אֵינֶ֥נּוּ אִתָּֽנוּ׃ כז וַיֹּ֛אמֶר עַבְדְּךָ֥ אָבִ֖י אֵלֵ֑ינוּ אַתֶּ֣ם
יְדַעְתֶּ֔ם כִּ֥י שְׁנַ֖יִם יָֽלְדָה־לִּ֥י אִשְׁתִּֽי׃ כח וַיֵּצֵ֤א הָֽאֶחָד֙ מֵֽאִתִּ֔י
וָאֹמַ֕ר אַ֖ךְ טָרֹ֣ף טֹרָ֑ף וְלֹ֥א רְאִיתִ֖יו עַד־הֵֽנָּה׃ כט וּלְקַחְתֶּ֧ם
גַּם־אֶת־זֶ֛ה מֵעִ֥ם פָּנַ֖י וְקָרָ֣הוּ אָס֑וֹן וְהֽוֹרַדְתֶּ֧ם אֶת־שֵׂיבָתִ֛י
בְּרָעָ֖ה שְׁאֹֽלָה׃ ל וְעַתָּ֗ה כְּבֹאִי֙ אֶל־עַבְדְּךָ֣ אָבִ֔י וְהַנַּ֖עַר אֵינֶ֣נּוּ
אִתָּ֑נוּ וְנַפְשׁ֖וֹ קְשׁוּרָ֥ה בְנַפְשֽׁוֹ׃

פרשת ויחי

פרק מז כח וַיְחִ֤י יַעֲקֹב֙ בְּאֶ֣רֶץ מִצְרַ֔יִם שְׁבַ֥ע עֶשְׂרֵ֖ה שָׁנָ֑ה וַיְהִ֤י
יְמֵֽי־יַעֲקֹב֙ שְׁנֵ֣י חַיָּ֔יו שֶׁ֣בַע שָׁנִ֔ים וְאַרְבָּעִ֖ים וּמְאַ֥ת שָׁנָֽה׃

כט וַיִּקְרְבוּ יְמֵי־יִשְׂרָאֵל לָמוּת וַיִּקְרָא | לִבְנוֹ לְיוֹסֵף וַיֹּאמֶר לוֹ
אִם־נָא מָצָאתִי חֵן בְּעֵינֶיךָ שִׂים־נָא יָדְךָ תַּחַת יְרֵכִי וְעָשִׂיתָ
עִמָּדִי חֶסֶד וֶאֱמֶת אַל־נָא תִקְבְּרֵנִי בְּמִצְרָיִם: ל וְשָׁכַבְתִּי
עִם־אֲבֹתַי וּנְשָׂאתַנִי מִמִּצְרַיִם וּקְבַרְתַּנִי בִּקְבֻרָתָם וַיֹּאמַר
אָנֹכִי אֶעֱשֶׂה כִדְבָרֶךָ: לא וַיֹּאמֶר הִשָּׁבְעָה לִי וַיִּשָּׁבַע לוֹ
וַיִּשְׁתַּחוּ יִשְׂרָאֵל עַל־רֹאשׁ הַמִּטָּה: פ [לוי] **פרק מח** א וַיְהִי
אַחֲרֵי הַדְּבָרִים הָאֵלֶּה וַיֹּאמֶר לְיוֹסֵף הִנֵּה אָבִיךָ חֹלֶה וַיִּקַּח
אֶת־שְׁנֵי בָנָיו עִמּוֹ אֶת־מְנַשֶּׁה וְאֶת־אֶפְרָיִם: ב וַיַּגֵּד לְיַעֲקֹב
וַיֹּאמֶר הִנֵּה בִּנְךָ יוֹסֵף בָּא אֵלֶיךָ וַיִּתְחַזֵּק יִשְׂרָאֵל וַיֵּשֶׁב
עַל־הַמִּטָּה: ג וַיֹּאמֶר יַעֲקֹב אֶל־יוֹסֵף אֵל שַׁדַּי נִרְאָה־אֵלַי
בְּלוּז בְּאֶרֶץ כְּנָעַן וַיְבָרֶךְ אֹתִי: [ישראל] ד וַיֹּאמֶר אֵלַי הִנְנִי
מַפְרְךָ וְהִרְבִּיתִךָ וּנְתַתִּיךָ לִקְהַל עַמִּים וְנָתַתִּי אֶת־הָאָרֶץ
הַזֹּאת לְזַרְעֲךָ אַחֲרֶיךָ אֲחֻזַּת עוֹלָם: ה וְעַתָּה שְׁנֵי־בָנֶיךָ
הַנּוֹלָדִים לְךָ בְּאֶרֶץ מִצְרַיִם עַד־בֹּאִי אֵלֶיךָ מִצְרַיְמָה לִי־הֵם
אֶפְרַיִם וּמְנַשֶּׁה כִּרְאוּבֵן וְשִׁמְעוֹן יִהְיוּ־לִי: ו וּמוֹלַדְתְּךָ אֲשֶׁר־
הוֹלַדְתָּ אַחֲרֵיהֶם לְךָ יִהְיוּ עַל שֵׁם אֲחֵיהֶם יִקָּרְאוּ בְּנַחֲלָתָם:
ז וַאֲנִי | בְּבֹאִי מִפַּדָּן מֵתָה עָלַי רָחֵל בְּאֶרֶץ כְּנַעַן בַּדֶּרֶךְ בְּעוֹד
כִּבְרַת־אֶרֶץ לָבֹא אֶפְרָתָה וָאֶקְבְּרֶהָ שָּׁם בְּדֶרֶךְ אֶפְרָת הִוא
בֵּית לָחֶם: ח וַיַּרְא יִשְׂרָאֵל אֶת־בְּנֵי יוֹסֵף וַיֹּאמֶר מִי־אֵלֶּה:
ט וַיֹּאמֶר יוֹסֵף אֶל־אָבִיו בָּנַי הֵם אֲשֶׁר־נָתַן־לִי אֱלֹהִים בָּזֶה
וַיֹּאמַר קָחֶם־נָא אֵלַי וַאֲבָרְכֵם:

פרשת שמות

פרק א א וְאֵלֶּה שְׁמוֹת בְּנֵי יִשְׂרָאֵל הַבָּאִים מִצְרָיְמָה אֵת יַעֲקֹב
אִישׁ וּבֵיתוֹ בָּאוּ: ב רְאוּבֵן שִׁמְעוֹן לֵוִי וִיהוּדָה: ג יִשָּׂשכָר
זְבוּלֻן וּבִנְיָמִן: ד דָּן וְנַפְתָּלִי גָּד וְאָשֵׁר: ה וַיְהִי כָּל־נֶפֶשׁ יֹצְאֵי

יֶרֶךְ־יַעֲקֹב שִׁבְעִים נָפֶשׁ וְיוֹסֵף הָיָה בְמִצְרָיִם׃ ו וַיָּמָת יוֹסֵף
וְכָל־אֶחָיו וְכֹל הַדּוֹר הַהוּא׃ ז וּבְנֵי יִשְׂרָאֵל פָּרוּ וַיִּשְׁרְצוּ וַיִּרְבּוּ
וַיַּעַצְמוּ בִּמְאֹד מְאֹד וַתִּמָּלֵא הָאָרֶץ אֹתָם׃ פ [לוי] ח וַיָּקָם
מֶלֶךְ־חָדָשׁ עַל־מִצְרָיִם אֲשֶׁר לֹא־יָדַע אֶת־יוֹסֵף׃ ט וַיֹּאמֶר
אֶל־עַמּוֹ הִנֵּה עַם בְּנֵי יִשְׂרָאֵל רַב וְעָצוּם מִמֶּנּוּ׃ י הָבָה
נִתְחַכְּמָה לוֹ פֶּן־יִרְבֶּה וְהָיָה כִּי־תִקְרֶאנָה מִלְחָמָה וְנוֹסַף
גַּם־הוּא עַל־שֹׂנְאֵינוּ וְנִלְחַם־בָּנוּ וְעָלָה מִן־הָאָרֶץ׃ יא וַיָּשִׂימוּ
עָלָיו שָׂרֵי מִסִּים לְמַעַן עַנֹּתוֹ בְּסִבְלֹתָם וַיִּבֶן עָרֵי מִסְכְּנוֹת
לְפַרְעֹה אֶת־פִּתֹם וְאֶת־רַעַמְסֵס׃ יב וְכַאֲשֶׁר יְעַנּוּ אֹתוֹ כֵּן
יִרְבֶּה וְכֵן יִפְרֹץ וַיָּקֻצוּ מִפְּנֵי בְּנֵי יִשְׂרָאֵל׃ [ישראל] יג וַיַּעֲבִדוּ
מִצְרַיִם אֶת־בְּנֵי יִשְׂרָאֵל בְּפָרֶךְ׃ יד וַיְמָרְרוּ אֶת־חַיֵּיהֶם
בַּעֲבֹדָה קָשָׁה בְּחֹמֶר וּבִלְבֵנִים וּבְכָל־עֲבֹדָה בַּשָּׂדֶה אֵת
כָּל־עֲבֹדָתָם אֲשֶׁר־עָבְדוּ בָהֶם בְּפָרֶךְ׃ טו וַיֹּאמֶר מֶלֶךְ מִצְרַיִם
לַמְיַלְּדֹת הָעִבְרִיֹּת אֲשֶׁר שֵׁם הָאַחַת שִׁפְרָה וְשֵׁם הַשֵּׁנִית
פּוּעָה׃ טז וַיֹּאמֶר בְּיַלֶּדְכֶן אֶת־הָעִבְרִיּוֹת וּרְאִיתֶן עַל־הָאָבְנָיִם
אִם־בֵּן הוּא וַהֲמִתֶּן אֹתוֹ וְאִם־בַּת הִוא וָחָיָה׃ יז וַתִּירֶאןָ
הַמְיַלְּדֹת אֶת־הָאֱלֹהִים וְלֹא עָשׂוּ כַּאֲשֶׁר דִּבֶּר אֲלֵיהֶן מֶלֶךְ
מִצְרָיִם וַתְּחַיֶּיןָ אֶת־הַיְלָדִים׃

פרשת וארא

פרק ו ב וַיְדַבֵּר אֱלֹהִים אֶל־מֹשֶׁה וַיֹּאמֶר אֵלָיו אֲנִי יְהוָה׃
ג וָאֵרָא אֶל־אַבְרָהָם אֶל־יִצְחָק וְאֶל־יַעֲקֹב בְּאֵל שַׁדָּי וּשְׁמִי
יְהוָה לֹא נוֹדַעְתִּי לָהֶם׃ ד וְגַם הֲקִמֹתִי אֶת־בְּרִיתִי אִתָּם
לָתֵת לָהֶם אֶת־אֶרֶץ כְּנָעַן אֵת אֶרֶץ מְגֻרֵיהֶם אֲשֶׁר־גָּרוּ
בָהּ׃ ה וְגַם ׀ אֲנִי שָׁמַעְתִּי אֶת־נַאֲקַת בְּנֵי יִשְׂרָאֵל אֲשֶׁר
מִצְרַיִם מַעֲבִדִים אֹתָם וָאֶזְכֹּר אֶת־בְּרִיתִי׃ [לוי] ו לָכֵן אֱמֹר

לִבְנֵֽי־יִשְׂרָאֵל֮ אֲנִ֣י יְהֹוָה֒ וְהוֹצֵאתִ֣י אֶתְכֶ֗ם מִתַּ֙חַת֙ סִבְלֹ֣ת
מִצְרַ֔יִם וְהִצַּלְתִּ֥י אֶתְכֶ֖ם מֵעֲבֹדָתָ֑ם וְגָאַלְתִּ֤י אֶתְכֶם֙ בִּזְר֣וֹעַ
נְטוּיָ֔ה וּבִשְׁפָטִ֖ים גְּדֹלִֽים׃ ז וְלָקַחְתִּ֨י אֶתְכֶ֥ם לִי֙ לְעָ֔ם וְהָיִ֥יתִי
לָכֶ֖ם לֵֽאלֹהִ֑ים וִֽידַעְתֶּ֗ם כִּ֣י אֲנִ֤י יְהֹוָה֙ אֱלֹהֵיכֶ֔ם הַמּוֹצִ֣יא
אֶתְכֶ֔ם מִתַּ֖חַת סִבְל֥וֹת מִצְרָֽיִם׃ ח וְהֵבֵאתִ֤י אֶתְכֶם֙ אֶל־
הָאָ֔רֶץ אֲשֶׁ֤ר נָשָׂ֙אתִי֙ אֶת־יָדִ֔י לָתֵ֣ת אֹתָ֔הּ לְאַבְרָהָ֥ם לְיִצְחָ֖ק
וּֽלְיַעֲקֹ֑ב וְנָתַתִּ֨י אֹתָ֥הּ לָכֶ֛ם מוֹרָשָׁ֖ה אֲנִ֥י יְהֹוָֽה׃ ט וַיְדַבֵּ֥ר
מֹשֶׁ֛ה כֵּ֖ן אֶל־בְּנֵ֣י יִשְׂרָאֵ֑ל וְלֹ֤א שָֽׁמְעוּ֙ אֶל־מֹשֶׁ֔ה מִקֹּ֣צֶר
ר֔וּחַ וּמֵעֲבֹדָ֖ה קָשָֽׁה׃ פ [ישראל] י וַיְדַבֵּ֥ר יְהֹוָ֖ה אֶל־מֹשֶׁ֥ה
לֵּאמֹֽר׃ יא בֹּ֣א דַבֵּ֔ר אֶל־פַּרְעֹ֖ה מֶ֣לֶךְ מִצְרָ֑יִם וִישַׁלַּ֥ח אֶת־
בְּנֵֽי־יִשְׂרָאֵ֖ל מֵאַרְצֽוֹ׃ יב וַיְדַבֵּ֣ר מֹשֶׁ֔ה לִפְנֵ֥י יְהֹוָ֖ה לֵאמֹ֑ר הֵ֤ן
בְּנֵֽי־יִשְׂרָאֵל֙ לֹא־שָׁמְע֣וּ אֵלַ֔י וְאֵיךְ֙ יִשְׁמָעֵ֣נִי פַרְעֹ֔ה וַאֲנִ֖י עֲרַ֥ל
שְׂפָתָֽיִם׃ פ יג וַיְדַבֵּ֣ר יְהֹוָה֮ אֶל־מֹשֶׁ֣ה וְאֶֽל־אַהֲרֹן֒ וַיְצַוֵּם֙
אֶל־בְּנֵ֣י יִשְׂרָאֵ֔ל וְאֶל־פַּרְעֹ֖ה מֶ֣לֶךְ מִצְרָ֑יִם לְהוֹצִ֥יא אֶת־בְּנֵֽי־
יִשְׂרָאֵ֖ל מֵאֶ֥רֶץ מִצְרָֽיִם׃

פרשת בא

פרק י א וַיֹּ֤אמֶר יְהֹוָה֙ אֶל־מֹשֶׁ֔ה בֹּ֖א אֶל־פַּרְעֹ֑ה כִּֽי־אֲנִ֞י
הִכְבַּ֤דְתִּי אֶת־לִבּוֹ֙ וְאֶת־לֵ֣ב עֲבָדָ֔יו לְמַ֗עַן שִׁתִ֛י אֹתֹתַ֥י אֵ֖לֶּה
בְּקִרְבּֽוֹ׃ ב וּלְמַ֡עַן תְּסַפֵּר֩ בְּאָזְנֵ֨י בִנְךָ֜ וּבֶן־בִּנְךָ֗ אֵ֣ת אֲשֶׁ֤ר
הִתְעַלַּ֙לְתִּי֙ בְּמִצְרַ֔יִם וְאֶת־אֹתֹתַ֖י אֲשֶׁר־שַׂ֣מְתִּי בָ֑ם וִידַעְתֶּ֖ם
כִּי־אֲנִ֥י יְהֹוָֽה׃ ג וַיָּבֹ֨א מֹשֶׁ֣ה וְאַהֲרֹן֮ אֶל־פַּרְעֹה֒ וַיֹּאמְר֣וּ אֵלָ֗יו
כֹּֽה־אָמַ֤ר יְהֹוָה֙ אֱלֹהֵ֣י הָֽעִבְרִ֔ים עַד־מָתַ֣י מֵאַ֔נְתָּ לֵעָנֹ֖ת מִפָּנָ֑י
שַׁלַּ֥ח עַמִּ֖י וְיַֽעַבְדֻֽנִי׃ [לוי] ד כִּ֛י אִם־מָאֵ֥ן אַתָּ֖ה לְשַׁלֵּ֣חַ אֶת־עַמִּ֑י
הִנְנִ֨י מֵבִ֥יא מָחָ֛ר אַרְבֶּ֖ה בִּגְבֻלֶֽךָ׃ ה וְכִסָּה֙ אֶת־עֵ֣ין הָאָ֔רֶץ וְלֹ֥א
יוּכַ֖ל לִרְאֹ֣ת אֶת־הָאָ֑רֶץ וְאָכַ֣ל ׀ אֶת־יֶ֣תֶר הַפְּלֵטָ֗ה הַנִּשְׁאֶ֙רֶת֙

לָכֶם֙ מִן־הַבָּרָ֔ד וְאָכַל֙ אֶת־כָּל־הָעֵ֔ץ הַצֹּמֵ֥חַ לָכֶ֖ם מִן־הַשָּׂדֶֽה׃
ו וּמָלְא֨וּ בָתֶּ֜יךָ וּבָתֵּ֣י כָל־עֲבָדֶ֗יךָ וּבָתֵּ֣י כָל־מִצְרַ֔יִם אֲשֶׁ֨ר
לֹֽא־רָא֤וּ אֲבֹתֶ֙יךָ֙ וַאֲב֣וֹת אֲבֹתֶ֔יךָ מִיּ֗וֹם הֱיוֹתָם֙ עַל־הָ֣אֲדָמָ֔ה
עַ֖ד הַיּ֣וֹם הַזֶּ֑ה וַיִּ֖פֶן וַיֵּצֵ֥א מֵעִ֥ם פַּרְעֹֽה׃ [ישראל] ז וַיֹּאמְר֩וּ
עַבְדֵ֨י פַרְעֹ֜ה אֵלָ֗יו עַד־מָתַי֙ יִהְיֶ֨ה זֶ֥ה לָ֙נוּ֙ לְמוֹקֵ֔שׁ שַׁלַּח֙ אֶת־
הָ֣אֲנָשִׁ֔ים וְיַֽעַבְד֖וּ אֶת־יְהֹוָ֣ה אֱלֹהֵיהֶ֑ם הֲטֶ֣רֶם תֵּדַ֔ע כִּ֥י אָבְדָ֖ה
מִצְרָֽיִם׃ ח וַיּוּשַׁ֞ב אֶת־מֹשֶׁ֤ה וְאֶֽת־אַהֲרֹן֙ אֶל־פַּרְעֹ֔ה וַיֹּ֣אמֶר
אֲלֵהֶ֔ם לְכ֖וּ עִבְד֣וּ אֶת־יְהֹוָ֣ה אֱלֹהֵיכֶ֑ם מִ֥י וָמִ֖י הַהֹלְכִֽים׃
ט וַיֹּ֣אמֶר מֹשֶׁ֔ה בִּנְעָרֵ֥ינוּ וּבִזְקֵנֵ֖ינוּ נֵלֵ֑ךְ בְּבָנֵ֨ינוּ וּבִבְנוֹתֵ֜נוּ
בְּצֹאנֵ֤נוּ וּבִבְקָרֵ֙נוּ֙ נֵלֵ֔ךְ כִּ֥י חַג־יְהֹוָ֖ה לָֽנוּ׃ י וַיֹּ֣אמֶר אֲלֵהֶ֗ם יְהִ֨י
כֵ֤ן יְהֹוָה֙ עִמָּכֶ֔ם כַּאֲשֶׁ֛ר אֲשַׁלַּ֥ח אֶתְכֶ֖ם וְאֶֽת־טַפְּכֶ֑ם רְא֕וּ כִּ֥י
רָעָ֖ה נֶ֥גֶד פְּנֵיכֶֽם׃ יא לֹ֣א כֵ֗ן לְכוּ־נָ֤א הַגְּבָרִים֙ וְעִבְד֣וּ אֶת־יְהֹוָ֔ה
כִּ֥י אֹתָ֖הּ אַתֶּ֣ם מְבַקְשִׁ֑ים וַיְגָ֣רֶשׁ אֹתָ֔ם מֵאֵ֖ת פְּנֵ֥י פַרְעֹֽה׃

פרשת בשלח

פרק יג יז וַיְהִ֗י בְּשַׁלַּ֣ח פַּרְעֹה֮ אֶת־הָעָם֒ וְלֹא־נָחָ֣ם אֱלֹהִ֗ים דֶּ֚רֶךְ
אֶ֣רֶץ פְּלִשְׁתִּ֔ים כִּ֥י קָר֖וֹב ה֑וּא כִּ֣י ׀ אָמַ֣ר אֱלֹהִ֗ים פֶּֽן־יִנָּחֵ֥ם
הָעָ֛ם בִּרְאֹתָ֥ם מִלְחָמָ֖ה וְשָׁ֥בוּ מִצְרָֽיְמָה׃ יח וַיַּסֵּ֨ב אֱלֹהִ֧ים ׀
אֶת־הָעָ֛ם דֶּ֥רֶךְ הַמִּדְבָּ֖ר יַם־ס֑וּף וַחֲמֻשִׁ֛ים עָל֥וּ בְנֵֽי־יִשְׂרָאֵ֖ל
מֵאֶ֥רֶץ מִצְרָֽיִם׃ יט וַיִּקַּ֥ח מֹשֶׁ֛ה אֶת־עַצְמ֥וֹת יוֹסֵ֖ף עִמּ֑וֹ כִּי֩
הַשְׁבֵּ֨עַ הִשְׁבִּ֜יעַ אֶת־בְּנֵ֤י יִשְׂרָאֵל֙ לֵאמֹ֔ר פָּקֹ֨ד יִפְקֹ֤ד אֱלֹהִים֙
אֶתְכֶ֔ם וְהַעֲלִיתֶ֧ם אֶת־עַצְמֹתַ֛י מִזֶּ֖ה אִתְּכֶֽם׃ כ וַיִּסְע֖וּ מִסֻּכֹּ֑ת
וַֽיַּחֲנ֣וּ בְאֵתָ֔ם בִּקְצֵ֖ה הַמִּדְבָּֽר׃ כא וַֽיהֹוָ֡ה הֹלֵךְ֩ לִפְנֵיהֶ֨ם יוֹמָ֜ם
בְּעַמּ֥וּד עָנָן֙ לַנְחֹתָ֣ם הַדֶּ֔רֶךְ וְלַ֛יְלָה בְּעַמּ֥וּד אֵ֖שׁ לְהָאִ֣יר לָהֶ֑ם
לָלֶ֖כֶת יוֹמָ֥ם וָלָֽיְלָה׃ כב לֹֽא־יָמִ֞ישׁ עַמּ֤וּד הֶֽעָנָן֙ יוֹמָ֔ם וְעַמּ֥וּד
הָאֵ֖שׁ לָ֑יְלָה לִפְנֵ֖י הָעָֽם׃ פ [לוי] **פרק יד** א וַיְדַבֵּ֥ר יְהֹוָ֖ה אֶל־

מֹשֶׁ֥ה לֵּאמֹֽר׃ ב דַּבֵּר֮ אֶל־בְּנֵ֣י יִשְׂרָאֵל֒ וְיָשֻׁ֗בוּ וְיַחֲנוּ֙ לִפְנֵי֙ פִּ֣י
הַחִירֹ֔ת בֵּ֥ין מִגְדֹּ֖ל וּבֵ֣ין הַיָּ֑ם לִפְנֵי֙ בַּ֣עַל צְפֹ֔ן נִכְח֥וֹ תַחֲנ֖וּ עַל־
הַיָּֽם׃ ג וְאָמַ֤ר פַּרְעֹה֙ לִבְנֵ֣י יִשְׂרָאֵ֔ל נְבֻכִ֥ים הֵ֖ם בָּאָ֑רֶץ סָגַ֥ר
עֲלֵיהֶ֖ם הַמִּדְבָּֽר׃ ד וְחִזַּקְתִּ֣י אֶת־לֵב־פַּרְעֹה֮ וְרָדַ֣ף אַחֲרֵיהֶם֒
וְאִכָּבְדָ֤ה בְּפַרְעֹה֙ וּבְכָל־חֵיל֔וֹ וְיָדְע֥וּ מִצְרַ֖יִם כִּֽי־אֲנִ֣י יְהֹוָ֑ה
וַיַּעֲשׂוּ־כֵֽן׃ [ישראל] ה וַיֻּגַּד֙ לְמֶ֣לֶךְ מִצְרַ֔יִם כִּ֥י בָרַ֖ח הָעָ֑ם וַ֠יֵּהָפֵ֠ךְ
לְבַ֨ב פַּרְעֹ֤ה וַעֲבָדָיו֙ אֶל־הָעָ֔ם וַיֹּֽאמְרוּ֙ מַה־זֹּ֣את עָשִׂ֔ינוּ כִּֽי־
שִׁלַּ֥חְנוּ אֶת־יִשְׂרָאֵ֖ל מֵעָבְדֵֽנוּ׃ ו וַיֶּאְסֹ֖ר אֶת־רִכְבּ֑וֹ וְאֶת־עַמּ֖וֹ
לָקַ֥ח עִמּֽוֹ׃ ז וַיִּקַּ֞ח שֵׁשׁ־מֵא֤וֹת רֶ֙כֶב֙ בָּח֔וּר וְכֹ֖ל רֶ֣כֶב מִצְרָ֑יִם
וְשָׁלִשִׁ֖ם עַל־כֻּלּֽוֹ׃ ח וַיְחַזֵּ֣ק יְהֹוָ֗ה אֶת־לֵ֤ב פַּרְעֹה֙ מֶ֣לֶךְ מִצְרַ֔יִם
וַיִּרְדֹּ֕ף אַחֲרֵ֖י בְּנֵ֣י יִשְׂרָאֵ֑ל וּבְנֵ֣י יִשְׂרָאֵ֔ל יֹצְאִ֖ים בְּיָ֥ד רָמָֽה׃

פרשת יתרו

פרק יח א וַיִּשְׁמַ֞ע יִתְר֨וֹ כֹהֵ֤ן מִדְיָן֙ חֹתֵ֣ן מֹשֶׁ֔ה אֵת֩ כָּל־אֲשֶׁ֨ר
עָשָׂ֤ה אֱלֹהִים֙ לְמֹשֶׁ֔ה וּלְיִשְׂרָאֵ֖ל עַמּ֑וֹ כִּֽי־הוֹצִ֧יא יְהֹוָ֛ה אֶת־
יִשְׂרָאֵ֖ל מִמִּצְרָֽיִם׃ ב וַיִּקַּ֗ח יִתְרוֹ֙ חֹתֵ֣ן מֹשֶׁ֔ה אֶת־צִפֹּרָ֖ה
אֵ֣שֶׁת מֹשֶׁ֑ה אַחַ֖ר שִׁלּוּחֶֽיהָ׃ ג וְאֵ֖ת שְׁנֵ֣י בָנֶ֑יהָ אֲשֶׁ֨ר שֵׁ֤ם
הָֽאֶחָד֙ גֵּֽרְשֹׁ֔ם כִּ֣י אָמַ֔ר גֵּ֣ר הָיִ֔יתִי בְּאֶ֖רֶץ נָכְרִיָּֽה׃ ד וְשֵׁ֥ם
הָאֶחָ֖ד אֱלִיעֶ֑זֶר כִּֽי־אֱלֹהֵ֤י אָבִי֙ בְּעֶזְרִ֔י וַיַּצִּלֵ֖נִי מֵחֶ֥רֶב פַּרְעֹֽה׃
[לוי] ה וַיָּבֹ֞א יִתְר֨וֹ חֹתֵ֥ן מֹשֶׁ֛ה וּבָנָ֥יו וְאִשְׁתּ֖וֹ אֶל־מֹשֶׁ֑ה אֶל־
הַמִּדְבָּ֗ר אֲשֶׁר־ה֛וּא חֹנֶ֥ה שָׁ֖ם הַ֥ר הָאֱלֹהִֽים׃ ו וַיֹּ֙אמֶר֙ אֶל־
מֹשֶׁ֔ה אֲנִ֛י חֹתֶנְךָ֥ יִתְר֖וֹ בָּ֣א אֵלֶ֑יךָ וְאִ֨שְׁתְּךָ֔ וּשְׁנֵ֥י בָנֶ֖יהָ עִמָּֽהּ׃
ז וַיֵּצֵ֨א מֹשֶׁ֜ה לִקְרַ֣את חֹֽתְנ֗וֹ וַיִּשְׁתַּ֙חוּ֙ וַיִּשַּׁק־ל֔וֹ וַיִּשְׁאֲל֥וּ
אִישׁ־לְרֵעֵ֖הוּ לְשָׁל֑וֹם וַיָּבֹ֖אוּ הָאֹֽהֱלָה׃ ח וַיְסַפֵּ֤ר מֹשֶׁה֙ לְחֹ֣תְנ֔וֹ
אֵת֩ כָּל־אֲשֶׁ֨ר עָשָׂ֤ה יְהֹוָה֙ לְפַרְעֹ֣ה וּלְמִצְרַ֔יִם עַ֖ל אוֹדֹ֣ת
יִשְׂרָאֵ֑ל אֵ֤ת כָּל־הַתְּלָאָה֙ אֲשֶׁ֣ר מְצָאָ֣תַם בַּדֶּ֔רֶךְ וַיַּצִּלֵ֖ם

יְהֹוָֽה׃ [ישראל] ט וַיִּ֣חַדְּ יִתְר֔וֹ עַ֚ל כׇּל־הַטּוֹבָ֔ה אֲשֶׁר־עָשָׂ֥ה יְהֹוָ֖ה
לְיִשְׂרָאֵ֑ל אֲשֶׁ֥ר הִצִּיל֖וֹ מִיַּ֥ד מִצְרָֽיִם׃ י וַיֹּאמֶר֮ יִתְרוֹ֒ בָּר֣וּךְ
יְהֹוָ֔ה אֲשֶׁ֨ר הִצִּ֥יל אֶתְכֶ֛ם מִיַּ֥ד מִצְרַ֖יִם וּמִיַּ֣ד פַּרְעֹ֑ה אֲשֶׁ֤ר
הִצִּיל֙ אֶת־הָעָ֔ם מִתַּ֖חַת יַד־מִצְרָֽיִם׃ יא עַתָּ֣ה יָדַ֔עְתִּי כִּֽי־גָד֥וֹל
יְהֹוָ֖ה מִכׇּל־הָאֱלֹהִ֑ים כִּ֣י בַדָּבָ֔ר אֲשֶׁ֥ר זָד֖וּ עֲלֵיהֶֽם׃ יב וַיִּקַּ֞ח
יִתְר֜וֹ חֹתֵ֥ן מֹשֶׁ֛ה עֹלָ֥ה וּזְבָחִ֖ים לֵֽאלֹהִ֑ים וַיָּבֹ֨א אַהֲרֹ֜ן וְכֹ֣ל ׀
זִקְנֵ֣י יִשְׂרָאֵ֗ל לֶאֱכׇל־לֶ֛חֶם עִם־חֹתֵ֥ן מֹשֶׁ֖ה לִפְנֵ֥י הָאֱלֹהִֽים׃

פרשת משפטים

פרק כא א וְאֵ֙לֶּה֙ הַמִּשְׁפָּטִ֔ים אֲשֶׁ֥ר תָּשִׂ֖ים לִפְנֵיהֶֽם׃ ב כִּ֤י
תִקְנֶה֙ עֶ֣בֶד עִבְרִ֔י שֵׁ֥שׁ שָׁנִ֖ים יַעֲבֹ֑ד וּבַּ֨שְּׁבִעִ֔ת יֵצֵ֥א לַחׇפְשִׁ֖י
חִנָּֽם׃ ג אִם־בְּגַפּ֥וֹ יָבֹ֖א בְּגַפּ֣וֹ יֵצֵ֑א אִם־בַּ֤עַל אִשָּׁה֙ ה֔וּא וְיָצְאָ֥ה
אִשְׁתּ֖וֹ עִמּֽוֹ׃ ד אִם־אֲדֹנָיו֙ יִתֶּן־ל֣וֹ אִשָּׁ֔ה וְיָלְדָה־ל֥וֹ בָנִ֖ים
א֣וֹ בָנ֑וֹת הָאִשָּׁ֣ה וִילָדֶ֗יהָ תִּהְיֶה֙ לַֽאדֹנֶ֔יהָ וְה֖וּא יֵצֵ֥א בְגַפּֽוֹ׃
ה וְאִם־אָמֹ֤ר יֹאמַר֙ הָעֶ֔בֶד אָהַ֙בְתִּי֙ אֶת־אֲדֹנִ֔י אֶת־אִשְׁתִּ֖י
וְאֶת־בָּנָ֑י לֹ֥א אֵצֵ֖א חׇפְשִֽׁי׃ ו וְהִגִּישׁ֤וֹ אֲדֹנָיו֙ אֶל־הָ֣אֱלֹהִ֔ים
וְהִגִּישׁוֹ֙ אֶל־הַדֶּ֔לֶת א֖וֹ אֶל־הַמְּזוּזָ֑ה וְרָצַ֨ע אֲדֹנָ֤יו אֶת־אׇזְנוֹ֙
בַּמַּרְצֵ֔עַ וַעֲבָד֖וֹ לְעֹלָֽם׃ ס [לוי] ז וְכִֽי־יִמְכֹּ֥ר אִ֛ישׁ אֶת־
בִּתּ֖וֹ לְאָמָ֑ה לֹ֥א תֵצֵ֖א כְּצֵ֥את הָעֲבָדִֽים׃ ח אִם־רָעָ֞ה בְּעֵינֵ֧י
אֲדֹנֶ֛יהָ אֲשֶׁר־לֹ֥א▽ יְעָדָ֖הּ וְהֶפְדָּ֑הּ לְעַ֥ם נׇכְרִ֛י לֹא־יִמְשֹׁ֥ל
לְמׇכְרָ֖הּ בְּבִגְדוֹ־בָֽהּ׃ ט וְאִם־לִבְנ֖וֹ יִֽיעָדֶ֑נָּה כְּמִשְׁפַּ֥ט הַבָּנ֖וֹת
יַעֲשֶׂה־לָּֽהּ׃ י אִם־אַחֶ֖רֶת יִֽקַּֽח־ל֑וֹ שְׁאֵרָ֛הּ כְּסוּתָ֥הּ וְעֹנָתָ֖הּ לֹ֥א
יִגְרָֽע׃ יא וְאִם־שְׁלׇשׁ־אֵ֔לֶּה לֹ֥א יַעֲשֶׂ֖ה לָ֑הּ וְיָצְאָ֥ה חִנָּ֖ם אֵ֥ין
כָּֽסֶף׃ ס [ישראל] יב מַכֵּ֥ה אִ֛ישׁ וָמֵ֖ת מ֥וֹת יוּמָֽת׃ יג וַאֲשֶׁר֙
לֹ֣א צָדָ֔ה וְהָאֱלֹהִ֖ים אִנָּ֣ה לְיָד֑וֹ וְשַׂמְתִּ֤י לְךָ֙ מָק֔וֹם אֲשֶׁ֥ר יָנ֖וּס

▽ ל֥וֹ

שָׁמָּה: ס יד וְכִי־יָזִד אִישׁ עַל־רֵעֵהוּ לְהָרְגוֹ בְעָרְמָה
מֵעִם מִזְבְּחִי תִּקָּחֶנּוּ לָמוּת: ס טו וּמַכֵּה אָבִיו וְאִמּוֹ
מוֹת יוּמָת: ס טז וְגֹנֵב אִישׁ וּמְכָרוֹ וְנִמְצָא בְיָדוֹ מוֹת
יוּמָת: ס יז וּמְקַלֵּל אָבִיו וְאִמּוֹ מוֹת יוּמָת: ס יח וְכִי־
יְרִיבֻן אֲנָשִׁים וְהִכָּה־אִישׁ אֶת־רֵעֵהוּ בְּאֶבֶן אוֹ בְאֶגְרֹף וְלֹא
יָמוּת וְנָפַל לְמִשְׁכָּב: יט אִם־יָקוּם וְהִתְהַלֵּךְ בַּחוּץ עַל־
מִשְׁעַנְתּוֹ וְנִקָּה הַמַּכֶּה רַק שִׁבְתּוֹ יִתֵּן וְרַפֹּא יְרַפֵּא:

פרשת תרומה

פרק כה א וַיְדַבֵּר יְהוָה אֶל־מֹשֶׁה לֵּאמֹר: ב דַּבֵּר אֶל־בְּנֵי
יִשְׂרָאֵל וְיִקְחוּ־לִי תְּרוּמָה מֵאֵת כָּל־אִישׁ אֲשֶׁר יִדְּבֶנּוּ
לִבּוֹ תִּקְחוּ אֶת־תְּרוּמָתִי: ג וְזֹאת הַתְּרוּמָה אֲשֶׁר תִּקְחוּ
מֵאִתָּם זָהָב וָכֶסֶף וּנְחֹשֶׁת: ד וּתְכֵלֶת וְאַרְגָּמָן וְתוֹלַעַת
שָׁנִי וְשֵׁשׁ וְעִזִּים: ה וְעֹרֹת אֵילִם מְאָדָּמִים וְעֹרֹת תְּחָשִׁים
וַעֲצֵי שִׁטִּים: [לוי] ו שֶׁמֶן לַמָּאֹר בְּשָׂמִים לְשֶׁמֶן הַמִּשְׁחָה
וְלִקְטֹרֶת הַסַּמִּים: ז אַבְנֵי־שֹׁהַם וְאַבְנֵי מִלֻּאִים לָאֵפֹד
וְלַחֹשֶׁן: ח וְעָשׂוּ לִי מִקְדָּשׁ וְשָׁכַנְתִּי בְּתוֹכָם: ט כְּכֹל אֲשֶׁר
אֲנִי מַרְאֶה אוֹתְךָ אֵת תַּבְנִית הַמִּשְׁכָּן וְאֵת תַּבְנִית כָּל־כֵּלָיו
וְכֵן תַּעֲשׂוּ: ס [ישראל] י וְעָשׂוּ אֲרוֹן עֲצֵי שִׁטִּים אַמָּתַיִם
וָחֵצִי אָרְכּוֹ וְאַמָּה וָחֵצִי רָחְבּוֹ וְאַמָּה וָחֵצִי קֹמָתוֹ: יא וְצִפִּיתָ
אֹתוֹ זָהָב טָהוֹר מִבַּיִת וּמִחוּץ תְּצַפֶּנּוּ וְעָשִׂיתָ עָלָיו זֵר זָהָב
סָבִיב: יב וְיָצַקְתָּ לּוֹ אַרְבַּע טַבְּעֹת זָהָב וְנָתַתָּה עַל אַרְבַּע
פַּעֲמֹתָיו וּשְׁתֵּי טַבָּעֹת עַל־צַלְעוֹ הָאֶחָת וּשְׁתֵּי טַבָּעֹת עַל־
צַלְעוֹ הַשֵּׁנִית: יג וְעָשִׂיתָ בַדֵּי עֲצֵי שִׁטִּים וְצִפִּיתָ אֹתָם זָהָב:
יד וְהֵבֵאתָ אֶת־הַבַּדִּים בַּטַּבָּעֹת עַל צַלְעֹת הָאָרֹן לָשֵׂאת
אֶת־הָאָרֹן בָּהֶם: טו בְּטַבְּעֹת הָאָרֹן יִהְיוּ הַבַּדִּים לֹא יָסֻרוּ
מִמֶּנּוּ: טז וְנָתַתָּ אֶל־הָאָרֹן אֵת הָעֵדֻת אֲשֶׁר אֶתֵּן אֵלֶיךָ:

פרשת תצוה

פרק כז כ וְאַתָּ֞ה תְּצַוֶּ֣ה ׀ אֶת־בְּנֵ֣י יִשְׂרָאֵ֗ל וְיִקְח֨וּ אֵלֶ֜יךָ שֶׁ֣מֶן
זַ֥יִת זָ֛ךְ כָּתִ֖ית לַמָּא֑וֹר לְהַעֲלֹ֥ת נֵ֖ר תָּמִֽיד׃ כא בְּאֹ֣הֶל מוֹעֵ֡ד
מִח֣וּץ לַפָּרֹ֜כֶת אֲשֶׁ֣ר עַל־הָעֵדֻ֗ת יַעֲרֹךְ֩ אֹת֨וֹ אַהֲרֹ֧ן וּבָנָ֛יו
מֵעֶ֥רֶב עַד־בֹּ֖קֶר לִפְנֵ֣י יְהֹוָ֑ה חֻקַּ֤ת עוֹלָם֙ לְדֹ֣רֹתָ֔ם מֵאֵ֖ת בְּנֵ֥י
יִשְׂרָאֵֽל׃ ס פרק כח א וְאַתָּ֡ה הַקְרֵ֣ב אֵלֶ֩יךָ֩ אֶת־אַהֲרֹ֨ן
אָחִ֜יךָ וְאֶת־בָּנָ֣יו אִתּ֗וֹ מִתּ֛וֹךְ בְּנֵ֥י יִשְׂרָאֵ֖ל לְכַהֲנוֹ־לִ֑י אַהֲרֹ֕ן
נָדָ֧ב וַאֲבִיה֛וּא אֶלְעָזָ֥ר וְאִֽיתָמָ֖ר בְּנֵ֥י אַהֲרֹֽן׃ ב וְעָשִׂ֥יתָ בִגְדֵי־
קֹ֖דֶשׁ לְאַהֲרֹ֣ן אָחִ֑יךָ לְכָב֖וֹד וּלְתִפְאָֽרֶת׃ ג וְאַתָּ֗ה תְּדַבֵּר֙ אֶל־
כָּל־חַכְמֵי־לֵ֔ב אֲשֶׁ֥ר מִלֵּאתִ֖יו ר֣וּחַ חָכְמָ֑ה וְעָשׂ֞וּ אֶת־בִּגְדֵ֧י
אַהֲרֹ֛ן לְקַדְּשׁ֖וֹ לְכַהֲנוֹ־לִֽי׃ ד וְאֵ֨לֶּה הַבְּגָדִ֜ים אֲשֶׁ֣ר יַעֲשׂ֗וּ
חֹ֤שֶׁן וְאֵפוֹד֙ וּמְעִ֔יל וּכְתֹ֥נֶת תַּשְׁבֵּ֖ץ מִצְנֶ֣פֶת וְאַבְנֵ֑ט וְעָשׂ֨וּ
בִגְדֵי־קֹ֜דֶשׁ לְאַהֲרֹ֥ן אָחִ֛יךָ וּלְבָנָ֖יו לְכַהֲנוֹ־לִֽי׃ ה וְהֵם֙ יִקְח֣וּ
אֶת־הַזָּהָ֔ב וְאֶת־הַתְּכֵ֖לֶת וְאֶת־הָֽאַרְגָּמָ֑ן וְאֶת־תּוֹלַ֥עַת הַשָּׁנִ֖י
וְאֶת־הַשֵּֽׁשׁ׃ פ [לוי] ו וְעָשׂ֖וּ אֶת־הָאֵפֹ֑ד זָ֠הָב תְּכֵ֨לֶת וְאַרְגָּמָ֜ן
תּוֹלַ֧עַת שָׁנִ֛י וְשֵׁ֥שׁ מָשְׁזָ֖ר מַעֲשֵׂ֥ה חֹשֵֽׁב׃ ז שְׁתֵּ֧י כְתֵפֹ֣ת חֹבְרֹ֗ת
יִהְיֶה־לּ֛וֹ אֶל־שְׁנֵ֥י קְצוֹתָ֖יו וְחֻבָּֽר׃ ח וְחֵ֤שֶׁב אֲפֻדָּתוֹ֙ אֲשֶׁ֣ר עָלָ֔יו
כְּמַעֲשֵׂ֖הוּ מִמֶּ֣נּוּ יִהְיֶ֑ה זָהָ֗ב תְּכֵ֧לֶת וְאַרְגָּמָ֛ן וְתוֹלַ֥עַת שָׁנִ֖י
וְשֵׁ֥שׁ מָשְׁזָֽר׃ ט וְלָ֣קַחְתָּ֔ אֶת־שְׁתֵּ֖י אַבְנֵי־שֹׁ֑הַם וּפִתַּחְתָּ֣
עֲלֵיהֶ֔ם שְׁמ֖וֹת בְּנֵ֥י יִשְׂרָאֵֽל׃ [ישראל] י שִׁשָּׁה֙ מִשְּׁמֹתָ֔ם עַ֖ל
הָאֶ֣בֶן הָאֶחָ֑ת וְאֶת־שְׁמ֞וֹת הַשִּׁשָּׁ֧ה הַנּוֹתָרִ֛ים עַל־הָאֶ֥בֶן
הַשֵּׁנִ֖ית כְּתוֹלְדֹתָֽם׃ יא מַעֲשֵׂ֣ה חָרַשׁ֮ אֶ֒בֶן֒ פִּתּוּחֵ֣י חֹתָ֗ם
תְּפַתַּח֙ אֶת־שְׁתֵּ֣י הָאֲבָנִ֔ים עַל־שְׁמֹ֖ת בְּנֵ֣י יִשְׂרָאֵ֑ל מֻסַבֹּ֛ת
מִשְׁבְּצ֥וֹת זָהָ֖ב תַּעֲשֶׂ֥ה אֹתָֽם׃ יב וְשַׂמְתָּ֞ אֶת־שְׁתֵּ֣י הָאֲבָנִ֗ים
עַ֚ל כִּתְפֹ֣ת הָאֵפֹ֔ד אַבְנֵ֥י זִכָּרֹ֖ן לִבְנֵ֣י יִשְׂרָאֵ֑ל וְנָשָׂא֩ אַהֲרֹ֨ן אֶת־
שְׁמוֹתָ֜ם לִפְנֵ֧י יְהֹוָ֛ה עַל־שְׁתֵּ֥י כְתֵפָ֖יו לְזִכָּרֹֽן׃

פרשת כי תשא

פרק ל יא וַיְדַבֵּר יְהוָה אֶל־מֹשֶׁה לֵּאמֹר: יב כִּי תִשָּׂא אֶת־רֹאשׁ
בְּנֵי־יִשְׂרָאֵל לִפְקֻדֵיהֶם וְנָתְנוּ אִישׁ כֹּפֶר נַפְשׁוֹ לַיהוָה בִּפְקֹד
אֹתָם וְלֹא־יִהְיֶה בָהֶם נֶגֶף בִּפְקֹד אֹתָם: יג זֶה | יִתְּנוּ כָּל־
הָעֹבֵר עַל־הַפְּקֻדִים מַחֲצִית הַשֶּׁקֶל בְּשֶׁקֶל הַקֹּדֶשׁ עֶשְׂרִים
גֵּרָה הַשֶּׁקֶל מַחֲצִית הַשֶּׁקֶל תְּרוּמָה לַיהוָה: [לוי] יד כֹּל הָעֹבֵר
עַל־הַפְּקֻדִים מִבֶּן עֶשְׂרִים שָׁנָה וָמָעְלָה יִתֵּן תְּרוּמַת יְהוָה:
טו הֶעָשִׁיר לֹא־יַרְבֶּה וְהַדַּל לֹא יַמְעִיט מִמַּחֲצִית הַשָּׁקֶל
לָתֵת אֶת־תְּרוּמַת יְהוָה לְכַפֵּר עַל־נַפְשֹׁתֵיכֶם: טז וְלָקַחְתָּ
אֶת־כֶּסֶף הַכִּפֻּרִים מֵאֵת בְּנֵי יִשְׂרָאֵל וְנָתַתָּ אֹתוֹ עַל־עֲבֹדַת
אֹהֶל מוֹעֵד וְהָיָה לִבְנֵי יִשְׂרָאֵל לְזִכָּרוֹן לִפְנֵי יְהוָה לְכַפֵּר
עַל־נַפְשֹׁתֵיכֶם: פ [ישראל] יז וַיְדַבֵּר יְהוָה אֶל־מֹשֶׁה לֵּאמֹר:
יח וְעָשִׂיתָ כִּיּוֹר נְחֹשֶׁת וְכַנּוֹ נְחֹשֶׁת לְרָחְצָה וְנָתַתָּ אֹתוֹ
בֵּין־אֹהֶל מוֹעֵד וּבֵין הַמִּזְבֵּחַ וְנָתַתָּ שָׁמָּה מָיִם: יט וְרָחֲצוּ
אַהֲרֹן וּבָנָיו מִמֶּנּוּ אֶת־יְדֵיהֶם וְאֶת־רַגְלֵיהֶם: כ בְּבֹאָם אֶל־
אֹהֶל מוֹעֵד יִרְחֲצוּ־מַיִם וְלֹא יָמֻתוּ אוֹ בְגִשְׁתָּם אֶל־הַמִּזְבֵּחַ
לְשָׁרֵת לְהַקְטִיר אִשֶּׁה לַיהוָה: כא וְרָחֲצוּ יְדֵיהֶם וְרַגְלֵיהֶם
וְלֹא יָמֻתוּ וְהָיְתָה לָהֶם חָק־עוֹלָם לוֹ וּלְזַרְעוֹ לְדֹרֹתָם:

פרשת ויקהל

פרק לה א וַיַּקְהֵל מֹשֶׁה אֶת־כָּל־עֲדַת בְּנֵי יִשְׂרָאֵל וַיֹּאמֶר
אֲלֵהֶם אֵלֶּה הַדְּבָרִים אֲשֶׁר־צִוָּה יְהוָה לַעֲשֹׂת אֹתָם: ב שֵׁשֶׁת
יָמִים תֵּעָשֶׂה מְלָאכָה וּבַיּוֹם הַשְּׁבִיעִי יִהְיֶה לָכֶם קֹדֶשׁ שַׁבַּת
שַׁבָּתוֹן לַיהוָה כָּל־הָעֹשֶׂה בוֹ מְלָאכָה יוּמָת: ג לֹא־תְבַעֲרוּ
אֵשׁ בְּכֹל מֹשְׁבֹתֵיכֶם בְּיוֹם הַשַּׁבָּת: פ [לוי] ד וַיֹּאמֶר מֹשֶׁה
אֶל־כָּל־עֲדַת בְּנֵי־יִשְׂרָאֵל לֵאמֹר זֶה הַדָּבָר אֲשֶׁר־צִוָּה יְהוָה

לֵאמֹֽר׃ ה קְח֨וּ מֵאִתְּכֶ֤ם תְּרוּמָה֙ לַֽיהוָ֔ה כֹּ֚ל נְדִ֣יב לִבּ֔וֹ יְבִיאֶ֕הָ
אֵ֖ת תְּרוּמַ֣ת יְהוָ֑ה זָהָ֥ב וָכֶ֖סֶף וּנְחֹֽשֶׁת׃ ו וּתְכֵ֧לֶת וְאַרְגָּמָ֛ן
וְתוֹלַ֥עַת שָׁנִ֖י וְשֵׁ֥שׁ וְעִזִּֽים׃ ז וְעֹרֹ֨ת אֵילִ֧ם מְאָדָּמִ֛ים וְעֹרֹ֥ת
תְּחָשִׁ֖ים וַעֲצֵ֥י שִׁטִּֽים׃ ח וְשֶׁ֖מֶן לַמָּא֑וֹר וּבְשָׂמִים֙ לְשֶׁ֣מֶן
הַמִּשְׁחָ֔ה וְלִקְטֹ֖רֶת הַסַּמִּֽים׃ ט וְאַ֙בְנֵי־שֹׁ֔הַם וְאַבְנֵ֖י מִלֻּאִ֑ים
לָאֵפ֖וֹד וְלַחֹֽשֶׁן׃ י וְכָל־חֲכַם־לֵ֖ב בָּכֶ֑ם יָבֹ֣אוּ וְיַעֲשׂ֔וּ אֵ֛ת כָּל־
אֲשֶׁ֥ר צִוָּ֖ה יְהוָֽה׃ [ישראל] יא אֶת־הַמִּשְׁכָּ֕ן אֶת־אָהֳל֖וֹ וְאֶת־
מִכְסֵ֑הוּ אֶת־קְרָסָיו֙ וְאֶת־קְרָשָׁ֔יו אֶת־בְּרִיחָ֕ו אֶת־עַמֻּדָ֖יו
וְאֶת־אֲדָנָֽיו׃ יב אֶת־הָאָרֹ֥ן וְאֶת־בַּדָּ֖יו אֶת־הַכַּפֹּ֑רֶת וְאֵ֖ת
פָּרֹ֥כֶת הַמָּסָֽךְ׃ יג אֶת־הַשֻּׁלְחָ֥ן וְאֶת־בַּדָּ֖יו וְאֶת־כָּל־כֵּלָ֑יו
וְאֵ֖ת לֶ֥חֶם הַפָּנִֽים׃ יד וְאֶת־מְנֹרַ֧ת הַמָּא֛וֹר וְאֶת־כֵּלֶ֖יהָ וְאֶת־
נֵרֹתֶ֑יהָ וְאֵ֖ת שֶׁ֥מֶן הַמָּאֽוֹר׃ טו וְאֶת־מִזְבַּ֤ח הַקְּטֹ֙רֶת֙ וְאֶת־
בַּדָּ֔יו וְאֵת֙ שֶׁ֣מֶן הַמִּשְׁחָ֔ה וְאֵ֖ת קְטֹ֣רֶת הַסַּמִּ֑ים וְאֶת־מָסַ֥ךְ
הַפֶּ֖תַח לְפֶ֥תַח הַמִּשְׁכָּֽן׃ טז אֵ֣ת ׀ מִזְבַּ֣ח הָעֹלָ֗ה וְאֶת־מִכְבַּ֤ר
הַנְּחֹ֙שֶׁת֙ אֲשֶׁר־ל֔וֹ אֶת־בַּדָּ֖יו וְאֶת־כָּל־כֵּלָ֑יו אֶת־הַכִּיֹּ֖ר וְאֶת־
כַּנּֽוֹ׃ יז אֵ֚ת קַלְעֵ֣י הֶֽחָצֵ֔ר אֶת־עַמֻּדָ֖יו וְאֶת־אֲדָנֶ֑יהָ וְאֵ֕ת מָסַ֖ךְ
שַׁ֥עַר הֶחָצֵֽר׃ יח אֶת־יִתְדֹ֧ת הַמִּשְׁכָּ֛ן וְאֶת־יִתְדֹ֥ת הֶחָצֵ֖ר
וְאֶת־מֵיתְרֵיהֶֽם׃ יט אֶת־בִּגְדֵ֥י הַשְּׂרָ֖ד לְשָׁרֵ֣ת בַּקֹּ֑דֶשׁ אֶת־
בִּגְדֵ֤י הַקֹּ֙דֶשׁ֙ לְאַהֲרֹ֣ן הַכֹּהֵ֔ן וְאֶת־בִּגְדֵ֥י בָנָ֖יו לְכַהֵֽן׃ כ וַיֵּצְא֛וּ
כָּל־עֲדַ֥ת בְּנֵֽי־יִשְׂרָאֵ֖ל מִלִּפְנֵ֥י מֹשֶֽׁה׃

פרשת פקודי

פרק לח כא אֵ֣לֶּה פְקוּדֵ֤י הַמִּשְׁכָּן֙ מִשְׁכַּ֣ן הָעֵדֻ֔ת אֲשֶׁ֥ר פֻּקַּ֖ד
עַל־פִּ֣י מֹשֶׁ֑ה עֲבֹדַת֙ הַלְוִיִּ֔ם בְּיַד֙ אִֽיתָמָ֔ר בֶּן־אַהֲרֹ֖ן הַכֹּהֵֽן׃
כב וּבְצַלְאֵ֛ל בֶּן־אוּרִ֥י בֶן־ח֖וּר לְמַטֵּ֣ה יְהוּדָ֑ה עָשָׂ֕ה אֵ֛ת כָּל־
אֲשֶׁר־צִוָּ֥ה יְהוָ֖ה אֶת־מֹשֶֽׁה׃ כג וְאִתּ֗וֹ אָהֳלִיאָ֛ב בֶּן־אֲחִֽיסָמָ֖ךְ

לְמַטֵּה־דָן חָרָשׁ וְחֹשֵׁב וְרֹקֵם בַּתְּכֵלֶת וּבָאַרְגָּמָן וּבְתוֹלַעַת
הַשָּׁנִי וּבַשֵּׁשׁ: ס [לוי] כד כָּל־הַזָּהָב הֶעָשׂוּי לַמְּלָאכָה
בְּכֹל מְלֶאכֶת הַקֹּדֶשׁ וַיְהִי | זְהַב הַתְּנוּפָה תֵּשַׁע וְעֶשְׂרִים
כִּכָּר וּשְׁבַע מֵאוֹת וּשְׁלֹשִׁים שֶׁקֶל בְּשֶׁקֶל הַקֹּדֶשׁ: כה וְכֶסֶף
פְּקוּדֵי הָעֵדָה מְאַת כִּכָּר וְאֶלֶף וּשְׁבַע מֵאוֹת וַחֲמִשָּׁה
וְשִׁבְעִים שֶׁקֶל בְּשֶׁקֶל הַקֹּדֶשׁ: כו בֶּקַע לַגֻּלְגֹּלֶת מַחֲצִית
הַשֶּׁקֶל בְּשֶׁקֶל הַקֹּדֶשׁ לְכֹל הָעֹבֵר עַל־הַפְּקֻדִים מִבֶּן עֶשְׂרִים
שָׁנָה וָמַעְלָה לְשֵׁשׁ־מֵאוֹת אֶלֶף וּשְׁלֹשֶׁת אֲלָפִים וַחֲמֵשׁ
מֵאוֹת וַחֲמִשִּׁים: כז וַיְהִי מְאַת כִּכַּר הַכֶּסֶף לָצֶקֶת אֵת אַדְנֵי
הַקֹּדֶשׁ וְאֵת אַדְנֵי הַפָּרֹכֶת מְאַת אֲדָנִים לִמְאַת הַכִּכָּר
כִּכָּר לָאָדֶן: [ישראל] כח וְאֶת־הָאֶלֶף וּשְׁבַע הַמֵּאוֹת וַחֲמִשָּׁה
וְשִׁבְעִים עָשָׂה וָוִים לָעַמּוּדִים וְצִפָּה רָאשֵׁיהֶם וְחִשַּׁק
אֹתָם: כט וּנְחֹשֶׁת הַתְּנוּפָה שִׁבְעִים כִּכָּר וְאַלְפַּיִם וְאַרְבַּע־
מֵאוֹת שָׁקֶל: ל וַיַּעַשׂ בָּהּ אֶת־אַדְנֵי פֶּתַח אֹהֶל מוֹעֵד וְאֵת
מִזְבַּח הַנְּחֹשֶׁת וְאֶת־מִכְבַּר הַנְּחֹשֶׁת אֲשֶׁר־לוֹ וְאֵת כָּל־כְּלֵי
הַמִּזְבֵּחַ: לא וְאֶת־אַדְנֵי הֶחָצֵר סָבִיב וְאֶת־אַדְנֵי שַׁעַר הֶחָצֵר
וְאֵת כָּל־יִתְדֹת הַמִּשְׁכָּן וְאֶת־כָּל־יִתְדֹת הֶחָצֵר סָבִיב: פרק
לט א וּמִן־הַתְּכֵלֶת וְהָאַרְגָּמָן וְתוֹלַעַת הַשָּׁנִי עָשׂוּ בִגְדֵי־שְׂרָד
לְשָׁרֵת בַּקֹּדֶשׁ וַיַּעֲשׂוּ אֶת־בִּגְדֵי הַקֹּדֶשׁ אֲשֶׁר לְאַהֲרֹן כַּאֲשֶׁר
צִוָּה יְהוָה אֶת־מֹשֶׁה:

פרשת ויקרא

פרק א א וַיִּקְרָא אֶל־מֹשֶׁה וַיְדַבֵּר יְהוָה אֵלָיו מֵאֹהֶל מוֹעֵד
לֵאמֹר: ב דַּבֵּר אֶל־בְּנֵי יִשְׂרָאֵל וְאָמַרְתָּ אֲלֵהֶם אָדָם כִּי־
יַקְרִיב מִכֶּם קָרְבָּן לַיהוָה מִן־הַבְּהֵמָה מִן־הַבָּקָר וּמִן־הַצֹּאן
תַּקְרִיבוּ אֶת־קָרְבַּנְכֶם: ג אִם־עֹלָה קָרְבָּנוֹ מִן־הַבָּקָר זָכָר

תָּמִים יַקְרִיבֶנּוּ אֶל־פֶּתַח אֹהֶל מוֹעֵד יַקְרִיב אֹתוֹ לִרְצֹנוֹ
לִפְנֵי יְהוָה: ד וְסָמַךְ יָדוֹ עַל רֹאשׁ הָעֹלָה וְנִרְצָה לוֹ לְכַפֵּר
עָלָיו: [לוי] ה וְשָׁחַט אֶת־בֶּן הַבָּקָר לִפְנֵי יְהוָה וְהִקְרִיבוּ
בְּנֵי אַהֲרֹן הַכֹּהֲנִים אֶת־הַדָּם וְזָרְקוּ אֶת־הַדָּם עַל־הַמִּזְבֵּחַ
סָבִיב אֲשֶׁר־פֶּתַח אֹהֶל מוֹעֵד: ו וְהִפְשִׁיט אֶת־הָעֹלָה וְנִתַּח
אֹתָהּ לִנְתָחֶיהָ: ז וְנָתְנוּ בְּנֵי אַהֲרֹן הַכֹּהֵן אֵשׁ עַל־הַמִּזְבֵּחַ
וְעָרְכוּ עֵצִים עַל־הָאֵשׁ: ח וְעָרְכוּ בְּנֵי אַהֲרֹן הַכֹּהֲנִים אֵת
הַנְּתָחִים אֶת־הָרֹאשׁ וְאֶת־הַפָּדֶר עַל־הָעֵצִים אֲשֶׁר עַל־
הָאֵשׁ אֲשֶׁר עַל־הַמִּזְבֵּחַ: ט וְקִרְבּוֹ וּכְרָעָיו יִרְחַץ בַּמָּיִם
וְהִקְטִיר הַכֹּהֵן אֶת־הַכֹּל הַמִּזְבֵּחָה עֹלָה אִשֵּׁה רֵיחַ־נִיחוֹחַ
לַיהוָה: ס [ישראל] י וְאִם־מִן־הַצֹּאן קָרְבָּנוֹ מִן־הַכְּשָׂבִים
אוֹ מִן־הָעִזִּים לְעֹלָה זָכָר תָּמִים יַקְרִיבֶנּוּ: יא וְשָׁחַט אֹתוֹ עַל
יֶרֶךְ הַמִּזְבֵּחַ צָפֹנָה לִפְנֵי יְהוָה וְזָרְקוּ בְּנֵי אַהֲרֹן הַכֹּהֲנִים אֶת־
דָּמוֹ עַל־הַמִּזְבֵּחַ סָבִיב: יב וְנִתַּח אֹתוֹ לִנְתָחָיו וְאֶת־רֹאשׁוֹ
וְאֶת־פִּדְרוֹ וְעָרַךְ הַכֹּהֵן אֹתָם עַל־הָעֵצִים אֲשֶׁר עַל־הָאֵשׁ
אֲשֶׁר עַל־הַמִּזְבֵּחַ: יג וְהַקֶּרֶב וְהַכְּרָעַיִם יִרְחַץ בַּמָּיִם וְהִקְרִיב
הַכֹּהֵן אֶת־הַכֹּל וְהִקְטִיר הַמִּזְבֵּחָה עֹלָה הוּא אִשֵּׁה רֵיחַ
נִיחֹחַ לַיהוָה:

פרשת צו

פרק ו א וַיְדַבֵּר יְהוָה אֶל־מֹשֶׁה לֵּאמֹר: ב צַו אֶת־אַהֲרֹן
וְאֶת־בָּנָיו לֵאמֹר זֹאת תּוֹרַת הָעֹלָה הִוא הָעֹלָה עַל מוֹקְדָה
עַל־הַמִּזְבֵּחַ כָּל־הַלַּיְלָה עַד־הַבֹּקֶר וְאֵשׁ הַמִּזְבֵּחַ תּוּקַד בּוֹ:
ג וְלָבַשׁ הַכֹּהֵן מִדּוֹ בַד וּמִכְנְסֵי־בַד יִלְבַּשׁ עַל־בְּשָׂרוֹ וְהֵרִים
אֶת־הַדֶּשֶׁן אֲשֶׁר תֹּאכַל הָאֵשׁ אֶת־הָעֹלָה עַל־הַמִּזְבֵּחַ
וְשָׂמוֹ אֵצֶל הַמִּזְבֵּחַ: [לוי] ד וּפָשַׁט אֶת־בְּגָדָיו וְלָבַשׁ בְּגָדִים

אֲחֵרִים וְהוֹצִיא אֶת־הַדֶּשֶׁן אֶל־מִחוּץ לַמַּחֲנֶה אֶל־מָקוֹם
טָהוֹר׃ ה וְהָאֵשׁ עַל־הַמִּזְבֵּחַ תּוּקַד־בּוֹ לֹא תִכְבֶּה וּבִעֵר
עָלֶיהָ הַכֹּהֵן עֵצִים בַּבֹּקֶר בַּבֹּקֶר וְעָרַךְ עָלֶיהָ הָעֹלָה וְהִקְטִיר
עָלֶיהָ חֶלְבֵי הַשְּׁלָמִים׃ ו אֵשׁ תָּמִיד תּוּקַד עַל־הַמִּזְבֵּחַ
לֹא תִכְבֶּה׃ ס [ישראל] ז וְזֹאת תּוֹרַת הַמִּנְחָה הַקְרֵב
אֹתָהּ בְּנֵי־אַהֲרֹן לִפְנֵי יְהוָה אֶל־פְּנֵי הַמִּזְבֵּחַ׃ ח וְהֵרִים מִמֶּנּוּ
בְּקֻמְצוֹ מִסֹּלֶת הַמִּנְחָה וּמִשַּׁמְנָהּ וְאֵת כָּל־הַלְּבֹנָה אֲשֶׁר
עַל־הַמִּנְחָה וְהִקְטִיר הַמִּזְבֵּחַ רֵיחַ נִיחֹחַ אַזְכָּרָתָהּ לַיהוָה׃
ט וְהַנּוֹתֶרֶת מִמֶּנָּה יֹאכְלוּ אַהֲרֹן וּבָנָיו מַצּוֹת תֵּאָכֵל בְּמָקוֹם
קָדֹשׁ בַּחֲצַר אֹהֶל־מוֹעֵד יֹאכְלוּהָ׃ י לֹא תֵאָפֶה חָמֵץ חֶלְקָם
נָתַתִּי אֹתָהּ מֵאִשָּׁי קֹדֶשׁ קָדָשִׁים הִוא כַּחַטָּאת וְכָאָשָׁם׃
יא כָּל־זָכָר בִּבְנֵי אַהֲרֹן יֹאכְלֶנָּה חָק־עוֹלָם לְדֹרֹתֵיכֶם מֵאִשֵּׁי
יְהוָה כֹּל אֲשֶׁר־יִגַּע בָּהֶם יִקְדָּשׁ׃

פרשת שמיני

פרק ט א וַיְהִי בַּיּוֹם הַשְּׁמִינִי קָרָא מֹשֶׁה לְאַהֲרֹן וּלְבָנָיו וּלְזִקְנֵי
יִשְׂרָאֵל׃ ב וַיֹּאמֶר אֶל־אַהֲרֹן קַח־לְךָ עֵגֶל בֶּן־בָּקָר לְחַטָּאת
וְאַיִל לְעֹלָה תְּמִימִם וְהַקְרֵב לִפְנֵי יְהוָה׃ ג וְאֶל־בְּנֵי יִשְׂרָאֵל
תְּדַבֵּר לֵאמֹר קְחוּ שְׂעִיר־עִזִּים לְחַטָּאת וְעֵגֶל וָכֶבֶשׂ בְּנֵי־
שָׁנָה תְּמִימִם לְעֹלָה׃ ד וְשׁוֹר וָאַיִל לִשְׁלָמִים לִזְבֹּחַ לִפְנֵי
יְהוָה וּמִנְחָה בְּלוּלָה בַשָּׁמֶן כִּי הַיּוֹם יְהוָה נִרְאָה אֲלֵיכֶם׃
ה וַיִּקְחוּ אֵת אֲשֶׁר צִוָּה מֹשֶׁה אֶל־פְּנֵי אֹהֶל מוֹעֵד וַיִּקְרְבוּ כָּל־
הָעֵדָה וַיַּעַמְדוּ לִפְנֵי יְהוָה׃ ו וַיֹּאמֶר מֹשֶׁה זֶה הַדָּבָר אֲשֶׁר־
צִוָּה יְהוָה תַּעֲשׂוּ וְיֵרָא אֲלֵיכֶם כְּבוֹד יְהוָה׃ [לוי] ז וַיֹּאמֶר
מֹשֶׁה אֶל־אַהֲרֹן קְרַב אֶל־הַמִּזְבֵּחַ וַעֲשֵׂה אֶת־חַטָּאתְךָ וְאֶת־
עֹלָתֶךָ וְכַפֵּר בַּעַדְךָ וּבְעַד הָעָם וַעֲשֵׂה אֶת־קָרְבַּן הָעָם וְכַפֵּר

בַּעֲדָם כַּאֲשֶׁר צִוָּה יְהוָה׃ ח וַיִּקְרַב אַהֲרֹן אֶל־הַמִּזְבֵּחַ וַיִּשְׁחַט
אֶת־עֵגֶל הַחַטָּאת אֲשֶׁר־לוֹ׃ ט וַיַּקְרִבוּ בְּנֵי אַהֲרֹן אֶת־הַדָּם
אֵלָיו וַיִּטְבֹּל אֶצְבָּעוֹ בַּדָּם וַיִּתֵּן עַל־קַרְנוֹת הַמִּזְבֵּחַ וְאֶת־
הַדָּם יָצַק אֶל־יְסוֹד הַמִּזְבֵּחַ׃ י וְאֶת־הַחֵלֶב וְאֶת־הַכְּלָיֹת
וְאֶת־הַיֹּתֶרֶת מִן־הַכָּבֵד מִן־הַחַטָּאת הִקְטִיר הַמִּזְבֵּחָה
כַּאֲשֶׁר צִוָּה יְהוָה אֶת־מֹשֶׁה׃ [ישראל] יא וְאֶת־הַבָּשָׂר וְאֶת־
הָעוֹר שָׂרַף בָּאֵשׁ מִחוּץ לַמַּחֲנֶה׃ יב וַיִּשְׁחַט אֶת־הָעֹלָה
וַיַּמְצִאוּ בְּנֵי אַהֲרֹן אֵלָיו אֶת־הַדָּם וַיִּזְרְקֵהוּ עַל־הַמִּזְבֵּחַ
סָבִיב׃ יג וְאֶת־הָעֹלָה הִמְצִיאוּ אֵלָיו לִנְתָחֶיהָ וְאֶת־הָרֹאשׁ
וַיַּקְטֵר עַל־הַמִּזְבֵּחַ׃ יד וַיִּרְחַץ אֶת־הַקֶּרֶב וְאֶת־הַכְּרָעָיִם
וַיַּקְטֵר עַל־הָעֹלָה הַמִּזְבֵּחָה׃ טו וַיַּקְרֵב אֵת קָרְבַּן הָעָם
וַיִּקַּח אֶת־שְׂעִיר הַחַטָּאת אֲשֶׁר לָעָם וַיִּשְׁחָטֵהוּ וַיְחַטְּאֵהוּ
כָּרִאשׁוֹן׃ טז וַיַּקְרֵב אֶת־הָעֹלָה וַיַּעֲשֶׂהָ כַּמִּשְׁפָּט׃

פרשת תזריע

פרק יב א וַיְדַבֵּר יְהוָה אֶל־מֹשֶׁה לֵּאמֹר׃ ב דַּבֵּר אֶל־בְּנֵי יִשְׂרָאֵל
לֵאמֹר אִשָּׁה כִּי תַזְרִיעַ וְיָלְדָה זָכָר וְטָמְאָה שִׁבְעַת יָמִים כִּימֵי
נִדַּת דְּוֺתָהּ תִּטְמָא׃ ג וּבַיּוֹם הַשְּׁמִינִי יִמּוֹל בְּשַׂר עָרְלָתוֹ׃
ד וּשְׁלֹשִׁים יוֹם וּשְׁלֹשֶׁת יָמִים תֵּשֵׁב בִּדְמֵי טָהֳרָה בְּכָל־קֹדֶשׁ
לֹא־תִגָּע וְאֶל־הַמִּקְדָּשׁ לֹא תָבֹא עַד־מְלֹאת יְמֵי טָהֳרָהּ׃
[לוי] ה וְאִם־נְקֵבָה תֵלֵד וְטָמְאָה שְׁבֻעַיִם כְּנִדָּתָהּ וְשִׁשִּׁים יוֹם
וְשֵׁשֶׁת יָמִים תֵּשֵׁב עַל־דְּמֵי טָהֳרָה׃ ו וּבִמְלֹאת | יְמֵי טָהֳרָהּ
לְבֵן אוֹ לְבַת תָּבִיא כֶּבֶשׂ בֶּן־שְׁנָתוֹ לְעֹלָה וּבֶן־יוֹנָה אוֹ־תֹר
לְחַטָּאת אֶל־פֶּתַח אֹהֶל־מוֹעֵד אֶל־הַכֹּהֵן׃ ז וְהִקְרִיבוֹ לִפְנֵי
יְהוָה וְכִפֶּר עָלֶיהָ וְטָהֲרָה מִמְּקֹר דָּמֶיהָ זֹאת תּוֹרַת הַיֹּלֶדֶת
לַזָּכָר אוֹ לַנְּקֵבָה׃ ח וְאִם־לֹא תִמְצָא יָדָהּ דֵּי שֶׂה וְלָקְחָה

שְׁתֵּי־תֹרִים אוֹ שְׁנֵי בְּנֵי יוֹנָה אֶחָד לְעֹלָה וְאֶחָד לְחַטָּאת
וְכִפֶּר עָלֶיהָ הַכֹּהֵן וְטָהֵרָה: פ [ישראל] **פרק יג** א וַיְדַבֵּר יְהֹוָה
אֶל־מֹשֶׁה וְאֶל־אַהֲרֹן לֵאמֹר: ב אָדָם כִּי־יִהְיֶה בְעוֹר־בְּשָׂרוֹ
שְׂאֵת אוֹ־סַפַּחַת אוֹ בַהֶרֶת וְהָיָה בְעוֹר־בְּשָׂרוֹ לְנֶגַע צָרָעַת
וְהוּבָא אֶל־אַהֲרֹן הַכֹּהֵן אוֹ אֶל־אַחַד מִבָּנָיו הַכֹּהֲנִים:
ג וְרָאָה הַכֹּהֵן אֶת־הַנֶּגַע בְּעוֹר־הַבָּשָׂר וְשֵׂעָר בַּנֶּגַע הָפַךְ |
לָבָן וּמַרְאֵה הַנֶּגַע עָמֹק מֵעוֹר בְּשָׂרוֹ נֶגַע צָרַעַת הוּא וְרָאָהוּ
הַכֹּהֵן וְטִמֵּא אֹתוֹ: ד וְאִם־בַּהֶרֶת לְבָנָה הִוא בְּעוֹר בְּשָׂרוֹ
וְעָמֹק אֵין־מַרְאֶהָ מִן־הָעוֹר וּשְׂעָרָה לֹא־הָפַךְ לָבָן וְהִסְגִּיר
הַכֹּהֵן אֶת־הַנֶּגַע שִׁבְעַת יָמִים: ה וְרָאָהוּ הַכֹּהֵן בַּיּוֹם הַשְּׁבִיעִי
וְהִנֵּה הַנֶּגַע עָמַד בְּעֵינָיו לֹא־פָשָׂה הַנֶּגַע בָּעוֹר וְהִסְגִּירוֹ
הַכֹּהֵן שִׁבְעַת יָמִים שֵׁנִית:

פרשת מצורע

פרק יד א וַיְדַבֵּר יְהֹוָה אֶל־מֹשֶׁה לֵּאמֹר: ב זֹאת תִּהְיֶה תּוֹרַת
הַמְּצֹרָע בְּיוֹם טָהֳרָתוֹ וְהוּבָא אֶל־הַכֹּהֵן: ג וְיָצָא הַכֹּהֵן
אֶל־מִחוּץ לַמַּחֲנֶה וְרָאָה הַכֹּהֵן וְהִנֵּה נִרְפָּא נֶגַע־הַצָּרַעַת
מִן־הַצָּרוּעַ: ד וְצִוָּה הַכֹּהֵן וְלָקַח לַמִּטַּהֵר שְׁתֵּי־צִפֳּרִים
חַיּוֹת טְהֹרוֹת וְעֵץ אֶרֶז וּשְׁנִי תוֹלַעַת וְאֵזֹב: ה וְצִוָּה הַכֹּהֵן
וְשָׁחַט אֶת־הַצִּפּוֹר הָאֶחָת אֶל־כְּלִי־חֶרֶשׂ עַל־מַיִם חַיִּים:
[לוי] ו אֶת־הַצִּפֹּר הַחַיָּה יִקַּח אֹתָהּ וְאֶת־עֵץ הָאֶרֶז וְאֶת־
שְׁנִי הַתּוֹלַעַת וְאֶת־הָאֵזֹב וְטָבַל אוֹתָם וְאֵת | הַצִּפֹּר הַחַיָּה
בְּדַם הַצִּפֹּר הַשְּׁחֻטָה עַל הַמַּיִם הַחַיִּים: ז וְהִזָּה עַל הַמִּטַּהֵר
מִן־הַצָּרַעַת שֶׁבַע פְּעָמִים וְטִהֲרוֹ וְשִׁלַּח אֶת־הַצִּפֹּר הַחַיָּה
עַל־פְּנֵי הַשָּׂדֶה: ח וְכִבֶּס הַמִּטַּהֵר אֶת־בְּגָדָיו וְגִלַּח אֶת־כָּל־
שְׂעָרוֹ וְרָחַץ בַּמַּיִם וְטָהֵר וְאַחַר יָבוֹא אֶל־הַמַּחֲנֶה וְיָשַׁב

מִח֥וּץ לְאָהֳל֖וֹ שִׁבְעַ֥ת יָמִֽים׃ ט וְהָיָה֩ בַיּ֨וֹם הַשְּׁבִיעִ֜י יְגַלַּ֣ח
אֶת־כָּל־שְׂעָר֗וֹ אֶת־רֹאשׁ֤וֹ וְאֶת־זְקָנוֹ֙ וְאֵת֙ גַּבֹּ֣ת עֵינָ֔יו וְאֶת־
כָּל־שְׂעָר֖וֹ יְגַלֵּ֑חַ וְכִבֶּ֣ס אֶת־בְּגָדָ֗יו וְרָחַ֧ץ אֶת־בְּשָׂר֛וֹ בַּמַּ֖יִם
וְטָהֵֽר׃ [ישראל] י וּבַיּ֣וֹם הַשְּׁמִינִ֗י יִקַּ֤ח שְׁנֵֽי־כְבָשִׂים֙ תְּמִימִ֔ם
וְכַבְשָׂ֥ה אַחַ֛ת בַּת־שְׁנָתָ֖הּ תְּמִימָ֑ה וּשְׁלֹשָׁ֣ה עֶשְׂרֹנִ֗ים סֹ֤לֶת
מִנְחָה֙ בְּלוּלָ֣ה בַשֶּׁ֔מֶן וְלֹ֥ג אֶחָ֖ד שָֽׁמֶן׃ יא וְהֶֽעֱמִ֞יד הַכֹּהֵ֣ן
הַֽמְטַהֵ֗ר אֵ֥ת הָאִ֛ישׁ הַמִּטַּהֵ֖ר וְאֹתָ֑ם לִפְנֵ֣י יְהוָ֔ה פֶּ֖תַח אֹ֥הֶל
מוֹעֵֽד׃ יב וְלָקַ֨ח הַכֹּהֵ֜ן אֶת־הַכֶּ֣בֶשׂ הָֽאֶחָ֗ד וְהִקְרִ֥יב אֹת֛וֹ
לְאָשָׁ֖ם וְאֶת־לֹ֣ג הַשָּׁ֑מֶן וְהֵנִ֥יף אֹתָ֛ם תְּנוּפָ֖ה לִפְנֵ֥י יְהוָֽה׃

פרשת אחרי מות

פרק טז א וַיְדַבֵּ֤ר יְהוָה֙ אֶל־מֹשֶׁ֔ה אַחֲרֵ֣י מ֔וֹת שְׁנֵ֖י בְּנֵ֣י אַהֲרֹ֑ן
בְּקָרְבָתָ֥ם לִפְנֵֽי־יְהוָ֖ה וַיָּמֻֽתוּ׃ ב וַיֹּ֨אמֶר יְהוָ֜ה אֶל־מֹשֶׁ֗ה
דַּבֵּר֮ אֶל־אַהֲרֹ֣ן אָחִיךָ֒ וְאַל־יָבֹ֤א בְכָל־עֵת֙ אֶל־הַקֹּ֔דֶשׁ מִבֵּ֖ית
לַפָּרֹ֑כֶת אֶל־פְּנֵ֨י הַכַּפֹּ֜רֶת אֲשֶׁ֤ר עַל־הָאָרֹן֙ וְלֹ֣א יָמ֔וּת כִּ֚י בֶּֽעָנָ֔ן
אֵרָאֶ֖ה עַל־הַכַּפֹּֽרֶת׃ ג בְּזֹ֛את יָבֹ֥א אַהֲרֹ֖ן אֶל־הַקֹּ֑דֶשׁ בְּפַ֧ר
בֶּן־בָּקָ֛ר לְחַטָּ֖את וְאַ֥יִל לְעֹלָֽה׃ ד כְּתֹֽנֶת־בַּ֨ד קֹ֜דֶשׁ יִלְבָּ֗שׁ
וּמִֽכְנְסֵי־בַד֮ יִהְי֣וּ עַל־בְּשָׂרוֹ֒ וּבְאַבְנֵ֥ט בַּד֙ יַחְגֹּ֔ר וּבְמִצְנֶ֥פֶת
בַּ֖ד יִצְנֹ֑ף בִּגְדֵי־קֹ֣דֶשׁ הֵ֔ם וְרָחַ֥ץ בַּמַּ֛יִם אֶת־בְּשָׂר֖וֹ וּלְבֵשָֽׁם׃
ה וּמֵאֵ֗ת עֲדַת֙ בְּנֵ֣י יִשְׂרָאֵ֔ל יִקַּ֛ח שְׁנֵֽי־שְׂעִירֵ֥י עִזִּ֖ים לְחַטָּ֑את
וְאַ֥יִל אֶחָ֖ד לְעֹלָֽה׃ ו וְהִקְרִ֧יב אַהֲרֹ֛ן אֶת־פַּ֥ר הַחַטָּ֖את אֲשֶׁר־
ל֑וֹ וְכִפֶּ֥ר בַּעֲד֖וֹ וּבְעַ֥ד בֵּיתֽוֹ׃ [לוי] ז וְלָקַ֖ח אֶת־שְׁנֵ֣י הַשְּׂעִירִ֑ם
וְהֶעֱמִ֤יד אֹתָם֙ לִפְנֵ֣י יְהוָ֔ה פֶּ֖תַח אֹ֥הֶל מוֹעֵֽד׃ ח וְנָתַ֧ן אַהֲרֹ֛ן
עַל־שְׁנֵ֥י הַשְּׂעִירִ֖ם גֹּרָל֑וֹת גּוֹרָ֤ל אֶחָד֙ לַֽיהוָ֔ה וְגוֹרָ֥ל אֶחָ֖ד
לַעֲזָאזֵֽל׃ ט וְהִקְרִ֤יב אַהֲרֹן֙ אֶת־הַשָּׂעִ֔יר אֲשֶׁ֨ר עָלָ֥ה עָלָ֛יו
הַגּוֹרָ֖ל לַֽיהוָ֑ה וְעָשָׂ֖הוּ חַטָּֽאת׃ י וְהַשָּׂעִ֗יר אֲשֶׁר֩ עָלָ֨ה עָלָ֤יו

הַגּוֹרָל לַעֲזָאזֵל יָעֳמַד־חַי לִפְנֵי יְהוָה לְכַפֵּר עָלָיו לְשַׁלַּח
אֹתוֹ לַעֲזָאזֵל הַמִּדְבָּרָה: יא וְהִקְרִיב אַהֲרֹן אֶת־פַּר הַחַטָּאת
אֲשֶׁר־לוֹ וְכִפֶּר בַּעֲדוֹ וּבְעַד בֵּיתוֹ וְשָׁחַט אֶת־פַּר הַחַטָּאת
אֲשֶׁר־לוֹ: [ישראל] יב וְלָקַח מְלֹא־הַמַּחְתָּה גַּחֲלֵי־אֵשׁ מֵעַל
הַמִּזְבֵּחַ מִלִּפְנֵי יְהוָה וּמְלֹא חָפְנָיו קְטֹרֶת סַמִּים דַּקָּה וְהֵבִיא
מִבֵּית לַפָּרֹכֶת: יג וְנָתַן אֶת־הַקְּטֹרֶת עַל־הָאֵשׁ לִפְנֵי יְהוָה
וְכִסָּה | עֲנַן הַקְּטֹרֶת אֶת־הַכַּפֹּרֶת אֲשֶׁר עַל־הָעֵדוּת וְלֹא
יָמוּת: יד וְלָקַח מִדַּם הַפָּר וְהִזָּה בְאֶצְבָּעוֹ עַל־פְּנֵי הַכַּפֹּרֶת
קֵדְמָה וְלִפְנֵי הַכַּפֹּרֶת יַזֶּה שֶׁבַע־פְּעָמִים מִן־הַדָּם בְּאֶצְבָּעוֹ:
טו וְשָׁחַט אֶת־שְׂעִיר הַחַטָּאת אֲשֶׁר לָעָם וְהֵבִיא אֶת־דָּמוֹ
אֶל־מִבֵּית לַפָּרֹכֶת וְעָשָׂה אֶת־דָּמוֹ כַּאֲשֶׁר עָשָׂה לְדַם הַפָּר
וְהִזָּה אֹתוֹ עַל־הַכַּפֹּרֶת וְלִפְנֵי הַכַּפֹּרֶת: טז וְכִפֶּר עַל־הַקֹּדֶשׁ
מִטֻּמְאֹת בְּנֵי יִשְׂרָאֵל וּמִפִּשְׁעֵיהֶם לְכָל־חַטֹּאתָם וְכֵן יַעֲשֶׂה
לְאֹהֶל מוֹעֵד הַשֹּׁכֵן אִתָּם בְּתוֹךְ טֻמְאֹתָם: יז וְכָל־אָדָם לֹא־
יִהְיֶה | בְּאֹהֶל מוֹעֵד בְּבֹאוֹ לְכַפֵּר בַּקֹּדֶשׁ עַד־צֵאתוֹ וְכִפֶּר
בַּעֲדוֹ וּבְעַד בֵּיתוֹ וּבְעַד כָּל־קְהַל יִשְׂרָאֵל:

פרשת קדושים

פרק יט א וַיְדַבֵּר יְהוָה אֶל־מֹשֶׁה לֵּאמֹר: ב דַּבֵּר אֶל־כָּל־עֲדַת
בְּנֵי־יִשְׂרָאֵל וְאָמַרְתָּ אֲלֵהֶם קְדֹשִׁים תִּהְיוּ כִּי קָדוֹשׁ אֲנִי
יְהוָה אֱלֹהֵיכֶם: ג אִישׁ אִמּוֹ וְאָבִיו תִּירָאוּ וְאֶת־שַׁבְּתֹתַי
תִּשְׁמֹרוּ אֲנִי יְהוָה אֱלֹהֵיכֶם: ד אַל־תִּפְנוּ אֶל־הָאֱלִילִם וֵאלֹהֵי
מַסֵּכָה לֹא תַעֲשׂוּ לָכֶם אֲנִי יְהוָה אֱלֹהֵיכֶם: [לוי] ה וְכִי תִזְבְּחוּ
זֶבַח שְׁלָמִים לַיהוָה לִרְצֹנְכֶם תִּזְבָּחֻהוּ: ו בְּיוֹם זִבְחֲכֶם יֵאָכֵל
וּמִמָּחֳרָת וְהַנּוֹתָר עַד־יוֹם הַשְּׁלִישִׁי בָּאֵשׁ יִשָּׂרֵף: ז וְאִם
הֵאָכֹל יֵאָכֵל בַּיּוֹם הַשְּׁלִישִׁי פִּגּוּל הוּא לֹא יֵרָצֶה: ח וְאֹכְלָיו

עֲוֺנ֖וֹ יִשָּׂ֑א כִּֽי־אֶת־קֹ֥דֶשׁ יְהֹוָ֖ה חִלֵּ֑ל וְנִכְרְתָ֛ה הַנֶּ֥פֶשׁ הַהִ֖וא
מֵעַמֶּֽיהָ׃ ט וּֽבְקֻצְרְכֶם֙ אֶת־קְצִ֣יר אַרְצְכֶ֔ם לֹ֥א תְכַלֶּ֛ה פְּאַ֥ת
שָׂדְךָ֖ לִקְצֹ֑ר וְלֶ֥קֶט קְצִֽירְךָ֖ לֹ֥א תְלַקֵּֽט׃ י וְכַרְמְךָ֙ לֹ֣א תְעוֹלֵ֔ל
וּפֶ֥רֶט כַּרְמְךָ֖ לֹ֣א תְלַקֵּ֑ט לֶֽעָנִ֤י וְלַגֵּר֙ תַּעֲזֹ֣ב אֹתָ֔ם אֲנִ֖י יְהֹוָ֥ה
אֱלֹהֵיכֶֽם׃ [ישראל] יא לֹ֖א תִּגְנֹ֑בוּ וְלֹא־תְכַחֲשׁ֥וּ וְלֹֽא־תְשַׁקְּר֖וּ
אִ֥ישׁ בַּעֲמִיתֽוֹ׃ יב וְלֹֽא־תִשָּׁבְע֥וּ בִשְׁמִ֖י לַשָּׁ֑קֶר וְחִלַּלְתָּ֛ אֶת־
שֵׁ֥ם אֱלֹהֶ֖יךָ אֲנִ֥י יְהֹוָֽה׃ יג לֹא־תַעֲשֹׁ֥ק אֶת־רֵֽעֲךָ֖ וְלֹ֣א תִגְזֹ֑ל
לֹֽא־תָלִ֞ין פְּעֻלַּ֥ת שָׂכִ֛יר אִתְּךָ֖ עַד־בֹּֽקֶר׃ יד לֹא־תְקַלֵּ֣ל חֵרֵ֔שׁ
וְלִפְנֵ֣י עִוֵּ֔ר לֹ֥א תִתֵּ֖ן מִכְשֹׁ֑ל וְיָרֵ֥אתָ מֵּאֱלֹהֶ֖יךָ אֲנִ֥י יְהֹוָֽה׃

פרשת אמור

פרק כא א וַיֹּ֤אמֶר יְהֹוָה֙ אֶל־מֹשֶׁ֔ה אֱמֹ֥ר אֶל־הַכֹּהֲנִ֖ים בְּנֵ֣י
אַהֲרֹ֑ן וְאָמַרְתָּ֣ אֲלֵהֶ֔ם לְנֶ֥פֶשׁ לֹֽא־יִטַּמָּ֖א בְּעַמָּֽיו׃ ב כִּ֚י אִם־
לִשְׁאֵר֔וֹ הַקָּרֹ֖ב אֵלָ֑יו לְאִמּ֣וֹ וּלְאָבִ֔יו וְלִבְנ֥וֹ וּלְבִתּ֖וֹ וּלְאָחִֽיו׃
ג וְלַאֲחֹת֤וֹ הַבְּתוּלָה֙ הַקְּרוֹבָ֣ה אֵלָ֔יו אֲשֶׁ֥ר לֹא־הָיְתָ֖ה לְאִ֑ישׁ
לָ֖הּ יִטַּמָּֽא׃ ד לֹ֥א יִטַּמָּ֖א בַּ֣עַל בְּעַמָּ֑יו לְהֵ֖חַלּֽוֹ׃ ה לֹֽא־יקרחה▽
קָרְחָה֙ בְּרֹאשָׁ֔ם וּפְאַ֥ת זְקָנָ֖ם לֹ֣א יְגַלֵּ֑חוּ וּבִ֨בְשָׂרָ֔ם לֹ֥א יִשְׂרְט֖וּ
שָׂרָֽטֶת׃ ו קְדֹשִׁ֤ים יִהְיוּ֙ לֵאלֹ֣הֵיהֶ֔ם וְלֹ֣א יְחַלְּל֔וּ שֵׁ֖ם אֱלֹהֵיהֶ֑ם
כִּ֩י אֶת־אִשֵּׁ֨י יְהֹוָ֜ה לֶ֧חֶם אֱלֹהֵיהֶ֛ם הֵ֥ם מַקְרִיבִ֖ם וְהָ֥יוּ קֹֽדֶשׁ׃
[לוי] ז אִשָּׁ֨ה זֹנָ֤ה וַחֲלָלָה֙ לֹ֣א יִקָּ֔חוּ וְאִשָּׁ֛ה גְּרוּשָׁ֥ה מֵאִישָׁ֖הּ
לֹ֣א יִקָּ֑חוּ כִּֽי־קָדֹ֥שׁ ה֖וּא לֵאלֹהָֽיו׃ ח וְקִדַּשְׁתּ֔וֹ כִּֽי־אֶת־לֶ֥חֶם
אֱלֹהֶ֖יךָ ה֣וּא מַקְרִ֑יב קָדֹשׁ֙ יִֽהְיֶה־לָּ֔ךְ כִּ֣י קָד֔וֹשׁ אֲנִ֥י יְהֹוָ֖ה
מְקַדִּשְׁכֶֽם׃ ט וּבַת֙ אִ֣ישׁ כֹּהֵ֔ן כִּ֥י תֵחֵ֖ל לִזְנ֑וֹת אֶת־אָבִ֙יהָ֙
הִ֣יא מְחַלֶּ֔לֶת בָּאֵ֖שׁ תִּשָּׂרֵֽף׃ ס י וְהַכֹּהֵן֩ הַגָּד֨וֹל מֵאֶחָ֜יו
אֲשֶׁר־יוּצַ֥ק עַל־רֹאשׁ֣וֹ ׀ שֶׁ֣מֶן הַמִּשְׁחָ֗ה וּמִלֵּ֥א אֶת־יָד֖וֹ לִלְבֹּ֣שׁ

▽ יִקְרְח֤וּ

אֶת־הַבְּגָדִים אֶת־רֹאשׁוֹ לֹא יִפְרָע וּבְגָדָיו לֹא יִפְרֹם: יא וְעַל
כָּל־נַפְשֹׁת מֵת לֹא יָבֹא לְאָבִיו וּלְאִמּוֹ לֹא יִטַּמָּא: יב וּמִן־
הַמִּקְדָּשׁ לֹא יֵצֵא וְלֹא יְחַלֵּל אֵת מִקְדַּשׁ אֱלֹהָיו כִּי נֵזֶר
שֶׁמֶן מִשְׁחַת אֱלֹהָיו עָלָיו אֲנִי יְהֹוָה: [ישראל] יג וְהוּא אִשָּׁה
בִבְתוּלֶיהָ יִקָּח: יד אַלְמָנָה וּגְרוּשָׁה וַחֲלָלָה זֹנָה אֶת־אֵלֶּה
לֹא יִקָּח כִּי אִם־בְּתוּלָה מֵעַמָּיו יִקַּח אִשָּׁה: טו וְלֹא־יְחַלֵּל
זַרְעוֹ בְּעַמָּיו כִּי אֲנִי יְהֹוָה מְקַדְּשׁוֹ:

פרשת בהר

פרק כה א וַיְדַבֵּר יְהֹוָה אֶל־מֹשֶׁה בְּהַר סִינַי לֵאמֹר: ב דַּבֵּר
אֶל־בְּנֵי יִשְׂרָאֵל וְאָמַרְתָּ אֲלֵהֶם כִּי תָבֹאוּ אֶל־הָאָרֶץ
אֲשֶׁר אֲנִי נֹתֵן לָכֶם וְשָׁבְתָה הָאָרֶץ שַׁבָּת לַיהֹוָה: ג שֵׁשׁ
שָׁנִים תִּזְרַע שָׂדֶךָ וְשֵׁשׁ שָׁנִים תִּזְמֹר כַּרְמֶךָ וְאָסַפְתָּ אֶת־
תְּבוּאָתָהּ: [לוי] ד וּבַשָּׁנָה הַשְּׁבִיעִת שַׁבַּת שַׁבָּתוֹן יִהְיֶה
לָאָרֶץ שַׁבָּת לַיהֹוָה שָׂדְךָ לֹא תִזְרָע וְכַרְמְךָ לֹא תִזְמֹר:
ה אֵת סְפִיחַ קְצִירְךָ לֹא תִקְצוֹר וְאֶת־עִנְּבֵי נְזִירֶךָ לֹא תִבְצֹר
שְׁנַת שַׁבָּתוֹן יִהְיֶה לָאָרֶץ: ו וְהָיְתָה שַׁבַּת הָאָרֶץ לָכֶם
לְאָכְלָה לְךָ וּלְעַבְדְּךָ וְלַאֲמָתֶךָ וְלִשְׂכִירְךָ וּלְתוֹשָׁבְךָ הַגָּרִים
עִמָּךְ: ז וְלִבְהֶמְתְּךָ וְלַחַיָּה אֲשֶׁר בְּאַרְצֶךָ תִּהְיֶה כָל־תְּבוּאָתָהּ
לֶאֱכֹל: ס [ישראל] ח וְסָפַרְתָּ לְךָ שֶׁבַע שַׁבְּתֹת שָׁנִים
שֶׁבַע שָׁנִים שֶׁבַע פְּעָמִים וְהָיוּ לְךָ יְמֵי שֶׁבַע שַׁבְּתֹת הַשָּׁנִים
תֵּשַׁע וְאַרְבָּעִים שָׁנָה: ט וְהַעֲבַרְתָּ שׁוֹפַר תְּרוּעָה בַּחֹדֶשׁ
הַשְּׁבִעִי בֶּעָשׂוֹר לַחֹדֶשׁ בְּיוֹם הַכִּפֻּרִים תַּעֲבִירוּ שׁוֹפָר בְּכָל־
אַרְצְכֶם: י וְקִדַּשְׁתֶּם אֵת שְׁנַת הַחֲמִשִּׁים שָׁנָה וּקְרָאתֶם
דְּרוֹר בָּאָרֶץ לְכָל־יֹשְׁבֶיהָ יוֹבֵל הִוא תִּהְיֶה לָכֶם וְשַׁבְתֶּם
אִישׁ אֶל־אֲחֻזָּתוֹ וְאִישׁ אֶל־מִשְׁפַּחְתּוֹ תָּשֻׁבוּ: יא יוֹבֵל הִוא

שְׁנַ֣ת הַחֲמִשִּׁ֔ים שָׁנָ֖ה תִּהְיֶ֣ה לָכֶ֑ם לֹ֣א תִזְרָ֔עוּ וְלֹ֤א תִקְצְרוּ֙
אֶת־סְפִיחֶ֔יהָ וְלֹ֥א תִבְצְר֖וּ אֶת־נְזִרֶֽיהָ׃ יב כִּ֚י יוֹבֵ֣ל הִ֔וא קֹ֖דֶשׁ
תִּהְיֶ֣ה לָכֶ֑ם מִ֨ן־הַשָּׂדֶ֔ה תֹּאכְל֖וּ אֶת־תְּבוּאָתָֽהּ׃ יג בִּשְׁנַ֥ת
הַיּוֹבֵ֖ל הַזֹּ֑את תָּשֻׁ֕בוּ אִ֖ישׁ אֶל־אֲחֻזָּתֽוֹ׃

פרשת בחקותי

פרק כו ג אִם־בְּחֻקֹּתַ֖י תֵּלֵ֑כוּ וְאֶת־מִצְוֺתַ֣י תִּשְׁמְר֔וּ וַעֲשִׂיתֶ֖ם
אֹתָֽם׃ ד וְנָתַתִּ֥י גִשְׁמֵיכֶ֖ם בְּעִתָּ֑ם וְנָתְנָ֤ה הָאָ֙רֶץ֙ יְבוּלָ֔הּ וְעֵ֥ץ
הַשָּׂדֶ֖ה יִתֵּ֥ן פִּרְיֽוֹ׃ ה וְהִשִּׂ֨יג לָכֶ֥ם דַּ֙יִשׁ֙ אֶת־בָּצִ֔יר וּבָצִ֖יר
יַשִּׂ֣יג אֶת־זָ֑רַע וַאֲכַלְתֶּ֤ם לַחְמְכֶם֙ לָשֹׂ֔בַע וִישַׁבְתֶּ֥ם לָבֶ֖טַח
בְּאַרְצְכֶֽם׃ [לוי] ו וְנָתַתִּ֤י שָׁלוֹם֙ בָּאָ֔רֶץ וּשְׁכַבְתֶּ֖ם וְאֵ֣ין מַחֲרִ֑יד
וְהִשְׁבַּתִּ֞י חַיָּ֤ה רָעָה֙ מִן־הָאָ֔רֶץ וְחֶ֖רֶב לֹא־תַעֲבֹ֥ר בְּאַרְצְכֶֽם׃
ז וּרְדַפְתֶּ֖ם אֶת־אֹיְבֵיכֶ֑ם וְנָפְל֥וּ לִפְנֵיכֶ֖ם לֶחָֽרֶב׃ ח וְרָדְפ֨וּ
מִכֶּ֤ם חֲמִשָּׁה֙ מֵאָ֔ה וּמֵאָ֥ה מִכֶּ֖ם רְבָבָ֣ה יִרְדֹּ֑פוּ וְנָפְל֧וּ אֹיְבֵיכֶ֛ם
לִפְנֵיכֶ֖ם לֶחָֽרֶב׃ ט וּפָנִ֣יתִי אֲלֵיכֶ֔ם וְהִפְרֵיתִ֣י אֶתְכֶ֔ם וְהִרְבֵּיתִ֖י
אֶתְכֶ֑ם וַהֲקִימֹתִ֥י אֶת־בְּרִיתִ֖י אִתְּכֶֽם׃ [ישראל] י וַאֲכַלְתֶּ֥ם יָשָׁ֖ן
נוֹשָׁ֑ן וְיָשָׁ֕ן מִפְּנֵ֥י חָדָ֖שׁ תּוֹצִֽיאוּ׃ יא וְנָתַתִּ֥י מִשְׁכָּנִ֖י בְּתוֹכְכֶ֑ם
וְלֹא־תִגְעַ֥ל נַפְשִׁ֖י אֶתְכֶֽם׃ יב וְהִתְהַלַּכְתִּי֙ בְּת֣וֹכְכֶ֔ם וְהָיִ֥יתִי
לָכֶ֖ם לֵאלֹהִ֑ים וְאַתֶּ֖ם תִּהְיוּ־לִ֥י לְעָֽם׃ יג אֲנִ֞י יְהוָ֣ה אֱלֹהֵיכֶ֗ם
אֲשֶׁ֨ר הוֹצֵ֤אתִי אֶתְכֶם֙ מֵאֶ֣רֶץ מִצְרַ֔יִם מִהְיֹ֥ת לָהֶ֖ם עֲבָדִ֑ים
וָאֶשְׁבֹּר֙ מֹטֹ֣ת עֻלְּכֶ֔ם וָאוֹלֵ֥ךְ אֶתְכֶ֖ם קֽוֹמְמִיּֽוּת׃

פרשת במדבר

פרק א א וַיְדַבֵּ֨ר יְהוָ֧ה אֶל־מֹשֶׁ֛ה בְּמִדְבַּ֥ר סִינַ֖י בְּאֹ֣הֶל מוֹעֵ֑ד
בְּאֶחָד֩ לַחֹ֨דֶשׁ הַשֵּׁנִ֜י בַּשָּׁנָ֣ה הַשֵּׁנִ֗ית לְצֵאתָ֛ם מֵאֶ֥רֶץ מִצְרַ֖יִם
לֵאמֹֽר׃ ב שְׂא֗וּ אֶת־רֹאשׁ֙ כָּל־עֲדַ֣ת בְּנֵֽי־יִשְׂרָאֵ֔ל לְמִשְׁפְּחֹתָ֖ם
לְבֵ֣ית אֲבֹתָ֑ם בְּמִסְפַּ֣ר שֵׁמ֔וֹת כָּל־זָכָ֖ר לְגֻלְגְּלֹתָֽם׃ ג מִבֶּ֨ן

עֶשְׂרִים שָׁנָה וָמַעְלָה כָּל־יֹצֵא צָבָא בְּיִשְׂרָאֵל תִּפְקְדוּ
אֹתָם לְצִבְאֹתָם אַתָּה וְאַהֲרֹן: ד וְאִתְּכֶם יִהְיוּ אִישׁ אִישׁ
לַמַּטֶּה אִישׁ רֹאשׁ לְבֵית־אֲבֹתָיו הוּא: [לוי] ה וְאֵלֶּה שְׁמוֹת
הָאֲנָשִׁים אֲשֶׁר יַעַמְדוּ אִתְּכֶם לִרְאוּבֵן אֱלִיצוּר בֶּן־שְׁדֵיאוּר:
ו לְשִׁמְעוֹן שְׁלֻמִיאֵל בֶּן־צוּרִישַׁדָּי: ז לִיהוּדָה נַחְשׁוֹן בֶּן־
עַמִּינָדָב: ח לְיִשָּׂשכָר נְתַנְאֵל בֶּן־צוּעָר: ט לִזְבוּלֻן אֱלִיאָב
בֶּן־חֵלֹן: י לִבְנֵי יוֹסֵף לְאֶפְרַיִם אֱלִישָׁמָע בֶּן־עַמִּיהוּד לִמְנַשֶּׁה
גַּמְלִיאֵל בֶּן־פְּדָהצוּר: יא לְבִנְיָמִן אֲבִידָן בֶּן־גִּדְעֹנִי: יב לְדָן
אֲחִיעֶזֶר בֶּן־עַמִּישַׁדָּי: יג לְאָשֵׁר פַּגְעִיאֵל בֶּן־עָכְרָן: יד לְגָד
אֶלְיָסָף בֶּן־דְּעוּאֵל: טו לְנַפְתָּלִי אֲחִירַע בֶּן־עֵינָן: טז אֵלֶּה
קריאֵי▽ הָעֵדָה נְשִׂיאֵי מַטּוֹת אֲבוֹתָם רָאשֵׁי אַלְפֵי יִשְׂרָאֵל
הֵם: [ישראל] יז וַיִּקַּח מֹשֶׁה וְאַהֲרֹן אֵת הָאֲנָשִׁים הָאֵלֶּה אֲשֶׁר
נִקְּבוּ בְּשֵׁמוֹת: יח וְאֵת כָּל־הָעֵדָה הִקְהִילוּ בְּאֶחָד לַחֹדֶשׁ
הַשֵּׁנִי וַיִּתְיַלְדוּ עַל־מִשְׁפְּחֹתָם לְבֵית אֲבֹתָם בְּמִסְפַּר שֵׁמוֹת
מִבֶּן עֶשְׂרִים שָׁנָה וָמַעְלָה לְגֻלְגְּלֹתָם: יט כַּאֲשֶׁר צִוָּה יְהוָה
אֶת־מֹשֶׁה וַיִּפְקְדֵם בְּמִדְבַּר סִינָי:

פרשת נשא

פרק ד כא וַיְדַבֵּר יְהוָה אֶל־מֹשֶׁה לֵּאמֹר: כב נָשֹׂא אֶת־רֹאשׁ בְּנֵי
גֵרְשׁוֹן גַּם־הֵם לְבֵית אֲבֹתָם לְמִשְׁפְּחֹתָם: כג מִבֶּן שְׁלֹשִׁים
שָׁנָה וָמַעְלָה עַד בֶּן־חֲמִשִּׁים שָׁנָה תִּפְקֹד אוֹתָם כָּל־הַבָּא
לִצְבֹא צָבָא לַעֲבֹד עֲבֹדָה בְּאֹהֶל מוֹעֵד: כד זֹאת עֲבֹדַת
מִשְׁפְּחֹת הַגֵּרְשֻׁנִּי לַעֲבֹד וּלְמַשָּׂא: [לוי] כה וְנָשְׂאוּ אֶת־יְרִיעֹת
הַמִּשְׁכָּן וְאֶת־אֹהֶל מוֹעֵד מִכְסֵהוּ וּמִכְסֵה הַתַּחַשׁ אֲשֶׁר־
עָלָיו מִלְמָעְלָה וְאֶת־מָסַךְ פֶּתַח אֹהֶל מוֹעֵד: כו וְאֵת קַלְעֵי

▽ קְרוּאֵי

הֶחָצֵ֜ר וְאֶת־מָסַ֣ךְ ׀ פֶּ֣תַח ׀ שַׁ֣עַר הֶחָצֵ֗ר אֲשֶׁ֨ר עַל־הַמִּשְׁכָּ֤ן
וְעַל־הַמִּזְבֵּ֙חַ֙ סָבִ֔יב וְאֵת֙ מֵיתְרֵיהֶ֔ם וְאֶת־כָּל־כְּלֵ֖י עֲבֹדָתָ֑ם
וְאֵ֨ת כָּל־אֲשֶׁ֧ר יֵעָשֶׂ֛ה לָהֶ֖ם וְעָבָֽדוּ׃ כז עַל־פִּי֩ אַהֲרֹ֨ן וּבָנָ֜יו
תִּֽהְיֶ֗ה כָּל־עֲבֹדַת֙ בְּנֵ֣י הַגֵּרְשֻׁנִּ֔י לְכָל־מַשָּׂאָ֖ם וּלְכֹ֣ל עֲבֹדָתָ֑ם
וּפְקַדְתֶּ֤ם עֲלֵהֶם֙ בְּמִשְׁמֶ֔רֶת אֵ֖ת כָּל־מַשָּׂאָֽם׃ כח זֹ֣את עֲבֹדַ֗ת
מִשְׁפְּחֹ֛ת בְּנֵ֥י הַגֵּרְשֻׁנִּ֖י בְּאֹ֣הֶל מוֹעֵ֑ד וּמִ֨שְׁמַרְתָּ֔ם בְּיַד֙ אִֽיתָמָ֔ר
בֶּן־אַהֲרֹ֖ן הַכֹּהֵֽן׃ ס [ישראל] כט בְּנֵ֖י מְרָרִ֑י לְמִשְׁפְּחֹתָ֥ם
לְבֵית־אֲבֹתָ֖ם תִּפְקֹ֥ד אֹתָֽם׃ ל מִבֶּן֩ שְׁלֹשִׁ֨ים שָׁנָ֜ה וָמַ֗עְלָה וְעַ֛ד
בֶּן־חֲמִשִּׁ֥ים שָׁנָ֖ה תִּפְקְדֵ֑ם כָּל־הַבָּא֙ לַצָּבָ֔א לַעֲבֹ֕ד אֶת־עֲבֹדַ֖ת
אֹ֥הֶל מוֹעֵֽד׃ לא וְזֹאת֙ מִשְׁמֶ֣רֶת מַשָּׂאָ֔ם לְכָל־עֲבֹדָתָ֖ם בְּאֹ֣הֶל
מוֹעֵ֑ד קַרְשֵׁי֙ הַמִּשְׁכָּ֔ן וּבְרִיחָ֖יו וְעַמּוּדָ֥יו וַאֲדָנָֽיו׃ לב וְעַמּוּדֵ֨י
הֶחָצֵ֜ר סָבִ֗יב וְאַדְנֵיהֶם֮ וִיתֵדֹתָם֮ וּמֵיתְרֵיהֶם֒ לְכָל־כְּלֵיהֶ֔ם
וּלְכֹ֖ל עֲבֹדָתָ֑ם וּבְשֵׁמֹ֣ת תִּפְקְד֔וּ אֶת־כְּלֵ֖י מִשְׁמֶ֥רֶת מַשָּׂאָֽם׃
לג זֹ֣את עֲבֹדַ֗ת מִשְׁפְּחֹת֙ בְּנֵ֣י מְרָרִ֔י לְכָל־עֲבֹדָתָ֖ם בְּאֹ֣הֶל מוֹעֵ֑ד
בְּיַד֙ אִֽיתָמָ֔ר בֶּן־אַהֲרֹ֖ן הַכֹּהֵֽן׃ [Some end here. Others continue]
לד וַיִּפְקֹ֨ד מֹשֶׁ֧ה וְאַהֲרֹ֛ן וּנְשִׂיאֵ֥י הָעֵדָ֖ה אֶת־בְּנֵ֣י הַקְּהָתִ֑י
לְמִשְׁפְּחֹתָ֖ם וּלְבֵ֥ית אֲבֹתָֽם׃ לה מִבֶּ֨ן שְׁלֹשִׁ֤ים שָׁנָה֙ וָמַ֔עְלָה
וְעַ֖ד בֶּן־חֲמִשִּׁ֣ים שָׁנָ֑ה כָּל־הַבָּא֙ לַצָּבָ֔א לַעֲבֹדָ֖ה בְּאֹ֥הֶל מוֹעֵֽד׃
לו וַיִּהְי֥וּ פְקֻדֵיהֶ֖ם לְמִשְׁפְּחֹתָ֑ם אַלְפַּ֕יִם שְׁבַ֥ע מֵא֖וֹת וַחֲמִשִּֽׁים׃
לז אֵ֣לֶּה פְקוּדֵי֙ מִשְׁפְּחֹ֣ת הַקְּהָתִ֔י כָּל־הָעֹבֵ֖ד בְּאֹ֣הֶל מוֹעֵ֑ד
אֲשֶׁ֨ר פָּקַ֤ד מֹשֶׁה֙ וְאַהֲרֹ֔ן עַל־פִּ֥י יְהֹוָ֖ה בְּיַד־מֹשֶֽׁה׃

פרשת בהעלותך

פרק ח א וַיְדַבֵּ֥ר יְהֹוָ֖ה אֶל־מֹשֶׁ֥ה לֵּאמֹֽר׃ ב דַּבֵּר֙ אֶֽל־אַהֲרֹ֔ן
וְאָמַרְתָּ֖ אֵלָ֑יו בְּהַעֲלֹֽתְךָ֙ אֶת־הַנֵּרֹ֔ת אֶל־מוּל֙ פְּנֵ֣י הַמְּנוֹרָ֔ה
יָאִ֖ירוּ שִׁבְעַ֥ת הַנֵּרֽוֹת׃ ג וַיַּ֤עַשׂ כֵּן֙ אַהֲרֹ֔ן אֶל־מוּל֙ פְּנֵ֣י

הַמְּנוֹרָ֔ה הֶעֱלָ֖ה נֵרֹתֶ֑יהָ כַּאֲשֶׁ֛ר צִוָּ֥ה יְהוָ֖ה אֶת־מֹשֶֽׁה׃ ד וְזֶ֨ה
מַעֲשֵׂ֤ה הַמְּנֹרָה֙ מִקְשָׁ֣ה זָהָ֔ב עַד־יְרֵכָ֥הּ עַד־פִּרְחָ֖הּ מִקְשָׁ֣ה
ה֑וא כַּמַּרְאֶ֗ה אֲשֶׁ֨ר הֶרְאָ֤ה יְהוָה֙ אֶת־מֹשֶׁ֔ה כֵּ֥ן עָשָׂ֖ה אֶת־
הַמְּנֹרָֽה׃ פ [לוי] ה וַיְדַבֵּ֥ר יְהוָ֖ה אֶל־מֹשֶׁ֥ה לֵּאמֹֽר׃ ו קַ֚ח
אֶת־הַלְוִיִּ֔ם מִתּ֖וֹךְ בְּנֵ֣י יִשְׂרָאֵ֑ל וְטִהַרְתָּ֖ אֹתָֽם׃ ז וְכֹה־תַעֲשֶׂ֤ה
לָהֶם֙ לְטַֽהֲרָ֔ם הַזֵּ֥ה עֲלֵיהֶ֖ם מֵ֣י חַטָּ֑את וְהֶעֱבִ֤ירוּ תַ֙עַר֙ עַל־
כָּל־בְּשָׂרָ֔ם וְכִבְּס֥וּ בִגְדֵיהֶ֖ם וְהִטֶּהָֽרוּ׃ ח וְלָֽקְחוּ֙ פַּ֣ר בֶּן־בָּקָ֔ר
וּמִנְחָת֔וֹ סֹ֖לֶת בְּלוּלָ֣ה בַשָּׁ֑מֶן וּפַר־שֵׁנִ֥י בֶן־בָּקָ֖ר תִּקַּ֥ח לְחַטָּֽאת׃
ט וְהִקְרַבְתָּ֙ אֶת־הַלְוִיִּ֔ם לִפְנֵ֖י אֹ֣הֶל מוֹעֵ֑ד וְהִ֨קְהַלְתָּ֔ אֶֽת־כָּל־
עֲדַ֖ת בְּנֵ֥י יִשְׂרָאֵֽל׃ [ישראל] י וְהִקְרַבְתָּ֥ אֶת־הַלְוִיִּ֖ם לִפְנֵ֣י יְהוָ֑ה
וְסָמְכ֧וּ בְנֵֽי־יִשְׂרָאֵ֛ל אֶת־יְדֵיהֶ֖ם עַל־הַלְוִיִּֽם׃ יא וְהֵנִיף֩ אַהֲרֹ֨ן
אֶת־הַלְוִיִּ֤ם תְּנוּפָה֙ לִפְנֵ֣י יְהוָ֔ה מֵאֵ֖ת בְּנֵ֣י יִשְׂרָאֵ֑ל וְהָי֕וּ לַעֲבֹ֖ד
אֶת־עֲבֹדַ֥ת יְהוָֽה׃ יב וְהַלְוִיִּם֙ יִסְמְכ֣וּ אֶת־יְדֵיהֶ֔ם עַ֖ל רֹ֣אשׁ
הַפָּרִ֑ים וַ֠עֲשֵׂה אֶת־הָאֶחָ֨ד חַטָּ֜את וְאֶת־הָאֶחָ֤ד עֹלָה֙ לַֽיהוָ֔ה
לְכַפֵּ֖ר עַל־הַלְוִיִּֽם׃ יג וְהַעֲמַדְתָּ֙ אֶת־הַלְוִיִּ֔ם לִפְנֵ֥י אַהֲרֹ֖ן וְלִפְנֵ֣י
בָנָ֑יו וְהֵנַפְתָּ֥ אֹתָ֛ם תְּנוּפָ֖ה לַֽיהוָֽה׃ יד וְהִבְדַּלְתָּ֙ אֶת־הַלְוִיִּ֔ם
מִתּ֖וֹךְ בְּנֵ֣י יִשְׂרָאֵ֑ל וְהָ֥יוּ לִ֖י הַלְוִיִּֽם׃

פרשת שלח

פרק יג א וַיְדַבֵּ֥ר יְהוָ֖ה אֶל־מֹשֶׁ֥ה לֵּאמֹֽר׃ ב שְׁלַח־לְךָ֣ אֲנָשִׁ֗ים
וְיָתֻ֙רוּ֙ אֶת־אֶ֣רֶץ כְּנַ֔עַן אֲשֶׁר־אֲנִ֥י נֹתֵ֖ן לִבְנֵ֣י יִשְׂרָאֵ֑ל אִ֨ישׁ אֶחָ֜ד
אִ֣ישׁ אֶחָ֞ד לְמַטֵּ֤ה אֲבֹתָיו֙ תִּשְׁלָ֔חוּ כֹּ֖ל נָשִׂ֥יא בָהֶֽם׃ ג וַיִּשְׁלַ֨ח
אֹתָ֥ם מֹשֶׁ֛ה מִמִּדְבַּ֥ר פָּארָ֖ן עַל־פִּ֣י יְהוָ֑ה כֻּלָּ֣ם אֲנָשִׁ֔ים רָאשֵׁ֥י
בְנֵֽי־יִשְׂרָאֵ֖ל הֵֽמָּה׃ [לוי] ד וְאֵ֖לֶּה שְׁמוֹתָ֑ם לְמַטֵּ֣ה רְאוּבֵ֔ן
שַׁמּ֖וּעַ בֶּן־זַכּֽוּר׃ ה לְמַטֵּ֣ה שִׁמְע֔וֹן שָׁפָ֖ט בֶּן־חוֹרִֽי׃ ו לְמַטֵּ֣ה
יְהוּדָ֔ה כָּלֵ֖ב בֶּן־יְפֻנֶּֽה׃ ז לְמַטֵּ֣ה יִשָּׂשכָ֔ר יִגְאָ֖ל בֶּן־יוֹסֵֽף׃

ח לְמַטֵּ֖ה אֶפְרָ֑יִם הוֹשֵׁ֖עַ בִּן־נֽוּן׃ ט לְמַטֵּ֥ה בִנְיָמִ֖ן פַּלְטִ֥י בֶּן־
רָפֽוּא׃ י לְמַטֵּ֣ה זְבוּלֻ֔ן גַּדִּיאֵ֖ל בֶּן־סוֹדִֽי׃ יא לְמַטֵּ֥ה יוֹסֵ֖ף לְמַטֵּ֣ה
מְנַשֶּׁ֑ה גַּדִּ֖י בֶּן־סוּסִֽי׃ יב לְמַטֵּ֣ה דָ֔ן עַמִּיאֵ֖ל בֶּן־גְּמַלִּֽי׃ יג לְמַטֵּ֣ה
אָשֵׁ֔ר סְת֖וּר בֶּן־מִֽיכָאֵֽל׃ יד לְמַטֵּ֖ה נַפְתָּלִ֑י נַחְבִּ֖י בֶּן־וָפְסִֽי׃
טו לְמַטֵּ֣ה גָ֔ד גְּאוּאֵ֖ל בֶּן־מָכִֽי׃ טז אֵ֚לֶּה שְׁמ֣וֹת הָאֲנָשִׁ֔ים אֲשֶׁר־
שָׁלַ֥ח מֹשֶׁ֖ה לָת֣וּר אֶת־הָאָ֑רֶץ וַיִּקְרָ֥א מֹשֶׁ֛ה לְהוֹשֵׁ֥עַ בִּן־נ֖וּן
יְהוֹשֻֽׁעַ׃ [ישראל] יז וַיִּשְׁלַ֤ח אֹתָם֙ מֹשֶׁ֔ה לָת֖וּר אֶת־אֶ֣רֶץ כְּנָ֑עַן
וַיֹּ֣אמֶר אֲלֵהֶ֗ם עֲל֥וּ זֶה֙ בַּנֶּ֔גֶב וַעֲלִיתֶ֖ם אֶת־הָהָֽר׃ יח וּרְאִיתֶ֥ם
אֶת־הָאָ֖רֶץ מַה־הִ֑וא וְאֶת־הָעָם֙ הַיֹּשֵׁ֣ב עָלֶ֔יהָ הֶחָזָ֥ק הוּא֙
הֲרָפֶ֔ה הַמְעַ֥ט ה֖וּא אִם־רָֽב׃ יט וּמָ֣ה הָאָ֗רֶץ אֲשֶׁר־הוּא֙ יֹשֵׁ֣ב
בָּ֔הּ הֲטוֹבָ֥ה הִ֖וא אִם־רָעָ֑ה וּמָ֣ה הֶעָרִ֗ים אֲשֶׁר־הוּא֙ יוֹשֵׁ֣ב
בָּהֵ֔נָּה הַבְּמַֽחֲנִ֖ים אִ֥ם בְּמִבְצָרִֽים׃ כ וּמָ֣ה הָאָ֡רֶץ הַשְּׁמֵנָ֨ה
הִ֜וא אִם־רָזָ֗ה הֲיֵֽשׁ־בָּ֥הּ עֵץ֙ אִם־אַ֔יִן וְהִ֨תְחַזַּקְתֶּ֔ם וּלְקַחְתֶּ֖ם
מִפְּרִ֣י הָאָ֑רֶץ וְהַ֨יָּמִ֔ים יְמֵ֖י בִּכּוּרֵ֥י עֲנָבִֽים׃

פרשת קרח

פרק טז א וַיִּקַּ֣ח קֹ֔רַח בֶּן־יִצְהָ֥ר בֶּן־קְהָ֖ת בֶּן־לֵוִ֑י וְדָתָ֨ן וַאֲבִירָ֜ם
בְּנֵ֧י אֱלִיאָ֛ב וְא֥וֹן בֶּן־פֶּ֖לֶת בְּנֵ֥י רְאוּבֵֽן׃ ב וַיָּקֻ֙מוּ֙ לִפְנֵ֣י מֹשֶׁ֔ה
וַאֲנָשִׁ֥ים מִבְּנֵֽי־יִשְׂרָאֵ֖ל חֲמִשִּׁ֣ים וּמָאתָ֑יִם נְשִׂיאֵ֥י עֵדָ֛ה קְרִאֵ֥י
מוֹעֵ֖ד אַנְשֵׁי־שֵֽׁם׃ ג וַיִּֽקָּהֲל֞וּ עַל־מֹשֶׁ֣ה וְעַֽל־אַהֲרֹ֗ן וַיֹּאמְר֣וּ
אֲלֵהֶם֮ רַב־לָכֶם֒ כִּ֤י כָל־הָֽעֵדָה֙ כֻּלָּ֣ם קְדֹשִׁ֔ים וּבְתוֹכָ֖ם יְהוָ֑ה
וּמַדּ֥וּעַ תִּֽתְנַשְּׂא֖וּ עַל־קְהַ֥ל יְהוָֽה׃ [לוי] ד וַיִּשְׁמַ֣ע מֹשֶׁ֔ה וַיִּפֹּ֖ל
עַל־פָּנָֽיו׃ ה וַיְדַבֵּ֨ר אֶל־קֹ֜רַח וְאֶל־כָּל־עֲדָתוֹ֮ לֵאמֹר֒ בֹּ֠קֶר וְיֹדַ֨ע
יְהוָ֧ה אֶת־אֲשֶׁר־ל֛וֹ וְאֶת־הַקָּד֖וֹשׁ וְהִקְרִ֣יב אֵלָ֑יו וְאֵ֛ת אֲשֶׁ֥ר
יִבְחַר־בּ֖וֹ יַקְרִ֥יב אֵלָֽיו׃ ו זֹ֖את עֲשׂ֑וּ קְחוּ־לָכֶ֣ם מַחְתּ֔וֹת קֹ֖רַח
וְכָל־עֲדָתֽוֹ׃ ז וּתְנ֣וּ־בָהֵ֣ן ׀ אֵ֡שׁ וְשִׂ֨ימוּ עֲלֵיהֶ֤ן ׀ קְטֹ֙רֶת֙ לִפְנֵ֣י

יְהוָה מָחָר וְהָיָה הָאִישׁ אֲשֶׁר־יִבְחַר יְהוָה הוּא הַקָּדוֹשׁ רַב־
לָכֶם בְּנֵי לֵוִי׃ [ישראל] ח וַיֹּאמֶר מֹשֶׁה אֶל־קֹרַח שִׁמְעוּ־נָא בְּנֵי
לֵוִי׃ ט הַמְעַט מִכֶּם כִּי־הִבְדִּיל אֱלֹהֵי יִשְׂרָאֵל אֶתְכֶם מֵעֲדַת
יִשְׂרָאֵל לְהַקְרִיב אֶתְכֶם אֵלָיו לַעֲבֹד אֶת־עֲבֹדַת מִשְׁכַּן
יְהוָה וְלַעֲמֹד לִפְנֵי הָעֵדָה לְשָׁרְתָם׃ י וַיַּקְרֵב אֹתְךָ וְאֶת־
כָּל־אַחֶיךָ בְנֵי־לֵוִי אִתָּךְ וּבִקַּשְׁתֶּם גַּם־כְּהֻנָּה׃ יא לָכֵן אַתָּה
וְכָל־עֲדָתְךָ הַנֹּעָדִים עַל־יְהוָה וְאַהֲרֹן מַה־הוּא כִּי תַלּוֹנוּ▽
עָלָיו׃ יב וַיִּשְׁלַח מֹשֶׁה לִקְרֹא לְדָתָן וְלַאֲבִירָם בְּנֵי אֱלִיאָב
וַיֹּאמְרוּ לֹא נַעֲלֶה׃ יג הַמְעַט כִּי הֶעֱלִיתָנוּ מֵאֶרֶץ זָבַת חָלָב
וּדְבַשׁ לַהֲמִיתֵנוּ בַּמִּדְבָּר כִּי־תִשְׂתָּרֵר עָלֵינוּ גַּם־הִשְׂתָּרֵר׃

פרשת חקת

פרק יט א וַיְדַבֵּר יְהוָה אֶל־מֹשֶׁה וְאֶל־אַהֲרֹן לֵאמֹר׃ ב זֹאת
חֻקַּת הַתּוֹרָה אֲשֶׁר־צִוָּה יְהוָה לֵאמֹר דַּבֵּר | אֶל־בְּנֵי
יִשְׂרָאֵל וְיִקְחוּ אֵלֶיךָ פָרָה אֲדֻמָּה תְּמִימָה אֲשֶׁר אֵין־בָּהּ
מוּם אֲשֶׁר לֹא־עָלָה עָלֶיהָ עֹל׃ ג וּנְתַתֶּם אֹתָהּ אֶל־אֶלְעָזָר
הַכֹּהֵן וְהוֹצִיא אֹתָהּ אֶל־מִחוּץ לַמַּחֲנֶה וְשָׁחַט אֹתָהּ לְפָנָיו׃
ד וְלָקַח אֶלְעָזָר הַכֹּהֵן מִדָּמָהּ בְּאֶצְבָּעוֹ וְהִזָּה אֶל־נֹכַח פְּנֵי
אֹהֶל־מוֹעֵד מִדָּמָהּ שֶׁבַע פְּעָמִים׃ ה וְשָׂרַף אֶת־הַפָּרָה
לְעֵינָיו אֶת־עֹרָהּ וְאֶת־בְּשָׂרָהּ וְאֶת־דָּמָהּ עַל־פִּרְשָׁהּ יִשְׂרֹף׃
ו וְלָקַח הַכֹּהֵן עֵץ אֶרֶז וְאֵזוֹב וּשְׁנִי תוֹלָעַת וְהִשְׁלִיךְ אֶל־תּוֹךְ
שְׂרֵפַת הַפָּרָה׃ [לוי] ז וְכִבֶּס בְּגָדָיו הַכֹּהֵן וְרָחַץ בְּשָׂרוֹ בַּמַּיִם
וְאַחַר יָבֹא אֶל־הַמַּחֲנֶה וְטָמֵא הַכֹּהֵן עַד־הָעָרֶב׃ ח וְהַשֹּׂרֵף
אֹתָהּ יְכַבֵּס בְּגָדָיו בַּמַּיִם וְרָחַץ בְּשָׂרוֹ בַּמָּיִם וְטָמֵא עַד־
הָעָרֶב׃ ט וְאָסַף | אִישׁ טָהוֹר אֵת אֵפֶר הַפָּרָה וְהִנִּיחַ מִחוּץ

▽ תַּלִּינוּ

לְמַחֲנֶה בְּמָקוֹם טָהוֹר וְהָיְתָה לַעֲדַת בְּנֵי־יִשְׂרָאֵל לְמִשְׁמֶרֶת
לְמֵי נִדָּה חַטָּאת הִוא: [ישראל] י וְכִבֶּס הָאֹסֵף אֶת־אֵפֶר
הַפָּרָה אֶת־בְּגָדָיו וְטָמֵא עַד־הָעָרֶב וְהָיְתָה לִבְנֵי יִשְׂרָאֵל
וְלַגֵּר הַגָּר בְּתוֹכָם לְחֻקַּת עוֹלָם: יא הַנֹּגֵעַ בְּמֵת לְכָל־נֶפֶשׁ
אָדָם וְטָמֵא שִׁבְעַת יָמִים: יב הוּא יִתְחַטָּא־בוֹ בַּיּוֹם הַשְּׁלִישִׁי
וּבַיּוֹם הַשְּׁבִיעִי יִטְהָר וְאִם־לֹא יִתְחַטָּא בַּיּוֹם הַשְּׁלִישִׁי וּבַיּוֹם
הַשְּׁבִיעִי לֹא יִטְהָר: יג כָּל־הַנֹּגֵעַ בְּמֵת בְּנֶפֶשׁ הָאָדָם אֲשֶׁר־
יָמוּת וְלֹא יִתְחַטָּא אֶת־מִשְׁכַּן יְהוָה טִמֵּא וְנִכְרְתָה הַנֶּפֶשׁ
הַהִוא מִיִּשְׂרָאֵל כִּי מֵי נִדָּה לֹא־זֹרַק עָלָיו טָמֵא יִהְיֶה עוֹד
טֻמְאָתוֹ בוֹ: יד זֹאת הַתּוֹרָה אָדָם כִּי־יָמוּת בְּאֹהֶל כָּל־הַבָּא
אֶל־הָאֹהֶל וְכָל־אֲשֶׁר בָּאֹהֶל יִטְמָא שִׁבְעַת יָמִים: טו וְכֹל
כְּלִי פָתוּחַ אֲשֶׁר אֵין־צָמִיד פָּתִיל עָלָיו טָמֵא הוּא: טז וְכֹל
אֲשֶׁר־יִגַּע עַל־פְּנֵי הַשָּׂדֶה בַּחֲלַל־חֶרֶב אוֹ בְמֵת אוֹ־בְעֶצֶם
אָדָם אוֹ בְקָבֶר יִטְמָא שִׁבְעַת יָמִים: יז וְלָקְחוּ לַטָּמֵא מֵעֲפַר
שְׂרֵפַת הַחַטָּאת וְנָתַן עָלָיו מַיִם חַיִּים אֶל־כֶּלִי:

פרשת בלק

פרק כב ב וַיַּרְא בָּלָק בֶּן־צִפּוֹר אֵת כָּל־אֲשֶׁר־עָשָׂה יִשְׂרָאֵל
לָאֱמֹרִי: ג וַיָּגָר מוֹאָב מִפְּנֵי הָעָם מְאֹד כִּי רַב־הוּא וַיָּקָץ
מוֹאָב מִפְּנֵי בְּנֵי יִשְׂרָאֵל: ד וַיֹּאמֶר מוֹאָב אֶל־זִקְנֵי מִדְיָן
עַתָּה יְלַחֲכוּ הַקָּהָל אֶת־כָּל־סְבִיבֹתֵינוּ כִּלְחֹךְ הַשּׁוֹר אֵת
יֶרֶק הַשָּׂדֶה וּבָלָק בֶּן־צִפּוֹר מֶלֶךְ לְמוֹאָב בָּעֵת הַהִוא:
[לוי] ה וַיִּשְׁלַח מַלְאָכִים אֶל־בִּלְעָם בֶּן־בְּעֹר פְּתוֹרָה אֲשֶׁר
עַל־הַנָּהָר אֶרֶץ בְּנֵי־עַמּוֹ לִקְרֹא־לוֹ לֵאמֹר הִנֵּה עַם יָצָא
מִמִּצְרַיִם הִנֵּה כִסָּה אֶת־עֵין הָאָרֶץ וְהוּא יֹשֵׁב מִמֻּלִי: ו וְעַתָּה
לְכָה־נָּא אָרָה־לִּי אֶת־הָעָם הַזֶּה כִּי־עָצוּם הוּא מִמֶּנִּי אוּלַי

אוּכַל נַכֶּה־בּוֹ וַאֲגָרְשֶׁנּוּ מִן־הָאָרֶץ כִּי יָדַעְתִּי אֵת אֲשֶׁר־
תְּבָרֵךְ מְבֹרָךְ וַאֲשֶׁר תָּאֹר יוּאָר׃ ז וַיֵּלְכוּ זִקְנֵי מוֹאָב וְזִקְנֵי
מִדְיָן וּקְסָמִים בְּיָדָם וַיָּבֹאוּ אֶל־בִּלְעָם וַיְדַבְּרוּ אֵלָיו דִּבְרֵי
בָלָק׃ [ישראל] ח וַיֹּאמֶר אֲלֵיהֶם לִינוּ פֹה הַלַּיְלָה וַהֲשִׁבֹתִי
אֶתְכֶם דָּבָר כַּאֲשֶׁר יְדַבֵּר יְהוָה אֵלָי וַיֵּשְׁבוּ שָׂרֵי־מוֹאָב
עִם־בִּלְעָם׃ ט וַיָּבֹא אֱלֹהִים אֶל־בִּלְעָם וַיֹּאמֶר מִי הָאֲנָשִׁים
הָאֵלֶּה עִמָּךְ׃ י וַיֹּאמֶר בִּלְעָם אֶל־הָאֱלֹהִים בָּלָק בֶּן־צִפֹּר
מֶלֶךְ מוֹאָב שָׁלַח אֵלָי׃ יא הִנֵּה הָעָם הַיֹּצֵא מִמִּצְרַיִם וַיְכַס
אֶת־עֵין הָאָרֶץ עַתָּה לְכָה קָבָה־לִּי אֹתוֹ אוּלַי אוּכַל לְהִלָּחֶם
בּוֹ וְגֵרַשְׁתִּיו׃ יב וַיֹּאמֶר אֱלֹהִים אֶל־בִּלְעָם לֹא תֵלֵךְ עִמָּהֶם
לֹא תָאֹר אֶת־הָעָם כִּי בָרוּךְ הוּא׃

פרשת פינחס

פרק כה י וַיְדַבֵּר יְהוָה אֶל־מֹשֶׁה לֵּאמֹר׃ יא פִּינְחָס בֶּן־אֶלְעָזָר
בֶּן־אַהֲרֹן הַכֹּהֵן הֵשִׁיב אֶת־חֲמָתִי מֵעַל בְּנֵי־יִשְׂרָאֵל בְּקַנְאוֹ
אֶת־קִנְאָתִי בְּתוֹכָם וְלֹא־כִלִּיתִי אֶת־בְּנֵי־יִשְׂרָאֵל בְּקִנְאָתִי׃
יב לָכֵן אֱמֹר הִנְנִי נֹתֵן לוֹ אֶת־בְּרִיתִי שָׁלוֹם׃ [לוי] יג וְהָיְתָה לּוֹ
וּלְזַרְעוֹ אַחֲרָיו בְּרִית כְּהֻנַּת עוֹלָם תַּחַת אֲשֶׁר קִנֵּא לֵאלֹהָיו
וַיְכַפֵּר עַל־בְּנֵי יִשְׂרָאֵל׃ יד וְשֵׁם אִישׁ יִשְׂרָאֵל הַמֻּכֶּה אֲשֶׁר
הֻכָּה אֶת־הַמִּדְיָנִית זִמְרִי בֶּן־סָלוּא נְשִׂיא בֵית־אָב לַשִּׁמְעֹנִי׃
טו וְשֵׁם הָאִשָּׁה הַמֻּכָּה הַמִּדְיָנִית כָּזְבִּי בַת־צוּר רֹאשׁ אֻמּוֹת
בֵּית־אָב בְּמִדְיָן הוּא׃ פ [ישראל] טז וַיְדַבֵּר יְהוָה אֶל־מֹשֶׁה
לֵּאמֹר׃ יז צָרוֹר אֶת־הַמִּדְיָנִים וְהִכִּיתֶם אוֹתָם׃ יח כִּי־צֹרְרִים
הֵם לָכֶם בְּנִכְלֵיהֶם אֲשֶׁר־נִכְּלוּ לָכֶם עַל־דְּבַר פְּעוֹר וְעַל־
דְּבַר כָּזְבִּי בַת־נְשִׂיא מִדְיָן אֲחֹתָם הַמֻּכָּה בְיוֹם־הַמַּגֵּפָה
עַל־דְּבַר פְּעוֹר׃ פרק כו א וַיְהִי אַחֲרֵי הַמַּגֵּפָה פ וַיֹּאמֶר

יְהוָה֙ אֶל־מֹשֶׁ֔ה וְאֶ֛ל אֶלְעָזָ֥ר בֶּן־אַהֲרֹ֛ן הַכֹּהֵ֖ן לֵאמֹֽר׃ ב שְׂא֞וּ
אֶת־רֹ֣אשׁ ׀ כָּל־עֲדַ֣ת בְּנֵֽי־יִשְׂרָאֵ֗ל מִבֶּ֨ן עֶשְׂרִ֥ים שָׁנָ֛ה וָמַ֖עְלָה
לְבֵ֣ית אֲבֹתָ֑ם כָּל־יֹצֵ֥א צָבָ֖א בְּיִשְׂרָאֵֽל׃ ג וַיְדַבֵּ֨ר מֹשֶׁ֜ה וְאֶלְעָזָ֧ר
הַכֹּהֵ֛ן אֹתָ֖ם בְּעַרְבֹ֣ת מוֹאָ֑ב עַל־יַרְדֵּ֥ן יְרֵח֖וֹ לֵאמֹֽר׃ ד מִבֶּ֛ן
עֶשְׂרִ֥ים שָׁנָ֖ה וָמָ֑עְלָה כַּאֲשֶׁ֨ר צִוָּ֤ה יְהוָה֙ אֶת־מֹשֶׁה֙ וּבְנֵ֣י
יִשְׂרָאֵ֔ל הַיֹּצְאִ֖ים מֵאֶ֥רֶץ מִצְרָֽיִם׃

פרשת מטות

פרק ל ב וַיְדַבֵּ֤ר מֹשֶׁה֙ אֶל־רָאשֵׁ֣י הַמַּטּ֔וֹת לִבְנֵ֥י יִשְׂרָאֵ֖ל לֵאמֹ֑ר
זֶ֣ה הַדָּבָ֔ר אֲשֶׁ֖ר צִוָּ֥ה יְהוָֽה׃ ג אִישׁ֩ כִּֽי־יִדֹּ֨ר נֶ֜דֶר לַיהוָ֗ה אֽוֹ־
הִשָּׁ֤בַע שְׁבֻעָה֙ לֶאְסֹ֤ר אִסָּר֙ עַל־נַפְשׁ֔וֹ לֹ֥א יַחֵ֖ל דְּבָר֑וֹ כְּכָל־
הַיֹּצֵ֥א מִפִּ֖יו יַעֲשֶֽׂה׃ ד וְאִשָּׁ֕ה כִּֽי־תִדֹּ֥ר נֶ֖דֶר לַיהוָ֑ה וְאָסְרָ֥ה
אִסָּ֛ר בְּבֵ֥ית אָבִ֖יהָ בִּנְעֻרֶֽיהָ׃ ה וְשָׁמַ֨ע אָבִ֜יהָ אֶת־נִדְרָ֗הּ וֶֽאֱסָרָהּ֙
אֲשֶׁ֤ר אָסְרָה֙ עַל־נַפְשָׁ֔הּ וְהֶחֱרִ֥ישׁ לָ֖הּ אָבִ֑יהָ וְקָ֙מוּ֙ כָּל־נְדָרֶ֔יהָ
וְכָל־אִסָּ֛ר אֲשֶׁר־אָסְרָ֥ה עַל־נַפְשָׁ֖הּ יָקֽוּם׃ ו וְאִם־הֵנִ֨יא אָבִ֣יהָ
אֹתָהּ֮ בְּי֣וֹם שָׁמְעוֹ֒ כָּל־נְדָרֶ֗יהָ וֶֽאֱסָרֶ֛יהָ אֲשֶׁר־אָסְרָ֥ה עַל־
נַפְשָׁ֖הּ לֹ֣א יָק֑וּם וַֽיהוָה֙ יִֽסְלַח־לָ֔הּ כִּֽי־הֵנִ֥יא אָבִ֖יהָ אֹתָֽהּ׃
ז וְאִם־הָי֤וֹ תִֽהְיֶה֙ לְאִ֔ישׁ וּנְדָרֶ֖יהָ עָלֶ֑יהָ א֚וֹ מִבְטָ֣א שְׂפָתֶ֔יהָ
אֲשֶׁ֥ר אָסְרָ֖ה עַל־נַפְשָֽׁהּ׃ ח וְשָׁמַ֥ע אִישָׁ֛הּ בְּי֥וֹם שָׁמְע֖וֹ
וְהֶחֱרִ֣ישׁ לָ֑הּ וְקָ֣מוּ נְדָרֶ֗יהָ וֶֽאֱסָרָ֛הּ אֲשֶׁר־אָסְרָ֥ה עַל־נַפְשָׁ֖הּ
יָקֻֽמוּ׃ ט וְ֠אִם בְּי֨וֹם שְׁמֹ֣עַ אִישָׁהּ֮ יָנִ֣יא אוֹתָהּ֒ וְהֵפֵ֗ר אֶת־נִדְרָהּ֙
אֲשֶׁ֣ר עָלֶ֔יהָ וְאֵת֙ מִבְטָ֣א שְׂפָתֶ֔יהָ אֲשֶׁ֥ר אָסְרָ֖ה עַל־נַפְשָׁ֑הּ
וַיהוָ֖ה יִֽסְלַֽח־לָֽהּ׃ [לוי] י וְנֵ֥דֶר אַלְמָנָ֖ה וּגְרוּשָׁ֑ה כֹּ֛ל אֲשֶׁר־
אָסְרָ֥ה עַל־נַפְשָׁ֖הּ יָק֥וּם עָלֶֽיהָ׃ יא וְאִם־בֵּ֥ית אִישָׁ֖הּ נָדָ֑רָה אוֹ־
אָסְרָ֥ה אִסָּ֛ר עַל־נַפְשָׁ֖הּ בִּשְׁבֻעָֽה׃ יב וְשָׁמַ֤ע אִישָׁהּ֙ וְהֶחֱרִ֣שׁ
לָ֔הּ לֹ֥א הֵנִ֖יא אֹתָ֑הּ וְקָ֙מוּ֙ כָּל־נְדָרֶ֔יהָ וְכָל־אִסָּ֖ר אֲשֶׁר־אָסְרָ֥ה

עַל־נַפְשָׁ֖הּ יָקֽוּם: יג וְאִם־הָפֵר֩ יָפֵ֨ר אֹתָ֥ם ׀ אִישָׁהּ֮ בְּי֣וֹם שָׁמְעוֹ֒
כָּל־מוֹצָ֨א שְׂפָתֶ֧יהָ לִנְדָרֶ֛יהָ וּלְאִסַּ֥ר נַפְשָׁ֖הּ לֹ֣א יָק֑וּם אִישָׁ֣הּ
הֲפֵרָ֔ם וַֽיהוָ֖ה יִֽסְלַֽח־לָֽהּ: [ישראל] יד כָּל־נֵ֛דֶר וְכָל־שְׁבֻ֥עַת אִסָּ֖ר
לְעַנֹּ֣ת נָ֑פֶשׁ אִישָׁ֥הּ יְקִימֶ֖נּוּ וְאִישָׁ֥הּ יְפֵרֶֽנּוּ: טו וְאִם־הַחֲרֵשׁ֩
יַחֲרִ֨ישׁ לָ֥הּ אִישָׁהּ֮ מִיּ֣וֹם אֶל־יוֹם֒ וְהֵקִים֙ אֶת־כָּל־נְדָרֶ֔יהָ א֥וֹ
אֶת־כָּל־אֱסָרֶ֖יהָ אֲשֶׁ֣ר עָלֶ֑יהָ הֵקִ֣ים אֹתָ֔ם כִּֽי־הֶחֱרִ֥שׁ לָ֖הּ
בְּי֥וֹם שָׁמְעֽוֹ: טז וְאִם־הָפֵ֥ר יָפֵ֛ר אֹתָ֖ם אַחֲרֵ֣י שָׁמְע֑וֹ וְנָשָׂ֖א
אֶת־עֲוֺנָֽהּ: יז אֵ֣לֶּה הַֽחֻקִּ֗ים אֲשֶׁ֨ר צִוָּ֤ה יְהוָה֙ אֶת־מֹשֶׁ֔ה בֵּ֥ין
אִ֖ישׁ לְאִשְׁתּ֑וֹ בֵּֽין־אָ֣ב לְבִתּ֔וֹ בִּנְעֻרֶ֖יהָ בֵּ֥ית אָבִֽיהָ:

פרשת מסעי

פרק לג א אֵ֜לֶּה מַסְעֵ֣י בְנֵֽי־יִשְׂרָאֵ֗ל אֲשֶׁ֥ר יָצְא֛וּ מֵאֶ֥רֶץ מִצְרַ֖יִם
לְצִבְאֹתָ֑ם בְּיַד־מֹשֶׁ֖ה וְאַהֲרֹֽן: ב וַיִּכְתֹּ֨ב מֹשֶׁ֜ה אֶת־מוֹצָאֵיהֶ֛ם
לְמַסְעֵיהֶ֖ם עַל־פִּ֣י יְהוָ֑ה וְאֵ֥לֶּה מַסְעֵיהֶ֖ם לְמוֹצָאֵיהֶֽם:
ג וַיִּסְע֤וּ מֵֽרַעְמְסֵס֙ בַּחֹ֣דֶשׁ הָֽרִאשׁ֔וֹן בַּחֲמִשָּׁ֥ה עָשָׂ֛ר י֖וֹם
לַחֹ֣דֶשׁ הָרִאשׁ֑וֹן מִמָּחֳרַ֣ת הַפֶּ֗סַח יָצְא֤וּ בְנֵֽי־יִשְׂרָאֵל֙ בְּיָ֣ד
רָמָ֔ה לְעֵינֵ֖י כָּל־מִצְרָֽיִם: [לוי] ד וּמִצְרַ֣יִם מְקַבְּרִ֗ים אֵת֩ אֲשֶׁ֨ר
הִכָּ֧ה יְהוָ֛ה בָּהֶ֖ם כָּל־בְּכ֑וֹר וּבֵאלֹ֣הֵיהֶ֔ם עָשָׂ֥ה יְהוָ֖ה שְׁפָטִֽים:
ה וַיִּסְע֥וּ בְנֵֽי־יִשְׂרָאֵ֖ל מֵרַעְמְסֵ֑ס וַֽיַּחֲנ֖וּ בְּסֻכֹּֽת: ו וַיִּסְע֖וּ מִסֻּכֹּ֑ת
וַיַּחֲנ֣וּ בְאֵתָ֔ם אֲשֶׁ֖ר בִּקְצֵ֥ה הַמִּדְבָּֽר: [ישראל] ז וַיִּסְעוּ֙ מֵֽאֵתָ֔ם
וַיָּ֙שָׁב֙ עַל־פִּ֣י הַחִירֹ֔ת אֲשֶׁ֥ר עַל־פְּנֵ֖י בַּ֣עַל צְפ֑וֹן וַֽיַּחֲנ֖וּ לִפְנֵ֥י
מִגְדֹּֽל: ח וַיִּסְעוּ֙ מִפְּנֵ֣י הַחִירֹ֔ת וַיַּעַבְר֥וּ בְתוֹךְ־הַיָּ֖ם הַמִּדְבָּ֑רָה
וַיֵּ֨לְכ֜וּ דֶּ֣רֶךְ שְׁלֹ֤שֶׁת יָמִים֙ בְּמִדְבַּ֣ר אֵתָ֔ם וַֽיַּחֲנ֖וּ בְּמָרָֽה: ט וַיִּסְעוּ֙
מִמָּרָ֔ה וַיָּבֹ֖אוּ אֵילִ֑מָה וּ֠בְאֵילִ֠ם שְׁתֵּ֨ים עֶשְׂרֵ֜ה עֵינֹ֥ת מַ֛יִם
וְשִׁבְעִ֥ים תְּמָרִ֖ים וַיַּחֲנוּ־שָֽׁם: י וַיִּסְע֖וּ מֵאֵילִ֑ם וַֽיַּחֲנ֖וּ עַל־
יַם־סֽוּף:

פרשת דברים

פרק א א אֵלֶּה הַדְּבָרִים אֲשֶׁר דִּבֶּר מֹשֶׁה אֶל־כָּל־יִשְׂרָאֵל
בְּעֵבֶר הַיַּרְדֵּן בַּמִּדְבָּר בָּעֲרָבָה מוֹל סוּף בֵּין־פָּארָן וּבֵין־
תֹּפֶל וְלָבָן וַחֲצֵרֹת וְדִי זָהָב׃ ב אַחַד עָשָׂר יוֹם מֵחֹרֵב דֶּרֶךְ
הַר־שֵׂעִיר עַד קָדֵשׁ בַּרְנֵעַ׃ ג וַיְהִי בְּאַרְבָּעִים שָׁנָה בְּעַשְׁתֵּי־
עָשָׂר חֹדֶשׁ בְּאֶחָד לַחֹדֶשׁ דִּבֶּר מֹשֶׁה אֶל־בְּנֵי יִשְׂרָאֵל כְּכֹל
אֲשֶׁר צִוָּה יְהוָה אֹתוֹ אֲלֵהֶם׃ [לוי] ד אַחֲרֵי הַכֹּתוֹ אֵת סִיחֹן
מֶלֶךְ הָאֱמֹרִי אֲשֶׁר יוֹשֵׁב בְּחֶשְׁבּוֹן וְאֵת עוֹג מֶלֶךְ הַבָּשָׁן
אֲשֶׁר־יוֹשֵׁב בְּעַשְׁתָּרֹת בְּאֶדְרֶעִי׃ ה בְּעֵבֶר הַיַּרְדֵּן בְּאֶרֶץ
מוֹאָב הוֹאִיל מֹשֶׁה בֵּאֵר אֶת־הַתּוֹרָה הַזֹּאת לֵאמֹר׃ ו יְהוָה
אֱלֹהֵינוּ דִּבֶּר אֵלֵינוּ בְּחֹרֵב לֵאמֹר רַב־לָכֶם שֶׁבֶת בָּהָר הַזֶּה׃
ז פְּנוּ | וּסְעוּ לָכֶם וּבֹאוּ הַר הָאֱמֹרִי וְאֶל־כָּל־שְׁכֵנָיו בָּעֲרָבָה
בָהָר וּבַשְּׁפֵלָה וּבַנֶּגֶב וּבְחוֹף הַיָּם אֶרֶץ הַכְּנַעֲנִי וְהַלְּבָנוֹן עַד־
הַנָּהָר הַגָּדֹל נְהַר־פְּרָת׃ [ישראל] ח רְאֵה נָתַתִּי לִפְנֵיכֶם אֶת־
הָאָרֶץ בֹּאוּ וּרְשׁוּ אֶת־הָאָרֶץ אֲשֶׁר נִשְׁבַּע יְהוָה לַאֲבֹתֵיכֶם
לְאַבְרָהָם לְיִצְחָק וּלְיַעֲקֹב לָתֵת לָהֶם וּלְזַרְעָם אַחֲרֵיהֶם׃
ט וָאֹמַר אֲלֵכֶם בָּעֵת הַהִוא לֵאמֹר לֹא־אוּכַל לְבַדִּי שְׂאֵת
אֶתְכֶם׃ י יְהוָה אֱלֹהֵיכֶם הִרְבָּה אֶתְכֶם וְהִנְּכֶם הַיּוֹם כְּכוֹכְבֵי
הַשָּׁמַיִם לָרֹב׃ יא יְהוָה אֱלֹהֵי אֲבוֹתֵכֶם יֹסֵף עֲלֵיכֶם כָּכֶם אֶלֶף
פְּעָמִים וִיבָרֵךְ אֶתְכֶם כַּאֲשֶׁר דִּבֶּר לָכֶם׃

פרשת ואתחנן

פרק ג כג וָאֶתְחַנַּן אֶל־יְהוָה בָּעֵת הַהִוא לֵאמֹר׃ כד אֲדֹנָי יֱהוִה
אַתָּה הַחִלּוֹתָ לְהַרְאוֹת אֶת־עַבְדְּךָ אֶת־גָּדְלְךָ וְאֶת־יָדְךָ
הַחֲזָקָה אֲשֶׁר מִי־אֵל בַּשָּׁמַיִם וּבָאָרֶץ אֲשֶׁר־יַעֲשֶׂה כְמַעֲשֶׂיךָ
וְכִגְבוּרֹתֶךָ׃ כה אֶעְבְּרָה־נָּא וְאֶרְאֶה אֶת־הָאָרֶץ הַטּוֹבָה

אֲשֶׁר בְּעֵבֶר הַיַּרְדֵּן הָהָר הַטּוֹב הַזֶּה וְהַלְּבָנֹן: [לוי] כו וַיִּתְעַבֵּר
יְהוָה בִּי לְמַעַנְכֶם וְלֹא שָׁמַע אֵלָי וַיֹּאמֶר יְהוָה אֵלַי רַב־
לָךְ אַל־תּוֹסֶף דַּבֵּר אֵלַי עוֹד בַּדָּבָר הַזֶּה: כז עֲלֵה | רֹאשׁ
הַפִּסְגָּה וְשָׂא עֵינֶיךָ יָמָּה וְצָפֹנָה וְתֵימָנָה וּמִזְרָחָה וּרְאֵה
בְעֵינֶיךָ כִּי־לֹא תַעֲבֹר אֶת־הַיַּרְדֵּן הַזֶּה: כח וְצַו אֶת־יְהוֹשֻׁעַ
וְחַזְּקֵהוּ וְאַמְּצֵהוּ כִּי־הוּא יַעֲבֹר לִפְנֵי הָעָם הַזֶּה וְהוּא יַנְחִיל
אוֹתָם אֶת־הָאָרֶץ אֲשֶׁר תִּרְאֶה: כט וַנֵּשֶׁב בַּגָּיְא מוּל בֵּית
פְּעוֹר: פ פרק ד א וְעַתָּה יִשְׂרָאֵל שְׁמַע אֶל־הַחֻקִּים וְאֶל־
הַמִּשְׁפָּטִים אֲשֶׁר אָנֹכִי מְלַמֵּד אֶתְכֶם לַעֲשׂוֹת לְמַעַן תִּחְיוּ
וּבָאתֶם וִירִשְׁתֶּם אֶת־הָאָרֶץ אֲשֶׁר יְהוָה אֱלֹהֵי אֲבֹתֵיכֶם
נֹתֵן לָכֶם: ב לֹא תֹסִפוּ עַל־הַדָּבָר אֲשֶׁר אָנֹכִי מְצַוֶּה אֶתְכֶם
וְלֹא תִגְרְעוּ מִמֶּנּוּ לִשְׁמֹר אֶת־מִצְוֹת יְהוָה אֱלֹהֵיכֶם אֲשֶׁר
אָנֹכִי מְצַוֶּה אֶתְכֶם: ג עֵינֵיכֶם הָרֹאֹת אֵת אֲשֶׁר־עָשָׂה
יְהוָה בְּבַעַל פְּעוֹר כִּי כָל־הָאִישׁ אֲשֶׁר הָלַךְ אַחֲרֵי בַעַל־
פְּעוֹר הִשְׁמִידוֹ יְהוָה אֱלֹהֶיךָ מִקִּרְבֶּךָ: ד וְאַתֶּם הַדְּבֵקִים
בַּיהוָה אֱלֹהֵיכֶם חַיִּים כֻּלְּכֶם הַיּוֹם: [ישראל] ה רְאֵה | לִמַּדְתִּי
אֶתְכֶם חֻקִּים וּמִשְׁפָּטִים כַּאֲשֶׁר צִוַּנִי יְהוָה אֱלֹהָי לַעֲשׂוֹת כֵּן
בְּקֶרֶב הָאָרֶץ אֲשֶׁר אַתֶּם בָּאִים שָׁמָּה לְרִשְׁתָּהּ: ו וּשְׁמַרְתֶּם
וַעֲשִׂיתֶם כִּי הִוא חָכְמַתְכֶם וּבִינַתְכֶם לְעֵינֵי הָעַמִּים אֲשֶׁר
יִשְׁמְעוּן אֵת כָּל־הַחֻקִּים הָאֵלֶּה וְאָמְרוּ רַק עַם־חָכָם וְנָבוֹן
הַגּוֹי הַגָּדוֹל הַזֶּה: ז כִּי מִי־גוֹי גָּדוֹל אֲשֶׁר־לוֹ אֱלֹהִים קְרֹבִים
אֵלָיו כַּיהוָה אֱלֹהֵינוּ בְּכָל־קָרְאֵנוּ אֵלָיו: ח וּמִי גּוֹי גָּדוֹל אֲשֶׁר־
לוֹ חֻקִּים וּמִשְׁפָּטִים צַדִּיקִם כְּכֹל הַתּוֹרָה הַזֹּאת אֲשֶׁר אָנֹכִי
נֹתֵן לִפְנֵיכֶם הַיּוֹם:

פרשת עקב

פרק ז יב וְהָיָה | עֵקֶב תִּשְׁמְעוּן אֵת הַמִּשְׁפָּטִים הָאֵלֶּה

וּשְׁמַרְתֶּם וַעֲשִׂיתֶם אֹתָם וְשָׁמַר יְהוָה אֱלֹהֶיךָ לְךָ אֶת־
הַבְּרִית וְאֶת־הַחֶסֶד אֲשֶׁר נִשְׁבַּע לַאֲבֹתֶיךָ: יג וַאֲהֵבְךָ
וּבֵרַכְךָ וְהִרְבֶּךָ וּבֵרַךְ פְּרִי־בִטְנְךָ וּפְרִי־אַדְמָתֶךָ דְּגָנְךָ וְתִירֹשְׁךָ
וְיִצְהָרֶךָ שְׁגַר־אֲלָפֶיךָ וְעַשְׁתְּרֹת צֹאנֶךָ עַל הָאֲדָמָה אֲשֶׁר־
נִשְׁבַּע לַאֲבֹתֶיךָ לָתֶת לָךְ: יד בָּרוּךְ תִּהְיֶה מִכָּל־הָעַמִּים
לֹא־יִהְיֶה בְךָ עָקָר וַעֲקָרָה וּבִבְהֶמְתֶּךָ: טו וְהֵסִיר יְהוָה מִמְּךָ
כָּל־חֹלִי וְכָל־מַדְוֵי מִצְרַיִם הָרָעִים אֲשֶׁר יָדַעְתָּ לֹא יְשִׂימָם
בָּךְ וּנְתָנָם בְּכָל־שֹׂנְאֶיךָ: טז וְאָכַלְתָּ אֶת־כָּל־הָעַמִּים אֲשֶׁר
יְהוָה אֱלֹהֶיךָ נֹתֵן לָךְ לֹא־תָחוֹס עֵינְךָ עֲלֵיהֶם וְלֹא תַעֲבֹד
אֶת־אֱלֹהֵיהֶם כִּי־מוֹקֵשׁ הוּא לָךְ: ס יז כִּי תֹאמַר בִּלְבָבְךָ
רַבִּים הַגּוֹיִם הָאֵלֶּה מִמֶּנִּי אֵיכָה אוּכַל לְהוֹרִישָׁם: יח לֹא
תִירָא מֵהֶם זָכֹר תִּזְכֹּר אֵת אֲשֶׁר־עָשָׂה יְהוָה אֱלֹהֶיךָ לְפַרְעֹה
וּלְכָל־מִצְרָיִם: יט הַמַּסֹּת הַגְּדֹלֹת אֲשֶׁר־רָאוּ עֵינֶיךָ וְהָאֹתֹת
וְהַמֹּפְתִים וְהַיָּד הַחֲזָקָה וְהַזְּרֹעַ הַנְּטוּיָה אֲשֶׁר הוֹצִאֲךָ יְהוָה
אֱלֹהֶיךָ כֵּן־יַעֲשֶׂה יְהוָה אֱלֹהֶיךָ לְכָל־הָעַמִּים אֲשֶׁר־אַתָּה יָרֵא
מִפְּנֵיהֶם: כ וְגַם אֶת־הַצִּרְעָה יְשַׁלַּח יְהוָה אֱלֹהֶיךָ בָּם עַד־
אֲבֹד הַנִּשְׁאָרִים וְהַנִּסְתָּרִים מִפָּנֶיךָ: כא לֹא תַעֲרֹץ מִפְּנֵיהֶם
כִּי־יְהוָה אֱלֹהֶיךָ בְּקִרְבֶּךָ אֵל גָּדוֹל וְנוֹרָא: [לוי] כב וְנָשַׁל יְהוָה
אֱלֹהֶיךָ אֶת־הַגּוֹיִם הָאֵל מִפָּנֶיךָ מְעַט מְעָט לֹא תוּכַל כַּלֹּתָם
מַהֵר פֶּן־תִּרְבֶּה עָלֶיךָ חַיַּת הַשָּׂדֶה: כג וּנְתָנָם יְהוָה אֱלֹהֶיךָ
לְפָנֶיךָ וְהָמָם מְהוּמָה גְדֹלָה עַד הִשָּׁמְדָם: כד וְנָתַן מַלְכֵיהֶם
בְּיָדֶךָ וְהַאֲבַדְתָּ אֶת־שְׁמָם מִתַּחַת הַשָּׁמָיִם לֹא־יִתְיַצֵּב אִישׁ
בְּפָנֶיךָ עַד הִשְׁמִדְךָ אֹתָם: כה פְּסִילֵי אֱלֹהֵיהֶם תִּשְׂרְפוּן בָּאֵשׁ
לֹא־תַחְמֹד כֶּסֶף וְזָהָב עֲלֵיהֶם וְלָקַחְתָּ לָךְ פֶּן תִּוָּקֵשׁ בּוֹ כִּי
תוֹעֲבַת יְהוָה אֱלֹהֶיךָ הוּא: כו וְלֹא־תָבִיא תוֹעֵבָה אֶל־בֵּיתֶךָ
וְהָיִיתָ חֵרֶם כָּמֹהוּ שַׁקֵּץ | תְּשַׁקְּצֶנּוּ וְתַעֵב | תְּתַעֲבֶנּוּ כִּי־

חֵרֶם הוּא: פ פרק ח א כָּל־הַמִּצְוָה אֲשֶׁר אָנֹכִי מְצַוְּךָ הַיּוֹם
תִּשְׁמְרוּן לַעֲשׂוֹת לְמַעַן תִּחְיוּן וּרְבִיתֶם וּבָאתֶם וִירִשְׁתֶּם
אֶת־הָאָרֶץ אֲשֶׁר־נִשְׁבַּע יְהוָה לַאֲבֹתֵיכֶם: ב וְזָכַרְתָּ אֶת־כָּל־
הַדֶּרֶךְ אֲשֶׁר הוֹלִיכְךָ יְהוָה אֱלֹהֶיךָ זֶה אַרְבָּעִים שָׁנָה בַּמִּדְבָּר
לְמַעַן עַנֹּתְךָ לְנַסֹּתְךָ לָדַעַת אֶת־אֲשֶׁר בִּלְבָבְךָ הֲתִשְׁמֹר
מצותו▽ אִם־לֹא: ג וַיְעַנְּךָ וַיַּרְעִבֶךָ וַיַּאֲכִלְךָ אֶת־הַמָּן אֲשֶׁר
לֹא־יָדַעְתָּ וְלֹא יָדְעוּן אֲבֹתֶיךָ לְמַעַן הוֹדִיעֲךָ כִּי לֹא עַל־
הַלֶּחֶם לְבַדּוֹ יִחְיֶה הָאָדָם כִּי עַל־כָּל־מוֹצָא פִי־יְהוָה יִחְיֶה
הָאָדָם: [ישראל] ד שִׂמְלָתְךָ לֹא בָלְתָה מֵעָלֶיךָ וְרַגְלְךָ לֹא
בָצֵקָה זֶה אַרְבָּעִים שָׁנָה: ה וְיָדַעְתָּ עִם־לְבָבֶךָ כִּי כַּאֲשֶׁר
יְיַסֵּר אִישׁ אֶת־בְּנוֹ יְהוָה אֱלֹהֶיךָ מְיַסְּרֶךָּ: ו וְשָׁמַרְתָּ אֶת־
מִצְוֹת יְהוָה אֱלֹהֶיךָ לָלֶכֶת בִּדְרָכָיו וּלְיִרְאָה אֹתוֹ: ז כִּי
יְהוָה אֱלֹהֶיךָ מְבִיאֲךָ אֶל־אֶרֶץ טוֹבָה אֶרֶץ נַחֲלֵי מָיִם עֲיָנֹת
וּתְהֹמֹת יֹצְאִים בַּבִּקְעָה וּבָהָר: ח אֶרֶץ חִטָּה וּשְׂעֹרָה וְגֶפֶן
וּתְאֵנָה וְרִמּוֹן אֶרֶץ־זֵית שֶׁמֶן וּדְבָשׁ: ט אֶרֶץ אֲשֶׁר לֹא
בְמִסְכֵּנֻת תֹּאכַל־בָּהּ לֶחֶם לֹא־תֶחְסַר כֹּל בָּהּ אֶרֶץ אֲשֶׁר
אֲבָנֶיהָ בַרְזֶל וּמֵהֲרָרֶיהָ תַּחְצֹב נְחֹשֶׁת: י וְאָכַלְתָּ וְשָׂבָעְתָּ
וּבֵרַכְתָּ אֶת־יְהוָה אֱלֹהֶיךָ עַל־הָאָרֶץ הַטֹּבָה אֲשֶׁר נָתַן־לָךְ:

פרשת ראה

פרק יא כו רְאֵה אָנֹכִי נֹתֵן לִפְנֵיכֶם הַיּוֹם בְּרָכָה וּקְלָלָה: כז אֶת־
הַבְּרָכָה אֲשֶׁר תִּשְׁמְעוּ אֶל־מִצְוֹת יְהוָה אֱלֹהֵיכֶם אֲשֶׁר
אָנֹכִי מְצַוֶּה אֶתְכֶם הַיּוֹם: כח וְהַקְּלָלָה אִם־לֹא תִשְׁמְעוּ
אֶל־מִצְוֹת יְהוָה אֱלֹהֵיכֶם וְסַרְתֶּם מִן־הַדֶּרֶךְ אֲשֶׁר אָנֹכִי
מְצַוֶּה אֶתְכֶם הַיּוֹם לָלֶכֶת אַחֲרֵי אֱלֹהִים אֲחֵרִים אֲשֶׁר לֹא־

▽ מִצְוֹתָיו

יְדַעְתֶּם׃ ס כט וְהָיָה כִּי יְבִיאֲךָ יְהוָה אֱלֹהֶיךָ אֶל־הָאָרֶץ
אֲשֶׁר־אַתָּה בָא־שָׁמָּה לְרִשְׁתָּהּ וְנָתַתָּה אֶת־הַבְּרָכָה עַל־
הַר גְּרִזִים וְאֶת־הַקְּלָלָה עַל־הַר עֵיבָל׃ ל הֲלֹא־הֵמָּה בְּעֵבֶר
הַיַּרְדֵּן אַחֲרֵי דֶּרֶךְ מְבוֹא הַשֶּׁמֶשׁ בְּאֶרֶץ הַכְּנַעֲנִי הַיֹּשֵׁב
בָּעֲרָבָה מוּל הַגִּלְגָּל אֵצֶל אֵלוֹנֵי מֹרֶה׃ לא כִּי אַתֶּם עֹבְרִים
אֶת־הַיַּרְדֵּן לָבֹא לָרֶשֶׁת אֶת־הָאָרֶץ אֲשֶׁר־יְהוָה אֱלֹהֵיכֶם
נֹתֵן לָכֶם וִירִשְׁתֶּם אֹתָהּ וִישַׁבְתֶּם־בָּהּ׃ [לוי] לב וּשְׁמַרְתֶּם
לַעֲשׂוֹת אֵת כָּל־הַחֻקִּים וְאֶת־הַמִּשְׁפָּטִים אֲשֶׁר אָנֹכִי נֹתֵן
לִפְנֵיכֶם הַיּוֹם׃ פרק יב א אֵלֶּה הַחֻקִּים וְהַמִּשְׁפָּטִים אֲשֶׁר
תִּשְׁמְרוּן לַעֲשׂוֹת בָּאָרֶץ אֲשֶׁר נָתַן יְהוָה אֱלֹהֵי אֲבֹתֶיךָ לְךָ
לְרִשְׁתָּהּ כָּל־הַיָּמִים אֲשֶׁר־אַתֶּם חַיִּים עַל־הָאֲדָמָה׃ ב אַבֵּד
תְּאַבְּדוּן אֶת־כָּל־הַמְּקֹמוֹת אֲשֶׁר עָבְדוּ־שָׁם הַגּוֹיִם אֲשֶׁר
אַתֶּם יֹרְשִׁים אֹתָם אֶת־אֱלֹהֵיהֶם עַל־הֶהָרִים הָרָמִים וְעַל־
הַגְּבָעוֹת וְתַחַת כָּל־עֵץ רַעֲנָן׃ ג וְנִתַּצְתֶּם אֶת־מִזְבְּחֹתָם
וְשִׁבַּרְתֶּם אֶת־מַצֵּבֹתָם וַאֲשֵׁרֵיהֶם תִּשְׂרְפוּן בָּאֵשׁ וּפְסִילֵי
אֱלֹהֵיהֶם תְּגַדֵּעוּן וְאִבַּדְתֶּם אֶת־שְׁמָם מִן־הַמָּקוֹם הַהוּא׃
ד לֹא־תַעֲשׂוּן כֵּן לַיהוָה אֱלֹהֵיכֶם׃ ה כִּי אִם־אֶל־הַמָּקוֹם
אֲשֶׁר־יִבְחַר יְהוָה אֱלֹהֵיכֶם מִכָּל־שִׁבְטֵיכֶם לָשׂוּם אֶת־שְׁמוֹ
שָׁם לְשִׁכְנוֹ תִדְרְשׁוּ וּבָאתָ שָּׁמָּה׃ [ישראל] ו וַהֲבֵאתֶם שָׁמָּה
עֹלֹתֵיכֶם וְזִבְחֵיכֶם וְאֵת מַעְשְׂרֹתֵיכֶם וְאֵת תְּרוּמַת יֶדְכֶם
וְנִדְרֵיכֶם וְנִדְבֹתֵיכֶם וּבְכֹרֹת בְּקַרְכֶם וְצֹאנְכֶם׃ ז וַאֲכַלְתֶּם־
שָׁם לִפְנֵי יְהוָה אֱלֹהֵיכֶם וּשְׂמַחְתֶּם בְּכֹל מִשְׁלַח יֶדְכֶם
אַתֶּם וּבָתֵּיכֶם אֲשֶׁר בֵּרַכְךָ יְהוָה אֱלֹהֶיךָ׃ ח לֹא תַעֲשׂוּן
כְּכֹל אֲשֶׁר אֲנַחְנוּ עֹשִׂים פֹּה הַיּוֹם אִישׁ כָּל־הַיָּשָׁר בְּעֵינָיו׃
ט כִּי לֹא־בָאתֶם עַד־עָתָּה אֶל־הַמְּנוּחָה וְאֶל־הַנַּחֲלָה אֲשֶׁר־

יְהוָ֥ה אֱלֹהֶ֖יךָ נֹתֵ֥ן לָֽךְ׃ י וַעֲבַרְתֶּם֮ אֶת־הַיַּרְדֵּן֒ וִֽישַׁבְתֶּ֣ם
בָּאָ֔רֶץ אֲשֶׁר־יְהוָ֥ה אֱלֹהֵיכֶ֖ם מַנְחִ֣יל אֶתְכֶ֑ם וְהֵנִ֨יחַ לָכֶ֧ם
מִכָּל־אֹיְבֵיכֶ֛ם מִסָּבִ֖יב וִֽישַׁבְתֶּם־בֶּֽטַח׃

פרשת שופטים

פרק טז יח שֹׁפְטִ֣ים וְשֹֽׁטְרִ֗ים תִּֽתֶּן־לְךָ֙ בְּכָל־שְׁעָרֶ֔יךָ אֲשֶׁ֨ר
יְהוָ֧ה אֱלֹהֶ֛יךָ נֹתֵ֥ן לְךָ֖ לִשְׁבָטֶ֑יךָ וְשָׁפְט֥וּ אֶת־הָעָ֖ם מִשְׁפַּט־
צֶֽדֶק׃ יט לֹא־תַטֶּ֣ה מִשְׁפָּ֔ט לֹ֥א תַכִּ֖יר פָּנִ֑ים וְלֹא־תִקַּ֣ח שֹׁ֔חַד
כִּ֣י הַשֹּׁ֗חַד יְעַוֵּר֙ עֵינֵ֣י חֲכָמִ֔ים וִֽיסַלֵּ֖ף דִּבְרֵ֥י צַדִּיקִֽם׃ כ צֶ֥דֶק
צֶ֖דֶק תִּרְדֹּ֑ף לְמַ֤עַן תִּֽחְיֶה֙ וְיָרַשְׁתָּ֣ אֶת־הָאָ֔רֶץ אֲשֶׁר־יְהוָ֥ה
אֱלֹהֶ֖יךָ נֹתֵ֥ן לָֽךְ׃ ס [לוי] כא לֹֽא־תִטַּ֥ע לְךָ֛ אֲשֵׁרָ֖ה כָּל־עֵ֑ץ
אֵ֗צֶל מִזְבַּ֛ח יְהוָ֥ה אֱלֹהֶ֖יךָ אֲשֶׁ֥ר תַּעֲשֶׂה־לָּֽךְ׃ כב וְלֹא־תָקִ֥ים לְךָ֖
מַצֵּבָ֑ה אֲשֶׁ֥ר שָׂנֵ֖א יְהוָ֥ה אֱלֹהֶֽיךָ׃ ס פרק יז א לֹא־תִזְבַּח֩
לַֽיהוָ֨ה אֱלֹהֶ֜יךָ שׁ֣וֹר וָשֶׂ֗ה אֲשֶׁ֨ר יִהְיֶ֥ה בוֹ֙ מ֔וּם כֹּ֖ל דָּבָ֣ר רָ֑ע
כִּ֧י תוֹעֲבַ֛ת יְהוָ֥ה אֱלֹהֶ֖יךָ הֽוּא׃ ס ב כִּֽי־יִמָּצֵ֤א בְקִרְבְּךָ֙
בְּאַחַ֣ד שְׁעָרֶ֔יךָ אֲשֶׁר־יְהוָ֥ה אֱלֹהֶ֖יךָ נֹתֵ֣ן לָ֑ךְ אִ֣ישׁ אוֹ־אִשָּׁ֗ה
אֲשֶׁ֨ר יַעֲשֶׂ֧ה אֶת־הָרַ֛ע בְּעֵינֵ֥י יְהוָֽה־אֱלֹהֶ֖יךָ לַעֲבֹ֥ר בְּרִיתֽוֹ׃
ג וַיֵּ֗לֶךְ וַֽיַּעֲבֹד֙ אֱלֹהִ֣ים אֲחֵרִ֔ים וַיִּשְׁתַּ֖חוּ לָהֶ֑ם וְלַשֶּׁ֣מֶשׁ ׀ א֣וֹ
לַיָּרֵ֗חַ א֛וֹ לְכָל־צְבָ֥א הַשָּׁמַ֖יִם אֲשֶׁ֥ר לֹא־צִוִּֽיתִי׃ ד וְהֻגַּד־לְךָ֖
וְשָׁמָ֑עְתָּ וְדָרַשְׁתָּ֣ הֵיטֵ֔ב וְהִנֵּ֤ה אֱמֶת֙ נָכ֣וֹן הַדָּבָ֔ר נֶעֶשְׂתָ֛ה
הַתּוֹעֵבָ֥ה הַזֹּ֖את בְּיִשְׂרָאֵֽל׃ ה וְהוֹצֵאתָ֣ אֶת־הָאִ֣ישׁ הַה֡וּא
א֩וֹ אֶת־הָאִשָּׁ֨ה הַהִ֜וא אֲשֶׁ֥ר עָ֠שׂוּ אֶת־הַדָּבָ֨ר הָרָ֤ע הַזֶּה֙ אֶל־
שְׁעָרֶ֔יךָ אֶת־הָאִ֕ישׁ א֖וֹ אֶת־הָאִשָּׁ֑ה וּסְקַלְתָּ֥ם בָּאֲבָנִ֖ים וָמֵֽתוּ׃
ו עַל־פִּ֣י ׀ שְׁנַ֣יִם עֵדִ֗ים א֛וֹ שְׁלֹשָׁ֥ה עֵדִ֖ים יוּמַ֣ת הַמֵּ֑ת לֹ֣א יוּמַ֔ת
עַל־פִּ֖י עֵ֥ד אֶחָֽד׃ ז יַ֣ד הָעֵדִ֞ים תִּֽהְיֶה־בּ֤וֹ בָרִֽאשֹׁנָה֙ לַהֲמִית֔וֹ
וְיַ֥ד כָּל־הָעָ֖ם בָּאַחֲרֹנָ֑ה וּבִעַרְתָּ֥ הָרָ֖ע מִקִּרְבֶּֽךָ׃ פ ח כִּ֣י יִפָּלֵא֩

מִמְּךָ דָבָר לַמִּשְׁפָּט בֵּין־דָּם | לְדָם בֵּין־דִּין לְדִין וּבֵין נֶגַע
לָנֶגַע דִּבְרֵי רִיבֹת בִּשְׁעָרֶיךָ וְקַמְתָּ וְעָלִיתָ אֶל־הַמָּקוֹם אֲשֶׁר
יִבְחַר יְהוָה אֱלֹהֶיךָ בּוֹ׃ ט וּבָאתָ אֶל־הַכֹּהֲנִים הַלְוִיִּם וְאֶל־
הַשֹּׁפֵט אֲשֶׁר יִהְיֶה בַּיָּמִים הָהֵם וְדָרַשְׁתָּ וְהִגִּידוּ לְךָ אֵת דְּבַר
הַמִּשְׁפָּט׃ י וְעָשִׂיתָ עַל־פִּי הַדָּבָר אֲשֶׁר יַגִּידוּ לְךָ מִן־הַמָּקוֹם
הַהוּא אֲשֶׁר יִבְחַר יְהוָה וְשָׁמַרְתָּ לַעֲשׂוֹת כְּכֹל אֲשֶׁר יוֹרוּךָ׃
[ישראל] יא עַל־פִּי הַתּוֹרָה אֲשֶׁר יוֹרוּךָ וְעַל־הַמִּשְׁפָּט אֲשֶׁר־
יֹאמְרוּ לְךָ תַּעֲשֶׂה לֹא תָסוּר מִן־הַדָּבָר אֲשֶׁר־יַגִּידוּ לְךָ יָמִין
וּשְׂמֹאל׃ יב וְהָאִישׁ אֲשֶׁר־יַעֲשֶׂה בְזָדוֹן לְבִלְתִּי שְׁמֹעַ אֶל־
הַכֹּהֵן הָעֹמֵד לְשָׁרֶת שָׁם אֶת־יְהוָה אֱלֹהֶיךָ אוֹ אֶל־הַשֹּׁפֵט
וּמֵת הָאִישׁ הַהוּא וּבִעַרְתָּ הָרָע מִיִּשְׂרָאֵל׃ יג וְכָל־הָעָם
יִשְׁמְעוּ וְיִרָאוּ וְלֹא יְזִידוּן עוֹד׃

פרשת כי תצא

פרק כא י כִּי־תֵצֵא לַמִּלְחָמָה עַל־אֹיְבֶיךָ וּנְתָנוֹ יְהוָה אֱלֹהֶיךָ
בְּיָדֶךָ וְשָׁבִיתָ שִׁבְיוֹ׃ יא וְרָאִיתָ בַּשִּׁבְיָה אֵשֶׁת יְפַת־תֹּאַר
וְחָשַׁקְתָּ בָהּ וְלָקַחְתָּ לְךָ לְאִשָּׁה׃ יב וַהֲבֵאתָהּ אֶל־תּוֹךְ בֵּיתֶךָ
וְגִלְּחָה אֶת־רֹאשָׁהּ וְעָשְׂתָה אֶת־צִפָּרְנֶיהָ׃ יג וְהֵסִירָה אֶת־
שִׂמְלַת שִׁבְיָהּ מֵעָלֶיהָ וְיָשְׁבָה בְּבֵיתֶךָ וּבָכְתָה אֶת־אָבִיהָ
וְאֶת־אִמָּהּ יֶרַח יָמִים וְאַחַר כֵּן תָּבוֹא אֵלֶיהָ וּבְעַלְתָּהּ וְהָיְתָה
לְךָ לְאִשָּׁה׃ יד וְהָיָה אִם־לֹא חָפַצְתָּ בָּהּ וְשִׁלַּחְתָּהּ לְנַפְשָׁהּ
וּמָכֹר לֹא־תִמְכְּרֶנָּה בַּכָּסֶף לֹא־תִתְעַמֵּר בָּהּ תַּחַת אֲשֶׁר
עִנִּיתָהּ׃ ס [לוי] טו כִּי־תִהְיֶיןָ לְאִישׁ שְׁתֵּי נָשִׁים הָאַחַת
אֲהוּבָה וְהָאַחַת שְׂנוּאָה וְיָלְדוּ־לוֹ בָנִים הָאֲהוּבָה וְהַשְּׂנוּאָה
וְהָיָה הַבֵּן הַבְּכֹר לַשְּׂנִיאָה׃ טז וְהָיָה בְּיוֹם הַנְחִילוֹ אֶת־בָּנָיו
אֵת אֲשֶׁר־יִהְיֶה לוֹ לֹא יוּכַל לְבַכֵּר אֶת־בֶּן־הָאֲהוּבָה עַל־פְּנֵי

בֶּן־הַשְּׂנוּאָה הַבְּכֹר׃ יז כִּי אֶת־הַבְּכֹר בֶּן־הַשְּׂנוּאָה יַכִּיר לָתֶת
לוֹ פִּי שְׁנַיִם בְּכֹל אֲשֶׁר־יִמָּצֵא לוֹ כִּי־הוּא רֵאשִׁית אֹנוֹ לוֹ
מִשְׁפַּט הַבְּכֹרָה׃ ס [ישראל] יח כִּי־יִהְיֶה לְאִישׁ בֵּן סוֹרֵר
וּמוֹרֶה אֵינֶנּוּ שֹׁמֵעַ בְּקוֹל אָבִיו וּבְקוֹל אִמּוֹ וְיִסְּרוּ אֹתוֹ וְלֹא
יִשְׁמַע אֲלֵיהֶם׃ יט וְתָפְשׂוּ בוֹ אָבִיו וְאִמּוֹ וְהוֹצִיאוּ אֹתוֹ אֶל־
זִקְנֵי עִירוֹ וְאֶל־שַׁעַר מְקֹמוֹ׃ כ וְאָמְרוּ אֶל־זִקְנֵי עִירוֹ בְּנֵנוּ
זֶה סוֹרֵר וּמֹרֶה אֵינֶנּוּ שֹׁמֵעַ בְּקֹלֵנוּ זוֹלֵל וְסֹבֵא׃ כא וּרְגָמֻהוּ
כָּל־אַנְשֵׁי עִירוֹ בָאֲבָנִים וָמֵת וּבִעַרְתָּ הָרָע מִקִּרְבֶּךָ וְכָל־
יִשְׂרָאֵל יִשְׁמְעוּ וְיִרָאוּ׃

פרשת כי תבוא

פרק כו א וְהָיָה כִּי־תָבוֹא אֶל־הָאָרֶץ אֲשֶׁר יְהוָה אֱלֹהֶיךָ
נֹתֵן לְךָ נַחֲלָה וִירִשְׁתָּהּ וְיָשַׁבְתָּ בָּהּ׃ ב וְלָקַחְתָּ מֵרֵאשִׁית |
כָּל־פְּרִי הָאֲדָמָה אֲשֶׁר תָּבִיא מֵאַרְצְךָ אֲשֶׁר יְהוָה אֱלֹהֶיךָ
נֹתֵן לָךְ וְשַׂמְתָּ בַטֶּנֶא וְהָלַכְתָּ אֶל־הַמָּקוֹם אֲשֶׁר יִבְחַר יְהוָה
אֱלֹהֶיךָ לְשַׁכֵּן שְׁמוֹ שָׁם׃ ג וּבָאתָ אֶל־הַכֹּהֵן אֲשֶׁר יִהְיֶה
בַּיָּמִים הָהֵם וְאָמַרְתָּ אֵלָיו הִגַּדְתִּי הַיּוֹם לַיהוָה אֱלֹהֶיךָ
כִּי־בָאתִי אֶל־הָאָרֶץ אֲשֶׁר נִשְׁבַּע יְהוָה לַאֲבֹתֵינוּ לָתֶת לָנוּ׃
[לוי] ד וְלָקַח הַכֹּהֵן הַטֶּנֶא מִיָּדֶךָ וְהִנִּיחוֹ לִפְנֵי מִזְבַּח יְהוָה
אֱלֹהֶיךָ׃ ה וְעָנִיתָ וְאָמַרְתָּ לִפְנֵי | יְהוָה אֱלֹהֶיךָ אֲרַמִּי אֹבֵד
אָבִי וַיֵּרֶד מִצְרַיְמָה וַיָּגָר שָׁם בִּמְתֵי מְעָט וַיְהִי־שָׁם לְגוֹי
גָּדוֹל עָצוּם וָרָב׃ ו וַיָּרֵעוּ אֹתָנוּ הַמִּצְרִים וַיְעַנּוּנוּ וַיִּתְּנוּ עָלֵינוּ
עֲבֹדָה קָשָׁה׃ ז וַנִּצְעַק אֶל־יְהוָה אֱלֹהֵי אֲבֹתֵינוּ וַיִּשְׁמַע
יְהוָה אֶת־קֹלֵנוּ וַיַּרְא אֶת־עָנְיֵנוּ וְאֶת־עֲמָלֵנוּ וְאֶת־לַחֲצֵנוּ׃
ח וַיּוֹצִאֵנוּ יְהוָה מִמִּצְרַיִם בְּיָד חֲזָקָה וּבִזְרֹעַ נְטוּיָה וּבְמֹרָא

גָּדֹל וּבְאֹתוֹת וּבְמֹפְתִים׃ ט וַיְבִאֵנוּ אֶל־הַמָּקוֹם הַזֶּה וַיִּתֶּן־
לָנוּ אֶת־הָאָרֶץ הַזֹּאת אֶרֶץ זָבַת חָלָב וּדְבָשׁ׃ י וְעַתָּה הִנֵּה
הֵבֵאתִי אֶת־רֵאשִׁית פְּרִי הָאֲדָמָה אֲשֶׁר־נָתַתָּה לִּי יְהוָה
וְהִנַּחְתּוֹ לִפְנֵי יְהוָה אֱלֹהֶיךָ וְהִשְׁתַּחֲוִיתָ לִפְנֵי יְהוָה אֱלֹהֶיךָ׃
יא וְשָׂמַחְתָּ בְכָל־הַטּוֹב אֲשֶׁר נָתַן־לְךָ יְהוָה אֱלֹהֶיךָ וּלְבֵיתֶךָ
אַתָּה וְהַלֵּוִי וְהַגֵּר אֲשֶׁר בְּקִרְבֶּךָ׃ ס [ישראל] יב כִּי תְכַלֶּה
לַעְשֵׂר אֶת־כָּל־מַעְשַׂר תְּבוּאָתְךָ בַּשָּׁנָה הַשְּׁלִישִׁת שְׁנַת
הַמַּעֲשֵׂר וְנָתַתָּה לַלֵּוִי לַגֵּר לַיָּתוֹם וְלָאַלְמָנָה וְאָכְלוּ בִשְׁעָרֶיךָ
וְשָׂבֵעוּ׃ יג וְאָמַרְתָּ לִפְנֵי יְהוָה אֱלֹהֶיךָ בִּעַרְתִּי הַקֹּדֶשׁ מִן־
הַבַּיִת וְגַם נְתַתִּיו לַלֵּוִי וְלַגֵּר לַיָּתוֹם וְלָאַלְמָנָה כְּכָל־מִצְוָתְךָ
אֲשֶׁר צִוִּיתָנִי לֹא־עָבַרְתִּי מִמִּצְוֺתֶיךָ וְלֹא שָׁכָחְתִּי׃ יד לֹא־
אָכַלְתִּי בְאֹנִי מִמֶּנּוּ וְלֹא־בִעַרְתִּי מִמֶּנּוּ בְּטָמֵא וְלֹא־נָתַתִּי
מִמֶּנּוּ לְמֵת שָׁמַעְתִּי בְּקוֹל יְהוָה אֱלֹהָי עָשִׂיתִי כְּכֹל אֲשֶׁר
צִוִּיתָנִי׃ טו הַשְׁקִיפָה מִמְּעוֹן קָדְשְׁךָ מִן־הַשָּׁמַיִם וּבָרֵךְ אֶת־
עַמְּךָ אֶת־יִשְׂרָאֵל וְאֵת הָאֲדָמָה אֲשֶׁר נָתַתָּה לָנוּ כַּאֲשֶׁר
נִשְׁבַּעְתָּ לַאֲבֹתֵינוּ אֶרֶץ זָבַת חָלָב וּדְבָשׁ׃

פרשת נצבים

פרק כט ט אַתֶּם נִצָּבִים הַיּוֹם כֻּלְּכֶם לִפְנֵי יְהוָה אֱלֹהֵיכֶם
רָאשֵׁיכֶם שִׁבְטֵיכֶם זִקְנֵיכֶם וְשֹׁטְרֵיכֶם כֹּל אִישׁ יִשְׂרָאֵל׃
י טַפְּכֶם נְשֵׁיכֶם וְגֵרְךָ אֲשֶׁר בְּקֶרֶב מַחֲנֶיךָ מֵחֹטֵב עֵצֶיךָ עַד
שֹׁאֵב מֵימֶיךָ׃ יא לְעָבְרְךָ בִּבְרִית יְהוָה אֱלֹהֶיךָ וּבְאָלָתוֹ אֲשֶׁר
יְהוָה אֱלֹהֶיךָ כֹּרֵת עִמְּךָ הַיּוֹם׃ [לוי] יב לְמַעַן הָקִים־אֹתְךָ
הַיּוֹם ׀ לוֹ לְעָם וְהוּא יִהְיֶה־לְּךָ לֵאלֹהִים כַּאֲשֶׁר דִּבֶּר־לָךְ
וְכַאֲשֶׁר נִשְׁבַּע לַאֲבֹתֶיךָ לְאַבְרָהָם לְיִצְחָק וּלְיַעֲקֹב׃ יג וְלֹא

אִתְּכֶם לְבַדְּכֶם אָנֹכִי כֹּרֵת אֶת־הַבְּרִית הַזֹּאת וְאֶת־הָאָלָה
הַזֹּאת׃ יד כִּי אֶת־אֲשֶׁר יֶשְׁנוֹ פֹּה עִמָּנוּ עֹמֵד הַיּוֹם לִפְנֵי יְהוָה
אֱלֹהֵינוּ וְאֵת אֲשֶׁר אֵינֶנּוּ פֹּה עִמָּנוּ הַיּוֹם׃ [ישראל] טו כִּי־אַתֶּם
יְדַעְתֶּם אֵת אֲשֶׁר־יָשַׁבְנוּ בְּאֶרֶץ מִצְרָיִם וְאֵת אֲשֶׁר־עָבַרְנוּ
בְּקֶרֶב הַגּוֹיִם אֲשֶׁר עֲבַרְתֶּם׃ טז וַתִּרְאוּ אֶת־שִׁקּוּצֵיהֶם וְאֵת
גִּלֻּלֵיהֶם עֵץ וָאֶבֶן כֶּסֶף וְזָהָב אֲשֶׁר עִמָּהֶם׃ יז פֶּן־יֵשׁ בָּכֶם
אִישׁ אוֹ־אִשָּׁה אוֹ מִשְׁפָּחָה אוֹ־שֵׁבֶט אֲשֶׁר לְבָבוֹ פֹנֶה הַיּוֹם
מֵעִם יְהוָה אֱלֹהֵינוּ לָלֶכֶת לַעֲבֹד אֶת־אֱלֹהֵי הַגּוֹיִם הָהֵם
פֶּן־יֵשׁ בָּכֶם שֹׁרֶשׁ פֹּרֶה רֹאשׁ וְלַעֲנָה׃ יח וְהָיָה בְּשָׁמְעוֹ אֶת־
דִּבְרֵי הָאָלָה הַזֹּאת וְהִתְבָּרֵךְ בִּלְבָבוֹ לֵאמֹר שָׁלוֹם יִהְיֶה־לִּי
כִּי בִּשְׁרִרוּת לִבִּי אֵלֵךְ לְמַעַן סְפוֹת הָרָוָה אֶת־הַצְּמֵאָה׃
יט לֹא־יֹאבֶה יְהוָה סְלֹחַ לוֹ כִּי אָז יֶעְשַׁן אַף־יְהוָה וְקִנְאָתוֹ
בָּאִישׁ הַהוּא וְרָבְצָה בּוֹ כָּל־הָאָלָה הַכְּתוּבָה בַּסֵּפֶר הַזֶּה
וּמָחָה יְהוָה אֶת־שְׁמוֹ מִתַּחַת הַשָּׁמָיִם׃ כ וְהִבְדִּילוֹ יְהוָה
לְרָעָה מִכֹּל שִׁבְטֵי יִשְׂרָאֵל כְּכֹל אָלוֹת הַבְּרִית הַכְּתוּבָה
בְּסֵפֶר הַתּוֹרָה הַזֶּה׃ כא וְאָמַר הַדּוֹר הָאַחֲרוֹן בְּנֵיכֶם אֲשֶׁר
יָקוּמוּ מֵאַחֲרֵיכֶם וְהַנָּכְרִי אֲשֶׁר יָבֹא מֵאֶרֶץ רְחוֹקָה וְרָאוּ
אֶת־מַכּוֹת הָאָרֶץ הַהִוא וְאֶת־תַּחֲלֻאֶיהָ אֲשֶׁר־חִלָּה יְהוָה
בָּהּ׃ כב גָּפְרִית וָמֶלַח שְׂרֵפָה כָל־אַרְצָהּ לֹא תִזָּרַע וְלֹא
תַצְמִחַ וְלֹא־יַעֲלֶה בָהּ כָּל־עֵשֶׂב כְּמַהְפֵּכַת סְדֹם וַעֲמֹרָה
אַדְמָה וצביים▽ אֲשֶׁר הָפַךְ יְהוָה בְּאַפּוֹ וּבַחֲמָתוֹ׃ כג וְאָמְרוּ
כָּל־הַגּוֹיִם עַל־מֶה עָשָׂה יְהוָה כָּכָה לָאָרֶץ הַזֹּאת מֶה חֳרִי
הָאַף הַגָּדוֹל הַזֶּה׃ כד וְאָמְרוּ עַל אֲשֶׁר עָזְבוּ אֶת־בְּרִית
יְהוָה אֱלֹהֵי אֲבֹתָם אֲשֶׁר כָּרַת עִמָּם בְּהוֹצִיאוֹ אֹתָם מֵאֶרֶץ

▽ וּצְבוֹיִם

מִצְרָיִם: כה וַיֵּלְכוּ וַיַּעַבְדוּ אֱלֹהִים אֲחֵרִים וַיִּשְׁתַּחֲווּ לָהֶם
אֱלֹהִים אֲשֶׁר לֹא־יְדָעוּם וְלֹא חָלַק לָהֶם: כו וַיִּחַר־אַף יְהוָה
בָּאָרֶץ הַהִוא לְהָבִיא עָלֶיהָ אֶת־כָּל־הַקְּלָלָה הַכְּתוּבָה בַּסֵּפֶר
הַזֶּה: כז וַיִּתְּשֵׁם יְהוָה מֵעַל אַדְמָתָם בְּאַף וּבְחֵמָה וּבְקֶצֶף
גָּדוֹל וַיַּשְׁלִכֵם אֶל־אֶרֶץ אַחֶרֶת כַּיּוֹם הַזֶּה: כח הַנִּסְתָּרֹת
לַיהוָה אֱלֹהֵינוּ וְהַנִּגְלֹת לָנוּ וּלְבָנֵינוּ עַד־עוֹלָם לַעֲשׂוֹת אֶת־
כָּל־דִּבְרֵי הַתּוֹרָה הַזֹּאת:

פרשת וילך

פרק לא א וַיֵּלֶךְ מֹשֶׁה וַיְדַבֵּר אֶת־הַדְּבָרִים הָאֵלֶּה אֶל־כָּל־
יִשְׂרָאֵל: ב וַיֹּאמֶר אֲלֵהֶם בֶּן־מֵאָה וְעֶשְׂרִים שָׁנָה אָנֹכִי
הַיּוֹם לֹא־אוּכַל עוֹד לָצֵאת וְלָבוֹא וַיהוָה אָמַר אֵלַי לֹא
תַעֲבֹר אֶת־הַיַּרְדֵּן הַזֶּה: ג יְהוָה אֱלֹהֶיךָ הוּא | עֹבֵר לְפָנֶיךָ
הוּא־יַשְׁמִיד אֶת־הַגּוֹיִם הָאֵלֶּה מִלְּפָנֶיךָ וִירִשְׁתָּם יְהוֹשֻׁעַ
הוּא עֹבֵר לְפָנֶיךָ כַּאֲשֶׁר דִּבֶּר יְהוָה: [לוי] ד וְעָשָׂה יְהוָה
לָהֶם כַּאֲשֶׁר עָשָׂה לְסִיחוֹן וּלְעוֹג מַלְכֵי הָאֱמֹרִי וּלְאַרְצָם
אֲשֶׁר הִשְׁמִיד אֹתָם: ה וּנְתָנָם יְהוָה לִפְנֵיכֶם וַעֲשִׂיתֶם לָהֶם
כְּכָל־הַמִּצְוָה אֲשֶׁר צִוִּיתִי אֶתְכֶם: ו חִזְקוּ וְאִמְצוּ אַל־תִּירְאוּ
וְאַל־תַּעַרְצוּ מִפְּנֵיהֶם כִּי | יְהוָה אֱלֹהֶיךָ הוּא הַהֹלֵךְ עִמָּךְ לֹא
יַרְפְּךָ וְלֹא יַעַזְבֶךָּ: ס [ישראל] ז וַיִּקְרָא מֹשֶׁה לִיהוֹשֻׁעַ
וַיֹּאמֶר אֵלָיו לְעֵינֵי כָל־יִשְׂרָאֵל חֲזַק וֶאֱמָץ כִּי אַתָּה תָּבוֹא
אֶת־הָעָם הַזֶּה אֶל־הָאָרֶץ אֲשֶׁר נִשְׁבַּע יְהוָה לַאֲבֹתָם לָתֵת
לָהֶם וְאַתָּה תַּנְחִילֶנָּה אוֹתָם: ח וַיהוָה הוּא | הַהֹלֵךְ לְפָנֶיךָ
הוּא יִהְיֶה עִמָּךְ לֹא יַרְפְּךָ וְלֹא יַעַזְבֶךָּ לֹא תִירָא וְלֹא תֵחָת:
ט וַיִּכְתֹּב מֹשֶׁה אֶת־הַתּוֹרָה הַזֹּאת וַיִּתְּנָהּ אֶל־הַכֹּהֲנִים בְּנֵי
לֵוִי הַנֹּשְׂאִים אֶת־אֲרוֹן בְּרִית יְהוָה וְאֶל־כָּל־זִקְנֵי יִשְׂרָאֵל:

י וַיְצַו מֹשֶׁה אוֹתָם לֵאמֹר מִקֵּץ | שֶׁבַע שָׁנִים בְּמֹעֵד שְׁנַת
הַשְּׁמִטָּה בְּחַג הַסֻּכּוֹת: יא בְּבוֹא כָל־יִשְׂרָאֵל לֵרָאוֹת אֶת־פְּנֵי
יְהוָה אֱלֹהֶיךָ בַּמָּקוֹם אֲשֶׁר יִבְחָר תִּקְרָא אֶת־הַתּוֹרָה הַזֹּאת
נֶגֶד כָּל־יִשְׂרָאֵל בְּאָזְנֵיהֶם: יב הַקְהֵל אֶת־הָעָם הָאֲנָשִׁים
וְהַנָּשִׁים וְהַטַּף וְגֵרְךָ אֲשֶׁר בִּשְׁעָרֶיךָ לְמַעַן יִשְׁמְעוּ וּלְמַעַן
יִלְמְדוּ וְיָרְאוּ אֶת־יְהוָה אֱלֹהֵיכֶם וְשָׁמְרוּ לַעֲשׂוֹת אֶת־כָּל־
דִּבְרֵי הַתּוֹרָה הַזֹּאת: יג וּבְנֵיהֶם אֲשֶׁר לֹא־יָדְעוּ יִשְׁמְעוּ
וְלָמְדוּ לְיִרְאָה אֶת־יְהוָה אֱלֹהֵיכֶם כָּל־הַיָּמִים אֲשֶׁר אַתֶּם
חַיִּים עַל־הָאֲדָמָה אֲשֶׁר אַתֶּם עֹבְרִים אֶת־הַיַּרְדֵּן שָׁמָּה
לְרִשְׁתָּהּ:

פרשת האזינו

פרק לב א הַאֲזִינוּ הַשָּׁמַיִם וַאֲדַבֵּרָה וְתִשְׁמַע הָאָרֶץ אִמְרֵי־
פִי: ב יַעֲרֹף כַּמָּטָר לִקְחִי תִּזַּל כַּטַּל אִמְרָתִי כִּשְׂעִירִם עֲלֵי־
דֶשֶׁא וְכִרְבִיבִים עֲלֵי־עֵשֶׂב: ג כִּי שֵׁם יְהוָה אֶקְרָא הָבוּ גֹדֶל
לֵאלֹהֵינוּ: [לוי] ד הַצּוּר תָּמִים פָּעֳלוֹ כִּי כָל־דְּרָכָיו מִשְׁפָּט אֵל
אֱמוּנָה וְאֵין עָוֶל צַדִּיק וְיָשָׁר הוּא: ה שִׁחֵת לוֹ לֹא בָּנָיו מוּמָם
דּוֹר עִקֵּשׁ וּפְתַלְתֹּל: ו הַלְיְהוָה תִּגְמְלוּ־זֹאת עַם נָבָל וְלֹא
חָכָם הֲלוֹא־הוּא אָבִיךָ קָּנֶךָ הוּא עָשְׂךָ וַיְכֹנְנֶךָ: [ישראל] ז זְכֹר
יְמוֹת עוֹלָם בִּינוּ שְׁנוֹת דֹּר וָדֹר שְׁאַל אָבִיךָ וְיַגֵּדְךָ זְקֵנֶיךָ
וְיֹאמְרוּ לָךְ: ח בְּהַנְחֵל עֶלְיוֹן גּוֹיִם בְּהַפְרִידוֹ בְּנֵי אָדָם יַצֵּב
גְּבֻלֹת עַמִּים לְמִסְפַּר בְּנֵי יִשְׂרָאֵל: ט כִּי חֵלֶק יְהוָה עַמּוֹ יַעֲקֹב
חֶבֶל נַחֲלָתוֹ: י יִמְצָאֵהוּ בְּאֶרֶץ מִדְבָּר וּבְתֹהוּ יְלֵל יְשִׁמֹן
יְסֹבְבֶנְהוּ יְבוֹנְנֵהוּ יִצְּרֶנְהוּ כְּאִישׁוֹן עֵינוֹ: יא כְּנֶשֶׁר יָעִיר קִנּוֹ
עַל־גּוֹזָלָיו יְרַחֵף יִפְרֹשׂ כְּנָפָיו יִקָּחֵהוּ יִשָּׂאֵהוּ עַל־אֶבְרָתוֹ:
יב יְהוָה בָּדָד יַנְחֶנּוּ וְאֵין עִמּוֹ אֵל נֵכָר:

פרשת וזאת הברכה

פרק לג א וְזֹ֣את הַבְּרָכָ֗ה אֲשֶׁ֨ר בֵּרַ֥ךְ מֹשֶׁ֛ה אִ֥ישׁ הָאֱלֹהִ֖ים
אֶת־בְּנֵ֣י יִשְׂרָאֵ֑ל לִפְנֵ֖י מוֹתֽוֹ׃ ב וַיֹּאמַ֗ר יְהֹוָ֞ה מִסִּינַ֥י בָּא֙
וְזָרַ֤ח מִשֵּׂעִיר֙ לָ֔מוֹ הוֹפִ֙יעַ֙ מֵהַ֣ר פָּארָ֔ן וְאָתָ֖ה מֵרִבְבֹ֣ת קֹ֑דֶשׁ
מִֽימִינ֕וֹ אֵ֥שְׁדָּ֖ת לָֽמוֹ׃ ג אַ֚ף חֹבֵ֣ב עַמִּ֔ים כָּל־קְדֹשָׁ֖יו בְּיָדֶ֑ךָ
וְהֵם֙ תֻּכּ֣וּ לְרַגְלֶ֔ךָ יִשָּׂ֖א מִדַּבְּרֹתֶֽיךָ׃ ד תּוֹרָ֥ה צִוָּה־לָ֖נוּ מֹשֶׁ֑ה
מוֹרָשָׁ֖ה קְהִלַּ֥ת יַעֲקֹֽב׃ ה וַיְהִ֥י בִישֻׁר֖וּן מֶ֑לֶךְ בְּהִתְאַסֵּף֙
רָ֣אשֵׁי עָ֔ם יַ֖חַד שִׁבְטֵ֥י יִשְׂרָאֵֽל׃ ו יְחִ֥י רְאוּבֵ֖ן וְאַל־יָמֹ֑ת
וִיהִ֥י מְתָ֖יו מִסְפָּֽר׃ ס ז וְזֹ֣את לִֽיהוּדָה֮ וַיֹּאמַר֒ שְׁמַ֤ע
יְהֹוָה֙ ק֣וֹל יְהוּדָ֔ה וְאֶל־עַמּ֖וֹ תְּבִיאֶ֑נּוּ יָדָיו֙ רָ֣ב ל֔וֹ וְעֵ֥זֶר מִצָּרָ֖יו
תִּהְיֶֽה׃ פ [לוי] ח וּלְלֵוִ֣י אָמַ֔ר תֻּמֶּ֥יךָ וְאוּרֶ֖יךָ לְאִ֣ישׁ חֲסִידֶ֑ךָ
אֲשֶׁ֤ר נִסִּיתוֹ֙ בְּמַסָּ֔ה תְּרִיבֵ֖הוּ עַל־מֵ֥י מְרִיבָֽה׃ ט הָאֹמֵ֞ר
לְאָבִ֣יו וּלְאִמּוֹ֮ לֹ֣א רְאִיתִיו֒ וְאֶת־אֶחָיו֙ לֹ֣א הִכִּ֔יר וְאֶת־בָּנָ֖ו
לֹ֣א יָדָ֑ע כִּ֤י שָֽׁמְרוּ֙ אִמְרָתֶ֔ךָ וּבְרִֽיתְךָ֖ יִנְצֹֽרוּ׃ י יוֹר֤וּ מִשְׁפָּטֶ֙יךָ֙
לְיַעֲקֹ֔ב וְתוֹרָתְךָ֖ לְיִשְׂרָאֵ֑ל יָשִׂ֤ימוּ קְטוֹרָה֙ בְּאַפֶּ֔ךָ וְכָלִ֖יל עַל־
מִזְבְּחֶֽךָ׃ יא בָּרֵ֤ךְ יְהֹוָה֙ חֵיל֔וֹ וּפֹ֥עַל יָדָ֖יו תִּרְצֶ֑ה מְחַ֨ץ מָתְנַ֧יִם
קָמָ֛יו וּמְשַׂנְאָ֖יו מִן־יְקוּמֽוּן׃ ס יב לְבִנְיָמִ֣ן אָמַ֔ר יְדִ֣יד
יְהֹוָ֔ה יִשְׁכֹּ֥ן לָבֶ֖טַח עָלָ֑יו חֹפֵ֤ף עָלָיו֙ כָּל־הַיּ֔וֹם וּבֵ֥ין כְּתֵפָ֖יו
שָׁכֵֽן׃ ס [ישראל] יג וּלְיוֹסֵ֣ף אָמַ֔ר מְבֹרֶ֥כֶת יְהֹוָ֖ה אַרְצ֑וֹ
מִמֶּ֤גֶד שָׁמַ֙יִם֙ מִטָּ֔ל וּמִתְּה֖וֹם רֹבֶ֥צֶת תָּֽחַת׃ יד וּמִמֶּ֖גֶד תְּבוּאֹ֣ת
שָׁ֑מֶשׁ וּמִמֶּ֖גֶד גֶּ֥רֶשׁ יְרָחִֽים׃ טו וּמֵרֹ֖אשׁ הַרְרֵי־קֶ֑דֶם וּמִמֶּ֖גֶד
גִּבְע֥וֹת עוֹלָֽם׃ טז וּמִמֶּ֗גֶד אֶ֚רֶץ וּמְלֹאָ֔הּ וּרְצ֥וֹן שֹׁכְנִ֖י סְנֶ֑ה
תָּבוֹ֙אתָה֙ לְרֹ֣אשׁ יוֹסֵ֔ף וּלְקָדְקֹ֖ד נְזִ֥יר אֶחָֽיו׃ יז בְּכ֨וֹר שׁוֹר֜וֹ
הָדָ֣ר ל֗וֹ וְקַרְנֵ֤י רְאֵם֙ קַרְנָ֔יו בָּהֶ֗ם עַמִּ֛ים יְנַגַּ֥ח יַחְדָּ֖ו אַפְסֵי־אָ֑רֶץ
וְהֵם֙ רִבְב֣וֹת אֶפְרַ֔יִם וְהֵ֖ם אַלְפֵ֥י מְנַשֶּֽׁה׃

TORAH READING FOR CHANUKAH

On the first day of חֲנֻכָּה begin וַיְהִי בְּיוֹם כַּלּוֹת (some begin וַיְדַבֵּר, Numbers 6:22) and continue until זֶה קָרְבַּן נַחְשׁוֹן בֶּן־עַמִּינָדָב following the indicated stops. On the second day and throughout the other days of חֲנֻכָּה (except the last day), the כֹּהֵן aliyah consists of the paragraph corresponding to the given day of חֲנֻכָּה (i.e. on the second day of חֲנֻכָּה, בַּיּוֹם הַשֵּׁנִי etc.) until מְלֵאָה קְטֹרֶת. The לֵוִי aliyah continues from פַּר אֶחָד until the end of the paragraph, and the יִשְׂרָאֵל aliyah consists of the following day's paragraph. On the last day of חֲנֻכָּה, begin בַּיּוֹם הַשְּׁמִינִי and continue until the end, following the indicated stops. For the קְרִיאַת הַתּוֹרָה for רֹאשׁ חֹדֶשׁ טֵבֵת, see page 911

יום א׳ של חנוכה

במדבר ז א וַיְהִי בְּיוֹם כַּלּוֹת מֹשֶׁה לְהָקִים אֶת־הַמִּשְׁכָּן
וַיִּמְשַׁח אֹתוֹ וַיְקַדֵּשׁ אֹתוֹ וְאֶת־כָּל־כֵּלָיו וְאֶת־הַמִּזְבֵּחַ וְאֶת־
כָּל־כֵּלָיו וַיִּמְשָׁחֵם וַיְקַדֵּשׁ אֹתָם׃ ב וַיַּקְרִיבוּ נְשִׂיאֵי יִשְׂרָאֵל
רָאשֵׁי בֵּית אֲבֹתָם הֵם נְשִׂיאֵי הַמַּטֹּת הֵם הָעֹמְדִים עַל־
הַפְּקֻדִים׃ ג וַיָּבִיאוּ אֶת־קָרְבָּנָם לִפְנֵי יְהֹוָה שֵׁשׁ־עֶגְלֹת
צָב וּשְׁנֵי־עָשָׂר בָּקָר עֲגָלָה עַל־שְׁנֵי הַנְּשִׂאִים וְשׁוֹר לְאֶחָד
וַיַּקְרִיבוּ אוֹתָם לִפְנֵי הַמִּשְׁכָּן׃ ד וַיֹּאמֶר יְהֹוָה אֶל־מֹשֶׁה
לֵּאמֹר׃ ה קַח מֵאִתָּם וְהָיוּ לַעֲבֹד אֶת־עֲבֹדַת אֹהֶל מוֹעֵד
וְנָתַתָּה אוֹתָם אֶל־הַלְוִיִּם אִישׁ כְּפִי עֲבֹדָתוֹ׃ ו וַיִּקַּח מֹשֶׁה
אֶת־הָעֲגָלֹת וְאֶת־הַבָּקָר וַיִּתֵּן אוֹתָם אֶל־הַלְוִיִּם׃ ז אֵת | שְׁתֵּי
הָעֲגָלוֹת וְאֵת אַרְבַּעַת הַבָּקָר נָתַן לִבְנֵי גֵרְשׁוֹן כְּפִי עֲבֹדָתָם׃
ח וְאֵת | אַרְבַּע הָעֲגָלֹת וְאֵת שְׁמֹנַת הַבָּקָר נָתַן לִבְנֵי מְרָרִי
כְּפִי עֲבֹדָתָם בְּיַד אִיתָמָר בֶּן־אַהֲרֹן הַכֹּהֵן׃ ט וְלִבְנֵי קְהָת
לֹא נָתָן כִּי־עֲבֹדַת הַקֹּדֶשׁ עֲלֵהֶם בַּכָּתֵף יִשָּׂאוּ׃ י וַיַּקְרִיבוּ
הַנְּשִׂאִים אֵת חֲנֻכַּת הַמִּזְבֵּחַ בְּיוֹם הִמָּשַׁח אֹתוֹ וַיַּקְרִיבוּ
הַנְּשִׂיאִם אֶת־קָרְבָּנָם לִפְנֵי הַמִּזְבֵּחַ׃ יא וַיֹּאמֶר יְהֹוָה אֶל־
מֹשֶׁה נָשִׂיא אֶחָד לַיּוֹם נָשִׂיא אֶחָד לַיּוֹם יַקְרִיבוּ אֶת־קָרְבָּנָם
לַחֲנֻכַּת הַמִּזְבֵּחַ׃ ס [לוי] יב וַיְהִי הַמַּקְרִיב בַּיּוֹם הָרִאשׁוֹן

אֶת־קָרְבָּנ֑וֹ נַחְשׁ֥וֹן בֶּן־עַמִּינָדָ֖ב לְמַטֵּ֥ה יְהוּדָֽה׃ יג וְקָרְבָּנ֞וֹ
קַֽעֲרַת־כֶּ֣סֶף אַחַ֗ת שְׁלֹשִׁ֣ים וּמֵאָה֮ מִשְׁקָלָהּ֒ מִזְרָ֤ק אֶחָד֙ כֶּ֔סֶף
שִׁבְעִ֥ים שֶׁ֖קֶל בְּשֶׁ֣קֶל הַקֹּ֑דֶשׁ שְׁנֵיהֶ֣ם ׀ מְלֵאִ֗ים סֹ֛לֶת בְּלוּלָ֥ה
בַשֶּׁ֖מֶן לְמִנְחָֽה׃ יד כַּ֥ף אַחַ֛ת עֲשָׂרָ֥ה זָהָ֖ב מְלֵאָ֥ה קְטֹֽרֶת׃
[ישראל] טו פַּ֣ר אֶחָ֞ד בֶּן־בָּקָ֗ר אַ֧יִל אֶחָ֛ד כֶּֽבֶשׂ־אֶחָ֥ד בֶּן־שְׁנָת֖וֹ
לְעֹלָֽה׃ טז שְׂעִיר־עִזִּ֥ים אֶחָ֖ד לְחַטָּֽאת׃ יז וּלְזֶ֣בַח הַשְּׁלָמִים֮
בָּקָ֣ר שְׁנַ֒יִם֒ אֵילִ֤ם חֲמִשָּׁה֙ עַתֻּדִ֣ים חֲמִשָּׁ֔ה כְּבָשִׂ֥ים בְּנֵי־שָׁנָ֖ה
חֲמִשָּׁ֑ה זֶ֛ה קָרְבַּ֥ן נַחְשׁ֖וֹן בֶּן־עַמִּינָדָֽב׃

יום ב׳ של חנוכה

יח בַּיּוֹם֙ הַשֵּׁנִ֔י הִקְרִ֖יב נְתַנְאֵ֣ל בֶּן־צוּעָ֑ר נְשִׂ֖יא יִשָּׂשכָֽר׃
יט הִקְרִ֨ב אֶת־קָרְבָּנ֜וֹ קַֽעֲרַת־כֶּ֣סֶף אַחַ֗ת שְׁלֹשִׁ֣ים וּמֵאָה֮
מִשְׁקָלָהּ֒ מִזְרָ֤ק אֶחָד֙ כֶּ֔סֶף שִׁבְעִ֥ים שֶׁ֖קֶל בְּשֶׁ֣קֶל הַקֹּ֑דֶשׁ
שְׁנֵיהֶ֣ם ׀ מְלֵאִ֗ים סֹ֛לֶת בְּלוּלָ֥ה בַשֶּׁ֖מֶן לְמִנְחָֽה׃ כ כַּ֥ף אַחַ֛ת
עֲשָׂרָ֥ה זָהָ֖ב מְלֵאָ֥ה קְטֹֽרֶת׃ [לוי] כא פַּ֣ר אֶחָ֞ד בֶּן־בָּקָ֗ר אַ֧יִל
אֶחָ֛ד כֶּֽבֶשׂ־אֶחָ֥ד בֶּן־שְׁנָת֖וֹ לְעֹלָֽה׃ כב שְׂעִיר־עִזִּ֥ים אֶחָ֖ד
לְחַטָּֽאת׃ כג וּלְזֶ֣בַח הַשְּׁלָמִים֮ בָּקָ֣ר שְׁנַ֒יִם֒ אֵילִ֤ם חֲמִשָּׁה֙
עַתֻּדִ֣ים חֲמִשָּׁ֔ה כְּבָשִׂ֥ים בְּנֵי־שָׁנָ֖ה חֲמִשָּׁ֑ה זֶ֛ה קָרְבַּ֥ן נְתַנְאֵ֖ל
בֶּן־צוּעָֽר׃

יום ג׳ של חנוכה

כד בַּיּוֹם֙ הַשְּׁלִישִׁ֔י נָשִׂ֖יא לִבְנֵ֣י זְבוּלֻ֑ן אֱלִיאָ֖ב בֶּן־חֵלֹֽן׃ כה קָרְבָּנ֞וֹ
קַֽעֲרַת־כֶּ֣סֶף אַחַ֗ת שְׁלֹשִׁ֣ים וּמֵאָה֮ מִשְׁקָלָהּ֒ מִזְרָ֤ק אֶחָד֙ כֶּ֔סֶף
שִׁבְעִ֥ים שֶׁ֖קֶל בְּשֶׁ֣קֶל הַקֹּ֑דֶשׁ שְׁנֵיהֶ֣ם ׀ מְלֵאִ֗ים סֹ֛לֶת בְּלוּלָ֥ה
בַשֶּׁ֖מֶן לְמִנְחָֽה׃ כו כַּ֥ף אַחַ֛ת עֲשָׂרָ֥ה זָהָ֖ב מְלֵאָ֥ה קְטֹֽרֶת׃
[לוי] כז פַּ֣ר אֶחָ֞ד בֶּן־בָּקָ֗ר אַ֧יִל אֶחָ֛ד כֶּֽבֶשׂ־אֶחָ֥ד בֶּן־שְׁנָת֖וֹ
לְעֹלָֽה׃ כח שְׂעִיר־עִזִּ֥ים אֶחָ֖ד לְחַטָּֽאת׃ כט וּלְזֶ֣בַח הַשְּׁלָמִים֮

בָּקָ֣ר שְׁנַ֒יִם֒ אֵילִ֤ם חֲמִשָּׁה֙ עַתֻּדִ֣ים חֲמִשָּׁ֔ה כְּבָשִׂ֥ים בְּנֵי־שָׁנָ֖ה
חֲמִשָּׁ֑ה זֶ֛ה קָרְבַּ֥ן אֱלִיאָ֖ב בֶּן־חֵלֹֽן׃

יום ד׳ של חנוכה

ל בַּיּוֹם֙ הָֽרְבִיעִ֔י נָשִׂ֖יא לִבְנֵ֣י רְאוּבֵ֑ן אֱלִיצ֖וּר בֶּן־שְׁדֵיאֽוּר׃
לא קָרְבָּנ֞וֹ קַֽעֲרַת־כֶּ֣סֶף אַחַ֗ת שְׁלֹשִׁ֣ים וּמֵאָה֮ מִשְׁקָלָהּ֒ מִזְרָ֤ק
אֶחָד֙ כֶּ֔סֶף שִׁבְעִ֥ים שֶׁ֖קֶל בְּשֶׁ֣קֶל הַקֹּ֑דֶשׁ שְׁנֵיהֶ֣ם ׀ מְלֵאִ֗ים
סֹ֛לֶת בְּלוּלָ֥ה בַשֶּׁ֖מֶן לְמִנְחָֽה׃ לב כַּ֥ף אַחַ֛ת עֲשָׂרָ֥ה זָהָ֖ב מְלֵאָ֥ה
קְטֹֽרֶת׃ [לוי] לג פַּ֣ר אֶחָ֞ד בֶּן־בָּקָ֗ר אַ֧יִל אֶחָ֛ד כֶּֽבֶשׂ־אֶחָ֥ד בֶּן־
שְׁנָת֖וֹ לְעֹלָֽה׃ לד שְׂעִיר־עִזִּ֥ים אֶחָ֖ד לְחַטָּֽאת׃ לה וּלְזֶ֣בַח
הַשְּׁלָמִים֮ בָּקָ֣ר שְׁנַ֒יִם֒ אֵילִ֤ם חֲמִשָּׁה֙ עַתֻּדִ֣ים חֲמִשָּׁ֔ה כְּבָשִׂ֥ים
בְּנֵי־שָׁנָ֖ה חֲמִשָּׁ֑ה זֶ֛ה קָרְבַּ֥ן אֱלִיצ֖וּר בֶּן־שְׁדֵיאֽוּר׃

יום ה׳ של חנוכה

לו בַּיּוֹם֙ הַחֲמִישִׁ֔י נָשִׂ֖יא לִבְנֵ֣י שִׁמְע֑וֹן שְׁלֻֽמִיאֵ֖ל בֶּן־צוּרִֽישַׁדָּֽי׃
לז קָרְבָּנ֞וֹ קַֽעֲרַת־כֶּ֣סֶף אַחַ֗ת שְׁלֹשִׁ֣ים וּמֵאָה֮ מִשְׁקָלָהּ֒ מִזְרָ֤ק
אֶחָד֙ כֶּ֔סֶף שִׁבְעִ֥ים שֶׁ֖קֶל בְּשֶׁ֣קֶל הַקֹּ֑דֶשׁ שְׁנֵיהֶ֣ם ׀ מְלֵאִ֗ים
סֹ֛לֶת בְּלוּלָ֥ה בַשֶּׁ֖מֶן לְמִנְחָֽה׃ לח כַּ֥ף אַחַ֛ת עֲשָׂרָ֥ה זָהָ֖ב מְלֵאָ֥ה
קְטֹֽרֶת׃ [לוי] לט פַּ֣ר אֶחָ֞ד בֶּן־בָּקָ֗ר אַ֧יִל אֶחָ֛ד כֶּֽבֶשׂ־אֶחָ֥ד
בֶּן־שְׁנָת֖וֹ לְעֹלָֽה׃ מ שְׂעִיר־עִזִּ֥ים אֶחָ֖ד לְחַטָּֽאת׃ מא וּלְזֶ֣בַח
הַשְּׁלָמִים֮ בָּקָ֣ר שְׁנַ֒יִם֒ אֵילִ֤ם חֲמִשָּׁה֙ עַתֻּדִ֣ים חֲמִשָּׁ֔ה כְּבָשִׂ֥ים
בְּנֵי־שָׁנָ֖ה חֲמִשָּׁ֑ה זֶ֛ה קָרְבַּ֥ן שְׁלֻמִיאֵ֖ל בֶּן־צוּרִֽישַׁדָּֽי׃

יום ו׳ של חנוכה

מב בַּיּוֹם֙ הַשִּׁשִּׁ֔י נָשִׂ֖יא לִבְנֵ֣י גָ֑ד אֶלְיָסָ֖ף בֶּן־דְּעוּאֵֽל׃ מג קָרְבָּנ֞וֹ
קַֽעֲרַת־כֶּ֣סֶף אַחַ֗ת שְׁלֹשִׁ֣ים וּמֵאָה֮ מִשְׁקָלָהּ֒ מִזְרָ֤ק אֶחָד֙ כֶּ֔סֶף
שִׁבְעִ֥ים שֶׁ֖קֶל בְּשֶׁ֣קֶל הַקֹּ֑דֶשׁ שְׁנֵיהֶ֣ם ׀ מְלֵאִ֗ים סֹ֛לֶת בְּלוּלָ֥ה
בַשֶּׁ֖מֶן לְמִנְחָֽה׃ מד כַּ֥ף אַחַ֛ת עֲשָׂרָ֥ה זָהָ֖ב מְלֵאָ֥ה קְטֹֽרֶת׃

[לוי] מה פַּר אֶחָד בֶּן־בָּקָר אַיִל אֶחָד כֶּבֶשׂ־אֶחָד בֶּן־שְׁנָתוֹ
לְעֹלָה: מו שְׂעִיר־עִזִּים אֶחָד לְחַטָּאת: מז וּלְזֶבַח הַשְּׁלָמִים
בָּקָר שְׁנַיִם אֵילִם חֲמִשָּׁה עַתֻּדִים חֲמִשָּׁה כְּבָשִׂים בְּנֵי־שָׁנָה
חֲמִשָּׁה זֶה קָרְבַּן אֶלְיָסָף בֶּן־דְּעוּאֵל:

יום ז׳ של חנוכה

מח בַּיּוֹם הַשְּׁבִיעִי נָשִׂיא לִבְנֵי אֶפְרָיִם אֱלִישָׁמָע בֶּן־עַמִּיהוּד:
מט קָרְבָּנוֹ קַעֲרַת־כֶּסֶף אַחַת שְׁלֹשִׁים וּמֵאָה מִשְׁקָלָהּ מִזְרָק
אֶחָד כֶּסֶף שִׁבְעִים שֶׁקֶל בְּשֶׁקֶל הַקֹּדֶשׁ שְׁנֵיהֶם | מְלֵאִים
סֹלֶת בְּלוּלָה בַשֶּׁמֶן לְמִנְחָה: נ כַּף אַחַת עֲשָׂרָה זָהָב מְלֵאָה
קְטֹרֶת: [לוי] נא פַּר אֶחָד בֶּן־בָּקָר אַיִל אֶחָד כֶּבֶשׂ־אֶחָד
בֶּן־שְׁנָתוֹ לְעֹלָה: נב שְׂעִיר־עִזִּים אֶחָד לְחַטָּאת: נג וּלְזֶבַח
הַשְּׁלָמִים בָּקָר שְׁנַיִם אֵילִם חֲמִשָּׁה עַתֻּדִים חֲמִשָּׁה כְּבָשִׂים
בְּנֵי־שָׁנָה חֲמִשָּׁה זֶה קָרְבַּן אֱלִישָׁמָע בֶּן־עַמִּיהוּד:

יום ח׳ של חנוכה

נד בַּיּוֹם הַשְּׁמִינִי נָשִׂיא לִבְנֵי מְנַשֶּׁה גַּמְלִיאֵל בֶּן־פְּדָהצוּר:
נה קָרְבָּנוֹ קַעֲרַת־כֶּסֶף אַחַת שְׁלֹשִׁים וּמֵאָה מִשְׁקָלָהּ
מִזְרָק אֶחָד כֶּסֶף שִׁבְעִים שֶׁקֶל בְּשֶׁקֶל הַקֹּדֶשׁ שְׁנֵיהֶם |
מְלֵאִים סֹלֶת בְּלוּלָה בַשֶּׁמֶן לְמִנְחָה: נו כַּף אַחַת עֲשָׂרָה
זָהָב מְלֵאָה קְטֹרֶת: [לוי] נז פַּר אֶחָד בֶּן־בָּקָר אַיִל אֶחָד
כֶּבֶשׂ־אֶחָד בֶּן־שְׁנָתוֹ לְעֹלָה: נח שְׂעִיר־עִזִּים אֶחָד לְחַטָּאת:
נט וּלְזֶבַח הַשְּׁלָמִים בָּקָר שְׁנַיִם אֵילִם חֲמִשָּׁה עַתֻּדִים
חֲמִשָּׁה כְּבָשִׂים בְּנֵי־שָׁנָה חֲמִשָּׁה זֶה קָרְבַּן גַּמְלִיאֵל בֶּן־
פְּדָהצוּר:

[ישראל] ס בַּיּוֹם הַתְּשִׁיעִי נָשִׂיא לִבְנֵי בִנְיָמִן אֲבִידָן בֶּן־גִּדְעֹנִי:
סא קָרְבָּנוֹ קַעֲרַת־כֶּסֶף אַחַת שְׁלֹשִׁים וּמֵאָה מִשְׁקָלָהּ מִזְרָק

אֶחָד כֶּסֶף שִׁבְעִים שֶׁקֶל בְּשֶׁקֶל הַקֹּדֶשׁ שְׁנֵיהֶם | מְלֵאִים
סֹלֶת בְּלוּלָה בַשֶּׁמֶן לְמִנְחָה: סב כַּף אַחַת עֲשָׂרָה זָהָב מְלֵאָה
קְטֹרֶת: סג פַּר אֶחָד בֶּן־בָּקָר אַיִל אֶחָד כֶּבֶשׂ־אֶחָד בֶּן־שְׁנָתוֹ
לְעֹלָה: סד שְׂעִיר־עִזִּים אֶחָד לְחַטָּאת: סה וּלְזֶבַח הַשְּׁלָמִים
בָּקָר שְׁנַיִם אֵילִם חֲמִשָּׁה עַתֻּדִים חֲמִשָּׁה כְּבָשִׂים בְּנֵי־שָׁנָה
חֲמִשָּׁה זֶה קָרְבַּן אֲבִידָן בֶּן־גִּדְעֹנִי:
סו בַּיּוֹם הָעֲשִׂירִי נָשִׂיא לִבְנֵי דָן אֲחִיעֶזֶר בֶּן־עַמִּישַׁדָּי:
סז קָרְבָּנוֹ קַעֲרַת־כֶּסֶף אַחַת שְׁלֹשִׁים וּמֵאָה מִשְׁקָלָהּ מִזְרָק
אֶחָד כֶּסֶף שִׁבְעִים שֶׁקֶל בְּשֶׁקֶל הַקֹּדֶשׁ שְׁנֵיהֶם | מְלֵאִים
סֹלֶת בְּלוּלָה בַשֶּׁמֶן לְמִנְחָה: סח כַּף אַחַת עֲשָׂרָה זָהָב מְלֵאָה
קְטֹרֶת: סט פַּר אֶחָד בֶּן־בָּקָר אַיִל אֶחָד כֶּבֶשׂ־אֶחָד בֶּן־שְׁנָתוֹ
לְעֹלָה: ע שְׂעִיר־עִזִּים אֶחָד לְחַטָּאת: עא וּלְזֶבַח הַשְּׁלָמִים
בָּקָר שְׁנַיִם אֵילִם חֲמִשָּׁה עַתֻּדִים חֲמִשָּׁה כְּבָשִׂים בְּנֵי־שָׁנָה
חֲמִשָּׁה זֶה קָרְבַּן אֲחִיעֶזֶר בֶּן־עַמִּישַׁדָּי:
עב בְּיוֹם עַשְׁתֵּי עָשָׂר יוֹם נָשִׂיא לִבְנֵי אָשֵׁר פַּגְעִיאֵל בֶּן־עָכְרָן:
עג קָרְבָּנוֹ קַעֲרַת־כֶּסֶף אַחַת שְׁלֹשִׁים וּמֵאָה מִשְׁקָלָהּ מִזְרָק
אֶחָד כֶּסֶף שִׁבְעִים שֶׁקֶל בְּשֶׁקֶל הַקֹּדֶשׁ שְׁנֵיהֶם | מְלֵאִים
סֹלֶת בְּלוּלָה בַשֶּׁמֶן לְמִנְחָה: עד כַּף אַחַת עֲשָׂרָה זָהָב מְלֵאָה
קְטֹרֶת: עה פַּר אֶחָד בֶּן־בָּקָר אַיִל אֶחָד כֶּבֶשׂ־אֶחָד בֶּן־שְׁנָתוֹ
לְעֹלָה: עו שְׂעִיר־עִזִּים אֶחָד לְחַטָּאת: עז וּלְזֶבַח הַשְּׁלָמִים
בָּקָר שְׁנַיִם אֵילִם חֲמִשָּׁה עַתֻּדִים חֲמִשָּׁה כְּבָשִׂים בְּנֵי־שָׁנָה
חֲמִשָּׁה זֶה קָרְבַּן פַּגְעִיאֵל בֶּן־עָכְרָן:
עח בְּיוֹם שְׁנֵים עָשָׂר יוֹם נָשִׂיא לִבְנֵי נַפְתָּלִי אֲחִירַע בֶּן־עֵינָן:
עט קָרְבָּנוֹ קַעֲרַת־כֶּסֶף אַחַת שְׁלֹשִׁים וּמֵאָה מִשְׁקָלָהּ מִזְרָק
אֶחָד כֶּסֶף שִׁבְעִים שֶׁקֶל בְּשֶׁקֶל הַקֹּדֶשׁ שְׁנֵיהֶם | מְלֵאִים

סֹ֛לֶת בְּלוּלָ֥ה בַשֶּׁ֖מֶן לְמִנְחָֽה׃ פ כַּ֥ף אַחַ֛ת עֲשָׂרָ֥ה זָהָ֖ב מְלֵאָ֥ה
קְטֹֽרֶת׃ פא פַּ֣ר אֶחָ֞ד בֶּן־בָּקָ֗ר אַ֧יִל אֶחָ֛ד כֶּֽבֶשׂ־אֶחָ֥ד בֶּן־שְׁנָת֖וֹ
לְעֹלָֽה׃ פב שְׂעִיר־עִזִּ֥ים אֶחָ֖ד לְחַטָּֽאת׃ פג וּלְזֶ֣בַח הַשְּׁלָמִים֮
בָּקָ֣ר שְׁנַ֒יִם֒ אֵילִ֤ם חֲמִשָּׁה֙ עַתֻּדִ֣ים חֲמִשָּׁ֔ה כְּבָשִׂ֥ים בְּנֵי־שָׁנָ֖ה
חֲמִשָּׁ֑ה זֶ֛ה קָרְבַּ֥ן אֲחִירַ֖ע בֶּן־עֵינָֽן׃
פד זֹ֣את ׀ חֲנֻכַּ֣ת הַמִּזְבֵּ֗חַ בְּיוֹם֙ הִמָּשַׁ֣ח אֹת֔וֹ מֵאֵ֖ת נְשִׂיאֵ֣י
יִשְׂרָאֵ֑ל קַעֲרֹ֨ת כֶּ֜סֶף שְׁתֵּ֣ים עֶשְׂרֵ֗ה מִֽזְרְקֵי־כֶ֙סֶף֙ שְׁנֵ֣ים עָשָׂ֔ר
כַּפּ֥וֹת זָהָ֖ב שְׁתֵּ֥ים עֶשְׂרֵֽה׃ פה שְׁלֹשִׁ֣ים וּמֵאָ֗ה הַקְּעָרָ֤ה הָֽאַחַת֙
כֶּ֔סֶף וְשִׁבְעִ֖ים הַמִּזְרָ֣ק הָאֶחָ֑ד כֹּ֚ל כֶּ֣סֶף הַכֵּלִ֔ים אַלְפַּ֥יִם
וְאַרְבַּע־מֵא֖וֹת בְּשֶׁ֥קֶל הַקֹּֽדֶשׁ׃ פו כַּפּ֨וֹת זָהָ֤ב שְׁתֵּים־עֶשְׂרֵה֙
מְלֵאֹ֣ת קְטֹ֔רֶת עֲשָׂרָ֧ה עֲשָׂרָ֛ה הַכַּ֖ף בְּשֶׁ֣קֶל הַקֹּ֑דֶשׁ כָּל־זְהַ֥ב
הַכַּפּ֖וֹת עֶשְׂרִ֥ים וּמֵאָֽה׃ פז כָּל־הַבָּקָ֨ר לָעֹלָ֜ה שְׁנֵ֧ים עָשָׂ֣ר
פָּרִ֗ים אֵילִ֤ם שְׁנֵים־עָשָׂר֙ כְּבָשִׂ֧ים בְּנֵי־שָׁנָ֛ה שְׁנֵ֥ים עָשָׂ֖ר
וּמִנְחָתָ֑ם וּשְׂעִירֵ֥י עִזִּ֛ים שְׁנֵ֥ים עָשָׂ֖ר לְחַטָּֽאת׃ פח וְכֹ֞ל בְּקַ֣ר ׀
זֶ֣בַח הַשְּׁלָמִ֗ים עֶשְׂרִ֣ים וְאַרְבָּעָה֮ פָּרִים֒ אֵילִ֤ם שִׁשִּׁים֙ עַתֻּדִ֣ים
שִׁשִּׁ֔ים כְּבָשִׂ֥ים בְּנֵי־שָׁנָ֖ה שִׁשִּׁ֑ים זֹ֚את חֲנֻכַּ֣ת הַמִּזְבֵּ֔חַ אַחֲרֵ֖י
הִמָּשַׁ֥ח אֹתֽוֹ׃ פט וּבְבֹ֨א מֹשֶׁ֜ה אֶל־אֹ֣הֶל מוֹעֵד֮ לְדַבֵּ֣ר אִתּוֹ֒
וַיִּשְׁמַ֨ע אֶת־הַקּ֜וֹל מִדַּבֵּ֣ר אֵלָ֗יו מֵעַ֤ל הַכַּפֹּ֙רֶת֙ אֲשֶׁר֙ עַל־אֲרֹ֣ן
הָעֵדֻ֔ת מִבֵּ֖ין שְׁנֵ֣י הַכְּרֻבִ֑ים וַיְדַבֵּ֖ר אֵלָֽיו׃ ח א וַיְדַבֵּ֥ר יְהוָ֖ה אֶל־
מֹשֶׁ֥ה לֵּאמֹֽר׃ ב דַּבֵּר֙ אֶֽל־אַהֲרֹ֔ן וְאָמַרְתָּ֖ אֵלָ֑יו בְּהַעֲלֹֽתְךָ֙ אֶת־
הַנֵּרֹ֔ת אֶל־מוּל֙ פְּנֵ֣י הַמְּנוֹרָ֔ה יָאִ֖ירוּ שִׁבְעַ֥ת הַנֵּרֽוֹת׃ ג וַיַּ֤עַשׂ
כֵּן֙ אַהֲרֹ֔ן אֶל־מוּל֙ פְּנֵ֣י הַמְּנוֹרָ֔ה הֶעֱלָ֖ה נֵרֹתֶ֑יהָ כַּאֲשֶׁ֛ר צִוָּ֥ה
יְהוָ֖ה אֶת־מֹשֶֽׁה׃ ד וְזֶ֨ה מַעֲשֵׂ֤ה הַמְּנֹרָה֙ מִקְשָׁ֣ה זָהָ֔ב עַד־
יְרֵכָ֥הּ עַד־פִּרְחָ֖הּ מִקְשָׁ֣ה הִ֑וא כַּמַּרְאֶ֗ה אֲשֶׁ֨ר הֶרְאָ֤ה יְהוָה֙
אֶת־מֹשֶׁ֔ה כֵּ֥ן עָשָׂ֖ה אֶת־הַמְּנֹרָֽה׃

TORAH READING FOR PURIM

Three people receive עֲלִיּוֹת on פּוּרִים.

שמות יז ח וַיָּבֹ֖א עֲמָלֵ֑ק וַיִּלָּ֥חֶם עִם־יִשְׂרָאֵ֖ל בִּרְפִידִֽם׃ ט וַיֹּ֨אמֶר
מֹשֶׁ֤ה אֶל־יְהוֹשֻׁ֙עַ֙ בְּחַר־לָ֣נוּ אֲנָשִׁ֔ים וְצֵ֖א הִלָּחֵ֣ם בַּעֲמָלֵ֑ק
מָחָ֗ר אָנֹכִ֤י נִצָּב֙ עַל־רֹ֣אשׁ הַגִּבְעָ֔ה וּמַטֵּ֥ה הָאֱלֹהִ֖ים בְּיָדִֽי׃
י וַיַּ֣עַשׂ יְהוֹשֻׁ֗עַ כַּאֲשֶׁ֤ר אָֽמַר־לוֹ֙ מֹשֶׁ֔ה לְהִלָּחֵ֖ם בַּעֲמָלֵ֑ק
וּמֹשֶׁה֙ אַהֲרֹ֣ן וְח֔וּר עָל֖וּ רֹ֥אשׁ הַגִּבְעָֽה׃ [לוי] יא וְהָיָ֗ה כַּאֲשֶׁ֨ר
יָרִ֥ים מֹשֶׁ֛ה יָד֖וֹ וְגָבַ֣ר יִשְׂרָאֵ֑ל וְכַאֲשֶׁ֛ר יָנִ֥יחַ יָד֖וֹ וְגָבַ֥ר עֲמָלֵֽק׃
יב וִידֵ֤י מֹשֶׁה֙ כְּבֵדִ֔ים וַיִּקְחוּ־אֶ֛בֶן וַיָּשִׂ֥ימוּ תַחְתָּ֖יו וַיֵּ֣שֶׁב עָלֶ֑יהָ
וְאַהֲרֹ֨ן וְח֜וּר תָּֽמְכ֣וּ בְיָדָ֗יו מִזֶּ֤ה אֶחָד֙ וּמִזֶּ֣ה אֶחָ֔ד וַיְהִ֥י יָדָ֛יו
אֱמוּנָ֖ה עַד־בֹּ֥א הַשָּֽׁמֶשׁ׃ יג וַיַּחֲלֹ֧שׁ יְהוֹשֻׁ֛עַ אֶת־עֲמָלֵ֥ק וְאֶת־
עַמּ֖וֹ לְפִי־חָֽרֶב׃ פ [ישראל] יד וַיֹּ֨אמֶר יְהֹוָ֜ה אֶל־מֹשֶׁ֗ה כְּתֹ֨ב
זֹ֤את זִכָּרוֹן֙ בַּסֵּ֔פֶר וְשִׂ֖ים בְּאָזְנֵ֣י יְהוֹשֻׁ֑עַ כִּֽי־מָחֹ֤ה אֶמְחֶה֙
אֶת־זֵ֣כֶר עֲמָלֵ֔ק מִתַּ֖חַת הַשָּׁמָֽיִם׃ טו וַיִּ֥בֶן מֹשֶׁ֖ה מִזְבֵּ֑חַ וַיִּקְרָ֥א
שְׁמ֖וֹ יְהֹוָ֥ה ׀ נִסִּֽי׃ טז וַיֹּ֗אמֶר כִּֽי־יָד֙ עַל־כֵּ֣ס יָ֔הּ מִלְחָמָ֥ה לַֽיהֹוָ֖ה
בַּעֲמָלֵ֑ק מִדֹּ֖ר דֹּֽר׃

TORAH READING FOR TISHA B'AV MORNING

Three people receive עֲלִיּוֹת on תִּשְׁעָה בְּאָב morning. The third person recites the הַפְטָרָה.

דברים ד כה כִּֽי־תוֹלִ֤יד בָּנִים֙ וּבְנֵ֣י בָנִ֔ים וְנוֹשַׁנְתֶּ֖ם בָּאָ֑רֶץ
וְהִשְׁחַתֶּ֗ם וַעֲשִׂ֤יתֶם פֶּ֙סֶל֙ תְּמ֣וּנַת כֹּ֔ל וַעֲשִׂיתֶ֥ם הָרַ֛ע
בְּעֵינֵֽי־יְהֹוָֽה־אֱלֹהֶ֖יךָ לְהַכְעִיסֽוֹ׃ כו הַעִידֹ֨תִי בָכֶ֜ם הַיּ֗וֹם אֶת־
הַשָּׁמַ֘יִם֮ וְאֶת־הָאָרֶץ֒ כִּֽי־אָבֹ֣ד תֹּאבֵדוּן֮ מַהֵר֒ מֵעַ֣ל הָאָ֗רֶץ
אֲשֶׁ֨ר אַתֶּ֜ם עֹבְרִ֧ים אֶת־הַיַּרְדֵּ֛ן שָׁ֖מָּה לְרִשְׁתָּ֑הּ לֹא־תַאֲרִיכֻ֤ן
יָמִים֙ עָלֶ֔יהָ כִּ֥י הִשָּׁמֵ֖ד תִּשָּׁמֵדֽוּן׃ כז וְהֵפִ֧יץ יְהֹוָ֛ה אֶתְכֶ֖ם
בָּעַמִּ֑ים וְנִשְׁאַרְתֶּם֙ מְתֵ֣י מִסְפָּ֔ר בַּגּוֹיִ֕ם אֲשֶׁ֧ר יְנַהֶ֛ג יְהֹוָ֖ה

אֶתְכֶם שָׁמָּה: כח וַעֲבַדְתֶּם־שָׁם אֱלֹהִים מַעֲשֵׂה יְדֵי אָדָם
עֵץ וָאֶבֶן אֲשֶׁר לֹא־יִרְאוּן וְלֹא יִשְׁמְעוּן וְלֹא יֹאכְלוּן וְלֹא
יְרִיחֻן: כט וּבִקַּשְׁתֶּם מִשָּׁם אֶת־יְהוָה אֱלֹהֶיךָ וּמָצָאתָ כִּי
תִדְרְשֶׁנּוּ בְּכָל־לְבָבְךָ וּבְכָל־נַפְשֶׁךָ: [לוי] ל בַּצַּר לְךָ וּמְצָאוּךָ כֹּל
הַדְּבָרִים הָאֵלֶּה בְּאַחֲרִית הַיָּמִים וְשַׁבְתָּ עַד־יְהוָה אֱלֹהֶיךָ
וְשָׁמַעְתָּ בְּקֹלוֹ: לא כִּי אֵל רַחוּם יְהוָה אֱלֹהֶיךָ לֹא יַרְפְּךָ וְלֹא
יַשְׁחִיתֶךָ וְלֹא יִשְׁכַּח אֶת־בְּרִית אֲבֹתֶיךָ אֲשֶׁר נִשְׁבַּע לָהֶם:
לב כִּי שְׁאַל־נָא לְיָמִים רִאשֹׁנִים אֲשֶׁר־הָיוּ לְפָנֶיךָ לְמִן־הַיּוֹם
אֲשֶׁר בָּרָא אֱלֹהִים | אָדָם עַל־הָאָרֶץ וּלְמִקְצֵה הַשָּׁמַיִם וְעַד־
קְצֵה הַשָּׁמָיִם הֲנִהְיָה כַּדָּבָר הַגָּדוֹל הַזֶּה אוֹ הֲנִשְׁמַע כָּמֹהוּ:
לג הֲשָׁמַע עָם קוֹל אֱלֹהִים מְדַבֵּר מִתּוֹךְ־הָאֵשׁ כַּאֲשֶׁר־
שָׁמַעְתָּ אַתָּה וַיֶּחִי: לד אוֹ | הֲנִסָּה אֱלֹהִים לָבוֹא לָקַחַת לוֹ גוֹי
מִקֶּרֶב גּוֹי בְּמַסֹּת בְּאֹתֹת וּבְמוֹפְתִים וּבְמִלְחָמָה וּבְיָד חֲזָקָה
וּבִזְרוֹעַ נְטוּיָה וּבְמוֹרָאִים גְּדֹלִים כְּכֹל אֲשֶׁר־עָשָׂה לָכֶם
יְהוָה אֱלֹהֵיכֶם בְּמִצְרַיִם לְעֵינֶיךָ: לה אַתָּה הָרְאֵתָ לָדַעַת כִּי
יְהוָה הוּא הָאֱלֹהִים אֵין עוֹד מִלְבַדּוֹ: [ישראל] לו מִן־הַשָּׁמַיִם
הִשְׁמִיעֲךָ אֶת־קֹלוֹ לְיַסְּרֶךָּ וְעַל־הָאָרֶץ הֶרְאֲךָ אֶת־אִשּׁוֹ
הַגְּדוֹלָה וּדְבָרָיו שָׁמַעְתָּ מִתּוֹךְ הָאֵשׁ: לז וְתַחַת כִּי אָהַב
אֶת־אֲבֹתֶיךָ וַיִּבְחַר בְּזַרְעוֹ אַחֲרָיו וַיּוֹצִאֲךָ בְּפָנָיו בְּכֹחוֹ הַגָּדֹל
מִמִּצְרָיִם: לח לְהוֹרִישׁ גּוֹיִם גְּדֹלִים וַעֲצֻמִים מִמְּךָ מִפָּנֶיךָ
לַהֲבִיאֲךָ לָתֶת־לְךָ אֶת־אַרְצָם נַחֲלָה כַּיּוֹם הַזֶּה: לט וְיָדַעְתָּ
הַיּוֹם וַהֲשֵׁבֹתָ אֶל־לְבָבֶךָ כִּי יְהוָה הוּא הָאֱלֹהִים בַּשָּׁמַיִם
מִמַּעַל וְעַל־הָאָרֶץ מִתָּחַת אֵין עוֹד: מ וְשָׁמַרְתָּ אֶת־חֻקָּיו
וְאֶת־מִצְוֹתָיו אֲשֶׁר אָנֹכִי מְצַוְּךָ הַיּוֹם אֲשֶׁר יִיטַב לְךָ וּלְבָנֶיךָ
אַחֲרֶיךָ וּלְמַעַן תַּאֲרִיךְ יָמִים עַל־הָאֲדָמָה אֲשֶׁר יְהוָה אֱלֹהֶיךָ
נֹתֵן לְךָ כָּל־הַיָּמִים:

Haftarah for Tisha B'Av

The blessing recited before the הַפְטָרָה is found on page 414, and the blessings after the הַפְטָרָה (until מָגֵן דָּוִד) are found on page 416.

ירמיה ח יג אָסֹף אֲסִיפֵם נְאֻם־יְהוָה אֵין עֲנָבִים בַּגֶּפֶן וְאֵין
תְּאֵנִים בַּתְּאֵנָה וְהֶעָלֶה נָבֵל וָאֶתֵּן לָהֶם יַעַבְרוּם: יד עַל־מָה
אֲנַחְנוּ יֹשְׁבִים הֵאָסְפוּ וְנָבוֹא אֶל־עָרֵי הַמִּבְצָר וְנִדְּמָה־שָּׁם
כִּי יְהוָה אֱלֹהֵינוּ הֲדִמָּנוּ וַיַּשְׁקֵנוּ מֵי־רֹאשׁ כִּי חָטָאנוּ לַיהוָה:
טו קַוֵּה לְשָׁלוֹם וְאֵין טוֹב לְעֵת מַרְפֵּה וְהִנֵּה בְעָתָה: טז מִדָּן
נִשְׁמַע נַחְרַת סוּסָיו מִקּוֹל מִצְהֲלוֹת אַבִּירָיו רָעֲשָׁה כָּל־
הָאָרֶץ וַיָּבוֹאוּ וַיֹּאכְלוּ אֶרֶץ וּמְלוֹאָהּ עִיר וְיֹשְׁבֵי בָהּ: יז כִּי
הִנְנִי מְשַׁלֵּחַ בָּכֶם נְחָשִׁים צִפְעֹנִים אֲשֶׁר אֵין־לָהֶם לָחַשׁ
וְנִשְּׁכוּ אֶתְכֶם נְאֻם־יְהוָה: יח מַבְלִיגִיתִי עֲלֵי יָגוֹן עָלַי לִבִּי
דַוָּי: יט הִנֵּה־קוֹל שַׁוְעַת בַּת־עַמִּי מֵאֶרֶץ מַרְחַקִּים הַיהוָה
אֵין בְּצִיּוֹן אִם־מַלְכָּהּ אֵין בָּהּ מַדּוּעַ הִכְעִסוּנִי בִּפְסִלֵיהֶם
בְּהַבְלֵי נֵכָר: כ עָבַר קָצִיר כָּלָה קָיִץ וַאֲנַחְנוּ לוֹא נוֹשָׁעְנוּ:
כא עַל־שֶׁבֶר בַּת־עַמִּי הָשְׁבָּרְתִּי קָדַרְתִּי שַׁמָּה הֶחֱזִקָתְנִי:
כב הַצֳרִי אֵין בְּגִלְעָד אִם־רֹפֵא אֵין שָׁם כִּי מַדּוּעַ לֹא עָלְתָה
אֲרֻכַת בַּת־עַמִּי: כג מִי־יִתֵּן רֹאשִׁי מַיִם וְעֵינִי מְקוֹר דִּמְעָה
וְאֶבְכֶּה יוֹמָם וָלַיְלָה אֵת חַלְלֵי בַת־עַמִּי: ט א מִי־יִתְּנֵנִי
בַמִּדְבָּר מְלוֹן אֹרְחִים וְאֶעֶזְבָה אֶת־עַמִּי וְאֵלְכָה מֵאִתָּם כִּי
כֻלָּם מְנָאֲפִים עֲצֶרֶת בֹּגְדִים: ב וַיַּדְרְכוּ אֶת־לְשׁוֹנָם קַשְׁתָּם
שֶׁקֶר וְלֹא לֶאֱמוּנָה גָּבְרוּ בָאָרֶץ כִּי מֵרָעָה אֶל־רָעָה | יָצָאוּ
וְאֹתִי לֹא־יָדָעוּ נְאֻם־יְהוָה: ג אִישׁ מֵרֵעֵהוּ הִשָּׁמֵרוּ וְעַל־
כָּל־אָח אַל־תִּבְטָחוּ כִּי כָל־אָח עָקוֹב יַעְקֹב וְכָל־רֵעַ רָכִיל
יַהֲלֹךְ: ד וְאִישׁ בְּרֵעֵהוּ יְהָתֵלּוּ וֶאֱמֶת לֹא יְדַבֵּרוּ לִמְּדוּ לְשׁוֹנָם

דַּבֵּר־שֶׁקֶר הַעֲוֵה נִלְאוּ׃ ה שִׁבְתְּךָ בְּתוֹךְ מִרְמָה בְּמִרְמָה
מֵאֲנוּ דַעַת־אוֹתִי נְאֻם־יְהוָה׃ ו לָכֵן כֹּה אָמַר יְהוָה צְבָאוֹת
הִנְנִי צוֹרְפָם וּבְחַנְתִּים כִּי־אֵיךְ אֶעֱשֶׂה מִפְּנֵי בַּת־עַמִּי׃ ז חֵץ
שָׁוחֵט▽ לְשׁוֹנָם מִרְמָה דִבֵּר בְּפִיו שָׁלוֹם אֶת־רֵעֵהוּ יְדַבֵּר
וּבְקִרְבּוֹ יָשִׂים אָרְבּוֹ׃ ח הַעַל־אֵלֶּה לֹא־אֶפְקָד־בָּם נְאֻם־יְהוָה
אִם בְּגוֹי אֲשֶׁר־כָּזֶה לֹא תִתְנַקֵּם נַפְשִׁי׃ ט עַל־הֶהָרִים
אֶשָּׂא בְכִי וָנֶהִי וְעַל־נְאוֹת מִדְבָּר קִינָה כִּי נִצְּתוּ מִבְּלִי־אִישׁ
עֹבֵר וְלֹא שָׁמְעוּ קוֹל מִקְנֶה מֵעוֹף הַשָּׁמַיִם וְעַד־בְּהֵמָה נָדְדוּ
הָלָכוּ׃ י וְנָתַתִּי אֶת־יְרוּשָׁלִַם לְגַלִּים מְעוֹן תַּנִּים וְאֶת־עָרֵי
יְהוּדָה אֶתֵּן שְׁמָמָה מִבְּלִי יוֹשֵׁב׃ יא מִי־הָאִישׁ הֶחָכָם וְיָבֵן
אֶת־זֹאת וַאֲשֶׁר דִּבֶּר פִּי־יְהוָה אֵלָיו וְיַגִּדָהּ עַל־מָה אָבְדָה
הָאָרֶץ נִצְּתָה כַמִּדְבָּר מִבְּלִי עֹבֵר׃ יב וַיֹּאמֶר יְהוָה עַל־עָזְבָם
אֶת־תּוֹרָתִי אֲשֶׁר נָתַתִּי לִפְנֵיהֶם וְלֹא־שָׁמְעוּ בְקוֹלִי וְלֹא־
הָלְכוּ בָהּ׃ יג וַיֵּלְכוּ אַחֲרֵי שְׁרִרוּת לִבָּם וְאַחֲרֵי הַבְּעָלִים אֲשֶׁר
לִמְּדוּם אֲבוֹתָם׃ יד לָכֵן כֹּה־אָמַר יְהוָה צְבָאוֹת אֱלֹהֵי
יִשְׂרָאֵל הִנְנִי מַאֲכִילָם אֶת־הָעָם הַזֶּה לַעֲנָה וְהִשְׁקִיתִים מֵי־
רֹאשׁ׃ טו וַהֲפִצוֹתִים בַּגּוֹיִם אֲשֶׁר לֹא יָדְעוּ הֵמָּה וַאֲבוֹתָם
וְשִׁלַּחְתִּי אַחֲרֵיהֶם אֶת־הַחֶרֶב עַד כַּלּוֹתִי אוֹתָם׃ טז כֹּה
אָמַר יְהוָה צְבָאוֹת הִתְבּוֹנְנוּ וְקִרְאוּ לַמְקוֹנְנוֹת וּתְבוֹאֶינָה
וְאֶל־הַחֲכָמוֹת שִׁלְחוּ וְתָבוֹאנָה׃ יז וּתְמַהֵרְנָה וְתִשֶּׂנָה עָלֵינוּ
נֶהִי וְתֵרַדְנָה עֵינֵינוּ דִּמְעָה וְעַפְעַפֵּינוּ יִזְּלוּ־מָיִם׃ יח כִּי קוֹל
נְהִי נִשְׁמַע מִצִּיּוֹן אֵיךְ שֻׁדָּדְנוּ בֹּשְׁנוּ מְאֹד כִּי־עָזַבְנוּ אָרֶץ כִּי
הִשְׁלִיכוּ מִשְׁכְּנוֹתֵינוּ׃ יט כִּי־שְׁמַעְנָה נָשִׁים דְּבַר־יְהוָה וְתִקַּח

▽ שָׁחוּט

אָזְנְכֶם דְּבַר־פִּיו וְלַמֵּדְנָה בְנוֹתֵיכֶם נֶהִי וְאִשָּׁה רְעוּתָהּ
קִינָה: כ כִּי־עָלָה מָוֶת בְּחַלּוֹנֵינוּ בָּא בְּאַרְמְנוֹתֵינוּ לְהַכְרִית
עוֹלָל מִחוּץ בַּחוּרִים מֵרְחֹבוֹת: כא דַּבֵּר כֹּה נְאֻם־יְהוָֹה
וְנָפְלָה נִבְלַת הָאָדָם כְּדֹמֶן עַל־פְּנֵי הַשָּׂדֶה וּכְעָמִיר מֵאַחֲרֵי
הַקֹּצֵר וְאֵין מְאַסֵּף: כב כֹּה | אָמַר יְהוָֹה אַל־יִתְהַלֵּל חָכָם
בְּחָכְמָתוֹ וְאַל־יִתְהַלֵּל הַגִּבּוֹר בִּגְבוּרָתוֹ אַל־יִתְהַלֵּל עָשִׁיר
בְּעָשְׁרוֹ: כג כִּי אִם־בְּזֹאת יִתְהַלֵּל הַמִּתְהַלֵּל הַשְׂכֵּל וְיָדֹעַ
אוֹתִי כִּי אֲנִי יְהוָֹה עֹשֶׂה חֶסֶד מִשְׁפָּט וּצְדָקָה בָּאָרֶץ כִּי־
בְאֵלֶּה חָפַצְתִּי נְאֻם־יְהוָֹה:

TORAH READING FOR FAST DAYS

Three people receive עֲלִיּוֹת on fast days. At מִנְחָה the third person recites the הַפְטָרָה. At the text in bold, the Reader should pause and the verses are recited aloud by the congregation. The Reader then repeats them and continues.

שמות לב יא וַיְחַל מֹשֶׁה אֶת־פְּנֵי יְהוָֹה אֱלֹהָיו וַיֹּאמֶר לָמָה יְהוָֹה
יֶחֱרֶה אַפְּךָ בְּעַמֶּךָ אֲשֶׁר הוֹצֵאתָ מֵאֶרֶץ מִצְרַיִם בְּכֹחַ גָּדוֹל
וּבְיָד חֲזָקָה: יב לָמָּה יֹאמְרוּ מִצְרַיִם לֵאמֹר בְּרָעָה הוֹצִיאָם
לַהֲרֹג אֹתָם בֶּהָרִים וּלְכַלֹּתָם מֵעַל פְּנֵי הָאֲדָמָה **שׁוּב מֵחֲרוֹן**
אַפֶּךָ וְהִנָּחֵם עַל־הָרָעָה לְעַמֶּךָ: יג זְכֹר לְאַבְרָהָם לְיִצְחָק
וּלְיִשְׂרָאֵל עֲבָדֶיךָ אֲשֶׁר נִשְׁבַּעְתָּ לָהֶם בָּךְ וַתְּדַבֵּר אֲלֵהֶם
אַרְבֶּה אֶת־זַרְעֲכֶם כְּכוֹכְבֵי הַשָּׁמָיִם וְכָל־הָאָרֶץ הַזֹּאת אֲשֶׁר
אָמַרְתִּי אֶתֵּן לְזַרְעֲכֶם וְנָחֲלוּ לְעֹלָם: יד וַיִּנָּחֶם יְהוָֹה עַל־
הָרָעָה אֲשֶׁר דִּבֶּר לַעֲשׂוֹת לְעַמּוֹ: [לוי] פ לד א וַיֹּאמֶר יְהוָֹה
אֶל־מֹשֶׁה פְּסָל־לְךָ שְׁנֵי־לֻחֹת אֲבָנִים כָּרִאשֹׁנִים וְכָתַבְתִּי
עַל־הַלֻּחֹת אֶת־הַדְּבָרִים אֲשֶׁר הָיוּ עַל־הַלֻּחֹת הָרִאשֹׁנִים

אֲשֶׁר שִׁבַּרְתָּ׃ ב וֶהְיֵה נָכוֹן לַבֹּקֶר וְעָלִיתָ בַבֹּקֶר אֶל־הַר סִינַי
וְנִצַּבְתָּ לִי שָׁם עַל־רֹאשׁ הָהָר׃ ג וְאִישׁ לֹא־יַעֲלֶה עִמָּךְ וְגַם־
אִישׁ אַל־יֵרָא בְּכָל־הָהָר גַּם־הַצֹּאן וְהַבָּקָר אַל־יִרְעוּ אֶל־מוּל
הָהָר הַהוּא׃ [ישראל] ד וַיִּפְסֹל שְׁנֵי־לֻחֹת אֲבָנִים כָּרִאשֹׁנִים
וַיַּשְׁכֵּם מֹשֶׁה בַבֹּקֶר וַיַּעַל אֶל־הַר סִינַי כַּאֲשֶׁר צִוָּה יְהוָה
אֹתוֹ וַיִּקַּח בְּיָדוֹ שְׁנֵי לֻחֹת אֲבָנִים׃ ה וַיֵּרֶד יְהוָה בֶּעָנָן וַיִּתְיַצֵּב
עִמּוֹ שָׁם וַיִּקְרָא בְשֵׁם יְהוָה׃ ו וַיַּעֲבֹר יְהוָה | עַל־פָּנָיו וַיִּקְרָא
יְהוָה | יְהוָה אֵל רַחוּם וְחַנּוּן אֶרֶךְ אַפַּיִם וְרַב־חֶסֶד וֶאֱמֶת׃
ז **נֹצֵר חֶסֶד לָאֲלָפִים נֹשֵׂא עָוֺן וָפֶשַׁע וְחַטָּאָה וְנַקֵּה** לֹא יְנַקֶּה
פֹּקֵד | עֲוֺן אָבוֹת עַל־בָּנִים וְעַל־בְּנֵי בָנִים עַל־שִׁלֵּשִׁים וְעַל־
רִבֵּעִים׃ ח וַיְמַהֵר מֹשֶׁה וַיִּקֹּד אַרְצָה וַיִּשְׁתָּחוּ׃ ט וַיֹּאמֶר
אִם־נָא מָצָאתִי חֵן בְּעֵינֶיךָ אֲדֹנָי יֵלֶךְ־נָא אֲדֹנָי בְּקִרְבֵּנוּ כִּי
עַם־קְשֵׁה־עֹרֶף הוּא **וְסָלַחְתָּ לַעֲוֺנֵנוּ וּלְחַטָּאתֵנוּ וּנְחַלְתָּנוּ׃**
י וַיֹּאמֶר הִנֵּה אָנֹכִי כֹּרֵת בְּרִית נֶגֶד כָּל־עַמְּךָ אֶעֱשֶׂה נִפְלָאֹת
אֲשֶׁר לֹא־נִבְרְאוּ בְכָל־הָאָרֶץ וּבְכָל־הַגּוֹיִם וְרָאָה כָל־הָעָם
אֲשֶׁר־אַתָּה בְקִרְבּוֹ אֶת־מַעֲשֵׂה יְהוָה כִּי־נוֹרָא הוּא אֲשֶׁר
אֲנִי עֹשֶׂה עִמָּךְ׃

Haftarah for Mincha on Fast Days

The blessing recited before the הַפְטָרָה is found on page 414, and the blessings after the הַפְטָרָה (until מָגֵן דָּוִד) are found on page 416.

ישעיה נה ו דִּרְשׁוּ יְהוָה בְּהִמָּצְאוֹ קְרָאֻהוּ בִּהְיוֹתוֹ קָרוֹב׃
ז יַעֲזֹב רָשָׁע דַּרְכּוֹ וְאִישׁ אָוֶן מַחְשְׁבֹתָיו וְיָשֹׁב אֶל־יְהוָה
וִירַחֲמֵהוּ וְאֶל־אֱלֹהֵינוּ כִּי־יַרְבֶּה לִסְלוֹחַ׃ ח כִּי לֹא מַחְשְׁבוֹתַי
מַחְשְׁבוֹתֵיכֶם וְלֹא דַרְכֵיכֶם דְּרָכָי נְאֻם יְהוָה׃ ט כִּי־גָבְהוּ שָׁמַיִם

מֵאָ֔רֶץ כֵּ֚ן גָּבְה֤וּ דְרָכַי֙ מִדַּרְכֵיכֶ֔ם וּמַחְשְׁבֹתַ֖י מִמַּחְשְׁבֹתֵיכֶֽם׃
י כִּ֡י כַּאֲשֶׁר֩ יֵרֵ֨ד הַגֶּ֜שֶׁם וְהַשֶּׁ֣לֶג מִן־הַשָּׁמַ֗יִם וְשָׁ֙מָּה֙ לֹ֣א יָשׁ֔וּב
כִּ֚י אִם־הִרְוָ֣ה אֶת־הָאָ֔רֶץ וְהוֹלִידָ֖הּ וְהִצְמִיחָ֑הּ וְנָ֤תַן זֶ֙רַע֙ לַזֹּרֵ֔עַ
וְלֶ֖חֶם לָאֹכֵֽל׃ יא כֵּ֣ן יִהְיֶ֤ה דְבָרִי֙ אֲשֶׁ֣ר יֵצֵ֣א מִפִּ֔י לֹֽא־יָשׁ֥וּב
אֵלַ֖י רֵיקָ֑ם כִּ֤י אִם־עָשָׂה֙ אֶת־אֲשֶׁ֣ר חָפַ֔צְתִּי וְהִצְלִ֖יחַ אֲשֶׁ֥ר
שְׁלַחְתִּֽיו׃ יב כִּֽי־בְשִׂמְחָ֣ה תֵצֵ֔אוּ וּבְשָׁל֖וֹם תּֽוּבָל֑וּן הֶהָרִ֣ים
וְהַגְּבָע֗וֹת יִפְצְח֤וּ לִפְנֵיכֶם֙ רִנָּ֔ה וְכָל־עֲצֵ֥י הַשָּׂדֶ֖ה יִמְחֲאוּ־
כָֽף׃ יג תַּ֤חַת הַנַּֽעֲצוּץ֙ יַעֲלֶ֣ה בְר֔וֹשׁ תחת▽ הַסִּרְפַּ֖ד יַעֲלֶ֣ה
הֲדַ֑ס וְהָיָ֤ה לַֽיהוָה֙ לְשֵׁ֔ם לְא֥וֹת עוֹלָ֖ם לֹ֥א יִכָּרֵֽת׃ נו א כֹּ֚ה
אָמַ֣ר יְהוָ֔ה שִׁמְר֥וּ מִשְׁפָּ֖ט וַעֲשׂ֣וּ צְדָקָ֑ה כִּֽי־קְרוֹבָ֤ה יְשׁוּעָתִי֙
לָב֔וֹא וְצִדְקָתִ֖י לְהִגָּלֽוֹת׃ ב אַשְׁרֵ֤י אֱנוֹשׁ֙ יַעֲשֶׂה־זֹּ֔את וּבֶן־
אָדָ֖ם יַחֲזִ֣יק בָּ֑הּ שֹׁמֵ֤ר שַׁבָּת֙ מֵֽחַלְּל֔וֹ וְשֹׁמֵ֥ר יָד֖וֹ מֵעֲשׂ֥וֹת
כָּל־רָֽע׃ ג וְאַל־יֹאמַ֣ר בֶּן־הַנֵּכָ֗ר הַנִּלְוָ֤ה אֶל־יְהוָה֙ לֵאמֹ֔ר
הַבְדֵּ֧ל יַבְדִּילַ֛נִי יְהוָ֖ה מֵעַ֣ל עַמּ֑וֹ וְאַל־יֹאמַר֙ הַסָּרִ֔יס הֵ֥ן אֲנִ֖י
עֵ֥ץ יָבֵֽשׁ׃ ד כִּי־כֹ֣ה ׀ אָמַ֣ר יְהוָ֗ה לַסָּֽרִיסִים֙ אֲשֶׁ֤ר יִשְׁמְרוּ֙
אֶת־שַׁבְּתוֹתַ֔י וּבָֽחֲר֖וּ בַּאֲשֶׁ֣ר חָפָ֑צְתִּי וּמַחֲזִיקִ֖ים בִּבְרִיתִֽי׃
ה וְנָתַתִּ֨י לָהֶ֜ם בְּבֵיתִ֤י וּבְחֽוֹמֹתַי֙ יָ֣ד וָשֵׁ֔ם ט֖וֹב מִבָּנִ֣ים וּמִבָּנ֑וֹת
שֵׁ֤ם עוֹלָם֙ אֶתֶּן־ל֔וֹ אֲשֶׁ֖ר לֹ֥א יִכָּרֵֽת׃ ו וּבְנֵ֣י הַנֵּכָ֗ר הַנִּלְוִ֤ים עַל־
יְהוָה֙ לְשָׁ֣רְת֔וֹ וּֽלְאַהֲבָה֙ אֶת־שֵׁ֣ם יְהוָ֔ה לִהְי֥וֹת ל֖וֹ לַעֲבָדִ֑ים
כָּל־שֹׁמֵ֤ר שַׁבָּת֙ מֵֽחַלְּל֔וֹ וּמַחֲזִיקִ֖ים בִּבְרִיתִֽי׃ ז וַהֲבִיאוֹתִ֞ים
אֶל־הַ֣ר קָדְשִׁ֗י וְשִׂמַּחְתִּים֙ בְּבֵ֣ית תְּפִלָּתִ֔י עוֹלֹתֵיהֶ֧ם וְזִבְחֵיהֶ֛ם
לְרָצ֖וֹן עַל־מִזְבְּחִ֑י כִּ֣י בֵיתִ֔י בֵּית־תְּפִלָּ֥ה יִקָּרֵ֖א לְכָל־הָעַמִּֽים׃
ח נְאֻם֙ אֲדֹנָ֣י יֱהוִ֔ה מְקַבֵּ֖ץ נִדְחֵ֣י יִשְׂרָאֵ֑ל ע֛וֹד אֲקַבֵּ֥ץ עָלָ֖יו
לְנִקְבָּצָֽיו׃

▽ וְתַ֥חַת ק׳

TORAH READING FOR ROSH CHODESH

Four people are called up on רֹאשׁ חֹדֶשׁ. On רֹאשׁ חֹדֶשׁ טֵבֵת, take out two סִפְרֵי תוֹרָה. From the first, read the קְרִיאַת הַתּוֹרָה for רֹאשׁ חֹדֶשׁ. Call up three עוֹלִים, combining the first two sections for the כֹּהֵן. This is followed by הַגְבָּהָה and גְלִילָה. Call up the fourth עוֹלֶה to the second סֵפֶר תּוֹרָה and read the appropriate section for that day of חֲנֻכָּה. Say חֲצִי קַדִּישׁ, followed by the second הַגְבָּהָה and גְלִילָה.

במדבר כח א וַיְדַבֵּר יְהוָה אֶל־מֹשֶׁה לֵּאמֹר׃ ב צַו אֶת־בְּנֵי
יִשְׂרָאֵל וְאָמַרְתָּ אֲלֵהֶם אֶת־קָרְבָּנִי לַחְמִי לְאִשַּׁי רֵיחַ נִיחֹחִי
תִּשְׁמְרוּ לְהַקְרִיב לִי בְּמוֹעֲדוֹ׃ ג וְאָמַרְתָּ לָהֶם זֶה הָאִשֶּׁה
אֲשֶׁר תַּקְרִיבוּ לַיהוָה כְּבָשִׂים בְּנֵי־שָׁנָה תְמִימִם שְׁנַיִם
לַיּוֹם עֹלָה תָמִיד׃ [לוי] ג וְאָמַרְתָּ לָהֶם זֶה הָאִשֶּׁה אֲשֶׁר
תַּקְרִיבוּ לַיהוָה כְּבָשִׂים בְּנֵי־שָׁנָה תְמִימִם שְׁנַיִם לַיּוֹם עֹלָה
תָמִיד׃ ד אֶת־הַכֶּבֶשׂ אֶחָד תַּעֲשֶׂה בַבֹּקֶר וְאֵת הַכֶּבֶשׂ
הַשֵּׁנִי תַּעֲשֶׂה בֵּין הָעַרְבָּיִם׃ ה וַעֲשִׂירִית הָאֵיפָה סֹלֶת
לְמִנְחָה בְּלוּלָה בְּשֶׁמֶן כָּתִית רְבִיעִת הַהִין׃ [ישראל] ו עֹלַת
תָּמִיד הָעֲשֻׂיָה בְּהַר סִינַי לְרֵיחַ נִיחֹחַ אִשֶּׁה לַיהוָה׃ ז וְנִסְכּוֹ
רְבִיעִת הַהִין לַכֶּבֶשׂ הָאֶחָד בַּקֹּדֶשׁ הַסֵּךְ נֶסֶךְ שֵׁכָר לַיהוָה׃
ח וְאֵת הַכֶּבֶשׂ הַשֵּׁנִי תַּעֲשֶׂה בֵּין הָעַרְבָּיִם כְּמִנְחַת הַבֹּקֶר
וּכְנִסְכּוֹ תַּעֲשֶׂה אִשֵּׁה רֵיחַ נִיחֹחַ לַיהוָה׃ פ ט וּבְיוֹם הַשַּׁבָּת
שְׁנֵי־כְבָשִׂים בְּנֵי־שָׁנָה תְּמִימִם וּשְׁנֵי עֶשְׂרֹנִים סֹלֶת מִנְחָה
בְּלוּלָה בַשֶּׁמֶן וְנִסְכּוֹ׃ י עֹלַת שַׁבַּת בְּשַׁבַּתּוֹ עַל־עֹלַת הַתָּמִיד
וְנִסְכָּהּ׃ פ [רביעי] יא וּבְרָאשֵׁי חָדְשֵׁיכֶם תַּקְרִיבוּ עֹלָה לַיהוָה
פָּרִים בְּנֵי־בָקָר שְׁנַיִם וְאַיִל אֶחָד כְּבָשִׂים בְּנֵי־שָׁנָה שִׁבְעָה
תְּמִימִם׃ יב וּשְׁלֹשָׁה עֶשְׂרֹנִים סֹלֶת מִנְחָה בְּלוּלָה בַשֶּׁמֶן
לַפָּר הָאֶחָד וּשְׁנֵי עֶשְׂרֹנִים סֹלֶת מִנְחָה בְּלוּלָה בַשֶּׁמֶן לָאַיִל
הָאֶחָד׃ יג וְעִשָּׂרֹן עִשָּׂרוֹן סֹלֶת מִנְחָה בְּלוּלָה בַשֶּׁמֶן לַכֶּבֶשׂ

הָאֶחָד עֹלָה רֵיחַ נִיחֹחַ אִשֶּׁה לַיהוָה׃ יד וְנִסְכֵּיהֶם חֲצִי הַהִין
יִהְיֶה לַפָּר וּשְׁלִישִׁת הַהִין לָאַיִל וּרְבִיעִת הַהִין לַכֶּבֶשׂ יָיִן
זֹאת עֹלַת חֹדֶשׁ בְּחָדְשׁוֹ לְחָדְשֵׁי הַשָּׁנָה׃ טו וּשְׂעִיר עִזִּים
אֶחָד לְחַטָּאת לַיהוָה עַל־עֹלַת הַתָּמִיד יֵעָשֶׂה וְנִסְכּוֹ׃

TORAH READINGS FOR THE THREE FESTIVALS

Torah Readings For Pesach

קריאה ליום הראשון של פסח

שמות יב כא וַיִּקְרָא מֹשֶׁה לְכָל־זִקְנֵי יִשְׂרָאֵל וַיֹּאמֶר אֲלֵהֶם
מִשְׁכוּ וּקְחוּ לָכֶם צֹאן לְמִשְׁפְּחֹתֵיכֶם וְשַׁחֲטוּ הַפָּסַח׃
כב וּלְקַחְתֶּם אֲגֻדַּת אֵזוֹב וּטְבַלְתֶּם בַּדָּם אֲשֶׁר־בַּסַּף וְהִגַּעְתֶּם
אֶל־הַמַּשְׁקוֹף וְאֶל־שְׁתֵּי הַמְּזוּזֹת מִן־הַדָּם אֲשֶׁר בַּסָּף וְאַתֶּם
לֹא תֵצְאוּ אִישׁ מִפֶּתַח־בֵּיתוֹ עַד־בֹּקֶר׃ כג וְעָבַר יהוה לִנְגֹּף
אֶת־מִצְרַיִם וְרָאָה אֶת־הַדָּם עַל־הַמַּשְׁקוֹף וְעַל שְׁתֵּי
הַמְּזוּזֹת וּפָסַח יהוה עַל־הַפֶּתַח וְלֹא יִתֵּן הַמַּשְׁחִית לָבֹא
אֶל־בָּתֵּיכֶם לִנְגֹּף׃ כד וּשְׁמַרְתֶּם אֶת־הַדָּבָר הַזֶּה לְחָק־לְךָ
וּלְבָנֶיךָ עַד־עוֹלָם׃ [לוי] כה וְהָיָה כִּי־תָבֹאוּ אֶל־הָאָרֶץ אֲשֶׁר
יִתֵּן יהוה לָכֶם כַּאֲשֶׁר דִּבֵּר וּשְׁמַרְתֶּם אֶת־הָעֲבֹדָה הַזֹּאת׃
כו וְהָיָה כִּי־יֹאמְרוּ אֲלֵיכֶם בְּנֵיכֶם מָה הָעֲבֹדָה הַזֹּאת לָכֶם׃
כז וַאֲמַרְתֶּם זֶבַח־פֶּסַח הוּא לַיהוה אֲשֶׁר פָּסַח עַל־בָּתֵּי
בְנֵי־יִשְׂרָאֵל בְּמִצְרַיִם בְּנָגְפּוֹ אֶת־מִצְרַיִם וְאֶת־בָּתֵּינוּ הִצִּיל
וַיִּקֹּד הָעָם וַיִּשְׁתַּחֲווּ׃ כח וַיֵּלְכוּ וַיַּעֲשׂוּ בְּנֵי יִשְׂרָאֵל כַּאֲשֶׁר

צִוָּ֧ה יְהוָ֛ה אֶת־מֹשֶׁ֥ה וְאַהֲרֹ֖ן כֵּ֥ן עָשֽׂוּ׃ ס [שלישי] כט וַיְהִ֣י ׀
בַּחֲצִ֣י הַלַּ֗יְלָה וַֽיהוָה֮ הִכָּ֣ה כָל־בְּכוֹר֒ בְּאֶ֣רֶץ מִצְרַ֔יִם מִבְּכֹ֤ר
פַּרְעֹה֙ הַיֹּשֵׁ֣ב עַל־כִּסְא֔וֹ עַ֚ד בְּכ֣וֹר הַשְּׁבִ֔י אֲשֶׁ֖ר בְּבֵ֣ית הַבּ֑וֹר
וְכֹ֖ל בְּכ֥וֹר בְּהֵמָֽה׃ ל וַיָּ֨קָם פַּרְעֹ֜ה לַ֗יְלָה ה֤וּא וְכָל־עֲבָדָיו֙
וְכָל־מִצְרַ֔יִם וַתְּהִ֛י צְעָקָ֥ה גְדֹלָ֖ה בְּמִצְרָ֑יִם כִּֽי־אֵ֣ין בַּ֔יִת אֲשֶׁ֥ר
אֵֽין־שָׁ֖ם מֵֽת׃ לא וַיִּקְרָא֩ לְמֹשֶׁ֨ה וּֽלְאַהֲרֹ֜ן לַ֗יְלָה וַיֹּ֙אמֶר֙ ק֤וּמוּ
צְּאוּ֙ מִתּ֣וֹךְ עַמִּ֔י גַּם־אַתֶּ֖ם גַּם־בְּנֵ֣י יִשְׂרָאֵ֑ל וּלְכ֛וּ עִבְד֥וּ אֶת־
יְהוָ֖ה כְּדַבֶּרְכֶֽם׃ לב גַּם־צֹאנְכֶ֨ם גַּם־בְּקַרְכֶ֥ם קְח֛וּ כַּאֲשֶׁ֥ר
דִּבַּרְתֶּ֖ם וָלֵ֑כוּ וּבֵֽרַכְתֶּ֖ם גַּם־אֹתִֽי׃ [בשבת רביעי] לג וַתֶּחֱזַ֤ק
מִצְרַ֙יִם֙ עַל־הָעָ֔ם לְמַהֵ֖ר לְשַׁלְּחָ֣ם מִן־הָאָ֑רֶץ כִּ֥י אָמְר֖וּ כֻּלָּ֥נוּ
מֵתִֽים׃ לד וַיִּשָּׂ֥א הָעָ֛ם אֶת־בְּצֵק֖וֹ טֶ֣רֶם יֶחְמָ֑ץ מִשְׁאֲרֹתָ֛ם
צְרֻרֹ֥ת בְּשִׂמְלֹתָ֖ם עַל־שִׁכְמָֽם׃ לה וּבְנֵֽי־יִשְׂרָאֵ֥ל עָשׂ֖וּ כִּדְבַ֣ר
מֹשֶׁ֑ה וַֽיִּשְׁאֲלוּ֙ מִמִּצְרַ֔יִם כְּלֵי־כֶ֛סֶף וּכְלֵ֥י זָהָ֖ב וּשְׂמָלֹֽת׃ לו
וַֽיהוָ֞ה נָתַ֨ן אֶת־חֵ֥ן הָעָ֛ם בְּעֵינֵ֥י מִצְרַ֖יִם וַיַּשְׁאִל֑וּם וַיְנַצְּל֖וּ
אֶת־מִצְרָֽיִם׃ פ [רביעי/בשבת חמישי] לז וַיִּסְע֧וּ בְנֵֽי־יִשְׂרָאֵ֛ל
מֵרַעְמְסֵ֖ס סֻכֹּ֑תָה כְּשֵׁשׁ־מֵא֨וֹת אֶ֧לֶף רַגְלִ֛י הַגְּבָרִ֖ים לְבַ֥ד
מִטָּֽף׃ לח וְגַם־עֵ֥רֶב רַ֖ב עָלָ֣ה אִתָּ֑ם וְצֹ֣אן וּבָקָ֔ר מִקְנֶ֖ה כָּבֵ֥ד
מְאֹֽד׃ לט וַיֹּאפ֨וּ אֶת־הַבָּצֵ֜ק אֲשֶׁ֨ר הוֹצִ֧יאוּ מִמִּצְרַ֛יִם עֻגֹ֥ת
מַצּ֖וֹת כִּ֣י לֹ֣א חָמֵ֑ץ כִּֽי־גֹרְשׁ֣וּ מִמִּצְרַ֗יִם וְלֹ֤א יָֽכְלוּ֙ לְהִתְמַהְמֵ֔הַּ
וְגַם־צֵדָ֖ה לֹא־עָשׂ֥וּ לָהֶֽם׃ מ וּמוֹשַׁב֙ בְּנֵ֣י יִשְׂרָאֵ֔ל אֲשֶׁ֥ר יָשְׁב֖וּ
בְּמִצְרָ֑יִם שְׁלֹשִׁ֣ים שָׁנָ֔ה וְאַרְבַּ֥ע מֵא֖וֹת שָׁנָֽה׃ מא וַיְהִ֗י מִקֵּץ֙
שְׁלֹשִׁ֣ים שָׁנָ֔ה וְאַרְבַּ֥ע מֵא֖וֹת שָׁנָ֑ה וַיְהִ֗י בְּעֶ֙צֶם֙ הַיּ֣וֹם הַזֶּ֔ה יָֽצְא֛וּ
כָּל־צִבְא֥וֹת יְהוָ֖ה מֵאֶ֥רֶץ מִצְרָֽיִם׃ מב לֵ֣יל שִׁמֻּרִ֥ים הוּא֙ לַֽיהוָ֔ה
לְהוֹצִיאָ֖ם מֵאֶ֣רֶץ מִצְרָ֑יִם הֽוּא־הַלַּ֤יְלָה הַזֶּה֙ לַֽיהוָ֔ה שִׁמֻּרִ֛ים
לְכָל־בְּנֵ֥י יִשְׂרָאֵ֖ל לְדֹרֹתָֽם׃ פ [חמישי/בשבת ששי] מג וַיֹּ֧אמֶר

יהוה אֶל־מֹשֶׁה וְאַהֲרֹן זֹאת חֻקַּת הַפָּסַח כָּל־בֶּן־נֵכָר לֹא־
יֹאכַל בּוֹ: מד וְכָל־עֶבֶד אִישׁ מִקְנַת־כָּסֶף וּמַלְתָּה אֹתוֹ אָז
יֹאכַל בּוֹ: מה תּוֹשָׁב וְשָׂכִיר לֹא־יֹאכַל בּוֹ: מו בְּבַיִת אֶחָד יֵאָכֵל
לֹא־תוֹצִיא מִן־הַבַּיִת מִן־הַבָּשָׂר חוּצָה וְעֶצֶם לֹא תִשְׁבְּרוּ־
בוֹ: מז כָּל־עֲדַת יִשְׂרָאֵל יַעֲשׂוּ אֹתוֹ: [בשבת שביעי] מח וְכִי־יָגוּר
אִתְּךָ גֵּר וְעָשָׂה פֶסַח לַיהוה הִמּוֹל לוֹ כָל־זָכָר וְאָז יִקְרַב
לַעֲשֹׂתוֹ וְהָיָה כְּאֶזְרַח הָאָרֶץ וְכָל־עָרֵל לֹא־יֹאכַל בּוֹ: מט
תּוֹרָה אַחַת יִהְיֶה לָאֶזְרָח וְלַגֵּר הַגָּר בְּתוֹכְכֶם: נ וַיַּעֲשׂוּ
כָּל־בְּנֵי יִשְׂרָאֵל כַּאֲשֶׁר צִוָּה יהוה אֶת־מֹשֶׁה וְאֶת־אַהֲרֹן כֵּן
עָשׂוּ: ס נא וַיְהִי בְּעֶצֶם הַיּוֹם הַזֶּה הוֹצִיא יהוה אֶת־בְּנֵי
יִשְׂרָאֵל מֵאֶרֶץ מִצְרַיִם עַל־צִבְאֹתָם:

מפטיר ליום הראשון והשני של פסח

After חצי קדיש (page 414), the מפטיר is read from the second ספר תורה on both the first and second days of פסח.

במדבר כח טז וּבַחֹדֶשׁ הָרִאשׁוֹן בְּאַרְבָּעָה עָשָׂר יוֹם לַחֹדֶשׁ
פֶּסַח לַיהוה: יז וּבַחֲמִשָּׁה עָשָׂר יוֹם לַחֹדֶשׁ הַזֶּה חָג שִׁבְעַת
יָמִים מַצּוֹת יֵאָכֵל: יח בַּיּוֹם הָרִאשׁוֹן מִקְרָא־קֹדֶשׁ כָּל־
מְלֶאכֶת עֲבֹדָה לֹא תַעֲשׂוּ: יט וְהִקְרַבְתֶּם אִשֶּׁה עֹלָה לַיהוה
פָּרִים בְּנֵי־בָקָר שְׁנַיִם וְאַיִל אֶחָד וְשִׁבְעָה כְבָשִׂים בְּנֵי שָׁנָה
תְּמִימִם יִהְיוּ לָכֶם: כ וּמִנְחָתָם סֹלֶת בְּלוּלָה בַשָּׁמֶן שְׁלֹשָׁה
עֶשְׂרֹנִים לַפָּר וּשְׁנֵי עֶשְׂרֹנִים לָאַיִל תַּעֲשׂוּ: כא עִשָּׂרוֹן עִשָּׂרוֹן
תַּעֲשֶׂה לַכֶּבֶשׂ הָאֶחָד לְשִׁבְעַת הַכְּבָשִׂים: כב וּשְׂעִיר חַטָּאת
אֶחָד לְכַפֵּר עֲלֵיכֶם: כג מִלְּבַד עֹלַת הַבֹּקֶר אֲשֶׁר לְעֹלַת
הַתָּמִיד תַּעֲשׂוּ אֶת־אֵלֶּה: כד כָּאֵלֶּה תַּעֲשׂוּ לַיּוֹם שִׁבְעַת
יָמִים לֶחֶם אִשֵּׁה רֵיחַ־נִיחֹחַ לַיהוה עַל־עוֹלַת הַתָּמִיד

יַעֲשֶׂה וְנִסְכּוֹ׃ כה וּבַיּוֹם הַשְּׁבִיעִי מִקְרָא־קֹדֶשׁ יִהְיֶה לָכֶם
כָּל־מְלֶאכֶת עֲבֹדָה לֹא תַעֲשׂוּ׃

הפטרה ליום הראשון של פסח

In some congregations, the הפטרה begins at בָּעֵת הַהִיא below (at the *).

יהושע ג ה וַיֹּאמֶר יְהוֹשֻׁעַ אֶל־הָעָם הִתְקַדָּשׁוּ כִּי מָחָר יַעֲשֶׂה
יְהוָה בְּקִרְבְּכֶם נִפְלָאוֹת׃ ו וַיֹּאמֶר יְהוֹשֻׁעַ אֶל־הַכֹּהֲנִים
לֵאמֹר שְׂאוּ אֶת־אֲרוֹן הַבְּרִית וְעִבְרוּ לִפְנֵי הָעָם וַיִּשְׂאוּ
אֶת־אֲרוֹן הַבְּרִית וַיֵּלְכוּ לִפְנֵי הָעָם׃
* יהושע ה ב בָּעֵת הַהִיא אָמַר יְהוָה אֶל־יְהוֹשֻׁעַ עֲשֵׂה לְךָ
חַרְבוֹת צֻרִים וְשׁוּב מֹל אֶת־בְּנֵי־יִשְׂרָאֵל שֵׁנִית׃ ג וַיַּעַשׂ־
לוֹ יְהוֹשֻׁעַ חַרְבוֹת צֻרִים וַיָּמָל אֶת־בְּנֵי יִשְׂרָאֵל אֶל־גִּבְעַת
הָעֲרָלוֹת׃ ד וְזֶה הַדָּבָר אֲשֶׁר־מָל יְהוֹשֻׁעַ כָּל־הָעָם הַיֹּצֵא
מִמִּצְרַיִם הַזְּכָרִים כֹּל | אַנְשֵׁי הַמִּלְחָמָה מֵתוּ בַמִּדְבָּר בַּדֶּרֶךְ
בְּצֵאתָם מִמִּצְרָיִם׃ ה כִּי־מֻלִים הָיוּ כָּל־הָעָם הַיֹּצְאִים וְכָל־
הָעָם הַיִּלֹּדִים בַּמִּדְבָּר בַּדֶּרֶךְ בְּצֵאתָם מִמִּצְרַיִם לֹא־מָלוּ׃ ו כִּי
| אַרְבָּעִים שָׁנָה הָלְכוּ בְנֵי־יִשְׂרָאֵל בַּמִּדְבָּר עַד־תֹּם כָּל־הַגּוֹי
אַנְשֵׁי הַמִּלְחָמָה הַיֹּצְאִים מִמִּצְרַיִם אֲשֶׁר לֹא־שָׁמְעוּ בְּקוֹל
יְהוָה אֲשֶׁר נִשְׁבַּע יְהוָה לָהֶם לְבִלְתִּי הַרְאוֹתָם אֶת־הָאָרֶץ
אֲשֶׁר נִשְׁבַּע יְהוָה לַאֲבוֹתָם לָתֶת לָנוּ אֶרֶץ זָבַת חָלָב וּדְבָשׁ׃
ז וְאֶת־בְּנֵיהֶם הֵקִים תַּחְתָּם אֹתָם מָל יְהוֹשֻׁעַ כִּי־עֲרֵלִים הָיוּ
כִּי לֹא־מָלוּ אוֹתָם בַּדָּרֶךְ׃ ח וַיְהִי כַּאֲשֶׁר־תַּמּוּ כָל־הַגּוֹי לְהִמּוֹל
וַיֵּשְׁבוּ תַחְתָּם בַּמַּחֲנֶה עַד חֲיוֹתָם׃ ס ט וַיֹּאמֶר יְהוָה
אֶל־יְהוֹשֻׁעַ הַיּוֹם גַּלּוֹתִי אֶת־חֶרְפַּת מִצְרַיִם מֵעֲלֵיכֶם וַיִּקְרָא
שֵׁם הַמָּקוֹם הַהוּא גִּלְגָּל עַד הַיּוֹם הַזֶּה׃ י וַיַּחֲנוּ בְנֵי־יִשְׂרָאֵל
בַּגִּלְגָּל וַיַּעֲשׂוּ אֶת־הַפֶּסַח בְּאַרְבָּעָה עָשָׂר יוֹם לַחֹדֶשׁ בָּעֶרֶב

בְּעַרְבוֹת יְרִיחוֹ׃ יא וַיֹּאכְלוּ מֵעֲבוּר הָאָרֶץ מִמָּחֳרַת הַפֶּסַח
מַצּוֹת וְקָלוּי בְּעֶצֶם הַיּוֹם הַזֶּה׃ יב וַיִּשְׁבֹּת הַמָּן מִמָּחֳרָת
בְּאָכְלָם מֵעֲבוּר הָאָרֶץ וְלֹא־הָיָה עוֹד לִבְנֵי יִשְׂרָאֵל מָן
וַיֹּאכְלוּ מִתְּבוּאַת אֶרֶץ כְּנַעַן בַּשָּׁנָה הַהִיא׃ ס יג וַיְהִי
בִּהְיוֹת יְהוֹשֻׁעַ בִּירִיחוֹ וַיִּשָּׂא עֵינָיו וַיַּרְא וְהִנֵּה־אִישׁ עֹמֵד
לְנֶגְדּוֹ וְחַרְבּוֹ שְׁלוּפָה בְּיָדוֹ וַיֵּלֶךְ יְהוֹשֻׁעַ אֵלָיו וַיֹּאמֶר לוֹ הֲלָנוּ
אַתָּה אִם־לְצָרֵינוּ׃ יד וַיֹּאמֶר ׀ לֹא כִּי אֲנִי שַׂר־צְבָא־יְהוָה
עַתָּה בָאתִי וַיִּפֹּל יְהוֹשֻׁעַ אֶל־פָּנָיו אַרְצָה וַיִּשְׁתָּחוּ וַיֹּאמֶר
לוֹ מָה אֲדֹנִי מְדַבֵּר אֶל־עַבְדּוֹ׃ טו וַיֹּאמֶר שַׂר־צְבָא יְהוָה אֶל־
יְהוֹשֻׁעַ שַׁל־נַעַלְךָ מֵעַל רַגְלֶךָ כִּי הַמָּקוֹם אֲשֶׁר אַתָּה עֹמֵד
עָלָיו קֹדֶשׁ הוּא וַיַּעַשׂ יְהוֹשֻׁעַ כֵּן׃ **יהושע ו** א וִירִיחוֹ סֹגֶרֶת
וּמְסֻגֶּרֶת מִפְּנֵי בְּנֵי יִשְׂרָאֵל אֵין יוֹצֵא וְאֵין בָּא׃

Some add:

יהושע ו כז וַיְהִי יְהוָה אֶת־יְהוֹשֻׁעַ וַיְהִי שָׁמְעוֹ בְּכָל־הָאָרֶץ׃

Continue with the blessings after the הפטרה on page 416.

קריאה ליום השני של פסח, וכן ליום הראשון של סוכות
ויום טוב שני

ויקרא כב כו וַיְדַבֵּר יְהוָה אֶל־מֹשֶׁה לֵּאמֹר׃ כז שׁוֹר אוֹ־כֶשֶׂב אוֹ־
עֵז כִּי יִוָּלֵד וְהָיָה שִׁבְעַת יָמִים תַּחַת אִמּוֹ וּמִיּוֹם הַשְּׁמִינִי
וָהָלְאָה יֵרָצֶה לְקָרְבַּן אִשֶּׁה לַיהוָה׃ כח וְשׁוֹר אוֹ־שֶׂה אֹתוֹ וְאֶת־
בְּנוֹ לֹא תִשְׁחֲטוּ בְּיוֹם אֶחָד׃ כט וְכִי־תִזְבְּחוּ זֶבַח־תּוֹדָה לַיהוָה
לִרְצֹנְכֶם תִּזְבָּחוּ׃ ל בַּיּוֹם הַהוּא יֵאָכֵל לֹא־תוֹתִירוּ מִמֶּנּוּ עַד־
בֹּקֶר אֲנִי יְהוָה׃ לא וּשְׁמַרְתֶּם מִצְוֹתַי וַעֲשִׂיתֶם אֹתָם אֲנִי יְהוָה׃
לב וְלֹא תְחַלְּלוּ אֶת־שֵׁם קָדְשִׁי וְנִקְדַּשְׁתִּי בְּתוֹךְ בְּנֵי יִשְׂרָאֵל
אֲנִי יְהוָה מְקַדִּשְׁכֶם׃ לג הַמּוֹצִיא אֶתְכֶם מֵאֶרֶץ מִצְרַיִם

לִהְי֥וֹת לָכֶ֖ם לֵֽאלֹהִ֑ים אֲנִ֖י יְהֹוָֽה׃ פ [בשבת לוי] כג א וַיְדַבֵּ֥ר
יְהֹוָ֖ה אֶל־מֹשֶׁ֥ה לֵּאמֹֽר׃ ב דַּבֵּ֞ר אֶל־בְּנֵ֤י יִשְׂרָאֵל֙ וְאָמַרְתָּ֣
אֲלֵהֶ֔ם מוֹעֲדֵ֣י יְהֹוָ֔ה אֲשֶׁר־תִּקְרְא֥וּ אֹתָ֖ם מִקְרָאֵ֣י קֹ֑דֶשׁ אֵ֥לֶּה
הֵ֖ם מוֹעֲדָֽי׃ ג שֵׁ֣שֶׁת יָמִים֮ תֵּעָשֶׂ֣ה מְלָאכָה֒ וּבַיּ֣וֹם הַשְּׁבִיעִ֗י
שַׁבַּ֤ת שַׁבָּתוֹן֙ מִקְרָא־קֹ֔דֶשׁ כָּל־מְלָאכָ֖ה לֹ֣א תַעֲשׂ֑וּ שַׁבָּ֥ת
הִוא֙ לַיהֹוָ֔ה בְּכֹ֖ל מוֹשְׁבֹתֵיכֶֽם׃ פ [לוי/בשבת שלישי] ד אֵ֚לֶּה
מוֹעֲדֵ֣י יְהֹוָ֔ה מִקְרָאֵ֖י קֹ֑דֶשׁ אֲשֶׁר־תִּקְרְא֥וּ אֹתָ֖ם בְּמוֹעֲדָֽם׃
ה בַּחֹ֣דֶשׁ הָרִאשׁ֗וֹן בְּאַרְבָּעָ֥ה עָשָׂ֛ר לַחֹ֖דֶשׁ בֵּ֣ין הָעַרְבָּ֑יִם פֶּ֖סַח
לַיהֹוָֽה׃ ו וּבַחֲמִשָּׁ֨ה עָשָׂ֥ר יוֹם֙ לַחֹ֣דֶשׁ הַזֶּ֔ה חַ֥ג הַמַּצּ֖וֹת לַיהֹוָ֑ה
שִׁבְעַ֥ת יָמִ֖ים מַצּ֥וֹת תֹּאכֵֽלוּ׃ ז בַּיּוֹם֙ הָֽרִאשׁ֔וֹן מִקְרָא־קֹ֖דֶשׁ
יִהְיֶ֣ה לָכֶ֑ם כָּל־מְלֶ֥אכֶת עֲבֹדָ֖ה לֹ֥א תַעֲשֽׂוּ׃ ח וְהִקְרַבְתֶּ֥ם אִשֶּׁ֛ה
לַיהֹוָ֖ה שִׁבְעַ֣ת יָמִ֑ים בַּיּ֤וֹם הַשְּׁבִיעִי֙ מִקְרָא־קֹ֔דֶשׁ כָּל־מְלֶ֥אכֶת
עֲבֹדָ֖ה לֹ֥א תַעֲשֽׂוּ׃ פ [בשבת רביעי/לוי בחוה"מ פסח] ט וַיְדַבֵּ֥ר
יְהֹוָ֖ה אֶל־מֹשֶׁ֥ה לֵּאמֹֽר׃ י דַּבֵּ֞ר אֶל־בְּנֵ֤י יִשְׂרָאֵל֙ וְאָמַרְתָּ֣ אֲלֵהֶ֔ם
כִּֽי־תָבֹ֣אוּ אֶל־הָאָ֗רֶץ אֲשֶׁ֤ר אֲנִי֙ נֹתֵ֣ן לָכֶ֔ם וּקְצַרְתֶּ֖ם אֶת־קְצִירָ֑הּ
וַהֲבֵאתֶ֥ם אֶת־עֹ֛מֶר רֵאשִׁ֥ית קְצִירְכֶ֖ם אֶל־הַכֹּהֵֽן׃ יא וְהֵנִ֧יף
אֶת־הָעֹ֛מֶר לִפְנֵ֥י יְהֹוָ֖ה לִֽרְצֹנְכֶ֑ם מִֽמָּחֳרַת֙ הַשַּׁבָּ֔ת יְנִיפֶ֖נּוּ
הַכֹּהֵֽן׃ יב וַעֲשִׂיתֶ֕ם בְּי֥וֹם הֲנִיפְכֶ֖ם אֶת־הָעֹ֑מֶר כֶּ֣בֶשׂ תָּמִ֧ים
בֶּן־שְׁנָת֛וֹ לְעֹלָ֖ה לַיהֹוָֽה׃ יג וּמִנְחָתוֹ֩ שְׁנֵ֨י עֶשְׂרֹנִ֜ים סֹ֣לֶת בְּלוּלָ֥ה
בַשֶּׁ֛מֶן אִשֶּׁ֥ה לַיהֹוָ֖ה רֵ֣יחַ נִיחֹ֑חַ וְנִסְכֹּ֥ה יַ֖יִן רְבִיעִ֥ת הַהִֽין׃
יד וְלֶחֶם֩ וְקָלִ֨י וְכַרְמֶ֜ל לֹ֣א תֹֽאכְל֗וּ עַד־עֶ֙צֶם֙ הַיּ֣וֹם הַזֶּ֔ה עַ֚ד
הֲבִ֣יאֲכֶ֔ם אֶת־קָרְבַּ֖ן אֱלֹהֵיכֶ֑ם חֻקַּ֤ת עוֹלָם֙ לְדֹרֹ֣תֵיכֶ֔ם בְּכֹ֖ל
מֹשְׁבֹתֵיכֶֽם׃ ס [שלישי/ביו"ט ובשבת חוה"מ חמישי] טו וּסְפַרְתֶּ֤ם
לָכֶם֙ מִמָּחֳרַ֣ת הַשַּׁבָּ֔ת מִיּוֹם֙ הֲבִ֣יאֲכֶ֔ם אֶת־עֹ֖מֶר הַתְּנוּפָ֑ה
שֶׁ֥בַע שַׁבָּת֖וֹת תְּמִימֹ֥ת תִּהְיֶֽינָה׃ טז עַ֣ד מִֽמָּחֳרַ֤ת הַשַּׁבָּת֙

הַשְּׁבִיעִ֔ת תִּסְפְּר֖וּ חֲמִשִּׁ֣ים י֑וֹם וְהִקְרַבְתֶּ֛ם מִנְחָ֥ה חֲדָשָׁ֖ה
לַיהֹוָֽה׃ יז מִמּוֹשְׁבֹ֨תֵיכֶ֜ם תָּבִ֣יאוּ ׀ לֶ֣חֶם תְּנוּפָ֗ה שְׁ֚תַּיִם שְׁנֵ֣י
עֶשְׂרֹנִ֔ים סֹ֣לֶת תִּהְיֶ֔ינָה חָמֵ֖ץ תֵּאָפֶ֑ינָה בִּכּוּרִ֖ים לַיהֹוָֽה׃
יח וְהִקְרַבְתֶּ֣ם עַל־הַלֶּ֗חֶם שִׁבְעַ֨ת כְּבָשִׂ֤ים תְּמִימִם֙ בְּנֵ֣י שָׁנָ֔ה
וּפַ֧ר בֶּן־בָּקָ֛ר אֶחָ֖ד וְאֵילִ֣ם שְׁנָ֑יִם יִהְי֤וּ עֹלָה֙ לַֽיהֹוָ֔ה וּמִנְחָתָם֙
וְנִסְכֵּיהֶ֔ם אִשֵּׁ֥ה רֵֽיחַ־נִיחֹ֖חַ לַֽיהֹוָֽה׃ יט וַעֲשִׂיתֶ֛ם שְׂעִיר־עִזִּ֥ים
אֶחָ֖ד לְחַטָּ֑את וּשְׁנֵ֧י כְבָשִׂ֛ים בְּנֵ֥י שָׁנָ֖ה לְזֶ֥בַח שְׁלָמִֽים׃
כ וְהֵנִ֣יף הַכֹּהֵ֣ן ׀ אֹתָ֡ם עַל֩ לֶ֨חֶם הַבִּכֻּרִ֤ים תְּנוּפָה֙ לִפְנֵ֣י יְהֹוָ֔ה
עַל־שְׁנֵ֖י כְּבָשִׂ֑ים קֹ֛דֶשׁ יִהְי֥וּ לַיהֹוָ֖ה לַכֹּהֵֽן׃ כא וּקְרָאתֶ֞ם בְּעֶ֣צֶם
׀ הַיּ֣וֹם הַזֶּ֗ה מִֽקְרָא־קֹ֙דֶשׁ֙ יִהְיֶ֣ה לָכֶ֔ם כָּל־מְלֶ֥אכֶת עֲבֹדָ֖ה
לֹ֣א תַעֲשׂ֑וּ חֻקַּ֥ת עוֹלָ֛ם בְּכָל־מוֹשְׁבֹתֵיכֶ֖ם לְדֹרֹתֵיכֶֽם׃
כב וּֽבְקֻצְרְכֶ֞ם אֶת־קְצִ֣יר אַרְצְכֶ֗ם לֹֽא־תְכַלֶּ֞ה פְּאַ֤ת שָׂדְךָ֙
בְּקֻצְרֶ֔ךָ וְלֶ֥קֶט קְצִירְךָ֖ לֹ֣א תְלַקֵּ֑ט לֶֽעָנִ֤י וְלַגֵּר֙ תַּעֲזֹ֣ב אֹתָ֔ם
אֲנִ֖י יְהֹוָ֥ה אֱלֹהֵיכֶֽם׃ פ [רביעי/בשבת ששי] כג וַיְדַבֵּ֥ר יְהֹוָ֖ה אֶל־
מֹשֶׁ֥ה לֵּאמֹֽר׃ כד דַּבֵּ֛ר אֶל־בְּנֵ֥י יִשְׂרָאֵ֖ל לֵאמֹ֑ר בַּחֹ֨דֶשׁ הַשְּׁבִיעִ֜י
בְּאֶחָ֣ד לַחֹ֗דֶשׁ יִהְיֶ֤ה לָכֶם֙ שַׁבָּת֔וֹן זִכְר֥וֹן תְּרוּעָ֖ה מִקְרָא־
קֹֽדֶשׁ׃ כה כָּל־מְלֶ֥אכֶת עֲבֹדָ֖ה לֹ֣א תַעֲשׂ֑וּ וְהִקְרַבְתֶּ֥ם אִשֶּׁ֖ה
לַיהֹוָֽה׃ ס כו וַיְדַבֵּ֥ר יְהֹוָ֖ה אֶל־מֹשֶׁ֥ה לֵּאמֹֽר׃ כז אַ֡ךְ בֶּעָשׂ֣וֹר
לַחֹדֶשׁ֩ הַשְּׁבִיעִ֨י הַזֶּ֜ה י֧וֹם הַכִּפֻּרִ֣ים ה֗וּא מִֽקְרָא־קֹ֜דֶשׁ יִהְיֶ֤ה
לָכֶם֙ וְעִנִּיתֶ֖ם אֶת־נַפְשֹׁתֵיכֶ֑ם וְהִקְרַבְתֶּ֥ם אִשֶּׁ֖ה לַיהֹוָֽה׃
כח וְכָל־מְלָאכָה֙ לֹ֣א תַעֲשׂ֔וּ בְּעֶ֖צֶם הַיּ֣וֹם הַזֶּ֑ה כִּ֣י י֤וֹם כִּפֻּרִים֙
ה֔וּא לְכַפֵּ֣ר עֲלֵיכֶ֔ם לִפְנֵ֖י יְהֹוָ֥ה אֱלֹהֵיכֶֽם׃ כט כִּ֤י כָל־הַנֶּ֙פֶשׁ֙ אֲשֶׁ֣ר
לֹֽא־תְעֻנֶּ֔ה בְּעֶ֖צֶם הַיּ֣וֹם הַזֶּ֑ה וְנִכְרְתָ֖ה מֵעַמֶּֽיהָ׃ ל וְכָל־הַנֶּ֗פֶשׁ
אֲשֶׁ֤ר תַּעֲשֶׂה֙ כָּל־מְלָאכָ֔ה בְּעֶ֖צֶם הַיּ֣וֹם הַזֶּ֑ה וְהַאֲבַדְתִּ֛י אֶת־
הַנֶּ֥פֶשׁ הַהִ֖וא מִקֶּ֥רֶב עַמָּֽהּ׃ לא כָּל־מְלָאכָ֖ה לֹ֣א תַעֲשׂ֑וּ חֻקַּ֥ת

עוֹלָם לְדֹרֹתֵיכֶם בְּכֹל מֹשְׁבֹתֵיכֶם: לב שַׁבַּת שַׁבָּתוֹן הוּא לָכֶם
וְעִנִּיתֶם אֶת־נַפְשֹׁתֵיכֶם בְּתִשְׁעָה לַחֹדֶשׁ בָּעֶרֶב מֵעֶרֶב עַד־
עֶרֶב תִּשְׁבְּתוּ שַׁבַּתְּכֶם: פ [חמישי/בשבת שביעי] לג וַיְדַבֵּר יְהוָה
אֶל־מֹשֶׁה לֵּאמֹר: לד דַּבֵּר אֶל־בְּנֵי יִשְׂרָאֵל לֵאמֹר בַּחֲמִשָּׁה
עָשָׂר יוֹם לַחֹדֶשׁ הַשְּׁבִיעִי הַזֶּה חַג הַסֻּכּוֹת שִׁבְעַת יָמִים
לַיהוָה: לה בַּיּוֹם הָרִאשׁוֹן מִקְרָא־קֹדֶשׁ כָּל־מְלֶאכֶת עֲבֹדָה
לֹא תַעֲשׂוּ: לו שִׁבְעַת יָמִים תַּקְרִיבוּ אִשֶּׁה לַיהוָה בַּיּוֹם
הַשְּׁמִינִי מִקְרָא־קֹדֶשׁ יִהְיֶה לָכֶם וְהִקְרַבְתֶּם אִשֶּׁה לַיהוָה
עֲצֶרֶת הִוא כָּל־מְלֶאכֶת עֲבֹדָה לֹא תַעֲשׂוּ: לז אֵלֶּה מוֹעֲדֵי
יְהוָה אֲשֶׁר־תִּקְרְאוּ אֹתָם מִקְרָאֵי קֹדֶשׁ לְהַקְרִיב אִשֶּׁה
לַיהוָה עֹלָה וּמִנְחָה זֶבַח וּנְסָכִים דְּבַר־יוֹם בְּיוֹמוֹ: לח מִלְּבַד
שַׁבְּתֹת יְהוָה וּמִלְּבַד מַתְּנוֹתֵיכֶם וּמִלְּבַד כָּל־נִדְרֵיכֶם וּמִלְּבַד
כָּל־נִדְבֹתֵיכֶם אֲשֶׁר תִּתְּנוּ לַיהוָה: לט אַךְ בַּחֲמִשָּׁה עָשָׂר יוֹם
לַחֹדֶשׁ הַשְּׁבִיעִי בְּאָסְפְּכֶם אֶת־תְּבוּאַת הָאָרֶץ תָּחֹגּוּ אֶת־
חַג־יְהוָה שִׁבְעַת יָמִים בַּיּוֹם הָרִאשׁוֹן שַׁבָּתוֹן וּבַיּוֹם הַשְּׁמִינִי
שַׁבָּתוֹן: מ וּלְקַחְתֶּם לָכֶם בַּיּוֹם הָרִאשׁוֹן פְּרִי עֵץ הָדָר כַּפֹּת
תְּמָרִים וַעֲנַף עֵץ־עָבֹת וְעַרְבֵי־נָחַל וּשְׂמַחְתֶּם לִפְנֵי יְהוָה
אֱלֹהֵיכֶם שִׁבְעַת יָמִים: מא וְחַגֹּתֶם אֹתוֹ חַג לַיהוָה שִׁבְעַת
יָמִים בַּשָּׁנָה חֻקַּת עוֹלָם לְדֹרֹתֵיכֶם בַּחֹדֶשׁ הַשְּׁבִיעִי תָּחֹגּוּ
אֹתוֹ: מב בַּסֻּכֹּת תֵּשְׁבוּ שִׁבְעַת יָמִים כָּל־הָאֶזְרָח בְּיִשְׂרָאֵל
יֵשְׁבוּ בַּסֻּכֹּת: מג לְמַעַן יֵדְעוּ דֹרֹתֵיכֶם כִּי בַסֻּכּוֹת הוֹשַׁבְתִּי
אֶת־בְּנֵי יִשְׂרָאֵל בְּהוֹצִיאִי אוֹתָם מֵאֶרֶץ מִצְרָיִם אֲנִי יְהוָה
אֱלֹהֵיכֶם: מד וַיְדַבֵּר מֹשֶׁה אֶת־מֹעֲדֵי יְהוָה אֶל־בְּנֵי יִשְׂרָאֵל:

חצי קדיש (page 414) is said. The מפטיר is read from the second ספר תורה: for the second day of פסח on page 914 and for the first two days of סוכות on page 955.

הפטרה ליום טוב שני של פסח

In some congregations, the הפטרה begins at וַיְצַו הַמֶּלֶךְ below (at the *).

מלכים ב׳ כג א וַיִּשְׁלַח הַמֶּלֶךְ וַיַּאַסְפוּ אֵלָיו כָּל־זִקְנֵי יְהוּדָה
וִירוּשָׁלָֽם׃ ב וַיַּעַל הַמֶּלֶךְ בֵּית־יהוה וְכָל־אִישׁ יְהוּדָה וְכָל־
יֹשְׁבֵי יְרוּשָׁלַם אִתּוֹ וְהַכֹּהֲנִים וְהַנְּבִיאִים וְכָל־הָעָם לְמִקָּטֹן
וְעַד־גָּדוֹל וַיִּקְרָא בְאָזְנֵיהֶם אֶת־כָּל־דִּבְרֵי סֵפֶר הַבְּרִית
הַנִּמְצָא בְּבֵית יהוה׃ ג וַיַּעֲמֹד הַמֶּלֶךְ עַל־הָעַמּוּד וַיִּכְרֹת
אֶת־הַבְּרִית ׀ לִפְנֵי יהוה לָלֶכֶת אַחַר יהוה וְלִשְׁמֹר מִצְוֺתָיו
וְאֶת־עֵדְוֺתָיו וְאֶת־חֻקֹּתָיו בְּכָל־לֵב וּבְכָל־נֶפֶשׁ לְהָקִים
אֶת־דִּבְרֵי הַבְּרִית הַזֹּאת הַכְּתֻבִים עַל־הַסֵּפֶר הַזֶּה וַיַּעֲמֹד
כָּל־הָעָם בַּבְּרִית׃ ד וַיְצַו הַמֶּלֶךְ אֶת־חִלְקִיָּהוּ הַכֹּהֵן הַגָּדוֹל
וְאֶת־כֹּהֲנֵי הַמִּשְׁנֶה וְאֶת־שֹׁמְרֵי הַסַּף לְהוֹצִיא מֵהֵיכַל
יהוה אֵת כָּל־הַכֵּלִים הָעֲשׂוּיִם לַבַּעַל וְלָאֲשֵׁרָה וּלְכֹל צְבָא
הַשָּׁמָיִם וַיִּשְׂרְפֵם מִחוּץ לִירוּשָׁלַם בְּשַׁדְמוֹת קִדְרוֹן וְנָשָׂא
אֶת עֲפָרָם בֵּית־אֵל׃ ה וְהִשְׁבִּית אֶת־הַכְּמָרִים אֲשֶׁר נָתְנוּ
מַלְכֵי יְהוּדָה וַיְקַטֵּר בַּבָּמוֹת בְּעָרֵי יְהוּדָה וּמְסִבֵּי יְרוּשָׁלָם
וְאֶת־הַמְקַטְּרִים לַבַּעַל לַשֶּׁמֶשׁ וְלַיָּרֵחַ וְלַמַּזָּלוֹת וּלְכֹל צְבָא
הַשָּׁמָיִם׃ ו וַיֹּצֵא אֶת־הָאֲשֵׁרָה מִבֵּית יהוה מִחוּץ לִירוּשָׁלַם
אֶל־נַחַל קִדְרוֹן וַיִּשְׂרֹף אֹתָהּ בְּנַחַל קִדְרוֹן וַיָּדֶק לְעָפָר
וַיַּשְׁלֵךְ אֶת־עֲפָרָהּ עַל־קֶבֶר בְּנֵי הָעָם׃ ז וַיִּתֹּץ אֶת־בָּתֵּי
הַקְּדֵשִׁים אֲשֶׁר בְּבֵית יהוה אֲשֶׁר הַנָּשִׁים אֹרְגוֹת שָׁם בָּתִּים
לָאֲשֵׁרָה׃ ח וַיָּבֵא אֶת־כָּל־הַכֹּהֲנִים מֵעָרֵי יְהוּדָה וַיְטַמֵּא
אֶת־הַבָּמוֹת אֲשֶׁר קִטְּרוּ־שָׁמָּה הַכֹּהֲנִים מִגֶּבַע עַד־בְּאֵר
שָׁבַע וְנִתַּץ אֶת־בָּמוֹת הַשְּׁעָרִים אֲשֶׁר־פֶּתַח שַׁעַר יְהוֹשֻׁעַ

שַׂר־הָעִ֑יר אֲשֶׁר־עַל־שְׂמֹ֥אול אִ֖ישׁ בְּשַׁ֥עַר הָעִֽיר׃ ט אַ֗ךְ לֹ֤א
יַֽעֲלוּ֙ כֹּהֲנֵ֣י הַבָּמ֔וֹת אֶל־מִזְבַּ֥ח יהוה בִּירוּשָׁלָ֑͏ִם כִּ֛י אִם־אָכְל֥וּ
מַצּ֖וֹת בְּת֥וֹךְ אֲחֵיהֶֽם׃
* מלכים ב׳ כג כא וַיְצַ֤ו הַמֶּ֙לֶךְ֙ אֶת־כָּל־הָעָ֣ם לֵאמֹ֔ר עֲשׂ֣וּ פֶ֔סַח
לַֽיהוָה אֱלֹהֵיכֶ֑ם כַּכָּת֕וּב עַ֖ל סֵ֥פֶר הַבְּרִ֖ית הַזֶּֽה׃ כב כִּ֣י לֹ֤א
נַֽעֲשָׂה֙ כַּפֶּ֣סַח הַזֶּ֔ה מִימֵי֙ הַשֹּׁ֣פְטִ֔ים אֲשֶׁ֥ר שָׁפְט֖וּ אֶת־יִשְׂרָאֵ֑ל
וְכֹ֗ל יְמֵ֛י מַלְכֵ֥י יִשְׂרָאֵ֖ל וּמַלְכֵ֥י יְהוּדָֽה׃ כג כִּ֣י אִם־בִּשְׁמֹנֶ֤ה
עֶשְׂרֵה֙ שָׁנָ֔ה לַמֶּ֖לֶךְ יֹאשִׁיָּ֑הוּ נַעֲשָׂ֞ה הַפֶּ֧סַח הַזֶּ֛ה לַֽיהוָ֖ה
בִּירוּשָׁלָֽ͏ִם׃ כד וְגַ֣ם אֶת־הָאֹב֣וֹת וְאֶת־הַיִּדְּעֹנִ֡ים וְאֶת־הַתְּרָפִ֣ים
וְאֶת־הַגִּלֻּלִים֩ וְאֵ֨ת כָּל־הַשִּׁקֻּצִ֜ים אֲשֶׁ֨ר נִרְאוּ֩ בְּאֶ֨רֶץ יְהוּדָ֜ה
וּבִירוּשָׁלַ֗͏ִם בִּעֵ֖ר יֹאשִׁיָּ֑הוּ לְמַ֨עַן הָקִ֜ים אֶת־דִּבְרֵ֤י הַתּוֹרָה֙
הַכְּתֻבִ֣ים עַל־הַסֵּ֔פֶר אֲשֶׁ֥ר מָצָ֛א חִלְקִיָּ֥הוּ הַכֹּהֵ֖ן בֵּ֥ית יהוה׃
כה וְכָמֹ֜הוּ לֹא־הָיָ֨ה לְפָנָ֥יו מֶ֙לֶךְ֙ אֲשֶׁר־שָׁ֤ב אֶל־יהוה֙ בְּכָל־
לְבָב֤וֹ וּבְכָל־נַפְשׁוֹ֙ וּבְכָל־מְאֹד֔וֹ כְּכֹ֖ל תּוֹרַ֣ת מֹשֶׁ֑ה וְאַחֲרָ֖יו
לֹא־קָ֥ם כָּמֹֽהוּ׃

Continue with the blessings after the הפטרה on page 416.

On each of the weekdays of חוֹל הַמּוֹעֵד פֶּסַח, two סִפְרֵי תוֹרָה are taken out of the Ark. Read the appropriate passage from the first סֵפֶר תּוֹרָה, calling up three עוֹלִים. This is followed by הַגְבָּהָה and גְּלִילָה. Call up the fourth עוֹלֶה to the second סֵפֶר תּוֹרָה and each day read the section beginning וְהִקְרַבְתֶּם on page 922. Say חֲצִי קַדִּישׁ, followed by the second הַגְבָּהָה and גְּלִילָה.

יום א׳ של חול המועד פסח

שמות יג א וַיְדַבֵּ֥ר יְהוָ֖ה אֶל־מֹשֶׁ֥ה לֵּאמֹֽר׃ ב קַדֶּשׁ־לִ֨י כָל־בְּכ֜וֹר
פֶּ֤טֶר כָּל־רֶ֙חֶם֙ בִּבְנֵ֣י יִשְׂרָאֵ֔ל בָּאָדָ֖ם וּבַבְּהֵמָ֑ה לִ֖י הֽוּא׃ ג וַיֹּ֨אמֶר
מֹשֶׁ֜ה אֶל־הָעָ֗ם זָכ֞וֹר אֶת־הַיּ֤וֹם הַזֶּה֙ אֲשֶׁ֨ר יְצָאתֶ֤ם מִמִּצְרַ֙יִם֙
מִבֵּ֣ית עֲבָדִ֔ים כִּ֚י בְּחֹ֣זֶק יָ֔ד הוֹצִ֧יא יְהוָ֛ה אֶתְכֶ֖ם מִזֶּ֑ה וְלֹ֥א
יֵאָכֵ֖ל חָמֵֽץ׃ ד הַיּ֖וֹם אַתֶּ֣ם יֹצְאִ֑ים בְּחֹ֖דֶשׁ הָאָבִֽיב׃ [לוי] ה וְהָיָ֣ה

כִּי־יְבִיאֲךָ יְהוָה אֶל־אֶרֶץ הַכְּנַעֲנִי וְהַחִתִּי וְהָאֱמֹרִי וְהַחִוִּי
וְהַיְבוּסִי אֲשֶׁר נִשְׁבַּע לַאֲבֹתֶיךָ לָתֶת לָךְ אֶרֶץ זָבַת חָלָב
וּדְבָשׁ וְעָבַדְתָּ אֶת־הָעֲבֹדָה הַזֹּאת בַּחֹדֶשׁ הַזֶּה: ו שִׁבְעַת
יָמִים תֹּאכַל מַצֹּת וּבַיּוֹם הַשְּׁבִיעִי חַג לַיהוָה: ז מַצּוֹת יֵאָכֵל
אֵת שִׁבְעַת הַיָּמִים וְלֹא־יֵרָאֶה לְךָ חָמֵץ וְלֹא־יֵרָאֶה לְךָ שְׂאֹר
בְּכָל־גְּבֻלֶךָ: ח וְהִגַּדְתָּ לְבִנְךָ בַּיּוֹם הַהוּא לֵאמֹר בַּעֲבוּר זֶה
עָשָׂה יְהוָה לִי בְּצֵאתִי מִמִּצְרָיִם: ט וְהָיָה לְךָ לְאוֹת עַל־
יָדְךָ וּלְזִכָּרוֹן בֵּין עֵינֶיךָ לְמַעַן תִּהְיֶה תּוֹרַת יְהוָה בְּפִיךָ כִּי
בְּיָד חֲזָקָה הוֹצִאֲךָ יְהוָה מִמִּצְרָיִם: י וְשָׁמַרְתָּ אֶת־הַחֻקָּה
הַזֹּאת לְמוֹעֲדָהּ מִיָּמִים יָמִימָה: פ [שלישי] יא וְהָיָה כִּי־
יְבִאֲךָ יְהוָה אֶל־אֶרֶץ הַכְּנַעֲנִי כַּאֲשֶׁר נִשְׁבַּע לְךָ וְלַאֲבֹתֶיךָ
וּנְתָנָהּ לָךְ: יב וְהַעֲבַרְתָּ כָל־פֶּטֶר־רֶחֶם לַיהוָה וְכָל־פֶּטֶר |
שֶׁגֶר בְּהֵמָה אֲשֶׁר יִהְיֶה לְךָ הַזְּכָרִים לַיהוָה: יג וְכָל־פֶּטֶר
חֲמֹר תִּפְדֶּה בְשֶׂה וְאִם־לֹא תִפְדֶּה וַעֲרַפְתּוֹ וְכֹל בְּכוֹר אָדָם
בְּבָנֶיךָ תִּפְדֶּה: יד וְהָיָה כִּי־יִשְׁאָלְךָ בִנְךָ מָחָר לֵאמֹר מַה־זֹּאת
וְאָמַרְתָּ אֵלָיו בְּחֹזֶק יָד הוֹצִיאָנוּ יְהוָה מִמִּצְרַיִם מִבֵּית
עֲבָדִים: טו וַיְהִי כִּי־הִקְשָׁה פַרְעֹה לְשַׁלְּחֵנוּ וַיַּהֲרֹג יְהוָה
כָּל־בְּכוֹר בְּאֶרֶץ מִצְרַיִם מִבְּכֹר אָדָם וְעַד־בְּכוֹר בְּהֵמָה עַל־
כֵּן אֲנִי זֹבֵחַ לַיהוָה כָּל־פֶּטֶר רֶחֶם הַזְּכָרִים וְכָל־בְּכוֹר בָּנַי
אֶפְדֶּה: טז וְהָיָה לְאוֹת עַל־יָדְכָה וּלְטוֹטָפֹת בֵּין עֵינֶיךָ כִּי
בְּחֹזֶק יָד הוֹצִיאָנוּ יְהוָה מִמִּצְרָיִם:

[רביעי] **במדבר כח** יט וְהִקְרַבְתֶּם אִשֶּׁה עֹלָה לַיהוָה פָּרִים בְּנֵי־
בָקָר שְׁנַיִם וְאַיִל אֶחָד וְשִׁבְעָה כְבָשִׂים בְּנֵי שָׁנָה תְּמִימִם
יִהְיוּ לָכֶם: כ וּמִנְחָתָם סֹלֶת בְּלוּלָה בַשָּׁמֶן שְׁלֹשָׁה עֶשְׂרֹנִים
לַפָּר וּשְׁנֵי עֶשְׂרֹנִים לָאַיִל תַּעֲשׂוּ: כא עִשָּׂרוֹן עִשָּׂרוֹן תַּעֲשֶׂה

לַכֶּ֖בֶשׂ הָֽאֶחָ֑ד לְשִׁבְעַ֖ת הַכְּבָשִֽׂים׃ כב וּשְׂעִ֥יר חַטָּ֖את אֶחָ֑ד
לְכַפֵּ֖ר עֲלֵיכֶֽם׃ כג מִלְּבַד֙ עֹלַ֣ת הַבֹּ֔קֶר אֲשֶׁ֖ר לְעֹלַ֣ת הַתָּמִ֑יד
תַּֽעֲשׂ֖וּ אֶת־אֵֽלֶּה׃ כד כָּאֵ֜לֶּה תַּעֲשׂ֤וּ לַיּוֹם֙ שִׁבְעַ֣ת יָמִ֔ים לֶ֛חֶם
אִשֵּׁ֥ה רֵֽיחַ־נִיחֹ֖חַ לַֽיהוָ֑ה עַל־עוֹלַ֧ת הַתָּמִ֛יד יֵעָשֶׂ֖ה וְנִסְכּֽוֹ׃
כה וּבַיּוֹם֙ הַשְּׁבִיעִ֔י מִקְרָא־קֹ֖דֶשׁ יִהְיֶ֣ה לָכֶ֑ם כָּל־מְלֶ֥אכֶת
עֲבֹדָ֖ה לֹ֥א תַעֲשֽׂוּ׃

If the second day of חוֹל הַמּוֹעֵד is a Sunday, read קַדֶּשׁ־לִי page 921.

יום ב׳ של חול המועד פסח

שמות כב כד אִם־כֶּ֣סֶף ׀ תַּלְוֶ֣ה אֶת־עַמִּ֗י אֶת־הֶֽעָנִי֙ עִמָּ֔ךְ לֹא־
תִהְיֶ֥ה ל֖וֹ כְּנֹשֶׁ֑ה לֹֽא־תְשִׂימ֥וּן עָלָ֖יו נֶֽשֶׁךְ׃ כה אִם־חָבֹ֥ל תַּחְבֹּ֖ל
שַׂלְמַ֣ת רֵעֶ֑ךָ עַד־בֹּ֥א הַשֶּׁ֖מֶשׁ תְּשִׁיבֶ֥נּוּ לֽוֹ׃ כו כִּ֣י הִ֤וא כְסוּתֹה֙
לְבַדָּ֔הּ הִ֥וא שִׂמְלָת֖וֹ לְעֹר֑וֹ בַּמֶּ֣ה יִשְׁכָּ֔ב וְהָיָה֙ כִּֽי־יִצְעַ֣ק אֵלַ֔י
וְשָׁמַעְתִּ֖י כִּֽי־חַנּ֥וּן אָֽנִי׃ ס [לוי] כז אֱלֹהִ֖ים לֹ֣א תְקַלֵּ֑ל
וְנָשִׂ֥יא בְעַמְּךָ֖ לֹ֥א תָאֹֽר׃ כח מְלֵאָתְךָ֥ וְדִמְעֲךָ֖ לֹ֣א תְאַחֵ֑ר
בְּכ֥וֹר בָּנֶ֖יךָ תִּתֶּן־לִּֽי׃ כט כֵּן־תַּעֲשֶׂ֥ה לְשֹׁרְךָ֖ לְצֹאנֶ֑ךָ שִׁבְעַ֤ת
יָמִים֙ יִהְיֶ֣ה עִם־אִמּ֔וֹ בַּיּ֥וֹם הַשְּׁמִינִ֖י תִּתְּנוֹ־לִֽי׃ ל וְאַנְשֵׁי־
קֹ֖דֶשׁ תִּהְי֣וּן לִ֑י וּבָשָׂ֨ר בַּשָּׂדֶ֤ה טְרֵפָה֙ לֹ֣א תֹאכֵ֔לוּ לַכֶּ֖לֶב
תַּשְׁלִכ֥וּן אֹתֽוֹ׃ ס כג א לֹ֥א תִשָּׂ֖א שֵׁ֣מַע שָׁ֑וְא אַל־
תָּ֤שֶׁת יָֽדְךָ֙ עִם־רָשָׁ֔ע לִהְיֹ֖ת עֵ֥ד חָמָֽס׃ ב לֹֽא־תִהְיֶ֥ה אַחֲרֵֽי־
רַבִּ֖ים לְרָעֹ֑ת וְלֹא־תַעֲנֶ֣ה עַל־רִ֗ב לִנְטֹ֛ת אַחֲרֵ֥י רַבִּ֖ים לְהַטֹּֽת׃
ג וְדָ֕ל לֹ֥א תֶהְדַּ֖ר בְּרִיבֽוֹ׃ ס ד כִּ֣י תִפְגַּ֞ע שׁ֧וֹר אֹֽיִבְךָ֛ א֥וֹ
חֲמֹר֖וֹ תֹּעֶ֑ה הָשֵׁ֥ב תְּשִׁיבֶ֖נּוּ לֽוֹ׃ ס ה כִּֽי־תִרְאֶ֞ה חֲמ֣וֹר
שֹׂנַאֲךָ֗ רֹבֵץ֙ תַּ֣חַת מַשָּׂא֔וֹ וְחָדַלְתָּ֖ מֵעֲזֹ֣ב ל֑וֹ עָזֹ֥ב תַּעֲזֹ֖ב
עִמּֽוֹ׃ ס [שלישי] ו לֹ֥א תַטֶּ֛ה מִשְׁפַּ֥ט אֶבְיֹנְךָ֖ בְּרִיבֽוֹ׃
ז מִדְּבַר־שֶׁ֖קֶר תִּרְחָ֑ק וְנָקִ֤י וְצַדִּיק֙ אַל־תַּהֲרֹ֔ג כִּ֥י לֹא־אַצְדִּ֖יק

רָשָֽׁע׃ ח וְשֹׁ֖חַד לֹ֣א תִקָּ֑ח כִּ֤י הַשֹּׁ֙חַד֙ יְעַוֵּ֣ר פִּקְחִ֔ים וִֽיסַלֵּ֖ף
דִּבְרֵ֥י צַדִּיקִֽים׃ ט וְגֵ֖ר לֹ֣א תִלְחָ֑ץ וְאַתֶּ֗ם יְדַעְתֶּם֙ אֶת־נֶ֣פֶשׁ
הַגֵּ֔ר כִּֽי־גֵרִ֥ים הֱיִיתֶ֖ם בְּאֶ֥רֶץ מִצְרָֽיִם׃ י וְשֵׁ֥שׁ שָׁנִ֖ים תִּזְרַ֣ע
אֶת־אַרְצֶ֑ךָ וְאָסַפְתָּ֖ אֶת־תְּבוּאָתָֽהּ׃ יא וְהַשְּׁבִיעִ֞ת תִּשְׁמְטֶ֣נָּה
וּנְטַשְׁתָּ֗הּ וְאָֽכְלוּ֙ אֶבְיֹנֵ֣י עַמֶּ֔ךָ וְיִתְרָ֕ם תֹּאכַ֖ל חַיַּ֣ת הַשָּׂדֶ֑ה כֵּֽן־
תַּעֲשֶׂ֥ה לְכַרְמְךָ֖ לְזֵיתֶֽךָ׃ יב שֵׁ֤שֶׁת יָמִים֙ תַּעֲשֶׂ֣ה מַעֲשֶׂ֔יךָ וּבַיּ֥וֹם
הַשְּׁבִיעִ֖י תִּשְׁבֹּ֑ת לְמַ֣עַן יָנ֗וּחַ שֽׁוֹרְךָ֙ וַחֲמֹרֶ֔ךָ וְיִנָּפֵ֥שׁ בֶּן־אֲמָתְךָ֖
וְהַגֵּֽר׃ יג וּבְכֹ֛ל אֲשֶׁר־אָמַ֥רְתִּי אֲלֵיכֶ֖ם תִּשָּׁמֵ֑רוּ וְשֵׁ֨ם אֱלֹהִ֤ים
אֲחֵרִים֙ לֹ֣א תַזְכִּ֔ירוּ לֹ֥א יִשָּׁמַ֖ע עַל־פִּֽיךָ׃ יד שָׁלֹ֣שׁ רְגָלִ֔ים תָּחֹ֥ג
לִ֖י בַּשָּׁנָֽה׃ טו אֶת־חַ֣ג הַמַּצּוֹת֮ תִּשְׁמֹר֒ שִׁבְעַ֣ת יָמִים֩ תֹּאכַ֨ל
מַצּ֜וֹת כַּאֲשֶׁ֣ר צִוִּיתִ֗ךָ לְמוֹעֵד֙ חֹ֣דֶשׁ הָֽאָבִ֔יב כִּי־ב֖וֹ יָצָ֣אתָ
מִמִּצְרָ֑יִם וְלֹא־יֵרָא֥וּ פָנַ֖י רֵיקָֽם׃ טז וְחַ֤ג הַקָּצִיר֙ בִּכּוּרֵ֣י מַעֲשֶׂ֔יךָ
אֲשֶׁ֥ר תִּזְרַ֖ע בַּשָּׂדֶ֑ה וְחַ֤ג הָֽאָסִף֙ בְּצֵ֣את הַשָּׁנָ֔ה בְּאָסְפְּךָ֥ אֶֽת־
מַעֲשֶׂ֖יךָ מִן־הַשָּׂדֶֽה׃ יז שָׁלֹ֥שׁ פְּעָמִ֖ים בַּשָּׁנָ֑ה יֵרָאֶה֙ כָּל־זְכ֣וּרְךָ֔
אֶל־פְּנֵ֖י הָאָדֹ֥ן ׀ יְהוָֽה׃ יח לֹֽא־תִזְבַּ֥ח עַל־חָמֵ֖ץ דַּם־זִבְחִ֑י וְלֹֽא־
יָלִ֥ין חֵֽלֶב־חַגִּ֖י עַד־בֹּֽקֶר׃ יט רֵאשִׁ֗ית בִּכּוּרֵי֙ אַדְמָ֣תְךָ֔ תָּבִ֕יא
בֵּ֖ית יְהוָ֣ה אֱלֹהֶ֑יךָ לֹֽא־תְבַשֵּׁ֥ל גְּדִ֖י בַּחֲלֵ֥ב אִמּֽוֹ׃

For רְבִיעִי read וְהִקְרַבְתֶּם on page 922 from the second סֵפֶר תּוֹרָה.

יום ג׳ של חול המועד פסח

שמות לד א וַיֹּ֤אמֶר יְהוָה֙ אֶל־מֹשֶׁ֔ה פְּסָל־לְךָ֛ שְׁנֵֽי־לֻחֹ֥ת אֲבָנִ֖ים
כָּרִאשֹׁנִ֑ים וְכָתַבְתִּי֙ עַל־הַלֻּחֹ֔ת אֶת־הַדְּבָרִ֔ים אֲשֶׁ֥ר הָי֛וּ עַל־
הַלֻּחֹ֥ת הָרִאשֹׁנִ֖ים אֲשֶׁ֥ר שִׁבַּֽרְתָּ׃ ב וֶהְיֵ֥ה נָכ֖וֹן לַבֹּ֑קֶר וְעָלִ֤יתָ
בַבֹּ֙קֶר֙ אֶל־הַ֣ר סִינַ֔י וְנִצַּבְתָּ֥ לִ֛י שָׁ֖ם עַל־רֹ֥אשׁ הָהָֽר׃ ג וְאִישׁ֙
לֹא־יַעֲלֶ֣ה עִמָּ֔ךְ וְגַם־אִ֥ישׁ אַל־יֵרָ֖א בְּכָל־הָהָ֑ר גַּם־הַצֹּ֤אן
וְהַבָּקָר֙ אַל־יִרְע֔וּ אֶל־מ֖וּל הָהָ֥ר הַהֽוּא׃ [לוי] ד וַיִּפְסֹ֡ל שְׁנֵֽי־

לֻחֹת אֲבָנִים כָּרִאשֹׁנִים וַיַּשְׁכֵּם מֹשֶׁה בַבֹּקֶר וַיַּעַל אֶל־הַר
סִינַי כַּאֲשֶׁר צִוָּה יְהוָה אֹתוֹ וַיִּקַּח בְּיָדוֹ שְׁנֵי לֻחֹת אֲבָנִים׃
ה וַיֵּרֶד יְהוָה בֶּעָנָן וַיִּתְיַצֵּב עִמּוֹ שָׁם וַיִּקְרָא בְשֵׁם יְהוָה׃
ו וַיַּעֲבֹר יְהוָה ׀ עַל־פָּנָיו וַיִּקְרָא יְהוָה ׀ יְהוָה אֵל רַחוּם וְחַנּוּן
אֶרֶךְ אַפַּיִם וְרַב־חֶסֶד וֶאֱמֶת׃ ז נֹצֵר חֶסֶד לָאֲלָפִים נֹשֵׂא עָוֺן
וָפֶשַׁע וְחַטָּאָה וְנַקֵּה לֹא יְנַקֶּה פֹּקֵד ׀ עֲוֺן אָבוֹת עַל־בָּנִים
וְעַל־בְּנֵי בָנִים עַל־שִׁלֵּשִׁים וְעַל־רִבֵּעִים׃ ח וַיְמַהֵר מֹשֶׁה
וַיִּקֹּד אַרְצָה וַיִּשְׁתָּחוּ׃ ט וַיֹּאמֶר אִם־נָא מָצָאתִי חֵן בְּעֵינֶיךָ
אֲדֹנָי יֵלֶךְ־נָא אֲדֹנָי בְּקִרְבֵּנוּ כִּי עַם־קְשֵׁה־עֹרֶף הוּא וְסָלַחְתָּ
לַעֲוֺנֵנוּ וּלְחַטָּאתֵנוּ וּנְחַלְתָּנוּ׃ י וַיֹּאמֶר הִנֵּה אָנֹכִי כֹּרֵת בְּרִית
נֶגֶד כָּל־עַמְּךָ אֶעֱשֶׂה נִפְלָאֹת אֲשֶׁר לֹא־נִבְרְאוּ בְכָל־הָאָרֶץ
וּבְכָל־הַגּוֹיִם וְרָאָה כָל־הָעָם אֲשֶׁר־אַתָּה בְקִרְבּוֹ אֶת־מַעֲשֵׂה
יְהוָה כִּי־נוֹרָא הוּא אֲשֶׁר אֲנִי עֹשֶׂה עִמָּךְ׃ [שלישי] יא שְׁמָר־לְךָ
אֵת אֲשֶׁר אָנֹכִי מְצַוְּךָ הַיּוֹם הִנְנִי גֹרֵשׁ מִפָּנֶיךָ אֶת־הָאֱמֹרִי
וְהַכְּנַעֲנִי וְהַחִתִּי וְהַפְּרִזִּי וְהַחִוִּי וְהַיְבוּסִי׃ יב הִשָּׁמֶר לְךָ פֶּן־
תִּכְרֹת בְּרִית לְיוֹשֵׁב הָאָרֶץ אֲשֶׁר אַתָּה בָּא עָלֶיהָ פֶּן־יִהְיֶה
לְמוֹקֵשׁ בְּקִרְבֶּךָ׃ יג כִּי אֶת־מִזְבְּחֹתָם תִּתֹּצוּן וְאֶת־מַצֵּבֹתָם
תְּשַׁבֵּרוּן וְאֶת־אֲשֵׁרָיו תִּכְרֹתוּן׃ יד כִּי לֹא תִשְׁתַּחֲוֶה לְאֵל
אַחֵר כִּי יְהוָה קַנָּא שְׁמוֹ אֵל קַנָּא הוּא׃ טו פֶּן־תִּכְרֹת בְּרִית
לְיוֹשֵׁב הָאָרֶץ וְזָנוּ ׀ אַחֲרֵי אֱלֹהֵיהֶם וְזָבְחוּ לֵאלֹהֵיהֶם וְקָרָא
לְךָ וְאָכַלְתָּ מִזִּבְחוֹ׃ טז וְלָקַחְתָּ מִבְּנֹתָיו לְבָנֶיךָ וְזָנוּ בְנֹתָיו
אַחֲרֵי אֱלֹהֵיהֶן וְהִזְנוּ אֶת־בָּנֶיךָ אַחֲרֵי אֱלֹהֵיהֶן׃ יז אֱלֹהֵי
מַסֵּכָה לֹא תַעֲשֶׂה־לָּךְ׃ יח אֶת־חַג הַמַּצּוֹת תִּשְׁמֹר שִׁבְעַת
יָמִים תֹּאכַל מַצּוֹת אֲשֶׁר צִוִּיתִךָ לְמוֹעֵד חֹדֶשׁ הָאָבִיב כִּי
בְּחֹדֶשׁ הָאָבִיב יָצָאתָ מִמִּצְרָיִם׃ יט כָּל־פֶּטֶר רֶחֶם לִי וְכָל־

מִקְנְךָ תִּזָּכָר פֶּטֶר שׁוֹר וָשֶׂה: כ וּפֶטֶר חֲמוֹר תִּפְדֶּה בְשֶׂה
וְאִם־לֹא תִפְדֶּה וַעֲרַפְתּוֹ כֹּל בְּכוֹר בָּנֶיךָ תִּפְדֶּה וְלֹא־יֵרָאוּ
פָנַי רֵיקָם: כא שֵׁשֶׁת יָמִים תַּעֲבֹד וּבַיּוֹם הַשְּׁבִיעִי תִּשְׁבֹּת
בֶּחָרִישׁ וּבַקָּצִיר תִּשְׁבֹּת: כב וְחַג שָׁבֻעֹת תַּעֲשֶׂה לְךָ בִּכּוּרֵי
קְצִיר חִטִּים וְחַג הָאָסִיף תְּקוּפַת הַשָּׁנָה: כג שָׁלֹשׁ פְּעָמִים
בַּשָּׁנָה יֵרָאֶה כָּל־זְכוּרְךָ אֶת־פְּנֵי הָאָדֹן | יְהֹוָה אֱלֹהֵי יִשְׂרָאֵל:
כד כִּי־אוֹרִישׁ גּוֹיִם מִפָּנֶיךָ וְהִרְחַבְתִּי אֶת־גְּבֻלֶךָ וְלֹא־יַחְמֹד
אִישׁ אֶת־אַרְצְךָ בַּעֲלֹתְךָ לֵרָאוֹת אֶת־פְּנֵי יְהֹוָה אֱלֹהֶיךָ שָׁלֹשׁ
פְּעָמִים בַּשָּׁנָה: כה לֹא־תִשְׁחַט עַל־חָמֵץ דַּם־זִבְחִי וְלֹא־יָלִין
לַבֹּקֶר זֶבַח חַג הַפָּסַח: כו רֵאשִׁית בִּכּוּרֵי אַדְמָתְךָ תָּבִיא בֵּית
יְהֹוָה אֱלֹהֶיךָ לֹא־תְבַשֵּׁל גְּדִי בַּחֲלֵב אִמּוֹ:

If the third day of חוֹל הַמּוֹעֵד is a Monday, read אִם כֶּסֶף תַּלְוֶה page 923.
For רְבִיעִי read וְהִקְרַבְתֶּם on page 922 from the second סֵפֶר תּוֹרָה.

יום ד׳ של חול המועד פסח

במדבר ט א וַיְדַבֵּר יְהֹוָה אֶל־מֹשֶׁה בְמִדְבַּר־סִינַי בַּשָּׁנָה הַשֵּׁנִית
לְצֵאתָם מֵאֶרֶץ מִצְרַיִם בַּחֹדֶשׁ הָרִאשׁוֹן לֵאמֹר: ב וְיַעֲשׂוּ
בְנֵי־יִשְׂרָאֵל אֶת־הַפָּסַח בְּמוֹעֲדוֹ: ג בְּאַרְבָּעָה עָשָׂר־יוֹם
בַּחֹדֶשׁ הַזֶּה בֵּין הָעַרְבַּיִם תַּעֲשׂוּ אֹתוֹ בְּמֹעֲדוֹ כְּכָל־חֻקֹּתָיו
וּכְכָל־מִשְׁפָּטָיו תַּעֲשׂוּ אֹתוֹ: ד וַיְדַבֵּר מֹשֶׁה אֶל־בְּנֵי יִשְׂרָאֵל
לַעֲשֹׂת הַפָּסַח: ה וַיַּעֲשׂוּ אֶת־הַפֶּסַח בָּרִאשׁוֹן בְּאַרְבָּעָה
עָשָׂר יוֹם לַחֹדֶשׁ בֵּין הָעַרְבַּיִם בְּמִדְבַּר סִינָי כְּכֹל אֲשֶׁר צִוָּה
יְהֹוָה אֶת־מֹשֶׁה כֵּן עָשׂוּ בְּנֵי יִשְׂרָאֵל: [לוי] ו וַיְהִי אֲנָשִׁים
אֲשֶׁר הָיוּ טְמֵאִים לְנֶפֶשׁ אָדָם וְלֹא־יָכְלוּ לַעֲשֹׂת־הַפֶּסַח
בַּיּוֹם הַהוּא וַיִּקְרְבוּ לִפְנֵי מֹשֶׁה וְלִפְנֵי אַהֲרֹן בַּיּוֹם הַהוּא:
ז וַיֹּאמְרוּ הָאֲנָשִׁים הָהֵמָּה אֵלָיו אֲנַחְנוּ טְמֵאִים לְנֶפֶשׁ אָדָם

לָמָּה נִגָּרַע לְבִלְתִּי הַקְרִיב אֶת־קָרְבַּן יְהוָה בְּמֹעֲדוֹ בְּתוֹךְ בְּנֵי
יִשְׂרָאֵל: ח וַיֹּאמֶר אֲלֵהֶם מֹשֶׁה עִמְדוּ וְאֶשְׁמְעָה מַה־יְצַוֶּה
יְהוָה לָכֶם: פ [שלישי] ט וַיְדַבֵּר יְהוָה אֶל־מֹשֶׁה לֵּאמֹר:
י דַּבֵּר אֶל־בְּנֵי יִשְׂרָאֵל לֵאמֹר אִישׁ אִישׁ כִּי־יִהְיֶה טָמֵא ׀
לָנֶפֶשׁ אוֹ בְדֶרֶךְ רְחֹקָה לָכֶם אוֹ לְדֹרֹתֵיכֶם וְעָשָׂה פֶסַח
לַיהוָה: יא בַּחֹדֶשׁ הַשֵּׁנִי בְּאַרְבָּעָה עָשָׂר יוֹם בֵּין הָעַרְבַּיִם
יַעֲשׂוּ אֹתוֹ עַל־מַצּוֹת וּמְרֹרִים יֹאכְלֻהוּ: יב לֹא־יַשְׁאִירוּ מִמֶּנּוּ
עַד־בֹּקֶר וְעֶצֶם לֹא יִשְׁבְּרוּ־בוֹ כְּכָל־חֻקַּת הַפֶּסַח יַעֲשׂוּ אֹתוֹ:
יג וְהָאִישׁ אֲשֶׁר־הוּא טָהוֹר וּבְדֶרֶךְ לֹא־הָיָה וְחָדַל לַעֲשׂוֹת
הַפֶּסַח וְנִכְרְתָה הַנֶּפֶשׁ הַהִוא מֵעַמֶּיהָ כִּי ׀ קָרְבַּן יְהוָה לֹא
הִקְרִיב בְּמֹעֲדוֹ חֶטְאוֹ יִשָּׂא הָאִישׁ הַהוּא: יד וְכִי־יָגוּר אִתְּכֶם
גֵּר וְעָשָׂה פֶסַח לַיהוָה כְּחֻקַּת הַפֶּסַח וּכְמִשְׁפָּטוֹ כֵּן יַעֲשֶׂה
חֻקָּה אַחַת יִהְיֶה לָכֶם וְלַגֵּר וּלְאֶזְרַח הָאָרֶץ:

For רְבִיעִי read וְהִקְרַבְתֶּם on page 922 from the second סֵפֶר תּוֹרָה.

קריאה לשבת חול המועד

שמות לג יב וַיֹּאמֶר מֹשֶׁה אֶל־יהוה רְאֵה אַתָּה אֹמֵר אֵלַי
הַעַל אֶת־הָעָם הַזֶּה וְאַתָּה לֹא הוֹדַעְתַּנִי אֵת אֲשֶׁר־תִּשְׁלַח
עִמִּי וְאַתָּה אָמַרְתָּ יְדַעְתִּיךָ בְשֵׁם וְגַם־מָצָאתָ חֵן בְּעֵינָי:
יג וְעַתָּה אִם־נָא מָצָאתִי חֵן בְּעֵינֶיךָ הוֹדִעֵנִי נָא אֶת־דְּרָכֶךָ
וְאֵדָעֲךָ לְמַעַן אֶמְצָא־חֵן בְּעֵינֶיךָ וּרְאֵה כִּי עַמְּךָ הַגּוֹי הַזֶּה:
יד וַיֹּאמַר פָּנַי יֵלֵכוּ וַהֲנִחֹתִי לָךְ: טו וַיֹּאמֶר אֵלָיו אִם־אֵין פָּנֶיךָ
הֹלְכִים אַל־תַּעֲלֵנוּ מִזֶּה: טז וּבַמֶּה ׀ יִוָּדַע אֵפוֹא כִּי־מָצָאתִי
חֵן בְּעֵינֶיךָ אֲנִי וְעַמֶּךָ הֲלוֹא בְּלֶכְתְּךָ עִמָּנוּ וְנִפְלֵינוּ אֲנִי
וְעַמְּךָ מִכָּל־הָעָם אֲשֶׁר עַל־פְּנֵי הָאֲדָמָה: פ [לוי] יז וַיֹּאמֶר
יהוה אֶל־מֹשֶׁה גַּם אֶת־הַדָּבָר הַזֶּה אֲשֶׁר דִּבַּרְתָּ אֶעֱשֶׂה
כִּי־מָצָאתָ חֵן בְּעֵינַי וָאֵדָעֲךָ בְּשֵׁם: יח וַיֹּאמַר הַרְאֵנִי נָא

אֶת־כְּבֹדֶךָ: יט וַיֹּאמֶר אֲנִי אַעֲבִיר כָּל־טוּבִי עַל־פָּנֶיךָ וְקָרָאתִי
בְשֵׁם יְהוָה לְפָנֶיךָ וְחַנֹּתִי אֶת־אֲשֶׁר אָחֹן וְרִחַמְתִּי אֶת־אֲשֶׁר
אֲרַחֵם: [שלישי] כ וַיֹּאמֶר לֹא תוּכַל לִרְאֹת אֶת־פָּנָי כִּי לֹא־
יִרְאַנִי הָאָדָם וָחָי: כא וַיֹּאמֶר יְהוָה הִנֵּה מָקוֹם אִתִּי וְנִצַּבְתָּ
עַל־הַצּוּר: כב וְהָיָה בַּעֲבֹר כְּבֹדִי וְשַׂמְתִּיךָ בְּנִקְרַת הַצּוּר
וְשַׂכֹּתִי כַפִּי עָלֶיךָ עַד־עָבְרִי: כג וַהֲסִרֹתִי אֶת־כַּפִּי וְרָאִיתָ
אֶת־אֲחֹרָי וּפָנַי לֹא יֵרָאוּ: פ [רביעי] לד א וַיֹּאמֶר יְהוָה אֶל־
מֹשֶׁה פְּסָל־לְךָ שְׁנֵי־לֻחֹת אֲבָנִים כָּרִאשֹׁנִים וְכָתַבְתִּי עַל־
הַלֻּחֹת אֶת־הַדְּבָרִים אֲשֶׁר הָיוּ עַל־הַלֻּחֹת הָרִאשֹׁנִים אֲשֶׁר
שִׁבַּרְתָּ: ב וֶהְיֵה נָכוֹן לַבֹּקֶר וְעָלִיתָ בַבֹּקֶר אֶל־הַר סִינַי וְנִצַּבְתָּ
לִי שָׁם עַל־רֹאשׁ הָהָר: ג וְאִישׁ לֹא־יַעֲלֶה עִמָּךְ וְגַם־אִישׁ
אַל־יֵרָא בְּכָל־הָהָר גַּם־הַצֹּאן וְהַבָּקָר אַל־יִרְעוּ אֶל־מוּל
הָהָר הַהוּא: [חמישי] ד וַיִּפְסֹל שְׁנֵי־לֻחֹת אֲבָנִים כָּרִאשֹׁנִים
וַיַּשְׁכֵּם מֹשֶׁה בַבֹּקֶר וַיַּעַל אֶל־הַר סִינַי כַּאֲשֶׁר צִוָּה יְהוָה
אֹתוֹ וַיִּקַּח בְּיָדוֹ שְׁנֵי לֻחֹת אֲבָנִים: ה וַיֵּרֶד יְהוָה בֶּעָנָן וַיִּתְיַצֵּב
עִמּוֹ שָׁם וַיִּקְרָא בְשֵׁם יְהוָה: ו וַיַּעֲבֹר יְהוָה | עַל־פָּנָיו וַיִּקְרָא
יְהוָה | יְהוָה אֵל רַחוּם וְחַנּוּן אֶרֶךְ אַפַּיִם וְרַב־חֶסֶד וֶאֱמֶת:
ז נֹצֵר חֶסֶד לָאֲלָפִים נֹשֵׂא עָוֺן וָפֶשַׁע וְחַטָּאָה וְנַקֵּה לֹא
יְנַקֶּה פֹּקֵד | עֲוֺן אָבוֹת עַל־בָּנִים וְעַל־בְּנֵי בָנִים עַל־שִׁלֵּשִׁים
וְעַל־רִבֵּעִים: ח וַיְמַהֵר מֹשֶׁה וַיִּקֹּד אַרְצָה וַיִּשְׁתָּחוּ: ט וַיֹּאמֶר
אִם־נָא מָצָאתִי חֵן בְּעֵינֶיךָ אֲדֹנָי יֵלֶךְ־נָא אֲדֹנָי בְּקִרְבֵּנוּ כִּי
עַם־קְשֵׁה־עֹרֶף הוּא וְסָלַחְתָּ לַעֲוֺנֵנוּ וּלְחַטָּאתֵנוּ וּנְחַלְתָּנוּ:
י וַיֹּאמֶר הִנֵּה אָנֹכִי כֹּרֵת בְּרִית נֶגֶד כָּל־עַמְּךָ אֶעֱשֶׂה נִפְלָאֹת
אֲשֶׁר לֹא־נִבְרְאוּ בְכָל־הָאָרֶץ וּבְכָל־הַגּוֹיִם וְרָאָה כָל־הָעָם
אֲשֶׁר־אַתָּה בְקִרְבּוֹ אֶת־מַעֲשֵׂה יְהוָה כִּי־נוֹרָא הוּא אֲשֶׁר

אָנֹכִי עֹשֶׂה עִמָּךְ׃ [ששי] יא שְׁמָר־לְךָ אֵת אֲשֶׁר אָנֹכִי מְצַוְּךָ
הַיּוֹם הִנְנִי גֹרֵשׁ מִפָּנֶיךָ אֶת־הָאֱמֹרִי וְהַכְּנַעֲנִי וְהַחִתִּי וְהַפְּרִזִּי
וְהַחִוִּי וְהַיְבוּסִי׃ יב הִשָּׁמֶר לְךָ פֶּן־תִּכְרֹת בְּרִית לְיוֹשֵׁב הָאָרֶץ
אֲשֶׁר אַתָּה בָּא עָלֶיהָ פֶּן־יִהְיֶה לְמוֹקֵשׁ בְּקִרְבֶּךָ׃ יג כִּי אֶת־
מִזְבְּחֹתָם תִּתֹּצוּן וְאֶת־מַצֵּבֹתָם תְּשַׁבֵּרוּן וְאֶת־אֲשֵׁרָיו
תִּכְרֹתוּן׃ יד כִּי לֹא תִשְׁתַּחֲוֶה לְאֵל אַחֵר כִּי יהוה קַנָּא
שְׁמוֹ אֵל קַנָּא הוּא׃ טו פֶּן־תִּכְרֹת בְּרִית לְיוֹשֵׁב הָאָרֶץ וְזָנוּ |
אַחֲרֵי אֱלֹהֵיהֶם וְזָבְחוּ לֵאלֹהֵיהֶם וְקָרָא לְךָ וְאָכַלְתָּ מִזִּבְחוֹ׃
טז וְלָקַחְתָּ מִבְּנֹתָיו לְבָנֶיךָ וְזָנוּ בְנֹתָיו אַחֲרֵי אֱלֹהֵיהֶן וְהִזְנוּ
אֶת־בָּנֶיךָ אַחֲרֵי אֱלֹהֵיהֶן׃ יז אֱלֹהֵי מַסֵּכָה לֹא תַעֲשֶׂה־לָּךְ׃
[שביעי] יח אֶת־חַג הַמַּצּוֹת תִּשְׁמֹר שִׁבְעַת יָמִים תֹּאכַל מַצּוֹת
אֲשֶׁר צִוִּיתִךָ לְמוֹעֵד חֹדֶשׁ הָאָבִיב כִּי בְּחֹדֶשׁ הָאָבִיב יָצָאתָ
מִמִּצְרָיִם׃ יט כָּל־פֶּטֶר רֶחֶם לִי וְכָל־מִקְנְךָ תִּזָּכָר פֶּטֶר שׁוֹר
וָשֶׂה׃ כ וּפֶטֶר חֲמוֹר תִּפְדֶּה בְשֶׂה וְאִם־לֹא תִפְדֶּה וַעֲרַפְתּוֹ
כֹּל בְּכוֹר בָּנֶיךָ תִּפְדֶּה וְלֹא־יֵרָאוּ פָנַי רֵיקָם׃ כא שֵׁשֶׁת יָמִים
תַּעֲבֹד וּבַיּוֹם הַשְּׁבִיעִי תִּשְׁבֹּת בֶּחָרִישׁ וּבַקָּצִיר תִּשְׁבֹּת׃
כב וְחַג שָׁבֻעֹת תַּעֲשֶׂה לְךָ בִּכּוּרֵי קְצִיר חִטִּים וְחַג הָאָסִיף
תְּקוּפַת הַשָּׁנָה׃ כג שָׁלֹשׁ פְּעָמִים בַּשָּׁנָה יֵרָאֶה כָּל־זְכוּרְךָ
אֶת־פְּנֵי הָאָדֹן | יהוה אֱלֹהֵי יִשְׂרָאֵל׃ כד כִּי־אוֹרִישׁ גּוֹיִם
מִפָּנֶיךָ וְהִרְחַבְתִּי אֶת־גְּבֻלֶךָ וְלֹא־יַחְמֹד אִישׁ אֶת־אַרְצְךָ
בַּעֲלֹתְךָ לֵרָאוֹת אֶת־פְּנֵי יהוה אֱלֹהֶיךָ שָׁלֹשׁ פְּעָמִים בַּשָּׁנָה׃
כה לֹא־תִשְׁחַט עַל־חָמֵץ דַּם־זִבְחִי וְלֹא־יָלִין לַבֹּקֶר זֶבַח חַג
הַפָּסַח׃ כו רֵאשִׁית בִּכּוּרֵי אַדְמָתְךָ תָּבִיא בֵּית יהוה אֱלֹהֶיךָ
לֹא־תְבַשֵּׁל גְּדִי בַּחֲלֵב אִמּוֹ׃

Continue with חצי קדיש on page 414. The מפטיר is read from the second ספר תורה. The מפטיר for שבת חול המועד פסח is the same as רביעי for the other days of חול המועד פסח, page 922.

הפטרה לשבת חול המועד פסח

יחזקאל לז א הָיְתָה עָלַי יַד־יהוה וַיּוֹצִאֵנִי בְרוּחַ יהוה וַיְנִיחֵנִי
בְּתוֹךְ הַבִּקְעָה וְהִיא מְלֵאָה עֲצָמוֹת: ב וְהֶעֱבִירַנִי עֲלֵיהֶם
סָבִיב | סָבִיב וְהִנֵּה רַבּוֹת מְאֹד עַל־פְּנֵי הַבִּקְעָה וְהִנֵּה
יְבֵשׁוֹת מְאֹד: ג וַיֹּאמֶר אֵלַי בֶּן־אָדָם הֲתִחְיֶינָה הָעֲצָמוֹת
הָאֵלֶּה וָאֹמַר אֲדֹנָי יֱהֹוִה אַתָּה יָדָעְתָּ: ד וַיֹּאמֶר אֵלַי הִנָּבֵא
עַל־הָעֲצָמוֹת הָאֵלֶּה וְאָמַרְתָּ אֲלֵיהֶם הָעֲצָמוֹת הַיְבֵשׁוֹת
שִׁמְעוּ דְּבַר־יהוה: ה כֹּה אָמַר אֲדֹנָי יֱהֹוִה לָעֲצָמוֹת הָאֵלֶּה
הִנֵּה אֲנִי מֵבִיא בָכֶם רוּחַ וִחְיִיתֶם: ו וְנָתַתִּי עֲלֵיכֶם גִּידִים
וְהַעֲלֵתִי עֲלֵיכֶם בָּשָׂר וְקָרַמְתִּי עֲלֵיכֶם עוֹר וְנָתַתִּי בָכֶם
רוּחַ וִחְיִיתֶם וִידַעְתֶּם כִּי־אֲנִי יהוה: ז וְנִבֵּאתִי כַּאֲשֶׁר צֻוֵּיתִי
וַיְהִי־קוֹל כְּהִנָּבְאִי וְהִנֵּה־רַעַשׁ וַתִּקְרְבוּ עֲצָמוֹת עֶצֶם אֶל־
עַצְמוֹ: ח וְרָאִיתִי וְהִנֵּה־עֲלֵיהֶם גִּדִים וּבָשָׂר עָלָה וַיִּקְרַם
עֲלֵיהֶם עוֹר מִלְמָעְלָה וְרוּחַ אֵין בָּהֶם: ט וַיֹּאמֶר אֵלַי הִנָּבֵא
אֶל־הָרוּחַ הִנָּבֵא בֶן־אָדָם וְאָמַרְתָּ אֶל־הָרוּחַ כֹּה־אָמַר |
אֲדֹנָי יֱהֹוִה מֵאַרְבַּע רוּחוֹת בֹּאִי הָרוּחַ וּפְחִי בַּהֲרוּגִים הָאֵלֶּה
וְיִחְיוּ: י וְהִנַּבֵּאתִי כַּאֲשֶׁר צִוָּנִי וַתָּבוֹא בָהֶם הָרוּחַ וַיִּחְיוּ
וַיַּעַמְדוּ עַל־רַגְלֵיהֶם חַיִל גָּדוֹל מְאֹד מְאֹד: יא וַיֹּאמֶר אֵלַי בֶּן־
אָדָם הָעֲצָמוֹת הָאֵלֶּה כָּל־בֵּית יִשְׂרָאֵל הֵמָּה הִנֵּה אֹמְרִים
יָבְשׁוּ עַצְמוֹתֵינוּ וְאָבְדָה תִקְוָתֵנוּ נִגְזַרְנוּ לָנוּ: יב לָכֵן הִנָּבֵא
וְאָמַרְתָּ אֲלֵיהֶם כֹּה־אָמַר אֲדֹנָי יֱהֹוִה הִנֵּה אֲנִי פֹתֵחַ אֶת־
קִבְרוֹתֵיכֶם וְהַעֲלֵיתִי אֶתְכֶם מִקִּבְרוֹתֵיכֶם עַמִּי וְהֵבֵאתִי
אֶתְכֶם אֶל־אַדְמַת יִשְׂרָאֵל: יג וִידַעְתֶּם כִּי־אֲנִי יהוה בְּפִתְחִי

אֶת־קִבְרוֹתֵיכֶם וּבְהַעֲלוֹתִי אֶתְכֶם מִקִּבְרוֹתֵיכֶם עַמִּי׃
יד וְנָתַתִּי רוּחִי בָכֶם וִחְיִיתֶם וְהִנַּחְתִּי אֶתְכֶם עַל־אַדְמַתְכֶם
וִידַעְתֶּם כִּי אֲנִי יְהוָה דִּבַּרְתִּי וְעָשִׂיתִי נְאֻם־יְהוָה׃

Continue with the blessings after the הפטרה on page 416.

קריאה לשביעי של פסח

שמות יג יז וַיְהִי בְּשַׁלַּח פַּרְעֹה אֶת־הָעָם וְלֹא־נָחָם אֱלֹהִים
דֶּרֶךְ אֶרֶץ פְּלִשְׁתִּים כִּי קָרוֹב הוּא כִּי | אָמַר אֱלֹהִים פֶּן־יִנָּחֵם
הָעָם בִּרְאֹתָם מִלְחָמָה וְשָׁבוּ מִצְרָיְמָה׃ יח וַיַּסֵּב אֱלֹהִים |
אֶת־הָעָם דֶּרֶךְ הַמִּדְבָּר יַם־סוּף וַחֲמֻשִׁים עָלוּ בְנֵי־יִשְׂרָאֵל
מֵאֶרֶץ מִצְרָיִם׃ יט וַיִּקַּח מֹשֶׁה אֶת־עַצְמוֹת יוֹסֵף עִמּוֹ כִּי
הַשְׁבֵּעַ הִשְׁבִּיעַ אֶת־בְּנֵי יִשְׂרָאֵל לֵאמֹר פָּקֹד יִפְקֹד אֱלֹהִים
אֶתְכֶם וְהַעֲלִיתֶם אֶת־עַצְמֹתַי מִזֶּה אִתְּכֶם׃ [בשבת לוי] כ וַיִּסְעוּ
מִסֻּכֹּת וַיַּחֲנוּ בְאֵתָם בִּקְצֵה הַמִּדְבָּר׃ כא וַיהוָה הֹלֵךְ לִפְנֵיהֶם
יוֹמָם בְּעַמּוּד עָנָן לַנְחֹתָם הַדֶּרֶךְ וְלַיְלָה בְּעַמּוּד אֵשׁ לְהָאִיר
לָהֶם לָלֶכֶת יוֹמָם וָלָיְלָה׃ כב לֹא־יָמִישׁ עַמּוּד הֶעָנָן יוֹמָם
וְעַמּוּד הָאֵשׁ לָיְלָה לִפְנֵי הָעָם׃ פ [לוי/בשבת שלישי] יד א וַיְדַבֵּר
יְהוָה אֶל־מֹשֶׁה לֵּאמֹר׃ ב דַּבֵּר אֶל־בְּנֵי יִשְׂרָאֵל וְיָשֻׁבוּ וְיַחֲנוּ
לִפְנֵי פִּי הַחִירֹת בֵּין מִגְדֹּל וּבֵין הַיָּם לִפְנֵי בַּעַל צְפֹן נִכְחוֹ
תַחֲנוּ עַל־הַיָּם׃ ג וְאָמַר פַּרְעֹה לִבְנֵי יִשְׂרָאֵל נְבֻכִים הֵם בָּאָרֶץ
סָגַר עֲלֵיהֶם הַמִּדְבָּר׃ ד וְחִזַּקְתִּי אֶת־לֵב־פַּרְעֹה וְרָדַף
אַחֲרֵיהֶם וְאִכָּבְדָה בְּפַרְעֹה וּבְכָל־חֵילוֹ וְיָדְעוּ מִצְרַיִם כִּי־אֲנִי
יְהוָה וַיַּעֲשׂוּ־כֵן׃ [בשבת רביעי] ה וַיֻּגַּד לְמֶלֶךְ מִצְרַיִם כִּי בָרַח
הָעָם וַיֵּהָפֵךְ לְבַב פַּרְעֹה וַעֲבָדָיו אֶל־הָעָם וַיֹּאמְרוּ מַה־זֹּאת
עָשִׂינוּ כִּי־שִׁלַּחְנוּ אֶת־יִשְׂרָאֵל מֵעָבְדֵנוּ׃ ו וַיֶּאְסֹר אֶת־רִכְבּוֹ
וְאֶת־עַמּוֹ לָקַח עִמּוֹ׃ ז וַיִּקַּח שֵׁשׁ־מֵאוֹת רֶכֶב בָּחוּר וְכֹל רֶכֶב

מִצְרַ֔יִם וְשָֽׁלִשִׁ֖ם עַל־כֻּלּֽוֹ׃ ח וַיְחַזֵּ֣ק יהוה אֶת־לֵ֣ב פַּרְעֹה֙ מֶ֣לֶךְ
מִצְרַ֔יִם וַיִּרְדֹּ֕ף אַחֲרֵ֖י בְּנֵ֣י יִשְׂרָאֵ֑ל וּבְנֵ֣י יִשְׂרָאֵ֔ל יֹצְאִ֖ים בְּיָ֥ד
רָמָֽה׃ [שלישי/בשבת חמישי] ט וַיִּרְדְּפ֨וּ מִצְרַ֜יִם אַחֲרֵיהֶ֗ם וַיַּשִּׂ֤יגוּ
אוֹתָם֙ חֹנִ֣ים עַל־הַיָּ֔ם כָּל־ס֗וּס רֶ֚כֶב פַּרְעֹ֔ה וּפָרָשָׁ֖יו וְחֵיל֑וֹ
עַל־פִּי֙ הַֽחִירֹ֔ת לִפְנֵ֖י בַּ֥עַל צְפֹֽן׃ י וּפַרְעֹ֖ה הִקְרִ֑יב וַיִּשְׂא֣וּ בְנֵֽי־
יִשְׂרָאֵ֣ל אֶת־עֵ֠ינֵיהֶם וְהִנֵּ֨ה מִצְרַ֜יִם ׀ נֹסֵ֣עַ אַחֲרֵיהֶ֗ם וַיִּֽירְאוּ֙
מְאֹ֔ד וַיִּצְעֲק֥וּ בְנֵֽי־יִשְׂרָאֵ֖ל אֶל־יהוה׃ יא וַיֹּאמְרוּ֮ אֶל־מֹשֶׁה֒
הֲֽמִבְּלִ֤י אֵין־קְבָרִים֙ בְּמִצְרַ֔יִם לְקַחְתָּ֖נוּ לָמ֣וּת בַּמִּדְבָּ֑ר מַה־
זֹּאת֙ עָשִׂ֣יתָ לָּ֔נוּ לְהוֹצִיאָ֖נוּ מִמִּצְרָֽיִם׃ יב הֲלֹא־זֶ֣ה הַדָּבָ֗ר אֲשֶׁר֩
דִּבַּ֨רְנוּ אֵלֶ֤יךָ בְמִצְרַ֙יִם֙ לֵאמֹ֔ר חֲדַ֥ל מִמֶּ֖נּוּ וְנַעַבְדָ֣ה אֶת־
מִצְרָ֑יִם כִּ֣י ט֥וֹב לָ֙נוּ֙ עֲבֹ֣ד אֶת־מִצְרַ֔יִם מִמֻּתֵ֖נוּ בַּמִּדְבָּֽר׃
יג וַיֹּ֨אמֶר מֹשֶׁ֣ה אֶל־הָעָם֮ אַל־תִּירָאוּ֒ הִֽתְיַצְּב֗וּ וּרְאוּ֙ אֶת־
יְשׁוּעַ֣ת יהוה אֲשֶׁר־יַעֲשֶׂ֥ה לָכֶ֖ם הַיּ֑וֹם כִּ֗י אֲשֶׁ֨ר רְאִיתֶ֤ם
אֶת־מִצְרַ֙יִם֙ הַיּ֔וֹם לֹ֥א תֹסִ֛פוּ לִרְאֹתָ֥ם ע֖וֹד עַד־עוֹלָֽם׃ יד יהוה
יִלָּחֵ֣ם לָכֶ֑ם וְאַתֶּ֖ם תַּחֲרִשֽׁוּן׃ פ [רביעי/בשבת ששי] טו וַיֹּ֤אמֶר
יהוה֙ אֶל־מֹשֶׁ֔ה מַה־תִּצְעַ֖ק אֵלָ֑י דַּבֵּ֥ר אֶל־בְּנֵֽי־יִשְׂרָאֵ֖ל וְיִסָּֽעוּ׃
טז וְאַתָּ֞ה הָרֵ֣ם אֶת־מַטְּךָ֗ וּנְטֵ֛ה אֶת־יָדְךָ֥ עַל־הַיָּ֖ם וּבְקָעֵ֑הוּ
וְיָבֹ֧אוּ בְנֵֽי־יִשְׂרָאֵ֛ל בְּת֥וֹךְ הַיָּ֖ם בַּיַּבָּשָֽׁה׃ יז וַאֲנִ֗י הִנְנִ֤י מְחַזֵּק֙
אֶת־לֵ֣ב מִצְרַ֔יִם וְיָבֹ֖אוּ אַחֲרֵיהֶ֑ם וְאִכָּבְדָ֤ה בְּפַרְעֹה֙ וּבְכָל־
חֵיל֔וֹ בְּרִכְבּ֖וֹ וּבְפָרָשָֽׁיו׃ יח וְיָדְע֥וּ מִצְרַ֖יִם כִּֽי־אֲנִ֣י יהוה בְּהִכָּֽבְדִ֣י
בְּפַרְעֹ֔ה בְּרִכְבּ֖וֹ וּבְפָרָשָֽׁיו׃ יט וַיִּסַּ֞ע מַלְאַ֣ךְ הָאֱלֹהִ֗ים הַהֹלֵךְ֙
לִפְנֵי֙ מַחֲנֵ֣ה יִשְׂרָאֵ֔ל וַיֵּ֖לֶךְ מֵאַחֲרֵיהֶ֑ם וַיִּסַּ֞ע עַמּ֤וּד הֶֽעָנָן֙
מִפְּנֵיהֶ֔ם וַֽיַּעֲמֹ֖ד מֵאַחֲרֵיהֶֽם׃ כ וַיָּבֹ֞א בֵּ֣ין ׀ מַחֲנֵ֣ה מִצְרַ֗יִם וּבֵין֙
מַחֲנֵ֣ה יִשְׂרָאֵ֔ל וַיְהִ֤י הֶֽעָנָן֙ וְהַחֹ֔שֶׁךְ וַיָּ֖אֶר אֶת־הַלָּ֑יְלָה וְלֹא־
קָרַ֥ב זֶ֛ה אֶל־זֶ֖ה כָּל־הַלָּֽיְלָה׃ כא וַיֵּ֨ט מֹשֶׁ֣ה אֶת־יָדוֹ֮ עַל־הַיָּם֒

וַיּ֣וֹלֶךְ יְהֹוָ֣ה ׀ אֶת־הַ֠יָּם בְּר֨וּחַ קָדִ֤ים עַזָּה֙ כׇּל־הַלַּ֔יְלָה וַיָּ֥שֶׂם
אֶת־הַיָּ֖ם לֶחָרָבָ֑ה וַיִּבָּקְע֖וּ הַמָּֽיִם׃ כב וַיָּבֹ֧אוּ בְנֵֽי־יִשְׂרָאֵ֛ל בְּת֥וֹךְ
הַיָּ֖ם בַּיַּבָּשָׁ֑ה וְהַמַּ֤יִם לָהֶם֙ חוֹמָ֔ה מִֽימִינָ֖ם וּמִשְּׂמֹאלָֽם׃
כג וַיִּרְדְּפ֤וּ מִצְרַ֙יִם֙ וַיָּבֹ֣אוּ אַחֲרֵיהֶ֔ם כֹּ֚ל ס֣וּס פַּרְעֹ֔ה רִכְבּ֖וֹ
וּפָרָשָׁ֑יו אֶל־תּ֖וֹךְ הַיָּֽם׃ כד וַֽיְהִי֙ בְּאַשְׁמֹ֣רֶת הַבֹּ֔קֶר וַיַּשְׁקֵ֤ף יְהֹוָה֙
אֶל־מַחֲנֵ֣ה מִצְרַ֔יִם בְּעַמּ֥וּד אֵ֖שׁ וְעָנָ֑ן וַיָּ֕הׇם אֵ֖ת מַחֲנֵ֥ה
מִצְרָֽיִם׃ כה וַיָּ֗סַר אֵ֚ת אֹפַ֣ן מַרְכְּבֹתָ֔יו וַֽיְנַהֲגֵ֖הוּ בִּכְבֵדֻ֑ת
וַיֹּ֣אמֶר מִצְרַ֗יִם אָנ֙וּסָה֙ מִפְּנֵ֣י יִשְׂרָאֵ֔ל כִּ֣י יְהֹוָ֔ה נִלְחָ֥ם לָהֶ֖ם
בְּמִצְרָֽיִם׃ פ [חמישי/בשבת שביעי] כו וַיֹּ֤אמֶר יְהֹוָה֙ אֶל־מֹשֶׁ֔ה
נְטֵ֥ה אֶת־יָדְךָ֖ עַל־הַיָּ֑ם וְיָשֻׁ֤בוּ הַמַּ֙יִם֙ עַל־מִצְרַ֔יִם עַל־רִכְבּ֖וֹ
וְעַל־פָּרָשָֽׁיו׃ כז וַיֵּט֩ מֹשֶׁ֨ה אֶת־יָד֜וֹ עַל־הַיָּ֗ם וַיָּ֨שׇׁב הַיָּ֜ם
לִפְנ֥וֹת בֹּ֙קֶר֙ לְאֵ֣יתָנ֔וֹ וּמִצְרַ֖יִם נָסִ֣ים לִקְרָאת֑וֹ וַיְנַעֵ֧ר יְהֹוָ֛ה
אֶת־מִצְרַ֖יִם בְּת֥וֹךְ הַיָּֽם׃ כח וַיָּשֻׁ֣בוּ הַמַּ֗יִם וַיְכַסּ֤וּ אֶת־הָרֶ֙כֶב֙
וְאֶת־הַפָּ֣רָשִׁ֔ים לְכֹל֙ חֵ֣יל פַּרְעֹ֔ה הַבָּאִ֥ים אַחֲרֵיהֶ֖ם בַּיָּ֑ם לֹֽא־
נִשְׁאַ֥ר בָּהֶ֖ם עַד־אֶחָֽד׃ כט וּבְנֵ֧י יִשְׂרָאֵ֛ל הָלְכ֥וּ בַיַּבָּשָׁ֖ה בְּת֣וֹךְ
הַיָּ֑ם וְהַמַּ֤יִם לָהֶם֙ חֹמָ֔ה מִימִינָ֖ם וּמִשְּׂמֹאלָֽם׃ ל וַיּ֨וֹשַׁע יְהֹוָ֜ה
בַּיּ֥וֹם הַה֛וּא אֶת־יִשְׂרָאֵ֖ל מִיַּ֣ד מִצְרָ֑יִם וַיַּ֤רְא יִשְׂרָאֵל֙ אֶת־
מִצְרַ֔יִם מֵ֖ת עַל־שְׂפַ֥ת הַיָּֽם׃ לא וַיַּ֨רְא יִשְׂרָאֵ֜ל אֶת־הַיָּ֣ד
הַגְּדֹלָ֗ה אֲשֶׁ֨ר עָשָׂ֤ה יְהֹוָה֙ בְּמִצְרַ֔יִם וַיִּֽירְא֥וּ הָעָ֖ם אֶת־יְהֹוָ֑ה
וַיַּֽאֲמִ֙ינוּ֙ בַּֽיהֹוָ֔ה וּבְמֹשֶׁ֖ה עַבְדּֽוֹ׃ פ טו א אָ֣ז יָשִֽׁיר־מֹשֶׁה֩ וּבְנֵ֨י
יִשְׂרָאֵ֜ל אֶת־הַשִּׁירָ֤ה הַזֹּאת֙ לַֽיהֹוָ֔ה וַיֹּאמְר֖וּ לֵאמֹ֑ר אָשִׁ֤ירָה
לַּֽיהֹוָה֙ כִּֽי־גָאֹ֣ה גָּאָ֔ה ס֥וּס וְרֹכְב֖וֹ רָמָ֥ה בַיָּֽם׃ ב עׇזִּ֤י וְזִמְרָת֙ יָ֔הּ
וַֽיְהִי־לִ֖י לִֽישׁוּעָ֑ה זֶ֤ה אֵלִי֙ וְאַנְוֵ֔הוּ אֱלֹהֵ֥י אָבִ֖י וַאֲרֹמְמֶֽנְהוּ׃
ג יְהֹוָ֖ה אִ֣ישׁ מִלְחָמָ֑ה יְהֹוָ֖ה שְׁמֽוֹ׃ ד מַרְכְּבֹ֥ת פַּרְעֹ֛ה וְחֵיל֖וֹ יָרָ֣ה
בַיָּ֑ם וּמִבְחַ֥ר שָׁלִשָׁ֖יו טֻבְּע֥וּ בְיַם־סֽוּף׃ ה תְּהֹמֹ֖ת יְכַסְיֻ֑מוּ יָרְד֥וּ

בִּמְצוֹלֹת כְּמוֹ־אָבֶן: ו יְמִינְךָ יְהוָה נֶאְדָּרִי בַּכֹּחַ יְמִינְךָ יְהוָה
תִּרְעַץ אוֹיֵב: ז וּבְרֹב גְּאוֹנְךָ תַּהֲרֹס קָמֶיךָ תְּשַׁלַּח חֲרֹנְךָ
יֹאכְלֵמוֹ כַּקַּשׁ: ח וּבְרוּחַ אַפֶּיךָ נֶעֶרְמוּ מַיִם נִצְּבוּ כְמוֹ־נֵד
נֹזְלִים קָפְאוּ תְהֹמֹת בְּלֶב־יָם: ט אָמַר אוֹיֵב אֶרְדֹּף אַשִּׂיג
אֲחַלֵּק שָׁלָל תִּמְלָאֵמוֹ נַפְשִׁי אָרִיק חַרְבִּי תּוֹרִישֵׁמוֹ יָדִי:
י נָשַׁפְתָּ בְרוּחֲךָ כִּסָּמוֹ יָם צָלֲלוּ כַּעוֹפֶרֶת בְּמַיִם אַדִּירִים:
יא מִי־כָמֹכָה בָּאֵלִם יְהוָה מִי כָּמֹכָה נֶאְדָּר בַּקֹּדֶשׁ נוֹרָא תְהִלֹּת
עֹשֵׂה פֶלֶא: יב נָטִיתָ יְמִינְךָ תִּבְלָעֵמוֹ אָרֶץ: יג נָחִיתָ בְחַסְדְּךָ
עַם־זוּ גָּאָלְתָּ נֵהַלְתָּ בְעָזְּךָ אֶל־נְוֵה קָדְשֶׁךָ: יד שָׁמְעוּ עַמִּים
יִרְגָּזוּן חִיל אָחַז יֹשְׁבֵי פְּלָשֶׁת: טו אָז נִבְהֲלוּ אַלּוּפֵי אֱדוֹם
אֵילֵי מוֹאָב יֹאחֲזֵמוֹ רָעַד נָמֹגוּ כֹּל יֹשְׁבֵי כְנָעַן: טז תִּפֹּל
עֲלֵיהֶם אֵימָתָה וָפַחַד בִּגְדֹל זְרוֹעֲךָ יִדְּמוּ כָּאָבֶן עַד־יַעֲבֹר
עַמְּךָ יְהוָה עַד־יַעֲבֹר עַם־זוּ קָנִיתָ: יז תְּבִאֵמוֹ וְתִטָּעֵמוֹ בְּהַר
נַחֲלָתְךָ מָכוֹן לְשִׁבְתְּךָ פָּעַלְתָּ יְהוָה מִקְּדָשׁ אֲדֹנָי כּוֹנְנוּ יָדֶיךָ:
יח יְהוָה | יִמְלֹךְ לְעֹלָם וָעֶד: יט כִּי בָא סוּס פַּרְעֹה בְּרִכְבּוֹ
וּבְפָרָשָׁיו בַּיָּם וַיָּשֶׁב יְהוָה עֲלֵהֶם אֶת־מֵי הַיָּם וּבְנֵי יִשְׂרָאֵל
הָלְכוּ בַיַּבָּשָׁה בְּתוֹךְ הַיָּם: פ כ וַתִּקַּח מִרְיָם הַנְּבִיאָה אֲחוֹת
אַהֲרֹן אֶת־הַתֹּף בְּיָדָהּ וַתֵּצֶאןָ כָל־הַנָּשִׁים אַחֲרֶיהָ בְּתֻפִּים
וּבִמְחֹלֹת: כא וַתַּעַן לָהֶם מִרְיָם שִׁירוּ לַיהוָה כִּי־גָאֹה גָּאָה
סוּס וְרֹכְבוֹ רָמָה בַיָּם: ס כב וַיַּסַּע מֹשֶׁה אֶת־יִשְׂרָאֵל
מִיַּם־סוּף וַיֵּצְאוּ אֶל־מִדְבַּר־שׁוּר וַיֵּלְכוּ שְׁלֹשֶׁת־יָמִים בַּמִּדְבָּר
וְלֹא־מָצְאוּ מָיִם: כג וַיָּבֹאוּ מָרָתָה וְלֹא יָכְלוּ לִשְׁתֹּת מַיִם
מִמָּרָה כִּי מָרִים הֵם עַל־כֵּן קָרָא־שְׁמָהּ מָרָה: כד וַיִּלֹּנוּ הָעָם
עַל־מֹשֶׁה לֵּאמֹר מַה־נִּשְׁתֶּה: כה וַיִּצְעַק אֶל־יְהוָה וַיּוֹרֵהוּ יְהוָה
עֵץ וַיַּשְׁלֵךְ אֶל־הַמַּיִם וַיִּמְתְּקוּ הַמָּיִם שָׁם שָׂם לוֹ חֹק וּמִשְׁפָּט

וְשָׁם נִסָּהוּ׃ כו וַיֹּאמֶר אִם־שָׁמוֹעַ תִּשְׁמַע לְקוֹל ׀ יְהוָה אֱלֹהֶיךָ
וְהַיָּשָׁר בְּעֵינָיו תַּעֲשֶׂה וְהַאֲזַנְתָּ לְמִצְוֺתָיו וְשָׁמַרְתָּ כָּל־חֻקָּיו
כָּל־הַמַּחֲלָה אֲשֶׁר־שַׂמְתִּי בְמִצְרַיִם לֹא־אָשִׂים עָלֶיךָ כִּי אֲנִי
יְהוָה רֹפְאֶךָ׃

מפטיר לשביעי של פסח

The first ספר תורה is lifted up (page 414) and מפטיר is read from the second ספר תורה:

במדבר כח וְהִקְרַבְתֶּם אִשֶּׁה עֹלָה לַיהוָה פָּרִים בְּנֵי־בָקָר שְׁנַיִם
וְאַיִל אֶחָד וְשִׁבְעָה כְבָשִׂים בְּנֵי שָׁנָה תְּמִימִם יִהְיוּ לָכֶם׃
כ וּמִנְחָתָם סֹלֶת בְּלוּלָה בַשָּׁמֶן שְׁלֹשָׁה עֶשְׂרֹנִים לַפָּר וּשְׁנֵי
עֶשְׂרֹנִים לָאַיִל תַּעֲשׂוּ׃ כא עִשָּׂרוֹן עִשָּׂרוֹן תַּעֲשֶׂה לַכֶּבֶשׂ הָאֶחָד
לְשִׁבְעַת הַכְּבָשִׂים׃ כב וּשְׂעִיר חַטָּאת אֶחָד לְכַפֵּר עֲלֵיכֶם׃ כג
מִלְּבַד עֹלַת הַבֹּקֶר אֲשֶׁר לְעֹלַת הַתָּמִיד תַּעֲשׂוּ אֶת־אֵלֶּה׃ כד
כָּאֵלֶּה תַּעֲשׂוּ לַיּוֹם שִׁבְעַת יָמִים לֶחֶם אִשֵּׁה רֵיחַ־נִיחֹחַ לַיהוָה
עַל־עוֹלַת הַתָּמִיד יֵעָשֶׂה וְנִסְכּוֹ׃ כה וּבַיּוֹם הַשְּׁבִיעִי מִקְרָא־
קֹדֶשׁ יִהְיֶה לָכֶם כָּל־מְלֶאכֶת עֲבֹדָה לֹא תַעֲשׂוּ׃

הפטרה לשביעי של פסח

שמואל ב׳ כב א וַיְדַבֵּר דָּוִד לַיהוָה אֶת־דִּבְרֵי הַשִּׁירָה
הַזֹּאת בְּיוֹם הִצִּיל יְהוָה אֹתוֹ מִכַּף כָּל־אֹיְבָיו וּמִכַּף
שָׁאוּל׃ ב וַיֹּאמַר יְהוָה סַלְעִי וּמְצֻדָתִי וּמְפַלְטִי־לִי׃ ג אֱלֹהֵי
צוּרִי אֶחֱסֶה־בּוֹ מָגִנִּי וְקֶרֶן יִשְׁעִי מִשְׂגַּבִּי וּמְנוּסִי מֹשִׁעִי
מֵחָמָס תֹּשִׁעֵנִי׃ ד מְהֻלָּל אֶקְרָא יְהוָה וּמֵאֹיְבַי אִוָּשֵׁעַ׃ ה כִּי
אֲפָפֻנִי מִשְׁבְּרֵי־מָוֶת נַחֲלֵי בְלִיַּעַל יְבַעֲתֻנִי׃ ו חֶבְלֵי שְׁאוֹל
סַבֻּנִי קִדְּמֻנִי מֹקְשֵׁי־מָוֶת׃ ז בַּצַּר־לִי אֶקְרָא יְהוָה וְאֶל־אֱלֹהַי
אֶקְרָא וַיִּשְׁמַע מֵהֵיכָלוֹ קוֹלִי וְשַׁוְעָתִי בְּאָזְנָיו׃ ח ותגעש ▽

▽ וַיִּתְגָּעַשׁ

וַתִּרְעַשׁ הָאָרֶץ מוֹסְדוֹת הַשָּׁמַיִם יִרְגָּזוּ וַיִּתְגָּעֲשׁוּ כִּי־חָרָה
לוֹ׃ ט עָלָה עָשָׁן בְּאַפּוֹ וְאֵשׁ מִפִּיו תֹּאכֵל גֶּחָלִים בָּעֲרוּ מִמֶּנּוּ׃
י וַיֵּט שָׁמַיִם וַיֵּרַד וַעֲרָפֶל תַּחַת רַגְלָיו׃ יא וַיִּרְכַּב עַל־כְּרוּב וַיָּעֹף
וַיֵּרָא עַל־כַּנְפֵי־רוּחַ׃ יב וַיָּשֶׁת חֹשֶׁךְ סְבִיבֹתָיו סֻכּוֹת חַשְׁרַת־
מַיִם עָבֵי שְׁחָקִים׃ יג מִנֹּגַהּ נֶגְדּוֹ בָּעֲרוּ גַּחֲלֵי־אֵשׁ׃ יד יַרְעֵם
מִן־שָׁמַיִם יְהוָה וְעֶלְיוֹן יִתֵּן קוֹלוֹ׃ טו וַיִּשְׁלַח חִצִּים וַיְפִיצֵם
בָּרָק ויהמם▽ ׃ טז וַיֵּרָאוּ אֲפִקֵי יָם יִגָּלוּ מֹסְדוֹת תֵּבֵל בְּגַעֲרַת
יְהוָה מִנִּשְׁמַת רוּחַ אַפּוֹ׃ יז יִשְׁלַח מִמָּרוֹם יִקָּחֵנִי יַמְשֵׁנִי
מִמַּיִם רַבִּים׃ יח יַצִּילֵנִי מֵאֹיְבִי עָז מִשֹּׂנְאַי כִּי אָמְצוּ מִמֶּנִּי׃
יט יְקַדְּמֻנִי בְּיוֹם אֵידִי וַיְהִי יְהוָה מִשְׁעָן לִי׃ כ וַיֹּצֵא לַמֶּרְחָב
אֹתִי יְחַלְּצֵנִי כִּי־חָפֵץ בִּי׃ כא יִגְמְלֵנִי יְהוָה כְּצִדְקָתִי כְּבֹר יָדַי
יָשִׁיב לִי׃ כב כִּי שָׁמַרְתִּי דַּרְכֵי יְהוָה וְלֹא רָשַׁעְתִּי מֵאֱלֹהָי׃
כג כִּי כָל־מִשְׁפָּטָו לְנֶגְדִּי וְחֻקֹּתָיו לֹא־אָסוּר מִמֶּנָּה׃ כד וָאֶהְיֶה
תָמִים לוֹ וָאֶשְׁתַּמְּרָה מֵעֲוֹנִי׃ כה וַיָּשֶׁב יְהוָה לִי כְּצִדְקָתִי כְּבֹרִי
לְנֶגֶד עֵינָיו׃ כו עִם־חָסִיד תִּתְחַסָּד עִם־גְּבוֹר תָּמִים תִּתַּמָּם׃
כז עִם־נָבָר תִּתָּבָר וְעִם־עִקֵּשׁ תִּתַּפָּל׃ כח וְאֶת־עַם עָנִי תּוֹשִׁיעַ
וְעֵינֶיךָ עַל־רָמִים תַּשְׁפִּיל׃ כט כִּי־אַתָּה נֵירִי יְהוָה וַיהוָה יַגִּיהַּ
חָשְׁכִּי׃ ל כִּי בְכָה אָרוּץ גְּדוּד בֵּאלֹהַי אֲדַלֶּג־שׁוּר׃ לא הָאֵל
תָּמִים דַּרְכּוֹ אִמְרַת יְהוָה צְרוּפָה מָגֵן הוּא לְכֹל הַחֹסִים
בּוֹ׃ לב כִּי מִי־אֵל מִבַּלְעֲדֵי יְהוָה וּמִי צוּר מִבַּלְעֲדֵי אֱלֹהֵינוּ׃
לג הָאֵל מָעוּזִּי חָיִל וַיַּתֵּר תָּמִים דרכו◂ ׃ לד מְשַׁוֶּה רגליו▸
כָּאַיָּלוֹת וְעַל־בָּמֹתַי יַעֲמִידֵנִי׃ לה מְלַמֵּד יָדַי לַמִּלְחָמָה וְנִחַת
קֶשֶׁת־נְחוּשָׁה זְרֹעֹתָי׃ לו וַתִּתֶּן־לִי מָגֵן יִשְׁעֶךָ וַעֲנֹתְךָ תַּרְבֵּנִי׃

▽ וַיָּהֹם

◂ דַּרְכִּי

▸ רַגְלַי

לז תַּרְחִיב צַעֲדִי תַּחְתֵּנִי וְלֹא מָעֲדוּ קַרְסֻלָּי׃ לח אֶרְדְּפָה אֹיְבַי
וָאַשְׁמִידֵם וְלֹא אָשׁוּב עַד־כַּלּוֹתָם׃ לט וָאֲכַלֵּם וָאֶמְחָצֵם וְלֹא
יְקוּמוּן וַיִּפְּלוּ תַּחַת רַגְלָי׃ מ וַתַּזְרֵנִי חַיִל לַמִּלְחָמָה תַּכְרִיעַ
קָמַי תַּחְתֵּנִי׃ מא וְאֹיְבַי תַּתָּה לִּי עֹרֶף מְשַׂנְאַי וָאַצְמִיתֵם׃
מב יִשְׁעוּ וְאֵין מֹשִׁיעַ אֶל־יהוה וְלֹא עָנָם׃ מג וְאֶשְׁחָקֵם כַּעֲפַר־
אֶרֶץ כְּטִיט־חוּצוֹת אֲדִקֵּם אֶרְקָעֵם׃ מד וַתְּפַלְּטֵנִי מֵרִיבֵי עַמִּי
תִּשְׁמְרֵנִי לְרֹאשׁ גּוֹיִם עַם לֹא־יָדַעְתִּי יַעַבְדֻנִי׃ מה בְּנֵי נֵכָר
יִתְכַּחֲשׁוּ־לִי לִשְׁמוֹעַ אֹזֶן יִשָּׁמְעוּ לִי׃ מו בְּנֵי נֵכָר יִבֹּלוּ וְיַחְגְּרוּ
מִמִּסְגְּרוֹתָם׃ מז חַי־יהוה וּבָרוּךְ צוּרִי וְיָרֻם אֱלֹהֵי צוּר יִשְׁעִי׃
מח הָאֵל הַנֹּתֵן נְקָמֹת לִי וּמוֹרִיד עַמִּים תַּחְתֵּנִי׃ מט וּמוֹצִיאִי
מֵאֹיְבָי וּמִקָּמַי תְּרוֹמְמֵנִי מֵאִישׁ חֲמָסִים תַּצִּילֵנִי׃ נ עַל־כֵּן
אוֹדְךָ יהוה בַּגּוֹיִם וּלְשִׁמְךָ אֲזַמֵּר׃ נא מגדיל▽ יְשׁוּעוֹת מַלְכּוֹ
וְעֹשֶׂה־חֶסֶד לִמְשִׁיחוֹ לְדָוִד וּלְזַרְעוֹ עַד־עוֹלָם׃

Continue with the blessings after the הפטרה on page 416.

קריאה ליום אחרון של פסח או שבועות, ולשמיני עצרת

If the last day of פסח or the second day of שבועות falls on שבת, start here. If it falls on a weekday, start with כָּל־הַבְּכוֹר on page 939. On שמיני עצרת start here.

דברים יד כב עַשֵּׂר תְּעַשֵּׂר אֵת כָּל־תְּבוּאַת זַרְעֶךָ הַיֹּצֵא
הַשָּׂדֶה שָׁנָה שָׁנָה׃ כג וְאָכַלְתָּ לִפְנֵי | יהוה אֱלֹהֶיךָ בַּמָּקוֹם
אֲשֶׁר־יִבְחַר לְשַׁכֵּן שְׁמוֹ שָׁם מַעְשַׂר דְּגָנְךָ תִּירֹשְׁךָ וְיִצְהָרֶךָ
וּבְכֹרֹת בְּקָרְךָ וְצֹאנֶךָ לְמַעַן תִּלְמַד לְיִרְאָה אֶת־יהוה
אֱלֹהֶיךָ כָּל־הַיָּמִים׃ כד וְכִי־יִרְבֶּה מִמְּךָ הַדֶּרֶךְ כִּי לֹא תוּכַל
שְׂאֵתוֹ כִּי־יִרְחַק מִמְּךָ הַמָּקוֹם אֲשֶׁר יִבְחַר יהוה אֱלֹהֶיךָ
לָשׂוּם שְׁמוֹ שָׁם כִּי יְבָרֶכְךָ יהוה אֱלֹהֶיךָ׃ כה וְנָתַתָּה בַּכָּסֶף
וְצַרְתָּ הַכֶּסֶף בְּיָדְךָ וְהָלַכְתָּ אֶל־הַמָּקוֹם אֲשֶׁר יִבְחַר יהוה
אֱלֹהֶיךָ בּוֹ׃ כו וְנָתַתָּה הַכֶּסֶף בְּכֹל אֲשֶׁר־תְּאַוֶּה נַפְשְׁךָ

▽ מִגְדּוֹל

בַּבָּקָר וּבַצֹּאן וּבַיַּיִן וּבַשֵּׁכָר וּבְכֹל אֲשֶׁר תִּשְׁאָלְךָ נַפְשֶׁךָ
וְאָכַלְתָּ שָּׁם לִפְנֵי יְהוָה אֱלֹהֶיךָ וְשָׂמַחְתָּ אַתָּה וּבֵיתֶךָ׃
כז וְהַלֵּוִי אֲשֶׁר־בִּשְׁעָרֶיךָ לֹא תַעַזְבֶנּוּ כִּי אֵין לוֹ חֵלֶק וְנַחֲלָה
עִמָּךְ׃ ס כח מִקְצֵה | שָׁלֹשׁ שָׁנִים תּוֹצִיא אֶת־כָּל־
מַעְשַׂר תְּבוּאָתְךָ בַּשָּׁנָה הַהִוא וְהִנַּחְתָּ בִּשְׁעָרֶיךָ׃ כט וּבָא
הַלֵּוִי כִּי אֵין־לוֹ חֵלֶק וְנַחֲלָה עִמָּךְ וְהַגֵּר וְהַיָּתוֹם וְהָאַלְמָנָה
אֲשֶׁר בִּשְׁעָרֶיךָ וְאָכְלוּ וְשָׂבֵעוּ לְמַעַן יְבָרֶכְךָ יְהוָה אֱלֹהֶיךָ
בְּכָל־מַעֲשֵׂה יָדְךָ אֲשֶׁר תַּעֲשֶׂה׃
[בשבת לוי ובשמיני עצרת חול] טו א מִקֵּץ שֶׁבַע־שָׁנִים תַּעֲשֶׂה
שְׁמִטָּה׃ ב וְזֶה דְּבַר הַשְּׁמִטָּה שָׁמוֹט כָּל־בַּעַל מַשֵּׁה יָדוֹ
אֲשֶׁר יַשֶּׁה בְּרֵעֵהוּ לֹא־יִגֹּשׂ אֶת־רֵעֵהוּ וְאֶת־אָחִיו כִּי־קָרָא
שְׁמִטָּה לַיהוָה׃ ג אֶת־הַנָּכְרִי תִּגֹּשׂ וַאֲשֶׁר יִהְיֶה לְךָ אֶת־אָחִיךָ
תַּשְׁמֵט יָדֶךָ׃ ד אֶפֶס כִּי לֹא יִהְיֶה־בְּךָ אֶבְיוֹן כִּי־בָרֵךְ יְבָרֶכְךָ
יְהוָה בָּאָרֶץ אֲשֶׁר יְהוָה אֱלֹהֶיךָ נֹתֵן־לְךָ נַחֲלָה לְרִשְׁתָּהּ׃
ה רַק אִם־שָׁמוֹעַ תִּשְׁמַע בְּקוֹל יְהוָה אֱלֹהֶיךָ לִשְׁמֹר לַעֲשׂוֹת
אֶת־כָּל־הַמִּצְוָה הַזֹּאת אֲשֶׁר אָנֹכִי מְצַוְּךָ הַיּוֹם׃ ו כִּי־יְהוָה
אֱלֹהֶיךָ בֵּרַכְךָ כַּאֲשֶׁר דִּבֶּר־לָךְ וְהַעֲבַטְתָּ גּוֹיִם רַבִּים וְאַתָּה
לֹא תַעֲבֹט וּמָשַׁלְתָּ בְּגוֹיִם רַבִּים וּבְךָ לֹא יִמְשֹׁלוּ׃ ס ז כִּי־
יִהְיֶה בְךָ אֶבְיוֹן מֵאַחַד אַחֶיךָ בְּאַחַד שְׁעָרֶיךָ בְּאַרְצְךָ אֲשֶׁר־
יְהוָה אֱלֹהֶיךָ נֹתֵן לָךְ לֹא תְאַמֵּץ אֶת־לְבָבְךָ וְלֹא תִקְפֹּץ
אֶת־יָדְךָ מֵאָחִיךָ הָאֶבְיוֹן׃ ח כִּי־פָתֹחַ תִּפְתַּח אֶת־יָדְךָ לוֹ
וְהַעֲבֵט תַּעֲבִיטֶנּוּ דֵּי מַחְסֹרוֹ אֲשֶׁר יֶחְסַר לוֹ׃ ט הִשָּׁמֶר
לְךָ פֶּן־יִהְיֶה דָבָר עִם־לְבָבְךָ בְלִיַּעַל לֵאמֹר קָרְבָה שְׁנַת־
הַשֶּׁבַע שְׁנַת הַשְּׁמִטָּה וְרָעָה עֵינְךָ בְּאָחִיךָ הָאֶבְיוֹן וְלֹא
תִתֵּן לוֹ וְקָרָא עָלֶיךָ אֶל־יְהוָה וְהָיָה בְךָ חֵטְא׃ י נָתוֹן תִּתֵּן
לוֹ וְלֹא־יֵרַע לְבָבְךָ בְּתִתְּךָ לוֹ כִּי בִּגְלַל | הַדָּבָר הַזֶּה יְבָרֶכְךָ

יְהוָ֣ה אֱלֹהֶ֗יךָ בְּכָל־מַעֲשֶׂ֔ךָ וּבְכֹ֖ל מִשְׁלַ֥ח יָדֶֽךָ׃ יא כִּ֛י לֹא־יֶחְדַּ֥ל
אֶבְי֖וֹן מִקֶּ֣רֶב הָאָ֑רֶץ עַל־כֵּ֞ן אָנֹכִ֤י מְצַוְּךָ֙ לֵאמֹ֔ר פָּ֠תֹחַ תִּפְתַּ֨ח
אֶת־יָדְךָ֜ לְאָחִ֧יךָ לַעֲנִיֶּ֛ךָ וּלְאֶבְיֹנְךָ֖ בְּאַרְצֶֽךָ׃ ס כִּֽי־יִמָּכֵ֨ר
לְךָ֜ אָחִ֣יךָ הָֽעִבְרִ֗י א֚וֹ הָֽעִבְרִיָּ֔ה וַעֲבָֽדְךָ֖ שֵׁ֣שׁ שָׁנִ֑ים וּבַשָּׁנָה֙
הַשְּׁבִיעִ֔ת תְּשַׁלְּחֶ֥נּוּ חָפְשִׁ֖י מֵעִמָּֽךְ׃ יג וְכִֽי־תְשַׁלְּחֶ֥נּוּ חָפְשִׁ֖י
מֵעִמָּ֑ךְ לֹ֥א תְשַׁלְּחֶ֖נּוּ רֵיקָֽם׃ יד הַעֲנֵ֤יק תַּעֲנִיק֙ ל֔וֹ מִצֹּ֣אנְךָ֔
וּמִגָּרְנְךָ֖ וּמִיִּקְבֶ֑ךָ אֲשֶׁ֧ר בֵּֽרַכְךָ֛ יְהוָ֥ה אֱלֹהֶ֖יךָ תִּתֶּן־לֽוֹ׃ טו וְזָכַרְתָּ֗
כִּ֣י עֶ֤בֶד הָיִ֙יתָ֙ בְּאֶ֣רֶץ מִצְרַ֔יִם וַֽיִּפְדְּךָ֖ יְהוָ֣ה אֱלֹהֶ֑יךָ עַל־כֵּ֞ן
אָנֹכִ֧י מְצַוְּךָ֛ אֶת־הַדָּבָ֥ר הַזֶּ֖ה הַיּֽוֹם׃ טז וְהָיָה֙ כִּֽי־יֹאמַ֣ר אֵלֶ֔יךָ
לֹ֥א אֵצֵ֖א מֵעִמָּ֑ךְ כִּ֤י אֲהֵֽבְךָ֙ וְאֶת־בֵּיתֶ֔ךָ כִּי־ט֥וֹב ל֖וֹ עִמָּֽךְ׃
יז וְלָקַחְתָּ֣ אֶת־הַמַּרְצֵ֗עַ וְנָתַתָּ֤ה בְאָזְנוֹ֙ וּבַדֶּ֔לֶת וְהָיָ֥ה לְךָ֖ עֶ֣בֶד
עוֹלָ֑ם וְאַ֥ף לַאֲמָתְךָ֖ תַּעֲשֶׂה־כֵּֽן׃ יח לֹא־יִקְשֶׁ֣ה בְעֵינֶ֗ךָ בְּשַׁלֵּֽחֲךָ֨
אֹת֤וֹ חָפְשִׁי֙ מֵֽעִמָּ֔ךְ כִּ֗י מִשְׁנֶה֙ שְׂכַ֣ר שָׂכִ֔יר עֲבָֽדְךָ֖ שֵׁ֣שׁ שָׁנִ֑ים
וּבֵֽרַכְךָ֙ יְהוָ֣ה אֱלֹהֶ֔יךָ בְּכֹ֖ל אֲשֶׁ֥ר תַּעֲשֶֽׂה׃

If the eighth day of Pesach or the second day of Shavuot is a weekday, begin here:

[בשבת שלישי] יט כָּל־הַבְּכ֡וֹר אֲשֶׁר֩ יִוָּלֵ֨ד בִּבְקָרְךָ֜ וּבְצֹֽאנְךָ֗ הַזָּכָ֔ר
תַּקְדִּ֖ישׁ לַיהוָ֣ה אֱלֹהֶ֑יךָ לֹ֤א תַעֲבֹד֙ בִּבְכֹ֣ר שׁוֹרֶ֔ךָ וְלֹ֥א תָגֹ֖ז
בְּכ֥וֹר צֹאנֶֽךָ׃ כ לִפְנֵי֩ יְהוָ֨ה אֱלֹהֶ֤יךָ תֹאכְלֶ֙נּוּ֙ שָׁנָ֣ה בְשָׁנָ֔ה
בַּמָּק֖וֹם אֲשֶׁר־יִבְחַ֣ר יְהוָ֑ה אַתָּ֖ה וּבֵיתֶֽךָ׃ כא וְכִֽי־יִהְיֶ֨ה ב֜וֹ
מ֗וּם פִּסֵּ֙חַ֙ א֣וֹ עִוֵּ֔ר כֹּ֖ל מ֣וּם רָ֑ע לֹ֣א תִזְבָּחֶ֔נּוּ לַיהוָ֖ה אֱלֹהֶֽיךָ׃
כב בִּשְׁעָרֶ֖יךָ תֹּאכְלֶ֑נּוּ הַטָּמֵ֤א וְהַטָּהוֹר֙ יַחְדָּ֔ו כַּצְּבִ֖י וְכָאַיָּֽל׃
כג רַ֥ק אֶת־דָּמ֖וֹ לֹ֣א תֹאכֵ֑ל עַל־הָאָ֥רֶץ תִּשְׁפְּכֶ֖נּוּ כַּמָּֽיִם׃ פ [לוי
לפסח ושבועות בחול – רביעי לשבת] טז א שָׁמוֹר֙ אֶת־חֹ֣דֶשׁ הָֽאָבִ֔יב
וְעָשִׂ֣יתָ פֶּ֔סַח לַיהוָ֖ה אֱלֹהֶ֑יךָ כִּ֞י בְּחֹ֣דֶשׁ הָֽאָבִ֗יב הוֹצִ֨יאֲךָ֜
יְהוָ֧ה אֱלֹהֶ֛יךָ מִמִּצְרַ֖יִם לָֽיְלָה׃ ב וְזָבַ֥חְתָּ פֶּ֛סַח לַיהוָ֥ה
אֱלֹהֶ֖יךָ צֹ֣אן וּבָקָ֑ר בַּמָּקוֹם֙ אֲשֶׁר־יִבְחַ֣ר יְהוָ֔ה לְשַׁכֵּ֥ן שְׁמ֖וֹ

שָׁם: ג לֹא־תֹאכַל עָלָיו חָמֵץ שִׁבְעַת יָמִים תֹּאכַל־עָלָיו
מַצּוֹת לֶחֶם עֹנִי כִּי בְחִפָּזוֹן יָצָאתָ מֵאֶרֶץ מִצְרַיִם לְמַעַן
תִּזְכֹּר אֶת־יוֹם צֵאתְךָ מֵאֶרֶץ מִצְרַיִם כֹּל יְמֵי חַיֶּיךָ:
[שלישי לפסח ושבועות בחול – רביעי לשמיני עצרת בחול – חמישי לשבת]
ד וְלֹא־יֵרָאֶה לְךָ שְׂאֹר בְּכָל־גְּבֻלְךָ שִׁבְעַת יָמִים וְלֹא־יָלִין מִן־
הַבָּשָׂר אֲשֶׁר תִּזְבַּח בָּעֶרֶב בַּיּוֹם הָרִאשׁוֹן לַבֹּקֶר: ה לֹא תוּכַל
לִזְבֹּחַ אֶת־הַפָּסַח בְּאַחַד שְׁעָרֶיךָ אֲשֶׁר־יְהוָה אֱלֹהֶיךָ נֹתֵן לָךְ:
ו כִּי אִם־אֶל־הַמָּקוֹם אֲשֶׁר־יִבְחַר יְהוָה אֱלֹהֶיךָ לְשַׁכֵּן שְׁמוֹ
שָׁם תִּזְבַּח אֶת־הַפֶּסַח בָּעָרֶב כְּבוֹא הַשֶּׁמֶשׁ מוֹעֵד צֵאתְךָ
מִמִּצְרָיִם: ז וּבִשַּׁלְתָּ וְאָכַלְתָּ בַּמָּקוֹם אֲשֶׁר יִבְחַר יְהוָה אֱלֹהֶיךָ
בּוֹ וּפָנִיתָ בַבֹּקֶר וְהָלַכְתָּ לְאֹהָלֶיךָ: ח שֵׁשֶׁת יָמִים תֹּאכַל
מַצּוֹת וּבַיּוֹם הַשְּׁבִיעִי עֲצֶרֶת לַיהוָה אֱלֹהֶיךָ לֹא תַעֲשֶׂה
מְלָאכָה: ס [רביעי לפסח ושבועות בחול – חמישי לשמיני עצרת
בחול – ששי לשבת] ט שִׁבְעָה שָׁבֻעֹת תִּסְפָּר־לָךְ מֵהָחֵל חֶרְמֵשׁ
בַּקָּמָה תָּחֵל לִסְפֹּר שִׁבְעָה שָׁבֻעוֹת: י וְעָשִׂיתָ חַג שָׁבֻעוֹת
לַיהוָה אֱלֹהֶיךָ מִסַּת נִדְבַת יָדְךָ אֲשֶׁר תִּתֵּן כַּאֲשֶׁר יְבָרֶכְךָ
יְהוָה אֱלֹהֶיךָ: יא וְשָׂמַחְתָּ לִפְנֵי | יְהוָה אֱלֹהֶיךָ אַתָּה וּבִנְךָ
וּבִתֶּךָ וְעַבְדְּךָ וַאֲמָתֶךָ וְהַלֵּוִי אֲשֶׁר בִּשְׁעָרֶיךָ וְהַגֵּר וְהַיָּתוֹם
וְהָאַלְמָנָה אֲשֶׁר בְּקִרְבֶּךָ בַּמָּקוֹם אֲשֶׁר יִבְחַר יְהוָה אֱלֹהֶיךָ
לְשַׁכֵּן שְׁמוֹ שָׁם: יב וְזָכַרְתָּ כִּי־עֶבֶד הָיִיתָ בְּמִצְרָיִם וְשָׁמַרְתָּ
וְעָשִׂיתָ אֶת־הַחֻקִּים הָאֵלֶּה: פ [חמישי לפסח ושבועות בחול – שביעי
לשבת] יג חַג הַסֻּכֹּת תַּעֲשֶׂה לְךָ שִׁבְעַת יָמִים בְּאָסְפְּךָ מִגָּרְנְךָ
וּמִיִּקְבֶךָ: יד וְשָׂמַחְתָּ בְּחַגֶּךָ אַתָּה וּבִנְךָ וּבִתֶּךָ וְעַבְדְּךָ וַאֲמָתֶךָ
וְהַלֵּוִי וְהַגֵּר וְהַיָּתוֹם וְהָאַלְמָנָה אֲשֶׁר בִּשְׁעָרֶיךָ: טו שִׁבְעַת
יָמִים תָּחֹג לַיהוָה אֱלֹהֶיךָ בַּמָּקוֹם אֲשֶׁר־יִבְחַר יְהוָה כִּי
יְבָרֶכְךָ יְהוָה אֱלֹהֶיךָ בְּכֹל תְּבוּאָתְךָ וּבְכֹל מַעֲשֵׂה יָדֶיךָ וְהָיִיתָ

אַ֖ךְ שָׂמֵֽחַ׃ טז שָׁל֣וֹשׁ פְּעָמִ֣ים ׀ בַּשָּׁנָ֡ה יֵרָאֶ֨ה כָל־זְכוּרְךָ֜ אֶת־
פְּנֵ֣י ׀ יְהוָ֣ה אֱלֹהֶ֗יךָ בַּמָּקוֹם֙ אֲשֶׁ֣ר יִבְחָ֔ר בְּחַ֧ג הַמַּצּ֛וֹת וּבְחַ֥ג
הַשָּׁבֻע֖וֹת וּבְחַ֣ג הַסֻּכּ֑וֹת וְלֹ֧א יֵרָאֶ֛ה אֶת־פְּנֵ֥י יְהוָ֖ה רֵיקָֽם׃
יז אִ֖ישׁ כְּמַתְּנַ֣ת יָד֑וֹ כְּבִרְכַּ֛ת יְהוָ֥ה אֱלֹהֶ֖יךָ אֲשֶׁ֥ר נָתַן־לָֽךְ׃

The מפטיר for יום שמיני של פסח is the same as Revi'i for the other days of חול המועד פסח, page 937.

הפטרה ליום האחרון של פסח

ישעיהו י לב ע֥וֹד הַיּ֖וֹם בְּנֹ֣ב לַעֲמֹ֑ד יְנֹפֵ֤ף יָדוֹ֙ הַ֣ר בית▽־צִיּ֔וֹן גִּבְעַ֖ת
יְרוּשָׁלִָֽם׃ ס לג הִנֵּ֤ה הָאָדוֹן֙ יְהוָ֣ה צְבָא֔וֹת מְסָעֵ֥ף פֻּארָ֖ה
בְּמַעֲרָצָ֑ה וְרָמֵ֤י הַקּוֹמָה֙ גְּדוּעִ֔ים וְהַגְּבֹהִ֖ים יִשְׁפָּֽלוּ׃ לד וְנִקַּ֛ף
סִבְכֵ֥י הַיַּ֖עַר בַּבַּרְזֶ֑ל וְהַלְּבָנ֖וֹן בְּאַדִּ֥יר יִפּֽוֹל׃ ס יא א וְיָצָ֥א
חֹ֖טֶר מִגֵּ֣זַע יִשָׁ֑י וְנֵ֖צֶר מִשָּׁרָשָׁ֥יו יִפְרֶֽה׃ ב וְנָחָ֥ה עָלָ֖יו ר֣וּחַ
יְהוָ֑ה ר֧וּחַ חָכְמָ֣ה וּבִינָ֗ה ר֤וּחַ עֵצָה֙ וּגְבוּרָ֔ה ר֥וּחַ דַּ֖עַת וְיִרְאַ֥ת
יְהוָֽה׃ ג וַהֲרִיח֖וֹ בְּיִרְאַ֣ת יְהוָ֑ה וְלֹֽא־לְמַרְאֵ֤ה עֵינָיו֙ יִשְׁפּ֔וֹט
וְלֹֽא־לְמִשְׁמַ֥ע אָזְנָ֖יו יוֹכִֽיחַ׃ ד וְשָׁפַ֤ט בְּצֶ֙דֶק֙ דַּלִּ֔ים וְהוֹכִ֥יחַ
בְּמִישׁ֖וֹר לְעַנְוֵי־אָ֑רֶץ וְהִכָּה־אֶ֙רֶץ֙ בְּשֵׁ֣בֶט פִּ֔יו וּבְר֥וּחַ שְׂפָתָ֖יו
יָמִ֥ית רָשָֽׁע׃ ה וְהָ֥יָה צֶ֖דֶק אֵז֣וֹר מָתְנָ֑יו וְהָאֱמוּנָ֖ה אֵז֥וֹר חֲלָצָֽיו׃
ו וְגָ֤ר זְאֵב֙ עִם־כֶּ֔בֶשׂ וְנָמֵ֖ר עִם־גְּדִ֣י יִרְבָּ֑ץ וְעֵ֨גֶל וּכְפִ֤יר וּמְרִיא֙
יַחְדָּ֔ו וְנַ֥עַר קָטֹ֖ן נֹהֵ֥ג בָּֽם׃ ז וּפָרָ֤ה וָדֹב֙ תִּרְעֶ֔ינָה יַחְדָּ֖ו יִרְבְּצ֣וּ
יַלְדֵיהֶ֑ן וְאַרְיֵ֖ה כַּבָּקָ֥ר יֹֽאכַל־תֶּֽבֶן׃ ח וְשִֽׁעֲשַׁ֥ע יוֹנֵ֖ק עַל־חֻ֣ר פָּ֑תֶן
וְעַל֙ מְאוּרַ֣ת צִפְעוֹנִ֔י גָּמ֖וּל יָד֥וֹ הָדָֽה׃ ט לֹֽא־יָרֵ֥עוּ וְלֹֽא־יַשְׁחִ֖יתוּ
בְּכָל־הַ֣ר קָדְשִׁ֑י כִּֽי־מָלְאָ֣ה הָאָ֗רֶץ דֵּעָה֙ אֶת־יְהוָ֔ה כַּמַּ֖יִם לַיָּ֥ם
מְכַסִּֽים׃ ס י וְהָיָה֙ בַּיּ֣וֹם הַה֔וּא שֹׁ֣רֶשׁ יִשַׁ֗י אֲשֶׁ֥ר עֹמֵ֛ד לְנֵ֥ס
עַמִּ֖ים אֵלָ֣יו גּוֹיִ֣ם יִדְרֹ֑שׁוּ וְהָיְתָ֥ה מְנֻחָת֖וֹ כָּבֽוֹד׃ ס יא וְהָיָ֣ה
בַּיּ֣וֹם הַה֗וּא יוֹסִ֨יף אֲדֹנָ֤י ׀ שֵׁנִית֙ יָד֔וֹ לִקְנ֖וֹת אֶת־שְׁאָ֣ר עַמּ֑וֹ

▽ בַּת־

אֲשֶׁר יִשָּׁאֵר מֵאַשּׁוּר וּמִמִּצְרַיִם וּמִפַּתְרוֹס וּמִכּוּשׁ וּמֵעֵילָם
וּמִשִּׁנְעָר וּמֵחֲמָת וּמֵאִיֵּי הַיָּם: יב וְנָשָׂא נֵס לַגּוֹיִם וְאָסַף נִדְחֵי
יִשְׂרָאֵל וּנְפֻצוֹת יְהוּדָה יְקַבֵּץ מֵאַרְבַּע כַּנְפוֹת הָאָרֶץ: יג וְסָרָה
קִנְאַת אֶפְרַיִם וְצֹרְרֵי יְהוּדָה יִכָּרֵתוּ אֶפְרַיִם לֹא־יְקַנֵּא אֶת־
יְהוּדָה וִיהוּדָה לֹא־יָצֹר אֶת־אֶפְרָיִם: יד וְעָפוּ בְכָתֵף פְּלִשְׁתִּים
יָמָּה יַחְדָּו יָבֹזּוּ אֶת־בְּנֵי־קֶדֶם אֱדוֹם וּמוֹאָב מִשְׁלוֹחַ יָדָם
וּבְנֵי עַמּוֹן מִשְׁמַעְתָּם: טו וְהֶחֱרִים יהוה אֵת לְשׁוֹן יַם־מִצְרַיִם
וְהֵנִיף יָדוֹ עַל־הַנָּהָר בַּעְיָם רוּחוֹ וְהִכָּהוּ לְשִׁבְעָה נְחָלִים
וְהִדְרִיךְ בַּנְּעָלִים: טז וְהָיְתָה מְסִלָּה לִשְׁאָר עַמּוֹ אֲשֶׁר יִשָּׁאֵר
מֵאַשּׁוּר כַּאֲשֶׁר הָיְתָה לְיִשְׂרָאֵל בְּיוֹם עֲלֹתוֹ מֵאֶרֶץ מִצְרָיִם:
יב א וְאָמַרְתָּ בַּיּוֹם הַהוּא אוֹדְךָ יהוה כִּי אָנַפְתָּ בִּי יָשֹׁב אַפְּךָ
וּתְנַחֲמֵנִי: ב הִנֵּה אֵל יְשׁוּעָתִי אֶבְטַח וְלֹא אֶפְחָד כִּי־עָזִּי
וְזִמְרָת יָהּ יהוה וַיְהִי־לִי לִישׁוּעָה: ג וּשְׁאַבְתֶּם־מַיִם בְּשָׂשׂוֹן
מִמַּעַיְנֵי הַיְשׁוּעָה: ד וַאֲמַרְתֶּם בַּיּוֹם הַהוּא הוֹדוּ לַיהוה קִרְאוּ
בִשְׁמוֹ הוֹדִיעוּ בָעַמִּים עֲלִילֹתָיו הַזְכִּירוּ כִּי נִשְׂגָּב שְׁמוֹ: ה זַמְּרוּ
יהוה כִּי גֵאוּת עָשָׂה מידעת▽ זֹאת בְּכָל־הָאָרֶץ: ו צַהֲלִי וָרֹנִּי
יוֹשֶׁבֶת צִיּוֹן כִּי־גָדוֹל בְּקִרְבֵּךְ קְדוֹשׁ יִשְׂרָאֵל:

Continue with the blessings after the הפטרה on page 416.

Torah Readings for Shavuot

קריאה ליום טוב ראשון של שבועות

שמות יט א בַּחֹדֶשׁ הַשְּׁלִישִׁי לְצֵאת בְּנֵי־יִשְׂרָאֵל מֵאֶרֶץ
מִצְרָיִם בַּיּוֹם הַזֶּה בָּאוּ מִדְבַּר סִינָי: ב וַיִּסְעוּ מֵרְפִידִים
וַיָּבֹאוּ מִדְבַּר סִינַי וַיַּחֲנוּ בַּמִּדְבָּר וַיִּחַן־שָׁם יִשְׂרָאֵל נֶגֶד

▽ מוּדַעַת

הָהָר: ג וּמֹשֶׁה עָלָה אֶל־הָאֱלֹהִים וַיִּקְרָא אֵלָיו יהוה מִן־
הָהָר לֵאמֹר כֹּה תֹאמַר לְבֵית יַעֲקֹב וְתַגֵּיד לִבְנֵי יִשְׂרָאֵל:
ד אַתֶּם רְאִיתֶם אֲשֶׁר עָשִׂיתִי לְמִצְרָיִם וָאֶשָּׂא אֶתְכֶם
עַל־כַּנְפֵי נְשָׁרִים וָאָבִא אֶתְכֶם אֵלָי: ה וְעַתָּה אִם־שָׁמוֹעַ
תִּשְׁמְעוּ בְּקֹלִי וּשְׁמַרְתֶּם אֶת־בְּרִיתִי וִהְיִיתֶם לִי סְגֻלָּה מִכָּל־
הָעַמִּים כִּי־לִי כָּל־הָאָרֶץ: ו וְאַתֶּם תִּהְיוּ־לִי מַמְלֶכֶת כֹּהֲנִים
וְגוֹי קָדוֹשׁ אֵלֶּה הַדְּבָרִים אֲשֶׁר תְּדַבֵּר אֶל־בְּנֵי יִשְׂרָאֵל:
[לוי] ז וַיָּבֹא מֹשֶׁה וַיִּקְרָא לְזִקְנֵי הָעָם וַיָּשֶׂם לִפְנֵיהֶם אֵת
כָּל־הַדְּבָרִים הָאֵלֶּה אֲשֶׁר צִוָּהוּ יהוה: ח וַיַּעֲנוּ כָל־הָעָם
יַחְדָּו וַיֹּאמְרוּ כֹּל אֲשֶׁר־דִּבֶּר יהוה נַעֲשֶׂה וַיָּשֶׁב מֹשֶׁה
אֶת־דִּבְרֵי הָעָם אֶל־יהוה: ט וַיֹּאמֶר יהוה אֶל־מֹשֶׁה הִנֵּה
אָנֹכִי בָּא אֵלֶיךָ בְּעַב הֶעָנָן בַּעֲבוּר יִשְׁמַע הָעָם בְּדַבְּרִי
עִמָּךְ וְגַם־בְּךָ יַאֲמִינוּ לְעוֹלָם וַיַּגֵּד מֹשֶׁה אֶת־דִּבְרֵי הָעָם
אֶל־יהוה: י וַיֹּאמֶר יהוה אֶל־מֹשֶׁה לֵךְ אֶל־הָעָם וְקִדַּשְׁתָּם
הַיּוֹם וּמָחָר וְכִבְּסוּ שִׂמְלֹתָם: יא וְהָיוּ נְכֹנִים לַיּוֹם הַשְּׁלִישִׁי
כִּי | בַּיּוֹם הַשְּׁלִשִׁי יֵרֵד יהוה לְעֵינֵי כָל־הָעָם עַל־הַר סִינָי:
יב וְהִגְבַּלְתָּ אֶת־הָעָם סָבִיב לֵאמֹר הִשָּׁמְרוּ לָכֶם עֲלוֹת בָּהָר
וּנְגֹעַ בְּקָצֵהוּ כָּל־הַנֹּגֵעַ בָּהָר מוֹת יוּמָת: יג לֹא־תִגַּע בּוֹ יָד
כִּי־סָקוֹל יִסָּקֵל אוֹ־יָרֹה יִיָּרֶה אִם־בְּהֵמָה אִם־אִישׁ לֹא יִחְיֶה
בִּמְשֹׁךְ הַיֹּבֵל הֵמָּה יַעֲלוּ בָהָר: [שלישי] יד וַיֵּרֶד מֹשֶׁה מִן־הָהָר
אֶל־הָעָם וַיְקַדֵּשׁ אֶת־הָעָם וַיְכַבְּסוּ שִׂמְלֹתָם: טו וַיֹּאמֶר
אֶל־הָעָם הֱיוּ נְכֹנִים לִשְׁלֹשֶׁת יָמִים אַל־תִּגְּשׁוּ אֶל־אִשָּׁה:
טז וַיְהִי בַיּוֹם הַשְּׁלִישִׁי בִּהְיֹת הַבֹּקֶר וַיְהִי קֹלֹת וּבְרָקִים
וְעָנָן כָּבֵד עַל־הָהָר וְקֹל שֹׁפָר חָזָק מְאֹד וַיֶּחֱרַד כָּל־הָעָם
אֲשֶׁר בַּמַּחֲנֶה: יז וַיּוֹצֵא מֹשֶׁה אֶת־הָעָם לִקְרַאת הָאֱלֹהִים

מִן־הַמַּחֲנֶה וַיִּתְיַצְּבוּ בְּתַחְתִּית הָהָר: יח וְהַר סִינַי עָשַׁן כֻּלּוֹ
מִפְּנֵי אֲשֶׁר יָרַד עָלָיו יהוה בָּאֵשׁ וַיַּעַל עֲשָׁנוֹ כְּעֶשֶׁן הַכִּבְשָׁן
וַיֶּחֱרַד כָּל־הָהָר מְאֹד: יט וַיְהִי קוֹל הַשֹּׁפָר הוֹלֵךְ וְחָזֵק מְאֹד
מֹשֶׁה יְדַבֵּר וְהָאֱלֹהִים יַעֲנֶנּוּ בְקוֹל: [רביעי] כ וַיֵּרֶד יְהוָה עַל־
הַר סִינַי אֶל־רֹאשׁ הָהָר וַיִּקְרָא יְהוָה לְמֹשֶׁה אֶל־רֹאשׁ
הָהָר וַיַּעַל מֹשֶׁה: כא וַיֹּאמֶר יהוה אֶל־מֹשֶׁה רֵד הָעֵד בָּעָם
פֶּן־יֶהֶרְסוּ אֶל־יהוה לִרְאוֹת וְנָפַל מִמֶּנּוּ רָב: כב וְגַם הַכֹּהֲנִים
הַנִּגָּשִׁים אֶל־יְהוָה יִתְקַדָּשׁוּ פֶּן־יִפְרֹץ בָּהֶם יְהוָה: כג וַיֹּאמֶר
מֹשֶׁה אֶל־יהוה לֹא־יוּכַל הָעָם לַעֲלֹת אֶל־הַר סִינָי כִּי־אַתָּה
הַעֵדֹתָה בָּנוּ לֵאמֹר הַגְבֵּל אֶת־הָהָר וְקִדַּשְׁתּוֹ: כד וַיֹּאמֶר
אֵלָיו יהוה לֶךְ־רֵד וְעָלִיתָ אַתָּה וְאַהֲרֹן עִמָּךְ וְהַכֹּהֲנִים
וְהָעָם אַל־יֶהֶרְסוּ לַעֲלֹת אֶל־יְהוָה פֶּן־יִפְרָץ־בָּם: כה וַיֵּרֶד
מֹשֶׁה אֶל־הָעָם וַיֹּאמֶר אֲלֵהֶם: ס כ א וַיְדַבֵּר אֱלֹהִים
אֵת כָּל־הַדְּבָרִים הָאֵלֶּה לֵאמֹר: ס ב אָנֹכִי יְהוָה אֱלֹהֶיךָ
אֲשֶׁר הוֹצֵאתִיךָ מֵאֶרֶץ מִצְרַיִם מִבֵּית עֲבָדִים: ג לֹא־יִהְיֶה
לְךָ אֱלֹהִים אֲחֵרִים עַל־פָּנָי: ד לֹא־תַעֲשֶׂה לְךָ פֶסֶל וְכָל־
תְּמוּנָה אֲשֶׁר בַּשָּׁמַיִם מִמַּעַל וַאֲשֶׁר בָּאָרֶץ מִתָּחַת וַאֲשֶׁר
בַּמַּיִם מִתַּחַת לָאָרֶץ: ה לֹא־תִשְׁתַּחֲוֶה לָהֶם וְלֹא תָעָבְדֵם
כִּי אָנֹכִי יְהוָה אֱלֹהֶיךָ אֵל קַנָּא פֹּקֵד עֲוֹן אָבֹת עַל־בָּנִים
עַל־שִׁלֵּשִׁים וְעַל־רִבֵּעִים לְשֹׂנְאָי: ו וְעֹשֶׂה חֶסֶד לַאֲלָפִים
לְאֹהֲבַי וּלְשֹׁמְרֵי מִצְוֹתָי: ס ז לֹא תִשָּׂא אֶת־שֵׁם־יְהוָה
אֱלֹהֶיךָ לַשָּׁוְא כִּי לֹא יְנַקֶּה יהוה אֵת אֲשֶׁר־יִשָּׂא אֶת־שְׁמוֹ
לַשָּׁוְא: פ ח זָכוֹר אֶת־יוֹם הַשַּׁבָּת לְקַדְּשׁוֹ: ט שֵׁשֶׁת יָמִים
תַּעֲבֹד וְעָשִׂיתָ כָּל־מְלַאכְתֶּךָ: י וְיוֹם הַשְּׁבִיעִי שַׁבָּת לַיהוָה
אֱלֹהֶיךָ לֹא־תַעֲשֶׂה כָל־מְלָאכָה אַתָּה | וּבִנְךָ וּבִתֶּךָ עַבְדְּךָ

וַאֲמָתְךָ֙ וּבְהֶמְתֶּ֔ךָ וְגֵרְךָ֖ אֲשֶׁ֥ר בִּשְׁעָרֶֽיךָ׃ יא כִּ֣י שֵֽׁשֶׁת־יָמִ֡ים
עָשָׂ֣ה יְהוָה֩ אֶת־הַשָּׁמַ֨יִם וְאֶת־הָאָ֜רֶץ אֶת־הַיָּם֙ וְאֶת־כָּל־
אֲשֶׁר־בָּ֔ם וַיָּ֖נַח בַּיּ֣וֹם הַשְּׁבִיעִ֑י עַל־כֵּ֗ן בֵּרַ֧ךְ יְהוָ֛ה אֶת־י֥וֹם
הַשַּׁבָּ֖ת וַֽיְקַדְּשֵֽׁהוּ׃ ס יב כַּבֵּ֥ד אֶת־אָבִ֖יךָ וְאֶת־אִמֶּ֑ךָ
לְמַ֙עַן֙ יַאֲרִכ֣וּן יָמֶ֔יךָ עַ֚ל הָאֲדָמָ֔ה אֲשֶׁר־יְהוָ֥ה אֱלֹהֶ֖יךָ נֹתֵ֥ן
לָֽךְ׃ יג לֹ֣א תִרְצָ֖ח לֹ֣א תִנְאָ֑ף לֹ֣א תִגְנֹ֔ב לֹ֥א תַעֲנֶ֥ה בְרֵעֲךָ֖ עֵ֥ד
שָֽׁקֶר׃ יד לֹ֥א תַחְמֹ֖ד בֵּ֣ית רֵעֶ֑ךָ לֹ֥א תַחְמֹ֞ד אֵ֣שֶׁת רֵעֶ֗ךָ וְעַבְדּ֤וֹ
וַאֲמָתוֹ֙ וְשׁוֹר֣וֹ וַחֲמֹר֔וֹ וְכֹ֖ל אֲשֶׁ֥ר לְרֵעֶֽךָ׃ [חמישי] טו וְכָל־הָעָם֩
רֹאִ֨ים אֶת־הַקּוֹלֹ֜ת וְאֶת־הַלַּפִּידִ֗ם וְאֵת֙ ק֣וֹל הַשֹּׁפָ֔ר וְאֶת־
הָהָ֖ר עָשֵׁ֑ן וַיַּ֤רְא הָעָם֙ וַיָּנֻ֔עוּ וַיַּֽעַמְד֖וּ מֵרָחֹֽק׃ טז וַיֹּֽאמְרוּ֙ אֶל־
מֹשֶׁ֔ה דַּבֵּר־אַתָּ֥ה עִמָּ֖נוּ וְנִשְׁמָ֑עָה וְאַל־יְדַבֵּ֥ר עִמָּ֛נוּ אֱלֹהִ֖ים
פֶּן־נָמֽוּת׃ יז וַיֹּ֨אמֶר מֹשֶׁ֣ה אֶל־הָעָם֮ אַל־תִּירָאוּ֒ כִּ֗י לְבַֽעֲבוּר֙
נַסּ֣וֹת אֶתְכֶ֔ם בָּ֖א הָאֱלֹהִ֑ים וּבַעֲב֗וּר תִּהְיֶ֧ה יִרְאָת֛וֹ עַל־
פְּנֵיכֶ֖ם לְבִלְתִּ֥י תֶחֱטָֽאוּ׃ יח וַיַּעֲמֹ֥ד הָעָ֖ם מֵרָחֹ֑ק וּמֹשֶׁה֙ נִגַּ֣שׁ
אֶל־הָעֲרָפֶ֔ל אֲשֶׁר־שָׁ֖ם הָאֱלֹהִֽים׃ ס יט וַיֹּ֤אמֶר יְהוָה֙
אֶל־מֹשֶׁ֔ה כֹּ֥ה תֹאמַ֖ר אֶל־בְּנֵ֣י יִשְׂרָאֵ֑ל אַתֶּ֣ם רְאִיתֶ֔ם כִּ֚י
מִן־הַשָּׁמַ֔יִם דִּבַּ֖רְתִּי עִמָּכֶֽם׃ כ לֹ֥א תַעֲשׂ֖וּן אִתִּ֑י אֱלֹ֤הֵי כֶ֙סֶף֙
וֵאלֹהֵ֣י זָהָ֔ב לֹ֥א תַעֲשׂ֖וּ לָכֶֽם׃ כא מִזְבַּ֣ח אֲדָמָה֮ תַּעֲשֶׂה־לִּי֒
וְזָבַחְתָּ֣ עָלָ֗יו אֶת־עֹלֹתֶ֙יךָ֙ וְאֶת־שְׁלָמֶ֔יךָ אֶת־צֹאנְךָ֖ וְאֶת־
בְּקָרֶ֑ךָ בְּכָל־הַמָּקוֹם֙ אֲשֶׁ֣ר אַזְכִּ֣יר אֶת־שְׁמִ֔י אָב֥וֹא אֵלֶ֖יךָ
וּבֵרַכְתִּֽיךָ׃ כב וְאִם־מִזְבַּ֤ח אֲבָנִים֙ תַּֽעֲשֶׂה־לִּ֔י לֹֽא־תִבְנֶ֥ה אֶתְהֶ֖ן
גָּזִ֑ית כִּ֧י חַרְבְּךָ֛ הֵנַ֥פְתָּ עָלֶ֖יהָ וַתְּחַלְלֶֽהָ׃ כג וְלֹֽא־תַעֲלֶ֥ה בְמַעֲלֹ֖ת
עַל־מִזְבְּחִ֑י אֲשֶׁ֛ר לֹֽא־תִגָּלֶ֥ה עֶרְוָתְךָ֖ עָלָֽיו׃

מפטיר לשבועות

The following מפטיר is read from the second ספר תורה on both days of שבועות:

במדבר כח כו וּבְיוֹם הַבִּכּוּרִים בְּהַקְרִיבְכֶם מִנְחָה חֲדָשָׁה
לַיהוָה בְּשָׁבֻעֹתֵיכֶם מִקְרָא־קֹדֶשׁ יִהְיֶה לָכֶם כָּל־מְלֶאכֶת
עֲבֹדָה לֹא תַעֲשׂוּ: כז וְהִקְרַבְתֶּם עוֹלָה לְרֵיחַ נִיחֹחַ לַיהוָה
פָּרִים בְּנֵי־בָקָר שְׁנַיִם אַיִל אֶחָד שִׁבְעָה כְבָשִׂים בְּנֵי שָׁנָה:
כח וּמִנְחָתָם סֹלֶת בְּלוּלָה בַשָּׁמֶן שְׁלֹשָׁה עֶשְׂרֹנִים לַפָּר
הָאֶחָד שְׁנֵי עֶשְׂרֹנִים לָאַיִל הָאֶחָד: כט עִשָּׂרוֹן עִשָּׂרוֹן לַכֶּבֶשׂ
הָאֶחָד לְשִׁבְעַת הַכְּבָשִׂים: ל שְׂעִיר עִזִּים אֶחָד לְכַפֵּר עֲלֵיכֶם:
לא מִלְּבַד עֹלַת הַתָּמִיד וּמִנְחָתוֹ תַּעֲשׂוּ תְּמִימִם יִהְיוּ־לָכֶם
וְנִסְכֵּיהֶם:

הפטרה ליום טוב ראשון של שבועות

א וַיְהִי | בִּשְׁלֹשִׁים שָׁנָה בָּרְבִיעִי בַּחֲמִשָּׁה לַחֹדֶשׁ וַאֲנִי
בְתוֹךְ־הַגּוֹלָה עַל־נְהַר־כְּבָר נִפְתְּחוּ הַשָּׁמַיִם וָאֶרְאֶה מַרְאוֹת
אֱלֹהִים: ב בַּחֲמִשָּׁה לַחֹדֶשׁ הִיא הַשָּׁנָה הַחֲמִישִׁית לְגָלוּת
הַמֶּלֶךְ יוֹיָכִין: ג הָיֹה הָיָה דְבַר־יְהוָה אֶל־יְחֶזְקֵאל בֶּן־בּוּזִי
הַכֹּהֵן בְּאֶרֶץ כַּשְׂדִּים עַל־נְהַר־כְּבָר וַתְּהִי עָלָיו שָׁם יַד־יְהוָה:
ד וָאֵרֶא וְהִנֵּה רוּחַ סְעָרָה בָּאָה מִן־הַצָּפוֹן עָנָן גָּדוֹל וְאֵשׁ
מִתְלַקַּחַת וְנֹגַהּ לוֹ סָבִיב וּמִתּוֹכָהּ כְּעֵין הַחַשְׁמַל מִתּוֹךְ
הָאֵשׁ: ה וּמִתּוֹכָהּ דְּמוּת אַרְבַּע חַיּוֹת וְזֶה מַרְאֵיהֶן דְּמוּת
אָדָם לָהֵנָּה: ו וְאַרְבָּעָה פָנִים לְאֶחָת וְאַרְבַּע כְּנָפַיִם לְאַחַת
לָהֶם: ז וְרַגְלֵיהֶם רֶגֶל יְשָׁרָה וְכַף רַגְלֵיהֶם כְּכַף רֶגֶל עֵגֶל
וְנֹצְצִים כְּעֵין נְחֹשֶׁת קָלָל: ח וידו▽ אָדָם מִתַּחַת כַּנְפֵיהֶם
עַל אַרְבַּעַת רִבְעֵיהֶם וּפְנֵיהֶם וְכַנְפֵיהֶם לְאַרְבַּעְתָּם: ט חֹבְרֹת

▽ וִידֵי

אִשָּׁה אֶל־אֲחוֹתָהּ כַּנְפֵיהֶם לֹא־יִסַּבּוּ בְלֶכְתָּן אִישׁ אֶל־עֵבֶר
פָּנָיו יֵלֵכוּ: י וּדְמוּת פְּנֵיהֶם פְּנֵי אָדָם וּפְנֵי אַרְיֵה אֶל־הַיָּמִין
לְאַרְבַּעְתָּם וּפְנֵי־שׁוֹר מֵהַשְּׂמֹאול לְאַרְבַּעְתָּן וּפְנֵי־נֶשֶׁר
לְאַרְבַּעְתָּן: יא וּפְנֵיהֶם וְכַנְפֵיהֶם פְּרֻדוֹת מִלְמָעְלָה לְאִישׁ
שְׁתַּיִם חֹבְרוֹת אִישׁ וּשְׁתַּיִם מְכַסּוֹת אֵת גְּוִיֹּתֵיהֶנָה: יב וְאִישׁ
אֶל־עֵבֶר פָּנָיו יֵלֵכוּ אֶל אֲשֶׁר יִהְיֶה־שָׁמָּה הָרוּחַ לָלֶכֶת יֵלֵכוּ
לֹא יִסַּבּוּ בְּלֶכְתָּן: יג וּדְמוּת הַחַיּוֹת מַרְאֵיהֶם כְּגַחֲלֵי־אֵשׁ
בֹּעֲרוֹת כְּמַרְאֵה הַלַּפִּדִים הִיא מִתְהַלֶּכֶת בֵּין הַחַיּוֹת וְנֹגַהּ
לָאֵשׁ וּמִן־הָאֵשׁ יוֹצֵא בָרָק: יד וְהַחַיּוֹת רָצוֹא וָשׁוֹב כְּמַרְאֵה
הַבָּזָק: טו וָאֵרֶא הַחַיּוֹת וְהִנֵּה אוֹפַן אֶחָד בָּאָרֶץ אֵצֶל הַחַיּוֹת
לְאַרְבַּעַת פָּנָיו: טז מַרְאֵה הָאוֹפַנִּים וּמַעֲשֵׂיהֶם כְּעֵין תַּרְשִׁישׁ
וּדְמוּת אֶחָד לְאַרְבַּעְתָּן וּמַרְאֵיהֶם וּמַעֲשֵׂיהֶם כַּאֲשֶׁר
יִהְיֶה הָאוֹפַן בְּתוֹךְ הָאוֹפָן: יז עַל־אַרְבַּעַת רִבְעֵיהֶן בְּלֶכְתָּם
יֵלֵכוּ לֹא יִסַּבּוּ בְּלֶכְתָּן: יח וְגַבֵּיהֶן וְגֹבַהּ לָהֶם וְיִרְאָה לָהֶם
וְגַבֹּתָם מְלֵאֹת עֵינַיִם סָבִיב לְאַרְבַּעְתָּן: יט וּבְלֶכֶת הַחַיּוֹת
יֵלְכוּ הָאוֹפַנִּים אֶצְלָם וּבְהִנָּשֵׂא הַחַיּוֹת מֵעַל הָאָרֶץ יִנָּשְׂאוּ
הָאוֹפַנִּים: כ עַל אֲשֶׁר יִהְיֶה־שָּׁם הָרוּחַ לָלֶכֶת יֵלֵכוּ שָׁמָּה
הָרוּחַ לָלֶכֶת וְהָאוֹפַנִּים יִנָּשְׂאוּ לְעֻמָּתָם כִּי רוּחַ הַחַיָּה
בָּאוֹפַנִּים: כא בְּלֶכְתָּם יֵלֵכוּ וּבְעָמְדָם יַעֲמֹדוּ וּבְהִנָּשְׂאָם מֵעַל
הָאָרֶץ יִנָּשְׂאוּ הָאוֹפַנִּים לְעֻמָּתָם כִּי רוּחַ הַחַיָּה בָּאוֹפַנִּים:
כב וּדְמוּת עַל־רָאשֵׁי הַחַיָּה רָקִיעַ כְּעֵין הַקֶּרַח הַנּוֹרָא נָטוּי
עַל־רָאשֵׁיהֶם מִלְמָעְלָה: כג וְתַחַת הָרָקִיעַ כַּנְפֵיהֶם יְשָׁרוֹת
אִשָּׁה אֶל־אֲחוֹתָהּ לְאִישׁ שְׁתַּיִם מְכַסּוֹת לָהֵנָּה וּלְאִישׁ
שְׁתַּיִם מְכַסּוֹת לָהֵנָּה אֵת גְּוִיֹּתֵיהֶם: כד וָאֶשְׁמַע אֶת־קוֹל
כַּנְפֵיהֶם כְּקוֹל מַיִם רַבִּים כְּקוֹל־שַׁדַּי בְּלֶכְתָּם קוֹל הֲמֻלָּה
כְּקוֹל מַחֲנֶה בְּעָמְדָם תְּרַפֶּינָה כַנְפֵיהֶן: כה וַיְהִי־קוֹל מֵעַל

לָרָקִ֫יעַ אֲשֶׁר עַל־רֹאשָׁם בְּעׇמְדָם תְּרַפֶּינָה כַנְפֵיהֶן׃ כו וּמִמַּ֫עַל
לָרָקִ֫יעַ אֲשֶׁר עַל־רֹאשָׁם כְּמַרְאֵה אֶבֶן־סַפִּיר דְּמוּת כִּסֵּא
וְעַל דְּמוּת הַכִּסֵּא דְּמוּת כְּמַרְאֵה אָדָם עָלָיו מִלְמָעְלָה׃
כז וָאֵרֶא | כְּעֵין חַשְׁמַל כְּמַרְאֵה־אֵשׁ בֵּית־לָהּ סָבִיב מִמַּרְאֵה
מׇתְנָיו וּלְמָעְלָה וּמִמַּרְאֵה מׇתְנָיו וּלְמַטָּה רָאִיתִי כְּמַרְאֵה־
אֵשׁ וְנֹגַהּ לוֹ סָבִיב׃ כח כְּמַרְאֵה הַקֶּשֶׁת אֲשֶׁר יִהְיֶה בֶעָנָן בְּיוֹם
הַגֶּשֶׁם כֵּן מַרְאֵה הַנֹּגַהּ סָבִיב הוּא מַרְאֵה דְּמוּת כְּבוֹד־יְהֹוָה
וָאֶרְאֶה וָאֶפֹּל עַל־פָּנַי וָאֶשְׁמַע קוֹל מְדַבֵּר׃
יחזקאל ג יב וַתִּשָּׂאֵנִי רוּחַ וָאֶשְׁמַע אַחֲרַי קוֹל רַעַשׁ גָּדוֹל בָּרוּךְ
כְּבוֹד־יְהֹוָה מִמְּקוֹמוֹ׃

Continue with the blessings after the הפטרה on page 416.

קריאה ליום טוב שני של שבועות

The קריאת התורה for the second day of שבועות is the same as that of the eighth day of פסח on page 937. The מפטיר is the same as that of the first day of שבועות (page 946).

הפטרה ליום טוב שני של שבועות

חבקוק ב כ וַיהֹוָה בְּהֵיכַל קׇדְשׁוֹ הַס מִפָּנָיו כׇּל־הָאָרֶץ׃

Many say the following יַצִּיב פִּתְגָם in the הפטרה.

יַצִּיב פִּתְגָם, לְאָת וּדְגָם, בְּרִבּוֹ רִבְבָן עִירִין. עֲנֵה אֲנָא, בְּמִנְיָנָא,
דְּפַסְלִין אַרְבְּעָה טוּרִין. קֳדָמוֹהִי, לְגוֹ מוֹהִי, נְגִיד וּנְפִיק נְהַר
דִּי נוּרִין. בְּטוּר תַּלְגָּא, נְהוֹר שְׁרָגָא, וְזִיקִין דִּי נוּר וּבְעוֹרִין.
בְּרָא וּסְכָא, מַה בַּחֲשׁוֹכָא, וְעִמֵּהּ שָׁרְיָין נְהוֹרִין. רְחִיקִין צְפָא,
בְּלָא שִׁטְפָא, וּגְלַיִן לֵהּ דְּמִטַּמְּרִין. בְּעֵית מִנֵּהּ, יָת הַרְמָנֵהּ,
וּבָתְרוֹהִי עֲדֵי גְּבָרִין. יְדָעֵי הִלְכְתָא, וּמַתְנִיתָא, וְתוֹסֶפְתָּא
סִפְרָא וְסִפְרִין. מֶלֶךְ חַיָּא, לְעָלְמַיָּא, יְמַגַּר עַם לְהוֹן מְשַׁחֲרִין.
אֲמִיר עֲלֵיהוֹן, כְּחָלָא יְהוֹן, וְלָא יִתְמְנוֹן הֵיךְ עַפְרִין. יְחַוְּרוּן
כְּעַן, לְהוֹן בְּקָעַן, יְטוּפוּן נַעֲוֵי חַמְרִין. רְעוּתְהוֹן הַב, וְאַפֵּיהוֹן
צְהַב, יְנַהֲרוּן כִּנְהוֹר צַפְרִין. לִי הַב תְּקַף, וְעֵינָךְ זְקַף, חֲזִי עָרָךְ
דְּבָךְ כָּפְרִין. יְהוֹן כְּתִבְנָא, בְּגוֹ לִבְנָא, כְּאַבְנָא יִשְׁתְּקוּן חָפְרִין.
כְּקָאֳמְנָא, וְתַרְגְּמָנָא, בְּמִלּוֹי דִּבְחִיר סַפְרִין. יְהוֹנָתָן, גְּבַר עִנְוְתָן,
בְּכֵן נִמְטִין אַפְרִין.

ג א תְּפִלָּ֖ה לַחֲבַקּ֣וּק הַנָּבִ֑יא עַ֖ל שִׁגְיֹנֽוֹת׃ ב יהוה שָׁמַ֣עְתִּי
שִׁמְעֲךָ֮ יָרֵ֒אתִי֒ יהוה פָּֽעָלְךָ֙ בְּקֶ֤רֶב שָׁנִים֙ חַיֵּ֔יהוּ בְּקֶ֥רֶב שָׁנִ֖ים
תּוֹדִ֑יעַ בְּרֹ֖גֶז רַחֵ֥ם תִּזְכּֽוֹר׃ ג אֱל֙וֹהַ֙ מִתֵּימָ֣ן יָב֔וֹא וְקָד֥וֹשׁ
מֵֽהַר־פָּארָ֖ן סֶ֑לָה כִּסָּ֤ה שָׁמַ֙יִם֙ הוֹד֔וֹ וּתְהִלָּת֖וֹ מָלְאָ֥ה הָאָֽרֶץ׃
ד וְנֹ֙גַהּ֙ כָּא֣וֹר תִּֽהְיֶ֔ה קַרְנַ֥יִם מִיָּד֖וֹ ל֑וֹ וְשָׁ֖ם חֶבְי֥וֹן עֻזֹּֽה׃ ה לְפָנָ֖יו
יֵ֣לֶךְ דָּ֑בֶר וְיֵצֵ֥א רֶ֖שֶׁף לְרַגְלָֽיו׃ ו עָמַ֣ד ׀ וַיְמֹ֣דֶד אֶ֗רֶץ רָאָה֙
וַיַּתֵּ֣ר גּוֹיִ֔ם וַיִּתְפֹּֽצְצוּ֙ הַרְרֵי־עַ֔ד שַׁח֖וּ גִּבְע֣וֹת עוֹלָ֑ם הֲלִיכ֥וֹת
עוֹלָ֖ם לֽוֹ׃ ז תַּ֣חַת אָ֔וֶן רָאִ֖יתִי אָהֳלֵ֣י כוּשָׁ֑ן יִרְגְּז֕וּן יְרִיע֖וֹת
אֶ֥רֶץ מִדְיָֽן׃ ס ח הֲבִנְהָרִים֙ חָרָ֣ה יהוה אִ֤ם בַּנְּהָרִים֙ אַפֶּ֔ךָ
אִם־בַּיָּ֖ם עֶבְרָתֶ֑ךָ כִּ֤י תִרְכַּב֙ עַל־סוּסֶ֔יךָ מַרְכְּבֹתֶ֖יךָ יְשׁוּעָֽה׃
ט עֶרְיָ֤ה תֵעוֹר֙ קַשְׁתֶּ֔ךָ שְׁבֻע֥וֹת מַטּ֖וֹת אֹ֣מֶר סֶ֑לָה נְהָר֖וֹת
תְּבַקַּע־אָֽרֶץ׃ י רָא֤וּךָ יָחִ֙ילוּ֙ הָרִ֔ים זֶ֥רֶם מַ֖יִם עָבָ֑ר נָתַ֤ן תְּהוֹם֙
קוֹל֔וֹ ר֖וֹם יָדֵ֥יהוּ נָשָֽׂא׃ יא שֶׁ֥מֶשׁ יָרֵ֖חַ עָ֣מַד זְבֻ֑לָה לְא֤וֹר חִצֶּ֙יךָ֙
יְהַלֵּ֔כוּ לְנֹ֖גַהּ בְּרַ֥ק חֲנִיתֶֽךָ׃ יב בְּזַ֖עַם תִּצְעַד־אָ֑רֶץ בְּאַ֖ף תָּד֥וּשׁ
גּוֹיִֽם׃ יג יָצָ֙אתָ֙ לְיֵ֣שַׁע עַמֶּ֔ךָ לְיֵ֖שַׁע אֶת־מְשִׁיחֶ֑ךָ מָחַ֤צְתָּ רֹּאשׁ֙
מִבֵּ֣ית רָשָׁ֔ע עָר֛וֹת יְס֥וֹד עַד־צַוָּ֖אר סֶֽלָה׃ ס יד נָקַ֤בְתָּ
בְמַטָּיו֙ רֹ֣אשׁ פְּרָזָ֔ו יִסְעֲר֖וּ לַהֲפִיצֵ֑נִי עֲלִ֣יצֻתָ֔ם כְּמוֹ־לֶאֱכֹ֥ל עָנִ֖י
בַּמִּסְתָּֽר׃ טו דָּרַ֥כְתָּ בַיָּ֖ם סוּסֶ֑יךָ חֹ֖מֶר מַ֥יִם רַבִּֽים׃ טז שָׁמַ֣עְתִּי ׀
וַתִּרְגַּ֣ז בִּטְנִ֗י לְקוֹל֙ צָלֲל֣וּ שְׂפָתַ֔י יָב֥וֹא רָקָ֛ב בַּעֲצָמַ֖י וְתַחְתַּ֣י
אֶרְגָּ֑ז אֲשֶׁ֤ר אָנ֙וּחַ֙ לְי֣וֹם צָרָ֔ה לַעֲל֖וֹת לְעַ֥ם יְגוּדֶֽנּוּ׃ יז כִּֽי־תְאֵנָ֣ה
לֹֽא־תִפְרָ֗ח וְאֵ֤ין יְבוּל֙ בַּגְּפָנִ֔ים כִּחֵשׁ֙ מַעֲשֵׂה־זַ֔יִת וּשְׁדֵמ֖וֹת
לֹא־עָ֣שָׂה אֹ֑כֶל גָּזַ֤ר מִמִּכְלָה֙ צֹ֔אן וְאֵ֥ין בָּקָ֖ר בָּרְפָתִֽים׃ יח וַאֲנִ֖י
בַּיהוה אֶעְל֑וֹזָה אָגִ֖ילָה בֵּאלֹהֵ֥י יִשְׁעִֽי׃ יט יֱהֹוִ֤ה אֲדֹנָי֙ חֵילִ֔י
וַיָּ֤שֶׂם רַגְלַי֙ כָּֽאַיָּל֔וֹת וְעַ֥ל בָּמוֹתַ֖י יַדְרִכֵ֑נִי לַמְנַצֵּ֖חַ בִּנְגִינוֹתָֽי׃

Continue with the blessings after the הפטרה on page 416.

Torah Readings for Sukkot

מפטיר ליום הראשון של סוכות, ויום טוב שני

The קריאת התורה for the first two days of סוכות is the same as that of the second day of פסח (page 916). The following מפטיר is then read from the second ספר תורה:

במדבר כט יב וּבַחֲמִשָּׁה עָשָׂר יוֹם לַחֹדֶשׁ הַשְּׁבִיעִי מִקְרָא־
קֹדֶשׁ יִהְיֶה לָכֶם כָּל־מְלֶאכֶת עֲבֹדָה לֹא תַעֲשׂוּ וְחַגֹּתֶם חַג
לַיהוָה שִׁבְעַת יָמִים: יג וְהִקְרַבְתֶּם עֹלָה אִשֵּׁה רֵיחַ נִיחֹחַ
לַיהוָה פָּרִים בְּנֵי־בָקָר שְׁלֹשָׁה עָשָׂר אֵילִם שְׁנָיִם כְּבָשִׂים
בְּנֵי־שָׁנָה אַרְבָּעָה עָשָׂר תְּמִימִם יִהְיוּ: יד וּמִנְחָתָם סֹלֶת
בְּלוּלָה בַשָּׁמֶן שְׁלֹשָׁה עֶשְׂרֹנִים לַפָּר הָאֶחָד לִשְׁלֹשָׁה עָשָׂר
פָּרִים שְׁנֵי עֶשְׂרֹנִים לָאַיִל הָאֶחָד לִשְׁנֵי הָאֵילִם: טו וְעִשָּׂרוֹן
עִשָּׂרוֹן לַכֶּבֶשׂ הָאֶחָד לְאַרְבָּעָה עָשָׂר כְּבָשִׂים: טז וּשְׂעִיר־
עִזִּים אֶחָד חַטָּאת מִלְּבַד עֹלַת הַתָּמִיד מִנְחָתָהּ וְנִסְכָּהּ:

הפטרה ליום הראשון של סוכות

זכריה הִנֵּה יוֹם־בָּא לַיהוָה וְחֻלַּק שְׁלָלֵךְ בְּקִרְבֵּךְ: ב וְאָסַפְתִּי
אֶת־כָּל־הַגּוֹיִם | אֶל־יְרוּשָׁלַםִ לַמִּלְחָמָה וְנִלְכְּדָה הָעִיר
וְנָשַׁסּוּ הַבָּתִּים וְהַנָּשִׁים תשגלנה▽ וְיָצָא חֲצִי הָעִיר בַּגּוֹלָה
וְיֶתֶר הָעָם לֹא יִכָּרֵת מִן־הָעִיר: ג וְיָצָא יהוה וְנִלְחַם בַּגּוֹיִם
הָהֵם כְּיוֹם הִלָּחֲמוֹ בְּיוֹם קְרָב: ד וְעָמְדוּ רַגְלָיו בַּיּוֹם־הַהוּא
עַל־הַר הַזֵּיתִים אֲשֶׁר עַל־פְּנֵי יְרוּשָׁלַםִ מִקֶּדֶם וְנִבְקַע הַר
הַזֵּיתִים מֵחֶצְיוֹ מִזְרָחָה וָיָמָּה גֵּיא גְּדוֹלָה מְאֹד וּמָשׁ חֲצִי
הָהָר צָפוֹנָה וְחֶצְיוֹ נֶגְבָּה: ה וְנַסְתֶּם גֵּיא־הָרַי כִּי־יַגִּיעַ גֵּי־
הָרִים אֶל־אָצַל וְנַסְתֶּם כַּאֲשֶׁר נַסְתֶּם מִפְּנֵי הָרַעַשׁ בִּימֵי
עֻזִּיָּה מֶלֶךְ־יְהוּדָה וּבָא יהוה אֱלֹהַי כָּל־קְדֹשִׁים עִמָּךְ: ו וְהָיָה

▽ תִּשָּׁכַבְנָה

בַּיּוֹם הַהוּא לֹא־יִהְיֶה אוֹר יְקָרוֹת יקפאון▽: ז וְהָיָה יוֹם־אֶחָד
הוּא יִוָּדַע לַיהוָה לֹא־יוֹם וְלֹא־לָיְלָה וְהָיָה לְעֵת־עֶרֶב יִהְיֶה־
אוֹר: ח וְהָיָה | בַּיּוֹם הַהוּא יֵצְאוּ מַיִם־חַיִּים מִירוּשָׁלַ͏ִם חֶצְיָם
אֶל־הַיָּם הַקַּדְמוֹנִי וְחֶצְיָם אֶל־הַיָּם הָאַחֲרוֹן בַּקַּיִץ וּבָחֹרֶף
יִהְיֶה: ט וְהָיָה יְהוָה לְמֶלֶךְ עַל־כָּל־הָאָרֶץ בַּיּוֹם הַהוּא יִהְיֶה
יְהוָה אֶחָד וּשְׁמוֹ אֶחָד: י יִסּוֹב כָּל־הָאָרֶץ כָּעֲרָבָה מִגֶּבַע
לְרִמּוֹן נֶגֶב יְרוּשָׁלָ͏ִם וְרָאֲמָה וְיָשְׁבָה תַחְתֶּיהָ לְמִשַּׁעַר בִּנְיָמִן
עַד־מְקוֹם שַׁעַר הָרִאשׁוֹן עַד־שַׁעַר הַפִּנִּים וּמִגְדַּל◦ חֲנַנְאֵל
עַד יִקְבֵי הַמֶּלֶךְ: יא וְיָשְׁבוּ בָהּ וְחֵרֶם לֹא יִהְיֶה־עוֹד וְיָשְׁבָה
יְרוּשָׁלַ͏ִם לָבֶטַח: ס יב וְזֹאת | תִּהְיֶה הַמַּגֵּפָה אֲשֶׁר יִגֹּף
יְהוָה אֶת־כָּל־הָעַמִּים אֲשֶׁר צָבְאוּ עַל־יְרוּשָׁלָ͏ִם הָמֵק | בְּשָׂרוֹ
וְהוּא עֹמֵד עַל־רַגְלָיו וְעֵינָיו תִּמַּקְנָה בְחֹרֵיהֶן וּלְשׁוֹנוֹ תִּמַּק
בְּפִיהֶם: יג וְהָיָה בַּיּוֹם הַהוּא תִּהְיֶה מְהוּמַת־יְהוָה רַבָּה בָּהֶם
וְהֶחֱזִיקוּ אִישׁ יַד רֵעֵהוּ וְעָלְתָה יָדוֹ עַל־יַד רֵעֵהוּ: יד וְגַם־
יְהוּדָה תִּלָּחֵם בִּירוּשָׁלָ͏ִם וְאֻסַּף חֵיל כָּל־הַגּוֹיִם סָבִיב זָהָב
וָכֶסֶף וּבְגָדִים לָרֹב מְאֹד: טו וְכֵן תִּהְיֶה מַגֵּפַת הַסּוּס הַפֶּרֶד
הַגָּמָל וְהַחֲמוֹר וְכָל־הַבְּהֵמָה אֲשֶׁר יִהְיֶה בַּמַּחֲנוֹת הָהֵמָּה
כַּמַּגֵּפָה הַזֹּאת: טז וְהָיָה כָּל־הַנּוֹתָר מִכָּל־הַגּוֹיִם הַבָּאִים
עַל־יְרוּשָׁלָ͏ִם וְעָלוּ מִדֵּי שָׁנָה בְשָׁנָה לְהִשְׁתַּחֲוֺת לְמֶלֶךְ יְהוָה
צְבָאוֹת וְלָחֹג אֶת־חַג הַסֻּכּוֹת: יז וְהָיָה אֲשֶׁר לֹא־יַעֲלֶה מֵאֵת
מִשְׁפְּחוֹת הָאָרֶץ אֶל־יְרוּשָׁלַ͏ִם לְהִשְׁתַּחֲוֺת לְמֶלֶךְ יְהוָה
צְבָאוֹת וְלֹא עֲלֵיהֶם יִהְיֶה הַגָּשֶׁם: יח וְאִם־מִשְׁפַּחַת מִצְרַיִם
לֹא־תַעֲלֶה וְלֹא בָאָה וְלֹא עֲלֵיהֶם תִּהְיֶה הַמַּגֵּפָה אֲשֶׁר יִגֹּף
יְהוָה אֶת־הַגּוֹיִם אֲשֶׁר לֹא יַעֲלוּ לָחֹג אֶת־חַג הַסֻּכּוֹת: יט

▽ וְקִפָּאוֹן

זֹאת תִּהְיֶה חַטַּאת מִצְרָיִם וְחַטַּאת כָּל־הַגּוֹיִם אֲשֶׁר לֹא
יַעֲלוּ לָחֹג אֶת־חַג הַסֻּכּוֹת: כ בַּיּוֹם הַהוּא יִהְיֶה עַל־מְצִלּוֹת
הַסּוּס קֹדֶשׁ לַיהוָה וְהָיָה הַסִּירוֹת בְּבֵית יהוה כַּמִּזְרָקִים
לִפְנֵי הַמִּזְבֵּחַ: כא וְהָיָה כָּל־סִיר בִּירוּשָׁלִַם וּבִיהוּדָה קֹדֶשׁ
לַיהוָה צְבָאוֹת וּבָאוּ כָּל־הַזֹּבְחִים וְלָקְחוּ מֵהֶם וּבִשְּׁלוּ בָהֶם
וְלֹא־יִהְיֶה כְנַעֲנִי עוֹד בְּבֵית־יהוָה צְבָאוֹת בַּיּוֹם הַהוּא:

Continue with the blessings after the הפטרה on page 416.

הפטרה ליום טוב שני של סוכות

מלכים א׳ ח ב וַיִּקָּהֲלוּ אֶל־הַמֶּלֶךְ שְׁלֹמֹה כָּל־אִישׁ יִשְׂרָאֵל
בְּיֶרַח הָאֵתָנִים בֶּחָג הוּא הַחֹדֶשׁ הַשְּׁבִיעִי: ג וַיָּבֹאוּ כֹּל
זִקְנֵי יִשְׂרָאֵל וַיִּשְׂאוּ הַכֹּהֲנִים אֶת־הָאָרוֹן: ד וַיַּעֲלוּ אֶת־אֲרוֹן
יהוה וְאֶת־אֹהֶל מוֹעֵד וְאֶת־כָּל־כְּלֵי הַקֹּדֶשׁ אֲשֶׁר בָּאֹהֶל
וַיַּעֲלוּ אֹתָם הַכֹּהֲנִים וְהַלְוִיִּם: ה וְהַמֶּלֶךְ שְׁלֹמֹה וְכָל־עֲדַת
יִשְׂרָאֵל הַנּוֹעָדִים עָלָיו אִתּוֹ לִפְנֵי הָאָרוֹן מְזַבְּחִים צֹאן
וּבָקָר אֲשֶׁר לֹא־יִסָּפְרוּ וְלֹא יִמָּנוּ מֵרֹב: ו וַיָּבִאוּ הַכֹּהֲנִים
אֶת־אֲרוֹן בְּרִית־יהוָה אֶל־מְקוֹמוֹ אֶל־דְּבִיר הַבַּיִת אֶל־קֹדֶשׁ
הַקֳּדָשִׁים אֶל־תַּחַת כַּנְפֵי הַכְּרוּבִים: ז כִּי הַכְּרוּבִים פֹּרְשִׂים
כְּנָפַיִם אֶל־מְקוֹם הָאָרוֹן וַיָּסֹכּוּ הַכְּרֻבִים עַל־הָאָרוֹן וְעַל־
בַּדָּיו מִלְמָעְלָה: ח וַיַּאֲרִכוּ הַבַּדִּים וַיֵּרָאוּ רָאשֵׁי הַבַּדִּים
מִן־הַקֹּדֶשׁ עַל־פְּנֵי הַדְּבִיר וְלֹא יֵרָאוּ הַחוּצָה וַיִּהְיוּ שָׁם עַד
הַיּוֹם הַזֶּה: ט אֵין בָּאָרוֹן רַק שְׁנֵי לֻחוֹת הָאֲבָנִים אֲשֶׁר הִנִּחַ
שָׁם מֹשֶׁה בְּחֹרֵב אֲשֶׁר כָּרַת יהוה עִם־בְּנֵי יִשְׂרָאֵל בְּצֵאתָם
מֵאֶרֶץ מִצְרָיִם: י וַיְהִי בְּצֵאת הַכֹּהֲנִים מִן־הַקֹּדֶשׁ וְהֶעָנָן
מָלֵא אֶת־בֵּית יהוָה: יא וְלֹא־יָכְלוּ הַכֹּהֲנִים לַעֲמֹד לְשָׁרֵת
מִפְּנֵי הֶעָנָן כִּי־מָלֵא כְבוֹד־יהוָה אֶת־בֵּית יהוָה: ס יב אָז

אָמַ֣ר שְׁלֹמֹ֔ה יְהוָ֣ה אָמַ֔ר לִשְׁכֹּ֖ן בָּעֲרָפֶֽל׃ יג בָּנֹ֥ה בָנִ֛יתִי בֵּ֥ית
זְבֻ֖ל לָ֑ךְ מָכ֥וֹן לְשִׁבְתְּךָ֖ עוֹלָמִֽים׃ יד וַיַּסֵּ֤ב הַמֶּ֙לֶךְ֙ אֶת־פָּנָ֔יו
וַיְבָ֕רֶךְ אֵ֖ת כָּל־קְהַ֣ל יִשְׂרָאֵ֑ל וְכָל־קְהַ֥ל יִשְׂרָאֵ֖ל עֹמֵֽד׃
טו וַיֹּ֗אמֶר בָּר֤וּךְ יְהוָה֙ אֱלֹהֵ֣י יִשְׂרָאֵ֔ל אֲשֶׁר֙ דִּבֶּ֣ר בְּפִ֔יו אֵ֖ת דָּוִ֣ד
אָבִ֑י וּבְיָד֥וֹ מִלֵּ֖א לֵאמֹֽר׃ טז מִן־הַיּ֗וֹם אֲשֶׁ֨ר הוֹצֵ֜אתִי אֶת־עַמִּ֣י
אֶת־יִשְׂרָאֵל֮ מִמִּצְרַיִם֒ לֹֽא־בָחַ֣רְתִּי בְעִ֗יר מִכֹּל֙ שִׁבְטֵ֣י יִשְׂרָאֵ֔ל
לִבְנ֣וֹת בַּ֔יִת לִהְי֥וֹת שְׁמִ֖י שָׁ֑ם וָאֶבְחַ֣ר בְּדָוִ֔ד לִהְי֖וֹת עַל־עַמִּ֥י
יִשְׂרָאֵֽל׃ יז וַיְהִ֕י עִם־לְבַ֖ב דָּוִ֣ד אָבִ֑י לִבְנ֣וֹת בַּ֔יִת לְשֵׁ֥ם יְהוָ֖ה
אֱלֹהֵ֥י יִשְׂרָאֵֽל׃ יח וַיֹּ֤אמֶר יְהוָה֙ אֶל־דָּוִ֣ד אָבִ֔י יַ֚עַן אֲשֶׁ֣ר הָיָ֣ה
עִם־לְבָבְךָ֔ לִבְנ֥וֹת בַּ֖יִת לִשְׁמִ֑י הֱטִיבֹ֕תָ כִּ֥י הָיָ֖ה עִם־לְבָבֶֽךָ׃
יט רַ֣ק אַתָּ֔ה לֹ֥א תִבְנֶ֖ה הַבָּ֑יִת כִּ֤י אִם־בִּנְךָ֙ הַיֹּצֵ֣א מֵחֲלָצֶ֔יךָ
הֽוּא־יִבְנֶ֥ה הַבַּ֖יִת לִשְׁמִֽי׃ כ וַיָּ֣קֶם יְהוָ֔ה אֶת־דְּבָר֖וֹ אֲשֶׁ֣ר דִּבֵּ֑ר
וָאָקֻ֡ם תַּחַת֩ דָּוִ֨ד אָבִ֜י וָאֵשֵׁ֣ב ׀ עַל־כִּסֵּ֣א יִשְׂרָאֵ֗ל כַּֽאֲשֶׁר֙ דִּבֶּ֣ר
יְהוָ֔ה וָאֶבְנֶ֣ה הַבַּ֔יִת לְשֵׁ֥ם יְהוָ֖ה אֱלֹהֵ֥י יִשְׂרָאֵֽל׃ כא וָאָשִׂ֨ם שָׁ֤ם
מָקוֹם֙ לָֽאָר֔וֹן אֲשֶׁר־שָׁ֖ם בְּרִ֣ית יְהוָ֑ה אֲשֶׁ֤ר כָּרַת֙ עִם־אֲבֹתֵ֔ינוּ
בְּהוֹצִיא֥וֹ אֹתָ֖ם מֵאֶ֥רֶץ מִצְרָֽיִם׃

Continue with the blessings after the הפטרה on page 416

יום א׳ של חול המועד סוכות

במדבר כט יז וּבַיּ֤וֹם הַשֵּׁנִי֙ פָּרִ֣ים בְּנֵי־בָקָ֔ר שְׁנֵ֖ים עָשָׂ֑ר אֵילִ֥ם
שְׁנַ֛יִם כְּבָשִׂ֥ים בְּנֵי־שָׁנָ֛ה אַרְבָּעָ֥ה עָשָׂ֖ר תְּמִימִֽם׃ יח וּמִנְחָתָ֣ם
וְנִסְכֵּיהֶ֡ם לַ֠פָּרִים לָאֵילִ֧ם וְלַכְּבָשִׂ֛ים בְּמִסְפָּרָ֖ם כַּמִּשְׁפָּֽט׃
יט וּשְׂעִיר־עִזִּ֥ים אֶחָ֖ד חַטָּ֑את מִלְּבַד֙ עֹלַ֣ת הַתָּמִ֔יד וּמִנְחָתָ֖הּ
וְנִסְכֵּיהֶֽם׃ [לוי] כ וּבַיּ֧וֹם הַשְּׁלִישִׁ֛י פָּרִ֥ים עַשְׁתֵּי־עָשָׂ֖ר אֵילִ֣ם
שְׁנָ֑יִם כְּבָשִׂ֧ים בְּנֵי־שָׁנָ֛ה אַרְבָּעָ֥ה עָשָׂ֖ר תְּמִימִֽם׃ כא וּמִנְחָתָ֣ם
וְנִסְכֵּיהֶ֡ם לַ֠פָּרִים לָאֵילִ֧ם וְלַכְּבָשִׂ֛ים בְּמִסְפָּרָ֖ם כַּמִּשְׁפָּֽט׃

כב וּשְׂעִיר חַטָּאת אֶחָד מִלְּבַד עֹלַת הַתָּמִיד וּמִנְחָתָהּ וְנִסְכָּהּ׃
[שלישי] כג וּבַיּוֹם הָרְבִיעִי פָּרִים עֲשָׂרָה אֵילִם שְׁנָיִם כְּבָשִׂים
בְּנֵי־שָׁנָה אַרְבָּעָה עָשָׂר תְּמִימִם׃ כד מִנְחָתָם וְנִסְכֵּיהֶם
לַפָּרִים לָאֵילִם וְלַכְּבָשִׂים בְּמִסְפָּרָם כַּמִּשְׁפָּט׃ כה וּשְׂעִיר־
עִזִּים אֶחָד חַטָּאת מִלְּבַד עֹלַת הַתָּמִיד מִנְחָתָהּ וְנִסְכָּהּ׃

For רְבִיעִי repeat the first two עֲלִיּוֹת.

יום ב׳ של חול המועד סוכות

במדבר כט כ וּבַיּוֹם הַשְּׁלִישִׁי פָּרִים עַשְׁתֵּי־עָשָׂר אֵילִם שְׁנָיִם
כְּבָשִׂים בְּנֵי־שָׁנָה אַרְבָּעָה עָשָׂר תְּמִימִם׃ כא וּמִנְחָתָם
וְנִסְכֵּיהֶם לַפָּרִים לָאֵילִם וְלַכְּבָשִׂים בְּמִסְפָּרָם כב וּשְׂעִיר
חַטָּאת אֶחָד מִלְּבַד עֹלַת הַתָּמִיד וּמִנְחָתָהּ וְנִסְכָּהּ׃ כַּמִּשְׁפָּט׃
[לוי] כג וּבַיּוֹם הָרְבִיעִי פָּרִים עֲשָׂרָה אֵילִם שְׁנָיִם כְּבָשִׂים
בְּנֵי־שָׁנָה אַרְבָּעָה עָשָׂר תְּמִימִם׃ כד מִנְחָתָם וְנִסְכֵּיהֶם
לַפָּרִים לָאֵילִם וְלַכְּבָשִׂים בְּמִסְפָּרָם כַּמִּשְׁפָּט׃ כה וּשְׂעִיר־
עִזִּים אֶחָד חַטָּאת מִלְּבַד עֹלַת הַתָּמִיד מִנְחָתָהּ וְנִסְכָּהּ׃
[שלישי] כו וּבַיּוֹם הַחֲמִישִׁי פָּרִים תִּשְׁעָה אֵילִם שְׁנָיִם כְּבָשִׂים
בְּנֵי־שָׁנָה אַרְבָּעָה עָשָׂר תְּמִימִם׃ כז וּמִנְחָתָם וְנִסְכֵּיהֶם
לַפָּרִים לָאֵילִם וְלַכְּבָשִׂים בְּמִסְפָּרָם כַּמִּשְׁפָּט׃ כח וּשְׂעִיר
חַטָּאת אֶחָד מִלְּבַד עֹלַת הַתָּמִיד וּמִנְחָתָהּ וְנִסְכָּהּ׃

For רְבִיעִי repeat the first two עֲלִיּוֹת.

יום ג׳ של חול המועד סוכות

במדבר כט כג וּבַיּוֹם הָרְבִיעִי פָּרִים עֲשָׂרָה אֵילִם שְׁנָיִם כְּבָשִׂים
בְּנֵי־שָׁנָה אַרְבָּעָה עָשָׂר תְּמִימִם׃ כד מִנְחָתָם וְנִסְכֵּיהֶם
לַפָּרִים לָאֵילִם וְלַכְּבָשִׂים בְּמִסְפָּרָם כַּמִּשְׁפָּט׃ כה וּשְׂעִיר־
עִזִּים אֶחָד חַטָּאת מִלְּבַד עֹלַת הַתָּמִיד מִנְחָתָהּ וְנִסְכָּהּ׃
[לוי] כו וּבַיּוֹם הַחֲמִישִׁי פָּרִים תִּשְׁעָה אֵילִם שְׁנָיִם כְּבָשִׂים

בְּנֵֽי־שָׁנָ֛ה אַרְבָּעָ֥ה עָשָׂ֖ר תְּמִימִֽם׃ כז וּמִנְחָתָ֣ם וְנִסְכֵּיהֶ֗ם
לַ֠פָּרִים לָאֵילִ֧ם וְלַכְּבָשִׂ֛ים בְּמִסְפָּרָ֖ם כַּמִּשְׁפָּֽט׃ כח וּשְׂעִ֥יר
חַטָּ֖את אֶחָ֑ד מִלְּבַד֙ עֹלַ֣ת הַתָּמִ֔יד וּמִנְחָתָ֖הּ וְנִסְכָּֽהּ׃
[שלישי] כט וּבַיּ֧וֹם הַשִּׁשִּׁ֛י פָּרִ֥ים שְׁמֹנָ֖ה אֵילִ֣ם שְׁנָ֑יִם כְּבָשִׂ֛ים
בְּנֵֽי־שָׁנָ֛ה אַרְבָּעָ֥ה עָשָׂ֖ר תְּמִימִֽם׃ ל וּמִנְחָתָ֣ם וְנִסְכֵּיהֶ֗ם
לַ֠פָּרִים לָאֵילִ֧ם וְלַכְּבָשִׂ֛ים בְּמִסְפָּרָ֖ם כַּמִּשְׁפָּֽט׃ לא וּשְׂעִ֥יר
חַטָּ֖את אֶחָ֑ד מִלְּבַד֙ עֹלַ֣ת הַתָּמִ֔יד מִנְחָתָ֖הּ וּנְסָכֶֽיהָ׃

For רְבִיעִי repeat the first two עֲלִיּוֹת.

יום ד׳ של חול המועד סוכות

במדבר כט כו וּבַיּ֧וֹם הַחֲמִישִׁ֛י פָּרִ֥ים תִּשְׁעָ֖ה אֵילִ֣ם שְׁנָ֑יִם כְּבָשִׂ֛ים
בְּנֵֽי־שָׁנָ֛ה אַרְבָּעָ֥ה עָשָׂ֖ר תְּמִימִֽם׃ כז וּמִנְחָתָ֣ם וְנִסְכֵּיהֶ֗ם לַ֠פָּרִים
לָאֵילִ֧ם וְלַכְּבָשִׂ֛ים בְּמִסְפָּרָ֖ם כַּמִּשְׁפָּֽט׃ כח וּשְׂעִ֥יר חַטָּ֖את אֶחָ֑ד
מִלְּבַד֙ עֹלַ֣ת הַתָּמִ֔יד וּמִנְחָתָ֖הּ וְנִסְכָּֽהּ׃ [לוי] כט וּבַיּ֧וֹם הַשִּׁשִּׁ֛י
פָּרִ֥ים שְׁמֹנָ֖ה אֵילִ֣ם שְׁנָ֑יִם כְּבָשִׂ֛ים בְּנֵֽי־שָׁנָ֛ה אַרְבָּעָ֥ה עָשָׂ֖ר
תְּמִימִֽם׃ ל וּמִנְחָתָ֣ם וְנִסְכֵּיהֶ֗ם לַ֠פָּרִים לָאֵילִ֧ם וְלַכְּבָשִׂ֛ים
בְּמִסְפָּרָ֖ם כַּמִּשְׁפָּֽט׃ לא וּשְׂעִ֥יר חַטָּ֖את אֶחָ֑ד מִלְּבַד֙ עֹלַ֣ת
הַתָּמִ֔יד מִנְחָתָ֖הּ וּנְסָכֶֽיהָ׃ ס [שלישי] לב וּבַיּ֧וֹם הַשְּׁבִיעִ֛י
פָּרִ֥ים שִׁבְעָ֖ה אֵילִ֣ם שְׁנָ֑יִם כְּבָשִׂ֛ים בְּנֵֽי־שָׁנָ֛ה אַרְבָּעָ֥ה עָשָׂ֖ר
תְּמִימִֽם׃ לג וּמִנְחָתָ֣ם וְנִסְכֵּהֶ֗ם לַ֠פָּרִים לָאֵילִ֧ם וְלַכְּבָשִׂ֛ים
בְּמִסְפָּרָ֖ם כְּמִשְׁפָּטָֽם׃ לד וּשְׂעִ֥יר חַטָּ֖את אֶחָ֑ד מִלְּבַד֙ עֹלַ֣ת
הַתָּמִ֔יד מִנְחָתָ֖הּ וְנִסְכָּֽהּ׃

For רְבִיעִי repeat the first two עֲלִיּוֹת.

קריאה להושענה רבה

במדבר כט כו וּבַיּ֧וֹם הַחֲמִישִׁ֛י פָּרִ֥ים תִּשְׁעָ֖ה אֵילִ֣ם שְׁנָ֑יִם
כְּבָשִׂ֛ים בְּנֵֽי־שָׁנָ֛ה אַרְבָּעָ֥ה עָשָׂ֖ר תְּמִימִֽם׃ כז וּמִנְחָתָ֣ם
וְנִסְכֵּיהֶ֗ם לַ֠פָּרִים לָאֵילִ֧ם וְלַכְּבָשִׂ֛ים בְּמִסְפָּרָ֖ם כַּמִּשְׁפָּֽט׃

כח וּשְׂעִ֥יר חַטָּ֖את אֶחָ֑ד מִלְּבַד֙ עֹלַ֣ת הַתָּמִ֔יד וּמִנְחָתָ֖הּ
וְנִסְכָּֽהּ׃ [לוי] כט וּבַיּ֧וֹם הַשִּׁשִּׁ֛י פָּרִ֥ים שְׁמֹנָ֖ה אֵילִ֣ם שְׁנָ֑יִם
כְּבָשִׂ֥ים בְּנֵֽי־שָׁנָ֛ה אַרְבָּעָ֥ה עָשָׂ֖ר תְּמִימִֽם׃ ל וּמִנְחָתָ֣ם
וְנִסְכֵּיהֶ֡ם לַ֠פָּרִים לָאֵילִ֧ם וְלַכְּבָשִׂ֛ים בְּמִסְפָּרָ֖ם כַּמִּשְׁפָּֽט׃
לא וּשְׂעִ֥יר חַטָּ֖את אֶחָ֑ד מִלְּבַד֙ עֹלַ֣ת הַתָּמִ֔יד מִנְחָתָ֖הּ
וּנְסָכֶֽיהָ׃ ס [שלישי] לב וּבַיּ֧וֹם הַשְּׁבִיעִ֛י פָּרִ֥ים שִׁבְעָ֖ה
אֵילִ֣ם שְׁנָ֑יִם כְּבָשִׂ֧ים בְּנֵֽי־שָׁנָ֛ה אַרְבָּעָ֥ה עָשָׂ֖ר תְּמִימִֽם׃
לג וּמִנְחָתָ֣ם וְנִסְכֵּהֶ֡ם לַ֠פָּרִים לָאֵילִ֧ם וְלַכְּבָשִׂ֛ים בְּמִסְפָּרָ֖ם
כְּמִשְׁפָּטָֽם׃ לד וּשְׂעִ֥יר חַטָּ֖את אֶחָ֑ד מִלְּבַד֙ עֹלַ֣ת הַתָּמִ֔יד
מִנְחָתָ֖הּ וְנִסְכָּֽהּ׃ ס [רביעי] כט וּבַיּ֧וֹם הַשִּׁשִּׁ֛י פָּרִ֥ים שְׁמֹנָ֖ה
אֵילִ֣ם שְׁנָ֑יִם כְּבָשִׂ֥ים בְּנֵֽי־שָׁנָ֛ה אַרְבָּעָ֥ה עָשָׂ֖ר תְּמִימִֽם׃
ל וּמִנְחָתָ֣ם וְנִסְכֵּיהֶ֡ם לַ֠פָּרִים לָאֵילִ֧ם וְלַכְּבָשִׂ֛ים בְּמִסְפָּרָ֖ם
כַּמִּשְׁפָּֽט׃ לא וּשְׂעִ֥יר חַטָּ֖את אֶחָ֑ד מִלְּבַד֙ עֹלַ֣ת הַתָּמִ֔יד
מִנְחָתָ֖הּ וּנְסָכֶֽיהָ׃ ס לב וּבַיּ֧וֹם הַשְּׁבִיעִ֛י פָּרִ֥ים שִׁבְעָ֖ה
אֵילִ֣ם שְׁנָ֑יִם כְּבָשִׂ֧ים בְּנֵֽי־שָׁנָ֛ה אַרְבָּעָ֥ה עָשָׂ֖ר תְּמִימִֽם׃
לג וּמִנְחָתָ֣ם וְנִסְכֵּהֶ֡ם לַ֠פָּרִים לָאֵילִ֧ם וְלַכְּבָשִׂ֛ים בְּמִסְפָּרָ֖ם
כְּמִשְׁפָּטָֽם׃ לד וּשְׂעִ֥יר חַטָּ֖את אֶחָ֑ד מִלְּבַד֙ עֹלַ֣ת הַתָּמִ֔יד
מִנְחָתָ֖הּ וְנִסְכָּֽהּ׃

קריאה לשבת חול המועד סוכות

The קריאת התורה for שבת חול המועד סוכות is the same as that of קריאת התורה שבת חול המועד פסח (page 927). The מפטיר is the קריאת התורה of the day of חול המועד סוכות on which שבת falls.

הפטרה לשבת חול המועד סוכות

יחזקאל לח יח וְהָיָ֣ה ׀ בַּיּ֣וֹם הַה֗וּא בְּי֨וֹם בּ֥וֹא גוֹג֙ עַל־אַדְמַ֣ת
יִשְׂרָאֵ֔ל נְאֻ֖ם אֲדֹנָ֣י יֱהֹוִ֑ה תַּעֲלֶ֥ה חֲמָתִ֖י בְּאַפִּֽי׃ יט וּבְקִנְאָתִ֥י
בְאֵשׁ־עֶבְרָתִ֖י דִּבַּ֑רְתִּי אִם־לֹ֣א ׀ בַּיּ֣וֹם הַה֗וּא יִהְיֶה֙ רַ֣עַשׁ גָּד֔וֹל

עַל אַדְמַת יִשְׂרָאֵל׃ כ וְרָעֲשׁוּ מִפָּנַי דְּגֵי הַיָּם וְעוֹף הַשָּׁמַיִם
וְחַיַּת הַשָּׂדֶה וְכָל־הָרֶמֶשׂ הָרֹמֵשׂ עַל־הָאֲדָמָה וְכֹל הָאָדָם
אֲשֶׁר עַל־פְּנֵי הָאֲדָמָה וְנֶהֶרְסוּ הֶהָרִים וְנָפְלוּ הַמַּדְרֵגוֹת
וְכָל־חוֹמָה לָאָרֶץ תִּפּוֹל׃ כא וְקָרָאתִי עָלָיו לְכָל־הָרַי חֶרֶב
נְאֻם אֲדֹנָי יֱהֹוִה חֶרֶב אִישׁ בְּאָחִיו תִּהְיֶה׃ כב וְנִשְׁפַּטְתִּי אִתּוֹ
בְּדֶבֶר וּבְדָם וְגֶשֶׁם שׁוֹטֵף וְאַבְנֵי אֶלְגָּבִישׁ אֵשׁ וְגָפְרִית
אַמְטִיר עָלָיו וְעַל־אֲגַפָּיו וְעַל־עַמִּים רַבִּים אֲשֶׁר אִתּוֹ׃
כג וְהִתְגַּדִּלְתִּי וְהִתְקַדִּשְׁתִּי וְנוֹדַעְתִּי לְעֵינֵי גּוֹיִם רַבִּים וְיָדְעוּ
כִּי־אֲנִי יְהֹוָה׃ ס לט א וְאַתָּה בֶן־אָדָם הִנָּבֵא עַל־גּוֹג
וְאָמַרְתָּ כֹּה אָמַר אֲדֹנָי יֱהֹוִה הִנְנִי אֵלֶיךָ גּוֹג נְשִׂיא רֹאשׁ
מֶשֶׁךְ וְתֻבָל׃ ב וְשֹׁבַבְתִּיךָ וְשִׁשֵּׁאתִיךָ וְהַעֲלִיתִיךָ מִיַּרְכְּתֵי
צָפוֹן וַהֲבִאוֹתִךָ עַל־הָרֵי יִשְׂרָאֵל׃ ג וְהִכֵּיתִי קַשְׁתְּךָ מִיַּד
שְׂמֹאולְךָ וְחִצֶּיךָ מִיַּד יְמִינְךָ אַפִּיל׃ ד עַל־הָרֵי יִשְׂרָאֵל תִּפּוֹל
אַתָּה וְכָל־אֲגַפֶּיךָ וְעַמִּים אֲשֶׁר אִתָּךְ לְעֵיט צִפּוֹר כָּל־כָּנָף
וְחַיַּת הַשָּׂדֶה נְתַתִּיךָ לְאָכְלָה׃ ה עַל־פְּנֵי הַשָּׂדֶה תִּפּוֹל כִּי
אֲנִי דִבַּרְתִּי נְאֻם אֲדֹנָי יֱהֹוִה׃ ו וְשִׁלַּחְתִּי־אֵשׁ בְּמָגוֹג וּבְיֹשְׁבֵי
הָאִיִּים לָבֶטַח וְיָדְעוּ כִּי־אֲנִי יְהֹוָה׃ ז וְאֶת־שֵׁם קָדְשִׁי אוֹדִיעַ
בְּתוֹךְ עַמִּי יִשְׂרָאֵל וְלֹא־אַחֵל אֶת־שֵׁם־קָדְשִׁי עוֹד וְיָדְעוּ
הַגּוֹיִם כִּי־אֲנִי יְהֹוָה קָדוֹשׁ בְּיִשְׂרָאֵל׃ ח הִנֵּה בָאָה וְנִהְיָתָה
נְאֻם אֲדֹנָי יֱהֹוִה הוּא הַיּוֹם אֲשֶׁר דִּבַּרְתִּי׃ ט וְיָצְאוּ יֹשְׁבֵי | עָרֵי
יִשְׂרָאֵל וּבִעֲרוּ וְהִשִּׂיקוּ בְּנֶשֶׁק וּמָגֵן וְצִנָּה בְּקֶשֶׁת וּבְחִצִּים
וּבְמַקֵּל יָד וּבְרֹמַח וּבִעֲרוּ בָהֶם אֵשׁ שֶׁבַע שָׁנִים׃ י וְלֹא־יִשְׂאוּ
עֵצִים מִן־הַשָּׂדֶה וְלֹא יַחְטְבוּ מִן־הַיְּעָרִים כִּי בַנֶּשֶׁק יְבַעֲרוּ־
אֵשׁ וְשָׁלְלוּ אֶת־שֹׁלְלֵיהֶם וּבָזְזוּ אֶת־בֹּזְזֵיהֶם נְאֻם אֲדֹנָי
יֱהֹוִה׃ ס יא וְהָיָה בַיּוֹם הַהוּא אֶתֵּן לְגוֹג | מְקוֹם־שָׁם קֶבֶר
בְּיִשְׂרָאֵל גֵּי הָעֹבְרִים קִדְמַת הַיָּם וְחֹסֶמֶת הִיא אֶת־הָעֹבְרִים

וְקָ֤בְרוּ שָׁ֨ם אֶת־גּ֜וֹג וְאֶת־כׇּל־הֲמוֹנֹ֗ה וְקָ֣רְא֔וּ גֵּ֖יא הֲמ֥וֹן גּֽוֹג׃ יב
וּקְבָרוּם֙ בֵּ֣ית יִשְׂרָאֵ֔ל לְמַ֖עַן טַהֵ֣ר אֶת־הָאָ֑רֶץ שִׁבְעָ֖ה חֳדָשִֽׁים׃
יג וְקָֽבְרוּ֙ כׇּל־עַ֣ם הָאָ֔רֶץ וְהָיָ֥ה לָהֶ֖ם לְשֵׁ֑ם י֚וֹם הִכָּ֣בְדִ֔י נְאֻ֖ם
אֲדֹנָ֥י יֱהֹוִֽה׃ יד וְאַנְשֵׁ֨י תָמִ֤יד יַבְדִּ֙ילוּ֙ עֹבְרִ֣ים בָּאָ֔רֶץ מְקַבְּרִ֣ים
אֶת־הָעֹבְרִ֗ים אֶת־הַנּֽוֹתָרִים֙ עַל־פְּנֵ֣י הָאָ֔רֶץ לְטַהֲרָ֑הּ מִקְצֵ֥ה
שִׁבְעָֽה־חֳדָשִׁ֖ים יַחְקֹֽרוּ׃ טו וְעָבְר֤וּ הָעֹֽבְרִים֙ בָּאָ֔רֶץ וְרָאָה֙ עֶ֣צֶם
אָדָ֔ם וּבָנָ֥ה אֶצְל֖וֹ צִיּ֑וּן עַ֣ד קָבְר֤וּ אֹתוֹ֙ הַֽמְקַבְּרִ֔ים אֶל־גֵּ֖יא הֲמ֥וֹן
גּֽוֹג׃ טז וְגַ֥ם שֶׁם־עִ֛יר הֲמוֹנָ֖ה וְטִהֲר֥וּ הָאָֽרֶץ׃

Continue with the blessings after the הפטרה on page 416.

מפטיר לשמיני עצרת ולשמחת תורה

The קריאת התורה for שמיני עצרת is the same as that of the eighth day of פסח, page 937.

במדבר כט לה בַּיּוֹם֙ הַשְּׁמִינִ֔י עֲצֶ֖רֶת תִּהְיֶ֣ה לָכֶ֑ם כׇּל־מְלֶ֥אכֶת
עֲבֹדָ֖ה לֹ֥א תַעֲשֽׂוּ׃ לו וְהִקְרַבְתֶּ֨ם עֹלָ֜ה אִשֵּׁ֨ה רֵ֤יחַ נִיחֹ֙חַ֙ לַיהֹוָ֔ה
פַּ֥ר אֶחָ֖ד אַ֣יִל אֶחָ֑ד כְּבָשִׂ֧ים בְּנֵי־שָׁנָ֛ה שִׁבְעָ֖ה תְּמִימִֽם׃
לז מִנְחָתָ֣ם וְנִסְכֵּיהֶ֗ם לַפָּ֨ר לָאַ֧יִל וְלַכְּבָשִׂ֛ים בְּמִסְפָּרָ֖ם כַּמִּשְׁפָּֽט׃
לח וּשְׂעִ֥יר חַטָּ֖את אֶחָ֑ד מִלְּבַד֙ עֹלַ֣ת הַתָּמִ֔יד וּמִנְחָתָ֖הּ וְנִסְכָּֽהּ׃
לט אֵ֛לֶּה תַּעֲשׂ֥וּ לַיהֹוָ֖ה בְּמוֹעֲדֵיכֶ֑ם לְבַ֨ד מִנִּדְרֵיכֶ֜ם וְנִדְבֹתֵיכֶ֗ם
לְעֹלֹתֵיכֶם֙ וּלְמִנְחֹ֣תֵיכֶ֔ם וּלְנִסְכֵּיכֶ֖ם וּלְשַׁלְמֵיכֶֽם׃ ל א וַיֹּ֥אמֶר
מֹשֶׁ֖ה אֶל־בְּנֵ֣י יִשְׂרָאֵ֑ל כְּכֹ֛ל אֲשֶׁר־צִוָּ֥ה יְהֹוָ֖ה אֶת־מֹשֶֽׁה׃

הפטרה לשמיני עצרת

מלכים א׳ ח נד וַיְהִ֣י ׀ כְּכַלּ֣וֹת שְׁלֹמֹ֗ה לְהִתְפַּלֵּל֙ אֶל־יְהֹוָ֔ה אֵ֛ת
כׇּל־הַתְּפִלָּ֥ה וְהַתְּחִנָּ֖ה הַזֹּ֑את קָ֞ם מִלִּפְנֵ֣י מִזְבַּ֤ח יְהֹוָה֙ מִכְּרֹ֣עַ
עַל־בִּרְכָּ֔יו וְכַפָּ֖יו פְּרֻשׂ֥וֹת הַשָּׁמָֽיִם׃ נה וַֽיַּעֲמֹ֕ד וַיְבָ֕רֶךְ אֵ֛ת

כָּל־קְהַל יִשְׂרָאֵל קוֹל גָּדוֹל לֵאמֹר: נו בָּרוּךְ יהוה אֲשֶׁר נָתַן
מְנוּחָה לְעַמּוֹ יִשְׂרָאֵל כְּכֹל אֲשֶׁר דִּבֵּר לֹא־נָפַל דָּבָר אֶחָד
מִכֹּל דְּבָרוֹ הַטּוֹב אֲשֶׁר דִּבֶּר בְּיַד מֹשֶׁה עַבְדּוֹ: נז יְהִי יהוה
אֱלֹהֵינוּ עִמָּנוּ כַּאֲשֶׁר הָיָה עִם־אֲבֹתֵינוּ אַל־יַעַזְבֵנוּ וְאַל־
יִטְּשֵׁנוּ: נח לְהַטּוֹת לְבָבֵנוּ אֵלָיו לָלֶכֶת בְּכָל־דְּרָכָיו וְלִשְׁמֹר
מִצְוֺתָיו וְחֻקָּיו וּמִשְׁפָּטָיו אֲשֶׁר צִוָּה אֶת־אֲבֹתֵינוּ: נט וְיִהְיוּ
דְבָרַי אֵלֶּה אֲשֶׁר הִתְחַנַּנְתִּי לִפְנֵי יהוה קְרֹבִים אֶל־יהוה
אֱלֹהֵינוּ יוֹמָם וָלָיְלָה לַעֲשׂוֹת | מִשְׁפַּט עַבְדּוֹ וּמִשְׁפַּט עַמּוֹ
יִשְׂרָאֵל דְּבַר־יוֹם בְּיוֹמוֹ: ס לְמַעַן דַּעַת כָּל־עַמֵּי הָאָרֶץ כִּי
יהוה הוּא הָאֱלֹהִים אֵין עוֹד: סא וְהָיָה לְבַבְכֶם שָׁלֵם עִם
יהוה אֱלֹהֵינוּ לָלֶכֶת בְּחֻקָּיו וְלִשְׁמֹר מִצְוֺתָיו כַּיּוֹם הַזֶּה: סב
וְהַמֶּלֶךְ וְכָל־יִשְׂרָאֵל עִמּוֹ זֹבְחִים זֶבַח לִפְנֵי יהוה: סג וַיִּזְבַּח
שְׁלֹמֹה אֵת זֶבַח הַשְּׁלָמִים אֲשֶׁר זָבַח לַיהוה בָּקָר עֶשְׂרִים
וּשְׁנַיִם אֶלֶף וְצֹאן מֵאָה וְעֶשְׂרִים אָלֶף וַיַּחְנְכוּ אֶת־בֵּית יהוה
הַמֶּלֶךְ וְכָל־בְּנֵי יִשְׂרָאֵל: סד בַּיּוֹם הַהוּא קִדַּשׁ הַמֶּלֶךְ אֶת־
תּוֹךְ הֶחָצֵר אֲשֶׁר לִפְנֵי בֵית־יהוה כִּי־עָשָׂה שָׁם אֶת־הָעֹלָה
וְאֶת־הַמִּנְחָה וְאֵת חֶלְבֵי הַשְּׁלָמִים כִּי־מִזְבַּח הַנְּחֹשֶׁת אֲשֶׁר
לִפְנֵי יהוה קָטֹן מֵהָכִיל אֶת־הָעֹלָה וְאֶת־הַמִּנְחָה וְאֵת חֶלְבֵי
הַשְּׁלָמִים: סה וַיַּעַשׂ שְׁלֹמֹה בָעֵת־הַהִיא | אֶת־הֶחָג וְכָל־
יִשְׂרָאֵל עִמּוֹ קָהָל גָּדוֹל מִלְּבוֹא חֲמָת | עַד־נַחַל מִצְרַיִם לִפְנֵי
יהוה אֱלֹהֵינוּ שִׁבְעַת יָמִים וְשִׁבְעַת יָמִים אַרְבָּעָה עָשָׂר יוֹם:
סו בַּיּוֹם הַשְּׁמִינִי שִׁלַּח אֶת־הָעָם וַיְבָרְכוּ אֶת־הַמֶּלֶךְ וַיֵּלְכוּ
לְאָהֳלֵיהֶם שְׂמֵחִים וְטוֹבֵי לֵב עַל כָּל־הַטּוֹבָה אֲשֶׁר עָשָׂה
יהוה לְדָוִד עַבְדּוֹ וּלְיִשְׂרָאֵל עַמּוֹ: ס ט א וַיְהִי כְּכַלּוֹת

שְׁלֹמֹה לִבְנוֹת אֶת־בֵּית־יְהוָה וְאֶת־בֵּית הַמֶּלֶךְ וְאֵת כָּל־
חֵשֶׁק שְׁלֹמֹה אֲשֶׁר חָפֵץ לַעֲשׂוֹת׃

Continue with the blessings after the הפטרה on page 416.

קריאה לשמחת תורה

דברים לג א וְזֹאת הַבְּרָכָה אֲשֶׁר בֵּרַךְ מֹשֶׁה אִישׁ הָאֱלֹהִים אֶת־
בְּנֵי יִשְׂרָאֵל לִפְנֵי מוֹתוֹ׃ ב וַיֹּאמַר יְהוָה מִסִּינַי בָּא וְזָרַח מִשֵּׂעִיר
לָמוֹ הוֹפִיעַ מֵהַר פָּארָן וְאָתָה מֵרִבְבֹת קֹדֶשׁ מִימִינוֹ אֵשְׁדָּת▽
לָמוֹ׃ ג אַף חֹבֵב עַמִּים כָּל־קְדֹשָׁיו בְּיָדֶךָ וְהֵם תֻּכּוּ לְרַגְלֶךָ יִשָּׂא
מִדַּבְּרֹתֶיךָ׃ ד תּוֹרָה צִוָּה־לָנוּ מֹשֶׁה מוֹרָשָׁה קְהִלַּת יַעֲקֹב׃
ה וַיְהִי בִישֻׁרוּן מֶלֶךְ בְּהִתְאַסֵּף רָאשֵׁי עָם יַחַד שִׁבְטֵי יִשְׂרָאֵל׃
ו יְחִי רְאוּבֵן וְאַל־יָמֹת וִיהִי מְתָיו מִסְפָּר׃ ס ז וְזֹאת
לִיהוּדָה וַיֹּאמַר שְׁמַע יְהוָה קוֹל יְהוּדָה וְאֶל־עַמּוֹ תְּבִיאֶנּוּ
יָדָיו רָב לוֹ וְעֵזֶר מִצָּרָיו תִּהְיֶה׃ פ [לוי] ח וּלְלֵוִי אָמַר תֻּמֶּיךָ
וְאוּרֶיךָ לְאִישׁ חֲסִידֶךָ אֲשֶׁר נִסִּיתוֹ בְּמַסָּה תְּרִיבֵהוּ עַל־מֵי
מְרִיבָה׃ ט הָאֹמֵר לְאָבִיו וּלְאִמּוֹ לֹא רְאִיתִיו וְאֶת־אֶחָיו לֹא
הִכִּיר וְאֶת־בָּנָו לֹא יָדָע כִּי שָׁמְרוּ אִמְרָתֶךָ וּבְרִיתְךָ יִנְצֹרוּ׃
י יוֹרוּ מִשְׁפָּטֶיךָ לְיַעֲקֹב וְתוֹרָתְךָ לְיִשְׂרָאֵל יָשִׂימוּ קְטוֹרָה
בְּאַפֶּךָ וְכָלִיל עַל־מִזְבְּחֶךָ׃ יא בָּרֵךְ יְהוָה חֵילוֹ וּפֹעַל יָדָיו תִּרְצֶה
מְחַץ מָתְנַיִם קָמָיו וּמְשַׂנְאָיו מִן־יְקוּמוּן׃ יב לְבִנְיָמִן אָמַר יְדִיד
יְהוָה יִשְׁכֹּן לָבֶטַח עָלָיו חֹפֵף עָלָיו כָּל־הַיּוֹם וּבֵין כְּתֵפָיו
שָׁכֵן׃ ס [שלישי] יג וּלְיוֹסֵף אָמַר מְבֹרֶכֶת יְהוָה אַרְצוֹ
מִמֶּגֶד שָׁמַיִם מִטָּל וּמִתְּהוֹם רֹבֶצֶת תָּחַת׃ יד וּמִמֶּגֶד תְּבוּאֹת
שָׁמֶשׁ וּמִמֶּגֶד גֶּרֶשׁ יְרָחִים׃ טו וּמֵרֹאשׁ הַרְרֵי־קֶדֶם וּמִמֶּגֶד
גִּבְעוֹת עוֹלָם׃ טז וּמִמֶּגֶד אֶרֶץ וּמְלֹאָהּ וּרְצוֹן שֹׁכְנִי סְנֶה

▽ אֵשׁ דָּת

תָּבוֹאתָה לְרֹאשׁ יוֹסֵף וּלְקָדְקֹד נְזִיר אֶחָיו: יז בְּכוֹר שׁוֹרוֹ הָדָר
לוֹ וְקַרְנֵי רְאֵם קַרְנָיו בָּהֶם עַמִּים יְנַגַּח יַחְדָּו אַפְסֵי־אָרֶץ וְהֵם
רִבְבוֹת אֶפְרַיִם וְהֵם אַלְפֵי מְנַשֶּׁה: ס [רביעי] יח וְלִזְבוּלֻן
אָמַר שְׂמַח זְבוּלֻן בְּצֵאתֶךָ וְיִשָּׂשכָר בְּאֹהָלֶיךָ: יט עַמִּים הַר־
יִקְרָאוּ שָׁם יִזְבְּחוּ זִבְחֵי־צֶדֶק כִּי שֶׁפַע יַמִּים יִינָקוּ וּשְׂפֻנֵי
טְמוּנֵי חוֹל: ס כ וּלְגָד אָמַר בָּרוּךְ מַרְחִיב גָּד כְּלָבִיא שָׁכֵן
וְטָרַף זְרוֹעַ אַף־קָדְקֹד: כא וַיַּרְא רֵאשִׁית לוֹ כִּי־שָׁם חֶלְקַת
מְחֹקֵק סָפוּן וַיֵּתֵא רָאשֵׁי עָם צִדְקַת יהוה עָשָׂה וּמִשְׁפָּטָיו
עִם־יִשְׂרָאֵל: ס [חמישי] כב וּלְדָן אָמַר דָּן גּוּר אַרְיֵה יְזַנֵּק
מִן־הַבָּשָׁן: כג וּלְנַפְתָּלִי אָמַר נַפְתָּלִי שְׂבַע רָצוֹן וּמָלֵא בִּרְכַּת
יהוה יָם וְדָרוֹם יְרָשָׁה: ס כד וּלְאָשֵׁר אָמַר בָּרוּךְ מִבָּנִים
אָשֵׁר יְהִי רְצוּי אֶחָיו וְטֹבֵל בַּשֶּׁמֶן רַגְלוֹ: כה בַּרְזֶל וּנְחֹשֶׁת
מִנְעָלֶךָ וּכְיָמֶיךָ דָּבְאֶךָ: כו אֵין כָּאֵל יְשֻׁרוּן רֹכֵב שָׁמַיִם בְּעֶזְרֶךָ
וּבְגַאֲוָתוֹ שְׁחָקִים:

*עלית כל הנערים

In many congregations, the children participate in the last עליה before calling up the חתן תורה. All the children gather on the בימה, a טלית is spread over them and they say the blessings aloud together with the עולה. After the blessing which follows the Reading, the whole congregation sing together:

בראשית מח הַמַּלְאָךְ הַגֹּאֵל אֹתִי מִכָּל־רָע יְבָרֵךְ אֶת־הַנְּעָרִים, וְיִקָּרֵא בָהֶם שְׁמִי וְשֵׁם אֲבֹתַי אַבְרָהָם וְיִצְחָק, וְיִדְגּוּ לָרֹב בְּקֶרֶב הָאָרֶץ:

Some add:

במדבר ו יְבָרֶכְךָ יהוה וְיִשְׁמְרֶךָ: יָאֵר יהוה פָּנָיו אֵלֶיךָ וִיחֻנֶּךָּ: יִשָּׂא יהוה פָּנָיו אֵלֶיךָ וְיָשֵׂם לְךָ שָׁלוֹם:

רשות לחתן תורה

Our custom is that the following is said by the גבאי to call up the חתן תורה to his עליה:

מֵרְשׁוּת הָאֵל הַגָּדוֹל הַגִּבּוֹר וְהַנּוֹרָא אֶפְתַּח פִּי בְּשִׁיר וּבְזִמְרָה לְהוֹדוֹת לְהַלֵּל לְדָר בִּנְהוֹרָא שֶׁהֶחֱיָנוּ וְקִיְּמָנוּ בְּיִרְאָתוֹ הַטְּהוֹרָה וְהִגִּיעָנוּ לִשְׂמֹחַ בְּשִׂמְחַת הַתּוֹרָה הַמְשַׂמַּחַת לֵב וְעֵינַיִם מְאִירָה הַמַּאֲרֶכֶת יָמִים וּמוֹסֶפֶת גְּבוּרָה לְאוֹהֲבֶיהָ וּלְשׁוֹמְרֶיהָ בְּצִוּוּי וְאַזְהָרָה. וּבְכֵן יְהִי רָצוֹן מִלִּפְנֵי הַגְּבוּרָה לָתֵת חַיִּים וָחֶסֶד וָנֵזֶר עֲטָרָה לְרַבִּי (פלוני ב״ר פלוני) הַנִּבְחָר לְהַשְׁלִים הַתּוֹרָה. עֲמֹד עֲמֹד עֲמֹד רַבִּי (פלוני ב״ר פלוני) חֲתַן הַתּוֹרָה וּבִשְׂכַר זֶה תִּזְכֶּה מֵאֵל נוֹרָא לִרְאוֹת בָּנִים וּבְנֵי בָנִים עוֹסְקִים בַּתּוֹרָה. יַעֲמֹד רַבִּי (פלוני ב״ר פלוני) חֲתַן הַתּוֹרָה.

קריאה לחתן תורה

דברים לג כז מְעֹנָה אֱלֹהֵי קֶדֶם וּמִתַּחַת זְרֹעֹת עוֹלָם וַיְגָרֶשׁ
מִפָּנֶיךָ אוֹיֵב וַיֹּאמֶר הַשְׁמֵד: כח וַיִּשְׁכֹּן יִשְׂרָאֵל בֶּטַח בָּדָד עֵין
יַעֲקֹב אֶל־אֶרֶץ דָּגָן וְתִירוֹשׁ אַף־שָׁמָיו יַעַרְפוּ־טָל: כט אַשְׁרֶיךָ
יִשְׂרָאֵל מִי כָמוֹךָ עַם נוֹשַׁע בַּיהוָה מָגֵן עֶזְרֶךָ וַאֲשֶׁר־חֶרֶב
גַּאֲוָתֶךָ וְיִכָּחֲשׁוּ אֹיְבֶיךָ לָךְ וְאַתָּה עַל־בָּמוֹתֵימוֹ תִדְרֹךְ: [בשבת
חתן תורה] ס **לד** א וַיַּעַל מֹשֶׁה מֵעַרְבֹת מוֹאָב אֶל־הַר
נְבוֹ רֹאשׁ הַפִּסְגָּה אֲשֶׁר עַל־פְּנֵי יְרֵחוֹ וַיַּרְאֵהוּ יְהוָה אֶת־
כָּל־הָאָרֶץ אֶת־הַגִּלְעָד עַד־דָּן: ב וְאֵת כָּל־נַפְתָּלִי וְאֶת־אֶרֶץ
אֶפְרַיִם וּמְנַשֶּׁה וְאֵת כָּל־אֶרֶץ יְהוּדָה עַד הַיָּם הָאַחֲרוֹן:
ג וְאֶת־הַנֶּגֶב וְאֶת־הַכִּכָּר בִּקְעַת יְרֵחוֹ עִיר הַתְּמָרִים עַד־צֹעַר:
ד וַיֹּאמֶר יְהוָה אֵלָיו זֹאת הָאָרֶץ אֲשֶׁר נִשְׁבַּעְתִּי לְאַבְרָהָם
לְיִצְחָק וּלְיַעֲקֹב לֵאמֹר לְזַרְעֲךָ אֶתְּנֶנָּה הֶרְאִיתִיךָ בְעֵינֶיךָ
וְשָׁמָּה לֹא תַעֲבֹר: ה וַיָּמָת שָׁם מֹשֶׁה עֶבֶד־יְהוָה בְּאֶרֶץ מוֹאָב
עַל־פִּי יְהוָה: ו וַיִּקְבֹּר אֹתוֹ בַגַּי בְּאֶרֶץ מוֹאָב מוּל בֵּית פְּעוֹר
וְלֹא־יָדַע אִישׁ אֶת־קְבֻרָתוֹ עַד הַיּוֹם הַזֶּה: ז וּמֹשֶׁה בֶּן־מֵאָה
וְעֶשְׂרִים שָׁנָה בְּמֹתוֹ לֹא־כָהֲתָה עֵינוֹ וְלֹא־נָס לֵחֹה: ח וַיִּבְכּוּ

בְנֵ֨י יִשְׂרָאֵ֧ל אֶת־מֹשֶׁ֛ה בְּעַרְבֹ֥ת מוֹאָ֖ב שְׁלֹשִׁ֣ים י֑וֹם וַיִּתְּמ֔וּ
יְמֵ֥י בְכִ֖י אֵ֥בֶל מֹשֶֽׁה׃ ט וִיהוֹשֻׁ֣עַ בִּן־נ֗וּן מָלֵא֙ ר֣וּחַ חָכְמָ֔ה כִּֽי־
סָמַ֥ךְ מֹשֶׁ֛ה אֶת־יָדָ֖יו עָלָ֑יו וַיִּשְׁמְע֨וּ אֵלָ֤יו בְּנֵֽי־יִשְׂרָאֵל֙ וַֽיַּעֲשׂ֔וּ
כַּאֲשֶׁ֛ר צִוָּ֥ה יהו֖ה אֶת־מֹשֶֽׁה׃ י וְלֹא־קָ֨ם נָבִ֥יא ע֛וֹד בְּיִשְׂרָאֵ֖ל
כְּמֹשֶׁ֑ה אֲשֶׁר֙ יְדָע֣וֹ יהו֔ה פָּנִ֖ים אֶל־פָּנִֽים׃ יא לְכָל־הָ֨אֹתֹ֜ת
וְהַמּֽוֹפְתִ֗ים אֲשֶׁ֤ר שְׁלָחוֹ֙ יהו֔ה לַעֲשׂ֖וֹת בְּאֶ֣רֶץ מִצְרָ֑יִם
לְפַרְעֹ֥ה וּלְכָל־עֲבָדָ֖יו וּלְכָל־אַרְצֽוֹ׃ יב וּלְכֹל֙ הַיָּ֣ד הַחֲזָקָ֔ה וּלְכֹ֖ל
הַמּוֹרָ֣א הַגָּד֑וֹל אֲשֶׁר֙ עָשָׂ֣ה מֹשֶׁ֔ה לְעֵינֵ֖י כָּל־יִשְׂרָאֵֽל׃

חֲזַק חֲזַק וְנִתְחַזֵּק

רשות לחתן בראשית

Our custom is that the following is said by the גבאי to call up the חתן בראשית to his עליה:

מֵרְשׁוּת מְרוֹמָם עַל כָּל בְּרָכָה וְשִׁירָה נוֹרָא עַל כָּל תְּהִלָּה וְזִמְרָה חֲכַם לֵבָב וְאַמִּיץ כֹּחַ וּגְבוּרָה מוֹשֵׁל עוֹלָם אֲדוֹן כָּל יְצִירָה וּמֵרְשׁוּת חֲבוּרַת צֶדֶק עֵדָה הַמְאֻשָּׁרָה קְבוּצִים פֹּה הַיּוֹם לְשִׂמְחַת תּוֹרָה וְנֶעֱצָרִים לְסַיֵּם וּלְהָחֵל בְּגִיל וּבְמוֹרָא עֲמֹד עֲמֹד רַבִּי (פלוני ב״ר פלוני) חֲתַן בְּרֵאשִׁית בָּרְאִיָּן נַעֲשֵׂית רִאשׁוֹן לְמִצְוָה גְּמוּרָה מָה רַב טוּבְךָ וּמַשְׂכֻּרְתְּךָ יְתֵרָה. יַעֲמֹד רַבִּי (פלוני ב״ר פלוני) חֲתַן בְּרֵאשִׁית.

קריאה לחתן בראשית

It is customary for the קהל to say aloud the passages marked by arrows, followed by the בעל קורא.

א בְּרֵאשִׁ֖ית בָּרָ֣א אֱלֹהִ֑ים אֵ֥ת הַשָּׁמַ֖יִם וְאֵ֥ת הָאָֽרֶץ׃ ב וְהָאָ֗רֶץ
הָיְתָ֥ה תֹ֙הוּ֙ וָבֹ֔הוּ וְחֹ֖שֶׁךְ עַל־פְּנֵ֣י תְה֑וֹם וְר֣וּחַ אֱלֹהִ֔ים מְרַחֶ֖פֶת
עַל־פְּנֵ֥י הַמָּֽיִם׃ ג וַיֹּ֥אמֶר אֱלֹהִ֖ים יְהִ֣י א֑וֹר וַֽיְהִי־אֽוֹר׃ ד וַיַּ֧רְא
אֱלֹהִ֛ים אֶת־הָא֖וֹר כִּי־ט֑וֹב וַיַּבְדֵּ֣ל אֱלֹהִ֔ים בֵּ֥ין הָא֖וֹר וּבֵ֥ין
הַחֹֽשֶׁךְ׃ ה וַיִּקְרָ֨א אֱלֹהִ֤ים ׀ לָאוֹר֙ י֔וֹם וְלַחֹ֖שֶׁךְ קָ֣רָא לָ֑יְלָה
◂ וַֽיְהִי־עֶ֥רֶב וַֽיְהִי־בֹ֖קֶר י֥וֹם אֶחָֽד׃ ◂ פ ו וַיֹּ֣אמֶר אֱלֹהִ֔ים יְהִ֥י
רָקִ֖יעַ בְּת֣וֹךְ הַמָּ֑יִם וִיהִ֣י מַבְדִּ֔יל בֵּ֥ין מַ֖יִם לָמָֽיִם׃ ז וַיַּ֣עַשׂ

אֱלֹהִים֮ אֶת־הָֽרָקִיעַ֒ וַיַּבְדֵּ֗ל בֵּ֤ין הַמַּ֙יִם֙ אֲשֶׁר֙ מִתַּ֣חַת לָֽרָקִ֔יעַ
וּבֵ֣ין הַמַּ֔יִם אֲשֶׁ֖ר מֵעַ֣ל לָֽרָקִ֑יעַ וַֽיְהִי־כֵֽן׃ ח וַיִּקְרָ֧א אֱלֹהִ֛ים
לָֽרָקִ֖יעַ שָׁמָ֑יִם וַֽיְהִי־עֶ֥רֶב וַֽיְהִי־בֹ֖קֶר י֥וֹם שֵׁנִֽי׃ פ ט וַיֹּ֣אמֶר
אֱלֹהִ֗ים יִקָּו֨וּ הַמַּ֜יִם מִתַּ֤חַת הַשָּׁמַ֙יִם֙ אֶל־מָק֣וֹם אֶחָ֔ד וְתֵרָאֶ֖ה
הַיַּבָּשָׁ֑ה וַֽיְהִי־כֵֽן׃ י וַיִּקְרָ֨א אֱלֹהִ֤ים ׀ לַיַּבָּשָׁה֙ אֶ֔רֶץ וּלְמִקְוֵ֥ה
הַמַּ֖יִם קָרָ֣א יַמִּ֑ים וַיַּ֥רְא אֱלֹהִ֖ים כִּי־טֽוֹב׃ יא וַיֹּ֣אמֶר אֱלֹהִ֗ים
תַּֽדְשֵׁ֤א הָאָ֙רֶץ֙ דֶּ֔שֶׁא עֵ֚שֶׂב מַזְרִ֣יעַ זֶ֔רַע עֵ֣ץ פְּרִ֞י עֹ֤שֶׂה פְּרִי֙
לְמִינ֔וֹ אֲשֶׁ֥ר זַרְעוֹ־ב֖וֹ עַל־הָאָ֑רֶץ וַֽיְהִי־כֵֽן׃ יב וַתּוֹצֵ֨א הָאָ֜רֶץ
דֶּ֠שֶׁא עֵ֣שֶׂב מַזְרִ֤יעַ זֶ֙רַע֙ לְמִינֵ֔הוּ וְעֵ֧ץ עֹֽשֶׂה־פְּרִ֛י אֲשֶׁ֥ר זַרְעוֹ־
ב֖וֹ לְמִינֵ֑הוּ וַיַּ֥רְא אֱלֹהִ֖ים כִּי־טֽוֹב׃ יג וַֽיְהִי־עֶ֥רֶב וַֽיְהִי־בֹ֖קֶר י֥וֹם
שְׁלִישִֽׁי׃ פ יד וַיֹּ֣אמֶר אֱלֹהִ֗ים יְהִ֤י מְאֹרֹת֙ בִּרְקִ֣יעַ הַשָּׁמַ֔יִם
לְהַבְדִּ֕יל בֵּ֥ין הַיּ֖וֹם וּבֵ֣ין הַלָּ֑יְלָה וְהָי֤וּ לְאֹתֹת֙ וּלְמ֣וֹעֲדִ֔ים
וּלְיָמִ֖ים וְשָׁנִֽים׃ טו וְהָי֤וּ לִמְאוֹרֹת֙ בִּרְקִ֣יעַ הַשָּׁמַ֔יִם לְהָאִ֖יר עַל־
הָאָ֑רֶץ וַֽיְהִי־כֵֽן׃ טז וַיַּ֣עַשׂ אֱלֹהִ֔ים אֶת־שְׁנֵ֥י הַמְּאֹרֹ֖ת הַגְּדֹלִ֑ים
אֶת־הַמָּא֤וֹר הַגָּדֹל֙ לְמֶמְשֶׁ֣לֶת הַיּ֔וֹם וְאֶת־הַמָּא֤וֹר הַקָּטֹן֙
לְמֶמְשֶׁ֣לֶת הַלַּ֔יְלָה וְאֵ֖ת הַכּוֹכָבִֽים׃ יז וַיִּתֵּ֥ן אֹתָ֛ם אֱלֹהִ֖ים
בִּרְקִ֣יעַ הַשָּׁמָ֑יִם לְהָאִ֖יר עַל־הָאָֽרֶץ׃ יח וְלִמְשֹׁל֙ בַּיּ֣וֹם וּבַלַּ֔יְלָה
וּֽלֲהַבְדִּ֔יל בֵּ֥ין הָא֖וֹר וּבֵ֣ין הַחֹ֑שֶׁךְ וַיַּ֥רְא אֱלֹהִ֖ים כִּי־טֽוֹב׃
יט וַֽיְהִי־עֶ֥רֶב וַֽיְהִי־בֹ֖קֶר י֥וֹם רְבִיעִֽי׃ פ כ וַיֹּ֣אמֶר אֱלֹהִ֔ים
יִשְׁרְצ֣וּ הַמַּ֔יִם שֶׁ֖רֶץ נֶ֣פֶשׁ חַיָּ֑ה וְעוֹף֙ יְעוֹפֵ֣ף עַל־הָאָ֔רֶץ עַל־פְּנֵ֖י
רְקִ֥יעַ הַשָּׁמָֽיִם׃ כא וַיִּבְרָ֣א אֱלֹהִ֔ים אֶת־הַתַּנִּינִ֖ם הַגְּדֹלִ֑ים וְאֵ֣ת
כָּל־נֶ֣פֶשׁ הַֽחַיָּ֣ה ׀ הָֽרֹמֶ֡שֶׂת אֲשֶׁר֩ שָׁרְצ֨וּ הַמַּ֜יִם לְמִֽינֵהֶ֗ם וְאֵ֨ת
כָּל־ע֤וֹף כָּנָף֙ לְמִינֵ֔הוּ וַיַּ֥רְא אֱלֹהִ֖ים כִּי־טֽוֹב׃ כב וַיְבָ֧רֶךְ אֹתָ֛ם
אֱלֹהִ֖ים לֵאמֹ֑ר פְּר֣וּ וּרְב֗וּ וּמִלְא֤וּ אֶת־הַמַּ֙יִם֙ בַּיַּמִּ֔ים וְהָע֖וֹף יִ֥רֶב
בָּאָֽרֶץ׃ כג וַֽיְהִי־עֶ֥רֶב וַֽיְהִי־בֹ֖קֶר י֥וֹם חֲמִישִֽׁי׃ פ כד וַיֹּ֣אמֶר
אֱלֹהִ֗ים תּוֹצֵ֨א הָאָ֜רֶץ נֶ֤פֶשׁ חַיָּה֙ לְמִינָ֔הּ בְּהֵמָ֥ה וָרֶ֛מֶשׂ וְחַיְתוֹ־

אֶ֖רֶץ לְמִינָ֑הּ וַֽיְהִי־כֵֽן׃ כה וַיַּ֣עַשׂ אֱלֹהִים֩ אֶת־חַיַּ֨ת הָאָ֜רֶץ
לְמִינָ֗הּ וְאֶת־הַבְּהֵמָה֙ לְמִינָ֔הּ וְאֵ֛ת כָּל־רֶ֥מֶשׂ הָֽאֲדָמָ֖ה לְמִינֵ֑הוּ
וַיַּ֥רְא אֱלֹהִ֖ים כִּי־טֽוֹב׃ כו וַיֹּ֣אמֶר אֱלֹהִ֔ים נַֽעֲשֶׂ֥ה אָדָ֛ם בְּצַלְמֵ֖נוּ
כִּדְמוּתֵ֑נוּ וְיִרְדּוּ֩ בִדְגַ֨ת הַיָּ֜ם וּבְע֣וֹף הַשָּׁמַ֗יִם וּבַבְּהֵמָה֙ וּבְכָל־
הָאָ֔רֶץ וּבְכָל־הָרֶ֖מֶשׂ הָֽרֹמֵ֥שׂ עַל־הָאָֽרֶץ׃ כז וַיִּבְרָ֨א אֱלֹהִ֤ים ׀
אֶת־הָֽאָדָם֙ בְּצַלְמ֔וֹ בְּצֶ֥לֶם אֱלֹהִ֖ים בָּרָ֣א אֹת֑וֹ זָכָ֥ר וּנְקֵבָ֖ה
בָּרָ֥א אֹתָֽם׃ כח וַיְבָ֣רֶךְ אֹתָם֮ אֱלֹהִים֒ וַיֹּ֨אמֶר לָהֶ֜ם אֱלֹהִ֗ים
פְּר֥וּ וּרְב֛וּ וּמִלְא֥וּ אֶת־הָאָ֖רֶץ וְכִבְשֻׁ֑הָ וּרְד֞וּ בִּדְגַ֤ת הַיָּם֙ וּבְע֣וֹף
הַשָּׁמַ֔יִם וּבְכָל־חַיָּ֖ה הָֽרֹמֶ֥שֶׂת עַל־הָאָֽרֶץ׃ כט וַיֹּ֣אמֶר אֱלֹהִ֗ים
הִנֵּה֩ נָתַ֨תִּי לָכֶ֜ם אֶת־כָּל־עֵ֣שֶׂב ׀ זֹרֵ֣עַ זֶ֗רַע אֲשֶׁר֙ עַל־פְּנֵ֣י
כָל־הָאָ֔רֶץ וְאֶת־כָּל־הָעֵ֛ץ אֲשֶׁר־בּ֥וֹ פְרִי־עֵ֖ץ זֹרֵ֣עַ זָ֑רַע לָכֶ֥ם
יִֽהְיֶ֖ה לְאָכְלָֽה׃ ל וּֽלְכָל־חַיַּ֣ת הָ֠אָרֶץ וּלְכָל־ע֨וֹף הַשָּׁמַ֜יִם וּלְכֹ֣ל
׀ רוֹמֵ֣שׂ עַל־הָאָ֗רֶץ אֲשֶׁר־בּוֹ֙ נֶ֣פֶשׁ חַיָּ֔ה אֶת־כָּל־יֶ֥רֶק עֵ֖שֶׂב
לְאָכְלָ֑ה וַֽיְהִי־כֵֽן׃ לא וַיַּ֤רְא אֱלֹהִים֙ אֶת־כָּל־אֲשֶׁ֣ר עָשָׂ֔ה וְהִנֵּה־
ט֖וֹב מְאֹ֑ד · וַֽיְהִי־עֶ֥רֶב וַֽיְהִי־בֹ֖קֶר י֥וֹם הַשִּׁשִּֽׁי׃ · פ · ב א וַיְכֻלּ֛וּ
הַשָּׁמַ֥יִם וְהָאָ֖רֶץ וְכָל־צְבָאָֽם׃ ב וַיְכַ֤ל אֱלֹהִים֙ בַּיּ֣וֹם הַשְּׁבִיעִ֔י
מְלַאכְתּ֖וֹ אֲשֶׁ֣ר עָשָׂ֑ה וַיִּשְׁבֹּת֙ בַּיּ֣וֹם הַשְּׁבִיעִ֔י מִכָּל־מְלַאכְתּ֖וֹ
אֲשֶׁ֥ר עָשָֽׂה׃ ג וַיְבָ֤רֶךְ אֱלֹהִים֙ אֶת־י֣וֹם הַשְּׁבִיעִ֔י וַיְקַדֵּ֖שׁ אֹת֑וֹ
כִּ֣י ב֤וֹ שָׁבַת֙ מִכָּל־מְלַאכְתּ֔וֹ אֲשֶׁר־בָּרָ֥א אֱלֹהִ֖ים לַעֲשֽׂוֹת׃ ·

The מפטיר for שמחת תורה is the same as that of שמיני עצרת on page 958.

הפטרה לשמחת תורה

יהושע א א וַיְהִ֗י אַחֲרֵ֛י מ֥וֹת מֹשֶׁ֖ה עֶ֣בֶד יְהוָ֑ה וַיֹּ֤אמֶר יְהוָה֙
אֶל־יְהוֹשֻׁ֣עַ בִּן־נ֔וּן מְשָׁרֵ֥ת מֹשֶׁ֖ה לֵאמֹֽר׃ ב מֹשֶׁ֥ה עַבְדִּ֖י מֵ֑ת
וְעַתָּה֩ ק֨וּם עֲבֹ֜ר אֶת־הַיַּרְדֵּ֣ן הַזֶּ֗ה אַתָּה֙ וְכָל־הָעָ֣ם הַזֶּ֔ה אֶל־
הָאָ֕רֶץ אֲשֶׁ֧ר אָנֹכִ֛י נֹתֵ֥ן לָהֶ֖ם לִבְנֵ֥י יִשְׂרָאֵֽל׃ ג כָּל־מָק֗וֹם אֲשֶׁ֨ר
תִּדְרֹ֧ךְ כַּף־רַגְלְכֶ֛ם בּ֖וֹ לָכֶ֣ם נְתַתִּ֑יו כַּאֲשֶׁ֥ר דִּבַּ֖רְתִּי אֶל־מֹשֶֽׁה׃

ד מֵהַמִּדְבָּר וְהַלְּבָנוֹן הַזֶּה וְעַד־הַנָּהָר הַגָּדוֹל נְהַר־פְּרָת כֹּל
אֶרֶץ הַחִתִּים וְעַד־הַיָּם הַגָּדוֹל מְבוֹא הַשָּׁמֶשׁ יִהְיֶה גְּבוּלְכֶם׃
ה לֹא־יִתְיַצֵּב אִישׁ לְפָנֶיךָ כֹּל יְמֵי חַיֶּיךָ כַּאֲשֶׁר הָיִיתִי עִם־
מֹשֶׁה אֶהְיֶה עִמָּךְ לֹא אַרְפְּךָ וְלֹא אֶעֶזְבֶךָּ׃ ו חֲזַק וֶאֱמָץ כִּי
אַתָּה תַּנְחִיל אֶת־הָעָם הַזֶּה אֶת־הָאָרֶץ אֲשֶׁר־נִשְׁבַּעְתִּי
לַאֲבוֹתָם לָתֵת לָהֶם׃ ז רַק חֲזַק וֶאֱמַץ מְאֹד לִשְׁמֹר לַעֲשׂוֹת
כְּכָל־הַתּוֹרָה אֲשֶׁר צִוְּךָ מֹשֶׁה עַבְדִּי אַל־תָּסוּר מִמֶּנּוּ יָמִין
וּשְׂמֹאול לְמַעַן תַּשְׂכִּיל בְּכֹל אֲשֶׁר תֵּלֵךְ׃ ח לֹא־יָמוּשׁ סֵפֶר
הַתּוֹרָה הַזֶּה מִפִּיךָ וְהָגִיתָ בּוֹ יוֹמָם וָלַיְלָה לְמַעַן תִּשְׁמֹר
לַעֲשׂוֹת כְּכָל־הַכָּתוּב בּוֹ כִּי־אָז תַּצְלִיחַ אֶת־דְּרָכֶךָ וְאָז
תַּשְׂכִּיל׃ ט הֲלוֹא צִוִּיתִיךָ חֲזַק וֶאֱמָץ אַל־תַּעֲרֹץ וְאַל־תֵּחָת
כִּי עִמְּךָ יהוה אֱלֹהֶיךָ בְּכֹל אֲשֶׁר תֵּלֵךְ׃ ס י וַיְצַו יְהוֹשֻׁעַ
אֶת־שֹׁטְרֵי הָעָם לֵאמֹר׃ יא עִבְרוּ | בְּקֶרֶב הַמַּחֲנֶה וְצַוּוּ אֶת־
הָעָם לֵאמֹר הָכִינוּ לָכֶם צֵידָה כִּי בְּעוֹד | שְׁלֹשֶׁת יָמִים
אַתֶּם עֹבְרִים אֶת־הַיַּרְדֵּן הַזֶּה לָבוֹא לָרֶשֶׁת אֶת־הָאָרֶץ
אֲשֶׁר יהוה אֱלֹהֵיכֶם נֹתֵן לָכֶם לְרִשְׁתָּהּ׃ ס יב וְלָרֽאוּבֵנִי
וְלַגָּדִי וְלַחֲצִי שֵׁבֶט הַמְנַשֶּׁה אָמַר יְהוֹשֻׁעַ לֵאמֹר׃ יג זָכוֹר
אֶת־הַדָּבָר אֲשֶׁר צִוָּה אֶתְכֶם מֹשֶׁה עֶבֶד־יהוה לֵאמֹר יהוה
אֱלֹהֵיכֶם מֵנִיחַ לָכֶם וְנָתַן לָכֶם אֶת־הָאָרֶץ הַזֹּאת׃ יד נְשֵׁיכֶם
טַפְּכֶם וּמִקְנֵיכֶם יֵשְׁבוּ בָּאָרֶץ אֲשֶׁר נָתַן לָכֶם מֹשֶׁה בְּעֵבֶר
הַיַּרְדֵּן וְאַתֶּם תַּעַבְרוּ חֲמֻשִׁים לִפְנֵי אֲחֵיכֶם כֹּל גִּבּוֹרֵי הַחַיִל
וַעֲזַרְתֶּם אוֹתָם׃ טו עַד אֲשֶׁר־יָנִיחַ יהוה | לַאֲחֵיכֶם כָּכֶם
וְיָרְשׁוּ גַם־הֵמָּה אֶת־הָאָרֶץ אֲשֶׁר־יהוה אֱלֹהֵיכֶם נֹתֵן לָהֶם
וְשַׁבְתֶּם לְאֶרֶץ יְרֻשַּׁתְכֶם וִירִשְׁתֶּם אוֹתָהּ אֲשֶׁר | נָתַן לָכֶם
מֹשֶׁה עֶבֶד יהוה בְּעֵבֶר הַיַּרְדֵּן מִזְרַח הַשָּׁמֶשׁ׃ טז וַיַּעֲנוּ

אֶת־יְהוֹשֻׁעַ לֵאמֹר כֹּל אֲשֶׁר־צִוִּיתָנוּ נַעֲשֶׂה וְאֶל־כָּל־אֲשֶׁר
תִּשְׁלָחֵנוּ נֵלֵךְ: יז כְּכֹל אֲשֶׁר־שָׁמַעְנוּ אֶל־מֹשֶׁה כֵּן נִשְׁמַע
אֵלֶיךָ רַק יִהְיֶה יְהוָה אֱלֹהֶיךָ עִמָּךְ כַּאֲשֶׁר הָיָה עִם־מֹשֶׁה: יח
כָּל־אִישׁ אֲשֶׁר־יַמְרֶה אֶת־פִּיךָ וְלֹא־יִשְׁמַע אֶת־דְּבָרֶיךָ לְכֹל
אֲשֶׁר־תְּצַוֶּנּוּ יוּמָת רַק חֲזַק וֶאֱמָץ:

Continue with the blessings after the הפטרה on page 416.

מי שברך

FOR A WORSHIPPER CALLED TO THE READING OF THE TORAH

מִי שֶׁבֵּרַךְ אֲבוֹתֵינוּ אַבְרָהָם יִצְחָק וְיַעֲקֹב הוּא יְבָרֵךְ אֶת (פלוני בֶּן פלוני) אֲשֶׁר עָלָה לַתּוֹרָה. הַקָּדוֹשׁ בָּרוּךְ הוּא יְבָרֵךְ אוֹתוֹ וְאֶת מִשְׁפַּחְתּוֹ (ביום טוב: וְיִזַכֵּהוּ לַעֲלוֹת לְרֶגֶל). וְיִשְׁלַח בְּרָכָה וְהַצְלָחָה בְּכָל מַעֲשֵׂה יָדָיו. וְנֹאמַר אָמֵן.

FOR A SICK PERSON

מִי שֶׁבֵּרַךְ אֲבוֹתֵינוּ אַבְרָהָם יִצְחָק וְיַעֲקֹב הוּא יְבָרֵךְ אֶת

For a male:

הַחוֹלֶה (פלוני בֶּן פלונית) אָנָא רְפָא אֹתוֹ הַמָּלֵא נָא רַחֲמִים עָלָיו לְהַחֲלִימוֹ וּלְהַחֲיוֹתוֹ וּשְׁלַח לוֹ

For a female:

הַחוֹלָה (פלונית בַּת פלונית) אָנָא רְפָא אֹתָהּ הַמָּלֵא נָא רַחֲמִים עָלֶיהָ לְהַחֲלִימָהּ וּלְהַחֲיוֹתָהּ וּשְׁלַח לָהּ

בִּמְהֵרָה רְפוּאָה שְׁלֵמָה בְּתוֹךְ שְׁאָר חוֹלֵי יִשְׂרָאֵל רְפוּאַת הַנֶּפֶשׁ וּרְפוּאַת הַגּוּף

On שַׁבָּת:

שַׁבָּת הִיא מִלִּזְעוֹק

On יוֹם טוֹב:

יוֹם טוֹב הוּא מִלִּזְעוֹק

וּרְפוּאָה קְרֹבָה לָבוֹא, וְנֹאמַר אָמֵן.

TORAH BLESSINGS

The עוֹלֶה says:

בָּרְכוּ אֶת יהוה הַמְבֹרָךְ.

The Congregation responds:

בָּרוּךְ יהוה הַמְבֹרָךְ לְעוֹלָם וָעֶד.

The עוֹלֶה continues:

בָּרוּךְ יהוה הַמְבֹרָךְ לְעוֹלָם וָעֶד. בָּרוּךְ אַתָּה יהוה אֱלֹהֵינוּ מֶלֶךְ הָעוֹלָם, אֲשֶׁר־בָּחַר בָּנוּ מִכָּל־הָעַמִּים, וְנָתַן לָנוּ אֶת־תּוֹרָתוֹ. בָּרוּךְ אַתָּה יהוה, נוֹתֵן הַתּוֹרָה.

After the reading, the עוֹלֶה says:

בָּרוּךְ אַתָּה יהוה אֱלֹהֵינוּ מֶלֶךְ הָעוֹלָם, אֲשֶׁר נָתַן־לָנוּ תּוֹרַת־אֱמֶת, וְחַיֵּי עוֹלָם נָטַע בְּתוֹכֵנוּ. בָּרוּךְ אַתָּה יהוה, נוֹתֵן הַתּוֹרָה.

One who has survived a situation of danger (safe arrival after a hazardous journey, release from captivity, or recovery from serious illness) says:

בָּרוּךְ אַתָּה יהוה אֱלֹהֵינוּ מֶלֶךְ הָעוֹלָם, הַגּוֹמֵל לְחַיָּבִים טוֹבוֹת, שֶׁגְּמָלַנִי כָּל־טוֹב.

The Congregation responds:

אָמֵן. מִי שֶׁגְּמָלְךָ כָּל־טוֹב, הוּא יִגְמָלְךָ כָּל־טוֹב, סֶלָה.

MEMORIAL PRAYER

For a man:

אֲדוֹן הָעוֹלָמִים זְכוֹר אֶת נִשְׁמַת (פלוני בֶּן פלוני) שֶׁהָלַךְ לְעוֹלָמוֹ, אָנָּא אַב הָרַחֲמִים וְהַסְּלִיחוֹת תְּהִי נַפְשׁוֹ צְרוּרָה בִּצְרוֹר הַחַיִּים, וּתְהִי מְנוּחָתוֹ כָּבוֹד, וְנֹאמַר אָמֵן.

For a woman:

אֲדוֹן הָעוֹלָמִים זְכוֹר אֶת נִשְׁמַת (פלונית בַּת פלוני) שֶׁהָלְכָה לְעוֹלָמָהּ, אָנָּא אַב הָרַחֲמִים וְהַסְּלִיחוֹת תְּהִי נַפְשָׁהּ צְרוּרָה בִּצְרוֹר הַחַיִּים, וּתְהִי מְנוּחָתָהּ כָּבוֹד, וְנֹאמַר אָמֵן.

THE JEWISH IDEA OF PRAYER

That following is an excerpt from the Companion to the ... Prayer Book ...

[illegible]

THE JEWISH IDEA OF PRAYER

Rabbi Lord Immanuel Jakobovits zt'l

The following is an excerpt from the Companion to the High Holydays Prayer Book, a compendium of writings by Rabbi Lord Jakobovits zt'l.

THE TRADITIONAL JEWISH CONCEPT of prayer embraces three distinct and essential characteristics: the text is fixed, as are the times for prayer; the compositions encompass teachings as well as petitions; and the liturgy (usually worded in the plural form) is intended for congregational rather than private recitation. These three essential characteristics provide the answer to the obvious problems raised by prayer: What purpose can be served by formulating our pleas to God? Does the all-knowing God who knows our needs better than we do require their articulation of what we feel in our hearts? Still more difficult theologically, how can we hope by prayer to change His will? Our very belief in the efficacy of our petitions would seem to challenge God's immutability, and even question His justice, since we should assume that whatever fate He decrees for man is essentially just; why, and how, therefore, do we seek to reverse it?

But such questions are based on a false, indeed pagan, understanding of prayer· as a means of pacifying and propitiating the deity and thus of earning its favours. It was against these perverse notions that the Hebrew Prophets directed their denunciations so fiercely when they fulminated against the heathen form of sacrifices, the original form of worship later replaced by prayer.

The Torah idea of sacrifice, *korban,* is meant to bring man near (from *karav)* to God. "Why (offer) *unto Me* the multitude of Your sacrifices; I am sated with the burnt-offerings of rams and the fat of animals" (Is. 1:11). God does not need our offerings; we need them. Prayer, if offered for the wrong motives, is likewise unacceptable: "And when you spread out your hands I will close my eyes from you, even when you multiply prayer I will not listen ..." (13).

Like sacrifices, prayer is intended to change man, not God. Its purpose is to cultivate a contrite heart, to promote feelings of humility and inadequacy, whilst encouraging reliance on Divine assistance. Through prayer, the worshipper becomes chastened, gains moral strength and intensifies the quest for spirituality, thereby turning himself into a person worthy of a response to his pleas.

Self-Improvement Through Prayer

If God has decreed the good fate for a man, He requires no prayer; and if there is no such decree how can prayer help to change the will of God in favour of a good decree? And similarly in reverse.

The answer is that the main purpose of prayer is not to change the will of the Holy One Blessed Be He, Heaven forfend. But through the prayer the worshipper himself becomes changed, for he rises to a more elevated and lofty level. And just as "a proselyte who becomes Jewish is like a new-born child" so does the Jew when he rises from step to step represents a new person. If the decree was issued on a certain person, then through prayer which crushes his heart he becomes someone else, who is no longer meant by the decree. (Joseph Albo, *Sepher Ha'Ikkarim* 1425)

The Hebrew for 'pray', unlike the English, is not synonymous with 'beg' or 'petition'. *Tephilah* derives from *hitpalel*, literally 'judge oneself'; one assesses one's own insignificance and one's impotence in relation to God's omnipotence. The reflexive form indicates that prayer is directed at oneself rather than at God. In short, Jewish prayer is intended to *impress* more than to *express* oneself. The harder I pray, the more convinced I become that only God can help me, and that I need His help. Prayer thereby turns me into a better and more deserving human being; in respect of all the favours for which I ask, I realize more and more my dependence on God and my own helplessness.

That is why in our tradition prayer is fixed. The virtues to be taught are changeless. The routine instruction provided by prayer is as vital and constant for spiritual health as daily bread is for physical sustenance.

Since prayer is primarily not a channel for emotional self-expression – of baring one's heart – but an instrument for the evocation of fundamental truths that are to stir our hearts, the impact of prayer is increased when the atmosphere in which it is offered is charged with the maximum solemnity and fervour. To this end, the corporate outpourings of a congregation are clearly more impressive than the private devotions of a lone worshipper. Hence the emphasis on public prayer. And hence also the profusion of teachings and declarations in the statutory liturgy, rather than mere petitions. The ultimate aim is primarily to ennoble the petitioner by making his dependence on God ever more manifest, with a correspondingly heightened realization of his own frailty.

THE ATMOSPHERE OF PRAYER

How Can God 'Dwell' In Synagogues?

When King Solomon consecrated the Temple he had built – the first permanent House of Divine Worship ever erected on earth – he uttered a superb prayer in which he alluded to one of the most perplexing religious problems: "But will God in very truth dwell on the earth? Behold, heaven and the heaven of heavens cannot contain You; how much less this house that I have built!" (I Kings 8:27).

We believe God is everywhere; infinite and omnipresent. How, then, can He be found and worshipped in 'synagogues' rather than anywhere else? Are we not just as near to Him in our homes, in the streets and fields, in the inner space of our hearts and the outer space of the universe beyond? Why, then, do we have to build Him temples and invest them with special sanctity? In what way are we closer to Him there than elsewhere?

The advances of science have given us many insights denied to former generations. Perhaps this problem, too, can be more easily understood and solved in the light of our present-day knowledge. The world is filled with a multitude of sounds carried on radio bands of different wave-lengths to every part of the universe. Thousands of radio stations constantly emit programmes of speech and song. And yet, despite the multitude of sounds surrounding us at all times, we hear none of them unless we tune in to a particular transmission on our radio receivers.

The human senses have only an extremely limited range of perception. Our ear, for instance, can hear only a tiny fraction of the sound waves (and none of the radio waves) in the air and make them audible to us. For a much larger range we need instruments, called radio sets, which transform ultrasound or electric waves so that we can hear them as sounds.

Spiritually we are constructed with similar limitations. Our human senses, made of flesh and blood, cannot perceive God, though He is everywhere around us. To transmit His Presence to us, to make us conscious of His infinite Being, we require special instruments, receiving sets called *synagogues,* through which the purely spiritual can register an impact on us.

A true house of worship has the capacity to make us sense Godliness, to enable us to hear His word, to cause us to experience His comfort. God *is* everywhere; but only in houses of God is He *felt* to be both receptive to our prayers and offering His blessings. Only there is His existence sufficiently amplified to enable us to realize that He dwells in our midst.

A radio set is a delicate apparatus, and it has to fulfil many technical requirements if it is to translate radio waves into audible sounds. A synagogue is a far more complex instrument. It seeks to transmute the intangible into something tangible; to make finite beings perceive the Infinite; to convert that which emanates from the Divine into terms sensible to humans.

To perform this unique function, a synagogue must satisfy many conditions, all designed to convey the Presence of God as a manifest reality. Inside it the worshipper is to find himself in an altogether different world, measured and constructed in purely spiritual dimensions. Its architecture, its seating arrangements, its melodies, its language, its decorum – in short, everything which makes up the totality of the worshipper's experience – must be distinct from the world outside. By means of these external tokens, those who enter a synagogue and participate in its services are to feel differently, think differently, talk differently and behave differently from the way they do anywhere else.

DEVOTION AT PRAYER

Detractors of rabbinic Judaism often decry its alleged legalism which stresses the letter of the law more than its spirit, and is unduly concerned with the mechanical performance of religious duties. Nothing refutes this canard more conclusively than the laws insisting on the proper devotion while praying. Devotion *(kavanah)* means both some comprehension of the meaning of the prayers one recites, and concentrating the mind while praying.

Genuinely Jewish prayer is a feast of spirituality. It is the antithesis of the cold formality of religious services favoured by some denominations which turn acts of worship, for officiants and worshippers alike, into performances rather than outpourings of the heart and most profoundly stirring experiences, ideally to be turned into daily, or at least weekly, events.

But even among the more pious regulars, prayers no longer have the electrifying grip of former generations. The knowledge of the Siddur and the *Machzor* has become ever more deficient just when familiarity with other rabbinic texts has expanded and intensified.

Modern Man's Lost Art of Prayer

"Modern man has lost the capacity to pray. Rare indeed are the individuals who can free their souls from the paralysing apathy of our days ... from the disastrous spell of rationalism and materialistic thoughts, to pray with deep devotion for the realisation of the ultimate purpose in life. The worshipper is conscious neither of the comforting and purifying power of prayer nor of its elevating and ennobling effects, for prayer fell victim to a culture estranged from God and became degraded to an act of mere habit." (Elie Munk, *The World of Prayer,* 1954)

All religious duties should be performed with due devotion and mental concentration. Nevertheless, at least according to some opinions, the absence of such devotion does not invalidate the act except in the case of prayer, where all authorities agree that some degree of concentration is required. Thus, particularly at the openings of the *Shema* and the *Amidah,* if these were recited without proper attention, they must be repeated. For, as the great Jewish moralist, Bachya ibn Pekudah of the 11th century put it, "Prayer without the heart is like a body without the spirit" *(Chovot HaLevavot).* This essential condition for the validity of prayer, or at least of some of them, is also included in all later codes of Jewish law (e.g. *Shulchan Aruch, Orach Chayim,* 61 and 101).

The importance of understanding one's prayers is such that worshippers ignorant of Hebrew may pray in the vernacular *(Sotah* 7:1). But Hebrew is still the preferred medium, and the answer to not knowing it is to learn it.

Also important for the effectiveness of prayer is the frame of mind out of which it is said. The Talmud urges that "one should never rise to pray in a mood of dejection, or indolence, or laughter, chatter, frivolity or idle talk, but only in a mood of joyful piety" *(Berachot* 31a).

The supreme form of prayer is synonymous with jubilation is also expressed at King Solomon's consecration of the Temple – the first permanent House of God ever built on earth – when he pleaded that God may hearken, above all else, 'to the singing and to the prayer' to be uttered there (I Kings 8:28).

Some of our synagogues might be rather empty if they were out of bounds to mourners. But the finest form of worship still enjoins: "Serve the Lord with gladness; enter His presence with singing" (Ps. 100:2).

Prayer requires constant effort and exercise. One who uses his legs only three times a year will find that he cannot walk properly even then, for his muscles will waste for lack of exercise. Similarly, he who prays only on Rosh Hashanah and Yom Kippur may find his prayers limping even on these days. Our Sages spoke of prayer as "A service, or labour, of the heart". Prayer means hard work and heart work: and a heart operation is a most delicate operation.

Operating On the Heart

"Imagine a heart-surgeon bending over his patient doing a cardiac operation and thinking not of his work but of the fees due to him. So is the worshipper who, while attending a Divine service, puts his mind on business matters instead of on his prayers. As a famous 17th-century Polish preacher expressed it: 'Is this a service of the heart, when the body is in the synagogue and the mind in the market?' " (Maggid of Koznitz)

For enhancing the fervour of our prayers, the Jewish tradition recommends both silence and crying out aloud in different contexts. This is based on what appear to be two contradictory biblical passages. The Talmud hails the example of Hannah when she pleaded for the gift of a child: 'Only her lips moved, but her voice could not be heard' (1 Sam 1:13) – which teaches that he who prays should pronounce the words with his lips without the voice being heard *(Berachot* 31a). By contrast, the citizens of Nineveh were told to 'cry mightily unto God' to avert their doom (Jonah 3:8) – implying that the voice should be raised in prayer (Ramban, end *Bo).*

Clearly, both practices apply, each according to circumstances. In general, Hannah's model should be followed, with prayers rendered in silence, though audible to one's own ears. Loud prayers should be avoided. Apart from disturbing other worshippers *(Tur Shulchan Aruch,* 111), such conduct suggests little faith, as if God could not hear silent prayer. It is also reminiscent of the false Prophets of Baal who cried out aloud when their sacrifice was spurned (I Kings 18:28; see *Berachot* 24b and Rashi). Another interesting reason for objecting to saying prayers aloud is "so as not to put sinners to shame" [by others hearing their confessions], just as the Torah (Lev. 6: 18) insists that sin-offerings and voluntary sacrifices be offered in the same place so that sinners would not be recognized *(Sotah* 32b).

But there are exceptions. They are made for those who cannot otherwise concentrate on their prayers. On Rosh Hashanah and Yom Kippur the practice is widespread, though not universally endorsed, to recite all prayers in a slightly raised voice *(Orach Chayim,* 11:3). Distracting the congregation need not then be feared, since all nowadays have Sidurim and *Machzorim (Mishnah Berurah,* 11).

On the other hand, the precedent in the Book of Jonah for loud utterances is intended for non-statutory compositions, such as the penitential and other poetic passages as well as songs of praise and rejoicing *(Aruch Hashulchan,* 111:8).

Ten Ways of Enhancing Kavanah

The *Sepher Derech Chayim (Venice,* 1618) page 67, lists ten items to enhance devotion at prayer:

1. *Torah.* Constant pursuit of Torah studies alone can engender the sincere intimacy with God which is conducive to praying with devotion and conviction.

2. *Novelty.* While the text remains fixed, every recitation of our prayers should have a freshness both of nuance and interpretation; otherwise it becomes routine and perfunctory. [In the same spirit, the Talmud teaches that studying a passage 100 times cannot be compared to studying it 101 times *(Chagigah* 9b) – each time one discovers some novel meaning.]

3. *Need.* Moments of great need, of crisis or danger, evoke the most ardent prayers.

4. *Language.* Pray in the language that is most familiar and meaningful. You should therefore practice speaking Hebrew with your friends so that it will become natural to you.

5. *Movement.* To sway the body during prayer distracts attention, whereas standing still increases it. The habit of swaying the body, founded on the verse: "All my bones shall say it" (Ps. 35: 10), refers only to Songs of Praise, the Blessings of the *Shema* and Torah study, but not to the *Amidah.* Experience proves that stand-

ing still enhances attention, just as a person would not plead before a mortal king whilst his body shakes like the trees in the forest before the wind.

6. *Voice.* Pray in soft tones to promote attention. Loudness distracts it. True, for those who cannot concentrate, a raised voice may help to preserve the awareness of praying, but it will not advance the attention to the meaning of the prayers.

7. *Preparation.* Before commencing the service, condition your mind by silent meditation – simply sitting still for a while, removing all mundane thoughts, and thinking of the greatness of the Creator and His wonders. In earlier times, the pious would spend an hour on such spiritual preparation before starting the service. *(Berachot,* 5:1).

8. *Entrance.* Do not proceed into the synagogue while the congregation recites the principal prayers so as not to interfere with the worshippers' concentration. Even in individual worship, be careful not to stand in a place where one is likely to be disturbed by passers-by.

9. *Neighbour.* Always try and render your prayers sitting near a pious person whose own devout manner of worship encourages emulation. By the same token, avoid a sinful neighbour since his presence may ensnare you to thoughts incompatible with the Divine presence.

10. *Time.* Set aside sufficient time to allow for prayers to be recited with due deliberation. A rushed service is bound to compromise the attention given to the meaning of your prayers. Sometimes it is difficult to keep pace with the speed of a public service and a slower tempo on your own may be preferable.

(Quoted in the *Siddur HaGRA* (the 'Gaon of Vilna'), Introduction from the *Sepher SHeLAH,* Amsterdam, 1598, p.250 b.)

PRAYING WITH A CONGREGATION

The importance of congregational prayer cannot be overstressed. In fact, virtually all standard texts are composed in the plural, and are meant primarily for public recitation. Even when recited privately or silently, they are meant to identify the individual worshipper with the community, and by extension with the entire House of Israel. Likewise, the most sacred parts of the service, such as *Kaddish, Kedusha* and the Reading of the Torah require a *minyan* of ten adult Jews making up a minimal 'congregation'. Otherwise these parts of the service must be altogether omitted.

Public prayer is different in essence and not just in degree from private prayer at several quite unrelated levels. It is not entirely an amplification of individual petitions or recitations, thereby enhancing their effectiveness.

1. Seeking blessings by prayer can be a purely selfish act. By merging one's wants with the congregation, public prayer eliminates this demerit (Moses Hasid, *Iggeret HaMussar,* 1717). This indeed is the characteristic difference between material and spiritual bounties. As the great chassidic teacher, R. Mendel of Kotsk (1788-1859) put it: "You [in the plural] shall serve the Lord ... and He will bless *your* [in the singular] bread. (Ex. 23:25) – one eats *alone,* by oneself (singular), but should pray (plural) in communion with all Israel, even *when alone*". The greatest Jewish poet and philosopher expressed a similar idea thus: "Praying only for oneself is like ... refusing to assist fellow-citizens in the repair of their walls ... In a congregation, one compensates for the defects of the other" (Yehuda Halevi, 1135, *Kuzari,* 3:19).

2. To pray for others is itself the highest form of neighbourly love. In a striking rule, the summary law code, *Kitzur Shulchan Aruch* (12:2), urges that before praying one should formally accept the commandment to 'Love your neighbour as yourself', and a special formula to that effect appears in several Siddur editions. Nothing demonstrates caring for others more than praying for them. Indeed, the Talmud *(Bava Kamma* 92a) declares without qualification: Whoever solicits mercy for the ailment of another with which he too is afflicted, his needs will be answered first, as evidenced by Abraham who prayed for the healing of Avimelech's childlessness (Gen. 20:17) was himself blessed and Sarah, his wife, bore him a child (21:1).

3. Each person is accountable both for his private deeds as an individual and also as a member of the society in which he lives. However, the individual and the community are subject to separate judgements. The *Shema* expresses this quite explicitly by using the plural in the passage dealing with reward and punishment (Deut. 11:13 and; see Rashi) and by limiting the illustrations to forms of retribution, such as promise of rain and plentiful harvests, and the warning of drought and exile rather than individual predicaments.

On Rosh Hashanah and Yom Kippur, this distinction between the status of the individual and that of the congregation is amplified in respect of all three aspects of the synagogue service:

i. The congregation may rely more fully on the Reader's public recitation. Altogether, at this season, extra care should be taken to choose a reader with the highest religious and moral virtues, imposing in appearance and preferably married and blessed with children, 'who can spontaneously pour out his heart and plead from the depth of his soul' *(Kitzur Shulchan Aruch,* 128:7);

ii. The essential blasts of the Shofar are repeated, first before *Musaph* (originally while seated – *teki'ot d'me'yushav)* for individual worshippers, and then again during the *Amidah* or its repetition (while standing – *d'me'umad)* for the congregation (see Maimonides, *Hil. Shofar,* 3:7);

iii. Similarly, the confession of sins, a biblical commandment unique to Yom Kippur, is recited privately at the end of the silent *Amidah,* and then in the middle of the public repetition by the reader collectively with the congregation.

UNDERSTANDING JEWISH PRAYER

Rabbi Lord Jonathan Sacks zt'l

1. INTRODUCTION

PRAYER IS THE LANGUAGE OF THE SOUL in conversation with GOD. It is the most intimate gesture of the religious life and the most transformative. The very fact that we can pray testifies to the deepest elements of Jewish faith: that the universe did not come into existence accidentally, nor are our lives destined to be bereft of meaning. The universe exists, and we exist, because someone – the One GOD, Author of all – brought us into existence with love. It is this belief more than any other that redeems life from solitude and fate from tragedy.

In prayer we speak to a presence vaster than the unfathomable universe, yet closer to us than we are to ourselves: the GOD beyond who is also the Voice within. Though language must fail when we try to describe a Being beyond all parameters of speech, language is all we have, and it is enough. For GOD who made the world with creative words, and who revealed His will through holy words, listens to our prayerful words. Language is the bridge joining us to Infinity.

Judah Halevi, the great eleventh-century poet, said that prayer is to the soul what food is to the body. Without prayer, something within us atrophies and dies. It is possible to have a life without prayer, just as it is possible to have a life without music, or love, or laughter, but it is a diminished thing, missing whole dimensions of experience. We need space within the soul to express our joy in being, our wonder at the universe, our hopes, our fears, our failures, our resolves, bringing our deepest thoughts as an offering to the One who listens, and listening, in turn, to the One who calls. Those who pray breathe a more expansive air: "In the prison of his days / Teach the free man how to praise."

The Siddur is the choral symphony the covenantal people has sung to GOD across forty centuries from the days of the patriarchs until present day. In it we hear the voices of Israel's prophets, priests and kings, its Sages and scholars, poets and philosophers, rationalists and mystics, singing in calibrated harmony. Its libretto weaves together texts from almost every part of the vast library of Jewish spirituality: Torah, the Prophets, the Writings, the classic compendia of the Oral Law – Mishnah, Midrash and Talmud – together with philosophical passages like Maimonides' Thirteen Principles of Faith and extracts from the Zohar, the key text of Jewish mysticism.

There is space in Judaism for private meditation, personal plea. But when we pray publicly we do so as members of a people who have served, spoken to, and wrestled with GOD for longer, in more varied circumstances than any other in history. We use the words of the greatest of those who came before us to make our prayers articulate and to join them to the prayers of others throughout the world and throughout the centuries.

Almost every age and major Jewish community has added something of its own: new words, prayers, customs and melodies. There are many different liturgies: Ashkenazi, Sephardi, Oriental, Yemenite, Italian, those of Rabbi Isaac Luria and the Vilna Gaon and others, each with its own subdivisions. The particular liturgy associated with British and Commonwealth Jewry is, in origin, German-Polish, and is distinct in several ways from the prayer books of Eastern Europe. Each tradition has a character of its own, to which Jewish law applies the principle *nahara nahara upashtei*: "Every river has its own course". Each of the historic traditions has its own integrity, its own channel through which words stream from earth to heaven.

This Introduction tells of how prayer came to take its present form, the distinct spiritual strands of which it is woven, the structures it has, and the path it takes in the journey of the spirit.

2. TWO SOURCES OF PRAYER

THE BEST-KNOWN PHRASE ABOUT Jewish religious worship is: "If you serve the LORD your GOD with all your heart (Deuteronomy 11:13) – what is [the sacrificial] service of the heart [*avodah she-be-lev*]? This is prayer" (*Ta'anit* 2a). Behind these simple words, lies a remarkable story.

Throughout the Hebrew Bible, we find two quite different forms of religious worship. One is prayer. Outside the Book of Psalms there are some 140 references to people praying; in 97 cases we are told the words they said. Abraham prays for the cities of the plain. Jacob prays for deliverance before confronting Esau. Hannah prays for a child. These prayers are direct, simple and spontaneous. They have no fixed formula, no set text. Some are very brief, like Moses' five-word prayer for his sister Miriam: "Please, GOD, heal her now". Others are long, like Moses' forty-day prayer for forgiveness of the people after the sin of the Golden Calf. There are no general rules: these prayers have no fixed time, place or liturgy. They are improvised as circumstance demands.

The other form – generally known as *avodah*, "service" – is sacrifice. Sacrifice could not be less like prayer. As set out from Exodus to Deuteronomy, the sacrificial service is minutely specified. It has its prescribed order: which offerings should be made, when, and by whom. It has a designated place: the Tabernacle in the wilderness, and later, the Temple in Jerusalem. There is no room for spontaneity. When two of Aaron's sons, Nadav and Avihu, make a spontaneous offering of incense, they die (Leviticus 10:1–2). The Mosaic books contain two set texts associated with the Sanctuary, the Priestly Blessing (Numbers 6:24–26) and the declaration made when bringing the first fruits (Deuteronomy 26:5–10). Certain sacrifices, such as sin-offerings, involved verbal confession. Psalms were sung in the Temple, and the Mishnah details the prayers said there. But the sacrificial act itself was wordless. It took place in silence.

So we have two quite different traditions, prayer and sacrifice: one spontaneous, the other rigorously legislated; one that could take place anywhere, at any time, by anyone; the other which could only happen in a set place and time in accordance with detailed and inflexible procedures. How did these two forms of worship become one?

The answer lies in the national crisis and renewal that occurred after the destruction of the First Temple by Nebuchadnezzar in 586 BCE. Psalm 137 has preserved a vivid record of the mood of near-despair among the exiles: "By the rivers of Babylon we sat and wept as we remembered Zion…How can we sing the LORD's songs in a strange land?" In exile in Babylon, Jews began to gather to expound the Torah, articulate a collective hope of return, and recall the Temple and its service. These assemblies (*kinishtu* in Babylonian, *Knesset* in Hebrew) were not substitutes for the Temple, rather they were reminders of it. The book of Daniel, set in Babylon, speaks of threefold daily prayer facing Jerusalem (Daniel 6:10). The loss of the Temple and the experience of exile led to the emergence of regular gatherings for study and prayer.

The next chapter in this story was written by Ezra (fifth century BCE) who, together with the statesman Nehemiah, reorganised Jewish life in Israel after the return from Babylon. Ezra ("the scribe") was a new type in history: the educator as hero. The Book of Nehemiah (8:1–9) contains a detailed description of the national assembly Ezra convened in Jerusalem, where he read the Torah aloud, with the help of the Levites who explained it to the people.

Ezra and Nehemiah were disturbed by the high degree of assimilation among the Jews who had remained in Israel. They knew that without a strong religious identity, the people would eventually disappear through intermingling with other nations and cultures. To guard against this, they set in motion far-reaching initiatives, including a national reaffirmation of the nation's covenant with GOD (Nehemiah 10). One of the most important developments was the first formulation of prayers, attributed by the Sages to Ezra and the Men of the Great Assembly. Maimonides suggests that one of their motives for so doing was to re-establish Hebrew as the national language: at that time, "Half of their children spoke the language of Ashdod or the language of the other peoples, and did not know how to speak the language of Judah" (Nehemiah 13:24; Laws of Prayer 1:4).

One of the results of this religious renewal was the birth, or growth, of the synagogue. During the Second Temple period, priests were divided into 24 groups, *mishmarot*, each of which served in the Temple for a week in a rota. They were accompanied by groups of local laypeople, *ma'amadot*, some of whom accompanied them to the Temple, others of whom stayed in their towns but said prayers to coincide with the sacrifices. Whether the synagogue developed from these *ma'amadot*, or whether its origins were earlier, by the time the Second Temple was destroyed in 70 CE, it was a well-established institution.

The synagogue was "one of the greatest revolutions in the history of religion and society" (M. Stern). It was the first place of worship made holy, not because of any historic association, nor because sacrifices were offered, but simply because people gathered there to study and pray. It embodied one of the great truths of monotheism: that the GOD of everywhere could be worshipped anywhere. After the loss of the Second Temple it became the home-in-exile of a scattered people. Every synagogue was a fragment of Jerusalem. And though the destruction of the Temple meant that sacrifices could no longer be offered, in their place came an offering of words, namely prayer.

The transition from sacrifice to prayer was not a sudden development. A thousand years earlier, in his speech at the dedication of the Temple, King Solomon had emphasised prayer rather than sacrifice (I Kings 8:12–53). Through Isaiah, God had said "My House shall be called *a house of prayer* for all peoples (Isaiah 56:7). The prophet Hosea had said: "Take words with you and return to the LORD... Instead of bulls we will pay [the offering of] our lips" (Hosea 14:3). Sacrifice was the external accompaniment of an inner act of heart and mind: thanksgiving, atonement, and so on. Therefore, though the outer act was no longer possible, the inner act remained. That is how sacrifice turned into prayer.

What had once been two quite different forms of worship now became one. Prayer took on the highly structured character of the sacrificial service, with fixed texts and times. The silence that had accompanied the sacrifice was transmuted into speech. Two traditions – prophetic prayer on the one hand, priestly sacrificial service on the other – merged and became one. That is the remarkable story behind the words, "What is the [sacrificial] service of the heart? This is prayer."

There is a series of arguments, spanning the centuries, about the nature of prayer. According to Maimonides, prayer is a biblical commandment; according to Nachmanides it is merely rabbinic. Two third-century teachers, Rabbi Jose, son of Rabbi Chanina, and Rabbi Joshua ben Levi, disagreed as to the origin of the prayers, the former holding that they were instituted by the patriarchs – Abraham initiating the morning prayer, Isaac the afternoon, and Jacob the evening service – while the latter held that they corresponded to the sacrifices. Centuries earlier, Rabban Gamliel and the Sages differed as to which was primary, the silent *Amidah* or the Reader's repetition. Each of these debates ultimately hinges on the question as to which of the two sources of prayer – the improvised prayers of the figures of the Bible or the sacrificial service of the Tabernacle and Temple – is the more fundamental.

In truth, there is no answer: prayer as we have known it for two millennia draws on both traditions. More remarkably, we honour both, because *each Amidah is said twice*, once silently by individuals, a second time aloud and publicly by the Leader. The silent *Amidah* recalls the prayers of individuals in the Bible, while the Leader's repetition recalls the sacrifice: hence there is no repetition of the evening *Amidah*, since there was no sacrifice in the evening. In prayer, two great streams of Jewish spirituality met and became one.

3. STRUCTURES OF PRAYER

THE HEBREW WORD FOR A PRAYER book, Siddur, means "order". At its height, prayer is an intensely emotional experience. The wonder of praise, the joy of thanksgiving, the passion of love, the trembling of awe, the broken-heartedness of confession, the yearning of hope – all these are part of the tonality of prayer. Yet Judaism is also, and supremely, a religion of the mind – for untutored emotion, like a river that bursts its banks, can be anarchic and destructive. The opening chapter of Genesis, with its account of creation, evokes a sense of order. Each day has its task; each life-form has its place; and the result (until the birth of sin) was harmony. Jewish prayer, therefore, has an order. Like a choral symphony, it has movements, each with its moods, its unfolding themes, its developmental logic. In this section, I analyse some of these structures.

The Siddur as it exists today is the result of some forty centuries of Jewish history. Yet the result is not mere bricolage, a patchwork of random additions. It is as if the composition of the prayer book has been shaped by an "invisible hand", a Divine inspiration that transcends the intentions of any particular author. Specifically, form mirrors substance. The shape of the prayers reveals the basic shape of the Jewish spirit as it has been moulded by its encounter with God. These are some of the structural features of the prayers.

A. From Universal to Particular

In general, sequences of Jewish prayer move from the universal to the particular. Grace after Meals, for example, begins with a blessing thanking God "who in His goodness feeds *the whole world*". The second blessing moves to particularities: Israel, liberation from slavery, "the covenant You sealed in our flesh", Torah and the commandments. We thank God "for the land [of Israel] and the food." The third is more narrowly focused still. It is about the holy city, Jerusalem.

The same pattern exists in the two blessings before the *Shema* in the morning and evening service. The first is about the universe ("who gives light to the earth", "who creates day and night"), and the second is about Torah, the specific bond of love between God and the Jewish people. Look and you will find many more examples in the Siddur. (The one exception is *Aleinu*, whose first paragraph is about Jewish particularity and whose second is a universal hope. On this, see below, on "mirror-image symmetry").

This movement from universal to particular is distinctively Jewish. Western culture, under the influence of Plato, has tended to move in the opposite direction, from the concrete instance to the general rule, valuing universals above particularities. Judaism is the great counter-Platonic narrative in Western civilization.

Moving from the universal to the particular, the prayer book mirrors the structure of the Torah itself. Genesis begins, in its first eleven chapters, with a description of the universal condition of humankind. Only in its twelfth chapter is there a call to an individual, Abraham, to leave his land, family and father's house and lead a life of righteousness through which "all the families of the earth shall be blessed".

There are universals of human behaviour: we call them the Noahide Laws. But we worship God in and through the particularity of our history, language and heritage. The highest love is not abstract but concrete. Those who truly love, cherish what makes the beloved different, unique, irreplaceable: that is the theme of the greatest of all books of religious love, *The Song of Songs*. That, we believe, is how God loves us.

B. Mirror-image Symmetry

Many Torah passages are constructed in the form of a mirror-image symmetry, technically known as *chiasmus*: a sequence with the form ABCCBA, where the second half reverses the order of the first. A precise example is the six-word commandment that forms the central element of the Noahide covenant (Genesis 9:6):

"[A] Who sheds [B] the blood [C] of man [C] by man [B] shall his blood [A] be shed."

This is more than a stylistic device. It is the expression of one of the Torah's most profound beliefs; namely, the reciprocal nature of justice. Those who do good are blessed with good. Those who do evil, suffer evil. What happens to us is a mirror image of what we do. Thus form mirrors substance: mirror-image symmetry is the literary equivalent of a just world.

Some prayers have a mirror-image structure. Most of the paragraphs of the *Amidah*, for example, finish the same way as they begin ("at the end of a blessing one should say something similar to its beginning", *Pesachim* 104a). So, for example, the sixteenth blessing begins, "Hear our voice" and ends "Who hears prayer". The eighteenth begins, "We thank You" and ends "To whom it is fitting to give thanks." The *Amidah* as a whole begins with a request to God to help us open our mouth in prayer. It ends with a request to God to help us close our mouth from deceitful speech.

According to Rav Joseph Soloveitchik, the first and last three blessings of the *Amidah* stand in a mirror-image relationship. The last uses the same key words as the first: kindness (*chessed*) and love (*ahavah*). The penultimate has the same subject as the second: the gift of life and the hidden miracles that surround us constantly. The seventeenth and third are both about holiness. Thus the end of the *Amidah* is a mirror-image of its beginning.

This explains why *Aleinu* – the prayer with which most services end – is constructed in a sequence opposite to all other prayers. Others move from the universal to the particular, but *Aleinu* reverses the order, beginning with a hymn to particularity ("Who has not made us like the nations of the world") and ending with one of the great prayers for universality, when "*all* mankind will call on Your name". *Aleinu* gives each service a chiastic structure. Previous prayers have been A–B (universal–particular); *Aleinu* is B–A (particular–universal).

As we will see, many of the other structuring principles are three-part series of the form A–B–A.

C. Praise, Request, Thanks

The Sages ruled that the *Amidah* – prayer par excellence – should follow a basic pattern of praise (*shevach*), request (*bakashah*), and acknowledgement or thanks (*hodayah*). This is how Maimonides puts it: "The obligation of prayer is that every person should daily, according to his ability, offer up supplication and prayer, first uttering *praises* of God, then with humble *supplication and petition* asking for all that he needs, and finally offering praise and *thanksgiving* to the Eternal for the benefits already bestowed on him in rich measure" (Laws of Prayer 1:2).

The *Amidah* is constructed on this template. Of its nineteen blessings, the first three express praise. The middle thirteen on weekdays are requests (we do not make requests in the *Amidah* on Shabbat or Festivals, which are times dedicated to thanking God for what we have, as opposed to asking Him for what we lack). The final three are acknowledgements. The same pattern can be seen in the blessings over the Torah at the beginning of the morning service (see below, *Fractals*).

D. Preparation, Prayer, Meditation

Prayer requires intense concentration, and this takes time. It is impossible to move directly from the stresses and preoccupations of everyday life into the presence of eternity. Nor should prayer end abruptly. It must be internalised if it is to leave its trace within us as we move back into our worldly pursuits. Maimonides writes that because prayer needs mental focus, "One should therefore sit awhile *before* beginning his prayers, so as to concentrate his mind. He should then pray in gentle tones, beseechingly, and not regard the service as a burden which he is carrying and which he will cast off before proceeding on his way. He should thus sit awhile *after* concluding the prayers, and only then leave. The ancient saints used to pause and meditate one hour before prayer and one hour after prayer, and spend an hour in prayer itself" (Laws of Prayer 4:16).

In the morning service, the Verses of Praise (*Pesukei de-Zimra*) are the preparation. In them, our thoughts gradually turn from the visible world to its invisible Creator. The *Shema, Amidah* and their surrounding blessings are prayer as such. The remainder of the service is our meditation as we leave the orbit of heaven and re-renter the gravitational field of earth.

E. Description, Experience, Recollection

It is one thing to describe an experience, another to live it. One of the striking features of the weekday morning service is its threefold repetition of the *Kedushah* ("Holy, holy, holy"), once before the *Shema* (known as *kedushat yotzer*); a second time during the Reader's repetition of the *Amidah*; and a third time during the prayer "A redeemer will come to Zion" (known as *kedushah de-Sidra*). The first and third are different from the second in that: 1. they do not require a *minyan*, and 2. they do not need to be said standing.

The *Kedushah* – one of the supreme moments of holiness in Jewish prayer – is constructed around the mystical visions of Isaiah and Ezekiel, of God enthroned in majesty, surrounded by angels singing His praises. In the first and third *Kedushot*, we *describe* the angelic order; in the second we *enact* it, using the same words, but this time in direct, not reported, speech (Geonim, Maimonides). The intensity of *Kedushah* is heightened by this three-movement form: first the anticipation and preparation, then the experience itself, and finally the recollection.

F. Private, Public, Private

The *Amidah* itself – especially on weekday mornings and afternoons – is constructed on a triadic pattern. First it is said silently by the members of the congregation as individuals. Next it is repeated publicly out loud by the Leader. This is then usually followed by private supplications (*Tachanun*), also said quietly. As I have suggested above, this is a way of re-enacting the two modes of spirituality from which prayer derives. The silent *Amidah* recalls the intensely personal prayers of the patriarchs and prophets. The public repetition represents the daily sacrifices offered by the priests in the Temple on behalf of all Israel (there is no repetition of the evening *Amidah* because there were no sacrifices at night). Thus the prayers weave priestly and prophetic, individual and collective voices, into a single three-movement sonata of great depth and resonance.

G. Fractals

We owe to the scientist Benoit Mandelbrot the concept of fractals, the discovery that phenomena in nature often display the same pattern at different levels of magnitude. A single rock looks like a mountain. Crystals, snowflakes and ferns are made up of elements that have the same shape as the whole. Fractal geometry is the scientific equivalent of the mystical ability to sense the great in the small: "To see a world in a grain of sand / And a Heaven in a wild flower, / Hold Infinity in the palm of your hand, and Eternity in an hour."

The first of the "request" prayers in the daily *Amidah* is a fractal. It replicates in miniature the structure of the *Amidah* as a whole (Praise–Request–Thanks). It begins with praise: "You favour man with knowledge and teach humanity understanding", moves to request: "Favour us with knowledge, understanding and insight", and ends with thanksgiving: "Blessed are You, O LORD, the gracious Giver of knowledge." You will find many other fractals in the Siddur.

The existence of fractals in the Siddur shows us how profoundly the structures of Jewish spirituality feed back time and again into the architectonics of prayer.

H. Midrashic Expansion

Midrash is the rabbinic investigation into the meaning of holy texts: the root *d-r-sh* means "to explore, enquire, explain, expound". It seeks out the inflections and innuendos of words, making explicit their implicit dimensions of meaning.

One example occurs in the *Nishmat* prayer on Shabbat morning (page 366). A key phrase in prayer, spoken by Moses and incorporated into the first paragraph of the *Amidah*, is "GOD, great, mighty and awesome" (Deuteronomy 10:17). *Nishmat* meditates on these four words, one by one:

GOD – in Your absolute power,
Great – in the glory of Your name,
Mighty – for ever,
Awesome – in Your awe-inspiring deeds.

Another is the passage on Shabbat morning following the phrase "who forms light and creates darkness, makes peace and creates all" (page 370). A brief prayer takes the last word, "all", and builds around it a fivefold set of variations: "*All* will thank You. *All* will praise You. *All* will declare: Nothing is holy as is the LORD. *All* will exalt You, Selah, You who form *all*".

Always look for apparent repetition in prayer – like the tenfold "Blessed" in "Blessed is He who spoke", the sixfold "True" after the *Shema*, or the sixfold "All" immediately after *Bar'chu* on Shabbat morning. Reiteration is never mere repetition. The prayer is inviting us to meditate on the multiple layers of meaning that may exist in a single word or phrase, as if words were diamonds and we were turning them this way and that to catch their multiple refractions of light.

I. Numerical Structures

As we have seen, many of the prayers have an obvious three-part structure, but in some cases this is repeated in great detail on a smaller scale, as in fractals.

The most striking example is the weekday *Amidah*, which is composed of three parts: praise–request–acknowledgement. The first and last of these are each constructed in threes: three blessings of praise at the beginning, and three of acknowledgement at the end. Less obvious is the fact that the middle thirteen blessings – "requests" – *also* share this structure. There are six individual requests, followed by six collective ones, each divided into two groups of three. The individual requests begin with three spiritual needs (understanding, repentance, forgiveness) followed by three material ones (deliverance from oppression, healing,prosperity). The collective requests begin with three political-historical elements (ingathering of exiles, restoration of judges, and an end to internal strife – the "slanderers"), followed by the three spiritual bases of nationhood (the righteous, Jerusalem, and the restoration of the Davidic monarchy). The thirteenth, "Hear our voice", stands outside this structure because it is not directed to any specific request but is, instead, a prayer that our prayers be heeded.

The number seven is also significant and always indicates holiness, as in the seventh day, Shabbat; the seventh month, Tishrei with its Days of Awe; the seventh year, the "year of release"; and the fiftieth year, the Jubilee, which follows seven cycles of seven years. Seven in Judaism is not a simple prime number. It is the *one-after-six*. Six represents the material, physical, secular. Ancient Mesopotamia, from which Abraham came, originally used a numerical system based on the number six. Western civilization still bears traces of this in the twenty-four hour day (2×6 hours of light, plus 2×6 of darkness); the sixty (10×6) minutes in an hour, and seconds in a minute; and the 360 degrees in a circle ($6 \times 6 \times 10$). All of these originated in astronomy, at which the ancient Mesopotamians excelled. Judaism acknowledges the six-part structure of time and space, but adds that God exists *beyond* time and space. Hence seven – the one beyond six – became the symbol of the holy.

Six, too, is not a simple number in Judaism. This becomes evident when we read the story of creation in Genesis 1 carefully. The first six days fall into two groups. On the first three, God created and separated *domains* (1: light and darkness, 2: upper and lower waters, 3: sea and dry land). On the second three God *populated* these domains, each with its appropriate objects or life-forms (4: sun, moon and stars, 5: birds and fish, 6: land animals and man). The seventh day, Shabbat, is *holy* because it stands *outside* nature and its causal-scientific laws.

Mirroring this pattern, the morning service is structured around the number seven: the three paragraphs of the *Shema*, surrounded by three blessings, leading to the seventh, the *Amidah*, which is the domain of the holy, where we stand directly in the presence of God. On holy days – Shabbat and Festivals – the *Amidah* has a sevenfold structure: the three opening and closing paragraphs, plus a middle paragraph dedicated to "the holiness of the day".

It follows that sixfold structures in the Siddur signal the universe and creation. Thus, on weekday mornings we say six psalms (145–150) in the Verses of Praise. *Kabbalat Shabbat* also contains six psalms, corresponding to the days of the week, before *Lecha Dodi*, which represents Shabbat itself. The blessing after the *Shema* repeats the keyword *Emet* ("true") six times to show how God's love is translated into redemptive activity in a this-worldly time and space.

Many prayers such as *El Adon* (page 374) and *Aleinu* are constructed in a pattern of fours: four-line verses, each of four words. Often these reflect Jewish mysticism with its four "worlds": *Asiyah* (Action), *Yetzirah* (Formation), *Beriah* (Creation) and *Atzilut* (Emanation).

Merkavah mysticism, based on Ezekiel's vision of the Divine chariot, is an important strand of early rabbinic prayer.

The number ten represents the "ten utterances with which the world was created" (the ten places in Genesis 1 where an act of creation is preceded by the words "God said"). That is why *Baruch She-amar*, the blessing before the creation section of the prayers, begins with a tenfold litany of phrases each beginning with the word "Blessed".

Fifteen represents the fifteen steps between the courtyards of the Temple, the fifteen Psalms beginning "A Song of Ascent", and the numerical value of the first two letters of God's holiest name. Hence there are fifteen expressions of praise in the paragraph *Yishtabach*; fifteen adjectives following "the Lord Your God, true" at the end of the *Shema* in the morning; fifteen psalms in the Verses of Praise on Shabbat and Festival mornings; and so on. There are also more intricate numerical patterns.

These are not mere aesthetic conventions like, for example, the fourteen-line sonnet form or the four-movement structure of a symphony. As always in Judaism there is a matching of form to content, structure to substance. The Sages understood – as did the ancient Greeks, amply confirmed by modern science – that *reality has a numerical structure*. Mirroring this structure in prayer, we evoke the sense of a world of order in which we are called on to respect differences and honour boundaries, accepting graciously the integrity of natural and moral law.

J. From Love to Awe

The supreme religious emotions are love and awe – in that order. We are commanded to "Love the Lord your God". We are also commanded to experience the feelings associated with the Hebrew word *yirah*, which means "awe, fear, reverence". This is how Maimonides puts it: "When a person contemplates His great and wondrous works and creatures and from them obtains a glimpse of His wisdom, which is incomparable and infinite, he will immediately love Him, praise Him, glorify Him, and long with an exceeding longing to know His great name… And when he ponders these matters, he will recoil frightened, and realise that he is a small creature, lowly and obscure, endowed with slight and slender intelligence, standing in the presence of Him who is perfect in knowledge" (*Yesodei HaTorah* 2:2).

The supreme expression of love in Judaism is the *Shema* with its injunction: "Love the Lord your God with all your heart, all your soul, and all your might." The supreme expression of awe is the *Amidah* prayer, when we stand consciously in the presence of God. The basic movement of the morning and evening prayers is first, to climb to the peak of love, the *Shema*, and from there to the summit of awe, the *Amidah*.

4. CREATION, REVELATION, REDEMPTION

One structural principle of the prayers deserves special attention, since it touches on the fundamentals of Jewish faith. In the twelfth century, Moses Maimonides enumerated the Thirteen Principles of Jewish Faith. They appear in the Siddur in two forms: the poem known as *Yigdal* (page 12) and a prose version after the end of the morning service (page 164).

Rabbi Shimon ben Tzemach Duran (1361–1444) pointed out that Maimonides' principles could be analysed and categorised into three themes: 1. the existence of God, the Creator (Principles 1–5: God's existence, unity, incorporeality and eternity, and that He alone is to be worshipped); 2. Divine revelation (Principles 6–9: prophecy, Moses' uniqueness, the God-given character of the Torah and its immutability), and 3. God's justice (Principles 10–13: God knows all, repays us according to our deeds, and will bring the messiah and the resurrection of the dead). The philosopher Franz Rosenzweig summarised these in three words: creation, revelation, redemption. Creation is the relationship between God and the universe. Revelation is the relationship between God and humanity. Redemption occurs when we apply revelation to creation.

The movement from creation to revelation to redemption is one of the great structural motifs of prayer. One example is the three blessings in the morning service, surrounding the *Shema* and leading up to the *Amidah* (pages 62–74). The first is about the *creation* of the universe in space and time; the second is about the *revelation* of the Torah; and the third is about the miracles of history, ending with the words, "who *redeemed* Israel".

The three paragraphs of the *Shema* display the same pattern. The first is about creation (God's unity and sovereignty), the second about revelation (acceptance of the commandments), and the third about redemption ("I am God your Lord who brought you out of the land of Egypt").

The weekday morning as a whole is constructed on this principle. First come the Verses of Praise, taken from the Book of Psalms, with their majestic vision of creation. Then follows the central section – the *Shema* and its blessings, leading to the *Amidah* – in which we sit, then stand, in the immediate presence of God (revelation). Finally we come to the concluding prayers with their central line, "A *redeemer* will come to Zion". The second paragraph of *Aleinu* is likewise a vision of redemption.

The pattern is repeated yet again in the Shabbat evening, morning and afternoon prayers. On Friday evening, in the central blessing of the *Amidah*, we speak of the Shabbat of creation ("the culmination of the creation of heaven and earth"). In the morning we refer to the Shabbat of revelation (when "Moses brought down in his hands the two tablets of stone"). In the afternoon we anticipate future redemption (when "You are one and Your name is one" and the people Israel are again "one nation on earth").

Rav Joseph Soloveitchik suggested that the same sequence is the basis for the threefold structure of the weekday *Amidah*: praise, request, thanks. Praise "emerges from an enraptured soul gazing at the *mysterium magnum* of creation", request "flows from an aching heart which finds itself in existential depths", and thanksgiving "is sung by the person who has attained, by the grace of God, redemption." Creation leads to praise, revelation to request, and redemption to thanksgiving.

In these multiple ways, prayer continually reiterates the basic principles of Jewish faith.

5. PRAYER AND STUDY

THERE IS ONE SPIRITUAL ACTIVITY that the Sages regarded as even higher than prayer: namely, study of Torah, God's word to humanity and His covenant with our ancestors and us (*Shabbat* 10a). The entire *Ethics of the Fathers* is a set of variations on the theme of a life devoted to Torah study. In prayer, we speak to God. Through Torah, God speaks to us. Praying, we speak. Studying, we listen.

From earliest times, the synagogue was a house of study as well as a house of prayer. Gatherings for study (perhaps around the figure of the prophet; see II Kings 4:23) may well have preceded formal prayer services by many centuries. Accordingly, interwoven with prayer are acts of study.

The most obvious is the public reading from the Torah, a central part of the Shabbat and Festival services, and in an abridged form on Monday and Thursday mornings and Shabbat afternoons. There are other examples. In the morning blessings before the Verses of Praise, there are two cycles of study, each in three parts: 1. Torah i.e. a passage from the Mosaic books; 2. Mishnah, the key document of the Oral Law; and 3. Talmud in the broadest sense (pages 14–16 and 24–32).

In the main section of prayer, the paragraph preceding the *Shema* is a form of blessing over Torah (see *Berachot* 11b), and the *Shema* itself represents Torah study (*Menachot* 99b). The last section of the weekday morning prayers (pages 136–138) was originally associated with the custom of studying ten verses from the prophetic books. *Kaddish*, which plays such a large part in the prayers, had its origin in the house of study as the conclusion of a *derashah*, a public exposition of biblical texts. The entire weekday morning service is thus an extended fugue between study and prayer.

This is dramatised in two key phrases: the first is *Shema Yisrael*, "Listen, Israel", God's word through Moses and the Torah, and the second is *Shema Koleinu*, "Listen to our voice", the paragraph within the *Amidah* that summarises all our requests (see above). These two phrases frame the great dialogue of study and prayer. Faith lives in these two acts of listening: ours to the call of God, God's to the cry of humankind.

6. PRAYER AND MYSTICISM

JEWISH MYSTICISM HAS PLAYED A major role in the prayer book. The most obvious examples are the passage from the Zohar, "Blessed is the name" (page 408), the Song of Glory (page 458) written by one of the medieval North European pietists, and the two songs written by the sixteenth-century Tzefat mystics associated with Rabbi Isaac Luria, "Beloved of the soul" (page 256) and "Come, my beloved" (page 266).

Less obviously, many of the early post-biblical prayers were deeply influenced by Hechalot ("Palace") and Merkavah ("Chariot") mysticism, two esoteric systems that charted the mysteries of creation, the angelic orders, and the innermost chambers of the Divine glory.

Undoubtedly, though, the most significant mystical contribution to the prayers is the *Kedushah*, said in three different forms, most notably during the Leader's repetition of the *Amidah*. We have noted the two major tributaries of prayer: the spontaneous prayers said by figures in the Hebrew Bible, and the sacrificial service in the Temple. Mysticism is the third, and its most sublime expression is the *Kedushah*, based on the mystical visions of Isaiah (6) and Ezekiel (1–3). There are times in the prayers when we are like prophets, others when we are like priests, but there is no more daring leap of faith than during the *Kedushah*, when we act out the role of angels singing praises to God in His innermost chambers.

Familiarity breeds inattention, and we can all too easily pass over the *Kedushah* without noticing its astonishing drama. "The ministering angels do not begin to sing praises in heaven until Israel sings praises down here on earth" (*Chullin* 91b). "You", said God through Isaiah, "are My witnesses" (Isaiah 43:10). Israel is "the people I formed for Myself that they might declare My praise" (43:21). We are God's angels on earth, His emissaries and ambassadors. The Jewish people, always small and vulnerable, have nonetheless been singled out for the most exalted mission ever entrusted to humankind: to be witnesses, in ourselves, to something beyond ourselves: to be God's "signal of transcendence" in a world in which His presence is often hidden.

This is a mystical idea, and like all mysticism it hovers at the edge of intelligibility. Mysticism is the attempt to say the unsayable, know the unknowable, to reach out in language to a reality that lies beyond the scope of language. Often in the course of history, mysticism has tended to devalue the world of the senses in favour of a more exalted realm of disembodied spirituality. Jewish mysticism did not take this course. Instead it chose to bathe our life on earth in the dazzling light of the Divine radiance (*zohar*, the title of Judaism's most famous mystical text).

7. RELIVING HISTORY

HISTORY, TOO, HAS LEFT ITS MARK on the Siddur. There are passages, indicated in the Commentary, that were born in the aftermath of tragedy or miraculous redemption. This edition of the Siddur also includes suggested orders of service for Yom Ha'Atzma'ut and Yom Yerushalayim, marking the birth of the State of Israel in 1948, and the Six Day War of 1967.

No less significantly, the synagogue service invites us at many points to re-enact history. The Verses of Praise begin with the song of celebration sung by King David when he brought the Ark to Jerusalem. The verses we sing when we take the Torah scroll from the Ark and return it recall the Israelites' journeys through the wilderness, when they carried the Ark with them. In one of the most fascinating transitions in the service, as we move from private meditation to public prayer (pages 358–362), we recall three epic moments of nation-formation: when David gathered the people to charge them with the task of building the Temple; when Ezra convened a national assembly to renew the covenant after the return from Babylonian exile; and when Moses led the Israelites through the Reed Sea. Even the three steps forward we take as we begin the *Amidah* recall the three biblical episodes in which people stepped forward (*vayigash*) as a prelude to prayer: Abraham pleading for the cities of the plain, Judah pleading with Joseph for Benjamin to be set free, and Elijah invoking God against the prophets of Baal on Mount Carmel.

We are a people defined by history. We carry our past with us. We relive it in ritual and prayer. We are not lonely individuals, disconnected with past and present. We are characters in the world's oldest continuous story, charged with writing its next chapter and handing it on to those who come after us. The Siddur is, among other things, a book of Jewish memory.

8. PRAYER AND FAITH

THE SIDDUR IS ALSO THE BOOK OF Jewish faith. Scholars of Judaism, noting that it contains little systematic theology, have sometimes concluded that it is a religion of deeds not creeds, acts not beliefs. They were wrong because they were searching in the wrong place. They were looking for a library of works like Moses Maimonides' *Guide for the Perplexed*. They should have looked instead at the prayer book. The home of Jewish belief is the Siddur.

At several points, the prayers have been shaped in response to theological controversy. The opening statement in the morning service after *Bar'chu*, "who forms light and creates darkness, makes peace and creates all", is a protest against dualism, which had a considerable following in the first centuries CE in the form of Gnosticism and Manichaeism. Its presence can be traced in the ancient documents discovered in the 1940s, the Dead Sea Scrolls and the Nag Hammadi codices. Against dualism, with its vision of perpetual cosmic struggle, Judaism insists that all reality derives from a single source.

The second paragraph of the *Amidah*, with its fivefold reference to the resurrection of the dead, reflects the ancient controversy between the Pharisees and Sadducees. The morning prayer, "My God, the soul You placed in me is pure" (page 16), may be directed against the Pauline doctrine of original sin. The Mishnah chapter, "With what wicks may we light?" (page 298), was probably inserted as part of the polemic against the Karaite sect. The Ten Commandments, said daily as part of the Temple service immediately after the *Shema*, was removed from the prayers when it was used by sectarians to argue that only these ten commandments were commanded by God.

The fact that Jewish faith was written into the prayers, rather than analysed in works of theology, is of immense significance. We do not analyse our faith: we pray it. We do not philosophise about truth: we sing it. Even Maimonides' Thirteen Principles of Jewish faith – the most famous creed in the history of Judaism – only entered the mainstream of Jewish consciousness when they were turned into a song and included in the Siddur as the hymn known as *Yigdal*. For Judaism, theology becomes real when it becomes prayer. We do not talk *about* God. We talk *to* God.

I have known many atheists. My doctoral supervisor, the late Sir Bernard Williams, described as the most brilliant mind in Britain, was one. He was a good, caring, deeply moral human being, but he could not understand my faith at all. For him, life was ultimately tragic. The universe was blind to our presence, deaf to our prayers, indifferent to our hopes. There is no meaning beyond that which human beings construct for themselves. We are dust on the surface of infinity.

I understood that vision, yet in the end I could not share his belief that it is somehow more honest to despair than to trust, to see existence as an accident rather than as invested with a meaning we strive to discover. Sir Bernard loved ancient Greece; I loved biblical Israel. Greece gave the world tragedy; Israel taught it hope. A people, a person, who can pray is one who, even in the darkest night of the soul, can never ultimately lose hope.

9. PRAYER AND SACRIFICE

THE CONNECTION BETWEEN PRAYER and sacrifice is deep. As we have seen, sacrifice is not the only forerunner of our prayers; many prayers were spoken by figures in the Bible. These were said without any accompanying offering. Yet the sacrificial system is a major tributary of the Jewish river of prayer. After the destruction of the Second Temple, prayer became a substitute for sacrifice. It is *avodah she-be-lev*, "the sacrificial service of the heart". Yet it is just this feature of the prayers that many find difficult to understand or find uplifting. What, then, was sacrifice?

The Hebrew word for sacrifice is *korban*, which comes from a root that means "to come, or bring close". The essential problem to which sacrifice is an answer is: how can we come close to God? This is a profound question – perhaps *the* question of the religious life – not simply because of the utter disparity between God's infinity and our finitude, but also because the very circumstances of life tend to focus our gaze downward to our needs rather than upward to our source. The Hebrew word for universe, *olam*, is connected to the verb meaning "to hide" (see Leviticus 4:13; Deuteronomy 22:1). The physical world is a place in which the presence of God is real, yet hidden. Our horizon of consciousness is foreshortened. We focus on our own devices and desires. We walk in God's light, but often our mind is on other things.

How then do we come close to God? By *an act of renunciation*; by giving something away; specifically, by giving something *back*. The sacrifices of the biblical age were ways in which the individual, or the nation as a whole, in effect said: what we have, God, is really Yours. The world exists because of You. *We* exist because of You. Nothing we have is ultimately ours. The fundamental gesture of sacrifice is, on the face of it, absurd. What we give to God is something that already belongs to Him. As King David said: "Who am I and who are my people that we should be able to give as generously as this? Everything comes from You, and we have given You only what comes from Your hand" (I Chronicles 29:14). Yet *to give back to* God is one of the most profound instincts of the soul. Doing so, we acknowledge our dependency. We cast off the carapace of self-absorption. That is why, in one of its most striking phrases, the Torah speaks of sacrifice as being *re'ach nichoach*, "sweet savour" to God.

One of the sweetest savours of parenthood is when a child, by now grown to maturity, brings a parent a gift to express his or her thanks. This too seems absurd. What can a child give a parent that remotely approximates what a parent gives a child, namely life itself? Yet it is so, and the reverse is also true. The cruellest thing a child can do is *not* to acknowledge his or her parents. The Talmud attributes to Rabbi Akiva the phrase *Avinu Malkeinu*, "Our Father, our King." Those two words encapsulate the essence of Jewish worship. God is King – Maker and Sovereign of the vast universe. Yet even before God is our King, He is our Father, our Parent, the One who brought us into being in love, who nurtured and sustained us, who taught us His ways, and who tenderly watches over our destiny. Sacrifice – the gift we bring to God – is the gift of the made to its Maker, the owned to its Owner, the child to its Parent. If creation is an act of love, sacrifice is an acknowledgement of that love.

The late Rav Joseph Soloveitchik emphasised the difference between *ma'aseh mitzvah*, the external act specified by a commandment, and *kiyyum mitzvah*, the actual fulfilment of a commandment. When the Temple stood, for example, a penitent would bring a guilt or sin-offering to atone for his sin: that was the external act. The fulfilment of the commandment, though, lay in confession and contrition, acts of the mind and will. In biblical times, the sacrificial order was the external act, but the internal act – acknowledgement, dependency, recognition, thanks, praise – was essential to its fulfilment. That is why Judaism was able to survive the destruction of the Temple and the cessation of the sacrificial order. The external act could no longer be performed, but the internal act remained. That is the link between sacrifice and prayer.

The difference between prayer-as-request and prayer-as-sacrifice is that request *seeks*, sacrifice *gives*. The prophets asked, usually on behalf of the people as a whole, for forgiveness, deliverance and blessing. The priests who offered sacrifices in the Temple asked for nothing. Sacrificial prayer is the giving back to God what God already owns: our lives, our days, our world. Prayer is creation's gift to its Creator.

The prophets were critical of the sacrificial system. They reserved for it some of their most lacerating prose. Yet none proposed its abolition, because what they opposed was not the sacrificial act, but the *ma'aseh* without the *kiyyum*, the outer act without the inner acknowledgement that gives the act its meaning and significance. The idea that God can be worshipped through externalities alone is pagan, and there is nothing worse than the intrusion of paganism into the domain of holiness itself. Then as now, the sign of paganism is the co-existence of religious worship with injustice and a lack of compassion in the dealings between the worshipper and the world.

Sacrifice, like prayer, is a transformative act. We should leave the synagogue, as our ancestors once left the Temple, seeing ourselves and the universe differently, freshly conscious that the world is God's work, the Torah God's word, our fellow believers God's children, and our fellow human beings God's image. We emerge re-focused and re-energised, for we have made the journey back to our source, to the One who gives life to all. Distant, we have come close. That is prayer as sacrifice, *korban*, giving back to God a token of what He has given us, thereby coming to see existence itself as a gift, to be celebrated and sanctified.

10. KAVANNAH: DIRECTING THE MIND

PRAYER IS MORE THAN SAYING CERtain words in the right order. It needs concentration, attention, engagement of mind and heart, the left and right hemispheres of the brain. Without devotion, said Rabbi Bachya ibn Pakuda, prayer is like a body without a soul. The key Hebrew word here is *kavannah* meaning mindfulness, intention, focus, direction of the mind. In the context of prayer, it means several different things.

The most basic level is *kavannah leshem mitzvah*, which means, having the intention to fulfil a *mitzvah*. This means that we do what we do, not for social or aesthetic reasons. We pray because we are commanded to pray. In general in Judaism there is a long-standing debate about whether the commandments require *kavannah*, but certainly prayer does, because it is supremely an act of the mind.

At a second level, *kavannah* means understanding the words (*perush ha-milim*). At least the most important sections of prayer require *kavannah* in this sense. Without it, the words we say would be mere sounds. Understanding the words is, of course, made much easier by the existence of translations and commentaries.

A third level relates to context. How

do I understand my situation when I pray? Maimonides states this principle as follows: "The mind should be *freed from all extraneous thoughts* and the one who prays should *realise that he is standing before the Divine presence*." These are essential elements of at least the *Amidah*, the prayer par excellence in which we are conscious of standing before God. That is why we take three steps forward at the beginning, and three back at the end – as if we were entering, then leaving, sacred space.

The fourth level of *kavannah* is not merely saying the words but meaning them, affirming them. Thus, for example, while saying the first paragraph of the *Shema*, we "accept of the yoke of the kingdom of heaven" – declaring our allegiance to God as the supreme authority in our lives. In the second paragraph, we "accept of the yoke of the commandments". The word *Amen* means roughly, "I affirm what has been said." In prayer we put ourselves into the words. We make a commitment. We declare our faith, our trust, our dependency. We mean what we say.

There are, of course, higher reaches of *kavannah*. Mystics and philosophers throughout the ages developed elaborate meditative practices before and during prayer. But at its simplest, *kavannah* is the practised harmony of word and thought, body and mind. This is how Judah Halevi described it:

"The tongue agrees with the thought, and does not overstep its bounds, does not speak in prayer in a mere mechanical way as the starling and the parrot, but every word is uttered thoughtfully and attentively. This moment forms the heart and thought of his time, while the other hours represent the way which leads to it. He looks forward to its approach, because while it lasts he resembles the spiritual beings, and is removed from mere animal existence. Those three times of daily prayer are the fruits of his day and night, and the Sabbath is the fruit of the week, because it has been appointed to establish the connection with the Divine spirit and to serve God in joy, not in sadness."

Of course it does not always happen. It is told that on one occasion Rabbi Levi Yitzchak of Berditchev went up to one of his followers after the prayers, held out his hand and said "Welcome home." "But I haven't been anywhere", said the disciple. "Your body hasn't been anywhere", said the Rebbe, "but your mind has been far away. That is why I wished it, 'Welcome home.'"

Rabbi Menachem Mendel of Kotzk once asked: "Why does it say in the *Shema*, 'These words shall be *on* your heart'? Should it not say, 'These words shall be *in* your heart'? The answer is that the heart is not always open. Therefore we should lay these words on our heart, so that when it opens, they will be there, ready to enter."

Prayer requires practice. That is implicit in defining prayer as *avodah shebe-lev*, "service of the heart". The word *avodah*, service, also means hard work, labour, strenuous activity. We have to work at prayer. But there are also times when the most inarticulate prayer, said from the heart, pierces the heavens. What matters is seriousness and honesty. "God is close to all who call on Him – to all who call on Him in truth."

11. JACOB'S LADDER

PRAYER IS A JOURNEY THAT HAS BEEN described in many ways. According to the mystics, it is a journey through the four levels of being – Action, Formation, Creation and Emanation. Rabbi Jacob Emden worked out an elaborate scheme in which the prayers represent a movement from the outer courtyards to the Holy of the Holies of the Temple in Jerusalem. According to everyone, the stages of prayer constitute an ascent and descent, reaching their highest level in the middle, in the *Shema* and *Amidah*.

The metaphor that, to me, captures the spirit of prayer more than any other is Jacob's dream in which, alone at night, fleeing danger, far from home, he saw a ladder stretching from earth to heaven with angels ascending and descending. He woke and said, "How awesome is this place! This is none other than the house of God; this is the gate to heaven" (Genesis 28:10–17).

Our Sages said that "this place" was Jerusalem. That is midrashic truth. But there is another meaning, the plain one, no less transfiguring. The verb the Torah uses, *vayifgah*, means "to happen upon, as if by chance". "This place" was any place. Any place, any time, even the dark of a lonely night, can be a place and time for prayer. If we have the strength to dream and then, awakening, refuse to let go of the dream, then here, now, where I stand, can be the gate to heaven.

Prayer is a ladder and we are the angels. If there is one theme sounded throughout the prayers, it is creation–revelation–redemption, or ascent–summit–descent. In the Verses of Praise, we climb from earth to heaven by meditating on creation. Like a Turner or Monet landscape, the psalms let us see the universe bathed in light, but *this* light is not the light of beauty but of holiness; the light the Sages say God made on the first day and "hid for the righteous in the life to come". Through some of the most magnificent poetry ever written, we see the world as God's masterpiece, suffused with His radiance, until we reach a crescendo in Psalm 150 with its thirteen-fold repetition of "Praise" in a mere thirty-seven words.

By the time we reach *Bar'chu* and the blessings of the *Shema* we have neared the summit. Now we are in heaven with the angels. We have reached revelation. The Divine presence is close, almost tangible. We speak of love in one of the most hauntingly beautiful of blessings, "Great love" with its striking phrase: "Our Father, merciful Father, the Merciful, have mercy on us". Now comes the great declaration of faith at the heart of prayer, the *Shema* with its passionate profession of the unity of God and the highest of all expressions of love, "with all your heart, with all your soul, and with all your might". Ending with a reference to the exodus, the *Shema* gives way to the *Emet* blessing with its emphasis on redemption, the exodus and the division of the sea. Then comes the *Amidah*, the supreme height of prayer. Three traditions fuse at this point: the silent *Amidah* said by individuals, reminding us of prophetic prayer; the Leader's repetition representing priestly worship and prayer as sacrifice; and then the *Kedushah*, prayer as a mystical experience.

From here, prayer begins its descent. First comes *Tachanun* in which we speak privately and intimately to the King. At this point, with a mixture of anguish and plea, we speak not of God's love for Israel but of Israel's defiant love of God: "Yet despite all this we did not forget You; please do not forget us." There is a direct reference back to the *Shema*: "Guardian of Israel, guard the remnant of Israel, and let not Israel perish who declare: *Shema Yisrael*".

Then comes *Ashrei* and the subsequent passages, similar to the Verses of Praise but this time with redemption, not creation, as their theme. The key verse is "A redeemer will come to Zion".

The section closes with a prayer that we may become agents of redemption as we re-engage with the world ("May it be Your will…that we keep Your laws in this world"). We are now back on earth, the service complete except for *Aleinu, Kaddish* and the Psalm of the Day. We are ready to re-enter life and its challenges.

What has prayer achieved? If we have truly prayed, we now know that the world did not materialise by chance. A single guiding will directed its apparent randomness. We know too that this will did not end there, but remains intimately involved with the universe, which He renews daily, and with humanity over whose destinies He presides. We have climbed the high ladder and have seen, if only dimly, how small some of our worries are. Our emotional landscape has been expanded. We have given voice to a whole range of emotions: thanks, praise, love, awe, guilt, repentance, remembrance, hope. As we leave the synagogue for the world outside, we now know that we are not alone; that God is with us; that we need not fear failure, for God forgives; that our hopes are not vain; that we are here for a purpose and there is work to do.

We are not the same after we have stood in the Divine presence as we were before. We have been transformed. We see the world in a different light. Perhaps we radiate a different light. We have spoken and listened to God. We have aligned ourselves with the moral energies of the universe. We have become, in Lurianic terminology, vessels for God's blessing. We are changed by prayer.

12. IS PRAYER ANSWERED?

IS PRAYER ANSWERED? IF GOD IS CHANGE-less, how can we change Him by what we say? Even discounting this, why do we need to articulate our requests? Surely God, who sees the heart, knows our wishes even before we do, without our having to put them into words. What we wish to happen is either right or wrong in the eyes of God. If it is right, God will bring it about even if we do not pray. If it is wrong, God will not bring it about even if we do. So why pray?

The classic Jewish answer is simple but profound. Without a vessel to contain a blessing, there can be no blessing. If we have no receptacle to catch the rain, the rain may fall, but we will have none to drink. If we have no radio receiver, the sound waves will flow, but we will be unable to convert them into sound. God's blessings flow continuously, but unless we make ourselves into a vessel for them, they will flow elsewhere. *Prayer is the act of turning ourselves into a vehicle for the Divine.*

Speaking from personal experience, and from many encounters with people for whom prayer was a lifeline, I know that our prayers are answered: not always in the *way* we expected, not always as quickly as we hoped, but *prayer is never in vain.* Sometimes the answer is No. If granting a request would do us or others harm, God will not grant it. But No is also an answer, and when God decides that something I have prayed for should not come to pass, then I pray for the wisdom to understand why. That too is part of spiritual growth: to accept graciously what we cannot or should not change. Nor is prayer a substitute for human effort: on the contrary, prayer is one of the most powerful sources of energy for human effort. God gives us the strength to achieve what we need to achieve, and to do what we were placed on earth to do.

Prayer changes the world because it changes us. At its height, it is a profoundly transformative experience. If we have truly prayed, we come in the course of time to know that the world was made, and we were made, for a purpose; that God, though immeasurably vast, is also intensely close; that "though my father and mother may reject me, God will gather me in"; that God is with us in our efforts, and that we do not labour in vain. We know too that we are part of the community of faith, and with us are four thousand years of history, and the prayers and hopes of those who came before us. However far we feel from God, He is there behind us, and all we have to do is turn to face Him. Faith is born and lives in prayer, and faith is the antidote to fear: "The Lord is the stronghold of my life – of whom shall I be afraid?"

It makes a difference to be brushed by the wings of eternity. Regular thrice-daily prayer works on us in ways not immediately apparent. As the sea smoothes the stone, as the repeated hammer-blows of the sculptor shape the marble, so prayer – cyclical, tracking the rhythms of time itself – gradually wears away the jagged edges of our character, turning it into a work of devotional art. We begin to see beauty of the created world. We locate ourselves as part of the story of our people. Slowly, we come to think less of the "I", more of the "We"; less of what we lack than of what we have; less of what we need from the world, more of what the world needs from us. Prayer is less about getting what we want than about learning what to want. Our priorities change; we become less angular; we learn the deep happiness that comes from learning to give praise and thanks. The world we build tomorrow is born in the prayers we say today.

When, at the end of his vision, Jacob opened his eyes, he said with a sense of awe: "Surely God is in this place and I did not know it." That is what prayer does. It opens our eyes to the wonder of the world. It opens our ears to the still, small voice of God. It opens our hearts to those who need our help. God exists where we pray. As Rabbi Menachem Mendel of Kotzk said: "God lives where we let Him in." And in that dialogue between the human soul and the Soul of the universe a momentous yet gentle strength is born.

KEYWORDS OF PRAYER

The names of God

The two key names, in prayer as in the Torah, are 1. the *Tetragrammaton*, יהוה, the "four letter" name, and 2. אֱלוֹהִים *Elohim*. They are different in meaning and tone. The Sages understood the Tetragrammaton as God's compassion. *Elohim* is God's attribute of justice.

Judah Halevi (*Kuzari*, IV:1) made a more fundamental distinction. The ancients used the word *El* or *Eloah* to designate a force of nature: the sun, the sea, the storm, and so on. These they personified as gods. Often, therefore, *el*, or *elil*, denotes an idol. In Hebrew, monotheism's mother tongue, *Elohim* in the plural means "the One who is the totality of powers, forces and causes in the universe". It refers to God as we experience Him in creation and its natural laws, as well as in justice and its moral laws (it sometimes also has a secular sense, meaning those who hold positions of power, usually judges).

The Tetragrammaton not only has a different meaning, it is also a word of a different grammatical type. It is God's *proper name*, standing in relation to Him as the names Abraham or Sarah attach to human beings (hence it is sometimes referred to as *Hashem*, "the name"). The use of a proper name in connection with God means that a direct relationship between us and heaven is possible. We can speak to God, and He listens. There is a direct connection between the Tetragrammaton and the word "You". Only a being that has a proper name can we address as "You". Hence, in prayer, "You" is always directed to the Tetragrammaton; *Elohim* goes with the third-person, "He". Thus *Elohim* signifies God-as-law, natural or moral. The Tetragrammaton refers to God as we encounter Him in intimacy, compassion and love.

Though I have followed convention, rendering the Tetragrammaton as "Lord", it should be remembered that "Lord" is not a *translation* but a *substitution*. So holy was the Divine name that it was used only in the Temple. In all other contexts, it was (and still is) pronounced as *Adonai*, which means "my Lord".

The use of the word *Eloheinu*, "*Our* God", signifies our acceptance of God as sole object of our worship. Formal acknowledgement of this fact – in the first line of the *Shema* – is a pledge of loyalty and service, called by the Sages, "Acceptance of the yoke of Divine kingship".

The word מֶלֶךְ "King" when applied to God means, first, that God is the sole ultimate Sovereign of the people Israel, who accepted His kingship and covenant at Mount Sinai. At that ceremony, God undertook to guide the Israelites' destiny, while the people accepted their vocation as "a kingdom of priests and a holy nation", bound by God's laws. The second and wider meaning is that God is Sovereign over the universe and all humanity – with whom, via Noah, He made a covenant after the Flood (Genesis 9). That covenant, with its seven laws, embodies the fundamental principles of human conduct under God. Though God's sovereignty is not yet recognised by all, it will be in the end of days. Hence our prayers often end with the prophecy of Zechariah (14:9), "Then the Lord shall be King over all the earth." The sovereignty of God is the ultimate sanction against tyranny. It implies that all human authority is delegated authority, to be exercised only within the constraints of the covenant.

Sometimes God is referred to as קוֹנֵה which, though I have followed convention by translating it as "Creator", literally means "Owner" of heaven and earth. This represents the idea that because God *created* the universe, He *owns* it. The world and its benefits do not belong to us. What we possess, we hold in trust from God. This is the legal basis of Divine sovereignty of the universe – similar to the ancient concept of "eminent domain" by which all ownership of land within a country is ultimately vested in its head of state. As Sovereign of the universe, God rules by right, not power.

Attributes of God

Many of the key terms descriptive of God are not precisely translatable because they presuppose the concept of covenant: an open-ended pledge between two or more parties to join their destinies together in a reciprocal bond of loyalty and love. The nearest human equivalents are: 1. the bond of marriage; 2. peace treaties between nations. The unique idea of the Torah is that such a covenant can exist between God and humanity.

Thus אֱמֶת, often translated as "true", actually means "faithful, one who acts in accord with his word, one who honours commitments and promises". חֶסֶד, translated as "lovingkindness", refers to the emotions and actions that flow from a covenantal bond, such as between husband

and wife, or between parents and children. It means *love translated into deed.*

There is no English word for צְדָקָה, which means both "justice" and "charity". צֶדֶק, often translated as "righteousness", means "distributive justice, equity" as opposed to מִשְׁפָּט, which means "legal or retributive justice". רַחֲמִים, which I have translated as "compassion", derives from the word *rechem*, meaning "a womb". It signifies the unconditional love of a mother for her child. חֵן ,"grace", means gratuitous kindness, which flows from the generosity of the giver, not the merits of the recipient.

קָדוֹשׁ *Holy.* In general, this means "separated, set apart, standing outside". Used of God, it means "He who stands outside nature" because He *made* nature. Used of the people of Israel (as in "a holy nation", Exodus 19:6) it means the people who stand outside the normal laws of nations – defined by land, language, race or political structure – because they are the sole nation whose constitutive *raison d'être* is to serve God as His witnesses to the world. Shabbat is holy time because it stands outside the normal concerns of the week. The Temple is holy space because it is dedicated to the service of God.

To stand in the presence of holiness, as in prayer, is to enter God's domain; that is, the place where His will rules, not ours. That is why prayer is like sacrifice, because both involve a psychological-spiritual act of renunciation. We renounce our will, accepting His. The Hebrew word for sacrifice, *korban*, means "coming, or bringing, close". Often, in non-Hebraic languages, the word "holy" implies distance and awe. In Judaism, the reverse is also true: Israel encounters holiness as a special closeness to God. This is experienced as both love and awe: love, because of our closeness to the Infinite; awe because of the exacting responsibilities this carries with it.

Other key terms

אָמֵן Saying "Amen" is what philosophers call a "performative utterance". It is a formal act of acceptance and affirmation, meaning: 1. we believe this to be true; or 2. we associate ourselves with what has been said. It functions in the Torah as an assent to an oath (e.g. in Deuteronomy 27:15–26). The root *'-m-n* has a range of senses, including "to believe, to trust, to care, to be faithful". In general, liturgical responses – such as "Blessed is He and blessed is His name" – form an essential link between the Reader and congregation, turning a prayer *on behalf of* the community into one assented to *by* the community. Special significance was attached by the Sages to the response during the recital of *Kaddish*, "May His great name be blessed for ever and all time". Indeed for them, the merit of saying *Kaddish* is precisely that it evokes this response from the community.

אַתָּה *You*: The gods of the ancient world were at best indifferent, at worst actively hostile, to human beings. The God of the philosophers – abstract, conceptual, the prime mover or necessary being – can be contemplated but not addressed. The difference between the God of the prophets and the God of the philosophers is that the former knows us, cares about us, listens to us (Judah Halevi, *Kuzari*). Without the word "You" there can be meditation, but not prayer. The central section of most forms of the *Amidah* begins with the word "You".

בָּרוּךְ *Blessed.* When applied to God it means: He is the *source* of all blessings, not only spiritual but also physical: health, livelihood, safety and security.

In prayer we learn to see our material enjoyments as GOD's blessing, belonging as they do to the world He created and pronounced good. The root *b-r-ch* also means: 1. to bow, bend the knee; 2. a pool or reservoir of water. What connects these is *downward movement.* A blessing is what, metaphorically, flows down to earth from heaven.

There are several categories of blessings in the Siddur: 1. blessings of acknowledgement, which are forms of praise and thanksgiving; 2. blessings over the performance of commandments, which are formal declarations of intent (*kavannah*) that the act we are about to perform is done because GOD has commanded us to do so; 3. blessings over enjoyments (food, drink, and so on), which are acts of redemption in the technical sense of buying something back for secular use that would otherwise be holy, and thus is not available for our personal benefit.

מִזְמוֹר *Mizmor* ("Psalm") is found 57 times as the heading of a psalm, and is used nowhere else in Tanach. Many believe it refers to a song written to be accompanied by musical instruments. תְּהִלָּה *Tehillah,* "song of praise", is used only once as superscription to a psalm (Psalm 145); despite this, the Book of Psalms as a whole is known to Jewish tradition as *Tehillim,* "Songs of Praise". Some psalms carry the name of the person who wrote it or to whom it was dedicated; others the occasion on which it was sung; yet others are musical directions. The term לַמְנַצֵּחַ *la-m'natze'ach* means "for the conductor, director of music, choir-master", and usually signals a choral work.

סֶלָה *Selah.* A word of unknown meaning. Some hold that it means "for ever"; others understand it as an affirmation, similar to the word "Amen". Yet others see it as a musical notation, a signalled pause, or an indication of the end of a passage.

עוֹלָם *Olam.* The word *olam* means both "universe" and "eternity" – the outermost limits of space and time. It may come from the same root as *ne'elam,* "hidden". This was understood by Jewish mystics, especially of the Lurianic school, as meaning that to create a universe, the Infinite had to contract or limit Himself, otherwise Infinity would leave no space for finitude. GOD is present in the physical universe but in a hidden way. We are, explains Nachmanides, surrounded by miracles. The world is filled with the radiance of GOD but to see it we have to open our eyes. Part of the purpose of prayer is, in this sense, to open our eyes.

שֵׁם *Name*: How GOD is perceived by human beings. When He is recognised as the supreme Sovereign, this is a "sanctification of the name". When He is forced to exile His people – and thus seen by the nations as if powerless to protect them – this is a "desecration of the name". The opening words of *Kaddish,* "Magnified and sanctified may His great name be", mean "May the sovereignty of GOD be ever more widely recognised by human beings". The closing words of *Aleinu,* "On that day GOD shall be One and His name One", refer to a time – the Messianic Age – when GOD will be recognised by all. GOD does not change; human recognition of GOD does. The use of the word "name" marks the distinction between GOD as He is, and as He is humanly perceived.

Other terms are explained within the Commentary.

GUIDE TO THE JEWISH YEAR AND PRAYER, INCORPORATING THE CUSTOMS OF THE UNITED SYNAGOGUE

Dayan Ivan Binstock

Introduction

The following guide is intended to offer direction to the laws and customs of prayer and the Jewish year, as practiced in the United Synagogue. A fuller version, with source references and illustrations, will be published separately.

GUIDE TO THE JEWISH YEAR

Ellul

1. Rosh Chodesh Ellul is always two days. 1st Ellul can fall on a Sunday, Monday, Wednesday or Friday.
2. When Rosh Chodesh starts on Sunday, replace the *Machar Chodesh* Haftarah with the regular *Re'eh* Haftarah, one of the seven haftarot of consolation. When Rosh Chodesh starts on Shabbat, the United Synagogue (US) custom is to replace the regular Haftarah with the Rosh Chodesh Haftarah (justified because the latter also contains a message of consolation). On Shabbat *Ki Tetze*, the *Re'eh* Haftarah is appended to the *Ki Tetze* Haftarah (they are adjacent passages in Isaiah).
3. From 1st Ellul, add Psalm 27 at the end of the evening and morning services. Sound the shofar (*Tekiah, Shevarim, Teruah, Tekiah*) before the morning reading until the day before the Eve of Rosh Hashanah.
4. 5th Ellul. Yahrzeit of Chief Rabbi Hart Lyon (died 26th August 1800).
5. On *Motza'ei* Shabbat prior to Rosh Hashanah, start saying *Selichot.* If Rosh Hashanah is on a Monday/Tuesday, *Selichot* begin on the preceding Motza'ei Shabbat.
6. *Selichot* continue every weekday until Yom Kippur. The original custom was to say *Selichot* before dawn. Most congregations say *Selichot* before Shacharit. If necessary, *Selichot* may be said the previous evening.
7. One praying without a minyan may say *Selichot* but should omit the '13 Middot'. Alternatively, one may say them as long as they are chanted in the *ta'amei hamikra* mode.

Erev Rosh Hashanah (29th Ellul)

8. The *Selichot* service is the longest of the year. A mourner in the week of Shivah may attend.
9. Omit *Tachanun* and Shofar blowing, even if Erev Rosh Hashanah is on Friday.
10. After Shacharit, it is customary to say *Hatarat Nedarim*, the annulment of vows, in front of an ad-hoc Bet Din of three adult males.
11. Other customs include visiting the cemetery and immersing in a mikva.
12. When Rosh Hashanah falls on Thursday, make *Eruv Tavshilin* (P. 642) to permit cooking on Friday for Shabbat.

Rosh Hashanah (1st and 2nd Tishrei)

13. The first day of Rosh Hashanah can fall on Monday, Tuesday, Thursday or Shabbat.
14. Rosh Hashanah can fall between 5th September and 5th October in the civil calendar.
15. Candle-lighting (P. 644). Two blessings are said: *Lehadlik Ner Shel Yom Tov* (or *Lehadlik Ner Shel Shabbat Veyom Tov* if on Shabbat) and *Shehecheyanu.* On a weekday, many women have the custom to say the blessings before lighting candles. Men lighting candles always do this.
16. Yom Tov Ma'ariv is conducted in the traditional melody. Insert the verse *Tik'u BaChodesh Shofar* (Psalms 81:4) before the Amidah. Following the Amidah, Kaddish *Titkabal.* If Rosh Hashanah starts on Friday night, Ma'ariv is preceded by the last two psalms of Kabbalat Shabbat (92 and 93), followed by Mourner's Kaddish. Insert the verse *Veshamru* (*Shemot* 9:16) before *Tik'u BaChodesh Shofar.* Say the Amidah with Shabbat additions. After the Amidah the congregation says *Veyechulu HaShamayim,* followed by *Me'ein Sheva* (the leader's summary of the Amidah). In *Magen Avot, HaMelech Hakadosh* replaces the phrase *HaEl HaKadosh.* The service concludes as per the Machzor.
17. In Kaddish, it is customary to replace the phrase *L'eyla Min Kol* with *L'eyla L'eyla Mikol,* although the original US custom was to retain *Min Kol.* If forgotten, one is not required to repeat Kaddish. US custom is not to change *Oseh Shalom* to *Oseh HaShalom.*
18. Amidah: From Rosh Hashanah to Yom Kippur add *Zochrenu LaChayim* in the first blessing; *Mi Kamocha* in the second; change the end of the third to *HaMelech HaKadosh*; add *Uchtov L'Chayim* in the penultimate blessing; change the final blessing's conclusion to *Osei HaShalom.* If forgotten, one is not required to repeat the Amidah. The exception is *HaMelech HaKadosh,* where one must repeat the entire Amidah unless the mistake is corrected straight away.
19. On the first night it is customary to greet people with the blessing of an inscription for a good year. To a man: *LeShana Tova Tichatev Vetechatem.* To a woman: *LeShana Tova Tichatevi Vetechatemi.*
20. At home, recite Kiddush in the traditional melody (P. 746) On Friday night, insert Shabbat additions. It is customary to dip challah in honey and, after eating, say a prayer for a sweet new year. The Talmud (*Keretot* 6a) mentions several significant

foods that are omens for a good and sweet year. The widespread custom is to dip a slice of apple in honey, make the blessing *Bore Peri Ha'Etz,* and after eating say the prayer for a sweet new year. *Ya'ale VeYavo* is added to *Birkat HaMazon.*

21. Shacharit: US custom is for officiants to wear a *kittel.* Morning blessings and *Pesukei de-Zimra* are said in the traditional melody. The Leader for Shacharit starts from *HaMelech.* In many communities, the custom is for him to start *HaMelech* from his place, then move to the Amud or Bima to continue with *Yoshev.* After *Yishtabach* some congregations open the Ark and say Psalm 130 responsively. The service continues as in the Machzor. In the repetition of the Amidah, the Ark is opened for some of the *piyyutim.* It is customary to stand at these points, if one is able. Following the Amidah, *Avinu Malkenu* (unless it is Shabbat). Kaddish *Titkabal.*
22. Torah reading: The '13 Middot' (Attributes of Mercy, P. 406) and the supplication following are said on weekdays but not Shabbat. Two Torah scrolls are taken from the Ark. The Torah reading is chanted in the Rosh Hashanah and Yom Kippur melody. Many have the custom that the *Oleh* makes the blessing in the same melody. First day: *Bereishit* 21:1-34. Second day: *Bereishit* 22:1-24.
23. Shofar: Hearing the shofar is a positive mitzvah of the Torah. The first 30 blasts sounded before Musaf are the minimum that one is required to hear. However, the custom of sounding 100 notes is now widespread (although the original US custom was only to sound 12 notes in the repetition of the Amidah)
24. Prior to the blowing, the custom is for the congregation to recite Psalm 47 seven times. The *Ba'al Toke'a* leads *Min HaMetzar.*
25. The *Ba'al Toke'a* is required to stand. It is the practice for the rabbi or a learned member of the congregation to stand next to him and call out the notes. The congregation may sit for the shofar sounds before Musaf, but usual practice is to stand.
26. The *Ba'al Toke'a* says two blessings: *Lishmo'a Kol Shofar* and *Shehecheyanu.*
27. To prevent distractions while performing the mitzvah of hearing the shofar, the congregation is not allowed to speak about unrelated matters until after the first 30 blasts. They should not speak about matters unrelated to prayer until after all 100 blasts.
28. The shofar is not blown on Shabbat, even where there is an Eruv.
29. Musaf: It is now customary in many US synagogues for the *Ba'al Musaf* to recite a preparatory prayer, *Hineni He'ani Mima'as,* before *Chatzi* Kaddish and the silent Amidah.
30. The fourth blessing in the repetition of the Amidah contains *Aleinu.* The Ark is opened and the Leader kneels and prostrates at *Va'anachu Kor'im.* In many communities the congregation does likewise. It is forbidden to prostrate on a bare stone floor; many do not prostrate on a wooden floor. Where there is no carpet, a piece of cloth or paper must be placed between one's head and the floor, or complete prostration should not take place.
31. Although the original US custom was not to have *Birkat Kohanim* (*Duchaning*) on Shabbat, it now takes place in many communities, even on Shabbat.

32. There are different customs regarding the final 40 Shofar blasts. The original practice (based on the *Shelah HaKadosh*) was to sound 30 notes during or after Kaddish *Titkabal* and the final 10 before *Aleinu* or *Adon Olam* to establish four stages for the Shofar blasts. Many communities now blow the final 40 in one session, during or after Kaddish *Titkabal*.
33. Mincha. As for Shabbat and Yom Tov. When a Shabbat, the first part of *Ha-azinu* is read. During the *Aseret Yemei Teshuva*, in the repetition of the Amidah it is customary for the Leader to pause before the additions *Zochrenu Lachayim, Mi Kamocha, Uchtom* and *Besefer Chayim*, to allow the congregation to say them first. *Avinu Malkenu* follows the repetition, except on Shabbat.
34. Following Mincha it is customary to say *Tashlich* by a source of flowing water. If Rosh Hashanah starts on Shabbat, *Tashlich* is said on the second day or on any weekday before Yom Kippur. If absolutely necessary, it can be said any day up to and including Hoshana Rabba.

Rosh Hashanah – Second Day

35. Candle-lighting and preparations for the meal take place after nightfall (see 308). On Sunday, the paragraph *Vatodi'enu* is added to the Amidah. On *Motza'ei* Shabbat, *Baruch HaMavdil Bein Kodesh LeKodesh* is said before candle-lighting.
36. On *Motza'ei* Shabbat, add the two Havdalah blessings to Kiddush (P. 746). At candle-lighting and at Kiddush, it is customary to wear a new garment or eat a new fruit for which the blessing *Shehecheyanu* would also apply. The blessing is made even if there is no new fruit or garment. If new fruit is available, the blessing *Borei Peri Ha'Etz* is made after Kiddush, before *HaMotzi*.
37. Ma'ariv, Shacharit, Musaf and Mincha parallel the first day, as do the Shofar blasts. The *Ba'al Toke'a* says *Shehecheyanu*. If the second day is Friday, omit *Avinu Malkenu* at Mincha.
38. *Motza'ei* Rosh Hashanah: Weekday Ma'ariv with the addition of *Ata Chonantanu* in the fourth blessing. In addition to the changes to the Amidah and Kaddish noted above (17 and 18), the eleventh blessing ends with *HaMelech HaMishpat*. One who forgets *HaMelech HaMishpat* is not required to repeat the Amidah. Havdalah is said over wine or grape juice.

***Aseret Yemei Teshuva* – Ten Days of Repentance**

39. Changes to Kaddish and Amidah as in notes 17 and 18. At Shacharit, after *Yishtabach* (P. 60) some congregations open the Ark and say Psalm 130 responsively. After the repetition of the Amidah in Shacharit and Mincha, add *Avinu Malkenu*, except on Friday afternoon and Shabbat.

***Tzom Gedalya* – Fast of Gedalya (3rd Tishrei)**

40. The fast commemorates the assassination of Gedalya ben Achikam, the Governor of Judea. His death, at the hand of fellow Jews, marked the end of Jewish self-government in Israel after the destruction of the First Temple.
41. If a Shabbat, the fast is postponed to Sunday.

42. The fast begins at dawn. One can eat or drink before dawn if one had intention to do so before going to sleep.
43. Although US custom is to recite *Selichot* on fast days in the repetition of the Amidah (see 182), on *Tzom Gedalya Selichot* are said before Shacharit, in common with other *Selichot* days. During the repetition of the Amidah, the Leader adds *Anenu* (P. 82) before *Refa'enu*. Following the Amidah, *Avinu Malkenu* (P. 98). Three men are called to the Torah and the regular portion for fast days is read (P. 908). During the Torah reading, it is customary for the congregation to say out loud, before the *Baal Koreh*: the last seven words of *Shemot* 32:12; the '13 Middot' (*Shemot* 34:6-7) until *Venake*; the last four words of *Shemot* 34:9.
44. Mincha: *Ashrei. Chatzi* Kaddish. The Torah is read as in the morning. Layning on fast days normally only takes place if six fasting men are present. The third *Oleh* reads the Haftarah (P. 909). After the Torah is returned to the Ark, *Chatzi* Kaddish. Weekday silent Amidah, with *Anenu* added in *Shema Kolenu* (P. 184). In the repetition, the Leader adds *Anenu* before *Refa'enu* (P. 178). After *Modim*, the Leader adds the paragraph relating to *Birkat Kohanim*, and *Sim Shalom* instead of *Shalom Rav*. Following the Amidah, the Ark is opened for *Avinu Malkenu*, P. 98. *Tachanun*. Kaddish *Titkabal. Aleinu*. Mourner's Kaddish.

Shabbat Shuva

45. Shabbat Shuva is named after the first word of the Haftarah, *Shuva*. If it falls on 3rd Tishrei, start Kabbalat Shabbat with *Mizmor Shir Leyom HaShabbat* (P. 270) and omit *Bameh Madlikin*. Otherwise it is a regular Friday night service, with the *Aseret Yemei Teshuva* additions in the Amidah. In *Magen Avot* (P. 294), *HaMelech HaKadosh* replaces *HaEl HaKadosh*.
46. Shacharit: Regular Shabbat service. After *Yishtabach* (P. 368) some congregations open the Ark and say Psalm 130 responsively. Amidah for Shabbat with the *Aseret Yemei Teshuva* additions. Torah reading is *Ha-azinu* or *Vayelech*. Haftarah: The original US custom was to read Hoshea 14:2-*10, Micah 7:18-20,* on *Vayelech* and *Hoshea 14:2-10, Joel 2:15-27* on *Ha-azinu*. Many communities now read Hoshea, Joel and Micah on either Shabbat but it is important to read the section from Joel before Micah as that is the order in which the books occur in Tanach. It is customary for the rabbi to read the Haftarah and deliver a sermon about repentance.

***Erev* Yom Kippur (9th Tishrei)**

47. *Selichot* are abbreviated. Weekday Shacharit. Psalm 100, *Avinu Malkenu, Tachanun* and Psalm 20 are omitted. However, if Yom Kippur is on Shabbat, *Avinu Malkenu* is said.
48. It is a mitzvah to eat and drink on this day.
49. One should ask for forgiveness from others because Yom Kippur atones for sins against others only if the person wronged has forgiven.
50. The custom of *Kapparot* should be performed with money, which is then distributed to charity.

51. It is customary for males to immerse in the mikva.
52. Most communities schedule Mincha early to allow time for a final meal (*Seuda Mafseket*) before the fast. Mincha is as for weekdays, with the *Aseret Yemei Teshuva* additions. After *Oseh HaShalom*, the *Viduy* confessional prayer is said. In the Leader's repetition, omit *Viduy*. Omit *Avinu Malkenu* and *Tachanun*.
53. The *Seuda Mafseket* must be finished at least a few minutes before sunset. It is customary for parents to bless their children.
54. Before lighting Yom Tov candles, one should also light a candle that will burn for the entire fast, so it can be used for Havdalah.
55. It is customary for those who have lost a close relative to also light a Yahrzeit candle.
56. It is customary for a married couple to light an additional candle (*Ner HaBari*) that will burn for the entire fast.
57. Candle-lighting: The blessings *Lehadlik Ner Shel Yom HaKippurim (Shabbat VeYom HaKippurim* if a Friday night) and *Shehecheyanu* are said after lighting.

Yom Kippur (10th Tishrei)

58. *Kol Nidrei.* Men put on their *tallit* before the *Kol Nidrei* service. The b'racha on the *tallit* must be made before sunset. Many married men will also wear a *kittel.* The Ark is opened and the rabbi and a senior member of the congregation each carry a Torah scroll to the Bima. (Some have a custom to use three scrolls.) It is customary to chant the verse *Or Zarua LaTzadik* (Psalm 97:11) while the scrolls are carried to the Bima. They are held on either side of the Leader. Before *Kol Nidrei*, the Leader or rabbi chants *BiShivah Shel Ma'la* three times. The Leader chants *Kol Nidrei* three times. The verses *Venislach* (*Bemidbar* 15:26), *Selach-Na* (*ibid.* 14:19) and *Vayomer* (*ibid.* 14:20) are chanted. The entire congregation says the *Shehecheyanu* blessing (except those who recited it at candle-lighting) and the scrolls are returned to the Ark.
59. When Yom Kippur is Friday night, US custom is to say *Shehecheyanu* after Mourner's Kaddish. Following the return of the scrolls to the Ark, the last two psalms of Kabbalat Shabbat (92 and 93) are said, followed by Mourner's Kaddish.
60. Ma'ariv: for Shabbat and Yom Tov. When saying the *Shema,* the line *Baruch Shem Kevod Malchuto* is said aloud. Before the Amidah, the verse *Ki Vayom HaZeh* (*Vayikra* 16:30) is said. Following the Amidah, *Selichot* and *Viduy* are said. The traditional practice in the US was that during *Selichot, El Melech Yoshev,* followed by the '13 Middot', was said only once. However, some communities include this more frequently. Following *Selichot, Avinu Malkenu,* Kaddish *Titkabal.*
61. The original US custom was for some worshippers to remain after the main service to recite *Shir HaYichud* for all the days of the week, or at least the one pertaining to the day of Yom Kippur.
62. Shacharit: Many men have the custom to wear a *kittel* under their *tallit.* US custom is for all officiants to wear a *kittel.* Morning Blessings and *Pesukei de-Zimra* are recited in the traditional melody. In many communities, *Anim Zemirot,* the Psalm for the Day and Psalm 27 are said before *Pesukei de-Zimra.* The Leader

for Shacharit starts from *HaMelech*. In many communities, the custom is for the *Ba'al Shacharit* to begin to chant *HaMelech* from his place and then move to the Amud or Bima to continue with *Yoshev*. After *Yishtabach* some congregations open the Ark and say Psalm 130 responsively. The order of service continues as in the Machzor (on Shabbat with the Shabbat additions.) In the repetition of the Amidah, the Ark is opened for some *piyyutim*. It is customary to stand at these points, unless it is difficult to do so. In all services, say the *Kedushah* of Musaf, *Na'aritzcha*. Originally, in the US, *Selichot* were added to Shacharit. Most communities today recite *Zechor Rachamecha* straight after *Ya'ale Veyavo*. Following the Amidah, *Avinu Malkenu* (except on Shabbat). Kaddish *Titkabal*.

63. Torah reading: The '13 Middot' (P. 406) and the supplication following are said (except on Shabbat). Two Torah scrolls are taken from the Ark. Torah reading is chanted in the special melody for Rosh Hashanah and Yom Kippur. Many have the custom that the *Oleh* makes his blessing with the melody of the Torah reading. *Vayikra* 15:1-34.
64. Yizkor: US custom is to say a memorial prayer for former Chief Rabbis whenever Yizkor is said. Many have the custom to leave the synagogue if they are not required to say Yizkor. It has become the practice to recite first the communal memorial prayers: for former Chief Rabbis, the Armed Services, Israeli soldiers and victims of terror, and victims of the Holocaust. After this, those who do not need to say personal Yizkor prayers can leave.
65. Musaf. It is customary for the *Ba'al Musaf* to recite a short preparatory prayer, *Hineni He'ani Mima'as*, before *Chatzi* Kaddish and the silent Amidah.
66. The fourth blessing in the repetition of the Amidah contains *Aleinu*. The Ark is opened and the Leader kneels and prostrates at the phrase *Va'anachu Kor'im*. In most communities, the congregation also kneel. This is followed by *piyyutim* describing the *Avoda*, the Yom Kippur Temple service, in which the Leader and congregation kneel three more times. In some communities, the rabbi or a senior congregant recites the passage *VehaKohanim* first, leading the congregation in kneeling, then the Leader repeats the passage. In other communities, everyone follows together with the Leader. For details of kneeling, see 30.
67. Kohanim say *Birkat Kohanim*, even on Shabbat.
68. Musaf concludes with Kaddish *Titkabal*. Omit *Ein Kelohenu* and Aleinu.
69. Mincha: Omit *Ashrei* and *Uva LeZion*. *Vayehi Binso'a Ha'Aron*. The Torah is taken out. Three men are called. Torah reading: *Vayikra* 18:1-30, in the regular tune. The third *Oleh* reads the Haftarah: Jonah and Micah 7:18-20. In some communities, a *Mi Sheberach* is made for the *Chatan Torah* and *Chatan Bereishit*, or they are given *Hagbahah* and *Gelilah*. After returning the Torah, *Chatzi* Kaddish. The silent Amidah is identical to Shacharit. The repetition includes *Kedushah* starting with *Na'aritzcha*, *Viduy* and the paragraph relating to *Birkat Kohanim*. US custom is to omit *Avinu Malkenu*.
70. *Ne'ilah*. The unique, fifth service of Yom Kippur. *Ashrei*, *Uva LeZion*. *Chatzi* Kaddish in the special *Ne'ilah* tune. In the Amidah, *Kotvenu* (inscribe us) is changed,

in all its conjugations, to *Chotmenu* (seal us). In the last blessing, *Sim Shalom* is said. *Al Chet* is replaced by a supplication on the frailty of man.

71. The Ark is open throughout the repetition of the Amidah. Many have the custom to stand for the whole service, if they can. Kedushah with *Na'aritzcha*. In *Selichot*, the traditional US practice was to say *El Melech Yoshev*, followed by the '13 Middot', only once. However, some communities include this more frequently. Following the repetition, *Avinu Malkenu* is said, even on Shabbat. In some communities, the whole of *Avinu Malkenu* is chanted responsively. This is followed by the responsive chanting of *Shema Yisrael* once, *Baruch Shem Kevod Malchuto* three times, and *HaShem Hu Ha'Elohim* seven times. Kaddish *Titkabal* follows. In many communities this is followed by a *Tekiah Gedola* and the singing of *LeShana HaBa Birushalayim*. However, some communities find that the decorum decreases after the shofar so instead they blow the shofar after Ma'ariv.
72. Ma'ariv. As for weekdays. *Ata Chonantanu* is added to *Amidah*. Kaddish *Titkabal*. Havdalah is made over wine or grape juice. A blessing is made on a candle that was lit (or kindled from a flame that was lit) before Yom Kippur.
73. On *Motza'ei Shabbat, Veyiten Lecha* (P. 588) precedes Havdalah, and Havdalah includes the blessing on spices.
74. It is customary to recite *Kiddush Levana* (P. 602) after the service.
75. It is customary to begin building the Sukkah that night.
76. Omit *Tachanun* between Yom Kippur and Sukkot.

Erev Sukkot (14th Tishrei)

77. The construction and decoration of the Sukkah should be completed before the festival. Likewise, the hadassim, aravot and lulav should be bound together before the festival.
78. When Sukkot falls on Thursday, make *Eruv Tavshilin* (P. 642) to permit cooking on Friday for Shabbat.

First Days of Sukkot (15th and 16th Tishrei)

79. Candle-lighting (P. 644): See 15.
80. Ma'ariv is conducted in the traditional melody. US custom is to say *Ma'aravot*, the poetic liturgical additions to the blessings before and after the Shema. Add *Vayedaber Moshe* before the Yom Tov Amidah.
81. On Friday night, begin with *Mizmor Shir Leyom HaShabbat* (P. 270). Omit *Ma'aravot*. Before the Amidah, add the Shabbat verse (*Veshamru*) and the Yom Tov verse (*Vayedaber Moshe*). After the Amidah, the congregation says *Vayechulu HaShamayim* and the Leader says *Me'ein Sheva* (P. 294). Omit *Bameh Madlikin*. If the second night of Sukkot is *Motza'ei* Shabbat, say *Ma'aravot* for the first night and add the paragraph *Vatodi'enu* in the Amidah.
82. Following Kaddish *Titkabal* on the first two nights of Yom Tov, US custom is to make Kiddush in the synagogue (without the blessing *Leishev BaSukkah*).
83. Kiddush in made in a shul Sukkah for the benefit of those who do not have

their own Sukkah. This is followed by *HaMotzi* on two challot, eating at least a *kezayit* (olive's bulk) of challah.

84. At home, some say a prayer before entering the Sukkah (P. 664). Kiddush is said in the traditional melody (P. 660) On the first night, the blessing *Leishev BaSukkah* precedes *Shehecheyanu.* On the second night, *Shehecheyanu* precedes *Leishev BaSukkah* (P. 662). On Friday night, add the Shabbat additions. When the second night of Sukkot is *Motza'ei* Shabbat, insert the Havdalah blessings before *Shehecheyanu.* Insert *Ya'ale Veyavo* in *Birkat HaMazon.*
85. Shacharit for Shabbat and Yom Tov (P. 322): The Leader begins from *Ha'El Beta'atzumot* (P. 366). After *Barchu,* say *HaMe'ir La'aretz,* or *HaKol Yoducha* on Shabbat. The Amidah for Yom Tov is said (P. 646), with Shabbat additions if it is also Shabbat.
86. After the repetition of the Amidah, the congregation takes the *lulav,* except on Shabbat. Many say a meditation beforehand (P. 616). Make the blessing *Al Netilat Lulav,* and *Shecheyanu* on the first day the *lulav* is taken.
87. Full Hallel, holding *lulav* and *etrog* (except on Shabbat). The following is US custom for the *Na'anu'im* or 'wavings' in Hallel: At *Hodu,* the Leader chants a line and the congregation respond each time with *Hodu LaShem Ki Tov Ki Le'Olam Chasdo.* Wave the *lulav* and *etrog* three times for each word of the verse, except God's name. On the first word, wave forward, then on subsequent words, wave right, back, left, up and down respectively. The leader only waves for the first two verses. The congregation waves each time the first verse is said in response. At *Ana HaShem Hoshi'a Na* wave the *lulav* and *etrog* three times in each direction, except God's name. On the first word, wave forward and right; third word: back and left; fourth word: up and down. When *Hodu LaShem Ki Tov* is said again, wave the *lulav* and *etrog* as before. Kaddish *Titkabal.*
88. *Ein Kamocha* (P. 404). US custom is to say the '13 Middot' (P. 406) and the supplication following (except on Shabbat). Two Torah scrolls are taken from the Ark. Torah reading: both days, *Vayikra* 22:26-23:44 (P. 916). Five men are called up, seven on Shabbat, as on Rosh Hashanah (see 22). Maftir is *Bemidbar* 29:12-16 (P. 949) for both days. *Hagbahah* and *Gelilah* are performed on the second Torah, followed by Haftarah. Haftarah: first day, Zechariah 14:1-21; second day, I Kings 8:2-21 (P. 949)
89. US custom is to omit the *piyyut, Ya Eli,* as opposed to the custom in other congregations.
90. Musaf: for festivals (P. 670). If also Shabbat, say the Shabbat additions. During the repetition of the Amidah, the *Kohanim* say *Birkat Kohanim.* In most communities, this occurs even on Shabbat, but the Kohanim do not chant on Shabbat. Some communities have preserved specific melodies for the *Kohen*-chants for each festival. After the repetition, the congregation take the *lulav.* The Ark is opened and a Torah is taken to the Bima. The Torah is normally held by an *Avel.* (Mourners do not walk round for the *Hoshanot* as this is associated with *Simcha,* rejoicing). The Leader leads the congregation chanting *Hoshanot* (P. 708) while encircling the Bima. The Torah is returned to the Ark.

91. On Shabbat, the *Hoshanot* circuit is not made. After the Amidah, the Ark is opened, no scroll is removed and the *Hoshana* for Shabbat (P. 712) is said.
92. Mincha: for Shabbat and Yom Tov. When Sukkot falls on Shabbat, the Torah is taken from the Ark and the beginning of *Vezot Hab'racha* (P. 897) is read. After returning the Torah to the Ark, the Leader says *Chatzi* Kaddish. The Yom Tov Amidah follows (P. 646). On Shabbat, say the Shabbat additions.
93. Second day: Candle-lighting and preparations for the meal are made after nightfall (see 308). If the first day was Shabbat, add the paragraph *Vatodi'enu* to the Amidah. On *Motza'ei* Shabbat, a woman says *Baruch HaMavdil Bein Kodesh LeKodesh* before candle-lighting.
94. If the second night is *Motza'ei* Shabbat, add the two Havdalah blessings to Kiddush (P. 746).
95. The second day service is the same as the first. *Shehecheyanu* is not made on the *lulav* unless the first day was Shabbat.

Chol Hamoed

96. Add *Ya'ale Veyavo* to the weekday Amidah and *Birkat HaMazon.* If it is forgotten, one must repeat the Amidah, but there is no need to repeat *Birkat HaMazon.*
97. On the first evening of Chol Hamoed, add *Ata Chonantanu* to the weekday Amidah. Make Havdalah in the synagogue on wine or grape juice.
98. US custom is for men to wear *tefillin*, without a b'racha, for Shacharit. Remove *tefillin* before Hallel so the *lulav* can be held without any interposition. The Leader should wear *tefillin*.
99. After Musaf, the congregation take their *lulavim* again. The Ark is opened and a Torah is taken to the Bima for *Hoshanot.* Since mourners do not join the circuit, the Torah is normally held by a mourner. The Leader chants *Hoshanot* and leads the congregation (P. 708) around the Bima. The Torah is returned to the Ark.

Shabbat Chol Hamoed

100. If Shabbat follows immediately after Yom Tov, Shabbat candles are lit from a pre-existing flame. Kabbalat Shabbat begins with *Mizmor Shir Leyom HaShabbat* (P. 270). Regular Friday night Ma'ariv follows, adding *Yaale Veyavo* in the Amidah. If Shabbat follows immediately after Yom Tov, omit *Bameh Madlikin* (P. 298). Make Kiddush in the synagogue.
101. Shacharit: The Leader begins at *Shochen Ad*, as on a regular Shabbat (P. 366). Add *Yaale Veyavo* to the Amidah. Full Hallel. It is customary to read *Kohelet.* If layned from a kosher Megillah, first say the berachot *Al Mikra Megillah* and *Shehecheyanu.* Following the Megillah, Mourner's Kaddish.
102. Haftarah blessings conclude with *Mekadesh HaShabbat VeYisrael VehaZemanim.*
103. *Chatzi* Kaddish before the Musaf Amidah concludes with the Yom Tov melody
104. Musaf is that for Yom Tov (P. 670), with Shabbat additions. Omit *Adir Adirenu* in Kedushah. Omit *Birkat Kohanim.*

105. After the Amidah, open the Ark (without removing any scrolls) and responsively chant the Shabbat *Hoshana* (P. 712).
106. Mincha: as for a regular Shabbat. Take the Torah from the Ark and read the start of *Vezot Hab'racha* (P. 897). After returning the Torah, *Chatzi* Kaddish, Amidah for Shabbat Mincha (P. 492) with *Ya'ale Veyavo*. After the repetition, omit *Tzidkatecha Tzedek*.

***Hoshana Rabba* (21st Tishrei)**

107. Shacharit: The Leader wears a kittel. *Berachot* and *Pesukei de-Zimra* are in the *Yamim Nora'im* melody. *Pesukei de-Zimra* for Shabbat and Yom Tov, including Psalm 100 (P. 332). After *Az Yashir* (P. 360), continue with *Yishtabach* (P. 58). Some congregations open the Ark and say Psalm 130 responsively. Add *Yaale Veyavo* to the weekday Shacharit Amidah. Men remove *tefillin* before Hallel and the congregation take their *lulavim*. Full Hallel. Some have the custom to remove the top two rings binding the *lulav* for more effective waving. Kaddish *Titkabal*.
108. Removal of the Torah from the Ark: with *Ein Kamocha*, the '13 Middot' (P. 406) and the supplication following. *Shema Yisrael* and *Echad Elohenu...Kadosh Venora Shemo* are chanted to the *Yamim Nora'im* tune. Torah reading (P. 954). Some have the custom to read in the *Yamim Nora'im* melody. *Chatzi* Kaddish. *Hagbahah* and *Gelilah*. The Torah is returned to the Ark. *Ashrei, Uva LeZion, Chatzi* Kaddish.
109. Musaf for Yom Tov (P. 670). Yom Tov *Kedushah* is said in the repetition but omit *Birkat Kohanim*. After the repetition of the Amidah, the congregation takes the *lulav*. The Ark is opened and seven Torah scrolls are taken to the Bima. The Leader leads the congregation in seven circuits of the Bima, holding *lulavim*, chanting *Hoshana* prayers (P. 715). One scroll is returned after each of the first six circuits. *Piyyutim* for rain follow. At the *piyyut, Ta'ane Emunim,* put down the *lulav* and take *Hoshanot* (a bundle of five willow branches). After chanting *Kol Mevaser Mevaser Ve'Omer* three times, beat the *Hoshanot* against a chair or the floor five times. The final scroll is returned. (Some return it immediately after the seventh circuit.) Kaddish *Titkabal*. Some have the custom to beat the *Hoshanot* after Kaddish *Titkabal*. *Ein Kelohenu, Pitum HaKetoret,* Kaddish *Derabbanan, Aleinu,* Mourner's Kaddish, Psalm for the Day, Psalm 27, Mourner's Kaddish.
110. When *Hoshana Rabba* falls on Wednesday, make *Eruv Tavshilin* (P. 642) to permit cooking on Friday for Shabbat.

***Shemini Atzeret* (22nd Tishrei)**

111. Candle-lighting (P. 644): See 15.
112. Yom Tov Ma'ariv is in the traditional melody. US custom is to say the *Ma'aravot*, see 80 above. In the Amidah (and in Kiddush) the Yom Tov is referred to as *HaShemini Chag HaAtzeret HaZeh*. Following the Amidah, Kaddish *Titkabal*.
113. When Shemini Atzeret is Friday night, begin Ma'ariv with *Mizmor Shir Leyom HaShabbat* (P. 270). Omit *Ma'aravot*. Before the Amidah, add the special verses for Shabbat (*Veshamru*) and for Yom Tov (*Vayedaber Moshe*). After the Ami-

dah, the congregation says *Vayechulu HaShamayim*, and the Leader says *Me'ein Sheva* (P. 294). Omit *Bameh Madlikin*.

114. Following Kaddish *Titkabal*, US custom is that Kiddush is made in the synagogue. *Aleinu*. Mourner's Kaddish. Psalm 27. Mourner's Kaddish. Yigdal.
115. Traditional Ashkenazi practice is to eat in the Sukkah on Shemini Atzeret, without a blessing, both in the evening and in the morning.
116. Shacharit: for Shabbat and Yom Tov (P. 322). The Leader for Shacharit begins from *Ha'El Beta'atzumot* (P. 366). After Barchu, *HaMe'ir La'aretz* is said, or *HaKol Yoducha* if it is Shabbat. The Amidah for Yom Tov is said (P. 646), with the additions for Shabbat on Shabbat. Full Hallel. Kaddish *Titkabal*. If Shabbat, the book of Kohelet is read after Hallel. If read from a kosher Megillah the blessings *Al Mikra Megillah* and *Shehecheyanu* are recited. Mourner's Kaddish follows the Megillah.
117. *Ein Kamocha* (P. 404) follows. US custom is to say the '13 Middot' (P. 406) and the supplication following, during the week but not on Shabbat. Two Torah scrolls are taken from the Ark.
118. Torah reading (P. 937) *Devarim* 14:22-16:17. US custom is to begin from *Aser Te'aser* even on weekdays. The *Levi* portion begins at 15:1; *Shelishi* at 15:19; *Revii* at 16:4 and *Chamishi* at 16:9.
119. Yizkor (see 64). US custom is not to say the *piyyut, Ya Eli*, as opposed to the custom in other congregations. *Ashrei*, and the Torah scrolls are returned to the Ark.
120. It is customary for the Leader to wear a kittel and to chant the *Chatzi* Kaddish before Musaf to the special *Geshem* melody. Before the Amidah (P. 670), an announcement is made for *Mashiv HaRuach Umorid HaGashem* to be said in the silent Amidah.
121. The Ark is opened, and the Leader begins the repetition and chants *Tefillat Geshem* (P. 702). During the repetition, the *Kohanim* say *Birkat Kohanim*. In most communities this occurs even on Shabbat, but the Kohanim do not chant on Shabbat. Some communities have preserved distinct melodies for the *Kohen*-chants for each festival.
122. Mincha: for Shabbat and Yom Tov. When Shemini Atzeret falls on Shabbat, the Torah is taken from the Ark and the beginning of *Vezot Hab'racha* (P. 897) is read. After returning the Torah, the Leader says *Chatzi* Kaddish. Yom Tov Amidah (P. 646), with the additions for Shabbat on Shabbat.
123. Some have a custom to recite a prayer before leaving the Sukkah for the last time.

Laws of *Mashiv HaRu'ach*

124. One begins reciting *Mashiv HaRuach* at Musaf on Shemini Atzeret and continues until Musaf on the first day of Pesach.
125. US custom is to say *Mashiv HaRuach Umorid Ha**Ga**shem*.
126. If one forgets to say *Mashiv HaRuach* in its proper place but realises before beginning the blessing *Mechaye HaMetim*, immediately say it and continue with the blessing. If one realizes the omission immediately after completing *Mechaye HaMetim*, say *Mashiv HaRuach* then continue with the following blessing. If

one realizes the omission after commencing the words *Ata Kadosh,* one must repeat the Amidah from the beginning.

127. If there is doubt whether one said *Mashiv HaRuach,* the presumption is as follows: within the first thirty days after Shemini Atzeret, one should assume that one omitted *Mashiv HaRuach.* After thirty days, one should assume that one said *Mashiv HaRuach.*

Simchat Torah (23rd Tishrei)

128. Candle-lighting and preparations for the meal made after nightfall (see 424). On *Motza'ei* Shabbat, a woman says *Baruch HaMavdil Bein Kodesh LeKodesh* before candle-lighting.
129. Yom Tov Ma'ariv is conducted in the traditional melody. US custom is to say the *Ma'aravot,* see 80 above. In the Amidah (and in Kiddush) the Yom Tov is referred to as *HaShemini Chag Ha'Atzeret HaZeh.* On *Motza'ei* Shabbat, add the paragraph *Vatodi'enu* to the middle section of the Amidah.
130. After Kaddish *Titkabal,* chant the verses of *Ata Hor'eta* responsively. The Ark is opened and all the Torah scrolls are removed. Seven *Hakafot* (circuits of the Bima) are performed, with singing and dancing. After the *Hakafot,* all the scrolls except one are returned to the Ark. The Leader chants *Shema Yisrael* and the rest of the ceremony for taking the Torah out of the Ark (P. 408). In communities where the Torah is not read on the night of Simchat Torah, the service continues as in 132 below.
131. After *Veya'azor,* three men are called to the Torah and the beginning of *Vezot Hab'racha* (P. 897) is read. In most congregations, *Chatzi* Kaddish follows. *Hagbahah* and *Gelilah* and the Torah is returned to the Ark.
132. Kiddush in the synagogue follows. When Simchat Torah is *Motza'ei* Shabbat, the blessings for Havdalah are inserted before *Shehecheyanu.*
133. Shacharit: for Shabbat and Yom Tov. US custom is to add the *piyyut, Nishmat Melumdei Morasha* before *Nishmat Kol Chai.*
134. The Leader for Shacharit begins from *Ha'El Beta'atzumot* (P. 366). After Barchu, *HaMe'ir La'aretz* is said. The Amidah for Yom Tov is said (P. 646). On Simchat Torah, the *Kohanim* do not *duchan* during Musaf. However, in many communities they *duchan* at Shacharit but omit *Vete'erav.* Full Hallel. After Kaddish *Titkabal,* the verses of *Ata Hor'eta* are chanted responsively. The Ark is opened and all the Torah scrolls are removed. Seven *Hakafot* (circuits of the Bima) are performed, with singing and dancing. After the *Hakafot,* all the scrolls except three are returned to the Ark.
135. Torah reading: *Vezot Hab'racha* is read, in cycles of five *aliyot,* until all males over the age of 13 have received an *aliyah.* In some communities, parallel readings are held to facilitate the *aliyot.* Some communities choose to call up several people together. If this is done, it is preferable that one person should make the b'racha.
136. *Kol HaNe'arim.* It is customary that all children participate in an *aliyah,* together with an adult. A canopy of multiple *tallitot* is spread over the children and the

Oleh. Following the reading of the portion from *Vezot Hab'racha,* it is customary to chant the verse *HaMal'ach HaGo'el* (*Bereishit* 48:16) in honour of the children.

137. *Chatan Torah.* It is customary to chant a poetic invocation, known as a *Reshut* (request for permission), prior to calling up the *Chatan Torah.* The text used in the US is an abbreviated version of that used in other communities. The melody is the same as for *Akdamut.* It is customary for the *Chatan Torah* to come to the Bima holding a Torah (which will be used for *Bereishit*), under a canopy of a *tallit,* accompanied by song. The canopy is held over him during the *aliyah.* In some communities, the *Chatan Torah* himself reads the portion, starting from *Me'ona* (*Devarim* 33:27). Following the *aliyah,* the *Bereishit* Torah is placed on the Bima and *Hagbahah* is performed on the first Torah.
138. *Chatan Bereishit.* Likewise, it is customary to chant a *Reshut* prior to calling up the *Chatan Bereishit.* The text used in the US is an abbreviated version of that used in other communities. It is customary for the *Chatan Bereishit* to come to the Bima under a canopy of a *tallit,* holding a Torah (which will be used for *Maftir*), accompanied by song. The *tallit* canopy is held over him during the *aliyah.* In some communities, the *Chatan Bereishit* himself reads the portion (*Bereishit* 1:1-2:3). It is customary to pause in the reading for the congregation to chant aloud *Veyehi Erev Vayehi Voker* for each day of creation, and to chant aloud the last three verses, starting with *Vayechulu HaShamayim.* The Maftir scroll is placed on the Bima and *Chatzi* Kaddish is said. Some have the custom to have all three scrolls on the Bima for the *Chatzi* Kaddish, in honour of Simchat Torah. *Hagbahah* and *Gelilah* are performed on the second Torah and the *Oleh* for Maftir is called.
139. After Haftarah, some communities chant *piyyutim,* such as *Sisu Vegilu Besimchat Torah.*
140. Musaf: for festivals (P. 670). The *Kohanim* do not say *Birkat Kohanim* because they are presumed to have drunk alcohol. The repetition of the Amidah is followed by Kaddish *Titkabal* and the service concludes as for a regular Shabbat and Yom Tov.
141. Mincha: for festivals.
142. Ma'ariv: for weekdays. Insert *Ata Chonantanu* in the fourth blessing of the Amidah. Say Havdalah over a cup of wine or grape juice; no blessing is made on spices or a flame.

Isru Chag (24th Tishrei)

143. Omit *Tachanun,* but say *Lamnatzeiach.* If Shabbat, omit *Tzidkatcha Tzedek.* On the Monday and Thursday morning Torah readings following Simchat Torah, US custom is to call the three *olim* to the first three days of creation.

Shabbat Bereishit

144. US custom is to follow the following breaks in the parasha: *Sheni,* 1:14. *Shelishi* 1:24. *Revii,* 2:4. *Chamishi,* 3:22. *Shishi,* 5:1. *Shevii,* 5:25. This Shabbat is always Shabbat Mevarchim.

145. Mincha. It is customary to say Psalm 104 (*Barchi Nafshi*, P. 506) followed by the 15 *Shir HaMa'alot* after Mincha (until *Shabbat HaGadol*), Mourner's Kaddish, Aleinu, Mourner's Kaddish.

Marcheshvan

146. Rosh Chodesh is two days. 1st Cheshvan (Marcheshvan) can fall on either Monday, Wednesday, Thursday or Shabbat.
147. When announcing the month on Shabbat Mevarchim, and writing in a Ketubah, the month is referred to as Marcheshvan.
148. It used to be the custom to make a *Mi Sheberach* on Shabbat Mevarchim for those who were going to be fasting on *BaHaB* – the first Monday, Thursday and following Monday of Marcheshvan.
149. 20th Marcheshvan. Yahrzeit of Chief Rabbi Lord Jonathan Sacks (died 7th November 2020).
150. 21st Marcheshvan. Yahrzeit of Chief Rabbi Lord Immanuel Jakobovits (died 31st October 1999).
151. 27th Marcheshvan. Yahrzeit of Chief Rabbi Solomon Hirschell (died 31st October 1842).
152. 28th Marcheshvan. Yahrzeit of Chief Rabbi Aaron Hart (died 21st November 1756).
153. In a regular year, Marcheshvan has 29 days (*Kesidra*). Sometimes it has 30 days (*Shelema*). If one is born on 30 Marcheshvan, their Bat/Bar Mitzvah takes place on 1st Kislev if there are only 29 days in Marcheshvan that year. If a death occurs on 30 Marcheshvan, the Yahrzeit is fixed according to the first year. If Marcheshvan has 30 days in the first year after the death, Yahrzeit will be on 30th Marcheshvan and in all years in which a 30th Marcheshvan occurs. In other years, Yahrzeit will be on 1st Kislev. If Marcheshvan has 29 days in the first year after death, Yahrzeit will be on 29th Marcheshvan and in all years in which no 30th Marcheshvan occurs. In all other years, Yahrzeit is on 30th Marcheshvan.

Kislev

154. Rosh Chodesh is one or two days. 1st Kislev can fall on any day except Shabbat.

Haftarah for Vayeitzei and Vayishlach

155. US custom is that the Vayeitzei Haftarah is Hoshea 12:13–14:10 (*Vayivrach Yaakov Sedei Aram*) and the Vayishlach Haftarah is Hoshea 11:7–12:12 (*Ve'ami Telu'im*).

Tal Umatar

156. In most years, during Ma'ariv on 4th December, one begins to say *Veten Tal Umatar Livracha* in the ninth *b'racha* of the Amidah, in place of *Veten B'racha*. In a year preceding a civil leap year, this begins one day later, on the night of 5th December. 5th December can fall between 3rd Kislev and 2nd Tevet.
157. If one forgets to say *Veten Tal* in its proper place but realises before saying God's

name in the blessing *Mevarech HaShanim*, one should immediately say *Veten Tal* and continue with the rest of the blessing. If one realises the omission after completing *Mevarech HaShanim*, one should say *Veten Tal* prior to the words *Ki Ata Shomei'a* in the blessing *Shomei'a Tefillah*. If one realises the omission after beginning *Retzei*, one must repeat the Amidah from the beginning of *Bareich Aleinu*. If one realises the omission after completing the Amidah, one must repeat the entire Amidah.

158. If there is doubt whether one properly said *Veten Tal*, the presumption is as follows: within the first 30 days, one should assume that it was forgotten. After 30 days, one should assume that it was said.
159. 21st Kislev. Yahrzeit of Chief Rabbi David Tevele Schiff (died 17th December 1791).
160. In a regular year, Kislev has 30 days (*Kesidra*). Sometimes, there are 29 days (*Chasera*). The observance of Bar/Bat Mitzvah and Yahrzeit parallels that of Marcheshvan above (see 153.)

Chanukah (25th Kislev – 2nd or 3rd Tevet)

161. The first day of Chanukah can fall on any day of the week except Tuesday.
162. Omit *Tachanun* at Mincha on Erev Chanukah. Add *Al HaNissim* to the Amidah in Ma'ariv, Shacharit and Mincha, and to the second blessing of *Birkat HaMazon*. If one forgets to say *Al HaNissim*, one does not repeat the Amidah or *Birkat HaMazon*.
163. The Menorah is kindled in the home as soon as possible after nightfall. The lights must burn for at least half an hour after nightfall. If not kindled at this time, one can kindle them any time until daybreak, but blessings are made only if other members of the household are awake. If kindled earlier, the lights must continue to burn for at least half an hour after nightfall.
164. On the first night, three blessings are said: *Lehadlik Ner Shel Chanukah, She'asa Nissim, Shehecheyanu* (P. 732) On subsequent nights, only the first two blessings are said. Each night, a new light is added to the left and the newest light is kindled first. The lights are kindled immediately after (but not during) the blessings.
165. In the Diaspora, the Menorah is generally lit indoors but near a window, if possible, so that it is visible to the general public as well.
166. After the lighting, it is customary to sing *HaNerot Hallalu* and *Maoz Tzur*.
167. Many have the custom for each member of the household to light their own Menorah, but the head of the household can light on behalf of the whole family.
168. Women are equally obligated to light the Menorah, though a married woman may choose to join with her husband's lighting. Nevertheless, she may light on behalf of her husband and others.
169. It is customary to also light the Menorah in the Synagogue, with blessings. When Mincha is followed by Ma'ariv, the Menorah is lit between Mincha and Ma'ariv. If Ma'ariv is taking place later, the Menorah is kindled before Ma'ariv. US custom is to chant Psalm 30 before singing *Maoz Tzur*. If it is not possible to leave the Menorah alight for half an hour after nightfall, it may be extinguished earlier.
170. Shacharit: The Menorah is kindled before the service, but without blessings.

Weekday Shacharit with the addition of *Al HaNissim* in the Amidah, as above. After the Amidah, omit *Tachanun* and say full Hallel. This is followed by *Chatzi* Kaddish and taking the Torah from the Ark. Three men are called to the Torah reading (P. 898–903). The Torah is returned to the Ark. *Ashrei. Uva LeTzion.* Omit *Lamnatzeiach.* Kaddish *Titkabal,* Aleinu, Mourner's Kaddish, Psalm for the Day, Psalm 30, Mourner's Kaddish. Some communities say a separate Mourner's Kaddish after the Psalm for the Day.

Shabbat Chanukah

171. Shabbat can be on any day of Chanukah except the fifth day.
172. At home, the Menorah is kindled before the Shabbat candles. (Some communities offer an earlier Friday Mincha, so that Mincha can be recited before lighting the Menorah.) It is customary not to sing *Maoz Tzur* at this point but to sing it before *Shalom Aleichem.* At least one of the lights of the Menorah must burn until half an hour after nightfall. Ideally, the Menorah is lit in the synagogue after Mincha, but if that would end up being later than sunset the Menorah may be lit before Mincha. Add *Al HaNissim* to the Shabbat Amidah.
173. Shacharit: Add *Al HaNissim* to the Shabbat Amidah. Full Hallel, followed by Kaddish *Titkabal.* Two Torah scrolls are taken out; three if it is also Rosh Chodesh Tevet.
174. Seven men are called to the weekly portion (normally *Miketz,* occasionally *Vayeshev*). The second Torah is placed on the Bima before *Chatzi* Kaddish. *Hagbahah* and *Gelilah* are performed on the first Torah, then the Oleh for the Maftir is called. The reading is the appropriate day's reading for Chanukah (P. 898–903). Haftarah: Zechariah 2:14-4:7. If there are two Shabbatot in Chanukah, Haftarah for the second Shabbat is I Kings 7:40-50 (the same as for *Vayakhel*). If Shabbat is Rosh Chodesh, add *Ya'ale Veyavo* as well as *Al HaNissim* to the Amidah and *Birkat HaMazon.*
175. Shacharit. Three Torah scrolls are taken from the Ark. A minimum of six men are called to the portion of the week. (It is usual to combine *Shishi* and *Shevii.*) The second Torah, for Rosh Chodesh, is placed on the Bima. *Hagbahah* and *Gelilah* are performed on the first Torah. The Oleh for *Shevii* is called and the Rosh Chodesh portion read (*Bemidbar* 28:9-15). The third Torah is placed on the Bima and *Chatzi* Kaddish is said on the second and third Torah scrolls. *Hagbahah* and *Gelilah* are performed on the second Torah, then the Oleh for Maftir is called and the day's portion for Chanukah is read. Following *Hagbahah* and *Gelilah,* Haftarah for Shabbat Chanukah is read.
176. The Shabbat service continues as usual. On Shabbat *Mevarchim,* the New Moon is blessed and announced. Add *Al HaNissim* to Musaf. Add Psalm 30 after the Psalm for Shabbat. On Rosh Chodesh, Psalm 30 is preceded by Psalm 104.
177. Mincha: Add *Al HaNissim* to the Amidah. *Motza'ei* Shabbat. Ma'ariv is said promptly so as not to delay the kindling of the Menorah. In the synagogue, the Menorah is kindled before Havdalah. At home, the usual custom is to kindle the Menorah after Havdalah.

Tevet

178. One or two days Rosh Chodesh. 1st Tevet can fall on any day except Thursday or Shabbat.
179. Rosh Chodesh. Add *Ya'ale Veyavo* as well as *Al HaNissim* to the Amidah and *Birkat HaMazon.* Shacharit. After the repetition of the Amidah full Hallel is said, followed by Kaddish *Titkabal.* Two Torah scrolls are taken from the Ark. Three men are called to the first Torah for the Rosh Chodesh portion (P. 911) The second Torah, for Chanukah, is placed on the Bima. *Hagbahah* and *Gelilah* are performed on the first Torah. The Oleh for *revii* is called and the Chanukah portion (day six or day seven) is read. The Leader says *Chatzi* Kaddish. *Hagbahah, Gelilah.* The Torah is returned to the Ark and the service continues as for a regular Rosh Chodesh, with the addition of *Al HaNissim* in Musaf. In a leap year, add the phrase *Ul'chaparat Pasha* in the Musaf Amidah.

Asara B'Tevet (Fast of 10th Tevet)

180. The fast commemorates the besieging of Jerusalem by Nebuchadnezer in the time of the First Temple that led to its capture and destruction.
181. The fast begins at dawn.
182. US custom is to recite *Selichot* in the repetition of the Amidah, after reciting the phrase, *Selach Lanu Malkenu Ki Chatanu, Mechal Lanu Malkenu Ki Fashanu* (P. 80). The Leader adds *Anenu* (P. 82) before *Refa'enu.* Following the Amidah, most congregations say *Avinu Malkenu* (P. 98). Tachanun. Three men are called to the Torah and the regular portion for fast days is read (P. 908).
183. Mincha: Regular Mincha for fast days. See 44. If the fast falls on a Friday, omit *Avinu Malkenu* and *Tachanun* and the fast continues to nightfall. Nevertheless, if the Friday evening service following the fast ends before nightfall, the Leader may drink the Kiddush wine in the synagogue if a child is not available.
184. In the civil calendar, the fast can be any time from 13th December to 10th January. Thus occasionally there are civil years in which the fast occurs twice and some years when it doesn't occur at all.
185. 29th Tevet. Yahrzeit of Chief Rabbi Nathan Marcus Adler (died 21st January 1890).

Shevat

186. One day Rosh Chodesh. Rosh Chodesh Shevat can fall on any day of the week except Sunday or Friday.
187. The second or third Shabbat of the month, Beshalach, is called Shabbat Shira when the Song of the Sea is read in a special melody. The custom is to stand for the Shira. In many synagogues, the Baal Koreh chants verses of the Shira responsively with the congregation.
188. 12th Shevat. Yahrzeit of Chief Rabbi Joseph Hertz (died 14th January 1946).

Tu B'Shevat (15th Shevat, New Year for Trees)

189. Omit *Tachanun* on this day and at Mincha on 14th Shevat. The Kabbalists of Safed instituted a custom of eating fruits particularly associated with the Land of Israel. In recent generations, the custom has arisen to eat a fruit that one has not yet enjoyed that season to make the blessing, *Shehecheyanu*.

Parashat Yitro

190. There are two sets of *Ta'amim* for the *Aseret Hadibrot: Ta'am Elyon and Ta'am Tachton*. US custom is to use *Ta'am Elyon* for Parashat Yitro and for the congregation to stand for the reading.
191. 23rd Shevat. Yahrzeit of Chief Rabbi Sir Israel Brodie (died 20th February 1979).

Parashat Shekalim

192. Shabbat Parashat Shekalim, Shabbat Mevarchim. The first of the *Arba Parashiyot*. On the Shabbat preceding Rosh Chodesh Adar (in a leap year, Rosh Chodesh Adar II), two Torah scrolls are taken from the Ark. The second Torah is placed on the Bima before *Chatzi* Kaddish. *Hagbahah* and *Gelilah* are performed on the first Torah, then the Oleh for the Maftir is called. The reading is Shemot 30:11-16. In a regular year, Parashat Shekalim coincides with Parashat Mishpatim. In a leap year, it coincides with Parashat Vaykhel, or occasionally Pekudei. Haftarah is II Kings 12:1-17. US custom is now not to say the *Yotzarot* for the *Arba Parashiyot*.
193. When Rosh Chodesh Adar (in a leap year, Rosh Chodesh Adar II) falls on Shabbat, three Torah scrolls are taken from the Ark. From the first scroll, a minimum of six men are called to the portion of the week. It is usual to combine *Shishi* and *Shevii*. The second Torah, for Rosh Chodesh, is placed on the Bima. *Hagbahah* and *Gelilah* are performed on the first Torah. The Oleh for *Shevii* is called and the Rosh Chodesh portion read (Bemidbar 28:9-15). The third Torah is placed on the Bima and *Chatzi* Kaddish is said on the second and third scrolls. *Hagbahah* and *Gelilah* are performed on the second Torah, then the Oleh for Maftir is called.

Adar Rishon

194. In a leap year, Adar I is added. There are two days Rosh Chodesh. When a bereavement has occurred in a leap year, the Yahrzeit is observed in a leap year in the appropriate Adar. If a bereavement occurred in a regular year, the Yahrzeit is observed in Adar I. Some observe in Adar II as well. A Bar or Bat Mitzvah is observed in Adar II.

***Zayin* Adar (7th Adar – Fast of the Chevra Kadisha)**

195. 7th Adar is traditionally regarded as the anniversary of both the birth and death of Moshe Rabenu. Many communities observe this day as the annual fast of the Chevra Kadisha. Following the fast a Seuda takes place. In a leap year, many hold the fast on 7th Adar Rishon. (This is because 7th Adar Rishon can never

fall on Shabbat, unlike 7th Adar Sheni.) If 7th Adar is a Friday, the Fast is held on the Thursday.

Purim Katan (14th Adar Rishon) and Shushan Purim Katan (15th Adar Rishon)

196. Omit *Tachanun* and *Lamnatzei'ach,* and omit *Tachanun* at Mincha on 13th Adar Rishon.

Parashat Shekalim. See 192 and 193 above.

Adar (or Adar Sheni)

197. Two days Rosh Chodesh. 1st Adar, or Adar Sheni, can fall on Monday, Wednesday, Friday or Shabbat.

Parashat Zachor

198. On the Shabbat before Purim, two Torah scrolls are taken from the Ark. The second Torah is placed on the Bima before *Chatzi* Kaddish. *Hagbahah* and *Gelilah* are performed on the first Torah, then the Oleh for the Maftir is called. The reading is Devarim 25:17-19. In a regular year, Parashat Zachor coincides with Tetzaveh. In a leap year, it coincides with Vayikra or Tzav. Hearing the Maftir for Parshat Zachor is a positive commandment from the Torah. It is not the practice for a Bar Mitzvah boy to read this Maftir. US custom is to read the word *Zeicher* with a *tzeireh* vowel on the first syllable, and not to repeat the word with a *segol* vowel.
199. Some communities arrange an extra reading of Parashat Zachor before Mincha for those (especially women) who were unable to hear it earlier.

Ta'anit Esther (Fast of Esther, 13th Adar or 13th Adar Sheni)

200. The fast begins at dawn. It is not as stringent as other fast days. US custom is to recite *Selichot* in the repetition of the Amidah. See 182 above.
201. Before Mincha it is customary to set out a collection plate for *Zecher LeMaChatzit Hashekel.* This charitable collection is separate to the *Matanot L'Evyonim* given on Purim. Contributions should be made before the Megillah is read on Purim morning.
202. Regular Mincha for fast days takes place with the Torah reading as in the morning, and the Haftarah for fast days (P. 909). During the silent Amidah, add *Anenu* in the *Shema Kolenu* blessing (P. 184). Omit *Avinu Malkenu* and *Tachanun.* When Purim falls on Sunday, Ta'anit Esther is brought forward to the previous Thursday. In such a case, recite *Avinu Malkenu* and *Tachanun* at Mincha.

Purim (14th Adar or 14th Adar Sheni)

203. Purim can fall on Sunday, Tuesday, Thursday or Friday.
204. *Al HaNissim* is added to the Amidah in Ma'ariv, Shacharit and Mincha, and the second blessing of *Birkat HaMazon.* If one forgets to say *Al HaNissim,* one does not repeat the Amidah or *Birkat HaMazon.*

205. Following Ma'ariv Amidah, Kaddish *Titkabal*. The Reader of Megillat Esther recites three blessings: *Al Mikra Megillah, She'asa Nisim* and *Shehecheyanu* (P. 738). Following the Megillah the concluding blessing, *Harav et Rivenu*, is said. The congregation say *Asher Heini*, then sing *Shoshanat Yaakov* (P. 738). Continue with *Vihi No'am* on *Motza'ei* Shabbat. *Ve'ata Kadosh*, full Kaddish (omitting the line *Titkabal*) and Aleinu. On *Motza'ei* Shabbat, *Veyiten Lecha* and Havdalah precede Aleinu.
206. Men and women are obligated to hear the reading of the Megillah.
207. Weekday Shacharit: No *Tachanun*. *Chatzi* Kaddish and the Torah is taken out. (Omit *El Erech Apayim* if Purim is on Thursday.) Three men are called up (P. 904). Following the returning of the Torah to the Ark, the Megillah is read, preceded by the three blessings as in the night-time. When making the *Shehecheyanu*, the Reader and all listening should have in mind the three other mitzvot of the day (see 218). Following the Megillah the concluding blessing, *Harav et Rivenu*, is said followed by *Shoshanat Yaakov* (P. 738). *Ashrei. Uva Letzion*. Kaddish *Titkabal*. The service concludes as in a normal weekday.
208. On Purim day one is commanded to fulfil the mitzvot of *Matanot L'Evyonim* (giving charity to at least two poor people); *Mishloach Manot* (sending gifts of at least two portions of ready-to-eat food to at least one person) and *Seudat Purim* (festive meal). The meal needs to commence before sunset. If concluded after nightfall, *Al HaNissim* is still added to *Birkat HaMazon*. While it is a mitzvah to drink on Purim, the *Chayei Adam* writes: "If one believes that drinking on Purim will interfere with one's performance of any mitzvah, such as reciting *Birkat Hamazon*, Mincha or Ma'ariv, or if one will behave in a boorish manner, it is preferable that one not drink."
209. Purim does not cancel a Shivah. In this respect, it is like Shabbat. Public mourning is not observed.

Shushan Purim (15th Adar or 15th Adar Sheni)

210. Omit *Tachanun* and *Lamnatzeiach*.
211. Public mourning is not observed (see 210).

Parashat Parah

212. On the penultimate Shabbat of Adar (Adar II in a leap year), two Torah scrolls are taken from the Ark. The second Torah is placed on the Bima before *Chatzi* Kaddish. *Hagbahah* and *Gelilah* are performed on the first Torah, then the Oleh for the Maftir is called. The reading is Bemidbar 19:1-22. In a regular year, Parashat Para coincides with Parashat Ki Tissa or Vayakhel or Vayakhel-Pekudei. In a leap year, it coincides with Tzav or Shemini. Haftarah is Ezekiel 36:16-38.

Parashat HaChodesh

213. On the final Shabbat of Adar (Adar II in a leap year), two Torah scrolls are taken from the Ark. The second Torah is placed on the Bima before *Chatzi* Kaddish. *Hagbahah* and *Gelilah* are performed on the first Torah, then the Oleh for the

Maftir is called. The reading is Shemot 12:1-20. In a regular year, Parashat Hachodesh coincides with Parashat Vayakhel-Pekudei, Pekudei or Vayikra. In a leap year, it coincides with Shemini or Tazria. Haftarah is Ezekiel 36:16-38.

214. When Rosh Chodesh Nisan falls on Shabbat, three Torah scrolls are taken from the Ark. From the first scroll, a minimum of six men are called to the portion of the week, which is Vayikra in a regular year or Tazria in a leap year. (It is usual to combine *Shishi* and *Shevii.*) The second Torah, for Rosh Chodesh, is placed on the Bima. *Hagbahah* and *Gelilah* are performed on the first Torah. The Oleh for *Shevii* is called and the Rosh Chodesh portion read (Bemidbar 28:9-15). The third Torah is placed on the Bima and *Chatzi* Kaddish is said on the second and third Sifrei Torah. *Hagbahah* and *Gelilah* are performed on the second Torah, then the Oleh for Maftir is called and Parashat Hachodesh is read.

Nisan

215. Rosh Chodesh Nisan is always one day and can be Sunday, Tuesday, Thursday or Shabbat.
216. During Nisan, omit *Tachanun* on weekday services and omit *Tzidkatecha* on Shabbat Mincha.
217. Although many communities refrain from reciting the memorial prayer *El Molei Rachamim* during Nisan, US custom is to always recite the briefer form of memorial prayer, *Adon Ha'olamim* (P. 970), which can be said throughout the year, even during Nisan.
218. Many have the custom to refrain from eating Matzah from Rosh Chodesh Nisan.
219. A bride and groom fast if their wedding day is on Rosh Chodesh Nisan. This is not the case on any other Rosh Chodesh.
220. During Nisan it is customary to make a blessing on the blossoms of fruit trees (P. 782).
221. Many communities raise charitable funds to provide for the needy for Pesach (*Ma'ot Chittin*).

Shabbat HaGadol

222. The Shabbat preceding Pesach is known as Shabbat HaGadol. In a regular year, it coincides with Parashat Tzav. In a leap year, it coincides with Metzora or Acharei. It is US custom for the rabbi to have Maftir. Haftarah (the last prophecy of the Bible) is Malachi 3:4-24. It is customary for the rabbi to give a shiur on an aspect of Pesach. Omit *Barchi Nafshi* at Mincha. Instead, recite the Haggada from *Avadim Hayinu* until *Lechaper al Avonotenu* followed by Kaddish *Derabbanan*.
223. On *Motza'ei* Shabbat HaGadol, omit *Vihi No'am* after Ma'ariv (unless Pesach starts on the following Shabbat).

Erev Pesach (14th Nisan)

224. As soon as possible after nightfall on 14th Nisan, the search for chametz (*Bedikat Chametz*) takes place. Many have the custom for a household member to hide ten pieces of chametz, to be found during the search. Before the search,

say the blessing *Al Biur Chametz* (P. 642). The search is customarily conducted with a candle, but a torch is also permitted. If Pesach falls on *Motza'ei* Shabbat, do *Bedikat Chametz* on Thursday night with a blessing.

225. After *Bedikat Chametz*, make the declaration *Kol Chamira* (P. 642), thereby renouncing ownership of any chametz, the whereabouts of which are unknown.
226. Shacharit. Omit *Mizmor Letoda* and *Lamnatzei'ach*.
227. First-born males are required to fast on the eve of Pesach (*Ta'anit Bechorot*) unless they attend a *siyum*, a celebratory meal to mark the completion of a unit of study, usually a tractate of the Talmud. The *siyum* is customarily held after Shacharit.
228. One may not eat Matzah.
229. One is forbidden from eating chametz from the end of the first third of the day. The ruling in the US is that the day is measured from sunrise to sunset.
230. One is forbidden to own chametz from the end of the fifth hour of the day. Any chametz in one's possession must be sold or disposed of before this time. The chametz collected in the search the previous night is burned. If burning is not possible, it should be made completely inedible in some other way. The declaration *Kol Chamira* (P. 642) is made before the end of the fifth hour.
231. If the first day of Pesach is Thursday, make *Eruv Tavshilin* (P. 642) to permit cooking on Friday for Shabbat.
232. Some have the custom in the afternoon to recite the verses relating to the order of the Pesach offering.
233. If the first day of Pesach is Sunday, the Fast of the Firstborn is on the previous Thursday. *Bedikat Chametz* occurs on Thursday night and chametz is burned on Friday morning, without the declaration of *Kol Chamira*. Specific arrangements for Shabbat and Erev Pesach are detailed in a special London Beth Din/US publication.

Pesach (15th–22nd Nisan)

234. Candle-lighting (P. 644) See 15.
235. On the second night, candle-lighting and preparations for the Seder are made after nightfall. On *Motza'ei* Shabbat, a woman says *Baruch HaMavdil Bein Kodesh LeKodesh* before candle-lighting.
236. Yom Tov Ma'ariv is conducted in the traditional melody. See 80 above.
237. When Pesach is Friday night, the service begins with *Mizmor Shir Leyom HaShabbat* (P. 270). Omit *Ma'aravot*. Before the Amidah, add the special verses for Shabbat (*Veshamru*) and for Yom Tov (*Vayedaber Moshe*). After the Amidah, the congregation says *Vayechulu HaShamayim*, but the Leader does not say *Me'ein Sheva* (P. 294). Omit *Bameh Madlikin*.
238. US custom is not to recite Hallel in the evening. Kiddush is not made in the synagogue on the first two nights of Yom Tov.
239. If the second night of Pesach is *Motza'ei* Shabbat, the *Ma'aravot* for the second night are said, (unlike other Yamim Tovim, when it would be normal to say the

Ma'aravot of the first night on *Motza'ei* Shabbat. This is because the *Ma'aravot* refer to the cutting of the Omer)

240. If either of the first two nights of Pesach are on *Motza'ei* Shabbat, the paragraph *Vatodi'enu* is added to the middle section of the Amidah.
241. Some communities will not count the Omer in the synagogue on the second night of Pesach and instead count at the Seder.
242. On the two nights of Pesach the custom is not to recite the full text of Prayers before Sleep (P. 244), just the *Hamapil* blessing and the first paragraph of the Shema.
243. Shacharit: for Shabbat and Yom Tov (P. 322) The Leader for Shacharit begins from *Ha'El Beta'atzumot* (P. 366) After Barchu, *HaMe'ir La'aretz* is said, or *Ha-Kol Yoducha* if it is Shabbat. Although most communities do not say the *Yotzarot,* the *Geula, Berach Dodi* (the *piyyut* inserted before *Ga'al Yisrael*) is said in most communities. The Amidah for Yom Tov is said (P. 646), with the additions for Shabbat on Shabbat. Full Hallel. Kaddish *Titkabal. Ein Kamocha* (P. 404). Our custom is to say the '13 Middot' (P. 406) and the supplication following, during the week but not on Shabbat. Two Torah scrolls are taken from the Ark.
244. Torah reading as for Yom Tov morning.
245. US custom is not to say the *piyyut, Ya Eli,* as opposed to the custom in other congregations. *Ashrei,* and the Torah scrolls are returned to the Ark.
246. It is customary for the Leader to wear a kittel and to chant *Chatzi* Kaddish before Musaf to the special melody for *Tal.* US custom is to continue to say *Mashiv Haruach* in the silent Amidah for Musaf on the first day. (P. 670).
247. The Ark is opened, and the Leader begins the repetition and chants *Tefillat Tal* (P. 696). From this point on, *Mashiv HaRuach* is no longer said. During the repetition of the Amidah, the *Kohanim* say *Birkat Kohanim*. In most communities, this takes place even on Shabbat, but the Kohanim do not chant on Shabbat. Some communities have preserved specific melodies for the *Kohen*-chants for each festival.

Sefirat Ha'Omer

248. One counts the Omer for a given day after nightfall. However, in many United Synagogues, the custom is to count on Friday night, even before nightfall.
249. The count should be made standing up.
250. One who forgets to count at night, may count during the following day, but without a blessing and resume counting with a blessing the following evening.
251. One who forgets to count for an entire 24-hour period, should continue to count, but without a blessing. If one is in doubt whether or not a count was made in a 24-hour period, the count can be continued with a blessing.
252. Regarding mourning practices during the Omer, see 273, 274 below.

Chol Hamoed

253. *Ya'ale Veyavo* is added to the weekday Amidah and *Birkat HaMazon.* If it is forgotten, one must repeat the Amidah, but if forgotten in *Birkat HaMazon* there is no need to repeat.
254. On the first evening of Chol Hamoed, *Ata Chonantanu* is added to the weekday Amidah. In the ninth blessing of the Amidah, we commence saying *Veten B'racha.* If one said *Veten Tal Umatar* in error, one must repeat the Amidah. If the mistake was realised before the Amidah was completed, one must go back to the ninth blessing, *Barech Aleinu.* The Omer is counted prior to Havdalah, which is made on wine or grape juice.
255. US custom is for men to wear *tefillin,* without a b'racha, during Shacharit on Chol Hamoed. The Leader should wear *tefillin.* On the first day of Chol Hamoed, *tefillin* are removed after the Torah reading as the reading refers to *tefillin.* On other days, remove them before Hallel.

Shabbat Chol Hamoed

256. If Shabbat follows immediately after Yom Tov, Shabbat candles are lit from a pre-existing flame. Kabbalat Shabbat begins with *Mizmor Shir Leyom HaShabbat* (P. 270). Regular Friday night Ma'ariv follows, adding of *Yaale Veyavo* in the Amidah. If Shabbat follows immediately after Yom Tov, omit *Bameh Madlikin* (P. 298). Count the Omer after Kiddush, before Aleinu.
257. The Leader for Shacharit begins at *Shochen Ad,* as on a regular Shabbat (P. 366). The *Geula, Berach Dodi* (the *piyyut* inserted before *Ga'al Yisrael*) is said in most communities. *Yaale Veyavo* is added to the Shabbat Shacharit Amidah. Half Hallel. After Hallel it is customary to read *Shir Hashirim.* If it is layned from a kosher Megillah, then the berachot *Al Mikra Megillah* and *Shehecheyanu* are said first. Following *Shir Hashirim,* Mourner's Kaddish is said.
258. The blessings after the Haftarah conclude, as on Shabbat, with *Mekadesh HaShabbat* with no reference to Yom Tov.
259. Musaf: for Yom Tov (P. 670) with the Shabbat additions. Omit *Adir Adirenu* in Kedushah. Omit *Birkat Kohanim.*
260. Mincha: for Shabbat and Yom Tov. The Torah is removed from the Ark and the beginning of the portion following Pesach is read. (*Shemini* or, in a leap year, *Acharei Mot* or *Kedoshim.*) Shabbat Amidah, with the addition of *Yaale Veyavo.* Omit *Tzidkatecha Tzedek.* Aleinu follows Kaddish *Titkabal.* On Motza'ei Shabbat, omit *Vihi Noam.* Count the Omer before *Veyiten Lecha.*

Last days of Pesach (21st and 22nd Nisan)

261. If the seventh day of Pesach is Friday, make *Eruv Tavshilin* (P. 642). As the last days do not constitute a separate Yom Tov (like Shemini Atzeret), omit the *Shehecheyanu* blessing when lighting candles and making Kiddush.
262. Yom Tov Ma'ariv is conducted as on the first nights. Omit *Ma'aravot* on Shabbat. Kiddush is made in the synagogue and the Omer is counted after Kiddush.
263. Shacharit: as the second day. The *Geula* is the poem by Yehuda Halevi, *Yom LeY-*

abasha. The Amidah for Yom Tov is said (P. 646), with the additions for Shabbat on Shabbat. Half Hallel. Kaddish *Titkabal*. If the seventh day is Shabbat, *Shir HaShirim* is read at this point. *Ein Kamocha* (P. 404). Our custom is to say the '13 Middot' (P. 406) and the supplication following, during the week but not on Shabbat. Two Torah scrolls are taken from the Ark.

264. Torah reading: seventh day, *Shemot* 13:17-15:26 (P. 931). As on *Parashat Beshalach*, the custom is to stand for the Shira. In many synagogues, the Baal Koreh chants verses of the Shira responsively with the congregation.
265. Musaf: for festivals (P. 670). During the repetition of the Amidah, the *Kohanim* say *Birkat Kohanim*. In most communities, this takes place even on Shabbat, but the Kohanim do not chant on Shabbat.
266. When the eighth night of Pesach is *Motza'ei* Shabbat, the *Ma'aravot* for the seventh night are substituted. On *Motza'ei* Shabbat, since Havdalah is said together with Kiddush, the Omer is counted before Kiddush.
267. Shacharit: 8th day as on 7th day. There is no *Geula* for the last day of Pesach. However, if there has been no Shabbat Chol Hamoed, the *Geula* for Shabbat Chol Hamoed is said on the last day. The Amidah for Yom Tov is said (P. 646), with the additions for Shabbat on Shabbat. Half Hallel. Kaddish *Titkabal*. If the eighth day is Shabbat, *Shir HaShirim* is read at this point. *Ein Kamocha* (P. 404) follows. Our custom is to say the '13 Middot' (P. 406) and the supplication following, during the week but not on Shabbat. Two Torah scrolls are taken from the Ark.
268. Torah reading: eighth day, *Devarim* 15:19-16:17. If the eighth day is Shabbat the reading begins from *Devarim* 14:22.
269. *Yekum Porkan* (on Shabbat) and prayers for the Royal Family and State of Israel, followed by Yizkor (see 64).
270. Musaf: for festivals (P. 670), as on 7th day (see 266).
271. Ma'ariv: for weekdays. In the fourth blessing of the Amidah, *Ata Chonantanu* is said. Havdalah is said over a cup of wine or grape juice. If the last day of Pesach is Shabbat, the blessings for spices and a flame are also said. Some have the custom to make Havdalah over beer rather than wine or grape juice.

Isru Chag (23rd Nisan)

272. *Lamnatzeiach* is said on *Isru Chag* but omit *Tachanun* for the remainder of the month of Nisan. Similarly, omit *Tzidkatecha Tzedek* at Mincha on the Shabbat after Pesach.

Laws of the Sefirat Ha'Omer Period

273. During this period, certain mourning rituals are observed: one abstains from holding weddings, having haircuts and shaving, listening to music. These practices commemorate the plague that killed the disciples of Rabbi Akiva during this time. The Ashkenazi community intensified these customs due to the massacres of the First Crusade in 1096.
274. Many customs exist regarding the duration of these observances during the Se-

fira period. US custom is to permit weddings from Isru Chag Pesach up to and including the first of Iyar, Lag B'Omer, and from Rosh Chodesh Sivan onwards.

Pirkei Avot (Ethics of the Fathers)

275. Pirkei Avot is recited at Mincha after the repetition of the Amidah, from the first Shabbat after Pesach until Rosh Hashanah. In most communities, Kaddish *Derabbanan* is said afterwards.

Haftarot

276. The Shabbat after Pesach in a regular year is *Shemini*. In a leap year, it is *Acharei Mot* and sometimes *Kedoshim*. There are various customs for the Haftarot for these Shabbatot. US custom is as follows: In a regular year, *Acharei Mot* and *Kedoshim* are always combined and Haftarah is from Amos 9:7, *Halo Chivnei Chushi'im* (which is listed in the Hertz chumash as the Haftarah for *Kedoshim* for Ashkenazim). In a leap year, *Acharei Mot* and *Kedoshim* are separate. If *Acharei Mot* is Shabbat HaGadol, the special Haftarah for Shabbat Hagadol is read. After Pesach, the Haftarah for *Kedoshim* is from Amos 9:7. If Shabbat Hagadol is *Metzora* then *Acharei Mot,* the first Shabbat after Pesach, is often Erev Rosh Chodesh or Rosh Chodesh, in which case the special Haftarot for those days are read. Haftarah for *Kedoshim* will then be Amos 9:7. In the rare situation where, in a leap year, the first day of Pesach is a Tuesday and the Shabbatot of *Acharei Mot* and *Kedoshim* occur after Pesach, US custom is to read Ezekiel 22:1-19 for *Acharei Mot* and from Amos 9:7 for *Kedoshim.* (In the 21st century, this occurs only five times: 2024, 2041, 2068, 2071, and 2095.)

Yom HaShoah (27th Nisan)

277. Israel designated 27th Nisan as *Yom HaShoah* (*Ugevurah*), Holocaust Memorial (and Warsaw Ghetto Uprising) Day. If it is a Friday, Yom HaShoah is observed on 26th Nisan. No special liturgy has been prescribed. Omit *Tachanun*, but say *Lamnatzeiach*. Many communities have established their own customs to mark this day. The US Machzor, *MiGalut LiGeulah,* contains ideas to give this day greater meaning.

Iyar

278. Rosh Chodesh Iyar is always two days. The first of Iyar can only fall on a Monday, Tuesday, Thursday or Shabbat.
279. If Rosh Chodesh Iyar is on Shabbat, even those who have refrained from a haircut and shaving from Pesach may groom in honour of Shabbat (though US custom is to only commence the mourning period from 2nd Iyar).
280. It used to be the custom to make a *Mi Sheberach* on Shabbat Mevarchim for those who were going to be fasting on *BaHaB* – the first Monday, Thursday and following Monday of Iyar.
281. Although when the State of Israel was established in 1948, 5th Iyar coincided with Friday 14th May, the Knesset subsequently decided to avoid the public ob-

servance of Yom Ha'Atzma'ut or Yom HaZikaron on a Friday, Shabbat or Sunday so as to minimise the desecration of Shabbat. Hence if 4th Iyar is a Sunday, Yom HaZikaron is observed on Monday 5th Iyar and Yom Ha'Atzma'ut on Tuesday 6th Iyar. If 5th Iyar is a Friday or Shabbat, Yom Ha'Atzma'ut is brought forward to Thursday 4th or Wednesday 3rd Iyar, and Yom HaZikaron is observed on Wednesday 3rd Iyar or Tuesday 2nd Iyar. Nevertheless, the Israeli Chief Rabbinate has ruled that *Tachanun* is omitted every year on 5th Iyar.

Yom HaZikaron (Israel's Memorial Day)

282. Recite *Tachanun* (except on 5th Iyar) and *Lamnatzeiach*. Many communities recite a memorial prayer for Israel's fallen soldiers and the victims of terror. See the *MiGalut LiGeulah* Machzor for further options. Omit *Tachanun* at Mincha.

Yom Ha'Atzma'ut (Israel's Independence Day)

283. Many congregations hold a communal, festive evening service on the night of Yom Ha'Atzma'ut. See the *MiGalut LiGeulah* Machzor.
284. Shacharit. After the repetition of the Amidah, omit *Tachanun*. Hallel is said. Some communities say Full Hallel with a *b'racha*. Some say Half Hallel, without a *b'racha*. Following Hallel, *Chatzi* Kaddish is said. If a Thursday, the Torah is read. Following the Torah reading or, on other days of the week, after *Chatzi* Kaddish, Isaiah 10:32–12:6 (Haftarah for 8th day Pesach) is read to the Haftarah tune, without blessings. Further details of the service are in the *MiGalut LiGeulah* Machzor.
285. Musical events to celebrate Yom Ha'Atzma'ut may take place on this day.

Pesach Sheni (14th Iyar)

286. US custom is that *Tachanun* is said on Pesach Sheni, and at Mincha on 13th Iyar.

Lag Ba'Omer (18th Iyar)

287. When Lag Ba'Omer falls on a Sunday, haircuts and shaving are permitted on the previous Friday in honour of Shabbat. Omit *Tachanun* (or *Tzidkatecha Tzedek*) at Mincha on Erev Lag Ba'Omer. The mourning restrictions of the Sefira period are lifted on this day, from nightfall. Weddings and musical events can be held from nightfall onwards. Once a celebratory event, involving music has begun on Lag Ba'Omer, it may continue even after nightfall.
288. Shabbat Mevarchim Sivan. In a regular year, the combined sidrot of Behar and Bechukotai are read. Haftarah is that of Bechukotai unless the Shabbat coincides with Erev Rosh Chodesh. On the Shabbat before Shavuot, US custom is to say *Av Harachamim*, even if it is Shabbat Mevarchim.

Yom Yerushalayim (28th Iyar)

289. Yom Yerushalayim can fall on Sunday, Monday, Wednesday or Friday. Omit *Tachanun* at Mincha the previous day. Many congregations hold a communal,

festive evening service on the night of Yom Yerushalayim. See the *MiGalut LiGeulah* Machzor.

290. Shacharit. After the repetition of the Amidah, omit *Tachanun*. Hallel is said. Some communities say Full Hallel with a *b'racha*. Some say Half Hallel without a *b'racha*. Following Hallel, *Chatzi* Kaddish is said. If a Monday, the Torah is read. For further details see the *MiGalut LiGeulah* Machzor.

291. Musical events to celebrate Yom Yerushalayim may take place on this day.

Sivan

292. Rosh Chodesh Sivan is always one day and can fall on Sunday, Tuesday, Wednesday or Friday. In the US the Sefira restrictions on weddings are lifted from Rosh Chodesh. Omit *Tachanun* (and *Tzidkatecha Tzedek*) from Rosh Chodesh until 8th Sivan.

293. 2nd Sivan is known as *Yom HaMeyuchas*.

294. 3rd to 5th Sivan are known as the *Shloshet Yemei Hagbala* (Three Days of Limitation).

Shavuot (6th and 7th Sivan)

295. Shavuot can fall on Sunday, Monday, Wednesday or Friday. When the first day of Shavuot is Friday, make *Eruv Tavshilin* (P. 642).

296. It is customary to decorate the synagogue with flowers and greenery in honour of the festival.

297. Whilst some communities delay Ma'ariv on the first night of Yom Tov until nightfall, the US, following many communities in Germany, did not accept this practice and continued to say Ma'ariv earlier, as on Erev Shabbat. Therefore, it is acceptable to hold Ma'ariv before nightfall, especially if this would facilitate greater participation in Torah study. Some communities start Mincha just before sunset and only daven Ma'ariv after sunset.

298. Candle lighting (P. 644). See 15.

299. Yom Tov Ma'ariv is conducted in the traditional melody. US custom is to say the *Ma'aravot*, see 80 above. Following the Amidah, Kaddish *Titkabal*. Kiddush is made in the synagogue.

300. If the first night of Shavuot is on *Motza'ei* Shabbat, the *Ma'aravot* for the first night are said and the paragraph *Vatodi'enu* is added to the middle section of the Amidah.

301. Many have the custom to eat dairy foods on Shavuot.

302. Many communities organise a *Tikun Leyl Shavuot* as an all-night Torah learning rather than saying the text of the published *Tikun*. Shacharit may begin before sunrise at the time of *Mi Sheyakir*. (In London, this is between 2.40 am and 3.31 am BST, depending on the time of year.)

303. If a man is available who has been asleep for part of the night, he should lead the community in berachot from *Al Netilat Yadayim* through to the end of *Hama'avir* (P. 12-20). If no such person is available, someone who has been awake the whole night may lead the berachot.

304. Shacharit: for Yom Tov (P. 322). The Leader begins from *Ha'El Beta'atzumot* (P. 366). After Barchu, say *HaMe'ir La'aretz*. Full Hallel. Kaddish *Titkabal. Ein Kamocha* (P. 404). Our custom is to say the '13 Middot' (P. 406) and the supplication following. Two Torah scrolls are taken from the Ark.
305. Torah reading: first day, *Shemot* 19:1-20:23 (P. 941). After the Cohen has been called but before he recites his b'racha, the *piyyut, Akdamut Milin,* is recited responsively by the Baal Koreh and the congregation. (In earlier generations, this was said after layning the first verse. This practice has been retained only for Haftarah on the second day of Yom Tov.) It is the custom to stand for the *Aseret HaDibrot*, which are layned with *Ta'am Elyon*. Some have the custom to honour the rabbi or a learned congregant with the Haftarah, given its mystical content. US custom is not to say the *piyyut, Ya Eli,* as opposed to the custom in other congregations.
306. Some have the custom to say the *piyyut, Az Shesh Me'ot,* in the repetition of Amidah after the *Korbanot*.
307. When the second night of Shavuot is Friday night, it is possible to bring in Shabbat early. Start service with *Mizmor Shir Leyom HaShabbat* (P. 270). Omit *Ma'aravot*. Before the Amidah, add the special verses for Shabbat (*Veshamru*) and for Yom Tov (*Vayedaber Moshe*). After the Amidah, the congregation says *Vayechulu HaShamayim* and *Me'ein Sheva* (P. 294). Omit *Bameh Madlikin*.
308. When the second night of Yom Tov is a weekday, the ideal practice is to wait until nightfall to recite Ma'ariv. In the summer, this presents difficulties for many congregations, so it is possible to light candles and recite Ma'ariv immediately after *plag hamincha* and cook food to be started to be eaten before sunset.
309. The book of Ruth is read after Hallel. If it is read from a kosher Megillah, the blessings *Al Mikra Megillah* and *Shehecheyanu* are recited. Mourner's Kaddish.
310. US custom is to insert the *piyyut Yetziv Pitgam* after the first verse of the Haftarah.
311. *Yekum Porkan* (on Shabbat) and the prayers for the Royal Family and State of Israel, followed by Yizkor (see 64).
312. After Yom Tov, Havdalah is said over a cup of wine or grape juice. If the second day of Shavuot is Shabbat, the blessings for spices and a flame are also said.

Isru Chag (8th Iyar)

313. Omit *Tachanun*, but say *Lamnatzei'ach*.
314. While some communities omit Tachanun for six days after Shavuot, corresponding to the days in the Temple when the festival offering could have been brought, US custom is to resume *Tachanun* on 9th Sivan. Nevertheless, if a burial took place before Shavuot, the Shivah is cancelled by Yom Tov and the second day of Yom Tov will count as seven days towards the Sheloshim.
315. When the first portion of *Parashat Naso* is read on Monday and Thursday mornings (and the previous Shabbat afternoon) US custom is to stop at chapter 4, verse 34 (not verse 38, which is the *Sheni* stop on Shabbat).
316. 20th Sivan is the anniversary of the start of the Chemlenitzki pogroms in 1648.

Before the Second World War, this day was widely observed as a day of *Selichot* and fasting.

Tammuz

317. Rosh Chodesh Tammuz is always two days. 1st Tammuz can fall on Sunday, Tuesday, Thursday or Friday.
318. In years when the second day of Shavuot is Shabbat, the sidrot of *Chukat* and *Balak* are combined and the Haftarah of *Balak* is read.

Fast of Tammuz (17th Tammuz)

319. The Mishna (*Ta'anit* 4:6) recounts five tragedies that occurred on this date: Moses broke the Tablets, the daily Tamid sacrifice was discontinued, the walls of Jerusalem were breached by Titus, Apostemos burned the Torah and an idol was placed in the Temple.
320. From 17th Tammuz to 9th Av is the period of mourning known as the Three Weeks. During this period, certain mourning rituals are observed: one abstains from holding weddings, haircuts and shaving, listening to music.
321. A wedding can take place on the eve of 17th Tammuz if no other date is available.
322. The fast begins at dawn. US custom is to recite *Selichot* in the repetition of the Amidah. See 182 above.
323. Mincha. The Torah reading, as in the morning, and Haftarah for fast days (P. 909). *Avinu Malkenu* as in the morning.
324. The three Shabbatot of the Three Weeks have special Haftarot know as the 'three Haftarot of rebuke', taken from Jeremiah 1, Jeremiah 2 and Isaiah 1. In most years, the Shabbatot correspond to Pinchas, Matot and Masay, and Devarim. Matot and Masay are normally combined. They are only separate in some leap years. (The last occasion was in 2014. The next occasions are 2035, 2038, 2052, 2062.) When Pinchas precedes 17th Tammuz, Haftarah is from I Kings 18 . If, in a regular year, the Haftarah from Kings is read in error on Pinchas, on the following week the Haftarot of both Jeremiah and Jeremiah 2 are read, as they are adjacent portions. If Rosh Chodesh Av falls on Shabbat, US custom is to read the Haftarah of Jeremiah.
325. 23rd Tammuz. Yahrzeit of Chief Rabbi Herman Adler (died 18th July 1911).
326. When Masay is read by itself, there is no objection to stopping at Sheni (Bemdibar 43:10), even though it is in the middle of the 42 journeys.
327. At Shacharit and Mincha weekday services, during the repetition of the Amidah there is a custom to intone the blessing, *Velirushalyim Ircha*, in the *Eicha* melody.

Menachem Av

328. Rosh Chodesh Av is always one day. 1st Av can fall on Monday, Wednesday, Friday or Shabbat. When announcing the month on Shabbat Mevarchim, and in writing a Ketubah, the month is referred to as Menachem Av.
329. From sunset before Rosh Chodesh Av, the period known as the Nine Days begins. One should not eat meat or poultry or drink wine or grape juice during

this period. Clothes are not laundered or ironed, and one generally minimises joyful activity. Meat and wine may be consumed on Shabbat and at a *Seudat Mitzvah* celebrating a *Brit* or *Pidyon Haben*. If a *siyum* is made concluding a tractate of Talmud, meat and wine can also be consumed.

330. US custom used to be that throughout the Three Weeks, a sadder tune was sung to *Lecha Dodi* during the Kabbalat Shabbat service. This has mostly died out but on Shabbat Chazon, the Shabbat before Tisha B'Av, *Lecha Dodi* is sung to the tune of *Eli Zion.*

331. Chapter 1, verse 12 of Parashat Devarim, *Eicha Esa Levadi,* is sung to the tune of *Eicha.* So as not to begin the portion on a mournful note, many communities will go back a verse when starting this portion (or end Rishon a verse earlier) The *Eicha* melody is also used from verse 2 in the Haftarah, except for the verses of consolation (Isaiah 1:9,16-19, 24-27). Haftarah is normally read by the rabbi (or senior member of the congregation).

332. *Av Harachamim* is said before Ashrei.

333. Both in the synagogue and at home, Havdalah is made on a cup of wine or grape juice which is given to a child to drink. If no child is available, the person making Havdalah may drink the wine or grape juice, but not share it with others.

334. Mincha on the eve of Tisha B'Av is held early so as to allow time to eat a meal before the fast and have the *Seuda Hamafseket* (final meal). Omit *Tachanun* at Mincha, and on Shabbat omit *Tzidkatcha Tzedek*.

335. The meal should consist of bread, one cooked item and a beverage. The traditional practice is to eat a boiled egg, water and bread dipped in ash. When Tisha B'Av falls on Sunday, or on Shabbat and is postponed to Sunday, there are no restrictions on the final meal, which may consist of even meat and wine. The restrictions of Tisha B'Av begin at sunset, even on Shabbat. When Tisha B'Av falls on Shabbat or Sunday, *Pirkei Avot* is omitted at Mincha.

Tisha B'Av (Fast of 9th Av)

336. The Mishna (*Ta'anit* 4:6) recounts five tragedies that occurred on this date: God decreed that the children of Israel would not be allowed to enter the land, the First Temple was destroyed, the Second Temple was destroyed, Beitar was captured, and Jerusalem was ploughed over.

337. Tisha B'Av can fall on a Sunday, Tuesday, Thursday or Shabbat, when the fast is postponed to Sunday.

338. On Tisha B'Av eating, drinking, washing, anointing, wearing leather shoes and marital relations are prohibited. One refrains from greeting people. Torah study is limited to passages associated with the destruction of the Temple and/or mourning.

339. Before Ma'ariv, the *Parochet* is removed in the synagogue in the place where prayers are being held. After *Barchu*, the congregation should sit on low chairs. The requirement to sit on low chairs continues until *Chatzot* (halachic midday) the following day. Ma'ariv is conducted in a mournful voice, incorporating the melody of *Eicha,* if possible. Kaddish *Titkabal.* The service continues with *Eicha*

and *Kinot.* If *Eicha* is read from a kosher Megillah, the blessing *Al Mikra Megillah* is made, but not *Shehecheyanu.* Continue with *Ve'ata Kadosh*, full Kaddish (omitting the line *Titkabal*), Aleinu, Mourners Kaddish.

340. If the fast occurs on *Motza'ei* Shabbat, *LeDavid Baruch* (P. 578) is not sung. *Baruch Hamavdil Bein Kodesh Lechol* should be said before performing any *melacha* and before changing into non-leather shoes, unless they are the kind that are worn on Shabbat as well. Omit Havdalah, as it is not possible to drink the wine. Nevertheless, the blessing *Borei Me'orei Ha'esh* is made over a candle before beginning *Eicha.* (If it was not said here, it can be said the entire night.) An extra *Kinah* is added, *Eich Mipi Vein Uvat.* After *Kinot*, omit *Vihi Noam* and *Veyiten Lecha.* Should anyone need to break their fast, Havdalah is made first. In this situation, use a beverage other than wine or grape juice.

341. In the morning, men do not wear *tallit* or *tefillin.* The *Tallit Katan* is donned without a *b'racha.* The usual morning blessings are made (including *She'asa Li Kol Tzorki* and *Oter Yisrael Betif'ara*). The tzitzit are not kissed for *Baruch She'amar* or during the *Shema.* In the repetition of the *Amidah,* add *Anenu.* Omit *Birkat Kohanim* from the *Amidah.* Omit *Avinu Malkenu.* On Thursday, omit *El Erech Apayim.* Three men are called to the Torah for the portion, *Ki Tolid Banim* (P. 904). The custom of saying *Baruch Dayan Ha'emet* by the *Oleh* or *Baal Koreh* has lapsed. Haftarah is read in the *Eicha* melody, except for the final two verses. After the Torah has been returned to the Ark, *Kinot* are recited. Some communities choose not to say the entire order of *Kinot* and instead recite a selection together with explanation and discussion. In this case, it is important that the core elements of the *Kinot* are said, commencing with *Kinot* from Kalir and concluding with *Zion Kinot.*

342. The *Parochet* is returned to the Ark before Mincha. Men put on *tallit* and *tefillin* with the usual blessings. The service begins with *Shir Shel Yom,* which was omitted in the morning, followed by Kaddish. Normal Mincha for a fast day follows with the omission of *Tachanun* and *Avinu Malkenu.* The prayer *Nachem* is added to the Amidah in the blessing *Velirushalayim Ircha.* Even someone who has not fasted should say *Nacheim.*

343. The fast ends at nightfall. It is possible to daven Ma'ariv before nightfall. On Sunday evening, Havdalah on wine or grape juice is made before breaking the fast, without the introductory verses and omitting the blessings on a flame or spices. *Kiddush Levana* (P. 602) is said, ideally, after breaking the fast.

344. The restrictions of the Nine Days remain in effect until halachic midday on 10th Av. However, if Tisha B'Av falls on Thursday, one may wash clothes, bathe, take a haircut and shave on Thursday night in order to prepare for Shabbat. If Tisha B'Av has been postponed from Shabbat to Sunday, the restrictions end when the fast is over, with the exception of eating meat and drinking wine (other than for Havdalah), which still apply the night after the fast.

Tu B'Av (15th Av)

345. 15th Av is a day of minor festivity. Omit *Tachanun* at Shacharit and Mincha, and at Mincha the previous afternoon.
346. The seven Shabbatot between Tisha B'Av and Rosh Hashanah are known as the 'seven haftarot of consolation', with prophetic messages of comfort taken from Isaiah. The first Shabbat is known as *Shabbat Nachamu* from the opening words of the Haftarah, Isaiah 40, *Nachamu Nachamu Ami.*

DAILY PRAYER

On Waking

347. The custom is to say *Modeh Ani Lefanecha* immediately on waking, even before washing the hands (P. 4).
348. Upon waking, one is required to wash hands. Some hold that one should not walk four *amot* (around 2 metres) prior to washing hands.
349. Hands should preferably be washed using a cup, but the absence of a cup does not disqualify the washing. The custom is to pour water from the cup onto the right hand, then the left. This is done three times.
350. The blessing *Al Netilat Yadayim* may be said before drying one's hands or afterward. The original US custom was to say this blessing in the synagogue at the beginning of the series of morning blessings (P. 12). If *Al Netilat Yadayim* is not said on washing, some have the custom to instead say *Reishit Chochma* (P. 4) and the succeeding verses.
351. The blessing of *Asher Yatzar* should be said each time after relieving oneself, after first having washed hands. It is recommended that in the morning, one should relieve oneself immediately after washing hands, then say *Al Netilat Yadayim* followed by *Asher Yatzar*. In the morning, it is permissible to say *Asher Yatzar* even without relieving oneself, as an expression of thanksgiving for a new day.
352. According to the Talmud, the blessing of *Elokai Neshama* (P. 16) should be said immediately upon wakening. US custom is to say *Elokai Neshama* as part of *Birchot HaTorah* or immediately after *Asher Yatzar*.
353. *Birchot HaTorah* are said either at home or in the synagogue before the *Birchot HaShachar*.

Tzitzit

354. Putting on a four-cornered garment with tzitzit attached fulfils a positive mitzvah from the Torah. The obligation applies only during the daytime. Since wearing tzitzit is a time-bound mitzvah, women are exempt.
355. The accepted practice is to wear a *tallit katan* all day long and to wear a *tallit gadol* (*tallit*) during Shacharit.
356. US custom is that someone who leads a service, or receives the honour of an *aliyah, Hagbahah, Gelilah* or *Peticha*, should also wear a *tallit*. Those who are 'standing *segan*' next to the Bima should also wear a *tallit*.

357. While many Ashkenazi men do not wear a *tallit* before marriage, US custom is for a boy to wear a *tallit* from the age of Bar Mitzvah.

358. One should put on the *tallit katan* whilst getting dressed. Ideally, one should first examine the strings of the tzitzit to ensure they are not torn. One should say the blessing of *Al Mitzvat Tzitzit* (p. 4) while standing, then immediately put on the garment. If one will soon put on a *tallit gadol* and have in mind the *tallit katan* when saying the blessing on the *tallit gadol*, one does not say the blessing on the *tallit katan*. If there will be a substantial interruption between putting on the *tallit katan* and putting on the *tallit gadol*, one should say the separate blessing on the *tallit katan*.

359. The blessing should be said from the time of *Mi Sheyakir* (see 384). If necessary, it can be said from dawn.

360. For the *tallit gadol*, one should ideally first examine the strings, stand, say the blessing *Lehitatef Batzitzit* and put it on. '*Lehitatef*' means to wrap oneself; one should initially wrap the *tallit gadol* around to cover one's shoulders and face for a few moments, after which it is sufficient that it be on the shoulders.

361. If one removes the *tallit gadol* for any reason, one should repeat the blessing when putting the *tallit* back on again. The blessing is not repeated if the *tallit gadol* is put on soon after taking it off and, either one was wearing a *tallit katan* all along, or one's original intention was to put the *tallit gadol* back on shortly.

Tefillin

362. Putting on *tefillin* fulfils two positive mitzvot from the Torah. The obligation applies only on weekdays. Since wearing *tefillin* is a time-bound mitzvah, women are exempt.

363. One puts on *tefillin* after the *tallit*, because *tefillin* are more holy and we follow the principle of "ascending in sanctity".

364. The *tefillin shel yad* is worn on the weaker arm, meaning that right-handed people wear it on the left arm, and vice versa.

365. The *tefillin* are put on standing up. The *tefillin shel yad* is put on first. One places the box on the biceps near the elbow joint, angled towards the heart, and says the blessing *LeHani'ach Tefillin*. One tightens the strap around the muscle and wraps the strap around the forearm seven times. Without speaking or otherwise becoming distracted, one places the *tefillin shel rosh* on the head, above the hairline, centred over the nose, and says the blessing *Al Mitzvat Tefillin*. One adjusts the straps so that the knot rests at the base of the skull and the two straps hang down in front of one's chest, and one says *Baruch Shem Kevod Malchuto Le'Olam Va'ed*. Finally, one wraps the strap of the *tefillin shel yad* around the fingers, while saying *Ve'erastich* (P. 8).

366. The box of the *tefillin shel yad* and the *tefillin shel rosh* must rest directly on the arm and head respectively, without any barrier between them. This rule does not apply to the straps of the tefillin.

367. One should regularly touch first the *tefillin shel yad* then the *tefillin shel rosh*, so as to remain conscious that one is wearing them. In particular, one should

touch the appropriate *tefillin* when saying the relevant verses of the Shema. It is also customary to touch them when saying *Potei'ach Et Yadecha* during *Ashrei*.

368. At a minimum, *tefillin* should be worn while saying the Shema and Amidah. They should not normally be removed before Kaddish *Titkabal*. It is best not to remove them until after the Mourner's Kaddish following Aleinu. In theory, one should wear *tefillin* all day. The custom, however, is to take off the *tefillin* after praying, because it is difficult to maintain a constant awareness of the *tefillin* and the requisite purity of mind and body throughout the day.

369. One removes the *tefillin* in the reverse order in which they were put on. Thus, one first unwinds the strap of the *tefillin shel yad* from one's fingers, then removes the *tefillin shel rosh* and wraps it in its box. One then unwinds the *tefillin shel yad* from the arm, removes it from the muscle and wraps the *tefillin* in its box. The entire process should be performed standing up.

Morning Blessings and *Pesukei de-Zimra*

370. According to the Talmud (*Berachot* 60b), Morning Blessings (*Birchot HaShachar*) were originally said in conjunction with the performance of the associated activity. Thus one would say the blessing of *Malbish Arumim* upon dressing, and say the blessing of *Zokef Kefufim* upon standing up. However, the custom now is to say all of the blessings together, in the synagogue.

371. The original US custom was for the Leader to include *Al Netilat Yadayim*, *Asher Yatzar* and *Birchot HaTorah* in the blessings said aloud by the Leader at the beginning of the service (P. 12). In most communities, the Leader starts *Birchot HaShachar* with *Asher Natan LaSechvi* (P. 16), and the other blessings are said by the congregation, either at home or at the synagogue before the service. The exception is on Shavuot morning if Shacharit immediately follows an all-night learning session. Because of uncertainties in obligation in reciting these blessings if one has been awake all night, the Leader starts from *Al Netilat Yadayim* and discharges the obligation on behalf of those listening.

372. The first line of the Shema, followed by *Baruch Shem Kevod Malchuto Le'Olam Va'ed*, is included in the section on sanctifying God's name (P. 22). If it is apparent that by the time the Shema and its blessings will be recited, the correct time for saying the Shema will have passed (see 384), all three paragraphs of the Shema are said at this point.

373. Following *Braita* of *Rabbi Yishmael*, Kaddish *Derabbanan* (P. 34) is said.

374. Saying Kaddish, *Barechu* and *Kedushah* requires the presence of a minyan (ten adult males).

375. It has become the practice in all United Synagogues to say Psalm 30 (P. 36), followed by Mourner's Kaddish, though this was not the original custom. Men hold the two front tzitzit of the *tallit* throughout *Baruch She'amar*, kiss them and release them at its conclusion.

376. US custom is to chant *Pesukei de-Zimra* in a particular melody for weekdays and a different melody for Shabbat and Yom Tov.

377. One should not speak unnecessarily from *Baruch She'Amar* until the end of

the Amidah. Certain responses are permitted, as detailed in the chart at the end of the Guide.

378. If one comes late to the synagogue, one may skip portions of *Pesukei de-Zimra* as follows:
379. If there is sufficient time, say *Baruch She'Amar*, Psalms 145-150 and *Yishtabach.*
380. If there is less time, say *Baruch She'Amar*, Psalms 145, 148, 150 and *Yishtabach.*
381. If there is less time, say *Baruch She'Amar*, Psalm 145 and *Yishtabach.*
382. If there is less time, omit *Pesukei de-Zimra* altogether. Complete the rest of the service with the congregation, then say *Pesukei de-Zimra* privately, omitting *Baruch She'Amar* and *Yishtabach.*

Morning Shema

383. Saying the three paragraphs of the Shema each morning fulfils a positive mitzvah from the Torah. Since saying the Shema is a time-bound mitzvah, women are exempt. Nevertheless, women are required to say the first verse to express their acceptance of *Ol Malchut Shamayim* (the yoke of the kingdom of Heaven). In accordance with Ashkenazi practice, women are permitted to say the Shema and its preceding and following blessings.
384. There is a set time period every morning during which the Shema may be said. The optimal time is immediately before sunrise. The normal time commences at *Mi Sheyakir*, when there is sufficient light to recognise an acquaintance from a distance of four *amot* (about 2 metres). The London Beth Din defines this technically as 12° solar depression. If necessary, the Shema may be said from dawn (16° solar depression). At the latest, the Shema must be said during the first quarter of the day. (In halachic terminology, this is up to the end of the 3rd 'halachic hour', where each 'hour' represents $\frac{1}{12}$ of the interval between sunrise and sunset.) After that, one is permitted to say the Shema with the blessings during the 4th 'halachic hour,' i.e. until the end of the first third of the day. After this time, some authorities say that the Shema should be said but without the blessings.
385. The Shema should be said with concentration and awe. Each word and syllable should be pronounced correctly and carefully, without slurring the consonants.
386. The custom is to cover the eyes with the right hand while saying the first verse, to promote concentration and avoid distraction.
387. It is customary to draw out one's pronunciation of the letters *Chet* and *Dalet* in the word *Echad* to emphasise God's sovereignty over creation.
388. The sentence *Baruch Shem Kevod Malchuto Le'Olam Va'ed* is said quietly because it does not appear in the biblical text of the Shema.
389. As discussed in 367 above, the custom is for men to touch the hand *tefillin* when saying *Ukeshartem Le'Ot Al Yadecha* and to touch the head *tefillin* when saying *Vehayu LeTotafot Bein Einecha.*
390. If one enters the synagogue and hears the congregation about to say the Shema, one is required to say the first verse of the Shema together with the congrega-

tion. If one is catching up with the davenning, they should cover their eyes at this point.

Shacharit Amidah

391. There is a set time period every morning during which the Shacharit Amidah may be said: in general, at or after sunrise. At the latest, the Amidah should be said during the first third of the day (measured from sunrise to sunset). If necessary, it is permitted to recite the Amidah after the first third of the day, but before midday.

392. One who needs to leave for work (or a journey) before sunrise is permitted to say the Amidah from daybreak. If one was not able to say the Amidah prior to midday, one should say the Mincha Amidah twice.

Havinenu

393. In cases of urgency, one is permitted to substitute a special paragraph, *Havinenu* (P. 96), for the 13 middle blessings of the Amidah, though not when *Veten Tal Umatar* is said. One says Havinenu while standing. One does not have to compensate with the full-length Amidah afterwards.

Repetition of the Amidah

394. During the repetition, the congregation is required to listen attentively and respond 'Amen.'

395. In order to begin the repetition, at least 9 men are required to be listening.

396. After *HaMevarech Et Amo Yisrael BaShalom,* US custom is to omit the verse *Yihyu LeRatzon Imrei-Fi,* both by the Leader and by the individual in his silent Amidah.

Kedushah

397. US custom is that while the Leader says Kedushah, the congregation are only required to say the biblical verses, *Kadosh*...; *Baruch*...and *Yimloch*... Nevertheless, it has become the practice that, whenever an expanded Kedushah is said, such as on Shacharit and Musaf on Shabbat, the congregation say the intermediate passages as well.

Tachanun

398. One should not speak between the Amidah and *Nefilat Apayim.*

399. *Nefilat Apayim* should be said sitting with one's head lowered against one's weaker forearm. However, if one is wearing *tefillin,* the head is lowered against the arm not wearing *tefillin.* The head is only lowered in the presence of a Sefer Torah. One should rest the head on a sleeve or *tallit,* rather than directly on the naked arm.

400. For days on which Tachanun is omitted, see P. 104.

Torah Reading

401. Before opening the Ark on Mondays and Thursdays, the supplication *El Erech Apayim* is said. US custom is to say both versions. For days on which *El Erech Apayim* is omitted, see P. 120.

402. US custom is not to say *Berich Shemei* on Mondays and Thursdays. The Ark remains open until after *Gadlu.*

403. US custom is that a person receiving an *aliyah* wears a *tallit.* The *Oleh* stands to the right of the Baal Koreh. There is a particular US custom for the melody for Torah reading.

404. If a Kohen is present, he is called first. If a Levi is present, he is called second. If no Levi is present, the same Kohen is called twice. Subsequent *aliyot* are given to a Yisrael. If no Kohen is present, a Yisrael or a Levi may be given the first *aliyah,* but a Levi is not called up after a Yisrael, or after another Levi.

405. A Kohen may be called up for Maftir, or for *acharon* if an additional *aliyah* is made.

406. During the week, if it is necessary to call up three Yisraelim, the Kohen may respectfully be asked to leave before the Yisrael makes his *b'racha* on his *aliyah.* He may return after the Yisrael has said *Barchu* and started his *b'racha* on the Torah. It occasionally happens that the rabbi or Baal Koreh is a Kohen. In this case, the Yisrael may be called in the presence of the Kohen, with the following formula: *Af Al Pi SheYesh Kan Kohen, Ya'amod Yisrael Bimkom Kohen.*

407. Priorities for an *aliyah* include: a bridegroom on his wedding day and the Shabbat preceding and following his wedding; a Bar Mitzvah; the father of a new baby; one commemorating a parent's Yahrzeit; one required to say *Birkat HaGomel.*

408. Following the Torah reading, *Chatzi* Kaddish, *Hagbahah* and *Gelilah.* On Monday and Thursday mornings, while the Torah is being wrapped, the Leader says the four paragraphs beginning *Yehi Ratzon Milifnei Avinu Shebashamayim,* and the congregation respond with Amen. All say *Achenu Kol Beit Yisrael* together. Omit these paragraphs on days when Tachanun is omitted. The Torah is returned to the Ark.

Mourner's Kaddish

409. The Mourner's Kaddish is generally said after specific Psalms at the beginning or end of a service. It is said by one who is in mourning for a relative or commemorating a relative's Yahrzeit. When no such person is present, Mourner's Kaddish is generally omitted, except after Aleinu at the end of Shacharit, when it is said by one whose parents have died or whose parents do no not object to the child saying Kaddish.

Mincha

410. There is a set time-period every afternoon during which Mincha may be said. The earliest time is one-half of a 'halachic hour' after midday (a 'halachic hour'

is $\frac{1}{12}$ of the day measured from sunrise to sunset). The latest the Amidah should be said is before sunset.

411. US custom is that the Leader wears a *tallit*.
412. US custom is to begin the Mincha Amidah with *HaShem Sefatai Tiftach* and not to precede it with *Ki Shem HaShem Ekra*.
413. Under extenuating circumstances, a *heicha kedushah* (literally 'half kedushah') may be said. Instead of the congregation saying their silent Amidah first, the Leader may begin saying the Amidah aloud, while the congregation say the Amidah quietly along with him. Kedushah is said with the congregation joining the Leader. After *Ha-El HaKadosh*, the Leader and congregation continue saying the Amidah quietly. Alternatively, the Leader may begin saying the Amidah aloud, while the congregation listen. Kedushah is said with the congregation responding. After the Leader finishes *Ha-El HaKadosh*, he continues his Amidah and the congregation say their own Amidah from the beginning.

Evening Shema and Ma'ariv

414. There is a specific time period during which the Shema may be said. Ideally, one should say the Shema from nightfall. It is preferable to say it before midnight, but one is permitted to say it until dawn. Some congregations hold Ma'ariv services early, with the result that the communal recitation of the Shema in Ma'ariv may be too early to fulfil the halachic obligation. Under such circumstances, one should repeat all three paragraphs of the Shema after nightfall. Ma'ariv cannot begin earlier than *Plag HaMincha* (1¼ variable hours before sunset).
415. US custom is that the Leader wears a *tallit*.

Bedtime Shema

416. As well as reciting the Shema during Ma'ariv, the first paragraph of the Shema is said before going to bed, preceded by the *HaMapil* blessing (P. 244). If Ma'ariv took place before nightfall, the three paragraphs of the Shema may be said at this time.

ROSH CHODESH PRAYER

417. On Rosh Chodesh, *Ya'ale Veyavo* is added to the 17th blessing of the Ma'ariv, Shacharit and Mincha Amidah. If one forgets to say it in Ma'ariv, one does not repeat the Amidah. If one forgets in Shacharit or Mincha, one must repeat the Amidah.
418. It is also added to the 3rd blessing of *Birkat HaMazon*. If forgotten after beginning the 4th blessing, one does not repeat *Birkat HaMazon*.
419. Shacharit: as for weekdays. Verses are added to the *Korbanot* section (P. 26). *Ya'ale Veyavo* is added to the Amidah. After the repetition, Half Hallel is said (except on Rosh Chodesh Tevet, which is also Chanukah, so whole Hallel is said), followed by Kaddish *Titkabal*.
420. Torah reading: P. 911. Four men are called up. The 2nd *aliyah* repeats the last

verse of the 1st *Aliyah* (other than on Rosh Chodesh Tevet, which is also Chanukah, when two scrolls are taken out; three aliyot are called for the Rosh Chodesh reading, one from the second Sefer from which the appropriate day of Chanukah is read). Half Kaddish is said and the Torah is returned to the Ark. *Ashrei. Uva LeZion*. Half Kaddish. *Tefillin* are removed. Musaf for Rosh Chodesh. US custom is to begin Musaf with *HaShem Sefatai Tiftach* and not to precede it with *Ki Shem HaShem Ekra*. The phrase *Ulechaparat Pasha* is added to the 4th blessing in a leap year, from Rosh Chodesh Marcheshvan to Rosh Chodesh Adar Sheni. In the repetition, the congregation respond with Amen to the phrases in the final paragraph of the 4th blessing, starting with *Letova Velivracha*.

Hallel

421. Hallel is said standing. The Leader recites the *b'racha Likro Et HaHallel*, then the congregation recites it. On Rosh Chodesh (other than Rosh Chodesh Tevet) and the last 6 days of Pesach, Half Hallel is said. On Yom Ha'Atzma'ut and Yom Yerushalayim some communities say Half Hallel without a *b'racha;* some say Full Hallel with a *b'racha*.
422. At the beginning of Psalm 118, the Leader chants each of the four verses aloud and the congregation respond each time with just *Hodu LaShem Ki Tov Ki Le'Olam Chasdo*.

SHABBAT PRAYER

Erev Shabbat

423. Mincha: As for weekdays. Omit *Tachanun*.

Shabbat Eve

Candle-lighting

424. There is a custom to give *tzedaka* before kindling the Shabbat lights. At least 2 candles are lit. Some have a custom to light a candle for each member of the household. The candles are lit, then the *b'racha Lehadlik Ner Shel Shabbat* (P. 254) is said with the eyes covered. Many women say a meditation before or after lighting candles. When men light candles, they may make the *b'racha* and then light.
425. Candles may be lit from *Plag HaMincha* (1¼ variable hours before sunset). The published latest candle-lighting time in the US is 15 minutes before sunset. At the latest, candles must be lit before sunset, at which time all *melacha* (weekday labour) must cease. Under exceptional circumstances, one may state that one is not yet bringing in Shabbat, light early, and continue doing *melacha* until just before sunset.
426. Candles must be lit in a place where one will benefit from the light. If one is not eating at home on Friday night, one should still normally light candles at home. If one is not sleeping at home, one should light candles where one sleeps.

Kabbalat Shabbat

427. Many congregations now sing *Yedid Nefesh* (P. 256) before Kabbalat Shabbat, though this never used to be the US custom.
428. It is permitted for a boy under Bar Mitzvah to lead Kabbalat Shabbat.
429. When saying the last verse of *Lecha Dodi,* the custom is to turn to face the door of the synagogue.
430. Mourners during their week of Shivah remain outside the synagogue during Kabbalat Shabbat. They are welcomed in, after the end of *Lecha Dodi.* An announcement is made, and the mourners are greeted with the words *HaMakom Yenachem Etchem Betoch She'ar Aveilei Zion Virushalayim* (P. 270).
431. The congregation recites Psalms 92 and 93, followed by Mourner's Kaddish. Someone observing a Yahrzeit on Shabbat says Kaddish at this point. US custom is to recite *Bameh Madlikin* (P. 298) after the Amidah.

Ma'ariv for Shabbat and Yom Tov

432. Omit *Vehu Rachum.* The conclusion of *Hashkivenu* is different from the weekday formula. If one mistakenly said the weekday version one does not have to repeat the blessing. Omit *Baruch HaShem Le'Olam.* It is customary to say *Veshamru* (P. 282) before the Amidah. If it is Yom Tov, one adds the verse relating to the festival, *Vayedaber Moshe* (P. 282). Half Kaddish is said in the traditional melody.
433. The Shabbat Ma'ariv Amidah is said (P. 284). US custom is that the phrase, *Veyanuchu Va,* is used for all the Amidot of Shabbat in the final paragraph of the 4th blessing. On Rosh Chodesh, add *Ya'ale Veyavo* to the 5th blessing (P. 288). On Chanukah, add *Al HaNissim* to the 6th blessing (P. 290).
434. Following the Amidah, the Leader and congregation say *Vayechulu* (P. 294). The Leader then says the abbreviated version of the Amidah, *B'racha Achat Me'ein Sheva.* There is no requirement to bow for *Baruch Ata HaShem.* Omit this prayer if the service is being held in a temporary location or if there is no Sefer Torah. US custom is that it is not necessary for the Leader to repeat the paragraph *Magen Avot.* Kaddish *Titkabal* is recited in the traditional melody. *Bameh Madlikin* (P. 298) is recited here and in most congregations Kaddish *Derabbanan* follows.
435. Kiddush is recited in the traditional melody. The wine or grape juice is given to a child under the age of Bar/Bat Mitzvah. If this is not possible, the person making Kiddush should drink a minimum of a *revi'it* of the wine.
436. From Shabbat Chol HaMoed Pesach until Shavuot, the Omer is counted at this point (by those communities who do not wait until nightfall to do so).
437. On returning home, the custom is to bless the children (P. 310) and sing *Shalom Aleichem* and *Eishet Chayil* (P. 310-312) before Kiddush. The Friday night Kiddush is a positive mitzvah from the Torah. Normally, one person makes Kiddush on behalf of everyone present. The two challot are covered during Kiddush. Following Kiddush, the hands are washed. Water is poured from a cup, twice on the right hand and twice on the left. If wine or grape juice is not available, we do not substitute another beverage. Instead, the hands are

washed before Kiddush and the blessing over wine is replaced with the blessing over bread. It is customary to sing *Zemirot* at the Shabbat table during the meal.

Shabbat day

438. *Tefillin* are not worn. In most communities, the service begins later than during the week. For much of the year, it may be necessary to say the Shema earlier, as the latest time (in London) to say Shema is 10.06 am in winter and it can be as early as 8.52 am in summer. Prayers begin as on weekdays, with special verses added in the *Korbanot* (P. 26). Following *Braita* of *Rabbi Yishmael*, Kaddish *Derabbanan* (P. 34). In some communities, the Psalm for Shabbat (P. 152) is said here. In other communities, it is said at the end of the service. Psalm 30. Mourners' Kaddish. *Pesukei de-Zimra* for Shabbat (P. 326). US custom is to chant *Pesukei de-Zimra* to a different melody on Shabbat and Yom Tov. The Leader for Shacharit begins with *Shochen Ad* (P. 366).
439. Shacharit is as for Shabbat and Yom Tov. After *Barechu*, the congregation says *Hakol Yoducha. El Adon* is normally sung. The Shabbat Amidah is said. On Rosh Chodesh, *Yaale Veyavo* is added in the 5th blessing. On Chanukah, *Al HaNissim* is added in the 6th blessing. The repetition of the Amidah follows the traditional melody. Following the Amidah, Kaddish *Titkabal* is said in the traditional melody. On Rosh Chodesh and Chanukah, Kaddish *Titkabal* is preceded with Half Hallel or Full Hallel, respectively.
440. Torah Reading. *Ein Kamocha* is chanted in the traditional melody. US custom, now, in most communities, is to say *Berich Shemei* (P. 408). Seven are called up, though additional individuals may be called. When 2 sidrot are read, the *revii* portion should span the 2 sidrot. After the final Aliyah, *Chatzi* Kaddish is said, either by the Leader or the *Baal Koreh*, in the traditional melody. Many communities do not make an individual *Mi Shebeirach* for an *Oleh* but instead recite a composite *Mi Shebeirach* before *Hagbahah*. There is a particular US tradition for the Haftarah melody. After the Haftarah and its blessings, the congregation says *Yekum Porkan* (P. 418), followed by the prayers for the Royal Family and State of Israel.
441. Memorial prayers for those observing a Yahrzeit on Shabbat or in the week ahead are normally said at this point. The custom in most United Synagogues is to use the abbreviated form of memorial prayer, *Adon Ha'Olamim* (P. 970), which may be said throughout the year. Other communities may use the full *El Malei Rachamim* prayer on regular Shabbatot, and the *Adon HaOlamim* on Shabbat Mevarchim, the *Arba Parshiot*, and those Shabbatot on which Tachanun would not be said if it were a weekday.
442. On a Shabbat immediately preceding Rosh Chodesh (except Rosh Chodesh Tishrei), *Birkat HaChodesh* (P. 424) is said. In some communities, the *Molad* is announced. The Leader takes the Sefer Torah at *Mi She'asa Nisim*. US custom is to announce the new month with the phrase *Yihye BaYom Ha…*(with the definite article). The announcement wording is on P. 1053.

443. In contrast to other communities, US custom is not to say *Av HaRachamim* except on 2 Shabbatot of the year: the Shabbat before Shavuot and the Shabbat before Tisha B'Av. *Ashrei* is said and the Torah is returned to the Ark. It is not regarded as a *hefsek* (unwarranted interruption in the service) for a sermon to be given at this point. *Chatzi* Kaddish.
444. Musaf. US custom is to begin the Amidah with *HaShem Sefatai Tiftach* and not to add *Ki Shem HaShem Ekra.* On Rosh Chodesh the 4th blessing is substituted with *Ata Yatzarta* (P. 440). On Chanukah, *Al HaNissim* is added to the 6th blessing. In the Kedushah in the repetition of the Amidah the original custom in the US was to say *Echad Hu Elo-henu.* This has lapsed in most communities. Following the Amidah, Kaddish *Titkabal* in the traditional melody. *Ein Keloheinu. Pitum HaKetoret.* Kaddish *Derabbanan. Aleinu.* Mourner's Kaddish. *Anim Zemirot.* Psalm of the day. On Rosh Chodesh, add Psalm 104, *Barechi Nafshi* (P. 154). From 1st Ellul to Shemini Atzeret, add Psalm 27. (Some communities say these before *Pesukei de-Zimra.*) Mourner's Kaddish. Adon Olam.
445. Shabbat Morning Kiddush should be made where one eats the Shabbat meal. If no wine or grape juice is available, one may say Kiddush over a cup of liquor or other beverage, but not over water or bread. There is a widespread practice just to consume *mezonot* with this Kiddush and to continue the meal later, even at another location, washing over 2 challot. When this occurs, a latter blessing, *B'racha Acharona* (P. 776) needs to be made over the wine/beverage and the *mezonot* before leaving the Kiddush.
446. Mincha: *Ashrei* and *Uva LeTzion* in the traditional melody. *Chatzi* Kaddish. *Va'ani Tefillati* (Psalms 69:14). Even if a Sefer Torah is not available, this verse is said. The Torah is taken from the Ark. Three are called up and the *rishon* of the following week's sidra is read. Omit *Chatzi* Kaddish. While the Torah is being wrapped the congregation sing Psalm 92 (*Mizmor Shir Leyom HaShabbat*) in the traditional melody. *Chatzi* Kaddish. Mincha Amidah. At the end of Kedushah, the Leader switches to the traditional melody for the Shabbat Mincha Amidah. On Rosh Chodesh, *Ya'ale Veyavo* is added to the 5th blessing (P. 498). On Chanukah, *Al HaNissim* is added to the 6th blessing (P. 500). After the repetition, the congregation says *Tzidkatecha* except on days when *Tachanun* is omitted. Kaddish *Titkabal.*
447. From Shabbat *Bereishit* to the Shabbat before Shabbat *HaGadol*, Psalm 104, *Barechi Nafshi* and the 15 *Shir HaMa'alot* Psalms (120-134) are said (P. 506-518), followed by Mourner's Kadddish. On Shabbat *HaGadol* the Haggada is recited from *Avadim Hayinu* to *Lechaper Al Avonotenu,* followed by Kaddish *Derabbanan* in many congregations. From Pesach to Rosh Hashanah, Pirkei Avot is said, followed by Kaddish *Derabbanan* in many congregations. Aleinu. Mourner's Kaddish.
448. Men and women are required to have a 3rd meal on Shabbat (*Se'uda Shlishit*). Ideally, one should wash on two challot, unless one is too full to eat bread in which case *Mezonot* or fruit may be substituted. After the meal, add *Retzei* to *Birkat HaMazon* even if the meal extends after nightfall.

Motza'ei Shabbat

449. US custom is to sing Psalms 144 and 67 in the traditional melody before Ma'ariv (P. 578). The custom in many communities is to add Psalms 121:2, *Ezri Me'im HaShem Osei Shamayim Va'aretz.*
450. Ma'ariv for weekdays (P. 202). In the 4th blessing of the Amidah, *Ata Chonantanu* is added (P. 216). On Rosh Chodesh, *Ya'ale Veyavo* (P. 222) is added to the 17th blessing. If either are forgotten, the Amidah is not repeated. After the Amidah, *Chatzi* Kaddish is said, followed by *Vihi No'am* and *Ve'ata Kadosh* (P. 582). followed by Kaddish *Titkabal.* If Yom Tov occurs before the coming Shabbat, omit *Vihi No'am* and *Ve'ata Kadosh.* On Chanukah, the Menorah is lit in the Synagogue after Kaddish *Titkabal.* Between Pesach and Shavuot, the Omer is counted at this point. The congregation says *Veyiten Lecha* (P. 588). It is not US custom to follow this with Mourner's Kaddish. Havdalah is made in the Synagogue. Aleinu. Mourner's Kaddish. From 1st Ellul to Shemini Atzeret add Psalm 27, followed by Mourner's Kaddish.
451. Between the 3rd and middle day of each month, say *Kiddush Levana,* the blessing on seeing the crescent of the new moon (P. 602). Ideally, it should be said on *Motza'ei Shabbat,* outside, with a minyan.
452. Havdalah is made at home using wine or grape juice, spices and a candle with at least two wicks (P. 608). If forgotten on *Motza'ei Shabbat,* Havdalah may be made until sunset on Tuesday, but only with wine or grape juice.
453. After Shabbat, one should eat a meal, the *Melave Malka,* as a way of marking the end of Shabbat.

LIFECYCLE EVENTS

***Brit Mila* (Circumcision)**

454. A boy is circumcised on the 8th day after birth, with the day of birth (from nightfall to sunset) counting as the 1st day. A boy born during *Bein HaShemashot* (twilight) is circumcised on the 8th day counting from nightfall, but not on a Shabbat. A circumcision takes place on Shabbat if it is definitely the 8th day and the baby has not been born through Caesarean section.
455. US custom is for the father to say the blessing *LeHachniso Bivrito Shel Avraham Avinu* immediately after the Mohel's blessing.
456. US custom (P. 802) is that the blessing after the circumcision follows the version *Asher Kidesh Yedid MiBeteni,* not *Kidash.* Similarly, later, the version is *Tzavei LeHatzil,* not *Tziva.*
457. The baby's mother may find it convenient to say *Birkat HaGomel* at the Brit.
458. The festive meal counts as a *Seudat Mitzvah.* As such, during the Nine Days, meat and wine can be consumed and on Erev Pesach, firstborns present are exempted from fasting.

Pidyon HaBen (Redemption of the Firstborn Son)

459. A firstborn male is redeemed on the 31st day after birth, with the day of birth counting as the 1st day. If the 31st day is Shabbat or Yom Tov, the ceremony is postponed until after nightfall. US custom is that a *Pidyon HaBen* can take place on Chol HaMoed.
460. A *Pidyon HaBen* is held for a natural firstborn son, but not if born by Caesarean section. If the mother has had previous miscarriages or stillbirths, a *Pidyon HaBen* is not performed. In case of early miscarriage, seek halachic advice. If either parent is a child of a Kohen or Levi, a *Pidyon HaBen* is not held.
461. The *Pidyon HaBen* (P. 810) is performed by the father giving the Kohen five silver *sela'im* – coins containing approximately 100 grams of silver. It is possible to use coins of any country, or other items such as a Kiddush cup, provided they contain the requisite amount of silver. It is not possible to use banknotes.
462. Holding the coins, the father makes two blessings, *Al Pidyon HaBen* and *Shehecheyanu,* and hands the coins to the Kohen.
463. A *Pidyon HaBen* can be performed even if the Brit has not yet taken place.
464. The festive meal counts as a *Seudat Mitzvah.* As such, during the Nine Days meat and wine can be consumed and on Erev Pesach firstborns present are exempted from fasting.
465. Slightly different versions of the ceremony occur when the father is absent, the father has died, the father is not Jewish, or when one is redeeming himself.

Zeved HaBat (Gift of a Daughter)

466. The original practice of naming a baby girl was to make a *Mi SheBeirach* after the father received an *aliyah* in the synagogue. The *Zeved HaBat* ceremony (P. 816), adopted from the Sephardi community, is increasing in popularity. It is performed either at home or in the synagogue.
467. The baby's mother may find it convenient to say *Birkat HaGomel* at the *Zeved HaBat.*

Bar and Bat Mitzvah

468. A boy becomes Bar Mitzvah when he is 13 years and 1 day old. A girl becomes Bat Mitzvah when she is 12 years and 1 day old. For example, one born on 5th Nisan would become Bat or Bar Mitzvah on 5th Nisan, 12 or 13 years later.
469. One born in Adar in a regular year becomes Bat or Bar Mitzvah in Adar Sheni if the 12th or 13th year is a leap year.
470. One born in Adar Rishon or Sheni in a leap year becomes Bat or Bar Mitzvah in the same Adar if that year is a leap year.
471. One born on 30th Cheshvan or 30th Kislev becomes Bat or Bar Mitzvah on 30th Cheshvan or 30th Kislev that year if that month has 30 days, otherwise it occurs on 1st Kislev or 1st Tevet.
472. After a Bar Mitzvah has his first *Aliyah* to the Torah, his father makes the blessing *Baruch Shepetarani* (P. 126). US custom is to say the blessing without *Shem Umalchut.* The blessing may similarly be said on a Bat Mitzvah.

Weddings

473. See notes 274 and 320 for details of when weddings cannot take place.

The burial service

474. For details, see the US publication, *Services For Use At The Cemetery.* US custom is to perform *keria* on the left side of one's clothing for children and on the right side for other relatives. On Chol HaMoed, only children perform *keria.* Other relatives do it after the festival.
475. *Tzidduk HaDin* is said on days that Tachanun is said. On days when Tachanun is omitted, Psalm 16 is substituted.
476. If one has not visited a cemetery for 30 days, *Asher Yatzar Etchem BaDin* is recited, normally just before the cortege enters the burial grounds. An *Onen* (mourner before the burial) is allowed to say the blessing.
477. US custom is to stop three times when accompanying the coffin to the grave, while reciting Psalm 91. On days when Tachanun is omitted, the stops are not made.
478. When filling the grave, the custom is that each participant fills at least three spadesful and does not hand the spade to the next participant.
479. Following *Vihi No'am* (P. 582), Burial Kaddish is said by the deceased's children. On days when Tachanun is omitted, the regular Mourner's Kaddish is substituted. US custom is to recite a Memorial Prayer followed by Mourner's Kaddish.

Prayer in a House of Mourning

480. Omit these prayers in a house of mourning during the Shivah:
    i. *Elohenu Velohe Avotenu* (P. 94)
    ii. *Tachanun* (P. 104)
    iii. *El Erech Apayim* (P. 120)
    iv. Psalm 20 (P. 134)
    v. *Pitum HaKetoret* (P. 452).
    vi. The verse *Vihi No'am* (P. 582).
    vii. Hallel on Rosh Chodesh. On Chanukah, those not mourning should say Hallel on returning home.
481. After Shacharit and Ma'ariv, it is customary to add Psalm 49 (P. 838) followed by Mourner's Kaddish. On days when Tachanun is omitted, Psalm 16 is substituted. It is customary to add a Memorial Prayer (P. 840). If Mishna is learned, it is followed by Kaddish *Derabbanan.*
482. For further details about prayers in a house of mourning, see the US *Sefer HaShivah.*

Yahrzeits

483. US custom is that even if a burial has been delayed, the Yahrzeit is always observed on the anniversary of the death, even in the first year. For Yahrzeits in

a leap year, see 194. For Yahrzeits on 30th Marcheshvan and 30th Kislev, see 153 and 160.

Milk after meat

484. US custom is to wait three hours after eating meat products before eating dairy products.

Shiur for *Challah*

485. US custom is to separate *Challah* with a blessing from dough made of at least 3.5 lb (1.6 kg) of flour.

PSALMS FOR SPECIAL OCCASIONS

The following Psalms may be recited on special occasions:

PSALM	PSALM NO.	PAGE
On the day of one's wedding	19	332
On the birth of a child	20	134
	139	822
For someone who is ill	23	574
	121	510
	130	516
	139	822
For safety in Israel	20	134
	120	508
	121	510
	125	512
On recovery from illness	6	112
	30	322
	103	820
Thanksgiving	95	258
	116	622
For guidance	139	822
For success	121	510
For repentance	90	338
For help in difficult times	20	134
	130	516
For travelling	91	582
In thanksgiving for being saved	124	512

The tables on this page provide the names of the months and the days of the week to be inserted into the blessing of the new month, *Birkat HaChodesh*, (P. 424) which takes place on the Shabbat prior to each new month starting in the Jewish calendar (with the exception of the month of Tishrei).

THE HEBREW MONTHS

תִּשְׁרֵי	Tishrei
מַרְחֶשְׁוָן	Marcheshvan
כִּסְלֵו	Kislev
טֵבֵת	Tevet
שְׁבָט	Shevat
אֲדָר	Adar
אֲדָר שֵׁנִי*	Adar Sheni
נִיסָן	Nisan
אִיָּר	Iyar
סִיוָן	Sivan
תַּמּוּז	Tamuz
מְנַחֵם אָב	Menachem Av
אֱלוּל	Ellul

*this month is added during a leap year in the Jewish calendar. See P. 1051 for a list of when leap years occur.

THE HEBREW DAYS OF THE WEEK

Weekdays	Hebrew Weekdays	Transliteration
Sunday	בַּיּוֹם הָרִאשׁוֹן	BaYom HaRishon
Monday	בַּיּוֹם הַשֵּׁנִי	BaYom HaSheini
Tuesday	בַּיּוֹם הַשְּׁלִישִׁי	BaYom HaShelishi
Wednesday	בַּיּוֹם הָרְבִיעִי	BaYom HaRevi'i
Thursday	בַּיּוֹם הַחֲמִישִׁי	BaYom HaChamishi
Friday	בַּיּוֹם הַשִּׁישִׁי	BaYom HaShishi
Shabbat	בְּיוֹם שַׁבַּת קֹדֶשׁ	BeYom Shabbat-Kodesh
Sunday & Monday	בַּיּוֹם הָרִאשׁוֹן וּבַיּוֹם הַשֵּׁנִי	BaYom HaRishon UvaYom HaSheini
Monday & Tuesday	בַּיּוֹם הַשֵּׁנִי וּבַיּוֹם הַשְּׁלִישִׁי	BaYom HaSheini UvaYom HaShelishi
Tuesday & Wednesday	בַּיּוֹם הַשְּׁלִישִׁי וּבַיּוֹם הָרְבִיעִי	BaYom HaShelishi UvaYom HaRevi'i
Wednesday & Thursday	בַּיּוֹם הָרְבִיעִי וּבַיּוֹם הַחֲמִישִׁי	BaYom HaRevi'i UvaYom HaChamishi
Thursday & Friday	בַּיּוֹם הַחֲמִישִׁי וּבַיּוֹם הַשִּׁישִׁי	BaYom HaChamishi UvaYom HaShishi
Friday & Shabbat	בַּיּוֹם הַשִּׁישִׁי וּבְיוֹם שַׁבַּת קֹדֶשׁ	BaYom HaShishi UveYom Shabbat-Kodesh
Shabbat & Sunday	בְּיוֹם שַׁבַּת קֹדֶשׁ וּלְמָחֳרָתוֹ בַּיּוֹם הָרִאשׁוֹן	BeYom Shabbat-Kodesh Ulemochorato BaYom HaRishon

RABBANAN KADDISH TRANSLITERATION

Mourner:

Yitgadal v'yitkadash sh'meh rabba. B'al'ma dee v'ra chiruteh, v'yamleech malchuteh, b'chayaychon, uv-yomaychon, uv-chayay dee chol beyt Yisra-el, ba-agala uvizman kareev, v'imru Amen.

All:

Y'heh sh'meh rabba mevarach l'alam ulal'mei al'ma-ya.

Mourner:

Yitbarach v'yishtabach v'yitpa-ar v'yitromam v'yitnaseh v'yit-hadar v'yitaleh v'yit-hallal sh'meh dee kudsha, b'reech hu. L'ela (Between Rosh Hashanah and Yom Kippur add: L'ela) min kol birchata v'sheerata tushb'chata v'nechemata, dee amiran b'al'ma, v'imru Amen.

Al Yisra-el, v'al rabbanan, v'al talmeedayhon, v'al kol talmeeday talmeedayhon, v'al kol man dee as'keen b'oryta dee b'atra haden v'dee bechol attar v'attar, yehay lehon ulchon sh'lama rabba, chinna v'chisda v'rachamin v'chayyin areecheen, umzona r'veecha, uforkana min kodam avuhon dee vishmaya, v'imru Amen.

Y'heh sh'lama rabba min sh'maya v'chayim tovim aleynu v'al kol Yisra-el, v'imru Amen.

Bow, take three steps back, then bow, first left, then right, then centre, while saying:

Oseh shalom bimromav, hu b'rachamav ya'aseh shalom, aleynu, v'al kol Yisra-el, v'imru Amen.

MOURNER'S KADDISH TRANSLITERATION

Mourner:

Yitgadal v'yitkadash sh'meh rabba. B'al'ma dee v'ra chiruteh, v'yamleech malchuteh, b'chayaychon, uv-yomaychon, uv-chayay dee chol beyt Yisra-el, ba-agala uvizman kareev, v'imru Amen.

All:

Y'heh sh'meh rabba mevarach l'alam ulal'mei al'ma-ya.

Mourner:

Yitbarach v'yishtabach v'yitpa-ar v'yitromam v'yitnaseh v'yit-hadar v'yitaleh v'yit-hallal sh'meh dee kudsha, b'reech hu. L'ela (Between Rosh Hashanah and Yom Kippur add: L'ela) min kol birchata v'sheerata tushb'chata v'nechemata, dee amiran b'al'ma, v'imru, Amen.

Y'heh sh'lama rabba min sh'maya v'chayim aleynu v'al kol Yisra-el v'imru Amen.

Bow, take three steps back, then bow, first left, then right, then centre, while saying:

Oseh shalom bimromav, hu ya'aseh shalom aleynu, v'al kol Yisra-el, v'imru Amen.